GREENS CIVIL COURT STATUTES

1992

GREENS CIVIL COURT STATUTES

1992

Divisions B C and D of The Parliament House Book

W GREEN/Sweet & Maxwell

EDINBURGH

1992

ISBN 0 414 01032 9

A catalogue record for this
book is available from the
British Library.

PRINTED IN GREAT BRITAIN BY
Butler and Tanner Ltd.,
Frome, Somerset

CONTENTS

The contents of this book are reproduced from the Parliament House Book which is published in looseleaf form and regularly updated by W. Green, the Scottish Law Publisher. The Parliament House Book contains all relevant statutory information on key areas in Scots Law.

Material in the Parliament House Book is set out in sections called Divisions. The first page of every Division lists its contents under the Division heading. The Division letters used in this book are those used for the equivalent Division in the Parliament House Book itself.

DIVISION B

Courts, Upper

(including House of Lords, Court of Session, Courts, General)

NOTE

For High Court of Justiciary, see Division E (Criminal Procedure).

Statutes

Statutory Instruments

For Acts of Sederunt, see Division C (Court of Session Practice). For Acts of Adjournal, see Division E (Criminal Procedure).

House of Lords Appeal Directions and Standing Orders

PAGE

Statutes

[1] Debtors (Scotland) Act 1838

(1 & 2 Vict. c. 114)

An Act to amend the Law of Scotland in matters relating to Personal Diligence, Arrestments, and Poindings

[16th August 1838]

NOTE

[1] Repealed so far as inconsistent with the Rules of Court by S.I. 1948 No. 1691 and S.I. 1965 No. 321.

1. [Repealed by the Administration of Justice (Scotland) Act 1933, Sched.]

2–15. [Repealed by the Debtors (Scotland) Act 1987, Sched. 8.]

16. [Superseded by Rules of Court 1965, rr. 70–74.]

Arrestment may be executed before executing the summons, but the summons must be executed and called within a limited period

17. By virtue of such warrant of arrestment, and also by virtue of letters of arrestment raised upon any libelled summons according to the present practice, it shall be competent before executing the warrant of citation to arrest the moveables, debts, and money belonging or owing to the defender until caution be found as aforesaid; and such arrestment shall be effectual, provided the warrant of citation shall be executed against the defender within twenty days after the date of the execution of the arrestment, and the summons called in court within twenty days after the diet of compearance, or where the expiry of the said period of twenty days after the diet of compearance falls within the vacation, or previous to the first calling day in the session next ensuing, provided the summons be called on the first calling day next thereafter; and if the warrant of citation shall not be executed and the summons called in manner above directed, the arrestment shall be null, without prejudice to the validity of any subsequent arrestment duly executed in virtue of the said warrant.

Arrestments against persons furth of the kingdom to be executed at the record office

18. From and after the said 31st day of December it shall not be competent to execute any arrestment as in the hands of a person furth of Scotland by service at the market cross of Edinburgh, and pier and shore of Leith, but such arrestment shall be executed by delivery of a schedule of arrestment at the record office of citations in the Court of Session, which delivery shall be made and the schedule registered and published in the same manner as charges are directed to be registered and published by the Court of Session Act 1825.

19. [Repealed by the Sheriff Courts (Scotland) Act 1907, Sched.]

Lord Ordinary in the Outer House may recall or restrict arrestments, subject to review

20. From and after the said 31st day of December it shall be competent to the Lord Ordinary in the Court of Session before whom any summons containing warrant of arrestment shall be enrolled as judge therein, or before whom any action on the dependence whereof letters of arrestment have been executed has been or shall be enrolled as judge therein, and to the Lord Ordinary on the Bills in time of vacation, on the application of the

Sheriff may recall or restrict arrestments, subject to review

[1] **21.** From and after the said 31st day of December it shall be competent for any sheriff from whose books a warrant of arrestment has been issued, on the petition of the debtor or defender duly intimated to the creditor or pursuer, to recall or to restrict such arrestment, on caution or without caution, as to the sheriff shall appear just; provided that the sheriff shall allow answers to be given in to the said petition, and shall proceed with the further disposal of the cause in the same manner as in summary causes, and his judgment shall be subject to review in the Court of Session.

NOTE

[1] For the interpretation of the term "sheriff" see the Sheriff Courts (Scotland) Act 1971, s.4, and the Interpretation Act 1978, Sched. 1.

Arrestments to prescribe in three years

[1] **22.**—(1) All arrestments shall hereafter prescribe in three years instead of five; and arrestments which shall be used upon a future or contingent debt shall prescribe in three years from the time when the debt shall become due and the contingency be purified.

(2) In the case of an arrestment which—

(*a*) secures a debt which is subject to a time to pay direction or a time to pay order; or

(*b*) is subject to an interim order under section 6(3) of the Debtors (Scotland) Act 1987 (order pending disposal of application for time to pay order),

there shall be disregarded, in computing the period at the end of which the arrestment prescribes, the period during which the time to pay direction, time to pay order or interim order is in effect.

(3) Nothing in this section shall apply to an earnings arrestment, a current maintenance arrestment or a conjoined arrestment order.

NOTE

[1] As amended by the Statute Law Revision Act 1893. Subss. (2) and (3) added by the Debtors (Scotland) Act 1987, Sched. 6, para. 3.

23–31. [Repealed by the Debtors (Scotland) Act 1987, Sched. 8.]

Citations, etc. One witness

[1] **32.** Extracts, citations, deliverances, schedules, and executions may be either printed or in writing, or partly both, and that more than one witness shall not be required for service or execution thereof.

NOTE

[1] "The enactment hereinbefore recited [*i.e.* the Debtors (Scotland) Act 1838, s.32] does and shall apply to all citations on all summonses, and to all cases whatsoever of services and execution, and more than one witness is not and shall not be required for service or execution in any case."—Citations (Scotland) Act 1846, s. 1. As amended by the Debtors (Scotland) Act 1987, Sched. 8.

33–34. [Repealed by the Statute Law Revision Act 1874.]

35. [Repealed by the Debtors (Scotland) Act 1987, Sched. 8.]

36. [Repealed by the Statute Law Revision Act 1874.]

SCHEDULES REFERRED TO IN THE FOREGOING ACT

[Repealed by the Debtors (Scotland) Act 1987, Sched. 8.]

[THE NEXT PAGE IS B 13]

[1] Attendance of Witnesses Act 1854

(17 & 18 Vict. c. 34)

An Act to enable the Courts of Law in England, Ireland, and Scotland, to issue Process to compel the Attendance of Witnesses out of their Jurisdiction, and to give effect to the service of such Process in any Part of the United Kingdom. [10th July 1854]

NOTE

[1] Repealed so far as authorising the issue of process by the High Court by the Supreme Court of Judicature (Consolidation) Act 1925, Sched. 6. Extended: see Evidence (Proceedings in Other Jurisdictions) Act 1975, s. 4.

[1] **1.** If, in any action or suit now or at any time hereafter depending in any of Her Majesty's Superior Courts of Common Law at Westminster or Dublin, or the Court of Session in Scotland, it shall appear to the court in which such action is pending, or, if such court is not sitting, to any judge of any of the said courts respectively, that it is proper to compel the personal attendance at any trial of any witness who may not be within the jurisdiction of the court in which such action is pending, it shall be lawful for such court or judge, if in his or their discretion it shall so seem fit, to order that a writ called a writ of subpoena *ad testificandum* or of subpoena *duces tecum* or warrant of citation shall issue in special form, commanding such witness to attend such trial, wherever he shall be within the United Kingdom, and the service of any such writ or process in any part of the United Kingdom shall be as valid and effectual to all intents and purposes as if same had been served within the jurisdiction of the Court from which it issues.

NOTE

[1] As amended by the Statute Law Revision Act 1892.

2. Every such writ shall have at foot thereof a statement or notice that the same is issued by the special order of the court or judge, as the case may be, and no such writ shall issue without such special order.

[1] **3.** In case any person so served shall not appear according to the exigency of such writ or process, it shall be lawful for the court out of which the same issued, upon proof made of the service thereof, and of such default, to the satisfaction of the said court, to transmit a certificate of such default under the seal of the same court, or under the hand of one of the judges or justices of the same, to any of Her Majesty's Superior Courts of Common Law at Westminster, in case such service was had in England, or in case such service was had in Scotland to the Court of Session at Edinburgh, or in case such service was had in Ireland, to any of Her Majesty's Superior Courts of Common Law at Dublin: and the court to which such certificate is so sent shall and may thereupon proceed against and punish the person so having made default in like manner as they might have done if such person had neglected or refused to appear in obedience to a writ of subpoena or other process issued out of such last-mentioned court.

NOTE

[1] As amended by the Statute Law Revision Act 1892.

4. None of the said courts shall in any case proceed against or punish any person for having made default by not appearing to give evidence in obedience to any writ of subpoena or other process issued under the powers given by this Act, unless it shall be made to appear to such court that a reasonable and sufficient sum of money to defray the expenses of coming and attending to give evidence, and of returning from giving such evidence, had been tendered to such person at the time when such writ of subpoena or process was served upon such person.

5. Nothing herein contained shall alter or affect the power of any of such courts to issue a commission for the examination of witnesses out of their jurisdiction, in any case in which, notwithstanding this Act, they shall think fit to issue such commission.

6. Nothing herein contained shall alter or affect the admissibility of any evidence at any trial where such evidence is now by law receivable, on the ground of any witness being beyond the jurisdiction of the court, but the admissibility of all such evidence shall be determined as if this Act had not passed.

[1] British Law Ascertainment Act 1859

(22 & 23 Vict. c. 63)

An Act to afford Facilities for the more certain Ascertainment of the Law Administered in one Part of Her Majesty's Dominions when pleaded in the Courts of another part thereof.

[13th August 1859]

NOTE

[1] Scottish procedure by petition saved by the Administration of Justice (Scotland) Act 1933, s. 6 (3) (*f*).

Courts in one part of Her Majesty's dominions may remit a case for the opinion in law of a court in any other part thereof

1. If in any action depending in any court within Her Majesty's dominions it shall be the opinion of such court that it is necessary or expedient, for the proper disposal of such action, to ascertain the law applicable to the facts of the case as administered in any other part of Her Majesty's dominions on any point on which the law of such other part of Her Majesty's dominions is different from that in which the court is situate, it shall be competent to the court in which such action may depend to direct a case to be prepared setting forth the facts, as these may be ascertained by verdict of a jury or other mode competent, or may be agreed upon by the parties, or settled by such person or persons as may have been appointed by the court for that purpose in the event of the parties not agreeing; and upon such case being approved of by such court or a judge thereof, they shall settle the questions of law arising out of the same on which they desire to have the opinion of another court, and shall pronounce an order remitting the same, together with the case, to the court in such other part of Her Majesty's dominions, being one of the superior courts thereof, whose opinion is desired upon the law administered by them as applicable to the facts set forth in such case, and desiring them to pronounce their opinion on the questions submitted to them in the terms of the Act; and it shall be competent to any of the parties to the action to present a petition to the court whose opinion is to be obtained, praying such last-mentioned court to hear parties or their counsel, and to pronounce their opinion thereon in terms of this Act, or to pronounce their opinion without hearing parties or counsel; and the court to which such petition shall be presented shall, if they think fit, appoint an early day for hearing parties or their counsel on such case, and shall thereafter pronounce their opinion upon the questions of law as administered by them which are submitted to them by the court; and in order to their pronouncing such opinion they shall be entitled to take such further procedure thereupon as to them shall seem proper.

Opinion to be authenticated and certified copy given

2. Upon such opinion being pronounced, a copy thereof, certified by an officer of such court, shall be given to each of the parties to the action by whom the same shall be required, and shall be deemed and held to contain a correct record of such opinion.

Opinion to be applied by the Court making the remit

3. It shall be competent to any of the parties to the action, after having obtained such certified copy of such opinion, to lodge the same with an officer of the court in which the action may be depending, who may have the official charge thereof, together with a notice of motion, setting forth that the party will, on a certain day named in such notice, move the court to apply the opinion contained in such certified copy thereof to the facts set forth in the case hereinbefore specified, and the said court shall thereupon apply such opinion to such facts, in the same manner as if the same had been pronounced by such court itself upon a case reserved for opinion of the court, or upon special verdict of a jury; or the said last-mentioned court shall, if it think fit, when the said opinion has been obtained before trial, order such opinion to be submitted to the jury with the other facts of the case as evidence, or conclusive evidence as the court may think fit, of the foreign law therein stated, and the said opinion shall be so submitted to the jury.

Her Majesty in Council or House of Lords on appeal may adopt or reject opinion

4. In the event of an appeal to Her Majesty in Council or to the House of Lords in any such action, it shall be competent to bring under the review of Her Majesty in Council or of the House of Lords the opinion pronounced as aforesaid by any courts whose judgments are reviewable by Her Majesty in Council or by the House of Lords, and Her Majesty in Council or that House may respectively adopt or reject such opinion of any court whose judgments are respectively reviewable by them, as the same shall appear to them to be well founded or not in law.

Interpretation of terms

[1] **5.** In the construction of this Act, the word "action" shall include every judicial proceeding instituted in any court, civil, criminal, or ecclesiastical; and the words "superior courts" shall include, in England, the Superior Courts of Law at the Royal Courts of Justice, the Lord Chancellor, the Lords Justices, the Master of the Rolls or any Vice-Chancellor, the Judge of the Court of Admiralty, the Judge Ordinary of the Court for Divorce and Matrimonial Causes, and the Judge of the Court of Probate; in Scotland, the High Court of Justiciary, and the Court of Session acting by either of its Divisions; in Ireland, the Superior Courts of Law at Belfast, the Master of the Rolls, and the Judge of the Admiralty Court; and in any other part of Her Majesty's dominions, the Superior Courts of Law or Equity therein.

NOTE

[1] As amended by the Supreme Court of Judicature (Consolidation) Act 1925, s.224(1) and S.R. & O. 1921 No. 1804: see the Supreme Court of Judicature Act (Consolidation) Act 1925, ss.18, 20–22 and 56(3) and the Judicature (Northern Ireland) Act 1978.

[THE NEXT PAGE IS B 19]

Appellate Jurisdiction Act 1876

(39 & 40 Vict. c. 59)

An Act for amending the Law in respect of the Appellate Jurisdiction of the House of Lords; and for other purposes.

[11th August 1876]

Preliminary

Short title

1. This Act may be cited for all purposes as the Appellate Jurisdiction Act 1876.

2. [Repealed by the Statute Law Revision Act 1894.]

Appeal

Cases in which appeal lies to House of Lords

[1] **3.** Subject as in this Act mentioned an appeal shall lie to the House of Lords from any order or judgment of any of the courts following; that is to say,

(1) Of Her Majesty's Court of Appeal in England; and

(2) Of any Court in Scotland from which error or an appeal at or immediately before the commencement of this Act lay to the House of Lords by common law or by statute; and

(3) [Repealed by the Northern Ireland Act 1962, Sched. 4.]

NOTE

[1] Excluded by the Foreign Compensation Act 1969, s. 3(8).

[THE NEXT PAGE IS B 20/1]

Form of appeal to House of Lords

4. Every appeal shall be brought by way of petition to the House of Lords, praying that the matter of the order or judgment appealed against may be reviewed before Her Majesty the Queen in her Court of Parliament, in order that the said Court may determine what of right, and according to the law and custom of this realm ought to be done in the subject-matter of such appeal.

Attendance of certain number of Lords of Appeal required at hearing and determination of appeals

5. An appeal shall not be heard and determined by the House of Lords unless there are present at such hearing and determination not less than three of the following persons, in this Act designated Lords of Appeal; that is to say,

(1) the Lord Chancellor of Great Britain for the time being; and

(2) the Lords of Appeal in Ordinary to be appointed as in this Act mentioned; and

(3) such Peers of Parliament as are for the time being holding or have held any of the offices in this Act described as high judicial offices.

Appointment of Lords of Appeal in Ordinary by Her Majesty

[1] **6.** For the purpose of aiding the House of Lords in the hearing and determination of appeals, Her Majesty may by letters patent appoint qualified persons to be Lords of Appeal in Ordinary.

A person shall not be qualified to be appointed by Her Majesty a Lord of Appeal in Ordinary unless he has been at or before the time of his appointment the holder for a period of not less than two years of some one or more of the offices in this Act described as high judicial offices, or has been at or before such time as aforesaid, for not less than 15 years,

(*a*) a person who has a Supreme Court qualification, within the meaning of section 71 of the Courts and Legal Services Act 1991;

(*b*) an advocate in Scotland, or a solicitor entitled to appear in the Court of Session and the High Court of Justiciary; or

(*c*) a practising member of the Bar of Northern Ireland.

Every Lord of Appeal in Ordinary shall hold his office during good behaviour but he may be removed from such office on the address of both Houses of Parliament.

Every Lord of Appeal in Ordinary, unless he is otherwise entitled to sit as a member of the House of Lords, shall by virtue and according to the date of his appointment be entitled during his life to rank as a Baron by such style as Her Majesty may be pleased to appoint, and shall be entitled to a writ of summons to attend, and to sit and vote in the House of Lords; his dignity as a Lord of Parliament shall not descend to his heirs.

On any Lord of Appeal in Ordinary vacating his office, by death, resignation or otherwise, Her Majesty may fill up the vacancy by the appointment of another qualified person.

A Lord of Appeal in Ordinary shall, if a Privy Councillor, be a member of the Judicial Committee of the Privy Council, and, subject to the due performance by a Lord of Appeal in Ordinary of his duties as to the hearing and determining of appeals in the House of Lords, it shall be his duty, being a Privy Councillor, to sit and act as a member of the Judicial Committee of the Privy Council.

NOTE

[1] As amended by the Statute Law Revision Act 1894; the Administration of Justice Act 1968, Sched.; the Judges' Remuneration Act 1965, Sched. 3; the Statute Law (Repeals) Act 1973, Sched., and the Courts and Legal Services Act 1990, Sched. 10, para. 1.

Supplemental Provisions

7. [Repealed by the Administration of Justice Act 1973, Sched. 4.]

Hearing and determination of appeals during prorogation of Parliament

[1] **8.** For preventing delay in the administration of justice, the House of

[THE NEXT PAGE IS B 21]

Lords may sit and act for the purpose of hearing and determining appeals, and also for the purpose of Lords of Appeal in Ordinary taking their seats and the oaths, during any prorogation of Parliament, at such time and in such manner as may be appointed by order of the House of Lords made during the preceding session of Parliament; and all orders and proceedings of the said House in relation to appeals and matters connected therewith during such prorogation, shall be as valid as if Parliament had been then sitting, but no business other than the hearing and determination of appeals and the matters connected therewith, and Lords of Appeal in Ordinary taking their seats and the oaths as aforesaid, shall be transacted by such House during such prorogation.

NOTE
[1] As amended by the Appellate Jurisdiction Act 1887, s. 1.

Hearing and determination of appeals during dissolution of Parliament

9. If on the occasion of a dissolution of Parliament Her Majesty is graciously pleased to think that it would be expedient, with a view to prevent delay in the administration of justice, to provide for the hearing and determination of appeals during such dissolution, it shall be lawful for Her Majesty, by writing under her Sign Manual, to authorise the Lords of Appeal in the name of the House of Lords to hear and determine appeals during the dissolution of Parliament, and for that purpose to sit in the House of Lords at such times as may be thought expedient; and upon such authority as aforesaid being given by Her Majesty, the Lords of Appeal may, during such dissolution, hear and determine appeals and act in all matters in relation thereto in the same manner in all respects as if their sittings were a continuation of the sittings of the House of Lords, and may in the name of the House of Lords exercise the jurisdiction of the House of Lords accordingly.

10. [Repealed by the Administration of Justice Act 1960, Sched. 4.]

Procedure under Act to supersede all other procedure

[1] **11.** An appeal shall not lie from any of the courts from which an appeal to the House of Lords is given by this Act, except in manner provided by this Act, and subject to such conditions as to the value of the subject-matter in dispute, and as to giving security for costs, and as to the time within which the appeal shall be brought, and generally as to all matters of practice and procedure, or otherwise, as may be imposed by orders of the House of Lords.

NOTE
[1] As amended by the Statute Law Revision Act 1894 and the Northern Ireland Act 1962, s. 1(5).

Certain cases excluded from appeal

[1] **12.** Except in so far as may be authorised by orders of the House of Lords an appeal shall not lie to the House of Lords from any court in Scotland in any case, which according to the law or practice hitherto in use, could not have been reviewed by that House, either in error or on appeal.

NOTE
[1] As amended by the Northern Ireland Act 1962, Sched. 4.

13. [Repealed by the Statute Law Revision Act 1883.]

14. [Repealed by the Statute Law Revision Act 1894 (c. 56); the Ecclesiastical Jurisdiction Measure 1963 (C.A.M. No. 1), Sched. 5; the Judges Remuneration Act 1965 (c. 61), Sched. 3; and the Administration of Justice Act 1968 (c. 5), Sched.]

15.–20. [Repealed by the Supreme Court of Judicature (Consolidation) Act 1925 (c. 49), Sched. 6.]

21. [Repealed by the Statute Law Revision Act 1883 (c. 39).]

22. [Repealed by the Administration of Justice Act 1925 (c. 28), Sched. 5.]

23. [Repealed by the Statute Law (Repeals) Act 1989 (c. 43), Sched. 1, Pt. VI.]

Repeal and Definitions

24. [Repealed by the Statute Law Revision Act 1883.]

Definitions

[1] **25.** In this Act, if not inconsistent with the context, the following expressions have the meaning hereinafter respectively assigned to them; that is to say,

"High judicial office" means any of the following offices: that is to say,

the office of Lord Chancellor of Great Britain, or of Judge of one of Her Majesty's superior courts of Great Britain and Ireland:

"Superior courts of Great Britain and Ireland" means and includes,—

As to England, Her Majesty's High Court of Justice and Her Majesty's Court of Appeal; and

As to Ireland, the superior courts of law and equity at Belfast; and

As to Scotland, the Court of Session.

NOTE

[1] As amended by the Statute Law Revision Act 1894, S.R. & O. 1921 No. 1804, the Administration of Justice Act 1965, Sched. 2 and the Justices of the Peace Act 1968, Sched. 5. See the Appellate Jurisdiction Act 1887, s.5.

[1] Bankers' Books Evidence Act 1879

(42 & 43 Vict. c. 11)

An Act to amend the law of evidence with respect to bankers' books.

[23rd May 1879]

NOTE

[1] Extended by the Companies Act 1948, s.432. See the Isle of Man Act 1979, s.12(3).

Short Title

1. This Act may be cited as the Bankers' Books Evidence Act 1879.

2. [Repealed by the Statute Law Revision Act 1894.]

Mode of proof of entries in bankers' books

[1] **3.** Subject to the provisions of this Act, a copy of any entry in a banker's book shall in all legal proceedings be received as *prima facie* evidence of such entry, and of the matters, transactions, and accounts therein recorded.

NOTE

[1] Disapplied by the Civil Evidence (Scotland) Act 1988, s.6(3).

Proof that book is a banker's book

[1] **4.** A copy of an entry in a banker's book shall not be received in evidence under this Act unless it be first proved that the book was at the time of the making of the entry one of the ordinary books of the bank, and that the entry was made in the usual and ordinary course of business, and that the book is in the custody or control of the bank.

Such proof may be given by a partner or officer of the bank, and may be given orally or by an affidavit sworn before any commissioner or person authorised to take affidavits.

NOTE

[1] Disapplied by the Civil Evidence (Scotland) Act 1988, s.6(3).

Verification of copy

[1] **5.** A copy of an entry in a banker's book shall not be received in evidence under this Act unless it be further proved that the copy has been examined with the original entry and is correct.

Such proof shall be given by some person who has examined the copy with the original entry, and may be given either orally or by an affidavit sworn before any commissioner or person authorised to take affidavits.

NOTE

[1] Disapplied by the Civil Evidence (Scotland) Act 1988, s.6(3).

Case in which banker, etc., not compellable to produce book, etc.

[1] **6.** A banker or officer of a bank shall not, in any legal proceeding to which the bank is not a party, be compellable to produce any banker's book the contents of which can be proved under this Act or under the Civil Evidence (Scotland) Act 1988, or to appear as a witness to prove the matters, transactions, and accounts therein recorded, unless by order of a judge made for special cause.

NOTE

[1] As amended by the Civil Evidence (Scotland) Act 1988, s.7(3).

Court or judge may order inspection

7. On the application of any party to a legal proceeding a court or judge may order that such party be at liberty to inspect and take copies of any entries in a banker's book for any of the purposes of such proceedings. An order under this section may be made either with or without summoning the bank or any other party, and shall be served on the bank three clear days before the same is to be obeyed, unless the court or judge otherwise directs.

Costs

8. The costs of any application to a court or judge under or for the purposes of this Act, and the costs of anything done or to be done under an order of a court or judge made under or for the purposes of this Act shall be in the discretion of the court or judge, who may order the same or any part thereof to be paid to any party by the bank, where the same have been occasioned by any default or delay on the part of the bank. Any such order against a bank may be enforced as if the bank was a party to the proceeding.

Interpretation of "bank", "banker" and "bankers' books"

[1] **9.**—(1) In this Act the expressions "bank" and "banker" mean—

[2] (*a*) an institution authorised under the Banking Act 1987 or a municipal bank within the meaning of that Act;

[3] (*aa*) a building society within the meaning of the Building Societies Act 1986;

(*b*) [Repealed by the Trustee Savings Banks Act 1985, Sched. 4.]

(*c*) the National Savings Bank; and

(*d*) the Post Office, in the exercise of its powers to provide banking services.

(2) Expressions in this Act relating to "bankers' books" include ledgers, day books, cash books, account books and other records used in the ordinary business of the bank, whether those records are in written form or are kept on microfilm, magnetic tape or any other form of mechanical or electronic data retrieval mechanism.

NOTES

[1] Substituted with savings for entries or transactions before 19th February 1982, by the Banking Act 1979, s.52(3) and Sched. 6, paras. 1 and 13.

[2] Substituted with savings for entries or transactions before 29th April 1988, by the Banking Act 1987, Sched. 6, para. 1.

[3] Inserted by the Building Societies Act 1986, Sched. 18, para. 1.

Interpretation of "legal proceeding", "court", "judge"

10. In this Act—

[1] The expression "legal proceeding" means any civil or criminal proceeding or inquiry in which evidence is or may be given, and includes an arbitration; and an application to, or an inquiry or other proceeding before, the Solicitors Disciplinary Tribunal or any body exercising functions in relation to solicitors in Scotland or Northern Ireland corresponding to the functions of that Tribunal.

The expression "the court" means the court, judge, arbitrator, persons, or person before whom a legal proceeding is held or taken;

The expression "a judge" means with respect to England a judge of the High Court of Justice, and with respect to Scotland a Lord Ordinary of the Outer House of the Court of Session, and with respect to Ireland a judge of the High Court in Ireland;

The judge of a county court may with respect to any action in such court exercise the powers of a judge under this act.

NOTE

[1] As amended by the Sclicitors Act 1974, s.86.

Computation of time

11. Sunday, Christmas Day, Good Friday, and any bank holiday shall be excluded from the computation of time under this Act.

[1] Citation Amendment (Scotland) Act 1882

(45 & 46 Vict. c. 77)

An Act to amend the law of citation in Scotland. [18th August 1882]

NOTE

[1] Applied: see the Licensing (Scotland) Act 1976, s.116.

Short title

1. This Act may be cited as the Citation Amendment (Scotland) Act 1882.

2. [Repealed by the Statute Law Revision Act 1898.]

Citation may be by registered letter

3. From and after the commencement of this Act—

In any civil action or proceeding in any court or before any person or body of persons having by law power to cite parties or witnesses, any summons or warrant of citation of a person, whether as a party or witness, or warrant of service or judicial intimation, may be executed in Scotland by an officer of the court from which such summons, warrant, or judicial intimation was issued, or other officer who, according to the present law and practice, might lawfully execute the same, or by an enrolled law-agent,[1] by sending to the known residence or place of business of the person upon whom such summons, warrant, or judicial intimation is to be served, or to his last known address, if it continues to be his legal domicile or proper place of citation, or to the office of the keeper of edictal citations,[2] where the summons, warrant, or judicial intimation is required to be sent to that office, a registered letter by post [3] containing the copy of the summons or petition or other document required by law in the particular case to be served, with the proper citation or notice subjoined thereto, or containing such other citation or notice as may be required in the circumstances, and such posting shall constitute a legal and valid citation, unless the person cited shall prove that such letter was not left or tendered at his known residence or place of business, or at his last known address if it continues to be his legal domicile or proper place of citation.

NOTES

[1] The Execution of Diligence (Scotland) Act 1926, s. 4—" For the purposes of section 3 of the Citation Amendment (Scotland) Act 1882, the expression 'enrolled law agent' shall mean—

(*a*) in the case of a summons, warrant or judicial intimation issued from the Court of Session, a law agent whose name is on the roll of law agents practising before such court kept in pursuance of section 12 of the Law Agents (Scotland) Act 1873; and

(*b*) in the case of a summons, warrant or judicial intimation issued from the sheriff court, a law agent whose name is on the roll, kept in pursuance of section 13 of the said Act, of law agents practising in any sheriff court of the sheriffdom in which the summons, warrant or judicial intimation is to be executed ". See also the Solicitors (Scotland) Act 1980, ss. 20 and 65.

[2] Functions of keeper of edictal citations now exercisable by clerks and officers of Court of Session: see S.R. & O. 1929 No. 588 and the Public Records (Scotland) Act 1937, s. 13 (1).

[3] Recorded delivery service now an alternative to registered post. See the Recorded Delivery Service Act 1962, s. 1.

Execution. Notice on back of letter. Letter not delivered to be returned to clerk of court

4. The following provisions shall apply to service by registered letter [1]:—

(1) The citation or notice subjoined to the copy or other citation or notice required in the circumstances shall specify the date of posting, and in cases where the party is not cited to a fixed diet, but to appear or lodge answers or other pleadings within a certain period, shall also state that the induciae or period for appearance or lodging answers or other pleadings is reckoned from that date:

(2) The induciae or period of notice shall be reckoned from twenty-four hours after the time of posting:

(3) The execution to be returned by the officer or law-agent shall be accompanied by the post office receipt for the registered letter. The execution returned by a law-agent shall for all purposes be equivalent to an execution by an officer of court. The execution may be in the form contained in the First Schedule hereto:

(4) On the back of such registered letter besides the address there shall be written or printed the following notice or a notice to the like effect:

This letter contains a citation to or intimation from [*specify the court*]. If delivery of the letter cannot be made, it is to be returned immediately to [*give the official name and office or place of business of the clerk of court*]:

If delivery of the letter be not made because the address cannot be found, or because the house or place of business at the address is shut up, or because the letter carrier is informed at the address that the person to whom the letter is addressed is not known there, or because the letter was refused, or because the address is not within a postal delivery district and the letter is not called for within twenty-four hours after its receipt at the post office of the place to which it is addressed, or for any other reason, the letter shall be immediately returned through the post office to the clerk of court, with the reason for the failure to deliver marked thereon, and the clerk shall make intimation to the party at whose instance the summons, warrant, or intimation was issued or obtained, and shall, where the order for service was made by a judge or magistrate, present the letter to a judge or magistrate of the court from which the summons, warrant, or intimation was issued, and he may, if he shall think fit, order service of new, either according to the present law and practice or in the manner herinbefore provided, and if need be substitute a new diet of appearance. Where the judge or magistrate is satisfied that the letter has been tendered at the proper address of the party or witness and refused, he may in the case of a witness, without waiting for the diet of appearance, issue second diligence to secure his attendance, and in the case of a party hold the tender equal to a good citation.

NOTE

[1] Recorded delivery service now an alternative to registered post. See the Recorded Delivery Service Act 1962, s. 1.

Fees

5. The fees for service under this Act shall be those contained in the Second Schedule hereto, and no other or higher fees shall be allowed on taxation.

Mode of service optional

6. It shall be lawful to execute summonses and warrants of citation, warrants of service, judicial intimations, either according to the existing law and practice or in the manner provided by this Act:

Provided that no higher fees shall be allowed on taxation than those contained in the Schedule hereto unless the judge or magistrate deciding the case shall be of opinion that it was not expedient in the interests of justice that such service should be made in the manner hereinbefore provided.

Definition

7. The word " person " shall include corporation, company, firm, or other body requiring to be cited or to receive intimation.

SCHEDULES

FIRST SCHEDULE

This summons or warrant of citation, or note of suspension, or petition, or other writ or citation executed [*or* intimated] by me [*insert name*] messenger at arms [*or* other officer or law agent] against [*or* to] [*insert name or names*] defender [*or* defenders, *or* respondent or respondents, *or* witness or witnesses, *or* haver or havers, *or otherwise as the case may be*], by posting on last, between the hours of and , at the post office of , a copy of the same to him [*or* them], with citation [*or* notice] subjoined, [*or* citation or notice where no copy is sent], in a registered letter [1] [*or* registered letters] addressed as follows, viz:

Signature of officer or agent.

NOTE

[1] Recorded delivery service now an alternative to registered post: see the Recorded Delivery Service Act 1962, s. 1.

SECOND SCHEDULE

Fees for Service or Citation by Registered Letter [1] for Returning Execution

[2] A. COURT OF SESSION

[3] B. INFERIOR COURTS

NOTES

[1] Recorded delivery service now an alternative to registered post: see the Recorded Delivery Service Act 1962, s. 1.

[2] Superseded. See Rules of Court, Chap. VII, I, 4.

[3] See S.I. 1971 No. 90 as amended by S.I. 1973 No. 461, S.I. 1975 No. 1148, S.I. 1976 No. 1119, S.I. 1978 Nos. 948 and 1167 and S.I. 1979 No. 1633.

Appellate Jurisdiction Act 1887

(50 & 51 Vict. c. 70)

An Act to amend the Appellate Jurisdiction Act 1876.

[16th September 1887]

Lord of Appeal may take his seat during prorogation

[1] **1.** Notwithstanding anything in the eighth section of the said Act contained, every Lord of Appeal shall be empowered to take his seat and the oaths at any such sitting of the House of Lords during prorogation.

NOTE

[1] " The said Act " means the Appellate Jurisdiction Act 1876; " any such sitting " means any sitting for hearing and determining appeals.

2. [Repealed by the Statute Law (Repeals) Act 1977.]

Amendment of 3 & 4 Will. 4. c. 41. 1833 c. 41

3. The Judicial Committee of the Privy Council as formed under the provisions of the first section of the Judicial Committee Act 1833 shall include such members of Her Majesty's Privy Council as are for the time being holding or have held any of the offices in the Appellate Jurisdiction Act 1876 and this Act, described as high judicial offices.

4. [Repealed by the Appellate Jurisdiction Act 1929, s. 1 (7).]

Amendment of 39 & 40 Vict. c. 59. s. 25

5. The expression " high judicial office " as defined in section 25 of the Appellate Jurisdiction Act 1876 shall be deemed to include the office of a Lord of Appeal in Ordinary and the office of a member of the Judicial Committee of the Privy Council.

Short title

6. This Act may be cited as the Appellate Jurisdiction Act 1887.

Foreign Jurisdiction Act 1890

(53 & 54 Vict. c. 37)

An Act to consolidate the Foreign Jurisdiction Acts.

[4th August 1890]

Whereas by treaty, capitulation, grant, usage, sufferance, and other lawful means, Her Majesty the Queen has jurisdiction within divers foreign countries, and it is expedient to consolidate the Acts relating to the exercise of Her Majesty's jurisdiction out of her dominions:

Exercise of jurisdiction in foreign country

1. It is and shall be lawful for Her Majesty the Queen to hold, exercise, and enjoy any jurisdiction which Her Majesty now has or may at any time hereafter have within a foreign country in the same and as ample a manner as if Her Majesty had acquired that jurisdiction by the cession or conquest of territory.

Exercise of jurisdiction over British subjects in countries without regular governments

2. Where a foreign country is not subject to any government from whom Her Majesty the Queen might obtain jurisdiction in the manner recited by this Act, Her Majesty shall by virtue of this Act have jurisdiction over Her Majesty's subjects for the time being resident in or resorting to that country, and that jurisdiction shall be jurisdiction of Her Majesty in a foreign country within the meaning of the other provisions of this Act.

Validity of acts done in pursuance of jurisdiction

3. Every act and thing done in pursuance of any jurisdiction of Her Majesty in a foreign country shall be as valid as if it had been done according to the local law then in force in that country.

Evidence as to existence or extent of jurisdiction in foreign country

4. If in any proceeding, civil or criminal, in a court in Her Majesty's dominions or held under the authority of Her Majesty any question arises as to the existence or extent of any jurisdiction of Her Majesty in a foreign country, a Secretary of State shall, on the application of the court, send to the court within a reasonable time his decision on the question, and his decision shall for the purposes of the proceeding be final.

(2) The court shall send to the Secretary of State, in a document under the seal of the court, or signed by a judge of the court, questions framed so as properly to raise the question, and sufficient answers to those questions shall be returned by the Secretary of State to the court, and those answers shall, on production thereof, be conclusive evidence of the matters therein contained.

Power to extend enactments in first schedule

5.—(1) It shall be lawful for Her Majesty the Queen in Council, if she thinks fit, by Order to direct that all or any of the enactments described in the first schedule to this Act, or any enactments for the time being in force amending or substituted for the same, shall extend, with or without any exceptions, adaptations, or modifications in the Order mentioned, to any foreign country in which for the time being Her Majesty has jurisdiction.

(2) Thereupon those enactments shall, to the extent of that jurisdiction, operate as if that country were a British possession, and as if Her Majesty in Council were the Legislature of that possession.

Power to send persons charged with offences for trial to a British possession

6.—(1) Where a person is charged with an offence cognisable by a British court in a foreign country, any person having authority derived from Her Majesty in that behalf may, by warrant, cause the person so charged to be sent for trial to any British possession for the time being appointed in that behalf by Order in Council, and upon the arrival of the person so charged in that British possession, such criminal court of that possession as is authorised in that behalf by Order in Council, or if no court is so authorised, the supreme criminal court of that possession, may cause him to be kept in safe and proper custody, and so soon as conveniently may be may inquire of, try, and determine the offence, and on conviction punish the offender according to the laws in force in that behalf within that possession in the same manner as if the offence had been committed within the jurisdiction of that criminal court.

Provided that—

(*a*) A person so charged may, before being so sent for trial, tender for examination to a British court in the foreign country where the offence is alleged to have been committed any competent witness whose evidence he deems material for his defence and whom he alleges himself unable to produce at the trial in the British possession:

(*b*) In such case the British court in the foreign country shall proceed in the examination and cross-examination of the witness as though he had been tendered at a trial before that court, and shall cause the evidence so taken to be reduced into writing, and shall transmit to the criminal court of the British possession by which the person charged is to be tried a copy of the evidence, certified as correct under the seal of the court before which the evidence was taken, or the signature of a judge of that court:

(*c*) Thereupon the court of the British possession before which the trial takes place shall allow so much of the evidence so taken as would have been admissible according to the law and practice of that court, had the witness been produced and examined at the trial, to be read and received as legal evidence at the trial:

(*d*) The court of the British possession shall admit and give effect to the law by which the alleged offender would have been tried by the British court in the foreign country in which his offence is alleged to have been committed, so far as that law relates to the criminality of the act alleged to have been committed, or the nature or degree of the offence, or the punishment thereof, if the law differs in those respects from the law in force in that British possession.

(2) Nothing in this section shall alter or repeal any law, statute, or usage by virtue of which any offence committed out of Her Majesty's dominions may, irrespectively of this Act, be inquired of, tried, determined, and punished within Her Majesty's dominions, or any part thereof.

Provision as to place of punishment of persons convicted

7. Where an offender convicted before a British court in a foreign country has been sentenced by that court to suffer death, penal servitude, imprisonment, or any other punishment, the sentence shall be carried into effect in such place as may be directed by Order in Council or be determined in accordance with directions given by Order in Council, and the conviction and sentence shall be of the same force in the place in which the sentence is so carried into effect as if the conviction had been made and the sentence passed by a competent court in that place.

Validity of acts done under Order in Council

8. Where, by Order in Council made in pursuance of this Act, any British court in a foreign country is authorised to order the removal or deportation of any person from that country, that removal or deportation, and any detention for the purposes thereof, according to the provisions of the Order in Council, shall be as lawful as if the order of the court were to have effect wholly within that country.

Power to asssign jurisdiction to British courts in cases within Foreign Jurisdiction Act

9. It shall be lawful for Her Majesty the Queen in Council, by order, to assign to or confer on any court in any British possession, or held under the authority of Her Majesty, any jurisdiction, civil or criminal, original or appellate, which may lawfully by Order in Council be assigned to or conferred on any British court in any foreign country, and to make such provisions and regulations as to Her Majesty in Council seem meet respecting the exercise of the jurisdiction so assigned or conferred, and respecting the enforcement and execution of the judgments, decrees, orders, and sentences of any such court, and respecting appeals therefrom.

Power to amend Orders in Council

10. It shall be lawful for Her Majesty the Queen in Council to revoke or vary any Order in Council made in pursuance of this Act.

Laying before Parliament, and effect of Orders in Council

[1] **11.** Every Order in Council made in pursuance of this Act shall be laid before both Houses of Parliament.

NOTE

[1] As amended by the Statute Law (Repeals) Act 1986, Sched., Pt. XII.

In what case Orders in Council void for repugnancy

12.—(1) If any Order in Council made in pursuance of this Act as respects any foreign country is in any respect repugnant to the provisions of any Act of Parliament extending to Her Majesty's subjects in that country, or repugnant to any order or regulation, made under the authority of any such Act of Parliament, or having in that country the force and effect of any such Act, it shall be read subject to that Act, order, or regulation, and shall, to the extent of such repugnancy, but not otherwise, be void.

(2) An Order in Council made in pursuance of this Act shall not be, or be deemed to have been, void on the ground of repugnancy to the law of England unless it is repugnant to the provisions of some such Act of Parliament, order, or regulation as aforesaid.

Provisions for protection of persons acting under Foreign Jurisdiction Acts

13.—(1) An action, suit, prosecution, or proceeding against any person for any act done in pursuance or execution or intended execution of this Act, or of any enactment repealed by this Act, or of any Order in Council made under this Act, or of any such jurisdiction of Her Majesty as is mentioned in this Act, or in respect of any alleged neglect or default in the execution of this Act, or of any such enactment, Order in Council, or jurisdiction as aforesaid, shall not lie or be instituted—

(*a*) In any court within Her Majesty's dominions, unless it is commenced within six months next after the act, neglect, or default complained of, or in case of a continuance of injury or damage within six months next after the ceasing thereof, or where the cause of action arose out of Her Majesty's dominions within six months after the parties to the action, suit, prosecution, or proceeding have been within the jurisdiction of the court in which the same is instituted; nor (*b*) In any of Her Majesty's courts without Her Majesty's dominions, unless the cause of action arose within the jurisdiction of that court, and the action is commenced within six months next after the act, neglect, or default complained of, or, in case of a continuance of injury or damage, within six months next after the ceasing thereof.

(2) In any such action, suit, or proceeding, tender of amends before the same was commenced may be pleaded in lieu of or in addition to any other plea. If the action, suit, or proceeding was commenced after such tender, or is proceeded with after payment into court of any money in satisfaction of the plaintiff's claim, and the plaintiff does not recover more than the sum tendered or paid, he shall not recover any costs incurred after such tender or payment, and the defendant shall be entitled to costs, to be taxed as between solicitor and client, as from the time of such tender or payment; but this provision shall not affect costs on any injunction in the action, suit, or proceeding.

14–15. [Repealed by the Statute Law (Repeals) Act 1973.]

Definitions

16. In this Act,—

The expression "foreign country" means any country or place out of Her Majesty's dominions:

The expression "British court in a foreign country" means any British court having jurisdiction out of Her Majesty's dominions in pursuance of an Order in Council whether made under any Act or otherwise:

The expression "jurisdiction" includes power.

17. [Repealed by the Statute Law (Repeals) Act 1973.]

18. [Repealed by the Statute Law (Repeals) Act 1986, Sched., Pt. IX.]

Short Title

[1] **19.**—(1) This Act may be cited as the Foreign Jurisdiction Act 1890.

NOTE

[1] As amended by the Statute Law Revision Act 1908.

---

[1] FIRST SCHEDULE

. . . .

NOTE

[1] Sched. 1 enumerates the Acts which may be extended by Order in Council under s. 5.

Supreme Court of Judicature Act 1891

(54 & 55 Vict. c. 53)

An Act to amend the Supreme Court of Judicature Acts.

[5th August 1891]

1, 2. [Repealed by the Supreme Court of Judicature (Consolidation) Act 1925, Sched. 6.]

Assessors in House of Lords

3. For the purpose of aiding the House of Lords in the hearing and determination of appeals in Admiralty actions, the House may, in any such appeal in which it may think it expedient to do so, call in the aid of one or more assessors specially qualified, and hear such appeal wholly or partially with the assistance of such assessors.

This section shall be carried into effect in pursuance of Orders made by the House of Lords.

4. [Repealed by the Supreme Court of Judicature (Consolidation) Act 1925, Sched. 6.]

Short titles and construction

[1] **5.** This Act may be cited as the Supreme Court of Judicature Act 1891.

NOTE

[1] As amended by the Supreme Court Act 1981, Sched. 7.

[1] Arbitration (Scotland) Act 1894

(57 & 58 Vict. c. 13)

An Act to amend the law of arbitration in Scotland.

[3rd July 1894]

NOTE

[1] Excluded by the Agricultural Holdings (Scotland) Act 1949, s. 75(1).

Reference to arbiter not named, etc., not to be invalid

[1] **1.** An agreement to refer to arbitration shall not be invalid or ineffectual by reason of the reference being to a person not named, or to a person to be named by another person, or to a person merely described as the holder for the time being of any office or appointment.

NOTE

[1] As amended by the Statute Law Revision Act 1908.

On failure to concur in nomination of single arbiter, court may appoint

2. Should one of the parties to an agreement to refer to a single arbiter refuse to concur in the nomination of such arbiter, and should no provision have been made for carrying out the reference in that event, or should such provision have failed, an arbiter may be appointed by the court, on the application of any party to the agreement, and the arbiter so appointed shall have the same powers as if he had been duly nominated by all the parties.

On failure of one party to nominate arbiter, court may appoint

3. Should one of the parties to an agreement to refer to two arbiters refuse to name an arbiter, in terms of the agreement, and should no provision have been made for carrying out the reference in that event, or should such provision have failed, an arbiter may be appointed by the court, on the application of the other party, and the arbiter so appointed shall have the same powers as if he had been duly nominated by the party so refusing.

Arbiters may devolve on oversmen unless otherwise agreed

[1] **4.** Unless the agreement to refer shall otherwise provide, arbiters shall have power to name an oversman on whom the reference shall be devolved in the event of their differing in opinion. Should the arbiters fail to agree in the nomination of an oversman, the court may on the application of any party to the agreement appoint an oversman. The decision of such oversman, whether he has been named by the arbiters or appointed by the court, shall be final.

NOTE

[1] As excluded by the Plant Varieties and Seeds Act 1964, s. 10.

Act not to apply to certain agreements

5. This Act shall not apply to any agreement, made before its passing, to refer to an arbiter not named or to be named by another person or merely described as the holder for the time being of an office or appointment, if any party to such agreement shall, before the passing of this Act, or within six months thereafter, have intimated to the other party by writing that he declines to be bound by such agreement.

Interpretation

[1] **6.** For the purposes of this Act the expression " the court " shall mean any sheriff having jurisdiction or any Lord Ordinary of the Court of Session: except that where—

(*a*) any arbiter appointed is; or

(*b*) in terms of the agreement to refer to arbitration an arbiter or oversman to be appointed must be,

a Senator of the College of Justice, " the court " shall mean the Inner House of the Court of Session.

NOTE

[1] As amended by the Law Reform (Miscellaneous Provisions) (Scotland) Act 1980, s. 17.

Extent of Act and short title

7. This Act shall apply to Scotland only, and may be cited as the Arbitration (Scotland) Act 1894.

[1] Nautical Assessors (Scotland) Act 1894

(57 & 58 Vict. c. 40)

An Act to provide for the attendance of assessors at the trial and hearing of maritime causes in the [Court of Session] and sheriff courts in Scotland, and in appeals to the House of Lords.

[17th August 1894]

NOTE

[1] Repealed in so far as inconsistent with Rules of Court by S.I. 1948 No. 1691 and S.I. 1965 No. 321: see Rules of Court 1965, rr. 37–46.

Short title

1. This Act may be cited as the Nautical Assessors (Scotland) Act 1894, and shall apply to Scotland only.

Appointment of assessors in Court of Session or Sheriff Court

2. In any action or proceeding in the Court of Session or in the sheriff court arising out of or relating to collision at sea, salvage, towage, or any other maritime matter, the court, if it thinks fit, may, and on the application of any party, shall, summon to its assistance at the trial, or at any subsequent hearing, whether on reclaiming note, appeal or otherwise, one or more persons of nautical skill and experience, who may be willing to sit with the court and act as assessor or assessors, but, where it is proposed to summon any person as an assessor, objection to him, either personally or in respect of his qualification, may be stated by any party to the action or proceeding, and shall be disposed of by the court.

Note to be made of questions submitted to assessors

3. The judge before whom any cause is tried with the assistance of an assessor or assessors summoned under the provisions of this Act, shall make a note of the questions submitted by him to such assessor or assessors, and of the answer or answers thereto.

List of assessors to be kept

[1] 4. The assessors shall be appointed from a list of persons approved for the purpose, as regards the Court of Session by the Lord President, and as regards the sheriff court by the sheriff [2] of the sheriffdom. Such lists shall be published as the Lord President, or the sheriff, as the case may be, shall direct, and shall be in force for three years only, but persons entered in any such list may be again approved in any subsequent list. It shall be lawful for the sheriff to defer the preparation of such a list until an application has been made to summon an assessor or assessors in an action depending in one of the courts of his sheriffdom.

NOTES

[1] For current List of Assessors, see *supra,* " Courts, Offices, etc."

[2] For the interpretation of the term " sheriff " see s. 7, *infra,* the Sheriff Courts (Scotland) Act 1971, s. 4, and the Interpretation Act 1978, Sched. 1.

Court of Session may frame Act of Sederunt

[1] 5. [The Court of Session may, by Act of Sederunt, prescribe such rules as it shall think fit with regard to the summoning and duties of assessors under this Act, and to their remuneration,] and such remuneration shall be treated as expenses in the action or proceeding, unless otherwise ordered by the court.

NOTE

[1] See the Administration of Justice (Scotland) Act 1933, Sched., which repeals the words in brackets.

Assessors in the House of Lords

6. For the hearing and determination of any appeal against a judgment of any Scottish court in any such action or proceeding as aforesaid, the House of Lords may, if it shall think it expedient to do so, call in the aid of one or more assessors specially qualified, and hear such appeal wholly or partially with the assistance of such assessor or assessors.

This section shall be carried into effect in pursuance of Orders made by the House of Lords.[1]

NOTE

[1] For these Orders see Division B, *supra.*

Definitions

[1] **7.** The expression "court" shall include the Lord Ordinary and either Division of the Court of Session, and the sheriff and sheriff substitute, but the expression "sheriff" shall not include sheriff substitute.

NOTE

[1] For the interpretation of the terms "sheriff" and "sheriff substitute" see the Sheriff Courts (Scotland) Act 1971, s.4(2) and the Interpretation Act 1978, Sched. 1.

[1] Evidence (Colonial Statutes) Act 1907

(7 Edw. 7, c. 16)

An Act to facilitate the admission in evidence of statutes passed by the legislatures of British possessions and protectorates including Cyprus. [21st August 1907]

NOTE

[1] See the Isle of Man Act 1979, s.12(1).

Proof of statutes of British possessions

[1] **1.**—(1) Copies of Acts, ordinances, and statutes passed (whether before or after the passing of this Act) by the Legislature of any British possession, and of orders, regulations, and other instruments issued or made, whether before or after the passing of this Act, under the authority of any such Act, ordinance, or statute, if purporting to be printed by the Government printer, shall be received in evidence by all courts of justice in the United Kingdom without any proof being given that the copies were so printed.

(2) If any person prints any copy or pretended copy of any such Act, ordinance, statute, order, regulation, or instrument which falsely purports to have been printed by the Government printer, or tenders in evidence any such copy or pretended copy which falsely purports to have been so printed, knowing that it was not so printed, he shall on conviction be liable to be sentenced to imprisonment for a period not exceeding twelve months.

(3) In this Act—

The expression "Government printer" means as respects any British possession, the printer purporting to be the printer authorised to print the Acts, ordinances, or statutes of the Legislature of that possession, or otherwise to be the Government printer of that possession:

The expression "British possession" means any part of His Majesty's dominions exclusive of the United Kingdom, and, where parts of those dominions are under both a central and a local Legislature, shall include both all parts under the central Legislature and each part under a local Legislature.

(4) Nothing in this Act shall affect the Colonial Laws Validity Act 1865.

(5) His Majesty may by Order in Council extend this Act to Cyprus and any British protectorate, and where so extended this Act shall apply as if Cyprus or the protectorate were a British possession, and with such other necessary adaptations as may be made by the Order.

NOTE

[1] As amended by S.R. & O. 1922 No. 183 and the Criminal Procedure (Scotland) Act 1975, s.221(2). Saved by the Civil Evidence (Scotland) Act 1988, s.10(3)(*c*).

Short title

2. This Act may be cited as the Evidence (Colonial Statutes) Act 1907.

Administration of Justice Act 1920

(10 & 11 Geo. 5, c. 81)

An Act to amend the law with respect to the Administration of Justice and to facilitate the Reciprocal Enforcement of Judgments and Awards in the United Kingdom and other parts of His Majesty's Dominions or Territories under His Majesty's protection. [23rd December 1920]

. . . .

[1] PART II—RECIPROCAL ENFORCEMENT OF JUDGMENTS IN THE UNITED KINGDOM AND IN OTHER PARTS OF HIS MAJESTY'S DOMINIONS

NOTE

[1] See the Foreign Judgments (Reciprocal Enforcement) Act 1933, s.7(1), and S.R. & O. 1933 No. 1073. Restricted by the Protection of Trading Interests Act 1980, s.5.

S.I. 1984 No. 129, as amended by S.I. 1985 No. 1994, consolidates the Orders in Council previously made extending Pt. II of the Act to the following territories, taking account of constitutional and nominal changes:

Anguilla
Antigua and Barbuda
Bahamas
Barbados
Belize
Bermuda
Botswana
British Indian Ocean Territory
British Virgin Islands
Cayman Islands
Christmas Island
Cocos (Keeling) Islands
Republic of Cyprus
Dominica
Falkland Islands
Fiji
The Gambia
Ghana
Gibraltar
Grenada
Guyana
Hong Kong
Jamaica
Kenya
Kiribati
Lesotho
Malawi
Malaysia
Malta
Mauritius
Montserrat
Newfoundland
New South Wales
New Zealand
Nigeria
Territory of Norfolk Island
Northern Territory of Australia
Papua New Guinea
Queensland
St. Christopher and Nevis
St. Helena
St. Lucia
St. Vincent and the Grenadines
Saskatchewan
Seychelles
Sierra Leone
Singapore
Solomon Islands
South Australia
Sovereign Base Areas of Akrotiri and Dhekelia in Cyprus
Sri Lanka
Swaziland
Tanzania
Tasmania
Trinidad and Tobago
Turks and Caicos Islands
Tuvalu
Uganda
Victoria
Western Australia
Zambia
Zimbabwe

See also the Civil Jurisdiction and Judgments Act 1982, s.18(7).

Enforcement in the United Kingdom of judgments obtained in superior courts in other British Dominions

[1] **9.**—(1) Where a judgment has been obtained in a superior court in any part of His Majesty's Dominions outside the United Kingdom to which this Part of this Act extends, the judgment creditor may apply to the High Court in England or Northern Ireland, or to the Court of Session in Scotland, at any time within twelve months after the date of the judgment, or such longer period as may be allowed by the court, to have the judgment registered in the court, and on any such application the court may, if in all the circumstances of the case they think it is just and convenient that the judgment should be enforced in the United Kingdom, and subject to the provisions of this section, order the judgment to be registered accordingly.

(2) No judgment shall be ordered to be registered under this section if—

(*a*) the original court acted without jurisdiction; or

(*b*) the judgment debtor, being a person who was neither carrying on business nor ordinarily resident within the jurisdiction of the original court, did not voluntarily appear or otherwise submit or agree to submit to the jurisdiction of that court; or

(*c*) the judgment debtor, being the defendant in the proceedings, was not duly served with the process of the original court and did not appear, notwithstanding that he was ordinarily resident or was carrying on business within the jurisdiction of that court or agreed to submit to the jurisdiction of that court; or

(*d*) the judgment was obtained by fraud; or

(*e*) the judgment debtor satisfies the registering court either that an appeal is pending, or that he is entitled and intends to appeal, against the judgment; or (*f*) the judgment was in respect of a cause of action which for reasons of public policy or for some other similar reason could not have been entertained by the registering court.

(3) Where a judgment is registered under this section—

(*a*) the judgment shall, as from the date of registration, be of the same force and effect, and proceedings may be taken thereon, as if it had been a judgment originally obtained or entered up on the date of registration in the registering court;

(*b*) the registering court shall have the same control and jurisdiction over the judgment as it has over similar judgments given by itself, but in so far only as relates to execution under this section;

(*c*) the reasonable costs of and incidental to the registration of the judgment (including the costs of obtaining a certified copy thereof from the original court and of the application for registration) shall be recoverable in like manner as if they were sums payable under the judgment.

[2] (4) Rules of court shall provide—

(*a*) service on the judgment debtor of notice of the registration of a judgment under this section; and

(*b*) enabling the registering court on an application by the judgment debtor to set aside the registration of a judgment under this section on such terms as the court thinks fit; and

(*c*) suspending the execution of a judgment registered under this section until the expiration of the period during which the judgment debtor may apply to have the registration set aside.

(5) In any action brought in any court in the United Kingdom on any judgment which might be ordered to be registered under this section, the plaintiff shall not be entitled to recover any costs of the action unless an application to register the judgment under this section has previously been refused, or unless the court otherwise orders.

NOTES

[1] As amended by S.R. & O. 1921 No. 1802.

[2] See Rules of Court, IV, 248 *et seq.*

Issue of certificates of judgments obtained in the United Kingdom

[1] **10.**—(1) Where—

(*a*) a judgment has been obtained in the High Court in England or Northern Ireland, or in the Court of Session in Scotland, against any person; and

(*b*) the judgment creditor wishes to secure the enforcement of the judgment in a part of Her Majesty's dominions outside the United Kingdom to which this Part of this Act extends,

the court shall, on an application made by the judgment creditor, issue to him a certified copy of the judgment.

(2) The reference in the preceding subsection to Her Majesty's dominions shall be construed as if that subsection had come into force in its present form at the commencement of this Act.

NOTE

[1] Substituted by the Civil Jurisdiction and Judgments Act 1982, s.35(2).

Power to make rules

11. Provision may be made by rules of court for regulating the practice and procedure (including scales of fees and evidence) in respect of proceedings of any kind under this Part of this Act.

Interpretation

12.—(1) In this Part of this Act, unless the context otherwise requires—

The expression "judgment" means any judgment or order given or made by a court in any civil proceedings, whether before or after the passing of this Act, whereby any sum of money is made payabie, and includes an award in proceedings on an arbitration if the award has, in pursuance of the law in force in the place where it was made, become enforceable in the same manner as a judgment given by a court in that place:

The expression "original court" in relation to any judgment means the court by which the judgment was given:

The expression "registering court" in relation to any judgment means the court by which the judgment was registered:

The expression "judgment creditor" means the person by whom the judgment was obtained, and includes the successors and assigns of that person:

The expression "judgment debtor" means the person against whom the judgment was given, and includes any person against whom the judgment is enforceable in the place where it was given.

(2) Subject to rules of court, any of the powers conferred by this Part of this Act on any court may be exercised by a judge of the court.

Power to apply Part II of Act to territories under His Majesty's protection

13. His Majesty may by Order in Council declare that this Part of this Act shall apply to any territory which is under His Majesty's protection, or in respect of which a mandate is being exercised by the Government of any part of His Majesty's dominions, as if that territory were part of His Majesty's dominions, and on the making of any such Order this Part of this Act shall, subject to the provisions of the Order, have effect accordingly.

Extent of Part II of Act

14.—(1) Where His Majesty is satisfied that reciprocal provisions have been made by the legislature of any part of His Majesty's dominions outside the United Kingdom for the enforcement within that part of His dominions of judgments obtained in the High Court in England, the Court of Session in Scotland, and the High Court in Ireland, His Majesty may by Order in Council declare that this Part of this Act shall extend to that part of His dominions, and on any such Order being made this Part of this Act shall extend accordingly.

(2) An Order in Council under this section may be varied or revoked by a subsequent Order.

[1] (3) Her Majesty may by Order in Council under this section consolidate any orders in Council under this section which are in force when the consolidating Order is made.

NOTE

[1] Added by the Civil Jurisdiction and Judgments Act 1982, s.35(3).

. . . . . .

PART III—MISCELLANEOUS

Short title, repeal, and application

21.—(1) This Act may be cited as the Administration of Justice Act 1920.

(2) [Repealed by the Statute Law Revision Act 1927.]

(3) This Act, except Part II thereof, applies only to England and Wales.

Execution of Diligence (Scotland) Act 1926

(16 & 17 Geo. 5, c. 16)

An Act to amend the law relating to the execution of diligence in Scotland. [8th July 1926]

Sheriff officer to have the powers of a messenger-at-arms in certain places

[1] **1.** In any sheriff court district in which there is no resident messenger-at-arms. or in any of the islands of Scotland, a sheriff officer duly authorised to practise in any part of the sheriffdom comprising such sheriff court district or island shall have all the powers of a messenger-at-arms in regard to the service of any summons, writ, citation or other proceeding, or to the execution of or diligence on, any decree, warrant or order.

NOTE

[1] As amended by the Debtors (Scotland) Act 1987, Sched. 6, para. 11.

Execution of arrestment or charge by registered letter in certain cases

[1] **2.**—(1) It shall be competent to execute by registered letter in accordance with the provisions hereinafter contained:—

(*a*) an arrestment proceeding on any warrant or decree of the sheriff in a summary cause, or

[2] (*b*) a charge upon a decree for payment of money, granted by the sheriff in a summary cause, if the place of execution is in any of the islands of Scotland or in any sheriff court district in which there is no resident sheriff officer, or is more than twelve miles distant from the seat of the court where such decree was granted.

(2) The following provisions shall apply to the execution by registered letter of an arrestment or charge in pursuance of the foregoing provisions of this section:—

(*a*) A registered letter containing the writ or other document to be served shall be sent by post to the known residence or place of business of the person in whose hands the arrestment is to be used (hereinafter referred to as the arrestee) or against whom the charge is to be executed (hereinafter referred to as the debtor) or to the last known address of such arrestee or debtor if it continues to be his legal domicile or proper place of citation:

(*b*) The registered letter may be sent by a sheriff officer who would be entitled to execute the arrestment or the charge according to the law and practice existing at the passing of this Act, or by a messenger-at-arms resident in the sheriffdom in which the place of execution is situated, or, if there is no sheriff officer or messenger-at-arms resident in the sheriffdom, by a law agent enrolled in such sheriffdom:

(*c*) On the back of the registered letter besides the address there shall be written or printed the following notice or a notice to the like effect:—"If delivery of this letter cannot be made, it is to be returned immediately to [give the name and address of law agent, messenger-at-arms, or sheriff officer concerned]":

(*d*) The execution to be returned shall be accompanied by the Post Office receipt for the registered letter:

(*e*) Delivery of a registered letter sent in accordance with the foregoing provisions shall constitute a valid arrestment in the hands of the arrestee, or a valid execution of the charge against the debtor as the case may be as at the time of such delivery, and where in any proceedings in which the validity of such arrestment or of such charge is in question there is produced an acknowledgment or certificate of the delivery of the registered letter issued by the Post Office in pursuance of any provision contained in a scheme made under section 28 of the Post Office Act 1969, the letter shall be presumed to have been delivered to the arrestee or to the debtor at the address and on the day specified in such acknowledgment or certificate, unless it shall be proved by the arrestee or the debtor or any person having an interest that the registered letter was never in fact delivered to or received by the arrestee or the debtor as the case may be, or any person with his authority, express or necessarily implied, or was so delivered on some other day:

(*f*) Where, in any proceedings in which the validity of any such arrestment or of such charge is in question, it is proved that the registered letter sent in pursuance of the foregoing provisions was duly tendered at the proper address of the arrestee or the debtor, but was refused by him or by some person with his authority, express or necessarily implied, the court may if it shall think fit hold such tender and refusal equivalent to delivery of the registered letter for the purposes of this section:

[3] (*g*) The provisions of rule 111 in Schedule 1 to the Sheriff Courts (Scotland) Act 1907 shall not apply to service of a schedule of arrestment in accordance with the foregoing provisions.

NOTES

[1] As amended by the Post Office Act 1969, Sched. 4, and the Sheriff Courts (Scotland) Act 1971, Sched. 1.

Recorded delivery service now an alternative to registered post. See the Recorded Delivery Service Act 1962, s.1.

[2] As amended by the Debtors (Scotland) Act 1987, Sched. 6, para. 12.

[3] As amended by S.I. 1992 No. 249 (effective 4th May 1992).

Authorisation by sheriff to do diligence in certain cases

3. Where an extract decree or warrant granted by any court in Scotland is presented to the sheriff within whose jurisdiction such decree or warrant requires to be executed, and the sheriff is satisfied that no messenger-at-arms or sheriff officer is reasonably available to execute such decree or warrant, the sheriff may, if he shall think fit, grant authority to any person whom he may deem suitable (but not including the law agent of the party presenting the extract decree or warrant) to execute such decree or warrant, and the person so authorised shall as regards any diligence or execution competent on such decree or warrant have all the powers of a messenger-at-arms or sheriff officer.

4. [See the Citation Amendment (Scotland) Act 1883, s.3, *supra*.]

Interpretation

[1] **5.** In this Act, unless the context otherwise requires, the expression "arrestment" shall include arrestment on the dependence, arrestment in security, and arrestment in execution, but shall not include arrestment to found jurisdiction; a [law agent[2]] shall be deemed to be enrolled in a sheriffdom if his name is on the roll, kept in pursuance of section 13 of the Law Agents (Scotland) Act 1873, of law agents practising in any of the sheriff courts in that sheriffdom.

NOTES

[1] As amended by the Sheriff Courts (Scotland) Act 1971, Scheds. 1 and 2.

[2] Now "solicitor": see the Solicitors (Scotland) Act 1980, s.65(2).

Regulations, forms and fees

6. The Court of Session may by Act of Sederunt make such regulations and prescribe such forms as may be necessary to give full effect to the provisions of this Act, and fix the fees payable to messengers-at-arms, sheriff officers or others in respect of anything done under this Act.

7. [Repealed by the Statute Law Revision Act 1950.]

Short title

8. This Act may be cited as the Execution of Diligence (Scotland) Act 1926.

Evidence (Foreign, Dominion and Colonial Documents) Act 1933

(23 & 24 Geo. 5, c. 4)

An Act to make further and better Provision with respect to the Admissibility in Evidence in the United Kingdom of entries contained in the Public Registers of other countries and with respect to the Proof by means of duly authenticated Official Certificates of entries in such Registers and in Consular Registers and of other matters. [29th March 1933]

Proof and effect of foreign, dominion and colonial registers and certain official certificates

[1] **1.**—(1) [Repealed by the Oaths and Evidence (Overseas Authorities and Countries) Act 1963, s. 5(2).]

[2] (2) An Order in Council made under section 5 of the Oaths and Evidence (Overseas Authorities and Countries) Act 1963 may provide that in all parts of the United Kingdom—

(*a*) a register of the country to which the Order relates, being such a register as is specified in the Order, shall be deemed to be a public register kept under the authority of the law of that country and recognised by the courts thereof as an authentic record, and to be a document of such a public nature as to be admissible as evidence of the matters regularly recorded therein;

(*b*) such matters as may be specified in the Order shall, if recorded in such a register, be deemed, until the contrary is proved, to be regularly recorded therein;

(*c*) subject to any conditions specified in the Order and to any requirements of rules of court a document purporting to be issued in the country to which the Order relates as an official copy of an entry in such a register as is so specified, and purporting to be authenticated as such in the manner specified in the Order as appropriate in the case of such a register, shall, without evidence as to the custody of the register or of inability to produce it and without any further or other proof, be received as evidence that the register contains such an entry;

(*d*) subject as aforesaid a certificate purporting to be given in the country to which the Order relates as an official certificate of any such class as is specified in the Order, and purporting to be signed by the officer, and to be authenticated in the manner, specified in the Order as appropriate in the case of a certificate of that class, shall be received as evidence of the facts stated in the certificate;

(*e*) no official document issued in the country to which the Order relates as proof of any matters for the proof of which provision is made by the Order shall, if otherwise admissible in evidence, be inadmissible by reason only that it is not authenticated by the process known as legalisation.

(3) Official books of record preserved in a central registry and containing entries copied from original registers may, if those entries were copied by officials in the course of their duty, themselves be treated for the purposes of this section as registers.

(4) In this section the expression "country" means a Dominion, the Isle of Man, any of the Channel Islands, a British colony or protectorate, a foreign country, a colony or protectorate of a foreign country, or any mandated territory:

Provided that where a part of a country is under both a local and a central legislature, an Order under this section may be made as well with respect to that part, as with respect to all the parts under that central legislature.

(5) [Repealed by the Oaths and Evidence (Overseas Authorities and Countries) Act 1963, s. 5(2).]

NOTES

[1] Saved by the Civil Evidence (Scotland) Act 1988, s.10(3)(*d*) and the Merchant Shipping (Liner Conferences) Act 1982, s.5(6). Oaths and Evidence (Overseas Authorities and Countries) Act 1963—"5.—(1) If Her Majesty in Council is satisfied as respects any country that—

(*a*) there exist in that country public registers kept under the authority of the law of that country and recognised by the courts of that country as authentic records, and

(*b*) that the registers are regularly and properly kept,

Her Majesty may by Order in Council make in respect of that country and all or any of those registers such provision as is specified in subsection (2) of section 1 of the Evidence (Foreign, Dominion and Colonial Documents) Act 1933.

(2) The foregoing subsection shall have effect in substitution for subsection (1) of the said section 1 . . . and subsection (4) of that section (interpretation of "country") shall apply for the interpretation of the foregoing subsection as it applies for the interpretation of the said

section 1; but any Order in Council made under the said section 1 and in force at the commencement of this Act shall continue in force until revoked, or as varied, by an Order in Council under this section."

The following Orders in Council have been made under the foregoing Acts:

	S.R. & O. or S.I.		S.R. & O. or S.I.
Aden	1965 No. 1527	Grenada	1966 No. 82
Australia (Commonwealth)	1938 No. 739	Guyana. *See* British Guiana, above.	
Antigua	1965 No. 312	Hong Kong	1962 No. 642
Bahamas	1961 No. 2041	Ireland (Republic)	1969 No. 1059
Barbados	1962 No. 641	Italy	1969 No. 145
Basutoland	1965 No. 1719	Jamaica	1962 No. 643
Bechuanaland	1965 No. 1720	Kenya	1965 No. 1712
Belgium	1933 No. 383	Lesotho. *See* Basutoland above.	
Belize. *See* British Honduras, below.		Luxembourg	1972 No. 116
Bermuda	1961 No. 2042	Mauritius	1961 No. 2048
Botswana. *See* Bechuanaland, above.		Montserrat	1962 No. 644
British Antarctic Territory	1962 No. 2605	Netherlands	1970 No. 284
British Guiana	1961 No. 2043	New Zealand	1959 No. 1306
British Honduras	1961 No. 2044	St. Helena	1961 No. 2049
British Indian Ocean Territory	1984 No. 857	St. Lucia	1965 No. 1721
Canada	1962 No. 2606	Sarawak	1961 No. 2050
Cayman Islands	1965 No. 313	Seychelles	1962 No. 2608
Denmark	1969 No. 144	Sierra Leone	1962 No. 2609
Dominica	1961 No. 2045	Swaziland	1965 No. 1865
Falkland Islands	1962 No. 2607	Tanganyika	1961 No. 2051
Fiji	1961 No. 2046	Tanzania. *See* Tanganyika, above and Zanzibar, below.	
France	1937 No. 515	Turks and Caicos Islands	1966 No. 83
Germany (Federal Republic)	1970 No. 819	Uganda	1961 No. 2052
Gibraltar	1961 No. 2047	U.S.A.	1969 No. 146
		Zanzibar	1961 No. 2053

[2] As amended by the Oaths and Evidence (Overseas Authorities and Countries) Act 1963, s. 5.

2. [Repealed by the British Nationality Act 1948, Sched. 4.]

Short title

3. This Act may be cited as the Evidence (Foreign, Dominion and Colonial Documents) Act 1933.

Foreign Judgments (Reciprocal Enforcement) Act 1933

(23 Geo. 5, c. 13)

An Act to make Provision for the Enforcement in the United Kingdom of Judgments given in Foreign Countries which accord reciprocal treatment to Judgments given in the United Kingdom, for facilitating the Enforcement in Foreign Countries of Judgments given in the United Kingdom, and for other purposes in connection with the matters aforesaid.

[13th April 1933]

[1] PART I.—REGISTRATION OF FOREIGN JUDGMENTS

NOTE

[1] Part I applied: see the Carriage of Goods by Road Act 1965, ss. 4, 11(2), the Merchant Shipping (Oil Pollution) Act 1971, s. 13(3), the Carriage by Railway Act 1972, s. 5(1)(3), the Merchant Shipping Act 1974, s. 6(4)(5), the Civil Aviation (Eurocontrol) Act 1983, s. 1 and the International Transport Conventions Act 1983, s. 6; extended by the Administration of

Justice Act 1956, s.51, the Nuclear Installations Act 1965, s.17(4) and the Carriage of Passengers by Road Act 1974, s.5; restricted by the Protection of Trading Interests Act 1980, s.5; saved by the Merchant Shipping (Liner Conferences) Act 1982, s.5(6). See also the Civil Jurisdiction and Judgments Act 1982, ss.18(7), 31(3) and 32(4).

Part I has been extended by Orders in Council to the following countries:

	S.R. & O. or S.I.
Australian Capital Territory	1955 No. 559
Austria	1962 No. 1339
Belgium	1936 No. 1169
Canada	1987 Nos. 468 and 2211, 1988 Nos. 1304 and 1853, 1989 No. 987 and 1991 No. 1724
France	1936 No. 609
Germany	1961 No. 1199
Guernsey	1973 No. 610
India	1958 No. 425
Isle of Man	1973 No. 611
Israel	1971 No. 1039
Italy	1973 No. 1894
Jersey	1973 No. 612
Netherlands	1969 No. 1062 1977 No. 2149
Norway	1962 No. 636
Pakistan	1958 No. 141
Surinam	1981 No. 735
Tonga	1980 No. 1523

See the Protection of Trading Interests Act 1980, s.5, for certain judgments which may not be registered under this Part.

Power to extend Part I of Act to foreign countries giving reciprocal treatment

[1] **1.**—[2] (1) If, in the case of any foreign country, Her Majesty is satisfied that, in the event of the benefits conferred by this Part of this Act being extended to, or to any particular class of, judgments given in the courts of that country or in any particular class of those courts, substantial reciprocity of treatment will be assured as regards the enforcement in that country of similar judgments given in similar courts of the United Kingdom, She may by Order in Council direct—

(*a*) that this Part of this Act shall extend to that country;

(*b*) that such courts of that country as are specified in the Order shall be recognised courts of that country for the purposes of this Part of this Act; and

(*c*) that judgments of any such recognised court, or such judgments of any class so specified, shall, if within subsection (2) of this section, be judgments to which this Part of this Act applies.

[2] (2) Subject to subsection (2A) of this section, a judgment of a recognised court is within this subsection if it satisfies the following conditions, namely—

(*a*) it is either final and conclusive as between the judgment debtor and the judgment creditor or requires the former to make an interim payment to the latter; and

(*b*) there is payable under it a sum of money, not being a sum payable in respect of taxes or other charges of a like nature or in respect of a fine or other penalty; and

(*c*) it is given after the coming into force of the Order in Council which made that court a recognised court.

[3] (2A) The following judgments of a recognised court are not within subsection (2) of this section—

(*a*) a judgment given by that court on appeal from a court which is not a recognised court;

[THE NEXT PAGE IS B 45]

(*b*) a judgment or other instrument which is regarded for the purposes of its enforcement as a judgment of that court but which was given or made in another country;

(*c*) a judgment given by that court in proceedings founded on a judgment of a court in another country and having as their object the enforcement of that judgment.

(3) For the purposes of this section, a judgment shall be deemed to be final and conclusive notwithstanding that an appeal may be pending against it, or that it may still be subject to appeal, in the courts of the country of the original court.

(4) His Majesty may by a subsequent Order in Council vary or revoke any Order previously made under this section.

[3] (5) Any Order in Council made under this section before its amendment by the Civil Jurisdiction and Judgments Act 1982 which deems any court of a foreign country to be a superior court of that country for the purposes of this Part of this Act shall (without prejudice to subsection (4) of this section) have effect from the time of that amendment as if it provided for that court to be a recognised court of that country for those purposes, and for any final and conclusive judgment of that court, if within subsection (2) of this section, to be a judgment to which this Part of this Act applies.

NOTES

[1] See S.I. 1987 No. 468, as amended by S.I. 1987 No. 2211, 1988 Nos. 1304 and 1853, and 1989 No. 987.

[2] Substituted by the Civil Jurisdiction and Judgments Act 1982, Sched. 10, para. 1.

[3] Inserted by the Civil Jurisdiction and Judgments Act 1982, Sched. 10, para. 1.

Application for, and effect of, registration of foreign judgment

[1] **2.**—(1) A person, being a judgment creditor under a judgment to which this Part of this Act applies, may apply to the High Court at any time within six years after the date of the judgment, or, where there have been proceedings by way of appeal against the judgment, after the date of the last judgment given in those proceedings, to have the judgment registered in the High Court, and on any such application the court shall, subject to proof of the prescribed matters and to the other provisions of this Act, order the judgment to be registered:

Provided that a judgment shall not be registered if at the date of the application—

(*a*) it has been wholly satisfied; or

(*b*) it could not be enforced by execution in the country of the original court.

(2) Subject to the provisions of this Act with respect to the setting aside of registration—

(*a*) a registered judgment shall, for the purposes of execution, be of the same force and effect; and

(*b*) proceedings may be taken on a registered judgment; and

(*c*) the sum for which a judgment is registered shall carry interest; and

(*d*) the registering court shall have the same control over the execution of a registered judgment;

as if the judgment had been a judgment originally given in the registering court and entered on the date of registration:

Provided that execution shall not issue on the judgment so long as, under this Part of this Act and the Rules of Court made thereunder, it is competent for any party to make an application to have the registration of the judgment set aside, or, where such an application is made, until after the application has been finally determined.

(3) [Repealed by the Administration of Justice Act 1977, Sched. 5.]

(4) If at the date of the application for registration the judgment of the original court has been partly satisfied, the judgment shall not be registered

in respect of the whole sum payable under the judgment of the original court, but only in respect of the balance remaining payable at that date.

(5) If, on an application for the registration of a judgment, it appears to the registering court that the judgment is in respect of different matters and that some, but not all, of the provisions of the judgment are such that if those provisions had been contained in separate judgments those judgments could properly have been registered, the judgment may be registered in respect of the provisions aforesaid but not in respect of any other provisions contained therein.

(6) In addition to the sum of money payable under the judgment of the original court, including any interest which by the law of the country of the original court becomes due under the judgment up to the time of registration, the judgment shall be registered for the reasonable costs of and incidental to registration, including the costs of obtaining a certified copy of the judgment from the original court.

NOTE

[1] See the Isle of Man Act 1979, s.4.

Rules of court

[1] **3.**—(1) The power to make rules of court under section 84 of the Supreme Court Act 1981 shall, subject to the provisions of this section, include power to make rules for the following purposes—

(*a*) For making provision with respect to the giving of security for costs by persons applying for the registration of judgments;

(*b*) For prescribing the matters to be proved on an application for the registration of a judgment and for regulating the mode of proving those matters;

(*c*) For providing for the service on the judgment debtor of notice of the registration of a judgment;

(*d*) For making provision with respect to the fixing of the period within which an application may be made to have the registration of the judgment set aside and with respect to the extension of the period so fixed;

(*e*) For prescribing the method by which any question arising under this Act whether a foreign judgment can be enforced by execution in the country of the original court, or what interest is payable under a foreign judgment under the law of the original court, is to be determined;

(*f*) For prescribing any matter which under this Part of this Act is to be prescribed.

(2) Rules made for the purposes of this Part of this Act shall be expressed to have, and shall have, effect subject to any such provisions contained in Orders in Council made under section one of this Act as are declared by the said Orders to be necessary for giving effect to agreements made between His Majesty and foreign countries in relation to matters with respect to which there is power to make rules of court for the purposes of this Part of this Act.

NOTE

[1] As amended by the Supreme Court Act 1981, Sched. 5. See the Isle of Man Act 1979, s.4(1). See S.I. 1987 No. 468, as amended by S.I. 1987 No. 2211, 1988 Nos. 1304 and 1853, and 1989 No. 987.

Cases in which registered judgments must, or may, be set aside

[1,2] **4.**—(1) On an application in that behalf duly made by any party against whom a registered judgment may be enforced, the registration of the judgment—

(*a*) shall be set aside if the registering court is satisfied—

(i) that the judgment is not a judgment to which this Part of this

Act applies or was registered in contravention of the foregoing provisions of this Act; or

(ii) that the courts of the country of the original court had no jurisdiction in the circumstances of the case; or

(iii) that the judgment debtor, being the defendant in the proceedings in the original court, did not (notwithstanding that process may have been duly served on him in accordance with the law of the country of the original court) receive notice of those proceedings in sufficient time to enable him to defend the proceedings and did not appear; or

(iv) that the judgment was obtained by fraud; or

(v) that the enforcement of the judgment would be contrary to public policy in the country of the registering court; or

(vi) that the rights under the judgment are not vested in the person by whom the application for registration was made;

(*b*) may be set aside if the registering court is satisfied that the matter in dispute in the proceedings in the original court had previously to the date of the judgment in the original court been the subject of a final and conclusive judgment by a court having jurisdiction in the matter.

[3] (2) For the purposes of this section the courts of the country of the original court shall, subject to the provisions of subsection (3) of this section, be deemed to have had jurisdiction—

(*a*) in the case of a judgment given in an action *in personam*—

(i) if the judgment debtor, being a defendant in the original court, submitted to the jurisdiction of that court by voluntarily appearing in the proceedings; or

(ii) if the judgment debtor was plaintiff in, or counter-claimed in, the proceedings in the original court; or

(iii) if the judgment debtor, being a defendant in the original court, had before the commencement of the proceedings agreed, in respect of the subject matter of the proceedings, to submit to the jurisdiction of that court or of the courts of the country of that court; or

(iv) if the judgment debtor, being a defendant in the original court, was at the time when the proceedings were instituted resident in, or being a body corporate had its principal place of business in, the country of that court; or

(v) if the judgment debtor, being a defendant in the original court, had an office or place of business in the country of that court and the proceedings in that court were in respect of a transaction effected through or at that office or place;

(*b*) in the case of a judgment given in an action of which the subject matter was immoveable property or in an action *in rem* of which the subject matter was moveable property, if the property in question was at the time of the proceedings in the original court situate in the country of that court;

(*c*) in the case of a judgment given in an action other than any such action as is mentioned in paragraph (*a*) or paragraph (*b*) of this subsection, if the jurisdiction of the original court is recognised by the law of the registering court.

[3] (3) Notwithstanding anything in subsection (2) of this section, the courts of the country of the original court shall not be deemed to have had jurisdiction—

(*a*) if the subject matter of the proceedings was immoveable property outside the country of the original court; or

(*c*) if the judgment debtor, being a defendant in the original proceedings, was a person who under the rules of public international law was entitled to immunity from the jurisdiction of the courts of the country of the original court and did not submit to the jurisdiction of that court.

NOTES

[1] See the Isle of Man Act 1979, s. 4 (1).

[2] Excluded by the Nuclear Installations Act 1965, s. 17 (4).

[3] Excluded by the Carriage by Railway Act 1972, s. 5 (2). As amended by the Civil Jurisdiction and Judgments Act 1982, Sched. 14, in relation to judgments registered on or after 24th August 1982.

Powers of registering court on application to set aside registration

[1] **5.**—(1) If, on an application to set aside the registration of a judgment, the applicant satisfies the registering court either that an appeal is pending, or that he is entitled and intends to appeal, against the judgment, the court, if it thinks fit, may, on such terms as it may think just, either set aside the registration or adjourn the application to set aside the registration until after the expiration of such period as appears to the court to be reasonably sufficient to enable the applicant to take the necessary steps to have the appeal disposed of by the competent tribunal.

(2) Where the registration of a judgment is set aside under the last foregoing subsection, or solely for the reason that the judgment was not at the date of the application for registration enforceable by execution in the country of the original court, the setting aside of the registration shall not prejudice a further application to register the judgment when the appeal has been disposed of or if and when the judgment becomes enforceable by execution in that country, as the case may be.

(3) Where the registration of a judgment is set aside solely for the reason that the judgment, notwithstanding that it had at the date of the application for registration been partly satisfied, was registered for the whole sum payable thereunder, the registering court shall, on the application of the judgment creditor, order judgment to be registered for the balance remaining payable at that date.

NOTE

[1] See the Isle of Man Act 1979, s. 4 (1).

Foreign judgments which can be registered not to be enforceable otherwise

6. No proceedings for the recovery of a sum payable under a foreign judgment, being a judgment to which this Part of this Act applies, other than proceedings by way of registration of the judgment, shall be entertained by any court in the United Kingdom.

Power to apply Part I of Act to British dominions, protectorates and mandated territories

7.—(1) His Majesty may by Order in Council direct that this Part of this Act shall apply to His Majesty's dominions outside the United Kingdom and to judgments obtained in the courts of the said dominions as it applies to foreign countries and judgments obtained in the courts of foreign countries, and, in the event of His Majesty so directing, this Act shall have effect accordingly and Part II of the Administration of Justice Act 1920 shall cease to have effect except in relation to those parts of the said dominions to which it extends at the date of the Order.

(2) If at any time after His Majesty has directed as aforesaid an Order in Council is made under section one of this Act extending Part I of this Act to any part of His Majesty's dominions to which the said Part II extends as aforesaid, the said Part II shall cease to have effect in relation to that part of His Majesty's dominions.

(3) References in this section to His Majesty's dominions outside the United Kingdom shall be construed as including references to any territories

which are under His Majesty's protection and to any territories in respect of which a mandate under the League of Nations has been accepted by His Majesty.

PART II.—MISCELLANEOUS AND GENERAL

General effect of certain foreign judgments

8.—(1) Subject to the provisions of this section, a judgment to which Part I of this Act applies or would have applied if a sum of money had been payable thereunder, whether it can be registered or not, and whether, if it can be registered, it is registered or not, shall be recognised in any court in the United Kingdom as conclusive between the parties thereto in all proceedings founded on the same cause of action and may be relied on by way of defence or counter-claim in any such proceedings.

(2) This section shall not apply in the case of any judgment—

(*a*) where the judgment has been registered and the registration thereof has been set aside on some ground other than—

(i) that a sum of money was not payable under the judgment; or

(ii) that the judgment had been wholly or partly satisfied; or

(iii) that at the date of the application the judgment could not be enforced by execution in the country of the original court; or

(*b*) where the judgment has not been registered, it is shewn (whether it could have been registered or not) that if it had been registered the registration thereof would have been set aside on an application for that purpose on some ground other than one of the grounds specified in paragraph (*a*) of this subsection.

(3) Nothing in this section shall be taken to prevent any court in the United Kingdom recognising any judgment as conclusive of any matter of law or fact decided therein if that judgment would have been so recognised before the passing of this Act.

Power to make foreign judgments unenforceable in United Kingdom if no reciprocity

[1] **9.**—(1) If it appears to His Majesty that the treatment in respect of recognition and enforcement accorded by the courts of any foreign country to judgments given in the courts of the United Kingdom is substantially less favourable than that accorded by the courts of the United Kingdom to judgments of the courts of that country, His Majesty may by Order in Council apply this section to that country.

(2) Except in so far as His Majesty may by Order in Council under this section otherwise direct, no proceedings shall be entertained in any court in the United Kingdom for the recovery of any sum alleged to be payable under a judgment given in a court of a country to which this section applies.

(3) His Majesty may by a subsequent Order in Council vary or revoke any Order previously made under this section.

NOTE

[1] As amended by the Civil Jurisdiction and Judgments Act 1982, Sched. 10, para. 2 and Sched. 14.

Provision for issue of copies of, and certificates in connection with, U.K. judgments

[1] **10.**—(1) Rules may make provision for enabling any judgment creditor wishing to secure the enforcement in a foreign country to which Part I of this Act extends of a judgment to which this subsection applies, to obtain, subject to any conditions specified in the rules—

(*a*) a copy of the judgment; and

(*b*) a certificate giving particulars relating to the judgment and the proceedings in which it was given.

(2) Subsection (1) applies to any judgment given by a court or tribunal in

the United Kingdom under which a sum of money is payable, not being a sum payable in respect of taxes or other charges of a like nature or in respect of a fine or other penalty.

(3) In this section "rules"—

(*a*) in relation to judgments given by a court, means rules of court;

(*b*) in relation to judgments given by any other tribunal, means rules or regulations made by the authority having power to make rules or regulations regulating the procedure of that tribunal.

NOTE

[1] Substituted by the Civil Jurisdiction and Judgments Act 1982, Sched. 10, para. 3.

Arbitration awards

[1] **10A.** The provisions of this Act, except sections 1(5) and 6, shall apply, as they apply to a judgment, in relation to an award in proceedings on an arbitration which has, in pursuance of the law in force in the place where it was made, become enforceable in the same manner as a judgment given by a court in that place.

NOTE

[1] Inserted by the Civil Jurisdiction and Judgments Act 1982, Sched. 10, para. 4.

Interpretation

[1] **11.**—[2] (1) In this Act, unless the context otherwise requires, the following expressions have the meanings hereby assigned to them respectively, that is to say—

"Appeal" includes any proceeding by way of discharging or setting aside a judgment or an application for a new trial or a stay of execution;

"Country of the original court"means the country in which the original court is situated;

"court", except in section 10 of this Act, includes a tribunal;

"Judgment" means a judgment or order given or made by a court in any civil proceedings, or a judgment or order given or made by a court in any criminal proceedings for the payment of a sum of money in respect of compensation or damages to an injured party;

"Judgment creditor" means the person in whose favour the judgment was given and includes any person in whom the rights under the judgment have become vested by succession or assignment or otherwise;

"Judgment debtor" means the person against whom the judgment was given, and includes any person against whom the judgment is enforceable under the law of the original court;

"Original court" in relation to any judgment means the court by which the judgment was given;

"Prescribed" means prescribed by rules of court;

"Registration" means registration under Part I of this Act, and the expressions "register" and "registered" shall be construed accordingly;

"Registering court" in relation to any judgment means the court to which an application to register the judgment is made.

(2) For the purposes of this Act, the expression "action *in personam*" shall not be deemed to include any matrimonial cause or any proceedings in connection with any of the following matters, that is to say, matrimonial matters, administration of the estates of deceased persons, bankruptcy, winding up of companies, lunacy or guardianship of infants.

NOTE

[1] As amended by the Courts Act 1971, Sched. 11. See the Isle of Man Act 1979, s.4(4).

[2] As amended by the Civil Jurisdiction and Judgments Act 1982, Sched. 10, para. 5 and Sched. 14.

Application to Scotland

[1] **12.** This Act in its application to Scotland shall have effect subject to the following modifications:—

[2] (*a*) For any reference to the High Court there shall be substituted a reference to the Court of Session:

(*b*) The Court of Session shall, subject to the provisions of subsection (2) of section 3 of this Act, have power by Act of Sederunt to make rules for the purposes specified in subsection (1) of the said section:

(*c*) Registration under Part I of this Act shall be effected by registering in the Books of Council and Session or in such manner as the Court of Session may by Act of Sederunt prescribe:

(*d*) [Repealed by the Civil Jurisdiction and Judgments Act 1982, Sched. 14.]

(*e*) For any reference to the entering of a judgment there shall be substituted a reference to the signing of the interlocutor embodying the judgment.

NOTES

[1] See the Isle of Man Act 1979, s.4(4).

[2] As amended by the Civil Jurisdiction and Judgments Act 1982, Sched. 14.

Application to Northern Ireland

[1] **13.** This Act in its application to Northern Ireland shall have effect subject to the following modifications:—

(*a*) References to the High Court shall, unless the context otherwise requires, be construed as references to the High Court in Northern Ireland.

[2] (*b*) For the references to section 99 of the Supreme Court of Judicature (Consolidation) Act 1925, there shall be substituted references to section 55 of the Judicature (Northern Ireland) Act 1978.

NOTES

[1] See the Isle of Man Act 1979, s.4(4).

[2] As amended by the Judicature (Northern Ireland) Act 1978, Sched. 5 and the Civil Jurisdiction and Judgments Act 1982, Sched. 14.

Short title

14. This Act may be cited as the Foreign Judgments (Reciprocal Enforcement) Act 1933.

Administration of Justice (Scotland) Act 1933

(23 & 24 Geo. 5, c. 41)

An Act to amend the Law of Scotland relating to the Court of Session and procedure therein, to the appointment of Officers in the said Court and the High Court of Justiciary, to criminal jury trials and to the Sheriffs and procedure in the Sheriff Court and with regard to solicitors' fees; and for purposes connected therewith. [28th July 1933]

PART I.—COURT OF SESSION

1. [Repealed by the Statute Law (Repeals) Act 1975.]

2–6. [Repealed by the Court of Session Act 1988, Sched. 2].

7. [Repealed by S.I. 1986 No. 1937.]

8. [Repealed by the Statute Law (Repeals) Act 1975.]

9–11. [Repealed by the Court of Session Act 1988, Sched. 2.]

12.—(1) [Repealed by the Age of Legal Capacity (Scotland) Act 1991, Sched. 2.]

(2) [Repealed by the Statute Law (Repeals) Act 1975.]

13–18. [Repealed by the Court of Session Act 1988, Sched. 2.]

[THE NEXT PAGE IS B 59]

PART II.—CRIMINAL JURY TRIALS, ETC.

19. [Repealed by the Criminal Procedure (Scotland) Act 1975, Sched. 10.]

20. [Repealed by the Criminal Procedure (Scotland) Act 1965, s.1(4).]

21. [Repealed by the Criminal Procedure (Scotland) Act 1975, Sched. 10.]

22. [Repealed by the Law Reform (Miscellaneous Provisions) (Scotland) Act 1980, Sched. 3.]

PART III.—OFFICERS OF THE HIGH COURT OF JUSTICIARY AND OF THE COURT OF SESSION

Appointment of clerks in the Court of Justiciary

23.—(1) The right of appointing any depute, assistant or other clerk in the Justiciary Office shall be vested in the Secretary of State and shall be exercised after consultation with the Lord Justice General.

(2) The duties of clerk of the High Court of Justiciary when sitting in Edinburgh or elsewhere may be performed by the Principal Clerk or by such depute, assistant, or other clerk in the Justiciary Office as the Lord Justice General may approve, and the said Principal Clerk and any such depute, assistant, or other clerk shall perform such duties in relation to the business of the said High Court as the Lord Justice-General may direct.

Appointment of officers of the Court of Session

24.—(1) Any enactment in force at the passing of this Act as to the number or appointment of the clerks of court shall cease to have effect and the Secretary of State shall, after consultation with the Lord President, appoint a Principal Clerk of Session and such other clerks and officers of the court as he may, with the sanction of the Treasury as to numbers, determine to be necessary to discharge the duties devolving, according to the law and practice existing immediately prior to the passing of this Act, on the whole staff of clerks in the Inner and Outer Houses and in the Bill Chamber and on the clerks to the judges, and such other clerks and officers shall, subject to the directions of the Lord President, be under the general supervision of the Principal Clerk of Session, and shall, subject as aforesaid, perform such duties in relation to the business of the court as the Principal Clerk may require.

(2) There shall be a Central Office of the court which shall comprise the clerks and officers appointed in pursuance of this section and which shall be divided into a General Department and a Petition Department. Causes initiated in the court by petition shall be assigned to the Petition Department and there shall be assigned to the General Department—

(*a*) causes initiated by summons in the court;
(*b*) special cases;
(*c*) causes brought before the court by appeal, removal, remit, stated case or other like process; and
(*d*) Exchequer causes.

(3) The Petition Department and the General Department shall be respectively responsible under the supervision of the Principal Clerk and subject to the directions of the Lord President, for the allocation among the Divisions of the Inner House or the Lords Ordinary, as the case may be, of the causes assigned to the said departments in pursuance of the foregoing subsection, and the General Department shall be responsible for the division of the causes initiated by summons among—

(*a*) the Ordinary Roll;
(*b*) the Admiralty and Commercial Roll; and
(*c*) the Consistorial Roll;
in accordance with any Act of Sederunt made under section 17 of this Act.

(4) The clerks and officers appointed in pursuance of this section shall be assigned by the Principal Clerk, subject to the directions of the Lord President and the provisions of any Act of Sederunt, to one or other of the aforesaid departments, provided always that any clerk or officer in the Central Office shall be capable of performing, and shall perform, any duty in relation to the business of the court as may be required by the Principal Clerk, subject to such directions and provisions as aforesaid.

(5) [Repealed by the Court of Session Act 1988, Sched. 2.]

(6) Any provision in an Act or an Act of Sederunt regarding the Principal Clerk of Session or the clerks of court shall apply to the Principal Clerk and to the clerks appointed in pursuance of this section in like manner as it applies to the Principal Clerk and to the clerks holding office at the passing of this Act, and any reference in any enactment to a depute, assistant or other clerk in the Court of Session or in the Bill Chamber, shall apply, in like manner as it applies to such depute, assistant or other clerk to the clerk required in pursuance of this section to perform the duties devolving on such depute, assistant or other clerk according to the law and practice existing immediately prior to the passing of this Act.

[1] (7) The right of appointing to the office of macer, which in accordance with the law and practice existing immediately prior to the passing of this Act was vested in His Majesty, shall be transferred to and vested in the Secretary of State, and shall be exercised on nomination by the Lord Advocate, and it shall be competent to the Secretary of State in pursuance of the power so vested in him to appoint the same persons to be macers in the High Court of Justiciary and in the Court of Session.

NOTE

[1] As amended by the Public Records (Scotland) Act 1937, s.16.

Appointment of Principal Clerk of Justiciary, etc.

[1] **25.** The right of appointing to the offices of Principal Clerk of Justiciary, Accountant of Court, Auditor of the Court of Session, shall be vested in the Secretary of State, and shall be exercised on nomination by the Lord Advocate.

NOTE

[1] As amended by the Public Records (Scotland) Act 1937, s.16.

Age limit for officers of High Court of Justiciary and Court of Session

26. A person appointed, in pursuance of the powers vested in the Secretary of State by this Part of this Act, to any office shall vacate his office on attaining the age of sixty-five years:

Provided that, where the Secretary of State after consultation with the Lord President considers it desirable in the public interest to retain any such person in office after he attains the age of sixty-five years, he may, with the approval of the Treasury, authorise the continuance in office of such person, up to such later age, not exceeding seventy years, as he may think fit.

Remuneration of officers of High Court of Justiciary and Court of Session

[1] **27.**—(1) The remuneration of the persons appointed to any office in pursuance of the powers vested in the Secretary of State by this Part of this Act, shall be of such amounts as the Secretary of State may, after consultation with the Lord President and with the concurrence of the Treasury,

from time to time, determine, and such remuneration shall be payable out of moneys provided by Parliament.

(2) The sole remuneration of the persons holding any office mentioned in the immediately preceding subsection (other than the office of Auditor of the Court of Session) shall be the remuneration determined in pursuance of the said subsection, and any fee or other sum paid or received, by virtue of his office, to or by any such person, other than such remuneration, shall be paid over and accounted for in such manner as the Treasury may direct.

NOTE

[1] As amended by the Statute Law (Repeals) Act 1981.

Regulations for admission of officers of High Court of Justiciary and Court of Session

[1] **28.** The Secretary of State may, after consultation with the Lord President and with the concurrence of the Treasury and the Civil Service Commissioners, make regulations prescribing the manner in which persons are to be admitted to any office the right of appointment to which is vested in the Secretary of State by this Part of this Act, and the principal civil service pension scheme within the meaning of section 2 of the Superannuation Act 1972 and for the time being in force shall apply in relation to persons appointed to any such office as it applies in relation to persons to whom section 1 of that Act applies.

NOTE

[1] As amended by the Superannuation Act 1972, Sched. 6.

29. [Repealed by the Superannuation Act 1972, Sched. 8.]

30. [Repealed by the Court of Session Act 1988, Sched. 2.]

PART IV.—SHERIFFS AND SHERIFF COURT

31. [Repealed by the Statute Law (Repeals) Act 1981.]

32. [Repealed by the Sheriff Courts (Scotland) Act 1971, Sched. 2.]

33. [Repealed by the Sheriffs' Pensions (Scotland) Act 1961, Sched. 2.]

34 and **35.** [Repealed by the Sheriff Courts (Scotland) Act 1971, Sched. 2.]

36. [Repealed by the Statute Law (Repeals) Act 1981.]

PART V.—MISCELLANEOUS

Agreements between solicitors as to sharing fees

37.—(1) An agreement between solicitors acting for the same client to share fees or profits shall be lawful if the following conditions are complied with but not otherwise:—

(i) The share payable under the agreement, by the solicitor to whom the fees or profits are due, to the other solicitor shall not exceed one-third.

(ii) The solicitor to whom such share is payable shall, not later than the time when he renders his account to the client, inform the client of the terms of the agreement.

(iii) The solicitor to whom such share is payable shall make no charge against the client for communications or correspondence with the other solicitor in the matter of the business to which the agreement relates.

(iv) The fees or profits to be shared under the agreement shall not include any charge in respect of clerk's writings.

(2) Section 41 of the Solicitors (Scotland) Act 1933, in so far as it relates to the legality of agreements between solicitors acting for the same client is hereby repealed.

38. [Repealed by the Fatal Accidents and Sudden Deaths Inquiry (Scotland) Act 1976, Sched. 2.]

Repeal

39. The enactments mentioned in the Schedule to this Act shall be repealed to the extent specified in the third column of that schedule: Provided that any Act of Sederunt in force at the passing of this Act made under any enactment so repealed shall have effect as if it had been made under this Act.

Interpretation

[1] **40.** In this Act unless the context otherwise requires:—

"The court" means the Court of Session, and, in any provision conferring a power on the court with regard to a cause before it, "the court" includes a reference to a division of the Inner House or to the Lord Ordinary.

"The Lord President" means the Lord President of the Court of Session.

The expression "cause" includes any petition, action, case, or proceeding whatsoever competent in the court.

The "Act of 1868" means the Court of Session Act 1868.

The expression "solicitor" has the like meaning as in the Solicitors (Scotland) Act 1933, provided that for the purpose of the construction of any provision of this Act with reference to any time prior to the 1st day of March, 1934, any reference to a solicitor shall be construed as a reference to a law agent as defined in the Law Agents (Scotland) Act 1873.

The expression "General Council of Solicitors in Scotland" means the General Council of Solicitors in Scotland constituted under the Solicitors (Scotland) Act 1933.

"Prescribed" means prescribed by Act of Sederunt under this Act.

NOTE

[1] As amended by the Court of Session Act 1988, Sched. 2.

Extent, short title and commencement

41.—(1) This Act shall extend to Scotland only, and may be cited as the Administration of Justice (Scotland) Act 1933.

(2) [Repealed by the Statute Law Revision Act 1950.]

(3) Any reference in any provision of this Act to the commencement of this Act shall be construed as a reference to the date when that provision comes into operation.

SCHEDULE

[Repealed by the Statute Law Revision Act 1950.]

Law Reform (Miscellaneous Provisions) (Scotland) Act 1940

(3 & 4 Geo. 6, c. 42)

An Act to amend the law of Scotland relating to enforcement of decrees *ad factum praestandum*, to solatium and damages, to contribution among joint wrongdoers, and to prorogation of the jurisdiction of the sheriff court; to amend and extend the Intestate Husband's Estate (Scotland) Acts 1911 and 1919; to make provision regarding the powers of the King's and Lord Treasurer's Remembrancer; to enable effect to be given to international conventions affecting Scottish courts; and to amend the law of Scotland relating to criminal procedure.

[17th July 1940]

Amendment of the law as to enforcement of decrees ad factum praestandum

1.—(1) No person shall be apprehended or imprisoned on account of his failure to comply with a decree *ad factum praestandum* except in accordance with the following provisions—

(i) On an application by the person in right of such a decree (hereinafter referred to as the applicant) to the court by which the decree was granted, the court may, if it is satisfied that the person against whom such decree was granted (hereinafter referred to as the respondent) is wilfully refusing to comply with the decree, grant warrant for his imprisonment for any period not exceeding six months;

(ii) Where the court is satisfied that a person undergoing imprisonment in pursuance of a warrant granted under this section has complied, or is no longer wilfully refusing to comply, with the decree, the court shall, notwithstanding any period specified in the warrant, order the immediate liberation of such person, and it shall be the duty of the applicant, as soon as he is satisfied that the decree has been complied with, forthwith to inform the clerk of the court of such compliance;

(iii) Imprisonment under a warrant granted under this subsection shall not operate to extinguish the obligation imposed by the decree on which the application proceeds;

(iv) The person on whose application a warrant for imprisonment has been granted under this subsection shall not be liable to aliment, or to contribute to the aliment of, the respondent while in prison.

(2) On any application in pursuance of the foregoing subsection, the court may, in lieu of granting warrant for imprisonment, recall the decree on which the application proceeds and make an order for the payment by the respondent to the applicant of a specified sum or make such other order as appears to the court to be just and equitable in the circumstances, including, in the case where the decree on which the application proceeds is a decree for delivery of corporeal moveables, a warrant to officers of court to search any premises in the occupation of the respondent or of such other person as may be named in the warrant, and to take possession of, and deliver to the applicant, any such moveables which may be found in such premises.

(3) Any warrant granted under the last foregoing subsection shall be deemed to include authority to open shut and lockfast places for the purpose of carrying the warrant into lawful execution.

(4) [Repealed by the Sheriff Courts (Scotland) Act 1971, Sched. 2.]

2. (1), (3) [Repealed by the Children Act 1975, Sched. 4, Pt. I.]
(2), (4) [Repealed by Damages (Scotland) Act 1976, Sched. 2.]

Contribution among joint wrongdoers

[1] **3.**—(1) Where in any action of damages in respect of loss or damage arising from any wrongful acts or negligent acts or omissions two or more persons are, in pursuance of the verdict of a jury or the judgment of a court found jointly and severally liable in damages or expenses, they shall be liable *inter se* to contribute to such damages or expenses in such proportions as the jury or the court, as the case may be, may deem just: Provided that nothing in this subsection shall affect the right of the person to whom such damages or expenses have been awarded to obtain a joint and several decree therefor against the persons so found liable.

(2) Where any person has paid any damages or expenses in which he has been found liable in any such action as aforesaid, he shall be entitled to recover from any other person who, if sued, might also have been held liable in respect of the loss or damage on which the action was founded, such contribution, if any, as the court may deem just.

(3) Nothing in this section shall—

(*a*) apply to any action in respect of loss or damage suffered before the commencement of this Act; or

(*b*) affect any contractual or other right of relief or indemnity or render enforceable any agreement for indemnity which could not have been enforced if this section had not been enacted.

NOTE

[1] See the Law Reform (Contributory Negligence) Act 1945, ss.1(3) and 5(*b*), the Public Utilities Street Works Act 1950, ss.19, 36(4), and the Limitation Act 1963, s.10(1). This section binds the Crown: see the Crown Proceedings Act 1947, ss.4(2), 43(*b*). See also the Prescription and Limitation (Scotland) Act 1973, s.20. Excluded by the Carriage of Goods by Road Act 1965, s.5. Applied by the Animals (Scotland) Act 1987, s.1(7). See the Consumer Protection Act 1987, s.6(1)(*b*).

Agreements to prorogate the jurisdiction of the sheriff court

4.—(1) Any provision or agreement in or in relation to a contract to which this section applies, whereby any party to such contract prorogates, or agrees to submit to, the jurisdiction of a particular sheriff court, shall be void.

[1] (2) This section applies to—

(*a*) any contract for the sale of an article; and

(*b*) and (*c*) [Repealed by the Consumer Credit Act 1974, Sched. 5.]

[2] (3) This section does not apply—

(*a*) in the case of an agreement entered into after the dispute in respect of which the agreement is intended to have effect has arisen; or

(*b*) where the contract is one referred to in Rule 3 of Schedule 8 to the Civil Jurisdiction and Judgments Act 1982.

NOTES

[1] As amended by the Hire-Purchase (Scotland) Act 1965, Sched. 5.

[2] Inserted by the Civil Jurisdiction and Judgments Act 1982, Sched. 12, Pt. II, para. 1.

5. [Repealed by the Succession (Scotland) Act 1964, s.1(1), Sched. 3.]

Provisions as to estate falling to Crown as ultimus haeres

[1] **6.**—(1) For removal of doubts it is hereby declared that when any estate shall have fallen to the Crown as *ultimus haeres*, the Secretary of State has the like right to uplift and ingather such estate in England and Wales as well as in Scotland as an executor nominate to whom confirmation has been granted as mentioned in section 1 of the Administration of Estates Act 1971.

(2) Where the Secretary of State is satisfied that any person has a legal right to any sum not exceeding £20 (exclusive of interest) which has been paid over to the said Secretary of State in pursuance of section 16 of the Court of Session Consignations (Scotland) Act 1895, or of section 10 of the Sheriff Courts Consignations (Scotland) Act 1893, it shall be lawful for the said Secretary of State to pay such sum to that person, without any order of the court:

Provided that nothing in this subsection shall authorise the said Secretary of State to pay any sum to which competing claims have been made.

NOTE

[1] As amended by the Administration of Estates Act 1971, Sched. 1 and S.I. 1974 No. 1274.

7. [Repealed by the State Immunity Act 1978, s. 24.]

8. [Repealed by the Criminal Procedure (Scotland) Act 1975, Sched. 10.]

9. [Repealed by the Summary Jurisdiction (Scotland) Act, 1954, Sched. 4.]

. . . . . .

Short title, extent and repeal

11.—(1) This Act may be cited as the Law Reform (Miscellaneous Provisions) (Scotland) Act 1940.

(2) Save as otherwise expressly provided, this Act shall extend to Scotland only.

(3) [Repealed by the Statute Law Revision Act 1950.]

Law Reform (Contributory Negligence) Act 1945

(8 & 9 Geo. 6, c. 28)

[1] An Act to amend the law relating to contributory negligence and for purposes connected therewith. [15th June 1945]

NOTE

[1] Applied to the Crown by the Crown Proceedings Act 1947, s. 4 (3). Extended by the Merchant Shipping Oil Pollution Act 1971, s. 1, and the Deposit of Poisonous Waste Act 1972, s. 2 (4).

Apportionment of liability in case of contributory negligence

[1] **1.**—(1) Where any person suffers damage as the result partly of his own fault and partly of the fault of any other person or persons, a claim in respect of that damage shall not be defeated by reason of the fault of the person suffering the damage, but the damages recoverable in respect thereof shall be reduced to such extent as the court thinks just and equitable having regard to the claimant's share in the responsibility for the damage:

Provided that—

(*a*) this subsection shall not operate to defeat any defence arising under a contract;

(*b*) where any contract or enactment providing for the limitation of liability is applicable to the claim, the amount of damages recoverable by the claimant by virtue of this subsection shall not exceed the maximum limit so applicable.

(2) Where damages are recoverable by any person by virtue of the foregoing subsection subject to such reduction as is therein mentioned, the court shall find and record the total damages which would have been recoverable if the claimant had not been at fault.

(3) [Repealed by the Civil Liability (Contribution) Act 1978, Sched. 2.]

[2] (4) Where any person dies as the result partly of his own fault and partly of the fault of any other person or persons, a claim by way dependant

of the first mentioned person for damages or solatium in respect of that person's death shall not be defeated by reason of his fault, but the damages or solatium recoverable shall be reduced to such extent as the court thinks just and equitable having regard to the share of the said person in the responsibility for his death.

(5) Where, in any case to which subsection (1) of this section applies, one of the persons at fault avoids liability to any other such person or his personal representative by pleading the Limitation Act 1939, or any other enactment limiting the time within which proceedings may be taken, he shall not be entitled to recover any damages or contributions from that other person or representative by virtue of the said subsection.

(6) Where any case to which subsection (1) of this section applies is tried with a jury, the jury shall determine the total damages which would have been recoverable if the claimant had not been at fault and the extent to which those damages are to be reduced.

(7) [Repealed by the Carriage by Air Act 1961, Sched. 2.]

NOTES

[1] Modified by the Control of Pollution Act 1974, s. 88 (4).

[2] As applicable to Scotland by s. 5 (*c*).

2. [Repealed by the National Insurance (Industrial Injuries) Act 1946, Sched. 9.]

Saving for Maritime Conventions Act 1911, and past cases

3.—(1) This Act shall not apply to any claim to which section 1 of the Maritime Conventions Act 1911 applies and that Act shall have effect as if this Act had not passed.

(2) This Act shall not apply to any case where the acts or omissions giving rise to the claim occurred before the passing of this Act.

Interpretation

[1] **4.** The following expressions have the meanings hereby respectively assigned to them, that is to say—

" court " means, in relation to any claim, the court or arbitrator by or before whom the claim falls to be determined;

" damage " includes loss of life and personal injury;

" fault " means negligence, breach of statutory duty or other act or omission which gives rise to a liability in tort or would, apart from this Act, give rise to the defence of contributory negligence.

NOTE

[1] As amended by the National Insurance (Industrial Injuries) Act 1946, Sched. 9, and the Fatal Accidents Act 1976, Sched. 2.

Application to Scotland

5. In the application of this Act to Scotland—

(*a*) the expression " dependant " means, in relation to any person, any person who would in the event of such first mentioned person's death through the fault of a third party be entitled to sue that third party for damages or solatium; and the expression " fault " means wrongful act, breach of statutory duty or negligent act or omission which gives rise to liability in damages, or would, apart from this Act, give rise to the defence of contributory negligence;

[1] (*b*) section 3 of the Law Reform (Miscellaneous Provisions) (Scotland) Act 1940 (contribution among joint wrongdoers) shall apply in any case where two or more persons are liable, or would

if they had all been sued be liable, by virtue of section 1(1) of this Act in respect of the damage suffered by any person.

NOTE
[1] Substituted by the Civil Liability (Contribution) Act 1978, Sched. 1.

. . . .

Short title and extent

7. This Act may be cited as the Law Reform (Contributory Negligence) Act 1945.

[1] Crown Proceedings Act 1947

(10 & 11 Geo. 6, c. 44)

An Act to amend the law relating to the civil liabilities and rights of the Crown and to civil proceedings by and against the Crown, to amend the law relating to the civil liabilities of persons other than the Crown in certain cases involving the affairs or property of the Crown, and for purposes connected with the matters aforesaid. [31st July 1947]

NOTE
[1] Applied by the Employment Protection Act 1975, Sched. 1, and the Occupiers' Liability (Scotland) Act 1960, s. 4.

[1] PART I.—SUBSTANTIVE LAW

NOTE
[1] Extended by the Plant Varieties and Seeds Act 1964, s. 14.

1. [Not applicable to Scotland.]

Liability of the Crown in tort

2.—(1) Subject to the provisions of this Act, the Crown shall be subject to all those liabilities in tort to which, if it were a private person of full age and capacity, it would be subject:—

(*a*) in respect of torts committed by its servants or agents;
(*b*) in respect of any breach of those duties which a person owes to his servants or agents at common law by reason of being their employer; and
(*c*) in respect of any breach of the duties attaching at common law to the ownership, occupation, possession or control of property:

Provided that no proceedings shall lie against the Crown by virtue of paragraph (*a*) of this subsection in respect of any act or omission of a servant or agent of the Crown unless the act or omission would apart from the provisions of this Act have given rise to a cause of action in tort against that servant or agent or his estate.

(2) Where the Crown is bound by a statutory duty which is binding also upon persons other than the Crown and its officers, then, subject to the provisions of this Act, the Crown shall, in respect of a failure to comply with that duty, be subject to all those liabilities in tort (if any) to which it would be so subject if it were a private person of full age and capacity.

(3) Where any functions are conferred or imposed upon an officer of the Crown as such either by any rule of the common law or by statute, and that officer commits a tort while performing or purporting to perform those

functions, the liabilities of the Crown in respect of the tort shall be such as they would have been if those functions had been conferred or imposed solely by virtue of instructions lawfully given by the Crown.

(4) Any enactment which negatives or limits the amount of the liability of any Government department or officer of the Crown in respect of any tort committed by that department or officer shall, in the case of proceedings against the Crown under this section in respect of a tort committed by that department or officer, apply in relation to the Crown as it would have applied in relation to that department or officer if the proceedings against the Crown had been proceedings against that department or officer.

(5) No proceedings shall lie against the Crown by virtue of this section in respect of anything done or omitted to be done by any person while discharging or purporting to discharge any responsibilities of a judicial nature vested in him, or any responsibilities which he has in connection with the execution of judicial process.

[1] (6) No proceedings shall lie against the Crown by virtue of this section in respect of any act, neglect or default of any officer of the Crown, unless that officer has been directly or indirectly appointed by the Crown and was at the material time paid in respect of his duties as an officer of the Crown wholly out of the Consolidated Fund of the United Kingdom, moneys provided by Parliament, or any Fund certified by the Treasury for the purposes of this subsection or was at the material time holding an office in respect of which the Treasury certify that the holder thereof would normally be so paid.

NOTE

[1] As amended by the Statute Law (Repeals) Act 1981.

Infringement of intellectual property rights

[1] **3.**—(1) Civil proceedings lie against the Crown for an infringement committed by a servant or agent of the Crown, with the authority of the Crown, of—

(*a*) a patent,
(*b*) a registered trade mark or registered service mark,
(*c*) the right in a registered design,
(*d*) design right, or
(*e*) copyright;

but save as provided by this subsection no proceedings lie against the Crown by virtue of this Act in respect of an infringement of any of those rights.

(2) Nothing in this section, or any other provision of this Act, shall be construed as affecting—

(*a*) the rights of a government department under section 55 of the Patents Act 1977, Schedule 1 to the Registered Designs Act 1949 or section 240 of the Copyright, Designs and Patents Act 1988 (Crown use of patents and designs), or
(*b*) the rights of the Secretary of State under section 22 of the Patents Act 1977 or section 5 of the Registered Designs Act 1949 (security of information prejudicial to defence or public safety).

NOTE

[1] Substituted by the Copyright, Designs and Patents Act 1988, Sched. 7, para. 4(1). Para. 4(2) provides:

"(2) In the application of sub-paragraph (1) to Northern Ireland—

(*a*) the reference to the Crown Proceedings Act 1947 is to that Act as it applies to the Crown in right of Her Majesty's Government in Northern Ireland, as well as to the Crown in right of Her Majesty's Government in the United Kingdom, and
(*b*) in the substituted section 3 as it applies in relation to the Crown in right of Her Majesty's Government in Northern Ireland, subsection (2)(*b*) shall be omitted."

Application of law as to indemnity, contribution, joint and several tortfeasors, and contributory negligence

4.—(1) Where the Crown is subject to any liability by virtue of this Part of this Act, the law relating to indemnity and contribution shall be enforceable by or against the Crown in respect of the liability to which it is so subject as if the Crown were a private person of full age and capacity.

(2) Without prejudice to the effect of the preceding subsection, Part II of the Law Reform (Married Women and Tortfeasors) Act 1935 (which

[THE NEXT PAGE IS B 69]

relates to proceedings against, and contribution between, joint and several tortfeasors), shall bind the Crown.

(3) Without prejudice to the general effect of section one of this Act, the Law Reform (Contributory Negligence) Act 1945 (which amends the law relating to contributory negligence), shall bind the Crown.

Liability in respect of Crown ships, etc.

[1] **5.**—(1) The provisions of sections 17 and 18 of the Merchant Shipping Act 1979 and of Schedule 4 to that Act (liability of shipowners and salvors) shall apply in relation to His Majesty's ships as they apply in relation to other ships.

(2) In this section "ships" has the same meaning as in those provisions.

NOTE

[1] Substituted by the Merchant Shipping Act 1978, Sched. 5, para. 3.

Application to Crown ships of rules as to division of loss, etc.

[1] **6.** The provisions of sections 1, 2 and 3 of the Maritime Conventions Act 1911 (which relate to the apportionment of damage or loss caused by vessels), shall apply in the case of vessels belonging to His Majesty as they apply in the case of other vessels.

NOTE

[1] Extended to hovercraft by S.I. 1972 No. 971.

Liability in respect of Crown docks, harbours, etc.

7.—(1) It is hereby declared that the provisions of the Merchant Shipping Acts 1894 to 1940, which limit the amount of the liability of the owners of docks and canals, and of harbour and conservancy authorities, apply for the purpose of limiting the liability of His Majesty in His capacity as the owner of any dock or canal, or in His capacity as a harbour or conservancy authority, and that all the relevant provisions of the said Acts have effect in relation to His Majesty accordingly.

(2) In this section the expressions "dock," "harbour," "owner," "harbour authority" and "conservancy authority" have respectively the same meanings as they have for the purposes of section two of the Merchant Shipping (Liability of Shipowners and Others) Act 1900.

(3) In this section references to His Majesty include references to any Government department and to any officer of the Crown in his capacity as such.

Salvage claims against the Crown, and Crown rights to salvage

[1] **8.**—(1) Subject to the provisions of this Act, the law relating to civil salvage, whether of life or property, except sections 551 to 554 of the Merchant Shipping Act 1894, or any corresponding provisions relating to aircraft, shall apply in relation to salvage services rendered after the commencement of this Act in assisting any of His Majesty's ships or aircraft, or in saving life therefrom, or in saving any cargo or apparel belonging to His Majesty in right of His Government in the United Kingdom, in the same manner as if the ship, aircraft, cargo or apparel belonged to a private person.

(2) Where after the commencement of this Act salvage services are rendered by or on behalf of His Majesty, whether in right of His Government in the United Kingdom or otherwise, His Majesty shall be entitled to claim salvage in respect of those services to the same extent as any other salvor, and shall have the same rights and remedies in respect of those services as any other salvor.

NOTE

[1] Extended to hovercraft by S.I. 1972 No. 971.

9. [Repealed by the Post Office Act 1969, Sched. 11.]

Provisions relating to the armed forces

[1] **10.**—(1) Nothing done or omitted to be done by a member of the armed forces of the Crown while on duty as such shall subject either him or the Crown to liability in tort for causing the death of another person, or for causing personal injury to another person, in so far as the death or personal injury is due to anything suffered by that other person while he is a member of the armed forces of the Crown if—

(*a*) at the time when that thing is suffered by that other person, he is either on duty as a member of the armed forces of the Crown or is, though not on duty as such, on any land, premises, ship, aircraft or vehicle for the time being used for the purposes of the armed forces of the Crown; and

(*b*) the Secretary of State certifies that his suffering that thing has been or will be treated as attributable to service for the purposes of entitlement to an award under the Royal Warrant, Order in Council or Order of His Majesty relating to the disablement or death of members of the force of which he is a member:

Provided that this subsection shall not exempt a member of the said forces from liability in tort in any case in which the court is satisfied that the act or omission was not connected with the execution of his duties as a member of those forces.

(2) No proceedings in tort shall lie against the Crown for death or personal injury due to anything suffered by a member of the armed forces of the Crown if—

(*a*) that thing is suffered by him in consequence of the nature or condition of any such land, premises, ship, aircraft or vehicle as aforesaid, or in consequence of the nature or condition of any equipment or supplies used for the purposes of those forces; and

(*b*) the Secretary of State certifies as mentioned in the preceding subsection;

nor shall any act or omission of an officer of the Crown subject him to liability in tort for death or personal injury, in so far as the death or personal injury is due to anything suffered by a member of the armed forces of the Crown being a thing as to which the conditions aforesaid are satisfied.

(3) A Secretary of State, if satisfied that it is the fact:—

(*a*) that a person was or was not on any particular occasion on duty as a member of the armed forces of the Crown; or

(*b*) that at any particular time any land, premises, ship, aircraft, vehicle, equipment or supplies was or was not, or were or were not, used for the purposes of the said forces;

may issue a certificate certifying that to be the fact; and any such certificate shall, for the purposes of this section, be conclusive as to the fact which it certifies.

NOTE

[1] As amended by S.I. 1953 No. 1198, S.I. 1964 No. 488, Ministry of Social Security Act 1966, s. 2(3), and S.I. 1968 No. 1699: extended by the Civil Defence (Armed Forces) Act 1954, s. 1(3); extended to hovercraft by S.I. 1972 No. 971. Repealed in respect of acts or omissions on or after 15th May 1987 by the Crown Proceedings (Armed Forces) Act 1987, subject to provision for its revival by order. See print of that Act, *infra*.

Saving in respect of acts done under prerogative and statutory powers

11.—(1) Nothing in Part I of this Act shall extinguish or abridge any powers or authorities which, if this Act had not been passed, would have been exercisable by virtue of the prerogative of the Crown, or any powers or authorities conferred on the Crown by any statute, and, in particular, nothing in the said Part I shall extinguish or abridge any powers or authorities exercisable by the Crown, whether in time of peace or of war, for the purpose of the defence of the realm or of training, or maintaining the efficiency of, any of the armed forces of the Crown.

[1] (2) Where in any proceedings under this Act it is material to determine whether anything was properly done or omitted to be done in the exercise of the prerogative of the Crown, a Secretary of State may, if satisfied that the act or omission was necessary for any such purpose as is mentioned in the last preceding subsection, issue a certificate to the effect that the act or omission was necessary for that purpose; and the certificate shall, in those proceedings, be conclusive as to the matter so certified.

NOTE

[1] As amended by S.I. 1964 No. 488.

Transitional provisions

12.—(1) When this Act comes into operation, the preceding provisions of this Part of this Act (except subsections (3) and (4) of section 5 thereof and any provision which is expressly related to the commencement of this Act) shall be deemed to have had effect as from the beginning of the 13th day of February 1947:

Provided that where by virtue of this subsection proceedings are brought against the Crown in respect of a tort alleged to have been committed on or after the said 13th day of February and before the commencement of this Act, the Crown may rely upon the appropriate provisions of the law relating to the limitation of time for bringing proceedings as if this Act had at all material times been in force.

(2) Where any civil proceedings brought before the commencement of this Act have not been finally determined, and the court for the time being seized of those proceedings is of opinion that having regard to the provisions of this section the Crown ought to be made a party to the proceedings for the purpose of disposing completely and effectually of the questions involved in the cause or matter before the court, the court may order that the Crown be made a party thereto upon such terms, if any, as the court thinks just, and may make such consequential orders as the court thinks expedient.

[1] Part II.—Jurisdiction and Procedure

NOTE

[1] Extended by the Taxes Management Act 1970, s. 100 (3), and the Finance Act 1975, Sched. 4.

The High Court

Civil proceedings in the High Court

13. Subject to the provisions of this Act, all such civil proceedings by or against the Crown as are mentioned in the First Schedule to this Act are hereby abolished, and all civil proceedings by or against the Crown in the High Court shall be instituted and proceeded with in accordance with rules of court and not otherwise.

In this section the expression " rules of court " means, in relation to any claim against the Crown in the High Court which falls within the jurisdiction of that court as a prize court, rules of court made under section 3 of the Prize Courts Act 1894.

14–20. [Not applicable to Scotland.]

Nature of relief

21.—(1) In any civil proceedings by or against the Crown the court shall, subject to the provisions of this Act, have power to make all such orders as it has power to make in proceedings between subjects, and otherwise to give such appropriate relief as the case may require:

Provided that:—

(*a*) where in any proceedings against the Crown any such relief is sought as might in proceedings between subjects be granted by way of injunction or specific performance, the court shall not grant an injunction or make an order for specific performance, but may in lieu thereof make an order declaratory of the rights of the parties; and

(*b*) in any proceedings against the Crown for the recovery of land or other property the court shall not make an order for the recovery of the land or the delivery of the property, but may in lieu thereof make an order declaring that the plaintiff is entitled as against the Crown to the land or property or to the possession thereof.

(2) The court shall not in any civil proceedings grant any injunction or make any order against an officer of the Crown if the effect of granting the injunction or making the order would be to give any relief against the Crown which could not have been obtained in proceedings against the Crown.

[1] Part III.—Judgments and Execution

NOTE

[1] Applied by the Finance Act 1975, Sched. 4.

24–25. [Not applicable to Scotland.]

Execution by the Crown

26.—(1) Subject to the provisions of this Act, any order made in favour of the Crown against any person in any civil proceedings to which the Crown is a party may be enforced in the same manner as an order made in an action between subjects, and not otherwise.

This subsection shall apply both in relation to proceedings pending at the commencement of this Act and in relation to proceedings instituted thereafter.

[1] (2) The exception in respect of taxes contained in section 4 of the Debtors (Scotland) Act 1880, from the enactment therein contained abolishing imprisonment for debt shall apply only in respect of death duties.

(3) Nothing in this section shall affect any procedure which immediately before the commencement of this Act was available for enforcing an order made in favour of the Crown in proceedings brought by the Crown for the recovery of any fine or penalty, or the forfeiture or condemnation of any goods, or the forfeiture of any ship or any share in a ship.

NOTE

[1] As applicable to Scotland by s. 49. As amended by the Finance Act 1972, Sched. 28, Pt. II.

27. [Not applicable to Scotland.]

Part IV.—Miscellaneous and Supplemental

Miscellaneous

28. [Not applicable to Scotland.]

Exclusion of proceedings in rem **against the Crown**

[1] **29.**—(1) Nothing in this Act shall authorise proceedings *in rem* in respect of any claim against the Crown, or the arrest, detention or sale of any

of His Majesty's ships or aircraft, or of any cargo or other property belonging to the Crown, or give to any person any lien on any such ship, aircraft, cargo or other property.

(2) Where proceedings *in rem* have been instituted in the High Court or in a county court against any such ship, aircraft, cargo or other property, the court may, if satisfied, either on an application by the plaintiff for an order under this subsection or an application by the Crown to set aside the proceedings, that the proceedings were so instituted by the plaintiff in the reasonable belief that the ship, aircraft, cargo or other property did not belong to the Crown, order that the proceedings shall be treated as if they were *in personam* duly instituted against the Crown in accordance with the provisions of this Act, or duly instituted against any other person whom the court regards as the proper person to be sued in the circumstances, and that the proceedings shall continue accordingly.

Any such order may be made upon such terms, if any, as the court thinks just; and where the court makes any such order it may make such consequential orders as the court thinks expedient.

NOTE

[1] Extended to hovercraft by S.I. 1972 No. 971.

Limitation of actions

[1, 2] **30.**—(1) Section 8 of the Maritime Conventions Act 1911 (which relates to the limitation of actions in respect of damage or loss caused to or by vessels and the limitation of actions in respect of salvage services), shall apply in the case of His Majesty's ships as it applies in the case of other vessels:

Provided that the said section 8, as applied by this section, shall have effect as if the words from " and shall, if satisfied " to the end of the said section 8 were omitted therefrom.

. . . .

(3) In this section the expression " ship " includes any boat or other description of vessel used in navigation, and the expression " His Majesty's ships " shall be construed accordingly.

NOTES

[1] Extended to hovercraft by S.I. 1972 No. 971.

[2] As amended by the Law Reform (Limitation of Actions, etc.) Act 1954, Sched.

Application to the Crown of certain statutory provisions

31.—(1) This Act shall not prejudice the right of the Crown to take advantage of the provisions of an Act of Parliament although not named therein; and it is hereby declared that in any civil proceedings against the Crown the provisions of any Act of Parliament which could, if the proceedings were between subjects, be relied upon by the defendant as a defence to the proceedings, whether in whole or in part, or otherwise, may, subject to any express provision to the contrary, be so relied upon by the Crown.

(2) Section 6 of the Debtors Act 1869 (which empowers the court in certain circumstances to order the arrest of a defendant about to quit England), shall, with any necessary modifications, apply to civil proceedings in the High Court by the Crown.

No abatement on demise of Crown

32. No claim by or against the Crown, and no proceedings for the enforcement of any such claim, shall abate or be affected by the demise of the Crown.

Abolition of certain writs

33. No writ of extent or of *diem clausit extremum* shall issue after the commencement of this Act.

34. [Repealed by the Administration of Justice Act 1977, Sched. 5.]

Supplemental

Rules of court, and county court rules

35.—(1) Any power to make rules of court or county court rules shall include power to make rules for the purpose of giving effect to the provisions of this Act, and any such rules may contain provisions to have effect in relation to any proceedings by or against the Crown in substitution for or by way of addition to any of the provisions of the rules applying to proceedings between subjects.

[1] (2) The following provisions shall apply as regards proceedings in the Court of Session or the sheriff court:—

(*a*) where decree in absence has been granted against the Crown the decree shall not be operative without the leave of the court obtained on an application of which notice has been given to the Crown;

(*b*) a person shall not be entitled to avail himself of any set-off or counter-claim in any proceedings by the Crown for the recovery of taxes, duties or penalties, or to avail himself in proceedings of any other nature by the Crown of any set-off or counter-claim arising out of a right or claim to repayment in respect of any taxes, duties or penalties;

(*c*) a person shall not be entitled without the leave of the court to avail himself of any set-off or counter-claim in any proceedings by the Crown if the subject-matter of the set-off or counter-claim does not relate to the Government department on whose behalf the proceedings are brought;

(*d*) the Crown, in any proceedings against a Government department, or against the Lord Advocate on behalf of a Government department, shall not, without the leave of the court, be entitled to avail itself of any set-off or counter-claim if the subject-matter thereof does not relate to that department.

(3) Provision may be made by rules of court for regulating any appeals to the High Court, whether by way of case stated or otherwise, under enactments relating to the revenue, and any rules made under this subsection may revoke any enactments or rules in force immediately before the commencement of this Act so far as they regulate any such appeals, and may make provision for any matters for which provision was made by any enactments or rules so in force.

NOTE

[1] As applicable to Scotland by s. 50.

Pending proceedings

36. Save as otherwise expressly provided, the provisions of this Act shall not affect proceedings by or against the Crown which have been instituted before the commencement of this Act.

[Remainder of section not applicable to Scotland.]

Financial provisions

37.—(1) Any expenditure incurred by or on behalf of the Crown in right of His Majesty's Government in the United Kingdom by reason of the passing of this Act shall be defrayed out of moneys provided by Parliament.

(2) Any sums payable to the Crown in right of His Majesty's Government in the United Kingdom by reason of the passing of this Act shall be paid into the Exchequer.

Interpretation

38.—(1) Any reference in this Act to the provisions of this Act shall, unless the context otherwise requires, include a reference to rules of court or county court rules made for the purposes of this Act.

(2) In this Act, except in so far as the context otherwise requires or it is otherwise expressly provided, the following expressions have the meanings hereby respectively assigned to them, that is to say:—

" Agent," when used in relation to the Crown, includes an independent contractor employed by the Crown;

" Civil proceedings " includes proceedings in the High Court or the county court for the recovery of fines or penalties, but does not include proceedings on the Crown side of the King's Bench Division;

" His Majesty's aircraft " does not include aircraft belonging to His Majesty otherwise than in right of His Government in the United Kingdom;

" His Majesty's ships " means ships of which the beneficial interest is vested in His Majesty or which are registered as Government ships for the purposes of the Merchant Shipping Acts 1894 to 1940, or which are for the time being demised or subdemised to or in the exclusive possession of the Crown, except that the said expression does not include any ship in which His Majesty is interested otherwise than in right of His Government in the United Kingdom unless that ship is for the time being demised or subdemised to His Majesty in right of His said Government or in the exclusive possession of His Majesty in that right;

" Officer," in relation to the Crown, includes any servant of His Majesty, and accordingly (but without prejudice to the generality of the foregoing provisions) includes a Minister of the Crown;

" Order " includes a judgment, decree, rule, award or declaration;

" Prescribed " means prescribed by rules of court or county court rules, as the case may be;

" Proceedings against the Crown " includes a claim by way of set-off or counter-claim raised in proceedings by the Crown;

" Ship " has the meaning assigned to it by section 742 of the Merchant Shipping Act 1894;

" Statutory duty " means any duty imposed by or under any Act of Parliament.

[1] (3) Any reference in this Act to His Majesty in His private capacity shall be construed as including a reference to His Majesty in right of His Duchy of Lancaster and to the Duke of Cornwall.

[2] (4) Any reference in Parts III, IV [or V] of this Act to civil proceedings by or against the Crown, or to civil proceedings to which the Crown is a party, shall be construed as including a reference to civil proceedings to which the [Lord Advocate], or any Government department, or any officer of the Crown as such is a party:

(5) [Repealed by the Armed Forces Act 1981, Sched. 5.]

(6) References in this Act to any enactment shall be construed as references to that enactment as amended by or under any other enactment, including this Act.

NOTES

[1] Extended by the Animals Act 1971, s. 12 (2), and the Health and Safety at Work, etc., Act 1974, s. 48 (6).

[2] As applicable to Scotland by s. 51.

Repeals, etc.

39.—(1) [Repealed by the Statute Law Revision Act 1950.]

(2) [Repealed by S.I. 1970 No. 1681.]

Savings

40.—(1) Nothing in this Act shall apply to proceedings by or against, or authorise proceedings in tort to be brought against His Majesty in his private capacity.

(2) Except as therein otherwise expressly provided, nothing in this Act shall:—

(*a*) affect the law relating to prize salvage, or apply to proceedings in causes or matters within the jurisdiction of the High Court as a prize court or to any criminal proceedings; or

(*b*) authorise proceedings to be taken against the Crown under or in accordance with this Act in respect of any alleged liability of the Crown arising otherwise than in respect of His Majesty's Government in the United Kingdom, or affect proceedings against the Crown in respect of any such alleged liability as aforesaid; or

(*c*) affect any proceedings by the Crown otherwise than in right of His Majesty's Government in the United Kingdom; or

(*d*) subject the Crown to any greater liabilities in respect of the acts or omissions of any independent contractor employed by the Crown than those to which the Crown would be subject in respect of such acts or omissions if it were a private person; or

(*e*) subject the Crown, in its capacity as a highway authority, to any greater liability than that to which a local authority is subject in that capacity; or

(*f*) affect any rules of evidence or any presumption relating to the extent to which the Crown is bound by any Act of Parliament; or

(*g*) affect any right of the Crown to demand a trial at bar or to control or otherwise intervene in proceedings affecting its rights, property or profits; or

(*h*) affect any liability imposed on the public trustee or on the Consolidated Fund of the United Kingdom by the Public Trustee Act 1906;

and, without prejudice to the general effect of the foregoing provisions, Part III of this Act shall not apply to the Crown except in right of His Majesty's Government in the United Kingdom.

(3) A certificate of a Secretary of State:—

(*a*) to the effect that any alleged liability of the Crown arises otherwise than in respect of His Majesty's Government in the United Kingdom;

(*b*) to the effect that any proceedings by the Crown are proceedings otherwise than in right of His Majesty's Government in the United Kingdom;

shall, for the purposes of this Act, be conclusive as to the matter so certified.

(4) Where any property vests in the Crown by virtue of any rule of law which operates independently of the acts or the intentions of the Crown, the Crown shall not by virtue of this Act be subject to any liabilities in tort by reason only of the property being so vested; but the provisions of this subsection shall be without prejudice to the liabilities of the Crown under this Act in respect of any period after the Crown or any person acting for the Crown has in fact taken possession or control of any such property, or entered into occupation thereof.

(5) This Act shall not operate to limit the discretion of the court to grant relief by way of mandamus in cases in which such relief might have been granted before the commencement of this Act, notwithstanding that by reason of the provisions of this Act some other and further remedy is available.

[1] PART V.—APPLICATION TO SCOTLAND

NOTE

[1] Applied by the Sex Discrimination Act 1975, s. 85(9), and the Race Relations Act 1976, s. 75(7).

Application of Act to Scotland

41. The provisions of this Part of this Act shall have effect for the purpose of the application of this Act to Scotland.

Exclusion of certain provisions

42. Section 1, Part II (except section 13 so far as relating to proceedings mentioned in the First Schedule) [*sic*] and section 21, Part III (except section 26) and section 28 of this Act shall not apply to Scotland.

Interpretation for purposes of application to Scotland

43. In the application of this Act to Scotland:—

(*a*) for any reference to the High Court (except a reference to that court as a prize court) there shall be substituted a reference to the Court of Session; for any reference to the county court there shall be substituted a reference to the sheriff court; the expression "plaintiff" means pursuer; the expression "defendant" means defender; the expression "county court rules" means Act of Sederunt applying to the sheriff court; and the expression "injunction" means interdict;

(*b*) the expression "tort" means any wrongful or negligent act or omission giving rise to liability in reparation, and any reference to liability or right or action or proceedings in tort shall be construed accordingly; and for any reference to Part II of the Law Reform (Married Women and Tortfeasors) Act 1935 there shall be substituted a reference to section 3 of the Law Reform (Miscellaneous Provisions) (Scotland) Act 1940.

Proceedings against the Crown in the sheriff court

[1] **44.** Subject to the provisions of this Act and to any enactment limiting the jurisdiction of the sheriff court (whether by reference to the subject-matter of the proceedings or otherwise) civil proceedings against the Crown may be instituted in the sheriff court in like manner as if the proceedings were against a subject:

Provided that where in any proceedings against the Crown in the sheriff court a certificate by the Lord Advocate is produced to the effect that the proceedings may involve an important question of law, or may be decisive of other cases, or are for other reasons more fit for trial in the Court of Session, the proceedings shall be remitted to the Court of Session, and where any proceedings have been so remitted to the Court of Session, and it appears to that court that the remit has occasioned additional expense to the pursuer, the court shall take account of the additional expense so occasioned in deciding any question as to expenses.

NOTE

[1] Proviso excluded by the Sex Discrimination Act 1975, s. 85(9) and the Race Relations Act 1976, s. 75(7).

Satisfaction of orders granted against the Crown in Scotland

[1] **45.**—(1) Where in any civil proceedings by or against the Crown or to which the Crown has been made a party, any order (including an award of expenses) is made by any court in favour of any person against the Crown or against a Government department or against an officer of the Crown as such, the clerk of court shall, on an application in that behalf made by or on behalf of that person at any time after the expiration of

21 days from the date of the order, or, in a case where there is an award of expenses and the expenses require to be taxed, at any time after taxation whichever is the later, issue to that person a certified copy of the order of the court.

(2) A copy of any such order may be served by the person in whose favour the order is made upon the person for the time being named in the record as the solicitor, or the person acting as solicitor, for the Crown or for the Government department or officer concerned.

(3) If the order decerns for the payment of any money by way of damages or otherwise or of any expenses, the appropriate Government department shall, subject as hereinafter provided, pay to the person entitled or to his solicitor the amount appearing from the order to be due to him together with the interest, if any, lawfully due thereon:

Provided that the court by which any such order as aforesaid is made or any court to which an appeal against the order lies may direct that, pending an appeal or otherwise, payment of the whole of any amount so payable, or any part thereof, shall be suspended.

(4) No such order as aforesaid shall warrant any diligence or execution against any person to enforce payment of any such money or expenses as aforesaid, and no person shall be individually liable under any order for the payment by the Crown, or any Government department or any officer of the Crown as such, of any such money or expenses.

NOTE

[1] See the Debtors (Scotland) Act 1987, ss.79(5) and 105.

Provisions as to arrestment

46. Arrestment in the hands of the Crown or of a Government department or of any officer of the Crown as such shall be competent in any case where arrestment in the hands of a subject would have been competent:

Provided that nothing in the foregoing provisions shall warrant the arrestment of:—

(*a*) [Repealed by the Debtors (Scotland) Act 1987, Sched. 8.]

(*b*) any money which is subject to the provisions of any enactment prohibiting or restricting assignation or charging or taking in execution;

(*c*) [Repealed by the Law Reform (Miscellaneous Provisions) (Scotland) Act 1985, s.49(*b*) and Sched. 4, with effect from 30th December 1985.]

Recovery of documents in possession of Crown

[1] **47.** Subject to and in accordance with Acts of Sederunt applying to the Court of Session and the sheriff court, commission and diligence for the recovery of documents in the possession of the Crown may be granted in any action whether or not the Crown is a party thereto, in like manner in all respects as if the documents were in the possession of a subject:

Provided that—

(i) this subsection shall be without prejudice to any rule of law which authorises or requires the withholding of any document on the ground that its disclosure would be injurious to the public interest; and

(ii) the existence of a document shall not be disclosed if, in the opinion of a Minister of the Crown, it would be injurious to the public interest to disclose the existence thereof.

NOTE

[1] Applied by the Administration of Justice (Scotland) Act 1972, s.1(4).

48. [Repealed by the Law Reform (Limitation of Actions, etc.) Act 1954, Sched.]

49–51. [Scottish application of ss.26, 35, 36 and 38 given effect to *supra.*]

PART VI.—EXTENT, COMMENCEMENT, SHORT TITLE, ETC.

Extent of Act

52. Subject to the provisions hereinafter contained with respect to Northern Ireland, this Act shall not affect the law enforced in courts elsewhere than in England and Scotland, or the procedure in any such courts.

. . . . . .

Short title and commencement

54.—(1) This Act may be cited as the Crown Proceedings Act 1947.

SCHEDULES

Section 13

FIRST SCHEDULE

PROCEEDINGS ABOLISHED BY THIS ACT

1.—(1) Latin informations and English informations.

(2) Writs of *capias ad respondendum*, writs of *subpœna ad respondendum*, and writs of appraisement.

(3) Writs of *scire facias*.

(4) Proceedings for the determination of any issue upon a writ of extent or of *diem clausit extremum*.

(5) Writs or summons under Part V of the Crown Suits Act 1865.

2.—(1) Proceedings against His Majesty by way of petition of right, including proceedings by way of petition of right intituled in the Admiralty Division under section 52 of the Naval Prize Act 1864.

(2) Proceedings against His Majesty by way of *monstrans de droit*.

. . . . . .

Law Reform (Personal Injuries) Act 1948

(11 & 12 Geo. 6, c.41)

An Act to abolish the defence of common employment, to amend the law relating to the measure of damages for personal injury or death, and for purposes connected therewith.

[30th June 1948]

Common employment

1.—(1) It shall not be a defence to an employer who is sued in respect of personal injuries caused by the negligence of a person employed by him, that that person was at the time the injuries were caused in common employment with the person injured.

(2) Accordingly the Employers' Liability Act 1880 shall cease to have effect, and is hereby repealed.

(3) Any provision contained in a contract of service or apprenticeship, or in an agreement collateral thereto (including a contract or agreement entered into before the commencement of this Act), shall be void in so far as it would have the effect of excluding or limiting any liability of the

employer in respect of personal injuries caused to the person employed or apprenticed by the negligence of persons in common employment with him.

Measure of damages

[1] **2.**—(1) In an action for damages for personal injuries (including any such action arising out of a contract), where this section applies there shall in assessing those damages be taken into account, against them, one half of the value of any rights which have accrued or probably will accrue to the injured person from the injuries in respect of—

(*a*) any of the relevant benefits, within the meaning of section 22 of the Social Security Act 1989, or

(*b*) any corresponding benefits payable in Northern Ireland,

for the five years beginning with the time when the cause of action accrued.

[2] (1A) This section applies in any case where the amount of the damages that would have been awarded apart from any reduction under subsection (1) above is less than the sum for the time being prescribed under paragraph 4(1) of Schedule 4 to the Social Security Act 1989 (recoupment of benefit: exception for small payments).

(2) [Repealed with effect from 3rd September 1990 by the Social Security Act 1989, Sched. 4, para. 22(3).]

(3) The reference in subsection (1) of this section to assessing the damages for personal injuries shall, in cases where the damages otherwise recoverable are subject to reduction under the law relating to contributory negligence or are limited by or under any Act or by contract, be taken as referring to the total damages which would have been recoverable apart from the reduction or limitation.

(4) In an action for damages for personal injuries (including any such action arising out of a contract), there shall be disregarded, in determining the reasonableness of any expenses, the possibility of avoiding those expenses or part of them by taking advantage of facilities available under the National Health Service Act 1977, or the National Health Service (Scotland) Act 1978, or of any corresponding facilities in Northern Ireland.

(5) [Repealed by the Fatal Accidents Act 1959, Sched.]

(5A) [Repealed by the Damages (Scotland) Act 1976, Sched. 2.]

[3] (6) For the purposes of this section disablement benefit in the form of a gratuity is to be treated as benefit for the period taken into account by the assessment of the extent of the disablement in respect of which it is payable.

NOTES

[1] As amended by the National Insurance Act 1971, Sched. 5, para. 1, the Social Security (Consequential Provisions) Act 1975, Sched. 2, the Social Security Pensions Act 1975, Sched. 4, the National Health Service Act 1977, Sched. 15, the National Health Service (Scotland) Act 1978, Sched. 16, the Health and Social Security Act 1984, Sched. 4, para. 1, the Social Security Act 1990, Sched. 1, para. 7, with effect from 13th July 1990, and by the Social Security Act 1989, Sched. 4, para. 22, with effect from 3rd September 1990.

[2] Inserted with effect from 3rd September 1990 by the Social Security Act 1989, Sched. 4, para. 22(2).

[3] As substituted by the Social Security (Consequential Provisions) Act 1975, Sched. 2.

Definition of "personal injury"

3. In this Act the expression "personal injury" includes any disease and any impairment of a person's physical or mental condition, and the expression "injured" shall be construed accordingly.

Application to Crown

4. This Act shall bind the Crown.

. . . .

Short title and commencement

6.—(1) This Act may be cited as the Law Reform (Personal Injuries) Act 1948.

(2) Section 1 and subsection (1) of section 2 of this Act shall apply only where the cause of action accrues on or after the day appointed[1] for the National Insurance (Industrial Injuries) Act 1946, to take effect; but subsections (4) and (5) of the said section 2 shall apply whether the cause of action accrued or the action was commenced before or after the commencement of this Act.

NOTE

[1] 5th July 1948: see S.I. 1948 No. 53.

Juries Act 1949

(12, 13 & 14 Geo. 6, c. 27)

An Act to provide for the making of payments in respect of jury service in Great Britain; to abolish special juries in Great Britain except in commercial causes tried in London; to abolish the privilege of landed persons in relation to jury trial in Scotland; . . . and for purposes connected with the matters aforesaid. [26th April 1949]

. . . .

PART II

SCOTLAND

Payments in respect of jury service in Scotland

24.—[1] (1) Subject to the provisions of this Part of this Act, a person who serves as a juror shall be entitled, in respect of his attendance at court for the purpose of performing jury service, to receive payments, at rates determined by the Secretary of State with the consent of the Minister for the Civil Service and subject to any prescribed conditions, by way of allowance—

(*a*) for travelling and subsistence; and

(*b*) for financial loss, where in consequence of his attendance for that purpose he has incurred any expenditure (other than on travelling and subsistence) to which he would not otherwise be subject or he has suffered any loss of earnings, or of benefit under the enactments relating to social security, which he would otherwise have made or received.

(2) For the purposes of this section, a person who, in obedience to a citation to serve on a jury, attends for service as a juror, shall be deemed to serve as a juror notwithstanding that he is not subsequently impanelled.

(3) A payment to which a person is entitled under this section is in this Part of this Act referred to as "a payment in respect of jury service".

NOTE

[1] Substituted by the Law Reform (Miscellaneous Provisions) (Scotland) Act 1980, Sched. 2.

Person by whom the amount of a payment is to be ascertained and paid

[1] **25.**—(1) The amount due to a person by way of a payment in respect of jury service shall be ascertained and paid—

(*a*) in the case of service at a sitting of the High Court of Justiciary at Edinburgh or in the Court of Session, by the Secretary of State or such other officer as may be prescribed;

(*b*) in the case of service at a sitting of the High Court of Justiciary other than at Edinburgh, or of the sheriff court, whether for a civil or a criminal trial, by the sheriff clerk of the county in which such sitting is held;

(*c*) [Repealed by the Law Reform (Miscellaneous Provisions) (Scotland) Act 1980, Sched. 3.]

(*d*) in the case of service on a jury summoned under the Lands Clauses Consolidation (Scotland) Act 1845, by the sheriff clerk of the court to which the petition to summon the jury is presented.

(2) The sums required for the making of payments in pursuance to paragraphs (*a*) and (*b*) of the last foregoing subsection shall be paid out of moneys provided by Parliament.

NOTE

[1] As amended by S.I. 1973 No. 643, 1974 No. 1274, the Law Reform (Miscellaneous Provisions) (Scotland) Act 1980, Scheds. 2 and 3, and the Criminal Justice (Scotland) Act 1987, Sched. 1, para. 1.

Fee payable by party applying for jury trial in civil cause

26.—[1] (1) Where an order is made—

(*a*) for the trial of any action by a jury in the Court of Session whether such action originated in that court or was removed thereto under section 30 of the Sheriff Courts (Scotland) Act 1907, or

(*b*) for the trial of any action by a jury in the sheriff court,

the person on whose application such order is made shall pay to the clerk of court such fee as may be fixed by an order made by the Secretary of State with the consent of the Treasury, and in the event of his failure to do so within such time as may be so fixed the court may recall the order.

(2) A fee payable in pursuance of the last foregoing subsection shall form part of the expenses of the action and shall be returned to the person who paid it in the event of the trial not being proceeded with and no person being cited to attend for service as a juror thereat.

NOTE

[1] As amended by the Divorce Jurisdiction, Court Fees and Legal Aid (Scotland) Act 1983, Sched. 1, para. 9 and Sched. 2.

. . . .

Abolition of special juries and special jurors

28.—(1) No issue or question shall be tried or determined by a special jury and no person shall be cited or summoned to serve as a special juror for the trial or determination of any issue or question, and any enactment requiring the preparation of a roll of special jurors or of a special jury book or the inclusion in a jury of special jurors shall cease to have effect.

(2) The privilege to which a landed person is entitled of being tried by a jury comprising a majority of landed persons is hereby abolished.

. . . .

30. [Repealed by the Statute Law (Repeals) Act 1978, Sched. 1.]

Discontinuance of terms "common jury" and "common juror"

31. As from the expiration of the month of September, 1949, the expressions "common jury" and "common juror" shall cease to be used.

Interpretation of Part II

32.—(1) In this Part of this Act the expression "prescribed" means prescribed by regulations made by the Secretary of State with the consent of the Treasury.

The power conferred by this subsection on the Secretary of State shall be exercisable by statutory instrument.

(2) Any reference in this Part of this Act to the Lands Clauses Consolidation (Scotland) Act 1845, or to any provision thereof shall be construed as including a reference to that Act or to that provision as the case may be, as incorporated in any Act whether public general or local.

Extent of Part II

33. This Part of this Act shall extend to Scotland only.

. . . .

PART IV

SHORT TITLE, ETC.

Short title, citation and repeal

35.—(1) This Act may be cited as the Juries Act 1949.

(2) [Repealed by the Juries Act 1974, s.22(4), Sched. 3.]

(3) [Repealed by the Statute Law (Repeals) Act 1978, Sched. 1.]

. . . . . .

Defamation Act 1952

(15 & 16 Geo. 6 and 1 Eliz. 2, c. 66)

[1] An Act to amend the law relating to libel and slander and other malicious falsehoods. [30th October 1952]

NOTE

[1] See general Scottish application provisions in s.14(*d*), *infra*.

1, 2. [Not applicable to Scotland.]

Actions for verbal injury

[1] **3.** In any action for verbal injury it shall not be necessary for the pursuer to aver or prove special damage if the words on which the action is founded are calculated to cause pecuniary damage to the pursuer.

NOTE

[1] As substituted for Scotland by s.14(*b*).

Unintentional defamation

4.—(1) A person who has published words alleged to be defamatory of another person may, if he claims that the words were published by him innocently in relation to that other person, make an offer of amends under this section; and in any such case—

(*a*) if the offer is accepted by the party aggrieved and is duly performed, no proceedings for libel or slander shall be taken or continued by that party against the person making the offer in respect of the publication in question (but without prejudice to any cause of action against any other person jointly responsible for that publication);

(*b*) if the offer is not accepted by the party aggrieved, then, except as otherwise provided by this section, it shall be a defence, in any proceedings by him for libel or slander against the person making the offer in respect of the publication in question, to prove that the words complained of were published by the defendant innocently in relation to the plaintiff and that the offer was made as soon as practicable after the defendant received notice that they were or might be defamatory of the plaintiff, and has not been withdrawn.

[1] (2) An offer of amends under this section must be expressed to be made for the purposes of this section, and must be accompanied by an affidavit specifying the facts relied upon by the person making it to show that the words in question were published by him innocently in relation to the party aggrieved; and for the purposes of a defence under paragraph (*b*) of subsection (1) of this section no evidence, other than evidence of facts specified in the affidavit, shall be admissible on behalf of that person to prove that the words were so published.

Nothing in this subsection shall be held to entitle a defender to lead evidence of any fact specified in the declaration unless notice of his intention to do so has been given in the defences.

(3) An offer of amends under this section shall be understood to mean an offer—

(*a*) in any case, to publish or join in the publication of a suitable correction of the words complained of, and a sufficient apology to the party aggrieved in respect of those words;

(*b*) where copies of a document or record containing the said words have been distributed by or with the knowledge of the person making the offer, to take such steps as are reasonably practicable on his part for

[THE NEXT PAGE IS B 85]

notifying persons to whom copies have been so distributed that the words are alleged to be defamatory of the party aggrieved.

(4) Where an offer of amends under this section is accepted by the party aggrieved—

(*a*) any question as to the steps to be taken in fulfilment of the offer as so accepted shall in default of agreement between the parties be referred to and determined by the High Court, whose decision thereon shall be final;

(*b*) the power of the court to make orders as to costs in proceedings by the party aggrieved against the person making the offer in respect of the publication in question, or in proceedings in respect of the offer under paragraph (*a*) of this subsection, shall include power to order the payment by the person making the offer to the party aggrieved of costs on an indemnity basis and any expenses reasonably incurred or to be incurred by that party in consequence of the publication in question;

and if no such proceedings as aforesaid are taken, the High Court may, upon application made by the party aggrieved, make any such order for the payment of such costs and expenses as aforesaid as could be made in such proceedings.

(5) For the purposes of this section words shall be treated as published by one person (in this subsection referred to as the publisher) innocently in relation to another person if and only if the following conditions are satisfied, that is to say—

(*a*) that the publisher did not intend to publish them of and concerning that other person, and did not know of circumstances by virtue of which they might be understood to refer to him; or

(*b*) that the words were not defamatory on the face of them, and the publisher did not know of circumstances by virtue of which they might be understood to be defamatory of that other person,

and in either case that the publisher exercised all reasonable care in relation to the publication; and any reference in this subsection to the publisher shall be construed as including a reference to any servant or agent of his who was concerned with the contents of the publication.

(6) Paragraph (*b*) of subsection (1) of this section shall not apply in relation to the publication by any person of words of which he is not the author unless he proves that the words were written by the author without malice.

NOTE

[1] As applied to Scotland by s. 14(*c*).

Justification

5. In an action for libel or slander in respect of words containing two or more distinct charges against the plaintiff, a defence of justification shall not fail by reason only that the truth of every charge is not proved if the words not proved to be true do not materially injure the plaintiff's reputation having regard to the truth of the remaining charges.

Fair comment

6. In an action for libel or slander in respect of words consisting partly of allegations of fact and partly of expression of opinion, a defence of fair comment shall not fail by reason only that the truth of every allegation of fact is not proved if the expression of opinion is fair comment having regard to such of the facts alleged or referred to in the words complained of as are proved.

Qualified privilege of newspapers

[1] **7.**—(1) Subject to the provisions of this section, the publication in a

newspaper of any such report or other matter as is mentioned in the Schedule to this Act shall be privileged unless the publication is proved to be made with malice.

(2) In an action for libel in respect of the publication of any such report or matter as is mentioned in Part II of the Schedule to this Act, the provisions of this section shall not be a defence if it is proved that the defendant has been requested by the plaintiff to publish in the newspaper in which the original publication was made a reasonable letter or statement by way of explanation or contradiction, and has refused or neglected to do so, or has done so in a manner not adequate or not reasonable having regard to all the circumstances.

(3) Nothing in this section shall be construed as protecting the publication of any matter the publication of which is prohibited by law, or of any matter which is not of public concern and the publication of which is not for the public benefit.

(4) Nothing in this section shall be construed as limiting or abridging any privilege subsisting (otherwise than by virtue of section 4 of the Law of Libel Amendment Act 1888) immediately before the commencement of this Act.

(5) In this section the expression "newspaper" means any paper containing public news or observations thereon, or consisting wholly or mainly of advertisements, which is printed for sale and is published in the United Kingdom either periodically or in parts or numbers at intervals not exceeding 36 days.

NOTE

[1] Applied by the Cable and Broadcasting Act 1984, s. 28(3).

8. [Not applicable to Scotland.]

Extension of certain defences to broadcasting

[1] **9.**—(1) Section 3 of the Parliamentary Papers Act 1840 (which confers protection in respect of proceedings for printing extracts from or abstracts of parliamentary papers) shall have effect as if the reference to printing included a reference to broadcasting by means of wireless telegraphy.

(2) Section 7 of this Act and section 3 of the Law of Libel Amendment Act 1888, as amended by this Act shall apply in relation to reports or matters broadcast by means of wireless telegraphy as part of any programme or service provided by means of a broadcasting station within the United Kingdom, and in relation to any broadcasting by means of wireless telegraphy of any such report or matter, as they apply in relation to reports and matters published in a newspaper and to publication in a newspaper; and subsection (2) of the said section 7 shall have effect, in relation to any such broadcasting, as if for the words "in the newspaper in which" there were substituted the words "in the manner in which".

(3) In this section "broadcasting station" means any station in respect of which a licence granted by the Postmaster General under the enactments relating to wireless telegraphy is in force, being a licence which (by whatever form of words) authorises the use of the station for the purpose of providing broadcasting services for general reception.

NOTE

[1] s. 9(2) explained by the Criminal Justice Act 1967, s. 5.

The reference to "Postmaster General" is to be construed as including a reference to the Secretary of State: see the Post Office Act 1969, s. 3(1) and S.I. 1974 No. 691.

Limitation on privilege at elections

10. A defamatory statement published by or on behalf of a candidate in any election to a local government authority or to Parliament shall not be deemed to be published on a privileged occasion on the ground that it is material to a question in issue in the election, whether or not the person by whom it is published is qualified to vote at the election.

Agreements for indemnity

11. An agreement for indemnifying any person against civil liability for libel in respect of the publication of any matter shall not be unlawful unless at the time of the publication that person knows that the matter is defamatory, and does not reasonably believe there is a good defence to any action brought upon it.

Evidence of other damages recovered by plaintiff

12. In any action for libel or slander the defendant may give evidence in mitigation of damages that the plaintiff has recovered damages, or has brought actions for damages, for libel or slander in respect of the publication of words to the same effect as the words on which the action is founded, or has received or agreed to receive compensation in respect of any such publication.

13. [Not applicable to Scotland.]

Application of Act to Scotland

14. This Act shall apply to Scotland subject to the following modifications, that is to say:—

(*a*) sections 1, 2, 8 and 13 shall be omitted;

(*b*) for section 3 there shall be substituted the following section—[see *supra*, s.3];

(*c*) subsection (2) of section 4 shall have effect as if at the end thereof there were added the words [see *supra*, s.4(2)];

(*d*) for any reference to libel, or to libel or slander, there shall be substituted a reference to defamation; the expression "plaintiff" means pursuer; the expression "defendant" means defender; for any reference to an affidavit made by any person there shall be substituted a reference to a written declaration signed by that person; for any reference to the High Court there shall be substituted a reference to the Court of Session or, if an action of defamation is depending in the sheriff court in respect of the publication in question, the sheriff[1]; the expression "costs" means expenses; and for any reference to a defence of justification there shall be substituted a reference to a defence of *veritas*.

NOTE

[1] For interpretation of the term "sheriff" see the Sheriff Courts (Scotland) Act 1971, s.4, and the Interpretation Act 1978, Sched. 1.

. . . .

Interpretation

[1] **16.**—(1) Any reference in this Act to words shall be construed as including a reference to pictures, visual images, gestures and other methods of signifying meaning.

(2) The provisions of Part III of the Schedule to this Act shall have effect for the purposes of the interpretation of that Schedule.

(3) In this Act "broadcasting by means of wireless telegraphy" means publication for general reception by means of wireless telegraphy within the meaning of the Wireless Telegraphy Act 1949, and "broadcast by means of wireless telegraphy" shall be construed accordingly.

(4) [Repealed by the Cable and Broadcasting Act 1984, Sched. 6.]

NOTE

[1] As amended by the Post Office Act 1969, Sched. 4.

Proceedings affected and saving

17.—(1) This Act applies for the purposes of any proceedings begun after the commencement of this Act, whenever the cause of action arose, but does not affect any proceedings begun before the commencement of this Act.

(2) Nothing in this Act affects the law relating to criminal libel.

Short title, commencement, extent and repeals

[1] **18.**—(1) This Act may be cited as the Defamation Act 1952, and shall come into operation one month after the passing of this Act.

(2) This Act shall not extend to Northern Ireland.

. . . . . .

NOTE

[1] As amended by the Northern Ireland Constitution Act 1973, Sched. 6.

SCHEDULE

NEWSPAPER STATEMENTS HAVING QUALIFIED PRIVILEGE

PART I

STATEMENTS PRIVILEGED WITHOUT EXPLANATION OR CONTRADICTION

1. A fair and accurate report of any proceedings in public of the legislature of any part of Her Majesty's dominions outside Great Britain.

2. A fair and accurate report of any proceedings in public of an international organisation of which the United Kingdom or Her Majesty's Government in the United Kingdom is a member, or of any international conference to which that government sends a representative.

3. A fair and accurate report of any proceedings in public of an international court.

[1] 4. A fair and accurate report of any proceedings before a court exercising jurisdiction throughout any part of Her Majesty's dominions outside the United Kingdom, or of any proceedings before a court-martial held outside the United Kingdom under the Naval Discipline Act, the Army Act 1955, or the Air Force Act 1955.

NOTE

[1] As amended by the Revision of the Army and Air Force Acts (Transitional Provisions) Act 1955, Sched. 2.

---

5. A fair and accurate report of any proceedings in public of a body or person appointed to hold a public inquiry by the government or legislature of any part of Her Majesty's dominions outside the United Kingdom.

6. A fair and accurate copy of or extract from any register kept in pursuance of any Act of Parliament which is open to inspection by the public, or of any other document which is required by the law of any part of the United Kingdom to be open to inspection by the public.

7. A notice or advertisement published by or on the authority of any court within the United Kingdom or any judge or officer of such a court.

PART II

STATEMENTS PRIVILEGED SUBJECT TO EXPLANATION OR CONTRADICTION

8. A fair and accurate report of the findings or decision of any of the following associations, or of any committee or governing body thereof, that is to say–

(*a*) an association formed in the United Kingdom for the purpose of promoting or encouraging the exercise of or interest in any art, science, religion or learning, and empowered by its constitution to exercise control over or adjudicate upon matters of interest or concern to the association, or the actions or conduct of any persons subject to such control or adjudication;

(*b*) an association formed in the United Kingdom for the purpose of promoting or safeguarding the interests of any trade, business, industry or profession, or of the persons carrying on or engaged in any trade, business, industry or profession, and empowered by its constitution to exercise control over or adjudicate upon matters connected with the trade, business, industry or profession, or the actions or conduct of those persons;

(*c*) an association formed in the United Kingdom for the purpose of promoting or safeguarding the interests of any game, sport or pastime to the playing or exercise of which members of the public are invited or admitted, and empowered by its constitution to exercise control over or adjudicate upon persons connected with or taking part in the game, sport or pastime,

being a finding or decision relating to a person who is a member of or is subject by virtue of any contract to the control of the association.

9. A fair and accurate report of the proceedings at any public meeting held in the United Kingdom, that is to say, a meeting bona fide and lawfully held for a lawful purpose and for the furtherance or discussion of any matter of public concern, whether the admission to the meeting is general or restricted.

10. A fair and accurate report of the proceedings at any meeting or sitting in any part of the United Kingdom of—

(*a*) any local authority or committee of a local authority or local authorities;

(*b*) any justice or justices of the peace acting otherwise than as a court exercising judicial authority;

(*c*) any commission, tribunal, committee or person appointed for the purposes of any inquiry by Act of Parliament, by Her Majesty or by a Minister of the Crown;

(*d*) any person appointed by a local authority to hold a local inquiry in pursuance of any Act of Parliament;

(*e*) any other tribunal, board, committee or body constituted by or under, and exercising functions under, an Act of Parliament,

not being a meeting or sitting admission to which is denied to representatives of newspapers and other members of the public.

11. A fair and accurate report of the proceedings at a general meeting of any company or association constituted, registered or certified by or under any Act of Parliament or incorporated by Royal Charter, not being a private company within the meaning of the Companies Act 1948.

12. A copy or fair and accurate report or summary of any notice, or other matter issued for the information of the public by or on behalf of any government department, officer of state, local authority or chief officer of police.

PART III

INTERPRETATION

[1] 13.—(1) In this Schedule the following expressions have the meanings hereby respectively assigned to them, that is to say:—

[2] "Act of Parliament" includes an Act of the Parliament of Northern Ireland, and the reference to the Companies Act 1948, includes a reference to any corresponding enactment of the Parliament of Northern Ireland;

"government department" includes a department of the Government of Northern Ireland;

"international court" means the International Court of Justice and any other judicial or arbitral tribunal deciding matters in dispute between States;

"legislature", in relation to any territory comprised in Her Majesty's dominions which is subject to a central and a local legislature, means either of those legislatures;

"local authority" means—

(*a*) any principal council, within the meaning of the Local Government Act 1972, any body falling within any paragraph of section 100J(1) of that Act and any local authority, within the meaning of the Local Government (Scotland) Act 1973;

(*b*) any authority or body to which the Public Bodies (Admission to Meetings) Act 1960 applies; and

(*c*) any authority or body to which sections 23 to 27 of the Local Government Act (Northern Ireland) 1972 apply;

and any reference to a committee of a local authority shall be construed in accordance with sub-paragraph (2) below.

"part of Her Majesty's dominions" means the whole of any territory within those dominions which is subject to a separate legislature.

(2) Any reference in this Schedule to a committee of a local authority includes a reference—

(*a*) to any committee or sub-committee in relation to which sections 100A to 100D of the Local Government Act 1972 apply by virtue of section 100E of that Act (whether or not also by virtue of section 100J of that Act); and

(*b*) to any committee or sub-committee in relation to which sections 50A to 50D of the Local Government (Scotland) Act 1973 apply by virtue of section 50E of that Act.

NOTES

[1] As amended by the Local Government (Access to Information) Act 1985, Sched. 2, para. 2, with effect from 1st April 1986.

[2] See the Northern Ireland Constitution Act 1973, Sched. 5, para. 1(1).

[1] 14. In relation to the following countries and territories, that is to say, India, The Republic of Ireland, any protectorate, protected state or trust territory within the meaning of the British Nationality Act 1948, any territory administered under the authority of a country mentioned in Schedule 3 to the British Nationality Act 1981, the Sudan and the New Hebrides, the provisions of this Schedule shall have effect as they have effect in relation to Her Majesty's dominions, and references therein to Her Majesty's dominions shall be construed accordingly.

NOTE

[1] As amended by the British Nationality Act 1981, Sched. 7.

Administration of Justice Act 1956

(4 & 5 Eliz. 2, c. 46)

An Act to amend the law relating to Admiralty jurisdiction, legal proceedings in connection with ships and aircraft and the arrest of ships and other property . . . and for purposes connected with the matters aforesaid. [5th July 1956]

. . . .

[1] Part V.—Admiralty Jurisdiction and Arrestment of Ships in Scotland

NOTE

[1] Extended with modifications by the Hovercraft Act 1968, s. 2. See Rules of Court, rr. 135–147.

Jurisdiction in relation to collisions, etc.

45.—(1) Subject to the provisions of this Part of this Act, any court having Admiralty jurisdiction shall have jurisdiction to entertain, as against any defender, an action to which this section applies if, but only if,—

(*a*) the defender has his habitual residence or a place of business in the area for which the court acts, or

(*b*) the cause of action arose in the area for which the court acts and either within inland waters or within the limits of a port, or (*c*) an action arising out of the same incident or series of incidents is proceeding in the court or has been heard and determined by the court, or

(*d*) the defender has prorogated the jurisdiction of the court, or

(*e*) a ship in which the defender owns one or more shares has been arrested (whether *ad fundandam jurisdictionem* or on the dependence of the action) within the area for which the court acts.

(2) Where an action to which this section applies is raised in a court having jurisdiction by virtue only of one or more of the provisions of the preceding subsection other than paragraph (*d*) thereof, and it appears to the court that cognate proceedings are depending in a competent court outside Scotland, the first mentioned court shall sist the action if so moved by any party thereto, and shall not recall the sist until satisfied that the cognate proceedings have been discontinued or have otherwise come to an end:

Provided that nothing in this subsection shall prevent the first mentioned court from entertaining any application as to diligence in the action.

[THE NEXT PAGE IS B 91]

In this subsection " cognate proceedings ", in relation to any action, means proceedings instituted, before the granting of warrant for service in the action, by the pursuer in the action against any other party to the action, being proceedings in respect of the same incident or series of incidents as those with which the action is concerned.

(3) This section applies to actions for payment of reparation arising out of one or more of the following incidents, that is to say—

(*a*) any collision between ships, or

(*b*) the carrying out of, or the omission to carry out, a manoeuvre in the case of one or more of two or more ships, or

(*c*) the non-compliance, on the part of one or more of two or more ships, with the collision regulations.

(4) In this section—

" inland waters " includes any part of the sea adjacent to the coast of the United Kingdom certified by the Secretary of State to be waters falling by international law to be treated as within the territorial sovereignty of Her Majesty apart from the operation of that law in relation to territorial waters;

" port " means any port, harbour, river, estuary, haven, dock, canal or other place so long as a person or body of persons is empowered by or under an Act or charter to make charges in respect of ships entering it or using the facilities therein, and " limits of a port " means the limits thereof as fixed by or under the Act in question or, as the case may be, by the relevant charter or custom;

" charges " means any charges with the exception of light dues, local light dues and any other charges in respect of lighthouses, buoys or beacons and of charges in respect of pilotage.

(5) For the avoidance of doubt it is hereby declared that any reference in this section to an action for payment of reparation does not include a reference to an action to make good a lien.

(6) Section 6 of the Sheriff Courts (Scotland) Act 1907 (as amended by any subsequent enactment), shall cease to have effect in relation to actions to which this section applies.

Exclusion of jurisdiction in cases falling within Rhine Convention

46. No court shall have jurisdiction to determine any claim or question certified by the Secretary of State to be a claim or question which, under the Rhine Navigation Convention, falls to be determined in accordance with the provisions thereof.

In this section " the Rhine Navigation Convention " means the Convention of 7th October 1868, as revised by any subsequent Convention.

Arrest of ships on the dependence of an action or in rem

47.—(1) Subject to the provisions of this section and section 50 of this Act, no warrant issued after the commencement of this Part of this Act for the arrest of property on the dependence of an action or *in rem* shall have effect as authority for the detention of a ship unless the conclusion in respect of which it is issued is appropriate for the enforcement of a claim to which this section applies, and, in the case of a warrant to arrest on the dependence of an action, unless either—

(*a*) the ship is the ship with which the action is concerned, or

(*b*) all the shares in the ship are owned by the defender against whom that conclusion is directed.

(2) This section applies to any claim arising out of one or more of the following, that is to say—

(*a*) damage done or received by any ship;

(*b*) loss of life or personal injury sustained in consequence of any defect in a ship or in her apparel or equipment, or of the wrongful act, neglect or default of the owners, charterers or persons in possession or control of a ship or of the master or crew thereof or of any other person for whose wrongful acts, neglects or defaults the owners, charterers or persons in possession or control of a ship are responsible, being an act, neglect or default in the navigation or management of the ship, in the loading, unloading or discharge of goods on, in or from the ship or in the embarkation, carriage or disembarkation of persons on, in or from the ship;

(*c*) salvage;

(*d*) any agreement relating to the use or hire of any ship whether by charterparty or otherwise;

(*e*) any agreement relating to the carriage of goods in any ship whether by charterparty or otherwise;

(*f*) loss of, or damage to, goods carried in any ship;

(*g*) general average;

(*h*) any bottomry bond;

(*i*) towage;

(*j*) pilotage;

(*k*) the supply of goods or materials to a ship for her operation or maintenance;

(*l*) the construction, repair or equipment of any ship;

(*m*) liability for dock charges or dues;

(*n*) liability for payment of wages (including any sum allotted out of wages under section 141 of the Merchant Shipping Act 1894, or adjudged under section 387 of that Act by a superintendent to be due by way of wages) of a master or member of the crew of a ship;

(*o*) master's disbursements, including disbursements made by shippers, charterers or agents on behalf of a ship or her owner;

(*p*) any dispute as to the ownership or right to possession of any ship or as to the ownership of any share in a ship;

(*q*) any dispute between co-owners of any ship as to the ownership, possession, employment or earnings of that ship;

(*r*) the mortgage or hypothecation of any ship or any share in a ship;

(*s*) any forfeiture or condemnation of any ship, or of goods which are being, or have been, carried, or have been attempted to be carried, in any ship, or for the restoration of a ship or any such goods after seizure.

(3) In any proceedings having a conclusion appropriate for the enforcement of any claim such as is mentioned in paragraphs (*p*) to (*s*) of the last preceding subsection a warrant may be issued—

(*a*) if the conclusion is a pecuniary conclusion, for the arrest of the ship on the dependence of the action; or

(*b*) in any other case (whether or not the claimant is entitled to a lien over the ship), for the arrest of the ship *in rem*;

but there shall not be issued in respect of any such conclusion as aforesaid (whether pecuniary or otherwise) a warrant to arrest, either in rem or on the dependence of the action, any ship other than the ship to which the conclusion relates.

(4) Subject to the preceding subsection, nothing in this section shall be taken to authorise—

(*a*) the use of an arrestment on the dependence of an action otherwise than in respect of a pecuniary conclusion, or

(*b*) the use of an arrestment in rem otherwise than in respect of a conclusion appropriate for the making good of a lien.

(5) A warrant for the arrest of a ship *in rem* issued by virtue of paragraph (*b*) of subsection (3) of this section in a case where the person in whose

favour it is issued is not entitled to a lien over the ship shall have effect as authority for the detention of the ship as security for the implementation of the decree of the court so far as it affects that ship:

Provided that the court may, on the application of any person having an interest, recall the arrestment if satisfied that sufficient bail or other security for such implementation has been found.

(6) Nothing in this section shall authorise the arrest, whether on the dependence of an action or in rem, of a ship while it is on passage.

(7) Nothing in this section shall authorise the arrest, whether on the dependence of an action or *in rem*, of a ship in respect of any claim against the Crown, or the arrest, detention or sale of any of Her Majesty's ships or Her Majesty's aircraft.

In this subsection "Her Majesty's ships" and "Her Majesty's aircraft" have the meanings assigned to them by subsection (2) of section 38 of the Crown Proceedings Act 1947.

(8) [Repealed by the Statute Law Revision Act 1963.]

Interpretation of Part V

48. In this Part of this Act, unless the context otherwise requires,—

(*a*) references to an action, a pursuer and a defender include respectively references to a counter-claim, the person making a counter-claim and the person against whom a counter-claim is made;

(*b*) any reference to a conclusion includes a reference to a crave, and "pecuniary conclusion" does not include a conclusion for expenses;

(*c*) any reference to a warrant to arrest property includes a reference to letters of arrestment and to a precept of arrestment;

(*d*) any reference to a lien includes a reference to any hypothec or charge;

(*e*) any reference to claims arising out of salvage includes a reference to such claims for services rendered in saving life from a ship or an aircraft or in preserving cargo, apparel or wreck as, under sections 544 to 546 of the Merchant Shipping Act 1894, or any Order in Council made under section 51 of the Civil Aviation Act 1949, are authorised to be made in connection with a ship or an aircraft; and

(*f*) the following expressions have the meanings hereby assigned to them respectively, that is to say—

"collision regulations" means regulations under section 418 of the Merchant Shipping Act 1894, or any such rules as are mentioned in subsection (1) of section 421 of that Act or any rules made under subsection (2) of the said section 421;

"goods" includes baggage;

"master" has the same meaning as in the Merchant Shipping Act 1894, and accordingly includes every person (except a pilot) having command or charge of a ship;

"ship" includes any description of vessel used in navigation not propelled by oars;

"towage" and "pilotage" in relation to an aircraft, mean towage and pilotage while the aircraft is waterborne.

Repeals

49.—(1) Section 165 of the Merchant Shipping Act 1894 (which imposes restrictions on proceedings for the recovery of wages of seamen and apprentices) shall cease to have effect and is hereby repealed.

(2) [Repealed by the Animal Health Act 1981, Sched. 6.]

Application and commencement of Part V

50.—(1) This Part of this Act shall apply to Scotland only.

[1] (2) This part of this Act shall come into operation on such day as the Secretary of State may appoint by order made by statutory instrument.

(3) Nothing in this Part of this Act shall affect any action in respect of which warrant for service has been granted before the commencement of this Part of this Act.

NOTE

[1] Came into operation 1st January 1957 (S.I. 1957 No. 2099).

Modification of Foreign Judgments (Reciprocal Enforcement) Act 1933, in relation to certain parts of Her Majesty's dominions

51. Where an Order in Council is made extending Part I of the Foreign Judgments (Reciprocal Enforcement) Act 1933 to a part of Her Majesty's dominions or other territory to which Part II of the Administration of Justice Act 1920 extends, the said Part I shall, in relation to that part of Her Majesty's dominions or other territory, have effect as if—

(*a*) [Repealed by the Civil Jurisdiction and Judgments Act 1982, Sched. 14.];

(*b*) the fact that a judgment was given before the coming into operation of the Order did not prevent it from being a judgment to which the said Part I applies, but the time limited for the registration of a judgment were, in the case of a judgment so given, twelve months from the date of the judgment or such longer period as may be allowed by the High Court in England and Wales, the Court of Session in Scotland, or the High Court in Northern Ireland;

(*c*) any judgment registered in any of the said courts under the said Part II before the coming into operation of the Order had been registered in that court under the said Part I and anything done in relation thereto under the said Part II or any rules of court or other provisions appliciable to the said Part II had been done under the said Part I or the corresponding rules of court or other provisions applicable to the said Part I.

. . . . . .

Short title, repeal, extent and commencement

57.—(1) This Act may be cited as the Administration of Justice Act 1956.

(3) This Act, except Part V and section 51 thereof, shall not extend to Scotland.

Interest on Damages (Scotland) Act 1958

(6 & 7 Eliz. 2, c. 61)

An Act to amend the law of Scotland relating to the power of the courts to order payment of interest on damages.

[1st August 1958]

Power of courts to grant interest on damages

1.—[1] (1) Where a court pronounces in interlocuter decerning for payment by any person of a sum of money as damages, the interlocutor may include decree for payment by that person of interest, at such rate or rates as may be specified in the interlocutor, on the whole or any part of that sum for the whole or any part of any period between the date when the right of action arose and the date of the interlocutor.

[1] (1A) Where a court pronounces an interlocutor decerning for payment of a sum which consists of or includes damages or solatium in respect of personal injuries sustained by the pursuer or any other person, then (without prejudice to the exercise of the power conferred by subsection (1) of this section in relation to any part of that sum which does not represent such damages or solatium) the court shall exercise that power so as to include in that sum interest on those damages and on that solatium or on such part of each as the court considers appropriate, unless the court is satisfied that there are reasons special to the case why no interest should be given in respect thereof.

[1] (1B) For the avoidance of doubt, it is hereby declared that where, in any action in which it is competent for the court to award interest under this Act, a tender is made in the course of the action, the tender shall, unless otherwise stated therein, be in full satisfaction of any claim to interest thereunder by any person in whose favour the tender is made; and in considering in any such action whether an award is equal to or greater than an amount tendered in the action, the court shall take account of the amount of any interest awarded under this Act, or such part of that interest as the court considers appropriate.

(2) Nothing in this section shall—

(*a*) authorise the granting of interest upon interest, or

(*b*) prejudice any other power of the court as to the granting of interest, or

(*c*) affect the running of any interest which apart from this section would run by virtue of any enactment or rule of law.

NOTE

[1] Substituted for subs. (1) by the Interest on Damages (Scotland) Act 1971, s. 1.

2. [Repealed with saving by the Law Reform (Miscellaneous Provisions) (Scotland) Act 1980, s. 11 (2) (*d*) and Sched. 3.]

Citation, interpretation, extent and commencement

3.—(1) This Act may be cited as the Interest on Damages (Scotland) Act 1958.

[1] (2) In this Act, " personal injuries " includes any disease and any impairment of a person's physical or mental condition.

(3) This Act shall extend to Scotland only, and shall not apply to any action commenced against any person before the passing of this Act.

NOTE

[1] Substituted by the Interest on Damages (Scotland) Act 1971, s. 1.

Recorded Delivery Service Act 1962

(10 & 11 Eliz. 2, c. 27)

An Act to authorise the sending by the recorded delivery service of certain documents and other things required or authorised to be sent by registered post; and for purposes connected therewith.

[3rd July 1962]

Recorded delivery service to be an alternative to registered post

1.—(1) Any enactment which requires or authorises a document or other thing to be sent by registered post (whether or not it makes any other provision in relation thereto) shall have effect as if it required or, as the case may be, authorised that thing to be sent by registered post or the recorded delivery service; and any enactment which makes any other provision in relation to the sending of a document or other thing by registered post or to a thing so sent shall have effect as if it made the like provision in relation to the sending of that thing by the recorded delivery service or, as the case may be, to a thing sent by that service.

(2) The Schedule to this Act shall have effect for the purpose of making consequential adaptations of the enactments therein mentioned.

[1] (3) Subject to the following subsection the Secretary of State may by order make such amendments of any enactment contained in a local or private Act (being an enactment to which this Act applies) as appear to him to be necessary or expedient in consequence of subsection (1) of this section.

[1] (4) Before making an order under this section, the Secretary of State shall, unless it appears to him to be impracticable to do so, consult with the person who promoted the Bill for the Act to which the order relates, or where it appears to the Secretary of State that some other person has succeeded to the promoter's interest in that Act, that other person.

(5) Any order under this section may be varied or revoked by a subsequent order thereunder, and the power to make any such order shall be exercisable by statutory instrument which shall be subject to annulment in pursuance of a resolution of either House of Parliament.

(6) This section shall not be construed as authorising the sending by the recorded delivery service of anything which under the Post Office Act 1953, or any instrument thereunder is not allowed to be sent by that service.

NOTE

[1] As amended by the Post Office Act 1969, s. 5, and S.I. 1974 No. 691.

Application and interpretation

2.—(1) Subject to the next following subsection, this Act applies to the following enactments, that is to say,—

(*a*) the provisions of any Act (whether public general, local or private) passed before or in the same Session as this Act;

(*b*) the provisions of any Church Assembly Measure so passed;

(*c*) the provisions of any agricultural marketing scheme made under the Agricultural Marketing Act 1958, before the passing of this Act or having effect as if made under that Act;

and, in the case of a provision which has been applied by or under any other enactment passed, or any instrument made under any enactment passed, before or in the same Session as this Act, applies to that provision as so applied, subject, however, in the case of an instrument made after the passing of this Act to any contrary intention appearing therein; and references in this Act (except this section) to any enactment shall be construed accordingly.

(2) This Act does not apply—

(*a*) to subsection (2) of section 9 of the Crown Proceedings Act 1947 (which enables proceedings to be brought against the Crown for loss of or damage to registered inland postal packets);

(*b*) to any enactment which, either as originally enacted or as amended by any subsequent enactment, requires or authorises a thing to be sent by the recorded delivery service as an alternative to registered post or makes provision in relation to a thing sent by that service;

(*c*) to the provisions of any Act of the Parliament of Northern Ireland or of any local or private Act which extends only to Northern Ireland.

(3) In this Act—

references to sending a document or other thing include references to serving, executing, giving or delivering it or doing any similar thing;

references to sending any thing by registered post include references to sending it by or in a registered letter or packet, whether the references are expressed in those terms or terms having the like effect and whether or not there is any mention of the post or pre-payment;

references to any thing sent by registered post or the recorded delivery service shall be construed accordingly; and

references to a local Act include references to any Act confirming a provisional order or scheme.

Extent

3.—(1) It is hereby declared that (subject to subsection (2) of the foregoing section) this Act extends to Northern Ireland.

(2) [Repealed by the Northern Ireland Constitution Act 1973, Sched. 6, Pt. I.]

(3) This Act, so far as it amends any enactment which extends to the Isle of Man or to any of the Channel Islands, or which applies in relation to persons of or belonging to any such island, shall extend to that island or, as the case may be, shall apply in like manner in relation to those persons.

Short title

4. This Act may be cited as the Recorded Delivery Service Act 1962.

SCHEDULE

Adaptation of Enactments

1. Any reference, however worded,—

(*a*) in any enactment the provisions of which apply to, or operate in consequence of the operation of, any enactment amended by section 1 of this Act; or

(*b*) in any enactment relating to the sending of documents or other things otherwise than by registered post or to documents or other things so sent;

to the registered post or to a registered letter or packet, shall be construed as including a reference to the recorded delivery service or to a letter or packet sent by that service; and any reference, however worded, in any such enactment to a Post Office receipt for a registered letter or to an acknowledgment of or certificate of delivery of a registered letter shall be construed accordingly.

2. The foregoing paragraph shall not be taken to prejudice the generality of subsection (1) of section 1 of this Act.

3. In the Citation Amendment (Scotland) Act 1882, the references in Schedule 2 to the post office charge for registration shall include references to the post office charge for sending by the recorded delivery service.

4. [Repealed by the Supreme Court Act 1981, Sched. 7.]

5. The requirement imposed by subsection (4) of section 9 of the Agricultural Marketing Act 1958, that every scheme under that Act shall be so framed as to secure that the notice mentioned in paragraph (*b*) of that subsection shall be served by registered post shall have effect as a requirement that that notice shall be served by registered post or by the recorded delivery service.

Law Reform (Husband and Wife) Act 1962

(10 & 11 Eliz. 2, c. 48)

An Act to amend the law with respect to civil proceedings between husband and wife. [1st August 1962]

. . . . . .

Proceedings between husband and wife in respect of delict

2.—(1) Subject to the provisions of this section, each of the parties to a marriage shall have the like right to bring proceedings against the other in respect of a wrongful or negligent act or omission, or for the prevention of a wrongful act, as if they were not married.

[1] (2) Where any such proceedings are brought by one of the parties to a marriage against the other during the subsistence of the marriage, the court may dismiss the proceedings if it appears that no substantial benefit would accrue to either party from the continuation thereof; and it shall be the duty of the court to consider at an early stage of the proceedings whether the power to dismiss the proceedings under this subsection should or should not be exercised.

(3) This section extends to Scotland only.

NOTE

[1] By s.21 of the Matrimonial Homes (Family Protection) (Scotland) Act 1981, this subsection does not apply to any proceedings brought before the court in pursuance of any provision of that Act.

Short title, repeal, interpretation, saving and extent

3.—(1) This Act may be cited as the Law Reform (Husband and Wife) Act 1962.

(2) [Repealed by the Statute Law (Repeals) Act 1974.]

(3) The references in subsection (1) of section 1 and subsection (1) of section 2 of this Act to the parties to a marriage include references to the persons who were parties to a marriage which has been dissolved.

(4) This Act does not apply to any cause of action which arose, or would but for the subsistence of a marriage have arisen, before the commencement of this Act.

(5) This Act does not extend to Northern Ireland.

Law Reform (Miscellaneous Provisions) (Scotland) Act 1968

(1968 c. 70)

An Act to . . . amend the law of evidence in civil proceedings in Scotland. . . . [25th October 1968]

. . . .

PART III

AMENDMENT OF THE LAW OF EVIDENCE IN CIVIL PROCEEDINGS

Restriction of rule of law requiring corroboration

9. [Repealed by the Civil Evidence (Scotland) Act 1988, Sched.]

Convictions, etc., as evidence in civil proceedings

Convictions as evidence in civil proceedings

[1] **10.**—(1) In any civil proceedings the fact that a person has been convicted of an offence by or before any court in the United Kingdom or by a court-martial there or elsewhere shall (subject to subsection (3) of this section) be admissible in evidence for the purpose of proving, where to do so is relevant to any issue in those proceedings, that he committed that offence, whether he was so convicted upon a plea of guilty or otherwise and whether or not he is a party to the civil proceedings; but no conviction other than a subsisting one shall be admissible in evidence by virtue of this section.

(2) In any civil proceedings in which by virtue of this section a person is proved to have been convicted of an offence by or before any court in the United Kingdom or by a court-martial there or elsewhere—

(*a*) he shall be taken to have committed that offence unless the contrary is proved, and

(*b*) without prejudice to the reception of any other admissible evidence for the purpose of identifying the facts which constituted that offence, the contents of any document which is admissible as evidence of the conviction, and the contents of the complaint, information, indictment or charge-sheet on which the person in question was convicted, shall be admissible in evidence for that purpose.

(3) Nothing in this section shall affect the operation of section 12 of this Act or any other enactment whereby a conviction or a finding of fact in any criminal proceedings is for the purposes of any other proceedings made conclusive evidence of any fact.

(4) Where in any civil proceedings the contents of any document are admissible in evidence by virtue of subsection (2) of this section, a copy of that document, or of the material part thereof, purporting to be certified or otherwise authenticated by or on behalf of the court or authority having custody of that document, shall be admissible in evidence and shall be taken to be a true copy of that document or part unless the contrary is shown.

[2] (5) Nothing in any of the following enactments, that is to say—

(*a*) section 13 of the Powers of Criminal Courts Act 1973 (under which a conviction leading to probation or discharge is to be disregarded except as therein mentioned);

(*b*) section 191 of the Criminal Procedure (Scotland) Act 1975 (which makes similar provision in respect of convictions on indictment in Scotland);

(*c*) section 8 of the Probation Act (Northern Ireland) 1950 (which corresponds to the said section 12) or any corresponding enactment of the Parliament of Northern Ireland for the time being in force,

shall affect the operation of this section; and for the purposes of this section any order made by a court of summary jurisdiction under section 383 of the said Act of 1975 shall be treated as a conviction.

(6) In this section "court-martial" means a court-martial constituted under the Army Act 1955, the Air Force Act 1955 or the Naval Discipline Act 1957 or a disciplinary court constituted under section 50 of the said Act of 1957, and in relation to a court-martial "conviction", as regards a court-martial constituted under either of the said Acts of 1955, means a finding of guilty which is, or falls to be treated as, a finding of the court duly confirmed and, as regards a court-martial or disciplinary court constituted under the said Act of 1957, means a finding of guilty which is, or falls to be treated as, the finding of the court, and "convicted" shall be construed accordingly.

NOTES

[1] Extended: see the Fair Trading Act 1973, s.36(1).

[2] As amended by the Powers of Criminal Courts Act 1973, Sched. 5, para. 32, and as read with the Interpretation Act 1978, s.17(2).

Findings of adultery and paternity as evidence in civil proceedings

[1] **11.**—(1) In any civil proceedings—

(*a*) the fact that a person has been found guilty of adultery in any matrimonial proceedings,

shall (subject to subsection (3) of this section) be admissible in evidence for the purpose of proving, where to do so is relevant to any issue in those civil proceedings, that he committed the adultery to which the finding relates, whether or not he offered any defence to the allegation of adultery and whether or not he is a party to the civil proceedings; but no finding other than a subsisting one shall be admissible in evidence by virtue of this section.

(2) In any civil proceedings in which by virtue of this section a person is proved to have been found guilty of adultery as mentioned in subsection (1)(*a*) of this section—

(*a*) he shall be taken to have committed the adultery to which the finding relates, unless the contrary is proved; and

(*b*) without prejudice to the reception of any other admissible evidence for the purpose of identifying the facts on which the finding was based, the contents of any document which was before the court, or which contains any pronouncement of the court, in the matrimonial proceedings in question shall be admissible in evidence for that purpose.

(3) Nothing in this section shall affect the operation of any enactment whereby a finding of fact in any matrimonial proceedings is for the purposes of any other proceedings made conclusive evidence of any fact.

[2] (4) Nothing in this section shall entitle the Court of Session to pronounce a decree of divorce without receiving evidence from the pursuer.

(5) Subsection (4) of section 10 of this Act shall apply for the purposes of this section as if the reference therein to subsection (2) were a reference to subsection (2) of this section.

(6) In this section—

(*a*) "matrimonial proceedings" means any consistorial action, any matrimonial cause in the High Court or a county court in England and Wales or in the High Court in Northern Ireland, or any appeal arising out of any such action or cause.

NOTES

[1] As amended by the Law Reform (Parent and Child) (Scotland) Act 1986, Sched. 2, with effect from 8th December 1986.

[2] As amended by the Divorce (Scotland) Act 1976, Sched. 1, para. 4.

Conclusiveness of convictions for purposes of defamation actions

12.—(1) In an action for defamation in which the question whether a person did or did not commit a criminal offence is relevant to an issue arising in the action, proof that, at the time when that issue falls to be determined, that person stands convicted of that offence shall be conclusive evidence that he committed that offence; and his conviction thereof shall be admissible in evidence accordingly.

(2) In any such action as aforesaid in which by virtue of this section a person is proved to have been convicted of an offence, the contents of any document which is admissible as evidence of the conviction, and the contents of the complaint, information, indictment, or charge-sheet on which that person was convicted, shall, without prejudice to the reception of any other admissible evidence for the purpose of identifying the facts which constituted that offence, be admissible in evidence for the purpose of identifying those facts.

(3) For the purposes of this section a person shall be taken to stand convicted of an offence if but only if there subsists against him a conviction of that offence by or before a court in the United Kingdom or by a court-martial there or elsewhere.

(4) Subsections (4) to (6) of section 10 of this Act shall apply for the purposes of this section as they apply for the purposes of that section, but as if in the said subsection (4) the reference to subsection (2) were a reference to subsection (2) of this section.

(5) The foregoing provisions of this section shall apply for the purposes of any action begun after the coming into operation of this section, whenever the cause of action arose, but shall not apply for the purposes of any action begun before such commencement or any appeal or other proceedings arising out of any such action.

Statements produced by computers as evidence in civil proceedings

13–16. [Repealed by the Civil Evidence (Scotland) Act 1988, Sched.]

[THE NEXT PAGE IS B 105]

General

Interpretation of Part III, saving, etc.

17.—[1] (1) In this Part of this Act "civil proceedings" includes, in addition to civil proceedings in any of the ordinary courts of law—

(*a*) civil proceedings before any other tribunal, except proceedings in relation to which the strict rules of evidence do not apply, and

(*b*) an arbitration, whether under an enactment or not, and "court" shall be construed accordingly.

(2) In this Part of this Act "consistorial action" does not include an action of aliment only between husband and wife raised in the Court of Session or an action of interim aliment raised in the sheriff court.

[2] (3) In this Part of this Act—

"document" includes in addition to a document in writing—

(*a*) any map, plan, graph or drawing;

(*b*) any photograph;

(*c*) any disc, tape, sound track or other device in which sounds or other data (not being visual images) are embodied so as to be capable (with or without the aid of some other equipment) of being reproduced therefrom; and

(*d*) any film, negative, tape or other device in which one or more visual images are embodied so as to be capable (as aforesaid) of being reproduced therefrom;

"film" includes a microfilm;

"statement" includes any representation of fact, whether made in words or otherwise.

(4) In this Part of this Act any reference to a copy of a document includes—

(*a*) in the case of a document falling within paragraph (*c*) but not (*d*) of the definition of "document" in subsection (3) of this section, a transcript of the sounds or other data embodied therein;

(*b*) in the case of a document falling within paragraph (*d*) but not (*c*) of that definition, a reproduction or still reproduction of the image or images embodied therein, whether enlarged or not;

(*c*) in the case of a document falling within both those paragraphs, such a transcript together with such a still reproduction; and

(*d*) in the case of a document not falling within the said paragraph (*d*) of which a visual image is embodied in a document falling within that paragraph, a reproduction of that image, whether enlarged or not;

and any reference to a copy of the material part of a document shall be construed accordingly.

(5) The clerk of any court having custody of any document shall, on the application of any person who wishes to rely, by virtue of section 10(2), section 11(2) or section 12(2) of this Act or any corresponding provision for the time being in force in any part of the United Kingdom outside Scotland, on the contents of that document in proceedings which he proposes to raise, or which are pending, in any court in the United Kingdom, and on payment by that person of such fee as may be prescribed by act of adjournal or act of sederunt, as the case may be, made with the approval of the Treasury, issue to that person a copy of that document, or of the material part thereof, certified or otherwise authenticated by or on behalf of the court.

(6) Nothing in this Part of this Act shall prejudice the operation of any agreement (whenever made) between the parties to any proceedings as to the evidence which is to be admissible (whether generally or for any particular purpose) in those proceedings.

NOTES

[1] Saved: see the Fair Trading Act 1973, s. 36(1)(4). Applied by the Value Added Tax Act 1983, s. 48(4)(*b*), and the Finance Act 1985, s. 10.

[2] As amended by the Civil Evidence (Scotland) Act 1988, Sched.

. . . . . .

Employer's Liability (Defective Equipment) Act 1969

(1969 c. 37)

An Act to make further provision with respect to the liability of an employer for injury to his employee which is attributable to any defect in equipment provided by the employer for the purposes of the employer's business; and for purposes connected with the matter aforesaid. [25th July 1969]

Extension of employer's liability for defective equipment

1.—(1) Where after the commencement of this Act—

(*a*) an employee suffers personal injury in the course of his employment in consequence of a defect in equipment provided by his employer for the purposes of the employer's business; and

(*b*) the defect is attributable wholly or partly to the fault of a third party (whether identified or not),

the injury shall be deemed to be also attributable to negligence on the part of the employer (whether or not he is liable in respect of the injury apart from this subsection), but without prejudice to the law relating to contributory negligence and to any remedy by way of contribution or in contract or otherwise which is available to the employer in respect of the injury.

(2) In so far as any agreement purports to exclude or limit any liability of an employer arising under subsection (1) of this section, the agreement shall be void.

(3) In this section—

"business" includes the activities carried on by any public body;

"employee" means a person who is employed by another person under a contract of service or apprenticeship and is so employed for the purposes of a business carried on by that other person, and "employer" shall be construed accordingly;

"equipment" includes any plant and machinery, vehicle, aircraft and clothing;

"fault" means negligence, breach of statutory duty or other act or omission which gives rise to liability in tort in England and Wales or which is wrongful and gives rise to liability in damages in Scotland; and

"personal injury" includes loss of life, any impairment of a person's physical or mental condition and any disease.

(4) This section binds the Crown, and persons in the service of the Crown shall accordingly be treated for the purposes of this section as employees of the Crown if they would not be so treated apart from this subsection.

Short title, commencement and extent

[1] **2.**—(1) This Act may be cited as the Employer's Liability (Defective Equipment) Act 1969.

(2) This Act shall come into force on the expiration of the period of three months beginning with the date on which it is passed.

. . . . . .

(4) This Act does not extend to Northern Ireland.

NOTE

[1] As amended by the Northern Ireland Constitution Act 1973, Sched. 6.

Administration of Justice (Scotland) Act 1972

(1972 c. 59)

An Act to confer extended powers on the courts in Scotland to order the inspection of documents and other property, and related matters; to enable an appeal to be taken to the House of Lords from an interlocutor of the Court of Session on a motion for a new trial; to enable a case to be stated on a question of law to the Court of Session in an arbitration; and to enable alterations to be made by act of sederunt in the rate of interest to be included in sheriff court decrees or extracts.

[9th August 1972]

Extended powers of courts to order inspection of documents and other property, etc.

[0] **1.**—[1] (1) Without prejudice to the existing powers of the Court of Session and of the sheriff court, those courts shall have power, subject to the provisions of subsection (4) of this section, to order the inspection, photographing, preservation, custody and detention of documents and other property (including, where appropriate, land) which appear to the court to be property as to which any question may relevantly arise in any existing civil proceedings before that court or in civil proceedings which are likely to be brought, and to order the production and recovery of any such property, the taking of samples thereof and the carrying out of any experiment thereon or therewith.

[2] (1A) Without prejudice to the existing powers of the Court of Session and of the sheriff court, those courts shall have power, subject to subsection (4) of this section, to order any person to disclose such information as he has as to the identity of any persons who appear to the court to be persons who—

(*a*) might be witnesses in any existing civil proceedings before that court or in civil proceedings which are likely to be brought; or

(*b*) might be defenders in any civil proceedings which appear to the court to be likely to be brought.

[3] (2) Notwithstanding any rule of law or practice to the contrary, the court may exercise the powers mentioned in subsection (1) or (1A) of this section—

(*a*) where proceedings have been commenced, on the application, at any time after such commencement, of a party to or minuter in the proceedings, or any other person who appears to the court to have an interest to be joined as such party or minuter;

(*b*) where proceedings have not been commenced, on the application at any time of a person who appears to the court to be likely to be a party to or minuter in proceedings which are likely to be brought;

unless there is special reason why the application should not be granted.

(3) The powers conferred on the Court of Session by section 16 of the Administration of Justice (Scotland) Act 1933 to regulate its own procedure and the powers conferred on that court by section 32 of the Sheriff Courts (Scotland) Act 1971 to regulate the procedure of the sheriff court shall include power to regulate and prescribe the procedure to be followed, and the form of any document to be used, in any application under the foregoing provisions of this section in a case where the application is in respect of proceedings which have not been commenced, and such incidental,

supplementary and consequential provisions as appear appropriate; and without prejudice to the said generality, the said powers shall include power to provide in such a case for the application to be granted *ex parte*, for the intimation of the application to such persons (if any) as the court thinks fit, and for the finding of caution where appropriate for any loss, damage or expenses which may be incurred as a result of the application.

(4) Nothing in this section shall affect any rule of law or practice relating to the privilege of witnesses and havers, confidentiality of communications and withholding or non-disclosure of information on the grounds of public interest; and section 47 of the Crown Proceedings Act 1947 (recovery of documents in possession of Crown) shall apply in relation to any application under this section in respect of a document or other property as it applied before the commencement of this section to an application for commission and diligence for the recovery of a document.

NOTES

[0] Extended by the Drug Trafficking Offences Act 1986, s.21(4), the Criminal Justice (Scotland) Act 1987, s.28(4), the Prevention of Terrorism (Temporary Provisions) Act 1989, Sched. 4, para. 19(5) and the Criminal Justice Act 1988, s.91(4). Applied by the Civil Jurisdiction and Judgments Act 1982, s.28.

[1] See the Law Reform (Miscellaneous Provisions) (Scotland) Act 1985, s.15(3), *infra*.

[2] Inserted by the Law Reform (Miscellaneous Provisions) (Scotland) Act 1985, s.19.

[3] As amended by the Law Reform (Miscellaneous Provisions) (Scotland) Act 1985, Sched. 2, para. 15.

2. [Repealed by the Court of Session Act 1988, Sched. 2.]

Power of arbiter to state case to Court of Session

[1] **3.**—(1) Subject to express provision to the contrary in an agreement to refer to arbitration, the arbiter or oversman may, on the application of a party to the arbitration, and shall, if the Court of Session on such an application so directs, at any stage in the arbitration state a case for the opinion of that court on any question of law arising in the arbitration.

(2) This section shall not apply to an arbitration under any enactment which confers a power to appeal to or state a case for the opinion of a court or tribunal in relation to that arbitration.

[2] (3) This section shall not apply to any form of arbitration relating to a trade dispute within the meaning of the Employment Protection Act 1975; to any other arbitration arising from a collective agreement within the meaning of the Trade Union and Labour Relations Act 1974; or to proceedings before the Industrial Arbitration Board.

(4) This section shall not apply in relation to an agreement to refer to arbitration made before the commencement of this Act.

NOTES

[1] Excluded: see the Local Government (Scotland) Act 1973, s.25(3) and the Electricity Act 1989, s.64(2).

[2] As amended by the Trade Union and Labour Relations Act 1974, Scheds. 3 and 5, and the Employment Act 1982, Sched. 3, para. 11.

Rate of interest in sheriff court decrees or extracts

4. The Court of Session may by act of sederunt direct that section 9 of the Sheriff Courts (Scotland) Extracts Act 1892 (interest included in sheriff court decree or extract), as that enactment has effect for the time being whether by virtue of this section or otherwise, shall be amended so as to substitute, for the rate of interest specified in that section, such rate as may be specified in the act of sederunt.

Short title, interpretation, commencement and extent

5.—(1) This Act may be cited as the Administration of Justice (Scotland) Act 1972.

(2) In this Act any reference to an enactment shall be construed as a reference to that enactment as amended by or under any other enactment.

[1] (3) Sections 1 and 3 of this Act shall come into operation on such day as the Secretary of State may by order made by statutory instrument appoint, and different days may be appointed for different purposes.

(4) This Act shall extend to Scotland only.

NOTE

[1] Ss.1 and 3 in operation on 2nd April 1973 (S.I. 1973 No. 339).

European Communities Act 1972

(1972 c. 68)

An Act to make provision in connection with the enlargement of the European Communities to include the United Kingdom, together with (for certain purposes) the Channel Islands, the Isle of Man and Gibraltar. [17th October 1972]

PART I

GENERAL PROVISIONS

Short title and interpretation

[1] **1.**—(1) This Act may be cited as the European Communities Act 1972.

(2) In this Act

"the Communities" means the European Economic Community, the European Coal and Steel Community and the European Atomic Energy Community;

"the Treaties" or "the Community Treaties" means, subject to subsection (3) below, the pre-accession treaties, that is to say, those described in Part I of Schedule 1 to this Act, taken with—

(*a*) the treaty relating to the accession of the United Kingdom to the European Economic Community and to the European Atomic Energy Community, signed at Brussels on the 22nd January 1972; and

(*b*) the decision, of the same date, of the Council of the European Communities relating to the accession of the United Kingdom to the European Coal and Steel Community; and

[2] (*c*) the treaty relating to the accession of the Hellenic Republic to the European Economic Community and to the European Atomic Energy Community, signed at Athens on 28th May 1979; and

[2] (*d*) the decision, of 24th May 1979, of the Council relating to the accession of the Hellenic Republic to the European Coal and Steel Community; and

[3] (*e*) the decisions, of 7th May 1985 and of 24th June 1988, of the Council on the Communities' system of own resources; and

[3] (*f*) the undertaking by the Representatives of the Governments of the member States, as confirmed at their meeting within the Council on 24th June 1988 in Luxembourg, to make payments to finance the Communities' general budget for the financial year 1988; and

[4] (*g*) the treaty relating to the accession of the Kingdom of Spain and the Portuguese Republic to the European Economic Community and to the European Atomic Energy Community, signed at Lisbon and Madrid on 12th June 1985; and

[4] (*h*) the decision, of 11th June 1985, of the Council relating to the accession of the Kingdom of Spain and the Portuguese Republic to the European Coal and Steel Community; and

[5] (*j*) the following provisions of the Single European Act signed at Luxembourg and The Hague on 17th and 28th February 1986, namely Title II (amendment of the treaties establishing the Communities) and, so far as they relate to any of the Communities or any Community institution, the preamble and Titles I (common provisions) and IV (general and final provisions);

and any other treaty entered into by any of the Communities, with or without any of the member States, or entered into, as a treaty ancillary to any of the treaties, by the United Kingdom;

and any expression defined in Schedule 1 to this Act has the meaning there given to it.

[THE NEXT PAGE IS B 111]

(3) If Her Majesty by Order in Council declares that a treaty specified in the Order is to be regarded as one of the Community Treaties as herein defined, the Order shall be conclusive that it is to be so regarded; but a treaty entered into by the United Kingdom after the 22nd January 1972, other than a pre-accession treaty to which the United Kingdom accedes on terms settled on or before that date, shall not be so regarded unless it is so specified, nor be so specified unless a draft of the Order in Council has been approved by resolution of each House of Parliament.

(4) For purposes of subsections (2) and (3) above, "treaty" includes any international agreement, and any protocol or annex to a treaty or international agreement.

NOTES

[1] As amended by the Interpretation Act 1978, Sched. 3.

[2] Added by the European Communities (Greek Accession) Act 1979, s. 1.

[3] Added by the European Communities (Finance) Act 1985, s. 1. Substituted by the European Communities (Finance) Act 1988, s. 1.

[4] Added by the European Communities (Spanish and Portuguese Accession) Act 1985, s. 1.

[5] Added by the European Communities (Amendment) Act 1986, s.1.

General implementation of Treaties

2.—(1) All such rights, powers, liabilities, obligations and restrictions from time to time created or arising by or under the Treaties, and all such remedies and procedures from time to time provided for by or under the Treaties, as in accordance with the Treaties are without further enactment to be given legal effect or used in the United Kingdom shall be recognised and available in law, and be enforced, allowed and followed accordingly; and the expression "enforceable Community right" and similar expressions shall be read as referring to one to which this subsection applies.

(2) Subject to Schedule 2 to this Act, at any time after its passing Her Majesty may by Order in Council, and any designated Minister or department may by regulations, make provision—

(*a*) for the purpose of implementing any Community obligation of the United Kingdom, or enabling any such obligation to be implemented, or of enabling any rights enjoyed or to be enjoyed by the United Kingdom under or by virtue of the Treaties to be exercised; or

(*b*) for the purpose of dealing with matters arising out of or related to any such obligation or rights or the coming into force, or the operation from time to time, of subsection (1) above;

and in the exercise of any statutory power or duty, including any power to give directions or to legislate by means of orders, rules, regulations or other subordinate instrument, the person entrusted with the power or duty may have regard to the objects of the Communities and to any such obligation or rights as aforesaid.

In this subsection "designated Minister or department" means such Minister of the Crown or government department as may from time to time be designated by Order in Council in relation to any matter or for any purpose, but subject to such restrictions or conditions (if any) as may be specified by the Order in Council.

(3) There shall be charged on and issued out of the Consolidated Fund or, if so determined by the Treasury, the National Loans Fund the amounts required to meet any Community obligation to make payments to any of the Communities or member States, or any Community obligation in respect of contributions to the capital or reserves of the European Investment Bank or in respect of loans to the Bank, or to redeem any notes or obligations issued or created in respect of any such Community obligation; and, except as otherwise provided by or under any enactment,—

(*a*) any other expenses incurred under or by virtue of the Treaties or this Act by any Minister of the Crown or government department may be paid out of moneys provided by Parliament; and (*b*) any sums received under or by virtue of the Treaties or this Act by any Minister of the Crown or government department, save for such sums as may be required for disbursements permitted by any other enactment, shall be paid into the Consolidated Fund or, if so determined by the Treasury, the National Loans Fund.

(4) The provision that may be made under subsection (2) above includes, subject to Schedule 2 to this Act, any such provision (of any such extent) as might be made by Act of Parliament, and any enactment passed or to be passed, other than one contained in this Part of this Act, shall be construed and have effect subject to the foregoing provisions of this section; but, except as may be provided by any Act passed after this Act, Schedule 2 shall have effect in connection with the powers conferred by this and the following sections of this Act to make Orders in Council and regulations.

[1] (5) And the references in that subsection to a Minister of the Crown or government department and to a statutory power or duty shall include a Minister or department of the Government of Northern Ireland and a power or duty arising under or by virtue of an Act of the Parliament of Northern Ireland.

(6) A law passed by the legislature of any of the Channel Islands or of the Isle of Man, or a colonial law (within the meaning of the Colonial Laws Validity Act 1865) passed or made for Gibraltar, if expressed to be passed or made in the implementation of the Treaties and of the obligations of the United Kingdom thereunder, shall not be void or inoperative by reason of any inconsistency with or repugnancy to an Act of Parliament, passed or to be passed, that extends to the Island or Gibraltar or any provision having the force and effect of an Act there (but not including this section), nor by reason of its having some operation outside the Island or Gibraltar; and any such Act or provision that extends to the Island or Gibraltar shall be construed and have effect subject to the provisions of any such law.

NOTE

[1] As amended by the Northern Ireland Constitution Act 1973, Sched. 6; "that subsection" means s. 2(2) of this Act.

Decisions on, and proof of, Treaties and Community instruments, etc.

[1] **3.**—(1) For the purposes of all legal proceedings any question as to the meaning or effect of any of the Treaties, or as to the validity, meaning or effect of any Community instrument, shall be treated as a question of law (and, if not referred to the European Court, be for determination as such in accordance with the principles laid down by and any relevant decision of the European Court or any court attached thereto).

(2) Judicial notice shall be taken of the Treaties, of the Official Journal of the Communities and of any decision of, or expression of opinion by, the European Court or any court attached thereto on any such question as aforesaid; and the Official Journal shall be admissible as evidence of any instrument or other act thereby communicated of any of the Communities or of any Community institution.

(3) Evidence of any instrument issued by a Community institution, including any judgment or order of the European Court or any court attached thereto, or of any document in the custody of a Community institution, or any entry in or extract from such a document, may be given in any legal proceedings by production of a copy certified as a true copy by an official of that institution; and any document purporting to be such a copy shall be received in evidence without proof of the official position or handwriting of the person signing the certificate.

(4) Evidence of any Community instrument may also be given in any legal proceedings—

(*a*) by production of a copy purporting to be printed by the Queen's Printer;

(*b*) where the instrument is in the custody of a government department (including a department of the Government of Northern Ireland), by production of a copy certified on behalf of the department to be a true copy by an officer of the department generally or specially authorised so to do;

[THE NEXT PAGE IS B 113]

and any document purporting to be such a copy as is mentioned in paragraph (*b*) above of an instrument in the custody of a department shall be received in evidence without proof of the official position or handwriting of the person signing the certificate, or of his authority to do so, or of the document being in the custody of the department.

(5) In any legal proceedings in Scotland evidence of any matter given in a manner authorised by this section shall be sufficient evidence of it.

NOTE

[1] As amended by the European Communities (Amendment) Act 1986, s.2.

. . . . . .

SCHEDULES

SCHEDULE 1

DEFINITIONS RELATING TO COMMUNITIES

PART I

THE PRE-ACCESSION TREATIES

1. The "E.C.S.C. Treaty", that is to say, the Treaty establishing the European Coal and Steel Community, signed at Paris on the 18th April 1951.

2. The "E.E.C. Treaty", that is to say, the Treaty establishing the European Economic Community, signed at Rome on the 25th March 1957.

3. The "Euratom Treaty", that is to say, the Treaty establishing the European Atomic Energy Community, signed at Rome on the 25th March 1957.

4. The Convention on certain Institutions common to the European Communities, signed at Rome on the 25th March 1957.

5. The Treaty establishing a single Council and a single Commission of the European Communities, signed at Brussels on the 8th April 1965.

6. The Treaty amending certain Budgetary Provisions of the Treaties establishing the European Communities and of the Treaty establishing a single Council and a single Commission of the European Communities, signed at Luxembourg on the 22nd April 1970.

7. Any treaty entered into before the 22nd January 1972 by any of the Communities (with or without any of the member States) or, as a treaty ancillary to any treaty included in this Part of this Schedule, by the member States (with or without any other country).

PART II

OTHER DEFINITIONS

"Economic Community", "Coal and Steel Community" and "Euratom" mean respectively the European Economic Community, the European Coal and Steel Community and the European Atomic Energy Community.

"Community customs duty" means, in relation to any goods, such duty of customs as may from time to time be fixed for those goods by directly applicable Community provision as the duty chargeable on importation into member States.

"Community institution" means any institution of any of the Communities or common to the Communities; and any reference to an institution of a particular Community shall include one common to the Communities when it acts for that Community, and similarly with references to a committee, officer or servant of a particular Community.

"Community instrument" means any instrument issued by a Community institution.

"Community obligation" means any obligation created or arising by or under the Treaties, whether an enforceable Community obligation or not.

"Enforceable Community right" and similar expressions shall be construed in accordance with section 2(1) of this Act.

"Entry date" means the date on which the United Kingdom becomes a member of the Communities.

"European Court" means the Court of Justice of the European Communities.

"Member", in the expression "member State", refers to membership of the Communities.

SCHEDULE 2

Provisions as to Subordinate Legislation

[1] 1.—(1) The powers conferred by section 2 (2) of this Act to make provision for the purposes mentioned in section 2 (2) (*a*) and (*b*) shall not include power—

(*a*) to make any provision imposing or increasing taxation; or

(*b*) to make any provision taking effect from a date earlier than that of the making of the instrument containing the provision; or

(*c*) to confer any power to legislate by means of orders, rules, regulations or other subordinate instrument, other than rules of procedure for any court or tribunal; or

(*d*) to create any new criminal offence punishable with imprisonment for more than two years or punishable on summary conviction with imprisonment for more than three months or with a fine of more than £400 (if not calculated on a daily basis) or with a fine of more than £100 a day.

(2) Sub-paragraph (1)(*c*) above shall not be taken to preclude the modification of a power to legislate conferred otherwise than under section 2(2), or the extension of any such power to purposes of the like nature as those for which it was conferred; and a power to give directions as to matters of administration is not to be regarded as a power to legislate within the meaning of sub-paragraph (1)(*c*).

NOTE

[1] As amended by the Criminal Law Act 1977, ss.32(3) and 65 (7).

2.—(1) Subject to paragraph 3 below, where a provision contained in any section of this Act confers power to make regulations (otherwise than by modification or extension of an existing power), the power shall be exercisable by statutory instrument.

(2) Any statutory instrument containing an Order in Council or regulations made in the exercise of a power so conferred, if made without a draft having been approved by resolution of each House of Parliament, shall be subject to annulment in pursuance of a resolution of either House.

3. Nothing in paragraph 2 above shall apply to any Order in Council made by the Governor of Northern Ireland or to any regulations made by a Minister or department of the Government of Northern Ireland; but where a provision contained in any section of this Act confers power to make such an Order in Council or regulations, then any Order in Council or regulations made in the exercise of that power, if made without a draft having been approved by resolution of each House of the Parliament of Northern Ireland, shall be subject to negative resolution within the meaning of section 41(6) of the Interpretation Act (Northern Ireland) 1954 as if the Order or regulations were a statutory instrument within the meaning of that Act.

. . . . . .

[THE NEXT PAGE IS B 116]

Litigants in Person (Costs and Expenses) Act 1975

(1975 c. 47)

An Act to make further provision as to the costs or expenses recoverable by litigants in person in civil proceedings.

[1st August 1975]

Costs or expenses recoverable

1. . . .

(2) Where in any proceedings to which this section applies, any costs or expenses of a party litigant are ordered to be paid by any other party to the proceedings or in any other way, there may, subject to rules of court, be allowed on the taxation or other determination of those costs or expenses sums in respect of work done, and any outlays and losses incurred, by the litigant in or in connection with the proceedings to which the order relates.

This subsection applies to civil proceedings—

(*a*) in the sheriff court, the Scottish Land Court, the Court of Session or the House of Lords on appeal from the Court of Session,

(*b*) before the Lands Tribunal for Scotland, or

(*c*) in or before any other court or tribunal specified in an order made under this subsection by the Lord Advocate.

(3) An order under subsection (1) or (2) above shall be made by statutory instrument and shall be subject to annulment in pursuance of a resolution of either House of Parliament.

(4) In this section "rules of court"—

(*a*) in relation to the Lands Tribunal or the Lands Tribunal for Scotland, means rules made under section 3 of the Lands Tribunal Act 1949,

. . . . . .

(*c*) in relation to any other tribunal specified in an order made under subsection (1) or (2) above, shall have the meaning given by the order as respects that tribunal.

. . . . . .

Short title, commencement and extent

2.—(1) This Act may be cited as the Litigants in Person (Costs and Expenses) Act 1975.

[1] (2) This Act shall come into operation—

. . . . . .

(*b*) in relation to Scotland, on such day as the Lord Advocate may by order made by statutory instrument appoint.

(3) An order under subsection (2) above—

(*a*) may appoint different days for different purposes, and

(*b*) may make such transitional provision as appears to the Lord Chancellor or, as the case may be, the Lord Advocate to be necessary or expedient.

. . . . . .

NOTE

[1] 1st October 1976 for civil proceedings in the sheriff court, the Scottish Land Court, the Court of Session, the House of Lords on Appeal from the Court of Session and the Lands Tribunal for Scotland in relation to Scotland: see S.I. 1976 No. 1432.

1st September 1980 for the remainder: see S.I. 1980 No. 1152.

[1] Damages (Scotland) Act 1976

(1976 c. 13)

An act to amend the law of Scotland relating to the damages recoverable in respect of deaths caused by personal injuries; to define the rights to damages in respect of personal injuries and death which are transmitted to an executor; to abolish rights to assythment; to make provision relating to the damages due to a pursuer for patrimonial loss caused by personal injuries whereby his expectation of life is diminished; and for purposes connected with the matters aforesaid. [13th April 1976]

NOTE
[1] See the Consumer Protection Act 1987, s. 6(2).

Rights of relatives of a deceased person

[0] **1.**—(1) Where a person dies in consequence of personal injuries sustained by him as a result of an act or omission of another person, being an act or omission giving rise to liability to pay damages to the injured person or his executor, then, subject to the following provisions of this Act, the person liable to pay those damages (in this section referred to as "the responsible person") shall also be liable to pay damages in accordance with this section to any relative of the deceased, being a relative within the meaning of Schedule 1 to this Act.

(2) No liability shall arise under this section if the liability to the deceased or his executor in respect of the act or omission has been excluded or discharged (whether by antecedent agreement or otherwise) by the deceased before his death, or is excluded by virtue of any enactment.

[1] (3) The damages which the responsible person shall be liable to pay to a relative of a deceased under this section shall (subject to the provisions of this Act) be such as will compensate the relative for any loss of support suffered by him since the date of the deceased's death or likely to be suffered by him as a result of the act or omission in question, together with any reasonable expense incurred by him in connection with the deceased's funeral.

[2] (4) If the relative is a member of the deceased's immediate family (within the meaning of section 10(2) of this Act) there shall be awarded, without prejudice to any claim under subsection (3) above, such sum of damages, if any, as the court thinks just by way of compensation for the loss of such non-patrimonial benefit as the relative might have been expected to derive from the deceased's society and guidance if he had not died; and a sum of damages such as is mentioned in this subsection shall be known as a "loss of society award".

[3] (5) In assessing for the purposes of this section the amount of any loss of support suffered by a relative of a deceased no account shall be taken of—

(*a*) any patrimonial gain or advantage which has accrued or will or may accrue to the relative from the deceased or from any other person by way of succession or settlement;

(*b*) any insurance money, benefit, pension or gratuity which has been, or will be or may be, paid as a result of the deceased's death;

and in this subsection—

"benefit" means benefit under the Social Security Act 1975 or the Social Security (Northern Ireland) Act 1975, and any payment by a friendly society or trade union for the relief or maintenance of a member's dependants;

"insurance money" includes a return of premiums; and

"pension" includes a return of contributions and any payment of a lump sum in respect of a person's employment.

(6) In order to establish loss of support for the purposes of this section it shall not be essential for a claimant to show that the deceased was, or might have become, subject to a duty in law to provide or contribute to the support of the claimant; but if any such fact is established it may be taken into account in determining whether, and if so to what extent, the deceased, if he had not died, would have been likely to provide or contribute to such support.

[4] (7) Except as provided in this section or in Part II of the Administration of Justice Act 1982 or under section 1 of the International Transport Conventions Act 1983 no person shall be entitled by reason of relationship to damages (including damages by way of solatium) in respect of the death of another person.

NOTES

[0] See the Consumer Protection Act 1987, s. 6(1)(*c*). Extended (*prosp.*): see the Antarctic Minerals Act 1989, s.13(1). Excluded by the Social Security Act 1989, s.22(4)(*d*).

[1] Extended: see the Administration of Justice Act 1982, s. 9(2).

[2] Saved by the International Transport Conventions Act 1983, Sched. 1, para. 1.

[3] Applied by the International Transport Conventions Act 1983, Sched. 1, para. 2.

[4] As amended by the Administration of Justice Act 1982, s. 14(1), and the International Transport Conventions Act 1983, Sched. 1, para. 4(*a*).

Rights transmitted to executor in respect of deceased person's injuries

2.—(1) Subject to subsection (3) below there shall be transmitted to the executor of a deceased person the like rights to damages in respect of personal injuries sustained by the deceased as were vested in him immediately before his death; and for the purpose of enforcing any such right the executor shall be entitled to bring an action or, if an action for that purpose had been brought by the deceased before his death and had not been concluded before then, to be sisted as pursuer in that action.

(2) For the purpose of subsection (1) above an action shall not be taken to be concluded while any appeal is competent or before any appeal timeously taken has been disposed of.

(3) There shall not be transmitted to the executor of a deceased person any right to damages in respect of personal injuries sustained by the deceased and vested in the deceased as aforesaid, being a right to damages—

(*a*) by way of solatium;

(*b*) by way of compensation for patrimonial loss attributable to any period after the deceased's death,

and accordingly the executor shall not be entitled to bring an action, or to be sisted as pursuer in any action brought by the deceased before his death, for the purpose of enforcing any such right.

Certain rights arising on death of another not transmissible

3. There shall not be transmitted to the executor of a deceased person any right which has accrued to the deceased before his death, being a right to—

(*a*) damages by way of solatium in respect of the death of any other person, under the law in force before the commencement of this Act;

(*b*) a loss of society award,

and accordingly the executor shall not be entitled to bring an action, or to be sisted as pursuer in any action brought by the deceased before his death, for the purpose of enforcing any such right.

Executor's claim not to be excluded by relatives' claims: and vice versa

[1] **4.** A claim by the executor of a deceased person for damages under

section 2 of this Act is not excluded by the making of a claim by a relative of the deceased for damages under section 1 of this Act; nor is a claim by a relative of a deceased person for damages under the said section 1 excluded by the making of a claim by the deceased's executor for damages under the said section 2.

NOTE

[1] As amended by the Administration of Justice Act 1982, s.14(2)(*a*).

5. [Repealed by the Administration of Justice Act 1982, s.14(2).]

Limitation of total amount of liability

[1] **6.**—[2] (1) Where in any action to which this section applies, so far as directed against any defender, it is shown that by antecedent agreement, compromise or otherwise, the liability arising in relation to that defender from the personal injuries in question had, before the deceased's death, been limited to damages of a specified or ascertainable amount, or where that liability is so limited by virtue of any enactment, nothing in this Act shall make the defender liable to pay damages exceeding that amount; and accordingly where in such an action there are two or more pursuers any damages to which they would respectively be entitled under this Act apart from the said limitation shall, if necessary, be reduced *pro rata*.

(2) Where two or more such actions are conjoined, the conjoined actions shall be treated for the purposes of this section as if they were a single action.

[3] (3) This section applies to any action in which, following the death of any person from personal injuries, damages are claimed—

(*a*) by the executor of the deceased, in respect of the injuries from which the deceased died;

(*b*) in respect of the death of the deceased, by any relative of his.

NOTES

[1] Excluded by the International Transport Conventions Act 1983, Sched. 1, para. 2.

[2] As amended by the Administration of Justice Act 1982, s.14(2)(*b*)(i).

[3] Added by the Administration of Justice Act 1982, s.14(2)(*b*)(ii).

Amendment of references in other Acts

7. In any Act passed before this Act, unless the context otherwise requires, any reference to solatium in respect of the death of any person (however expressed) shall be construed as a reference to a loss of society award within the meaning of section 1 of this Act; and any reference to a dependant of a deceased person, in relation to an action claiming damages in respect of the deceased person's death, shall be construed as including a reference to a relative of the deceased person within the meaning of this Act.

Abolition of right of assythment

8. After the commencement of this Act no person shall in any circumstances have a right to assythment, and accordingly any action claiming that remedy shall (to the extent that it does so) be incompetent.

Damages due to injured person for patrimonial loss caused by personal injuries whereby expectation of life is diminished

9.—(1) This section applies to any action for damages in respect of personal injuries sustained by the pursuer where his expected date of death is earlier than it would have been if he had not sustained the injuries.

(2) In assessing, in any action to which this section applies, the amount of any patrimonial loss in respect of the period after the date of decree—

(*a*) it shall be assumed that the pursuer will live until the date when he would have been expected to die if he had not sustained the injuries (hereinafter referred to as the "notional date of death");

(*b*) the court may have regard to any amount, whether or not it is an amount related to earnings by the pursuer's own labour or other gainful activity, which in its opinion the pursuer, if he had not sustained the injuries in question, would have received in the period up to his notional date of death by way of benefits in money or money's worth, being benefits derived from sources other than the pursuer's own estate;

(*c*) the court shall have regard to any diminution of any such amount as aforesaid by virtue of expenses which in the opinion of the court the pursuer, if he had not sustained the injuries in question, would reasonably have incurred in the said period by way of living expenses.

Interpretation

10.—(1) In this Act, unless the context otherwise requires—

"loss of society award" has the meaning assigned to it by section 1(4) of this Act;

"personal injuries" includes any disease or any impairment of a person's physical or mental condition;

"relative", in relation to a deceased person, has the meaning assigned to it by Schedule 1 to this Act.

[1] (2) References in this Act to a member of a deceased person's immediate family are references to any relative of his who falls within subparagraph (*a*) (*aa*) (*b*) or (*c*) of paragraph 1 of Schedule 1 to this Act.

(3) References in this Act to any other Act are references to that Act as amended, extended or applied by any other enactment, including this Act.

NOTE

[1] As amended by the Administration of Justice Act 1982, s.14(4).

Repeals

11. The enactments specified in Schedule 2 to this Act are hereby repealed to the extent specified in relation thereto in the third column of that Schedule.

Citation, application to Crown, commencement and extent

12.—(1) This Act may be cited as the Damages (Scotland) Act 1976.

(2) This Act binds the Crown.

(3) This Act shall come into operation on the expiration of one month beginning with the day on which it is passed.

(4) Nothing in this Act affects any proceedings commenced before this Act comes into operation.

(5) This Act extends to Scotland only.

SCHEDULES

Section 1 SCHEDULE 1

DEFINITION OF "RELATIVE"

1. In this Act "relative" in relation to a deceased person includes—
   (*a*) any person who immediately before the deceased's death was the spouse of the deceased;
   [1] (*aa*) any person, not being the spouse of the deceased, who was, immediately before the deceased's death, living with the deceased as husband or wife;
   (*b*) any person who was a parent of child of the deceased;
   (*c*) any person not falling within paragraph (*b*) above who was accepted by the deceased as a child of his family;
   (*d*) any person who was an ascendant or descendant (other than a parent or child) of the deceased;
   (*e*) any person who was, or was the issue of, a brother, sister, uncle or aunt of the deceased; and
   (*f*) any person who, having been a spouse of the deceased, had ceased to be so by virtue of a divorce;

but docs not include any other person.

NOTE

[1] Inserted by the Administration of Justice Act 1982, s.14(4).

2. In deducing any relationship for the purposes of the foregoing paragraph—
   (*a*) any relationship by affinity shall be treated as a relationship by consanguinity; any relationship of the half blood shall be treated as a relationship of the whole blood; and the stepchild of any person shall be treated as his child; and
   [1] (*b*) section 1(1) of the Law Reform (Parent and Child) (Scotland) Act 1986 shall apply; and any reference (however expressed) in this Act to a relative shall be construed accordingly.

NOTE

[1] As amended by the Law Reform (Parent and Child) (Scotland) Act 1986, Sched. 1, para. 15, with effect from 8th December 1986.

. . . . . .

Law Reform (Miscellaneous Provisions) (Scotland) Act 1980

(1980 c. 55)

An Act to make new provision for Scotland as respects the law relating to the qualification of jurors; to amend the law relating to jury service in Scotland; to make further provision for Scotland in respect of prior rights in the estates of deceased persons; to dispense with caution as regards certain executors-dative; to provide a procedure whereby an heir of provision may establish entitlement to act as trustee; to amend provisions of the Judicial Factors Act 1849 and the Trusts (Scotland) Act 1961 relating to the actings of judicial factors; to remove an obligation to preserve inventories of the estates of deceased persons in Scotland; to make further provision in respect of performance of the duties of sheriff principal; to amend the law relating to the jurisdiction and powers of the sheriff court; to empower Senators of the

College of Justice to act as arbiters and oversmen in commercial disputes; to make further provision in respect of awards of compensation by the Lands Tribunal for Scotland; to remove the right of a vexatious litigant to appeal against a Lord Ordinary's refusal to allow the institution of legal proceedings; to amend the law relating to the jurisdiction of the Court of Session in actions for reduction; . . . to amend provisions of the Marriage (Scotland) Act 1977 relating to the validity of marriages; to amend the provisions of the Prescription and Limitation (Scotland) Act 1973 relating to limitation of actions; to amend the law relating to the constitution and powers of the Scottish Solicitors' Discipline Tribunal; to make further provision as regards Scottish solicitors' clients' accounts; to enable amendments to be made to provisions of the Legal Aid (Scotland) Act 1967 relating to contributions from assisted persons; . . . and for connected purposes.

[29th October 1980]

Juries

Qualification of jurors

1.—(1) Subject to subsections (2) and (3) below, every person who—

(*a*) is for the time being registered as a parliamentary or local government elector;

(*b*) is not less than eighteen nor more than sixty-five years of age;

(*c*) has been ordinarily resident in the United Kingdom the Channel Islands or the Isle of Man for any period of at least five years since attaining the age of thirteen years; and

(*d*) is not among the persons listed in Part I of Schedule 1 to this Act, being persons hereby declared ineligible for, nor among those listed in Part II of that Schedule, being persons hereby declared disqualified from, jury service,

shall be qualified and liable to serve as a juror in any Scottish court, civil or criminal.

(2) A person who is qualified under subsection (1) above but is among the persons listed in Part III of Schedule 1 to this Act, being persons hereby declared excusable as of right from jury service, shall be excused therefrom on any occasion where, having been cited to attend for jury service he—

(*a*) attends in compliance with the citation and intimates to the court his right and desire to be so excused; or

(*b*) before the date on which he is cited first to attend, gives written notice of his right and desire to be so excused to the clerk of court issuing the citation.

(3) Without prejudice to subsection (2) above, a person who is qualified under subsection (1) above but is among the persons listed in Group C of Part III of Schedule 1 to this Act shall be excused from jury service on any occasion where he has been cited to attend for such service but his commanding officer certifies to the clerk of the court issuing the citation that it would be prejudicial to the efficiency of the force of which the person is a member were the person required to be absent from duty.

(4) The fact that any person serving on the jury chosen for a particular trial (whether before or after the coming into force of this Act) is, under subsection (1) above, ineligible or not qualified for or disqualified from jury service, or was under section 1 of the Jurors (Scotland) Act 1825 not qualified for such service, (as the case may be), shall not in itself affect the validity of any verdict returned by that jury in the trial.

(5) A person cited to attend for jury service and not excused under subsection (2) or (3) above may, if he shows to the satisfaction of the clerk of court issuing the citation that there is good reason why he should be excused from attending in compliance with the citation, be excused by that clerk of court from so attending.

(6) Without prejudice to—

(*a*) the preceding provisions of this section;

(*b*) [Repealed by the Court of Session Act 1988, Sched. 2.]

(*c*) section 100(1) or 133 of the Criminal Procedure (Scotland) Act 1975,

the court before which a person is cited to attend for jury service may excuse that person from that jury service.

[THE NEXT PAGE IS B 123]

Fining of jurors for non-attendance

2.—(1) Persons cited to attend for jury service in any civil proceedings may, unless they have been excused in respect thereof under section 1 of this Act, be fined up to £200 if they fail to attend in compliance with the citation.

(2) A fine imposed under subsection (1) above may, on application, be remitted—

(*a*) by a Lord Ordinary where imposed in the Court of Session;

(*b*) [Repealed by the Statute Law (Repeals) Act 1986, Sched., Pt. I.]

and no court fees or expenses shall be exigible in respect of any such application.

(3) [See *infra*, the Criminal Procedure (Scotland) Act 1975, s. 99.]

Offences in connection with jury service

3.—[1] (1) Subject to subsection (2) below, a person who—

(*a*) having been cited to attend for jury service, falsely claims to be a person excusable as of right from such service shall be guilty of an offence and shall be liable, on summary conviction, to a fine not exceeding level 3 on the standard scale;

(*b*) knowing that he is a person ineligible, or not qualified, for jury service, serves on a jury shall be guilty of an offence and shall be liable, on summary conviction, to a fine not exceeding level 3 on the standard scale; or

(*c*) knowing that he is a person disqualified from jury service, serves on a jury shall be guilty of an offence and shall be liable, on summary conviction, to a fine not exceeding level 5 on the standard scale.

(2) Subsection (1) above shall not apply to a person ineligible for jury service by reason of being among the persons listed in Group C of Part I of Schedule 1 to this Act.

NOTE

[1] As amended by virtue of the Criminal Procedure (Scotland) Act 1975, s. 289G.

Trusts, factors and succession

Prior rights in estate of deceased person

4. [See *infra,* the Succession (Scotland) Act 1964, ss. 9 and 9A.]

Finding of caution by intestate's spouse

5. In section 2 of the Confirmation of Executors (Scotland) Act 1823 (court to regulate caution to be found), for the words "executors-nominate; and in" there shall be substituted the words—

"(*a*) an executor-nominate; or

(*b*) an intestate's spouse who shall be executor-dative and has right, by virtue of sections 8 and 9(2) of the Succession (Scotland) Act 1964, to the whole estate.

In".

Procedure whereby heir of provision may establish entitlement to act as trustee

6. Without prejudice to section 37(1)(*d*) of the Succession (Scotland) Act 1964, sections 27 to 50 of the Titles to Land Consolidation (Scotland) Act 1868 (with such amendments as had been made to them prior to the coming into force of the said Act of 1964) are hereby revived—

(*c*) in so far as they provide; and

(*b*) the purpose only of providing,

a procedure whereby the heir of a last surviving trustee in a trust, called as heir of provision in the trust destination, may establish his entitlement to act as trustee by having himself served as heir in general to the last surviving trustee.

Amendment of Judicial Factors Act 1849

7. [See *infra*, the Judicial Factors Act 1849, ss.5 and 19.]

Amendment of section 2 of Trusts (Scotland) Act 1961

8. [See *infra*, the Trusts (Scotland) Act 1961, s.2.]

Removal of obligation to preserve inventories

9. In section 12 of the Customs, Inland Revenue, and Savings Banks Act 1877 (transmission and custody of inventories in Scotland)—

(*a*) for the words "Controller of Legacy and Succession Duties, at his office in" there shall be substituted the words "Registrar, Capital Taxes Office at";

(*b*) the words from "instead" to "same at his office in Edinburgh" shall cease to have effect; and

(*c*) for the words "Controller of Legacy and Succession Duties in" there shall be substituted the words "Registrar, Capital Taxes Office at".

Sheriff court

Performance of duties of sheriff principal

10. [See *infra*, the Sheriff Courts (Scotland) Act 1971, ss.10 and 11.]

No jury trial in civil actions in sheriff court

11.—[1] (1) It shall not be competent to appoint a civil action to be tried before a jury in the sheriff court.

(2) [Repealed by the Statute Law (Repeals) Act 1989, Sched. 1, Pt. 1.]

NOTE

[1] As amended by the Statute Law (Repeals) Act 1989, Sched. 1, Pt. 1.

12. [Repealed by the Bankruptcy (Scotland) Act 1985, Sched. 8.]

Jurisdiction of sheriff court in proceedings relating to trusts

13. [See *infra*, the Trusts (Scotland) Act 1921, ss.22 to 24A.]

Power of sheriff to appoint judicial factor

14. [See *infra*, the Judicial Factors (Scotland) Act 1880, ss.3 and 4.]

Jurisdiction of sheriff court in suspension of charges

15. [See *infra*, the Sheriff Courts (Scotland) Act 1907, s.5(5) and Sched. 1.]

Remit from sheriff court to Court of Session

16. [See *infra*, the Sheriff Courts (Scotland) Act 1971, s.37.]

Miscellaneous

Power of judges to act as arbiters

17.—(1) A Senator of the College of Justice may, if in all the circumstances he thinks fit, accept appointment as arbiter, or as oversman, by or by virtue of an arbitration agreement where the dispute appears to him to be of a commercial character:

Provided that he shall not accept such appointment unless the Lord President of the Court of Session has informed him that, having regard to the state of business in that court, he can be made available to do so.

(2) The fees payable for the services of a Senator of the College of Justice as arbiter or oversman shall be—

(*a*) payable in the Court of Session; and

(*b*) of such amount as the Secretary of State may, with the consent of the Treasury, by order made by statutory instrument prescribe.

(3) Any jurisdiction which is exercisable, other than under the Arbitration (Scotland) Act 1894, by the Court of Session in relation to arbiters and oversmen shall in relation to a Senator of the College of Justice appointed as arbiter or oversman be exercisable by the Inner House of that court.

(4) In section 6 of the said Act of 1894 (interpretation), at the end there shall be added the words—

": except that where—

(*a*) any arbiter appointed is; or

(*b*) in terms of the agreement to refer to arbitration an arbiter or oversman to be appointed must be,

a Senator of the College of Justice, 'the court' shall mean the Inner House of the Court of Session.".

(5) An order under subsection (2)(*b*) above shall be subject to annulment in pursuance of a resolution of either House of Parliament.

Interest on awards of compensation by Lands Tribunal for Scotland

18. A sum awarded as compensation by the Lands Tribunal for Scotland may, if the Tribunal so determine, carry interest as from the date of the award at the same rate as would apply (in the absence of any such statement as is provided for in Rule 66 of the Act of Sederunt (Rules of Court, consolidation and amendment) 1965), in the case of a decree or extract in an action commenced on that date in the Court of Session if interest were included in or exigible under that decree or extract:

Provided that this section shall not affect

(*a*) any existing enactment or rule of law whereby and in accordance with which a sum so awarded may carry interest;

(*b*) any case in which the hearing has begun before the coming into force of this section.

Vexatious litigants

19. After section 1 of the Vexatious Actions (Scotland) Act 1898, there shall be inserted the following section—

"**1A.** A decision of the Lord Ordinary to refuse leave, under section 1 of this Act, to institute legal proceedings shall be final.".

Jurisdiction in actions for reduction

20. The Court of Session shall have jurisdiction to entertain an action for reduction of any decree granted by a Scottish court whether or not the court would have jurisdiction to do so apart from this section and whether the decree was granted before or after the coming into force of this section.

. . . . . .

Amendment of Marriage (Scotland) Act 1977

22.—(1) [See *infra*, the Marriage (Scotland) Act 1977, ss.6, 8, 13 and 23A.]

(2) The said Act of 1977 shall be deemed for all purposes to have had effect as if it had originally been enacted as amended by subsection (1) above.

Amendment of Prescription and Limitation (Scotland) Act 1973

23. [See *infra*, the Prescription and Limitation (Scotland) Act 1973, s.19A.]

. . . . . .

Solicitors' clients' accounts

25. [See *infra*, the Solicitors (Scotland) Act 1980, ss.36, 42 and 65.]

Contributions from persons receiving legal aid

26. [Repealed by the Legal Aid (Scotland) Act 1987, Sched. 5.]

General

Expenses

27. There shall be defrayed out of moneys provided by Parliament any increase attributable to this Act in the sums payable out of moneys so provided under any other enactment.

Amendments and repeals

28.—(1) The enactments mentioned in Schedule 2 to this Act shall have effect subject to the amendments respectively specified in that Schedule, being minor amendments or amendments consequential on the provisions of this Act.

(2) [Repealed by the Statute Law (Repeals) Act 1989, Sched. 1, Pt. 1.]

Short title, extent and commencement

29.—(1) This Act may be cited as the Law Reform (Miscellaneous Provisions) (Scotland) Act 1980 and extends to Scotland only.

[1] (2) This Act, except this section, shall come into force on such date as the Secretary of State may by order made by statutory instrument appoint; and different dates may be appointed for, or for different purposes of, different provisions.

NOTE

[1] The Act came into operation on 22nd December 1980: see S.I. 1980 No. 1726.

SCHEDULES

Section 1 SCHEDULE 1

INELIGIBILITY FOR AND DISQUALIFICATION AND EXCUSAL FROM JURY SERVICE

PART I

PERSONS INELIGIBLE

GROUP A

The Judiciary

(*a*) Lords of Appeal;

(*b*) Senators of the College of Justice;
(*c*) sheriffs;
(*d*) Justices of the Peace;
(*e*) stipendiary magistrates;
(*f*) the chairman or president, the vice-chairman or vice-president and the registrar or assistant registrar of any tribunal; and
(*g*) persons who, at any time within the ten years immediately preceding the date at which their eligibility, in terms of section 1 of this Act, for jury service is being considered, have come within any description listed above in this group.

GROUP B

Others concerned with the administration of justice

(*a*) Advocates and solicitors, whether or not in actual practice as such;
(*b*) advocates' clerks;
(*c*) apprentices of, and legal trainees employed by, solicitors;
(*d*) officers and staff of any court if their work is wholly or mainly concerned with the day-to-day administration of the court;
(*e*) persons employed as shorthand writers in any court;
(*f*) Clerks of the Peace and their deputies;
(*g*) Inspectors of Constabulary appointed by Her Majesty;
(*h*) assistant inspectors of constabulary appointed by the Secretary of State;
(*i*) constables of any police force (including constables engaged on central service within the meaning of section 38 of the Police (Scotland) Act 1967);
(*j*) constables of any constabulary maintained under statute;
(*k*) persons employed in any capacity by virtue of which they have the powers and privileges of police constables;
(*l*) special constables;
(*m*) police cadets;
(*n*) persons employed under section 9 of the said Act of 1967 for the assistance of the constables of a police force;
(*o*) officers of, and members of visiting committees for, prisons, remand centres, detention centres, borstal institutions and young offenders institutions;
(*p*) procurators fiscal within the meaning of section 462(1) of the Criminal Procedure (Scotland) Act 1975, and persons employed as clerks and assistants to such procurators fiscal;
(*q*) messengers at arms and sheriff officers;
(*r*) members of children's panels;
(*s*) reporters appointed under section 36 of the Social Work (Scotland) Act 1968 and staffs;
(*t*) directors of social work appointed under section 3 of the said Act of 1968 and persons employed to assist such directors in the performance of such of their functions as relate to probation schemes within the meaning of section 27 of that Act;
(*u*) members of the Parole Board for Scotland;
[1] (*v*) members of local review committees established by virtue of section 18(5) of the Prisons (Scotland) Act 1989; and
(*w*) persons who, at any time within the five years immediately preceding the date at which their eligibility, in terms of section 1 of this Act, for jury service is being considered, have come within any description listed above in this Group.

NOTE
[1] As amended by the Prisons (Scotland) Act 1989, Sched. 2, para. 17, with effect from 16th February 1990.

GROUP C

The mentally disordered

(Expressions used in this Group are to be construed in accordance with the Mental Health (Scotland) Act 1960.)
(*a*) Persons who are receiving medical treatment for mental disorder and either—
(i) are, for the purposes of that treatment, resident in a hospital; or
(ii) attend on more than one day of each week to receive that treatment;
(*b*) persons incapable by reason of mental disorder of adequately managing and administering their property and affairs and for whom a *curator bonis* has accordingly been appointed; and
(*c*) persons for the time being in guardianship under section 25 of the said Act of 1960.

PART II

PERSONS DISQUALIFIED

(*a*) Persons who have at any time been sentenced in the United Kingdom, the Channel Islands or the Isle of Man—
  (i) to imprisonment for life or for a term of five years or more; or
  (ii) to be detained during Her Majesty's pleasure, during the pleasure of the Secretary of State or during the pleasure of the Governor of Northern Ireland;

(*b*) persons who have at any time in the United Kingdom, the Channel Islands or the Isle of Man—
  (i) served any part of a sentence of imprisonment or detention, being a sentence for a term of 3 months or more; or
  (ii) been detained in a borstal institution,

and who are not rehabilitated persons for the purposes of the Rehabilitation of Offenders Act 1974.

PART III

PERSONS EXCUSABLE AS OF RIGHT

GROUP A

Parliament

(*a*) Peers and peeresses entitled to receive writs of summons to attend the House of Lords;
(*b*) members of the House of Commons;
(*c*) officers of the House of Lords; and
(*d*) officers of the House of Commons.

GROUP B

European Assembly

Representatives to the Assembly of the European Comrmunities.

GROUP C

The Forces

Full-time serving members of—
(*a*) any of Her Majesty's naval, military or air forces;
(*b*) the Women's Royal Naval Service;
(*c*) Queen Alexandra's Royal Naval Nursing Service; or
(*d*) any Voluntary Aid Detachment serving with the Royal Navy.

GROUP D

Medical and similar professions

The following, if actually practising their profession and registered (whether fully or otherwise), enrolled or certified under the enactments relating to that profession—
(*a*) medical practitioners;
(*b*) dentists;
(*c*) nurses;
(*d*) midwives;
(*e*) pharmaceutical chemists; and
(*f*) veterinary surgeons and veterinary practitioners.

GROUP E

Ministers of religion, etc.

(*a*) persons in holy orders;

(*b*) regular ministers of any religious denomination; and
(*c*) vowed members of any religious order living in a monastery, convent or religious community.

GROUP F

Others

(*a*) Persons whose obedience to the citation for jury service would result in their serving, or duly attending for service, more than once in any period of five years; and
(*b*) persons excused by the direction of any court from jury service during a period which has not terminated.

[1] SCHEDULES 2 AND 3

NOTE
[1] The minor and consequential amendments and repeals made by these Schedules have been given effect to in the Acts printed in *The Parliament House Book*.

---

[1] Contempt of Court Act 1981

(1981 c. 49)

NOTE
[1] Shown as applied to Scotland: see s.21(4).

An Act to amend the law relating to contempt of court and related matters. [27th July 1981]

Strict liability

The strict liability rule

1.—In this Act "the strict liability rule" means the rule of law whereby conduct may be treated as a contempt of court as tending to interfere with the course of justice in particular legal proceedings regardless of intent to do so.

Limitations of scope of strict liability

2.—[1] (1) The strict liability rule applies only in relation to publications, and for this purpose "publication" includes any speech, writing, programme included in a programme service or other communication in whatever form, which is addressed to the public at large or any section of the public.

(2) The strict liability rule applies only to a publication which creates a substantial risk that the course of justice in the proceedings in question will be seriously impeded or prejudiced.

(3) The strict liability rule applies to a publication only if the proceedings in question are active within the meaning of this section at the time of the publication.

(4) Schedule 1 applies for determining the times at which proceedings are to be treated as active within the meaning of this section.

[2] (5) In this section "programme service" has the same meaning as in the Broadcasting Act 1990.

NOTES
[1] As amended by the Cable and Broadcasting Act 1984, Sched. 5, para. 39(1), and (with effect from 1st January 1991) the Broadcasting Act 1990, Sched. 20, para. 31(1).
[2] Inserted by the Broadcasting Act 1990, Sched. 20, para. 31(1), with effect from 1st January 1991.

Defence of innocent publication or distribution

3.—(1) A person is not guilty of contempt of court under the strict liability rule as the publisher of any matter to which that rule applies if at the time of publication (having taken all reasonable care) he does not know and has no reason to suspect that relevant proceedings are active.

(2) A person is not guilty of contempt of court under the strict liability rule as the distributor of a publication containing any such matter if at the time of distribution (having taken all reasonable care) he does not know that it contains such matter and has no reason to suspect that it is likely to do so.

(3) The burden of proof of any fact tending to establish a defence afforded by this section to any person lies upon that person.

(4) Section 11 of the Administration of Justice Act 1960 is repealed.

Contemporary reports of proceedings

4.—(1) Subject to this section a person is not guilty of contempt of court under the strict liability rule in respect of a fair and accurate report of legal proceedings held in public, published contemporaneously and in good faith.

(2) In any such proceedings the court may, where it appears to be necessary for avoiding a substantial risk of prejudice to the administration of justice in those proceedings, or in any other proceedings pending or imminent, order that the publication of any report of the proceedings, or any part of the proceedings, be postponed for such period as the court thinks necessary for that purpose.

(3) For the purposes of subsection (1) of this section . . . a report of proceedings shall be treated as published contemporaneously—

(*a*) in the case of a report of which publication is postponed pursuant to an order under subsection (2) of this section, if published as soon as practicable after that order expires;

(*b*) in the case of a report of committal proceedings of which publication is permitted by virtue only of subsection (3) of section 8 of the Magistrates' Courts Act 1980, if published as soon as practicable after publication is so permitted.

(4) . . .

Discussion of public affairs

5.—A publication made as or as part of a discussion in good faith of public affairs or other matters of general public interest is not to be treated as a contempt of court under the strict liability rule if the risk of impediment or prejudice to particular legal proceedings is merely incidental to the discussion.

Savings

6.—Nothing in the foregoing provisions of this Act—

(*a*) prejudices any defence available at common law to a charge of contempt of court under the strict liability rule;

(*b*) implies that any publication is punishable as contempt of court under that rule which would not be so punishable apart from those provisions;

(*c*) restricts liability for contempt of court in respect of conduct intended to impede or prejudice the administration of justice.

. . . . . .

Other aspects of law and procedure

Confidentiality of jury's deliberations

8.—(1) Subject to subsection (2) below, it is a contempt of court to obtain, disclose or solicit any particulars of statements made, opinions expressed, arguments advanced or votes cast by members of a jury in the course of their deliberations in any legal proceedings.

(2) This section does not apply to any disclosure of any particulars—

(*a*) in the proceedings in question for the purpose of enabling the jury to arrive at their verdict, or in connection with the delivery of that verdict, or;

(*b*) in evidence in any subsequent proceedings for an offence alleged to have been committed in relation to the jury in the first mentioned proceedings,

or to the publication of any particulars so disclosed.

(3) . . .

Use of tape recorders

9.—(1) Subject to subsection (4) below, it is a contempt of court—

(*a*) to use in court, or bring into court for use, any tape recorder or other instrument for recording sound, except with the leave of the court;

(*b*) to publish a recording of legal proceedings made by means of any such instrument, or any recording derived directly or indirectly from it, by playing it in the hearing of the public or any section of the public, or to dispose of it or any recording so derived, with a view to such publication;

(*c*) to use any such recording in contravention of any conditions of leave granted under paragraph (*a*).

(2) Leave under paragraph (*a*) of subsection (1) may be granted or refused at the discretion of the court, and if granted may be granted subject to such conditions as the court thinks proper with respect to the use of any recording made pursuant to the leave; and where leave has been granted the court may at the like discretion withdraw or amend it either generally or in relation to any particular part of the proceedings.

(3) Without prejudice to any other power to deal with an act of contempt under paragraph (*a*) of subsection (1), the court may order the instrument, or any recording made with it, or both, to be forfeited; and any object so forfeited shall (unless the court otherwise determines on application by a person appearing to be the owner) be sold or otherwise disposed of in such manner as the court may direct.

(4) This section does not apply to the making or use of sound recordings for purposes of official transcripts of proceedings.

Sources of information

10. No court may require a person to disclose, nor is any person guilty of contempt of court for refusing to disclose, the source of information contained in a publication for which he is responsible, unless it be established to the satisfaction of the court that disclosure is necessary in the interests of justice or national security or for the prevention of disorder or crime.

Publication of matters exempted from disclosure in court

11. In any case where a court (having power to do so) allows a name or other matter to be withheld from the public in proceedings before the court, the court may give such directions prohibiting the publication of that name or matter in connection with the proceedings as appear to the court to be necessary for the purpose for which it was so withheld.

. . . . . .

Legal aid

13.—(1)–(3) [Repealed by the Legal Aid Act 1988, Sched. 6.]

(4) [Repealed by the Legal Aid (Scotland) Act 1986, Sched. 5.]

(5) This section is without prejudice to any other enactment by virtue of which legal aid may be granted in or for purposes of civil or criminal proceedings.

NOTE

[1] See s.21(2) as to coming into force of this section.

. . . . . .

Penalties for contempt and kindred offences

Penalties for contempt of court in Scottish proceedings

15.—(1) In Scottish proceedings, when a person is committed to prison for contempt of court the committal shall (without prejudice to the power of the court to order his earlier discharge) be for a fixed term.

[1] (2) The maximum penalty which may be imposed by way of imprisonment or fine for contempt of court in Scottish proceedings shall be two years' imprisonment or a fine or both, except that—

(*a*) where the contempt is dealt with by the sheriff in the course of or in connection with proceedings other than criminal proceedings on indictment, such penalty shall not exceed three months' imprisonment or a fine of level 4 on the standard scale or both; and

(*b*) where the contempt is dealt with by the district court, such penalty shall not exceed 60 days' imprisonment or a fine of level 4 on the standard scale or both.

(3) Section 207 (restriction on detention of young offenders) and sections 175 to 178 (persons suffering from mental disorder) of the Criminal Procedure (Scotland) Act 1975 shall apply in relation to persons found guilty of contempt of court in Scottish proceedings as they apply in relation to persons convicted of offences, except—

(*a*) where subsection (2)(*a*) above applies, when sections 415 and 376 to 379 of the said Act shall so apply; and

(*b*) where subsection (2)(*b*) above applies, when section 415 of the said Act and subsection (5) below shall apply.

(4) Until the commencement of section 45 of the Criminal Justice (Scotland) Act 1980, in subsection (3) above for the references to section 207 and section 415 of the Criminal Procedure (Scotland) Act 1975 there shall be substituted respectively references to sections 207 and 208 and sections 415 and 416 of that Act.

(5) Where a person is found guilty by a district court of contempt of court and it appears to the court that he may be suffering from mental disorder, it shall remit him to the sheriff in the manner provided by section 286 of the Criminal Procedure (Scotland) Act 1975 and the sheriff shall, on such remit being made, have the like power to make an order under section 376(1) of the said Act in respect of him as if he had been convicted by the sheriff of an offence, or in dealing with him may exercise the like powers as the court making the remit.

[2] (6) For the purposes of section 22 of the Prisons (Scotland) Act 1989 (release on licence of prisoners serving determinate sentences) a penalty of a period of imprisonment imposed for contempt of court shall be treated as a sentence of imprisonment within the meaning of that Act.

NOTES

[1] As amended by the Criminal Justice Act 1982, Sched. 7, and the Criminal Procedure (Scotland) Act 1975, s.289G.

[2] Added by the Criminal Justice (Scotland) Act 1987, Sched. 1, para. 19, and as amended by the Prisons (Scotland) Act 1989, Sched. 2, para. 18, with effect from 16th February 1990.

. . . . . .

Supplemental

. . . . . .

Interpretation

[1] **19.** In this Act—

"court" includes any tribunal or body exercising the judicial power of the State, and "legal proceedings" shall be construed accordingly;

"publication" has the meaning assigned by subsection (1) of section 2, and "publish" (except in section 9) shall be construed accordingly;

"Scottish proceedings" means proceedings before any court, including the Courts-Martial Appeal Court, the Restrictive Practices Court and the Employment Appeal Tribunal, sitting in Scotland, and includes proceedings before the House of Lords in the exercise of any appellate jurisdiction over proceedings in such a court;

"the strict liability rule" has the meaning assigned by section 1;

"superior court" means the Court of Appeal, the High Court, the Crown Court, the Courts-Martial Appeal Court, the Restrictive Practices Court, the Employment Appeal Tribunal and any other court exercising in relation to its proceedings powers equivalent to those of the High Court, and includes the House of Lords in the exercise of its appellate jurisdiction.

NOTE

[1] As amended by the Cable and Broadcasting Act 1984, Sched. 5, para. 39(2), and the Broadcasting Act 1990, Sched. 20, para. 31(2) and Sched. 21.

Tribunals of Inquiry

20.—(1) In relation to any tribunal to which the Tribunals of Inquiry (Evidence) Act 1921 applies, and the proceedings of such a tribunal, the provisions of this Act (except subsection (3) of section 9) apply as they apply in relation to courts and legal proceedings; and references to the course of justice or the administration of justice in legal proceedings shall be construed accordingly.

(2) The proceedings of a tribunal established under the said Act shall be treated as active within the meaning of section 2 from the time when the tribunal is appointed until its report is presented to Parliament.

Short title, commencement and extent

21.—(1) This Act may be cited as the Contempt of Court Act 1981.

(2) The provisions of this Act relating to legal aid in England and Wales shall come into force on such day as the Lord Chancellor may appoint by order made by statutory instrument; and the provisions of this Act relating to legal aid in Scotland and Northern Ireland shall come into force on such day or days as the Secretary of State may so appoint.

Different days may be appointed under this subsection in relation to different courts.

(3) Subject to subsection (2), this Act shall come into force at the expiration of the period of one month beginning with the day on which it is passed.

(4) Sections 7, 8(3), 12, 13(1) to (3), 14, 16, 17 and 18, Parts I and III of Schedule 2 and Schedules 3 and 4 of this Act do not extend to Scotland.

(5) . . .

SCHEDULES

Section 2

SCHEDULE 1

TIMES WHEN PROCEEDINGS ARE ACTIVE FOR PURPOSES OF SECTION 2

Preliminary

1. In this Schedule "criminal proceedings" means proceedings against a person in respect of an offence, not being appellate proceedings or proceedings commenced by motion for committal or attachment in England and Wales or Northern Ireland; and "appellate proceedings" means proceedings on appeal from or for the review of the decision of a court in any proceedings.

2. Criminal, appellate and other proceedings are active within the meaning of section 2 at the times respectively prescribed by the following paragraphs of this Schedule; and in relation to proceedings in which more than one of the steps described in any of those paragraphs is taken, the reference in that paragraph is a reference to the first of those steps.

Criminal proceedings

3. Subject to the following provisions of this Schedule, criminal proceedings are active from the relevant initial step specified in paragraph 4 until concluded as described in paragraph 5.

4. The initial steps of criminal proceedings are:—
   (*a*) arrest without warrant;
   (*b*) the issue, or in Scotland the grant, of a warrant for arrest;
   (*c*) the issue of a summons to appear, or in Scotland the grant of a warrant to cite;
   (*d*) the service of an indictment or other document specifying the charge;
   (*e*) except in Scotland, oral charge.

5. Criminal proceedings are concluded—
   (*a*) by acquittal or, as the case may be, by sentence;
   (*b*) by any other verdict, finding, order or decision which puts an end to the proceedings;
   (*c*) by discontinuance or by operation of law.

6. The reference in paragraph 5(*a*) to sentence includes any order or decision consequent on conviction or finding of guilt which disposes of the case, either absolutely or subject to future events, and a deferment of sentence under section 1 of the Powers of Criminal Courts Act 1973, section 219 or 432 of the Criminal Procedure (Scotland) Act 1975 or Article 14 of the Treatment of Offenders (Northern Ireland) Order 1976.

7. Proceedings are discontinued within the meaning of paragraph 5(*c*)—
   (*a*) in England and Wales or Northern Ireland, if the charge or summons is withdrawn or a *nolle prosequi* entered;
   (*b*) in Scotland, if the proceedings are expressly abandoned by the prosecutor or are deserted *simpliciter*;
   (*c*) in the case of proceedings in England and Wales or Northern Ireland commenced by arrest without warrant, if the person arrested is released, otherwise than on bail, without having been charged.

8. Criminal proceedings before a court-martial or standing civilian court are not concluded until the completion of any review of finding or sentence.

9. Criminal proceedings in England and Wales or Northern Ireland cease to be active if an order is made for the charge to lie on the file, but become active again if leave is later given for the proceedings to continue.

[1] 10. Without prejudice to paragraph 5(*b*) above, criminal proceedings against a person cease to be active—
   (*a*) if the accused is found to be under a disability such as to render him unfit to be tried or unfit to plead or, in Scotland, is found to be insane in bar of trial; or
   (*b*) if a hospital order is made in his case under section 51(5) of the Mental Health Act 1983 or paragraph (*b*) of subsection (2) of section 62 of the Mental Health Act (Northern Ireland) 1961 or, in Scotland, where a transfer order ceases to have effect by virtue of section 73(1) of the Mental Health (Scotland) Act 1984,

but become active again if they are later resumed.

NOTE

[1] As amended by the Mental Health Act 1983, Sched. 4, para. 57(*c*), and the Mental Health (Scotland) Act 1984, Sched. 3, para. 48.

---

11. Criminal proceedings against a person which become active on the issue or the grant of a warrant for his arrest cease to be active at the end of the period of twelve months beginning with the date of the warrant unless he has been arrested within that period, but become active again if he is subsequently arrested.

Other proceedings at first instance

12. Proceedings other than criminal proceedings and appellate proceedings are active from the time when arrangements for the hearing are made or, if no such arrangements are previously made, from the time the hearing begins, until the proceedings are disposed of or discontinued or withdrawn; and for the purpose of this paragraph any motion or application

made in or for the purposes of any proceedings, and any pre-trial review in the county court, is to be treated as a distinct proceeding.

13. In England and Wales or Northern Ireland arrangements for the hearing of proceedings to which paragraph 12 applies are made within the meaning of that paragraph—

(*a*) in the case of proceedings in the High Court for which provision is made by rules of court for setting down for trial, when the case is set down;

(*b*) in the case of any proceedings, when a date for the trial or hearing is fixed.

14. In Scotland arrangements for the hearing of proceedings to which paragraph 12 applies are made within the meaning of that paragraph—

(*a*) in the case of an ordinary action in the Court of Session or in the sheriff court, when the Record is closed;

(*b*) in the case of a motion or application, when it is enrolled or made;

(*c*) in any other case, when the date for a hearing is fixed or a hearing is allowed.

Appellate proceedings

15. Appellate proceedings are active from the time when they are commenced—

(*a*) by application for leave to appeal or apply for review, or by notice of such an application;

(*b*) by notice of appeal or of application for review;

(*c*) by other originating process,

until disposed of or abandoned, discontinued or withdrawn.

16. Where, in appellate proceedings relating to criminal proceedings, the court—

(*a*) remits the case to the court below; or

(*b*) orders a new trial or a *venire de novo*, or in Scotland grants authority to bring a new prosecution,

any further or new proceedings which result shall be treated as active from the conclusion of the appellate proceedings.

Sections 13, 14

SCHEDULE 2

AMENDMENTS

PART I

[Repealed by the Legal Aid Act 1988, Sched. 6.]

. . . . . .

PART II

[Repealed by the Legal Aid (Scotland) Act 1986, Sched. 5.]

[1] Civil Jurisdiction and Judgments Act 1982

(1982 c. 27)

NOTE

[1] The extensive prospective amendments made by the Civil Jurisdiction and Judgments Act 1991, the text of which is printed *infra*, will be given effect when that Act is brought into force.

An Act to make further provision about the jurisdiction of courts and tribunals in the United Kingdom and certain other territories and about the recognition and enforcement of judgments given in the United Kingdom or elsewhere; to provide for the modification of certain provisions relating to legal aid; and for connected purposes. [13th July 1982]

[1] PART I

IMPLEMENTATION OF THE CONVENTIONS

NOTE

[1] Saved by the Merchant Shipping (Liner Conferences) Act 1982, s.5(6).

Main implementing provisions

Interpretation of references to the Conventions and Contracting States

1.—(1) In this Act—

"the 1968 Convention" means the Convention on jurisdiction and the enforcement of judgments in civil and commercial matters (including the Protocol annexed to that Convention), signed at Brussels on 27th September 1968;

"the 1971 Protocol" means the Protocol on the interpretation of the 1968 Convention by the European Court, signed at Luxembourg on 3rd June 1971;

"the Accession Convention" means the Convention on the accession to the 1968 Convention and the 1971 Protocol of Denmark, the Republic of Ireland and the United Kingdom, signed at Luxembourg on 9th October 1978;

"the Conventions" means the 1968 Convention, the 1971 Protocol and the Accession Convention.

(2) In this Act, unless the context otherwise requires—

(*a*) references to, or to any provision of, the 1968 Convention or the 1971 Protocol are references to that Convention, Protocol or provision as amended by the Accession Convention; and

(*b*) any reference to a numbered Article is a reference to the Article so numbered of the 1968 Convention, and any reference to a sub-division of a numbered Article shall be construed accordingly.

(3) In this Act "Contracting State" means—

(*a*) one of the original parties to the 1968 Convention (Belgium, the Federal Republic of Germany, France, Italy, Luxembourg and the Netherlands); or

(*b*) one of the parties acceding to that Convention under the Accession Convention (Denmark, the Republic of Ireland and the United Kingdom),

being a state in respect of which the Accession Convention has entered into force in accordance with Article 39 of that Convention.

The Conventions to have the force of law

2.—(1) The Conventions shall have the force of law in the United Kingdom, and judicial notice shall be taken of them.

(2) For convenience of reference there are set out in Schedules 1, 2 and 3 respectively the English texts of—

(*a*) the 1968 Convention as amended by Titles II and III of the Accession Convention;

(*b*) the 1971 Protocol as amended by Title IV of the Accession Convention; and

(*c*) Titles V and VI of the Accession Convention (transitional and final provisions),

being texts prepared from the authentic English texts referred to in Articles 37 and 41 of the Accession Convention.

Interpretation of the Conventions

3.—(1) Any question as to the meaning or effect of any provision of the Conventions shall, if not referred to the European Court in accordance with the 1971 Protocol, be determined in accordance with the principles laid down by and any relevant decision of the European Court.

(2) Judicial notice shall be taken of any decision of, or expression of opinion by, the European Court on any such question.

(3) Without prejudice to the generality of subsection (1), the following reports (which are reproduced in the Official Journal of the Communities), namely—

(*a*) the reports by Mr. P. Jenard on the 1968 Convention and the 1971 Protocol; and

(*b*) the report by Professor Peter Schlosser on the Accession Convention,

may be considered in ascertaining the meaning or effect of any provision of the Conventions and shall be given such weight as is appropriate in the circumstances.

Supplementary provisions as to recognition and enforcement of judgments

Enforcement of judgments other than maintenance orders

[1] **4.**—(1) A judgment, other than a maintenance order, which is the subject of an application under Article 31 for its enforcement in any part of the United Kingdom shall, to the extent that its enforcement is authorised by the appropriate court, be registered in the prescribed manner in that court.

In this subsection " the appropriate court " means the court to which the application is made in pursuance of Article 32 (that is to say, the High Court or the Court of Session).

(2) Where a judgment is registered under this section, the reasonable costs or expenses of and incidental to its registration shall be recoverable as if they were sums recoverable under the judgment.

(3) A judgment registered under this section shall, for the purposes of its enforcement, be of the same force and effect, the registering court shall have in relation to its enforcement the same powers, and proceedings for or with respect to its enforcement may be taken, as if the judgment had been originally given by the registering court and had (where relevant) been entered.

(4) Subsection (3) is subject to Article 39 (restriction on enforcement where appeal pending or time for appeal unexpired), to section 7 and to any provision made by rules of court as to the manner in which and conditions subject to which a judgment registered under this section may be enforced.

NOTE

[1] Saved: see s. 18 (7), *infra*.

Recognition and enforcement of maintenance orders

[1] **5.**—(1) The function of transmitting to the appropriate court an application under Article 31 for the recognition or enforcement in the United Kingdom of a maintenance order shall be discharged—

(*a*) as respects England and Wales and Scotland, by the Secretary of State;

(*b*) as respects Northern Ireland, by the Lord Chancellor.

In this subsection " the appropriate court " means the magistrates' court or sheriff court having jurisdiction in the matter in accordance with the second paragraph of Article 32.

(2) Such an application shall be determined in the first instance by the prescribed officer of that court.

(3) Where on such an application the enforcement of the order is authorised to any extent, the order shall to that extent be registered in the prescribed manner in that court.

(4) A maintenance order registered under this section shall, for the purposes of its enforcement, be of the same force and effect, the registering court shall have in relation to its enforcement the same powers, and proceedings for or with respect to its enforcement may be taken, as if the order had been originally made by the registering court.

(5) Subsection (4) is subject to Article 39 (restriction on enforcement where appeal pending or time for appeal unexpired), to section 7 and to any provision made by rules of court as to the manner in which and conditions subject to which an order registered under this section may be enforced.

(6) A maintenance order which by virtue of this section is enforceable by a magistrates' court in England and Wales or Northern Ireland shall be enforceable in the same manner as an affiliation order made by that court.

(7) The payer under a maintenance order registered under this section in a magistrates' court in England and Wales or Northern Ireland shall give notice of any changes of address to the clerk of that court.

A person who without reasonable excuse fails to comply with this subsection shall be guilty of an offence and liable on summary conviction to a fine not exceeding £50.

NOTE

[1] Saved: see s. 18 (7), *infra*.

Appeals under Article 37, second paragraph and Article 41

6.—(1) The single further appeal on a point of law referred to in Article 37, second paragraph and Article 41 in relation to the recognition or enforcement of a judgment other than a maintenance order lies—

(*a*) . . .

(*b*) in Scotland, to the Inner House of the Court of Session.

(2) . . .

(3) The single further appeal on a point of law referred to in Article 37, second paragraph and Article 41 in relation to the recognition or enforcement of a maintenance order lies—

(*a*) . . .

(*b*) in Scotland, to the Inner House of the Court of Session;

(*c*) . . .

Interest on registered judgments

7.—(1) Subject to subsection (4), where in connection with an application for registration of a judgment under section 4 or 5 the applicant shows—

(*a*) that the judgment provides for the payment of a sum of money; and

(*b*) that in accordance with the law of the Contracting State in which the judgment was given interest on that sum is recoverable under the judgment from a particular date or time,

the rate of interest and the date or time from which it is so recoverable shall be registered with the judgment and, subject to any provision made under subsection (2), the debt resulting, apart from section 4 (2), from the registration of the judgment shall carry interest in accordance with the registered particulars.

(2) Provision may be made by rules of court as to the manner in which and the periods by reference to which any interest payable by virtue of subsection (1) is to be calculated and paid, including provision for such interest to cease to accrue as from a prescribed date.

(3) Costs or expenses recoverable by virtue of section 4(2) shall carry interest as if they were the subject of an order for the payment of costs or expenses made by the registering court on the date of registration.

(4) Interest on arrears of sums payable under a maintenance order registered under section 5 in a magistrates' court in England and Wales or Northern Ireland shall not be recoverable in that court, but without prejudice to the operation in relation to any such order of section 2A of the Maintenance Orders Act 1958 or section 11A of the Maintenance and Affiliation Orders Act (Northern Ireland) 1966 (which enable interest to be recovered if the order is re-registered for enforcement in the High Court).

(5) Except as mentioned in subsection (4), debts under judgments registered under section 4 or 5 shall carry interest only as provided by this section.

Currency of payment under registered maintenance orders

8.—(1) Sums payable in the United Kingdom under a maintenance order by virtue of its registration under section 5, including any arrears so payable, shall be paid in the currency of the United Kingdom.

(2) Where the order is expressed in any other currency, the amounts shall be converted on the basis of the exchange rate prevailing on the date of registration of the order.

(3) For the purposes of this section, a written certificate purporting to be signed by an officer of any bank in the United Kingdom and stating the exchange rate prevailing on a specified date shall be evidence, and in Scotland sufficient evidence, of the facts stated.

Other supplementary provisions

Provisions supplementary to Title VII of 1968 Convention

[1] **9.**—(1) The provisions of Title VII of the 1968 Convention (relationship between that convention and other conventions to which Contracting States are or may become parties) shall have effect in relation to—

(*a*) any statutory provision, whenever passed or made, implementing any such other convention in the United Kingdom; and

(*b*) any rule of law so far as it has the effect of so implementing any such other convention,

as they have effect in relation to that other convention itself.

(2) Her Majesty may by Order in Council declare a provision of a convention entered into by the United Kingdom to be a provision whereby the United Kingdom assumed an obligation of a kind provided for in Article 59 (which allows a Contracting State to agree with a third State to withhold recognition in certain cases from a judgment given by a court in another Contracting State which took jurisdiction on one of the grounds mentioned in the second paragraph of Article 3).

NOTE

[1] See S.I. 1987 No. 468 (Canada), as amended by S.I. 1987 No. 2211, 1988 Nos. 1304 and 1853, and 1989 No. 987.

Allocation within U.K. of jurisdiction with respect to trusts and consumer contracts

10.—(1) The provisions of this section have effect for the purpose of allocating within the United Kingdom jurisdiction in certain proceedings in respect of which the 1968 Convention confers jurisdiction on the courts of the United Kingdom generally and to which section 16 does not apply.

(2) Any proceedings which by virtue of Article 5(6) (trusts) are brought in the United Kingdom shall be brought in the courts of the part of the United Kingdom in which the trust is domiciled.

(3) Any proceedings which by virtue of the first paragraph of Article 14 (consumer contracts) are brought in the United Kingdom by a consumer on the ground that he is himself domiciled there shall be brought in the courts of the part of the United Kingdom in which he is domiciled.

Proof and admissibility of certain judgments and related documents

11.—(1) For the purposes of the 1968 Convention—

(*a*) a document, duly authenticated, which purports to be a copy of a judgment given by a court of a Contracting State other than the United Kingdom shall without further proof be deemed to be a true copy, unless the contrary is shown; and

(*b*) the original or a copy of any such document as is mentioned in Article 46(2) or 47 (supporting documents to be produced by a party seeking recognition or enforcement of a judgment) shall be evidence, and in Scotland sufficient evidence, of any matter to which it relates.

(2) A document purporting to be a copy of a judgment given by any such court as is mentioned in subsection (1)(*a*) is duly authenticated for the purposes of this section if it purports—

(*a*) to bear the seal of that court; or

(*b*) to be certified by any person in his capacity as a judge or officer of that court to be a true copy of a judgment given by that court.

(3) Nothing in this section shall prejudice the admission in evidence of any document which is admissible apart from this section.

Provision for issue of copies of, and certificates in connection with, U.K. judgments

12. Rules of court may make provision for enabling any interested party wishing to secure under the 1968 Convention the recognition or enforcement in another Contracting State of a judgment given by a court in the United Kingdom to obtain, subject to any conditions specified in the rules—

(*a*) a copy of the judgment; and

(*b*) a certificate giving particulars relating to the judgment and the proceedings in which it was given.

Modifications to cover authentic instruments and court settlements

[1] **13.**—(1) Her Majesty may by Order in Council provide that—

(*a*) any provision of this Act relating to the recognition or enforcement in the United Kingdom or elsewhere of judgments to which the 1968 Convention applies; and

(*b*) any other statutory provision, whenever passed or made, so relating,

shall apply, with such modifications as may be specified in the Order, in relation to documents and settlements within Title IV of the 1968 Convention (authentic instruments and court settlements enforceable in the same manner as judgments) as if they were judgments to which that Convention applies.

(2) An Order in Council under this section may make different provision in relation to different descriptions of documents and settlements.

(3) Any Order in Council under this section shall be subject to annulment in pursuance of a resolution of either House of Parliament.

NOTE

[1] See the Debtors (Scotland) Act 1987, ss.15(3)(*e*), 73 and 106(*h*).

Modifications consequential on revision of the Conventions

14.—(1) If at any time it appears to Her Majesty in Council that Her Majesty's Government in the United Kingdom have agreed to a revision of any of the Conventions, including in particular any revision connected with the accession to the 1968 Convention of one or more further states, Her Majesty may by Order in Council make such modifications of this Act or any other statutory provision, whenever passed or made, as Her Majesty considers appropriate in consequence of the revision.

(2) An Order in Council under this section shall not be made unless a draft of the Order has been laid before Parliament and approved by a resolution of each House of Parliament.

(3) In this section " revision " means an omission from, addition to or alteration of any of the Conventions and includes replacement of any of the Conventions to any extent by another convention, protocol or other description of international agreement.

Interpretation of Part I and consequential amendments

15.—(1) In this Part, unless the context otherwise requires—

" judgment " has the meaning given by Article 25;

" maintenance order " means a maintenance judgment within the meaning of the 1968 Convention;

" payer ", in relation to a maintenance order, means the person liable to make the payments for which the order provides;

" prescribed " means prescribed by rules of court.

(2) References in this Part to a judgment registered under section 4 or 5 include, to the extent of its registration, references to a judgment so registered to a limited extent only.

(3) . . .

(4) The enactments specified in Part I of Schedule 12 shall have effect with the amendments specified there, being amendments consequential on this Part.

PART II

JURISDICTION, AND RECOGNITION AND ENFORCEMENT OF JUDGMENTS, WITHIN UNITED KINGDOM

Allocation within U.K. of jurisdiction in certain civil proceedings

16.—(1) The provisions set out in Schedule 4 (which contains a modified version of Title II of the 1968 Convention) shall have effect for determining, for each part of the United Kingdom, whether the courts of law of that part, or any particular court of law in that part, have or has jurisdiction in proceedings where—

(*a*) the subject-matter of the proceedings is within the scope of the 1968 Convention as determined by Article 1 (whether or not the Convention has effect in relation to the proceedings); and

(*b*) the defendant or defender is domiciled in the United Kingdom or the proceedings are of a kind mentioned in Article 16 (exclusive jurisdiction regardless of domicile).

(2) In Schedule 4 modifications of Title II of the 1968 Convention are indicated as follows—

(*a*) modifications by way of omission are indicated by dots; and

(*b*) within each Article words resulting from modifications by way of addition or substitution are printed in heavy type.

(3) In determining any question as to the meaning or effect of any provision contained in Schedule 4—

(*a*) regard shall be had to any relevant principles laid down by the European Court in connection with Title II of the 1968 Convention and to any relevant decision of that court as to the meaning or effect of any provision of that Title; and

(*b*) without prejudice to the generality of paragraph (*a*), the reports mentioned in section 3 (3) may be considered and shall, so far as relevant, be given such weight as is appropriate in the circumstances.

(4) The provisions of this section and Schedule 4 shall have effect subject to the 1968 Convention and to the provisions of section 17.

(5) In section 15 (1) (*a*) of the Maintenance Orders Act 1950 (domestic proceedings in which initial process may be served in another part of the United Kingdom), after sub-paragraph (v) there shall be added—

" (vi) Article 5 (2) of Schedule 4 to the Civil Jurisdiction and Judgments Act 1982; or ".

Exclusion of certain proceedings from Schedule 4

17.—(1) Schedule 4 shall not apply to proceedings of any description listed in Schedule 5 or to proceedings in Scotland under any enactment which confers jurisdiction on a Scottish court in respect of a specific subject-matter on specific grounds.

(2) Her Majesty may by Order in Council—

(*a*) add to the list in Schedule 5 any description of proceedings in any part of the United Kingdom; and

(*b*) remove from that list any description of proceedings in any part of the United Kingdom (whether included in the list as originally enacted or added by virtue of this subsection).

(3) An Order in Council under subsection (2)—

(*a*) may make different provisions for different descriptions of proceedings, for the same description of proceedings in different courts or for different parts of the United Kingdom; and

(*b*) may contain such transitional and other incidental provisions as appear to Her Majesty to be appropriate.

(4) An Order in Council under subsection (2) shall not be made unless a draft of the Order has been laid before Parliament and approved by a resolution of each House of Parliament.

Enforcement of U.K. judgments in other parts of U.K.

18.—(1) In relation to any judgment to which this section applies—

(*a*) Schedule 6 shall have effect for the purpose of enabling any money provisions contained in the judgment to be enforced in a part of the United Kingdom other than the part in which the judgment was given; and

(*b*) Schedule 7 shall have effect for the purpose of enabling any non-money provisions so contained to be so enforced.

(2) In this section " judgment " means any of the following (references to the giving of a judgment being construed accordingly)—

(*a*) any judgment or order (by whatever name called) given or made by a court of law in the United Kingdom;

(*b*) any judgment or order not within paragraph (*a*) which has been entered in England and Wales or Northern Ireland in the High Court or a county court;

(*c*) any document which in Scotland has been registered for execution in the Books of Council and Session or in the sheriff court books kept for any sheriffdom;

(*d*) any award or order made by a tribunal in any part of the United Kingdom which is enforceable in that part without an order of a court of law;

(*e*) an arbitration award which has become enforceable in the part of the United Kingdom in which it was given in the same manner as a judgment given by a court of law in that part;

and, subject to the following provisions of this section, this section applies to all such judgments.

(3) Subject to subsection (4), this section does not apply to—

(*a*) a judgment given in proceedings in a magistrates' court in England and Wales or Northern Ireland;

(*b*) a judgment given in proceedings other than civil proceedings;
[1] (*ba*) a judgment given in the exercise of jurisdiction in relation to insolvency law, within the meaning of section 426 of the Insolvency Act 1986;
(*c*) a judgment given in proceedings relating to—
(i), (ii) [Repealed by the Insolvency Act 1985, Sched. 10, Pt. IV.]
(iii) the obtaining of title to administer the estate of a deceased person.

(4) This section applies, whatever the nature of the proceedings in which it is made, to—
(*a*) a decree issued under section 13 of the Court of Exchequer (Scotland) Act 1856 (recovery of certain rent-charges and penalties by process of the Court of Session);
(*b*) an order which is enforceable in the same manner as a judgment of the High Court in England and Wales by virtue of section 16 of the Contempt of Court Act 1981 or section 140 of the Supreme Court Act 1981 (which relate to fines for contempt of court and forfeiture of recognisances).

[2] (4A) This section does not apply as respects the enforcement in Scotland of orders made by the High Court in England and Wales under or for the purposes of the Drug Trafficking Offences Act 1986 or Part VI of the Criminal Justice Act 1988 (confiscation of the proceeds of offences) or as respects the enforcement in England and Wales of orders made by the Court of Session under or for the purposes of Part I of the Criminal Justice (Scotland) Act 1987.

(5) This section does not apply to so much of any judgment as—
(*a*) is an order to which section 16 of the Maintenance Orders Act 1950 applies (and is therefore an order for whose enforcement in another part of the United Kingdom provision is made by Part II of that Act);
(*b*) concerns the status or legal capacity of an individual;
(*c*) relates to the management of the affairs of a person not capable of managing his own affairs;
(*d*) is a provisional (including protective) measure other than an order for the making of an interim payment;

and except where otherwise stated references to a judgment to which this section applies are to such a judgment exclusive of any such provisions.

(6) The following are within subsection (5)(*b*), but without prejudice to the generality of that provision—
(*a*) a decree of judicial separation or of separation;
[3](*b*) any order which is a Part I order for the purposes of the Family Law Act 1986.

(7) This section does not apply to a judgment of a court outside the United Kingdom which falls to be treated for the purposes of its enforcement as a judgment of a court of law in the United Kingdom by virtue of registration under Part II of the Administration of Justice Act 1920, Part I of the Foreign Judgments (Reciprocal Enforcement) Act 1933, Part I of the Maintenance Orders (Reciprocal Enforcement) Act 1972 or section 4 or 5 of this Act.

(8) A judgment to which this section applies, other than a judgment within paragraph (*e*) of subsection (2), shall not be enforced in another part of the United Kingdom except by way of registration under Schedule 6 or 7.

NOTES

[1] Inserted by the Insolvency Act 1985, Sched. 8, para. 36, and as amended by the Insolvency Act 1986, Sched. 14.

[2] Inserted by the Drug Trafficking Offences Act 1986, s.39. As amended by the Criminal Justice (Scotland) Act 1987, s.45(3), and the Criminal Justice Act 1988, Sched. 15, para. 82.

[3] As substituted by the Courts and Legal Services Act 1990, Sched. 16, para. 41.

Recognition of U.K. judgments in other parts of U.K.

19.—(1) A judgment to which this section applies given in one part of the United Kingdom shall not be refused recognition in another part of the

United Kingdom solely on the ground that, in relation to that judgment, the court which gave it was not a court of competent jurisdiction according to the rules of private international law in force in that other part.

(2) Subject to subsection (3), this section applies to any judgment to which section 18 applies.

(3) This section does not apply to—

(*a*) the documents mentioned in paragraph (*c*) of the definition of "judgment" in section 18(2);

(*b*) the awards and orders mentioned in paragraphs (*d*) and (*e*) of that definition;

(*c*) the decrees and orders referred to in section 18(4).

PART III

JURISDICTION IN SCOTLAND

Rules to jurisdiction in Scotland

20.—(1) Subject to Parts I and II and to the following provisions of this Part, Schedule 8 has effect to determine in what circumstances a person may be sued in civil proceedings in the Court of Session or in a sheriff court.

(2) Nothing in Schedule 8 affects the competence as respects subject-matter or value of the Court of Session or of the sheriff court.

(3) Section 6 of the Sheriff Courts (Scotland) Act 1907 shall cease to have effect to the extent that it determines jurisdiction in relation to any matter to which Schedule 8 applies.

(4) In Schedule 8—

(*a*) words resulting from modifications of Title II of the 1968 Convention, by way of addition or substitution, and provisions not derived from that Title are printed in heavy type; and

(*b*) the marginal notes show, where appropriate, of which provision of Title II a provision of Schedule 8 is a modified version.

(5) In determining any question as to the meaning or effect of any provision contained in Schedule 8 and derived to any extent from Title II of the 1968 Convention—

(*a*) regard shall be had to any relevant principles laid down by the European Court in connection with Title II of the 1968 Convention and to any relevant decision of that court as to the meaning or effect of any provision of that Title; and

(*b*) without prejudice to the generality of paragraph (*a*), the reports mentioned in section 3(3) may be considered and shall, so far as relevant, be given such weight as is appropriate in the circumstances.

Continuance of certain existing jurisdictions

21.—(1) Schedule 8 does not affect—

(*a*) the operation of any enactment which confers jurisdiction on a Scottish court in respect of a specific subject-matter on specific grounds;

(*b*) without prejudice to the foregoing generality, the jurisdiction of any court in respect of any matter mentioned in Schedule 9.

(2) Her Majesty may by Order in Council—

(*a*) add to the list in Schedule 9 any description of proceedings; and

(*b*) remove from that list any description of proceedings (whether included in the list as originally enacted or added by virtue of this subsection).

(3) An Order in Council under subsection (2) may—

(*a*) make different provision for different descriptions of proceedings or for the same description of proceedings in different courts; and

(*b*) contain such transitional and other incidental provisions as appear to Her Majesty to be appropriate.

(4) An Order in Council under subsection (2) shall not be made unless a draft of the Order has been laid before Parliament and approved by a resolution of each House of Parliament.

Supplementary provisions

22.—(1) Nothing in Schedule 8 shall prevent a court from declining jurisdiction on the ground of *forum non conveniens*.

(2) Nothing in Schedule 8 affects the operation of any enactment or rule of law under which a court may decline to exercise jurisdiction because of the prorogation by parties of the jurisdiction of another court.

[THE NEXT PAGE IS B 145]

(3) For the avoidance of doubt, it is declared that nothing in Schedule 8 affects the *nobile officium* of the Court of Session.

(4) Where a court has jurisdiction in any proceedings by virtue of Schedule 8, that court shall also have jurisdiction to determine any matter which—

(*a*) is ancillary or incidental to the proceedings; or

(*b*) requires to be determined for the purposes of a decision in the proceedings.

Savings and consequential amendments

23.—(1) Nothing in Schedule 8 shall affect—

(*a*) the power of any court to vary or recall a maintenance order granted by that court;

(*b*) the power of a sheriff court under section 22 of the Maintenance Orders Act 1950 (discharge and variation of maintenance orders registered in sheriff courts) to vary or discharge a maintenance order registered in that court under Part II of that Act; or

(*c*) the power of a sheriff court under section 9 of the Maintenance Orders (Reciprocal Enforcement) Act 1972 (variation and revocation of maintenance orders registered in United Kingdom courts) to vary or revoke a registered order within the meaning of Part I of that Act.

(2) The enactments specified in Part II of Schedule 12 shall have effect with the amendments specified there, being amendments consequential on Schedule 8.

PART IV

MISCELLANEOUS PROVISIONS

Provisions relating to jurisdiction

Interim relief and protective measures in cases of doubtful jurisdiction

24. . . .

(2) Any power of a court in Scotland to grant protective measures pending the decision of any hearing shall apply to a case where—

(*a*) the subject of the proceedings includes a question as to the jurisdiction of the court to entertain them; or

(*b*) the proceedings involve the reference of a matter to the European Court under the 1971 Protocol.

(3) Subsections (1) and (2) shall not be construed as restricting any power to grant interim relief or protective measures which a court may have apart from this section.

. . . . . .

Provisional and protective measures in Scotland in the absence of substantive proceedings

27.—(1) The Court of Session may, in any case to which this subsection applies—

(*a*) subject to subsection (2)(*c*), grant a warrant for the arrestment of any assets situated in Scotland;

(*b*) subject to subsection (2)(*c*), grant a warrant of inhibition over any property situated in Scotland; and (*c*) grant interim interdict.

(2) Subsection (1) applies to any case in which—

(*a*) proceedings have been commenced but not concluded, or, in relation to paragraph (*c*) of that subsection, are to be commenced, in another Contracting State or in England and Wales or Northern Ireland;

(*b*) the subject-matter of the proceedings is within the scope of the 1968 Convention as determined by Article 1; and

(*c*) in relation to paragraphs (*a*) and (*b*) of subsection (1), such a warrant could competently have been granted in equivalent proceedings before a Scottish court;

but it shall not be necessary, in determining whether proceedings have been commenced for the purpose of paragraph (*a*) of this subsection, to show that any document has been served on or notice given to the defender.

(3) Her Majesty may by Order in Council confer on the Court of Session power to do anything mentioned in subsection (1) or in section 28 in relation to proceedings of any of the following descriptions, namely—

(*a*) proceedings commenced otherwise than in a Contracting State;

(*b*) proceedings whose subject-matter is not within the scope of the 1968 Convention as determined by Article 1;

(*c*) arbitration proceedings;

(*d*) in relation to subsection (1)(*c*) or section 28, proceedings which are to be commenced otherwise than in a Contracting State.

(4) An Order in Council under subsection (3)—

(*a*) may confer power to do only certain of the things mentioned in subsection (1) or in section 28;

(*b*) may make different provision for different classes of proceedings, for proceedings pending in different countries or courts outside the United Kingdom or in different parts of the United Kingdom, and for other different circumstances; and

(*c*) may impose conditions or restrictions on the exercise of any power conferred by the Order.

(5) Any Order in Council under subsection (3) shall be subject to annulment in pursuance of a resolution of either House of Parliament.

Application of s. 1 of Administration of Justice (Scotland) Act 1972

[1] **28.** When any proceedings have been brought, or are likely to be brought, in another Contracting State or in England and Wales or Northern Ireland in respect of any matter which is within the scope of the 1968 Convention as determined in Article 1, the Court of Session shall have the like power to make an order under section 1 of the Administration of Justice (Scotland) Act 1972 as amended by the Law Reform (Miscellaneous Provisions) (Scotland) Act 1985 as if the proceedings in question had been brought, or were likely to be brought, in that court.

NOTE

[1] As amended by the Law Reform (Miscellaneous Provisions) (Scotland) Act 1985, Sched. 2, para. 24, with effect from 8th December 1986.

. . . .

Proceedings in England and Wales or Northern Ireland for torts to immovable property

30.—(1) The jurisdiction of any court in England and Wales or Northern Ireland to entertain proceedings for trespass to, or any other tort affecting, immovable property shall extend to cases in which the property in question is situated outside that part of the United Kingdom unless the proceedings are principally concerned with a question of the title to, or the right to possession of, that property.

(2) Subsection (1) has effect subject to the 1968 Convention and to the provisions set out in Schedule 4.

Provisions relating to recognition and enforcement of judgments

Overseas judgments given against states, etc.

31.—(1) A judgment given by a court of an overseas country against a state other than the United Kingdom or the state to which that court belongs shall be recognised and enforced in the United Kingdom if, and only if—

(*a*) it would be so recognised and enforced if it had not been given against a state; and

[THE NEXT PAGE IS B 147]

(*b*) that court would have had jurisdiction in the matter if it had applied rules corresponding to those applicable to such matters in the United Kingdom in accordance with sections 2 to 11 of the State Immunity Act 1978.

(2) References in subsection (1) to a judgment given against a state include references to judgments of any of the following descriptions given in relation to a state—

(*a*) judgments against the government, or a department of the government, of the state but not (except as mentioned in paragraph (*c*)) judgments against an entity which is distinct from the executive organs of government;

(*b*) judgments against the sovereign or head of state in his public capacity;

(*c*) judgments against any such separate entity as is mentioned in paragraph (*a*) given in proceedings relating to anything done by it in the exercise of the sovereign authority of the state.

[1] (3) Nothing in subsection (1) shall affect the recognition or enforcement in the United Kingdom of a judgment to which Part I of the Foreign Judgments (Reciprocal Enforcement) Act 1933 applies by virtue of section 4 of the Carriage of Goods by Road Act 1965, section 17(4) of the Nuclear Installations Act 1965, section 13(3) of the Merchant Shipping (Oil Pollution) Act 1971, section 6 of the International Transport Conventions Act 1983 or section 5 of the Carriage of Passengers by Road Act 1974.

(4) Sections 12, 13 and 14(3) and (4) of the State Immunity Act 1978 (service of process and procedural privileges) shall apply to proceedings for the recognition or enforcement in the United Kingdom of a judgment given by a court of an overseas country (whether or not that judgment is within subsection (1) of this section) as they apply to other proceedings.

(5) In this section "state", in the case of a federal state, includes any of its constituent territories.

NOTE

[1] As amended by the International Transport Conventions Act 1983, s.11(2).

Overseas judgments given in proceedings brought in breach of agreement for settlement of disputes

32.—(1) Subject to the following provisions of this section, a judgment given by a court of an overseas country in any proceedings shall not be recognised or enforced in the United Kingdom if—

(*a*) the bringing of those proceedings in that court was contrary to an agreement under which the dispute in question was to be settled otherwise than by proceedings in the courts of that country; and

(*b*) those proceedings were not brought in that court by, or with the agreement of, the person against whom the judgment was given; and

(*c*) that person did not counterclaim in the proceedings or otherwise submit to the jurisdiction of that court.

(2) Subsection (1) does not apply where the agreement referred to in paragraph (*a*) of that subsection was illegal, void or unenforceable or was incapable of being performed for reasons not attributable to the fault of the party bringing the proceedings in which the judgment was given.

(3) In determining whether a judgment given by a court of an overseas country should be recognised or enforced in the United Kingdom, a court in the United Kingdom shall not be bound by any decision of the overseas court relating to any of the matters mentioned in subsection (1) or (2).

[1] (4) Nothing in subsection (1) shall affect the recognition or enforcement in the United Kingdom of—

(*a*) a judgment which is required to be recognised or enforced there under the 1968 Convention;

(*b*) a judgment to which Part I of the Foreign Judgments (Reciprocal Enforcement) Act 1933 applies by virtue of section 4 of the Carriage of Goods by Road Act 1965, section 17(4) of the Nuclear Installations Act 1965, section 13(3) of the Merchant Shipping (Oil Pollution) Act 1971, section 6 of the International Transport Conventions At 1983, section 5 of the Carriage of Passengers by Road Act 1974 or section 6(4) of the Merchant Shipping Act 1974.

NOTE

[1] As amended by the International Transport Conventions Act 1983, s.11(2).

. . . . . .

Minor amendments relating to overseas judgments

35.—(1) The Foreign Judgments (Reciprocal Enforcement) Act 1933 shall have effect with the amendments specified in Schedule 10, being amendments whose main purpose is to enable Part I of that Act to be applied to judgments of courts other than superior courts, to judgments providing for interim payments and to certain arbitration awards.

(2) For section 10 of the Administration of Justice Act 1920 (issue of certificates of judgments obtained in the United Kingdom) there shall be substituted—

"10.—(1) Where—

(*a*) a judgment has been obtained in the High Court in England or Northern Ireland, or in the Court of Session in Scotland, against any person; and

(*b*) the judgment creditor wishes to secure the enforcement of the judgment in a part of Her Majesty's dominions outside the United Kingdom to which this part of this Act extends,

the court shall, on an application made by the judgment creditor, issue to him a certified copy of the judgment.

(2) The reference in the preceding subsection to Her Majesty's dominions shall be construed as if that subsection had come into force in its present form at the commencement of this Act.".

(3) [See print of the Administration of Justice Act 1920, s.14, *supra*.]

Registration of maintenance orders in Northern Ireland

36.—(1) Where—

(*a*) a High Court order or a Court of Session order has been registered in the High Court of Justice in Northern Ireland ("the Northern Ireland High Court") under Part II of the Maintenance Orders Act 1950; or

(*b*) a county court order, a magistrates' court order or a sheriff court order has been registered in a court of summary jurisdiction in Northern Ireland under that Part,

an application may be made to the original court for the registration of the order in, respectively, a court of summary jurisdiction in Northern Ireland or the Northern Ireland High Court.

(2) In subsection (1) "the original court", in relation to an order, means the court by which the order was made.

(3) Section 2 (except subsection (6A)) and section 2A of the Maintenance Orders Act 1958 shall have effect for the purposes of an application under subsection (1), and subsections (2), (3), (4) and (4A) of section 5 of that Act shall have effect for the purposes of the cancellation of a registration made on such an application, as if—

(*a*) "registration" in those provisions included registration in the appropriate Northern Ireland court ("registered" being construed accordingly);

(*b*) any reference in those provisions to a High Court order or a magistrates' court order included, respectively, a Court of Session order or a sheriff court order; and

(*c*) any other reference in those provisions to the High Court or a magistrates' court included the Northern Ireland High Court or a court of summary jurisdiction in Northern Ireland.

[THE NEXT PAGE IS B149]

(4) . . .

(5) A court of summary jurisdiction in Northern Ireland shall have jurisdiction to hear a complaint by or against a person residing outside Northern Ireland for the discharge or variation of an order registered in Northern Ireland under this section; and where such a complaint is made against a person residing outside Northern Ireland, then, if he resides in England and Wales or Scotland, section 15 of the Maintenance Orders Act 1950 (which relates to the service of process on persons residing in those countries) shall have effect in relation to the complaint as it has effect in relation to the proceedings therein mentioned.

(6) The enactments specified in Part III of Schedule 12 shall have effect with the amendments specified there, being amendments consequential on this section.

Minor amendments relating to maintenance orders

37.—(1) The enactments specified in Schedule 11 shall have effect with the amendments specified there, being amendments whose main purpose is as follows—

Part I—to extend certain enforcement provisions to lump sum maintenance orders;

Part II—to provide for the recovery of interest according to the law of the country of origin in the case of maintenance orders made in other jurisdiction and registered in the High Court;

Part III—to extend the Maintenance Orders (Reciprocal Enforcement) Act 1972 to cases where the payer under a maintenance order is not resident within the jurisdiction but has assets there.

(2) . . .

Overseas judgments counteracting an award of multiple damages

38.—(1) Section 7 of the Protection of Trading Interests Act 1980 (which enables provision to be made by Order in Council for the enforcement in the United Kingdom on a reciprocal basis of overseas judgments directed to counteracting a judgment for multiple damages given in a third country) shall be amended as follows.

(2) In subsection (1) for "judgments given under any provision of the law of that country corresponding to that section" there shall be substituted "judgments of any description specified in the Order which are given under any provision of the law of that country relating to the recovery of sums paid or obtained pursuant to a judgment for multiple damages within the meaning of section 5(3) above, whether or not that provision corresponds to section 6 above".

(3) After subsection (1) there shall be inserted—

"(1A) Such an Order in Council may, as respects judgments to which it relates—

(*a*) make different provisions for different descriptions of judgment; and

(*b*) impose conditions or restrictions on the enforcement of judgments of any description.".

Jurisdiction, and recognition and enforcement of judgments, as between United Kingdom and certain territories

Application of provisions corresponding to 1968 Convention in relation to certain territories

39.—(1) Her Majesty may by Order in Council make provision corresponding to the provisions made by the 1968 Convention as between the Contracting States to that Convention, with such modifications as appear to Her Majesty to be appropriate, for regulating, as between the United

Kingdom and any of the territories mentioned in subsection (2), the jurisdiction of courts and the recognition and enforcement of judgments.

(2) The territories referred to in subsection (1) are—

(*a*) the Isle of Man;
(*b*) any of the Channel Islands;
(*c*) Gibraltar;
(*d*) the Sovereign Base Areas of Akrotiri and Dhekelia (that is to say the areas mentioned in section 2(1) of the Cyprus Act 1960).

(3) An Order in Council under this section may contain such supplementary and incidental provisions as appear to Her Majesty to be necessary or expedient, including in particular provisions corresponding to or applying any of the provisions of Part I with such modifications as may be specified in the Order.

(4) Any Order in Council under this section shall be subject to annulment in pursuance of a resolution of either House of Parliament.

Legal Aid

Power to modify enactments relating to legal aid etc.

40. . . .

(2) [Repealed by the Legal Aid (Scotland) Act 1986, Sched. 5.]

(3) . . .

PART V

SUPPLEMENTARY AND GENERAL PROVISIONS

Domicile

Domicile of individuals

[1] **41.**—(1) Subject to Article 52 (which contains provisions for determining whether a party is domiciled in a Contracting State), the following provisions of this section determine, for the purposes of the 1968 Convention and this Act, whether an individual is domiciled in the United Kingdom or in a particular part of, or place in, the United Kingdom or in a state other than a Contracting State.

(2) An individual is domiciled in the United Kingdom if and only if—

(*a*) he is resident in the United Kingdom; and
(*b*) the nature and circumstances of his residence indicate that he has a substantial connection with the United Kingdom.

(3) Subject to subsection (5), an individual is domiciled in a particular part of the United Kingdom if and only if—

(*a*) he is resident in that part; and
(*b*) the nature and circumstances of his residence indicate that he has a substantial connection with that part.

(4) An individual is domiciled in a particular place in the United Kingdom if and only if he—

(*a*) is domiciled in the part of the United Kingdom in which that place is situated; and
(*b*) is resident in that place.

(5) An individual who is domiciled in the United Kingdom but in whose case the requirements of subsection (3)(*b*) are not satisfied in relation to any particular part of the United Kingdom shall be treated as domiciled in the part of the United Kingdom in which he is resident.

(6) In the case of an individual who—

(*a*) is resident in the United Kingdom, or in a particular part of the United Kingdom; and
(*b*) has been so resident for the last three months or more,

the requirements of subsection (2) (*b*) or, as the case may be, subsection (3) (*b*) shall be presumed to be fulfilled unless the contrary is proved.

(7) An individual is domiciled in a state other than a Contracting State if and only if—

(*a*) he is resident in that state; and

(*b*) the nature and circumstances of his residence indicate that he has a substantial connection with that state.

Domicile and seat of corporation or association

42.—(1) For the purposes of this Act the seat of a corporation or association (as determined by this section) shall be treated as its domicile.

(2) The following provisions of this section determine where a corporation or association has its seat—

(*a*) for the purpose of Article 53 (which for the purposes of the 1968 Convention equates the domicile of such a body with its seat); and

(*b*) for the purposes of this Act other than the provisions mentioned in section 43 (1) (*b*) and (*c*).

(3) A corporation or association has its seat in the United Kingdom if and only if—

(*a*) it was incorporated or formed under the law of a part of the United Kingdom and has its registered office or some other official address in the United Kingdom; or

(*b*) its central management and control is exercised in the United Kingdom.

(4) A corporation or association has its seat in a particular part of the United Kingdom if and only if it has its seat in the United Kingdom and—

(*a*) it has its registered office or some other official address in that part; or

(*b*) its central management and control is exercised in that part; or

(*c*) it has a place of business in that part.

(5) A corporation or association has its seat in a particular place in the United Kingdom if and only if it has its seat in the part of the United Kingdom in which that place is situated and—

(*a*) it has its registered office or some other official address in that place; or

(*b*) its central management and control is exercised in that place; or

(*c*) it has a place of business in that place.

(6) Subject to subsection (7), a corporation or association has its seat in a state other than the United Kingdom if and only if—

(*a*) it was incorporated or formed under the law of that state and has its registered office or some other official address there; or

(*b*) its central management and control is exercised in that state.

(7) A corporation or association shall not be regarded as having its seat in a Contracting State other than the United Kingdom if it is shown that the courts of that state would not regard it as having its seat there.

(8) In this section—

" business " includes any activity carried on by a corporation or association, and " place of business " shall be construed accordingly;

" official address ", in relation to a corporation or association, means an address which it is required by law to register, notify or maintain for the purpose of receiving notices or other communications.

Seat of corporation or association for purposes of Article 16 (2) and related provisions

43.—(1) The following provisions of this section determine where a corporation or association has its seat for the purposes of—

(*a*) Article 16 (2) (which confers exclusive jurisdiction over proceedings relating to the formation or dissolution of such bodies, or to the decisions of their organs);

(*b*) Articles 5A and 16 (2) in Schedule 4; and

(*c*) Rules 2 (12) and 4 (1) (*b*) in Schedule 8.

(2) A corporation or association has its seat in the United Kingdom if and only if—

(*a*) it was incorporated or formed under the law of a part of the United Kingdom; or

(*b*) its central management and control is exercised in the United Kingdom.

(3) A corporation or association has its seat in a particular part of the United Kingdom if and only if it has its seat in the United Kingdom and—

(*a*) subject to subsection (5), it was incorporated or formed under the law of that part; or

(*b*) being incorporated or formed under the law of a state other than the United Kingdom, its central management and control is exercised in that part.

(4) A corporation or association has its seat in a particular place in Scotland if and only if it has its seat in Scotland and—

(*a*) it has its registered office or some other official address in that place; or

(*b*) it has no registered office or other official address in Scotland, but its central management and control is exercised in that place.

(5) A corporation or association incorporated or formed under—

(*a*) an enactment forming part of the law of more than one part of the United Kingdom; or

(*b*) an instrument having effect in the domestic law of more than one part of the United Kingdom,

shall, if it has a registered office, be taken to have its seat in the part of the United Kingdom in which that office is situated, and not in any other part of the United Kingdom.

(6) Subject to subsection (7), a corporation or association has its seat in a Contracting State other than the United Kingdom if and only if—

(*a*) it was incorporated or formed under the law of that state; or

(*b*) its central management and control is exercised in that state.

(7) A corporation or association shall not be regarded as having its seat in a Contracting State other than the United Kingdom if—

(*a*) it has its seat in the United Kingdom by virtue of subsection (2) (*a*); or

(*b*) it is shown that the courts of that other state would not regard it for the purposes of Article 16 (2) as having its seat there.

(8) In this section " official address " has the same meaning as in section 42.

Persons deemed to be domiciled in the United Kingdom for certain purposes

44.—(1) This section applies to—

(*a*) proceedings within Section 3 of Title II of the 1968 Convention (insurance contracts), and

(*b*) proceedings within Section 4 of that Title (consumer contracts).

(2) A person who, for the purposes of proceedings to which this section applies arising out of the operations of a branch, agency or other establishment in the United Kingdom, is deemed for the purposes of the 1968 Convention to be domiciled in the United Kingdom by virtue of—

(*a*) Article 8, second paragraph (insurers); or

(*b*) Article 13, second paragraph (suppliers of goods, services or credit to consumers),

shall, for the purposes of those proceedings, be treated for the purposes of this Act as so domiciled and as domiciled in the part of the United Kingdom in which the branch, agency or establishment in question is situated.

Domicile of trusts

45.—(1) The following provisions of this section determine, for the purposes of the 1968 Convention and this Act, where a trust is domiciled.

(2) A trust is domiciled in the United Kingdom if and only if it is by virtue of subsection (3) domiciled in a part of the United Kingdom.

(3) A trust is domiciled in a part of the United Kingdom if and only if the system of law of that part is the system of law with which the trust has its closest and most real connection.

Domicile and seat of the Crown

46.—(1) For the purposes of this Act the seat of the Crown (as determined by this section) shall be treated as its domicile.

(2) The following provisions of this section determine where the Crown has its seat—

(*a*) for the purposes of the 1968 Convention (in which Article 53 equates the domicile of a legal person with its seat); and

(*b*) for the purposes of this Act..

(3) Subject to the provisions of any Order in Council for the time being in force under subsection (4)—

(*a*) the Crown in right of Her Majesty's government in the United Kingdom has its seat in every part of, and every place in, the United Kingdom; and

(*b*) the Crown in right of Her Majesty's government in Northern Ireland has its seat in, and in every place in, Northern Ireland.

(4) Her Majesty may by Order in Council provide that, in the case of proceedings of any specified description against the Crown in right of Her Majesty's government in the United Kingdom, the Crown shall be treated for the purposes of the 1968 Convention and this Act as having its seat in, and in every place in, a specified part of the United Kingdom and not in any other part of the United Kingdom.

(5) An Order in Council under subsection (4) may frame a description of proceedings in any way, and in particular may do so by reference to the government department or officer of the Crown against which or against whom they fall to be instituted.

(6) Any Order in Council made under this section shall be subject to annulment in pursuance of a resolution of either House of Parliament.

(7) Nothing in this section applies to the Crown otherwise than in right of Her Majesty's government in the United Kingdom or Her Majesty's government in Northern Ireland.

Other supplementary provisions

Modifications occasioned by decisions of European Court as to meaning or effect of Conventions

47.—(1) Her Majesty may by Order in Council—

(*a*) make such provision as Her Majesty considers appropriate for the purpose of bringing the law of any part of the United Kingdom into accord with the Conventions as affected by any principle laid down by the European Court in connection with the Conventions or by any decision of that court as to the meaning or effect of any provision of the Conventions; or

(*b*) make such modifications of Schedule 4 or Schedule 8, or of any other statutory provision affected by any provision of either of those Schedules, as Her Majesty considers appropriate in view of any principle laid down by the European Court in connection with Title II of the 1968 Convention or of any decision of that court as to the meaning or effect of any provision of that Title.

(2) The provision which may be made by virtue of paragraph (*a*) of subsection (1) includes such modifications of this Act or any other statutory

provision, whenever passed or made, as Her Majesty considers appropriate for the purpose mentioned in that paragraph.

(3) The modifications which may be made by virtue of paragraph (*b*) of subsection (1) include modifications designed to produce divergence between any provision of Schedule 4 or Schedule 8 and a corresponding provision of Title II of the 1968 Convention as affected by any such principle or decision as is mentioned in that paragraph.

(4) An Order in Council under this section shall not be made unless a draft of the Order has been laid before Parliament and approved by a resolution of each House of Parliament.

Matters for which rules of court may provide

48.—(1) Rules of court may make provision for regulating the procedure to be followed in any court in connection with any provision of this Act or the Conventions.

(2) Rules of court may make provision as to the manner in which and the conditions subject to which a certificate or judgment registered in any court under any provision of this Act may be enforced, including provision for enabling the court or, in Northern Ireland the Enforcement of Judgments Office, subject to any conditions specified in the rules, to give directions about such matters.

(3) . . .

(4) Nothing in this section shall be taken as derogating from the generality of any power to make rules of court conferred by any other enactment.

Saving for powers to stay, sist, strike out or dismiss proceedings

49. Nothing in this Act shall prevent any court in the United Kingdom from staying, sisting, striking out or dismissing any proceedings before it, on the ground of *forum non conveniens* or otherwise, where to do so is not inconsistent with the 1968 Convention.

General

Interpretation: general

50. In this Act, unless the context otherwise requires—

" the Accession Convention " has the meaning given by section 1 (1);

" Article " and references to sub-divisions of numbered Articles are to be construed in accordance with section 1 (2) (*b*);

" association " means an unincorporated body of persons;

" Contracting State " has the meaning given by section 1 (3);

" the 1968 Convention " has the meaning given by section 1 (1), and references to that Convention and to provisions of it are to be construed in accordance with section 1 (2) (*a*);

" the Conventions " has the meaning given by section 1 (1);

" corporation " means a body corporate, and includes a partnership subsisting under the law of Scotland;

" court ", without more, includes a tribunal;

" court of law ", in relation to the United Kingdom, means any of the following courts, namely—

(*a*) the House of Lords,

(*b*) in England and Wales or Northern Ireland, the Court of Appeal, the High Court, the Crown Court, a county court and a magistrates' court,

(*c*) in Scotland, the Court of Session and a sheriff court;

" the Crown " is to be construed in accordance with section 51 (2);

"enactment" includes an enactment comprised in Northern Ireland legislation;

"judgment", subject to sections 15(1) and 18(2) and to paragraph 1 of Schedules 6 and 7, means any judgment or order (by whatever name called) given or made by a court in any civil proceedings;

"magistrates' court", in relation to Northern Ireland, means a court of summary jurisdiction;

"modifications" includes additions, omissions and alterations;

"overseas country" means any country or territory outside the United Kingdom;

"part of the United Kingdom" means England and Wales, Scotland or Northern Ireland;

"the 1971 Protocol" has the meaning given by section 1(1), and references to that Protocol and to provisions of it are to be construed in accordance with section 1(2)(*a*);

"rules of court", in relation to any court, means rules, orders or regulations made by the authority having power to make rules, orders or regulations regulating the procedure of that court, and includes—
- (*a*) in Scotland, Acts of Sederunt;
- (*b*) in Northern Ireland, Judgment Enforcement Rules;

"statutory provision" means any provision contained in an Act, or in any Northern Ireland legislation, or in—
- (*a*) subordinate legislation (as defined in section 21(1) of the Interpretation Act 1978); or
- (*b*) any instrument of a legislative character made under any Northern Ireland legislation;

"tribunal"—
- (*a*) means a tribunal of any description other than a court of law;
- (*b*) in relation to an overseas country, includes, as regards matters relating to maintenance within the meaning of the 1968 Convention, any authority having power to give, enforce, vary or revoke a maintenance order.

Application to Crown

51.—(1) This Act binds the Crown.

(2) In this section and elsewhere in this Act references to the Crown do not include references to Her Majesty in Her private capacity or to Her Majesty in right of Her Duchy of Lancaster or to the Duke of Cornwall.

Extent

52.—(1) This Act extends to Northern Ireland.

(2) Without prejudice to the power conferred by section 39, Her Majesty may by Order in Council direct that all or any of the provisions of this Act apart from that section shall extend, subject to such modifications as may be specified in the Order, to any of the following territories, that is to say—
- (*a*) the Isle of Man;
- [1] (*b*) any of the Channel Islands;
- (*c*) Gibraltar;
- (*d*) the Sovereign Base Areas of Akrotiri and Dhekelia (that is to say the areas mentioned in section 2(1) of the Cyprus Act 1960).

NOTE

[1] See S.I. 1983 No. 607.

Commencement, transitional provisions and savings

53.—(1) This Act shall come into force in accordance with the provisions of Part I of Schedule 13.

(2) The transitional provisions and savings contained in Part II of that Schedule shall have effect in relation to the commencement of the provisions of this Act mentioned in that Part.

Repeals

54. The enactments mentioned in Schedule 14 are hereby repealed to the extent specified in the third column of that Schedule.

Short title

55. This Act may be cited as the Civil Jurisdiction and Judgments Act 1982.

SCHEDULES

Section 2(2)

SCHEDULE 1

TEXT OF 1968 CONVENTION, AS AMENDED

Arrangement of Provisions

CONVENTION ON JURISDICTION AND THE ENFORCEMENT OF JUDGMENTS IN CIVIL AND COMMERCIAL MATTERS

Preamble

The High Contracting Parties to the Treaty establishing the European Economic Community;

Desiring to implement the provisions of Article 220 of that Treaty by virtue of which they undertook to secure the simplification of formalities governing the reciprocal recognition and enforcement of judgments of courts or tribunals;

Anxious to strengthen in the Community the legal protection of persons therein established;

Considering that it is necessary for this purpose to determine the international jurisdiction of their courts, to facilitate recognition and to introduce an expeditious procedure for securing the enforcement of judgments, authentic instruments and court settlements;

Have decided to conclude this Convention and to this end have designated as their Plenipotentiaries:

(Designations of Plenipotentiaries of the original six Contracting States)

Who, meeting within the Council, having exchanged their Full Powers, found in good and due form,

Have agreed as follows:

TITLE I

Scope

Article 1

This Convention shall apply in civil and commercial matters whatever the nature of the court or tribunal. It shall not extend, in particular, to revenue, customs or administrative matters.

The Convention shall not apply to:

(1) the status or legal capacity of natural persons, rights in property arising out of a matrimonial relationship, wills and succession;

(2) bankruptcy, proceedings relating to the winding-up of insolvent companies or other legal persons, judicial arrangements, compositions and analogous proceedings;

(3) social security;

(4) arbitration.

TITLE II

Jurisdiction

Section 1

General provisions

Article 2

Subject to the provisions of this Convention, persons domiciled in a Contracting State shall, whatever their nationality, be sued in the courts of that State.

Persons who are not nationals of the State in which they are domiciled shall be governed by the rules of jurisdiction applicable to nationals of that State.

Article 3

Persons domiciled in a Contracting State may be sued in the courts of another Contracting State only by virtue of the rules set out in Sections 2 to 6 of this Title.

In particular the following provisions shall not be applicable as against them:

. . . . . .

—in the United Kingdom:	the rules which enable jurisdiction to be founded on: (*a*) the document instituting the proceedings having been served on the defendant during his temporary presence in the United Kingdom; or (*b*) the presence within the United Kingdom of property belonging to the defendant; or (*c*) the seizure by the plaintiff of property situated in the United Kingdom.

Article 4

If the defendant is not domiciled in a Contracting State, the jurisdiction of the courts of each Contracting State shall, subject to the provisions of Article 16, be determined by the law of that State.

As against such a defendant, any person domiciled in a Contracting State may, whatever his nationality, avail himself in that State of the rules of jurisdiction there in force, and in particular those specified in the second paragraph of Article 3, in the same way as the nationals of that State.

Section 2

Special Jurisdiction

Article 5

A person domiciled in a Contracting State may, in another Contracting State, be sued:

(1) in matters relating to a contract, in the courts for the place of performance of the obligation in question;

(2) in matters relating to maintenance, in the courts for the place where the maintenance creditor is domiciled or habitually resident or, if the matter is ancillary to proceedings concerning the status of a person, in the court which, according to its own law, has jurisdiction to entertain those proceedings, unless that jurisdiction is based solely on the nationality of one of the parties;

(3) in matters relating to tort, delict or quasi-delict, in the courts for the place where the harmful event occurred;

(4) as regards a civil claim for damages or restitution which is based on an act giving rise to criminal proceedings, in the court seised of those proceedings, to the extent that that court has jurisdiction under its own law to entertain civil proceedings;

(5) as regards a dispute arising out of the operations of a branch, agency or other establishment, in the courts for the place in which the branch, agency or other establishment is situated;

(6) in his capacity as settlor, trustee or beneficiary of a trust created by the operation of a statute, or by a written instrument, or created orally and evidenced in writing, in the courts of the Contracting State in which the trust is domiciled;

(7) as regards a dispute concerning the payment of remuneration claimed in respect of the salvage of a cargo or freight, in the court under the authority of which the cargo or freight in question:

(*a*) has been arrested to secure such payment, or

(*b*) could have been so arrested, but bail or other security has been given;

provided that this provision shall apply only if it is claimed that the defendant has an interest in the cargo or freight or had such an interest at the time of salvage.

Article 6

A person domiciled in a Contracting State may also be sued:

(1) where he is one of a number of defendants, in the courts for the place where any one of them is domiciled;

(2) as a third party in an action on a warranty or guarantee or in any other third party proceedings, in the court seised of the original proceedings, unless these were instituted solely with the object of removing him from the jurisdiction of the court which would be competent in his case;

(3) on a counterclaim arising from the same contract or facts on which the original claim was based, in the court in which the original claim is pending.

Article 6A

Where by virtue of this Convention a court of a Contracting State has jurisdiction in actions relating to liability arising from the use or operation of a ship, that court, or any other court substituted for this purpose by the internal law of that State, shall also have jurisdiction over claims for limitation of such liability.

Section 3

Jurisdiction in matters relating to insurance

Article 7

In matters relating to insurance, jurisdiction shall be determined by this Section, without prejudice to the provisions of Articles 4 and 5 (5).

Article 8

An insurer domiciled in a Contracting State may be sued:

(1) in the courts of the State where he is domiciled, or

(2) in another Contracting State, in the courts for the place where the policy-holder is domiciled, or

(3) if he is a co-insurer, in the courts of a Contracting State in which proceedings are brought against the leading insurer.

An insurer who is not domiciled in a Contracting State but has a branch, agency or other establishment in one of the Contracting States shall, in disputes arising out of the operations of the branch, agency or establishment, be deemed to be domiciled in that State.

Article 9

In respect of liability insurance or insurance of immovable property, the insurer may in addition be sued in the courts for the place where the harmful event occurred. The same applies if movable and immovable property are covered by the same insurance policy and both are adversely affected by the same contingency.

Article 10

In respect of liability insurance, the insurer may also, if the law of the court permits it, be joined in proceedings which the injured party has brought against the insured.

The provisions of Articles 7, 8 and 9 shall apply to actions brought by the injured party directly against the insurer, where such direct actions are permitted.

If the law governing such direct actions provides that the policy-holder or the insured may be joined as a party to the action, the same court shall have jurisdiction over them.

Article 11

Without prejudice to the provisions of the third paragraph of Article 10, an insurer may bring proceedings only in the courts of the Contracting State in which the defendant is domiciled, irrespective of whether he is the policy-holder, the insured or a beneficiary.

The provisions of this Section shall not affect the right to bring a counterclaim in the court in which, in accordance with this Section, the original claim is pending.

Article 12

The provisions of this Section may be departed from only by an agreement on jurisdiction:

(1) which is entered into after the dispute has arisen, or

(2) which allows the policy-holder, the insured or a beneficiary to bring proceedings in courts other than those indicated in this Section, or

(3) which is concluded between a policy-holder and an insurer, both of whom are at the time of conclusion of the contract domiciled or habitually resident in the same Contracting State, and which has the effect of conferring jurisdiction on the courts of that State even if the harmful event were to occur abroad, provided that such an agreement is not contrary to the law of that State, or

(4) which is concluded with a policy-holder who is not domiciled in a Contracting State, except in so far as the insurance is compulsory or relates to immovable property in a Contracting State, or

(5) which relates to a contract of insurance in so far as it covers one or more of the risks set out in Article 12A.

Article 12A

The following are the risks referred to in Article 12 (5):

(1) Any loss of or damage to

(*a*) sea-going ships, installations situated offshore or on the high seas, or aircraft, arising from perils which relate to their use for commercial purposes,

(*b*) goods in transit other than passengers' baggage where the transit consists of or includes carriage by such ships or aircraft;

(2) Any liability, other than for bodily injury to passengers or loss of or damage to their baggage,

(*a*) arising out of the use or operation of ships, installations or aircraft as referred to in (1) (*a*) above in so far as the law of the Contracting State in which such aircraft are registered does not prohibit agreements on jurisdiction regarding insurance of such risks,

(*b*) for loss or damage caused by goods in transit as described in (1) (*b*) above;

(3) Any financial loss connected with the use or operation of ships, installations or aircraft as referred to in (1) (*a*) above, in particular loss of freight or charter-hire;

(4) Any risk or interest connected with any of those referred to in (1) to (3) above.

Section 4

Jurisdiction over consumer contracts

Article 13

In proceedings concerning a contract concluded by a person for a purpose which can be regarded as being outside his trade or profession, hereinafter called the " consumer ", jurisdiction shall be determined by this Section, without prejudice to the provisions of Articles 4 and 5 (5), if it is:

(1) a contract for the sale of goods on instalment credit terms, or

(2) a contract for a loan repayable by instalments, or for any other form of credit, made to finance the sale of goods, or

(3) any other contract for the supply of goods or a contract for the supply of services and

(*a*) in the State of the consumer's domicile the conclusion of the contract was preceded by a specific invitation addressed to him or by advertising, and

(*b*) the consumer took in that State the steps necessary for the conclusion of the contract.

Where a consumer enters into a contract with a party who is not domiciled in a Contracting State but has a branch, agency or other establishment in one of the Contracting States, that party shall, in disputes arising out of the operations of the branch, agency or establishment, be deemed to be domiciled in that State.

This Section shall not apply to contracts of transport.

Article 14

A consumer may bring proceedings against the other party to a contract either in the courts of the Contracting State in which that party is domiciled or in the courts of the Contracting State in which he is himself domiciled.

Proceedings may be brought against a consumer by the other party to the contract only in the courts of the Contracting State in which the consumer is domiciled.

These provisions shall not affect the right to bring a counter-claim in the court in which, in accordance with this Section, the original claim is pending.

Article 15

The provisions of this Section may be departed from only by an agreement:

(1) which is entered into after the dispute has arisen,

or

(2) which allows the consumer to bring proceedings in courts other than those indicated in this Section,

or

(3) which is entered into by the consumer and the other party to the contract, both of whom are at the time of conclusion of the contract domiciled or habitually resident in the same Contracting State, and which confers jurisdiction on the courts of that State, provided that such an agreement is not contrary to the law of that State.

Section 5

Exclusive jurisdiction

Article 16

The following courts shall have exclusive jurisdiction, regardless of domicile:

(1) in proceedings which have as their object rights *in rem* in, or tenancies of, immovable property, the courts of the Contracting State in which the property is situated;

(2) in proceedings which have as their object the validity of the constitution, the nullity or the dissolution of companies or other legal persons or associations of natural or legal persons, or the decisions of their organs, the courts of the Contracting State in which the company, legal person or association has its seat;

(3) in proceedings which have as their object the validity of entries in public registers, the courts of the Contracting State in which the register is kept;

(4) in proceedings concerned with the registration or validity of patents, trade marks, designs, or other similar rights required to be deposited or registered, the courts of the Contracting State in which the deposit or registration has been applied for, has taken place or is under the terms of an international convention deemed to have taken place;

(5) in proceedings concerned with the enforcement of judgments, the courts of the Contracting State in which the judgment has been or is to be enforced.

Section 6

Prorogation of jurisdiction

Article 17

If the parties, one or more of whom is domiciled in a Contracting State, have agreed that a court or the courts of a Contracting State are to have jurisdiction to settle any disputes which have arisen or which may arise in connection with a particular legal relationship, that court or those courts shall have exclusive jurisdiction. Such an agreement conferring jurisdiction shall be either in writing or evidenced in writing or, in international trade or commerce, in a form which accords with practices in that trade or commerce of which the parties are or ought to have been aware. Where such an agreement is concluded by parties, none of whom is domiciled in a Contracting State, the courts of other Contracting States shall have no jurisdiction over their disputes unless the court or courts chosen have declined jurisdiction.

The court or courts of a Contracting State on which a trust instrument has conferred jurisdiction shall have exclusive jurisdiction in any proceedings brought against a settlor, trustee or beneficiary, if relations between these persons or their rights or obligations under the trust are involved.

Agreements or provisions of a trust instrument conferring jurisdiction shall have no legal force if they are contrary to the provisions of Articles 12 or 15, or if the courts whose jurisdiction they purport to exclude have exclusive jurisdiction by virtue of Article 16.

If an agreement conferring jurisdiction was concluded for the benefit of only one of the parties, that party shall retain the right to bring proceedings in any other court which has jurisdiction by virtue of this Convention.

Article 18

Apart from jurisdiction derived from other provisions of this Convention, a court of a Contracting State before whom a defendant enters an appearance shall have jurisdiction. This rule shall not apply where appearance was entered solely to contest the jurisdiction, or where another court has exclusive jurisdiction by virtue of Article 16.

Section 7

Examination as to jurisdiction and admissibility

Article 19

Where a court of a Contracting State is seised of a claim which is principally concerned with a matter over which the courts of another Contracting State have exclusive jurisdiction by virtue of Article 16, it shall declare of its own motion that it has no jurisdiction.

Article 20

Where a defendant domiciled in one Contracting State is sued in a court of another Contracting State and does not enter an appearance, the court shall declare of its own motion that it has no jurisdiction unless its jurisdiction is derived from the provisions of this Convention.

The court shall stay the proceedings so long as it is not shown that the defendant has been able to receive the document instituting the proceedings or an equivalent document in sufficient time to enable him to arrange for his defence, or that all necessary steps have been taken to this end.

The provisions of the foregoing paragraph shall be replaced by those of Article 15 of the Hague Convention of 15 November 1965 on the Service Abroad of Judicial and Extrajudicial Documents in Civil or Commercial Matters, if the document instituting the proceedings or notice thereof had to be transmitted abroad in accordance with that Convention.

Section 8

Lis Pendens—Related actions

Article 21

Where proceedings involving the same cause of action and between the same parties are brought in the courts of different Contracting States, any court other than the court first seised shall of its own motion decline jurisdiction in favour of that court.

A court which would be required to decline jurisdiction may stay its proceedings if the jurisdiction of the other court is contested.

Article 22

Where related actions are brought in the courts of different Contracting States, any court other than the court first seised may, while the actions are pending at first instance, stay its proceedings.

A court other than the court first seised may also, on the application of one of the parties, decline jurisdiction if the law of that court permits the consolidation of related actions and the court first seised has jurisdiction over both actions.

For the purposes of this Article, actions are deemed to be related where they are so closely connected that it is expedient to hear and determine them together to avoid the risk of irreconcilable judgments resulting from separate proceedings.

Article 23

Where actions come within the exclusive jurisdiction of several courts, any court other than the court first seised shall decline jurisdiction in favour of that court.

Section 9

Provisional, including protective, measures

Article 24

Application may be made to the courts of a Contracting State for such provisional, including protective, measures as may be available under the law of that State, even if, under this Convention, the courts of another Contracting State have jurisdiction as to the substance of the matter.

TITLE III

Recognition and Enforcement

Article 25

For the purposes of this Convention, " judgment " means any judgment given by a court or tribunal of a Contracting State, whatever the judgment may be called, including a decree, order, decision or writ of execution, as well as the determination of costs or expenses by an officer of the court.

Section 1

Recognition

Article 26

A judgment given in a Contracting State shall be recognised in the other Contracting States without any special procedure being required.

Any interested party who raises the recognition of a judgment as the principal issue in a dispute may, in accordance with the procedures provided for in Sections 2 and 3 of this Title, apply for a decision that the judgment be recognised.

If the outcome of proceedings in a court of a Contracting State depends on the determination of an incidental question of recognition that court shall have jurisdiction over that question.

Article 27

A judgment shall not be recognised:

(1) if such recognition is contrary to public policy in the State in which recognition is sought;

(2) where it was given in default of appearance, if the defendant was not duly served with the document which instituted the proceedings or with an equivalent document in sufficient time to enable him to arrange for his defence;

(3) if the judgment is irreconcilable with a judgment given in a dispute between the same parties in the State in which recognition is sought;

(4) if the court of the State in which the judgment was given, in order to arrive at its judgment, has decided a preliminary question concerning the status or legal capacity of natural persons, rights in property arising out of a matrimonial relationship, wills or succession in a way that conflicts with a rule of the private international law of the State in which the recognition is sought, unless the same result would have been reached by the application of the rules of private international law of that State;

(5) if the judgment is irreconcilable with an earlier judgment given in a non-Contracting State involving the same cause of action and between the same parties, provided that this latter judgment fulfils the conditions necessary for its recognition in the State addressed.

Article 28

Moreover, a judgment shall not be recognised if it conflicts with the provisions of Sections 3, 4 or 5 of Title II, or in a case provided for in Article 59.

In its examination of the grounds of jurisdiction referred to in the foregoing paragraph, the court or authority applied to shall be bound by the findings of fact on which the court of the State in which the judgment was given based its jurisdiction.

Subject to the provisions of the first paragraph, the jurisdiction of the court of the State in which the judgment was given may not be reviewed; the test of public policy referred to in Article 27 (1) may not be applied to the rules relating to jurisdiction.

Article 29

Under no circumstances may a foreign judgment be reviewed as to its substance.

Article 30

A court of a Contracting State in which recognition is sought of a judgment given in another Contracting State may stay the proceedings if an ordinary appeal against the judgment has been lodged.

A court of a Contracting State in which recognition is sought of a judgment given in Ireland or the United Kingdom may stay the proceedings if enforcement is suspended in the State in which the judgment was given by reason of an appeal.

Section 2

Enforcement

Article 31

A judgment given in a Contracting State and enforceable in that State shall be enforced in another Contracting State when, on the application of any interested party, the order for its enforcement has been issued there.

However, in the United Kingdom, such a judgment shall be enforced in England and Wales, in Scotland, or in Northern Ireland when, on the application of any interested party, it has been registered for enforcement in that part of the United Kingdom.

Article 32

The application shall be submitted:

. . . . .

— in the United Kingdom:

(1) in England and Wales, to the High Court of Justice, or in the case of a maintenance judgment to the Magistrates' Court on transmission by the Secretary of State;

(2) in Scotland, to the Court of Session, or in the case of a maintenance judgment to the Sheriff Court on transmission by the Secretary of State;

(3) in Northern Ireland, to the High Court of Justice, or in the case of a maintenance judgment to the Magistrates' Court on transmission by the Secretary of State.

The jurisdiction of local courts shall be determined by reference to the place of domicile of the party against whom enforcement is sought. If he is not domiciled in the State in which enforcement is sought, it shall be determined by reference to the place of enforcement.

Article 33

The procedure for making the application shall be governed by the law of the State in which enforcement is sought.

The applicant must give an address for service of process within the area of jurisdiction of the court applied to. However, if the law of the State in which enforcement is sought does not provide for the furnishing of such an address, the applicant shall appoint a representative *ad litem*.

The documents referred to in Articles 46 and 47 shall be attached to the application.

Article 34

The court applied to shall give its decision without delay; the party against whom enforcement is sought shall not at this stage of the proceedings be entitled to make any submissions on the application.

The application may be refused only for one of the reasons specified in Articles 27 and 28.

Under no circumstances may the foreign judgment be reviewed as to its substance.

Article 35

The appropriate officer of the court shall without delay bring the decision given on the application to the notice of the applicant in accordance with the procedure laid down by the law of the State in which enforcement is sought.

Article 36

If enforcement is authorised, the party against whom enforcement is sought may appeal against the decision within one month of service thereof.

If that party is domiciled in a Contracting State other than that in which the decision authorising enforcement was given, the time for appealing shall be two months and shall run from the date of service, either on him in person or at his residence. No extension of time may be granted on account of distance.

Article 37

An appeal against the decision authorising enforcement shall be lodged in accordance with the rules governing procedure in contentious matters:

. . . .

— in the United Kingdom:

(1) in England and Wales, with the High Court of Justice, or in the case of a maintenance judgment with the Magistrates' Court;

(2) in Scotland, with the Court of Session, or in the case of a maintenance judgment with the Sheriff Court;

(3) in Northern Ireland, with the High Court of Justice, or in the case of a maintenance judgment with the Magistrates' Court.

The judgment given on the appeal may be contested only:

. . . .

— in the United Kingdom, by a single further appeal on a point of law.

Article 38

The court with which the appeal under the first paragraph of Article 37 is lodged may, on the application of the appellant, stay the proceedings if an ordinary appeal has been lodged against the judgment in the State in which that judgment was given or if the time for such an appeal has not yet expired; in the latter case, the court may specify the time within which such an appeal is to be lodged.

Where the judgment was given in Ireland or the United Kingdom, any form of appeal available in the State in which it was given shall be treated as an ordinary appeal for the purposes of the first paragraph.

The court may also make enforcement conditional on the provision of such security as it shall determine.

Article 39

During the time specified for an appeal pursuant to Article 36 and until any such appeal has been determined, no measures of enforcement may be taken other than protective measures taken against the property of the party against whom enforcement is sought.

The decision authorising enforcement shall carry with it the power to proceed to any such protective measures.

Article 40

If the application for enforcement is refused, the applicant may appeal:

. . . .

— in the United Kingdom:

(1) in England and Wales, to the High Court of Justice, or in the case of a maintenance judgment to the Magistrates' Court;

(2) in Scotland, to the Court of Session, or in the case of a maintenance judgment to the Sheriff Court;

(3) in Northern Ireland, to the High Court of Justice, or in the case of a maintenance judgment to the Magistrates' Court.

The party against whom enforcement is sought shall be summoned to appear before the appellate court. If he fails to appear, the provisions of the second and third paragraphs of Article 20 shall apply even where he is not domiciled in any of the Contracting States.

Article 41

A judgment given on an appeal provided for in Article 40 may be contested only:

. . . .

— in the United Kingdom, by a single further appeal on a point of law.

Article 42

Where a foreign judgment has been given in respect of several matters and enforcement cannot be authorised for all of them, the court shall authorise enforcement for one or more of them.

An applicant may request partial enforcement of a judgment.

Article 43

A foreign judgment which orders a periodic payment by way of a penalty shall be enforceable in the State in which enforcement is sought only if the amount of the payment has been finally determined by the courts of the State in which the judgment was given.

Article 44

An applicant who, in the State in which the judgment was given, has benefited from complete or partial legal aid or exemption from costs or expenses, shall be entitled, in the procedures provided for in Articles 32 to 35, to benefit from the most favourable legal aid or the most extensive exemption from costs or expenses provided for by the law of the State addressed.

An applicant who requests the enforcement of a decision given by an administrative authority in Denmark in respect of a maintenance order may, in the State addressed, claim the benefits referred to in the first paragraph if he presents a statement from the Danish Ministry of Justice to the effect that he fulfils the economic requirements to qualify for the grant of complete or partial legal aid or exemption from costs or expenses.

Article 45

No security, bond or deposit, however described, shall be required of a party who in one Contracting State applies for enforcement of a judgment given in another Contracting State on the ground that he is a foreign national or that he is not domiciled or resident in the State in which enforcement is sought.

Section 3

Common provisions

Article 46

A party seeking recognition or applying for enforcement of a judgment shall produce:

(1) a copy of the judgment which satisfies the conditions necessary to establish its authenticity;

(2) in the case of a judgment given in default, the original or a certified true copy of the document which establishes that the party in default was served with the document instituting the proceedings or with an equivalent document.

Article 47

A party applying for enforcement shall also produce:

(1) documents which establish that, according to the law of the State in which it has been given, the judgment is enforceable and has been served;

(2) where appropriate, a document showing that the applicant is in receipt of legal aid in the State in which the judgment was given.

Article 48

If the documents specified in Article 46 (2) and Article 47 (2) are not produced, the court may specify a time for their production, accept equivalent documents or, if it considers that it has sufficient information before it, dispense with their production.

If the court so requires, a translation of the documents shall be produced; the translation shall be certified by a person qualified to do so in one of the Contracting States.

Article 49

No legalisation or other similar formality shall be required in respect of the documents referred to in Articles 46 or 47 or the second paragraph of Article 48, or in respect of a document appointing a representative *ad litem.*

TITLE IV

Authentic Instruments and Court Settlements

Article 50

A document which has been formally drawn up or registered as an authentic instrument and is enforceable in one Contracting State shall, in another Contracting State, have an order for its enforcement issued there, on application made in accordance with the procedures provided for in Article 31 *et seq.* The application may be refused only if enforcement of the instrument is contrary to public policy in the State in which enforcement is sought.

The instrument produced must satisfy the conditions necessary to establish its authenticity in the State of origin.

The provisions of Section 3 of Title III shall apply as appropriate.

Article 51

A settlement which has been approved by a court in the course of proceedings and is enforceable in the State in which it was concluded shall be enforceable in the State in which enforcement is sought under the same conditions as authentic instruments.

TITLE V

General Provisions

Article 52

In order to determine whether a party is domiciled in the Contracting State whose courts are seised of the matter, the court shall apply its internal law.

If a party is not domiciled in the State whose courts are seised of the matter, then, in order to determine whether the party is domiciled in another Contracting State, the court shall apply the law of that State.

The domicile of a party shall, however, be determined in accordance with his national law if, by that law, his domicile depends on that of another person or on the seat of an authority.

Article 53

For the purposes of this Convention, the seat of a company or other legal person or association of natural or legal persons shall be treated as its domicile. However, in order to determine that seat, the court shall apply its rules of private international law.

In order to determine whether a trust is domiciled in the Contracting State whose courts are seised of the matter, the court shall apply its rules of private international law.

TITLE VI

Transitional Provisions

Article 54

The provisions of this Convention shall apply only to legal proceedings instituted and to documents formally drawn up or registered as authentic instruments after its entry into force.

However, judgments given after the date of entry into force of this Convention in proceedings instituted before that date shall be recognised and enforced in accordance with the provisions of Title III if jurisdiction was founded upon rules which accorded with those provided for either in Title II of this Convention or in a convention concluded between the State of origin and the State addressed which was in force when the proceedings were instituted.

TITLE VII

RELATIONSHIP TO OTHER CONVENTIONS

Article 55

Subject to the provisions of the second paragraph of Article 54, and of Article 56, this Convention shall, for the States which are parties to it, supersede the following conventions concluded between two or more of them:

. . . . . .

— the Convention between the United Kingdom and the French Republic providing for the Reciprocal Enforcement of Judgments in Civil and Commercial Matters, with Protocol, signed at Paris on 18 January 1934;
— the Convention between the United Kingdom and the Kingdom of Belgium providing for the Reciprocal Enforcement of Judgments in Civil and Commercial Matters, with Protocol, signed at Brussels on 2 May 1934;

. . . . . .

— the Convention between the United Kingdom and the Federal Republic of Germany for the Reciprocal Recognition and Enforcement of Judgments in Civil and Commercial Matters, signed at Bonn on 14 July 1960;

. . . . . .

— the Convention between the United Kingdom and the Republic of Italy for the Reciprocal Recognition and Enforcement of Judgments in Civil and Commercial Matters, signed at Rome on 7 February 1964, with amending Protocol signed at Rome on 14 July 1970;
— the Convention between the United Kingdom and the Kingdom of the Netherlands providing for the Reciprocal Recognition and Enforcement of Judgments in Civil Matters, signed at The Hague on 17 November 1967;

. . . . . .

Article 56

The Treaty and the conventions referred to in Article 55 shall continue to have effect in relation to matters to which this Convention does not apply.

They shall continue to have effect in respect of judgments given and documents formally drawn up or registered as authentic instruments before the entry into force of this Convention.

Article 57

This Convention shall not affect any conventions to which the Contracting States are or will be parties and which, in relation to particular matters, govern jurisdiction or the recognition or enforcement of judgments.

This Convention shall not affect the application of provisions which, in relation to particular matters, govern jurisdiction or the recognition or enforcement of judgments and which are or will be contained in acts of the Institutions of the European Communities or in national laws harmonised in implementation of such acts.

(Article 25 (2) of the Accession Convention provides:

"With a view to its uniform interpretation, paragraph 1 of Article 57 shall be applied in the following manner:

(*a*) The 1968 Convention as amended shall not prevent a court of a Contracting State which is a party to a convention on a particular matter from assuming jurisdiction in accordance with that convention, even where the defendant is domiciled in another Contracting State which is not a party to that convention. The court shall, in any event, apply Article 20 of the 1968 Convention as amended.

(*b*) A judgment given in a Contracting State in the exercise of jurisdiction provided for in a convention on a particular matter shall be recognised and enforced in the other Contracting States in accordance with the 1968 Convention as amended.

Where a convention on a particular matter to which both the State of origin and the State addressed are parties lays down conditions for the recognition or enforcement of judgments, those conditions shall apply. In any event, the provisions of the 1968 Convention as amended which concern the procedures for recognition and enforcement of judgments may be applied.")

. . . .

Article 59

This Convention shall not prevent a Contracting State from assuming, in a convention on the recognition and enforcement of judgments, an obligation towards a third State not to recognise judgments given in other Contracting States against defendants domiciled or habitually resident in the third State where, in cases provided for in Article 4, the judgment could only be founded on a ground of jurisdiction specified in the second paragraph of Article 3.

However, a Contracting State may not assume an obligation towards a third State not to recognise a judgment given in another Contracting State by a court basing its jurisdiction on the presence within that State of property belonging to the defendant, or the seizure by the plaintiff of property situated there:

(1) if the action is brought to assert or declare proprietary or possessory rights in that property, seeks to obtain authority to dispose of it, or arises from another issue relating to such property, or,

(2) if the property constitutes the security for a debt which is the subject-matter of the action.

TITLE VIII

Final Provisions

Article 60

This Convention shall apply to the European territories of the Contracting States, including Greenland, to the French overseas departments and territories, and to Mayotte.

The Kingdom of the Netherlands may declare at the time of signing or ratifying this Convention or at any later time, by notifying the Secretary-General of the Council of the European Communities, that this Convention shall be applicable to the Netherlands Antilles. In the absence of such declaration, proceedings taking place in the European territory of the Kingdom as a result of an appeal in cassation from the judgment of a court in the Netherlands Antilles shall be deemed to be proceedings taking place in the latter court.

Notwithstanding the first paragraph, this Convention shall not apply to:

(1) the Faroe Islands, unless the Kingdom of Denmark makes a declaration to the contrary,

(2) any European territory situated outside the United Kingdom for the international relations of which the United Kingdom is responsible, unless the United Kingdom makes a declaration to the contrary in respect of any such territory.

Such declarations may be made at any time by notifying the Secretary-General of the Council of the European Communities.

Proceedings brought in the United Kingdom on appeal from courts in one of the territories referred to in subparagraph (2) of the third paragraph shall be deemed to be proceedings taking place in those courts.

Proceedings which in the Kingdom of Denmark are dealt with under the law on civil procedure for the Faroe Islands (*lov for Faerøerne om rettens pleje*) shall be deemed to be proceedings taking place in the courts of the Faroe Islands.

Article 61

This Convention shall be ratified by the signatory States. The instruments of ratification shall be deposited with the Secretary-General of the Council of the European Communities.

Article 62

This Convention shall enter into force on the first day of the third month following the deposit of the instrument of ratification by the last signatory State to take this step.

Article 63

The Contracting States recognise that any State which becomes a member of the European Economic Community shall be required to accept this Convention as a basis for the negotiations between the Contracting States and that State necessary to ensure the implementation of the last paragraph of Article 220 of the Treaty establishing the European Economic Community.

The necessary adjustments may be the subject of a special convention between the Contracting States of the one part and the new Member State of the other part.

Article 64

The Secretary-General of the Council of the European Communities shall notify the signatory States of:

(*a*) the deposit of each instrument of ratification;
(*b*) the date of entry into force of this Convention;
(*c*) any declaration received pursuant to Article 60;
(*d*) any declaration received pursuant to Article IV of the Protocol;
(*e*) any communication made pursuant to Article VI of the Protocol.

Article 65

The Protocol annexed to this Convention by common accord of the Contracting States shall form an integral part thereof.

Article 66

This Convention is concluded for an unlimited period.

Article 67

Any Contracting State may request the revision of this Convention. In this event, a revision conference shall be convened by the President of the Council of the European Communities.

Article 68

This Convention, drawn up in a single original in the Dutch, French, German, and Italian languages, all four texts being equally authentic, shall be deposited in the archives of the Secretariat of the Council of the European Communities. The Secretary-General shall transmit a certified copy to the Government of each signatory State.

(Signatures of Plenipotentiaries of the original six Contracting States)

ANNEXED PROTOCOL

Article I

Any person domiciled in Luxembourg who is sued in a court of another Contracting State pursuant to Article 5 (1) may refuse to submit to the jurisdiction of that court. If the defendant does not enter an appearance the court shall declare of its own motion that it has no jurisdiction.

An agreement conferring jurisdiction, within the meaning of Article 17, shall be valid with respect to a person domiciled in Luxembourg only if that person has expressly and specifically so agreed.

Article II

Without prejudice to any more favourable provisions of national laws, persons domiciled in a Contracting State who are being prosecuted in the criminal courts of another Contracting State of which they are not nationals for an offence which was not intentionally committed may be defended by persons qualified to do so, even if they do not appear in person.

However, the court seised of the matter may order appearance in person; in the case of failure to appear, a judgment given in the civil action without the person concerned having had the opportunity to arrange for his defence need not be recognised or enforced in the other Contracting States.

Article III

In proceedings for the issue of an order for enforcement, no charge, duty or fee calculated by reference to the value of the matter in issue may be levied in the State in which enforcement is sought.

Article IV

Judicial and extrajudicial documents drawn up in one Contracting State which have to be served on persons in another Contracting State shall be transmitted in accordance with the procedures laid down in the conventions and agreements concluded between the Contracting States.

Unless the State in which service is to take place objects by declaration to the Secretary-General of the Council of the European Communities, such documents may also be sent by the appropriate public officers of the State in which the document has been drawn up directly to the appropriate public officers of the State in which the addressee is to be found. In this case the officer of the State of origin shall send a copy of the document to the officer of the State addressed who is competent to forward it to the addressee. The document shall be forwarded in the manner specified by the law of the State addressed. The forwarding shall be recorded by a certificate sent directly to the officer of the State of origin.

. . . .

Article V B

In proceedings involving a dispute between the master and a member of the crew of a sea-going ship registered in Denmark or in Ireland, concerning remuneration or other conditions of service, a court in a Contracting State shall establish whether the diplomatic or consular officer responsible for the ship has been notified of the dispute. It shall stay the proceedings so long as he has not been notified. It shall of its own motion decline jurisdiction if the officer, having been duly notified, has exercised the powers accorded to him in the matter by a consular convention, or in the absence of such a convention, has, within the time allowed, raised any objection to the exercise of such jurisdiction.

Article V C

Articles 52 and 53 of this Convention shall, when applied by Article 69 (5) of the Convention for the European Patent for the Common Market, signed at Luxembourg on 15 December 1975, to the provisions relating to " residence " in the English text of that Convention, operate as if " residence " in that text were the same as " domicile " in Articles 52 and 53.

Article V D

Without prejudice to the jurisdiction of the European Patent Office under the Convention on the Grant of European Patents, signed at Munich on 5 October 1973, the courts of each Contracting State shall have exclusive jurisdiction, regardless of domicile, in proceedings concerned with the registration or validity of any European patent granted for that State which is not a Community patent by virtue of the provisions of Article 86 of the Convention for the European Patent for the Common Market, signed at Luxembourg on 15 December 1975.

Article VI

The Contracting States shall communicate to the Secretary-General of the Council of the European Communities the text of any provisions of their laws which amend either those articles of their laws mentioned in the Convention or the lists of courts specified in Section 2 of Title III of the Convention.

Section 2 (2)

SCHEDULE 2

Text of 1971 Protocol, as Amended

Article 1

The Court of Justice of the European Communities shall have jurisdiction to give rulings on the interpretation of the Convention on Jurisdiction and the Enforcement of Judgments in Civil and Commercial Matters and of the Protocol annexed to that Convention, signed at Brussels on 27 September 1968, and also on the interpretation of the present Protocol.

The Court of Justice of the European Communities shall also have jurisdiction to give rulings on the interpretation of the Convention on the Accession of the Kingdom of Denmark, Ireland and the United Kingdom of Great Britain and Northern Ireland to the Convention of 27 September 1968 and to this Protocol.

Article 2

The following courts may request the Court of Justice to give preliminary rulings on questions of interpretation:

. . . . .

— in the United Kingdom: the House of Lords and courts to which application has been made under the second paragraph of Article 37 or under Article 41 of the Convention;

(2) the courts of the Contracting States when they are sitting in an appellate capacity;

(3) in the cases provided for in Article 37 of the Convention, the courts referred to in that Article.

Article 3

(1) Where a question of interpretation of the Convention or of one of the other instruments referred to in Article 1 is raised in a case pending before one of the courts listed in Article 2 (1), that court shall, if it considers that a decision on the question is necessary to enable it to give judgment, request the Court of Justice to give a ruling thereon.

(2) Where such a question is raised before any court referred to in Article 2 (2) or (3), that court may, under the conditions laid down in paragraph (1), request the Court of Justice to give a ruling thereon.

Article 4

(1) The competent authority of a Contracting State may request the Court of Justice to give a ruling on a question of interpretation of the Convention or of one of the other instruments referred to in Article 1 if judgments given by courts of that State conflict with the interpretation given either by the Court of Justice or in a judgment of one of the courts of another Contracting State referred to in Article 2 (1) or (2). The provisions of this paragraph shall apply only to judgments which have become *res judicata.*

(2) The interpretation given by the Court of Justice in response to such a request shall not affect the judgments which gave rise to the request for interpretation.

(3) The Procurators-General of the Courts of Cassation of the Contracting States, or any other authority designated by a Contracting State, shall be entitled to request the Court of Justice for a ruling on interpretation in accordance with paragraph (1).

(4) The Registrar of the Court of Justice shall give notice of the request to the Contracting States, to the Commission and to the Council of the European Communities; they shall then be entitled within two months of the notification to submit statements of case or written observations to the Court.

(5) No fees shall be levied or any costs or expenses awarded in respect of the proceedings provided for in this Article.

Article 5

(1) Except where this Protocol otherwise provides, the provisions of the Treaty establishing the European Economic Community and those of the Protocol on the Statute of the Court of Justice annexed thereto, which are applicable when the Court is requested to give a preliminary ruling, shall also apply to any proceedings for the interpretation of the Convention and the other instruments referred to in Article 1.

(2) The Rules of Procedure of the Court of Justice shall, if necessary, be adjusted and supplemented in accordance with Article 188 of the Treaty establishing the European Economic Community.

Article 6

This Protocol shall apply to the European territories of the Contracting States, including Greenland to the French overseas departments and territories, and to Mayotte.

The Kingdom of the Netherlands may declare at the time of signing or ratifying this Protocol or at any later time, by notifying the Secretary-General of the Council of the European Communities, that this Protocol shall be applicable to the Netherlands Antilles.

Notwithstanding the first paragraph, this Protocol shall not apply to:

(1) the Faroe Islands, unless the Kingdom of Denmark makes a declaration to the contrary,

(2) any European territory situated outside the United Kingdom for the international relations of which the United Kingdom is responsible, unless the United Kingdom makes a declaration to the contrary in respect of any such territory.

Such declarations may be made at any time by notifying the Secretary-General of the Council of the European Communities.

Article 7

This Protocol shall be ratified by the signatory States. The instruments of ratification shall be deposited with the Secretary-General of the Council of the European Communities.

Article 8

This Protocol shall enter into force on the first day of the third month following the deposit of the instrument of ratification by the last signatory State to take this step; provided that it shall at the earliest enter into force at the same time as the Convention of 27 September 1968 on Jurisdiction and the Enforcement of Judgments in Civil and Commercial Matters.

Article 9

The Contracting States recognise that any State which becomes a member of the European Economic Community, and to which Article 63 of the Convention on Jurisdiction and the Enforcement of Judgments in Civil and Commercial Matters applies, must accept the provisions of this Protocol, subject to such adjustments as may be required.

Article 10

The Secretary-General of the Council of the European Communities shall notify the signatory States of:

(*a*) the deposit of each instrument of ratification;

(*b*) the date of entry into force of this Protocol;

(*c*) any designation received pursuant to Article 4 (3);

(*d*) any declaration received pursuant to Article 6.

Article 11

The Contracting States shall communicate to the Secretary-General of the Council of the European Communities the texts of any provisions of their laws which necessitate an amendment to the list of courts in Article 2 (1).

Article 12

This Protocol is concluded for an unlimited period.

Article 13

Any Contracting State may request the revision of this Protocol. In this event, a revision conference shall be convened by the President of the Council of the European Communities.

Article 14

This Protocol, drawn up in a single original in the Dutch, French, German and Italian languages, all four texts being equally authentic, shall be deposited in the archives of the

Secretariat of the Council of the European Communities. The Secretary-General shall transmit a certified copy to the Government of each signatory State.

Section 2 (2)

SCHEDULE 3

Text of Titles V and VI of Accession Convention

TITLE V

Transitional Provisions

Article 34

(1) The 1968 Convention and the 1971 Protocol, with the amendments made by this Convention, shall apply only to legal proceedings instituted and to authentic instruments formally drawn up or registered after the entry into force of this Convention in the State of origin and, where recognition or enforcement of a judgment or authentic instrument is sought, in the State addressed.

(2) However, as between the six Contracting States to the 1968 Convention, judgments given after the date of entry into force of this Convention in proceedings instituted before that date shall be recognised and enforced in accordance with the provisions of Title III of the 1968 Convention as amended.

(3) Moreover, as between the six Contracting States to the 1968 Convention and the three States mentioned in Article 1 of this Convention, and as between those three States, judgments given after the date of entry into force of this Convention between the State of origin and the State addressed in proceedings instituted before that date shall also be recognised and enforced in accordance with the provisions of Title III of the 1968 Convention as amended if jurisdiction was founded upon rules which accorded with the provisions of Title II, as amended, or with provisions of a convention concluded between the State of origin and the State addressed which was in force when the proceedings were instituted.

Article 35

If the parties to a dispute concerning a contract had agreed in writing before the entry into force of this Convention that the contract was to be governed by the law of Ireland or of a part of the United Kingdom, the courts of Ireland or of that part of the United Kingdom shall retain the right to exercise jurisdiction in the dispute.

. . . .

TITLE VI

Final Provisions

Article 37

The Secretary-General of the Council of the European Communities shall transmit a certified copy of the 1968 Convention and of the 1971 Protocol in the Dutch, French, German and Italian languages to the Governments of the Kingdom of Denmark, Ireland and the United Kingdom of Great Britain and Northern Ireland.

The texts of the 1968 Convention and the 1971 Protocol, drawn up in the Danish, English and Irish languages, shall be annexed to this Convention. The texts drawn up in the Danish, English and Irish languages shall be authentic under the same conditions as the original texts of the 1968 Convention and the 1971 Protocol.

Article 38

This Convention shall be ratified by the signatory States. The instruments of ratification shall be deposited with the Secretary-General of the Council of the European Communities.

Article 39

This Convention shall enter into force, as between the States which shall have ratified it, on

the first day of the third month following the deposit of the last instrument of ratification by the original Member States of the Community and one new Member State.

It shall enter into force for each new Member State which subsequently ratifies it on the first day of the third month following the deposit of its instrument of ratification.

Article 40

The Secretary-General of the Council of the European Communities shall notify the signatory States of:

(*a*) the deposit of each instrument of ratification,

(*b*) the dates of entry into force of this Convention for the Contracting States.

Article 41

This Convention, drawn up in a single original in the Danish, Dutch, English, French, German, Irish and Italian languages, all seven texts being equally authentic, shall be deposited in the archives of the Secretariat of the Council of the European Communities. The Secretary-General shall transmit a certified copy to the Government of each signatory State.

Section 16

[1] SCHEDULE 4

Title II of 1968 Convention as Modified for Allocation of Jurisdiction Within U.K.

NOTE

[1] For explanation of modifications see s. 16 (2). Excluded: see s. 17 and Sched. 5.

TITLE II

Jurisdiction

Section 1

General Provisions

Article 2

Subject to the provisions of this **Title,** persons domiciled in a **part of the United Kingdom** shall . . . be sued in the courts of that **part.**

. . . .

Article 3

Persons domiciled in a **part of the United Kingdom** may be sued in the courts of another **part of the United Kingdom** only by virtue of the rules set out in Sections 2, **4, 5 and** 6 of this Title.

. . . .

Section 2

Special jurisdiction

Article 5

A person domiciled in a **part of the United Kingdom** may, in another **part of the United Kingdom,** be sued:

(1) in matters relating to a contract, in the courts for the place of performance of the obligation in question;

(2) in matters relating to maintenance, in the courts for the place where the maintenance creditor is domiciled or habitually resident or, if the matter is ancillary to proceedings concerning the status of a person, in the court which, according to its own law, has jurisdiction to entertain those proceedings, unless that jurisdiction is based solely on the nationality of one of the parties;

(3) in matters relating to tort, delict or quasi-delict, in the courts for the place where the harmful event occurred **or in the case of a threatened wrong is likely to occur;**

(4) as regards a civil claim for damages or restitution which is based on an act giving rise to criminal proceedings, in the court seised of those proceedings, to the extent that that court has jurisdiction under its own law to entertain civil proceedings;

(5) as regards a dispute arising out of the operations of a branch, agency or other establishment, in the courts for the place in which the branch, agency or other establishment is situated;

(6) in his capacity as a settlor, trustee or beneficiary of a trust created by the operation of a statute, or by a written instrument, or created orally and evidenced in writing, in the courts of the **part of the United Kingdom** in which the trust is domiciled;

(7) as regards a dispute concerning the payment of remuneration claimed in respect of the salvage of a cargo or freight, in the court under the authority of which the cargo or freight in question

(*a*) has been arrested to secure such payment, or

(*b*) could have been so arrested, but bail or other security has been given;

provided that this provision shall apply only if it is claimed that the defendant has an interest in the cargo or freight or had such an interest at the time of salvage;

(8) in proceedings—

(a) concerning a debt secured on immovable property; or

(b) which are brought to assert, declare or determine proprietary or possessory rights, or rights of security, in or over movable property, or to obtain authority to dispose of movable property,

in the courts of the part of the United Kingdom in which the property is situated.

Article 5A

Proceedings which have as their object a decision of an organ of a company or other legal person or of an association of natural or legal persons may, without prejudice to the other provisions of this Title, be brought in the courts of the part of the United Kingdom in which that company, legal person or association has its seat.

Article 6

A person domiciled in a **part of the United Kingdom** may, **in another part of the United Kingdom,** also be sued;

(1) where he is one of a number of defendants, in the courts for the place where any one of them is domiciled;

(2) as a third party in an action on a warranty or guarantee or in any other third party proceedings, in the court seised of the original proceedings, unless these were instituted solely with the object of removing him from the jurisdiction of the court which would be competent in his case;

(3) on a counterclaim arising from the same contract or facts on which the original claim was based, in the court in which the original claim is pending.

Article 6A

Where by virtue of this **Title** a court of a **part of the United Kingdom** has jurisdiction in actions relating to liability arising from the use or operation of a ship, that court, or any other court substituted for this purpose by the internal law of that **part**, shall also have jurisdiction over claims for limitation of such liability.

. . . .

Section 4

Jurisdiction over consumer contracts

Article 13

In proceedings concerning a contract concluded by a person for a purpose which can be regarded as being outside his trade or profession, hereinafter called " the consumer ", jurisdiction shall be determined by this Section, without prejudice to the provisions of Articles . . . 5 (5) **and (8) (b),** if it is:

(1) a contract for the sale of goods on instalment credit terms, or

(2) a contract for a loan repayable by instalments, or for any other form of credit, made to finance the sale of goods, or

(3) any other contract for the supply of goods or a contract for the supply of services and . . . the consumer took in **the part of the United Kingdom in which he is domiciled** the steps necessary for the conclusion of the contract.

. . . .

This Section shall not apply to contracts of transport **or insurance.**

Article 14

A consumer may bring proceedings against the other party to a contract either in the courts of the **part of the United Kingdom** in which that party is domiciled or in the courts of the **part of the United Kingdom** in which he is himself domiciled.

Proceedings may be brought against a consumer by the other party to the contract only in the courts of the **part of the United Kingdom** in which the consumer is domiciled.

These provisions shall not affect the right to bring a counterclaim in the court in which, in accordance with this Section, the original claim is pending.

Article 15

The provisions of this Section may be departed from only by an agreement:

(1) which is entered into after the dispute has arisen,
or

(2) which allows the consumer to bring proceedings in courts other than those indicated in this Section,
or

(3) which is entered into by the consumer and the other party to the contract, both of whom are at the time of conclusion of the contract domiciled or habitually resident in the same **part of the United Kingdom,** and which confers jurisdiction on the courts of that **part,** provided that such an agreement is not contrary to the law of that **part.**

Section 5

Exclusive jurisdiction

Article 16

The following courts shall have exclusive jurisdiction, regardless of domicile:

(1) in proceedings which have as their object rights *in rem* in, or tenancies of, immovable property, the courts of the **part of the United Kingdom** in which the property is situated;

(2) in proceedings which have as their object the validity of the constitution, the nullity or the dissolution of companies or other legal persons or associations of natural or legal persons . . . the courts of the **part of the United Kingdom** in which the company, legal person or association has its seat;

(3) in proceedings which have as their object the validity of entries in public registers, the courts of the **part of the United Kingdom** in which the register is kept;

. . . .

(5) in proceedings concerned with the enforcement of judgments, the courts of the **part of the United Kingdom** in which the judgment has been or is to be enforced.

Section 6

Prorogation of jurisdiction

Article 17

If the parties . . . have agreed that a court or the courts of a **part of the United Kingdom** are to have jurisdiction to settle any disputes which have arisen or which may arise in connection with a particular legal relationship, **and, apart from this Schedule, the agreement would be effective to confer jurisdiction under the law of that part,** that court or those courts shall have . . . jurisdiction . . .

The court or courts of a **part of the United Kingdom** on which a trust instrument has conferred jurisdiction shall have . . . jurisdiction in any proceedings brought against a settlor, trustee or beneficiary, if relations between these persons or their rights or obligations under the trust are involved.

Agreements or provisions of a trust instrument conferring jurisdiction shall have no legal force if they are contrary to the provisions of Article . . . 15, or if the courts whose jurisdiction they purport to exclude have exclusive jurisdiction by virtue of Article 16.

. . . .

Article 18

Apart from jurisdiction derived from other provisions of this **Title,** a court of a **part of the United Kingdom** before whom a defendant enters an appearance shall have jurisdiction. This rule shall not apply where appearance was entered solely to contest the jurisdiction, or where another court has exclusive jurisdiction by virtue of Article 16.

Section 7

Examination as to jurisdiction and admissibility

Article 19

Where a court of a **part of the United Kingdom** is seised of a claim which is principally concerned with a matter over which the courts of another **part of the United Kingdom** have exclusive jurisdiction by virtue of Article 16, it shall declare of its own motion that it has no jurisdiction.

Article 20

Where a defendant domiciled in one **part of the United Kingdom** is sued in a court of another **part of the United Kingdom** and does not enter an appearance, the court shall declare of its own motion that it has no jurisdiction unless its jurisdiction is derived from the provisions of this **Title.**

The court shall stay the proceedings so long as it is not shown that the defendant has been able to receive the document instituting the proceedings or an equivalent document in sufficient time to enable him to arrange for his defence, or that all necessary steps have been taken to this end.

. . . .

Section 9

Provisional, including protective, measures

Article 24

Application may be made to the courts of a **part of the United Kingdom** for such provisional, including protective, measures as may be available under the law of that **part,** even if, under this **Title,** the courts of another **part of the United Kingdom** have jurisdiction as to the substance of the matter.

Section 17

SCHEDULE 5

Proceedings Excluded from Schedule 4

Proceedings under the Companies Acts

[1] 1. Proceedings for the winding up of a company under the Insolvency Act 1986 or the Companies Act (Northern Ireland) 1960, or proceedings relating to a company as respects which jurisdiction is conferred on the court having winding up jurisdiction under either of those Acts.

NOTE

[1] As amended by the Insolvency Act 1986, Sched. 14.

Patents, trade marks, designs and similar rights

[1] 2. Proceedings concerned with the registration or validity of patents, trade marks, designs or other similar rights required to be deposited or registered.

NOTE

[1] See the Patents, Designs and Marks Act 1986, Sched. 2, Pt. I, para. 1(2)(j).

Protection of Trading Interests Act 1980

3. Proceedings under section 6 of the Protection of Trading Interests Act 1980 (recovery of sums paid or obtained pursuant to a judgment for multiple damages).

Appeals etc. from tribunals

4. Proceedings on appeal from, or for review of, decisions of tribunals.

Maintenance and similar payments to local and other public authorities

5. Proceedings for, or otherwise relating to, an order under any of the following provisions—

[11] (*a*) paragraph 23 of Schedule 2 to the Children Act 1989, section 80 of the Social Work (Scotland) Act 1968 or section 156 of the Children and Young Persons Act (Northern Ireland) 1968 (contributions in respect of children in care, etc.);

(*b*) section 49 or 50 of the Child Care Act 1980, section 81 of the Social Work (Scotland) Act 1968 or section 159 of the Children and Young Persons Act (Northern Ireland) 1968 (applications for, or for variation of, affiliation orders in respect of children in care, etc.);

(*c*) section 43 of the National Assistance Act 1948, section 18 of the Supplementary Benefits Act 1976, section 24 of the Social Security Act 1986, or any enactment applying in Northern Ireland and corresponding to it, Article 101 of the Health and Personal Social Services (Northern Ireland) Order 1972 or Article 23 of the Supplementary Benefits (Northern Ireland) Order 1977 (recovery of cost of assistance or benefit from person liable to maintain the assisted person);

[1](*d*) section 44 of the National Assistance Act 1948, section 19 of the Supplementary Benefits Act 1976, section 25 of the Social Security Act 1986 or any enactment applying in Northern Ireland and corresponding to it, Article 102 of the Health and Personal Social Services (Northern Ireland) Order 1972 or Article 24 of the Supplementary Benefits (Northern Ireland) Order 1977 (applications for, or for variation of, affiliation orders in respect of children for whom assistance or benefit provided).

NOTES

[11] As amended by the Children Act 1989, Sched. 13, para. 47 with effect from 14th October 1991.

[1] As amended by the Social Security Act 1986, Sched. 10, para. 55(*a*) and (*b*).

Proceedings under certain conventions, etc.

6. Proceedings brought in any court in pursuance of—
(*a*) any statutory provision which, in the case of any convention to which Article 57 applies (conventions relating to specific matters which override the general rules in the 1968 Convention), implements the convention or makes provision with respect to jurisdiction in any field to which the convention relates; and
(*b*) any rule of law so far as it has the effect of implementing any such convention.

Certain Admiralty proceedings in Scotland

7. Proceedings in Scotland in an Admiralty cause where the jurisdiction of the Court of Session or, as the case may be, of the sheriff is based on arrestment *in rem* or *ad fundandam jurisdictionem* of a ship, cargo or freight.

Register of aircraft mortgages

8. Proceedings for the rectification of the register of aircraft mortgages kept by the Civil Aviation Authority.

Continental Shelf Act 1964

[1] 9. Proceedings brought in any court in pursuance of an order under section 23 of the Oil and Gas (Enterprise) Act 1982.

NOTE
[1] As amended by the Oil and Gas Enterprise Act 1982, Sched. 3, para. 42.

Proceedings concerning financial services agencies

[1] 10. Proceedings such as are mentioned in section 188 of the Financial Services Act 1986.

NOTE
[1] Inserted by the Financial Services Act 1986, s.188(2). As amended by the Companies Act 1989, s.200(2).

Section 18

SCHEDULE 6

ENFORCEMENT OF U.K. JUDGMENTS (MONEY PROVISIONS)

Preliminary

1. In this Schedule—
"judgment" means any judgment to which section 18 applies and references to the giving of a judgment shall be construed accordingly;
"money provision" means a provision for the payment of one or more sums of money;
"prescribed" means prescribed by rules of court.

Certificates in respect of judgments

2.—(1) Any interested party who wishes to secure the enforcement in another part of the United Kingdom of any money provisions contained in a judgment may apply for a certificate under this Schedule.

(2) The application shall be made in the prescribed manner to the proper officer of the original court, that is to say—
(*a*) in relation to a judgment within paragraph (*a*) of the definition of "judgment" in section 18(2), the court by which the judgment or order was given or made;
(*b*) in relation to a judgment within paragraph (*b*) of that definition, the court in which the judgment or order is entered;
(*c*) in relation to a judgment within paragraph (*c*) of that definition, the court in whose books the document is registered;

(*d*) in relation to a judgment within paragraph (*d*) of that definition, the tribunal by which the award or order was made;

(*e*) in relation to a judgment within paragraph (*e*) of that definition, the court which gave the judgment or made the order by virtue of which the award has become enforceable as mentioned in that paragraph.

3. A certificate shall not be issued under this Schedule in respect of a judgment unless under the law of the part of the United Kingdom in which the judgment was given—

(*a*) either—

(i) the time for bringing an appeal against the judgment has expired, no such appeal having been brought within that time; or

(ii) such an appeal having been brought within that time, that appeal has been finally disposed of; and

(*b*) enforcement of the judgment is not for the time being stayed or suspended, and the time available for its enforcement has not expired.

4.—(1) Subject to paragraph 3, on an application under paragraph 2 the proper officer shall issue to the applicant a certificate in the prescribed form—

(*a*) stating the sum or aggregate of the sums (including any costs or expenses) payable under the money provisions contained in the judgment, the rate of interest, if any, payable thereon and the date or time from which any such interest began to accrue;

(*b*) stating that the conditions specified in paragraph 3(*a*) and (*b*) are satisfied in relation to the judgment; and

(*c*) containing such other particulars as may be prescribed.

(2) More than one certificate may be issued under this Schedule (simultaneously or at different times) in respect of the same judgment.

[THE NEXT PAGE IS B 181]

Registration of certificates

5.—(1) Where a certificate has been issued under this Schedule in any part of the United Kingdom, any interested party may, within six months from the date of its issue, apply in the prescribed manner to the proper officer of the superior court in any other part of the United Kingdom for the certificate to be registered in that court.

(2) In this paragraph " superior court " means, in relation to England and Wales or Northern Ireland, the High Court and, in relation to Scotland, the Court of Session.

(3) Where an application is duly made under this paragraph to the proper officer of a superior court, he shall register the certificate in that court in the prescribed manner.

General effect of registration

6.—(1) A certificate registered under this Schedule shall, for the purposes of its enforcement, be of the same force and effect, the registering court shall have in relation to its enforcement the same powers, and proceedings for or with respect to its enforcement may be taken, as if the certificate had been a judgment originally given in the registering court and had (where relevant) been entered.

(2) Sub-paragraph (1) is subject to the following provisions of this Schedule and to any provision made by rules of court as to the manner in which and the conditions subject to which a certificate registered under this Schedule may be enforced.

Costs or expenses

7. Where a certificate is registered under this Schedule, the reasonable costs or expenses of and incidental to the obtaining of the certificate and its registration shall be recoverable as if they were costs or expenses stated in the certificate to be payable under a money provision contained in the original judgment.

Interest

8.—(1) Subject to any provision made under sub-paragraph (2), the debt resulting, apart from paragraph 7, from the registration of the certificate shall carry interest at the rate, if any, stated in the certificate from the date or time so stated.

(2) Provision may be made by rules of court as to the manner in which and the periods by reference to which any interest payable by virtue of sub-paragraph (1) is to be calculated and paid, including provision for such interest to cease to accrue as from a prescribed date.

(3) All such sums as are recoverable by virtue of paragraph 7 carry interest as if they were the subject of an order for costs or expenses made by the registering court on the date of registration of the certificate.

(4) Except as provided by this paragraph sums payable by virtue of the registration of a certificate under this Schedule shall not carry interest.

Stay or sisting of enforcement in certain cases

9. Where a certificate in respect of a judgment has been registered under this Schedule, the registering court may, if it is satisfied that any person against whom it is sought to enforce the certificate is entitled and intends to apply under the law of the part of the United Kingdom in which the judgment was given for any remedy which would result in the setting aside or quashing of the judgment, stay (or, in Scotland, sist) proceedings for the enforcement of the certificate, on such terms as it thinks fit, for such period as appears to the court to be reasonably sufficient to enable the application to be disposed of.

Cases in which registration of a certificate must or may be set aside

10. Where a certificate has been registered under this Schedule, the registering court—

(*a*) shall set aside the registration if, on an application made by any interested party, it is satisfied that the registration was contrary to the provisions of this Schedule;

(*b*) may set aside the registration if, on an application so made, it is satisfied that the matter in dispute in the proceedings in which the judgment in question was given had previously been the subject of a judgment by another court or tribunal having jurisdiction in the matter.

Section 18

SCHEDULE 7

Enforcement of U.K. Judgments (Non-Money Provisions)

Preliminary

1. In this Schedule—

" judgment " means any judgment to which section 18 applies and references to the giving of a judgment shall be construed accordingly;

" non-money provision " means a provision for any relief or remedy not requiring payment of a sum of money;

" prescribed " means prescribed by rules of court.

Certified copies of judgments

2.—(1) Any interested party who wishes to secure the enforcement in another part of the United Kingdom of any non-money provisions contained in a judgment may apply for a certified copy of the judgment.

(2) The application shall be made in the prescribed manner to the proper officer of the original court, that is to say—

(*a*) in relation to a judgment within paragraph (*a*) of the definition of " judgment " in section 18 (2), the court by which the judgment or order was given or made;

(*b*) in relation to a judgment within paragraph (*b*) of that definition, the court in which the judgment or order is entered;

(*c*) in relation to a judgment within paragraph (*c*) of that definition, the court in whose books the document is registered;

(*d*) in relation to a judgment within paragraph (*d*) of that definition, the tribunal by which the award or order was made;

(*e*) in relation to a judgment within paragraph (*e*) of that definition, the court which gave the judgment or made the order by virtue of which the award has become enforceable as mentioned in that paragraph.

3. A certified copy of a judgment shall not be issued under this Schedule unless under the law of the part of the United Kingdom in which the judgment was given—

(*a*) either—

(i) the time for bringing an appeal against the judgment has expired no such appeal having been brought within that time; or

(ii) such an appeal having been brought within that time, that appeal has been finally disposed of; and

(*b*) enforcement of the judgment is not for the time being stayed or suspended, and the time available for its enforcement has not expired.

4.—(1) Subject to paragraph 3, on an application under paragraph 2 the proper officer shall issue to the applicant—

(*a*) a certified copy of the judgment (including any money provisions or excepted provisions which it may contain); and

(*b*) a certificate stating that the conditions specified in paragraph 3 (*a*) and (*b*) are satisfied in relation to the judgment.

(2) In sub-paragraph (1) (*a*) " excepted provision " means any provision of a judgment which is excepted from the application of section 18 by subsection (5) of that section.

(3) There may be issued under this Schedule (simultaneously or at different times)—

(*a*) more than one certified copy of the same judgment; and

(*b*) more than one certificate in respect of the same judgment.

Registration of judgments

5.—(1) Where a certified copy of a judgment has been issued under this Schedule in any part of the United Kingdom, any interested party may apply in the prescribed manner to the superior court in any other part of the United Kingdom for the judgment to be registered in that court.

(2) In this paragraph " superior court " means, in relation to England and Wales or Northern Ireland, the High Court and, in relation to Scotland, the Court of Session.

(3) An application under this paragraph for the registration of a judgment must be accompanied by—

(*a*) a certified copy of the judgment issued under this Schedule; and

(*b*) a certificate issued under paragraph 4 (1) (*b*) in respect of the judgment not more than six months before the date of the application.

(4) Subject to sub-paragraph (5), where an application under this paragraph is duly made to a superior court, the court shall order the whole of the judgment as set out in the certified copy to be registered in that court in the prescribed manner.

(5) A judgment shall not be registered under this Schedule by the superior court in any part of the United Kingdom if compliance with the non-money provisions contained in the judgment would involve a breach of the law of that part of the United Kingdom.

General effect of registration

6.—(1) The non-money provisions contained in a judgment registered under this Schedule shall, for the purposes of their enforcement, be of the same force and effect, the registering court shall have in relation to their enforcement the same powers, and proceedings for or with respect to their enforcement may be taken, as if the judgment containing them had been originally given in the registering court and had (where relevant) been entered.

(2) Sub-paragraph (1) is subject to the following provisions of this Schedule and to any provision made by rules of court as to the manner in which and conditions subject to which the non-money provisions contained in a judgment registered under this Schedule may be enforced.

Costs or expenses

7.—(1) Where a judgment is registered under this Schedule, the reasonable costs or expenses of and incidental to—

(*a*) the obtaining of the certified copy of the judgment and of the necessary certificate under paragraph 4(1)(*b*) in respect of it; and

(*b*) the registration of the judgment,

shall be recoverable as if on the date of registration there had also been registered in the registering court a certificate under Schedule 6 in respect of the judgment and as if those costs or expenses were costs or expenses stated in that certificate to be payable under a money provision contained in the judgment.

(2) All such sums as are recoverable by virtue of sub-paragraph (1) shall carry interest as if they were the subject of an order for costs or expenses made by the registering court on the date of registration of the judgment.

Stay or sisting of enforcement in certain cases

8. Where a judgment has been registered under this Schedule, the registering court may, if it is satisfied that any person against whom it is sought to enforce the judgment is entitled and intends to apply under the law of the part of the United Kingdom in which the judgment was given for any remedy which would result in the setting aside or quashing of the judgment, stay (or, in Scotland, sist) proceedings for the enforcement of the judgment, on such terms as it thinks fit, for such period as appears to the court to be reasonably sufficient to enable the application to be disposed of.

Cases in which registered judgment must or may be set aside

9. Where a judgment has been registered under this Schedule, the registering court—

(*a*) shall set aside the registration if, on an application made by any interested party, it is satisfied that the registration was contrary to the provisions of this Schedule;

(*b*) may set aside the registration if, on an application so made, it is satisfied that the matter in dispute in the proceedings in which the judgment was given had previously been the subject of a judgment by another court or tribunal having jurisdiction in the matter.

Section 20

[1] SCHEDULE 8

Rules as to Jurisdiction in Scotland

NOTE

[1] For explanation of modifications see s.20(4). Excluded: see s.21 and Sched. 9.

General

[Article 2] 1. Subject to the **following Rules,** persons shall be sued in the courts **for the place where they are domiciled.**

Special jurisdiction

[Article 5] [1] 2. **Subject to Rules 3 (jurisdiction over consumer contracts), 4 (exclusive jurisdiction) and 5 (prorogation)** a person may **also** be sued—

(1) **where he has no fixed residence, in a court within whose jurisdiction he is personally cited;**

[Article 5 (1)] (2) in matters relating to a contract, in the courts for the place of performance of the obligation in question;

[Article 5 (3)] (3) in matters relating to delict or quasi-delict, in the courts for the place where the harmful event occurred;

[Article 5 (4)] (4) as regards a civil claim for damages or restitution which is based on an act giving rise to criminal proceedings, in the court seised of those proceedings to the extent that that court has jurisdiction to entertain civil proceedings;

[Article 5 (2)] (5) in matters relating to maintenance, in the courts for the place where the maintenance creditor is domiciled or habitually resident or, if the matter is ancillary to proceedings concerning the status of a person, in the court which has jurisdiction to entertain those proceedings, **provided that an action of affiliation and aliment shall be treated as a matter relating to maintenance which is not ancillary to proceedings concerning the status of a person, and provided also that—**

(a) where a local authority exercises its power to raise an action under section 44(7)(a) of the National Assistance Act 1948 or under section 81(1) of the Social Work (Scotland) Act 1968; and

(b) where the Secretary of State exercises his power to raise an action under section 19(8)(a) of the Supplementary Benefits Act 1976;

this Rule shall apply as if the reference to the maintenance creditor were a reference to the mother of the child;

[Article 5 (5)] (6) as regards a dispute arising out of the operations of a branch, agency or other establishment, in the courts for the place in which the branch, agency or other establishment is situated;

[Article 5 (6)] (7) in his capacity as settlor, trustee or beneficiary of a trust **domiciled in Scotland** created by the operation of a statute, or by a written instrument, or created orally and evidenced in writing, in the **Court of Session, or the appropriate sheriff court within the meaning of section 24A of the Trusts (Scotland) Act 1921;**

(8) **where he is not domiciled in the United Kingdom, in the courts for any place where—**

(a) any moveable property belonging to him has been arrested; or

(b) any immoveable property in which he has any beneficial interest is situated;

(9) **in proceedings which are brought to assert, declare or determine proprietary or possessory rights, or rights of security, in or over moveable property, or to obtain authority to dispose of moveable property, in the courts for the place where the property is situated;**

(10) **in the proceedings for interdict, in the courts for the place where it is alleged that the wrong is likely to be committed;**

(11) **in proceedings concerning a debt secured over immoveable property, in the courts for the place where the property is situated;**

(12) **in proceedings which have as their object a decision of an organ of a company or other legal person or of an association of natural or legal persons, in the courts for the place where that company, legal person or association has its seat;**

(13) **in proceedings concerning an arbitration which is conducted in Scotland or in which the procedure is governed by Scots law, in the Court of Session;**

(14) **in proceedings principally concerned with the registration in the United Kingdom or the validity in the United Kingdom of patents, trade marks, designs or other similar rights required to be deposited or registered, in the Court of Session;**

[Article 6] (15) (*a*) where he is one of a number of **defenders,** in the courts for the place where any one of them is domiciled;

(*b*) as a third party in an action on a warranty or guarantee or in any other third party proceedings, in the court seised of the original proceedings, unless these were instituted solely with the object of removing him from the jurisdiction of the court which would be competent in his case;

(*c*) on a counterclaim arising from the same contract or facts on which the original claim was based, in the court in which the original claim is pending.

NOTE

[1] As amended by the Law Reform (Husband and Wife) (Scotland) Act 1984, Sched. 1, para. 7. Subpara. (14), see the Patents, Designs and Marks Act 1986, Sched. 2, Pt. 1, para. 1(2)(j).

Jurisdiction over consumer contracts

3.—(1) In proceedings concerning a contract concluded by a person for a purpose which can be regarded as being outside his trade or profession, hereinafter called the "consumer", **subject to Rule 4 (exclusive jurisdiction),** jurisdiction shall be determined by this **Rule** if it is— [Article 13]

(*a*) a contract for the sale of goods on instalment credit terms; or

(*b*) a contract for a loan repayable by instalments, or for any other form of credit, made to finance the sale of goods; or

(*c*) any other contract for the supply of goods or a contract for the supply of services, **if—**

(i) the consumer took in **Scotland** the steps necessary for the conclusion of the contract; **or**

(ii) **proceedings are brought in Scotland by virtue of section 10(3).**

(2) This **Rule** shall not apply to contracts of transport **or contracts of insurance.**

(3) A consumer may bring proceedings against the other party to a contract **only in—** [Article 14]

(*a*) the courts **for the place** in which that party is domiciled;

(*b*) the courts **for the place** in which he is himself domiciled; **or**

(*c*) **any court having jurisdiction by virtue of Rule 2(6) or (9).**

(4) Proceedings may be brought against a consumer by the other party to the contract only in the courts **for the place where** the consumer is domiciled **or any court having jurisdiction under Rule 2(9).**

(5) **Nothing in this Rule** shall affect the right to bring a counterclaim in the court in which, **in accordance with this Rule,** the original claim is pending.

(6) The provisions of this **Rule** may be departed from only by an agreement— [Article 15(1) and (2)]

(*a*) which is entered into after the dispute has arisen; or

(*b*) which allows the consumer to bring proceedings in **a court** other than **a court** indicated in this **Rule.**

Exclusive jurisdiction

4.—(1) **Notwithstanding anything contained in any of Rules 1 to 3 above or 5 to 8 below,** the following courts shall have exclusive jurisdiction— [Article 16]

(*a*) in proceedings which have as their object rights *in rem* in, or tenancies of, immoveable property, the courts **for the place where** the property is situated; [Article 16(1)]

(*b*) in proceedings which have as their object the validity of the constitution, the nullity or the dissolution of companies or other legal persons or associations of natural or legal persons, the courts **for the place where** the company, legal person or association has its seat; [Article 16(2)]

[1] (*c*) in proceedings (other than proceedings under section 16 of the Abolition of Domestic Rates Etc. (Scotland) Act 1987) which have as their object the validity of entries in public registers, the courts **for the place where** the register is kept; [Article 16(3)]

(*d*) in proceedings concerned with the enforcement of judgments, the courts **for the place where** the judgment has been or is to be enforced. [Article 16(5)]

[2](2) **Nothing in paragraph (1)(c) above affects jurisdiction in any proceedings concerning the validity of entries in registers of patents, trade marks, designs, or other similar rights required to be deposited or registered.**

(3) **No court shall exercise jurisdiction in a case where immoveable property, the seat of a body mentioned in paragraph (1)(b) above, a public register or the place where a judgment has**

been or is to be enforced is situated outside Scotland and where paragraph (1) above would apply if the property, seat, register or, as the case may be, place of enforcement were situated in Scotland.

NOTES

[1] As amended by the Abolition of Domestic Rates Etc. (Scotland) Act 1987, s.16(8).
[2] See the Patents, Designs and Marks Act 1986, Sched. 2, Pt. I, para. 1(2)(j).

Prorogation of jurisdiction

[Article 17(1)] 5.—(1) If the parties have agreed that a court is to have jurisdiction to settle any disputes which have arisen or which may arise in connection with a particular legal relationship, that court shall have exclusive jurisdiction.

[Article 17(1)] (2) Such an agreement conferring jurisdiction shall be either in writing or evidenced in writing or, in trade or commerce, in a form which accords with practices in that trade or commerce of which the parties are or ought to have been aware.

[Article 17(2)] (3) The court on which a trust instrument has conferred jurisdiction shall have exclusive jurisdiction in any proceedings brought against a settlor, trustee or beneficiary, if relations between these persons or their rights or obligations under the trust are involved.

(4) **Where an agreement or a trust instrument confers jurisdiction on the courts of the United Kingdom or of Scotland, proceedings to which paragraph (1) or, as the case may be, (3) above applies may be brought in any court in Scotland.**

[Article 17(3)] (5) Agreements or provisions of a trust instrument conferring jurisdiction shall have no legal force if the courts whose jurisdiction they purport to exclude have exclusive jurisdiction by virtue of **Rule 4 or where Rule 4(3) applies.**

[Article 18] 6.—(1) Apart from jurisdiction derived from other provisions of this **Schedule,** a court before whom a defender enters an appearance shall have jurisdiction.

(2) This Rule shall not apply where appearance was entered solely to contest jurisdiction, or where another court has exclusive jurisdiction by virtue of **Rule 4 or where Rule 4(3) applies.**

Examination as to jurisdiction and admissibility

[Article 19] 7. Where a court is seised of a claim which is principally concerned with a matter over which **another court has** exclusive jurisdiction by virtue of **Rule 4, or where it is precluded from exercising jurisdiction by Rule 4(3),** it shall declare of its own motion that it has no jurisdiction.

[Article 20] 8. Where **in any case a court has no jurisdiction which is compatible with this Act, and the defender** does not enter an appearance, the court shall declare of its own motion that it has no jurisdiction.

Section 21

SCHEDULE 9

PROCEEDINGS EXCLUDED FROM SCHEDULE 8

[1] 1. Proceedings concerning the status or legal capacity of natural persons (including proceedings for separation) other than proceedings which consist solely of proceedings of affiliation and aliment.

2. Proceedings for regulating the custody of children.

[2] 3. Proceedings relating to guardianship of children and all proceedings relating to the management of the affairs of persons who are incapable of managing their own affairs.

4. Proceedings in respect of sequestration in bankruptcy; or the winding up of a company or other legal person; or proceedings in respect of a judicial arrangement or judicial composition with creditors.

5. Proceedings relating to a company where, by any enactment, jurisdiction in respect of those proceedings is conferred on the court having jurisdiction to wind it up.

6. Admiralty causes in so far as the jurisdiction is based on arrestment *in rem* or *ad fundandam jurisdictionem* of a ship, cargo or freight.

7. Commissary proceedings.

8. Proceedings for the rectification of the register of aircraft mortgages kept by the Civil Aviation Authority.

9. Proceedings under section 7(3) of the Civil Aviation (Eurocontrol) Act 1962 (recovery of charges for air navigation services and proceedings for damages against Eurocontrol).

[3] 10. Proceedings brought in pursuance of an order under section 23 of the Oil and Gas (Enterprise) Act 1982.

11. Proceedings under section 6 of the Protection of Trading Interests Act 1980 (recovery of sums paid or obtained pursuant to a judgment for multiple damages).

12. Appeals from or review of decisions of tribunals.

13. Proceedings which are not in substance proceedings in which a decree against any person is sought.

14. Proceedings brought in any court in pursuance of—

(*a*) any statutory provision which, in the case of any convention to which Article 57 applies (conventions relating to specific matters which override the general rules in the 1968 Convention), implements the convention; and

(*b*) any rule of law so far as it has the effect of implementing any such convention.

NOTES

[1] As amended by the Family Law (Scotland) Act 1985, Sched. 2.

[2] As amended by the Age of Legal Capacity (Scotland) Act 1991, Sched. 1, para. 38.

[3] As amended by the Oil and Gas Enterprise Act 1982, Sched. 3, para. 43.

[THE NEXT PAGE IS B 187]

Section 35(1) SCHEDULE 10

AMENDMENTS OF FOREIGN JUDGMENTS (RECIPROCAL ENFORCEMENT) ACT 1933

[Amendments to the said Act reprinted *supra* have been given effect.]

Section 37(1) SCHEDULE 11

MINOR AMENDMENTS RELATING TO MAINTENANCE ORDERS

PART I

ENFORCEMENT OF LUMP SUM ORDERS

[Amendments to Acts reprinted in *The Parliament House Book* have been given effect.]

. . . .

Maintenance Orders Act 1958 (c. 39)

2.—(1) Section 2 of the Maintenance Orders Act 1958 (registration of orders) is amended as follows.

(2) In subsection (3) (registration of magistrates' court order for enforcement in the High Court), for the words from "shall" onwards (which require the court to be satisfied that not less than a certain number of periodical payments are in arrears) substitute "may, if it thinks fit, grant the application".

(3) After subsection (3) insert—

"(3A) Without prejudice to subsection (3) of this section, where a magistrates' court order provides both for the payment of a lump sum and for the making of periodical payments, a person entitled to receive a lump sum under the order who considers that, so far as it relates to that sum, the order could be more effectively enforced if it were registered may apply to the original court for the registration of the order so far as it so relates, and the court may, if it thinks fit, grant the application.

(3B) Where an application under subsection (3A) of this section is granted in the case of a magistrates' court order, the provisions of this Part of this Act shall have effect in relation to that order as if so far as it relates to the payment of a lump sum it were a separate order.".

. . . .

PART II

RECOVERY OF INTEREST ON ARREARS

. . . .

Maintenance Orders Act 1958 (c. 39)

6.—(1) The Maintenance Orders Act 1958 is amended as follows.

(2) After section 2 insert—

"Interest on sums recoverable under certain orders registered in the High Court

2A.—(1) Where, in connection with an application under section 2(3) of this Act for the registration of a magistrates' court order, the applicant shows in accordance with rules of court—

(*a*) that the order, though deemed for the purposes of section 1 of this Act to have been made by a magistrates' court in England, was in fact made in another part of the United Kingdom or in a country or territory outside the United Kingdom; and

(*b*) that, as regards any sum for whose payment the order provides, interest on that sum at a particular rate is, by the law of that part or of that country or territory, recoverable under the order from a particular date or time,

then, if the original court grants the application and causes a certified copy of the order to be sent to the prescribed officer of the High Court under section 2(4)(*c*) of this Act, it shall also cause to be sent to him a certificate in the prescribed form showing, as regards that sum, the rate of interest so recoverable and the date or time from which it is so recoverable.

(2) The officer of the court who receives a certificate sent to him under the preceding subsection shall cause the certificate to be registered in that court together with the order to which it relates.

(3) Where an order is registered together with a certificate under this section, then, subject to any provision made under the next following subsection, sums payable under the order shall carry interest at the rate specified in the certificate from the date or time so specified.

(4) Provision may be made by rules of court as to the manner in which and the periods by reference to which any interest payable by virtue of subsection (3) is to be calculated and paid, including provision for such interest to cease to accrue as from a prescribed date.

(5) Except as provided by this section sums payable under registered orders shall not carry interest.".

(3) In section 3(1) of that Act (enforcement of registered orders), after "Subject to the provisions of "insert" section 2A of this Act and".

. . . . . .

Part III

Reciprocal Enforcement Founded on Presence of Assets

. . . . . .

Sections 15(4), 23(2) and 36(6)

SCHEDULE 12

Consequential Amendments

. . . . . .

Part II

Amendments Consequential on Schedule 8

[Amendments to Acts reprinted in *The Parliament House Book* have been given effect.]

. . . . . .

Consumer Credit Act 1974 (c. 39)

4. In section 141 of the Consumer Credit Act 1974 the following subsections shall be substituted for subsection (3)—

"(3) In Scotland the sheriff court shall have jurisdiction to hear and determine any action referred to in subsection (1) and such an action shall not be brought in any other court.

(3A) Subject to subsection (3B) an action which is brought in the sheriff court by virtue of subsection (3) shall be brought only in one of the following courts, namely—

(*a*) the court for the place where the debtor or hirer is domiciled (within the meaning of section 41 or 42 of the Civil Jurisdiction and Judgments Act 1982);

(*b*) the court for the place where the debtor or hirer carries on business; and

(*c*) where the purposes of the action is to assert, declare or determine proprietary or possessory rights, or rights of security, in or over moveable property, or to obtain authority to dispose of moveable property, the court for the place where the property is situated.

(3B) Subsection (3A) shall not apply—

(*a*) where Rule 3 of Schedule 8 to the said Act of 1982 applies; or

(*b*) where the jurisdiction of another court has been prorogated by an agreement entered into after the dispute has arisen.".

PART III

AMENDMENTS CONSEQUENTIAL ON SECTION 36

. . . .

Maintenance Orders Act 1958 (c. 39)

2. In section 23(2) of the Maintenance Orders Act 1958 (provisions which extend to Scotland and Northern Ireland) after "section 2" insert "section 2A".

. . . .

Section 53

SCHEDULE 13

COMMENCEMENT, TRANSITIONAL PROVISIONS AND SAVINGS

PART I

COMMENCEMENT

Provisions coming into force on Royal Assent

1. The following provisions come into force on Royal Assent:

Provision	*Subject-matter*
section 53(1) and Part I of this Schedule.	Commencement.
section 55	Short title.

Provisions coming into force six weeks after Royal Assent

2. The following provisions come into force at the end of the period of six weeks beginning with the day on which this Act is passed:

Provision	*Subject-matter*
section 24(1)(*a*), (2)(*a*) and (3).	Interim relief and protective measures in cases of doubtful jurisdiction.
section 29	Service of county court process outside Northern Ireland.
section 30	Proceedings in England and Wales or Northern Ireland for torts to immovable property.
section 31	Overseas judgments given against states.
section 32	Overseas judgments given in breach of agreement for settlement of disputes.
section 33	Certain steps not to amount to submission to jurisdiction of overseas court.
section 34	Certain judgments a bar to further proceedings on the same cause of action.
section 35(3)	Consolidation of Orders in Council under section 14 of the Administration of Justice Act 1920.
section 38	Overseas judgments counteracting an award of multiple damages.
section 40	Power to modify enactments relating to legal aid, etc.
section 49	Saving for powers to stay, sist, strike out or dismiss proceedings.
section 50	Interpretation: general.
section 51	Application to Crown.
section 52	Extent.

[THE NEXT PAGE IS B 193]

Provision	*Subject-matter*
paragraphs 7 to 10 of Part II of this Schedule and section 53 (2) so far as relates to those paragraphs.	Transitional provisions and savings.
section 54 and Schedule 14 so far as relating to the repeal of provisions in section 4 of the Foreign Judgments (Reciprocal Enforcement) Act 1933.	Repeals consequential on sections 32 and 33.

Provisions coming into force on a day to be appointed

3.—(1) The other provisions of this Act come into force on such day as the Lord Chancellor and the Lord Advocate may appoint by order made by statutory instrument.

(2) Different days may be appointed under this paragraph for different purposes.

PART II

TRANSITIONAL PROVISIONS AND SAVINGS

Section 16 and Schedule 4

1.—(1) Section 16 and Schedule 4 shall not apply to any proceedings begun before the commencement of that section.

(2) Nothing in section 16 or Schedule 4 shall preclude the bringing of proceedings in any part of the United Kingdom in connection with a dispute concerning a contract if the parties to the dispute had agreed before the commencement of that section that the contract was to be governed by the law of that part of the United Kingdom.

Section 18 and Schedule 6 and associated repeals

2.—(1) In relation to a judgment a certificate whereof has been registered under the 1868 Act or the 1882 Act before the repeal of that Act by this Act, the 1868 Act or, as the case may be, the 1882 Act shall continue to have effect notwithstanding its repeal.

(2) Where by virtue of sub-paragraph (1) the 1882 Act continues to have effect in relation to an order to which section 47 of the Fair Employment (Northern Ireland) Act 1976 (damages etc. for unfair discrimination) applies, that section shall continue to have effect in relation to that order notwithstanding the repeal of that section by this Act.

(3) A certificate issued under Schedule 6 shall not be registered under that Schedule in a part of the United Kingdom if the judgment to which that certificate relates is the subject of a certificate registered in that part under the 1868 Act or the 1882 Act.

(4) In this paragraph—

" the 1868 Act " means the Judgments Extension Act 1868;

" the 1882 Act " means the Inferior Courts Judgments Extension Act 1882;

" judgment " has the same meaning as in section 18.

Section 18 and Schedule 7

3. Schedule 7 and, so far as it relates to that Schedule, section 18 shall not apply to judgments given before the coming into force of that section.

Section 19

4. Section 19 shall not apply to judgments given before the commencement of that section.

Section 20 and Schedule 8

5. Section 20 and Schedule 8 shall not apply to any proceedings begun before the commencement of that section.

Section 26

6. The power conferred by section 26 shall not be exercisable in relation to property arrested before the commencement of that section or in relation to bail or other security given—

(*a*) before the commencement of that section to prevent the arrest of property; or
(*b*) to obtain the release of property arrested before the commencement of that section; or
(*c*) in substitution (whether directly or indirectly) for security given as mentioned in sub-paragraph (*a*) or (*b*).

Section 31

7. Section 31 shall not apply to any judgment—
(*a*) which has been registered under Part II of the Administration of Justice Act 1920 or Part I of the Foreign Judgments (Reciprocal Enforcement) Act 1933 before the time when that section comes into force; or
(*b*) in respect of which proceedings at common law for its enforcement have been finally determined before that time.

Section 32 and associated repeal

8.—(1) Section 32 shall not apply to any judgment—
(*a*) which has been registered under Part II of the Administration of Justice Act 1920, Part I of the Foreign Judgments (Reciprocal Enforcement) Act 1933 or Part I of the Maintenance Orders (Reciprocal Enforcement) Act 1972 before the time when that section comes into force; or
(*b*) in respect of which proceedings at common law for its enforcement have been finally determined before that time.

(2) Section 4 (3) (*b*) of the Foreign Judgments (Reciprocal Enforcement) Act 1933 shall continue to have effect, notwithstanding its repeal by this Act, in relation to a judgment registered under Part I of that Act before the commencement of section 32.

Section 33 and associated repeal

9.—(1) Section 33 shall not apply to any judgment—
(*a*) which has been registered under Part II of the Administration of Justice Act 1920 or Part I of the Foreign Judgments (Reciprocal Enforcement) Act 1933 before the time when that section comes into force; or
(*b*) in respect of which proceedings at common law for its enforcement have been finally determined before that time.

(2) The repeal by this Act of words in section 4 (2) (*a*) (i) of the Foreign Judgments (Reciprocal Enforcement) Act 1933 shall not affect the operation of that provision in relation to a judgment registered under Part I of that Act before the commencement of section 33.

Section 34

10. Section 34 shall not apply to judgments given before the commencement of that section.

Section 54 SCHEDULE 14

REPEALS

[Repeals affecting Acts reprinted in *The Parliament House Book* have been given effect.]

Administration of Justice Act 1982

(1982 c. 53)

An Act to make further provision with respect to the administration of justice and matters connected therewith; to amend the law relating to actions for damages for personal injuries, including injuries resulting in death, and to abolish certain actions for loss of services; . . . [28th October 1982]

. . . . . .

[1] PART II

DAMAGES FOR PERSONAL INJURIES ETC.—SCOTLAND

NOTE

[1] In force 1st January 1983, except for ss.12 and 14(2), which came into force on 1st September 1984: s.76(3), (4) and (11) and S.I. 1984 No. 1287. See the Consumer Protection Act 1987, s.6(1)(*d*).

Damages in respect of services

7. Where a person (in this Part of this Act referred to as "the injured person")—

(*a*) has sustained personal injuries, or

(*b*) has died in consequence of personal injuries sustained,

as a result of an act or omission of another person giving rise to liability in any person (in this Part of this Act referred to as "the responsible person") to pay damages, the responsible person shall also be liable to pay damages in accordance with the provisions of sections 8 and 9 of this Act.

Services rendered to injured person

8.—(1) Where necessary services have been rendered to the injured person by a relative in consequence of the injuries in question, then, unless the relative has expressly agreed in the knowledge that an action for damages has been raised or is in contemplation that no payment should be made in respect of those services, the responsible person shall be liable to pay to the injured person by way of damages such sum as represents reasonable remuneration for those services and repayment of reasonable expenses incurred in connection therewith.

[1] (2) The injured person shall be under an obligation to account to the relative for any damages recovered from the responsible person under subsection (1) above.

[1] (3) Where, at the date of an award of damages in favour of the injured person, it is likely that necessary services will, after that date, be rendered to him by a relative in consequence of the injuries in question, then, unless the relative has expressly agreed that no payment shall be made in respect of those services, the responsible person shall be liable to pay to the injured person by way of damages such sum as represents—

(*a*) reasonable remuneration for those services; and
(*b*) reasonable expenses which are likely to be incurred in connection therewith.

[1] (4) The relative shall have no direct right of action in delict against the responsible person in respect of any services or expenses referred to in this section.

NOTE

[1] As substituted for former subs. (2) by the Law Reform (Miscellaneous Provisions) (Scotland) Act 1990, s.69(1). S. 69(2) provides:

"Without prejudice to Parts II and III of the Prescription and Limitation (Scotland) Act 1973, this section shall apply to rights accruing both before and after the date appointed for its coming into force [1st March 1991], but shall not affect any proceedings commenced before that date."

Services to injured person's relative

9.—(1) The responsible person shall be liable to pay to the injured person a reasonable sum by way of damages in respect of the inability to render the personal services referred to in subsection (3) below.

(2) Where the injured person has died, any relative of his entitled to damages in respect of loss of support under section 1(3) of the Damages (Scotland) Act 1976 shall be entitled to include as a head of damage under that section a reasonable sum in respect of the loss to him of the personal services mentioned in subsection (3) below.

(3) The personal services referred to in subsections (1) and (2) above are personal services—

(*a*) which were or might have been expected to have been rendered by the injured person before the occurrence of the act or omission giving rise to liability,
(*b*) of a kind which, when rendered by a person other than a relative, would ordinarily be obtainable on payment, and
(*c*) which the injured person but for the injuries in question might have been expected to render gratuitously to a relative.

(4) Subject to subsection (2) above, the relative shall have no direct right of action in delict against the responsible person in respect of the personal services mentioned in subsection (3) above.

Assessment of damages for personal injuries

10. Subject to any agreement to the contrary, in assessing the amount of damages payable to the injured person in respect of personal injuries there shall not be taken into account so as to reduce that amount—

(*a*) any contractual pension or benefit (including any payment by a friendly society or trade union);
(*b*) any pension or retirement benefit payable from public funds other than any pension or benefit to which section 2(1) of the Law Reform (Personal Injuries) Act 1948 applies;
(*c*) any benefit payable from public funds, in respect of any period after the date of the award of damages, designed to secure to the injured person or any relative of his a minimum level of subsistence;
(*d*) any redundancy payment under the Employment Protection (Consolidation) Act 1978, or any payment made in circumstances corresponding to those in which a right to a redundancy payment would have accrued if section 81 of that Act had applied;
(*e*) any payment made to the injured person or to any relative of his by the injured person's employer following upon the injuries in question where the recipient is under an obligation to reimburse the employer in the event of damages being recovered in respect of those injuries;
(*f*) subject to paragraph (iv) below, any payment of a benevolent character made to the injured person or to any relative of his by any person following upon the injuries in question;

but there shall be taken into account—

(i) any remuneration or earnings from employment;

(ii) any unemployment benefit;

(iii) any benefit referred to in paragraph (*c*) above payable in respect of any period prior to the date of the award of damages;

(iv) any payment of a benevolent character made to the injured person or to any relative of his by the responsible person following on the injuries in question, where such a payment is made directly and not through a trust or other fund from which the injured person or his relatives have benefited or may benefit.

Maintenance at public expense to be taken into account in assessment of damages: Scotland

11. In an action for damages for personal injuries (including any such action arising out of a contract) any saving to the injured person which is attributable to his maintenance wholly or partly at public expense in a hospital, nursing home or other institution shall be set off against any income lost by him as a result of the injuries.

[THE NEXT PAGE IS B 197]

Award of provisional damages for personal injuries: Scotland

12.—(1) This section applies to an action for damages for personal injuries in which—

(*a*) there is proved or admitted to be a risk that at some definite or indefinite time in the future the injured person will, as a result of the act or omission which gave rise to the cause of the action, develop some serious disease or suffer some serious deterioration in his physical or mental condition; and

(*b*) the responsible person was, at the time of the act or omission giving rise to the cause of the action,

(i) a public authority or public corporation; or

(ii) insured or otherwise indemnified in respect of the claim.

(2) In any case to which this section applies, the court may, on the application of the injured person, order—

(*a*) that the damages referred to in subsection (4)(*a*) below be awarded to the injured person; and

(*b*) that the injured person may apply for the further award of damages referred to in subsection (4)(*b*) below,

and the court may, if it considers it appropriate, order that an application under paragraph (*b*) above may be made only within a specified period.

(3) Where an injured person in respect of whom an award has been made under subsection (2)(*a*) above applies to the court for an award under subsection (2)(*b*) above, the court may award to the injured person the further damages referred to in subsection (4)(*b*) below.

(4) The damages referred to in subsections (2) and (3) above are—

(*a*) damages assessed on the assumption that the injured person will not develop the disease or suffer the deterioration in his condition; and

(*b*) further damages if he develops the disease or suffers the deterioration.

(5) Nothing in this section shall be construed—

(*a*) as affecting the exercise of any power relating to expenses including a power to make rules of court relating to expenses; or

(*b*) as prejudicing any duty of the court under any enactment or rule of law to reduce or limit the total damages which would have been recoverable apart from any such duty.

(6) The Secretary of State may, by order, provide that categories of defenders shall, for the purposes of paragraph (*b*) of subsection (1) above, become or cease to be responsible persons, and may make such modifications of that paragraph as appear to him to be necessary for the purpose.

And an order under this subsection shall be made by statutory instrument subject to annulment in pursuance of a resolution of either House of Parliament.

Supplementary

13.—(1) In this Part of this Act, unless the context otherwise requires—

"personal injuries" includes any disease or any impairment of a person's physical or mental condition;

"relative", in relation to the injured person, means—

(*a*) the spouse or divorced spouse;

(*b*) any person, not being the spouse of the injured person, who was, at the time of the act or omission giving rise to liability in the responsible person, living with the injured person as husband or wife;

(*c*) any ascendant or descendant;

(*d*) any brother, sister, uncle or aunt; or any issue of any such person;

(*e*) any person accepted by the injured person as a child of his family.

In deducing any relationship for the purposes of the foregoing definition—

(*a*) any relationship by affinity shall be treated as a relationship by consanguinity; any relationship of the half blood shall be treated as a relationship of the whole blood; and the stepchild of any person shall be treated as his child; and

[1] (*b*) section 1(1) of the Law Reform (Parent and Child) (Scotland) Act 1986 shall apply; and any reference (howsoever expressed) in this Part of this Act to a relative shall be construed accordingly.

(2) Any reference in this Part of this Act to a payment, benefit or pension shall be construed as a reference to any such payment, benefit or pension whether in cash or in kind.

(3) This Part of this Act binds the Crown.

NOTE

[1] As amended by the Law Reform (Parent and Child) (Scotland) Act 1986, Sched. 1, para. 19, with effect from 8th December 1986.

Amendment and repeal of enactments

14.—(1), (2), (4) [Amendments to the Damages (Scotland) Act 1976 are incorporated in the print of that Act, *supra*.]

(3) Notwithstanding section 73(5) of this Act, where an action to which section 5 of that Act applies has been raised and has not, prior to the commencement of subsection (2) above, been disposed of, the court shall not dismiss the action on the ground only that the pursuer has failed to serve notice of the action as required by subsection (6) of the said section 5.

. . . .

PART IX

GENERAL AND SUPPLEMENTARY

Transitional provisions and savings

73. . . .

(5) Without prejudice to the provisions of Parts II and III of the Prescription and Limitation (Scotland) Act 1973, Part II of this Act shall apply to rights of action which accrued before, as well as rights of action which accrue after, the coming into operation of that Part of this Act; but nothing in Part II of this Act other than the repeal of section 5 of the Damages (Scotland) Act 1976 shall affect any proceedings commenced before that Part of this Act comes into operation.

. . . .

Extent

77. . . .

(3) Part II of this Act and section 26 above extend to Scotland only . . .

. . . .

Citation

78. This Act may be cited as the Administration of Justice Act 1982.

[1] Law Reform (Miscellaneous Provisions) (Scotland) Act 1985

(1985 c. 73)

An Act to amend the law of Scotland in respect of . . . certain courts and their powers; evidence and procedure; . . .

[30th October 1985]

NOTE

[1] Of the provisions reprinted here, s.22 came into force on 30th December 1985 and ss.14, 15 and 19 on 8th December 1986: see s.60(3), reprinted in Division E, *infra*, and S.I. 1986 No. 1945.

. . . .

Provisions relating to civil jurisdiction and procedure

Remit from Court of Session to sheriff

14. The Court of Session may in relation to an action before it which could competently have been brought before a sheriff remit the action (at its own instance or on the application of any of the parties to the action) to the sheriff within whose jurisdiction the action could have been brought, where, in the opinion of the court, the nature of the action makes it appropriate to do so.

Withdrawal of privilege against self-incrimination in certain proceedings relating to intellectual property

[0] **15.**—(1) In any proceedings to which this subsection applies a person shall not be excused, by reason that to do so would tend to expose him to proceedings for a related offence or for the recovery of a related penalty—

(*a*) from answering any questions put to him in the first mentioned proceedings; or

(*b*) from complying with any order made in those proceedings.

(2) Subsection (1) above applies to civil proceedings in the Court of Session or the sheriff court—

(*a*) for infringement of rights pertaining to any intellectual property or for passing off;

(*b*) brought to obtain disclosure of information relating to any infringement of such rights or to any passing off; and

(*c*) brought to prevent any apprehended infringement of such rights or any apprehended passing off.

(3) The proceedings referred to in subsection (2) above include—

(*a*) proceedings on appeal arising out of these proceedings;

(*b*) proceedings under section 1(1) of the Administration of Justice (Scotland) Act 1972 (provision in relation to the power of the court to order inspection of documents and other property etc.) which relate to civil proceedings falling within subsection (2) above which are likely to be brought.

(4) No statement or admission made by a person—

(*a*) in answering a question put to him in any proceedings to which subsection (1) above applies; or

(*b*) in complying with any order made in such proceedings,

shall in proceedings for any related offence, or for the recovery of any related penalty, be admissible in evidence against him:

Provided that this subsection shall not render any such statement or admission inadmissible against him in proceedings for perjury or contempt of court.

(5) In this section—

[1] "intellectual property" means any patent, trade mark, copyright or design right, registered design, technical or commercial information or other intellectual property;

"related offence", in relation to any proceedings to which subsection (1) above applies, means—

(*a*) in the case of proceedings within subsection (2)(*a*) or (*b*)—

(i) any offence committed by or in the course of the infringement or passing off to which those proceedings relate; or

(ii) any offence not within sub-paragraph (i) committed in connection with that infringement or passing off, being an offence involving fraud or dishonesty;

(*b*) in the case of proceedings within subsection (2)(*c*), any offence revealed by the facts on which the pursuer relies in those proceedings;

"related penalty", in relation to any proceedings to which subsection (1) above applies, means—

(*a*) in the case of proceedings within subsection (2)(*a*) or (*b*), any penalty incurred in respect of anything done or omitted in connection with the infringement or passing off to which those proceedings relate;

(*b*) in the case of proceedings within subsection (2)(*c*), any penalty incurred in respect of any act or omission revealed by the facts on which the pursuer relies in those proceedings.

NOTES

[0] Applied by the Copyright, Designs and Patents Act 1988, ss.296(6) and 298(4).

[1] See the Patents, Designs and Marks Act 1986, Sched. 2, para. 1(2)(*h*). As amended by the Copyright, Designs and Patents Act 1988, Sched. 7, para. 32. "Copyright" extended to "topography right" by S.I. 1987 No. 1497.

. . . . . .

Disclosure of names in certain proceedings

19. [New s.1(1A) of the Administration of Justice (Scotland) Act 1972 is inserted in the print of that Act, *supra*.]

Other provisions relating to courts

. . . . . .

Re-employment of retired judges

22.—(1) If it appears to the Lord President of the Court of Session that it is expedient as a temporary measure to make an appointment under this section in order to facilitate the disposal of business in the Court of Session or the High Court of Justiciary he may, with the consent of the Secretary of State, appoint a person who—

(*a*) has held office as a judge of the Court of Session; or

(*b*) has held office as a Lord of Appeal in Ordinary and who, at the time of his appointment as a Lord of Appeal in Ordinary, was eligible for appointment as a judge in the Court of Session,

and, in either case, has not reached the age of 75 years, to act as a judge of the Court of Session and High Court of Justiciary during such period or on such occasions as the Lord President thinks fit but, subject to subsection (4) below, a period during which or occasion on which a person may so act, shall not extend beyond or be after he reaches the age of 75 years.

(2) A person while acting under this section shall, subject to subsection (3) below, be treated for all purposes as, and accordingly may perform any of the functions of, a judge of the court in which he is acting.

(3) A person shall not, by virtue of subsection (2) above, be treated as a judge of the Court of Session or the High Court of Justiciary for the purposes of any statutory provision or rule of law relating to—

(*a*) the appointment, retirement, removal or disqualification of judges of that court (including, without prejudice to the foregoing generality, any statutory provision or rule of law relating to the number of judges who may be appointed);

(*b*) the tenure of office and oaths to be taken by such judges;

(*c*) the remuneration, allowances or pensions of such judges.

(4) Notwithstanding the expiry of any period for which a person is appointed by virtue of subsection (1) above to act as a judge of the Court of Session and High Court of Justiciary—

(*a*) he may attend at the court for the purpose of continuing to deal with, giving judgment in, or dealing with any matter relating to, any case begun before him while acting as a judge of that court; and

(*b*) for that purpose, and for the purpose of any proceedings arising out of any such case or matter, he shall be treated as being or, as the case may be, having been, a judge of that court.

(5) The Secretary of State may pay to, or in respect of, a person appointed under subsection (1) above such remuneration or allowances as he may, with the consent of the Treasury, determine.

. . . . . .

[1] Debtors (Scotland) Act 1987

(1987 c. 18)

An Act to make new provision with regard to Scotland for an extension of time for payment of debts; to amend the law relating to certain diligencies; to make provision in respect of messengers-at-arms and sheriff officers; and for connected purposes.

[15th May 1987]

NOTE

[1] Excluded by the Companies Act 1989, s.161(4).

Arrangement of Sections

Part I

Extension of Time to Pay Debts

Time to pay directions on granting decree

Section

Time to pay orders following charge or diligence

Miscellaneous

PART II

POINDINGS AND WARRANT SALES

Poinding

Removal, damage or destruction of poinded articles

Warrant sales

Articles belonging to third parties or in common ownership

Supplementary

PART III

DILIGENCE AGAINST EARNINGS

Introduction

Earnings arrestments

PART I

EXTENSION OF TIME TO PAY DEBTS

Time to pay directions on granting decree

Time to pay directions

1.—(1) Subject to subsections (3) to (5) below and to section 14 of this Act, the court, on granting decree for payment of any principal sum of money may, on an application by the debtor, direct that any sum decerned for in the decree (including any interest claimed in pursuance of subsections (6) and (7) below) or any expenses in relation to which the decree contains a finding as to liability or both such sum and such expenses shall be paid—

(*a*) by such instalments, commencing at such time after the date of intimation by the creditor to the debtor of an extract of the decree containing the direction, payable at such intervals; or

(*b*) as a lump sum at the end of such period following intimation as mentioned in paragraph (*a*) above,

as the court may specify in the direction.

(2) A direction under subsection (1) above shall be known as a "time to pay direction".

(3) Where a court grants a decree which contains a finding as to liability for expenses but does not at the same time make a time to pay direction, then (whether or not the decree also decerns for payment of the expenses), it shall not at any time thereafter be competent for the court to make a time to pay direction in relation to those expenses.

(4) Where a court grants a decree which contains a finding as to liability for expenses and makes a time to pay direction in relation to those expenses but—

(*a*) does not decern for payment of the expenses; or

(*b*) decerns for payment of the expenses as taxed by the auditor of court but does not specify the amount of those expenses, in relation to so much of the time to pay direction as relates to the expenses, the reference in subsection (1) above to the date of intimation of an extract of the decree containing the direction shall be treated as a reference to the date of intimation of an extract of a decree decerning for payment of the expenses, being an extract specifying their amount.

[0] (5) It shall not be competent for the court to make a time to pay direction—

(*a*) where the sum of money (exclusive of any interest and expenses) decerned for exceeds £10,000 or such amount as may be prescribed in regulations made by the Lord Advocate;

(*b*) where the decree contains an award of a capital sum on divorce or on the granting of a declarator of nullity of marriage;

(*c*) in connection with a maintenance order;

(*d*) in an action by or on behalf of the Inland Revenue for payment of any sum recoverable in respect of tax or as if it were tax;

(*e*) in an action by or on behalf of a rating authority for payment of rates;

[1] (*ee*) in an action by or on behalf of a—

(i) levying authority for the payment of any community charge or community water charge within the meaning of section 26 of the Abolition of Domestic Rates Etc. (Scotland) Act 1987 (which defines terms used in that Act) or any amount payable under section 18(3) (payment of community charges in respect of backdated period, with surcharge and interest) of that Act; or

(ii) regional or islands council for payment of any amount payable as a civil penalty under section 17(10) or (11) (failure to provide information to a registration officer) of that Act; or

(*f*) in an action for payment of—

(i) any duty due under the Betting and Gaming Duties Act 1981;

(ii) car tax due under the Car Tax Act 1983; or

(iii) value added tax due under the Value Added Tax Act 1983 or any sum recoverable as if it were value added tax.

(6) Without prejudice to section 2(5) of this Act, interest payable under a decree containing a time to pay direction (other than interest awarded as a specific sum in the decree) shall not be recoverable by the creditor except in accordance with subsection (7) below.

(7) A creditor who wishes to recover interest to which subsection (6) above applies shall serve a notice on the debtor, not later than the date prescribed by Act of Sederunt occurring—

(*a*) in the case of a direction under subsection (1)(*a*) above, before the date when the last instalment of the debt concerned (other than such interest) is payable under the direction;

(*b*) in the case of a direction under subsection (1)(*b*) above, before the end of the period specified in the direction,

stating that he is claiming such interest and specifying the amount of the interest claimed.

(8) Any sum paid by a debtor under a time to pay direction shall not be ascribed to interest claimed in pursuance of subsections (6) and (7) above until the debt concerned (other than such interest) has been discharged.

NOTES

[0] Amended (*prosp.*) by the Child Support Act 1991, Sched. 5, para. 8(2).

[1] Inserted by the Abolition of Domestic Rates Etc. (Scotland) Act 1987, s.33(*a*).

Effect of time to pay direction on diligence

2.—(1) While a time to pay direction is in effect, it shall not be competent—

(*a*) to serve a charge for payment; or

(*b*) to commence or execute any of the following diligences—

(i) an arrestment and action of furthcoming or sale;

(ii) a poinding and sale;

(iii) an earnings arrestment;
(iv) an adjudication for debt,

to enforce payment of the debt concerned.

(2) While a time to pay direction is in effect an arrestment used on the dependence of the action or in security of the debt concerned shall remain in effect—

(*a*) if it has not been recalled; and
(*b*) to the extent that it has not been restricted under subsection (3) below,

but, while the direction is in effect, it shall not be competent to commence an action of furthcoming or sale following on such an arrestment.

(3) The court may, on making a time to pay direction, recall or restrict an arrestment of the kind described in subsection (2) above.

(4) If an arrestment of the kind described in subsection (2) above is in effect, the court may order that the making of a time to pay direction and the recall or restriction of the arrestment shall be subject to the fulfilment by the debtor of such conditions within such period as the court thinks fit; and, where the court so orders, it shall postpone granting decree until such fulfilment or the end of that period, whichever is the earlier.

(5) Where a time to pay direction is recalled or ceases to have effect, otherwise than—

(*a*) under section 12(2)(*a*) of this Act; or
(*b*) by reason of the debt concerned being paid or otherwise extinguished,

the debt in so far as it remains outstanding and interest thereon, whether or not awarded as a specific sum in the decree, shall, subject to any enactment or rule of law to the contrary, become enforceable by any diligence mentioned in subsection (1)(*b*) above.

Variation and recall of time to pay direction and arrestment

3.—(1) The court which granted a decree containing a time to pay direction may, on an application by the debtor or the creditor—

(*a*) vary or recall the direction if it is satisfied that it is reasonable to do so; or
(*b*) if an arrestment in respect of the debt concerned is in effect, recall or restrict the arrestment.

(2) If an arrestment in respect of the debt concerned is in effect, the court may order that any variation, recall or restriction under subsection (1) above shall be subject to the fulfilment by the debtor of such conditions as the court thinks fit.

(3) The clerk of court or sheriff clerk shall as soon as is reasonably practicable intimate a variation under subsection (1) above to the debtor and to the creditor, and the variation shall come into effect on the date of such intimation.

Lapse of time to pay direction

4.—(1) If, on the day on which an instalment payable under a time to pay direction becomes due, there remains unpaid a sum, due under previous instalments, of not less than the aggregate of two instalments, the direction shall cease to have effect.

(2) If at the end of the period of three weeks immediately following the day on which the last instalment payable under a time to pay direction becomes due, any part of the debt concerned remains outstanding, the direction shall cease to have effect.

(3) If any sum payable under a time to pay direction under section 1(1)(*b*) of this Act remains unpaid 24 hours after the end of the period specified in the direction, the direction shall cease to have effect.

(4) Where—

(*a*) a decree for payment of a principal sum of money contains a finding as to liability for expenses and decree for payment of the expenses is subsequently granted; and

(*b*) a time to pay direction is made in relation to both the principal sum and the expenses,

if under subsections (1) to (3) above the direction ceases to have effect in relation to the sum payable under either of the decrees, the direction shall also cease to have effect in relation to the sum payable under the other decree.

Time to pay orders following charge or diligence

Time to pay orders

5.—(1) Subject to section 14 of this Act, this section applies to a debt due under a decree or other document in respect of which—

(*a*) a charge for payment has been served on the debtor;

(*b*) an arrestment has been executed; or

(*c*) an action of adjudication for debt has been commenced.

(2) Subject to subsections (4) and (5) below, the sheriff may, on an application by the debtor, make an order that a debt to which this section applies (including any interest claimed in pursuance of subsections (6) and (7) below) so far as outstanding, shall be paid—

(*a*) by such instalments, commencing at such time after the date of intimation in accordance with section 7(4) of this Act by the sheriff clerk to the debtor of the order under this subsection, payable at such intervals; or

(*b*) as a lump sum at the end of such period following intimation as mentioned in paragraph (*a*) above,

as the sheriff may specify in the order.

(3) An order under subsection (2) above shall be known as a "time to pay order".

(4) It shall not be competent for the sheriff to make a time to pay order—

(*a*) where the amount of the debt outstanding at the date of the making of the application under subsection (2) above (exclusive of any interest) exceeds £10,000 or such amount as may be prescribed in regulations made by the Lord Advocate;

(*b*) where, in relation to the debt, a time to pay direction or a time to pay order has previously been made (whether such direction or order is in effect or not);

(*c*) where, in relation to the debt, a summary warrant has been granted;

(*d*) in relation to a debt including any sum recoverable by or on behalf of the Inland Revenue in respect of tax or as if it were tax;

(*e*) in relation to a debt including rates payable to a rating authority;

[1] (*ee*) in relation to a debt including any sum due to—

(i) a levying authority in respect of any community charge or community water charge within the meaning of section 26 of the Abolition of Domestic Rates Etc. (Scotland) Act 1987 (which defines terms used in that Act) or any amount payable under section 18(3) (payment of community charges in respect of backdated period, with surcharge and interest) of that Act; or

(ii) a regional or islands council in respect of any amount payable as a civil penalty under section 17(10) or (11) (failure to provide information to a registration officer) of that Act; or

(*f*) in relation to a debt including—

(i) any duty due under the Betting and Gaming Duties Act 1981;

(ii) car tax due under the Car Tax Act 1983; or

(iii) value added tax due under the Value Added Tax Act 1983 or any sum recoverable as if it were value added tax.

(5) Where in respect of a debt to which this section applies—

(*a*) there has been a poinding of articles belonging to the debtor and a warrant of sale has been granted in respect of them but has not been executed;

(*b*) moveable property of the debtor has been arrested and in respect of the arrested property—

(i) a decree in an action of furthcoming has been granted but has not been enforced; or

(ii) a warrant of sale has been granted but the warrant has not been executed; or

(*c*) a decree in an action of adjudication for debt has been granted and the creditor has, with the debtor's consent or acquiescence, entered into possession of any property adjudged by the decree or has obtained a decree of maills and duties, or a decree of removing or ejection, in relation to any such property,

it shall not be competent for the sheriff to make a time to pay order in respect of that debt until the diligence has been completed or has otherwise ceased to have effect.

(6) Without prejudice to section 9(12) of this Act, interest payable under a decree for payment of a debt in respect of which a time to pay order has been made (other than interest awarded as a specific sum in the decree) shall not be recoverable by the creditor except in accordance with subsection (7) below.

(7) A creditor who wishes to recover interest to which subsection (6) above applies shall serve a notice on the debtor not later than the date prescribed by Act of Sederunt occurring—

(*a*) in the case of an order under subsection (2)(*a*) above, before the date when the last instalment of the debt (other than such interest) is payable under the order;

(*b*) in the case of an order under subsection (2)(*b*) above, before the end of the period specified in the order,

stating that he is claiming such interest and specifying the amount of the interest claimed.

(8) Any sum paid by a debtor under a time to pay order shall not be ascribed to interest claimed in pursuance of subsections (6) and (7) above until the debt concerned (other than such interest) has been discharged.

NOTE

[1] Inserted by the Abolition of Domestic Rates Etc. (Scotland) Act 1987, s.33(*b*).

Application for time to pay order

6.—(1) An application for a time to pay order shall specify, to the best of the debtor's knowledge, the amount of the debt outstanding as at the date of the making of the application and shall include an offer to pay it—

(*a*) by specified instalments, payable at specified intervals; or

(*b*) as a lump sum at the end of a specified period.

(2) The sheriff clerk's duty under section 96(2)(*b*) of this Act to assist the debtor in the completion of certain forms shall, in relation to a form of application for a time to pay order, consist of a duty to assist him in the completion of the form in accordance with proposals for payment made by the debtor.

(3) On receipt of an application for a time to pay order, the sheriff shall, if the application is properly made and unless it appears to him that the making of a time to pay order would not be competent, make an interim order sisting diligence as provided for in section 8(1) of this Act.

(4) The sheriff may, where the debtor is unable to furnish the necessary information, make an order requiring the creditor, within such period as may be specified therein, to furnish to the sheriff such particulars of the decree or other document under which the debt is payable as may be prescribed by Act of Sederunt.

(5) If a creditor fails to comply with an order under subsection (4) above the sheriff may, after giving the creditor an opportunity to make representations, make an order recalling or extinguishing any existing diligence, and interdicting the creditor from executing diligence, for the recovery of the debt.

(6) Where the sheriff makes an interim order under subsection (3) above, the sheriff clerk shall as soon as is reasonably practicable—

(*a*) serve a copy of the application for the time to pay order on the creditor informing him that he may object to the granting of the application within a period of 14 days after the date of service; and

(*b*) serve on the creditor a copy of the interim order and of any order under subsection (4) above.

Disposal of application

7.—(1) If no objection is made in pursuance of section 6(6)(*a*) of this Act, the sheriff shall make a time to pay order in accordance with the application.

(2) If such an objection is made, the sheriff shall not dispose of the application without first—

[THE NEXT PAGE IS B 209]

(*a*) giving the debtor an opportunity to make representations; and
(*b*) if agreement is not reached as to whether a time to pay order should be made or as to its terms, giving the parties an opportunity to be heard.

(3) Where the sheriff refuses to make a time to pay order, he shall recall any interim order under section 6(3) of this Act.

(4) The sheriff clerk shall as soon as is reasonably practicable—
(*a*) intimate the decision of the sheriff on an application for a time to pay order (including any recall of an interim order under subsection (3) above) to the debtor and the creditor; and
(*b*) if the sheriff has made a time to pay order, inform the creditor of the date when he intimated that fact to the debtor.

Effect of interim order on diligence

8.—(1) While an interim order under section 6(3) of this Act is in effect it shall not be competent in respect of the debt—
(*a*) to grant a warrant of sale of articles which, before or after the making of the interim order, have been poinded, and any application for such warrant of sale (other than an application for an order under section 21(1)(*b*) of this Act) which is pending when the interim order comes into effect shall fall;
(*b*) to execute an earnings arrestment;
(*c*) where an arrestment of property belonging to the debtor (other than an arrestment of earnings in the hands of his employer) has been executed before or after the making of the interim order, to commence an action of furthcoming or sale, or to grant decree in any such action which has already been commenced, in pursuance of that arrestment;
(*d*) to commence an action of adjudication for debt or, if such an action has already been commenced, to take any steps other than the registration of a notice of litigiosity in connection with the action, the obtaining and extracting of a decree in the action, the registration of an abbreviate of adjudication and the completion of title to property adjudged by the decree.

(2) An interim order under section 6(3) of this Act shall come into effect on intimation to the creditor under section 6(6)(*b*) of this Act and shall remain in effect until intimation of the sheriff's decision on the application for a time to pay order is made to the debtor and the creditor under section 7(4)(*a*) of this Act.

(3) For the purposes of section 27 of this Act, the period during which such an interim order is in effect shall be disregarded in calculating the period during which a poinding to which the interim order applies remains in effect.

Effect of time to pay order on diligence

9.—(1) While a time to pay order is in effect, it shall not be competent—
(*a*) to serve a charge for payment; or
(*b*) to commence or execute any of the following diligences—
(i) an arrestment and action of furthcoming or sale;
(ii) a poinding and sale;
(iii) an earnings arrestment;
(iv) an adjudication for debt,

to enforce payment of the debt concerned.

(2) On making a time to pay order, the sheriff in respect of the debt—
(*a*) shall make an order recalling any existing earnings arrestment;
(*b*) where the debt is being enforced by a conjoined arrestment order, shall—
(i) if he, or another sheriff sitting in the same sheriff court, made the conjoined arrestment order, vary it so as to exclude the

debt or, where no other debt or maintenance is being enforced by the order, recall the order;

(ii) if a sheriff sitting in another sheriff court made the conjoined arrestment order, require intimation of the time to pay order to be made to a sheriff sitting there who shall so vary or, as the case may be, recall the conjoined arrestment order;

(*c*) where an action of adjudication for debt has been commenced, shall make an order prohibiting the taking of any steps other than the registration of a notice of litigiosity in connection with the action, the obtaining and extracting of a decree in the action, the registration of an abbreviate of adjudication and the completion of title to property adjudged by the decree;

(*d*) may make an order recalling a poinding;

(*e*) may make an order recalling or restricting any arrestment other than an arrestment of the debtor's earnings in the hands of his employer.

(3) If a poinding or such an arrestment as is mentioned in subsection (2)(*e*) above is in effect, the sheriff may order that the making of a time to pay order or the recall of the poinding or the recall or restriction of the arrestment shall be subject to the fulfilment by the debtor of such conditions as the sheriff thinks fit.

(4) Where the sheriff does not exercise the powers conferred on him by subsection (2)(*d*) or (*e*) above to recall a diligence, he shall order that no further steps shall be taken by the creditor in the diligence concerned other than, in the case of a poinding, applying for an order under section 21(1) of this Act or making a report of the execution of the poinding under section 22 of this Act.

(5) Any order made under subsection (2) or (4) above shall specify the diligence in relation to which it is made.

(6) The sheriff shall not make an order under subsection (2)(*d*) or (*e*) above without first giving the creditor an opportunity to make representations.

(7) The sheriff clerk shall, at the same time as he makes intimation under section 7(4)(*a*) of this Act—

(*a*) intimate any order under subsection (2) or (4) above to the debtor and the creditor and the order shall come into effect on such intimation being made to the creditor;

(*b*) intimate any order under subsection (2)(*a*) or (*b*) above to the employer.

(8) While an order under subsection (4) above is in effect it shall not be competent to grant—

(*a*) a warrant (other than an order under section 21(1)(*b*) of this Act) to sell articles which have been poinded;

(*b*) a decree of furthcoming or sale of arrested property.

(9) For the purposes of section 27 of this Act, the period during which an order under subsection (4) above is in effect shall be disregarded in calculating the period during which a poinding to which the order applies remains in effect.

(10) Where, before the making of a time to pay order in respect of a debt, a charge to pay that debt has been served—

(*a*) if the period for payment specified in the charge has not expired, the charge shall lapse on the making of the order;

(*b*) if that period has expired, nothing in the time to pay order nor in any order under this section shall affect retrospectively the effect of the charge in the constitution of apparent insolvency within the meaning of section 7 of the Bankruptcy (Scotland) Act 1985.

(11) If, when a time to pay order in relation to a debt is made, any diligence enforcing it is in effect which is not specified in an order under subsection (2) or (4) above, the diligence shall remain in effect unless and until it is recalled under section 10(4) of this Act.

(12) Where a time to pay order is recalled or ceases to have effect, otherwise than—

(*a*) under section 12(2)(*a*) of this Act; or

(*b*) by the debt payable under the order being paid or otherwise extinguished,

the debt in so far as it remains outstanding (including interest thereon, whether or not awarded as a specific sum in the decree) shall, subject to any enactment or rule of law to the contrary, become enforceable by any diligence mentioned in subsection (1)(*b*) above; and, notwithstanding section 25 of this Act, in this subsection "diligence" includes, where the debt was, immediately before the time to pay order was made, being enforced by a poinding in any premises, another poinding in those premises.

Variation and recall of time to pay order and arrestment

10.—(1) The sheriff may, on an application by the debtor or the creditor—

(*a*) vary or recall a time to pay order if he is satisfied that it is reasonable to do so; or

(*b*) if a poinding or an arrestment in respect of the debt is in effect, recall the poinding or recall or restrict the arrestment.

(2) If a poinding or an arrestment in respect of the debt is in effect, the sheriff may order that any variation, recall or restriction under subsection (1) above shall be subject to the fulfilment by the debtor of such conditions as the sheriff thinks fit.

(3) The sheriff clerk shall as soon as is reasonably practicable intimate a variation under subsection (1) above to the debtor and to the creditor, and the variation shall come into effect on the date of such intimation.

(4) Where, after a time to pay order has been made, it comes to the knowledge of the sheriff that the debt to which the order applies is being enforced by any of the diligences mentioned in section 9(1)(*b*) of this Act which was in effect when the time to pay order was made, the sheriff, after giving all interested parties an opportunity to be heard, may make—

(*a*) an order recalling the time to pay order; or

(*b*) any of the orders mentioned in subsection (2) or (4) of section 9 of this Act; and that section shall, subject to any necessary modifications, apply for the purposes of an order made under this paragraph as it applies for the purposes of an order made under either of those subsections.

Lapse of time to pay order

11.—(1) If, on the day on which an instalment payable under a time to pay order becomes due, there remains unpaid a sum, due under previous instalments, of not less than the aggregate of two instalments, the order shall cease to have effect.

(2) If at the end of the period of three weeks immediately following the day on which the last instalment payable under a time to pay order becomes due, any part of the debt payable under the order remains outstanding, the order shall cease to have effect.

(3) If any sum payable under a time to pay order under section 5(2)(*b*) of this Act remains unpaid 24 hours after the end of the period specified in the order, the order shall cease to have effect.

Miscellaneous

Sequestration and insolvency

12.—(1) While a time to pay direction or a time to pay order is in effect, the creditor shall not be entitled to found on the debt concerned in presenting, or in concurring in the presentation of, a petition for the sequestration of the debtor's estate.

(2) A time to pay direction or a time to pay order shall cease to have effect—

(*a*) on the granting of an award of sequestration of the debtor's estate;

(*b*) on the granting by the debtor of a voluntary trust deed whereby his estate is conveyed to a trustee for the benefit of his creditors generally; or

(*c*) on the entering by the debtor into a composition contract with his creditors.

Saving of creditor's rights and remedies

13.—(1) No right or remedy of a creditor to enforce his debt shall be affected by—

(*a*) a time to pay direction;

(*b*) a time to pay order; or

(*c*) an interim order under section 6(3) of this Act,

except as expressly provided in this Part of this Act.

(2) The recall—

(*a*) on the making of a time to pay direction or an order under section 3(1) of this Act, of an arrestment; or

(*b*) on the making of a time to pay order or an order under section 10(1) of this Act, of an arrestment or a poinding,

shall not prevent the creditor therein from being ranked by virtue of that arrestment of poinding pari passu under paragraph 24 of Schedule 7 to the Bankruptcy (Scotland) Act 1985 on the proceeds of any other arrestment or poinding.

Circumstances where direction or order not competent or no longer effective

14.—(1) It shall be competent to make a time to pay direction or a time to pay order only in relation to a debtor who is an individual and only if, and to the extent that, the debtor is liable for payment of the debt concerned in either or both of the following capacities—

(*a*) personally;

(*b*) as a tutor of an individual or as a judicial factor loco tutoris, curator bonis or judicial factor loco absentis on an individual's estate.

(2) A time to pay direction or a time to pay order shall cease to have effect on the death of the debtor or on the transmission of the obligation to pay the debt concerned during his lifetime to another person.

(3) Where a time order for the payment by instalments of a sum owed under a regulated agreement or a security has been made under section 129(2)(*a*) of the Consumer Credit Act 1974 it shall not thereafter be competent to make a time to pay direction or a time to pay order in relation to that sum.

Interpretation of Part I

15.—(1) In this Part of this Act—

"adjudication for debt" does not include—

(*a*) an adjudication on a debitum fundi; or

(*b*) an adjudication under section 23 of the Conveyancing (Scotland) Act 1924 (adjudication to recover arrears of ground annual);

"poinding" does not include poinding of the ground, and "poinded" shall be construed accordingly.

(2) In sections 1 to 4 of this Act—

"the court" means the Court of Session or the sheriff;

"the debt concerned" means the sum or expenses in respect of which a time to pay direction is made.

[1] (3) In sections 5 to 14 of this Act—

"debt" means the sum due by a debtor under a decree or other document (including any interest thereon and any expenses decerned for), and any expenses of diligence used to recover such sum which are chargeable against the debtor, but does not include—

(*a*) any sum due under an order of court in criminal proceedings;
(*b*) maintenance, whether due at the date of application for the time to pay order or not, or any capital sum awarded on divorce or on the granting of a declarator of nullity of marriage or any other sum due under a decree awarding maintenance or such a capital sum; or
(*c*) any fine imposed—
(i) for contempt of court;
(ii) under any enactment, for professional misconduct; or
(iii) for failure to implement an order under section 91 of the Court of Session Act 1868 (orders for specific performance of statutory duty);

"decree or other document" means—
(*a*) a decree of the Court of Session or the sheriff;
(*b*) an extract of a document which is registered for execution in the Books of Council and Session or the sheriff court books;
(*c*) an order or determination which by virtue of any enactment is enforceable as if it were an extract registered decree arbitral bearing a warrant for execution issued by the sheriff;
(*d*) a civil judgment granted outside Scotland by a court, tribunal or arbiter which by virtue of any enactment or rule of law is enforceable in Scotland; and
(*e*) a document or settlement which by virtue of an Order in Council made under section 13 of the Civil Jurisdiction and Judgments Act 1982 is enforceable in Scotland,

but does not include a maintenance order or a summary warrant;

"sheriff"—
(*a*) in relation to a debt constituted by decree granted by a sheriff, means that sheriff or another sheriff sitting in the same sheriff court;
(*b*) in any other case, means the sheriff having jurisdiction—
(i) in the place where the debtor is domiciled;
(ii) if the debtor is not domiciled in Scotland, in a place in Scotland where he carries on business; or
(iii) if the debtor does not carry on business in Scotland, in a place where he has property which is not exempt from diligence;

and, for the purposes of sub-paragraphs (i) and (ii) above, the debtor's domicile shall be determined in accordance with section 41 of the Civil Jurisdiction and Judgments Act 1982.

NOTE
[1] Amended (*prosp.*) by the Child Support Act 1991, Sched. 5, para. 8(3).

PART II

POINDINGS AND WARRANT SALES

Poinding

Articles exempt from poinding

16.—(1) The following articles belonging to a debtor shall be exempt from poinding at the instance of a creditor in respect of a debt due to him by the debtor—
(*a*) clothing reasonably required for the use of the debtor or any member of his household;
(*b*) implements, tools of trade, books or other equipment reasonably required for the use of the debtor or any member of his household in the practice of the debtor's or such member's profession, trade or business, not exceeding in aggregate value £500 or such amount as may be prescribed in regulations made by the Lord Advocate;
(*c*) medical aids or medical equipment reasonably required for the use of the debtor or any member of his household;

(*d*) books or other articles reasonably required for the education or training of the debtor or any member of his household not exceeding in aggregate value £500 or such amount as may be prescribed in regulations made by the Lord Advocate;

(*e*) toys for the use of any child who is a member of the debtor's household;

(*f*) articles reasonably required for the care or upbringing of a child who is a member of the debtor's household.

(2) The following articles belonging to a debtor shall be exempt from poinding if they are at the time of the poinding in a dwellinghouse and are reasonably required for the use in the dwellinghouse of the person residing there or a member of his household—

(*a*) beds or bedding;
(*b*) household linen;
(*c*) chairs or settees;
(*d*) tables;
(*e*) food;
(*f*) lights or light fittings;
(*g*) heating appliances;
(*h*) curtains;
(*j*) floor coverings;
(*k*) furniture, equipment or utensils used for cooking, storing or eating food;
(*l*) refrigerators;
(*m*) articles used for cleaning, mending, or pressing clothes;
(*n*) articles used for cleaning the dwellinghouse;
(*o*) furniture used for storing—
  (i) clothing, bedding or household linen;
  (ii) articles used for cleaning the dwellinghouse; or
  (iii) utensils used for cooking or eating food;
(*p*) articles used for safety in the dwellinghouse;
(*q*) tools used for maintenance or repair of the dwellinghouse or of household articles.

(3) The Lord Advocate may by regulations add to the list set out in subsection (2) above, or delete or vary any of the items contained in that list.

(4) If, on an application made within 14 days after the date of the execution of the poinding—

(*a*) by the debtor or any person who owns a pointed article in common with the debtor; or

(*b*) by any person in possession of a poinded article,

the sheriff is satisfied that the article is exempt from poinding under this section, he shall make an order releasing the article from the poinding.

Restrictions on times when poinding may be executed

17.—(1) No poinding shall be executed on Sunday, Christmas Day, New Year's Day, Good Friday or such other day as may be prescribed by Act of Sederunt.

(2) The execution of a poinding shall not—

(*a*) be commenced before 8 a.m. or after 8 p.m.; or

(*b*) be continued after 8 p.m.,

unless the officer of court has obtained prior authority from the sheriff for such commencement or continuation; and any rule of law which prohibits poindings outwith the hours of daylight shall cease to have effect.

Power of entry for execution of poinding

18.—(1) Subject to subsection (2) below, notwithstanding any warrant authorising him to open shut and lockfast places, an officer of court shall not enter a dwellinghouse to execute a poinding if, at the time of his intended entry, there appears to him to be nobody, or only children under the age of 16 years, present there unless, at least four days before the date of his intended entry, he has served notice on the debtor specifying that date.

(2) If it appears to the sheriff, on an application made to him by the officer of court (which shall not require to be intimated to the debtor), that the requirement of service under this section would be likely to prejudice the execution of the poinding he may dispense with such service.

Value of articles which may be poinded and presumption as to ownership

19.—(1) The officer of court shall be entitled to poind articles only to the extent necessary to ensure that the sum recoverable at the time of the sale would be realised if they were sold at the values fixed under section 20(4) of this Act.

(2) In executing a poinding, an officer of court shall be entitled to proceed on the assumption that any article in the possession of the debtor is owned by him unless the officer of court knows or ought to know that the contrary is the case.

(3) The officer of court shall not be precluded from relying on the assumption mentioned in subsection (2) above by reason only of one or both of the following circumstances—

(*a*) that the articles belongs to a class which is commonly held under a hire, hire-purchase or conditional sale agreement or on some other limited title of possession;

(*b*) that an assertion has been made that the article is not owned by the debtor.

Poinding procedure

20.—(1) The procedure in a poinding shall be in accordance with this section and section 21 of this Act.

(2) Before executing the poinding, the officer of court shall—

(*a*) exhibit to any person present the warrant to poind and the certificate of execution of the charge relating thereto;

(*b*) demand payment of the sum recoverable from the debtor, if he is present, or any person present appearing to the officer of court to be authorised to act for the debtor; and

(*c*) make enquiry of any person present as to the ownership of the articles proposed to be poinded, and in particular whether there are any persons who own any articles in common with the debtor,

but it shall not be necessary for the officer of court to make public proclamation of the poinding or to read publicly the extract decree containing the warrant to poind and the execution of the charge relating thereto.

(3) The officer of court shall be accompanied at the poinding by one witness.

(4) The poinded articles shall be valued by the officer of court according to the price which they would be likely to fetch if sold on the open market unless he considers that the articles are such that a valuation by a professional valuer or other suitably skilled person is advisable, in which case he may arrange for such a valuation.

(5) The officer of court shall prepare a schedule (referred to in this Part of this Act as "the poinding schedule"), in the form prescribed by Act of Sederunt, which shall specify—

(*a*) the identity of the creditor and of the debtor;

(*b*) the articles poinded, and their respective values;

(*c*) the sum recoverable; and

(*d*) the place where the poinding was executed.

(6) On completion of the valuation the officer of court shall—

(*a*) along with the witness sign the poinding schedule;

(*b*) deliver the poinding schedule to any person in possession of the articles or—

(i) where the poinding was executed in a dwellinghouse or other premises, leave it in the premises; or

(ii) in any other case, deliver it to premises occupied by that person;

(*c*) if the person in possession of the articles is not the debtor and it is reasonably practicable, serve a copy of it by post on the debtor;

(*d*) inform the debtor (if present) of his right to redeem poinded articles under section 21(4) of this Act;

(*e*) inform any person present who owns any poinded article in common with the debtor of his right to redeem poinded articles under section 41(2) and (3)(*a*) of this Act; and

(*f*) inform the debtor (if present) and any person present who owns any poinded article in common with the debtor, or who is in possession of any poinded article, of his right to apply for an order releasing articles from poinding under section 16(4), 23(1) or 41(3)(*b*) of this Act.

(7) The officer of court shall leave poinded articles at the place where they were poinded, except that where that place is not a dwellinghouse or other premises, if he considers it necessary for their security or the preservation of their value and there is insufficient time to obtain an order under section 21(1)(*a*) of this Act, he shall remove them at the creditor's expense—

(*a*) to the nearest convenient premises belonging to the debtor or to the person in possession of the articles; or

(*b*) if no such premises are available, to the nearest suitable secure premises.

Poinding procedure—further provisions

21.—(1) The sheriff, on an application by the creditor, the officer of court or the debtor intimated in accordance with subsection (2) below, may at any time after the execution of a poinding make an order—

(*a*) for the security of any of the poinded articles; or

(*b*) in relation to any of the articles which are of a perishable nature or which are likely to deteriorate substantially and rapidly in condition or value, for their immediate disposal and, in the event of their disposal by sale, for payment of the proceeds of sale to the creditor or for consignation of the proceeds in court until the diligence is completed or otherwise ceases to have effect,

and a decision of the sheriff under paragraph (*b*) above for the immediate disposal of articles shall not be subject to appeal.

(2) An application for an order under subsection (1)(*b*) above—

(*a*) by the creditor or the officer of court, shall be intimated by him to the debtor;

(*b*) by the debtor, shall be intimated to the creditor or the officer of court,

at the time when it is made.

(3) It shall not be competent for an officer of court in executing a poinding to examine a person on oath as to the ownership of any article.

(4) Subject to subsection (1)(*b*) above, the debtor shall be entitled, within 14 days after the date of execution of the poinding, to redeem any poinded article at the value fixed under section 20(4) of this Act; and the officer of court shall mention any such redemption in his report under section 22 of this Act or, if he has already made that report, shall report the redemption as soon as is reasonably practicable to the sheriff.

(5) The officer of court shall, on receiving payment from the debtor for the redemption under subsection (4) above of a poinded article, grant a receipt in the form prescribed by Act of Sederunt to the debtor; and the receipt shall operate as a release of the article from the poinding.

(6) Subject to section 29(2)(*b*) of this Act, the revaluation in the same

poinding of an article which has been valued under section 20(4) of this Act shall not be competent.

(7) A poinding shall be deemed to have been executed on the date when the poinding schedule has been delivered, or left on the premises, in pursuance of section 20(6)(*b*) of this Act.

(8) Subject to subsection (9) below, at any time before the execution of a poinding on behalf of a creditor, an officer of court shall, if requested to do so by any other creditor who has delivered to him a warrant to poind, conjoin that creditor in the poinding.

(9) It shall not be competent for an officer of court to conjoin a creditor in a poinding in respect of a debt for which the creditor holds a summary warrant.

Report of execution of poinding

22.—(1) The officer of court shall, within a period of 14 days after the date of execution of the poinding (or such longer period as the sheriff on cause shown may allow on an application by the officer of court) make to the sheriff in the form prescribed by Act of Sederunt a report of the execution of the poinding which shall be signed by the officer of court and the witness who attended the poinding.

(2) The officer of court shall note in the report under subsection (1) above any assertion made before the submission of the report that any poinded article does not belong to the debtor.

(3) The sheriff may refuse to receive a report on the ground that it has not been made and signed in accordance with subsection (1) above, and if the sheriff refuses to receive a report on that ground the poinding shall cease to have effect.

(4) The sheriff clerk shall intimate a refusal under subsection (3) above—

(*a*) to the debtor; and

(*b*) if he is a different person from the debtor, to the person in possession of the poinded articles.

(5) Any rule of law whereby the sheriff may refuse to receive a report of the execution of a poinding on a ground other than one specified in subsection (3) above shall cease to have effect.

Release of poinded article on ground of undue harshness

23.—(1) The sheriff may, on an application made within 14 days after the date of execution of a poinding by the debtor or any person in possession of a poinded article, make an order releasing an article from the poinding if it appears to the sheriff that its continued inclusion in the poinding or its sale under warrant of sale would be unduly harsh in the circumstances.

(2) Where the sheriff has made an order under subsection (1) above he may, notwithstanding section 25 of this Act, on an application by the creditor or by an officer of court on his behalf, authorise the poinding of other articles belonging to the debtor on the same premises.

Invalidity, cessation and recall of poinding

24.—(1) If, at any time before the sale of the poinded articles, the sheriff is satisfied that the poinding is invalid or has ceased to have effect he shall, on his own initiative or on an application by the debtor, make an order declaring that to be the case, and may make such consequential order as appears to him to be necessary in the circumstances.

(2) Without prejudice to section 16(4) of this Act, it shall not be competent for the sheriff to make an order under subsection (1) above on the ground that any poinded article is exempt from poinding under that section.

(3) At any time before an application is made under section 30 of this Act for a warrant of sale, the sheriff may, on an application by the debtor, recall a poinding on any of the following grounds—

(*a*) that it would be unduly harsh in the circumstances for a warrant of sale of the poinded articles to be granted;
(*b*) that the aggregate of the values of the poinded articles fixed under section 20(4) of this Act was substantially below the aggregate of the prices which they would have been likely to fetch if sold on the open market; or
(*c*) that the likely aggregate proceeds of sale of the poinded articles would not exceed the expenses likely to be incurred in the application for warrant of sale and in any steps required to be taken under this Part of this Act in execution of such a warrant, on the assumption that that application and such steps are unopposed.

(4) The sheriff shall not grant an application on the ground mentioned in subsection (3)(*c*) above if an order for further poinding of articles belonging to the debtor has been authorised under section 23(2), 28(6) or 29(2), or has become competent by reason of section 9(12), 28(2), 40(5) or 41(6), of this Act.

(5) The sheriff shall not make an order under subsection (1) above, recall a poinding or refuse an application under this section without first giving the debtor and the creditor—
(*a*) an opportunity to make representations; and
(*b*) if either party wishes to be heard, an opportunity to be heard.

(6) The sheriff clerk shall intimate to the debtor any order made under subsection (1) above by the sheriff on his own initiative.

Second poinding in same premises

25. Subject to sections 9(12), 23(2), 28(2) and (6), 29(2), 40(5) and 41(6) of this Act, where articles are poinded in any premises (whether or not the poinding is valid), another poinding in those premises to enforce the same debt shall not be competent except in relation to articles which have been brought on to the premises since the execution of the first poinding.

Sist of proceedings in poinding of mobile homes

26.—(1) Where a caravan, houseboat or other moveable structure which is the only or principal residence of the debtor or another person has been poinded the sheriff, on an application by the debtor or that other person made at any time after the execution of the poinding and before the granting of a warrant of sale, may order that for such period as he shall specify no further steps shall be taken in the poinding.

(2) In calculating under section 27(1) or (2) of this Act the period during which a poinding in respect of which an order has been made under subsection (1) above shall remain effective, there shall be disregarded the period specified in the order.

Duration of poinding

27.—(1) Subject to subsections (2), (3) and (5)(*a*) below, a poinding shall cease to have effect on the expiry of a period of one year after the date of execution of the poinding, unless before such expiry an application has been made under section 30(1) of this Act for a warrant of sale in relation to the poinded articles.

(2) The sheriff, on an application by the creditor or by an officer of court on his behalf made before the expiry of the period mentioned in subsection (1) above and before an application has been made under section 30(1) of this Act, may extend that period—
(*a*) where he considers that, if the said period is extended, the debtor is likely to comply with an agreement between the creditor and the debtor for the payment of the sum recoverable by instalments or otherwise; or
(*b*) to enable further proceedings to be taken in the diligence where the termination of the poinding would prejudice the creditor and the

creditor cannot be held responsible for the circumstances giving rise to the need for the extension,

for such further period as he considers reasonable in the circumstances.

(3) The sheriff may grant further extensions under subsection (2) above, on application being made to him before the expiry of the previously extended period.

(4) The decision of the sheriff under subsection (2) above shall not be subject to appeal, and shall be intimated to the debtor by the sheriff clerk.

(5) Where, within the period mentioned in subsection (1) above or within that period as extended under subsection (2) above, an application is made—

(*a*) under subsection (2) above—

(i) if the application is made on the ground referred to in paragraph (*a*) of that subsection, the poinding shall, if the date of disposal of the application is later than 14 days before the poinding is due to expire, continue to have effect until 14 days after that disposal;

(ii) in any other case, the poinding shall continue to have effect until the disposal of the application;

(*b*) under section 30 of this Act for a warrant of sale, the poinding shall, if the sheriff refuses to grant a warrant of sale, continue to have effect—

(i) until the period for leave to appeal has expired without an application for leave having been made;

(ii) where an application for leave to appeal is made, until leave has been refused or the application has been abandoned;

(iii) where leave to appeal has been granted, until the period for an appeal has expired without an appeal being made; or

(iv) where an appeal against the decision is made, until the matter has been finally determined or the appeal has been abandoned; or

(*c*) under section 30 of this Act for a warrant of sale, the poinding shall, if the sheriff grants a warrant of sale, continue to have effect—

(i) if the articles are sold, or ownership passes to the creditor under section 37(6) of this Act, until the date of such sale or such ownership passing; or

(ii) if the articles are sold, or ownership does not pass to the creditor, until the expiry of the period specified for the warrant sale in the warrant of sale.

(6) Without prejudice to subsection (7) below, if a report has been made to the sheriff under section 36(2) of this Act, the poinding shall continue to have effect for a period of six months after the date when the latest such report was made.

(7) Where, within the period specified for the warrant sale in the warrant of sale, or within the period mentioned in subsection (6) above, an application is made under section 35 of this Act for a variation of the warrant of sale, the poinding shall cease to have effect—

(*a*) if the sheriff refuses to grant a variation—

(i) when the period for leave to appeal has expired without an application for leave having been made;

(ii) where an application for leave to appeal is made, when leave has been refused or the application has been abandoned;

(iii) where leave to appeal has been granted, when the period for an appeal has expired without an appeal being made; or

(iv) where an appeal against the decision is made, when the matter has been finally determined in favour of the sheriff's decision or the appeal has been abandoned,

or on such later date as the sheriff may direct;

(*b*) if the sheriff grants a variation—

(i) where the articles are sold, or ownership passes to the creditor under section 37(6) of this Act in the period specified for the warrant sale in the warrant of sale as so varied, on the date of the warrant sale or of ownership so passing;

(ii) where the articles are not sold and ownership does not pass to the creditor within that period, on the expiry of that period.

Removal, damage or destruction of pointed articles

Removal of poinded articles

28.—(1) The debtor or the person in possession of poinded articles may move them to another location if—

(*a*) the creditor or an officer of court on behalf of the creditor has consented in writing to their removal; or

(*b*) the sheriff, on an application by the debtor or the person in possession, has authorised their removal.

(2) Where poinded articles have been removed under subsection (1) above, an officer of court may, under the same warrant to poind, again poind any of the articles so removed and, notwithstanding section 25 of this Act, any articles which were not so removed, whether or not they were previously poinded; and, on the execution of any such further poinding, the original poinding shall be deemed to have been abandoned.

(3) The removal, except in accordance with this Part of this Act, from any premises of poinded articles by—

(*a*) the debtor; or

(*b*) any person, other than the creditor or an officer of court, who knows that the articles have been poinded,

shall be a breach of the poinding and may be dealt with as a contempt of court.

(4) Where articles have been removed from premises otherwise than in accordance with this Part of this Act, the sheriff, on an application by the creditor—

(*a*) may, subject to subsection (5) below, make an order requiring the person in possession of the articles to restore them to the premises from which they were removed within a period specified in the order; and

(*b*) if an order under paragraph (*a*) above is not complied with, and it appears to the sheriff that the articles are likely to be found in premises specified in the application, may grant a warrant to officers of court—

(i) to search for the articles in those premises; and

(ii) to restore the articles to the premises from which they were removed or to make such other arrangements for their security as the sheriff may direct,

and such a warrant shall be authority to open shut and lockfast places for the purpose of its execution.

(5) Where it appears to the sheriff, on an application made to him by any person having an interest, that any article which has been removed from premises otherwise than in accordance with this Part of this Act has been acquired for value and without knowledge of the poinding, he shall—

(*a*) refuse an order under subsection (4)(*a*) above relating to that article;

(*b*) recall any such order which he has already made; and

(*c*) make an order releasing the article from the poinding.

(6) Where articles have been removed from premises otherwise than in accordance with this Part of this Act in circumstances in which the debtor is at fault the sheriff, on an application by the creditor or by an officer of court on his behalf, may, notwithstanding section 25 of this Act, authorise the poinding of other articles belonging to the debtor in the same premises.

(7) The removal of poinded articles to another location shall not have the effect of releasing the articles from the poinding.

Unlawful acts relating to poinded articles

29.—(1) The wilful damage or destruction of poinded articles by—

(*a*) the debtor; or

(*b*) any person, other than the creditor or an officer of court, who knows that the articles have been poinded,

shall be a breach of the poinding and may be dealt with as a contempt of court.

(2) Where poinded articles have been damaged or destroyed the sheriff, on an application by the creditor or by the officer of court on his behalf, may—

(*a*) where the debtor has been at fault, authorise the poinding of other articles belonging to the debtor in the premises in which the original poinding took place; and

(*b*) in any case, authorise the revaluation of any damaged article in accordance with section 20(4) of this Act.

(3) Where a third party, knowing that an article has been poinded—

(*a*) wilfully damages or destroys it; or

(*b*) removes it from premises in breach of a poinding, and—

(i) it is damaged, destroyed, lost or stolen; or

(ii) it is acquired from or through him by another person without knowledge of the poinding and for value,

the sheriff may order the third party to consign the sum mentioned in subsection (4) below in court until the completion of the sale or until the poinding otherwise ceases to have effect.

(4) The sum to be consigned in court under subsection (3) above shall be—

(*a*) where the article has been damaged but not so damaged as to make it worthless, a sum equal to the difference between the value of the article fixed under section 20(4) of this Act and the value of the article as so damaged;

(*b*) in any other case, a sum equal to the value fixed under that section.

(5) Any sum consigned in court under subsection (3) above shall, on the completion of the sale or on the poinding otherwise ceasing to have effect, be paid to the creditor to the extent necessary to meet the sum recoverable, any surplus thereof being paid to the debtor.

Warrant sales

Application for warrant of sale

30.—(1) A creditor shall not be entitled to sell articles poinded by him unless, on an application by him or by an officer of court on his behalf, the sheriff has granted a warrant under this section (referred to in this Act as a "warrant of sale").

(2) The sheriff may refuse to grant a warrant of sale—

(*a*) on his own initiative or on an objection by the debtor—

(i) on the ground that the poinding is invalid or has ceased to have effect;

(ii) on a ground mentioned in section 24(3)(*b*) or (*c*) of this Act;

(*b*) on an objection by the debtor, on the ground that the granting of the application would be unduly harsh in the circumstances.

(3) The creditor or officer of court, when making an application under subsection (1) above, shall serve a copy thereof on the debtor together with a notice in the form prescribed by Act of Sederunt informing him—

(*a*) that he may object to the application within 14 days after the date when it was made; and

(*b*) of his right to redeem poinded articles under section 33(2) of this Act.

(4) The sheriff shall not—

(*a*) refuse to grant a warrant of sale on his own initiative; or

(*b*) dispose of an application under subsection (1) above where the debtor has objected thereto in accordance with subsection (3)(*a*) above,

without first giving the parties an opportunity to be heard.

(5) It shall not be competent for the sheriff to refuse to grant a warrant of sale on the ground that any poinded article is exempt from poinding under section 16 of this Act.

(6) Where the sheriff refuses to grant a warrant of sale, the sheriff clerk shall intimate that refusal to the debtor and, if he is a different person from the debtor, to the person in possession of the poinded articles.

(7) A sale under a warrant of sale shall be known as a "warrant sale".

Provisions of warrant of sale

31.—(1) Every warrant of sale shall provide that the warrant sale shall be by public auction and shall specify the location of the sale in accordance with section 32 of this Act.

(2) A warrant of sale shall—

(*a*) appoint an officer of court to make arrangements for the warrant sale in accordance with the warrant;

(*b*) specify a period within which the warrant sale shall take place; and

(*c*) empower the officer of court to open shut and lockfast places for the purpose of executing the warrant.

(3) Where the warrant of sale provides for the sale to be held in premises other than an auction room, it shall appoint to conduct the warrant sale—

(*a*) if the aggregate of the values of the poinded articles fixed under section 20(4) of this Act exceeds £1,000 or such other sum as may be prescribed by Act of Sederunt and a person who carries on business as an auctioneer is available, that person;

(*b*) in any other case, the officer of court appointed under subsection (2) above or another suitable person.

(4) A warrant of sale which provides for the warrant sale to be held in premises other than where the poinded articles are situated shall also empower the officer of court appointed by the warrant to remove the poinded articles to such premises for the sale.

Location of sale

32.—(1) The warrant of sale shall not provide for the warrant sale to be held in a dwellinghouse except with the consent in writing, in a form to be prescribed by Act of Sederunt, of the occupier thereof and, if he is not the occupier, of the debtor.

(2) Subject to subsection (3) below, where articles are poinded in a dwellinghouse and any consent required under subsection (1) above is not given, the warrant of sale shall provide for the warrant sale to be held in an auction room specified in the warrant.

(3) Where—

(*a*) articles are poinded in a dwellinghouse and any consent required under subsection (1) above is not given; and

(*b*) it appears to the sheriff that, if the sale were to be held in an auction room, the likely proceeds of the warrant sale would not exceed the expenses of the application for warrant of sale and the expenses likely to be incurred in any steps required to be taken under this Part of this Act in the execution of the warrant on the assumption that that application and any such steps are unopposed,

if the creditor is able to offer suitable premises in which the warrant sale could be held, the warrant of sale shall, subject to subsection (1) above and subsections (4) and (5) below, provide for the sale to be held in those premises, but otherwise the sheriff shall refuse to grant a warrant of sale.

(4) Subject to subsection (5) below, the warrant of sale shall not provide for the sale to be held in premises (other than a dwellinghouse or an auction room) which are occupied by a person other than the debtor or the creditor except with the consent in writing, in a form to be prescribed by Act of Sederunt, of the occupier thereof.

(5) Where the occupier of premises (other than a dwellinghouse or an auction room) where poinded articles are situated does not give his consent under subsection (4) above to the holding of the warrant sale in those premises, the warrant of sale may, if the sheriff considers that it would be unduly costly to require the removal of the poinded articles to other premises for sale, nevertheless provide that the warrant sale shall be held in the premises where they are situated.

(6) In this section "occupier", in relation to premises where there are two or more occupiers, means each of them.

Release or redemption of poinded articles after warrant

33.—(1) Where a warrant sale is to be held in premises other than where the poinded articles are situated, the officer of court may, in pursuance of section 31(4) of this Act, remove to those premises only such poinded articles as, if sold at their values fixed under section 20(4) of this Act, would realise in total the sum recoverable at the time of the sale; and shall release the remaining poinded articles from the poinding.

(2) Subject to section 21(1) of this Act, the debtor may, within seven days after the date when a copy of an application for warrant of sale has been served on him, redeem any poinded article by paying to the officer of court a sum equal to its value fixed under section 20(4) of this Act.

(3) The officer of court shall, on receiving payment from the debtor under subsection (2) above, grant a receipt in the form prescribed by Act of Sederunt to the debtor; and the receipt shall operate as a release of the article from the poinding.

(4) The creditor and the debtor may by agreement release articles from the poinding.

(5) Any release or redemption of poinded articles under this section—

(*a*) shall be mentioned in the next subsequent application (if any) which is made for warrant of sale or for variation of warrant of sale; or

(*b*) if it takes place after an application for warrant of sale (or variation thereof) has been made and before it has been disposed of, shall be reported as soon as is reasonably practicable by the officer of court to the sheriff; or

(*c*) in any other case, shall be mentioned in any report of sale.

Intimation and publication of sale

34.—(1) The officer of court appointed under section 31(2)(*a*) of this Act to make arrangements for the warrant sale shall—

(*a*) as soon as is reasonably practicable intimate to the debtor and, if the person in possession of the poinded articles is not the debtor, to that person, the date arranged for the warrant sale; and

(*b*) not later than the date of intimation under paragraph (*a*) above, serve a copy of the warrant of sale on the debtor and any such person.

(2) Where the warrant sale is not to be held in the premises where the poinded articles are situated, the officer of court referred to in subsection (1) above shall, not less than seven days before the date arranged for the removal of the poinded articles from those premises, intimate to the debtor and, if he is not the debtor, to the person in possession of the poinded articles—

(*a*) the place where the sale is to be held; and

(*b*) the date arranged for the removal.

(3) The sheriff clerk shall arrange for such particulars of the warrant of sale as are prescribed by Act of Sederunt to be displayed on the walls of court.

(4) The warrant sale shall be advertised by public notice and, where the sale is to be held otherwise than in an auction room, the public notice shall be as directed by the warrant of sale.

(5) Where the warrant sale is to be held in premises not belonging to the debtor, the public notice under subsection (4) above shall not name him or disclose that the articles for sale are poinded articles.

(6) Where the warrant sale is to be held in premises other than the debtor's premises or an auction room, any public notice of the sale shall state that the articles to be sold do not belong to the occupier of the premises where the sale is to be held.

Alteration of arrangements for sale

35.—(1) Where, for any reason for which neither the creditor nor the officer of court is responsible, the arrangements made for the warrant sale cannot be implemented in accordance with the provisions of the warrant of sale, the sheriff may, on an application by the creditor or by the officer of court on his behalf, grant a variation of the warrant of sale.

(2) Subject to subsection (3) below, the sheriff may, on his own initiative or on an objection by the debtor, refuse to grant an application under subsection (1) above on the ground that—

(*a*) the poinding is invalid or has ceased to have effect; or

(*b*) the proposed variation is unsuitable.

(3) It shall not be competent for the sheriff to refuse to grant an application under subsection (1) above on the ground that any poinded article is exempt from poinding under section 16 of this Act.

(4) Section 32 of this Act shall apply to a warrant of sale as varied under this section.

(5) A creditor or officer of court who makes an application under subsection (1) above shall at the same time—

(*a*) serve on the debtor a copy thereof together with a notice in the form prescribed by Act of Sederunt, informing him that he may object to the application within seven days after the date of such service; and

(*b*) serve on any other person in possession of the poinded articles a copy of the application.

(6) The sheriff shall not—

(*a*) refuse to grant a variation under subsection (1) above on his own initiative; or

(*b*) dispose of an application under that subsection where the debtor has objected thereto in accordance with subsection (5) above,

without first giving the parties an opportunity to be heard.

(7) On granting a variation under subsection (1) above, the sheriff may make such consequential orders as he thinks fit including, where appropriate—

(*a*) an order requiring service on the debtor, and on any other person in possession of the poinded articles, of the warrant of sale as varied;

(*b*) the retaking of any steps in the diligence which have already been taken.

(8) Where the sheriff refuses to grant a variation under subsection (1) above, the sheriff clerk shall intimate that refusal to the debtor and to any other person in possession of the poinded articles.

(9) Subject to subsection (10) below and without prejudice to section 36(3) of this Act, after intimation has been given under section 34 of this Act to the debtor of the date arranged for the warrant sale or for the removal for sale of the poinded articles from the premises where they are situated, the creditor or officer of court shall not be entitled to arrange a new date for the sale of for such removal.

(10) Where, for any reason for which neither the creditor nor the officer of court is responsible, it is not possible for the warrant sale or, as the case may be, the removal for sale of the poinded articles from the premises where they are situated, to take place on the date arranged for it, the creditor may instruct the officer of court to arrange a new date in accordance with subsection (11) below, and the officer of court shall intimate the new date to the debtor and to any other person in possession of the poinded articles.

(11) The new date arranged under subsection (10) above—

(*a*) shall not in any case be less than seven days after the date of intimation under that subsection; and

(*b*) in the case of a new date arranged for a warrant sale, shall be a date within the period specified in the warrant of sale as the period within which the sale is required to be held.

Payment agreements after warrant of sale

36.—(1) Without prejudice to section 35(1) and (10) of this Act, in order to enable the sum recoverable to be paid by instalments or otherwise in accordance with an agreement between the creditor and the debtor, the creditor may, after the granting of a warrant of sale, cancel the arrangements for the warrant sale on not more than two occasions.

(2) The creditor or the officer or court on his behalf shall as soon as is reasonably practicable after any agreement of the kind referred to in subsection (1) above has been entered into make a report of the agreement to the sheriff.

(3) Where, following cancellation of the warrant sale in pursuance of subsection (1) above, the debtor is in breach of the agreement—

(*a*) if the provisions of the original warrant of sale still allow, the creditor may instruct the officer of court to make arrangements for the warrant sale in accordance with those provisions;

(*b*) if, for any reason for which neither the creditor nor the officer of court is responsible, arrangements for the warrant sale cannot be implemented in accordance with the provisions of the original warrant of sale, the sheriff may, on an application by the creditor or by the officer of court on his behalf made within six months after the date when the report was made under subsection (2) above, grant a variation of the warrant of sale under section 35(1) of this Act.

(4) For the purposes of subsection (3) above, the original warrant of sale shall be deemed to have specified that the sale is required to be held within the period of six months after the date when the latest report was made under subsection (2) above.

The warrant sale

37.—(1) Where the warrant of sale does not appoint as auctioneer the officer of court appointed under section 31(2)(*a*) of this Act to conduct the warrant sale, that officer—

(*a*) shall attend the sale and keep a record of any articles which are sold and the amount for which they are sold and of any articles whose ownership passes to the creditor under subsection (6) below; and

(*b*) if the sale is to be held in premises other than an auction room, shall supervise the sale.

(2) Where the officer of court appointed under section 31(2)(*a*) of this Act is appointed as auctioneer to conduct the sale, he shall be attended at the sale by one witness.

(3) In the warrant sale there shall be no reserve price unless the creditor chooses to have one and, if he does so choose, it shall not exceed the value of the article fixed under section 20(4) of this Act.

(4) The value of a poinded article fixed under section 20(4) of this Act and the reserve price, if any, fixed by the creditor under subsection (3) above need not be disclosed to any person bidding for the article.

(5) In the warrant sale any poinded article exposed for sale may be purchased by—

(*a*) any creditor, including the creditor on whose behalf the poinding was executed; or

(*b*) a person who owns the article in common with the debtor.

(6) Subject to subsection (7) below and without prejudice to the rights of any third party, where the sum recoverable has not been realised by the warrant sale, ownership of a poinded article which remains unsold after being exposed for sale shall pass to the creditor.

(7) Without prejudice to the rights of any third party, where the warrant sale is held in premises belonging to the debtor, the ownership of a poinded article which has passed to the creditor under subsection (6) above shall revert to the debtor unless the creditor uplifts the article by 8 p.m. (or such other time as may be prescribed by Act of Sederunt)—

(*a*) if the premises are a dwellinghouse in which the debtor is residing, on the day when the sale is completed;

(*b*) in any other case, on the third working day following that day,

and the officer of court may remain on or re-enter any premises (whether open, shut or lockfast) for the purpose of enabling the creditor to uplift any such article.

(8) For the purposes of subsection (7) above "working day" means a day which is not—

Saturday;
Sunday;
1st or 2nd January;
Good Friday;
Easter Monday;
25th or 26th December;
a public holiday in the area in which the premises are situated.

(9) Subject to subsection (10) below, where at the warrant sale any article is unsold or is sold at a price below the value fixed under section 20(4) of this Act, the debtor shall be credited with an amount equal to that valuation.

(10) Where—

(*a*) any damaged article has been revalued under section 20(4) of this Act on the authority of the sheriff given under section 29(2) of this Act;

(*b*) the damage was not caused by the fault of the debtor; and

(*c*) no order has been made under section 29(3) of this Act requiring a third party to consign a sum in respect of the article, or such an order has been made but has not been complied with,

the amount credited to the debtor under subsection (9) above shall be an amount equal to the original valuation and not the revaluation referred to in paragraph (*a*) above.

Disposal of proceeds of sale

38. The officer of court appointed under section 31(2)(*a*) of this Act shall dispose of the proceeds of the warrant sale—

(*a*) by paying to the creditor the proceeds so far as necessary to meet the sum recoverable (subject to any agreement between the officer of court and the creditor relating to the fees or outlays of the officer of court) or, if the sheriff so directs, by consigning such proceeds in court; and

(*b*) by paying to the debtor any surplus remaining after the sum recoverable has been paid or, if the debtor cannot be found, by consigning such surplus in court.

Report of warrant sale

39.—(1) The officer of court appointed under section 31(2)(*a*) of this Act shall within a period of 14 days after the date of completion of the warrant sale make to the sheriff a report in the form prescribed by Act of Sederunt (referred to in this Part of this Act as "the report of sale") setting out—

(*a*) any articles which have been sold and the amount for which they have been sold;

(*b*) any articles which remain unsold;

(*c*) the expenses chargeable against the debtor under Schedule 1 to this Act;

(*d*) any surplus paid to the debtor; and

(*e*) any balance due by or to the debtor.

(2) The report of sale shall be signed by the officer of court and, if a witness was required to attend at the sale under section 37(2) of this Act, by that witness.

(3) If an officer of court—

(*a*) without reasonable excuse makes a report of sale after the expiry of the period mentioned in subsection (1) above; or

(*b*) wilfully refuses or delays to make a report of sale after the expiry of that period,

the sheriff may, without prejudice to his right to report the matter to the Court of Session or the sheriff principal under section 79(1)(*b*) of this Act, make an order that the officer of court shall be liable for the expenses chargeable against the debtor under Schedule 1 to this Act, either in whole or in part.

(4) The report of sale shall be remitted by the sheriff to the auditor of court who shall—

(*a*) tax the expenses chargeable against the debtor under Schedule 1 to this Act;

(*b*) certify the balance due by or to the debtor following the poinding and sale; and

(*c*) make a report to the sheriff,

but shall not alter the amount of the expenses or of the balance referred to in paragraph (*b*) above without first giving all interested persons an opportunity to make representations.

(5) On receipt of the auditor's report, the sheriff may make an order—

(*a*) declaring the balance due by or to the debtor, as certified by the auditor;

(*b*) declaring such a balance after making modifications to the balance as so certified; or

(*c*) if he is satisfied that there has been a substantial irregularity in the poinding and sale (other than the making of the report of sale after the expiry of the period mentioned in subsection (1) above), declaring the poinding and sale to be void, in which case (subject to subsection (9) below) he may make such consequential order as appears to him to be necessary in the circumstances,

and the sheriff clerk shall intimate the sheriff's order under this subsection to the debtor.

(6) The sheriff shall not make an order under subsection (5)(*b*) or (*c*) above without first giving all interested persons an opportunity to be heard.

(7) The auditor of court shall not be entitled to charge a fee in respect of his report.

(8) The report of sale and the auditor's report shall be retained by the sheriff clerk for the period prescribed by Act of Sederunt and during that period they shall be open for inspection in the sheriff clerk's office by any interested person on payment of such fee as may be prescribed in an order made under section 2 of the Courts of Law Fees (Scotland) Act 1895.

(9) An order under subsection (5)(*c*) above shall not affect the title of a person to any article acquired by him at the warrant sale, or subsequently, in good faith and for value.

(10) Any rule of law whereby the sheriff may refuse to receive the report of sale shall cease to have effect.

Articles belonging to third parties or in common ownership

Release from poinding of articles belonging to third party

40.—(1) An officer of court may, at any time after the execution of a poinding and before the warrant sale, release an article from the poinding if—

(*a*) he is satisfied that the article belongs to a third party; and

(*b*) the debtor or other person in possession of the article does not deny that it belongs to the third party.

(2) Where, on an application made to him by a third party, at any time after the execution of a poinding and before the warrant sale, the sheriff is satisfied that a pointed article belongs to that third party, he shall make an order releasing it from the poinding.

(3) The making of an application under subsection (2) above shall not prejudice the taking of any other proceedings by the third party for the recovery of a poinded article belonging to him, and an order of the sheriff under that subsection shall not be binding in any other proceedings.

(4) The release of a poinded article under subsection (1) above—

(*a*) shall be mentioned in the next subsequent application (if any) which is made for warrant of sale or for variation of warrant of sale; or

(*b*) if it takes place after an application for warrant of sale (or variation thereof) has been made and before it has been disposed of, shall be reported as soon as is reasonably practicable by the officer of court to the sheriff; or

(*c*) in any other case, shall be mentioned in any report of sale.

(5) Where an article has been released from a poinding under this section, an officer of court may, notwithstanding section 25 of this Act, poind other articles belonging to the debtor in the same premises.

Poinding and sale of articles in common ownership

41.—(1) Articles which are owned in common by a debtor and a third party may be poinded and disposed of in accordance with this Part of this Act in satisfaction of the debts of that debtor.

(2) Where, at any time after the execution of a poinding and before the warrant sale, a third party—

(*a*) claims that a poinded article is owned in common by the debtor and himself; and

(*b*) pays to the officer of court a sum equal to the value of the debtor's interest in the article,

the officer of court may, unless the debtor (or the person in possession of the article, if not the debtor) denies the claim, release the article from the poinding.

(3) If, on an application made by a third party, at any time after the execution of a poinding and before the warrant sale, the sheriff is satisfied that a poinded article is owned in common by the debtor and that third party and either—

(*a*) the third party undertakes to pay to the officer of court a sum equal to the value of the debtor's interest in the article; or

(*b*) the sheriff is satisfied that the continued poinding of that article or its sale under warrant of sale would be unduly harsh to the third party in the circumstances,

he shall make an order releasing the article from the poinding.

(4) A release under subsection (2) above or where subsection (3)(*a*) above applies shall not become effective until the granting by the officer of court of a receipt for payment in accordance therewith, when the debtor's interest in the released article shall be transferred to the third party.

(5) A release of a poinded article under subsection (2) above—

(*a*) shall be mentioned in the next subsequent application (if any) which is made for warrant of sale or for variation of warrant of sale; or (*b*) if it takes place after an application for warrant of sale (or variation thereof) has been made and before it has been disposed of, shall be reported as soon as is reasonably practicable by the officer of court to the sheriff; or

(*c*) in any other case, shall be mentioned in any report of sale.

(6) Where an article is released in pursuance of subsection (3)(*b*) above from a poinding, an officer of court may, notwithstanding section 25 of this Act, poind other articles belonging to the debtor in the same premises.

(7) This subsection applies where, at any time after the execution of a poinding, a third party claims that any of the poinded articles is owned in common by the debtor and himself but does not seek release of the article from the poinding, and either—

(*a*) the claim is admitted by the creditor and the debtor; or

(*b*) the claim is not admitted by both the creditor and the debtor, but the sheriff, on an application made to him, is satisfied that the claim is valid.

(8) Where subsection (7) above applies, the creditor shall pay to the third party—

(*a*) if the article is sold, the fraction of the proceeds of sale (or of the value of that article fixed under section 20(4) of this Act, whichever is the greater) which corresponds to the third party's interest in the article;

(*b*) if ownership of the article passes to the creditor in default of sale, the fraction of the value of the article fixed under section 20(4) of this Act which corresponds to the third party's interest in the article.

Supplementary

Certain proceedings under Part II to postpone further steps in the diligence

42.—(1) Where an application under any of the provisions of this Act listed in subsection (3) below has been made, it shall be not be competent during a relevant period to grant a warrant of sale in respect of the poinded articles, to remove them for sale or to hold a warrant sale.

(2) Where subsection (1) above applies, a relevant period shall be disregarded in calculating—

(*a*) the period within which a warrant sale is required to be held under section 31(2)(*b*) of this Act; or

(*b*) the period on the expiry of which the poinding ceases to have effect under section 27 of this Act.

(3) The provisions referred to in subsection (1) above are—

(*a*) section 16(4), 23(1), 40(2) or 41(3) (release of poinded articles);

(*b*) section 24(1) or (3) (invalidity, cessation or recall of poinding);

(*c*) section 26(1) (sist of proceedings in poinding of mobile homes);

(*d*) section 28(4) (restoration of articles removed without consent or authority);

(*e*) section 28(5) (recall of order under section 28(4)).

(4) In subsections (1) and (2) above "a relevant period" means—

(*a*) the period while the application is pending;

(*b*) where the application has been disposed of by the sheriff—

(i) the period during which an application for leave to appeal may be made;

(ii) where an application for leave to appeal is made, the period until leave has been refused or the application has been abandoned;

(iii) where leave to appeal has been granted, the period during which an appeal may be made; or

(iv) where an appeal against the decision is made, the period until the matter has been finally determined or the appeal has been abandoned.

Conjoining of further poinding with original poinding

43.—(1) Subject to subsection (2) below, where a report of a further poinding by the same creditor to enforce the same debt executed in pursuance of section 9(12), 23(2), 28(2) or (6), 29(2), 40(5) or 41(6) of this Act has been received under section 22 of this Act, the sheriff shall, on an application made to him by the creditor or by an officer of court on his behalf, make an order conjoining the further poinding with the original poinding.

(2) It shall not be competent for the sheriff to make an order under subsection (1) above—

(*a*) where a warrant of sale has been granted in respect of the original poinding or the further poinding;

(*b*) until 14 days after the date of execution of the further poinding; or

(*c*) while an application under this Part of this Act in relation to the further poinding is pending or, where such an application has been disposed of by the sheriff—

(i) until the period for leave to appeal has expired without an application for leave having been made;

(ii) where an application for leave to appeal is made, until leave has been refused or the application has been abandoned;

(iii) where leave to appeal has been granted, until the period for an appeal has expired without an appeal being made; or

(iv) where an appeal against the decision is made, until the matter has been finally determined or the appeal has been abandoned.

(3) Where the sheriff makes an order under subsection (1) above, it shall not thereafter be competent for him to grant any application for warrant of sale relating to the original poinding which is pending when the order is made.

(4) The effect of an order under subsection (1) above shall be that thereafter the further poinding shall be treated for all purposes as if it were part of the original poinding, except that the references to a poinding being invalid or having ceased to have effect in sections 24(1), 30(2)(*a*)(i) and 35(2)(*a*) of this Act shall be construed as references to either poinding being invalid or having ceased to have effect.

(5) The decision of the sheriff under subsection (1) above shall not be subject to appeal.

Expenses of poinding and sale

44. Schedule 1 to this Act shall have effect for the purposes of determining the liability, as between the creditor and the debtor, for expenses incurred in serving a charge and in the process of poinding and warrant sale.

Interpretation of Part II

45. In this Part of this Act—

"dwellinghouse" includes a caravan, a houseboat and any structure adapted for use as a residence;

"the poinding schedule" means the schedule provided for in section 20(5) of this Act;

"the report of sale" means the report provided for in section 39(1) of this Act;

"the sum recoverable" means the total of—

(*a*) the amount outstanding of the sum due by the debtor under the decree or other document on which the diligence proceeds (including any interest thereon and any expenses decerned for);

(*b*) any sum due under section 93(5) of this Act; and

(*c*) any expenses which have been incurred in serving a charge and in the process of poinding and sale which are chargeable against the debtor under Schedule 1 to this Act.

PART III

DILIGENCE AGAINST EARNINGS

Introduction

New diligences against earnings

46.—(1) The following diligences against earnings of a debtor in the hands of his employer shall replace the diligence of arrestment and action of furthcoming against such earnings—

(*a*) a diligence, to be known as an "earnings arrestment", to enforce the payment of any ordinary debt which is due as at the date of execution of the diligence;

(*b*) a diligence, to be known as a "current maintenance arrestment", to enforce the payment of current maintenance;

(*c*) an order, to be known as a "conjoined arrestment order", to enforce the payment of two or more debts owed to different creditors against the same earnings.

(2) Any rule of law whereby there is exempted from arrestment of earnings of a debtor in the hands of his employer a reasonable amount for the subsistence of the debtor and his dependants shall cease to have effect.

Earnings arrestments

General effect of earnings arrestment

47.—(1) Subject to section 69 of this Act, an earnings arrestment shall have the effect of requiring the employer of a debtor, while the arrestment is in effect, to deduct a sum calculated in accordance with section 49 of this Act from the debtor's net earnings on every pay-day and, as soon as is reasonably practicable, to pay any sum so deducted to the creditor.

(2) Subject to sections 59 (priority among arrestments), 62 (relationship of conjoined arrestment order with certain other arrestments) and 90 (provisions relating to charges for payment) of this Act, an earnings arrestment—

(*a*) shall come into effect on the date of its execution, being the date on which a schedule in the form prescribed by Act of Sederunt (to be known as an "earnings arrestment schedule") is served on the employer; and

(*b*) shall remain in effect until the debt recoverable has been paid or otherwise extinguished, the debtor has ceased to be employed by the employer, or the arrestment has been recalled or abandoned by the creditor or has for any other reason ceased to have effect.

Debt recoverable by earnings arrestment

48.—(1) Subject to subsections (2) and (3) below, the debt recoverable by an earnings arrestment shall consist of the following sums, in so far as outstanding—

(*a*) any ordinary debt and any expenses due under the decree or other document on which the earnings arrestment proceeds;

(*b*) any interest on those sums which has accrued at the date of execution of the earnings arrestment; and

(*c*) the expenses incurred in executing the earnings arrestment and the charge which preceded it.

(2) In relation to arrears of maintenance, the ordinary debt referred to in subsection (1)(*a*) above shall be the amount of those arrears less any sum which the debtor is entitled to deduct from that amount under any enactment in respect of income tax.

(3) Any sum mentioned in subsection (1) above shall be included in the debt recoverable only if, and to the extent that, it is specified in the earnings arrestment schedule.

(4) It shall be competent for a creditor to enforce payment of more than one debt payable to him by the same debtor by means of a single earnings arrestment, whether the arrestment is executed in pursuance of the same warrant or of two or more different warrants authorising diligence.

Deductions from net earnings to be made by employer

49.—(1) The sum to be deducted under section 47 of this Act on any pay-day shall be—

(*a*) where the debtor's earnings are payable weekly, the sum specified in column 2 of Table A in Schedule 2 to this Act opposite the band in column 1 of that Table within which his net earnings payable on that pay-day fall;

(*b*) where his earnings are payable monthly, the sum specified in column 2 of Table B in that Schedule opposite the band in column 1 of that Table within which his net earnings payable on that pay-day fall;

(*c*) where his earnings are payable at regular intervals of a whole number of weeks or months, the sum arrived at by—

(i) calculating what would be his weekly or monthly net earnings by dividing the net earnings payable to him on the pay-day by that whole number (of weeks or months, as the case may be);

(ii) ascertaining the sum specified in column 2 of Table A (if the whole number is of weeks) or of Table B (if the whole number is of months) in Schedule 2 to this Act opposite the band in column 1 of that Table within which the notional net earnings calculated under sub-paragraph (i) above fall; and

(iii) multiplying that sum by the whole number (of weeks or months, as the case may be).

(2) Where the debtor's earnings are payable at regular intervals other than at intervals to which subsection (1) above applies, the sum to be deducted on any pay-day under section 47 of this Act shall be arrived at by—

(*a*) calculating what would be his daily net earnings by dividing the net earnings payable to him on the pay-day by the number of days in the interval;

(*b*) ascertaining the sum specified in column 2 of Table C in Schedule 2 to this Act opposite the band in column 1 of that Table within which the notional net earnings calculated under paragraph (*a*) above fall; and

(*c*) multiplying that sum by the number of days in the interval.

(3) Where the debtor's earnings are payable at irregular intervals, the sum to be deducted on any pay-day under section 47 of this Act shall be arrived at by—

(*a*) calculating what would be his daily net earnings by dividing the net earnings payable to him on the pay-day—

(i) by the number of days since earnings were last paid to him; or

(ii) if the earnings are the first earnings to be paid to him by the employer, by the number of days since he commenced his employment with the employer;

(*b*) taking the sum specified in column 2 of Table C in Schedule 2 to this Act opposite the band in column 1 of that Table within which the notional net earnings calculated under paragraph (*a*) above fall; and

(*c*) multiplying that sum by the number of days mentioned in paragraph (*a*) above.

(4) Where on the same pay-day there are paid to the debtor both earnings payable at regular intervals and earnings which are not payable at regular intervals, for the purpose of arriving at the sum to be deducted on that pay-day under section 47 of this Act, all those earnings shall be aggregated and treated as earnings payable at the regular interval.

(5) Where earnings payable to a debtor at regular intervals are paid to him on one pay-day and earnings which are not payable at regular intervals are paid to him on a different pay-day, the sum to be deducted on each of those pay-days under section 47 of this Act in respect of those earnings which are not paid at regular intervals shall be 20 per cent. of the net earnings paid to him on that pay-day.

(6) Where earnings are paid to a debtor by two or more series of payments at regular intervals—

(*a*) if the intervals are of different lengths—

(i) for the purpose of arriving at the sum to be deducted under section 47 of this Act, whichever of subsections (1) and (2) above is appropriate shall apply to the series with the shortest interval; and

(ii) in relation to the earnings paid in any other series, the said sum shall be 20 per cent. of the net earnings;

(*b*) if the intervals are of the same length and payments in more than one series are payable on the same day—

(i) the payments in those series shall be aggregated and whichever of subsections (1) and (2) above is appropriate shall apply to the aggregate; and

(ii) paragraph (*a*)(ii) above shall apply to every other series;

(*c*) if the intervals are of the same length and no two payments are payable on the same day paragraph (*a*)(i) above shall apply to such series as the employer may choose, and paragraph (*a*)(ii) above shall apply to every other series.

(7) The Lord Advocate may, by regulations, vary—

(*a*) Tables A, B and C of Schedule 2 to this Act;

(*b*) the percentage specified in subsections (5) and (6)(*a*)(ii) above,

and such regulations may make different provision for different cases.

(8) Subject to section 69(1) and (2) of this Act, regulations under subsection (7) above shall not apply in relation to an existing earnings arrestment unless and until the creditor or the debtor intimates the making of the regulations to the employer in the form prescribed by Act of Sederunt.

Review of earnings arrestment

50.—(1) If the sheriff is satisfied that an earnings arrestment is invalid or has ceased to have effect he shall, on an application by the debtor or the person on whom the earnings arrestment schedule was served, make an order declaring that to be the case, and may make such consequential order as appears to him to be necessary in the circumstances; and the sheriff clerk shall intimate any order under this subsection to the debtor, the creditor and the person on whom the earnings arrestment schedule was served.

(2) An order under subsection (1) above declaring that an arrestment is invalid or has ceased to have effect shall not be subject to appeal.

(3) The sheriff, on an application by the debtor, the creditor or the employer, may make an order determining any dispute as to the operation of an earnings arrestment.

(4) Without prejudice to section 57(5) of this Act, the sheriff, when making an order under subsection (3) above, may order—

(*a*) the reimbursement of any payment made in the operation of the arrestment which ought not to have been made; or

(*b*) the payment of any sum which ought to have been paid in the operation of the arrestment but which has not been paid.

(5) An order under subsection (4) above shall require the person against whom it is made to pay interest on the sum to be paid by him under the order at the specified rate from such date as the sheriff shall specify in the order.

Current maintenance arrestments

General effect of current maintenance arrestment

51.—(1) Subject to sections 58(2) and 69 of this Act, a current maintenance arrestment shall have the effect of requiring the employer of the debtor while the arrestment is in effect to deduct a sum calculated in accordance with section 53 of this Act from the debtor's net earnings on every pay-day and as soon as is reasonably practicable to pay any sum so deducted to the creditor.

(2) Subject to sections 59 to 62 of this Act, a current maintenance arrestment—

(*a*) shall come into effect on the date of its execution, being the date on which a schedule in the form prescribed by Act of Sederunt (to be known as a "current maintenance arrestment schedule") is served on the employer of the debtor; and

(*b*) shall remain in effect until the debtor has ceased to be employed by the employer concerned, or the arrestment has been recalled or abandoned by the creditor or has ceased to have effect under section 55(8) of this Act or for any other reason.

(3) The expenses incurred in executing a current maintenance arrestment shall be recoverable from the debtor as an ordinary debt.

(4) Subject to section 52(2)(*b*) of this Act, a current maintenance arrestment schedule shall specify the maintenance payable by the debtor expressed as a daily rate.

(5) For the purposes of subsection (4) above the daily rate shall be arrived at—

(*a*) where the maintenance is paid monthly, by multiplying the monthly rate by 12 and dividing it by 365;

(*b*) where it is paid quarterly, by multiplying the quarterly rate by four and dividing it by 365.

(6) No interest shall accrue on any arrears of the maintenance which arise while a current maintenance arrestment is in effect.

Enforcement of 2 or more obligations to pay maintenance

52.—(1) This section applies where one or more maintenance orders are in effect which provide for the payment by the same debtor to the same person (whether for his own benefit or for another person's) of maintenance in respect of more than one individual.

(2) Where this section applies—

(*a*) all or any of the obligations to pay maintenance may be enforced by a single current maintenance arrestment against the same earnings; and

(*b*) in that case, the current maintenance arrestment schedule shall specify one daily rate of maintenance, being the aggregate of the daily rates calculated in accordance with section 51(5) of this Act.

Deductions from net earnings to be made by employer

53.—(1) The sum to be deducted from a debtor's net earnings on a pay-day under section 51 of this Act shall be whichever is the lesser of the amounts mentioned in paragraphs (*a*) and (*b*) of subsection (2) below, less any sum which the debtor is entitled to deduct under any enactment in respect of income tax.

(2) The amounts referred to in subsection (1) above are—

(*a*) subject to subsections (3) and (5) below, a sum arrived at by multiplying the daily rate of maintenance (as specified in the current maintenance arrestment schedule) by the number of days—

(i) since the last pay-day when a deduction was made in respect of the arrestment; or

(ii) if there was no such pay-day, since the date of execution of the arrestment; or

(*b*) any net earnings in so far as they exceed the sum of £5 per day for the number of days mentioned in paragraph (*a*) above.

(3) The sum specified in subsection (2)(*b*) above may be varied by regulations made by the Lord Advocate and such regulations may make different provision for different cases.

(4) Subject to section 69(1) and (2) of this Act, regulations under subsection (3) above shall not apply to an existing current maintenance arrestment unless and until the creditor or the debtor intimates the making of the regulations to the employer in the form prescribed by Act of Sederunt.

(5) An employer operating a current maintenance arrestment shall be entitled, but shall not be required, to apply a change in the small maintenance payments limits before the creditor or the debtor intimates the change to the employer in the form prescribed by Act of Sederunt.

[1] (6) For the purposes of subsection (5) above, the small maintenance payment limits are the rates mentioned in section 351(2) of the Income and Corporation Taxes Act 1988.

NOTE

[1] As amended by the Income and Corporation Taxes Act 1988, Sched. 29.

Current maintenance arrestment to be preceded by default

54.—[1] (1) Subject to subsections (2) and (3) below, a current maintenance arrestment schedule may be served in pursuance of a maintenance order which is subsisting at the date of such service only if—

(*a*) the creditor has intimated to the debtor in the manner prescribed by Act of Sederunt—

(i) in the case of an order mentioned in paragraph (*a*) or (*b*) of the definition of "maintenance order" in section 106 of this Act, the making of the order;

(ii) in the case of an order mentioned in paragraph (*c*), (*e*), (*f*), (*g*) or (*h*) thereof, the registration mentioned in the paragraph concerned;

(iii) in the case of an order mentioned in paragraph (*d*) thereof, the confirmation of the order mentioned in that paragraph;

(*b*) at least four weeks have elapsed since the date of intimation under paragraph (*a*) above; and

(*c*) except where section 56 of this Act applies, at the time when it is proposed to serve the schedule, a sum not less than the aggregate of three instalments of maintenance remains unpaid.

(2) Subsection (1) above shall not apply where—

(*a*) the maintenance order is one that has been registered in Scotland as mentioned in paragraph (*c*), (*e*), (*f*) or (*g*) of the said definition; and

(*b*) a certificate of arrears (within the meaning of section 21 of the Maintenance Orders (Reciprocal Enforcement) Act 1972) was produced to the court in Scotland which registered the order to the effect that at the time at which the certificate was issued the debtor was in arrears in his payment of instalments under the order.

(3) Where a current maintenance arrestment which was validly executed has ceased to have effect otherwise than by virtue of its recall under section 55(2) of this Act, the creditor may within three months after the date when the arrestment ceased to have effect execute another current maintenance arrestment without complying with subsection (1) above.

NOTE

[1] Amended (*prosp.*) by the Child Support Act 1991, Sched. 5, para. 8(4).

Review and termination of current maintenance arrestment

55.—(1) If the sheriff is satisfied, on an application by the debtor or the person on whom the current maintenance arrestment schedule was served, that a current maintenance arrestment is invalid or has ceased to have effect, he shall make an order declaring that to be the case, and may make such consequential order as appears to him to be necessary in the circumstances.

(2) If the sheriff is satisfied, on an application by the debtor, that the debtor is unlikely to default again in paying maintenance, he may make an order recalling a current maintenance arrestment.

(3) The sheriff clerk shall intimate any order made under subsection (1) or (2) above to the debtor, the creditor and the person on whom the current maintenance arrestment schedule was served.

(4) An order under subsection (1) above declaring that an arrestment is invalid or has ceased to have effect or under subsection (2) above shall not be subject to appeal.

(5) The sheriff, on an application by the debtor, the creditor or the employer, may make an order determining any dispute as to the operation of a current maintenance arrestment.

(6) Without prejudice to section 57(5) of this Act, the sheriff, when making an order under subsection (5) above, may order—

(*a*) the reimbursement of any payment made in the operation of the arrestment which ought not to have been made;

(*b*) the payment of any sum which ought to have been paid in the operation of the arrestment but which has not been paid.

(7) An order under subsection (6) above shall require the person against whom it is made to pay interest on the sum to be paid by him under the order at the specified rate, and such interest shall be payable as from such date as the sheriff shall specify in the order.

(8) A current maintenance arrestment shall cease to have effect—

(*a*) on the coming into effect of an order or decree which varies, supersedes or recalls a maintenance order which is being enforced by the arrestment;

(*b*) on an obligation to pay maintenance under a maintenance order being so enforced ceasing or ceasing to be enforceable in Scotland.

(9) In the case of an order mentioned in paragraph (*c*), (*e*), (*f*) or (*g*) of the definition of "maintenance order" in section 106 of this Act, the reference in subsection (8)(*a*) above to the coming into effect of an order or decree shall be construed as a reference to the registration of the order in Scotland.

Effect of new maintenance order on current maintenance arrestment

56.—(1) Where a maintenance order (referred to in this section as "the earlier order") which is being enforced by a current maintenance arrestment is varied or superseded by an order or decree granted by a court in Scotland (referred to in this section as "the later order"), the later order may include a condition that it shall not come into effect until the earlier of—

(*a*) the expiry of such period specified in the later order as the court considers necessary to allow notice to be given to the employer that the earlier order has been varied or superseded; or

(*b*) the service of a new current maintenance arrestment schedule in pursuance of the later order.

(2) Subsection (1) above shall not apply where the earlier order includes an order for the payment of aliment for the benefit of a spouse and the later order includes an order for the payment of a periodical allowance on divorce or on the granting of a declarator of nullity of marriage for the benefit of that spouse.

General

Failure to comply with arrestment, manner of payment and creditor's duty when arrestment ceases to have effect

57.—(1) Subject to section 69(4) of this Act, where an employer fails to comply with an earnings arrestment or a current maintenance arrestment—

(*a*) he shall be liable to pay to the creditor any sum which he would have paid to him under section 47(1) or 51(1) of this Act if he had so complied; and

(*b*) he shall not be entitled to recover any sum which he has paid to the debtor in contravention of the arrestment.

(2) Subject to subsection (3) below, a creditor shall not be entitled to refuse to accept payment under section 47(1) or 51(1) of this Act which is tendered by cheque or by such other method as may be prescribed by Act of Sederunt.

(3) If a cheque tendered in payment under section 47(1) or 51(1) of this Act is dishonoured or for any other reason the method of payment used by the employer is ineffectual, the creditor may insist that the payment concerned and any future payment under that provision shall be tendered in cash.

(4) Where—

(*a*) the debt recoverable under an earnings arrestment is paid or otherwise extinguished;

(*b*) a current maintenance arrestment ceases to have effect under section 55(8) above; or

(*c*) the debt being enforced by an earnings arrestment ceases to be enforceable by diligence,

the creditor shall, as soon as is reasonably practicable, intimate that fact to the employer.

(5) Where an event mentioned in subsection (4) above occurs, any sum paid by an employer—

(*a*) under an earnings arrestment, in excess of the debt recoverable; or

(*b*) under a current maintenance arrestment, in excess of the sum to be deducted under section 51(1) of this Act,

shall be recoverable by the debtor from the creditor with interest on that sum at the specified rate.

(6) Without prejudice to subsection (5) above, where a creditor has failed to comply with subsection (4) above the sheriff, on an application by the debtor, may make an order requiring the creditor to pay to the debtor an amount not exceeding twice the amount recoverable by the debtor under the said subsection (5).

Simultaneous operation of earnings and current maintenance arrestment

58.—(1) Subject to subsection (2) below, one earnings arrestment and one current maintenance arrestment may be in effect simultaneously against earnings payable to the same debtor by the same employer.

(2) If on any pay-day the net earnings of the debtor are less than the total of the sums required to be paid under sections 47(1) and 51(1) of this Act, the employer shall—

(*a*) first operate the earnings arrestment; and

(*b*) secondly operate the current maintenance arrestment against the balance of the net earnings in accordance with section 53(1) of this Act.

Priority among arrestments

59.—(1) While an earnings arrestment is in effect, any other earnings arrestment against the earnings of the same debtor payable by the same employer shall not be competent.

(2) While a current maintenance arrestment is in effect, any other current maintenance arrestment against the earnings of the same debtor payable by the same employer shall not be competent.

(3) Where an employer receives on the same day two or more earnings arrestment schedules or two or more current maintenance arrestment schedules relating to earnings payable by him to the same debtor—

(*a*) if the employer receives the schedules at different times and he is aware of the respective times of receipt, only the earnings arrestment or, as the case may be, the current maintenance arrestment to which the first schedule he received relates shall have effect;

(*b*) in any other case, only such one of the earnings arrestments or, as the case may be, current maintenance arrestments as he shall choose shall have effect.

(4) Where a creditor (referred to in this section as "the second creditor") serves on an employer an earnings arrestment schedule or, as the case may be, a current maintenance arrestment schedule and, by virtue of this section, the arrestment to which that schedule relates does not come into effect, the employer shall as soon as is reasonably practicable give the following information to the second creditor regarding any other earnings arrestment or current maintenance arrestment in effect against the earnings of the same debtor payable by the same employer—

(*a*) the name and address of the creditor;

(*b*) the date and place of execution; and

(*c*) the debt recoverable specified in the earnings arrestment schedule or, as the case may be, the daily rate of maintenance specified in the current maintenance arrestment schedule.

(5) If the employer fails without reasonable excuse to give information to the second creditor under subsection (4) above, the sheriff, on an application by the second creditor, may order the employer to give the required information to the second creditor.

Conjoined arrestment orders

Conjoined arrestment orders: general provision

60.—(1) This section applies where at the date of an application under subsection (2) below—

(*a*) there is in effect against the earnings of a debtor in the hands of a single employer an earnings arrestment or a current maintenance arrestment or (under section 58 of this Act) both; and

(*b*) a creditor, who may be a creditor already enforcing a debt by an arrestment mentioned above, (referred to in this section as "a qualified creditor") would be entitled, but for section 59(1) or (2) of this Act, to enforce his debt by executing an earnings arrestment or a current maintenance arrestment.

(2) Subject to subsection (4) below, where this section applies the sheriff, on an application made by a qualified creditor, shall make a conjoined arrestment order.

(3) A conjoined arrestment order shall—

(*a*) recall any arrestment mentioned in subsection (1)(*a*) above so that it shall cease to have effect on the coming into effect of the order; and

(*b*) require the employer concerned, while the order is in effect, to deduct a sum calculated in accordance with section 63 of this Act from the debtor's net earnings on any pay-day and to pay it as soon as is reasonably practicable to the sheriff clerk.

(4) It shall not be competent to make a conjoined arrestment order—

(*a*) where all the debts concerned are maintenance payable by the same debtor to the same person (whether for his own benefit or for another person's) so that, if the existing current maintenance arrestment were abandoned, they could all be enforced under section 52(2)(*a*) of this Act; or

(*b*) where there are only two debts, one an ordinary debt and one maintenance, so that they could be enforced under section 58(1) of this Act (one earnings arrestment and one current maintenance arrestment); or

(*c*) where the same person is the creditor or person to whom any maintenance is payable (as described in paragraph (*a*) above) in relation to all the debts sought to be enforced by the order.

(5) A conjoined arrestment order—

(*a*) shall come into effect seven days after a copy of it has been served on the employer under subsection (7) below; and

(*b*) shall remain in effect until a copy of an order recalling the conjoined arrestment order has been served on the employer under section 66(7) of this Act or the debtor ceases to be employed by him.

(6) A conjoined arrestment order shall be in the form prescribed by Act of Sederunt, and—

(*a*) where an ordinary debt is to be enforced, the order shall specify the amount recoverable in respect of the debt under the order; and

(*b*) where current maintenance is to be enforced, the order shall specify the maintenance expressed as a daily rate or, as the case may be, as an aggregate of the daily rates; and subsection (5) of section 51 of this Act shall apply for the purposes of this paragraph as it applies for the purposes of subsection (4) of that section.

(7) The sheriff clerk shall as soon as is reasonably practicable serve a copy of the conjoined arrestment order on the employer and the debtor, and on the creditor in every arrestment mentioned in subsection (1)(*a*) above.

(8) A decision of the sheriff making a conjoined arrestment order shall not be subject to appeal.

(9) Subject to section 69(4) of this Act, where an employer fails to comply with a conjoined arrestment order—

(*a*) the employer shall be liable to pay to the sheriff clerk any sum which he would have paid if he had so complied;

(*b*) the employer shall not be entitled to recover any sum which he has paid to the debtor in contravention of the order; and

(*c*) the sheriff, on an application by the sheriff clerk, may grant warrant for diligence against the employer for recovery of the sums which appear to the sheriff to be due.

Amount recoverable under conjoined arrestment order

61.—(1) Subject to subsection (2) below, the amount recoverable under any conjoined arrestment order in respect of an ordinary debt shall consist of the following sums, in so far as outstanding—

(*a*) any sum (including expenses) due under the decree or other document on which the creditor founds or, as the case may be, under section 51(3) of this Act;

(*b*) any interest on that sum which had accrued at the date of execution of the arrestment or, where no arrestment was executed, at the date of the making of the conjoined arrestment order; and

(*c*) where an earnings arrestment has been executed, the expenses of executing it and the charge which preceded it.

(2) Any sum mentioned in subsection (1) above shall be recoverable only if and to the extent that—

(*a*) it was specified in an earnings arrestment schedule in respect of an arrestment which is recalled under subsection (3)(*a*) of section 60 of this Act; or

(*b*) it is specified in the application under subsection (2) of that section.

(3) Where an obligation to pay maintenance is enforced by a conjoined arrestment order, no interest shall accrue on any arrears of maintenance which arise while the order is in effect.

(4) Subject to subsection (5) below, a creditor who makes an application under section 60(2) of this Act shall be entitled to recover as an ordinary debt under any conjoined arrestment order which is made his expenses in connection with the application to the extent that they are specified in the application.

(5) There shall not be recoverable under subsection (4) above any expenses incurred in serving an earnings arrestment schedule or a current

maintenance arrestment schedule on the employer after the date of the application.

Relationship of conjoined arrestment order with earnings and current maintenance arrestments

62.—(1) While a conjoined arrestment order is in effect, it shall not be competent to execute any earnings arrestment or current maintenance arrestment or for the sheriff to grant any other conjoined arrestment order against the earnings of the same debtor payable by the same employer.

(2) If, while a conjoined arrestment order is in effect, a creditor whose debt is not being enforced by it serves an earnings arrestment schedule or a current maintenance arrestment schedule, against earnings payable to the debtor, on the employer, the employer shall as soon as is reasonably practicable inform that creditor which court made the order.

(3) If, after an application is made under section 60(2) of this Act for a conjoined arrestment order and before any such order comes into effect, an earnings arrestment or a current maintenance arrestment against earnings payable by the employer to the debtor comes into effect under section 58(1) of this Act—

(*a*) the arrestment shall cease to have effect when the conjoined arrestment order comes into effect; and

(*b*) the employer shall, as soon as is reasonably practicable after the service of a copy of the conjoined arrestment order on him under section 60(7) of this Act, inform the creditor on whose behalf the arrestment was executed which court made the order.

(4) If an employer fails without reasonable excuse to give information to a creditor under subsection (2) or (3) above, the sheriff, on an application by the creditor, may order the employer to give the required information to the creditor.

(5) Where a conjoined arrestment order is in effect, the sheriff, on an application made by a creditor whose debt is not being enforced by the order and who, but for the order, would be entitled to enforce his debt by an earnings arrestment or a current maintenance arrestment, shall make an order varying the conjoined arrestment order so that the creditor's debt is included among the debts enforced by the conjoined arrestment order; and section 61(1), (2), (4) and (5) of this Act shall apply in relation to an application under this subsection as it applies in relation to an application under section 60 of this Act.

(6) The sheriff clerk shall as soon as is reasonably practicable serve a copy of an order under subsection (5) above on the debtor, the employer and the other creditors whose debts are being enforced by the conjoined arrestment order.

(7) Subject to section 69(2) of this Act, an order under subsection (5) above shall come into effect seven days after a copy of it has been served on the employer under subsection (6) above.

(8) Section 60(6) of this Act shall apply to a conjoined arrestment order as varied under subsection (5) above as it applies to a conjoined arrestment order mentioned in that section.

(9) A decision of the sheriff under subsection (5) above shall not be subject to appeal.

Sum payable by employer under conjoined arrestment order

63.—(1) Subject to section 69(3) of this Act, this section shall have effect for the purpose of determining the sum to be deducted on a pay-day and paid to the sheriff clerk under a conjoined arrestment order.

(2) Where all the debts are ordinary debts, the said sum shall be the sum which the employer would pay under section 47(1) of this Act if the debts were one debt being enforced on the pay-day by an earnings arrestment.

(3) Where all the debts are current maintenance, the sum shall be whichever is the lesser of the amounts mentioned in paragraphs (*a*) and (*b*) of

subsection (4) below, less any sum which the debtor is entitled to deduct under any enactment in respect of income tax.

(4) The amounts referred to in subsection (3) above are—

(*a*) the aggregate of the sums arrived at by multiplying each of the daily rates of maintenance (as specified in the conjoined arrestment order) by the number of days—

(i) since the last pay-day when a deduction from earnings was made by the employer under section 51(1) or 60(3)(*b*) of this Act in respect of the maintenance obligation; or

(ii) if there was no such previous pay-day, since the date when the conjoined arrestment order or any order under section 62(5) of this Act varying it came into effect; or

(*b*) any net earnings in so far as they exceed the sum of £5 per day for the number of days mentioned in paragraph (*a*) above.

(5) Where one or more of the debts are ordinary debts, and one or more are current maintenance, the sum shall be the aggregate of the following—

(*a*) the sum which the employer would pay under section 47(1) of this Act if the ordinary debt was being enforced on the pay-day by an earnings arrestment (where there is more than one ordinary debt, treating the aggregate amount of them as if it were one debt); and

(*b*) in relation to the debts which are current maintenance, the sum which would be payable under subsection (3) above if all the debts were current maintenance and so much of the debtor's net earnings as are left after deduction of the sum provided for in paragraph (*a*) above were his whole net earnings.

(6) The sum specified in subsection (4)(*b*) above may be varied by regulations made by the Lord Advocate and such regulations may make different provision for different cases.

(7) The sheriff clerk shall intimate to the employer operating a conjoined arrestment order, in the form prescribed by Act of Sederunt, the making of regulations under section 49(7) of this Act or subsection (6) above; and subject to section 69(1) and (2) of this Act, such regulations shall not apply to the conjoined arrestment order until such intimation.

(8) An employer operating a conjoined arrestment order in relation to current maintenance shall be entitled, but shall not be required, to apply a change in the small maintenance payments limits before the sheriff clerk intimates the change to the employer in the form prescribed by Act of Sederunt.

[1] (9) For the purposes of subsection (8) above, the small maintenance payment limits are the rates mentioned in section 351(2) of the Income and Corporation Taxes Act 1988.

(10) Subject to subsection (11) below, the sheriff clerk shall not be entitled to refuse to accept payment by the employer under section 60(3)(*b*) of this Act which is tendered by cheque or by such other method as may be prescribed by Act of Sederunt.

(11) If a cheque tendered in payment under section 60(3)(*b*) of this Act is dishonoured or for any other reason the method of payment used is ineffectual, the sheriff clerk may insist that the payment for which the cheque was tendered and any future payment by the employer under the conjoined arrestment order shall be tendered in cash.

NOTE

[1] As amended by the Income and Corporation Taxes Act 1988, Sched. 29.

Disbursement by sheriff clerk of sums received from employer

64. Sums paid to the sheriff clerk under section 60(3)(*b*) of this Act shall be disbursed by him to the creditors whose debts are being enforced by the conjoined arrestment order in accordance with Schedule 3 to this Act.

Operation of conjoined arrestment order

65.—(1) The sheriff may make an order determining any dispute as to the operation of a conjoined arrestment order, on an application by—

(*a*) the debtor;
(*b*) a creditor whose debt is being enforced by the order;
(*c*) the employer; or
(*d*) the sheriff clerk.

(2) Without prejudice to subsection (6) below, the sheriff, when making an order under subsection (1) above, may order—

(*a*) the reimbursement of any payment made in the operation of the conjoined arrestment order which ought not to have been made; or
(*b*) the payment of any sum which ought to have been paid in the operation of the conjoined arrestment order but which has not been paid.

(3) An order under subsection (2) above shall require the person against whom it is made to pay interest on the sum to be paid by him under the order at the specified rate from such date as the sheriff shall specify in the order.

(4) Where an ordinary debt is being enforced by a conjoined arrestment order, the creditor shall, as soon as is reasonably practicable after the debt recoverable has been paid or otherwise extinguished, or the debt has ceased to be enforceable by diligence, intimate that fact to the sheriff clerk.

(5) Where current maintenance is being enforced by a conjoined arrestment order, the creditor shall, as soon as is reasonably practicable after any obligation to pay such maintenance has ceased or has ceased to be enforceable by diligence, intimate that fact to the sheriff clerk.

(6) Any sum received by a creditor under a conjoined arrestment order in respect of—

(*a*) an ordinary debt, after the debt has been paid or otherwise extinguished or has ceased to be enforceable by diligence; or
(*b*) current maintenance after the obligation to pay such maintenance has ceased or has ceased to be enforceable by diligence;

shall be recoverable by the sheriff clerk from the creditor with interest on that sum at the specified rate.

(7) Without prejudice to subsection (6) above, where the creditor has failed to comply with subsection (4) or (5) above the sheriff may, on an application by the debtor, make an order requiring the creditor to pay to the debtor an amount not exceeding twice the amount recoverable by the sheriff clerk under subsection (6) above.

(8) Any amount recovered from a creditor by the sheriff clerk under subsection (6) above shall be disbursed by him to the creditors whose debts are being enforced by the conjoined arrestment order in accordance with Schedule 3 to this Act or, if there are no such creditors, shall be paid to the debtor.

Recall and variation of conjoined arrestment order

66.—(1) The sheriff shall make an order recalling a conjoined arrestment order—

(*a*) on an application by any of the persons mentioned in subsection (2) below, if he is satisfied—
  (i) that the conjoined arrestment order is invalid;
  (ii) that all the ordinary debts being enforced by the order have been paid or otherwise extinguished or have ceased to be enforceable by diligence and that all the obligations to pay current maintenance being so enforced have ceased or have ceased to be enforceable by diligence; or
  (iii) that the debtor's estate has been sequestrated; or
(*b*) on an application for recall of the order by all the creditors whose debts are being enforced by the order.

(2) The persons referred to in subsection (1)(*a*) above are—

(*a*) the debtor;

(*b*) any creditor whose debt is being enforced by the order;
(*c*) the person on whom a copy of the order or an order varying the order was served under section 60(7) or 62(6) of this Act;
(*d*) the sheriff clerk;
(*e*) if the debtor's estate has been sequestrated, the interim trustee appointed under section 13 of the Bankruptcy (Scotland) Act 1985 or the permanent trustee in the sequestration.

(3) Where the sheriff recalls a conjoined arrestment order under subsection (1) above, he may make such consequential order as appears to him to be necessary in the circumstances.

(4) Where—
(*a*) any ordinary debt being enforced by a conjoined arrestment order is paid or otherwise extinguished or ceases to be enforceable by diligence; or
(*b*) current maintenance is being so enforced and—
  (i) an order or decree comes into effect which varies, supersedes or recalls the maintenance order which is being enforced; or
  (ii) the obligation to pay maintenance has ceased or has ceased to be enforceable in Scotland,

the sheriff, on an application by the debtor, any creditor whose debt is being enforced by the conjoined arrestment order, the employer or the sheriff clerk, may make an order varying the conjoined arrestment order appropriately.

(5) In the case of an order mentioned in paragraph (*c*), (*e*), (*f*) or (*g*) of the definition of "maintenance order" in section 106 of this Act, the reference in subsection (4)(*b*)(i) above to the coming into effect of an order shall be construed as a reference to the registration of the order in Scotland.

(6) The sheriff may vary a conjoined arrestment order to give effect to a request by a creditor whose debt is being enforced by the order that it should cease to be so enforced.

(7) The sheriff clerk shall as soon as is reasonably practicable serve a copy of any order under subsection (1), (3), (4) or (6) above on the debtor, the employer (or, where he is not the employer, the person mentioned in subsection (2)(*c*) above), any creditor whose debt is being enforced by the conjoined arrestment order and, if the conjoined arrestment order has been recalled on the ground of the sequestration of the debtor's estate, the interim trustee or the permanent trustee in the sequestration, if known to the sheriff clerk.

(8) Subject to section 103(6) of this Act, an order under subsection (3) above shall not come into effect until a copy of the order has been served on the employer under subsection (7) above.

(9) An order under subsection (1) above shall not come into effect until a copy of the order has been served on the employer under subsection (7) above and shall not be subject to appeal.

(10) An order under subsection (4) or (6) above shall come into effect seven days after a copy of the order has been served on the employer under subsection (7) above.

Supplementary provisions

Equalisation of diligences not to apply

67. Paragraph 24 of Schedule 7 to the Bankruptcy (Scotland) Act 1985 (equalisation of arrestments and poindings used within 60 days before, and four months after, apparent insolvency) shall not apply in relation to an earnings arrestment, a current maintenance arrestment or a conjoined arrestment order.

Diversion of arrested earnings to Secretary of State

68. After section 25 of the Social Security Act 1986 there shall be inserted the following section—

"**Diversion of arrested earnings to Secretary of State**

25A.—(1) Where in Scotland a creditor who is enforcing a maintenance order or an alimentary bond or agreement by a current maintenance arrestment or a conjoined arrestment order is in receipt of income support, the creditor may in writing authorise the Secretary of State to receive any sums payable under the arrestment or order until the creditor ceases to be in receipt of income support or in writing withdraws the authorisation, whichever occurs first.

(2) On intimation by the Secretary of State—

(*a*) to the employer operating the current maintenance arrestment; or

(*b*) to the sheriff clerk operating the conjoined arrestment order;

of an authorisation under subsection (1) above, the employer or sheriff clerk shall, until notified by the Secretary of State that the authorisation has ceased to have effect, pay to the Secretary of State any sums which would otherwise be payable under the arrestment or order to the creditor.".

Restriction on liability of employer in operating diligence against earnings

69.—(1) An employer operating an earnings arrestment or a current maintenance arrestment or a conjoined arrestment order shall be entitled to apply regulations made under section 49(7), 53(3) or 63(6) of this Act before receiving intimation under section 49(8), 53(4) or 63(7) of this Act of the making of the regulations.

(2) Where a pay-day occurs within a period of seven days after the date of—

(*a*) service on the employer of an earnings arrestment schedule or a current maintenance arrestment schedule or a copy of a conjoined arrestment order or of a variation thereof; or

(*b*) intimation under section 49(8), 53(4) or 63(7) of this Act to the employer of the making of regulations,

the employer shall be entitled, but shall not be required, on that day to operate the arrestment or order or, as the case may be, to give effect to the regulations.

(3) Where, in accordance with subsection (2) above, the employer on a pay-day (referred to below as "the previous pay-day")—

(*a*) does not operate an earnings arrestment, current maintenance arrestment or conjoined arrestment order; or

(*b*) does not give effect to regulations,

he shall not include in any sum deducted from the net earnings of the debtor on a subsequent pay-day under the arrestment or order any sum in respect of the debtor's net earnings on the previous pay-day.

(4) No claim may be made by—

(*a*) the debtor or the creditor against the employer in respect of any deduction which has, or ought to have, been made by the employer from the debtor's net earnings, or any payment which has been, or ought to have been, made by him, under an earnings arrestment or a current maintenance arrestment; or

(*b*) the debtor, the sheriff clerk or any creditor against the employer in respect of any such deduction or payment which has been, or ought to have been, made under a conjoined arrestment order,

more than one year after the date when the deduction or payment has, or ought to have, been made.

(5) The employer shall not be liable to the debtor for any deduction made by him from the debtor's net earnings—

(*a*) under an earnings arrestment unless and until he receives intimation—

(i) from the creditor under section 57(4) of this Act that the debt recoverable has been paid or otherwise extinguished or has ceased to be enforceable by diligence;

(ii) from the sheriff clerk under section 9(7)(*b*) or 50(1) of this Act that an order has been made recalling the arrestment or, as the case may be, declaring that it is invalid or has ceased to have effect;
(iii) that the debtor's estate has been sequestrated; or
(iv) from the creditor that he has abandoned the arrestment;

(*b*) under a current maintenance arrestment unless and until he receives intimation—
(i) from the creditor under section 57(4) of this Act that the arrestment has ceased to have effect;
(ii) from the sheriff clerk under section 55(3) of this Act that an order has been made recalling the arrestment or declaring that the arrestment is invalid or has ceased to have effect;
(iii) that the debtor's estate has been sequestrated; or
(iv) from the creditor that he has abandoned the arrestment.

Execution and intimation of copies

70.—(1) When an officer of court serves an earnings arrestment schedule or a current maintenance arrestment schedule on the employer of the debtor he shall, if reasonably practicable, intimate a copy of the schedule to the debtor.

(2) Failure to intimate a copy of the schedule to the debtor shall not by itself render the arrestment invalid.

(3) Service of any such schedule shall be by registered or recorded delivery letter or, if such letter cannot be delivered, by any other competent mode of service.

(4) The certificate of execution of an earnings arrestment or a current maintenance arrestment shall be signed by the officer of court who effected the service.

(5) Section 17(1) of this Act shall apply to the service of an earnings arrestment schedule, a current maintenance arrestment schedule or a conjoined arrestment order as it applies to the execution of a poinding except where such service is by post.

Employer's fee for operating diligence against earnings

71. On any occasion on which an employer makes a payment to a creditor under an earnings arrestment or a current maintenance arrestment or to the sheriff clerk under a conjoined arrestment order, he may charge the debtor a fee of 50 pence or such other sum as may be prescribed in regulations made by the Lord Advocate which shall be deductible from the amount of the debtor's net earnings after any deduction has been made from them under section 47, 51 or 60 of this Act.

Effect of sequestration on diligence against earnings

[1] **72.**—(1) This section shall have effect where a debtor's estate is sequestrated.

(2) Any existing earnings arrestment, current maintenance arrestment or, subject to subsection (3) below, conjoined arrestment order shall cease to have effect on the date of sequestration.

(3) Any sum paid by the employer to the sheriff clerk under a conjoined arrestment order on a pay-day occurring before the date of sequestration shall be disbursed by the sheriff clerk under section 64 of this Act notwithstanding that the date of disbursement is after the date of sequestration.

(4) The execution of an earnings arrestment or the making of a conjoined arrestment order shall not be competent after the date of sequestration to enforce a debt in respect of which the creditor is entitled to make a claim in the sequestration.

(5) In this section "date of sequestration" has the same meaning as in section 12(4) of the Bankruptcy (Scotland) Act 1985.

NOTE

[1] Amended (*prosp.*) by the Child Support Act 1991, Sched. 5, para. 8(5).

Interpretation of Part III

73.—[1] (1) In this Part of this Act—

"creditor", in relation to maintenance, means the payee specified in the maintenance order or orders or anyone deriving title from the payee;

"current maintenance" means maintenance being deducted from earnings in accordance with section 53(1) or 63(3) or (5) of this Act;

"debt recoverable" has the meaning given in section 48(1) of this Act;

"decree or other document" means—

(*a*) a decree of the Court of Session or the sheriff or a document registered for execution in the Books of Council and Session or the sheriff court books;

(*b*) a summary warrant, a warrant for civil diligence or a bill protested for non-payment by a notary public;

(*c*) an order or determination which by virtue of any enactment is enforceable as if it were an extract registered decree arbitral bearing a warrant for execution issued by the sheriff;

(*d*) a civil judgment granted outside Scotland by a court, tribunal or arbiter which by virtue of any enactment or rule of law is enforceable in Scotland; or

(*e*) a document or settlement which by virtue of an Order in Council made under section 13 of the Civil Jurisdiction and Judgments Act 1982 is enforceable in Scotland,

on which, or on an extract of which, an earnings arrestment, a current maintenance arrestment or a conjoined arrestment order is founded;

"earnings" has the meaning given in subsection (2) below;

"employer" means any person who pays earnings to a debtor under a contract of service or apprenticeship, but—

(*a*) in relation to any sum payable as a pension within the meaning of subsection (2)(*c*) below, means the person paying that sum; and

(*b*) where the employee is an officer of the Crown, means, subject to subsection (5) below, the chief officer in Scotland of the department or other body concerned,

and "employee", "employed" and "employment" shall be construed accordingly;

"net earnings" means the earnings which remain payable to the debtor after the employer has deducted any sum which he is required to deduct in respect of—

(*a*) income tax;

(*b*) primary class 1 contributions under Part I of the Social Security Act 1975;

(*c*) amounts deductible under any enactment, or in pursuance of a request in writing by the debtor, for the purposes of a superannuation scheme within the meaning of the Wages Councils Act 1979;

"ordinary debt" means any debt (including a fine or any sum due under an order of court in criminal proceedings in respect of which a warrant for civil diligence has been issued, arrears of maintenance and the expenses of current maintenance arrestments) other than current maintenance;

"pay-day" means a day on which the employer of a debtor pays earnings to the debtor;

"sheriff", in relation to an application—

(*a*) under section 50(1), or (3), 55(1), (2) or (5) or 57(6) of this Act, means the sheriff having jurisdiction—

(i) over the place where the earnings arrestment or the current maintenance arrestment to which the application relates was executed; or

(ii) if that place is unknown to the applicant, over an established place of business of the debtor's employer;

(*b*) under section 59(5) or 62(4), means the sheriff having jurisdiction over the place where a creditor serves an earnings arrestment or a current maintenance arrestment schedule in relation to an arrestment which is not competent by reason of section 59 or 62 of this Act;

(*c*) under section 60(2), means the sheriff having jurisdiction over the place where the existing earnings arrestment or current maintenance arrestment or either such arrestment was executed;

(*d*) under section 60(9)(*c*), 62(5), 65 or 66 means the sheriff who made the conjoined arrestment order;

"specified rate", in relation to interest—

(*a*) included in a decree, order or extract, means the rate specified in such decree, order or extract (or deemed to be so specified by virtue of section 9 of the Sheriff Courts (Scotland) Extracts Act 1892);

(*b*) not included in a decree, order or extract, means the rate for the time being specified by virtue of that section.

(2) Subject to subsection (3) below, in this Part of this Act "earnings" means any sums payable to the debtor—

(*a*) as wages or salary;

(*b*) as fees, bonuses, commission or other emoluments payable under a contract of service or apprenticeship;

(*c*) as a pension, including a pension declared to be alimentary, an annuity in respect of past services, (whether or not the services were rendered to the person paying the annuity), and any periodical payments of compensation for the loss, abolition, relinquishment, or diminution in earnings of any office or employment; or

(*d*) as statutory sick pay.

(3) The following shall not be treated as earnings—

(*a*) a pension or allowance payable in respect of disablement or disability;

(*b*) any sum the assignation of which is precluded by section 203 of the Army Act 1955 or section 203 of the Air Force Act 1955, or any like sum payable to a member of the naval forces of the Crown, or to a member of any women's service administered by the Defence Council;

(*c*) in relation to the enforcement by an earnings arrestment of a debt other than maintenance, the wages of a seaman (other than a member of the crew of a fishing boat);

(*d*) any occupational pension payable under any enactment which precludes the assignation of the pension or exempts it from diligence;

(*e*) a pension, allowance or benefit payable under any enactment relating to social security;

(*f*) a guaranteed minimum pension within the meaning of the Social Security Pensions Act 1975;

(*g*) a redundancy payment within the meaning of section 81(1) of the Employment Protection (Consolidation) Act 1978.

(4) In subsection (3)(*c*) above—

(*a*) "seaman" has the same meaning as in section 742 of the Merchant Shipping Act 1894;

(*b*) "fishing boat" has the meaning given to it in section 370 of that Act as modified by section 744 thereof.

(5) Any question arising as to who is the chief officer in Scotland of a department or body referred to in paragraph (*b*) of the definition of "employer" in subsection (1) above shall be referred to and determined by the Minister for the Civil Service, and a document purporting to set out a determination of the Minister and signed by an official of the Minister shall be sufficient evidence of that determination.

NOTE

[1] Amended (*prosp.*) by the Child Support Act 1991, Sched. 5, para. 8(6).

PART IV

RECOVERY OF RATES AND TAXES ETC.

[Amendments to Acts reprinted in *The Parliament House Book* have been given effect.]

. . . .

Recovery of rates and taxes etc.

74.—(1) The enactments mentioned in Schedule 4 to this Act shall have effect subject to the amendments specified therein.

(2) A poinding and sale in pursuance of a summary warrant shall be proceeded with in accordance with Schedule 5 to this Act.

(3) No person shall be imprisoned for failure to pay rates or any tax.

(4) Section 248 of the Local Government (Scotland) Act 1947 (priority of claims for rates over other claims) is hereby repealed.

(5) The following provisions of the Exchequer Court (Scotland) Act 1856 are hereby repealed—

(*a*) in section 28 (extracts of exchequer decrees), the words from "except that" to the end;

(*b*) sections 29 to 34 (special modes of diligence for the enforcement of Crown debts);

(*c*) section 36 (effects of deceased Crown debtor may be attached by arrestment or poinding);

(*d*) section 42 (preference of Crown over other creditors).

. . . .

PART VI

WARRANTS FOR DILIGENCE AND CHARGES FOR PAYMENT

Effect of warrants for diligence in extract decrees and other documents

87.—(1) Every extract of a decree for the payment of money, or among other things for the payment of money, which is pronounced by—

(*a*) the Court of Session;

(*b*) the High Court of Justiciary; or

(*c*) the Court of Teinds,

shall contain a warrant in the form prescribed by Act of Sederunt or, as the case may be, by Act of Adjournal.

(2) The warrant referred to in subsection (1) above shall have the effect of authorising—

(*a*) in relation to an ordinary debt, the charging of the debtor to pay to the creditor within the period specified in the charge the sum specified in the extract and any interest accrued on the sum and, in the event of failure to make such payment within that period, the execution of an earnings arrestment and the poinding of articles belonging to the debtor and, if necessary for the purpose of executing the poinding, the opening of shut and lockfast places;

(*b*) in relation to an ordinary debt, an arrestment other than an arrestment of the debtor's earnings in the hands of his employer; and

(*c*) if the decree consists of or includes a maintenance order, a current maintenance arrestment in accordance with Part III of this Act.

(3) In section 7(1) of the Sheriff Courts (Scotland) Extracts Act 1892 (import of the warrant for execution), for the words from "it shall" to the end there shall be substituted the following words—

"the said warrant shall have the effect of authorising—

(*a*) in relation to an ordinary debt within the meaning of the Debtors (Scotland) Act 1987, the charging of the debtor to pay to the creditor within the period specified in the charge the sum specified in the extract and any interest accrued on the sum and, in the event of failure to make such payment within that period, the execution of an earnings arrestment and the poinding of articles belonging to the debtor and, if necessary for the purpose of executing the poinding, the opening of shut and lockfast places;

(*b*) in relation to an ordinary debt within the meaning of the Debtors (Scotland) Act 1987, an arrestment other than an arrestment of the debtor's earnings in the hands of his employer; and

(*c*) if the decree consists of or includes a maintenance order within the meaning of the Debtors (Scotland) Act 1987, a current maintenance arrestment in accordance with Part III of that Act.".

(4) For section 3 of the Writs Execution (Scotland) Act 1877 there shall be substituted the following section—

"Power to execute diligence by virtue of warrant

3. The warrant inserted in an extract of a document registered in the Books of Council and Session or in sheriff court books which contains an obligation to pay a sum of money shall have the effect of authorising—

(*a*) in relation to an ordinary debt within the meaning of the Debtors (Scotland) Act 1987, the charging of the debtor to pay to the creditor within the period specified in the charge the sum specified in the extract and any interest accrued on the sum and, in the event of failure to make such payment within that period, the execution of an earnings arrestment and the poinding of articles belonging to the debtor and, if necessary for the purpose of executing the poinding, the opening of shut and lockfast places;

[THE NEXT PAGE IS B 249]

(*b*) in relation to an ordinary debt within the meaning of the Debtors (Scotland) Act 1987, an arrestment other than an arrestment of the debtor's earnings in the hands of his employer; and

(*c*) if the document is a maintenance order within the meaning of the Debtors (Scotland) Act 1987, a current maintenance arrestment in accordance with Part III of that Act.".

(5) An extract of a decree in an action of poinding of the ground shall contain a warrant in the form prescribed by Act of Sederunt which shall have the effect of authorising a poinding of the ground.

Warrants for diligence: special cases

88.—(1) This section applies where a creditor has acquired by assignation intimated to the debtor, confirmation as executor, or otherwise a right to—

(*a*) a decree;

(*b*) an obligation contained in a document an extract of which, after the document has been registered in the Books of Council and Session or in sheriff court books, may be obtained containing warrant for execution;

(*c*) an order or determination which by virtue of any enactment is enforceable as if it were an extract registered decree arbitral bearing a warrant for execution issued by a sheriff,

either directly or through a third party from a person in whose favour the decree, order or determination was granted or who was the creditor in the obligation contained in the document.

(2) Where this section applies, the creditor who has acquired a right as mentioned in subsection (1) above may apply to the appropriate clerk for a warrant having the effect of authorising the execution at the instance of that creditor of any diligence authorised by an extract of the decree or document or by the order or determination, as the case may be.

(3) The applicant under subsection (2) above shall submit to the appropriate clerk—

(*a*) an extract of the decree or of the document registered as mentioned in subsection (1)(*b*) above or a certified copy of the order or determination; and

(*b*) the assignation (along with evidence of its intimation to the debtor), confirmation as executor or other document establishing the applicant's right.

(4) The appropriate clerk shall grant the warrant applied for under subsection (2) above if he is satisfied that the applicant's right is established.

(5) Where—

(*a*) a charge has already been served in pursuance of the decree, order, determination or registered document; and

(*b*) the applicant under subsection (2) above submits with his application the certificate of execution of the charge in addition to the documents mentioned in subsection (3) above,

a warrant granted under subsection (4) above shall authorise the execution at the instance of the applicant of diligence in pursuance of that charge.

(6) For the purposes of this section, "the appropriate clerk" shall be—

(*a*) in the case of a decree granted by the Court of Session or a document registered (whether before or after such acquisition) in the Books of Council and Session, a clerk of court of the Court of Session;

(*b*) in the case of a decree granted by the High Court of Justiciary, a clerk of Justiciary;

(*c*) in the case of a decree granted by a sheriff or a document registered (whether before or after such acquisition) in the books of a sheriff court, the sheriff clerk of that sheriff court;

(*d*) in the case of such an order or determination as is mentioned in subsection (1)(*c*) above, any sheriff clerk.

Abolition of letters of horning, horning and poinding, poinding, and caption

89. The granting of letters of horning, letters of horning and poinding, letters of poinding and letters of caption shall cease to be competent.

Provisions relating to charges for payment

90.—(1) Subject to subsection (2) below, the execution of a poinding or an earnings arrestment shall not be competent unless a charge for payment has been served on the debtor and the period for payment specified in the charge has expired without payment being made.

(2) Subsection (1) above shall not apply to a poinding or an earnings arrestment executed in pursuance of a summary warrant.

(3) The period for payment specified in any charge for payment served in pursuance of a warrant for execution shall be 14 days if the person on whom it is served is within the United Kingdom and 28 days if he is outside the United Kingdom or his whereabouts are unknown.

(4) Any such charge shall be in the form prescribed by Act of Sederunt or Act of Adjournal.

(5) Subject to subsection (6) below, where any such charge has been served, it shall not be competent to execute a poinding or an earnings arrestment by virtue of that charge more than two years after the date of such service.

(6) A creditor may reconstitute his right to execute a poinding or an earnings arrestment by the service of a further charge for payment.

(7) No expenses incurred in the service of a further charge for payment within the period of two years after service of the first charge shall be chargeable against the debtor.

(8) Registration of certificates of execution of charges for payment in a register of hornings shall cease to be competent.

Enforcement of certain warrants and precepts of sheriff anywhere in Scotland

91.—(1) The following may be executed anywhere in Scotland—

(*a*) a warrant for execution contained in an extract of a decree granted by a sheriff;

(*b*) a warrant for execution inserted in an extract of a document registered in sheriff court books;

(*c*) a summary warrant;

(*d*) a warrant of a sheriff for arrestment on the dependence of an action or in security;

(*e*) a precept (issued by a sheriff clerk) of arrestment in security of a liquid debt the term of payment of which has not arrived.

(2) A warrant or precept mentioned in subsection (1) above may be executed by a sheriff officer of—

(*a*) the court which granted it; or

(*b*) the sheriff court district in which it is to be executed.

PART VII

MISCELLANEOUS AND GENERAL

General provision relating to liability for expenses in court proceedings

92.—(1) Subject to subsection (2) below, a debtor shall not be liable to a creditor, nor a creditor to a debtor, for any expenses incurred by the other party in connection with an application, any objections to an application, or a hearing, under any provision of this Act.

(2) If—

(*a*) an application under any provision of this Act is frivolous;

(*b*) such an application is opposed on frivolous grounds; or (*c*) a party requires a hearing under any provision of this Act to be held on frivolous grounds,

the sheriff may award a sum of expenses, not exceeding £25 or such amount as may be prescribed in regulations made by the Lord Advocate, against the party acting frivolously in favour of the other party.

(3) Subsections (1) and (2) above do not apply to—

(*a*) expenses of poinding and sale for which provision is made in Schedule 1 to this Act or paragraphs 25 to 34 of Schedule 5 to this Act; or

(*b*) expenses incurred—

(i) under section 1 of this Act;

(ii) in connection with an appeal under any provision of this Act; or

(iii) by or against a person other than the debtor or a creditor in connection with an application under any provision of this Act.

Recovery from debtor of expenses of certain diligences

93.—(1) Subject to subsections (3) and (5) below, any expenses chargeable against the debtor which are incurred in—

(*a*) a poinding and sale (including the service of the charge preceding it);

(*b*) the service of an earnings arrestment schedule (including the service of the charge preceding it);

(*c*) an application for, or for inclusion in, a conjoined arrestment order under section 60(2) or 62(5) of this Act,

shall be recoverable from the debtor by the diligence concerned but not by any other legal process, and any such expenses which have not been recovered by the time the diligence is completed or otherwise ceases to have effect shall cease to be chargeable against the debtor.

(2) Subject to subsection (5) below, any expenses chargeable against the debtor which are incurred in the service of a schedule of arrestment and in an action of furthcoming or sale shall be recoverable from the debtor out of the arrested property; and the court shall grant a decree in the action of furthcoming for payment of the balance of any expenses not so recovered.

(3) The sheriff shall grant decree for payment of—

(*a*) any expenses awarded by him against the debtor in favour of the creditor under paragraph 8 or 11 of Schedule 1 or paragraph 30 or 33 of Schedule 5 to this Act; or

(*b*) any additional sum of expenses awarded by him against the debtor in favour of the creditor under paragraph 9 of Schedule 1 or paragraph 31 of Schedule 5 to this Act.

(4) Subsection (5) below applies where any diligence mentioned in subsection (1) or (2) above is—

(*a*) recalled under section 9(2)(*a*), (*d*) or (*e*) of this Act in relation to a time to pay order;

(*b*) in effect immediately before the date of sequestration (within the meaning of the Bankruptcy (Scotland) Act 1985) of the debtor's estate;

(*c*) in effect immediately before the presentation of a petition for an administration order under Part II of the Insolvency Act 1986;

(*d*) in effect against property of the debtor immediately before a floating charge attaches to all or part of that property under section 53(7) or 54(6) of that Act;

(*e*) in effect immediately before the commencement of the winding up, under Part IV or V of that Act, of the debtor;

(*f*) rendered unenforceable by virtue of the creditor entering into a composition contract or acceding to a trust deed for creditors or by virtue of the subsistence of a protected trust deed within the meaning of Schedule 5 to the Bankruptcy (Scotland) Act 1985; or

(*g*) recalled by a conjoined arrestment order.

(5) Where this subsection applies—

(*a*) the expenses of the diligence which were chargeable against the debtor shall remain so chargeable; and

(*b*) if the debtor's obligation to pay the expenses is not discharged under or by virtue of the time to pay order, sequestration, administration order, receivership, winding up, composition contract, trust deed for creditors or conjoined arrestment order, those expenses shall be recoverable by further diligence in pursuance of the warrant which authorised the original diligence.

(6) The expenses incurred in the execution of a current maintenance arrestment shall be recoverable by any diligence other than a current maintenance arrestment, and shall be so recoverable in pursuance of the warrant which authorised the current maintenance arrestment.

Ascription of sums recovered by diligence or while diligence is in effect

94.—(1) This section applies to any sums recovered by any of the following diligences—

(*a*) a poinding and sale;

(*b*) an earnings arrestment;

(*c*) an arrestment and action of furthcoming or sale; or

(*d*) a conjoined arrestment order in so far as it enforces an ordinary debt,

or paid to account of the sums recoverable by the diligence while the diligence is in effect.

(2) A sum to which this section applies shall be ascribed to the following in the order in which they are mentioned—

(*a*) the expenses already incurred in respect of—

(i) the diligence;

(ii) any previous diligence the expenses of which are chargeable against and recoverable from the debtor under section 93(5) of this Act;

(iii) the execution of a current maintenance arrestment;

(*b*) any interest, due under the decree or other document on which the diligence proceeds, which has accrued at the date of execution of the poinding, earnings arrestment or arrestment, or in the case of an ordinary debt included in a conjoined arrestment order which has accrued at the date of application under section 60(2) or 62(5) of this Act;

(*c*) any sum (including any expenses) due under the decree or other document, other than any expenses or interest mentioned in paragraphs (*a*) and (*b*) above.

Certain diligences terminated by payment or tender of full amount owing

95.—(1) Any of the following diligences—

(*a*) a poinding and sale;

(*b*) an earnings arrestment;

(*c*) an arrestment and action of furthcoming or sale,

shall cease to have effect if the full amount recoverable thereby is paid to the creditor, an officer of court, or any other person who has authority to receive payment on behalf of the creditor, or is tendered to any of those persons and the tender is not accepted within a reasonable time.

(2) Any rule of law whereby any diligence mentioned in subsection (1) above ceases to have effect on payment or tender of the sum due under the decree or other document is hereby abolished.

Provisions to assist debtor in proceedings under Act

96.—(1) No fees shall be payable by a debtor in connection with—

(*a*) any application by him;

(*b*) objections by him to an application by any other person; or

(*c*) a hearing held,

under any provision of this Act, to any officer of any office or department connected with the Court of Session or the sheriff court the expenses of which are paid wholly or partly out of the Consolidated Fund or out of money provided by Parliament.

(2) The sheriff clerk shall, if requested by the debtor—

(*a*) provide him with information as to the procedures available to him under this Act; and

(*b*) without prejudice to subsection (2) of section 6 of this Act, assist him in the completion of any form required in connection with any proceedings under this Act,

but the sheriff clerk shall not be liable for any error or omission by him in performing the duties imposed on him by this subsection or that subsection.

Lay representation

97. In relation to any proceedings before the sheriff under any provision of this Act, the power conferred on the Court of Session by section 32 of the Sheriff Courts (Scotland) Act 1971 (power of Court of Session to regulate civil procedure in sheriff court) shall extend to the making of rules permitting a party to such proceedings, in such circumstances as may be specified in the rules, to be represented by a person who is neither an advocate nor a solicitor.

Legal aid

98. At the end of Part II of Schedule 2 to the Legal Aid (Scotland) Act 1986 (proceedings for which civil legal aid shall not be available) there shall be added the following paragraphs—

"4. Subject to paragraph 5 below, civil legal aid shall not be available in relation to proceedings at first instance under the Debtors (Scotland) Act 1987, other than proceedings in connection with an application under section 1(1) or 3(1) of that Act to a Lord Ordinary or to the sheriff in an ordinary cause.

5. Nothing in paragraph 4 above shall preclude any third party to proceedings under the Debtors (Scotland) Act 1987 from obtaining legal aid in connection with those proceedings.".

Sequestration for rent or feuduty and arrestments other than arrestments of earnings

99.—(1) Sections 16 to 18, 23 and 26 of this Act shall apply to a landlord's or superior's right of hypothec and its enforcement by a sequestration for rent or feuduty as they apply to a poinding.

(2) Section 16 of this Act shall apply to an arrestment other than an arrestment of a debtor's earnings in the hands of his employer as it applies to a poinding.

Obligations ad factum praestandum

100.—(1) An obligation ad factum praestandum which is contained in a document registered in the Books of Council and Session or in sheriff court books shall not by virtue of that registration be enforceable by imprisonment.

(2) A charge for the purpose of enforcing an obligation ad factum praestandum which is contained in an extract of a decree or of a document registered as aforesaid shall not be competent.

Adjudication for debt

101. It shall not be competent for a creditor to bring an action of adjudication for debt (other than an action under section 23(5) of the Conveyancing (Scotland) Act 1924) to enforce a debt payable under a liquid document of debt unless—

(*a*) the debt has been constituted by decree; or
(*b*) the debt is a debitum fundi; or
(*c*) the document of debt or, if the document is a bill of exchange or a promissory note, a protest of the bill or note, has been registered for execution in the Books of Council and Session or in sheriff court books.

Procedure in diligence proceeding on extract of registered document etc.

102.—(1) The Court of Session may by Act of Sederunt—
(*a*) regulate and prescribe the procedure and practice in; and
(*b*) prescribe the form of any document to be used in, or for the purposes of,

diligence of a kind specified in subsection (2) below.

(2) The diligences referred to in subsection (1) above are diligences proceeding—
(*a*) on an extract of a document which has been registered for execution in the Books of Council and Session or in sheriff court books; or
(*b*) on an order or a determination which by virtue of any enactment is to be treated as if it were so registered.

Appeals

103.—(1) Subject to subsection (9) below and sections 21(1), 27(4), 43(5), 50(2), 55(4), 60(8), 62(9) and 66(9) of this Act and paragraphs 6(1), 11(4) and 14(5) of Schedule 5 thereto, an appeal may be made against any decision of the sheriff under this Act but only on a question of law and with the leave of the sheriff; and section 38 of the Sheriff Courts (Scotland) Act 1971 (appeal in summary causes) shall not apply to any appeal or any further appeal taken under this Act.

(2) Any appeal against a decision of the sheriff under subsection (1) above must be made within a period of 14 days from the date when leave to appeal against the decision was granted.

(3) An appeal may be made against any decision of the Lord Ordinary on an application under section 1(1) or 3(1) of this Act but only on a question of law and with the leave of the Lord Ordinary.

(4) Subject to subsections (6) and (7) below, any decision of the sheriff or of the Lord Ordinary under this Act shall take effect as soon as it is made and shall remain in effect unless and until it is reversed on appeal and either—
(*a*) the period allowed for further appeal has expired without an appeal being made; or
(*b*) if such a further appeal has been made, the matter has been finally determined in favour of the reversal of the sheriff's or Lord Ordinary's decision.

(5) No decision reversing a decision of the sheriff or Lord Ordinary under this Act shall have retrospective effect.

(6) A decision or order of the sheriff under any provision of this Act mentioned in subsection (7) below shall not take effect—
(*a*) until the period for leave to appeal specified in rules of court has expired without an application for leave having been made;
(*b*) where an application for leave to appeal is made, until leave has been refused or the application has been abandoned;
(*c*) where leave to appeal has been granted, until the period for an appeal has expired without an appeal being made; or
(*d*) where an appeal against the decision is made, until the matter has been finally determined or the appeal has been abandoned.

(7) The provisions of this Act referred to in subsection (6) above are—
(*a*) section 16(4);
(*b*) section 23(1);

(*c*) section 24(1) except in so far as it relates to orders declaring that a poinding is invalid or has ceased to have effect;
(*d*) section 24(3);
(*e*) section 30;
(*f*) section 35(1);
(*g*) section 39(5)(*b*) and (*c*);
(*h*) section 40(2);
(*j*) section 41(3);
(*k*) section 50(1) except in so far as it relates to orders declaring that an arrestment is invalid or has ceased to have effect;
(*l*) section 50(4);
(*m*) section 55(1) except in so far as it relates to orders declaring that an arrestment is invalid or has ceased to have effect;
(*n*) section 55(6);
(*o*) section 65(2);
(*p*) section 66(3);
(*q*) paragraphs 1(4), 7(1), 8(1) and (3), 21(2) and 22(3) of Schedule 5.

(8) A court to which an appeal under this Act or a further appeal is made may—

(*a*) before it disposes of the appeal, make such interim order; and
(*b*) on determining the appeal, make such supplementary order,

as it thinks necessary or reasonable in the circumstances.

(9) This section does not apply to any decision of a court under Part V of this Act.

Regulations

104.—(1) Regulations under this Act shall be made by statutory instrument and shall, except as provided in subsection (2) below, be subject to annulment in pursuance of a resolution of either House of Parliament.

(2) No regulation shall be made under paragraph 1(2) of Schedule 1 or paragraph 25(2) of Schedule 5 to this Act unless a draft of it has been laid before, and approved by a resolution of, each House of Parliament.

Application to Crown

105. Without prejudice to the Crown Proceedings Act 1947, this Act shall bind the Crown acting in its capacity as a creditor or employer.

Interpretation

[1] **106.** In this Act—

"current maintenance" has the meaning given to it in section 73(1) of this Act;

"earnings" has the meaning given to it in section 73(2) of this Act;

"employer" has the meaning given to it in section 73(1) of this Act;

"levying authority" has the meaning assigned to it in paragraph 1 of Schedule 2 to the Abolition of Domestic Rates Etc. (Scotland) Act 1987 and, in relation to community water charges, means the regional or islands council;

"maintenance" means periodical sums payable under a maintenance order;

"maintenance order" means—

(*a*) an order granted by a court in Scotland for payment of a periodical allowance on divorce or on the granting of a declarator of nullity of marriage, or for aliment;
(*b*) an order under section 43 or 44 of the National Assistance Act 1948, section 23 or 24 of the Ministry of Social Security Act 1966, section 80 or 81 of the Social Work (Scotland) Act 1968, section 11(3) of the Guardianship Act 1973, section 18 or 19 of the Supplementary Benefits Act 1976, section 50 or 51 of the Child Care Act 1980 or section 24 or 25 of the Social Security Act 1986;

(*c*) an order of a court in England and Wales or Northern Ireland registered in Scotland under Part II of the Maintenance Orders Act 1950;
(*d*) a provisional order of a reciprocating country which is confirmed by a court in Scotland under Part I of the Maintenance Orders (Reciprocal Enforcement) Act 1972;
(*e*) an order of a reciprocating country which is registered in Scotland under that Part of that Act;
(*f*) an order registered in Scotland under Part II, or under an Order in Council made in pursuance of Part III, of that Act;
(*g*) an order registered in Scotland under section 5 of the Civil Jurisdiction and Judgments Act 1982; or
(*h*) an alimentary bond or agreement (including a document providing for the maintenance of one party to a marriage by the other after the marriage has been dissolved or annulled)—
(i) registered for execution in the Books of Council and Session or sheriff court books; or
(ii) registered in Scotland under an Order in Council made under section 13 of the Civil Jurisdiction and Judgments Act 1982;

"net earnings" has the meaning given to it in section 73(1) of this Act;
"officer of court" means a messenger-at-arms or a sheriff officer;
"ordinary debt" has the meaning given to it in section 73(1) of this Act;
"summary warrant" means a summary warrant granted under or by virtue of paragraph 7 of Schedule 2 to the Abolition of Domestic Rates Etc. (Scotland) Act 1987 or any of the enactments mentioned in Schedule 4 to this Act;
"warrant of sale" has the meaning given in section 30 of this Act.

NOTE
[1] As amended by the Abolition of Domestic Rates Etc. (Scotland) Act 1987, s.33(*c*). Amended (*prosp.*) by the Child Support Act 1991, Sched. 5, para. 8(7).

Financial provisions

107.—(1) Any sums recovered by the Lord Advocate under section 79(6)(*b*) or 80(9) of this Act shall be paid by him into the Consolidated Fund.

(2) There shall be paid out of money provided by Parliament—
(*a*) any fees or outlays payable under section 78(4) or 79(4) of this Act;
(*b*) any expenses payable by the Lord Advocate under section 79(6)(*a*) of this Act; and
(*c*) any increase attributable to this Act in the sums payable out of money so provided under any other Act.

Minor and consequential amendments, transitional provisions and repeals

108.—(1) The amendments specified in Schedule 6 to this Act, being minor amendments or amendments consequential on the provisions of this Act, shall have effect.

(2) The transitional provisions contained in Schedule 7 to this Act shall have effect.

(3) The enactments mentioned in columns 1 and 2 of Schedule 8 to this Act are repealed to the extent specified in column 3 thereof.

Short title, commencement and extent

109.—(1) This Act may be cited as the Debtors (Scotland) Act 1987.

[1] (2) This Act (except this section) shall come into force on such day as the Lord Advocate may by order made by statutory instrument appoint, and different days may be so appointed for different purposes and for different provisions.

(3) This Act extends to Scotland only.

NOTE
[1] The following dates of commencement have been prescribed:
2nd November 1987: ss. 75, 76, 97 (S.I. 1987 No. 1838).
30th November 1988: all remaining provisions (S.I. 1988 No. 1818).

SCHEDULES

Section 44

SCHEDULE 1

Expenses of Poinding and Sale

Expenses chargeable against the debtor

1.—(1) Subject to paragraphs 2, 3 and 5 to 7 below, there shall be chargeable against the debtor any expenses incurred—

(*a*) subject to section 90(7) of this Act, in serving a charge;
(*b*) in serving a notice under section 18 of this Act before entering a dwellinghouse for the purpose of executing a poinding;
(*c*) in executing a poinding under section 20 of this Act;
(*d*) in making a report under section 21(4) of this Act of the redemption by the debtor of any poinded article;
(*e*) in granting a receipt under section 21(5) of this Act for payment for redemption under subsection (4) of that section;
(*f*) in making a report under section 22 of this Act of the execution of a poinding, but not in applying for an extension of time for the making of such a report;
(*g*) in applying for a warrant of sale under section 30(1) of this Act;
(*h*) in granting a receipt under section 33(3) of this Act for payment for the redemption of any poinded article;
(*j*) in making a report under section 33(5)(*b*) of this Act of the release or redemption of poinded articles;
(*k*) in making intimation, serving a copy of the warrant of sale and giving public notice under section 34 of this Act;
(*l*) in removing any articles for sale in pursuance of a warrant of sale;
(*m*) in making arrangements for, conducting and supervising a warrant sale;
(*n*) where the arrangements for a sale have been cancelled under section 36(1) of this Act, in returning poinded articles to any premises from which they have been removed for sale;
(*o*) in making a report of an agreement under section 36(2) of this Act;
(*p*) subject to section 39(3) of this Act, in making a report of sale under that section;
(*q*) in granting a receipt under section 41(4) of this Act for payment for the release from a poinding of any article which is owned in common;
(*r*) in making a report under section 41(5)(*b*) of this Act of the release of any such article;
(*s*) in opening shut and lockfast places in the execution of the diligence;
(*t*) by a solicitor in instructing an officer of court to take any of the steps specified in this sub-paragraph.

(2) The Lord Advocate may by regulations add to, delete or vary any of the steps specified in sub-paragraph (1) above.

2. Where a warrant of sale is varied under section 35 of this Act, there shall be chargeable against the debtor the expenses incurred in the application for the variation and the execution of the warrant of sale as varied but, subject to paragraph 4 below, not in the application for, and the execution of, the original warrant of sale.

3. Where arrangements for a sale are cancelled under subsection (1) of section 36 of this Act, if new arrangements are made for the sale in the circumstances mentioned in subsection (3)(*a*) of that section, there shall be chargeable against the debtor the expenses incurred in the making of the new arrangements but not in the making of the arrangements which have been cancelled.

4. Where a warrant of sale is varied under section 35 of this Act and the sheriff has awarded an additional sum of expenses under paragraph 9 below in the application for the original warrant of sale, that sum shall be chargeable against the debtor.

5. Subject to paragraph 6 below, where any such further poinding as is mentioned in section 28(2) of this Act has been executed, there shall be chargeable against the debtor the expenses incurred in that poinding but not the expenses incurred in the original poinding.

6. Where any such further poinding as is mentioned in subsection (2) of section 28 of this Act has been executed and—

(*a*) the creditor has, as a condition of his consenting to the removal of the poinded articles under subsection (1)(*a*) of that section, required the debtor to undertake liability for the expenses incurred in the original poinding; or

(*b*) the sheriff has, when authorising the removal of the poinded articles under subsection (1)(*b*) of that section, directed that the debtor shall be liable for those expenses,

there shall be chargeable against the debtor the expenses incurred in both poindings.

7. Where a new date is arranged under section 35(10) of this Act for the holding of a warrant sale or for the removal of poinded articles for sale, there shall be chargeable against the debtor the expenses incurred in connection with arranging the new date but not those incurred in connection with arranging the original date.

Circumstances where liability for expenses is at the discretion of the sheriff

8. The liability for any expenses incurred by the creditor or the debtor—

(*a*) in an application by the creditor or an officer of court to the sheriff under any provision of Part II of this Act, other than an application for a warrant of sale under section 30(1) of this Act or an application for variation of a warrant of sale under section 35(1) of this Act; or

(*b*) in implementing an order under—

(i) section 21(1) of this Act (order for security or immediate disposal of poinded articles); or

(ii) section 28(4) to (6) or 29 of this Act (orders dealing with unauthorised removal, damage or destruction of poinded articles),

shall be as determined by the sheriff.

Calculation of amount chargeable against debtor under the foregoing provisions

9. Expenses—

(*a*) chargeable against the debtor by virtue of any of paragraphs 1 to 6 above in respect of an application under Part II of this Act; or

(*b*) awarded by the sheriff against the debtor in favour of the creditor in a determination under paragraph 8 above in respect of an application other than an application under section 28(4) to (6) or 29 of this Act,

shall be calculated, whether or not the application is opposed by the debtor, as if it were unopposed, except that, if the debtor opposes the application on grounds which appear to the sheriff to be frivolous, the sheriff may award an additional sum of expenses, not exceeding £25 or such amount as may be prescribed in regulations made by the Lord Advocate, against the debtor.

Circumstances where no expenses are due to or by either party

10. Subject to paragraph 11 below, the debtor shall not be liable to the creditor nor the creditor to the debtor for any expenses incurred by the other party in connection with—

(*a*) an application by the debtor to the sheriff under any provision of Part II of this Act;

(*b*) any objections to such an application;

(*c*) a hearing held by virtue of section 24(5), 30(4), 35(6) or 39(6) of this Act.

11. If—

(*a*) an application mentioned in paragraph 10(*a*) above is frivolous;

(*b*) such an application is opposed on frivolous grounds; or

(*c*) a party requires a hearing held by virtue of any of the provisions mentioned in paragraph 10(*c*) above to be held on frivolous grounds,

the sheriff may award a sum of expenses, not exceeding £25 or such amount as may be prescribed in regulations made by the Lord Advocate, against the party acting frivolously in favour of the other party.

Supplementary

12. Any expenses chargeable against the debtor by virtue of any provision of this Schedule shall be recoverable out of the proceeds of sale.

Section 49

SCHEDULE 2

Deductions to be Made under Earnings Arrestment

Table A: Deductions from Weekly Earnings

Net earnings	Deduction
Not exceeding £35	Nil
Exceeding £35 but not exceeding £40	£1
Exceeding £40 but not exceeding £45	£2
Exceeding £45 but not exceeding £50	£3
Exceeding £50 but not exceeding £55	£4
Exceeding £55 but not exceeding £60	£5
Exceeding £60 but not exceeding £65	£6
Exceeding £65 but not exceeding £70	£7
Exceeding £70 but not exceeding £75	£8
Exceeding £75 but not exceeding £80	£9
Exceeding £80 but not exceeding £85	£10
Exceeding £85 but not exceeding £90	£11
Exceeding £90 but not exceeding £95	£12
Exceeding £95 but not exceeding £100	£13
Exceeding £100 but not exceeding £110	£15
Exceeding £110 but not exceeding £120	£17
Exceeding £120 but not exceeding £130	£19
Exceeding £130 but not exceeding £140	£21
Exceeding £140 but not exceeding £150	£23
Exceeding £150 but not exceeding £160	£26
Exceeding £160 but not exceeding £170	£29
Exceeding £170 but not exceeding £180	£32
Exceeding £180 but not exceeding £190	£35
Exceeding £190 but not exceeding £200	£38
Exceeding £200 but not exceeding £220	£46
Exceeding £220 but not exceeding £240	£54
Exceeding £240 but not exceeding £260	£63
Exceeding £260 but not exceeding £280	£73
Exceeding £280 but not exceeding £300	£83
Exceeding £300	£83 in respect of the first £300 plus 50 per cent of the remainder

Table B: Deductions from Monthly Earnings

Net earnings	Deduction
Not exceeding £152	Nil
Exceeding £152 but not exceeding £170	£5
Exceeding £170 but not exceeding £185	£8
Exceeding £185 but not exceeding £200	£11
Exceeding £200 but not exceeding £220	£14
Exceeding £220 but not exceeding £240	£18
Exceeding £240 but not exceeding £260	£22
Exceeding £260 but not exceeding £280	£26
Exceeding £280 but not exceeding £300	£30
Exceeding £300 but not exceeding £320	£34
Exceeding £320 but not exceeding £340	£38
Exceeding £340 but not exceeding £360	£42
Exceeding £360 but not exceeding £380	£46
Exceeding £380 but not exceeding £400	£50
Exceeding £400 but not exceeding £440	£58
Exceeding £440 but not exceeding £480	£66

Exceeding £480 but not exceeding £520	£74
Exceeding £520 but not exceeding £560	£82
Exceeding £560 but not exceeding £600	£90
Exceeding £600 but not exceeding £640	£98
Exceeding £640 but not exceeding £680	£109
Exceeding £680 but not exceeding £720	£121
Exceeding £720 but not exceeding £760	£133
Exceeding £760 but not exceeding £800	£145
Exceeding £800 but not exceeding £900	£180
Exceeding £900 but not exceeding £1000	£220
Exceeding £1000 but not exceeding £1100	£262
Exceeding £1100 but not exceeding £1200	£312
Exceeding £1200 but not exceeding £1300	£362
Exceeding £1300	£362 in respect of the first £1300 plus 50 per cent of the remainder

Table C: Deductions Based on Daily Earnings

Net earnings	Deduction
Not exceeding £5	Nil
Exceeding £5 but not exceeding £6	£0.15
Exceeding £6 but not exceeding £7	£0.30
Exceeding £7 but not exceeding £8	£0.45
Exceeding £8 but not exceeding £9	£0.60
Exceeding £9 but not exceeding £10	£1.00
Exceeding £10 but not exceeding £11	£1.20
Exceeding £11 but not exceeding £12	£1.40
Exceeding £12 but not exceeding £13	£1.60
Exceeding £13 but not exceeding £14	£1.80
Exceeding £14 but not exceeding £15	£2.00
Exceeding £15 but not exceeding £17	£2.40
Exceeding £17 but not exceeding £19	£2.70
Exceeding £19 but not exceeding £21	£3.20
Exceeding £21 but not exceeding £23	£3.70
Exceeding £23 but not exceeding £25	£4.30
Exceeding £25 but not exceeding £27	£5.00
Exceeding £27 but not exceeding £30	£6.00
Exceeding £30 but not exceeding £33	£7.00
Exceeding £33 but not exceeding £36	£8.50
Exceeding £36 but not exceeding £39	£10.00
Exceeding £39 but not exceeding £42	£11.50
Exceeding £42	£11.50 in respect of the first £42 plus 50 per cent of the remainder

Section 64

SCHEDULE 3

Disbursements by Sheriff Clerks under Conjoined Arrestment Order

1. Where all the debts are ordinary debts, in every disbursement by the sheriff clerk each creditor shall be paid the same proportion of the amount of his debt.

2. Where all the debts are current maintenance, then, in any such disbursement, if the sum available for disbursement is—

(*a*) sufficient to satisfy every creditor in respect of the amount of maintenance to be deducted in respect of his debt on that pay-day, each creditor shall be paid that amount;

(*b*) insufficient to satisfy every creditor in respect of the amount of maintenance specified in paragraph (*a*) above, each creditor shall be paid the same proportion of that amount.

3. Subject to paragraph 4 below, where the debts comprise both ordinary debts and current maintenance, then, in any such disbursement—

(*a*) if only one of the debts is an ordinary debt, the creditor in that debt shall be paid the sum which would be payable to him if the debt were being enforced by an earnings arrestment;

(*b*) if more than one of the debts is an ordinary debt, each of the creditors in those debts, out of the sum which would be payable to a creditor if the debt were a single debt being enforced by an earnings arrestment, shall be paid the same proportion of the amount of his debt;

(*c*) if only one of the debts is current maintenance, the creditor in that debt shall be paid the sum which would be payable to him under section 51 of this Act if the debt were being enforced by a current maintenance arrestment;

(*d*) if more than one of the debts is current maintenance, each of the creditors in those debts shall receive a payment in accordance with paragraph 2 of this Schedule.

4. If the sum available for any disbursement is insufficient to enable the provisions of paragraph 3 above to operate both in relation to the ordinary debts and the current maintenance, priority shall be given in the disbursement to the ordinary debts.

5. For the purposes of this Schedule, the amount of an ordinary debt—

(*a*) of a creditor whose debt was being enforced by an earnings arrestment which was recalled under section 60(3) of this Act, shall be the amount specified in the earnings arrestment schedule;

(*b*) of any other creditor, shall be the amount specified in the conjoined arrestment order or the order under section 62(5) of this Act.

. . . . . .

Section 74(1)

SCHEDULE 4

Recovery of Rates and Taxes etc.

The Local Government (Scotland) Act 1947 (c. 43)

1.—(1) For section 247 there shall be substituted the following sections—

"**Recovery of rates**

247.—(1) Subject to subsections (4) and (5) below, arrears of rates may be recovered by a rating authority by diligence—

(*a*) authorised by a summary warrant granted under subsection (2) below; or

(*b*) in pursuance of a decree granted in an action for payment

(2) Subject to subsection (4) below, the sheriff, on an application by the rating authority accompanied by a certificate by the rating authority—

(*a*) stating that none of the persons specified in the application has paid the rates due by him;

(*b*) stating that the authority has given written notice to each such person requiring him to make payment of the amount due by him within a period of 14 days after the date of the giving of the notice;

(*c*) stating that the said period of 14 days has expired without payment of the said amount; and

(*d*) specifying the amount due and unpaid by each such person,

shall grant a summary warrant in a form prescribed by Act of Sederunt authorising the recovery by any of the diligences mentioned in subsection (3) below of the amount remaining due and unpaid along with a surcharge of 10 per cent. (or such percentage as may be prescribed) of that amount.

(3) The diligences referred to in subsection (2) above are—

(*a*) a poinding and sale in accordance with Schedule 5 to the Debtors (Scotland) Act 1987;
(*b*) an earnings arrestment;
(*c*) an arrestment and action of furthcoming or sale.

(4) It shall not be competent for the sheriff to grant a summary warrant under subsection (2) above in respect of rates due by a debtor if an action has already been commenced for the recovery of those rates; and, without prejudice to subsection (5) below, on the commencing of an action for the recovery of rates, any existing summary warrant in so far as it relates to the recovery of those rates shall cease to have effect.

(5) It shall not be competent to commence an action for the recovery of rates if, in pursuance of a summary warrant, any of the diligences mentioned in subsection (3) above for the recovery of those rates has been executed.

(6) In any proceedings for the recovery of rates, whether by summary warrant or otherwise, no person shall be entitled to found upon failure of the rating authority or any other authority to comply with any provision of this Part of this Act relating to the date by which something shall be done, not being a provision in this section or a provision regulating the diligence.

(7) Regulations under subsection (2) above shall be made by statutory instrument and shall be subject to annulment in pursuance of a resolution of either House of Parliament.

Sheriff officer's fees and outlays

247A.—(1) Subject to subsection (2) below and without prejudice to paragraphs 25 to 34 of Schedule 5 to the Debtors (Scotland) Act 1987 (expenses of poinding and sale), the sheriff officer's fees, together with the outlays necessarily incurred by him, in connection with the execution of a summary warrant shall be chargeable against the debtor.

(2) No fee shall be chargeable by the sheriff officer against the debtor for collecting, and accounting to the rating authority for, sums paid to him by the debtor in respect of the amount owing.".

(2) In section 250, for the words from "warrant" to "in payment" where third occurring there shall be substituted the words—

"a summary warrant in a form prescribed by Act of Sederunt authorising the recovery by any of the diligences mentioned in section 247(3) of this Act of the amount remaining due and unpaid".

The Taxes Management Act 1970 (c. 9)

2. For section 63 there shall be substituted the following sections—

"**Recovery of tax in Scotland**

63.—(1) Subject to subsection (3) below, in Scotland, where any tax is due and has not been paid, the sheriff, on an application by the collector accompanied by a certificate by the collector—

(*a*) stating that none of the persons specified in the application has paid the tax due by him;
(*b*) stating that the collector has demanded payment under section 60 of this Act from each such person of the amount due by him;
(*c*) stating that 14 days have elapsed since the date of such demand without payment of the said amount; and
(*d*) specifying the amount due and unpaid by each such person,

shall grant a summary warrant in a form prescribed by Act of Sederunt authorising the recovery, by any of the diligences mentioned in subsection (2) below, of the amount remaining due and unpaid.

(2) The diligences referred to in subsection (1) above are—

(*a*) a poinding and sale in accordance with Schedule 5 to the Debtors (Scotland) Act 1987;
(*b*) an earnings arrestment;
(*c*) an arrestment and action of furthcoming or sale.

[1] (3) Paragraph (*c*) of subsection (1) above shall not apply to an application under that subsection insofar as it relates to sums due in respect of—

(*a*) deductions of income tax which any person specified in the application was liable to make under section 203 of the principal Act (pay as you earn); or
(*b*) deductions required to be made under section 559 of the principal Act (subcontractors in the construction industry) by any person specified in the application.

[2] (4) In this section references to amounts of tax due and references to sums due in respect of deductions include references to amounts which are deemed to be—

(*a*) amounts of tax which the person is liable to pay by virtue of the Income Tax (Employments) Regulations 1973; or

(*b*) amounts which the person is liable to pay by virtue of the Income Tax (Sub-Contractors in the Construction Industry) Regulations 1975.

NOTES

[1] As amended by the Finance Act 1989, s.154(2).

[2] Inserted by the Finance Act 1989, s.154(3).

Sheriff officer's fees and outlays

63A.—(1) Subject to subsection (2) below and without prejudice to paragraphs 25 to 34 of Schedule 5 to the Debtors (Scotland) Act 1987 (expenses of poinding and sale), the sheriff officer's fees, together with the outlays necessarily incurred by him, in connection with the execution of a summary warrant shall be chargeable against the debtor.

[THE NEXT PAGE IS B 263]

Court of Session - ADVANTAGES

(1)

Actions where Ct. of S. has exclusive J.:-

1) Some status cases eg actions of declarator of marriage, nullity etc
2) Actions of adjudication
3) Actions of reduction
4) Company actions where paid up share-capital exceeds £120K
5) Most applications relating to the administration of Scottish trusts except basic administration matters
6) Actions of proving the Tenor - only necessary to proceed with such an action where that document is crucial
7) Intellectual Property applications
8) Supervisory jurisdiction
9) Petitions for recall/restrict inhibitions

(2) where width of remedy is important - sh's J. is limited to sheriffdom.

1) INTERDICTS - If want an interdict to cover whole of Scotland then go to Ct. of S.

2) Extended powers of citation of witnesses - if want to compel witnesses outside Scotland you should go to Ct. of S. Longer process in sh. ct.

(3) EMERGENCY REMEDIES - available of emergency remedy

1) Inhibitions - accessability of inhibitions through Ct of S. They are immediately available on dependence of Ct. of S action. Counsel will ask for warrant to inhibit on summons.

~~other~~ Warranted IW sent to Edinburgh + bill for letters for inhibition is prepared. Last vestige of J. of royal cts. in Scotland, Bill presented to signet at Ct. of S. Principal IW then must be registered to inhibit sale of property belonging to D. Thereafter bill + IW must be returned to agent + personally served on D.

- considerable time lapse if actions outwith Edinburgh, can take a couple of hours in Edinburgh

2) Provisional Measures - Civil Jurisdiction + Judgements Act 1982 s.27+28
- applies where an action has been commenced in a contracting state or in Eng. + Wales. Ct. of S. ONLY can grant warrant to arrest or inhibit on basis of actions raised in other contracting state

3) Scottish 'Anton Piller' orders
- ct. can order search + seizure of documents in civil actions
- an AP order is an ideal example of how Ct. of S. has made use of existing procedure - R.84

1983 decision decided that Ct. of S. not only had power to grant commission + diligence but could do so where no intimation given to haver. Normally opportunity must be given to haver to give up documents

GO TO B275

(2) No fee shall be chargeable by the sheriff officer against the debtor for collecting, and accounting to the collector for, sums paid to him by the debtor in respect of the amount owing.".

The Car Tax Act 1983 9(c. 53)

3. In paragraph 3(2) of Schedule 1 (recovery of car tax), for the words from "and (*b*)" to the end there shall be substituted the following sub-paragraphs—

"(3) In respect of Scotland, where any tax is due and has not been paid, the sheriff, on an application by the Commissioners accompanied by a certificate by the Commissioners—

(*a*) stating that none of the persons specified in the application has paid the tax due from him;

(*b*) stating that payment of the amount due from each such person has been demanded from him; and

(*c*) specifying the amount due from and unpaid by each such person,

shall grant a summary warrant in a form prescribed by Act of Sederunt authorising the recovery, by any of the diligences mentioned in sub-paragraph (4) below, of the amount remaining due and unpaid.

(4) The diligences referred to in sub-paragraph (3) above are—

(*a*) a poinding and sale in accordance with Schedule 5 to the Debtors (Scotland) Act 1987;

(*b*) an earnings arrestment;

(*c*) an arrestment and action of furthcoming or sale.

(5) Subject to sub-paragraph (6) below and without prejudice to paragraphs 25 to 34 of Schedule 5 to the Debtors (Scotland) Act 1987 (expenses of poinding and sale), the sheriff officer's fees, together with the outlays necessarily incurred by him, in connection with the execution of a summary warrant shall be chargeable against the debtor.

(6) No fee shall be chargeable by the sheriff officer against the debtor for collecting, and accounting to the Commissioners for, sums paid to him by the debtor in respect of the amount owing.

(7) Regulations under this Schedule may make provision for anything which the Commissioners may do under sub-paragraphs (3) to (6) above to be done by an officer of the Commissioners holding such rank as the regulations may specify.".

The Value Added Tax Act 1983 (c. 55)

4. In paragraph 6(4) of Schedule 7 (recovery of value added tax), for the words from "and (*b*)" to the end there shall be substituted the following sub-paragraphs—

"(5) In respect of Scotland, where any tax or any sum recoverable as if it were tax is due and has not been paid, the sheriff, on an application by the Commissioners accompanied by a certificate by the Commissioners—

(*a*) stating that none of the persons specified in the application has paid the tax or other sum due from him;

(*b*) stating that payment of the amount due from each such person has been demanded from him; and

(*c*) specifying the amount due from and unpaid by each such person,

shall grant a summary warrant in a form prescribed by Act of Sederunt authorising the recovery, by any of the diligences mentioned in sub-paragraph (6) below, of the amount remaining due and unpaid.

(6) The diligences referred to in sub-paragraph (5) above are—

(*a*) a poinding and sale in accordance with Schedule 5 to the Debtors (Scotland) Act 1987;

(*b*) an earnings arrestment;

(*c*) an arrestment and action of furthcoming or sale.

(7) Subject to sub-paragraph (8) below and without prejudice to paragraphs 25 to 34 of Schedule 5 to the Debtors (Scotland) Act 1987 (expenses of poinding and sale), the sheriff officer's fees, together with the outlays necessarily incurred by him, in connection with the execution of a summary warrant shall be chargeable against the debtor.

(8) No fee shall be chargeable by the sheriff officer against the debtor for collecting, and accounting to the Commissioners for, sums paid to him by the debtor in respect of the amount owing.

(9) The Commissioners may by regulations make provision for anything which the Commissioners may do under sub-paragraphs (5) to (8) above to be done by an officer of the Commissioners holding such rank as the regulations may specify.".

Section 74

SCHEDULE 5

Poindings and Sales in Pursuance of Summary Warrants

Articles exempt from poinding

1.—(1) The following articles belonging to a debtor shall be exempt from poinding at the instance of a creditor in respect of a debt due to him by the debtor—

(*a*) clothing reasonably required for the use of the debtor or any member of his household;

(*b*) implements, tools of trade, books or other equipment reasonably required for the use of the debtor or any member of his household in the practice of the debtor's or such member's profession, trade or business, not exceeding in aggregate value £500 or such amount as may be prescribed in regulations made by the Lord Advocate;

(*c*) medical aids or medical equipment reasonably required for the use of the debtor or any member of his household;

(*d*) books or other articles reasonably required for the education or training of the debtor or any member of his household not exceeding in aggregate value £500 or such amount as may be prescribed in regulations made by the Lord Advocate;

(*e*) toys for the use of any child who is a member of the debtor's household;

(*f*) articles reasonably required for the care or upbringing of a child who is a member of the debtor's household.

(2) The following articles belonging to a debtor shall be exempt from poinding if they are at the time of the poinding in a dwellinghouse and are reasonably required for the use in the dwellinghouse of the person residing there or a member of his household—

(*a*) beds or bedding;

(*b*) household linen;

(*c*) chairs or settees;

(*d*) tables;

(*e*) food;

(*f*) lights or light fittings;

(*g*) heating appliances;

(*h*) curtains;

(*j*) floor coverings;

(*k*) furniture, equipment or utensils used for cooking, storing or eating food;

(*l*) refrigerators;

(*m*) articles used for cleaning, mending, or pressing clothes;

(*n*) articles used for cleaning the dwellinghouse;

(*o*) furniture used for storing—

(i) clothing, bedding or household linen;

(ii) articles used for cleaning the dwellinghouse; or

(iii) utensils used for cooking or eating food;

(*p*) articles used for safety in the dwellinghouse;

(*q*) tools used for maintenance or repair of the dwellinghouse or of household articles.

(3) The Lord Advocate may by regulations add to the list set out in sub-paragraph (2) above, or delete or vary any of the items contained in that list.

(4) If, on an application made within 14 days after the date of the execution of the poinding—

(*a*) by the debtor or any person who owns a poinded article in common with the debtor; or

(*b*) by any person in possession of a poinded article,

the sheriff is satisfied that the article is exempt from poinding under this paragraph, he shall make an order releasing the article from the poinding.

Restrictions on time when poinding may be executed

2.—(1) No poinding shall be executed on Sunday, Christmas Day, New Year's Day, Good Friday or such other day as may be prescribed by Act of Sederunt.

(2) The execution of a poinding shall not—

(*a*) be commenced before 8 a.m. or after 8 p.m.; or

(*b*) be continued after 8 p.m.,

unless the sheriff officer has obtained prior authority from the sheriff for such commencement or continuation; and any rule of law which prohibits poindings outwith the hours of daylight shall cease to have effect.

Power of entry for execution of poinding

3.—(1) Subject to sub-paragraph (2) below, notwithstanding any warrant authorising him to open shut and lockfast places, a sheriff officer shall not enter a dwellinghouse to execute a poinding if, at the time of his intended entry, there appears to him to be nobody, or only children under the age of 16 years, present there unless, at least four days before the date of his intended entry, he has served notice on the debtor specifying that date.

(2) If it appears to the sheriff, on an application made to him by the sheriff officer (which shall not require to be intimated to the debtor), that the requirement of service under this paragraph would be likely to prejudice the execution of the poinding he may dispense with such service.

Value of articles which may be poinded and presumption as to ownership

4.—(1) The sheriff officer shall be entitled to poind articles only to the extent necessary to ensure that the sum recoverable and the likely expenses chargeable against the debtor under paragraphs 25 to 34 below would be realised if they were sold at the value fixed under paragraph 5(4) below.

(2) In executing a poinding, a sheriff officer shall be entitled to proceed on the assumption that any article in the possession of the debtor is owned by him unless the sheriff officer knows or ought to know that the contrary is the case.

(3) The sheriff officer shall not be precluded from relying on the assumption mentioned in sub-paragraph (2) above by reason only of one or both of the following circumstances—

(*a*) that the article belongs to a class which is commonly held under a hire, hire-purchase or conditional sale agreement or on some other limited title of possession;

(*b*) that an assertion has been made that the article is not owned by the debtor.

Poinding procedure

5.—(1) The procedure in a poinding shall be in accordance with this paragraph and paragraph 6 below.

(2) Before executing the poinding, the sheriff officer shall—

(*a*) exhibit to any person present the summary warrant or, if the warrant does not identify the debtor, a certified copy of the warrant together with a statement certified by the creditor that the summary warrant applies to the debtor;

(*b*) demand payment of the sum recoverable from the debtor, if he is present, or any person present appearing to the sheriff officer to be authorised to act for the debtor; and

(*c*) make enquiry of any person present as to the ownership of the articles proposed to be poinded, and in particular whether there are any persons who own any articles in common with the debtor.

(3) The sheriff officer shall be accompanied at the poinding by one witness.

(4) The poinded articles shall be valued by the sheriff officer according to the price which they would be likely to fetch if sold on the open market unless he considers that the articles are such that a valuation by a professional valuer or other suitably skilled person is advisable, in which case he may arrange for such a valuation.

(5) The sheriff officer shall prepare a schedule (referred to in this Schedule as "the poinding schedule"), in the form prescribed by Act of Sederunt, which shall specify—

(*a*) the identity of the creditor and of the debtor;

(*b*) the articles poinded, and their respective values;

(*c*) the sum recoverable; and

(*d*) the place where the poinding was executed.

(6) On completion of the valuation the sheriff officer shall—

(*a*) along with the witness sign the poinding schedule;

(*b*) deliver the poinding schedule to any person in possession of the articles or—

(i) where the poinding was executed in a dwellinghouse or other premises, leave it in the premises, or

(ii) in any other case, deliver it to premises occupied by that person;

(*c*) if the person in possession of the articles is not the debtor and it is reasonably practicable, serve a copy of it by post on the debtor;

(*d*) inform the debtor (if present) of his right to redeem poinded articles under paragraph 6(4) below;

(*e*) inform any person present who owns any poinded article in common with the debtor of his right to redeem poinded articles under paragraph 22(2) and (3) below; and

(*f*) inform the debtor (if present) and any person present who owns any poinded article in common with the debtor, or who is in possession of any poinded article, of his right to apply for an order releasing articles from poinding under paragraph 1(4) above or paragraph 7(1) or 22(3)(*b*) below.

(7) The sheriff officer shall leave pointed articles at the place where they were poinded, except that where that place is not a dwellinghouse or other premises, if he considers it necessary for their security or the preservation of their value and there is insufficient time to obtain an order under paragraph 6(1)(*a*) below, he shall remove them at the creditor's expense—

(*a*) to the nearest convenient premises belonging to the debtor or to the person in possession of the articles; or

(*b*) if no such premises are available, to the nearest suitable secure premises.

6.—(1) The sheriff, on an application by the creditor, the sheriff officer or the debtor intimated in accordance with sub-paragraph (2) below, may at any time after the execution of a poinding make an order—

(*a*) for the security of any of the poinded articles; or

(*b*) in relation to any of the articles which are of a perishable nature or which are likely to deteriorate substantially and rapidly in condition or value, for their immediate disposal and, in the event of their disposal by sale, for payment of the proceeds of sale to the creditor or for consignation of the proceeds in court until the diligence is completed or otherwise ceases to have effect,

and a decision of the sheriff under paragraph (*b*) above for the immediate disposal of articles shall not be subject to appeal.

(2) An application for an order under sub-paragraph (1)(*b*) above—

(*a*) by the creditor or the sheriff officer, shall be intimated by him to the debtor;

(*b*) by the debtor, shall be intimated to the creditor or the officer of court,

at the time when it is made.

(3) It shall not be competent for a sheriff officer in executing a poinding to examine a person on oath as to the ownership of any article.

(4) Subject to sub-paragraph (1)(*b*) above, the debtor shall be entitled, within 14 days after the date of execution of the poinding, to redeem any poinded article at the value fixed under paragraph 5(4) above.

(5) The sheriff officer shall, on receiving payment from the debtor for the redemption under sub-paragraph (4) above of a poinded article, grant a receipt in the form prescribed by Act of Sederunt to the debtor; and the receipt shall operate as a release of the article from the poinding.

(6) Subject to paragraph 13(2)(*b*) below, the revaluation in the same poinding of an article which has been valued under paragraph 5(4) above shall not be competent.

(7) A poinding shall be deemed to have been executed on the date when the poinding schedule has been delivered, or left on the premises, in pursuance of paragraph 5(6)(*b*) above.

(8) At any time before the execution of a poinding on behalf of a creditor, a sheriff officer shall, if requested to do so by any other creditor who has exhibited to him a summary warrant authorising the poinding of articles belonging to the debtor, conjoin that creditor in the poinding.

Release of poinded article on ground of undue harshness

7.—(1) The sheriff may, on an application made within 14 days after the date of execution of a poinding by the debtor or any person in possession of a poinded article, make an order releasing an article from the poinding if it appears to the sheriff that its continued inclusion in the poinding or its sale under the summary warrant would be unduly harsh in the circumstances.

(2) Where the sheriff has made an order under subsection (1) above he may, notwithstanding paragraph 9 below, on an application by the creditor or by a sheriff officer on his behalf, authorise the poinding of other articles belonging to the debtor on the same premises.

Invalidity, cessation and recall of poinding

8.—(1) If, at any time before the sale of the poinded articles, the sheriff is satisfied that the poinding is invalid or has ceased to have effect he shall, on his own initiative or on an application by the debtor, make an order declaring the poinding to be void, and may make such consequential order as appears to him to be necessary in the circumstances.

(2) Without prejudice to paragraph 1(4) above, it shall not be competent for the sheriff to make an order under sub-paragraph (1) above on the ground that any poinded article is exempt from poinding under that paragraph.

(3) At any time before intimation is given to the debtor under paragraph 16 below of the date arranged for the removal of the poinded articles for sale or, if the articles are to be sold in the premises where they are situated, the date arranged for the sale, the sheriff may, on an application by the debtor, recall a poinding on any of the following grounds—

(*a*) that it would be unduly harsh in the circumstances for the poinded articles to be sold under the summary warrant;

(*b*) that the aggregate of the values of the poinded articles fixed under paragraph 5(4) above was substantially below the aggregate of the prices which they would have been likely to fetch if sold on the open market; or

(*c*) that the likely aggregate proceeds of sale of the poinded articles would not exceed the expenses likely to be incurred in the taking of further steps in the diligence, on the assumption that such steps are unopposed.

(4) The sheriff shall not grant an application on the ground mentioned in sub-paragraph (3)(*c*) above if an order for further poinding of articles belonging to the debtor has been authorised under paragraph 7(2) above or paragraphs 12(6) or 13(2) below, or has become competent by reason of paragraph 12(2), 21(4) or 22(5) below.

(5) The sheriff shall not make an order under sub-paragraph (1) above, recall a poinding or refuse an application under this paragraph without first giving the debtor and the creditor—

(*a*) an opportunity to make representations; and

(*b*) if either party wishes to be heard, an opportunity to be heard.

(6) The sheriff clerk shall intimate to the debtor any order made under sub-paragraph (1) above by the sheriff on his own initiative.

Second poinding in same premises

9. Subject to paragraph 7(2) above and paragraphs 12(2) and (6), 13(2), 21(4) and 22(5) below, where articles are poinded in any premises (whether or not the poinding is valid), another poinding in those premises to enforce the same debt shall not be competent except in relation to articles which have been brought on to the premises since the execution of the first poinding.

Sist of proceedings in poinding of mobile homes

10.—(1) Where a caravan, houseboat or other moveable structure which is the only or principal residence of the debtor or another person has been poinded the sheriff, on an application by the debtor or that other person made at any time after the execution of the poinding and before intimation is given to the debtor under paragraph 16 below of the date arranged for the removal of the poinded articles for sale or, if the articles are to be sold in the premises where they are situated, the date arranged for the sale, may order that for such period as he shall specify no further steps shall be taken in the poinding.

(2) In calculating under paragraph 11(1) or (2) below the period during which a poinding in respect of which an order has been made under sub-paragraph (1) above shall remain effective, there shall be disregarded the period specified in the order.

Duration of poinding

11.—(1) Subject to sub-paragraphs (2), (3) and (5) below, a poinding shall cease to have effect on the expiry of a period of one year after the date of execution of the poinding.

(2) The sheriff, on an application by the creditor or by a sheriff officer on his behalf made before the expiry of the period mentioned in sub-paragraph (1) above, may extend that period—

(*a*) where he considers that, if the said period is extended, the debtor is likely to comply with an agreement between the creditor and the debtor for the payment of the sum recoverable by instalments or otherwise; or

(*b*) to enable further proceedings to be taken in the diligence where the termination of the poinding would prejudice the creditor and the creditor cannot be held responsible for the circumstances giving rise to the need for the extension,

for such further period as he considers reasonable in the circumstances.

(3) The sheriff may grant further extensions under sub-paragraph (2) above, on application being made to him before the expiry of the previously extended period.

(4) The decision of the sheriff under sub-paragraph (2) above shall not be subject to appeal, and shall be intimated to the debtor by the sheriff clerk.

(5) Where, within the period mentioned in sub-paragraph (1) above or within that period as extended under sub-paragraph (2) above, an application is made under sub-paragraph (2) above, the poinding shall continue to have effect until the disposal of the application.

Removal, damage or destruction of pointed articles

12.—(1) The debtor or the person in possession of poinded articles may move them to another location if—

(*a*) the creditor or a sheriff officer on behalf of the creditor has consented in writing to their removal; or

(*b*) the sheriff, on an application by the debtor or the person in possession, has authorised their removal.

(2) Where poinded articles have been removed under sub-paragraph (1) above, a sheriff officer may, under the same warrant to poind, again poind any of the articles so removed and, notwithstanding paragraph 9 above, any articles which were not so removed, whether or not they were previously poinded; and, on the execution of any such further poinding, the original poinding shall be deemed to have been abandoned.

(3) The removal, except in accordance with this Schedule, from any premises of poinded articles by—

(*a*) the debtor; or

(*b*) any person, other than the creditor or a sheriff officer, who knows that the articles have been poinded,

shall be a breach of the poinding and may be dealt with as a contempt of court.

(4) Where articles have been removed from premises otherwise than in accordance with this Schedule, the sheriff, on an application by the creditor—

(*a*) may, subject to sub-paragraph (5) below, make an order requiring the person in possession of the articles to restore them to the premises from which they were removed within a period specified in the order; and

(*b*) if an order under paragraph (*a*) above is not complied with, and it appears to the sheriff that the articles are likely to be found in premises specified in the application, may grant a warrant to sheriff officers—

(i) to search for the articles in those premises; and

(ii) to restore the articles to the premises from which they were removed or to make such other arrangements for their security as the sheriff may direct,

and such a warrant shall be authority to open shut and lockfast places for the purpose of its execution.

(5) Where it appears to the sheriff, on an application made to him by any person having an interest, that any article which has been removed from premises otherwise than in accordance with this Schedule has been acquired for value and without knowledge of the poinding, he shall—

(*a*) refuse an order under sub-paragraph (4)(*a*) above relating to that article;

(*b*) recall any such order which he has already made; and

(*c*) make an order releasing the article from the poinding.

(6) Where articles have been removed from premises otherwise than in accordance with this Schedule in circumstances in which the debtor is at fault the sheriff, on an application by the creditor or by a sheriff officer on his behalf, may, notwithstanding paragraph 9 above, authorise the poinding of other articles belonging to the debtor in the same premises.

(7) The removal of poinded articles to another location shall not have the effect of releasing the articles from the poinding.

13.—(1) The wilful damage or destruction of poinded articles by—

(*a*) the debtor; or

(*b*) any person, other than the creditor or a sheriff officer, who knows that the articles have been poinded,

shall be a breach of the poinding and may be dealt with as a contempt of court.

(2) Where poinded articles have been damaged or destroyed the sheriff, on an application by the creditor or by the sheriff officer on his behalf, may—

(*a*) where the debtor has been at fault, authorise the poinding of other articles belonging to the debtor in the premises in which the original poinding took place; and

(*b*) in any case, authorise the revaluation of any damaged article in accordance with paragraph 5(4) above.

(3) Where a third party, knowing that an article has been poinded—

(*a*) wilfully damages or destroys it; or

(*b*) removes it from premises in breach of a poinding, and—

(i) it is damaged, destroyed, lost or stolen; or

(ii) it is acquired from or through him by another person without knowledge of the poinding and for value,

the sheriff may order the third party to consign the sum mentioned in sub-paragraph (4) below in court until the completion of the sale or until the poinding otherwise ceases to have effect.

(4) The sum to be consigned in court under sub-paragraph (3) above shall be—

(*a*) where the article has been damaged but not so damaged as to make it worthless, a sum equal to the difference between the value of the article fixed under paragraph 5(4) above and the value of the article as so damaged;

(*b*) in any other case, a sum equal to the value fixed under that paragraph.

(5) Any sum consigned in court under sub-paragraph (3) above shall, on the completion of the sale or on the poinding otherwise ceasing to have effect, be paid to the creditor to the extent necessary to meet the sum recoverable, any surplus thereof being paid to the debtor.

Arrangements for sale

14.—(1) A sale in pursuance of a summary warrant shall be by public auction.

(2) A sale in pursuance of a summary warrant shall not be held in a dwellinghouse except with the consent in writing, in a form to be prescribed by Act of Sederunt, of the occupier thereof and, if he is not the occupier, of the debtor.

(3) Subject to sub-paragraph (4) below, the sale shall not be held in premises (other than a dwellinghouse or an auction room) which are occupied by a person other than the debtor or the creditor except with the consent in writing, in a form to be prescribed by Act of Sederunt, of the occupier thereof.

(4) Where the occupier of premises (other than a dwellinghouse or an auction room) where poinded articles are situated does not give his consent under sub-paragraph (3) above to the holding of the sale in those premises, the sheriff may, if on an application by the creditor or the sheriff officer he considers that it would be unduly costly to require the removal of the poinded articles to other premises for sale, nevertheless order that the sale shall be held in the premises where they are situated.

(5) The decision of the sheriff under sub-paragraph (4) above shall not be subject to appeal.

(6) In this paragraph "occupier", in relation to premises where there are two or more occupiers, means each of them.

Release or redemption of poinded articles

15.—(1) Where a sale of poinded articles is to be held in premises other than where the poinded articles are situated, the sheriff officer may remove to those premises only such poinded articles as, if sold at their values fixed under paragraph 5(4) above, would realise in total the sum recoverable and the likely expenses chargeable against the debtor under paragraphs 25 to 34 below; and shall release the remaining poinded articles from the poinding.

(2) Subject to paragraph 6(1) above, the debtor may, within seven days after the date when intimation is given to him under paragraph 16 below of the date arranged for the removal of the poinded articles for sale or, if the articles are to be sold in the premises where they are situated, the date arranged for the sale, redeem any poinded article by paying to the officer of court a sum equal to its value fixed under paragraph 5(4) above.

(3) The sheriff officer shall, on receiving payment from the debtor under sub-paragraph (2) above, grant a receipt in the form prescribed by Act of Sederunt to the debtor; and the receipt shall operate as a release of the article from the poinding.

(4) The creditor and the debtor may by agreement release articles from the poinding.

Intimation and publication of sale

16.—(1) The sheriff officer who makes arrangements for the sale of the poinded articles shall—

(*a*) as soon as is reasonably practicable intimate to the debtor and, if the person in possession of the poinded articles is not the debtor, to that person, the date and place arranged for the sale; and

(*b*) where the sale is not to be held in the premises where the poinded articles are situated, intimate to the debtor and, if he is not the debtor, to the person in possession of the poinded articles, not less than 14 days before the date arranged for the removal of the poinded articles from those premises, the date arranged for the removal.

(2) The sheriff officer shall, at the same time as he intimates the date arranged for the sale under sub-paragraph (1) above, send such particulars of the arrangements for the sale as are prescribed by Act of Sederunt to the sheriff clerk of the sheriff court within whose jurisdiction the articles were poinded; and the sheriff clerk shall arrange for those particulars to be displayed on the walls of court.

(3) The sale shall be advertised by public notice.

(4) Where the sale is to be held in premises not belonging to the debtor, the public notice under sub-paragraph (3) above shall not name him or disclose that the articles for sale are poinded articles.

(5) Where the sale is to be held in premises other than the debtor's premises or an auction room, any public notice of the sale shall state that the articles to be sold do not belong to the occupier of the premises where the sale is to be held.

Alteration of arrangements for sale

17.—(1) Subject to sub-paragraph (2) below and without prejudice to sub-paragraph (5) below, after intimation has been given under paragraph 16(1) above to the debtor of the date arranged for the sale or for the removal for sale of the poinded articles from the premises where they are situated, the creditor or sheriff officer shall not be entitled to arrange a new date for the sale or for such removal.

(2) Where, for any reason for which neither the creditor nor the sheriff officer is responsible, it is not possible for the sale or, as the case may be, the removal for sale of the poinded articles from the premises where they are situated, to take place on the date arranged for it, the creditor may instruct the sheriff officer to arrange a new date in accordance with sub-paragraph (3) below, and the sheriff officer shall intimate the new date to the debtor and to any other person in possession of the poinded articles.

(3) The new date arranged under sub-paragraph (2) above shall not be less than seven days after the date of intimation under that sub-paragraph.

(4) Without prejudice to sub-paragraph (2) above, in order to enable the sum recoverable to be paid by instalments or otherwise in accordance with an agreement between the creditor and the debtor, the creditor may, after intimation has been given under paragraph 16 above of the date arranged for the sale, cancel the arrangements for the sale on not more than two occasions.

(5) Where, following cancellation of the sale in pursuance of sub-paragraph (4) above, the debtor is in breach of the agreement, the creditor may instruct the sheriff officer to make arrangements for the sale of the poinded articles at any time while they remain poinded.

The sale

18.—(1) In the sale there shall be no reserve price unless the creditor chooses to have one and, if he does so choose, it shall not exceed the value of the article fixed under paragraph 5(4) above.

(2) The value of a poinded article fixed under paragraph 5(4) above and the reserve price, if any, fixed by the creditor under sub-paragraph (1) above need not be disclosed to any person bidding for the article.

(3) In the sale any poinded article exposed for sale may be purchased by—

(*a*) any creditor, including the creditor on whose behalf the poinding was executed; or

(*b*) a person who owns the article in common with the debtor.

(4) Subject to sub-paragraph (5) below and without prejudice to the rights of any third party, where the sum recoverable has not been realised by the sale, ownership of a poinded article which remains unsold after being exposed for sale shall pass to the creditor.

(5) Without prejudice to the rights of any third party, where the sale is held in premises belonging to the debtor, the ownership of a poinded article which has passed to the creditor under sub-paragraph (4) above shall revert to the debtor unless the creditor uplifts the article by 8 p.m. (or such other time as may be prescribed by Act of Sederunt)—

(*a*) if the premises are a dwellinghouse in which the debtor is residing, on the day when the sale is completed;

(*b*) in any other case, on the third working day following that day,

and the sheriff officer may remain on or re-enter any premises (whether open, shut or lockfast) for the purpose of enabling the creditor to uplift any such article.

(6) For the purposes of sub-paragraph (5) above "working day" means a day which is not—
Saturday;
Sunday;
1st or 2nd January;
Good Friday;
Easter Monday;
25th or 26th December;
a public holiday in the area in which the premises are situated.

(7) Subject to sub-paragraph (8) below, where at the sale any article is unsold or is sold at a price below the value fixed under paragraph 5(4) above, the debtor shall be credited with an amount equal to that valuation.

(8) Where—

(*a*) any damaged article has been revalued under paragraph 5(4) above on the authority of the sheriff given under paragraph 13(2) above;

(*b*) the damage was not caused by the fault of the debtor; and

(*c*) no order has been made under paragraph 13(3) above requiring a third party to consign a sum in respect of the article, or such an order has been made but has not been complied with,

the amount credited to the debtor under sub-paragraph (7) above shall be an amount equal to the original valuation and not the revaluation referred to in paragraph (*a*) above.

Disposal of proceeds of sale

19. The sheriff officer who arranges the sale shall dispose of the proceeds of the sale—

(*a*) by paying to the creditor the proceeds so far as necessary to meet the sum recoverable (subject to any agreement between the sheriff officer and the creditor relating to the fees or outlays of the officer of court); and

(*b*) by paying to the debtor any surplus remaining after the sum recoverable has been paid or, if the debtor cannot be found, by consigning such surplus in court.

Report of sale

20.—(1) The sheriff officer who arranged the sale shall within a period of 14 days after the date of completion of the sale send to the creditor a report of the sale in the form prescribed by Act of Sederunt setting out—

(*a*) any articles which have been sold and the amount for which they have been sold;

(*b*) any articles which remain unsold;

(*c*) the expenses of the diligence chargeable against the debtor;

(*d*) any surplus paid to the debtor; and

(*e*) any balance due by or to the debtor;

and the sheriff officer shall, within the same period, send a copy of the report to the debtor.

(2) The report of sale shall be signed by the sheriff officer.

(3) The creditor and the debtor may have the report of sale taxed by the auditor of court of the sheriff court within whose jurisdiction the articles were poinded.

Articles belonging to third parties or in common ownership

21.—(1) A sheriff officer may, at any time after the execution of a poinding and before the sale of the poinded articles, release an article from the poinding if—

(*a*) he is satisfied that the article belongs to a third party; and

(*b*) the debtor or other person in possession of the article does not deny that it belongs to the third party.

(2) Where, on an application made to him by a third party, at any time after the execution of a poinding and before the sale of the poinded articles, the sheriff is satisfied that a poinded article belongs to that third party, he shall make an order releasing it from the poinding.

(3) The making of an application under sub-paragraph (2) above shall not prejudice the taking of any other proceedings by the third party for the recovery of a poinded article belonging to him, and an order of the sheriff under that sub-paragraph shall not be binding in any other proceedings.

(4) Where an article has been released from a poinding under this paragraph, a sheriff officer may, notwithstanding paragraph 9 above, poind other articles belonging to the debtor in the same premises.

22.—(1) Articles which are owned in common by a debtor and a third party may be poinded and disposed of in accordance with this Schedule in satisfaction of the debts of that debtor.

(2) Where, at any time after the execution of a poinding and before the sale of the poinded articles, a third party—

(*a*) claims that a poinded article is owned in common by the debtor and himself; and

(*b*) pays to the sheriff officer a sum equal to the value of the debtor's interest in the article,

the sheriff officer may, unless the debtor (or the person in possession of the article, if not the debtor) denies the claim, release the article from the poinding.

(3) If, on an application made by a third party, at any time after the execution of a poinding and before the sale of the poinded articles, the sheriff is satisfied that a poinded article is owned in common by the debtor and that third party and either—

(*a*) the third party undertakes to pay to the sheriff officer a sum equal to the value of the debtor's interest in the article; or

(*b*) the sheriff is satisfied that the continued poinding of that article or its sale under summary warrant would be unduly harsh to the third party in the circumstances,

he shall make an order releasing the article from the poinding.

(4) A release under sub-paragraph (2) above or where sub-paragraph (3)(*a*) above applies shall not become effective until the granting by the sheriff officer of a receipt for payment in accordance therewith, when the debtor's interest in the released article shall be transferred to the third party.

(5) Where an article is released in pursuance of sub-paragraph (3)(*b*) above from a poinding, a sheriff officer may, notwithstanding paragraph 9 above, poind other articles belonging to the debtor in the same premises.

(6) This sub-paragraph applies where, at any time after the execution of a poinding, a third party claims that any of the poinded articles is owned in common by the debtor and himself but does not seek release of the article from the poinding, and either—

(*a*) the claim is admitted by the creditor and the debtor; or

(*b*) the claim is not admitted by both the creditor and the debtor, but the sheriff, on an application made to him, is satisfied that the claim is valid.

(7) Where sub-paragraph (6) above applies, the creditor shall pay to the third party—

(*a*) if the article is sold, the fraction of the proceeds of sale (or of the value of that article fixed under paragraph 5(4) above, whichever is the greater) which corresponds to the third party's interest in the article;

(*b*) if ownership of the article passes to the creditor in default of sale, the fraction of the value of the article fixed under paragraph 5(4) above which corresponds to the third party's interest in the article.

Certain proceedings under this Schedule to postpone further steps in the diligence

23.—(1) Where an application under any of the provisions of this Schedule listed in sub-paragraph (2) below has been made—

(*a*) it shall be not be competent during a relevant period to remove the poinded articles for sale or to hold a sale;

(*b*) a relevant period shall be disregarded in calculating the period on the expiry of which the poinding ceases to have effect under paragraph 11 above.

(2) The provisions referred to in sub-paragraph (1) above are—

(*a*) paragraph 1(4), 7(1), 21(2) or 22(3) (release of poinded articles);

(*b*) paragraph 8(1) or (3) (invalidity, cessation or recall of poinding);

(*c*) paragraph 10(1) (sist of proceedings in poinding of mobile homes);

(*d*) paragraph 12(4) (restoration of articles removed without consent or authority);

(*e*) paragraph 12(5) (recall of order under paragraph 12(4)).

(3) In sub-paragraph (1) above "a relevant period" means—

(*a*) the period while the application is pending;

(*b*) where the application has been disposed of by the sheriff—

(i) the period during which an application for leave to appeal may be made;

(ii) where an application for leave to appeal is made, the period until leave has been refused or the application has been abandoned;

(iii) where leave to appeal has been granted, the period during which an appeal may be made; or

(iv) where an appeal against the decision is made, the period until the matter has been finally determined or the appeal has been abandoned.

Power to enter premises and open shut and lockfast places

24. A summary warrant shall contain a warrant authorising a sheriff officer to enter premises in the occupancy of the debtor in order to execute the poinding or the sale, or the removal and sale of the poinded articles and, for any of those purposes, to open shut and lockfast places.

Expenses chargeable against the debtor

25.—(1) Subject to paragraphs 26 to 29 below, there shall be chargeable against the debtor any expenses incurred—

(*a*) in serving a notice under paragraph 3 above before entering a dwellinghouse for the purpose of executing a poinding;

(*b*) in executing a poinding under paragraph 5 above;
(*c*) in granting a receipt under sub-paragraph (5) of paragraph 6 above for payment for redemption under sub-paragraph (4) thereof;
(*d*) in granting a receipt under paragraph 15(3) above for payment for the redemption of any poinded article;
(*e*) in making intimation, sending particulars of the arrangements for the sale to the sheriff clerk and giving public notice under paragraph 16 above;
(*f*) in removing any poinded articles for sale;
(*g*) in making arrangements for and conducting a sale;
(*h*) where the arrangements for a sale have been cancelled under paragraph 17(4) above, in returning poinded articles to any premises from which they have been removed for sale;
(*j*) in making a report of sale under paragraph 20 above;
(*k*) in granting a receipt under paragraph 22(4) above for payment for the release from a poinding of any article which is owned in common;
(*l*) in opening shut and lockfast places in the execution of the diligence;
(*m*) by a solicitor in instructing a sheriff officer to take any of the steps specified in this sub-paragraph.

(2) The Lord Advocate may by regulations add to, delete or vary any of the steps specified in sub-paragraph (1) above.

26. Where arrangements for a sale are cancelled under sub-paragraph (4) of paragraph 17 above, if new arrangements are made for the sale in the circumstances mentioned in sub-paragraph (5) thereof, there shall be chargeable against the debtor the expenses incurred in the making of the new arrangements but not in the making of the arrangements which have been cancelled.

27. Subject to paragraph 28 below, where any such further poinding as is mentioned in paragraph 12(2) above has been executed, there shall be chargeable against the debtor the expenses incurred in that poinding but not the expenses incurred in the original poinding.

28. Where any such further poinding as is mentioned in sub-paragraph (2) of paragraph 12 above has been executed and—
(*a*) the creditor has, as a condition of his consenting to the removal of the poinded articles under sub-paragraph (1)(*a*) of that paragraph, required the debtor to undertake liability for the expenses incurred in the original poinding; or
(*b*) the sheriff has, when authorising the removal of the poinded articles under sub-paragraph (1)(*b*) of that paragraph, directed that the debtor shall be liable for those expenses,

there shall be chargeable against the debtor the expenses incurred in both poindings.

29. Where a new date is arranged under paragraph 17(2) above for the holding of a sale or for the removal of poinded articles for sale, there shall be chargeable against the debtor the expenses incurred in connection with arranging the new date but not those incurred in connection with arranging the original date.

Circumstances where liability for expenses is at the discretion of the sheriff

30. The liability for any expenses incurred by the creditor or the debtor—
(*a*) in an application by the creditor or a sheriff officer to the sheriff under any provision of this Schedule; or
(*b*) in implementing an order under—
(i) paragraph 6(1) above (order for security or immediate disposal of poinded articles); or
(ii) paragraph 12(4) to (6) or 13 above (orders dealing with unauthorised removal, damage or destruction of poinded articles),

shall be as determined by the sheriff.

Calculation of amount chargeable against debtor under the foregoing provisions

31. Expenses awarded by the sheriff against the debtor in favour of the creditor in a determination under paragraph 30 above in respect of an application other than an application under paragraph 12(4) to (6) or 13 above shall be calculated, whether or not the application is opposed by the debtor, as if it were unopposed, except that, if the debtor opposes the application on grounds which appear to the sheriff to be frivolous, the sheriff may award an

additional sum of expenses, not exceeding £25 or such amount as may be prescribed in regulations made by the Lord Advocate, against the debtor.

Circumstances where no expenses are due to or by either party

32. Subject to paragraph 33 below, the debtor shall not be liable to the creditor nor the creditor to the debtor for any expenses incurred by the other party in connection with—
(*a*) an application by the debtor to the sheriff under any provision of this Schedule;
(*b*) any objections to such an application;
(*c*) a hearing held by virtue of paragraph 8(5) above.

33. If—
(*a*) an application mentioned in paragraph 32(*a*) above is frivolous;
(*b*) such an application is opposed on frivolous grounds; or
(*c*) a party requires a hearing mentioned in paragraph 32(*c*) above to be held on frivolous grounds,
the sheriff may award a sum of expenses, not exceeding £25 or such amount as may be prescribed in regulations made by the Lord Advocate, against the party acting frivolously in favour of the other party.

Supplementary

34. Any expenses chargeable against the debtor by virtue of any provision of this Schedule shall be recoverable out of the proceeds of sale.

[1] 35. In this Schedule—
"creditor" means—
(*a*) for the purposes of section 247 of the Local Government (Scotland) Act 1947, a rating authority;
(*b*) for the purposes of section 63 of the Taxes Management Act 1970, any collector of taxes;
(*c*) for the purposes of paragraph 3 of Schedule 1 to the Car Tax Act 1983 and paragraph 6 of Schedule 7 to the Value Added Tax Act 1983, the Commissioners of Customs and Excise;
(*d*) for the purposes of—
(i) paragraph 7 of Schedule 2 to the Abolition of Domestic Rates Etc. (Scotland) Act 1987, the levying authority;
(ii) that paragraph as read with section 17(10) or (11) of that Act, the regional or islands council;
"dwellinghouse" includes a caravan, a houseboat and any structure adapted for use as a residence;
"the poinding schedule" means the schedule provided for in paragraph 5(5) above;
"the sum recoverable"—
(*a*) for the purposes of the said section 247, includes the surcharge recoverable thereunder but excludes interest;
(*b*) for the purposes of the said section 63, includes interest.

NOTE
[1] As amended by the Abolition of Domestic Rates Etc. (Scotland) Act 1987, s.33(*d*).

SCHEDULE 6

MINOR AND CONSEQUENTIAL AMENDMENTS

General amendment

1. Any reference in any enactment to an order being enforceable in like manner as a recorded decree arbitral shall be construed as a reference to such an order being enforceable in like manner as an extract registered decree arbitral bearing a warrant for execution issued by the sheriff court of any sheriffdom in Scotland.

Specific amendments

[Amendments to Acts reprinted in *The Parliament House Book* have been given effect.]

BUT A.P. order occurs where no intimation given - used where you think evidence would be destroyed
- sh. ct. has no power to grant this type of order

(4) VALUE ISSUES - value of claim - lower value £1500. Over this concurrent).
- generally incompetent to raise actions for less than £1500 in Ct. of S.

Higher the value the more likely it is to go to Ct. of S. Papers could be sent to counsel to obtain a preliminary note on choice of).

(5) ATTRACTIVE PROCEDURAL FEATURES

1) ADJUSTMENT - adjustment procedure is probably one of least satisfactory aspects of sh. ct. procedure

2) MOTION - in Ct. of S. Rule of Ct. 57 - motions which are not opposed proceed on basis of written case basically a letter
- extremely efficient in terms of expense

3) Summary decree - R89B - summary decree even where case has been defended, if ct. holds that the defence as initially lodged does not form a defence
- puts a damper on skeleton defences which in sh. ct. have to wait to close of record

4) Jury Trials

5) Optional Procedure in reparation cases - R.188E-P
- Rolls Royce of reparation action - introduced in 1985 + now most significant way of proceeding
- all actions for personal injury where P. elects for this. P. waives right for jury trial.
- procedural differences are that optional procedure has its own form of summons where pleader must briefly states facts relied on as cause of accident. In addition P. must mention the legal arguments in a short form

GO TO B279

Section 108(2) SCHEDULE 7

TRANSITIONAL PROVISIONS

1. Notwithstanding the repeal by this Act of subsection (4) of section 36 of the Sheriff Courts (Scotland) Act 1971—
   (*a*) any direction made under that subsection which is in force immediately before the commencement of that repeal shall continue in force; and
   (*b*) any summary cause action for payment which is pending immediately before such commencement shall proceed and be disposed of,

as if this Act had not been passed.

2. The sheriff may refuse to make a time to pay order if, on an objection being duly made in pursuance of section 6(6)(*a*) of this Act, he is satisfied that a direction has been made under section 36(4) of the said Act of 1971 whereby the debt concerned was payable by instalments, but the right to pay by instalments has ceased by reason of failure to pay an instalment.

3. Without prejudice to paragraphs 4 to 6 of this Schedule, a warrant issued before the commencement of Part VI of this Act, for the enforcement by diligence of an obligation to pay money, contained in an extract of a decree of the Court of Session or the sheriff court or of a document which has been registered in the Books of Council and Session or in sheriff court books shall be treated as if it were a warrant contained in such a decree granted after the commencement of that Part.

4. Nothing in Part II of this Act shall affect a poinding which is in effect immediately before the commencement of that Part; and further proceedings in such a poinding and in any warrant sale to follow thereon shall be in accordance with the law in force immediately before such commencement.

5. Nothing in this Act shall affect an arrestment of earnings in the hands of an employer which has been executed before the commencement of Part III of this Act nor preclude the bringing of an action of furthcoming in pursuance of such an arrestment or the granting of a decree in any such action.

6. Where an arrestment of a debtor's earnings in the hands of an employer which has been executed before the commencement of Part III of this Act has effect in relation to earnings payable on the first pay-day occurring after such commencement, the execution of an earnings arrestment or a current maintenance arrestment against earnings payable to the debtor by the employer shall not be competent until after that pay-day.

7.—(1) Subject to sub-paragraph (2) below, a summary warrant granted before the commencement of Schedules 4 and 5 to this Act under or by virtue of any of the enactments to which this paragraph applies shall be deemed to authorise only the following diligences—
   (*a*) a poinding and sale in accordance with the said Schedule 5;
   (*b*) an earnings arrestment; and
   (*c*) an arrestment other than an arrestment of the debtor's earnings in the hands of his employer.

(2) If at the commencement of those Schedules diligence executed in pursuance of a warrant referred to in sub-paragraph (1) above is in effect, that diligence shall proceed as if this Act had not been passed.

(3) This paragraph applies to the following enactments—
   (*a*) section 247 of the Local Government (Scotland) Act 1947;
   (*b*) section 63 of the Taxes Management Act 1970;
   (*c*) section 33 of the Finance Act 1972;
   (*d*) paragraph 16(2) of Schedule 7 to the Finance Act 1972;
   (*e*) paragraph 3 of Schedule 1 to the Car Tax Act 1983;
   (*f*) paragraph 6 of Schedule 7 to the Value Added Tax Act 1983.

8.—(1) Where before the commencement of paragraphs 21 and 23 of Schedule 6 to this Act—
   (*a*) a warrant has been granted under any of the enactments to which this paragraph applies; and
   (*b*) no diligence has been executed in pursuance of the warrant,

the warrant shall cease to have effect.

(2) Where before the commencement of the said paragraphs 21 and 23—

(*a*) a warrant has been granted under any of the enactments to which this paragraph applies; and

(*b*) diligence has been executed in pursuance of the warrant,

the diligence shall proceed as if this Act had not been passed.

(3) This paragraph applies to the following enactments—

(*a*) section 253 of the Customs and Excise Act 1952;

(*b*) paragraph 10 of Schedule 2 to the Betting and Gaming Duties Act 1972;

(*c*) section 117 of the Customs and Excise Management Act 1979;

(*d*) section 29 of the Betting and Gaming Duties Act 1981.

9.—(1) The provisions of this Act relating to the liability for the expenses of a diligence shall not apply in relation to a diligence to which this paragraph applies.

(2) Section 93(1) or (2) of this Act shall not prevent a creditor taking proceedings in court to recover any expenses of a diligence to which this paragraph applies which are chargeable against the debtor.

(3) Notwithstanding section 95 of this Act, a diligence to which this paragraph applies shall cease to have effect on payment or tender of the sum due under the decree or other document.

(4) This paragraph applies to the following diligences—

(*a*) a poinding and sale;

(*b*) an arrestment and action of furthcoming or sale;

in effect at the commencement of sections 93 and 95 of this Act.

10. Until the commencement of the repeal of the Supplementary Benefits Act 1976 by Schedule 11 to the Social Security Act 1986 the said Act of 1976 shall have effect as if there were inserted after section 18 of that Act the new section set out in section 68 of this Act with the following modifications—

(*a*) for "25A" there shall be substituted "18A"; and

(*b*) for references to income support there shall be substituted references to supplementary benefit.

Section 108

SCHEDULE 8

REPEALS

[Repeals affecting *The Parliament House Book* have been given effect.]

Crown Proceedings (Armed Forces) Act 1987

(1987 c. 25)

An Act to repeal section 10 of the Crown Proceedings Act 1947 and to provide for the revival of that section in certain circumstances. [15th May 1987]

Repeal of s.10 of the Crown Proceedings Act 1947

1. Subject to section 2 below, section 10 of the Crown Proceedings Act 1947 (exclusions from liability in tort in cases involving the armed forces) shall cease to have effect except in relation to anything suffered by a person in consequence of an act or omission committed before the date on which this Act is passed.

Revival of s.10

2.—(1) Subject to the following provisions of this section, the Secretary of State may, at any time after the coming into force of section 1 above, by order—

(*a*) revive the effect of section 10 of the Crown Proceedings Act 1947 either for all purposes or for such purposes as may be described in the order; or (*b*) where that section has effect for the time being in pursuance of an order made by virtue of paragraph (*a*) above, provide for that section to cease to have effect either for all of the purposes for which it so has effect or for such of them as may be so described.

(2) The Secretary of State shall not make an order reviving the effect of the said section 10 for any purposes unless it appears to him necessary or expedient to do so—

(*a*) by reason of any imminent national danger or of any great emergency that has arisen; or

(*b*) for the purposes of any warlike operations in any part of the world outside the United Kingdom or of any other operations which are or are to be carried out in connection with the warlike activity of any persons in any such part of the world.

(3) Subject to subsection (4) below, an order under this section describing purposes for which the effect of the said section 10 is to be revived, or for which that section is to cease to have effect, may describe those purposes by reference to any matter whatever and may make different provision for different cases, circumstances or persons.

(4) Nothing in any order under this section shall revive the effect of the said section 10, or provide for that section to cease to have effect, in relation to anything suffered by a person in consequence of an act or omission committed before the date on which the order comes into force.

(5) The power to make an order under this section shall be exercisable by statutory instrument subject to annulment in pursuance of a resolution of either House of Parliament.

Consequential adaptations of existing enactments etc.

3.—(1) Except in so far as an order under section 2 above otherwise provides, any reference to section 10 of the Crown Proceedings Act 1947 in any Act passed, or subordinate legislation made, before the passing of this Act shall be construed as a reference to that section as it from time to time has effect by virtue of this Act.

(2) Subsection (1) above shall apply, as it applies to express references to the said section 10—

(*a*) to the references to that section which are comprised in the references in the said Act of 1947 to or to the provisions of that Act itself; and

(*b*) to any other references to the said section 10 which are comprised in references to that Act, in references to enactments generally or in references to any description of enactments.

(3) In this section "subordinate legislation" has the same meaning as in the Interpretation Act 1978.

Expenses

4. There shall be paid out of money provided by Parliament any expenses incurred by a Minister of the Crown or Government department in consequence of the provisions of this Act.

Short title, interpretation and extent

5.—(1) This Act may be cited as the Crown Proceedings (Armed Forces) Act 1987.

(2) For the purposes of the application of any provision of this Act in relation to subsection (2) of section 10 of the Crown Proceedings Act 1947 references in this Act to anything suffered by any person in consequence of an act or omission committed before a particular date shall include references to anything which—

(*a*) would not, apart from this subsection, be regarded as suffered in consequence of an act or omission; but

(b) is suffered in consequence of the nature or condition at a time before that date of any land, premises, ship, aircraft, hovercraft, or vehicle or of any equipment or supplies.

(3) This Act shall extend to Northern Ireland.

Consumer Protection Act 1987

(1987 c. 43)

An Act to make provision with respect to the liability of persons for damage caused by defective products; to consolidate with amendments the Consumer Safety Act 1978 and the Consumer Safety (Amendment) Act 1986; to make provision with respect to the giving of price indications; to amend Part I of the Health and Safety at Work etc. Act 1974 and sections 31 and 80 of the Explosives Act 1875; to repeal the Trade Descriptions Act 1972 and the Fabrics (Misdescription) Act 1913; and for connected purposes. [15th May 1987]

ARRANGEMENT OF SECTIONS

PART I

PRODUCT LIABILITY

Section

[THE NEXT PAGE IS B 279]

- no formal adjustment period unless ct. decides that it is appropriate. Obligation on each party to lodge all documents on which it intends to rely within 14 days of order allowing proof

- can proceed by way of affidavits, part. attractive in diminishing costs of bringing action where no. of witnesses.

6) Commercial Causes - R. 148 - 151F

7) Interim damages

Court of Session - Petition Procedure

The distinction between actions initiated by summons + those initiated by petition can be stated thus:-

- the object of a summons is to enforce a P's legal right against a D. who resists it, or to protect a legal right which the D. is infringing; the object of a petition, on other hand, is to obtain from the administrative J. of the ct, power to do something or to require something to be done. The contentious character of proceedings initiated by summons necessitated of higher degree of formality

- Petition may be served on many people but unusual for answers, or defences, to be lodged except in cases of supervision + interdict or custody of children. Proofs on petitions are rare. Many Pet. involve the appointment of a person to office

- Caveats are maintained with an index

- CAVEAT - anyone apprehensive of an action of interdict being raised against him + an interim interdict being applied for in his absence, may lodge a caveat with sh. cl. or Depute Principal Clerk of Session in the Ct. of S. where caveats are kept in the Pet. dept.

A caveat is a written request for notice in the event of such an application being made

- caveat endures 12 months - on expiry of period a fresh caveat may be lodged GO TO B307

PART II

CONSUMER SAFETY

[Not reprinted.]

PART III

MISLEADING PRICE INDICATIONS

[Not reprinted.]

PART IV

ENFORCEMENT OF PARTS II AND III

[Not reprinted.]

PART V

MISCELLANEOUS AND SUPPLEMENTAL

PART I

PRODUCT LIABILITY

Purpose and construction of Part I

1.—(1) This Part shall have effect for the purpose of making such provision as is necessary in order to comply with the product liability Directive and shall be construed accordingly.

(2) In this Part, except in so far as the context otherwise requires—

"agricultural produce" means any produce of the soil, of stock-farming or of fisheries;

"dependant" and "relative" have the same meaning as they have in, respectively, the Fatal Accidents Act 1976 and the Damages (Scotland) Act 1976;

"producer", in relation to a product, means—

(*a*) the person who manufactured it;

(*b*) in the case of a substance which has not been manufactured but has been won or abstracted, the person who won or abstracted it;

(*c*) in the case of a product which has not been manufactured, won or abstracted but essential characteristics of which are attributable to an industrial or other process having been carried out (for example, in relation to agricultural produce), the person who carried out that process;

"product" means any goods or electricity and (subject to subsection (3) below) includes a product which is comprised in another product, whether by virtue of being a component part or raw material or otherwise; and "the product liability Directive" means the Directive of the Council of the European Communities, dated 25th July 1985, (No. 85/374/EEC) on the approximation of the laws, regulations and administrative provisions of the member States concerning liability for defective products.

(3) For the purposes of this Part a person who supplies any product in which products are comprised, whether by virtue of being component parts or raw materials, or otherwise, shall not be treated by reason only of his supply of that product as supplying any of the products so comprised.

Liability for defective products

2.—(1) Subject to the following provisions of this Part, where any damage is caused wholly or partly by a defect in a product, every person to whom subsection (2) below applies shall be liable for the damage.

(2) This subsection applies to—

(*a*) the producer of the product;

(*b*) any person who, by putting his name on the product or using a trade mark or other distinguishing mark in relation to the product, has held himself out to be the producer of the product;

(*c*) any person who has imported the product into a member State from a place outside the member States in order, in the course of any business of his, to supply it to another.

(3) Subject as aforesaid, where any damage is caused wholly or partly by a defect in a product, any person who supplied the product (whether to the person who suffered the damage, to the producer of any product in which the product in question is comprised or to any other person) shall be liable for the damage if—

(*a*) the person who suffered the damage requests the supplier to identify one or more of the persons (whether still in existence or not) to whom subsection (2) above applies in relation to the product;

(*b*) that request is made within a reasonable period after the damage occurs and at a time when it is not reasonably practicable for the person making the request to identify all those persons; and

(*c*) the supplier fails, within a reasonable period after receiving the request, either to comply with the request or to identify the person who supplied the product to him.

(4) Neither subsection (2) nor subsection (3) above shall apply to a person in respect of any defect in any game or agricultural produce if the only supply of the game or produce by that person to another was at a time when it had not undergone an industrial process.

(5) Where two or more persons are liable by virtue of this Part for the same damage, their liability shall be joint and several.

(6) This section shall be without prejudice to any liability arising otherwise than by virtue of this Part.

Meaning of "defect"

3.—(1) Subject to the following provisions of this section, there is a defect in a product for the purposes of this Part if the safety of the product is not such as persons generally are entitled to expect; and for those purposes "safety", in relation to a product, shall include safety with respect to products comprised in that product and safety in the context of risks of damage to property, as well as in the context of risks of death or personal injury.

(2) In determining for the purposes of subsection (1) above what persons generally are entitled to expect in relation to a product all the circumstances shall be taken into account, including—

(*a*) the manner in which, and purposes for which, the product has been marketed, its get-up, the use of any mark in relation to the product and any instructions for, or warnings with respect to, doing or refraining from doing anything with or in relation to the product;

(*b*) what might reasonably be expected to be done with or in relation to the product; and

(*c*) the time when the product was supplied by its producer to another;

and nothing in this section shall require a defect to be inferred from the fact alone that the safety of a product which is supplied after that time is greater than the safety of the product in question.

Defences

4.—(1) In any civil proceedings by virtue of this Part against any person ("the person proceeded against") in respect of a defect in a product it shall be a defence for him to show—

(*a*) that the defect is attributable to compliance with any requirement imposed by or under any enactment or with any Community obligation; or

(*b*) that the person proceeded against did not at any time supply the product to another; or

(*c*) that the following conditions are satisfied, that is to say—

(i) that the only supply of the product to another by the person proceeded against was otherwise than in the course of a business of that person's; and

(ii) that section 2(2) above does not apply to that person or applies to him by virtue only of things done otherwise than with a view to profit; or

(*d*) that the defect did not exist in the product at the relevant time; or

(*e*) that the state of scientific and technical knowledge at the relevant time was not such that a producer of products of the same description as the product in question might be expected to have discovered the defect if it had existed in his products while they were under his control; or

(*f*) that the defect—

(i) constituted a defect in a product ("the subsequent product") in which the product in question had been comprised; and

(ii) was wholly attributable to the design of the subsequent product or to compliance by the producer of the product in question with instructions given by the producer of the subsequent product.

(2) In this section "the relevant time", in relation to electricity, means the time at which it was generated, being a time before it was transmitted or distributed, and in relation to any other product, means—

(*a*) if the person proceeded against is a person to whom subsection (2) of section 2 above applies in relation to the product, the time when he supplied the product to another;

(*b*) if that subsection does not apply to that person in relation to the product, the time when the product was last supplied by a person to whom that subsection does apply in relation to the product.

Damage giving rise to liability

5.—(1) Subject to the following provisions of this section, in this Part "damage" means death or personal injury or any loss or damage to any property (including land).

(2) A person shall not be liable under section 2 above in respect of any defect in a product for the loss of or any damage to the product itself or for the loss of or any damage to the whole or any part of any product which has been supplied with the product in question comprised in it.

(3) A person shall not be liable under section 2 above for any loss of or damage to any property which, at the time it is lost or damaged, is not—

(*a*) of a description of property ordinarily intended for private use, occupation or consumption; and

(*b*) intended by the person suffering the loss or damage mainly for his own private use, occupation or consumption.

(4) No damages shall be awarded to any person by virtue of this part in respect of any loss of or damage to any property if the amount which would fall to be so awarded to that person, apart from this subsection and any liability for interest, does not exceed £275.

. . .

(8) Subsections (5) to (7) above shall not extend to Scotland.

Application of certain enactments etc.

6—(1) Any damage for which a person is liable under section 2 above shall be deemed to have been caused—

(*a*) for the purposes of the Fatal Accidents Act 1976, by that person's wrongful act, neglect or default;

(*b*) for the purposes of section 3 of the Law Reform (Miscellaneous Provisions) (Scotland) Act 1940 (contribution among joint wrongdoers), by that person's wrongful act or negligent act or omission;

(*c*) for the purposes of section 1 of the Damages (Scotland) Act 1976 (rights of relatives of a deceased), by that person's act or omission; and

(*d*) for the purposes of Part II of the Administration of Justice Act 1982 (damages for personal injuries, etc.—Scotland), by an act or omission giving rise to liability in that person to pay damages.

(2) Where—

(*a*) a person's death is caused wholly or partly by a defect in a product, or a person dies after suffering damage which has been so caused;

(*b*) a request such as mentioned in paragraph (*a*) of subsection (3) of section 2 above is made to a supplier of the product by that person's personal representatives or, in the case of a person whose death is caused wholly or partly by the defect, by any dependant or relative of that person; and

(*c*) the conditions specified in paragraphs (*b*) and (*c*) of that subsection are satisfied in relation to that request.

this Part shall have effect for the purposes of the Law Reform (Miscellaneous Provisions) Act 1934, the Fatal Accidents Act 1976 and the Damages (Scotland) Act 1976 as if liability of the supplier to that person under that subsection did not depend on that person having requested the supplier to identify certain persons or on the said conditions having been satisfied in relation to a request made by that person.

(3) Section 1 of the Congenital Disabilities (Civil Liability) Act 1976 shall have effect for the purposes of this Part as if—

(*a*) a person were answerable to a child in respect of an occurrence caused wholly or partly by a defect in a product if he is or has been liable under section 2 above in respect of any effect of the occurrence on a parent of the child, or would be so liable if the occurrence caused a parent of the child to suffer damage;

(*b*) the provisions of this Part relating to liability under section 2 above applied in relation to liability by virtue of paragraph (*a*) above under the said section 1; and

(*c*) subsection (6) of the said section 1 (exclusion of liability) were omitted.

(4) Where any damage is caused partly by a defect in a product and partly by the fault of the person suffering the damage, the Law Reform (Contributory Negligence) Act 1945 and section 5 of the Fatal Accidents Act 1976 (contributory negligence) shall have effect as if the defect were the fault of every person liable by virtue of this Part for the damage caused by the defect.

(5) in subsection (4) above "fault" has the same meaning as in the said Act of 1945.

(6) Schedule 1 to this Act shall have effect for the purpose of amending the Limitation Act 1980 and the Prescription and Limitation (Scotland) Act 1973 in their application in relation to the bringing of actions by virtue of this Part.

(7) It is hereby declared that liability by virtue of this Part is to be treated as liability in tort for the purposes of any enactment conferring jurisdiction on any court with respect to any matter.

(8) Nothing in this Part shall prejudice the operation of section 12 of the Nuclear Installations Act 1965 (rights to compensation for certain breaches of duties confined to rights under that Act).

Prohibition of exclusions from liability

7. The liability of a person by virtue of this Part to a person who has suffered damage caused wholly or partly by a defect in a product, or to a dependant or relative of such a person, shall not be limited or excluded by any contract term, by any notice or by any other provision.

Power to modify Part I

8.—(1) Her Majesty may by Order in Council make such modifications of this Part and of any other enactment (including an enactment contained in the following Parts of this Act, or in an Act passed after this Act) as appear to Her Majesty in Council to be necessary or expedient in consequence of any modification of the product liability Directive which is made at any time after the passing of this Act.

(2) An Order in Council under subsection (1) above shall not be submitted to Her Majesty in Council unless a draft of the Order has been laid before, and approved by a resolution of, each House of Parliament.

Application of Part I to Crown

9.—(1) Subject to subsection (2) below, this Part shall bind the Crown.

(2) The Crown shall not, as regards the Crown's liability by virtue of this Part, be bound by this Part further than the Crown is made liable in tort or in reparation under the Crown Proceedings Act 1947, as that Act has effect from time to time.

. . . . . .

PART V

MISCELLANEOUS AND SUPPLEMENTAL

Interpretation

45.—(1) In this Act, except in so far as the context otherwise requires—

"aircraft" includes gliders, balloons and hovercraft;

"business" includes a trade or profession and the activities of a professional or trade association or of a local authority or other public authority;

"conditional sale agreement", "credit—sale agreement" and "hire-purchase agreement" have the same meanings as in the Consumer Credit Act 1974 but as if in the definitions in that Act "goods" had the same meaning as in this Act;

. . .

"gas" has the same meaning as in Part I of the Gas Act 1986;

"goods" includes substances, growing crops and things comprised in

land by virtue of being attached to it and any ship, aircraft or vehicle;
"information" includes accounts, estimates and returns;

. . .

"mark" and "trade mark" have the same meanings as in the Trade Marks Act 1938;

. . .

[1] "motor vehicle" has the same meaning as in the Road Traffic Act 1988;

. . .

"personal injury" includes any disease and any other impairment of a person's physical or mental condition;

"premises" includes any place and any ship, aircraft or vehicle;

. . .

"records" includes any books or documents and any records in non-documentary form;

. . .

"ship" includes any boat and any other description of vessel used in navigation;

. . .

"substance" means any natural or artificial substance, whether in solid, liquid or gaseous form or in the form of a vapour, and includes substances that are comprised in or mixed with other goods;

"supply" and cognate expressions shall be construed in accordance with section 46 below;

. . .

(4) Section 68(2) of the Trade Marks Act 1938 (construction of references to use of a mark) shall apply for the purposes of this Act as it applies for the purposes of that Act.

(5) In Scotland, any reference in this Act to things comprised in land by virtue of being attached to it is a reference to moveables which have become heritable by accession to heritable property.

NOTE

[1] As amended by the Road Traffic (Consequential Provisions) Act 1988.

Meaning of "supply"

46.—(1) Subject to the following provisions of this section, references in this Act to supplying goods shall be construed as references to doing any of the following, whether as principal or agent, that is to say—

(*a*) selling, hiring out or lending the goods;
(*b*) entering into a hire-purchase agreement to furnish the goods;
(*c*) the performance of any contract for work and materials to furnish the goods;
(*d*) providing the goods in exchange for any consideration (including trading stamps) other than money;
(*e*) providing the goods in or in connection with the performance of any statutory function; or
(*f*) giving the goods as a prize or otherwise making a gift of the goods;

and, in relation to gas or water, those references shall be construed as including references to providing the service by which the gas or water is made available for use.

(2) For the purposes of any reference in this Act to supplying goods, where a person ("the ostensible supplier") supplies goods to another person ("the customer") under a hire-purchase agreement, conditional sale agreement or credit-sale agreement or under an agreement for the hiring of goods (other than a hire-purchase agreement) and the ostensible supplier—

(*a*) carries on the business of financing the provision of goods for others by means of such agreements; and
(*b*) in the course of that business acquired his interest in the goods supplied to the customer as a means of financing the provision of them for the customer by a further person ("the effective supplier").

the effective supplier and not the ostensible supplier shall be treated as supplying the goods to the customer.

(3) Subject to subsection (4) below, the performance of any contract by the erection of any building or structure on any land or by the carrying out of any other building works shall be treated for the purposes of this Act as a supply of goods in so far as, but only in so far as, it involves the provision of any goods to any person by means of their incorporation into the building, structure or works.

(4) Except for the purposes of, and in relation to, notices to warn or any provision made by or under Part III of this Act, references in this Act to supplying goods shall not include references to supplying goods comprised in land where the supply is effected by the creation or disposal of an interest in the land.

(5) Except in Part I of this Act references in this Act to a person's supplying goods shall be confined to references to that person's supplying goods in the course of a business of his, but for the purposes of this subsection it shall be immaterial whether the business is a business of dealing in the goods.

(6) For the purposes of subsection (5) above goods shall not be treated as supplied in the course of a business if they are supplied, in pursuance of an obligation arising under or in connection with the insurance of the goods, to the person with whom they were insured.

. . .

(8) Where any goods have at any time been supplied by being hired out or lent to any person, neither a continuation or renewal of the hire or loan (whether on the same or different terms) nor any transaction for the transfer after that time of any interest in the goods to the person to whom they were hired or lent shall be treated for the purposes of this Act as a further supply of the goods to that person.

(9) A ship, aircraft or motor vehicle shall not be treated for the purposes of this Act as supplied to any person by reason only that services consisting in the carriage of goods or passengers in that ship, aircraft or vehicle, or in its use for any other purpose, are provided to that person in pursuance of an agreement relating to the use of the ship, aircraft or vehicle for a particular period or for particular voyages, flights or journeys.

Savings for certain privileges

47.—(1) Nothing in this Act shall be taken as requiring any person to produce any records if he would be entitled to refuse to produce those records in any proceedings in any court on the grounds that they are the subject of legal professional privilege or, in Scotland, that they contain a confidential communication made by or to an advocate or solicitor in that capacity, or as authorising any person to take possession of any records which are in the possession of a person who would be so entitled.

(2) Nothing in this Act shall be construed as requiring a person to answer any question or give any information if to do so would incriminate that person or that person's spouse.

. . . .

Short title, commencement and transitional provision

50.—(1) This Act may be cited as the Consumer Protection Act 1987.

[1] (2) This Act shall come into force on such day as the Secretary of State may by order made by statutory instrument appoint, and different days may be so appointed for different provisions or for different purposes.

. . .

(4) An order under subsection (2) above bringing a provision into force may contain such transitional provision in connection with the coming into force of that provision as the Secretary of State considers appropriate.

. . .

(7) Nothing in this Act or in any order under subsection (2) above shall make any person liable by virtue of Part I of this Act for any damage caused wholly or partly by a defect in a product which was supplied to any person by its producer before the coming into force of Part I of this Act.

(8) Expressions used in subsection (7) above and in Part I of this Act have the same meanings in that subsection as in that Part.

NOTE

[1] Part I was brought into force on 1st March 1988 by S.I. 1987 No. 1680.

SCHEDULES

. . . .

Section 6

[1] SCHEDULE 1

NOTE

[1] The amendments made by this Schedule to the Prescription and Limitation (Scotland) Act 1973 are now shown in the print of that Act in Division J of *The Parliament House Book*.

Consumer Arbitration Agreements Act 1988

(1988 c. 21)

An Act to extend to consumers certain rights as regards agreements to refer future differences to arbitration and for purposes connected therewith. [28th June 1988]

. . . .

Scotland

Arbitration agreements: Scotland

6.—(1) In the case of a consumer contract to which, by virtue of subsections (2) to (4) of section 15 of the Act of 1977 (scope of Part II of that Act), sections 16 to 18 of that Act apply, an agreement to refer future differences arising out of the contract to arbitration cannot, if it is a domestic arbitration agreement, be enforced against the consumer in respect of a relevant difference so arising except—

(*a*) with his written consent given after that difference has arisen; or

(*b*) where, subject to subsection (2) below, he has submitted to arbitration in pursuance of the agreement (whether or not the arbitration was in respect of that difference); or

(*c*) by virtue of an order under section 7 below in respect of that difference.

(2) In determining for the purposes of subsection (1)(*b*) above whether the consumer has submitted to arbitration, any arbitration which takes place in consequence of an order of the court under section 7 below shall be disregarded.

Power of court to disapply section 6 where no detriment to consumer

7.—[1] (1) Subject to subsection (4) below, the Court of Session or the sheriff ("the court") may, on an application made after a relevant difference has arisen, order that section 6 above shall not apply as respects that difference.

(2) No such order shall be made unless the court is satisfied that it would not be detrimental to the interests of the consumer were the difference to be referred to arbitration in pursuance of the arbitration agreement.

(3) In determining for the purposes of subsection (2) above whether there would be any detriment to the consumer's interests, the court shall have regard to all factors appearing to be relevant, including, in particular, the availability of legal aid and the relative amounts of any expenses which he might incur—

(*a*) if the difference is referred to arbitration; and

(*b*) if it is determined by proceedings before a court.

(4) No order shall be made under subsection (1) above where, if (disregarding the arbitration agreement) the difference were to be resolved by civil proceedings in the sheriff court, the form of summary cause process to be used for the purposes of those proceedings would be that of a small claim.

NOTE

[1] An application to the sheriff under this subsection shall be made by summary application (S.I. 1989 No. 80).

Construction of sections 6 and 7

8.—(1) In sections 6 and 7 above "consumer" and "consumer contract" have the meanings assigned to those expressions by section 25(1) of the Act of 1977 and "domestic arbitration agreement" has the same meaning as in section 1 of the Arbitration Act 1975.

(2) For the purposes of sections 6 and 7 above a difference is "relevant" where, if (disregarding the arbitration agreement) it were to be resolved by civil proceedings in the sheriff court—

(*a*) the form of process to be used for the purposes of those proceedings would be that of a summary cause; or

(*b*) the proceedings would come within such description of proceedings as may, by order, be specified by the Secretary of State for the purposes of this paragraph.

(3) The power to make an order under paragraph (*b*) of subsection (2) above shall be exercisable by statutory instrument made with the concurrence of the Lord Advocate; but no order shall be so made unless a draft has been laid before, and approved by resolution of, each House of Parliament.

Supplementary

Short title, commencement, interpretation and extent

9.—(1) This Act may be cited as the Consumer Arbitration Agreements Act 1988.

[1] (2) This Act shall have effect in relation to contracts made on or after such day as the Secretary of State may by order made by statutory instrument appoint; and different days may be so appointed for different provisions and different purposes.

(3) In this Act "the Act of 1977" means the Unfair Contract Terms Act 1977.

(4) Sections 1 to 5 above do not extend to Scotland, sections 6 to 8 extend to Scotland only, and this Act, apart from sections 6 to 8, extends to Northern Ireland.

NOTE

[1] S.I. 1988 No. 2291 provides that the appointed day is 1st February 1989.

Civil Evidence (Scotland) Act 1988

(1988 c. 32)

An Act to make fresh provision in relation to civil proceedings in Scotland regarding corroboration of evidence and the admissibility of hearsay and other evidence; and for connected purposes. [29th July 1988]

ARRANGEMENT OF SECTIONS

Rule requiring corroboration abolished

1.—(1) In any civil proceedings the court or, as the case may be, the jury, if satisfied that any fact has been established by evidence in those proceedings, shall be entitled to find that fact proved by that evidence notwithstanding that the evidence is not corroborated.

(2) Any rule of law whereby any evidence may be taken to be corroborated by a false denial shall cease to have effect.

Admissibility of hearsay

2.—(1) In any civil proceedings—

(*a*) evidence shall not be excluded solely on the ground that it is hearsay;

(*b*) a statement made by a person otherwise than in the course of the proof shall be admissible as evidence of any matter contained in the statement of which direct oral evidence by that person would be admissible; and

(*c*) the court, or as the case may be the jury, if satisfied that any fact has been established by evidence in those proceedings, shall be entitled to find that fact proved by the evidence notwithstanding that the evidence is hearsay.

(2) Nothing in this section shall affect the admissibility of any statement as evidence of the fact that the statement was made.

(3) In paragraph (*e*) of section 5 of the Court of Session Act 1988 (power to make provision as regards the Court of Session for admission of written statements etc. in lieu of parole evidence), for the words "the admission in lieu of parole evidence of written statements (including affidavits) and reports, on such conditions as may be prescribed" there shall be substituted the words "written statements (including affidavits) and reports, admissible under section 2(1)(*b*) of the Civil Evidence (Scotland) Act 1988, to be received in evidence, on such conditions as may be prescribed, without being spoken to by a witness".

(4) [The substituted s.32(1)(*e*) of the Sheriff Courts (Scotland) Act 1971 is shown in the print of that Act.]

Statement as evidence as to credibility

3. In any civil proceedings a statement made otherwise than in the course of the proof by a person who at the proof is examined as to the statement shall be admissible as evidence in so far as it tends to reflect favourably or unfavourably on that person's credibility.

Leading of additional evidence

4.—(1) For the purposes of section 2 or 3 above, any person may at the proof, with leave of the court, at any time before the commencement of closing submissions—

(*a*) be recalled as a witness whether or not he has been present in court since giving evidence initially; or

(*b*) be called as an additional witness whether or not he has been present in court during the proof (or during any other part of the proceedings).

(2) Nothing in section 3 of the Evidence (Scotland) Act 1840 (presence in court not to disqualify witnesses in certain cases) shall apply as respects a witness called or recalled under subsection (1) above.

Document as part of business records

5.—(1) Unless the court otherwise directs, a document may in any civil proceedings be taken to form part of the records of a business or undertaking if it is certified as such by a docquet purporting to be signed by an officer of the business or undertaking to which the records belong; and a statement contained in any document certified as aforesaid may be received in evidence without being spoken to by a witness.

(2) For the purposes of this section, a facsimile of a signature shall be treated as a signature.

Production of copy document

6.—(1) For the purposes of any civil proceedings, a copy of a document, purporting to be authenticated by a person responsible for the making of the copy, shall, unless the court otherwise directs, be—

(*a*) deemed a true copy; and

(*b*) treated for evidential purposes as if it were the document itself.

(2) In subsection (1) above, "copy" includes a transcript or reproduction.

(3) Sections 3 to 5 of the Bankers' Books Evidence Act 1879 (mode of proof of entries in bankers' books, proof that book is a bankers' book and verification of copy of entry in such a book) shall not apply to civil proceedings.

Statement not contained in business records

7.—(1) In any civil proceedings, the evidence of an officer of a business or undertaking that any particular statement is not contained in the records of the business or undertaking shall be admissible as evidence of that fact whether or not the whole or any part of the records have been produced in the proceedings.

(2) The evidence referred to in subsection (1) above may, unless the court otherwise directs, be given by means of the affidavit of the officer.

(3) In section 6 of the Bankers' Books Evidence Act 1879 (case in which banker not compellable to produce book), after the word "Act" there shall be inserted the word "or under the Civil Evidence (Scotland) Act 1988".

Evidence in actions concerning family relationships, etc.

8.—(1) In any action to which this subsection applies (whether or not appearance has been entered for the defender), no decree or judgment in favour of the pursuer shall be pronounced until the grounds of action have been established by evidence.

(2) Subsection (1) above applies to actions for divorce, separation or declarator of marriage, nullity of marriage, legitimacy, legitimation, illegitimacy, parentage or non-parentage.

(3) Subject to subsection (4) below, in any action for divorce, separation or declarator of marriage or nullity of marriage, the evidence referred to in

subsection (1) above shall consist of or include evidence other than that of a party to the marriage (or alleged or purported marriage).

[1] (4) The Lord Advocate may by order made by statutory instrument provide that subsection (3) above shall not apply, or shall apply subject to such modifications as may be specified in the order, in respect of such class or classes of action as may be so specified.

(5) No order shall be made under this section unless a draft of the order has been laid before Parliament and has been approved by resolution of each House.

NOTE

[1] See S.I. 1989 No. 582, printed in Division K.

Interpretation

9. In this Act, unless the context otherwise requires—

"business" includes trade or profession;

"civil proceedings" includes, in addition to such proceedings in any of the ordinary courts of law—

(*a*) any hearing by the sheriff under section 42 of the Social Work (Scotland) Act 1968 of an application for a finding as to whether grounds for the referral of a child's case to a children's hearing are established, except in so far as the application relates to a ground mentioned in section 32(2)(*g*) of that Act (commission by the child of an offence);

(*b*) any arbitration, whether or not under an enactment, except in so far as, in relation to the conduct of the arbitration, specific provision has been made as regards the rules of evidence which are to apply;

(*c*) any proceedings before a tribunal or inquiry, except in so far as, in relation to the conduct of proceedings before the tribunal or inquiry, specific provision has been made as regards the rules of evidence which are to apply; and

(*d*) any other proceedings conducted wholly or mainly in accordance with rules of procedure agreed between the parties themselves (or as respects which it would have been open to them to agree such rules had they wished to do so) except in so far as any such agreement makes specific provision as regards the rules of evidence which are to apply;

"court" shall be construed in accordance with the definition of "civil proceedings";

"document" includes, in addition to a document in writing,—

(*a*) any map, plan, graph or drawing;

(*b*) any photograph;

(*c*) any disc, tape, sound track or other device in which sounds or other data (not being visual images) are recorded so as to be capable (with or without the aid of some other equipment) of being reproduced therefrom; and

(*d*) any film, negative, tape or other device in which one or more visual images are recorded so as to be capable (as aforesaid) of being reproduced therefrom;

"film" includes a microfilm;

"hearsay" includes hearsay of whatever degree;

"made" includes "allegedly made";

"proof" includes trial or other hearing of evidence, proof on commission and any continued proof;

"records" means records in whatever form;

"statement" includes any representation (however made or expressed) of fact or opinion but does not include a statement in a precognition; and

"undertaking" includes any public or statutory undertaking, any local authority and any government department.

Repeals and application

10.—(1) The enactments specified in columns 1 and 2 of the Schedule to this Act are hereby repealed to the extent specified in column 3 of the Schedule.

(2) This Act shall apply to proceedings whether commenced before or after the date of its coming into force (but not to proceedings in which proof commenced before that date).

(3) Nothing in this Act shall affect the operation of the following enactments—

(*a*) section 2 of the Documentary Evidence Act 1868 (mode of proving certain documents);

(*b*) section 2 of the Documentary Evidence Act 1882 (documents printed under superintendence of Stationery Office);

(*c*) section 1 of the Evidence (Colonial Statutes) Act 1907 (proof of statutes of certain legislatures);

(*d*) section 1 of the Evidence (Foreign, Dominion and Colonial Documents) Act 1933 (proof and effect of registers and official certificates of certain countries); and

(*e*) section 5 of the Oaths and Evidence (Overseas Authorities and Countries) Act 1963 (provision in respect of public registers of other countries).

Citation, commencement and extent

11.—(1) This Act may be cited as the Civil Evidence (Scotland) Act 1988.

[1] (2) This Act shall come into force on such day as the Lord Advocate may by order made by statutory instrument appoint.

(3) This Act shall extend to Scotland only.

NOTE

[1] S.I. 1989 No. 556 provides for the provisions of this Act to come into force on 3rd April 1989.

Section 10(1)

SCHEDULE

ENACTMENTS REPEALED

Chapter	Short Title	Extent of repeal
11 Geo. 4. & 1 Will. 4. c. 69.	The Court of Session Act 1830.	Section 36.
15 & 16 Vict. c. 27.	The Evidence (Scotland) Act 1852.	Section 3.
1966 c. 19.	The Law Reform (Miscellaneous Provisions) (Scotland) Act 1966.	Section 7.
1968 c. 70	The Law Reform (Miscellaneous Provisions) (Scotland) Act 1968.	Section 9. Sections 13 to 16. In section 17(3), the definition of "computer".
1983 c. 12.	The Divorce Jurisdiction, Court Fees and Legal Aid (Scotland) Act 1983.	Section 2. In Schedule 1, paragraph 2.
1986 c. 9	The Law Reform (Parent and Child) (Scotland) Act 1986.	Section 7(4).

Court of Session Act 1988

(1988 c. 36)

An Act to consolidate, with amendments to give effect to recommendations of the Scottish Law Commission, certain enactments relating to the constitution, administration and procedure of the Court of Session and procedure on appeal therefrom to the House of Lords; and to repeal, in accordance with recommendations of the Scottish Law Commission, certain enactments relating to the aforesaid matters which are no longer of practical utility. [29th July 1988]

ARRANGEMENT OF SECTIONS

Part IV

Other Causes

Consistorial causes

Appeals to House of Lords

PART VI

MISCELLANEOUS PROVISIONS

PART VII

SUPPLEMENTARY

PART I

CONSTITUTION AND ADMINISTRATION OF THE COURT

Number of judges of Court

1.—[1] (1) Subject to subsections (2), (3) and (4) below, the maximum number of judges of the Court of Session (hereinafter in this Act referred to as "the Court") shall be 25.

(2) Her Majesty may by Order in Council from time to time amend subsection (1) above so as to increase or further increase the maximum number of persons who may be appointed as judges of the Court.

(3) No recommendation shall be made to Her Majesty in Council to make an order under this section unless a draft of the order has been laid before Parliament and approved by resolution of each House of Parliament.

(4) No vacancy arising among the judges of the Court shall be filled unless the Secretary of State, with the concurrence of the Treasury, is satisfied that the state of business in the Court requires that the vacancy should be filled.

(5) There shall be paid out of the Consolidated Fund any increase attributable to the provisions of this section in the sums which, under any other enactment, are payable out of that Fund.

NOTE

[1] As amended by S.I. 1991 No. 2884, with effect from 19th December 1991.

Composition of Court

2.[—(1)] The Court shall be composed of an Inner House and an Outer House constituted in accordance with the following provisions of this section.

(2) Subject to subsection (3) below, the Inner House shall be composed of two Divisions, namely, the First Division comprising the Lord President

and three senior judges of the Court, and the Second Division comprising the Lord Justice Clerk and three other senior judges of the Court.

[1] (3) The Lord President may from time to time direct any three judges of the Court to sit as an extra Division of the Inner House for the purpose of hearing and disposing of causes pending before the Inner House, and the senior judge present shall preside and shall sign any judgment or interlocutor pronounced by the extra Division; and any reference in this Act or in any other enactment to a Division of the Inner House shall be construed as including a reference to such an extra Division.

(4) The quorum for a Division of the Inner House shall be three judges.

(5) The Outer House shall be composed of the judges of the Court (other than the judges of the Inner House while they are sitting in the Inner House) sitting singly, and any reference in this Act or in any other enactment to a Lord Ordinary shall be construed as a reference to a judge sitting singly in the Outer House.

[2] (6) Subject to subsection (7) below, a vacancy arising in a Division of the Inner House shall be filled by the appointment of the senior Lord Ordinary.

(7) Subsection (6) above shall not apply in the case of such a vacancy arising by reason of the death or resignation of the Lord President or the Lord Justice Clerk.

NOTES

[1] Amended (*prosp.*) by the Law Reform (Miscellaneous Provisions) (Scotland) Act 1990, Sched. 4, para. 4(2).

[2] Substituted (*prosp.*) by *ibid.*

Exchequer causes

[1] **3.** One of the judges of the Court who usually sits as a Lord Ordinary shall be appointed by the Court by act of sederunt to act as Lord Ordinary in exchequer causes, and no other judge shall so act unless and until such judge is appointed in his place:

Provided that, in the event of the absence or inability of the Lord Ordinary in exchequer causes for whatever reason, any of his duties may be performed by any other Lord Ordinary acting in his place.

NOTE

[1] Amended (*prosp.*) by the Law Reform (Miscellaneous Provisions) (Scotland) Act 1990, Sched. 4, para. 4(3).

Power of judges to act in cases relating to rates and taxes

4.—(1) A judge of the Court shall not be incapable of acting as such in any proceedings by reason of being, as one of a class of ratepayers, taxpayers or persons of any other description, liable in common with others to pay, or contribute to, or benefit from, any rate or tax which may be increased, reduced or in any way affected by those proceedings.

(2) In this section "rate or tax" means any rate, tax, duty or assessment, whether public, general or local, and includes—

(*a*) any fund formed from the proceeds of any such rate, tax, duty or assessment; and

(*b*) any fund applicable for purposes the same as, or similar to, those for which the proceeds of any such rate, tax, duty or assessment are or might be applied.

PART II

GENERAL POWERS OF THE COURT IN RELATION TO PROCEDURE

Power to regulate procedure etc. by act of sederunt

5. The Court shall have power by act of sederunt—

(*a*) to regulate and prescribe the procedure and practice to be followed in various categories of causes in the Court or in execution or diligence following on such causes, whether originating in the said Court or brought there by way of appeal, removal, remit, stated case, or other like process, and any matters incidental or relating to any such procedure or practice including (but without prejudice to the foregoing generality) the manner in which, the time within which, and the conditions on which any interlocutor of a Lord Ordinary may be submitted to the review of the Inner House, or any application to the Court, or any thing required or authorised to be done in relation to any such causes as aforesaid shall or may be made or done;

(*b*) to prescribe the form of any summons, defence, petition, answer, writ, pleading, extract of a decree or other document whatsoever to be used in, or for the purposes of, any such causes as aforesaid, or in, or for the purposes of, execution or diligence following on such causes and the manner in which, and the person by whom, any such summons, petition, writ, pleading, extract of a decree or document shall be signed or authenticated;

(*c*) to prescribe the manner in which, the time within which, and the conditions on which any verdict of a jury may be submitted to the review of the Inner House on any ground set out in section 29 of this Act;

(*d*) to regulate the production and recovery of documents;

[1] (*e*) to provide in any category of causes before the Court, for written statements (including affidavits) and reports, admissible under section 2(1)(*b*) of the Civil Evidence (Scotland) Act 1988, to be received in evidence, on such conditions as may be prescribed, without being spoken to by a witness;

(*f*) to provide for the payment into Court and the investment or application of sums of money awarded in any action of damages in the Court to a pupil or a minor;

[2] (*g*) to regulate the fees of solicitors practising before the Court (other than such fees as the Secretary of State may regulate under or by virtue of section 33 of the Legal Aid (Scotland) Act 1986);

(*h*) to regulate the expenses which may be awarded to parties in causes before the Court;

(*i*) to regulate the summoning, remuneration, and duties of assessors;

(*j*) to fix the ordinary sessions of the Court and to regulate the days on which and times at which the Court shall sit;

(*k*) to prescribe the matters with which the vacation judge may deal;

(*l*) to make such regulations as may be necessary to carry out the provisions of this Act or of any Act conferring powers or imposing duties on the Court or relating to proceedings therein; and

(*m*) to modify, amend or repeal any provision of any enactment including this Act relating to matters with respect to which an act of sederunt may be made under this Act.

NOTES

[1] As amended by the Civil Evidence (Scotland) Act 1988, s.2(3).

[2] Repealed (*prosp.*) by the Law Reform (Miscellaneous Provisions) (Scotland) Act 1990, Sched. 9.

Allocation of business etc. by act of sederunt

6. With a view to securing that causes coming before the Court may be heard and determined with as little delay as is possible, and to the simplifying of procedure and the reduction of expense in causes before the Court, the Court shall, in the exercise of the powers conferred on it by section 5 of this Act, provide by act of sederunt—

(i) for the classification of the causes brought into the Court according to the manner in which they are initiated, and for the institution of (a) an Ordinary Roll; (b) an Admiralty and Commercial Roll; and (c) a Consistorial Roll; and the assignment to the Consistorial Roll of all consistorial causes and to the Ordinary Roll or to the Admiralty and Commercial Roll of all other causes initiated by summons, according to the subject matter of such causes;

(ii) for the allocation of the causes before the Inner House among the Divisions thereof and of the causes before the Outer House among the Lords Ordinary;

(iii) for enabling the enforcement of a maritime lien over a ship by an action *in rem* directed against the ship and all persons interested therein without naming them and concluding for the sale of the ship and the application of the proceeds in extinction *pro tanto* of the lien, and for enabling arrestment of the ship on the dependence of such an action, and for the regulation of the procedure in any such action;

(iv) for enabling the inclusion, in any such action as is mentioned in paragraph (iii) above, of conclusions *in personam* against the registered owners of the vessel, whether their names are or are not known to the pursuer, and the granting of decree in any such action containing such conclusions against any compearing defender;

(v) for the inclusion in defences to any action of any counter claim arising out of the matters on which the action is based, to the effect of enabling such counter claim to be enforced without a separate action being raised;

(vi) for enabling trustees under any trust deed to obtain the direction of the Court on questions relating to the investment, distribution, management or administration of the trust estate, or the exercise of any power vested in, or the performance of any duty imposed on, the trustees notwithstanding that such direction may affect contingent interests in the trust estate, whether of persons in existence at, or of persons who may be born after, the date of the direction;

(vii) for enabling arrestment *ad fundandam jurisdictionem* to proceed on a warrant contained in the summons in like manner as arrestment on the dependence of the action.

Fees on remit to accountants etc.

7. The Court shall have power to regulate from time to time the fees which shall be payable to any accountant or person of skill to whom any remit is made in the course of any judicial proceedings before the Court.

Rules Council

8.—(1) The Rules Council established under section 18 of the Administration of Justice (Scotland) Act 1933 shall continue and shall consist of the Lord President *ex officio* two other judges of the Court to be appointed by the Lord President, five members of the Faculty of Advocates to be appointed by the Faculty, and five solicitors, of whom not less than two shall be solicitors practising before the Court, to be appointed by the Council of the Law Society of Scotland.

(2) The members of the Rules Council, other than the Lord President, shall, so long as they retain the respective qualifications set out in subsection (1) above, hold office for three years and be eligible for reappointment.

(3) Any vacancy in the membership of the Rules Council occurring by death, resignation, or other cause prior to the expiry of three years from the date of appointment of the member whose office is so vacated shall be filled by the appointment by the person or body by whom that member was appointed of another person possessing the same qualification:

Provided that any person appointed in pursuance of this subsection to fill a vacancy shall remain a member of the council only until the expiry of three years from the date of the appointment of the member whose office is so vacated.

(4) The Rules Council may from time to time frame rules regarding any of the matters relating to the Court, being matters which the Court is empowered to regulate by act of sederunt, and shall submit any rules so framed to the Court, and the Court shall consider such rules and, if

approved, embody them (with or without amendment) in an act of sederunt.

(5) At any meeting of the Rules Council seven members shall form a quorum.

Part III

Ordinary Actions

Proof

Allowing of proof by Lord Ordinary

9. The Lord Ordinary may allow a proof—

(*a*) in any action, other than an action enumerated in section 11 of this Act, without the consent of both parties and without reporting to and obtaining the leave of the Inner House;

(*b*) in any action enumerated as aforesaid, if the parties to the action consent thereto or if special cause is shown.

Evidence on commission in Outer House

10. The Lord Ordinary may grant commission in any action—

(*a*) to any person competent to take and report in writing the depositions of havers;

(*b*) to take and report in writing the evidence of any witness who is resident beyond the jurisdiction of the Court, or who, by reason of age, infirmity or sickness, is unable to attend the diet of proof or trial:

Provided that nothing in this section shall affect the existing practice in regard to granting commission for the examination of aged and infirm witnesses to take their evidence to lie *in retentis* before a proof or, as the case may be, trial has been allowed.

Jury actions

11. Subject to section 9(*b*) of this Act, the following actions if remitted to probation shall be tried by jury—

(*a*) an action of damages for personal injuries;

(*b*) an action for libel or defamation;

(*c*) an action founded on delinquency or quasi delinquency, where the conclusion is for damages only and expenses; and

(*d*) an action of reduction on the ground of incapacity, essential error, or force and fear;

and such an action which has been ordered by the Lord Ordinary to be tried by jury is hereafter in this Act referred to as a jury action.

Trial by jury

Summoning of jury

12. The jurors for the trial of issues in a jury action shall be summoned by virtue of an authority or precept signed by a Lord Ordinary or by any clerk of court officiating either in the Outer House or Inner House, and issued to the sheriff principal.

Selection of jury

13.—(1) The jurors for the trial of any jury action shall be 12 persons selected in open court by ballot in accordance with the following provisions of this section from the list of persons summoned to attend the Court for that purpose.

(2) The clerk of court shall cause the name of each person so summoned to be written on a separate piece of paper, all the pieces being of the same

size, and shall cause the pieces to be rolled up as nearly as may be in the same shape, and to be put into a box or glass and mixed; and the clerk shall draw out the said pieces one by one from the box or glass.

(3) Each party to the action may challenge the selection of any juror whose name has been drawn in the ballot, and may, without assigning any reason, challenge the selection of not more than 4 jurors; and any challenges for an assigned reason may be made at any time during the selection of the jury.

Application for view by jury

14. Any party to a jury action may apply to a Lord Ordinary to allow the jury to view any property heritable or moveable relevant to the action; and, where the Lord Ordinary considers that it is proper and necessary for the jury to view that property, he may grant the application.

Illness or death of juror during trial

15. Where in the course of the trial of any jury action in the Court the presiding judge is satisfied that any member of the jury is, by reason of illness, unable to continue to serve on the jury or ought, for any other reason, to be discharged from further service on the jury, it shall be lawful for the judge to discharge such member, and in any such case or in any case where in the course of such a jury trial, a member of the jury dies, the remaining members of the jury (if they are not less than 10 in number) shall in all respects be deemed to constitute the jury for the purpose of the trial and any verdict returned by them whether unanimous or by majority shall be of the like force and effect as a unanimous verdict or a verdict by majority of the whole number of the jury.

Trial to proceed despite objection to opinion and direction of judge

16. Notwithstanding any objection being taken in the course of the trial in any jury action to the opinion and direction of the presiding judge, the trial shall proceed and the jury shall return their verdict and assess damages where necessary.

Return of verdict

17.—(1) At the end of his charge to the jury the presiding judge shall direct the jury to select someone to speak for them when returning their verdict.

(2) The jury impanelled to try any jury action may at any time return a verdict by a majority of their members, and if the jury, after they have been enclosed for 3 hours, are unable to agree upon a verdict or to return a verdict by a majority, the presiding judge may discharge the jury without their having given a verdict and, on the jury being discharged, shall order the action to be tried by another jury.

(3) The verdict when returned shall be declared orally by the juror selected as aforesaid in open court and taken down in writing by the clerk of court before the jury is discharged.

(4) Where the jury in an action which concludes for damages finds a verdict for the pursuer they shall also assess the amount of the damages.

(5) Subject to Part V of this Act, the verdict of the jury shall be final so far as relating to the facts found by them.

Judgment

Lord Ordinary's judgment final in Outer House

18. Every interlocutor of the Lord Ordinary shall be final in the Outer House, subject however to the review of the Inner House in accordance with this Act.

Part IV

Other Causes

Consistorial causes

Lord Advocate as party to action for nullity of marriage or divorce

19.—(1) The Lord Advocate may enter appearance as a party in any action of declarator of nullity of marriage or for divorce, and he may lead such proof and maintain such pleas as he thinks fit, and the Court shall, whenever it considers it necessary for the proper disposal of any such action, direct that the action shall be brought to the notice of the Lord Advocate in order that he may determine whether he should enter appearance therein.

(2) No expenses shall be claimable by or against the Lord Advocate in any action in which he has entered appearance under this section.

Orders with respect to children

20.—(1) In any action for divorce, judicial separation or declarator of nullity of marriage, the Court may make, with respect to any child of the marriage to which the action relates, such order (including an interim order) as it thinks fit relating to parental rights, and may vary or recall such order.

(2) In this section—

(*a*) "child" and "parental rights" have the same meaning as in section 8 of the Law Reform (Parent and Child) (Scotland) Act 1986; and

(*b*) "child of the marriage" includes any child who—

(i) is the child of both parties to the marriage; or

(ii) is the child of one party to the marriage and has been accepted as a child of the family by the other party.

Exchequer causes

Exchequer causes to have precedence

21. Exchequer causes shall at all times take precedence of and have preference over all other causes in the Court.

Lord Advocate to sue and be sued on behalf of the Crown

22. Except where any enactment otherwise provides, all exchequer causes brought—

(*a*) on behalf of the Crown, shall be at the instance of the Lord Advocate;

(*b*) by any person alleging any ground of action against the Crown, shall be directed against the Lord Advocate.

Lord Advocate may be heard last

23. In all exchequer causes, the Lord Advocate shall, in pleading on behalf of the Crown, have the privilege of being heard last.

Appeal to House of Lords

24. An appeal may be brought to the House of Lords against the judgment of the Inner House in an exchequer cause as if it were a judgment of the Inner House on the whole merits of the cause in an ordinary action.

Petitions

Disposal of petitions initiated in Outer House

25.—(1) The Lord Ordinary before whom any cause initiated by a petition comes shall have power to dispose of the petition himself.

(2) For the purpose of disposing of such a cause, the Lord Ordinary may make such investigation and require such assistance from professional person or persons of science or of skill as he thinks fit.

(3) On any such cause coming before him, the Lord Ordinary may grant commission to take the depositions of havers and the evidence of witnesses as provided in section 10 of this Act with respect to an action.

Summary trials

Summary trials

26.—(1) The parties to any dispute or question to which this section applies may present a petition in the Outer House setting out the dispute or question and craving that it may be decided by a particular Lord Ordinary, and any such petition shall stand referred to such Lord Ordinary for his determination of the dispute or question.

(2) The parties to any action in dependence in the Outer House not affecting the status of any person may agree by joint minute, or in such other manner as may be prescribed, that the provisions of this section shall apply to the action, and thereafter those provisions shall apply accordingly.

(3) Provision shall be made by act of sederunt under this Act for securing that causes under this section shall be disposed of with as little delay as possible.

(4) This section shall apply to any dispute or question not affecting the status of any person which might competently be the subject of any cause in the Outer House, or which might competently have been the subject of any such cause but for section 7 of the Sheriff Courts (Scotland) Act 1907.

Special cases

Special cases

27.—(1) Where any parties interested, whether personally or in some fiduciary or official capacity, in the decision of a question of law are agreed upon the facts, and are in dispute only on the law applicable to those facts, it shall be competent for them without raising any proceedings, or at any stage of any proceeding, to present to the Inner House a case (in this section referred to as a special case) signed by their counsel setting out the facts upon which they are so agreed and the question of law arising from those facts; and the parties may ask the Court either for its opinion or for its judgment on that question of law.

(2) The Court may, if it thinks fit, in case of difficulty or importance or of equal division, appoint a special case to be reheard by a larger court under section 36 of this Act.

(3) The Court shall dispose of all questions of expenses arising in a special case.

(4) Any judgment pronounced by the Court by virtue of this section shall be extractible in common form.

(5) Any judgment pronounced by the Court by virtue of this section shall be liable to review by the House of Lords unless such review is excluded by consent of all the parties to the special case.

Part V

Appeal and Review

Reclaiming

Reclaiming

28. Any party to a cause initiated in the Outer House either by a summons or a petition who is dissatisfied with an interlocutor pronounced by the Lord Ordinary may, except as otherwise prescribed, reclaim against that interlocutor within such period after the interlocutor is pronounced, and in such manner, as may be prescribed.

Review in jury actions

Application for new trial

29.—(1) Any party who is dissatisfied with the verdict of the jury in any jury action may, subject to such conditions and in such manner as may be prescribed, apply to the Inner House for a new trial on the ground—

(*a*) of misdirection by the judge;
(*b*) of the undue admission or rejection of evidence;
(*c*) that the verdict is contrary to the evidence;
(*d*) of excess or inadequacy of damages; or
(*e*) of *res noviter veniens ad notitiam*;

or on such other ground as is essential to the justice of the cause.

(2) The Inner House on hearing an application under this section may, subject to section 30 of this Act and any act of sederunt, grant or refuse a new trial.

(3) If the Court, on an application for a new trial on the ground that the verdict is contrary to the evidence, after hearing parties is unanimously of the opinion that the verdict under review is contrary to the evidence, and that it has before it all the evidence that could be reasonably expected to be obtained relevant to the cause, it may set aside the verdict and, in place of granting a new trial, may enter judgment for the party unsuccessful at the trial.

Restrictions on granting of application for new trial

30.—(1) Where an application for a new trial is made on the ground of the undue admission of evidence, and the Court is of the opinion that the exclusion of that evidence could not have led to a different verdict than that actually returned, it shall refuse to grant a new trial.

(2) Where an application for a new trial is made on the ground of the undue rejection of documentary evidence, and it appears to the Court from the documents themselves that they ought not to have affected the result at which the jury by their verdict have arrived, it may refuse to grant a new trial.

(3) Where the Court, on an application for a new trial made to it, is of opinion that the only ground for granting a new trial is either excess of damages or such inadequacy of damages as to show that a new trial is essential to the justice of the cause, it may grant a new trial restricted to the question of the amount of damages only.

(4) No verdict of a jury shall be discharged or set aside upon an application for a new trial, unless in conformity with the opinion of a majority of the judges hearing the application, and in case of equal division judgment shall be given in conformity with the verdict.

Verdict may be returned subject to opinion of Inner House on point reserved

31.—(1) Where in a jury action the presiding judge has directed the jury upon any matter of law, any party against whom the verdict is returned may apply to the Inner House to enter the verdict for him.

(2) The Inner House may, on an application made to it by a party under subsection (1) above—

(*a*) where it is of opinion that the direction of the presiding judge was erroneous and that the party making the application was truly entitled to the verdict in whole or in part, direct the verdict to be entered for that party in whole or in part, either absolutely or on such terms as it may think fit; or (*b*) where it is of opinion that it is necessary, set aside the verdict and order a new trial; or

(*c*) refuse the application.

Appeals and transmissions from sheriff

Appeals

32.—(1) Where an appeal is taken to the Court from the judgment of the sheriff principal or sheriff under section 28 of the Sheriff Courts (Scotland) Act 1907, the record may, with the leave of the Court, be amended at any time on such conditions as to the Court seem proper.

(2) On any such appeal the Court may, if it thinks fit, remit the cause to the sheriff principal or sheriff with instructions.

(3) On any such appeal the Court may, if necessary, order proof or additional proof to be taken in accordance with section 37 of this Act and shall thereafter, or without any such order if no such proof or additional proof is necessary, give judgment on the merits of the cause.

(4) Where such an appeal is taken to the Court from the judgment of the sheriff principal or sheriff proceeding on a proof, the Court shall in giving judgment distinctly specify in its interlocutor the several facts material to the cause which it finds to be established by the proof, and express how far its judgment proceeds on the matter of facts so found, or on matter of law, and the several points of law which it means to decide.

(5) The judgment of the Court on any such appeal shall be appealable to the House of Lords only on matters of law.

Transmissions from sheriff to Court on ground of contingency

33.—(1) The Court shall, on an application made to it, if it is of the opinion that there is contingency between a sheriff court cause and a cause depending before it, grant warrant to the clerk of the sheriff court cause for transmission of that cause to the Court.

(2) In subsection (1) above "sheriff court cause" means a cause depending before the sheriff principal or the sheriff.

Review by suspension

Suspension of decrees of Court granted in absence

34. It shall be competent for any party to bring proceedings in manner prescribed for the suspension of any decree in absence granted in the Court.

Suspension of sheriff court decree

35.—(1) It shall be competent in any proceedings for the suspension of a decree of a sheriff for that sheriff or the Court to regulate all matters relating to interim possession.

(2) The Court may in any such proceedings remit the cause to the sheriff with instructions; but no such remit shall be made, except in the case of the suspension of a decree in absence, without hearing counsel or receiving a written answer on the part of the respondent.

(3) The Court may in granting suspension find the petitioner entitled to his expenses both in the sheriff court and in the Court.

(4) In this section "sheriff" includes sheriff principal.

Rehearing and additional proof in Inner House

Rehearing by larger court of causes pending in Inner House

36. Where a division of the Inner House before whom a cause is pending—

(*a*) considers the cause to be one of difficulty or importance; or (*b*) is equally divided in opinion on the cause (whether on a question of law or fact),

it may appoint the cause to be reheard by such larger court as is necessary for the proper disposal of the cause.

Additional proof ordered by Inner House

37. Where proof has been ordered by the Inner House, the proof shall be taken before any one of the judges of the Inner House to whom the Inner House may think fit to remit the case, and the ruling of that judge upon the admissibility of evidence in the course of taking the proof shall be subject to review by the Inner House in the discussion of the report of the proof; and where the Inner House alters any finding of that judge rejecting evidence, it may, if it thinks fit, remit the case to have that evidence taken.

Evidence on commission in Inner House

38. In any cause coming before it, the Inner House may grant commission to take the depositions of havers and the evidence of witnesses as provided in section 10 of this Act with respect to an action.

Judgment in Inner House

Inner House judgment final in Court of Session

39. The judgment pronounced by the Inner House shall in all causes be final in the Court.

Appeals to House of Lords

Appealable interlocutors

40.—(1) Subject to the provisions of any other Act restricting or excluding an appeal to the House of Lords and of sections 27(5) and 32(5) of this Act, it shall be competent to appeal from the Inner House to the House of Lords—

(*a*) without the leave of the Inner House, against a judgment on the whole merits of the cause, or against an interlocutory judgment where there is a difference of opinion among the judges or where the interlocutory judgment is one sustaining a dilatory defence and dismissing the action;

(*b*) with the leave of the Inner House, against any interlocutory judgment other than one falling within paragraph (*a*) above.

(2) An interlocutor of the Court granting or refusing a new trial, on an application under section 29 of this Act, shall be appealable without the leave of the Court to the House of Lords; and on such an appeal the House of Lords shall have the same powers as the Court had on the application and in particular the powers specified in sections 29(3) and 30(3) of this Act.

(3) It shall be incompetent to appeal to the House of Lords against an interlocutor of a Lord Ordinary unless the interlocutor has been reviewed by the Inner House.

(4) On an appeal under this section all the prior interlocutors in the cause shall be submitted to the review of the House of Lords.

Interim possession, execution and expenses

41.—(1) On an appeal to the House of Lords under section 40 of this Act, a copy of the petition of appeal shall be laid by the respondent before the Inner House which may regulate all matters relating to interim possession, execution and expenses already incurred as it thinks fit, having regard to the interests of the parties to the cause as they may be affected by the upholding or reversal of the judgment against which the appeal has been taken.

(2) It shall not be competent by appeal to the House of Lords in respect of regulations made under subsection (1) above to stop the execution of those regulations; but when the House of Lords hears the appeal under section 40 of this Act, it may make such order or give such judgment respecting any matter which has been done or taken place in pursuance or in consequence of the regulations as it thinks fit.

House of Lords may make order on payment of interest

42. The House of Lords in hearing an appeal under section 40 of this Act may make such order with regard to payment of interest, simple or compound, by any of the parties, as it thinks fit.

Interest and expenses where appeal dismissed for want of prosecution

43. Where an appeal to the House of Lords under section 40 of this Act is dismissed for want of prosecution, the Inner House may, on an application made to it by any respondent in the appeal, order the appellant to pay to that respondent such interest, simple or compound, as it thinks fit, together with the expenses which have been incurred in consequence of the appeal.

PART VI

MISCELLANEOUS PROVISIONS

Selection of judges for trial of election petitions

44.—(1) The judges to be placed on the rota for the trial of parliamentary election petitions in Scotland under Part III of the Representation of the People Act 1983 in each year shall be selected, in such manner as the Lord President may direct, from the judges of the Court exclusive of any who are members of the House of Lords.

(2) Notwithstanding the expiry of the year for which a judge has been placed on the rota, he may act as if that year had not expired for the purpose of continuing to deal with, giving judgment in, or dealing with any ancillary matter relating to, any case with which he may have been concerned during that year.

(3) Any judge placed on the rota shall be eligible to be placed on the rota again in the succeeding or any subsequent year.

Restoration of possession and specific performance

[1] **45.** The Court may, on application by summary petition—

(*a*) order the restoration of possession of any real or personal property of the possession of which the petitioner may have been violently or fraudulently deprived; and

(*b*) order the specific performance of any statutory duty, under such conditions and penalties (including fine and imprisonment, where consistent with the enactment concerned) in the event of the order not being implemented, as to the Court seem proper.

NOTE

[1] Extended by the Harbours, Piers and Ferries (Scotland) Act 1937, s.22(4), S.I. 1955 No. 1752, the Housing and Town Development (Scotland) Act 1957, s.16(3)(*b*), the Town and Country Planning (Scotland) Act 1972, s.260(7), the Civil Aviation Act 1982, s.78(7), the Road Traffic Regulation Act 1984, ss.70(2) and 93(4)(*b*), and the Capital Transfer Tax Act 1984, s.26(6). See the Financial Services Act 1986, ss.13(3), 111(2), 128(3), 192(5), 192(6) as amended and Sched. 11, paras. 7(3) and 33(5), and the Companies Act 1989, ss.29(6) (*prosp.*), 35(6), 36(6), 40(3), 166(8), 167(5) and Sched. 14, para. 7(1). See also the Outer Space Act 1986, s.8(3), the Debtors (Scotland) Act 1987, s.15(3)(*c*)(iii), the Antarctic Minerals Act 1989, s.7(2) (*prosp.*), and the Food Safety Act 1990, s.40(3).

Specific relief may be granted in interdict proceedings

46. Where a respondent in any application or proceedings in the Court, whether before or after the institution of such proceedings or application, has done any act which the Court might have prohibited by interdict, the Court may ordain the respondent to perform any act which may be necessary for reinstating the petitioner in his possessory right, or for granting specific relief against the illegal act complained of.

Interim interdict and other interim orders

47.—(1) In any cause containing a conclusion or a crave for interdict or liberation, the Division of the Inner House or the Lord Ordinary (as the case may be) may, on the motion of any party to the cause, grant interim interdict or liberation; and it shall be competent for the Division of the Inner House or the Lord Ordinary before whom any cause in which interim interdict has been granted is pending to deal with any breach of the interim interdict without the presentation of a petition and complaint.

(2) In any cause in dependence before the Court, the Court may, on the motion of any party to the cause, make such order regarding the interim possession of any property to which the cause relates, or regarding the subject matter of the cause, as the Court may think fit.

(3) Every interim act, warrant and decree granted during the dependence of a cause in the Court shall, unless the Court otherwise directs, be extractible *ad interim*.

Right of audience of solicitor before the court

[1] **48.**—(1) Any solicitor who has, by virtue of section 25A (rights of audience) of the Solicitors (Scotland) Act 1980 a right of audience in relation to the Court of Session shall have the same right of audience in that court as is enjoyed by an advocate.

(2) Any solicitor shall have a right of audience—

(*a*) before the vacation judge; and

(*b*) in such other circumstances as may be prescribed.

NOTE

[1] Ss. 48 and 48A substituted for former s. 48 by the Law Reform (Miscellaneous Provisions) (Scotland) Act 1990, Sched. 8, para. 38.

Further provision as to rights of audience

[1] **48A.** Any person who has complied with the terms of a scheme approved under section 26 of the Law Reform (Miscellaneous Provisions) (Scotland) Act 1990 (consideration of applications made under section 25) shall have such rights of audience before the court as may be specified in an act of sederunt made under subsection (7)(*a*) of that section.

NOTE

[1] Ss.48 and 48A substituted for former s. 48 by the Law Reform (Miscellaneous Provisions) (Scotland) Act 1990, Sched. 8, para. 38.

Subscription of bill for letters of inhibition

49.—(1) Subject to subsection (2) below, the subscription by such of the clerks of session as may be prescribed of a bill craving warrant for the signeting of letters of inhibition shall be sufficient warrant for that purpose without the subscription of the bill by a Lord Ordinary.

(2) Where in the case of any such bill a doubt or difficulty occurs to the clerk of session, he shall report the matter to a Lord Ordinary, and where a matter is so reported the subscription of the bill by the Lord Ordinary shall be necessary.

Copy of interlocutor granting commission and diligence to be equivalent to formal extract

50. A copy of an interlocutor, pronounced by a Lord Ordinary or the Inner House granting commission and diligence, which is certified by a clerk of court shall have the same force and effect as a formal extract of the interlocutor.

Part VII

Supplementary

Interpretation

51. In this Act unless the context otherwise requires—

"action" means a cause initiated by a summons;

"the Court" means the Court of Session and, in any provision conferring a power on the Court with regard to a cause before it, means, as the case may be, a Division of the Inner House, a Division sitting with an additional judge or judges or a Lord Ordinary;

"enactment" includes an act of sederunt;

"the Inner House" means, in any provision conferring power on it, a Division thereof;

"the Lord President" means the Lord President of the Court of Session;

"prescribed" means prescribed by act of sederunt;

"solicitor" has the same meaning as in section 65(1) of the Solicitors (Scotland) Act 1980.

[THE NEXT PAGE IS B 307]

INHIBITIONS – an I. is a preventative diligence prohibiting the party inhibited from contracting any debt or granting any deed by which any of his heritable prop. may be alienated

– widely used remedy on dependence of an action where D. is not an institution of substance + there is no insurance co. in background.

Consequential amendments, repeals and savings

52.—(1) The enactments specified in Schedule 1 to this Act shall have effect subject to the amendments specified in that Schedule, being amendments consequential upon the provisions of this Act.

(2) The enactments mentioned in Part I of Schedule 2 to this Act are hereby repealed to the extent specified in the third column of that Schedule; and Parts II and III of that Schedule respectively show the extent to which the aforesaid enactments are re-enacted (with or without amendment) in this Act or are repealed without re-enactment as being no longer of practical utility or being spent or unnecessary.

(3) Notwithstanding section 24 of this Act, no appeal shall be allowed to the House of Lords against a decision of the Court on an appeal relating to estate duty except with the leave of the Court.

(4) In so far as any appointment, act of sederunt or regulations made under any enactment repealed and re-enacted by this Act, or any other thing done under any such enactment, could have been made or done under a corresponding provision of this Act, it shall not be invalidated by the repeals effected by this section but shall have effect as if made or done under that corresponding provision.

(5) Where any Act or any document refers, either expressly or by implication, to an enactment repealed and re-enacted by this Act, the reference shall, except where the context otherwise requires, be construed as a reference to the corresponding provision of this Act.

(6) Nothing in this section shall be taken as prejudicing the operation of sections 16 and 17 of the Interpretation Act 1978 (general savings and repeal and re-enactment).

Short title, commencement and extent

53.—(1) This Act may be cited as the Court of Session Act 1988.

(2) This Act shall come into force on the expiry of the period of two months beginning with the date on which it is passed.

(3) This Act extends to Scotland only.

SCHEDULES

SCHEDULE 1

Section 52(1)

MINOR AMENDMENTS

. . . .

The Sheriff Courts (Scotland) Act 1907 (c. 51).

[New ss.38B and 38C of the Sheriff Courts (Scotland) Act 1907 are shown in the print of that Act.]

SCHEDULE 2

Section 52(2).

REPEALS

PART I

ENACTMENTS REPEALED

Chapter	Short Title	Extent of repeal
1594 c. 22.	The Declinature Act 1594.	The whole Act.
1672 c. 6.	The Summons Execution Act 1672.	The whole Act.
1681 c. 79.	The Declinature Act 1681.	The whole Act so far as relating to the Court of Session.

Chapter	Short Title	Extent of repeal
48 Geo. 3. c. 151.	The Court of Session Act 1808.	The whole Act.
50 Geo. 3. c. 112.	The Court of Session Act 1810.	The whole Act.
53 Geo. 3. c. 64.	The Court of Session Act 1813.	The whole Act.
55 Geo. 3. c. 42.	The Jury Trials (Scotland) Act 1815.	Sections 1 to 19. In section 20 the words "by the clerk of the jury court" where they occur for the second time. Sections 21 to 41.
59 Geo. 3. c. 35.	The Jury Trials (Scotland) Act 1819.	The whole Act.
59 Geo. 3. c. 45.	The Court of Session Act 1819.	The whole Act.
1 & 2 Geo. 4. c. 38.	The Court of Session Act 1821.	The whole Act except section 32.
6 Geo. 4. c. 22.	The Jurors (Scotland) Act 1825.	Sections 17 and 19.
6 Geo. 4. c. 120.	The Court of Session Act 1825.	Sections 1 to 52. In section 53 the words from the beginning to "sixty days; and" and the words "or sited". Section 54.
11 Geo. 4 & 1 Wm. 4 c. 69.	The Court of Session Act 1830.	Sections 1 to 3. Section 9. Section 11. Sections 15 and 16. Section 19. Section 29, so far as relating to the Court of Session, and the proviso. Section 35. Section 37. Section 40
2 & 3 Wm. 4. c. 5.	The Court of Session Act 1832.	The whole Act.
7 Wm. 4 & 1 Vict. c. 14.	The Jury Trials (Scotland) Act 1837.	The whole Act.
1 & 2 Vict. c. 86.	The Court of Session (No. 1) Act 1838.	The whole Act.
1 & 2 Vict. c. 118.	The Court of Session (No. 2) Act 1838.	The whole Act except section 27.
2 & 3 Vict. c. 36.	The Court of Session Act 1839.	Section 1.
13 & 14 Vict. c. 36.	The Court of Session Act 1850.	The whole Act except section 16.
19 & 20 Vict. c. 56.	The Exchequer Court (Scotland) Act 1856.	Sections 2 to 4. Section 13. In section 14 the words from "and such application" to "proper". Sections 15 and 16. Sections 19 to 23. Sections 25 to 28. Section 44. Schedule G.
20 & 21 Vict. c. 18.	The Bill Chamber Procedure Act 1857.	The whole Act.
20 & 21 Vict. c. 56.	The Court of Session Act 1857.	The whole Act.
24 & 25 Vict. c. 86.	The Conjugal Rights (Scotland) Amendment Act 1861.	The whole Act except sections 6 and 20.
29 & 30 Vict. c. 112.	The Evidence (Scotland) Act 1866.	The whole Act.

Chapter	Short Title	Extent of repeal
31 & 32 Vict. c. 100.	The Court of Session Act 1868.	Section 10. Sections 12 and 13. Section 14 in so far as it relates to summonses and petitions. Sections 15 and 44. In section 45 the words from "or at" to "such trial"). Section 46. In section 47 the words from "where the trial" to "town". Sections 50 and 101.
31 & 32 Vict. c. 125.	The Parliamentary Elections Act 1868.	The whole Act.
40 & 41 Vict. c. 11.	The Jurisdiction in Rating Act 1877.	In section 3, in the definition of "judge" the words "As to Scotland, any judge of the High Court of Session; and".
42 & 43 Vict. c. 75.	The Parliamentary Elections and Corrupt Practices Act 1879.	The whole Act.
46 & 47 Vict. c. 51.	The Corrupt and Illegal Practices Prevention Act 1883.	The whole Act.
52 & 53 Vict. c. 54.	The Clerks of Session (Scotland) Regulation Act 1889.	Sections 6 and 7. Section 9. Section 12.
10 Edw. 7 & 1 Geo. 5. c. 31.	The Jury Trials Amendment (Scotland) Act 1910.	The whole Act.
18 & 19 Geo. 5. c. 34.	The Reorganisation of Offices (Scotland) Act 1928.	Sections 8 and 9.
23 & 24 Geo. 5. c. 41.	The Administration of Justice (Scotland) Act 1933.	Sections 2 to 6. Sections 9 to 11. Sections 13 to 18. In section 24, subsection (5). Section 30. In section 40, the definition of "consistorial cause".
12 13 & 14 Geo. 6. c. 10.	The Administration of Justice (Scotland) Act 1948.	The whole Act.
12 & 13 Geo. 6. c. 27.	The Juries Act 1949.	Schedule 1 so far as relating to the Court of Session Act 1868.
1968 c. 5.	The Administration of Justice Act 1968.	The whole Act so far as relating to Scotland.
1972 c. 59.	The Administration of Justice (Scotland) Act 1972.	Section 2.
1977 c. 38.	The Administration of Justice Act 1977.	Section 29(1).
1980 c. 55.	The Law Reform (Miscellaneous Provisions) (Scotland) Act 1980.	Section 1(6)(b).
1983 c. 12.	The Divorce Jurisdiction, Court Fees and Legal Aid (Scotland) Act 1983.	In Schedule 1, paragraphs 5 and 8.
1985 c. 6.	The Companies Act 1985.	In section 425(5) the words from "in pursuance" to "1933".
1985 c. 73.	The Law Reform (Miscellaneous Provisions) (Scotland) Act 1985.	In Schedule 2, paragraph 8.
1986 c. 9.	The Law Reform (Parent and Child) (Scotland) Act 1986.	In Schedule 1, paragraph 2.
1986 c. 45.	The Insolvency Act 1986.	In section 120(2) the words from "in pursuance" to the end. In section 162(2) the words from "in pursuance" to "1933".
1986 c. 55.	The Family Law Act 1986.	In Schedule 1, paragraph 1.

Part II

Repealed Enactments which are Re-enacted

Chapter	Short Title	Extent of repeal
48 Geo. 3 c. 151.	The Court of Session Act 1808	Section 15 except the words "to which such Lords Ordinary belong". Section 17 except the words "or any four of the judges thereof". Sections 18 to 20.
50 Geo. 3 c. 112.	The Court of Session Act 1810.	In section 32 the words from "three judges" to "inner house".
53 Geo. 3 c. 64.	The Court of Session Act 1813.	In section 17 the words from "the endorsation" to the end.
55 Geo. 3 c. 42.	The Jury Trials (Scotland) Act 1815.	Section 1. Section 5. In section 6, the proviso. In section 7 the words from "notwithstanding" to "when necessary". Section 8 except the words "or judges" and "or by the judge admiral respectively". In section 21 the words from "in challenging" to the end. In section 29 the words from the beginning to "be allowed". Section 33 except the words from "to be afterwards" to the end.
59 Geo. 3 c. 45.	The Court of Session Act 1819.	Section 1 in so far as it enables the senior Lord Ordinary to fill a vacancy arising in the Inner House.
1 & 2 Geo. 4. c. 38.	The Court of Session Act 1821.	Section 1 except the words "advocation and" and "either for the lord ordinary on the bills or".
6 Geo. 4 c. 120.	The Court of Session Act 1825.	Section 1. Section 5 so far as relating to appeal to the House of Lords. In section 17 the words from "every interlocutor" to the end. In section 21 the words from "the judgment" to the end. Section 23. Section 28 except the words from "all actions on account of any injury to moveables" to "seduction", from "all actions on the responsibility" to "nuisance" and from "all actions on policies" to the end and except so far as relating to the jury court and Court of Admiralty. In section 40 the words from the beginning to "in the interlocutor" and from "and further" to "of the case" but only in relation to proofs in sheriff courts. In section 46 the words from "and in the event" to the end.
1 & 2 Vict. c. 86.	The Court of Session (No. 1) Act 1838.	In section 4 the words from "in all cases" to "interim possession". In section 5 the words from the beginning to "Session".
13 & 14 Vict. c. 36.	The Court of Session Act 1850.	Section 25. Section 28 except the words "without the necessity of such special allowance". Section 35. Section 42.

Chapter	Short Title	Extent of repeal
19 & 20 Vict. c. 56.	The Exchequer Court (Scotland) Act 1856.	Sections 2 and 3. Section 20. Sections 22 and 23. Section 25.
20 & 21 Vict. c. 56.	The Court of Session Act 1857.	Section 5 so far as relating to petitions. Section 6 so far as relating to petitions.
24 & 25 Vict. c. 86.	The Conjugal Rights (Scotland) Amendment Act 1861.	Sections 8 and 9. In section 13, the proviso.
29 & 30 Vict. c. 112.	The Evidence (Scotland) Act 1866.	Section 1 in so far as it authorises the taking of proof before the Lord Ordinary. Section 2. Section 3 except the words from "and where" to the end. Section 4. Section 6.
31 & 32 Vict. c. 100.	The Court of Session Act 1868.	Section 36. Section 44 except the words from "and if" to the end. Section 59. Section 60 except the words from "the printed" to "or to direct that". In section 61 the words from the beginning to "verdict". Sections 62 and 63. Section 72 so far as relating to appeals from the sheriff, except the words "although such law is not pleaded on the record". Section 74 so far as relating to transmission of sheriff court causes. Section 89. In section 91 the words from the beginning to "seem proper". In section 92, the last sentence. Section 100(2).
31 & 32 Vict. c. 125.	The Parliamentary Elections Act 1868.	Section 58.
40 & 41 Vict. c. 11.	The Jurisdiction in Rating Act 1877.	In section 3, in the definition of "judge" the words "As to Scotland, any judge of the High Court of Session, and".
42 & 43 Vict. c. 75.	The Parliamentary Elections and Corrupt Practices Act 1879.	Section 2.
46 & 47 Vict. c. 51.	The Corrupt and Illegal Practices Prevention Act 1883.	Section 42.
10 Edw. 7 & 1 Geo. 5 c. 31.	The Jury Trials Amendment (Scotland) Act 1910.	Section 2.
23 & 24 Geo. 5 c. 41.	The Administration of Justice (Scotland) Act 1933.	Section 2(1). Section 3(2). Section 4 so far as it relates to the regulation of the powers of the vacation judge by act of sederunt. In section 6, subsections (4) and (7). In section 10, subsections (1) and (6) to (8). In section 11, subsections (1) and (2). Section 14 so far as providing competence for reclaiming. Section 15 so far as relating to power to prescribe form of extract of decree. Sections 16 and 17. Section 18 except proviso (i) to subsection (3). Section 24(5).

Chapter	Short Title	Extent of repeal
12, 13 and 14. Geo. 6. c. 10.	The Administration of Justice (Scotland) Act 1948.	Section 1 except the words from "when" to "thirteen". Sections 2 and 3.
12 & 13 Geo. 6. c. 27.	The Juries Act 1949.	Schedule 1 so far as relating to the Court of Session Act 1868.
1968 c. 5.	The Administration of Justice Act 1968.	Section 1 so far as relating to Scotland.
1972 c. 59.	The Administration of Justice (Scotland) Act 1972.	Section 2.
1977 c. 38.	The Administration of Justice Act 1977.	Section 29(1).
1983 c. 12.	The Divorce Jurisdiction, Court Fees and Legal Aid (Scotland) Act 1983.	In Schedule 1, paragraph 8.
1985 c. 73.	The Law Reform (Miscellaneous Provisions) (Scotland) Act 1985.	In Schedule 2, paragraph 8.
1986 c. 9.	The Law Reform (Parent and Child) (Scotland) Act 1986.	In Schedule 1, paragraph 2.

Part III

Repealed Enactments which are not Re-enacted

Chapter	Short Title	Extent of repeal
1594 c. 22.	The Declinature Act 1594.	The whole Act.
1672 c. 6.	The Summons Execution Act 1672.	The whole Act.
1681 c. 79.	The Declinature Act 1681.	The whole Act so far as relating to the Court of Session.
48 Geo. 3 c. 151.	The Court of Session Act 1808.	Section 1. Section 4. Section 6. Section 10. Section 13. In section 15 the words "to which such Lords Ordinary belong". In section 17 the words "or any four of the judges thereof". Section 21.
50 Geo. 3 c. 112.	The Court of Session Act 1810.	Section 11. Section 13. Sections 18 to 25. Sections 28 to 30. Section 32 except the words from "three judges" to "inner house". Sections 33 to 38. Section 48. Sections 51 and 52. The Schedules.
53 Geo. 3 c. 64.	The Court of Session Act 1813.	Section 1. Section 7. Section 14. Section 17 except the words from "the endorsation" to the end.
55 Geo. 3 c. 42.	The Jury Trials (Scotland) Act 1815.	Section 6 except the proviso. Section 7 except the words from "notwithstanding" to "when necessary". In section 8 the words "or judges" and "or by the judge admiral respectively". Section 9. Section 12.

Chapter	Short Title	Extent of repeal
		Sections 15 to 17. Section 19. In section 20 the words "by the clerk of the jury court" where they occur for the second time. In section 21 the words from the beginning to "Provided always that". Section 22. Section 23. Section 28. In section 29 the words after "be allowed". In section 33 the words from "to be afterwards" to the end. Section 39. Section 41.
59 Geo. 3 c. 35.	The Jury Trials (Scotland) Act 1819.	Sections 7 to 9. Sections 13 and 14. Section 17. Section 19. Sections 26 and 27. Section 35.
59 Geo. 3 c. 45.	The Court of Session Act 1819.	Section 1 except in so far as it enables the senior Lord Ordinary to fill a vacancy arising in the Inner House. Section 3. Section 6.
1 & 2 Geo. 4 c. 38.	The Court of Session Act 1821.	In section 1 the words "advocation and" and "either for the Lord Ordinary on the bills or". Section 3. Section 9. Sections 11 to 14. Section 18. Section 24. Sections 26 and 27. Sections 29 to 31.
6 Geo. 4 c. 22.	The Jurors (Scotland) Act 1825.	Sections 17 and 19.
6 Geo. 4 c. 120.	The Court of Session Act 1825.	Section 5 except so far as relating to appeal to the House of Lords. Sections 11 and 12. In section 17 the words from the beginning to "in part; and". Section 20. In section 21 the words from the beginning to "expenses; and". Section 22. Sections 24 to 26. In section 28 the words from "all actions on account of any injury to moveables" to "seduction", from "all actions on the responsibility" to "nuisance" and from "all actions on policies" to the end and that section so far as relating to the jury court and the Court of Admiralty. Section 33. Section 35. Section 40 so far as relating to proofs in inferior courts other than sheriff courts and in that section the words from "Provided however" to "repealed" and from "but it is" to the end.

Chapter	Short Title	Extent of repeal
		Section 44. Section 45. In section 46 the words from the beginning to "other division". Sections 47 and 48. Sections 51 and 52. In section 53 the words from the beginning to "sixty days; and" and the words "or cited".
11 Geo. 4 & 1 Will. 4 c. 69.	The Court of Session Act 1830.	Sections 1 to 3. Section 9. Section 11. Sections 15 and 16. Section 19. Section 29, so far as relating to the Court of Session, and the proviso. Section 35. Section 37. Section 40.
2 & 3 Will. 4 c. 5.	The Court of Session Act 1832.	The whole Act.
7 Will. 4 & 1 Vict. c. 14.	The Jury Trials (Scotland) Act 1837.	The whole Act.
1 & 2 Vict. c. 86.	The Court of Session (No. 1) Act 1838.	Section 4 except the words from "in all cases" to "interim possession". In section 5 the words from "by lodging" to the end. Section 6.
1 & 2 Vict. c. 118.	The Court of Session (No. 2) Act 1838.	Section 1. Section 4. Section 14. Section 17. Section 21. Section 24. Section 26. Sections 28 and 29. The Schedule.
2 & 3 Vict. c. 36.	The Court of Session Act 1839.	Section 1.
13 & 14 Vict. c. 36.	The Court of Session Act 1850.	Section 5. Sections 7 and 8. Sections 17 to 20. Sections 22 and 23. Sections 26 and 27. In section 28 the words "without the necessity of such special allowance". Section 29. Section 32. Section 36. Sections 39 to 41. Sections 44 to 53. Schedule (B).
19 & 20 Vict. c. 56.	The Exchequer Court (Scotland) Act 1856.	Section 4. Section 13. In section 14 the words from "and such application" to "proper". Sections 15 and 16. Section 19. Sections 26 to 28. Section 44. Schedule G.
20 & 21 Vict. c. 18.	The Bill Chamber Procedure Act 1857.	The whole Act.

Chapter	Short Title	Extent of repeal
20 & 21 Vict. c. 56.	The Court of Session Act 1857.	Section 5 so far as relating to applications and reports. Section 6 so far as relating to applications and reports. Section 8.
24 & 25 Vict. c. 86.	The Conjugal Rights (Scotland) Amendment Act 1861.	Section 10. Section 13 except the proviso. Section 19.
29 & 30 Vict. c. 112.	The Evidence (Scotland) Act 1866.	Section 1 except in so far as it authorises the taking of proof before the Lord Ordinary. In section 3 the words from "and where" to the end.
31 & 32 Vict. c. 100.	The Court of Session Act 1868.	Section 10. Sections 12 and 13. Section 14 in so far as it relates to summonses and petitions. Sections 15 to 17. Sections 20 to 22. Sections 25 and 26. Sections 28 to 30. Section 32. Sections 34 and 35. Sections 37 and 38. Sections 40 and 41. Section 43. In section 44 the words from "and if" to the end. In section 45 the words from "or at" to "such trial)". Section 46. In section 47 the words from "where the trial" to "town". Section 50. Sections 52 and 53. Sections 56 to 58. In section 60 the words from "the printed" to "or to direct that". In section 61 the words from "but this" to the end. Sections 65 to 71. In section 72 the words "although such law is not pleaded on the record" and that section except so far as relating to appeals from the sheriff. Section 73. Section 74 except so far as relating to transmission of sheriff court causes. Sections 76 to 88. Section 90. In section 91 the words from "and such petitions" to the end. Section 92 except the last sentence. Section 93. Sections 95 to 99. Section 100(1). Section 101.
31 & 32 Vict. c. 125.	The Parliamentary Elections Act 1868.	Section 1.
42 & 43 Vict. c. 75.	The Parliamentary Elections and Corrupt Practices Act 1879.	Section 1.
46 & 47 Vict. c. 51.	The Corrupt and Illegal Practices Prevention Act 1883.	Section 65.

Chapter	Short Title	Extent of repeal
52 & 53 Vict. c. 54.	The Clerks of Session (Scotland) Regulation Act 1889.	Sections 6 and 7. Section 9. Section 12.
10 Edw. 7 & 1 Geo. 5 c. 31.	The Jury Trials Amendment (Scotland) Act 1910.	Sections 3 and 4.
18 & 19 Geo. 5. c. 34.	The Reorganisation of Offices (Scotland) Act 1928.	Sections 8 and 9.
23 & 24 Geo. 5. c. 41.	The Administration of Justice (Scotland) Act 1933.	Section 2(2). Section 3(1). Section 4 except so far as it relates to the regulation of the powers of the vacation judge by act of sederunt. Section 5. In section 6, subsections (1) to (3) and (5) and (6). Section 9. In section 10, subsections (2) to (5). Section 11(3). Section 13. Section 14 so far as relating to procedure. Section 15 except so far as relating to power to prescribe form of extract of decree. In section 18(3), proviso (i). Section 30. In section 40, the definition of "consistorial cause".
12, 13 & 14 Geo. 6. c. 10.	The Administration of Justice (Scotland) Act 1948.	In section 1 the words from "when" to "thirteen". Section 5.
1968 c. 5.	The Administration of Justice Act 1968.	Section 2.
1980 c. 55.	The Law Reform (Miscellaneous Provisions) (Scotland) Act 1980.	Section 1(6)(b).
1983 c. 12.	The Divorce Jurisdiction, Court Fees and Legal Aid (Scotland) Act 1983.	In Schedule 1, paragraph 5.
1985 c. 6.	The Companies Act 1985.	In section 425(5) the words from "in pursuance" to "1933".
1986 c. 45.	The Insolvency Act 1986.	In section 120(2) the words from "in pursuance" to the end. In section 162(2) the words from "in pursuance" to 1933".
1986 c. 55.	The Family Law Act 1986.	In Schedule 1, paragraph 1.

Social Security Act 1989

(1989 c. 24)

An Act to . . . to provide for the recovery, out of certain compensation payments, of amounts determined by reference to payments of benefit; . . . and for connected purposes.

[21st July 1989]

. . . . . .

Recovery from damages etc. of sums equivalent to benefit

Recovery of sums equivalent to benefit from compensation payments in respect of accidents, injuries and diseases

22.—(1) A person (the "compensator") making a compensation payment, whether on behalf of himself or another, in consequence of an accident, injury or disease suffered by any other person (the "victim") shall not do so until the Secretary of State has furnished him with a certificate of total benefit and shall then—

(*a*) deduct from the payment an amount, determined in accordance with the certificate of total benefit, equal to the gross amount of any relevant benefits paid or likely to be paid to or for the victim during the relevant period in respect of that accident, injury or disease;

(*b*) pay to the Secretary of State an amount equal to that which is required to be so deducted; and

(*c*) furnish the person to whom the compensation payment is or, apart from this section, would have been made (the "intended recipient") with a certificate of deduction.

(2) Any right of the intended recipient to receive the compensation payment in question shall be regarded as satisfied to the extent of the amount certified in the certificate of deduction.

[1] (3) In this section—

"benefit" means any benefit under—

(*a*) the Social Security Acts 1975 to 1988, or

(*b*) the Old Cases Act,

and the "relevant benefits" are such of those benefits as may be prescribed for the purposes of this section;

"certificate of total benefit" means a certificate given by the Secretary of State in accordance with Schedule 4 to this Act;

"certificate of deduction" means a certificate given by the compensator specifying the amount which he has deducted and paid to the Secretary of State in pursuance of subsection (1) above;

"compensation payment" means any payment falling to be made (whether voluntarily, or in pursuance of a court order or an agreement, or otherwise)—

(*a*) to or in respect of the victim in consequence of the accident, injury or disease in question, and

(*b*) either

(i) by or on behalf of a person who is, or is alleged to be, liable to any extent in respect of that accident, injury or disease, or

(ii) in pursuance of a compensation scheme for motor accidents,

but does not include benefit for an exempt payment or so much of any payment as is referable to costs incurred by any person;

"compensation scheme for motor accidents" means any scheme or arrangement under which funds are available for the payment of compensation in respect of motor accidents caused, or alleged to have been caused, by uninsured or unidentified persons;

"compensator", "victim" and "intended recipient" shall be construed in accordance with subsection (1) above;

"costs", in relation to proceedings in Scotland, means expenses;

"payment" means payment in money or money's worth, and cognate expressions shall be construed accordingly;

"relevant period" means—

(*a*) in the case of a disease, the period of 5 years beginning with the date on which the victim first claims a relevant benefit in consequence of the disease; or

(*b*) in any other case, the period of 5 years immediately following the day on which the accident or injury in question occurred;

but where before the end of that period the compensator makes a compensation payment in final discharge of any claim made by or in respect of the victim and arising out of the accident, injury or disease, the relevant period shall end on the date on which that payment is made.

(4) For the purposes of this section the following are the "exempt payments"—

(*a*) any small payment, as defined in paragraph 4 of Schedule 4 to this Act;

(*b*) any payment made to or for the victim under section 35 of the Powers of Criminal Courts Act 1973 or section 58 of the Criminal Justice (Scotland) Act 1980;

(*c*) any payment to the extent that it is made—

(i) in consequence of an action under the Fatal Accidents Act 1976; or

(ii) in circumstances where, had an action been brought, it would have been brought under that Act;

(*d*) any payment to the extent that it is made in respect of a liability arising by virtue of section 1 of the Damages (Scotland) Act 1976;

(*e*) without prejudice to section 6(4) of the Vaccine Damage Payments Act 1979 (which provides for the deduction of any such payment in the assessment of any award of damages), any payment made under that Act to or in respect of the victim;

(*f*) any award of compensation made to or in respect of the victim by the Criminal Injuries Compensation Board under section 111 of the Criminal Justice Act 1988;

(*g*) any payment made in the exercise of a discretion out of property held subject to a trust in a case where no more than 50 per cent. by value of the capital contributed to the trust was directly or indirectly provided by persons who are, or are alleged to be, liable in respect of—

(i) the accident, injury or disease suffered by the victim in question; or

(ii) the same or any connected accident, injury or disease suffered by another;

(*h*) any payment made out of property held for the purposes of any prescribed trust (whether the payment also falls within paragraph (*g*) above or not);

(*j*) any payment made to the victim by an insurance company within the meaning of the Insurance Companies Act 1982 under the terms of any contract of insurance entered into between the victim and the company before—

(i) the date on which the victim first claims a relevant benefit in consequence of the disease in question; or

(ii) the occurrence of the accident or injury in question;

(*k*) any redundancy payment falling to be taken into account in the assessment of damages in respect of an accident, injury or disease.

(5) The Secretary of State may by regulations provide that any prescribed payment shall be an exempt payment for the purposes of this section.

(6) Except as provided by any other enactment, in the assessment of damages in respect of an accident, injury or disease the amount of any relevant benefits paid or likely to be paid shall be disregarded.

(7) Schedule 4 to this Act shall have effect for the purpose of supplementing the provisions of this section; and this section shall have effect subject to the provisions of that Schedule.

(8) This section and that Schedule shall apply in relation to any compensation payment made after the coming into force of this section to the extent that it is made in respect of—

(*a*) an accident or injury occurring on or after 1st January 1989; or

(*b*) a disease, if the victim's first claim for a relevant benefit in consequence of the disease is made on or after that date.

NOTE

[1] As amended by the Social Security Act 1990, Sched. 1, para. 1(1)–(3).

. . . .

Short title, commencement and extent

33.—(1) This Act may be cited as the Social Security Act 1989; and this Act, other than section 25, and the Social Security Acts 1975 to 1988 may be cited together as the Social Security Acts 1975 to 1989.

[1] (2) Apart from the provisions specified in subsection (3) below, this Act shall come into force on such day as the Secretary of State may by order appoint; and different days may be so appointed for different provisions or different purposes of the same provision. . . .

(5) Paragraph 12 of Schedule 4 does not extend to Scotland. . . .

NOTE

[1] The following dates of commencement (so far as relevant) have been prescribed:

18th January 1990: s.22(3), (4) (part), (5) (part), (7) (part) and Sched. 4, paras. 1(2) (part), 4 (part), 11 (part), 13 (part), 17(4) and (10) (part), 21(2) (part) (S.I. 1990 Nos. 102, 312).

25th January 1990: s.22(7) (part) and Sched. 4, para. 15(1)(*a*)(i) and (*b*) (part) (S.I. 1990 No. 312).

1st March 1990: s.22(4) (remainder) (S.I. 1990 No. 102).

2nd April 1990: s.22(7) (part) and Sched. 4, para. 13 (remainder) (S.I. 1990 No. 102).

9th July 1990: s.22(7) (part) and Sched. 4, paras. 3, 14, 15(1)(*a*) and (*b*) (remainder), 16, 17(4)(*b*) (remainder), 21 (remainder) (S.I. 1990 Nos. 102, 132).

3rd September 1990: s.22 (remainder) and Sched. 4 (remainder) (S.I. 1990 No. 102).

. . . . . .

SCHEDULES

. . . . . .

Section 22

[1] SCHEDULE 4

RECOVERY OF SUMS EQUIVALENT TO BENEFIT FROM COMPENSATION PAYMENTS IN RESPECT OF ACCIDENTS ETC: SUPPLEMENTARY PROVISION

NOTE

[1] As amended by the Social Security Act 1990, Sched. 1, paras. 1(4)–5(2) and 6.

PART I

INTERPRETATION

1.—(1) In this Schedule—

"the recoupment provisions" means the provisions of section 22 of this Act and this Schedule;

"the relevant deduction" means the deduction required to be made from the compensation payment in question by virtue of the recoupment provisions;

"the relevant payment" means the payment required to be made to the Secretary of State by virtue of the recoupment provisions;

"the total benefit" means the gross amount referred to in section 22(1)(*a*) of this Act.

(2) If, after making the relevant deduction from the compensation payment, there would be no balance remaining for payment to the intended recipient, any reference in this Schedule to the making of the compensation payment shall be construed in accordance with regulations.

(3) Expressions used in this Schedule and in section 22 of this Act have the same meaning in this Schedule as they have in that section.

PART II

PAYMENTS, DEDUCTIONS AND CERTIFICATES

Time for making payment to Secretary of State

2. The compensator's liability to make the relevant payment arises immediately before the making of the compensation payment, and he shall make the relevant payment before the end of the period of 14 days following the day on which the liability arises.

The certificate of total benefit

3.—(1) It shall be for the compensator to apply to the Secretary of State for the certificate of total benefit and he may, subject to sub-paragraph (5) below, from time to time apply for fresh certificates.

(2) The certificate of total benefit shall specify—

(*a*) the amount which has been, or is likely to be, paid on or before a specified date by way of any relevant benefit which is capable of forming part of the total benefit;

(*b*) where applicable—

(i) the rate of any relevant benefit which is, has been, or is likely to be paid after the date so specified and which would be capable of forming part of the total benefit; and

(ii) the intervals at which any such benefit is paid and the period for which it is likely to be paid;

(*c*) the amounts (if any) which, by virtue of the recoupment provisions, are to be treated as increasing the total benefit; and

(*d*) the aggregate amount of any relevant payments made on or before a specified date (reduced by so much of that amount as has been paid by the Secretary of State to the intended recipient before that date in consequence of the recoupment provisions).

(3) On issuing a certificate of total benefit, the Secretary of State shall be taken to have certified the total benefit as at every date for which it is possible to calculate an amount that would, on the basis of the information so provided, be the total benefit as at that date, on the assumption that payments of benefit are made on the days on which they first become payable.

(4) The Secretary of State may estimate, in such manner as he thinks fit, any of the amounts, rates or periods specified in the certificate of total benefit.

(5) A certificate of total benefit shall remain in force until such date as may be specified in the certificate for that purpose and no application for a fresh certificate shall be made before that date.

(6) Where a certificate ceases to be in force, the Secretary of State may issue a fresh certificate, whether or not an application has been made to him for such a certificate.

(7) The compensator shall not make the compensation payment at any time when there is no certificate of total benefit in force in respect of the victim, unless his liability to make the relevant deduction and the relevant payment has ceased to be enforceable by virtue of paragraph 15 below.

Exemption from deduction in cases involving small payments

4.—(1) Regulations may make provision exempting persons from liability to make the relevant deduction or the relevant payment in prescribed cases where the amount of the compensation payment in question, or the aggregate amount of two or more connected compensation payments, does not exceed the prescribed sum.

(2) Regulations may make provision for cases where an amount has been deducted and paid to the Secretary of State which, by virtue of regulations under sub-paragraph (1) above, ought not to have been so deducted and paid, and any such regulations may, in particular, provide for him to pay that amount to the intended recipient or the compensator or to pay a prescribed part of it to each of them.

(3) The reference in section 22(4)(*a*) of this Act to a "small payment" is a reference to a payment from which by virtue of this paragraph no relevant deduction falls to be made.

(4) For the purposes of this paragraph—

(*a*) two or more compensation payments are "connected" if each is made to or in respect of the same victim and in respect of the same accident, injury or disease; and

(*b*) any reference to a compensation payment is a reference to a payment which would be such a payment apart from section 22(4)(*a*) of this Act.

Multiple compensation payments

5.—(1) This paragraph applies where—

(*a*) a compensation payment has been made (an "earlier payment") to or in respect of the victim; and

(*b*) subsequently another such payment (a "later payment") falls to be made to or in respect of the same victim in respect of the same accident, injury or disease (whether by the same or another compensator).

(2) In determining the amount of the relevant deduction and payment required to be made in connection with the later payment, the amount referred to in section 22(1)(*a*) of this Act shall be reduced by the amount of any relevant payment made in connection with the earlier payment, or, if more than one, the aggregate of those relevant payments.

(3) In relation to the later payment, the compensator shall take the amount of the reduction required by sub-paragraph (2) above to be such as may be specified under paragraph 3(2)(*d*) above in the certificate of total benefit issued to him in connection with that later payment.

(4) In any case where—

(*a*) the relevant payment made in connection with an earlier payment is not reflected in the certificate of total benefit in force in relation to a later payment, and

(*b*) in consequence, the aggregate of the relevant payments made in relation to the later payment and every earlier payment exceeds what it would have been had that relevant payment been so reflected,

the Secretary of State shall pay the intended recipient an amount equal to the excess.

(5) In determining any rights and liabilities in respect of contribution or indemnity, relevant payments shall be treated as damages paid to or for the intended recipient in respect of the accident, injury or disease in question.

[THE NEXT PAGE IS B 321]

Collaboration between compensators

6.—(1) This paragraph applies where compensation payments in respect of the same accident, injury or disease fall (or apart from the recoupment provisions would fall) to be made to or in respect of the same victim by two or more compensators.

(2) Where this paragraph applies, any two or more of those compensators may give the Secretary of State notice that they are collaborators in respect of compensation payments in respect of that victim and that accident, injury or disease.

(3) Where such a notice is given and any of the collaborators makes a relevant payment in connection with such a compensation payment, each of the other collaborators shall be treated as if the aggregate amount of relevant payments specified in his certificate of total benefit, as in force at the time of that relevant payment, or in a fresh certificate which does not purport to reflect the payment, were increased by the amount of that payment.

Structured settlements

7.—(1) This paragraph applies where—

(*a*) in final settlement of a person's claim, an agreement is entered into—

(i) for the making of periodical payments (whether of an income or capital nature) to or in respect of the victim; or

(ii) for the making of such payments and one or more lump sum payments; and

(*b*) apart from this paragraph, those payments would fall to be regarded for the purposes of the recoupment provisions as compensation payments.

(2) Where this paragraph applies, the recoupment provisions (other than this paragraph) shall have effect on the following assumptions, that is to say—

(*a*) the relevant period in the case of the compensator in question shall be taken to end (if it has not previously done so) on the day of settlement;

(*b*) the compensator in question shall be taken—

(i) to have been liable to make on that day a single compensation payment of the amount referred to in section 22(1)(*a*) of this Act (reduced or increased in accordance with such of the recoupment provisions as would have applied in the case of a payment on that day); and

(ii) to have made from that single payment a relevant deduction of an amount equal to it; and

(*c*) the payments under the agreement referred to in sub-paragraph (1) above shall be taken to be exempt payments.

(3) The intended recipient shall not by virtue of anything in this paragraph become entitled to be paid any sum, whether by the compensator or the Secretary of State, and if on a review or appeal under paragraph 16 or 18 below it appears that the amount paid by a compensator in pursuance of this paragraph was either greater or less than it ought to have been, then—

(*a*) any excess shall be repaid to the compensator instead of to the intended recipient; but

(*b*) any deficiency shall be paid to the Secretary of State by the intended recipient.

(4) Where any further compensation payment falls to be made to or in respect of the victim otherwise than under the agreement in question, sub-paragraph (2)(*a*) above shall be disregarded for the purpose of determining the end of the relevant period in relation to that further payment.

(5) In any case where—

(*a*) the person making the periodical payments (the "secondary party") does so in pursuance of arrangements entered into with another (as in a case where an insurance company purchases an annuity for the victim from another such company), and

(*b*) apart from those arrangements, that other ("the primary party") would have been regarded as the compensator,

then for the purposes of the recoupment provisions, the primary party shall be regarded as the compensator and the secondary party shall not be so regarded.

(6) In determining for the purposes of this paragraph whether any periodical payments would fall to be regarded as compensation payments, section 22(4)(*a*) of this Act shall be disregarded.

(7) In this paragraph "the day of settlement" means—

(*a*) if the agreement referred to in sub-paragraph (1) above is approved by a court, the day on which that approval is given; and

(*b*) in any other case, the day on which that agreement is entered into.

Insolvency

8.—(1) Where the intended recipient is subject to a bankruptcy order, nothing in the Insolvency Act 1986 shall affect the operation of the recoupment provisions.

(2) Where the estate of the intended recipient is sequestrated, the relevant deduction from the compensation payment shall not form part of the whole estate of the debtor, within the meaning of section 31(8) of the Bankruptcy (Scotland) Act 1985.

Protection of legal aid charges

9.—(1) In any case where—

(*a*) the compensation payment is subject to any charge under the Legal Aid Act 1974 or the Legal Aid Act 1988, and

(*b*) after the making of the relevant deduction, the balance of the compensation payment is insufficient to satisfy that charge,

the Secretary of State shall make such a payment as will secure that the deficiency is made good to the extent of the relevant payment.

(2) Where the Secretary of State makes a payment under this paragraph, then, for the purposes of paragraph 3 above, the amount of the payment shall be treated as increasing the total benefit.

(3) In the application of this paragraph to Scotland, references in sub-paragraph (1) to a charge under the Acts specified shall be construed as references to any provisions of the Legal Aid (Scotland) Act 1986 for the repayment to the Scottish Legal Aid Fund of sums paid by it on behalf of the intended recipient in respect of the proceedings in which the compensation payment is made.

Overpaid benefits

10. In any case where—

(*a*) during the relevant period, there has, in respect of the accident, injury or disease, been paid to or for the victim any relevant benefit to which he was not entitled ("the overpaid benefit"), and

(*b*) the amount of the relevant payment is such that, after taking account of the rest of the total benefit, there remains an amount which represents the whole or any part of the overpaid benefit,

then, notwithstanding anything in section 53 of the 1986 Act or any regulations under that section, the receipt by the Secretary of State of the relevant payment shall be treated as the recovery of the whole or, as the case may be, that part of the overpaid benefit.

Death

11. In the case of any compensation payment the whole or part of which is made—

(*a*) in consequence of an action under the Fatal Accidents Act 1976, or

(*b*) in circumstances where, had an action been brought, it would have been brought under that Act, or

(*c*) in respect of a liability arising by virtue of section 1 of the Damages (Scotland) Act 1976,

regulations may make provision for estimating or calculating the portion of the payment which is to be regarded as so made for the purposes of section 22(4)(*c*) or (*d*) of this Act.

. . . .

PART III

ADMINISTRATION AND ADJUDICATION

Provision of information

13.—(1) Any person who is, or is alleged to be, liable in respect of an accident, injury or disease, or any person acting on his behalf, shall furnish the Secretary of State with the prescribed information relating to any person seeking compensation, or in respect of whom compensation is sought, in respect of that accident, injury or disease.

(2) Any person who claims a relevant benefit or who has been in receipt of such a benefit or, if he has died, the personal representatives of such a person, shall furnish the Secretary of State with the prescribed information relating to any accident, injury or disease suffered by that person.

(2A) A person who makes any payment (whether a compensation payment or not) on behalf of himself or another—

(*a*) in consequence of any accident, injury or disease suffered, or any damage to property sustained, by any other person, or

(*b*) which is referable to any costs, or, in Scotland, expenses, incurred by any such other person by reason of such an accident, injury, disease or damage,

shall, if the Secretary of State so requests him in writing, furnish the Secretary of State with such particulars relating to the size and composition of the payment as may be specified in the request.

(3) Any person—

(*a*) who is the employer of a person who suffers or has suffered an accident, injury or disease, or

(*b*) who has been the employer of such a person at any time during the relevant period, shall furnish the Secretary of State with the prescribed information relating to the payment of statutory sick pay in respect of that person.

(4) In sub-paragraph (3) above "employer" has the same meaning as it has in Part I of the 1982 Act.

(5) Any person furnishing information under this paragraph shall do so in the prescribed manner, at the prescribed place and within the prescribed time.

Applications for certificates of total benefit

14.—(1) If at any time before he makes the compensation payment in question the compensator applies to the Secretary of State in accordance with paragraph 3 above for a certificate of total benefit relating to the victim in question—

(*a*) the Secretary of State shall furnish him with such a certificate before the end of the period of four weeks, or such other number of weeks as may be prescribed, following the day on which the application is, or is deemed in accordance with regulations to be, received; and

(*b*) any certificate so furnished shall, in particular, specify for the purposes of paragraph 3(2)(*a*) above a date not earlier than the date of the application.

(2) Where the Secretary of State furnishes any person with a certificate of total benefit, he shall also provide the information contained in that certificate to the person who appears to him to be the victim in relation to the compensation payment in question.

(3) The victim may apply to the Secretary of State for particulars of the manner in which any amount, rate or period specified in a certificate of total benefit has been determined.

Liability of compensator unenforceable if certificate not issued within time limit

15.—(1) The liability of the compensator to make the relevant deduction and payment relating to the first compensation payment after the default date shall not be enforceable if—

(*a*) he has made a request under paragraph 14(1) above which—

(i) accurately states the prescribed particulars relating to the victim and the accident, injury or disease in question; and

(ii) specifies the name and address of the person to whom the certificate is to be sent;

(*b*) he has in his possession a written acknowledgment, sent to him in accordance with regulations, of the receipt of the request; and

(*c*) the Secretary of State does not, within the time limit referred to in paragraph 14(1) above, send the certificate to the person specified in the request as the person to whom the certificate is to be sent, at the address so specified;

and accordingly, where those liabilities cease to be enforceable, nothing in the recoupment provisions shall prevent the compensator from making that compensation payment.

(2) In any case where—

(*a*) the liability to make the relevant deduction and payment becomes unenforceable by virtue of this paragraph, but

(*b*) the compensator nevertheless makes that deduction and payment,

he shall be treated for all purposes as if the liability had remained enforceable.

(3) Where the compensator, in reliance on this paragraph, does not make the relevant deduction and payment, then—

(*a*) he shall within 14 days of the default date give the Secretary of State notice of that fact together with such other particulars as may be prescribed; and

(*b*) in determining the amount of the relevant deduction and payment to be made in connection with any subsequent compensation payment made by the same or any other compensator, the amount which, apart from this paragraph, would have fallen to be deducted and paid by him shall continue to form part of the total benefit and shall not be treated as if it had been paid.

(4) If, in the opinion of the Secretary of State, circumstances have arisen which adversely affect normal methods of communication—

(*a*) he may by order provide that no liability shall become unenforceable by virtue of this paragraph during a specified period not exceeding three months; and

(*b*) he may continue any such order in force for further periods not exceeding three months at a time.

(5) In this paragraph "the default date" means the date on which the time limit mentioned in sub-paragraph (1)(*c*) above expires.

Review of certificates of total benefit

16.—(1) The Secretary of State may review any certificate of total benefit if he is satisfied that it was issued in ignorance of, or was based on a mistake as to, some material fact or that a mistake (whether in computation or otherwise) has occurred in its preparation.

(2) On any such review the Secretary of State may either—

(*a*) confirm the certificate, or

(*b*) issue a fresh certificate containing such variations as he considers appropriate,

but he shall not so vary the certificate as to increase the total benefit.

(3) In any case where—

(*a*) one or more relevant payments have been made, and

(*b*) in consequence of a review under this paragraph, it appears that the aggregate amount so paid exceeds the amount that ought to have been paid,

the Secretary of State shall pay the intended recipient an amount equal to the excess.

Appeals

17.—(1) An appeal shall lie in accordance with this paragraph against any certificate of total benefit at the instance of the compensator, the victim or the intended recipient, on the ground—

(*a*) that any amount, rate or period specified in the certificate is incorrect, or

(*b*) that benefit paid or payable otherwise than in consequence of the accident, injury or disease in question has been brought into account.

(2) No appeal shall be brought under this paragraph until—

(*a*) the claim giving rise to the compensation payment has been finally disposed of; and

(*b*) the relevant payment, or where more than one such payment may fall to be made, the final relevant payment, has been made.

(3) Notwithstanding sub-paragraph (2) above, where—

(*a*) an award of damages ("provisional damages") has been made under or by virtue of—

(i) section 32A(2)(*a*) of the Supreme Court Act 1981, or

(ii) section 12(2)(*a*) of the Administration of Justice Act 1982, or

(iii) section 51(2)(*a*) of the County Courts Act 1984, and

(*b*) the relevant payment or, where more than one such payment falls to be made, the final relevant payment in relation to the provisional damages so awarded has been made,

an appeal may be brought under this paragraph against any certificate of total benefit by reference to which the amount of that relevant payment, or any of those relevant payments, was made.

(4) Regulations may—

(*a*) make provision as to the manner in which, and the time within which, appeals under this paragraph are to be brought, and

(*b*) make provision for the purpose of enabling any such appeal to be treated as an application for review under paragraph 16 above,

and regulations under paragraph (*b*) above may, in particular, provide that the circumstances in which such a review may be carried out shall not be restricted to those specified in paragraph 16 above.

(5) If any of the medical questions arises for determination on an appeal under this paragraph, the Secretary of State shall refer that question to a medical appeal tribunal, whose determination shall be binding, for the purposes of the appeal, on any social security appeal tribunal to whom a question is referred under sub-paragraph (7) below.

(6) A medical appeal tribunal, in determining any of the medical questions, shall take into account any decision of any court relating to the same, or any similar, issue arising in connection with the accident, injury or disease in question.

(7) If any question concerning any amount, rate or period specified in the certificate of total benefit arises for determination on an appeal under this paragraph, the Secretary of State shall refer that question to a social security appeal tribunal, but where any medical questions arising on the appeal have been referred to a medical appeal tribunal—

(*a*) he shall not refer any question to the social security appeal tribunal until he has received the determination of the medical appeal tribunal on the questions referred to them; and

(*b*) he shall notify the social security appeal tribunal of the determinations of the medical appeal tribunal.

(8) On a reference under sub-paragraph (7) above a social security appeal tribunal may either—

(*a*) confirm the amounts, rates and periods specified in the certificate of total benefit; or

(*b*) specify any increases, reductions or other variations which are to be made on the issue of the fresh certificate under sub-paragraph (9) below.

(9) When the Secretary of State has received the determinations of the tribunals on the questions referred to them under sub-paragraphs (5) and (7) above, he shall in accordance with those determinations either—

(*a*) confirm the certificate against which the appeal was brought, or

(*b*) issue a fresh certificate.

(10) Regulations may make provision with respect to the procedure for the reference under this paragraph of questions to medical appeal tribunals or social security appeal tribunals.

(11) An appeal shall lie to a Commissioner at the instance of the Secretary of State, the compensator, the victim or the intended recipient from a decision of a medical appeal tribunal or a social security appeal tribunal under this paragraph on the ground that the decision was erroneous in point of law; and for the purposes of appeals under this sub-paragraph—

(*a*) section 101(5), (5A) and (5B) of the principal Act shall apply in relation to an appeal from the decision of a social security appeal tribunal; and

(*b*) section 112(3) of that Act shall apply in relation to an appeal from the decision of a medical appeal tribunal.

(12) In this paragraph "the medical questions" means—

(*a*) any question whether, as the result of a particular occurrence, a person suffered an injury, sickness or disease;

(*b*) any question as to the period for which a person suffered any injury, sickness or disease.

Recovery in consequence of an appeal

18.—(1) Where it appears, in consequence of an appeal under paragraph 17 above, that the aggregate amount of the relevant payment or payments actually made exceeds the amount that ought to have been paid, the Secretary of State shall pay the intended recipient an amount equal to that excess.

(2) Where it appears, in consequence of such an appeal, that the aggregate amount of the relevant payment or payments actually made is less than the amount that ought to have been paid, the intended recipient shall pay the Secretary of State an amount equal to the deficiency.

(3) Without prejudice to any other method of enforcement, an amount payable under sub-paragraph (2) above may be recovered by deduction from any benefits which are prescribed benefits for the purposes of section 53 of the 1986 Act (recovery of overpayments).

Recovery of relevant payment in cases of default

19.—(1) This paragraph applies in any case where the compensator has made a compensation payment but—

(*a*) has not requested a certificate of total benefit in respect of the victim, or

(*b*) if he has done so, has not made the relevant payment within the time limit imposed by paragraph 2 above.

(2) Where this paragraph applies, the Secretary of State may—

(*a*) if no certificate of total benefit has been issued to the compensator, issue to him such a certificate and a demand for the relevant payment to be made forthwith, or

(*b*) if a certificate of total benefit has been issued to the compensator, issue to him a copy of that certificate and such a demand,

and that relevant payment shall, to the extent that it does not exceed the amount of the compensation payment, be recoverable by the Secretary of State from the compensator.

(3) Any amount recoverable under this paragraph shall—

(*a*) if the compensator resides or carries on business in England and Wales and a county court so orders, be recoverable by execution issued from the county court or otherwise as if it were payable under an order of that court; or

(*b*) if the compensator resides or carries on business in Scotland, be enforced in like manner as an extract registered decree arbitral bearing a warrant for execution issued by the sheriff court of any sheriffdom in Scotland.

(4) A document bearing a certificate which—

(*a*) is signed by a person authorised in that behalf by the Secretary of State, and

(*b*) states that the document, apart from the certificate, is a record of the amount recoverable under this paragraph,

shall be conclusive evidence that that amount is so recoverable; and a certificate purporting to be signed as aforesaid shall be deemed to be so signed unless the contrary is proved.

(5) Where this paragraph applies in relation to two or more connected compensators, the Secretary of State may proceed against them as if they were jointly and severally liable for an amount equal to the difference between—

(*a*) the total benefit determined in accordance with the latest connected certificate of total benefit issued to any of them, and

(*b*) the aggregate amount of any connected relevant payments previously made.

(6) Nothing in sub-paragraph (5) above authorises the recovery from any person of an amount in excess of the compensation payment by virtue of which this paragraph applies to him (or, if there are two or more such payments which are connected, the aggregate amount of those payments).

(7) In sub-paragraphs (5) and (6) above, "connected" means relating to the same victim and the same accident, injury or disease.

. . . .

PART IV

MISCELLANEOUS

Persons in Northern Ireland

20A.—(1) Where, immediately before making a compensation payment to or in respect of a victim, the compensator—

(*a*) is not resident and does not have a place of business in Great Britain, but

(*b*) is resident or has a place of business in Northern Ireland,

the Great Britain provisions shall apply as if at that time he were resident or had a place of business in the relevant part of Great Britain.

(2) Where, immediately before making a Northern Ireland compensation payment to or in respect of a Northern Ireland victim, the Northern Ireland compensator—

(*a*) is not resident and does not have a place of business in Northern Ireland, but

(*b*) is resident or has a place of business in any part of Great Britain,

the Northern Ireland provisions shall apply as if at that time he were resident or had a place of business in Northern Ireland.

(3) Where an address in Northern Ireland is the first address notified in writing to the compensator by or on behalf of the victim as his residence (or, if the victim has died, by or on behalf of the intended recipient as the victim's last residence) then—

(*a*) the compensator shall apply, as a Northern Ireland compensator, for a Northern Ireland certificate in accordance with the Northern Ireland provisions (and shall not make any separate application for a certificate of total benefit);

(*b*) any Northern Ireland certificate which is issued to the compensator in relation to the victim and the accident, injury or disease in question—

(i) shall contain a statement that it is to be treated as including a certificate of total benefit so issued by the Secretary of State and that any relevant payment required to be made to him by reference thereto is to be paid to the Northern Ireland Department as his agent; and

(ii) shall be taken to include such a certificate of total benefit; and

(*c*) any payment made by the compensator to the Northern Ireland Department in pursuance of such a Northern Ireland certificate shall be applied—

(i) first towards discharging his liability under the Northern Ireland provisions, and

(ii) then, as respects any remaining balance, towards discharging his liability under the Great Britain provisions,

in respect of the relevant victim and that accident, injury or disease.

(4) Where an address in any part of Great Britain is the first address notified in writing to the Northern Ireland compensator by or on behalf of the Northern Ireland victim as his residence (or, if the Northern Ireland victim has died, by or on behalf of the Northern Ireland intended recipient as the Northern Ireland victim's last residence) then—

(*a*) the Northern Ireland compensator shall apply, as a compensator, for a certificate of total benefit in accordance with the Great Britain provisions (and shall not make any separate application for a Northern Ireland certificate);

(*b*) any certificate of total benefit which is issued to the Northern Ireland compensator in relation to the Northern Ireland victim and the accident, injury or disease in question—

(i) shall contain a statement that it is to be treated as including a Northern Ireland certificate so issued by the Northern Ireland Department and that any Northern Ireland relevant payment required to be made to that Department by reference thereto is to be paid to the Secretary of State as its agent; and

(ii) shall be taken to include such a Northern Ireland certificate; and

(*c*) any payment made by the Northern Ireland compensator to the Secretary of State in pursuance of such a certificate shall be applied—

(i) first towards discharging his liability under the Great Britain provisions, and

(ii) then, as respects any remaining balance, towards discharging his liability under the Northern Ireland provisions,

in respect of the relevant victim and that accident, injury or disease.

(5) For the purposes of sub-paragraph (1) above, "the relevant part of Great Britain," in relation to a compensator, means—

(*a*) if the compensator has been notified in writing—

(i) by or on behalf of the victim, or

(ii) where the victim has died, by or on behalf of the intended recipient,

that the victim is or was at any time resident at an address in any part of Great Britain, that part of Great Britain (or, if more than one such notification has been given, the part in which he was so notified that the victim was most recently so resident); or

(*b*) in any other case, such part of Great Britain as the Secretary of State may determine in accordance with regulations.

(6) In this paragraph—

"the Great Britain provisions" means the recoupment provisions, other than this paragraph;

"Northern Ireland certificate" means a certificate of total benefit, within the meaning of the Northern Ireland provisions;

"Northern Ireland compensation payment" means a compensation payment, within the meaning of the Northern Ireland provisions;

"Northern Ireland compensator" means a compensator, within the meaning of the Northern Ireland provisions;

"the Northern Ireland Department" has the same meaning as it has in the principal Act;

"the Northern Ireland intended recipient" means the intended recipient, within the meaning of the Northern Ireland provisions, in relation to a Northern Ireland compensation payment;

"the Northern Ireland provisions" means any legislation corresponding to the recoupment provisions (other than this paragraph) and having effect in Northern Ireland;

"Noıthern Ireland relevant payment" means a relevant payment, within the meaning of the Northern Ireland provisions;

"Northern Ireland victim" means a person who is the victim, within the meaning of the Northern Ireland provisions, in relation to a Northern Ireland compensation payment;

"the relevant victim" means the person who is the victim or the Northern Ireland victim (or both), as the case may be.

(7) This paragraph extends to Northern Ireland.

Foreign compensators: duties of intended recipient

21.—(1) Where, immediately before the making of the compensation payment, the compensator is not resident and does not have a place of business in any part of the United Kingdom, any deduction, payment or other thing which would, apart from this paragraph, fall to be made or done under the recoupment provisions by the compensator shall instead be made or done by the intended recipient and references to the compensator shall be construed accordingly.

(2) The Secretary of State may by regulations make such provision as he considers expedient for the purpose of modifying the recoupment provisions in their application in such a case.

Modification of Law Reform (Personal Injuries) Act 1948

22.—(1) In section 2 of the Law Reform (Personal Injuries) Act 1948, in subsection (1) (which requires that, in assessing damages, half of certain benefits shall be brought into account against loss of profits or earnings)—

(*a*) after the word "contract)," there shall be inserted the words "where this section applies";

(*b*) for the words from "against any loss" to "from the injuries" there shall be substituted the words "against them"; and

(*c*) for the words from "therefrom" onwards there shall be substituted the words "from the injuries in respect of—

(*a*) any of the relevant benefits, within the meaning of section 22 of the Social Security Act 1989, or

(*b*) any corresponding benefits payable in Northern Ireland,

for the five years beginning with the time when the cause of action accrued."

(2) After that subsection there shall be inserted—

"(1A) This section applies in any case where the amount of the damages that would have been awarded apart from any reduction under subsection (1) above is less than the sum for the time being prescribed under paragraph 4(1) of Schedule 4 to the Social Security Act 1989 (recoupment of benefit: exception for small payments)."

(3) Subsection (2) of that section (disregard of increase for constant attendance) shall cease to have effect.

Modification of Bankruptcy (Scotland) Act 1985

23. In section 31 of the Bankruptcy (Scotland) Act 1985 (vesting of debtor's estate at date of sequestration) in subsection (8) after the words "subsection (9) below" there shall be inserted the words "and to paragraph 8(2) of Schedule 4 to the Social Security Act 1989."

Interest on damages: reductions in respect of relevant payments

24. In assessing the amount of interest payable in respect of an award of damages, the amount of the award shall be treated as reduced by a sum equal to the amount of the relevant payment (if any) required to be made in connection with the payment of the damages and—

(*a*) in England and Wales, if both special and general damages are awarded, any such reductions shall be treated as made first against the special damages and then, as respects any remaining balance, against the general damages; and

(*b*) in Scotland, if damages are awarded both for patrimonial loss and for solatium, any such reductions shall be treated as made first against the damages for patrimonial loss and then, as respects any remaining balance, against the damages for solatium.

Law Reform (Miscellaneous Provisions) (Scotland) Act 1990

(1990 c. 40)

An Act, as respects Scotland, . . . to provide as to rights of audience in courts of law, legal services and judicial appointments, and for the establishment and functions of an ombudsman in relation to legal services; . . . and to make certain other miscellaneous reforms of the law. [1st November 1990]

. . . . . .

[1] Part II

Legal Services

NOTE

[1] Pt. II shall come into force on a day or days to be appointed: s.75(2).

. . . . . .

Rights of audience

24–30. [*See* Division F.]

Rules of conduct

Rules of conduct etc.

31.—(1) Any rule, whether made before or after the coming into force of this section, whereby an advocate is prohibited from forming a legal relationship with another advocate or with any other person for the purpose of their jointly offering professional services to the public shall have no effect unless it is approved by the Lord President and the Secretary of State; and before approving any such rule the Secretary of State shall consult the Director in accordance with section 40 of this Act.

(2) Where it appears to the Faculty of Advocates that any rule of conduct in relation to the exercise of an advocate's right of audience in the Court of Session is more restrictive than the equivalent rule in relation to the exercise of the equivalent right in the sheriff court, they may submit that rule to the Secretary of State for his approval, and the Secretary of State shall consult the Director in accordance with section 40 of this Act, and thereafter, having—

(*a*) considered any advice tendered to him by the Director;

(*b*) compared the rule applicable in the Court of Session with the equivalent rule applicable in the sheriff court; and

(*c*) considered whether the interests of justice require that there should be such a rule in the Court of Session,

he may approve or refuse to approve the rule.

. . . . . .

Complaints in relation to legal services

33–34. [*See* Division F.]

Judicial appointments

Judicial appointments

35.—(1) Paragraphs 1 to 3 of Schedule 4 to this Act shall have effect in relation to the eligibility of sheriffs principal, sheriffs and solicitors to be appointed as judges of the Court of Session.

(2) Paragraph 4 of the said Schedule shall have effect in relation to the appointment of—

(*a*) members of the Inner House of the Court of Session; and

(*b*) a Lord Ordinary of that Court to be the Lord Ordinary in exchequer causes.

(3) Notwithstanding any provision in any enactment, if it appears expedient to the Secretary of State he may, in accordance with the provisions of paragraphs 5 to 11 of the said Schedule, and after consulting the Lord President, appoint persons to act as temporary judges of the Court of Session.

(4) Section 3 (constitution of Scottish Land Court) of the Small Landholders (Scotland) Act 1911 shall have effect subject to the amendments mentioned in paragraph 12 of the said Schedule.

Solicitors' and counsel's fees

Solicitors' and counsel's fees

36.—(1) An advocate and the person instructing him may agree, in relation to a litigation undertaken on a speculative basis, that, in the event of the litigation being successful, the advocate's fee shall be increased by such percentage as may, subject to subsection (2) below, be agreed.

(2) The percentage increase which may be agreed under subsection (1) above shall not exceed such limit as the court may, after consultation with the Dean of the Faculty of Advocates, prescribe by act of sederunt.

. . . . . .

Interpretation of Part II

44. In this Part of this Act, unless the context otherwise requires—

"advocate" means a member of the Faculty of Advocates practising as such;

"the Director" means the Director General of Fair Trading;
"Lord President" means the Lord President of the Court of Session;
"solicitor" has the same meaning as in section 65(1) of the 1980 Act; and
"the 1980 Act" means the Solicitors (Scotland) Act 1980.

. . . . . .

Part IV

Miscellaneous Reforms

. . . . . .

Blood and other samples in civil proceedings

Blood and other samples in civil proceedings

70.—(1) In any civil proceedings to which this section applies, the court may (whether or not on application made to it) request a party to the proceedings—

(*a*) to provide a sample of blood or other body fluid or of body tissue for the purpose of laboratory analysis;

(*b*) to consent to the taking of such a sample from a child in relation to whom the party has power to give such consent.

(2) Where a party to whom a request under subsection (1) above has been made refuses or fails—

(*a*) to provide or, as the case may be, to consent to the taking of, a sample as requested by the court, or

(*b*) to take any step necessary for the provision or taking of such a sample,

the court may draw from the refusal or failure such adverse inference, if any, in relation to the subject matter of the proceedings as seems to it to be appropriate.

(3) [Amendments to section 6 of the Law Reform (Parent and Child) (Scotland) Act 1986 are given effect in the print of that Act, *infra*, Division K.]

[1] (4) This section applies to any civil proceedings brought in the Court of Session or the sheriff court—

(*a*) on or after the date of the commencement of this section; or

(*b*) before the said date in a case where the proof has not by that date begun.

NOTE

[1] This section was brought into force on 1st January 1991 by s.75(3).

. . . . . .

SCHEDULE 4

Judicial Appointments

Appointments of sheriffs principal, sheriffs and solicitors as judges of the Court of Session

1. The following categories of person shall, in accordance with this paragraph and paragraphs 2 and 3 below, be eligible to be appointed as judges of the Court of Session—

(*a*) sheriffs principal and sheriffs who have held office as such for a continuous period of not less than five years; and

(*b*) solicitors who, by virtue of section 25A (rights of audience) of the Solicitors (Scotland) Act 1980, have for a continuous period of not less than 5 years had a right of audience in both the Court of Session and the High Court of Justiciary.

2. Paragraph 1(*a*) above shall not confer any eligibility for appointment as a judge of the Court of Session on a temporary sheriff principal or sheriff appointed under section 11 (temporary sheriffs principal and sheriffs) of the Sheriff Courts (Scotland) Act 1971 who is not otherwise eligible for appointment as a judge of the Court of Session.

3. Paragraphs 1 and 2 above are without prejudice to any eligibility to be appointed as a judge of the Court of Session conferred on any category of persons by any other enactment.

Further provision as to Inner House and exchequer causes

4.—(1) The Court of Session Act 1988 shall be amended as follows.

(2) In section 2 (composition of court)—

(*a*) in subsection (3), for the words "the senior judge present shall preside and shall" there shall be substituted the words "shall direct one of those judges to preside and to"; and

(*b*) for subsection (6) there shall be substituted the following subsection—

"(6) Subject to subsection (7) below, where a vacancy arises in a Division of the Inner House the Lord President and the Lord Justice Clerk, with the consent of the Secretary of State and after such consultation with judges as appears to them to be appropriate in the particular circumstances, shall appoint a Lord Ordinary to fill that vacancy.".

(3) In section 3 (exchequer causes), for the words "Court by Act of Sederunt" there shall be substituted the words "Lord President."

Temporary judges

5. Any person who is eligible under—

(*a*) paragraph 1 above; or

(*b*) any other enactment,

for appointment as a judge of the Court of Session may be appointed as a temporary judge under section 35(3) of this Act for such period as the Secretary of State may determine, but, subject to paragraph 9 below, no such appointment shall extend beyond the date on which the person reaches the age of 75 years.

6. Subject to paragraph 7 below, a person appointed as a temporary judge under the said section 35(3) shall, while so acting, be treated for all purposes as, and accordingly may perform any of the functions of, a judge of the Court in which he is acting.

7. Subject to paragraph 8 below, a person shall not, by virtue of paragraph 6 above, be treated as a judge of the Court of Session for the purposes of any other enactment or rule of law relating to—

(*a*) the appointment, tenure of office, retirement, removal or disqualification of judges of that Court, including, without prejudice to the generality of the foregoing, any enactment or rule of law relating to the number of judges who may be appointed; and

(*b*) the remuneration, allowances or pensions of such judges.

8. A person appointed to be a temporary judge of the Court of Session shall, by virtue of such appointment, be a temporary Lord Commissioner of Justiciary in Scotland.

9. Notwithstanding the expiry of any period for which a person is appointed under the said section 35(3) to act as a judge—

(*a*) he may attend at the Court of Session or the High Court of Justiciary for the purpose of continuing to deal with, giving judgment in, or dealing with any matter relating to, any case begun before him while acting as a judge of either Court; and

(*b*) for that purpose, and for the purpose of any proceedings arising out of any such case or matter, he shall be treated as being or, as the case may be, having been, a judge of the relevant Court.

10. The Secretary of State may pay to a person appointed under the said section 35(3) such remuneration as he may, with the consent of the Treasury, determine.

11. The appointment of a person to act as a temporary judge under the said section 35(3) is without prejudice to—

(*a*) any appointment held by him as a sheriff principal or sheriff; or

(*b*) his continuing with any business or professional occupation not inconsistent with his acting as a judge.

. . . . . .

Civil Jurisdiction and Judgments Act 1991

(1991 c. 12)

An Act to give effect to the Convention on jurisdiction and the enforcement of judgments in civil and commercial matters, including the Protocol annexed thereto, opened for signature at Lugano on 16th September 1988; and for purposes connected therewith. [9th May 1991]

ARRANGEMENT OF SECTIONS

Implementation and interpretation of the Lugano Convention

1.—(1) The Civil Jurisdiction and Judgments Act 1982 (in this Act referred to as "the 1982 Act") shall have effect with the insertion of the following after section 3—

"**The Lugano Convention to have the force of law**

3A.—(1) The Lugano Convention shall have the force of law in the United Kingdom, and judicial notice shall be taken of it.

(2) For convenience of reference there is set out in Schedule 3C the English text of the Lugano Convention.

Interpretation of the Lugano Convention

3B.—(1) In determining any question as to the meaning or effect of a provision of the Lugano Convention, a court in the United Kingdom shall, in accordance with Protocol No. 2 to that Convention, take account of any principles laid down in any relevant decision delivered by a court of any other Lugano Contracting State concerning provisions of the Convention.

(2) Without prejudice to any practice of the courts as to the matters which may be considered apart from this section, the report on the Lugano Convention by Mr. P. Jenard and Mr. G. Möller (which is reproduced in the Official Journal of the Communities of 28th July 1990) may be considered in ascertaining the meaning or effect of any provision of the Convention and shall be given such weight as is appropriate in the circumstances."

(2) In section 9 of that Act, after subsection (1) (which, as amended, will govern the relationship between other conventions and the 1968 and Lugano Conventions) there shall be inserted—

"(1A) Any question arising as to whether it is the Lugano Convention or any of the Brussels Conventions which applies in the circumstances of a particular case falls to be determined in accordance with the provisions of Article 54B of the Lugano Convention."

(3) After Schedule 3B to that Act there shall be inserted the Schedule 3C set out in Schedule 1 to this Act.

Interpretation of the 1982 Act

2.—(1) Section 1 of the 1982 Act (interpretation of references to the Conventions and Contracting States) shall be amended in accordance with the following provisions of this section.

(2) In subsection (1), in the definition of "the Conventions", for the words "the Conventions" there shall be substituted the words "the Brussels Conventions".

(3) At the end of that subsection there shall be added—

" 'the Lugano Convention' means the Convention on jurisdiction and the enforcement of judgments in civil and commercial matters (including the Protocols annexed to that Convention) opened for signature at Lugano on 16th September 1988 and signed by the United Kingdom on 18th September 1989."

(4) In subsection (2), for paragraph (*b*) (citation of Articles) there shall be substituted—

"(*b*) any reference in any provision to a numbered Article without more is a reference—

(i) to the Article so numbered of the 1968 Convention, in so far as the provision applies in relation to that Convention, and

(ii) to the Article so numbered of the Lugano Convention, in so far as the provision applies in relation to that Convention,

and any reference to a sub-division of a numbered Article shall be construed accordingly."

(5) In subsection (3) (definition of "Contracting State") for the words "In this Act 'Contracting State' means—" there shall be substituted the words—

"In this Act—

'Contracting State', without more, in any provision means—

(*a*) in the application of the provision in relation to the Brussels Conventions, a Brussels Contracting State; and

(*b*) in the application of the provision in relation to the Lugano Convention, a Lugano Contracting State;

'Brussels Contracting State' means—".

(6) At the end of that subsection there shall be added—

" 'Lugano Contracting State' means one of the original parties to the Lugano Convention, that is to say—

Austria, Belgium, Denmark, Finland, France, the Federal Republic of Germany, the Hellenic Republic, Iceland, the Republic of Ireland, Italy, Luxembourg, the Netherlands, Norway, Portugal, Spain, Sweden, Switzerland and the United Kingdom,

being a State in relation to which that Convention has taken effect in accordance with paragraph 3 or 4 of Article 61."

Other amendments of the 1982 Act

3. The 1982 Act shall have effect with the amendments specified in Schedule 2 to this Act, which are either consequential on the amendments made by sections 1 and 2 above or otherwise for the purpose of implementing the Lugano Convention.

Application to the Crown

4. The amendments of the 1982 Act made by this Act bind the Crown in accordance with the provisions of section 51 of that Act.

Short title, interpretation, commencement and extent

5.—(1) This Act may be cited as the Civil Jurisdiction and Judgments Act 1991.

(2) In this Act—

"the 1982 Act" means the Civil Jurisdiction and Judgments Act 1982;

"the Lugano Convention" has the same meaning as it has in the 1982 Act by virtue of section 2(3) above.

(3) This Act shall come into force on such day as the Lord Chancellor and the Lord Advocate may appoint in an order made by statutory instrument.

(4) This Act extends to Northern Ireland.

SCHEDULES

SCHEDULE 1

SCHEDULE TO BE INSERTED AS SCHEDULE 3C TO THE 1982 ACT

SCHEDULE 3C

Section 3A(2) TEXT OF THE LUGANO CONVENTION

ARRANGEMENT OF PROVISIONS

CONVENTION

ON JURISDICTION AND THE ENFORCEMENT OF JUDGMENTS IN CIVIL AND COMMERCIAL MATTERS

Preamble

The High Contracting Parties to this Convention,

Anxious to strengthen in their territories the legal protection of persons therein established,

Considering that it is necessary for this purpose to determine the international jurisdiction of their courts, to facilitate recognition and to introduce an expeditious procedure for securing the enforcement of judgments, authentic instruments and court settlements,

Aware of the links between them, which have been sanctioned in the economic field by the free trade agreements concluded between the European Economic Community and the States members of the European Free Trade Association,

Taking into account the Brussels Convention of 27 September 1968 on jurisdiction and the enforcement of judgments in civil and commercial matters, as amended by the Accession Conventions under the successive enlargements of the European Communities,

Persuaded that the extension of the principles of that Convention to the States parties to this instrument will strengthen legal and economic co-operation in Europe,

Desiring to ensure as uniform an interpretation as possible of this instrument,

Have in this spirit decided to conclude this Convention and

Have agreed as follows:

TITLE I

Scope

Article 1

This Convention shall apply in civil and commercial matters whatever the nature of the court or tribunal. It shall not extend, in particular, to revenue, customs or administrative matters.

The Convention shall not apply to:

1. the status or legal capacity of natural persons, rights in property arising out of a matrimonial relationship, wills and succession;
2. bankruptcy, proceedings relating to the winding-up of insolvent companies or other legal persons, judicial arrangements, compositions and analogous proceedings;
3. social security;
4. arbitration.

TITLE II

Jurisdiction

Section 1

General Provisions

Article 2

Subject to the provisions of this Convention, persons domiciled in a Contracting State shall, whatever their nationality, be sued in the courts of that State.

Persons who are not nationals of the State in which they are domiciled shall be governed by the rules of jurisdiction applicable to nationals of that State.

Article 3

Persons domiciled in a Contracting State may be sued in the courts of another Contracting State only by virtue of the rules set out in Sections 2 to 6 of this Title.

In particular the following provisions shall not be applicable as against them:

—in Belgium: Article 15 of the civil code (Code civil—Burgerlijk Wetboek) and Article 638 of the judicial code (Code judiciaire—Gerechtelijk Wetboek),
—in Denmark: Article 246(2) and (3) of the law on civil procedure (Lov om rettens pleje),
—in the Federal Republic of Germany: Article 23 of the code of civil procedure (Zivilprozeßordnung),
—in Greece: Article 40 of the code of civil procedure (Κώδικας πολιτικής δικονομίας),
—in France: Articles 14 and 15 of the civil code (Code civil),
—in Ireland: the rules which enable jurisdiction to be founded on the document instituting the proceedings having been served on the defendant during his temporary presence in Ireland,
—in Iceland: Article 77 of the Civil Proceedings Act (lög um meðferð einkamála í héraði),
—in Italy: Articles 2 and 4, Nos 1 and 2 of the code of civil procedure (Codice di procedura civile),
—in Luxembourg: Articles 14 and 15 of the civil code (Code civil),
—in the Netherlands: Articles 126(3) and 127 of the code of civil procedure (Wetboek van Burgerlijke Rechtsvordering),
—in Norway: Section 32 of the Civil Proceedings Act (tvistemålsloven),
—in Austria: Article 99 of the Law on Court Jurisdiction (Jurisdiktionsnorm),
—in Portugal: Articles 65(1)(c), 65(2) and 65A(c) of the code of civil procedure (Código de Processo Civíl) and Article 11 of the code of labour procedure (Código de Processo de Trabalho),
—in Switzerland: le for du lieu du séquestre/Gerichtsstand des Arrestortes/foro del luogo del sequestro within the meaning of Article 4 of the loi fédérale sur le droit international privé/Bundesgesetz über das internationale Privatrecht/legge federale sul diritto internazionale privato,
—in Finland: the second, third and fourth sentences of Section 1 of Chapter 10 of the Code of Judicial Procedure (oikeudenkäymiskaari/rättegångsbalken),
—in Sweden: the first sentence of Section 3 of Chapter 10 of the Code of Judicial Procedure (Rättegångsbalken),
—in the United Kingdom: the rules which enable jurisdiction to be founded on:
(a) the document instituting the proceedings having been served on the defendant during his temporary presence in the United Kingdom; or
(b) the presence within the United Kingdom of property belonging to the defendant; or
(c) the seizure by the plaintiff of property situated in the United Kingdom.

Article 4

If the defendant is not domiciled in a Contracting State, the jurisdiction of the courts of each Contracting State shall, subject to the provisions of Article 16, be determined by the law of that State.

As against such a defendant, any person domiciled in a Contracting State may, whatever his nationality, avail himself in that State of the rules of jurisdiction there in force, and in particular those specified in the second paragraph of Article 3, in the same way as the nationals of that State.

Section 2

Special Jurisdiction

Article 5

A person domiciled in a Contracting State may, in another Contracting State, be sued:

1. in matters relating to a contract, in the courts for the place of performance of the obligation in question; in matters relating to individual contracts of employment, this

place is that where the employee habitually carries out his work, or if the employee does not habitually carry out his work in any one country, this place shall be the place of business through which he was engaged;

2. in matters relating to maintenance, in the courts for the place where the maintenance creditor is domiciled or habitually resident or, if the matter is ancillary to proceedings concerning the status of a person, in the court which, according to its own law, has jurisdiction to entertain those proceedings, unless that jurisdiction is based solely on the nationality of one of the parties;
3. in matters relating to tort, delict or quasi-delict, in the courts for the place where the harmful event occurred;
4. as regards a civil claim for damages or restitution which is based on an act giving rise to criminal proceedings, in the court seised of those proceedings, to the extent that that court has jurisdiction under its own law to entertain civil proceedings;
5. as regards a dispute arising out of the operations of a branch, agency or other establishment, in the courts for the place in which the branch, agency or other establishment is situated;
6. in his capacity as settlor, trustee or beneficiary of a trust created by the operation of a statute, or by a written instrument, or created orally and evidenced in writing, in the courts of the Contracting State in which the trust is domiciled;
7. as regards a dispute concerning the payment of remuneration claimed in respect of the salvage of a cargo or freight, in the court under the authority of which the cargo or freight in question:

   (*a*) has been arrested to secure such payment,

   or

   (*b*) could have been so arrested, but bail or other security has been given;

   provided that this provision shall apply only if it is claimed that the defendant has an interest in the cargo or freight or had such an interest at the time of salvage.

Article 6

A person domiciled in a Contracting State may also be sued:

1. where he is one of a number of defendants, in the courts for the place where any one of them is domiciled;
2. as a third party in an action on a warranty or guarantee or in any other third party proceedings, in the court seised of the original proceedings, unless these were instituted solely with the object of removing him from the jurisdiction of the court which would be competent in his case;
3. on a counterclaim arising from the same contract or facts on which the original claim was based, in the court in which the original claim is pending;
4. in matters relating to a contract, if the action may be combined with an action against the same defendant in matters relating to rights *in rem* in immovable property, in the court of the Contracting State in which the property is situated.

Article 6A

Where by virtue of this Convention a court of a Contracting State has jurisdiction in actions relating to liability arising from the use or operation of a ship, that court, or any other court substituted for this purpose by the internal law of that State, shall also have jurisdiction over claims for limitation of such liability.

Section 3

Jurisdiction in Matters Relating to Insurance

Article 7

In matters relating to insurance, jurisdiction shall be determined by this Section, without prejudice to the provisions of Articles 4 and 5(5).

Article 8

An insurer domiciled in a Contracting State may be sued:

1. in the courts of the State where he is domiciled; or
2. in another Contracting State, in the courts for the place where the policy-holder is domiciled; or

3. if he is a co-insurer, in the courts of a Contracting State in which proceedings are brought against the leading insurer.

An insurer who is not domiciled in a Contracting State but has a branch, agency or other establishment in one of the Contracting States shall, in disputes arising out of the operations of the branch, agency or establishment, be deemed to be domiciled in that State.

Article 9

In respect of liability insurance or insurance of immovable property, the insurer may in addition be sued in the courts for the place where the harmful event occurred. The same applies if movable and immovable property are covered by the same insurance policy and both are adversely affected by the same contingency.

Article 10

In respect of liability insurance, the insurer may also, if the law of the court permits it, be joined in proceedings which the injured party has brought against the insured.

The provisions of Articles 7, 8 and 9 shall apply to actions brought by the injured party directly against the insurer, where such direct actions are permitted.

If the law governing such direct actions provides that the policy-holder or the insured may be joined as a party to the action, the same court shall have jurisdiction over them.

Article 11

Without prejudice to the provisions of the third paragraph of Article 10, an insurer may bring proceedings only in the courts of the Contracting State in which the defendant is domiciled, irrespective of whether he is the policy-holder, the insured or a beneficiary.

The provisions of this Section shall not affect the right to bring a counterclaim in the court in which, in accordance with this Section, the original claim is pending.

Article 12

The provisions of this Section may be departed from only by an agreement on jurisdiction:

1. which is entered into after the dispute has arisen; or
2. which allows the policy-holder, the insured or a beneficiary to bring proceedings in courts other than those indicated in this Section; or
3. which is concluded between a policy-holder and an insurer, both of whom are at the time of conclusion of the contract domiciled or habitually resident in the same Contracting State, and which has the effect of conferring jurisdiction on the courts of that State even if the harmful event were to occur abroad, provided that such an agreement is not contrary to the law of the State; or
4. which is concluded with a policy-holder who is not domiciled in a Contracting State, except in so far as the insurance is compulsory or relates to immovable property in a Contracting State; or
5. which relates to a contract of insurance in so far as it covers one or more of the risks set out in Article 12A.

Article 12A

The following are the risks referred to in Article 12(5):

1. any loss of or damage to:
   (*a*) sea-going ships, installations situated offshore or on the high seas, or aircraft, arising from perils which relate to their use for commercial purposes;
   (*b*) goods in transit other than passengers' baggage where the transit consists of or includes carriage by such ships or aircraft;
2. any liability, other than for bodily injury to passengers or loss of or damage to their baggage;
   (*a*) arising out of the use or operation of ships, installations or aircraft as referred to in (1)(*a*) above in so far as the law of the Contracting State in which such aircraft are registered does not prohibit agreements on jurisdiction regarding insurance of such risks;
   (*b*) for loss or damage caused by goods in transit as described in (1)(*b*) above;
3. any financial loss connected with the use or operation of ships, installations or aircraft as referred to in (1)(*a*) above, in particular loss of freight or charter-hire;
4. any risk or interest connected with any of those referred to in (1) to (3) above.

Section 4

Jurisdiction over Consumer Contracts

Article 13

In proceedings concerning a contract concluded by a person for a purpose which can be regarded as being outside his trade or profession, hereinafter called "the consumer," jurisdiction shall be determined by this Section, without prejudice to the provisions of Articles 4 and 5(5), if it is:

1. a contract for the sale of goods on instalment credit terms; or
2. a contract for a loan repayable by instalments, or for any other form of credit, made to finance the sale of goods; or
3. any other contract for the supply of goods or a contract for the supply of services, and
   (*a*) in the State of the consumer's domicile the conclusion of the contract was preceded by a specific invitation addressed to him or by advertising, and
   (*b*) the consumer took in that State the steps necessary for the conclusion of the contract.

Where a consumer enters into a contract with a party who is not domiciled in a Contracting State but has a branch, agency or other establishment in one of the Contracting States, that party shall, in disputes arising out of the operations of the branch, agency or establishment, be deemed to be domiciled in that State.

This Section shall not apply to contracts of transport.

Article 14

A consumer may bring proceedings against the other party to a contract either in the courts of the Contracting State in which that party is domiciled or in the courts of the Contracting State in which he is himself domiciled.

Proceedings may be brought against a consumer by the other party to the contract only in the courts of the Contracting State in which the consumer is domiciled.

These provisions shall not affect the right to bring a counterclaim in the court in which, in accordance with this Section, the original claim is pending.

Article 15

The provisions of this Section may be departed from only by an agreement:

1. which is entered into after the dispute has arisen; or
2. which allows the consumer to bring proceedings in courts other than those indicated in this Section; or
3. which is entered into by the consumer and the other party to the contract, both of whom are at the time of conclusion of the contract domiciled or habitually resident in the same Contracting State, and which confers jurisdiction on the courts of that State, provided that such an agreement is not contrary of the law of that State.

Section 5

Exclusive Jurisdiction

Article 16

The following courts shall have exclusive jurisdiction, regardless of domicile:

1. (*a*) in proceedings which have as their object rights *in rem* in immovable property or tenancies of immovable property, the courts of the Contracting State in which the property is situated;
   (*b*) however, in proceedings which have as their object tenancies of immovable property concluded for temporary private use for a maximum period of six consecutive months, the courts of the Contracting State in which the defendant is domiciled shall also have jurisdiction, provided that the tenant is a natural person and neither party is domiciled in the Contracting State in which the property is situated;

2. in proceedings which have as their object the validity of the constitution, the nullity or the dissolution of companies or other legal persons or associations of natural or legal persons, or the decisions of their organs, the courts of the Contracting State in which the company, legal person or association has its seat;
3. in proceedings which have as their object the validity of entries in public registers, the court of the Contracting State in which the register is kept;
4. in proceedings concerned with the registration or validity of patents, trade marks, designs, or other similar rights required to be deposited or registered, the courts of the Contracting State in which the deposit or registration has been applied for, has taken place or is under the terms of an international convention deemed to have taken place;
5. in proceedings concerned with the enforcement of judgments, the courts of the Contracting State in which the judgment has been or is to be enforced.

Section 6

Prorogation of Jurisdiction

Article 17

1. If the parties, one or more of whom is domiciled in a Contracting State, have agreed that a court or the courts of a Contracting State are to have jurisdiction to settle any disputes which have arisen or which may arise in connection with a particular legal relationship, that court or those courts shall have exclusive jurisdiction. Such an agreement conferring jurisdiction shall be either:

(*a*) in writing or evidenced in writing, or

(*b*) in a form which accords with practices which the parties have established between themselves, or

(*c*) in international trade or commerce, in a form which accords with a usage of which the parties are or ought to have been aware and which in such trade or commerce is widely known to, and regularly observed by, parties to contracts of the type involved in the particular trade or commerce concerned.

Where such an agreement is concluded by parties, none of whom is domiciled in a Contracting State, the courts of other Contracting States shall have no jurisdiction over their disputes unless the court or courts chosen have declined jurisdiction.

2. The court or courts of a Contracting State on which a trust instrument has conferred jurisdiction shall have exclusive jurisdiction in any proceedings brought against a settlor, trustee or beneficiary, if relations between these persons or their rights or obligations under the trust are involved.

3. Agreements or provisions of a trust instrument conferring jurisdiction shall have no legal force if they are contrary to the provisions of Article 12 or 15, or if the courts whose jurisdiction they purport to exclude have exclusive jurisdiction by virtue of Article 16.

4. If an agreement conferring jurisdiction was concluded for the benefit of only one of the parties, that party shall retain the right to bring proceedings in any other court which has jurisdiction by virtue of this Convention.

5. In matters relating to individual contracts of employment an agreement conferring jurisdiction shall have legal force only if it is entered into after the dispute has arisen.

Article 18

Apart from jurisdiction derived from other provisions of this Convention, a court of a Contracting State before whom a defendant enters an appearance shall have jurisdiction. This rule shall not apply where appearance was entered solely to contest the jurisdiction, or where another court has exclusive jurisdiction by virtue of Article 16.

Section 7

Examination as to Jurisdiction and Admissibility

Article 19

Where a court of a Contracting State is seised of a claim which is principally concerned with a matter over which the courts of another Contracting State have exclusive jurisdiction by virtue of Article 16, if shall declare of its own motion that it has no jurisdiction.

Article 20

Where a defendant domiciled in one Contracting State is sued in a court of another Contracting State and does not enter an appearance, the court shall declare of its own motion that it has no jurisdiction unless its jurisdiction is derived from the provisions of this Convention.

The court shall stay the proceedings so long as it is not shown that the defendant has been able to receive the document instituting the proceedings or an equivalent document in sufficient time to enable him to arrange for his defence, or that all necessary steps have been taken to this end.

The provisions of the foregoing paragraph shall be replaced by those of Article 15 of the Hague Convention of 15 November 1965 on the service abroad of judicial and extrajudicial documents in civil or commercial matters, if the document instituting the proceedings or notice thereof had to be transmitted abroad in accordance with that Convention.

Section 8

***Lis Pendens*—Related Actions**

Article 21

Where proceedings involving the same cause of action and between the same parties are brought in the courts of different Contracting States, any court other than the court first seised shall of its own motion stay its proceedings until such time as the jurisdiction of the court first seised is established.

Where the jurisdiction of the court first seised is established, any court other than the court first seised shall decline jurisdiction in favour of that court.

Article 22

Where related actions are brought in the courts of different Contracting States, any court other than the court first seised may, while the actions are pending at first instance, stay its proceedings.

A court other than the court first seised may also, on the application of one of the parties, decline jurisdiction if the law of that court permits the consolidation of related actions and the court first seised has jurisdiction over both actions.

For the purposes of this Article, actions are deemed to be related where they are so closely connected that it is expedient to hear and determine them together to avoid the risk of irreconcilable judgments resulting from separate proceedings.

Article 23

Where actions come within the exclusive jurisdiction of several courts, any court other than the court first seised shall decline jurisdiction in favour of that court.

Section 9

Provisional, Including Protective, Measures

Article 24

Application may be made to the courts of a Contracting State for such provisional, including protective, measures as may be available under the law of that State, even if, under this Convention, the courts of another Contracting State have jurisdiction as to the substance of the matter.

TITLE III

RECOGNITION AND ENFORCEMENT

Article 25

For the purposes of this Convention, "judgment" means any judgment given by a court or tribunal of a Contracting State, whatever the judgment may be called, including a decree, order, decision or writ of execution, as well as the determination of costs or expenses by an officer of the court.

Section 1

Recognition

Article 26

A judgment given in a Contracting State shall be recognised in the other Contracting States without any special procedure being required.

Any interested party who raises the recognition of a judgment as the principal issue in a dispute may, in accordance with the procedure provided for in Sections 2 and 3 of this Title, apply for a decision that the judgment be recognised.

If the outcome of proceedings in a court of a Contracting State depends on the determination of an incidental question of recognition that court shall have jurisdiction over that question.

Article 27

A judgment shall not be recognised:

1. if such recognition is contrary to public policy in the State in which recognition is sought;
2. where it was given in default of appearance, if the defendant was not duly served with the document which instituted the proceedings or with an equivalent document in sufficient time to enable him to arrange for his defence;
3. if the judgment is irreconcilable with a judgment given in a dispute between the same parties in the State in which recognition is sought;
4. if the court of the State of origin, in order to arrive at its judgment, has decided a preliminary question concerning the status or legal capacity of natural persons, rights in property arising out a matrimonial relationship, wills or succession in a way that conflicts with a rule of the private international law of the State in which the recognition is sought, unless the same result would have been reached by the application of the rules of private international law of that State;
5. if the judgment is irreconcilable with an earlier judgment given in a non-contracting State involving the same cause of action and between the same parties, provided that this latter judgment fulfils the conditions necessary for its recognition in the State addressed.

Article 28

Moreover, a judgment shall not be recognised if it conflicts with the provisions of Section 3, 4 or 5 of Title II or in a case provided for in Article 59.

A judgment may furthermore be refused recognition in any case provided for in Article 54B(3) or 57(4).

In its examination of the grounds of jurisdiction referred to in the foregoing paragraphs, the court or authority applied to shall be bound by the findings of fact on which the court of the State of origin based its jurisdiction.

Subject to the provisions of the first and second paragraphs, the jurisdiction of the court of the State of origin may not be reviewed; the test of public policy referred to in Article 27(1) may not be applied to the rules relating to jurisdiction.

Article 29

Under no circumstances may a foreign judgment be reviewed as to its substance.

Article 30

A court of a Contracting State in which recognition is sought of a judgment given in another Contracting State may stay the proceedings if an ordinary appeal against the judgment has been lodged.

A court of a Contracting State in which recognition is sought of a judgment given in Ireland or the United Kingdom may stay the proceedings if enforcement is suspended in the State of origin by reason of an appeal.

Section 2

Enforcement

Article 31

A judgment given in a Contracting State and enforceable in that State shall be enforced in another Contracting State when, on the application of any interested party, it has been declared enforceable there.

However, in the United Kingdom, such a judgment shall be enforced in England and Wales, in Scotland, or in Northern Ireland when, on the application of any interested party, it has been registered for enforcement in that part of the United Kingdom.

Article 32

1. The application shall be submitted:
— in Belgium, to the tribunal de première instance or rechtbank van eerste aanleg,
— in Denmark, to the byret,
— in the Federal Republic of Germany, to the presiding judge of a chamber of the Landgericht,
— in Greece, to the μονομελές πρωτοδικείο,
— in Spain, to the Juzgado de Primera Instancia,
— in France, to the presiding judge of the tribunal de grande instance,
— in Ireland, to the High Court,
— in Iceland, to the héraðsdómari,
— in Italy, to the corte d'appello,
— in Luxembourg, to the presiding judge of the tribunal d'arrondissement,
— in the Netherlands, to the presiding judge of the arrondissementsrechtbank,
— in Norway, to the herredsrett or byrett as namsrett,
— in Austria, to the Landesgericht or the Kreisgericht,
— in Portugal, to the Tribunal Judicial de Círculo,
— in Switzerland:
(*a*) in respect of judgments ordering the payment of a sum of money, to the juge de la mainlevée/Rechsöffnungsrichter/giudice competente a pronunciare sul rigetto dell'opposizione, within the framework of the procedure governed by Articles 80 and 81 of the loi fédérale sur la poursuite pour dettes et la faillite/ Bundesgesetz über Schuldbetreibung und Konkurs/legge federale sulla esecuzione e sul fallimento;
(*b*) in respect of judgments ordering a performance other than the payment of a sum of money, to the juge cantonal d'exequatur compétent/zuständiger kantonaler Vollstreckungsrichter/giudice cantonale competente a pronunciare l'exequatur,
— in Finland, to the ulosotonhaltija/överexekutor,
— in Sweden, to the Svea hovrätt,
— in the United Kingdom:
(*a*) in England and Wales, to the High Court of Justice, or in the case of a maintenance judgment to the Magistrates' Court on transmission by the Secretary of State;
(*b*) in Scotland, to the Court of Session, or in the case of a maintenance judgment to the Sheriff Court on transmission by the Secretary of State;
(*c*) in Northern Ireland, to the High Court of Justice, or in the case of a maintenance judgment to the Magistrates' Court on transmission by the Secretary of State.

2. The jurisdiction of local courts shall be determined by reference to the place of domicile of the party against whom enforcement is sought. If he is not domiciled in the State in which enforcement is sought, it shall be determined by reference to the place of enforcement.

Article 33

The procedure for making the application shall be governed by the law of the State in which enforcement is sought.

The applicant must give an address for service of process within the area of jurisdiction of the court applied to. However, if the law of the State in which enforcement is sought does not provide for the furnishing of such an address, the applicant shall appoint a representative *ad litem*.

The documents referred to in Articles 46 and 47 shall be attached to the application.

Article 34

The court applied to shall give its decision without delay: the party against whom enforcement is sought shall not at this stage of the proceedings be entitled to make any submissions on the application.

The application may be refused only for one of the reasons specified in Articles 27 and 28.

Under no circumstances may the foreign judgment be reviewed as to its substance.

Article 35

The appropriate officer of the court shall without delay bring the decision given on the application to the notice of the applicant in accordance with the procedure laid down by the law of the State in which enforcement is sought.

Article 36

If enforcement is authorised, the party against whom enforcement is sought may appeal against the decision within one month of service thereof.

If the party is domiciled in a Contracting State other than that in which the decision authorising enforcement was given, the time for appealing shall be two months and shall run from the date of service, either on him in person or at his residence. No extension of time may be granted on account of distance.

Article 37

1. An appeal against the decision authorising enforcement shall be lodged in accordance with the rules governing procedure in contentious matters:
— in Belgium, with the tribunal de première instance or rechtbank van eerste aanleg,
— in Denmark, with the landsret,
— in the Federal Republic of Germany, with the Oberlandesgericht,
— in Greece, with the έφετείο,
— in Spain, with the Audiencia Provincial,
— in France, with the cour d'appel,
— in Ireland, with the High Court,
— in Iceland, with the héraðsdómari,
— in Italy, with corte d'appello,
— in Luxembourg, with the Cour supérieure de justice sitting as a court of civil appeal,
— in the Netherlands, with the arrondissementsrechtbank,
— in Norway, with the lagmannsrett,
— in Austria, with the Landesgericht or the Kreisgericht,
— in Portugal, with the Tribunal da Relação,
— in Switzerland, with the tribunal cantonal / Kantonsgericht / tribunale cantonale,
— in Finland, with hovioikeus/hovrätt,
— in Sweden, with the Svea hovrätt,
— in the United Kingdom:
(*a*) in England and Wales, with the High Court of Justice, or in the case of a maintenance judgment with the Magistrates' Court;
(*b*) in Scotland, with the Court of Session, or in the case of a maintenance judgment with the Sheriff Court;
(*c*) in Northern Ireland, with the High Court of Justice, or in the case of a maintenance judgment with the Magistrates' Court.

2. The judgment given on the appeal may be contested only:
— in Belgium, Greece, Spain, France, Italy, Luxembourg and in the Netherlands, by an appeal in cassation,
— in Denmark, by an appeal to the højesteret, with the leave of the Minister of Justice,
— in the Federal Republic of Germany, by a Rechtsbeschwerde,
— in Ireland, by an appeal on a point of law to the Supreme Court,
— in Iceland, by an appeal to the Hæstiréttur,
— in Norway, by an appeal (kjæremal or anke) to the Hoyesteretts Kjæremålsutvalg or Hoyesterett,
— in Austria, in the case of an appeal, by a Revisionsrekurs and, in the case of opposition proceedings, by a Berufung with the possibility of a Revision,
— in Portugal, by an appeal on a point of law,

— in Switzerland, by a recours de droit public devant le tribunal fédéral / staatsrechtliche Beschwerde beim Bundesgericht / ricorso di diritto pubblico davanti al tribunale federale,
— in Finland, by an appeal to the korkein oikeus / högsta domstolen,
— in Sweden, by an appeal to the högsta domstolen,
— in the United Kingdom, by a single further appeal on a point of law.

Article 38

The court with which the appeal under the first paragraph of Article 37 is lodged may, on the application of the appellant, stay the proceedings if an ordinary appeal has been lodged against the judgment in the State of origin or if the time for such an appeal has not yet expired; in the latter case, the court may specify the time within which such an appeal is to be lodged.

Where the judgment was given in Ireland or the United Kingdom, any form of appeal available in the State of origin shall be treated as an ordinary appeal for the purposes of the first paragraph.

The court may also make enforcement conditional on the provision of such security as it shall determine.

Article 39

During the time specified for an appeal pursuant to Article 36 and until any such appeal has been determined, no measures of enforcement may be taken other than protective measures taken against the property of the party against whom enforcement is sought.

The decision authorising enforcement shall carry with it the power to proceed to any such protective measures.

Article 40

1. If the application for enforcement is refused, the applicant may appeal:
— in Belgium, to the cour d'appel or hof van beroep,
— in Denmark, to the landsret,
— in the Federal Republic of Germany, to the Oberlandesgericht,
— in Greece, to the ἐφετεῖο,
— in Spain, to the Audiencia Provincial,
— in France, to the cour d'appel,
— in Ireland, to the High Court,
— in Iceland, to the héraðsdómari
— in Italy, to the corte d'appello,
— in Luxembourg, to the Cour supérieure de justice sitting as a court of civil appeal,
— in the Netherlands, to the gerechtshof,
— in Norway, to the lagmannsrett,
— in Austria, to the Landesgericht or the Kreisgericht,
— in Portugal, to the Tribunal da Relação,
— in Switzerland, to the tribunal cantonal / Kantonsgericht / tribunale cantonale,
— in Finland, to the hovioikeus / hovrätt,
— in Sweden, to the Svea hovrätt,
— in the United Kingdom:
(*a*) in England and Wales, to the High Court of Justice, or in the case of a maintenance judgment to the Magistrates' Court;
(*b*) in Scotland, to the Court of Session, or in the case of a maintenance judgment to the Sheriff Court;
(*c*) in Northern Ireland, to the High Court of Justice, or in the case of a maintenance judgment to the Magistrates' Court.

2. The party against whom enforcement is sought shall be summoned to appear before the appellate court. If he fails to appear, the provisions of the second and third paragraphs of Article 20 shall apply even where he is not domiciled in any of the Contracting States.

Article 41

A judgment given on an appeal provided for in Article 40 may be contested only:
— in Belgium, Greece, Spain, France, Italy, Luxembourg and in the Netherlands, by an appeal in cassation,

— in Denmark, by an appeal to the højesteret, with the leave of the Minister of Justice,
— in the Federal Republic of Germany, by a Rechtsbeschwerde,
— in Ireland, by an appeal on a point of law to the Supreme Court,
— in Iceland, by an appeal to the Hæstiréttur,
— in Norway, by an appeal (kjæremål or anke) to the Hoyesteretts kjæremålsutvalg or Hoyesterett,
— in Austria, by a Revisionsrekurs,
— in Portugal, by an appeal on a point of law,
— in Switzerland, by a recours de droit public devant le tribunal fédéral / staatsrechtliche Beschwerde beim Bundesgericht / ricorso di diritto pubblico davanti al tribunale federale,
— in Finland, by an appeal to the korkein oikeus / högsta domstolen,
— in Sweden, by an appeal to the högsta domstolen,
— in the United Kingdom, by a single further appeal on a point of law.

Article 42

Where a foreign judgment has been given in respect of several matters and enforcement cannot be authorised for all of them, the court shall authorise enforcement for one or more of them.

An applicant may request partial enforcement of a judgment.

Article 43

A foreign judgment which orders a periodic payment by way of a penalty shall be enforceable in the State in which enforcement is sought only if the amount of the payment has been finally determined by the courts of the State of origin.

Article 44

An applicant who, in the State of origin, has benefited from complete or partial legal aid or exemption from costs or expenses, shall be entitled, in the procedures provided for in Articles 32 to 35, to benefit from the most favourable legal aid or the most extensive exemption from costs or expenses provided for by the law of the State addressed.

However, an applicant who requests the enforcement of a decision given by an administrative authority in Denmark or in Iceland in respect of a maintenance order may, in the State addressed, claim the benefits referred to in the first paragraph if he presents a statement from, respectively, the Danish Ministry of Justice or the Icelandic Ministry of Justice to the effect that he fulfils the economic requirements to qualify for the grant of complete or partial legal aid or exemption from costs or expenses.

Article 45

No security, bond or deposit, however described, shall be required of a party who in one Contracting State applies for enforcement of a judgment given in another Contracting State on the ground that he is a foreign national or that he is not domiciled or resident in the State in which enforcement is sought.

Section 3

Common Provisions

Article 46

A party seeking recognition or applying for enforcement of a judgment shall produce:

1. a copy of the judgment which satisfies the conditions necessary to establish its authenticity;
2. in the case of a judgment given in default, the original or a certified true copy of the document which establishes that the party in default was served with the document instituting the proceedings or with an equivalent document.

Article 47

A party applying for enforcement shall also produce:

1. documents which establish that, according to the law of the State of origin, the judgment is enforceable and has been served;
2. where appropriate, a document showing that the applicant is in receipt of legal aid in the State of origin.

Article 48

If the documents specified in Article 46(2) and Article 47(2) are not produced, the court may specify a time for their production, accept equivalent documents or, if it considers that it has sufficient information before it, dispense with their production.

If the court so requires, a translation of the documents shall be produced; the translation shall be certified by a person qualified to do so in one of the Contracting States.

Article 49

No legislation or other similar formality shall be required in respect of the documents referred to in Article 46 or 47 or the second paragraph of Article 48, or in respect of a document appointing a representative *ad litem*.

TITLE IV

Authentic Instruments and Court Settlements

Article 50

A document which has been formally drawn up or registered as an authentic instrument and is enforceable in one Contracting State shall, in another Contracting State, be declared enforceable there, on application made in accordance with the procedures provided for in Articles 31 *et seq*. The application may be refused only if enforcement of the instrument is contrary to public policy in the State addressed.

The instrument produced must satisfy the conditions necessary to establish its authenticity in the State of origin.

The provisions of Section 3 of Title III shall apply as appropriate.

Article 51

A settlement which has been approved by a court in the course of proceedings and is enforceable in the State in which it was concluded shall be enforceable in the State addressed under the same conditions as authentic instruments.

TITLE V

General Provisions

Article 52

In order to determine whether a party is domiciled in the Contracting State whose courts are seised of a matter, the court shall apply its internal law.

If a party is not domiciled in the State whose courts are seised of the matter, then, in order to determine whether the party is domiciled in another Contracting State, the court shall apply the law of that State.

Article 53

For the purposes of this Convention, the seat of a company or other legal person or association of natural or legal persons shall be treated as its domicile. However, in order to determine that seat, the court shall apply its rules of private international law.

In order to determine whether a trust is domiciled in the Contracting State whose courts are seised of the matter, the court shall apply its rules of private international law.

TITLE VI

Transitional Provisions

Article 54

The provisions of this Convention shall apply only to legal proceedings instituted and to documents formally drawn up or registered as authentic instruments after its entry into force in the State of origin and, where recognition or enforcement of a judgment or authentic instrument is sought, in the State addressed.

However, judgments given after the date of entry into force of this Convention between the State of origin and the State addressed in proceedings instituted before that date shall be recognised and enforced in accordance with the provisions of Title III if jurisdiction was founded upon rules which accorded with those provided for either in Title II of this Convention or in a convention concluded between the State of origin and the State addressed which was in force when the proceedings were instituted.

If the parties to a dispute concerning a contract had agreed in writing before the entry into force of this Convention that the contract was to be governed by the law of Ireland or of a part of the United Kingdom, the courts of Ireland or of that part of the United Kingdom shall retain the right to exercise jurisdiction in the dispute.

Article 54A

For a period of three years from the entry into force of this Convention for Denmark, Greece, Ireland, Iceland, Norway, Finland and Sweden, respectively, jurisdiction in maritime matters shall be determined in these States not only in accordance with the provisions of Title II, but also in accordance with the provisions of paragraphs 1 to 7 following. However, upon the entry into force of the International Convention relating to the arrest of sea-going ships, signed at Brussels on 10 May 1952, for one of these States, these provisions shall cease to have effect for that State.

1. A person who is domiciled in a Contracting State may be sued in the courts of one of the States mentioned above in respect of a maritime claim if the ship to which the claim relates or any other ship owned by him has been arrested by judicial process within the territory of the latter State to secure the claim, or could have been so arrested there but bail or other security has been given, and either:
   (*a*) the claimant is domiciled in the latter State; or
   (*b*) the claim arose in the latter State; or
   (*c*) the claim concerns the voyage during which the arrest was made or could have been made; or
   (*d*) the claim arises out of a collision or out of damage caused by a ship to another ship or to goods or persons on board either ship, either by the execution or non-execution of a manoeuvre or by the non-observance of regulations; or
   (*e*) the claim is for salvage; or
   (*f*) the claim is in respect of a mortgage or hypothecation of the ship arrested.
2. A claimant may arrest either the particular ship to which the maritime claim relates, or any other ship which is owned by the person who was, at the time when the maritime claim arose, the owner of the particular ship. However, only the particular ship to which the maritime claim relates may be arrested in respect of the maritime claims set out in 5.(*o*), (*p*) or (*q*) of this Article.
3. Ships shall be deemed to be in the same ownership when all the shares therein are owned by the same person or persons.
4. When in the case of a charter by demise of a ship the charterer alone is liable in respect of a maritime claim relating to that ship, the claimant may arrest that ship or any other ship owned by the charterer, but no other ship owned by the owner may be arrested in respect of such claim. The same shall apply to any case in which a person other than the owner of a ship is liable in respect of a maritime claim relating to that ship.
5. The expression "maritime claim" means a claim arising out of one or more of the following:
   (*a*) damage caused by any ship either in collision or otherwise;
   (*b*) loss of life or personal injury caused by any ship or occurring in connection with the operation of any ship;
   (*c*) salvage;
   (*d*) agreement relating to the use or hire of any ship whether by charterparty or otherwise;

(*e*) agreement relating to the carriage of goods in any ship whether by charterparty or otherwise;
(*f*) loss of or damage to goods including baggage carried in any ship;
(*g*) general average;
(*h*) bottomry;
(*i*) towage;
(*j*) pilotage;
(*k*) goods or materials wherever supplied to a ship for her operation or maintenance;
(*l*) construction, repair or equipment of any ship or dock charges and dues;
(*m*) wages of masters, officers or crew;
(*n*) master's disbursements, including disbursements made by shippers, charterers or agents on behalf of a ship or her owner;
(*o*) dispute as to the title to or ownership of any ship;
(*p*) disputes between co-owners of any ship as to the ownership, possession, employment or earnings of that ship;
(*q*) the mortgage or hypothecation of any ship.

6. In Denmark, the expression "arrest" shall be deemed, as regards the maritime claims referred to in 5.(*o*) and (*p*) of this Article, to include a "forbud," where that is the only procedure allowed in respect of such a claim under Articles 646 to 653 of the law on civil procedure (lov om rettens pleje).
7. In Iceland, the expression "arrest" shall be deemed, as regards the maritime claims referred to in 5.(*o*) and (*p*) of this Article, to include a "lögbann," where that is the only procedure allowed in respect of such a claim under Chapter III of the law on arrest and injunction (lög um kyrrsetningu og lögbann).

TITLE VII

RELATIONSHIP TO THE BRUSSELS CONVENTION AND TO OTHER CONVENTIONS

Article 54B

1. This Convention shall not prejudice the application by the Member States of the European Communities of the Convention on Jurisdiction and the Enforcement of Judgments in Civil and Commercial Matters, signed at Brussels on 27 September 1968 and of the Protocol on interpretation of that Convention by the Court of Justice, signed at Luxembourg on 3 June 1971, as amended by the Conventions of Accession to the said Convention and the said Protocol by the States acceding to the European Communities, all of these Conventions and the Protocol being hereinafter referred to as the "Brussels Convention."

2. However, this Convention shall in any event be applied:
(*a*) in matters of jurisdiction, where the defendant is domiciled in the territory of a Contracting State which is not a member of the European Communities, or where Article 16 or 17 of this Convention confers a jurisdiction on the courts of such a Contracting State;
(*b*) in relation to a *lis pendens* or to related actions as provided for in Articles 21 and 22, when proceedings are instituted in a Contracting State which is not a member of the European Communities and in a Contracting State which is a member of the European Communities;
(*c*) in matters of recognition and enforcement, where either the State of origin or the State addressed is not a member of the European Communities.

3. In addition to the grounds provided for in Title III recognition or enforcement may be refused if the ground of jurisdiction on which the judgment has been based differs from that resulting from this Convention and recognition or enforcement is sought against a party who is domiciled in a Contracting State which is not a member of the European Communities, unless the judgment may otherwise be recognised or enforced under any rule of law in the State addressed.

Article 55

Subject to the provisions of the second paragraph of Article 54 and of Article 56, this Convention shall, for the States which are parties to it, supersede the following conventions concluded between two or more of them:

— the Convention between the Swiss Confederation and France on jurisdiction and enforcement of judgments in civil matters, signed at Paris on 15 June 1869,

— the Treaty between the Swiss Confederation and Spain on the mutual enforcement of judgments in civil or commercial matters, signed at Madrid on 19 November 1896,
— the Convention between the Swiss Confederation and the German Reich on the recognition and enforcement of judgments and arbitration awards, signed at Berne on 2 November 1929,
— the Convention between Denmark, Finland, Iceland, Norway and Sweden on the recognition and enforcement of judgments, signed at Copenhagen on 16 March 1932,
— the Convention between the Swiss Confederation and Italy on the recognition and enforcement of judgments, signed at Rome on 3 January 1933,
— the Convention between Sweden and the Swiss Confederation on the recognition and enforcement of judgments and arbitral awards, signed at Stockholm on 15 January 1936,
— the Convention between the Kingdom of Belgium and Austria on the reciprocal recognition and enforcement of judgments and authentic instruments relating to maintenance obligations, signed at Vienna on 25 October 1957,
— the Convention between the Swiss Confederation and Belgium on the recognition and enforcement of judgments and arbitration awards, signed at Berne on 29 April 1959,
— the Convention between the Federal Republic of Germany and Austria on the reciprocal recognition and enforcement of judgments, settlements and authentic instruments in civil and commercial matters, signed at Vienna on 6 June 1959,
— the Convention between the Kingdom of Belgium and Austria on the reciprocal recognition and enforcement of judgments, arbitral awards and authentic instruments in civil and commercial matters, signed at Vienna on 16 June 1959,
— the Convention between Austria and the Swiss Confederation on the recognition and enforcement of judgments, signed at Berne on 16 December 1960,
— the Convention between Norway and the United Kingdom providing for the reciprocal recognition and enforcement of judgments in civil matters, signed at London on 12 June 1961,
— the Convention between the United Kingdom and Austria providing for the reciprocal recognition and enforcement of judgments in civil and commercial matters, signed at Vienna on 14 July 1961, with amending Protocol signed at London on 6 March 1970,
— the Convention between the Kingdom of the Netherlands and Austria on the reciprocal recognition and enforcement of judgments and authentic instruments in civil and commercial matters, signed at The Hague on 6 February 1963,
— the Convention between France and Austria on the recognition and enforcement of judgments and authentic instruments in civil and commercial matters, signed at Vienna on 15 July 1966,
— the Convention between Luxembourg and Austria on the recognition and enforcement of judgments and authentic instruments in civil and commercial matters, signed at Luxembourg on 29 July 1971,
— the Convention between Italy and Austria on the recognition and enforcement of judgments in civil and commercial matters, of judicial settlements and of authentic instruments, signed at Rome on 16 November 1971,
— the Convention between Norway and the Federal Republic of Germany on the recognition and enforcement of judgments and enforceable documents, in civil and commercial matters, signed at Oslo on 17 June 1977,
— the Convention between Denmark, Finland, Iceland, Norway and Sweden on the recognition and enforcement of judgments in civil matters, signed at Copenhagen on 11 October 1977,
— the Convention between Austria and Sweden on the recognition and enforcement of judgments in civil matters, signed at Stockholm on 16 September 1982,
— the Convention between Austria and Spain on the recognition and enforcement of judgments, settlements and enforceable authentic instruments in civil and commercial matters, signed at Vienna on 17 February 1984,
— the Convention between Norway and Austria on the recognition and enforcement of judgments in civil matters, signed at Vienna on 21 May 1984, and
— the Convention between Finland and Austria on the recognition and enforcement of judgments in civil matters, signed at Vienna on 17 November 1986.

Article 56

The Treaty and the conventions referred to in Article 55 shall continue to have effect in relation to matters to which this Convention does not apply.

They shall continue to have effect in respect of judgments given and documents formally drawn up or registered as authentic instruments before the entry into force of this Convention.

Article 57

1. This Convention shall not affect any conventions to which the Contracting States are or will be parties and which, in relation to particular matters, govern jurisdiction or the recognition or enforcement of judgments.

2. This Convention shall not prevent a court of a Contracting State which is party to a convention referred to in the first paragraph from assuming jurisdiction in accordance with that convention, even where the defendant is domiciled in a Contracting State which is not a party to that convention. The court hearing the action shall, in any event, apply Article 20 of this Convention.

3. Judgments given in a Contracting State by a court in the exercise of jurisdiction provided for in a convention referred to in the first paragraph shall be recognised and enforced in the other Contracting States in accordance with Title III of this Convention.

4. In addition to the grounds provided for in Title III, recognition or enforcement may be refused if the State addressed is not a contracting party to a convention referred to in the first paragraph and the person against whom recognition or enforcement is sought is domiciled in that State, unless the judgment may otherwise be recognised or enforced under any rule of law in the State addressed.

5. Where a convention referred to in the first paragraph to which both the State of origin and the State addressed are parties lays down conditions for the recognition or enforcement of judgments, those conditions shall apply. In any event, the provisions of this Convention which concern the procedures for recognition and enforcement of judgments may be applied.

Article 58

(None)

Article 59

This Convention shall not prevent a Contracting State from assuming, in a convention on the recognition and enforcement of judgments, an obligation towards a third State not to recognise judgments given in other Contracting States against defendants domiciled or habitually resident in the third State where, in cases provided for in Article 4, the judgment could only be founded on a ground of jurisdiction specified in the second paragraph of Article 3.

However, a Contracting State may not assume an obligation towards a third State not to recognise a judgment given in another Contracting State by a court basing its jurisdiction on the presence within that State of property belonging to the defendant, or the seizure by the plaintiff of property situated there:

1. if the action is brought to assert or declare proprietary or possessory rights in that property, seeks to obtain authority to dispose of it, or arises from another issue relating to such property, or
2. if the property constitutes the security for a debt which is the subject-matter of the action.

TITLE VIII

Final Provisions

Article 60

The following may be parties to this Convention:

(*a*) States which, at the time of the opening of this Convention for signature, are members of the European Communities or of the European Free Trade Association;

(*b*) States which, after the opening of this Convention for signature, become members of the European Communities or of the European Free Trade Association;

(*c*) States invited to accede in accordance with Article 62(1)(b).

Article 61

1. This Convention shall be opened for signature by the States members of the European Communities or of the European Free Trade Association.

2. The Convention shall be submitted for ratification by the signatory States. The instruments of ratification shall be deposited with the Swiss Federal Council.

3. The Convention shall enter into force on the first day of the third month following the date on which two States, of which one is a member of the European Communities and the other a member of the European Free Trade Association, deposit their instruments of ratification.

4. The Convention shall take effect in relation to any other signatory State on the first day of the third month following the deposit of its instrument of ratification.

Article 62

1. After entering into force this Convention shall be open to accession by:
   (*a*) the States referred to in Article 60(*b*);
   (*b*) other States which have been invited to accede upon a request made by one of the Contracting States to the depositary State. The depositary State shall invite the State concerned to accede only if, after having communicated the contents of the communications that this State intends to make in accordance with Article 63, it has obtained the unanimous agreement of the signatory States and the Contracting States referred to in Article 60(*a*) and (*b*).

2. If an acceding State wishes to furnish details for the purposes of Protocol No. 1, negotiations shall be entered into to that end. A negotiating conference shall be convened by the Swiss Federal Council.

3. In respect of an acceding State, the Convention shall take effect on the first day of the third month following the deposit of its instrument of accession.

4. However, in respect of an acceding State referred to in paragraph 1(*a*) or (*b*), the Convention shall take effect only in relations between the acceding State and the Contracting States which have not made any objections to the accession before the first day of the third month following the deposit of the instrument of accession.

Article 63

Each acceding State shall, when depositing its instrument of accession, communicate the information required for the application of Articles 3, 32, 37, 40, 41 and 55 of this Convention and furnish, if need be, the details prescribed during the negotiations for the purposes of Protocol No. 1.

Article 64

1. This Convention is concluded for an initial period of five years from the date of its entry into force in accordance with Article 61(3), even in the case of States which ratify it or accede to it after that date.

2. At the end of the initial five-year period, the Convention shall be automatically renewed from year to year.

3. Upon the expiry of the initial five-year period, any Contracting State may, at any time, denounce the Convention by sending a notification to the Swiss Federal Council.

4. The denunciation shall take effect at the end of the calendar year following the expiry of a period of six months from the date of receipt by the Swiss Federal Council of the notification of denunciation.

Article 65

The following are annexed to this Convention:
— a Protocol No. 1, on certain questions of jurisdiction, procedure and enforcement,
— a Protocol No. 2, on the uniform interpretation of the Convention,
— a Protocol No. 3, on the application of Article 57.

These Protocols shall form an integral part of the Convention.

Article 66

Any Contracting State may request the revision of this Convention. To that end, the Swiss Federal Council shall issue invitations to a revision conference within a period of six months from the date of the request for revision.

Article 67

The Swiss Federal Council shall notify the States represented at the Diplomatic Conference of Lugano and the States who have later acceded to the Convention of:

(*a*) the deposit of each instrument of ratification or accession;
(*b*) the dates of entry into force of this Convention in respect of the Contracting States;
(*c*) any denunciation received pursuant to Article 64;
(*d*) any declaration received pursuant to Article Ia of Protocol No. 1;
(*e*) any declaration received pursuant to Article Ib of Protocol No. 1;
(*f*) any declaration received pursuant to Article IV of Protocol No. 1;
(*g*) any communication made pursuant to Article VI of Protocol No. 1.

Article 68

This Convention, drawn up in a single original in the Danish, Dutch, English, Finnish, French, German, Greek, Icelandic, Irish, Italian, Norwegian, Portuguese, Spanish and Swedish languages, all fourteen texts being equally authentic, shall be deposited in the archives of the Swiss Federal Council. The Swiss Federal Council shall transmit a certified copy to the Government of each State represented at the Diplomatic Conference of Lugano and to the Government of each acceding State.

PROTOCOL NO. 1

ON CERTAIN QUESTIONS OF JURISDICTION, PROCEDURE AND ENFORCEMENT

The High Contracting Parties have agreed upon the following provisions, which shall be annexed to the Convention:

Article I

Any person domiciled in Luxembourg who is sued in a court of another Contracting State pursuant to Article 5(1) may refuse to submit to the jurisdiction of that court. If the defendant does not enter an appearance the court shall declare of its own motion that it has no jurisdiction.

An agreement conferring jurisdiction, within the meaning of Article 17, shall be valid with respect to a person domiciled in Luxembourg only if that person has expressly and specifically so agreed.

Article Ia

1. Switzerland reserves the right to declare, at the time of depositing its instrument of ratification, that a judgment given in another Contracting State shall be neither recognised nor enforced in Switzerland if the following conditions are met:

(*a*) the jurisdiction of the court which has given the judgment is based only on Article 5(1) of this Convention; and
(*b*) the defendant was domiciled in Switzerland at the time of the introduction of the proceedings; for the purposes of this Article, a company or other legal person is considered to be domiciled in Switzerland if it has its registered seat and the effective centre of activities in Switzerland; and
(*c*) the defendant raises an objection to the recognition or enforcement of the judgment in Switzerland, provided that he has not waived the benefit of the declaration foreseen under this paragraph.

2. This reservation shall not apply to the extent that at the time recognition or enforcement is sought a derogation has been granted from Article 59 of the Swiss Federal Constitution. The Swiss Government shall communicate such derogations to the signatory States and the acceding States.

3. This reservation shall cease to have effect on 31 December 1999. It may be withdrawn at any time.

Article Ib

Any Contracting State may, by declaration made at the time of signing or of deposit of its instrument of ratification or of accession, reserve the right, notwithstanding the provisions of Article 28, not to recognise and enforce judgments given in the other Contracting States if the jurisdiction of the court of the State of origin is based, pursuant to Article 16(1)(*b*), exclusively on the domicile of the defendant in the State of origin, and the property is situated in the territory of the State which entered the reservation.

Article II

Without prejudice to any more favourable provisions of national laws, persons domiciled in a Contracting State who are being prosecuted in the criminal courts of another Contracting State of which they are not nationals for an offence which was not intentionally committed may be defended by persons qualified to do so, even if they do not appear in person.

However, the court seised of the matter may order appearance in person; in the case of failure to appear, a judgment given in the civil action without the person concerned having had the opportunity to arrange for his defence need not be recognised or enforced in the other Contracting States.

Article III

In proceedings for the issue of an order for enforcement, no charge, duty or fee calculated by reference to the value of the matter in issue may be levied in the State in which enforcement is sought.

Article IV

Judicial and extrajudicial documents drawn up in one Contracting State which have to be served on persons in another Contracting State shall be transmitted in accordance with the procedures laid down in the conventions and agreements concluded between the Contracting States.

Unless the State in which service is to take place objects by declaration to the Swiss Federal Council, such documents may also be sent by the appropriate public officers of the State in which the document has been drawn up directly to the appropriate public officers of the State in which the addressee is to be found. In this case the officer of the State of origin shall send a copy of the document to the officer of the State applied to who is competent to forward it to the addressee. The document shall be forwarded in the manner specified by the law of the State applied to. The forwarding shall be recorded by a certificate sent directly to the officer of the State of origin.

Article V

The jurisdiction specified in Articles 6(2) and 10 in actions on a warranty or guarantee or in any other third party proceedings may not be resorted to in the Federal Republic of Germany, in Spain, in Austria and in Switzerland. Any person domiciled in another Contracting State may be sued in the courts:

- — of the Federal Republic of Germany, pursuant to Articles 68, 72, 73 and 74 of the code of civil procedure (Zivilprozeβordnung) concerning third-party notices,
- — of Spain, pursuant to Article 1482 of the civil code,
- — of Austria, pursuant to Article 21 of the code of civil procedure (Zivilprozeβordnung) concerning third-party notices,
- — of Switzerland, pursuant to the appropriate provisions concerning third-party notices of the cantonal codes of civil procedure.

Judgments given in the other Contracting States by virtue of Article 6(2) or Article 10 shall be recognised and enforced in the Federal Republic of Germany, in Spain, in Austria and in Switzerland in accordance with Title III. Any effects which judgments given in these States may have on third parties by application of the provisions in the preceding paragraph shall also be recognised in the other Contracting States.

Article Va

In matters relating to maintenance, the expression "court" includes the Danish, Icelandic and Norwegian administrative authorities.

In civil and commercial matters, the expression "court" includes the Finnish ulosotonhaltija / överexekutor.

Article Vb

In proceedings involving a dispute between the master and a member of the crew of a sea-going ship registered in Denmark, in Greece, in Ireland, in Iceland, in Norway, in Portugal or in Sweden concerning remuneration or other conditions of service, a court in a Contracting State shall establish whether the diplomatic or consular officer responsible for the ship has been notified of the dispute. It shall stay the proceedings so long as he has not been notified. It shall of its own motion decline jurisdiction if the officer, having been duly notified, has exercised the powers accorded to him in the matter by a consular convention, or in the absence of such a convention has, within the time allowed, raised any objection to the exercise of such jurisdiction.

Article Vc

(None)

Article Vd

Without prejudice to the jurisdiction of the European Patent Office under the Convention on the grant of European patents, signed at Munich on 5 October 1973, the courts of each Contracting State shall have exclusive jurisdiction, regardless of domicile, in proceedings concerned with the registration or validity of any European patent granted for that State which is not a Community patent by virtue of the provision of Article 86 of the Convention for the European patent for the common market, signed at Luxembourg on 15 December 1975.

Article VI

The Contracting States shall communicate to the Swiss Federal Council the text of any provisions of their laws which amend either those provisions of their laws mentioned in the Convention or the lists of courts specified in Section 2 of Title III.

PROTOCOL NO. 2

ON THE UNIFORM INTERPRETATION OF THE CONVENTION

Preamble

The High Contracting Parties,
Having regard to Article 65 of this Convention,
Considering the substantial link between this Convention and the Brussels Convention,
Considering that the Court of Justice of the European Communities by virtue of the Protocol of 3 June 1971 has jurisdiction to give rulings on the interpretation of the provisions of the Brussels Convention,
Being aware of the rulings delivered by the Court of Justice of the European Communities on the interpretation of the Brussels Convention up to the time of signature of this Convention,
Considering that the negotiations which led to the conclusion of the Convention were based on the Brussels Convention in the light of these rulings,
Desiring to prevent, in full deference to the independence of the courts, divergent interpretations and to arrive at as uniform an interpretation as possible of the provisions of the Convention, and of these provisions and those of the Brussels Convention which are substantially reproduced in this Convention,

Have agreed as follows:

Article 1

The courts of each Contracting State shall, when applying and interpreting the provisions of the Convention, pay due account to the principles laid down by any relevant decision delivered by courts of the other Contracting States concerning provisions of this Convention.

Article 2

1. The Contracting Parties agree to set up a system of exchange of information concerning judgments delivered pursuant to this Convention as well as relevant judgments under the Brussels Convention. This system shall comprise:
- transmission to a central body by the competent authorities of judgments delivered by courts of last instance and the Court of Justice of the European Communities as well as judgments of particular importance which have become final and have been delivered pursuant to this Convention or the Brussels Convention,
- classification of these judgments by the central body including, as far as necessary, the drawing-up and publication of translations and abstracts,
- communication by the central body of the relevant documents to the competent national authorities of all signatories and acceding States to the Convention and to the Commission of the European Communities.

2. The central body is the Registrar of the Court of Justice of the European Communities.

Article 3

1. A Standing Committee shall be set up for the purposes of this Protocol.
2. The Committee shall be composed of representatives appointed by each signatory and acceding State.
3. The European Communities (Commission, Court of Justice and General Secretariat of the Council) and the European Free Trade Association may attend the meetings as observers.

Article 4

1. At the request of a Contracting Party, the depositary of the Convention shall convene meetings of the Committee for the purpose of exchanging views on the functioning of the Convention and in particular on:
- the development of the case-law as communicated under the first paragraph first indent of Article 2,
- the application of Article 57 of the Convention.

2. The Committee, in the light of these exchanges, may also examine the appropriateness of starting on particular topics a revision of the Convention and make recommendations.

PROTOCOL NO. 3

On the Application of Article 57

The High Contracting Parties have agreed as follows:
1. For the purposes of the Convention, provisions which, in relation to particular matters, govern jurisdiction or the recognition or enforcement of judgments and which are, or will be, contained in acts of the institutions of the European Communities shall be treated in the same way as the conventions referred to in paragraph 1 of Article 57.
2. If one Contracting State is of the opinion that a provision contained in an act of the institutions of the European Communities is incompatible with the Convention, the Contracting States shall promptly consider amending the Convention pursuant to Article 66, without prejudice to the procedure established by Protocol No. 2.

SCHEDULE 2

Other Amendments of the 1982 Act

1. The words "Brussels Conventions" shall be substituted for the word "Conventions" wherever occurring in section 2 (the Conventions to have the force of law) and section 3 (interpretation of the Conventions).

2. In section 4(1) (enforcement of judgments other than maintenance orders) and section 5(1) (recognition and enforcement of maintenance orders) after the words "an application under Article 31" there shall be inserted the words "of the 1968 Convention or of the Lugano Convention".

3. In section 6 (appeals under Article 37, second paragraph and Article 41)—
(*a*) in subsection (1), after the words "referred to" there shall be inserted the words "in the 1968 Convention and the Lugano Convention"; and

(*b*) in subsection (3), after the words "referred to" there shall be inserted the words "in each of those Conventions".

4. In section 9 (provisions supplementary to Title VII of the 1968 Convention) in subsection (1)—

(*a*) after the words "Title VII of the 1968 Convention" there shall be inserted the words "and, apart from Article 54B, of Title VII of the Lugano Convention"; and

(*b*) for the words "that convention" there shall be substituted the words "the Convention in question".

5. In section 10 (allocation within UK of jurisdiction in proceedings with respect to trusts and consumer contracts in respect of which in 1968 Convention confers jurisdiction on UK courts generally) in subsection (1), after the words "the 1968 Convention" there shall be inserted the words "or the Lugano Convention".

6. In section 11 (proof and admissibility of certain judgments and related documents for the purposes of the 1968 Convention) in subsection (1), after the words "For the purposes of the 1968 Convention" there shall be inserted the words "and the Lugano Convention".

7. In section 12 (provision for issue of copies of, and certificates in connection with, UK judgments for purposes of the 1968 Convention) after the words "the 1968 Convention" there shall be inserted the words "or the Lugano Convention".

8. In section 13 (modifications to cover authentic instruments and court settlements) in subsection (1)—

(*a*) after the words "the 1968 Convention" in paragraph (*a*) there shall be inserted the words "or the Lugano Convention";

(*b*) after the words "Title IV of the 1968 Convention" there shall be inserted the words "or, as the case may be, Title IV of the Lugano Convention"; and

(*c*) for the words "that Convention" there shall be substituted the words "the Convention in question".

9. In section 14 (modifications consequential on revision of the Conventions)—

(*a*) for the words "any of the Conventions," wherever occurring in subsections (1) and (3), there shall be substituted the words "the Lugano Convention or any of the Brussels Conventions"; and

(*b*) in subsection (1), after the words "any revision connected with the accession to" there shall be inserted the words "the Lugano Convention or".

10. In section 15 (interpretation of Part I)—

(*a*) in subsection (1), in the definition of "maintenance order," after the words "maintenance judgment within the meaning of the 1968 Convention" there shall be inserted the words "or, as the case may be, the Lugano Convention"; and

(*b*) in subsection (3), after the words "authorised or required by the 1968 Convention" there shall be inserted the words "the Lugano Convention".

11. In section 16 (allocation within UK of jurisdiction in certain civil proceedings)—

(*a*) in paragraph (*a*) of subsection (1), for the words "the Convention" there shall be substituted the words "that or any other Convention";

(*b*) in paragraph (*b*) of that subsection, after the words "Article 16" there shall be inserted the words "of the 1968 Convention"; and

(*c*) in subsection (4), after the words "subject to the 1968 Convention" there shall be inserted the words "and the Lugano Convention".

12. The words "Brussels or Lugano Contracting State" shall be substituted for the words "Contracting State" wherever occurring in each of the following provisions, that is to say—

(*a*) in subsections (1)(*a*) and (3)(*a*) of section 25 (interim relief in England and Wales or Northern Ireland in the absence of substantive proceedings);

(*b*) in subsections (2)(*a*) and (3)(*a*) and (*d*) of section 27 (which makes for Scotland similar provision to that made by section 25 for England and Wales); and

(*c*) in section 28 (application of section 1 of the Administration of Justice (Scotland) Act 1972);

and, in section 25(1)(*b*), for the words "the Convention" there shall be substituted the words "that or any other Convention".

13. In section 30 (proceedings in England and Wales or Northern Ireland for torts to immovable property) in subsection (2), after the words "subject to the 1968 Convention" there shall be inserted the words "and the Lugano Convention".

14. In section 32 (overseas judgments given in proceedings brought in breach of agreement for settlement of disputes) in subsection (4) (saving for judgments required to be recognised or enforced in UK under the 1968 Convention etc) in paragraph (*a*), after the words "under the 1968 Convention" there shall be inserted the words "or the Lugano Convention".

15. In section 33 (certain steps not to amount to submission to the jurisdiction of an overseas court) in subsection (2) (saving for judgments required to be recognised or enforced in England and Wales or Northern Ireland under the 1968 Convention) after the words "under the 1968 Convention" there shall be inserted the words "or the Lugano Convention".

16. In section 41 (determination of domicile of individuals for the purposes of the 1968 Convention etc) in subsection (1), after the words "for the purposes of the 1968 Convention" there shall be inserted the words "the Lugano Convention".

17. In section 42 (domicile and seat of corporation or association) in subsection (2)(*a*), after the words "for the purposes of the 1968 Convention" there shall be inserted the words "or, as the case may be, the Lugano Convention".

18. In section 43 (seat of corporation or association for purposes of Article 16(2) and related provisions) in subsection (1)(*a*), after the words "Article 16(2)" there shall be inserted the words "of the 1968 Convention or of the Lugano Convention".

19.—(1) In section 44 (persons deemed to be domiciled in UK for certain purposes) in subsection (1)—

(*a*) in paragraph (*a*) (which provides that the section applies to proceedings within Section 3 of Title II of the 1968 Convention) after the words "the 1968 Convention" there shall be inserted the words "or Section 3 of Title II of the Lugano Convention"; and

(*b*) in paragraph (*b*) (proceedings within Section 2 of that Title) for the words "that Title" there shall be substituted the words "Title II of either of those Conventions".

(2) In subsection (2) of that section, after the words "is deemed for the purposes of the 1968 Convention" there shall be inserted the words "or, as the case may be, of the Lugano Convention".

20. In section 45 (domicile of trusts) in subsection (1), after the words "for the purposes of the 1968 Convention" there shall be inserted the words "the Lugano Convention".

21.—(1) In section 46 (domicile and seat of the Crown) in subsection (2)(*a*), after the words "for the purposes of the 1968 Convention" there shall be inserted the words "and the Lugano Convention" and for the words "(in which" there shall be substituted the words "(in each of which".

(2) In subsection (4) of that section (Order in Council with respect to seat of the Crown) after the words "for the purposes of the 1968 Convention" there shall be inserted the words "the Lugano Convention".

22. In section 47 (modifications occasioned by decisions of the European Court as to meaning or effect of the Conventions) for the word "Conventions," wherever occurring, there shall be substituted the words "Brussels Conventions".

23. In section 48 (matters for which rules of court may provide)—

(*a*) in subsection (1), for the words "or the Conventions" there shall be substituted the words "the Lugano Convention or the Brussels Conventions"; and

(*b*) in subsection (3), for the words "the Conventions" there shall be substituted the words "the Lugano Convention, the Brussels Conventions".

24. In section 49 (saving for powers to stay, sist, strike out of dismiss proceedings where to do so is not inconsistent with the 1968 Convention) after the words "the 1968 Convention" there shall be inserted the words "or, as the case may be, the Lugano Convention".

25. In section 50 (general interpretation) the following definitions shall be inserted at the appropriate places—

" 'Brussels Contracting State' has the meaning given by section 1(3)";

" 'the Brussels Conventions' has the meaning given by section 1(1)";

" 'Lugano Contracting State' has the meaning given by section 1(3)";

" 'the Lugano Convention' has the meaning given by section 1(1)";

and the entry relating to "the Conventions" is hereby repealed.

[THE NEXT PAGE IS B 501]

House of Lords Appeal Directions and Standing Orders

Form of Appeal Directions as to Procedure and Standing Orders applicable to Civil Appeals from the Court of Appeal in England; the Court of Session in Scotland; the Court of Appeal in Northern Ireland; the High Court of Justice in England and Wales and the High Court of Justice in Northern Ireland 1988

TABLE OF CONTENTS

I—Petitions For Leave To Appeal

Leave To Appeal

Court of Appeal in England & Court of Appeal in Northern Ireland

[1] **1.1** Leave to appeal is required before an appeal from an order of either of these Courts may be presented to the House of Lords.

1.2 An application for leave to appeal must first be made to the Court of Appeal. If leave is refused, a petition for leave to appeal may be presented to the House of Lords.

Court of Session in Scotland

1.3 Leave to appeal from an interlocutor of this Court is not normally required. However the following statutory provisions contain a requirement for leave in certain circumstances—

Building (Scotland) Act 1959, section 16(3);
Caravan Sites and Control of Development Act 1960, section 32(2)(*b*);
Tribunals and Inquiries Act 1971, section 13(6)(*c*);
Aircraft & Shipbuilding Industries Act 1977, Schedule 7, paragraph 9(2);

Estate Agents Act 1979, section 7(6);
Transport Act 1985, section 9(9);
Banking Act 1987, section 31(4); and
[2] Court of Session Act 1988, section 40(1)(*b*).

High Court of Justice in England & Wales & in Northern Ireland

[3] **1.4** In certain proceedings an appeal from an order of these Courts may be brought direct to the House of Lords. Leave to appeal is required and a petition for such leave should be presented to the House.

Cross-appeals

1.5 The presentation of an appeal does not entitle a respondent to present a cross-appeal. A respondent to an appeal who wishes to reverse or vary an order of the Court of Appeal must first obtain leave to cross-appeal. Application for leave to cross-appeal must first be made to the Court of Appeal. If leave is refused, an application for leave to cross-appeal may be made to the House of Lords.

NOTES

[1] See the Administration of Justice (Appeals) Act 1934 and the Judicature (Northern Ireland) Act 1978.

[2] See *The Laws of Scotland*, Stair Memorial Encyclopaedia, Vol. 6, para. 829.

[3] See Pt. II of the Administration of Justice Act 1969. See also paras. 6.1–6.6.

Time Limits

[1] **2.1** A petition for leave to appeal must be lodged in the Judicial Office within one month of the date on which an order appealed from was made. The order appealed from is the substantive order complained of.

Out of time petitions

2.2 A petition lodged after the prescribed time limit has expired must be drafted as out of time.

2.3 A petition for leave to appeal out of time should first set out the reasons why the petition was not lodged within the time limit. The reasons should not normally exceed a paragraph in length.

NOTE

[1] For definition of lodgment see para. 40.1. See Standing Order II, *infra*. For extension of time in legal aid cases, see paras. 25.3 and 25.4.

Lodging Of Petition

Form of petition

[1] **3.1** A petition for leave to appeal should briefly set out the facts and points of law involved in the appeal. It should conclude with a summary of the reasons why leave to appeal should be granted.

3.2 A petition must be signed by the petitioners or their agents.

Title

3.3 Petitions for leave to appeal to the House of Lords carry the same title as the cause in the court below, but the parties are described as petitioners and respondents.

Service

3.4 A copy of the petition must be served on the respondents or their agents, either by delivery in person or by first class post. A certificate of such service must be endorsed on the back of the original petition and signed.

Lodgment

3.5 The original petition must be lodged in the Judical Office together with a copy of the order appealed from and, if separate, a copy of the order of the Court of Appeal refusing leave to appeal to the House of Lords. If the order is not immediately available, the petition should be lodged in time and the order lodged as soon as possible thereafter.

Appearance for respondents

3.6 Respondents or their agents should enter appearance to a petition for leave as soon as they have received service. They should enter their name and address at the Judicial Office, either in person or by post. Those respondents who intend to take no part in the proceedings before the House should notify the Judicial Office, in writing, of that fact. Communications concerning the petition will be sent only to those who have entered appearance.

NOTE

[1] For style see Appendix A. For preparation of documents see para. 37.

APPEAL COMMITTEE

4.1 On presentation to the House a petition for leave will be referred to an Appeal Committee.

Additional papers

4.2 The following additional papers, for use by the Appeal Committee, must be lodged within one week of lodgment of the petition—

(*a*) four copies of the petition;
(*b*) four copies of the order appealed from;
(*c*) if separate, four copies of the order of the court below refusing leave to appeal to the House of Lords;
[1] (*d*) five copies of the official transcript of the judgment of the court below;
(*e*) five copies of the order of the court of first instance;
[1] (*f*) five copies of the official transcript of the judgment of the court of first instance.

4.3 There is no need for these papers to be bound.

4.4 Where the necessary papers are not lodged within three months of presentation of the petition, and no good reason for such failure is given, the petition may, at the direction of the Principal Clerk, be referred to an Appeal Committee without the papers.

Admissibility of petitions

4.5 The Appeal Committee will consider whether the petition is admissible. Petitions are not admissible if they fall into one of the following categories—

(*a*) petitions for leave to appeal to the House of Lords against a refusal by the Court of Appeal to grant leave to appeal to that Court from a judgment of a lower court;
(*b*) petitions for leave to appeal to the House of Lords against a refusal by the Court of Appeal or a Divisional Court of the Queen's Bench Division to grant an *ex parte* application for leave to apply for judicial review under Order 53 of the Rules of the Supreme Court;
(*c*) petitions for leave to appeal to the House of Lords barred by paragraph 13(4) of Schedule 11, and by paragraph 7(4) of Schedule 22, to the Housing Act 1985;
(*d*) petitions for leave to appeal to the House of Lords brought by a petitioner in respect of whom the High Court has made an order under section 42 of the Supreme Court Act 1981 (restriction of vexatious legal proceedings) unless leave to present such a petition has been granted by the High Court or a judge thereof pursuant to that section.

4.6 If the members of the Appeal Committee are unanimously of the opinion that a petition is not admissible, parties will be notified that the petition is dismissed.

4.7 If a petition is admissible, the Appeal Committee will consider whether or not leave to appeal should be given. The particular facts and circumstances of each petition will be taken into account.

4.8 The Appeal Committee does not give reasons for a decision. In broad terms, leave to appeal may be refused if a petition does not raise an arguable point of law of general public importance. If the Appeal Committee is unanimously of the opinion that leave should be refused, parties will be notified of that result.

Respondents' objections

4.9 If the Appeal Committee takes the provisional view that leave to appeal should be given or given upon terms, the respondents will be invited to lodge objections to the petition, briefly setting out reasons why the petition should not be allowed or making other relevant submissions as to the terms upon which leave should be granted. The petitioner will be notified of any proposed terms and may submit observations, which must be served on the respondents.

4.10 Seven copies of the objections should be lodged in the Judicial Office by the date specified in the notification that objections may be lodged. A copy should be served on the other parties.

4.11 If, having considered any objections submitted by the respondents, the Appeal Committee is unanimous that leave to appeal should be given, parties will be notified of that result.

4.12 Where the Appeal Committee is not unanimous, or where further argument is required, the petition will be referred for an oral hearing.

Oral hearing

4.13 If a petition is referred for an oral hearing, the petitioners and all respondents who have entered appearance will be notified of the probable date of meeting of the Appeal Committee, before whom the parties are directed to attend. However no guarantee can be given that the date notified will be adhered to. Once referred for an oral hearing a petition may be listed at any time, possibly at short notice.

4.14 Parties may be heard before the Appeal Committee by counsel, by agent or in person, but only one may be heard on each side. With the exception of leading counsel's advice prepared for the legal aid authorities, only junior counsel's fees are allowed on taxation for this or any other stage of the petition for leave procedure.

4.15 If counsel is briefed, the Judicial Office must be notified of the name.

4.16 Authorities should not normally be cited before the Appeal Committee.

Appeal Committee order

4.17 The Minutes of Proceedings of the House, containing the decision of the Appeal Committee, are sent to all parties.

4.18 A formal order of the Appeal Committee is only issued on written request, and on payment of a fee. An Appeal Committee order is not required for taxation of costs in the House of Lords.

NOTE

[1] If the judgment has been published in a report which is ordinarily received in court, copies of the report may be lodged in lieu of transcripts. Transcripts of judgments in draft or judge's notes are not acceptable.

Costs

5.1 Where a petition for leave to appeal is determined without an oral hearing, costs may be awarded as follows—

[1] (*a*) to a legally aided petitioner, reasonable costs incurred in preparing papers for the Appeal Committee;

[1] (*b*) to a legally aided respondent, only those costs necessarily incurred in attending the client, attending the petitioner's agents, perusing the petition and entering appearance;

[2] (*c*) to an unassisted respondent where the petitioner is legally aided, payment out of the Legal Aid Fund (pursuant to section 18 of the Legal Aid Act 1988) of costs as specified at (*b*) above;

(*d*) to a respondent whether neither party is legally aided, costs as specified at (*b*) above.

Where costs are sought under (*c*) or (*d*) above, application must be made in writing to the Judicial Office before the bill is lodged.

5.2 Where a petition for leave to appeal is referred for an oral hearing and is dismissed, application for costs must be made by the respondent at the end of the hearing. No order for costs will be made unless requested at that time.

5.3 Where a petition for leave to appeal is allowed, costs of the petition will be costs in the ensuing appeal.

NOTES

[1] See "Forms of Bills of Costs in the House of Lords," *infra* at p. **B** 530.

[2] In Scotland, for the Legal Aid Act 1988, read Legal Aid (Scotland) Act 1986.

"Leap Frog" Petitions

6.1 Where a certificate has been granted by the High Court under section 12 of the Administration of Justice Act 1969, a petition for leave to appeal to the House of Lords may be lodged by any or all of the parties to the proceedings. The petition should indicate whether the High Court certificate was granted under section 12(3)(*a*) or 12(3)(*b*) of the Act.

[1] **6.2** A petition must be lodged within one month of the date on which the certificate was granted by the High Court. Where further time is required for lodging a petition, a request must be made in writing before the original time expires. The request must give reasons for the time to be extended and must be accompanied by three copies of the official transcript of the High Court judgment.

6.3 If there is any party not joining in the petition the petitioners must notify that party in writing. They must endorse on the back of the petition a certificate that such notice has been given.

6.4 One copy of the High Court's certificate must be lodged with the petition.

6.5 The following additional papers, for use by the Appeal Committee, must be lodged within one week of the lodgment of the petition—

(*a*) four copies of the petition;

(*b*) four copies of the order appealed from;

(*c*) where separate, four copies of the High Court's certificate;

[2] (*d*) five copies of the official transcript of the judgment of the High Court.

6.6 A "leap frog" petition will be considered by an Appeal Committee without an oral hearing. Parties will be notified of the Committee's decision.

NOTES

[1] For definition of lodgment, see para. 40.1. For extension of time in legal aid cases, see paras. 25.3 and 25.4.

[2] If the judgment has been published in a report which is ordinarily received in court, copies of the report may be lodged in lieu of transcripts. Transcripts of judgments in draft are not acceptable.

Fees

[1] **7.1** No fee is payable at any stage of a petition for leave to appeal, except when an Appeal Committee order is requested. Fees are payable on the taxation of a bill of costs.

NOTE

[1] See para. 4.18.

II—Appeals

Time Limits

8.1 Unless the time for appealing is otherwise limited by statute or by an order of the House or of the court below, a petition of appeal must be lodged in the Judicial Office within three months of the date on which the order appealed from was made. The order appealed from is the substantive order complained of.

Out of time appeals

8.2 Where an appeal is not lodged within the time allowed, a petition for leave to present an appeal out of time may be lodged, together with the appropriate fee. Such petition will be dealt with in accordance with Direction 29.

Use Of London Agents

9.1 Solicitors outside London may appoint London agents. Those who decide not to do so should note that any additional costs incurred as a result of that decision may be disallowed on taxation.

Presentation Of Appeal

Form of petition of appeal

10.1 For style of petition see Appendix C. For preparation of documents see Direction 37.

10.2 Where leave to appeal has been obtained, a petition of appeal must be signed by the appellants or their agents. Where leave is not required (that is, in most Scottish appeals) a petition must be signed, and certified as reasonable, by two counsel. In certain Scottish appeals a further certificate is also required.

Title

10.3 Petitions of appeal to the House of Lords carry the same title as the cause in the court below, but the parties are described as appellants and respondents.

Service

[1] **10.4** A copy of the petition of appeal must be served on the respondents or their agents, either by delivery in person or by first class post. A certificate of such service must be endorsed on the back of the original petition and signed.

Presentation of petition of appeal

10.5 The original petition, and five copies, must be lodged in the Judicial Office together with the appropriate fee.

10.6 Presentation of a petition to the House is recorded in the Minutes of Proceedings.

Appearance for respondents

10.7 Respondent's agents should enter appearance to an appeal as soon as they have received service of the petition of appeal. They should enter their name and address at the Judicial Office, either in person or by post, together with the appropriate fee. Those respondents who intend to take no part in the proceedings before the House should notify the Judicial Office, in writing, of that fact. Communications concerning the appeal will be sent only to those who have entered appearance.

NOTE

[1] For style see Appendix C.

Security For Costs

[1] **11.1** Appellants must give security for costs by payment into the House of Lords Security Fund Account of the appropriate sum within one week of the presentation of an appeal. Failure to do so will result in the appeal being dismissed.

11.2 No interest is payable on security money.

Waiver of security

11.3 If all the respondents agree to security for costs being waived, the appellants may lodge, together with the appropriate fee, a form of consent to a waiver signed by the respondents. Thereafter an order will be made releasing the appellants from the obligation to pay security. Consent must be lodged within one week of the presentation of an appeal. A form of consent should be obtained from the Judicial Office.

[2] **11.4** The following classes of appellant are not required to give security for costs and no waiver is necessary—

(i) an appellant who has been granted a legal aid certificate;

(ii) an appellant in an appeal under the Child Abduction and Custody Act 1985;

(iii) a cross-appellant;

(iv) a Minister or Government department

NOTES

[1] See Standing Order VI (1).

[2] See Standing Order VI (2).

Statement Of Facts And Issues

[1] **12.1** The appellants must prepare a statement of the facts and issues involved in the appeal. The appellants should draw up the statement and submit it to the respondents for discussion. Wherever possible, the statement lodged should be a single document agreed between the parties. It should not contain material more appropriately included in a case.

12.2 Where, after consultation, the parties are unable to adopt an agreed statement, the respondents may prepare their own statement which should be appended to that of the appellants under the title "Respondents' statement of facts and issues." If the respondents neither agree to a joint statement nor produce a statement of their own for attachment to the appellants' statement, the appellants may lodge their statement with a certificate to the effect that the respondents have been offered an opportunity to join in preparation of the statement.

12.3 The statement need not set out or summarise the judgments of the lower courts, nor set out statutory provisions, nor contain an account of the proceedings below. It may be assumed that the statement will be read in conjunction with the documents in the Appendix. Moreover, attention is drawn to the remarks of Lord Diplock in *M.V. Yorke Motors* v. *Edwards* [1982] 1 W.L.R. 444; [1982] 1 All E.R. 1024.

12.4 For form of statement see Direction 37.

NOTE

[1] For the lodging of the statement, see para. 14. See also para. 16.

APPENDIX

[1] **13.1** The appellants must also prepare and lodge an appendix containing documents used in evidence or recording proceedings in the courts below. This should be done in consultation with the respondents, and the contents of the appendix must be agreed between the parties.

13.2 The cost of preparing the appendix is borne in the first instance by the appellants, though it will ultimately be subject to the decision of the House as to the costs of the appeal.

Contents of appendix

13.3 The appendix should contain only such documents, or such extracts from documents, as are clearly necessary for the support and understanding of the argument of the appeal. No document which was not used in evidence or does not record proceedings relevant to the action in the courts below may be included. Authorities must not be included except after consultation with the Judicial Office. Transcripts of arguments in the courts below must not be included unless:

(*a*) any party relies on remarks by a judge; or

(*b*) the arguments refer to facts which are admitted by all parties and as to which no evidence was called.

13.4 The appendix may consist of one or more parts. Part I should contain:—

(*a*) formal originating documents;

(*b*) case stated (if any);

(*c*) judgments of the decisions at first instance and on appeal together with copies of the Orders of all Courts. Unbound parts of the Law Reports or the Weekly Law Reports should be used, if available; otherwise the All England Reports, Tax Cases, Simons' Tax Cases, Reports of Patent Cases and Lloyds List Reports may be used. In appeals from Scotland, Session Cases should be used where available; failing that, Scots Law Times may be used. Where at the time of preparation of the appendix a judgment of a court below is not published in one of the reports listed above, a transcript must be included. If it then becomes available by the time the bound case is lodged, the published version should be substituted for the transcript. Where a judgment is published after the lodging of the bound case but before the hearing of the appeal, six copies should be submitted to the Judicial Office as soon as possible. Judgments in draft are not accepted;

(*d*) the relevant statutory provisions including Statutory Instruments. If the printed Act or set of Regulations is conveniently small, it should be used. If the statutory provisions are bulky or numerous, the relevant provisions only should be copied;

(*e*) any crucial document on which the action is founded, such as a will, contract, map, plan etc, or the relevant extract from such a document.

13.5 Other documents should be included in Part II of the appendix (and subsequent parts if, owing to bulk, the material is more conveniently made up into more than one volume).

13.6 For form of appendix see Direction 37.

Documents in readiness at hearing

13.7 Any documents disputed between the parties, and any documents which are not included in the appendix but which may be required at the hearing, should be held in readiness and, subject to leave being given, may be introduced at an appropriate moment. Six copies are required. The other parties must be given notice of any documents which will be held in readiness at the hearing.

Respondents' additional documents

13.8 Where the appellants decline to include in the appendix any documents which the respondents consider necessary for their argument of the appeal, the respondents must prepare and reproduce them at their own cost. The respondents' additional documents must be produced in the same form as, and paginated consecutively with, the appendix. The costs of such preparation will ultimately be subject to the decision of the House as to the costs of the appeal.

Examination of appendix

13.9 The appendix (and, where applicable, respondents' additional documents) is for the use of all parties. As soon as a proof is available it should be examined against the originals by all parties, if possible at one joint examination.

13.10 As soon as practicable after the examination a final proof of the appendix and any additional documents should be provided to each party.

Scottish record

[2] **13.11** Appellants in Scottish appeals should include the Record and Interlocutors in Part I of the appendix.

NOTES

[1] For lodging of the Appendix, see para. 14.

[2] See Standing Order VII (2).

LODGING OF STATEMENT AND APPENDIX

Time limits

[1] **14.1** The statement and appendix must be lodged by the appellants within six weeks of the presentation of the appeal.

Petitions for extension of time

[2] **14.2** If the appellants are unable to prepare the statement and appendix within the time specified, they may petition for an extension of that time, indicating the reasons for the request. Applications may usually be made for an extension of one to six weeks, and the petition must specify the date to which extension is requested. The extension granted in recess by Standing Order IX does not apply to time extended on petition, but if the date specified is likely to fall in a recess, the petition may request extension until "[date specified] or the third sitting day of the next ensuing meeting of the House."

14.3 A petition for extension of time must be signed by the appellants. It must be submitted to those respondents who have entered appearance, for the endorsement of their consent. The petition, together with the appropriate fee, must be lodged before the expiration of the time allowed for lodgment of the statement and appendix.

14.4 It is expected that respondents will not unreasonably withhold consent to a petition for extension of time. If consent is refused the petition must be endorsed with a certificate that it has been served on the respondents. The petition will then be referred to an Appeal Committee for hearing. In that event six copies of the petition must be lodged, together with the appropriate fee.

14.5 In most circumstances up to three extensions of time will be granted. Subsequent petitions may, at the direction of the Principal Clerk, be referred to an Appeal Committee.

Lodgment

14.6 The appellants should deposit in the Judicial Office, together with the appropriate fee, six copies of the statement, six copies of Part I of the appendix and 15 copies of each subsequent part of the appendix.

NOTES

[1] See Standing Order VII(1). For extensions of this time see below. For extension in a legal aid case see paras. 25.3 and 25.4. See also para. 40.1.

[2] For style see Appendix D. A *pro forma* is available from the Judicial Office.

Setting Down For Hearing

15.1 When lodging the statement and appendix the appellants must apply to set the appeal down for hearing, on payment of the appropriate fee.

Allocation of time

15.2 Within seven days of the setting down of the appeal each party should notify the Judicial Office of the time, in hours, which counsel consider necessary for each address which it is proposed should be made on behalf of that party.

15.3 Subject to any directions which may be given at or prior to the hearing counsel will be expected to confine their submissions to the time indicated in their estimates. Arrangements for hearings will be made on that basis.

Appellants' And Respondents' Cases

16.1 As soon as possible after the setting down of the appeal, and in any event no later than two weeks before the proposed date of hearing, the appellants and respondents should lodge their own cases.

16.2 Parties are reminded that once an appeal has been set down for hearing, that is on lodgment of the statement and appendix, it may be called at any time.

16.3 A case should be a succinct statement of a party's argument in the appeal. It should omit the material contained in the statement of facts and issues and should be confined to the heads of argument which counsel propose to submit at the hearing.

16.4 If either party are abandoning any point taken below, this should be made plain in the case. Equally if they intend to apply in the course of the hearing for leave to introduce a new point not taken below, this should be indicated in their case and the Judicial Office should be informed. If such a point involves the introduction of fresh evidence, application for leave must be made either in the case or by lodging a petition for leave to adduce the fresh evidence.

[1] **16.5** If a party intend to invite the House to depart from one of its own decisions, this intention must be clearly stated in a separate paragraph of the case, to which special attention must be drawn. The intention must also be restated as one of the reasons. A respondent who wishes to contend that a decision of the court below should be affirmed on grounds other than those relied on by that court, must set out the grounds for that contention in the case.

[2] **16.6** All cases must conclude with a numbered summary of the reasons upon which the argument is founded, and must bear the signature of at least one counsel who has appeared in the court below or who will be briefed for the hearing before the House.

16.7 Counsel should take note of the speech of Lord Diplock in *Roberts Petroleum Limited* v. *Bernard Kenny* [1983] 2 A.C. 192 as to the citing of unreported cases. Leave to cite unreported cases should be sought at the hearing and "will only be granted on counsel giving an assurance that the transcript contains a statement of some principle of law, relevant to an issue in the appeal to the House, that is binding on the Court of Appeal and of which the substance, as distinct from the mere choice of phraseology, is not to be found in any judgment of that court that has appeared in one of the generalised or specialised series of Reports". Unreported cases should not be included in documents lodged.

16.8 The lodgment of a case carries the right to be heard by two counsel, one of whom may be leading counsel. Unless otherwise ordered upon application at the hearing, only two counsel's fees are allowed on taxation.

Separate cases

16.9 All the appellants must join in one case, and all the respondents must similarly join unless it can be shown that the interests of one or more of the respondents are distinct from those of the remainder. In the latter event the respondents' agents first lodging their case must give a certificate by letter in one of the following forms:—

(*a*) "We as agents for the respondent(s) (*name particular parties*) certify that opportunity has been offered by us for joining in one case to the respondent(s) (*name particular parties*) whose interests are, in our opinion, similar to those set out in the case lodged by us".

(*b*) "We, as agents for the respondent(s) (*name particular parties*) certify that the interests represented in the case lodged by us are, in our opinion, distinct from those of the remaining respondent(s)".

16.10 When one of the foregoing certificates has been given, all remaining respondents wishing to lodge a case must respectively petition to do so in respect of each of their separate cases. Such petitions (which must be lodged with the appropriate fee) must be consented to by the appellants, and must set out the reasons for separate lodgment.

16.11 Parties whose interests in the appeal are passive (*e.g.* stake-holders, trustees, executors, etc.) are not required to lodge a separate case but should ensure that their position is explained in one of the cases lodged.

Joint cases

16.12 The lodgment of a joint case on behalf of both appellants and respondents may be permitted in certain circumstances.

Lodgment of cases

16.13 Each party must lodge in the Judicial Office six copies of their case. The respondents must also (where applicable) lodge six copies of their additional documents if supplementary to Part I of the appendix (15 copies if supplementary to any other part of the appendix).

Exchange of cases

16.14 As soon as the cases have been prepared, all parties must exchange cases. The number of cases should be sufficient to meet the requirements of counsel and agents but should not usually exceed eight.

NOTES

[1] See para. 16.6.

[2] See Standing Order VII (3).

Bound Volumes

17.1 As soon as cases have been exchanged, and in any event no later than one week before the proposed date of hearing, the appellants must lodge (in addition to the documents earlier lodged) 15 bound volumes. Each should contain:—

(*a*) the petition(s) of appeal;
(*b*) the petition(s) of cross appeal (if any);
(*c*) the statement of facts and issues;
(*d*) the appellants' and respondents' cases;
(*e*) Part I of the appendix;
(*f*) respondents' additional documents (if any and if supplementary to Part I of the appendix).

17.2 For form of bound volumes see Direction 37.

17.3 To enable the appellants to lodge the bound volumes, the respondents must provide them with 15 further copies of their case and, where applicable, with 15 further copies of the additional documents.

17.4 Respondents should arrange with the appellants for the binding of such volumes as the respondents' counsel and agents may require.

Notice Of Hearing

18.1 In arranging the dates for the hearing of an appeal the Judicial Office will endeavour to suit the convenience of all parties and to that end provisional dates are arranged sometime in advance. However no guarantee can be given that these dates will be adhered to and once an appeal has been set down it may be called in at any time, possibly at short notice. Counsel, agents and parties should, in any event, hold themselves in readiness during the week prior to, and the week following, the provisional date arranged.

18.2 Agents receive formal notification shortly before the hearing.

18.3 The Judicial Office must be informed as early as possible of the names of counsel briefed.

Authorities

19.1 At least a week before the hearing of the appeal agents for all parties should forward to the Judicial Office a list, drawn up by junior counsel, of the law reports, text books and other authorities on which they rely.

19.2 The list should be in two parts. Part I should contain only those authorities which counsel definitely intend to cite before the House. Copies of these authorities will be made available to each member of the Appellate Committee at the hearing. Part II should contain any authorities which in the opinion of counsel might be called for in the course of the appeal but which counsel themselves do not intend to cite. Copies of these will be available only to the chairman of the Committee.

19.3 Lists should indicate by reference those particular passages of the authorities on which counsel rely.

19.4 Where a case is not reported in the *Law Reports* or *Session Cases*, references to other recognised reports should be given. In Revenue appeals *Tax Cases* may be cited but, wherever possible, references to the case in the *Law Reports* or *Session Cases* should also be given.

[1] **19.5** The House of Lords Library can arrange for copies of certain authorities to be made available at the hearing. Parties must themselves provide six copies of any other authority or of unreported cases. They must similarly provide copies of any authority of which adequate notice has not been given.

19.6 In certain circumstances parties may prefer to provide photocopies of all their authorities. In that event, the particular passages relied on should be indicated by highlighting. Parties are requested to use small, flexible covers in preference to heavy binders.

NOTE

[1] See Appendix G. On the use of unreported cases, see para. 16.7.

Costs

Submissions at the hearing

20.1 If counsel wish to seek an order other than that costs be awarded to the successful party, submissions to that effect should be made at the hearing immediately after the conclusion of the argument.

Submissions at judgment

20.2 Leave may be given to a party to make such submissions at the judgment in the House. Prior notice of intention to make submissions on costs must be given in writing to the Judicial Office, at least two clear days before the judgment, stating the nature of the order sought. A copy of the submissions must be sent to the agents for the other party or parties to the appeal.

20.3 Where one party is legally aided and where, in the event of proceedings being decided in favour of the unassisted party, the unassisted party intends to apply for costs under section 18 of the Legal Aid Act 1988, the Legal Aid Board should be informed.

Judgment

21.1 Agents will be notified of the date of judgment, which is delivered in the Chamber of the House. One junior only of counsel for each party or group of parties who have lodged a case is required to attend when judgment is delivered, and only a junior's fee will be allowed on taxation.

21.2 The opinions of the Lords of Appeal may be made available to each party a short while before judgment is given, usually at 10.30 am when judgment is to be given at 2.00 pm. In that event a strict embargo applies until after judgment has been delivered.

Order Of The House

Draft order

22.1 After the House has given judgment, drafts of the order of the House are sent to all parties who lodged a case. The drafts must be returned to the Judicial Office within one week of the date of receipt (unless otherwise directed) either approved or with suggested amendments. If substantial amendments are proposed, they must be submitted to the agents for the other parties, who should indicate their approval or disagreement, both to the agents submitting the proposals and to the Judicial Office. Where the amendments proposed are contrary to the questions put to the House, a petition should be lodged.

Final order

22.2 The agents for the successful parties taking up the judgment are notified when the final order is ready for issue. The appropriate fee is payable on collection of the certified copy.

22.3 Prints of the final order are sent free of charge to the agents for all parties who have entered appearance.

Bills Of Costs

23.1 Bills of costs for taxation must be lodged within three months from the date of the final judgment or the decision of the Appeal Committee. If an extension of the three month period is required, application should be made to the Taxing Officer in writing before the original time expires. If no application is made a bill lodged out of time will be accepted only in exceptional circumstances.

23.2 The directions relating to taxation, and the form of bill to be lodged, are available on request from the Judicial Office.

Disposal Of Security Money

24.1 Where the appellants are ordered to pay the costs of the appeal, unless otherwise agreed, respondents' costs are first satisfied, either in whole or in part, by direct payment to the respondents from money deposited in the Security Fund.

24.2 If the total amount of the respondents' costs as allowed can be so satisfied any balance of the money in the Security Fund is remitted to the party who paid it in.

24.3 If the respondents' costs are in part satisfied by such payment, the certificate of taxation which is forwarded to the respondents takes account of the amount so paid.

24.4 Where more than one bill of respondents' costs require payment by the appellants, and the money deposited as security is insufficient to satisfy all the bills, the money is divided between the bills in proportion to their amounts as allowed.

24.5 Where the appellants are not ordered to pay the costs of the appeal, money paid into the Security Fund is returned to them when the final order has been issued.

24.6 If an appeal is withdrawn before setting down, or is dismissed for want of prosecution or if the respondent fails to lodge a bill of costs within three months, the appellants may make written application to the Clerk of the Parliaments for the return to them of money deposited in the Security Fund. Such application must be accompanied by the written consent of all the respondents who have entered appearance. If any respondents refuse consent, the appellants may send them a written demand that they lodge a bill of costs within four weeks from the date of such notice; and, if the Clerk of the Parliaments is satisfied that such a demand was duly sent and, if the said respondent fails to lodge a bill of costs within the time specified, the money deposited in the Security Fund will be returned to the appellants.

III—Miscellaneous

Legal Aid

25.1 The House of Lords does not grant legal aid. Application should be made to the appropriate Area Office of the Legal Aid Board, or, in Northern Ireland, to the Legal Aid Committee, or, in Scotland, to the Scottish Legal Aid Board.

25.2 A party to whom a certificate is issued must immediately lodge the certificate, or a copy of it, in the Judicial Office. An emergency certificate, or subsequent amendments, and the authority for leading counsel, must also be lodged.

[1] **25.3** Where a prospective petitioner or appellant has applied for legal aid, the Judicial Office must be informed in writing within the original time limit for lodging the petition. The period within which a petition may be lodged will then be extended to one month after the final determination of the legal aid application. The prospective petitioner or appellant must also give notice in writing to the other parties to the proposed petition. Failure to comply with this direction will result in a petition being out of time.

[2] **25.4** Where a respondent to an appeal has applied for legal aid, the Judicial Office must be informed within the original time limit for lodging the statement and appendix. The period will then be extended to six weeks after the final determination of the legal aid application.

NOTES

[1] For petitions for leave, see para. 2. For petitions of appeal, see para. 8.

[2] See para. 14.

Cross-Appeals

[1] **26.1** The presentation of an appeal does not entitle a respondent to present a cross-appeal. Leave is required.

[2] **26.2** A petition of cross-appeal must be presented within six weeks of the presentation of the original appeal.

26.3 Argument in respect of a cross-appeal must be included by each party in their case in the original appeal. Such an inclusive case must clearly state that it is lodged in respect of both the original and cross-appeals.

26.4 Documents in respect of the original appeal and the cross-appeal should be included in one appendix. Lodgment of the statement and appendix, and setting down for hearing, are the responsibility of the original appellants.

NOTES

[1] See para. 1.5.

[2] See Standing Order VIII. For style of petition, see Appendix C.

Consolidation And Conjoinder

27.1 Where the issues in two or more appeals are similar, it may be appropriate for them to be consolidated or conjoined. Consolidation of two or more appeals results in them being carried on as a single cause with one set of counsel and one case on each side and a single appendix. Conjoinder is a looser linking of two or more appeals. The most usual form of conjoinder results in one case and one set of counsel for each of the respective appellants and for each of the respective respondents in two or more appeals, and with one appendix common to both or all the conjoined appeals. However a number of variations are possible.

[1] **27.2** Applications to consolidate or to conjoin appeals and other incidental applications must be made by petition. All parties should ensure that their requirements are covered by the petition.

27.3 The petition should be signed by the agents for all petitioners and must be submitted to the agents for all the other parties who have entered appearance for the endorsement of their consent. If consent is refused, the petition must be endorsed with a certificate that it has been served on the agents in question.

[2] **27.4** If all parties consent to or join in the petition, one copy only of the petition should be lodged, together with the appropriate fee. If any party refuses his consent, six copies of the petition should be lodged, together with the appropriate fee. In that event the petition will be referred to an Appeal Committee.

NOTES

[1] For style, see Appendix E.

[2] See para. 29.

Withdrawal Of Petitions

Petitions for leave to appeal

28.1 A petition for leave to appeal may be withdrawn by writing to the Principal Clerk, stating that the parties to the petition have agreed how the costs should be settled. The respondents should notify the Judicial Office of their agreement.

Petitions of appeal

28.2 An appeal which has not been set down for hearing may be withdrawn by writing to the Principal Clerk, stating that the parties to the appeal have agreed the costs of the appeal. The nature of the agreement should be indicated. Where appropriate, the letter should also indicate how the security money should be disposed of. Written notification must also be given to the respondents who must notify the Judicial Office of their agreement to the withdrawal of the appeal and who must confirm that the costs have been agreed.

28.3 An appeal which has been set down for hearing may only be withdrawn by order of the House on petition. Such petition, which may include submissions on costs, must be submitted for their consent to those respondents who have entered appearance. The petition should be lodged with the appropriate fee.

Opposed Incidental Petitions

29.1 Unless the Principal Clerk directs otherwise, opposed incidental petitions (including any interlocutory petition which relates to any petition of appeal) will be referred to an Appeal Committee.

29.2 Six copies of the petition must be lodged together with the appropriate fee. The original petition should bear a certificate of service on the other parties.

29.3 If an oral hearing is ordered the parties may apply at that time to hand in affidavits and such other documents as they may wish. Six copies will be required. Copies of such documents must be served on the other parties before the oral hearing.

New Submissions

30.1 If, after the conclusion of the argument of an appeal, a party wishes to bring to the notice of the House new circumstances which have arisen and which might affect the decision or order of the House, application must be made forthwith for leave to make new submissions. The application should indicate the circumstances and the submissions it is desired to make, and a copy must be sent to the agents for the other parties to the appeal.

Abatement Through Death

31.1 In the event of the death of a party to an appeal notice in writing must be given immediately both to the Clerk of the Parliaments and to the other parties. The appeal abates as from the date of death and cannot proceed until a petition for revivor has been agreed to by the House.

[1] **31.2** A petition for revivor must be lodged, together with the appropriate fee, within three months of the date of death. It must be accompanied by an affidavit explaining the circumstances in which the petition for revivor is lodged. The petition must be endorsed with a certificate of service on the respondents.

31.3 If abatement takes place after the case for the deceased person has been lodged and before the appeal has been heard, the appellants must lodge a supplemental case setting out the orders of the House on revivor and information as to the newly added parties.

NOTE

[1] See Standing Orders XI.

Defect Through Bankruptcy

32.1 If a party to an appeal is adjudicated bankrupt immediate notice must be given in writing to the other parties and to the Clerk of the Parliaments, who must also be provided with a certified copy of the Bankruptcy Order. The appeal cannot proceed until a petition to render the appeal effective has been agreed to by the House.

32.2 Such a petition must be lodged within three months of the date of the notice.

[1] **32.3** The form of petition and the procedure for a supplemental case follows that for abatement.

NOTE

[1] See Standing Order XI and para. 31.

Appeal Against Order For Revocation Of Patent

33.1 These Directions apply to any appeal direct from the High Court in pursuance of sections 12 and 13 of the Administration of Justice Act 1969, from an order for the revocation of a patent made under section 32 or 61 of the Patents Act 1949 or under section 72 of the Patents Act 1977.

33.2 Notice of intention to present an appeal, with a copy of the petition of appeal, must be served on the Comptroller-General of Patents, Designs and Trade Marks, as well as on the respondents.

33.3 If, at any time before the appeal comes on for hearing, the respondents decide not to appear on the appeal or not to oppose it, they must forthwith serve notice of this decision on the Comptroller and on the appellants. Any such notice served on the Comptroller must be accompanied by a copy of the petition under the said section 32 or of the pleadings in the action and the affidavits filed therein.

33.4 The Comptroller must, within 14 days of receiving notice of the respondents' decision, serve on the appellant and lodge in the Judicial Office a notice stating whether or not he intends to appear on the appeal.

33.5 The Comptroller may appear and be heard in opposition to the appeal:—

(*a*) in any case where he has given notice of his intention to appear, and

(*b*) in any other case (including in particular a case where the respondents withdraw opposition to the appeal during the hearing) if the House so directs or allows.

33.6 The House will make such orders for the postponement or adjournment of the hearing of the appeal as may appear necessary for the purpose of giving effect to the provisions of these Directions.

Interveners

[1] **34.1** Participation in a cause as an intervener in a court below does not entitle a person to intervene in the House of Lords. Application for leave to intervene must be made by petition, lodged together with the appropriate fee. The petition should be certified with the consent of the parties in the case. If consent is refused, the petition should be endorsed with a certificate of service on the parties. All petitions for leave to intervene, whether opposed by the parties or not, will be referred to an Appeal Committee.

NOTE
[1] See para. 29.

Exhibits

35.1 Parties who require exhibits (such as machines in a patent action) to be available for inspection at the hearing must apply to the Judicial Office for permission for the exhibits to be brought to the House before the hearing.

Nautical Assessors

[1] **36.1** Any party to an appeal in an Admiralty action or maritime cause may apply in writing to the Clerk of the Parliaments for nautical assessors to attend the hearing.

36.2 The fees payable to nautical assessors are those payable in the Admiralty Court and the Court of Appeal.

NOTE
[1] See Standing Order XV.

PREPARATION OF DOCUMENTS

General

37.1 Documents which are not clearly legible or which are not produced in the form specified will not be accepted.

37.2 The Judicial Office can give advice as to the form and content of documents for lodging. Parties are advised to consult the office at all stages of preparation and should submit proofs for approval where appropriate.

37.3 Appendix F shows the numbers of documents usually required for the hearing of an appeal.

37.4 All formal documents should be produced on good quality A4 paper, bound on the left and using both sides of the paper.

Form of statement and case

37.5 The statement and case should be produced with letters down the inside margin. The outside margin should carry references to the relevant pages of the appendix.

37.6 The front page of the statement should carry the references of every law report of the cause in the courts below. A head-note summary should be given, whether or not the cause has been reported.

37.7 The front page of the statement should carry an indication of the time occupied by the cause in each court below.

37.8 The statement should be signed by counsel on both sides, and their names clearly indicated. Where the statement is not agreed to by all parties it should be signed by counsel for the appellants and should indicate that the respondents have been given due facilities for joining in the statement.

37.9 Each party's case should be signed by their counsel.

Form of appendix

37.10 The appendix should be bound with plastic comb binding, in limp cornflower blue covers, of Fibrex board.

37.11 All documents must be numbered and each part of the appendix must contain a list of its contents.

37.12 Documents should be reproduced economically and in the minimum number necessary for the purposes of the appeal.

37.13 Documents of an unsuitable size or form for binding with the other documents—such as maps, booklets—should be inserted in pockets at the back of the appropriate volume.

Form of bound volumes

37.14 The bound volumes should be bound in the same manner as the appendix. They should contain cut out indices for each of the items listed in Direction 16.1, tabbed with the name of the document on the front sheet of each. The front cover should carry a list of the contents and the names of the agents for all parties. The short title of the cause should be given on a strip affixed to the plastic spine. Each volume should include a few blank pages at either end.

DISPOSAL OF DOCUMENTS

38.1 All petitions and supporting documents lodged become the property of the House. However if application is made in writing within fourteen days of the determination of an appeal, or a petition for leave to appeal, documents other than the original petition may, at the direction of the Principal Clerk, be returned to the parties.

PAYMENTS AND DEPOSITS

39.1 Payments of fees and deposits of security money may be made in cash or by bankers draft or cheque. Drafts and cheques for fees must be made payable to "House of Lords Account". Drafts and cheques for security money must be made payable to "House of Lords Security Fund Account". Personal cheques are not accepted.

Lodgment

[1] **40.1** "Lodgment" and "lodging" mean delivery to a member of the Judicial Office staff, either in person during opening hours or by post. Where the time for lodging a document expires on a Saturday, Sunday, Bank holiday or any other day on which the Judicial Office is closed, it will be received if it is lodged on the first day on which the Office is again open.

40.2 Communications may be transmitted by facsimile, and the cost of such transmission will be allowed on taxation, only where urgent circumstances make this appropriate. No document which is to be presented to the House or on which a fee is payable may be so transmitted.

40.3 Any agent who attends the Judicial Office to lodge papers must be fully conversant with the matter to be dealt with.

NOTE

[1] See also Standing Order IX.

[THE NEXT PAGE IS B 519]

Standing Orders

Standing Order No. 14 of the House of Lords relating to Public Business

Recall of the House, 20th May 1970

14.—(1) If, during any adjournment of the House, the Lord Chancellor is satisfied that the public interest requires that the House should meet at a time earlier than that appointed, he may signify that he is so satisfied and notice shall be given and thereupon the House shall meet at the time stated in the notice, as if it had been duly adjourned to that time.

(2) If the Lord Chancellor is unable to act for the purposes of this Standing Order, the Chairman of Committees, after consultation with Her Majesty's Government, may act in his stead.

(3) Notwithstanding any adjournment of the House, the House may meet for judicial business at a time earlier than that appointed if the Lord Chancellor or, in his absence, the senior Lord of Appeal in Ordinary, is satisfied that it should do so and has signified that he is so satisfied and has given notice to such Lords as he thinks fit.

Standing Order No. 82 of the House of Lords relating to Public Business

Appellate and Appeal Committees, 20th May 1970, 28th January 1984

82.—(1) For the purposes of its appellate jurisdiction, the House shall have Appellate and Appeal Committees, of which all Lords qualified under the Appellate Jurisdiction Acts 1876 and 1887 shall be members.

(2) These Committeees shall be:—

(*a*) two Appellate Committees, which shall hear any cause or matter referred to them and shall report thereon to the House;

(*b*) two Appeal Committees, which shall consider any petition or application for leave to appeal that may be referred to them and any matter relating thereto, or to causes depending, or formerly depending, in this House, and shall report thereon to the House.

(3) In any criminal matter, or in any matter concerning extradition, an Appeal Committee may take decisions and give directions on behalf of the House.

(4) In any Appellate or Appeal Committee the Chair shall be taken by the Lord Chancellor or, in his absence, by the senior Lord of Appeal in Ordinary present, such seniority being determined in accordance with the Commission for the time being appointing Speakers for the purpose of the hearing and determination of Appeals.

(5) For the purposes of section 8 of the Appellate Jurisdiction Act 1876, any Appellate Committee may sit and act while Parliament is prorogued.

Standing Orders of the House of Lords regulating Judicial Business, made in pursuance of the Appellate Jurisdiction Act 1876 and subsequent enactments

I

Time limited for presenting appeals. ORDERED, that no petition of appeal be received by this House unless the same be lodged in the Parliament Office for presentation to the House within the period of three months from the date of the last order or interlocutor appealed from.

II

Leave to appeal from the Courts of Appeal. ORDERED, that, in all appeals from the Court of Appeal, the Court of Appeal in Northern Ireland or the

Court of Session in Scotland in which the leave of the House is required under the provisions of any Act of Parliament, a petition for leave to appeal be lodged in the Parliament Office within one month from the date of the last order or judgment appealed from, and that such petition be referred to an Appeal Committee to consider whether such leave should be granted.

III

Leave to appeal from the High Court. ORDERED, that, in all cases where application is made for leave for an appeal to be brought direct to the House from the High Court of Justice in England and Wales or from the High Court of Justice in Northern Ireland—

(*a*) a petition for such leave, together with the certificate granted by the High Court under section 12 of the Administration of Justice Act 1969, be lodged in the Parliament Office within one month from the date of the grant of such certificate or within such extended time as in any particular case the House may allow;

(*b*) any such petition, and any application for extension of time or other incidental matter, be referred to an Appeal Committee for their consideration and report.

IV

Appeals to be signed and certified by counsel. ORDERED, that, except in cases where leave to appeal has been granted under the provisions of any Act of Parliament, all petitions of appeal be signed, and the reasonableness thereof certified by two counsel.

V

Order of service. ORDERED, that the order of service issued upon the presentation of an appeal for service on the respondent or his solicitor be returned to the Parliament Office, together with an affidavit of due service entered thereon, within the time limited by Standing Order No. VII for the appellant to lodge his cases, unless within that period all the Respondents shall have lodged their cases; in default the appeal to stand dismissed.

VI

(1) *Security for costs.* ORDERED, that in all appeals the appellants do give security for costs by paying into the House of Lords Security Fund Account within one week of the presentation of the appeal such sum as shall be authorised from time to time by the House, to be subject to the order of the House with regard to the costs of the appeal.

On default by the appellants in complying with the above conditions, the appeal to stand dismissed.

(2) *Exemptions.* ORDERED, that this Standing Order shall not apply (*a*) to appellants who have been granted legal aid, (*b*) to appellants in appeals under the Child Abduction and Custody Act 1985, or (*c*) to a minister or Government department.

VII

(1) *Time for lodging statement.* ORDERED, that the statement and the appendix thereto be lodged in the Parliament Office within six weeks from the date of the presentation of the appeal to the House; and the appeal be set down for hearing on the first sitting day thereafter; on default by the appellant, the appeal to stand dismissed.

(2) *Scottish Appeals.* ORDERED, that in all appeals from Scotland the appellant in the appendix shall lay before this House a copy of the record

as authenticated by the Deputy Principal Clerk of Session or a Clerk of Session delegated by him; together with a supplement containing an account, without argument or statement of other facts, of the further steps which have been taken in the cause since the record was completed, and containing also copies of the interlocutors or parts of interlocutors complained of; and each party shall in his case lay before the House a copy of the case presented by him to the Court of Session, if any such case was presented there, with a short summary of any additional reasons upon which he means to insist; and if there shall have been no case presented to the Court of Session then each party shall set forth in his case the reasons upon which he founds his argument, as shortly and succinctly as possible.

(3) *Statement to be signed by counsel.* ORDERED, that the statement be signed by one or more counsel for each party, who shall have attended as counsel in the Court below, or shall purpose attending as counsel at the hearing in this House.

VIII

Cross-appeals. ORDERED, that all cross-appeals be presented to the House within the period allowed by Standing Order No. VII for lodging the statement in the original appeal.

IX

Expiry of time during recess. ORDERED, with regard to appeals in which the periods under Standing Orders Nos. V, VI, VII and VIII expire during the recess of the House, that such periods be extended to the third sitting day of the next ensuing meeting of the House.

Provided that if the House is recalled in pursuance of Public Business Standing Order No. 14 or Proclamation, any day on which the House sits pursuant to such recall is not a sitting day for the purposes of this Standing Order.

X

Legal aid. ORDERED, that where a party to an appeal has applied for legal aid, and the application has not been determined before the expiration of the periods of time limited by Standing Orders Nos. I, II or III such periods of time shall be extended until one month after the final refusal of the application or the issue of a certificate.

XI

Abatement or defect. ORDERED, that in the event of abatement by death or defect through bankruptcy, an appeal shall not stand dismissed for default under Standing Orders Nos. V, VI or VII, provided that notice of such abatement or defect be given by a letter from the appellant's agent addressed to the Clerk of the Parliaments and lodged in the Judicial Office prior to the expiration of the period limited by the Standing Order under which the appeal would otherwise have stood dismissed.

Revivor, etc. ORDERED, that all appeals marked on the cause list of the House as abated or defective shall stand dismissed unless, within three months from the date of the notice to the Clerk of the Parliaments of abatement or defect, if the House be then sitting, or, if not, then not later than the third sitting day of the next ensuing sittings of the House, a petition shall be presented to the House for reviving the appeal or for rendering the same effective.

Supplemental case. ORDERED, that when an appeal has abated or become defective after the cases have been lodged, and it is subsequently revived or rendered effective, a supplemental case shall be lodged by the appellant setting forth the order or orders made by the House reviving the appeal or rendering the same effective.

The like rule shall be observed by the appellant and respondent respectively, where any person or persons shall, by leave of the House, upon petition or otherwise, be added as a party or parties to the said appeal after the cases in such appeal shall have been lodged.

XII

Certificate of leave or difference of opinion in Scottish appeals. ORDERED, that when any petition of appeal shall be presented to this House from any interlocutory judgment of either division of the Lords of Session in Scotland, the counsel who shall sign the said petition, or two of the counsel for the party or parties in the court below, shall sign a certificate or declaration, stating either that leave was given by that division of the judges pronouncing such interlocutory judgment to the appellant or appellants to present such petition of appeal, or that there was a difference of opinion amongst the judges of the said division pronouncing such interlocutory judgment.

XIII

Taxation of costs. ORDERED, that the Clerk of the Parliaments shall appoint such person as he may think fit as Taxing Officer, and in all cases in which this House shall make any order for payment of costs by any party or parties in any cause, the amount thereof to be certified by the Clerk of the Parliaments, the Taxing Officer shall tax the bill of costs so ordered to be paid, and ascertain the amount thereof, and report the same to the Clerk of the Parliaments or Clerk Assistant: And it is further ordered, that the same fees shall be demanded from and paid by the party applying for such taxation for and in respect thereof as are now charged or shall be authorised from time to time by the House; and such fees shall be added at the foot of the said bill of costs as taxed. And the Clerk of the Parliaments or Clerk Assistant may give a certificate of such costs, expressing the amount so reported to him as aforesaid, and in his certificate, as well as in the Taxing Officer's report, regard shall be had to any sum that has been paid in to the security fund account of the House, as directed by Standing Order No. VI; and the amount in money certified by him in such certificate shall be the sum to be demanded and paid under or by virtue of such order as aforesaid for payment of costs.

XIV

Fees. ORDERED, that fees be taken in this House on the documents specified in the Schedule hereto, that the fees to be charged shall be such as shall be authorised from time to time by the House, and that none of the said documents be issued from, or received at the Parliament Office, unless it shall have been endorsed by the Accountant and Receiver of Fees with the date of lodgment and the amount of fee paid.

SCHEDULE

Interlocutory petitions referred to an Appeal Committee (including the Report thereon).
" petition of appeal.
" notice of appearance.
" waiver of security for costs.
" petition not referred to Appeal Committee.
" joint petition (from each party thereto).

" application to set down for hearing.
" petition to withdraw appeal after setting down.
" final judgment.

XV

Nautical assessors. (1) ORDERED, that the parties, or either party, to an appeal may apply by letter to the Clerk of the Parliaments requesting, upon grounds stated in the letter, the attendance of nautical assessors, or the Lord Chancellor or the Lord Speaker may, in the absence of any application by the parties, direct the attendance of nautical assessors.

(2) ORDERED, that in each appeal in which the attendance of nautical assessors is required, there shall be two assessors, to be selected by the Lord Chancellor or the Lord Speaker and of whom one shall be an Officer, active or retired, of Her Majesty's Navy, and the other an Elder Brother of the Corporation of Trinity House.

(3) ORDERED, that the fees to be paid to each assessor for each day or part of a day's attendance shall be such as shall be authorised from time to time by the House.

(4) ORDERED, that assessors, other than Elder Brethren of the Corporation of Trinity House, shall, in addition to the attendance fee, be paid reasonable sums in respect of travelling expenses and subsistence.

(5) ORDERED, that the amount of such fees and expenses, failing any special order of the House on the subject, shall be paid by the party against whom costs are awarded, or by his agent, into the House of Lords Account immediately after the determination of the appeal.

APPENDIX A

(See Direction No. 3)

Form of Petition for Leave to Appeal

In the House of Lords.

On Appeal from Her Majesty's Court of Appeal (England)[1]
(Set out title of cause)[2]

To the Right Honourable the House of Lords

THE HUMBLE PETITION OF *(set out full name(s) and address(es) of Petitioner(s))* SHEWETH—
That [set out briefly in numbered paragraphs such facts and arguments as may be necessary to enable the Appeal Committee to report to the House whether leave to appeal should be granted].

YOUR PETITIONER(S) HUMBLY SUBMIT(S) that leave to appeal to your Lordships' House should be granted for the following among other

REASONS

(*Here give numbered reasons, generally summarising the foregoing arguments.*)

And your Petitioner(s) will ever pray.

(*Signature of petitioner(s) or petitioner's agents.*)

Form of Certificate of Service to be endorsed on the back of the original Petition for Leave to Appeal

I/We, Messrs , of , [agents for] the Petitioner(s) within-named, hereby certify that on the day of we served [Messrs. , of , agents for] , the within-named Respondent(s) with a correct copy of the aforegoing Petition, and with a notice that on the day of , or as soon after as conveniently may be, the Petition for leave to appeal would be presented to the House of Lords on behalf of the Petitoner(s).

(*Signature of petitioner(s) or petitioners' agents.*)

NOTES

[1] Or the relevant court.

[2] Petitions for leave to appeal to the House of Lords carry the same title as in the court below.

APPENDIX B

(See Direction No. 2)

Form of Petition for Leave to Appeal out of time

In the House of Lords.

ON APPEAL FROM HER MAJESTY'S COURT OF APPEAL (ENGLAND)[1]

(*Set out title of cause*)[2]

To the Right Honourable the House of Lords.

THE HUMBLE PETITION OF [*set out full name(s) and address(es) of Petitioner(s)*] PRAYING FOR LEAVE TO APPEAL NOTWITHSTANDING THAT THE TIME LIMITED BY STANDING ORDER NO. II HAS EXPIRED SHEWETH—

That (*set out briefly in numbered paragraphs the reasons why the petition was not lodged in time*).

That (*continue as indicated, in Appendix A*).

NOTES

[1] Or the relevant court.

[2] Petitions for Leave to appeal to the House of Lords carry the same title as in the court below.

APPENDIX C

(See Directions Nos. 14 and 22)

Form of Petition of Appeal or Cross-appeal

In the House of Lords.

ON APPEAL FROM HER MAJESTY'S COURT OF APPEAL (ENGLAND)[1]

between:

(*Set out title of cause*) [2]

To the Right Honourable the House of Lords.

THE HUMBLE PETITION and (CROSS-)APPEAL OF (*set out the full name(s) and address(es) of the Appellant(s)*).

YOUR PETITIONER(S) humbly pray(s) that the matter of the order (interlocutor(s)) set forth in the Schedule hereto (*if partly appealed against insert the words*:—so far as therein stated to be appealed against) may be reviewed before Her Majesty the

Queen, in Her Court of Parliament, and that the said Order (Interlocutor(s)) (*if partly appealed against insert the words:*—so far as aforesaid) may be reversed, varied or altered, [and that (*if specific relief is asked for, it should be so stated*)] or that the petitioner(s) may have such other relief in the premises as to Her Majesty the Queen, in Her Court of Parliament, may seem meet; and that (*set out the full names of the respondent(s)*) mentioned in the schedule to the appeal, may be ordered to lodge such case [3] as they may be advised, and the circumstances of the cause may require, in answer to this (cross-)appeal; and that service of such order on the solicitors in the cause of the said respondent(s) may be deemed good service.

To be signed here (see Direction No. 16).

NOTES

[1] Or the relevant court.

[2] Appeals to the House of Lords carry the same title as in the court below. In a petition of cross-appeal, the original respondent in the House of Lords lodging the cross-appeal should be designated the cross-appellant and the original appellant should be designated the cross-respondent.

[3] See Directions, paras. 16.9–16.11 as to lodgment of separate respondents' cases.

THE SCHEDULE ABOVE REFERRED TO

From HER MAJESTY'S COURT of APPEAL (ENGLAND)

(*or other Court*)

In a certain cause (*or other matter*) wherein A was (were) plaintiff(s) (*or other designation*) and B was (were) defendant(s) (*or other designation*). (*The names of all parties to the action, whether originally in the cause or added by subsequent order, must be given.*)

(*When the whole order or interlocutor is appealed against the following wording should be used.*)

The order (or interlocutor(s)) of (state court and date of order or interlocutor(s)) appealed from is (are) in the words following:—

[The whole of the order or interlocutor(s), including the recital, must be set forth. The order or interlocutor(s) must be underlined, with the exception of the recital which should not be underlined. If the order or interlocutor includes leave to appeal to the House of Lords, that part should not be underlined.]

(*When a part only of the order or interlocutor is appealed against, the following wording should be used.*)

The order, (or interlocutor(s)) of (state court and date of order or interlocutor(s)) referred to in the above prayer is (are) in the words following, the portion(s) complained of being underlined:—

[The whole of the order or interlocutor(s), including the recital, must be set forth, the part(s) complained of being underlined. The remainder, including the recital, should not be underlined.]

[Where leave to appeal has been granted by a subsequent order of the court or by order of the House on report from the Appeal Committee, that order must also be set out (not underlined).]

(*The following must be added when leave to appeal is not required under the provisions of any Act of Parliament (see Direction No. 16)*).

We humbly conceive this to be a proper case to be heard before your Lordships by way of appeal.

Signatures of two counsel.

(*The special certificate required by S.O. XII in certain Scottish appeals must also be added if necessary.*)

Form of Certificate of Service to be endorsed on the back of the original Petition of Appeal

We, Messrs , of , agents for the (cross-)appellant(s) within-named, hereby certify that on the day of we served Messrs of , agents for , the within-named respondent(s) with a correct copy of the aforegoing appeal, and with notice that on the day of , or as soon after as conveniently may be, the petition for leave to appeal would be presented to the House of Lords on behalf of the (cross-)appellant(s).

(*Signature of appellant(s) or appellants' agents.*)

APPENDIX D

(See Direction No. 14)

Form of Petition for Extension of Time to Lodge Statement

In the House of Lords.

ON APPEAL FROM HER MAJESTY'S COURT OF APPEAL (ENGLAND) [1]

between

To the Right Honourable the House of Lords.

THE HUMBLE PETITION of the appellants SHEWETH—

That your petitioners presented a petition of appeal on the day of 19 complaining of an order of the Court of Appeal dated the day of 19 .

That the time allowed by Standing Order No. VII for the appellants to lodge the statement and appendix and to set down the cause for hearing will expire/originally expired [2] on the day of 19 .

That the House, pursuant to a petition from the appellants, granted an extension of time in which to lodge the case and the appendix and set down the cause for hearing to the day of 19 .[2]

That the House, pursuant to a further petition from the appellants, granted a second extension of time until the day of 19 .[2]

That the petitioners will be unable to lodge the statement and appendix by the said date for the following reasons:—

(*Set out brief reasons.*)

THEREFORE YOUR PETITIONERS HUMBLY PRAY

That your Lordships will be pleased to grant an extension of time until the day of 19 to lodge the statement and appendix and set down the cause for hearing.

And your petitioners will ever pray.

(*Signature of agents.*)
Agents for the appellants

Set out below name and address of appellant's agents.

We consent to the prayer of the above petition.

(*Signature of agents.*)
Agents for the Respondents

NOTES

[1] Or relevant court.

[2] Delete as appropriate.

APPENDIX E

(See Direction No. 27)

Form of Petition for Consolidation, Conjoinder, etc.

In the House of Lords.

ON APPEAL FROM (*name relevant court below*).

BETWEEN

and

AND BETWEEN

and

To the Right Honourable the House of Lords.

THE HUMBLE PETITION of (name of appellant(s)) SHEWETH

That your petitioner(s) presented (a) petition(s) of appeal on the day of 19 complaining of (an) order(s) of the (*name relevant court below*) dated the day of 19 .

That your petitioners (*name appellants in other appeal(s), if different*) presented (a) petition(s) of appeal on the day of 19 complaining of (an) order(s) of the (*name relevant court below*) dated the day of 19 .

That the same matters of law are raised in each of the appeals (and that the appeals of the (*name relevant parties*) to (*name relevant court below*) were heard and argued together and one judgment was delivered in respect of the (two) appeals).

That it is expedient that (your petitioners') said appeals be consolidated/conjoined.

YOUR PETITIONERS THEREFORE HUMBLY PRAY

(*Consolidation*)

1. That the said appeals may be consolidated and that they be allowed to lodge one statement and appendix applicable to the (*insert relevant number*) appeals and that the respondents have leave to lodge one case in respect of the appeals.

or

(*Conjoinder*)

1. That the said appeals may be conjoined and that they be allowed to lodge separate statements and one appendix in respect of the (*insert relevant number*) appeals and that the respondents have leave to lodge separate cases in respect of the appeals or that such other order may be made with a view to the convenient conduct of the said appeals as to your Lordships may seem meet.[1]

And your petitioners will ever pray

Agents for the (co-)petitioners
Agents for the co-petitioners

We consent to the prayer of the above petition

Agents for the respondents
Agents for the respondents
etc.

NOTE

[1] Or other variation as required. Agents should consult the Judicial Office.

APPENDIX F

Numbers of Documents Normally Required for the Hearing of an Appeal

(The numbers shown below are the minimum specifically laid down in the Directions. Actual requirements must be subject to agreement, to the number of parties, counsel and agents concerned, and to the special circumstances of each appeal. Copies for the use of the party originating the documents are in addition to the numbers indicated.)

Appellants must provide:	*For Judicial Office*	*For other side*
(1) Petition of appeal	original and 5 on lodgment 15 in bound volumes	2 on service
(2) Statement	6 on lodgment 15 in bound volumes	as arranged
(3) Case	6 on setting down 15 in bound volumes	as arranged on exchange
(4) Appendix Part I	6 on setting down 15 in bound volumes	1 advance copy: otherwise as arranged
(5) Appendix Part II and subsequent Parts	15 on setting down	1 advance copy: otherwise as arranged

Appellants must provide:	*For Judicial Office*	*For other side*
(6) Bound volumes	15 (after exchange of case)	as arranged
Respondents must provide:		
(1) Case	6 on lodgment	as arranged on exchange 15 for bound volumes for the House
(2) Respondents' additional documents (if any)...................................	6 (if supplementary to part 1 of the appendix) 15 on lodgment (if supplementary to part 2 or any other part of the appendix)	15 for bound volumes (if supplementary to part I of appendix)

APPENDIX G

(See Direction No. 44)

AUTHORITIES

The House of Lords Library has five sets of the following authorities:—

Law Reports from 1866
The English Reports
Weekly Law Reports
All England Reports
Criminal Appeal Reports
Reports of Patent Cases
Session Cases
Tax Cases
Statutes
European Court Reports
Lloyds Law Reports

The Library has one set of each of the following:—

Anglo American Law Review
British Yearbook of International Law
Cambridge Law Journal
Canadian Rights Reporter
Common Market Law Reports
Common Market Law Review
Criminal Appeal Reports (Sentencing)
Criminal Law Review
Crown Office Digest
Estates Gazette Law Reports (from 1985)
European Human Rights Law Journal
European Human Rights Law Reports
European Law Digest
European Law Review
Family Law Reports
Financial Law Reports
Fleet Street Reports
Halsburys Laws and Statutes
Housing Law Reports
Human Rights Law Journal
Immigration Appeal Reports
Industrial Cases Reports

Industrial Relations Law Reports
Industrial Tribunal Reports 1967–78
International and Comparative Law Quarterly
Irish Jurist 1848–1866, 1935–1965
Irish Jurist Reports
Irish Law Reports
Journal of Legal History
Journal of Social Welfare Law
The Jurist-Reports of Cases in Law and Equity (1838–1866)
Justice of the Peace Reports
Law Quarterly Review
Law Times Reports
Legislative Studies Quarterly
Local Government Review Reports
Modern Law Review
Northern Ireland Law Reports
Northern Ireland Legal Quarterly (From Vol. 34 1983)
Northern Ireland Statutes
Oxford Journal of Legal Studies
Planning and Compensation Reports (1963–67)
Property and Compensation Reports (1968–)
Public Law (British Journal of Administrative Law)
Road Traffic Reports
Rydes Rating Cases 1956–1979
Scots Law Times
Scottish Criminal Case Reports (From 1983)
Scottish Jurist 1829–1873
Scottish Law Reporter 1865–1924
Scottish Planning Law and Practice
Simons Tax Cases (From 1981)
Solicitors Journal
Times Law Reports
Weekly Notes (1866–1952)
Weekly Reporter (1852–1906)

APPENDIX H

[[1] *Fees and Security Money*]

NOTE
[1] As amended, 9th April 1991.

---

(1) Judicial Fees

	£
Petition of appeal	60
Notice of appearance	7
Waiver of security for costs	15
Petition not referred to Appeal Committee (including incidental petition to conjoin or consolidate)	30
Petition referred to Appeal Committee (including report thereon)	35
Joint petition (from each party thereto)	15
Application to set down for hearing	320
Final judgment	35

(2) Taxing Fee

The fees payable upon the sums allowed by the Taxing Officer are as follows:—

(1) On bills taxed on or after 1 April 1983, where the amount allowed does not exceed £500, a flat rate of £25 be charged.

(2) On bills taxed on or after 1 April 1983, where the amount allowed exceeds £500, for every £1 or fraction of £1 an amount of 5p be charged.

(3) On the withdrawal of a bill of costs which has been lodged for taxation, such fee as may be reasonable having regard to the amount of work done:
Provided that the fee shall not exceed the amount payable under paragraphs (1) or (2) above if the bill had been allowed in full.

(3) Security Money

Security for costs, to be paid by appellant 12,000

Forms of Bills of Costs applicable to Judicial Taxations in the House of Lords in Civil Appeals from the Court of Appeal in England; the High Court of Justice in England and Wales; the Court of Session in Scotland; the Court of Appeal in Northern Ireland . . . 1988.

This edition of the Forms of Bills of Costs applicable to Judicial Taxations in the House of Lords supersedes all previous editions. The new scale will apply in respect of petitions for leave to appeal presented after 7th July 1988 or an entitlement to costs created by orders or judgments made on or after 1st October 1988 but excluding item 4(a) where a petition for leave has been presented prior to 7th July 1988.

(1) Directions for the Taxation of Bills of Costs in the House of Lords

Lodgment

[1] **1.** Bills of costs for taxation must be lodged within three months of:
(i) the date of the final judgment
(ii) the date on which a petition for leave to appeal is before an Appeal Committee.

NOTE

[1] As amended, 23rd November 1989. The practice direction of 11th June 1990 emphasises this time limit and further provides:

"In future these directions will be strictly adhered to. A bill presented for taxation outside the time limit in respect of which no application for an extension of time has been received, will only be accepted in exceptional circumstances."

Extension of time

[1] **2.** If an extension of the three month period is required application must be made in writing to the Taxing Officer before the expiry of the period. Agents wishing to lodge bills outside the time limits mentioned at (1) above should seek in writing the approval of the Taxing Officer and state the reasons for the delay.

NOTE

[1] The practice direction of 11th June 1990 emphasises this time limit and further provides:

"In future these directions will be strictly adhered to. A bill presented for taxation outside the time limit in respect of which no application for an extension of time has been received, will only be accepted in exceptional circumstances."

Documents

3. Except for counsel's brief and a breakdown of the instructions item where necessary, no documents are required to be lodged with the bill before taxation. Agents are nevertheless at liberty to lodge any papers that they think may assist the Taxing Officer.

Endorsement

4. The bill must be endorsed before lodgment with a certificate of service on the agents for parties entitled to be represented at the taxation and to whom a notice of appointment to tax will be sent after the bill has been lodged.

Agents for successful unassisted parties, whose costs have been ordered to be paid out of the Legal Aid Fund pursuant to the Legal Aid Act 1974, must lodge a copy of the bill with the appropriate Legal Aid Area Committee and endorse the bill accordingly.

Appointment for taxation

5. The Taxing Officer, who is the Principal Clerk of the Judicial Office, will give to the party beginning the proceedings, and to any other party entitled to be heard in the taxation proceeding, not less than seven days' notice of the day and time appointed for taxation. Only the agent who had carriage of the matter in the House of Lords or his deputy may attend the taxation.

A request for a provisional taxation should be made at the time of lodgment.

(Taxations are conducted in the Principal Clerk's Room (Room 22, First Floor, West Front).)

Taxing Officer's discretion

6. It is within the discretion of the Taxing Officer to allow further charges in relation to items not mentioned in the scale.

Form of bill

7. *In drawing the bill the items should be numbered in accordance with the scale and, where possible, similarly worded.* Agents are required to adhere to the items shown in the scale. Anything not otherwise provided for should be either inserted at a convenient point in the bill or included in the instructions item. The standard three column bill paper should be used.

Legal aid

8.—(i) Items relating to the issue etc. of legal aid orders should be included in the correct chronological order, but not numbered.

(ii) Where costs are to be taxed both *inter partes* and under the Second Schedule to the Legal Aid Act 1974, or the Second Schedule to the Legal Aid, Advice and Assistance (Northern Ireland) Order 1981, a suitable bill should be drawn.

[THE NEXT PAGE IS B 531]

Allocatur

9. Forms of allocatur can be obtained from the Taxing Clerk on taxation and must be returned within one month of the date of taxation, signed by all agents who attended the taxation, together with the completed bill. (See example at the end of these notes.)

Vouching

10. Unless covered by a certificate of discharge (see below), receipted vouchers must be produced on completion of the bill. Counsel's fee notes must be receipted except in the case of legal aid bills. (Agents wishing to vouch and complete bills are asked to inform the Taxing Clerk in advance.)

Certificate of discharge

11. A certificate in the following form must be accepted as evidence of payment of any disbursement not exceeding £200 (other than fees to counsel) providing the paying party does not require otherwise and subject to any direction to the contrary that may be given by the Taxing Officer:

We A. B. & Co.,

Hereby certify that all disbursements listed in the taxed bill in the matter of C. v. D. which individually do not exceed £200 (other than those relating to Counsel's fees) have been duly discharged.

(*signed*)

A. B. & Co.

Summary

12. The summary when completed should show the total amount taxed-off profit costs. Where, in the substance of the bill, an amount on which VAT is due has been reduced, the VAT should be recalculated before the summary is prepared.

Statutory deduction in respect of:
Legal Aid Fund and Northern Ireland Legal Aid Fund

13. Solicitors and counsel acting under civil aid certificates, are entitled to receive from the above mentioned funds such costs, disbursements and fees as are allowed on a taxation under the Second Schedule to the Legal Aid Act 1974, or under the Second Schedule to the Legal Aid, Advice and Assistance (Northern Ireland) Order 1981, subject to the statutory deduction of 5 *per centum* of counsel's fees and profit costs, or 10 *per centum* if the taxation was held before 1st January 1988. Where an order for taxation is made on or after 29th July 1988 no deduction is made.

Taxing fee

14.—(i) On bills where the amount allowed does not exceed £500, a flat rate of £25.

(ii) On bills where the amount allowed exceeds £500, for every £1 or fraction of £1 an amount of 5p.

(Drafts and cheques for taxing fees are payable to the "House of Lords Account")

Certificates

15. (*a*) *Civil.* When the taxing fee has been paid, a certificate of taxation for the costs as allowed is forwarded to the agents who lodged the bill, except in the case of respondents whose costs can be wholly satisfied from moneys deposited as security (see Dir. 48(i) (Civil)).

(*b*) *Criminal.* Where the costs have been ordered to be paid out of central funds or where costs are paid under legal aid orders issued by the Registrar of the Court of Appeal (Criminal Division) the certificate and counsel's fee notes are sent to the Supreme Court Accounts Office to settle the certificated amounts with the agents and counsel direct.

(*c*) *Courts-Martial*. Where costs are payable to the Secretary of State for Defence in respect of an appeal from the Courts-Martial Appeal Court the certificate is sent direct to the Ministry of Defence to settle as in (*b*) above.

(*d*) *Criminal (Northern Ireland)*. Where the costs are payable in accordance with section 41 of the Criminal Appeal (Northern Ireland) Act 1980 the certificates are sent to the Northern Ireland Office to settle as in (*b*) above.

Costs of litigants in person

16. The amount which may be allowed to a litigant in person who has properly taken time from work is not to exceed all loss actually sustained or, where no loss has been sustained, £6.25 per hour, subject in either case to a maximum for any particular item of two thirds of the sum which in the opinion of the Taxing Officer would have been allowed for that item if a litigant had been represented by a solicitor.

Agreement of costs

17. The Taxing Officer should be informed in writing when costs have been agreed between the parties.

Review of taxation in the House of Lords

18. An appeal lies on principle but not on quantum and such appeal must be made within 14 days of the taxation. (A copy of the review procedure is available on request from the Taxing Clerk.)

(*These forms should be read in conjunction with the Form of Appeal, Directions as to Procedure and Standing Orders applicable to Civil Appeals to the House of Lords.*)

Interest

[1] **19.**—(i) With effect from 1st January 1990 interest is chargeable on orders made in respect of *inter partes* costs and orders for costs in favour of successful unassisted parties. The rate of interest will be in accordance with the provisions of the Judgment Act 1838 as amended by statutory instrument and interest will accrue from the day on which the order of the House is made.

(ii) In addition to his other powers it shall be within the discretion of the Taxing Officer to vary the period for which interest is allowed, in any case where the circumstances make it appropriate to do so.

NOTE

[1] Inserted, 23rd November 1989.

(2) Forms of Bills of Costs in the House of Lords

. . . . . .

(APPELLANT/RESPONDENT—SCOTTISH: EDINBURGH ACCOUNT)

In the House of Lords.

On Appeal from the Court of Session in Scotland.

Between:

v.

APPELLANT'S/RESPONDENT'S BILL OF COSTS EDINBURGH AGENT'S ACCOUNT

	Appellant's bill £	Respondent's bill £
Petition of appeal: attending counsel		
9.(*a*) (i) Attending counsel settling petition, signing petition.[1]		
(ii) Care and attention		
(*b*) Travelling and waiting		
(*c*) Paid counsel's fees		
Incidental petitions		
10. *(see London agent's account)*		

[THE NEXT PAGE IS B 533]

	Appellant's bill £	*Respondent's bill* £

Documentation

11. (*a*) (i) Drawing list of documents for appendix; attending other parties; attending copy of judge's opinion; drawing case for counsel to settle; attending counsel; attending exchange and perusal; attending printer with instructions for binding and printing[1]

(ii) Care and attention ....

(*b*) Travelling and waiting ....

(*c*) Paid counsel's fees ....

(*d*) Paid printer's account ....

(*e*) Paid carriage to London ....

Note

[1] Enter cost of work properly itemised.

Consultation

12. (*a*) (i) Attending consultation ....

(ii) Care and attention ....

(*b*) Travelling and waiting ....

(*c*) Paid counsel's fees ....

Hearing/judgment

13. (*a*) (i) Attending counsel in respect of brief, list of authorities and refreshers, attending appellant/respondent informing them of the judgment, perusing draft judgment[1] ....

(ii) Care and attention ....

(*b*) Travelling and waiting ....

(*c*) Paid counsel's fees ....

(*d*) Paid counsel's refresher fees ....

Instructions

14. Preparation for hearing before the Appellate Committee. (This item should include an itemised breakdown of any work done not otherwise provided for necessarily or properly done in preparing for the hearing. Letters written and telephone calls will generally be allowed on a unit basis of six minutes each. An actual time charge may be allowed for letters of substance and telephone calls that properly amount to an attendance.) ....

Taxation of costs

15. Preparing this account (where allowable)[1] ....

Note

[1] Add net total of this account to summary of London agents account.

(APPELLANT/RESPONDENT—SCOTTISH: LONDON ACCOUNT)

LONDON AGENT'S ACCOUNT

Petition of Appeal

Incidental Petitions

16. (*a*) (i) Drawing petition, attending serving, perusing and lodging ....

(ii) Care and attention ....

(*b*) Travelling and waiting ....

(*c*) Paid fee ....
(*if the petition was heard by the Appeal Committee*)

(*d*) Attending and preparing hearing before Appeal Committee ....

	Appellant's bill £	*Respondent's bill* £
Documentation		
17. (*a*) (i) Attending receipt of case from Edinburgh agent. Attending lodging and setting down; attending exchange and perusal (if exchanged in London) attending printer with instructions for printing and binding; (if printed in London) attending Judicial Office with proofs[1]		
(ii) Care and attention		
(*b*) Travelling and waiting		
(*c*) Paid fees		
(*d*) Paid printer's account		
Hearing/judgment		
18. (*a*) (i) Attending Edinburgh agent in respect of list of authorities; attending lodging[1]		
(ii) Care and attention		
(*b*) Travelling and waiting		
(*c*) (i) Attending Appellate Committee when part/fully heard. Attending delivery of judgment and informing Edinburgh agent[1 2]		
(ii) Care and attention		
(*d*) Travelling and waiting		
(*e*) Paid counsel's judgment fee[3]		
(*f*) Paid fee		
Taxation of costs		
19. (*a*) (i) Preparing the bill (where allowable) and preparing for and attending taxation		
(ii) Care and attention		
(*b*) Travelling and waiting		

Notes

[1] Enter cost of work properly itemised.

[2] Separate entries for each day of heating.

[3] Junior counsel only.

(3) Allocaturs and Summaries of Bills of Costs

(*1*) *Allocatur*

In the House of Lords

Between ....

v.

....

APPELLANT'S/RESPONDENT'S[1] COSTS

Amount of profit costs and disbursements claimed ....

Less taxed off disbursements and profit costs .... ———

Total ....

Add VAT (on amounts allowed which attract VAT) .... ———

Total allowed ....

Taxing fee on total allowed (see Direction 14)[2] .... ———

Amount to be certified .... ═══

.... *Agent for the appellant*

.... *Agent for the respondent*

JUDICIAL TAXING OFFICE,
HOUSE OF LORDS.

Notes

[1] Delete where applicable.

[2] Taxing fee payable to "House of Lords Account".

(2) *Summary for inter partes bills, for bills payable out of central funds and where legal aid certificates have been granted under Part II of the Legal Aid Act 1974.*

Taxed off			*Value Added Tax*[1]	*Disburse-ments*	*Profit costs*
Disbs.	Profit costs				
		Page 1			
		Page 2			
		Page 3			
		Page 4			
		Taxed off			
		Add VAT on profit costs at 15%			
		Add disbursements			
		Add VAT on disbursements at 15%			
		Total			
		Taxing fee 5%			

(3) *Summary for legal aid bill*

Taxed off			*Value Added Tax*[1]	*Disburse-ments*	*Profit costs*
Disbs.	Profit costs				
		Page 1			
		Page 2			
		Page 3			
		Page 4			
		Taxed off			
		Add VAT on 95% of profit costs at 15%			
		Add Counsel's fees			
		Add VAT on 95% of counsel's fees at 15%			
		Other disbursements			
		Add VAT on other disbursements			
		Total			
		Taxing fee 5%			
		Legal aid summary			
		Profit costs			
		VAT on 95% profit costs at 15%[2 3]			
		Counsel's fees ...			
		VAT on 95% counsel's fees at 15%[2 3]			
		Other disbursements			
		VAT on other disbursements ..			

Notes

[1] Value added tax on disbursements as allowed.

[2] Where the taxation took place before 1st January 1988 VAT should be calculated on 90% of these sums.

[3] Where the order for taxation is made on or after 29th July 1988 VAT should be calculated on 100% of these sums.

DIVISION C

Court of Session Practice

Rules of Court

Other Acts of Sederunt

Service of Documents Abroad

Court of Session Practice Notes

Digest of Court of Session Practice

Rules of Court

Act of Sederunt (Rules of Court, consolidation and amendment) 1965

(S.I. 1965 No. 321)

[10th November 1964]

The Lords of Council and Session, under and by virtue of the provisions of the Administration of Justice (Scotland) Act 1933 considering that the Rules of Court enacted by the Act of Sederunt, and that it is desirable to make further amendments and to consolidate the Rules as so amended, do hereby enact and declare that the Rules attached hereto and embodied herein are approved as rules of the Court of Session in place of the Rules enacted and amended as aforesaid, and shall come into force on 4th May 1965.

And the Lords do further enact and declare as follows:—

[1] (1) The provisions of any Act of Parliament or Act of Sederunt relating to any of the matters regulated or prescribed by these Rules are hereby repealed, in so far as inconsistent with the provisions of these Rules, as from 15th June 1965.

[1] (2) Where any *induciae* or other period of time appointed or allowed by order of court or by pre-existing law and practice for taking any step of procedure is still current on 15th June 1965, such *induciae* or other period of time shall continue to be in force notwithstanding the provisions of these Rules.

[1] (3) If in any cause in dependence on 15th June 1965, it is shown to the Court that the enforcement in any particular of the provisions of these Rules would be productive of hardship or injustice to any of the parties, the Court may grant such relief as may be necessary to prevent such hardship or injustice.

[1] (4) From and after 15th June 1965, the Court may in its discretion relieve any party from the consequences of any failure to comply with the provisions of these Rules which is shown to be due to mistake, oversight or other cause, not being wilful non-observance of the same, on such terms and conditions as shall appear to be just; and in any such case the Court may make such order as may be just by way of extension of time, lodging or amendment of papers or otherwise so as to enable the cause to proceed as if such failure had not happened.

This Act may be cited as the Act of Sederunt (Rules of Court, consolidation and amendment) 1965.

NOTE

[1] As amended by S.I. 1965 No. 1090.

CHAPTER I

General

SECTION 1—VACATION JUDGE

Powers

[1] **1.**—(*a*) Subject to the provisions contained in these Rules, it shall be competent for a vacation judge, whenever necessary or convenient during vacation or recess, to deal with:

(i) any matter which might competently be disposed of from day to day by the Petition Judge;

(ii) any motion in a cause initiated by summons and depending in the Outer House;

(iii) any application in a cause depending in the Outer House which might, in accordance with these Rules, competently be disposed of during session by a Lord Ordinary sitting in chambers;

(iv) any motion in a cause depending before the Inner House, provided that the motion does not affect the merits of the cause;

(v) any motion for approval of a Report by the Auditor of Court (including objections, if any, thereto), as well in causes depending before the Inner House, as in causes depending before the Outer House; and

(vi) the taking of evidence under Rule 100.

(*b*) A vacation judge shall not be bound to dispose of any motion, application, or other matter, if in his opinion such motion, application, or other matter can more conveniently be postponed until the meeting of the Court after the vacation or recess.

NOTE

[1] As amended by S.I. 1987 No. 1206.

SECTION 2—SOLICITORS AND NOTARIES PUBLIC

Admission

2.—[1] (*a*) All petitions under sections 14 and 15 of the Solicitors (Scotland) Act 1933 (in this section referred to as "the Act of 1933") shall be presented to the court by the clerk to the examiners appointed by the Council of the Law Society of Scotland (in this section referred to as "the Council"), and there shall be payable to the said clerk by any applicant the following fees:

(i) For the preparation of and carrying through the petition under section 14 of the Act of 1933, including the issue of the certificate of fitness by the Council, certificate of exemption from the Society's examinations, obtaining the interlocutor of admission, extract thereof and certificate of enrolment, where the applicant holds the certificate of the Council—£30.

(ii) the preparation and carrying through the petition under the said section 14 including the issue and obtaining of the certificates and other documents mentioned in head (i), where the applicant holds a qualified certificate of the Council—£40.

(iii) For obtaining the interlocutor of admission of an applicant under section 15 of the Act of 1933, including extract thereof of certificate of enrolment—£10.

(*b*) Where a petition for admission as a law agent has been presented to the court prior to the first day of March 1934, and the examiners of law agents have signed a report to the court thereon to the effect that the applicant has complied with the requirements for admission and is duly qualified to be admitted as a law agent in terms of the Law Agents (Scotland) Act 1873, and relative amending Acts, the court may, without a further petition being presented, admit the applicant as a solicitor and cause his name to be enrolled as such in terms of section 15 of the Act of 1933; provided that, where a period of seven or more years has elapsed since the date of the report of the examiners, the applicant shall lodge with the clerk to the examiners an affidavit setting forth his occupation since the date of the report, and shall also furnish any further particulars which the Council may require, and the Council may make such further or additional report on the said petition as they may consider proper.

NOTE

[1] Substituted by S.I. 1971 No. 1714 and as amended by S.I. 1976 No. 867.

Registration and enrolment of solicitors

3.—[1] (*a*) A register shall be kept by the Registrar of Solicitors under the Solicitors' (Scotland) Acts 1933 to 1958 for the registration and enrolment of persons admitted as solicitors.

[2] (*b*) Every solicitor whose name is for the time being included in the Roll or Register of Solicitors shall pay to the Registrar annually a fee of £10 in respect of the cost of maintaining the Roll or Register, which fee shall be payable on the first day of November in each year, provided that no fee shall be payable by a solicitor for the period between the date of his enrolment and the thirty-first day of October occurring immediately thereafter.

NOTES

[1] Substituted by S.I. 1968 No. 1971 and as amended by S.I. 1976 No. 867.

[2] As amended by S.I. 1979 No. 1410.

Admission of solicitors as notaries public

4.—(*a*) All petitions to be admitted a notary public shall be framed and presented by the Clerk to the Admission of Notaries Public who shall obtain the Royal Authority for the petitioner's admission by a presentation; and the said Clerk shall administer the oath of office, keep the roll of notaries, and prepare and issue all commissions as notary public.

[1] (*b*) On presentation of any such petition the fee payable to the said Clerk shall be £9·45; and, in addition, intrants shall make payment of the fee fund dues, and dues of presentation.

(*c*) The said Clerk shall supply each notary public on his admission with a duly certified and docqueted protocol book of ninety-one folios.

NOTE

[1] As amended by the Decimal Currency Act 1969, s. 10 (1).

Appeals under paragraphs 2 (2) and 3 (4) of the Fifth Schedule to the Act of 1949 and sections 3 (2) and 17 (3) of the Act of 1958

5.—(*a*) Appeals under paragraphs 2 (2) and 3 (4) of the Fifth Schedule to the Solicitors' (Scotland) Act 1949 (in this section referred to as " the Act of 1949 ") and sections 3 (2) and 17 (3) of the Solicitors' (Scotland) Act 1958 (in this section referred to as " the Act of 1958 ") shall be by petition to the Inner House. Any such petition shall be lodged in the Petition Department, not later than fourteen days in the case of an appeal under paragraph 2 (2) of the Fifth Schedule to the Act of 1949, and not later than twenty-one days in the case of appeals under sections 3 (2) and 17 (3) of the Act of 1958 from the date when the decision appealed against shall have been intimated to the petitioner and shall set forth the decision appealed against and state the date on which it was intimated to the petitioner, and shall contain an articulate statement in numbered paragraphs of the facts relevant to the disposal of the petition.

(*b*) On the petition being so lodged it shall be brought before one or other Division in Chambers, and the Division may, without hearing parties, order service of the petition on the Council and intimation in the Minute Book and allow the Council to lodge Answers thereto within seven days after service.

(*c*) The court shall thereafter proceed in the petition summarily in such manner as shall be necessary and proper.

(*d*) Any petitioner may at any time after lodging a petition abandon the same by giving notice of abandonment to all persons upon whom the petition may have been served.

Applications under paragraphs 1 (3) of the Fifth Schedule and 5 (5) of the Sixth Schedule to the Act of 1949

6. Applications under paragraph 1 (3) to the Fifth Schedule and paragraph 5 (5) of the Sixth Schedule to the Act of 1949 shall be by petition to the Inner House. Any such petition shall be lodged in the Petition Department (in the case of applications under paragraph 5 (5) of the Sixth Schedule to the Act of 1949 within fourteen days after a notice under sub-paragraph (3) of paragraph 5 of that Schedule has been served and stating the date on which the notice was served on the petitioner) and shall contain an articulate statement in numbered paragraphs of the facts relevant to the disposal of the petition. On the petition being so lodged paragraphs (*b*), (*c*) and (*d*) of Rule 7 shall apply.

Appeals under section 7 of the Act of 1958

7.—(*a*) Appeals under section 7 of the Act of 1958 by persons aggrieved by a decision of the Discipline Tribunal [1] shall be by petition to the Inner House.

(*b*) Any such petition shall be lodged in the Petition Department not later than twenty-one days from the date on which the decision of the Discipline Tribunal shall have been intimated to the petitioner and shall set forth the decision appealed against and state the date on which it was intimated to the petitioner and shall contain an articulate statement in numbered paragraphs of the facts relevant to the disposal of the petition.

(*c*) On the petition being so lodged it shall be brought before one or other Division in chambers and the Division may, without hearing parties, make such order for intimation and service as may be necessary, including intimation to the Discipline Tribunal (who shall, however, not be regarded as parties to the cause except as after-mentioned) ordaining the Tribunal to lodge in process within the period of the *induciae* the Findings appealed against, together with the documents lodged by either party and (if available) the notes of the evidence adduced before and heard by the Discipline Tribunal.

(*d*) The court shall thereafter proceed in the petition summarily in such manner as shall be necessary and proper.

(*e*) Where the petitioner is the person or one of the persons who complained of the solicitor's alleged professional misconduct the court may order him to give security for expenses (including the cost of extending the notes of evidence adduced before and heard by the Discipline Tribunal) as a condition of proceeding with the petition.

(*f*) Any petitioner may at any time after lodging a petition abandon the same by giving notice of abandonment to all persons upon whom the petition may have been served.

(*g*) The court may substitute any other punishment for that inflicted by a finding appealed against, or make any order in relation thereto it may think fit.

NOTE

[1] Formerly the Discipline Committee: see the Solicitors (Scotland) Act 1980, ss. 10 and 54.

Applications under section 29 of the Act of 1933, paragraph 5 (2) and paragraph 6 of the Sixth Schedule to the Act of 1949 and section 15 of the Act of 1958

8.—(*a*) Applications under section 29 of the Act of 1933, paragraph 5 (2) and paragraph 6 of the Sixth Schedule to the Act of 1949 and section 15 of the Act of 1958 shall be by petition to the Inner House. The petition shall contain an articulate statement of the facts in numbered paragraphs relevant to the petition and shall be lodged in the Petition Department.

(*b*) On the petition being so lodged it shall be brought before one or other Division in Chambers, and the Division may, without hearing parties, order service of the petition on the Respondent and intimation in the Minute Book and allow him to lodge Answers thereto within seven days after service.

(*c*) The court shall thereafter proceed in the petition summarily in such manner as shall be necessary and proper.

Petitions under section 6(1)(a) of the Act of 1958

9.—(*a*) Petitions under section 6(1)(*a*) of the Act of 1958 shall be presented in the Inner House and lodged in the Petition Department and shall contain an articulate statement of the facts necessary to show cause why the applicant's name should be restored to the Roll of Solicitors.

(*b*) On the petition being so lodged it shall be brought before one or other Division in chambers and the Division may, without hearing parties, make such order for intimation and service as may be necessary, the Discipline Committee and the Council both being deemed to be the Respondents in the petition.

(*c*) Paragraphs (*c*) and (*d*) of Rule 7 shall thereafter apply.

Remit for further enquiry

10. In any proceedings under any of the preceding rules of this section, the court may, if it thinks necessary or expedient in the interests of justice, remit to any person to make further enquiry into the facts, or to take further evidence and to report to the court.

Deprivation of office of notary public

11. Where an order has been made by the court causing a solicitor who is also a notary public to be struck off the roll of solicitors, or suspending him from practice, the court may also deprive him of his office of notary public, or suspend him from discharging his said office, as the case may be; and, in the event of a person who has been struck off the roll of solicitors and has been deprived of his office of notary public in terms of this rule, having his name restored to the roll of solicitors under section 6(1) of the Act of 1958, the court may grant warrant to the Keeper of the Roll or Register of Notaries Public to restore his name to the said roll or register as a notary public.

Section 3—Offices of Court

The General and other offices of the Court

12.—(*a*) The Central Office of the Court (generally referred to in these Rules as "the Office of Court") shall combine and comprise:

1. The General Department;
2. The Petition Department;
3. The Extracts Department; and
4. The Teind Office;

but shall not include the offices of the Accountant of Court or the Auditor of Court.

(*b*) The General Department and the Petition Department shall be under the charge of a Deputy Principal Clerk of Session; the Extracts Department shall be under the charge of a Depute Clerk of Session, who shall be known as the Extractor of the Court of Session, and the Teind Office shall be under the charge of a Clerk of Session, who shall be known as the Teind Clerk, all acting under the directions of the Principal Clerk of Session in consultation with the Lord President.

(*c*) Any reference to the Principal Extractor or to his office in any Act of Parliament, or in any Order made pursuant to an Act of Parliament or in any Act of Sederunt shall be construed as a reference to the Extractor or to his Department.

Distribution of business

13.—[1] (*a*) To the General Department there shall belong all processes in:

(i) causes originating in the Court of Session and initiated by summons and simplified divorce application;

(ii) appeals from inferior courts, remits from sheriff courts, appeals under particular statutes, and stated cases or special cases, including references and submissions under particular statutes;

(iii) causes transmitted from any inferior court to the Court of Session *ob contingentiam*; and

(iv) appeals under the Lands Valuation and Rating Acts.

(*b*) To the Petition Department there shall belong all processes in causes originating in the Court of Session and initiated by petition.

(*c*) To the Teind Office there shall belong all processes which by statute or practice have been dealt with by the Teind Court and the Lord Ordinary on Teinds.

(*d*) All bonds of caution and consignation receipts in any process shall be lodged with or transmitted to the Accountant of Court.

NOTE

[1] As amended by S.I. 1982 No. 1679.

Section 4—The Rolls

Keeper of the Rolls

14. The rolls of court shall be kept by the Principal Clerk of Session as Keeper of the Rolls with the assistance of the Deputy Principal Clerk of Session and in consultation with the Lord President, the Lord Justice-Clerk and the senior Lord Ordinary in the Outer House.

Classification of causes in the General Department

15. In the records kept in the Offices of Court, all causes belonging to the General Department shall be classified as (i) ordinary causes, (ii) admiralty and commercial causes, and (iii) consistorial causes.

Putting out causes for hearing or trial

16.—(*a*) Subject to the provisions contained in these Rules, it shall be the duty of the Keeper of the Rolls to cause lists to be prepared of all causes sent to procedure roll in the Outer House, and of all causes sent to the summar and short rolls in the Inner House, and also of all causes in which proofs, jury trials, or special hearings have been fixed in terms of the immediately succeeding rule, and to put out such causes for hearing or trial before such Lord Ordinary, or before such Division as may be convenient; provided always that any continued adjustment of record or pleadings, and any continued motion, in either the Outer or the Inner House, shall, if possible, be put out before the Division or Lord Ordinary by whom the continuation was granted; and that if the merits of a cause have once been discussed in whole or in part before a particular Division or a particular Lord Ordinary, the cause shall, if possible, be put out for any further hearing, or for proof, or jury trial, before the same Division or Lord Ordinary, as the case may be.

(*b*) Causes put out in the printed rolls of court for hearing in any roll or at any diet shall be so put out in the printed rolls issued not later than the second day before the day on which the cause is to be heard.

Fixing diets for proofs, jury trials, and special hearings in the Outer House

17. When a proof is allowed, or an issue or issues approved, or when a

[THE NEXT PAGE IS C 9]

cause is appointed to be heard at a special diet, the court shall not itself proceed to fix the diet for the proof or jury trial or special hearing, but shall leave the date of such diet blank in the interlocutor. The Keeper of the Rolls shall, in the case of a proof, as soon as convenient after the lodging in process of copies of the Closed Record as required by Rule 91 (*e*), or in the case of a jury trial, as soon as convenient after the approval of an issue or issues, publish such causes in the Rolls of Court and in consultation with the parties assign a day or days for the proof or jury trial, and shall cause the blank in the interlocutor to be filled in accordingly and to be initialled by the Clerk in charge of the process.

Printing and publishing of rolls

18.—(*a*) The daily rolls, the minute-book, the teind minute-book and the record of edictal citations shall be published, and delivered to subscribers, under directions made from time to time by the Lord President.

SECTION 5—THE PROCESS

Form, size, etc., of papers forming the process

19.—(*a*) In all causes originating in the Court of Session, and initiated by summons or petition, the principal summons or petition shall be on the official printed forms, and may be filled in in writing, typescript, or print, and shall be backed with the official printed backing.

(*b*) All special cases originating in the Court of Session, all written appeals, all stated or special cases and generally all writs whereby any cause first comes to depend before the Inner House, may be in writing, typescript or print or other suitable method of reproduction approved by the court and shall, if in writing, be written on process paper, or, if in typescript or print, be typed or printed on paper of a texture not less durable than process paper and of a like size.

(*c*) All steps of process lodged in any cause depending before the Court of Session, whether originating there or appealed or remitted to that court from any inferior court, may be in writing, typescript, or print; and shall, if in writing, be written on process paper, or, if in typescript or print, be typed or printed on paper of a texture not less durable than process paper, and of a like size.

(*d*) All the writs and documents mentioned in the three immediately preceding paragraphs of this rule shall be folded and backed lengthwise, and shall bear on the first page and on the backing a delimited square space for the serial letter and number assigned to the principal writ on lodging, and the backings of all the writs and documents mentioned in the two immediately preceding paragraphs of this rule shall be of cartridge paper or paper of similar durability.

Steps of process

20. A process shall consist of an Inventory of Process, the principal writ, an interlocutor sheet, a duplicate inventory of process, a copy of the principal writ certified by the solicitor lodging the same, a motion sheet and a minute of proceedings. Each of these steps of process (other than the principal writ and the certified copy thereof) shall consist of at least four pages of process paper. If productions are lodged at the same time, there shall also be lodged an inventory of such productions. No minute of proceedings need be lodged in any petition unless and until answers have been lodged.

Intimation of lodging documents

21. The solicitor lodging a step of process shall give written intimation of such lodging to the solicitor of the other party; and the clerks shall not mark any step as received until a certificate of intimation has been endorsed thereon, provided that no intimation need be given of the lodging of an open or closed record, or the original writ or defences or answers.

Writs on which interlocutor has to be signed

22. Every petition, note, principal copy issues, or counter issues, and the like, on which any interlocutor, order, verdict, or authentication falls to be written for signature, shall have annexed a sheet of process paper on which such interlocutor, order, verdict or authentication may be written and signed.

Lost summonses, etc.

23. Where a summons, petition, or other original writ or pleading or interlocutor sheet is lost or destroyed, a copy thereof, proved in the cause to the satisfaction of the court, and authenticated in such manner as the court shall require, may be substituted, and shall be held equivalent to the original for the purposes of the action, including the use of diligence.

Duplicate inventory of process

24. The duplicate inventory of process shall be written up by the solicitor lodging the steps of process or productions at the time of lodging. The process number of each production in the process shall be marked opposite its number in the inventory of productions by the solicitor when he lodges the same.

Productions

25. Each production consisting of more than one sheet shall be securely fastened together and backed up by the solicitor lodging the same, and each production shall be marked at lodging with the serial letter and number assigned to the principal writ. Copies of productions for the use of the court shall be lodged within 48 hours of the date of the proof or jury trial.

Copies and reproductions of documents and notes of evidence

26.—(*a*) All records, petitions, answers, proofs, or other documents which require to be copied for the use of the court, may be either printed or typewritten or reproduced by any other process approved by the court. The clerks shall refuse to accept any reproduction which does not conform to a standard approved by the court in size, spacing, lettering, legibility, quality of paper, or otherwise, and any party tendering a document which is so refused by the clerks of court shall have the right to appeal in writing to the Principal Clerk of Session; provided that, where such appeal is refused, the Principal Clerk of Session may extend the time for lodging; and the decision of the said Principal Clerk sustaining or refusing such appeal, or granting or refusing an extension of time, shall be final.

(*b*) In all causes initiated in the Inner House, and in all causes reclaimed or appealed to the Inner House, at least ten copies or reproductions of the record, petition and answers, appeal, stated or special case, as the case may be, and also (in the case of motions for review by the Inner House) of the interlocutor or interlocutors reclaimed against shall be lodged in the appropriate Department at the same time as the cause is submitted to the Inner House; and ten copies or reproductions of any documents or notes of evidence or opinions which it is desired to submit for the consideration of the court, shall be lodged in the General or Petition Department, as the case may be, as soon as possible thereafter. The party lodging any of the documents referred to in this paragraph shall at the same time deliver to the solicitor for the opposite party, unless otherwise agreed between the parties, ten copies thereof.

Interlocutors ordering or allowing papers to be given in

27.—(*a*) In all interlocutors ordering or allowing papers from both or either of the parties a time shall be fixed for giving in the same, which time may be prorogated, provided that before the elapse thereof a motion shall be enrolled for such prorogation; and no prorogation shall be granted in any instance, except on cause shown.

(*b*) Every paper produced in process, in terms of an interlocutor ordering or allowing the same to be given in, shall have prefixed thereto a full copy of the interlocutor ordering or allowing such paper and a copy of any interlocutor prorogating the time originally allowed.

Signature of papers

[1] **28.**—(1) Except as otherwise provided in these Rules and subject to paragraph (2) below, petitions to the court and all defences, answers, notes, minutes and other papers in causes depending before the court shall be signed by an advocate or a solicitor who has a right of audience in the Court of Session, who shall be looked upon as the drawer thereof and shall be answerable for what they contain.

(2) A minute of amendment, answers to a minute of amendment, a minute of sist, a minute of transference, a minute of objection to a minute of transference, and a note of objection to a report of the Auditor shall not require any signature.

NOTE

[1] As amended by S.I. 1991 No. 2483, with effect from 25th November 1991.

Papers not to be received after due date

29. Before marking any paper as lodged the clerks shall examine the copy interlocutor or interlocutors ordered to be prefixed, and shall not in any instance receive and mark any paper after the lapse of the day on which it is receivable. The Clerks of Court shall mark the true date of lodgment on every paper (not being a production) given into process.

Interlocutors

[1] **30.**—(1) Subject to Rule 93A, an interlocutor may be written by the clerk of court and shall be signed by the judge, or by the presiding judge, of the court pronouncing it, and an extract of an interlocutor that is not so signed shall be void and of no effect.

(2) The judge who signs an interlocutor may on cause shown correct or alter it at any time before extract.

[2] (3) During vacation or recess the judge, or presiding judge, may sign an interlocutor in respect of a cause heard or tried before him during session.

NOTES

[1] Substituted by S.I. 1984 No. 472.

[2] Added by S.I. 1986 No. 1937.

Certain writs not borrowable

31.—(*a*) The principal writ by which a process is commenced in the Court of Session shall remain constantly in the office of court, subject to inspection by any party interested, and shall on no account be lent out; provided always that:

(i) this rule shall not apply to the copy of such writ, certified as provided in Rule 20 which may be lent out when required;

(ii) this rule is without prejudice to the general right of a defender to borrow the principal Summons and any productions lodged therewith upon entering appearance, in terms of Rules 86 and 87; the same being in that case returnable in accordance with the provisions of said rules;

(iii) each party may, after the record is closed, borrow his own principal writ for the purpose of writing on it and authenticating such amendments as may have been made, and similarly when any amendment has been allowed by the court;

(iv) this rule shall not apply in the case of a party intending to do diligence on the dependence of the action.

(*b*) The minute of proceedings shall only be borrowable for transmission to the auditor of court.

Borrowing and returning process

32.—(*a*) The Clerks of Court shall, except as after-mentioned, receive back no process or part of a process without at once either comparing it with the principal inventory and receipt in presence of the solicitor or his clerk and scoring the receipt; or, in the case of a partial return, marking on the principal inventory the numbers so returned; or otherwise, if the whole numbers borrowed be not then returned, or if the process be bulky so that it cannot at the time be conveniently examined, the Clerks of Court shall not receive back such process or part of a process without a separate slip or note accompanying the same, dated and signed or initialled by the solicitor or his clerk, specifying the numbers so returned; and it shall be the duty of the Clerks of Court in all cases where they receive back a process or part of a process without at once scoring the receipt or making a marking on the inventory as aforesaid, to examine the same before the close of the following business day at latest, and to give notice to the solicitor of any inaccuracy in the slip or note aforesaid; and if no notice to the solicitor be delivered or put into the post office in the course of such following day, stating that such slip or note is inaccurate, the accuracy thereof shall be presumed, and the solicitor shall be equally exonered as if the receipt had been scored, or a marking made as aforesaid.

(*b*) The solicitor returning the whole or any part of a process shall see that the numbers so returned are previously arranged in their regular order according to the inventory and the Clerks of Court may refuse to receive any process or part of a process the numbers of which are not so arranged.

Transmission of Records

[1] **32A.**—(*a*) The Register of Acts and Decreets for each year shall, within six months from the end of that year, be transmitted by the Extractor of the Court of Session to the Keeper of the Records for permanent custody.

[2] (*b*) Every process in which final extract has been issued and every unextracted process shall, subject to the following paragraph, be transmitted to the Keeper of Records on the expiration of a period of five years from the date of the last interlocutor pronounced in the cause, or in any cause where no interlocutor has been pronounced, from the date of the calling of that cause.

(*c*) No process of a petition for appointment of a judicial factor, *curator bonis*, factor *loco tutoris* or *loco absentis*, or for liquidation of a company, shall be transmissible under this rule unless the factor, curator or liquidator, as the case may be, has been granted a final discharge by the court.

NOTES

[1] Added by S.I. 1976 No. 745.

[2] As amended by S.I. 1982 No. 1825.

Index of processes

33. All persons having interest in a process in the custody of the Keeper of the Records shall have access to the index and also to exhibition of the process on payment of fees to be charged at the rates after specified.

Retransmission of unextracted process to Office of Court

34.—(*a*) Where a person having interest in an unextracted process in the custody of the Keeper of the Records shall require any such process to be retransmitted to the Office of Court, in either Department, it shall be retransmitted accordingly and an entry shall be made in a book to be kept in the department of the Keeper of the Records recording the retransmission, which shall be signed by the clerk who receives the process.

(*b*) No process, or part of a process, shall be allowed to be borrowed by any person while the process remains in the custody of the Keeper of the Registers and Records; provided that when any person having interest desires to borrow any process, or part of a process, in such custody, he shall be entitled to have the process retransmitted to the Offices of Court in terms of the immediately preceding section.

[1] (*c*) The fee for retransmission of a process shall be £1·05.

NOTE

[1] As amended by the Decimal Currency Act 1969, s.10(1).

Certified copy interlocutors and steps of process

[1] **35.** The Keeper of the Records may allow inspection of the indices.

[THE NEXT PAGE IS C 13]

and may issue to any person desiring the same certified or " plain " copies of any interlocutors or steps of process on payment of the fees hereinafter provided, namely:

For inspection of the indices of a single office 10p
For inspection of the indices of the whole offices 25p
For inspection of a process 37p

Certified Official Copies

For each sheet of 250 words or part thereof of all typed or written certified official copies 15p

This fee is exclusive of fees of writing.

For each page or part thereof reproduced by photography 10p

Excerpts of " Plain " Copies

For typed or written excerpts or copies whether complete or partial per sheet of 250 words or part thereof 10p
For photographed excerpts or copies whether complete or partial per page or part thereof 10p
For excerpts or copies made by the public in addition to the fee for inspection, each sheet of 250 words or part thereof 3p

NOTE
[1] As amended by the Decimal Currency Act 1969, s. 10 (1).

SECTION 6—TAXES UPON FUNDS *in Manibus Curiae*

Certificate by officer of Inland Revenue

36.—(1) No decree, warrant or order for payment to any person of any money consigned in name of the Accountant of Court in terms of the Court of Session Consignations (Scotland) Act 1895 or any part thereof, (2) no decree, warrant or order for payment of any consigned money or for transfer or conveyance to any person of any stocks, shares, or other property, heritable or moveable, in any process for the distribution of the estate of any deceased, pending in the Court of Session, and (3) unless where appropriate procedure has been taken for the continued administration of any lapsed trust, intestate estate, partnership estate, or other estate, moveable or heritable, no decree for exoneration and discharge of any judicial factor appointed by the said court for the purpose of administering and distributing such trust or other estates, shall issue until there is lodged with the Clerk of Court a certificate by the proper officer in the Department of Inland Revenue that all income tax, estate duty, legacy duty, succession duty, and any other duty payable thereon to the Commissioners of Inland Revenue has been paid and satisfied to the Department; provided that in an action of multiple poinding it shall not be a condition precedent to the issue of a Certificate by the Commissioners of Inland Revenue under (2) above that all income tax, estate duty, etc., exigible on the estate of a deceased claimant has been paid. The clerks of court shall not present for the signature of the court any such decree, warrant or order as aforesaid, without the provisions of the above section having been first complied with.

SECTION 7—ASSESSORS

Nautical assessors and assessors in any proceedings under the Patents Act 1949 or the Patents Act 1977

[1] **37.** In any cause arising out of or relating to a collision at sea, salvage, towage, or any other maritime matter, and in any proceedings under the Patents Act 1949 or the Patents Act 1977 the court, if it shall think fit, may, and on the application of any party to the cause shall, summon to its

assistance at the trial, or proof, or at any hearing in the cause, whether in the Outer or Inner House, a specially qualified assessor to sit with the court and act as assessor at such trial, proof, or hearing, but where it is proposed to summon any person as an assessor, objection to him, either personally or in respect of his qualification, may be stated by any party to the cause and shall be disposed of by the court.

NOTE

[1] As amended by S.I. 1978 No. 955.

Assessors in other causes

38. In any cause other than those to which the immediately foregoing rule applies, the court may, on the joint motion of parties, summon to its assistance at the trial or proof or at any hearing, whether in the Outer or Inner House, a specially qualified assessor, who shall be selected either by the parties and named in the said joint motion, or by the court if the parties shall leave the selection of the assessor to the court, to sit with the court and act as assessor at such trial, proof, or hearing.

Application for assessor to be summoned

39. In any cause, whether falling under Rule 37 or Rule 38, an application for an assessor at the instance of the parties to the cause or any one or more of the parties shall be made by motion; provided that:—

(*a*) All such motions shall be enrolled at least fourteen days before the date of the trial, proof or hearing, at which the presence of such assessor is desired.

(*b*) Where the application is at the instance of the parties jointly, the motion shall be signed on behalf of all the parties and shall be disposed of as a motion which is not marked " opposed " by any of the parties.

(*c*) The party or parties enrolling the motion shall at the time of such enrolment lodge in process for the use of the assessor a copy of the closed record or other papers setting forth the pleadings in the cause: and where an assessor is to be summoned *ex proprio motu* of the Court, such copy of the closed record or other pleadings shall be lodged in process by the pursuer or petitioner as the case may be, unless the court shall otherwise direct.

Where the court decides to summon an assessor ex proprio motu

40. In any cause to which Rule 37 applies, if the court shall think that the cause is one in which the presence of an assessor is desirable although none of the parties may have moved to that effect, the court shall hear parties before summoning the assessor.

Interlocutor ordering assessor to be summoned

41. Upon a motion for an assessor selected and named by the parties being granted, or upon the court deciding *ex proprio motu* to summon an assessor, or upon a motion for an assessor to be selected by the court being granted, the court by interlocutor shall order the assessor to be summoned to attend the trial, proof or hearing, as the case may be, and shall remit to the Principal Clerk of Session to arrange for the attendance of such assessor.

Expert evidence when assessor summoned

42. It shall not be competent, at any trial or proof in a cause in which an assessor is summoned to sit, to lead evidence by more than one witness for each side of expert opinion on any matter within the special qualifications of the assessor; and in the event of any question arising at the trial or proof with regard to the application of this rule, the decision of the judge presiding at the trial or proof shall be final; provided that the court may, on the motion of either party enrolled not later than fourteen days before the date of the trial or proof, on special cause shewn, allow the examination of a greater number of witnesses to expert opinion. The provisions of this rule are without prejudice to the special provisions of Rule 146.

Number of assessors

43. For any trial, proof, or hearing in the Outer House one assessor only shall be summoned; for any trial or proof before one of the Judges of the Inner House or for any hearing in the Inner House whether on reclaiming motion, appeal, or otherwise, the number of assessors to be summoned shall be one, or more than one, as the court shall think fit.

Remuneration of assessors

[1] **44.**—(*a*) The remuneration of an assessor other than a nautical assessor or an assessor in any proceedings under the Patents Act 1949 or the Patents Act 1977 shall be such fees and expenses as the court shall in each cause determine.

(*b*) The remuneration to be paid to an assessor, whether nautical or otherwise, shall, unless the court otherwise directs, be treated as expenses in the cause.

(*c*) A motion for an assessor to be summoned shall only be granted on condition that the party or parties making the motion shall consign in the name of the Accountant of Court such sum to meet the fees and expenses of the assessor as the court may determine: and, when an assessor is to be summoned *ex proprio motu* of the court, such consignation shall be made by the pursuer or petitioner as the case may be, unless the court shall otherwise direct.

NOTE

[1] As amended by S.I. 1978 No. 955.

Note to be made of questions submitted to assessor

45. In every cause the judge who presides at the trial, proof, or hearing at which an assessor attends shall make a note of the questions submitted to such assessor and of the answer or answers thereto, and shall cause the same to be lodged in process.

Special provisions applicable to nautical assessors

46. In any cause arising out of or relating to a collision at sea, salvage, towage or any other maritime matter, the following provisions shall apply:—

(*a*) Nautical assessors shall be selected from a list of persons approved for the purpose by the Lord President. Such list shall be kept by the Principal Clerk of Session and shall be published as the Lord President shall direct and shall be in force for three years only; but persons entered in any such list may be again approved in any subsequent list.

[1] (*b*) The remuneration of every person attending as a nautical assessor shall be £6·30 a day for each day on which he so attends and also for any Sunday over which he is necessarily detained at the seat of the court, besides subsistence and travelling expenses. In the case of an assessor resident out of Scotland he shall be entitled to charge for a day for coming and a day for returning at the above rate; but other assessors shall not be entitled to a fee for travelling days unless owing to the distance of their ordinary residence from the seat of the court, it is impossible with reasonable convenience to travel on the day or days on which they are required to sit in court.

NOTE

[1] As amended by the Decimal Currency Act 1969, s.10(1).

SECTION 8—MESSENGERS-AT-ARMS

47.–62. [Revoked by S.I. 1988 No. 2097.]

SECTION 9—EXTRACTS

Form of extract

63.—(1) An extract of a decree of the court may be—
(*a*) partly or wholly written, or
(*b*) typewritten, or
(*c*) printed, or
(*d*) lithographed, or
(*e*) photographed.

(2) Every such extract shall—
(*a*) be signed on the last page by the extractor, and
(*b*) have each page impressed with the extractor's seal or stamp, and
(*c*) have any alteration authenticated by the initials of the extractor or assistant extractor.

NOTE
[1] Substituted by S.I. 1986 No. 1937.

Expenses to include dues of extract

63A. Any interlocutor awarding a lump sum by way of modified expenses shall be treated as also awarding, in addition to that sum, the dues of any extract required to enforce the award, and the extractor shall include in the extract the amount of those dues.

NOTE
[1] Added by S.I. 1986 No. 1937.

Extract not a bar to review

63B. Review by the Inner House of an interlocutor of the Outer House shall not be prevented by reason only that extract has been issued before the expiry of the reclaiming days.

NOTE
[1] Added by S.I. 1986 No. 1937.

64. In every extract of a decree pronounced or to be pronounced by the Court of Session on which execution may competently proceed there shall

[THE NEXT PAGE IS C 19]

be included a warrant for execution in the following terms, *viz.*:—"and the said Lords grant warrant for all lawful execution hereon".

65. The following provisions shall apply to the short form of warrant for execution added to said extracts: It shall be lawful by virtue of said warrant to arrest the readiest goods gear debts and sums of money of the debtor or obligant mentioned in said extract in payment and satisfaction of the sum or sums of money or obligation or obligations therein specified; as also charge the debtor or obligant therein mentioned to pay the sum or sums of money or to perform the obligation or obligations therein specified within the appropriate days of charge under pain of poinding (and also under the pain of imprisonment where the debt or obligation is of such a nature as the payment or implement thereof may be enforced by imprisonment), the terms of payment or implement being first come and bygone; and if a debtor fail to obey the said charge then so far as competent to apprise poind and distrain all his readiest goods gear and other effects in payment and satisfaction of the said sum or sums or obligation or obligations; and, if necessary for effecting the said poinding, to open shut and lockfast places.

66. Where interest is included in or exigible under a decree or extract, it shall be deemed to be at the rate of five [seven][1] [eleven][2] [twelve][3] [fifteen][4] per centum per annum, unless otherwise stated.

NOTES

[1] "In the case of any decree or extract in an action commenced on or after 6th January 1970, . . . " S.I. 1969 No. 1819.

[2] "In the case of any decree or extract in an action commenced on or after 7th January 1975, . . . " S.I. 1974 No. 2090.

[3] "In relation to any decree pronounced or extracted after" 5th April 1983: S.I. 1983 No. 398.

[4] "In relation to any decree pronounced or extracted after" 15th August 1985: S.I. 1985 No. 1178.

67. Execution on said extracts shall be carried out by Messengers-at-Arms or other officers entitled to execute diligence thereon.

68. The Officer's execution of charge shall be as nearly as the circumstances permit in the terms shown in Form 44.

Section 10—Service, Intimation and Citation

[1] **68A.** In any cause in which it shall be competent to serve or intimate any document or to cite any person by recorded delivery, such service, intimation or citation, when made by recorded delivery, shall only be competent and effective by such mode if it is made by recorded delivery first class service.

NOTE

[1] Added by S.I. 1968 No. 1150.

Section 11—Sittings of the Court

NOTE

[1] Added by S.I. 1987 No. 2160.

Sessions of court

68B.—(1) There shall be three sessions of the court, namely—

(*a*) a winter session;

(*b*) a spring session; and

(*c*) a summer session,

the dates of which shall be such as the Lord President shall direct annually.

(2) The Lord President may, if at any time he considers the business of the court so requires, direct that a session of the court shall be extended for such period as may be necessary.

Sederunt days

68C.—(1) A day on which the court sits during session under Rule 68D(1) shall be a sederunt day.

(2) The Lord President may by direction provide that such days in vacation as he may specify in the direction shall be sederunt days.

Sittings during session

68D.—(1) Subject to the following paragraphs of this Rule, the court shall sit on Tuesday, Wednesday, Thursday and Friday of each week during session at such times as the Lord President may direct.

(2) The court shall not sit during session—

(*a*) subject to paragraph (3), on such public holidays; or

(*b*) on such other days in exceptional circumstances,

as the Lord President may direct.

(3) A Division or Lord Ordinary may sit—

(*a*) on a Monday where it is considered necessary to hear and determine a cause; or

(*b*) on a Saturday, Sunday or public holiday to hear and determine a matter of urgency.

Sittings during vacation

68E.—(1) During vacation one or more of the judges of the court, other than the Lord President and the Lord Justice-Clerk, shall act from time to time as vacation judge sitting in court or in chambers.

(2) A vacation judge shall deal with the business of the vacation judge under Rule 1 on such days and at such times as may be convenient, subject to any direction of the Lord President.

(3) A Division or Lord Ordinary may sit during vacation, whether or not on a sederunt day, to conclude a hearing commenced in session.

(4) A Division may sit during vacation, whether or not on a sederunt day, to hear and determine urgent Inner House business which cannot competently be heard and determined by the vacation judge.

Lord Ordinary in exchequer causes

68F. The Lord Ordinary in exchequer causes may hear and determine an exchequer cause whether during a session of the court or in vacation.

Exercise of powers of Lord President by Lord Justice-Clerk

68G. In the absence of the Lord President, the Lord Justice-Clerk may exercise a power conferred on the Lord President in this section to make directions.

[1] SECTION 12—CAVEATS

NOTE

[1] Added by S.I. 1990 No. 2118.

Orders against which caveats may be lodged

68H. A person may lodge a caveat against—

(*a*) *interim* interdict sought in an action before he has lodged defences;

(*b*) any other *interim* order sought in any action before the time within which appearance may be entered has expired;

(*c*) any *interim* order sought in a petition before he has lodged answers; provided that, for the purposes of this rule, an order under section 1 of the Administration of Justice (Scotland) Act 1972 granted in terms of the prayer, or part of the prayer, of a petition shall not be regarded as an *interim* order;

(*d*) an order for intimation, service and advertisement of a petition to wind up a company or for the appointment of an administrator to a company; or

(*e*) an order for intimation, service and advertisement of a petition for his sequestration.

Form, lodging and renewal of caveats

68I.—(1) A caveat shall be in Form 72 and shall be lodged in the Petition Department.

(2) A caveat shall remain in force for a period of one year from the date of lodging, and may be renewed on its expiry for a further period of a year and yearly thereafter.

[1] Section 13—Fiats

NOTE

[1] Added by S.I. 1991 No. 2483, with effect from 25th November 1991.

Application for fiats

68J.—(1) All applications for fiats shall be presented to the Outer House and lodged in the General Department and shall, subject to sub-paragraph (2) of this rule, be determined by the Deputy Principal Clerk or an officer delegated by him.

(2) Where a fiat is refused, the application may on request be placed before a Lord Ordinary who may authorise or refuse the granting of a fiat; and the decision of the Lord Ordinary shall be final and not subject to review.

(3) An application for a fiat on the dependence of an action in which a claim to which section 19 of the Family Law (Scotland) Act 1985 applies is made shall be placed before a Lord Ordinary; and the decision of the Lord Ordinary shall be final and not subject to review.

CHAPTER II

Ordinary Actions

SECTION 1—SUMMONS, CITATION, CALLING

Initiation of proceedings

69. Save as hereinafter provided, all causes originating in the Court of Session shall be commenced in the Outer House either by summons or by petition.

Form of summons

[1] **70.**—(1) All summonses shall be on the official printed form (Form 1), which, along with the official printed backing thereon, shall be filled in and completed either in manuscript, typescript or print; provided that:—

(*a*) The conclusions shall be stated in one or more of the short forms exemplified in Form 2, or in such similar short form as the circumstances may require.

(*b*) There shall be annexed to every summons a statement in the form of an articulate numbered condescendence of the averments of fact which form the grounds of the pursuer's claim, and there shall also be annexed to every summons a note of the pursuer's pleas-in-law.

[2] (*c*) A condescendence shall include averments stating—

(i) the ground of jurisdiction of the court, unless jurisdiction would arise only if the defender prorogated the jurisdiction of the court (without contesting jurisdiction);

(ii) where appropriate, whether there is reason to believe that there exists an agreement prorogating the jurisdiction of a court in a particular country; and

(iii) whether proceedings involving the same cause of action are in subsistence between the parties in a country to which the Convention in Schedule 1 to the Civil Jurisdiction and Judgments Act 1982 applies, unless the court has exclusive jurisdiction.

(2) A summons may include—

(*a*) a warrant of inhibition which shall have the same effect as letters of inhibition;

(*b*) if the summons concludes for payment of money, a warrant to arrest the moveable property belonging to or owing to the defender.

NOTES

[1] As amended by S.I. 1984 No. 472.

[2] Inserted by S.I. 1986 No. 1941. As amended by S.I. 1987 No. 1206.

Designation of defender furth of Scotland

71. In any summons against a party not therein designed as resident or carrying on business within Scotland, the pursuer shall either state the defender's known residence or place of business, or set forth expressly that the defender's residence and place of business are unknown to the pursuer.

Induciae *in summons*

[1] **72.**—(1) Subject to Rule 75, the *induciae* in a summons shall be—

(*a*) in the case of citation within Europe, 21 days after the date of execution of service;

(*b*) in the case of personal citation under Rule 74B(1)(*d*) or (*e*) outside Europe, 21 days after the date of execution of service; and

(*c*) in any other case of citation outside Europe, 42 days after the date of execution of service.

(2) Where citation is executed in Scotland by registered or recorded delivery letter, the *induciae* shall be reckoned from 24 hours after the date of posting.

(3) An application to shorten or extend the *induciae* made after signeting of the summons but before service shall be subject to the following provisions of this paragraph:—

(*a*) the application shall be made by motion;
(*b*) the application shall be heard before a Lord Ordinary in chambers at which the solicitor for the applicant shall attend; and
(*c*) the decision of the Lord Ordinary shall be final.

NOTE
[1] Substituted by S.I. 1986 No. 1941.

Signature of summons and letters

73.—[1] (*a*) All summonses shall be signed by the pursuer's solicitor, being a solicitor entitled to practice before the Court of Session, and to his signature there shall be appended his business address; and no further or other signature shall be required.

(*b*) All letters passing the signet and all applications to the Petition Department for warrants under the Debtors (Scotland) Act 1838 or otherwise shall be signed by a solicitor entitled to practice before the Court of Session and no further or other signature shall be required.

NOTE
[1] As amended by S.I. 1991 No. 2483, with effect from 25th November 1991.

Signeting; service; diligence to found jurisdiction and on dependence, recall of arrestment or inhibition

[1] **74.** All summonses shall pass the signet and no summons shall bear any date but the date of signeting which shall be held to be the date of the summons; when signeted, the summons shall not only be warrant for service on the defender or defenders, but shall also be warrant (i) for arrestment to found jurisdiction, (ii) for any competent form of diligence by way of inhibition on the dependence or of arrestment on the dependence, or *in rem*, or to dismantle a ship, or (iii) in consistorial causes, for any of the intimations referred to in Rule 155; provided that application be made therefor before the summons is signeted by filling in the blank in the official printed form of summons after the words "warrant for".

(*a*) In the case of the service of a summons or other writ by registered or recorded delivery letter, the citation and execution thereof shall, as nearly as may be, be in the forms shewn in Form 3.

[1a](*b*) In the event of the defender or his known solicitor accepting service and dispensing with the *induciae*, the *induciae* shall be deemed to expire on the day on which the pursuer receives intimation of such acceptance and dispensation.

(*c*) When both warrant for arrestment to found jurisdiction and warrant for arrestment or inhibition on the dependence are contained in the summons as signeted it shall not be necessary for the messenger-at-arms to serve separate schedules; but it shall be competent to combine in one schedule the arrestments to found jurisdiction and the arrestments on the dependence.

(*d*) Where warrant for diligence on the dependence of the action is not obtained when the summons is signeted, it shall be competent for the pursuer to apply for such warrant at any stage of the proceedings by motion to the Lord Ordinary. A certified copy of the interlocutor granting warrant for diligence on the dependence shall be sufficient authority for service of the appropriate schedules.

[2] (*e*) The warrant for inhibition contained in the summons in terms of this rule shall have the like force and effect as letters of inhibition, and the summons, containing such warrant and the execution thereof, may be registered in the Register of Inhibitions and Adjudications. Notice of said summons may also be registered in terms of section 155 of the Titles to Land Consolidation (Scotland) Act 1868, and Schedule (PP) thereof, and the registration thereof shall have the like force and effect as registration of a notice under said last-mentioned section and schedule.

(*f*) Where a minute of amendment is lodged by the pursuer in terms of Rule 92(*c*) calling in an additional or substitute defender it shall be competent for the pursuer to apply for warrant to use any form of diligence by way of arrestment or inhibition which might have been competent on the dependence of a separate action. Such application shall be made by appending to the minute "Warrant for (arrestment to found jurisdiction, or arrestment or inhibition on the dependence, or all of them, or arrestment *in rem* or to dismantle a ship as the case may be) applied for" and shall be granted by the clerk who receives the minute when lodged by adding the words "warrant granted as craved" and adhibiting his signature together with the date below those words. Such warrant shall be equivalent to the like warrant in a signeted summons. The registration of the warrant of inhibition and execution thereof or notice thereof as the case may be shall be made in accordance with the provisions of paragraph (*e*) of this rule and shall then have the force and effect as therein mentioned.

[1a,3](*g*) Any application for the recall of any arrestment or inhibition used on the dependence of an action or for authority to move an arrested vessel made in a cause before calling shall be made by motion. The deputy principal clerk, or a clerk instructed by him, shall bring the application before a Lord Ordinary in chambers, making intimation to the parties of the place and hour. The clerk shall be accompanied by counsel, solicitor or both counsel and solicitor for each party. The solicitor or counsel for the pursuer shall produce to the Lord Ordinary the principal summons bearing the signet. The Lord Ordinary may either recall or restrict such arrestment or inhibition, on caution or without caution, and dispose of the question of expenses; provided that his judgment shall be subject to the review of the Inner House by a reclaiming motion, without leave, within seven days from the date thereof.

[3] (*h*) Any application for the recall of any arrestment or inhibition used on the dependence of an action or for authority to move an arrested vessel made after calling shall be made by motion to the Outer House or Inner House, according as the cause depends before one or the other, or to the Vacation Judge; provided that the judgment of the Lord Ordinary or Vacation Judge shall be subject to the review of the Inner House, by a reclaiming motion, without leave, within seven days from the date thereof.

(*i*) It shall not be necessary that any messenger-at-arms or sheriff-officer serving a summons or other writ or order of court shall have the original document in his hands at the time of such service, provided that a copy of the summons or other writ certified as correct by the solicitor in the cause or a certified copy of the order of court shall at the time be in possession of such messenger or officer, and shall be exhibited to the party on whom the service is made, if required.

NOTES

[1] As amended by S.I. 1986 No. 1941.

[1a] As amended by S.I. 1991 No. 2483, with effect from 25th November 1991.

[2] As amended by S.I. 1984 No. 472.

[3] As amended by S.I. 1990 No. 705.

Citation and service

[1] **74A.**—(1) Subject to paragraph (2) and Rule 74B, citation in any action shall be executed either—

(*a*) personally; or
(*b*) if the person executing the citation after due inquiry has reasonable grounds for believing that the defender—
(i) is residing at a particular dwelling place but is unavailable, by leaving the citation in the hands of a person, or depositing it, in the dwelling place; or
(ii) carries on business at a particular place, by leaving the citation at, or depositing it in that place; or
(iii) being a company, has a registered office at a particular place, by leaving the citation at, or depositing it in, that place; or
(*c*) by post.

(2) Where the place where a defender resides cannot be ascertained or citation cannot be successfully effected in accordance with a method permitted under paragraph (1), citation shall be made edictally in accordance with Rule 75.

(3) All citations or other writs or orders of the court served on any person shall be signed and dated by the person executing service and the service so executed shall be certified by means of a form of execution signed and dated by that person stating the manner of service.

(4) Any citation that is executed personally under sub-paragraph (*a*) or by leaving the citation under sub-paragraph (*b*) of paragraph (1) shall—
(*a*) be served on the defender or at his dwelling place, registered office or place of business by a messenger-at-arms who shall explain its purpose to the defender, or other person with whom he leaves it whose name and designation he shall ascertain and enter in the execution;
(*b*) be witnessed by one witness signing the citation and certificate of execution which shall state his occupation and address;
[2] (*c*) where left with a person other than the defender, be placed in a sealed envelope (bearing the notice in paragraph (6)) by the messenger-at-arms together with the summons or other document served.

(5) A citation executed by post shall be effected by means of—
(*a*) a messenger-at-arms; or
[3] (*b*) a solicitor,
posting a copy of the summons with citation in the terms set out in Form 3 by registered or recorded delivery letter addressed to the defender and having on the face of the envelope the notice set out in paragraph (6).

(6) The notice mentioned in paragraph (5) shall be in the following terms:—

"This letter contains a citation to or intimation from the Court of Session, Scotland. If delivery of the letter cannot be made it is to be returned immediately to the Deputy Principal Clerk of Session, 2 Parliament Square, Edinburgh."

(7) On a citation being executed by post, the solicitor who executed it shall complete and return the execution in the terms set out in Form 3.

(8) Any citation executed by post is a valid citation unless and until the defender proves that the letter was not tendered or left at his address.

NOTES

[1] Inserted by S.I. 1984 No. 472 and as amended by S.I. 1985 No. 1600, 1986 No. 1941 and 1990 No. 705.

[2] As amended by S.I. 1991 No. 1157.

[3] As amended by S.I. 1991 No. 2483, with effect from 25th November 1991.

Citation and service furth of the United Kingdom

[1] **74B.**—(1) Citation and service in any cause on a defender in a country furth of the United Kingdom may be made by any of the following methods of service if permitted under a convention providing for service in that country, or, insofar as permitted by the laws of that country—

(*a*) by post;
(*b*) through the central, or other appropriate, authority of the country in which the defender is to be found, at the request of the Foreign Office;
(*c*) through a British consular officer in the country in which the defender is to be found, at the request of the Foreign Office;
(*d*) by an *huissier*, other judicial officer or competent official in the country in which the defender is to be found, at the request of a messenger-at-arms; and
(*e*) personal citation by the pursuer or his agent.

(2) Where the place where a defender resides cannot be ascertained or citation cannot be successfully effected in accordance with a method permitted under paragraph (1), citation shall be made edictally in accordance with Rule 75.

(3) Where citation is by post—
(*a*) it shall be executed by means of—
(i) a messenger-at-arms; or
[2] (ii) a solicitor,
posting a copy of the summons with citation in Form 3 by registered or recorded delivery letter addressed to the defender and having on the face of the envelope the notice set out in Rule 74A(6); and
(*b*) on being executed, the pursuer shall lodge a certificate of execution in Form 3 (with such modification as may be necessary) together with a certificate of delivery or such evidence of actual delivery to the defender or to his place of residence as the court may require.

(4) Where citation is through a central or other appropriate authority of, or through a British consular officer in, another country, at the request of the Foreign Office, the pursuer shall—
(*a*) send a copy of the summons, with a request for execution of the citation by the method indicated in the request, to the Secretary of State for Foreign and Commonwealth Affairs; and
(*b*) lodge a certificate signed by the authority serving the citation that it has been, and stating the manner in which it was, executed, together with, where appropriate, a translation into English.

(5) Where citation is by an *huissier*, other judicial officer or competent official at the request of a messenger-at-arms—
(*a*) the messenger-at-arms shall send a copy of the summons with a request for execution of the citation by the method indicated in the request, to the official in the country in which the citation is to be executed; and
(*b*) the pursuer shall lodge a certificate signed by the official serving the citation that it has been, and stating the manner in which it was, executed, together with, where appropriate, a translation into English.

(6) Where citation is executed personally by the pursuer or his agent—
(*a*) a copy of the summons shall be served with a citation;
(*b*) the pursuer shall lodge a certificate of execution, together with, where appropriate, a translation into English; and
(*c*) the service shall be witnessed by a witness signing the citation and certificate of execution which shall state his occupation and address.

(7) Where citation is to be executed in a country where English is not an official language—
(*a*) the copy of the summons shall be served together with a translation in an official language of that country; and

[THE NEXT PAGE IS C 23]

(*b*) for the notice under paragraph (3)(*a*), there shall be a translation in an official language of that country.

(8) A translation under paragraph (4)(*b*), (5)(*b*) or (7)(*a*) shall be certified as a correct translation by the person making it; and the certificate must contain the full name, address and qualification of the translator.

NOTES
[1] Inserted by S.I. 1986 No. 1941.
[2] As amended by S.I. 1991 No. 2483, with effect from 25th November 1991.

Edictal citation and citation by advertisement

[1] **75.**—(1) This Rule applies, and edictal citation shall be made, where the place where the defender resides cannot be ascertained or citation cannot be successfully effected in accordance with a method permitted under Rule 74A(1) or 74B(1).

(2) Where citation is sought to be made edictally, a motion shall be enrolled when the summons is presented for signet craving the court—

(*a*) to grant warrant to cite the defender edictally;

(*b*) for an order for citation of the defender by the publication, in a specified newspaper circulating in the area of last known address of the defender or elsewhere, of an advertisement, or for an order to dispense with advertisement; and

(*c*) where there are no averments in the condescendence, stating what steps have been taken to trace the defender.

[2] (3) A motion under paragraph (2) made before calling shall be heard in chambers at which the solicitor or counsel for the pursuer shall appear.

(4) Where an order is made for advertisement, the advertisement shall be in Form 4A.

(5) Where citation has been made by advertisement, there shall be lodged in process a copy of the newspaper containing the advertisement.

(6) Where citation is to be made edictally, citation shall be made at the office of the extractor of the Court of Session in Form 4.

(7) The *induciae* for edictal citation shall be six months from the date of service on the extractor of the Court of Session or, where there is citation by advertisement, the date on which the advertisement is published.

(8) Where the same summons is to be served edictally at the same time on two or more persons, such service may be made by delivery at the office of the extractor of one copy of the summons provided that it bears on its face that it is delivered for all of such persons.

NOTES
[1] Substituted by S.I. 1986 No. 1941. As amended by S.I. 1987 No. 1206.
[2] As amended by S.I. 1991 No. 2483, with effect from 25th November 1991.

Intimation to connected persons

[1] **75A.**—(1) This rule applies to any action in which following the death of any person from personal injuries, damages are claimed—

(*a*) by the executor of the deceased, in respect of the injuries from which the deceased died;

(*b*) in respect of the death of the deceased, by any relative of his.

(2) In this rule, "relative" has the same meaning as in the Damages (Scotland) Act 1976.

(3) In any action to which this rule applies, the pursuer shall aver in the summons as appropriate—

(*a*) that he is the only person with a title to sue the defender in respect of the injuries or death;

(*b*) that there are other persons having a title to sue the defender in respect of the injuries or death, being the persons specified in the warrant for intimation;

(*c*) that there are other such persons in respect of whom intimation should be dispensed with on the ground either—

(i) that the pursuer does not know their names or whereabouts and cannot reasonably ascertain them; or
(ii) that they are not likely to be awarded more than the sum of £200.

(4) In a case where the pursuer makes averments under sub-paragraph (*c*) of paragraph (3), he shall apply to the court by motion for an order dispensing with intimation in accordance with those averments.

(5) The court may in respect of any person specified in a motion enrolled under paragraph (4) grant any such motion or may refuse it with or without conditions (including a condition that such advertisement be made in such manner and in such place and at such times as may be specified in the order), and in doing so shall have regard to—
(*a*) the desirability of avoiding multiplicity of actions;
(*b*) the expense likely to be incurred in ascertaining the name or the whereabouts of any such person;
(*c*) the inconvenience or difficulty of taking steps to ascertain the name or the whereabouts of any such person.

(6) In a case where the pursuer makes averments under sub-paragraph (*b*) of paragraph (3), a warrant for intimation shall be endorsed on the official printed form of summons in the following terms—

"Warrant to intimate to (name and address) as a person who is believed to have a title to sue the defender in an action based on (the injuries from which the late (name and former address) died) *or* (the death of the late (name and former address))."

and intimation shall be made to the person specified in the warrant in the form set out in Form 5A or as nearly as may be in that form, together with a copy of the summons.

(7) In a case where at any stage of the proceedings, intimation on any person requires to be made by the pursuer in consequence of—
(*a*) an order under paragraph (5);
(*b*) an order of the court made on being informed of the name and whereabouts of any person in respect of whom intimation has been dispensed with under paragraph (3)(*c*)(i), or on a motion in that behalf at the instance of a party to the action other than the pursuer,

the interlocutor shall include a warrant for intimation, and intimation shall be made by serving the interlocutor on the person or persons named in the warrant for intimation, together with a copy of the summons, or of the open or closed record as the case may be.

(8) Rule 76 shall apply to the execution of a warrant under this rule as it applies to the execution of a warrant under that rule with the substitution for the reference to Form 5 of a reference to Form 5A.

(9) Any person upon whom intimation is made in accordance with this rule may apply to the court within 21 days after intimation or such longer period as the court thinks fit to be sisted as an additional pursuer to the action, and on so doing shall lodge in process either—
(*a*) a minute craving leave of the court to be sisted to the action, to adopt the existing grounds of action, and to amend the conclusions, condescendence, and pleas-in-law; or
(*b*) a minute craving leave of the court to be sisted to the action and setting out a separate conclusion, averments and pleas-in-law.

(10) On lodging a minute under paragraph (9), the minuter shall intimate the minute to all other parties to the action, who may lodge answers thereto within 14 days after such intimation or such longer period as the court thinks fit; and the court may grant, with or without conditions, or refuse, the crave of the minute after such further procedure, if any, as it thinks fit.

(11) If any person upon whom intimation is made in accordance with this rule does not apply to be sisted as an additional pursuer to the action, and subsequently raises a separate action against the same defender in

respect of the same injuries or death, and would apart from this rule be awarded the expenses or part of the expenses of that action, he shall not be awarded those expenses except on cause shown.

NOTE

[1] Added by S.I. 1976 No. 2020, substituted by S.I. 1984 No. 920 and amended by S.I. 1986 No. 1941. The Rule originally numbered 75A (service in certain actions founded on delict), introduced by S.I. 1971 No. 1215, was revoked by S.I. 1986 No. 1941.

Intimation to heritable creditors

[1] **76.** In any action relating to heritage it shall not be necessary to call as a defender any person by reason only of any interest he may have as the holder of a heritable security over such heritage, but intimation of the action shall be made to such a person; and accordingly in such case the official printed form of summons shall be filled up so as to contain a warrant for such intimation in the following terms as nearly as may be:—

"Warrant to intimate to (name and address) as a person who is believed to be a heritable creditor of the defender";

such warrant may be executed contemporaneously with, or after, the citation of the defender, by any messenger-at-arms, or by the pursuer's solicitor, by serving personally or by posting a registered or recorded delivery letter addressed to such person and containing a copy of the summons with intimation subjoined in the terms as nearly as may be of Form 5.

NOTE

[1] As amended by S.I. 1991 No. 2483, with effect from 25th November 1991.

Certificates of execution

77. All certificates of execution or intimation of a summons shall be written thereon.

Calling of summons

78.—[1] (*a*) In order that a summons may be called during session, it shall be lodged for calling in the General Department not later than 1 p.m. on the day before that on which it is to be called, provided always that the *induciae* of such summons expire on or before the day on which it is to be so called.

(*b*) In order that a summons may be called during vacation, it shall be lodged for calling as aforesaid not later than 1 p.m. on the second day preceding any calling day, of which notice will be given in the printed rolls prior to the commencement of each vacation, provided always that the *induciae* of such summons expire on or before such calling day.

(*c*) As lodged, every summons shall be accompanied by a slip containing the instance. If there are more than two pursuers, the slip shall contain only the name and designation of the pursuer first named with the words "and others"; and, if the defenders are more than three, it shall contain the name and designation of the defender first named with the words "and others as per roll", referring to a separate roll of all the defenders, which roll shall be lodged along with the summons itself. In naming and designing a pursuer or defender who is a body of persons, such as a trust or partnership, whether individual members are also parties or not, it shall be sufficient to use the collective name of such body, *e.g.* the testamentary trustees of the late A.B., the firm or partnership of A.B. and Company or A.B. and Son, as the case may be.

[2] (*d*) Each step of the process, lodged along with the summons, shall be marked on the backing thereof with the same letter and number as shall be given to the summons itself.

(*e*) The calling of any summons shall be published on the walls and in the printed rolls of court on the day on which the summons is called.

NOTES

[1] See Practice Notes, 1976, No. 3.

[2] As amended by S.I. 1990 No. 705.

Motions for interim orders

[1] **79.**—[2] (1) If in any cause initiated by a summons which includes a conclusion for interim interdict, the pursuer desires to move therefor before the calling of the summons or after the calling of the summons but before lodging of defences, it shall not be necessary to present a separate petition for suspension and interdict, but the summons when signeted may forthwith be lodged in the General Department and a motion enrolled craving interim interdict in terms of the conclusions of the summons. The same procedure shall then be followed *mutatis mutandis* as is prescribed with regard to interim orders in petitions by Rule 236, provided (1) that the Deputy Principal Clerk or the clerk instructed by him shall report to the Lord Ordinary before any order is made whether a caveat has been lodged for any of the defenders, and (2) that, if the Lord Ordinary so determines, the *induciae* for service of the summons may be shortened in terms of Rule 72(3).

(2) Paragraph (1) shall also apply in any cause in which a motion is made for any interim order—

(*a*) before calling; and
(*b*) other than a motion for an interim order for which intimation is required under any enactment.

(3) [Revoked by S.I. 1990 No. 2118.]

NOTES

[1] As amended by S.I. 1984 No. 499.

[2] As amended by S.I. 1986 No. 1941.

Protestation for not calling summons

80.—(*a*) If a pursuer shall not lodge his summons for calling on the day on which the *induciae* expire, or on one of the three sederunt days next ensuing if in session, or, if in vacation on the first ensuing calling-day, or, failing a calling day, on the first sederunt day after vacation, the defender may proceed by way of protestation in the same form and to the same effect as under present practice, provided that written intimation of intention to make protestation shall be given by the defender's solicitor so as to reach the pursuer's solicitor at his office before protestation is made.

[1] (*b*) Where protestation is put up in the minute book for not calling any summons, and warrant is issued for extract thereof, such extract shall contain a decerniture for £3·15 of protestation money, as expenses; provided that a pursuer may be reponed against a protestation for not calling at any time not later than ten days after the same has been given out for extract, whether extract shall have issued or not, by lodging with the clerk, for calling, his summons, with the relative documents, accompanied by the receipt of the solicitor for the defender for the said sum of £3·15 of protestation money, or consigning the money itself in the hands of the clerk, for the use of the solicitor for the defender, and payable to him on demand.

(*c*) When protestation is put up in the minute-book for not calling any summons, the Extractor of the Court of Session shall be bound to score the same on production to him of a certificate from the Deputy Principal Clerk that the summons has been duly lodged for calling; and, after the granting of such certificate, the procedure will be regularly and immediately followed out in calling the same.

NOTE

[1] As amended by the Decimal Currency Act 1969, s.10(1).

Section 2—Appearance, Defences and Counter-claims

Appearance

[1] **81.**—(1) The defender may enter appearance within three days after the day on which the summons has called by requesting a clerk of session in the appropriate section in the General Department to mark on the summons the names of the counsel (or solicitor who has a right of audience in the Court of Session) and solicitor who are acting for him or that he appears for himself.

(1A) On receipt of the intimation referred to in paragraph (1), the clerk of session shall mark on the summons the names of the defender's counsel (or solicitor who has a right of audience in the Court of Session) and solicitor or that he appears for himself.

(1B) On entering appearance, the defender shall give written intimation to the pursuer that appearance has been entered.

(2) The entering of appearance shall not be taken to imply acceptance of the jurisdiction of the court.

NOTE

[1] As amended by S.I. 1986 No. 1941 and (with effect from 25th November 1991) S.I. 1991 No. 2483.

Party appearing not to state objections to execution of summonses, etc.

82. No party appearing in any action or proceeding in the Court of Session shall be entitled to state any objection to the regularity of the execution or service as against himself of the summons or other pleading or writ whereby he is convened.

Defences

83.—(*a*) Defences may be lodged on any day after the day on which the summons is called, but not later than the fourteenth day after the day on which the summons is called, or, if such fourteenth day is in vacation or recess, on the first calling day or sederunt day, whichever is earlier; provided that, if defences are lodged earlier than the said fourteenth day or first calling day or sederunt day, notice in writing shall be given to the pursuer on the day of lodging that such defences have been lodged.

(*b*) Defences shall be in the form of articulate numbered answers to the condescendence annexed to the summons, and there shall be annexed to such defences a note of the defender's pleas-in-law.

(*c*) [Revoked by S.I. 1990 No. 705.]

(*d*) On lodging defences, the defender's solicitor shall send a copy thereof to the pursuer's solicitor.

[1] (*e*) Where a defender intends to contest the jurisdiction of the court, he must—

(i) lodge defences relating only to the question of jurisdiction in the first instance; and if unsuccessful, be allowed to amend his defences to defend on the substantive issues of the action within such time as the court may allow; or

(ii) lodge defences relating to both jurisdiction and the substantive issues of the action without submitting to the jurisdiction of the court.

NOTE

[1] Added by S.I. 1986 No. 1941.

Counter-claim

84.—(*a*) It shall be competent for a defender either in his defences as lodged, or at adjustment, or, subject to such conditions, if any, as to expenses or otherwise as the court may think just, by way of amendment at any later stage of the case at which amendment is competent, to counter-claim against the pursuer in respect of any matter forming part of, or arising out of the grounds of, the pursuer's action, or the decision of which is necessary for the determination of the question in controversy between the parties, or which, if the pursuer had been a person not otherwise subject to the jurisdiction of the court, might competently have formed the subject of an action against such pursuer in which jurisdiction would have arisen *ex reconventione*; provided that, in any case, the counter-claim is such as might have formed matter of a separate action, and that, if such separate action had been raised, it would not have been necessary to call as defender thereto any person other than the pursuer.

(*b*) Any such counter-claim shall be headed "Counter-claim for the Defender", and shall be preceded by the conclusion or conclusions, in the like short form or forms as exemplified with regard to the conclusions of a summons in Form 2 in the Appendix, which, if the counter-claim had been enforced by a separate action, would have been appropriately used in the summons in such separate action. The counter-claim shall also contain an articulate numbered statement of facts setting forth the facts on which the counter-claim is founded. Such statement of facts may incorporate by reference any matter contained in the defences. The note of pleas-in-law for the defender shall include any pleas which may be necessary to support the counter-claim.

(*c*) On lodging defences containing a counter-claim, or on a counter-claim being included in the defences at adjustment, or on a counter-claim being incorporated in a closed record by way of amendment it shall be competent for the defender to apply for warrant to use any form of diligence by way of arrestment or inhibition which might have been competent on the dependence of a separate action brought to enforce the matter of the counter-claim. Such application shall be made by appending to the conclusion or conclusions which precede the counter-claim the words "Warrant for (*arrestment or inhibition on the dependence, or both, or arrestment* in rem *or to dismantle a ship, as the case may be*) applied for", and shall be granted by the clerk who receives the defences when lodged, or who receives the record as closed or as closed anew after amendment, adding the words "Warrant granted as craved", and adhibiting his signature, together with the date, below those words. Such warrant shall be equivalent to the like warrant in a signeted summons. The registration of the warrant of inhibition

[THE NEXT PAGE IS C 27]

and execution thereof or notice thereof, as the case may be shall be made in accordance with the provisions of paragraph (*e*) of Rule 74 and shall then have the force and effect as therein mentioned.

(*d*) The right of a pursuer to abandon his action shall not be affected on account of a counter-claim by the defender; but any expenses payable by the pursuer as a condition of, or in consequence of, such abandonment shall be exclusive of the expenses of the counter-claim.

(*e*) It shall be competent for a defender who has counter-claimed in manner aforesaid to abandon his counter-claim on condition of paying any expenses occasioned to the pursuer by the counter-claim.

(*f*) Notwithstanding abandonment by the pursuer, the defender may insist on his counter-claim, and the proceedings therein shall continue in dependence as if the counter-claim were a separate action.

(*g*) A counter-claim may be heard and tried along with, or before, or after, the claim in the pursuer's summons, as the court may consider just and expedient in the circumstances; and, if evidence is led with regard to either claim separately from the other, such evidence shall, so far as competent and relevant, be evidence with regard to the other claim.

(*h*) Any interlocutor or decree, which would have been competent in a separate action brought to enforce the conclusions stated in the counter-claim may competently be pronounced on the counter-claim.

(*j*) Procedure by way of counter-claim shall not be applicable to consistorial causes, but shall apply in the case of counter-claims concluding for declarator, or for production and reduction of any writ founded on by the pursuer.

(*k*) Answers to a counter-claim may be lodged by the pursuer not later than the fourteenth day after the day on which the counter-claim is lodged.

Third party notices

85.— [1] (1) Where in any action, a defender claims that he has any right of contribution, relief, or indemnity against any person who is not already a party to the action, or that a person whom the pursuer is not bound to call as a defender should be made a party to the action along with the defender in respect that such person is either solely liable or jointly or jointly and severally liable with the defender to the pursuer in respect of the subject-matter of the action, the defender may set forth in his defences or in a separate statement of facts the grounds upon which he maintains that any such person (hereinafter called a third party) is liable to him by way of contribution, relief, or indemnity, or should be made a party to the action. The defences or statement of facts shall also contain appropriate pleas-in-law directed against such third party. Thereafter the defender may enrol the cause for the purpose of obtaining an order of court for the service of a third party notice upon such third party. The court shall have complete discretion to grant or refuse such order. If it be granted, it shall be competent to such third party, within 28 days after service or such other period as the court may on cause shown appoint, to appear and lodge answers. Averments directed against a third party shall ordinarily be made prior to the closing of the record, but may, in the discretion of the court and subject to such conditions as the court may attach, be made at a later stage, but in no event later than the commencement of the trial or hearing of the cause on its merits, by amendment of the record. Subject as aforesaid, the amendment of the record with a view to bringing in a third party shall apply to a cause remitted from the sheriff court to the Court of Session as to a cause originating in the Court of Session. A third party notice shall be as nearly as may be in one or other of the forms shown in Form 7 in the Appendix; and the answers by a third party shall be headed ' Answers for E.F. Third Party in the action at the instance of A.B. Pursuer against C.D. Defender '; and the following provisions shall apply to the procedure under such third party notice;

(*a*) The third party notice shall be served upon the third party in any manner in which a summons may competently be served upon a defender and shall be accompanied by a copy of the summons and defences, or the record, if any. A copy of the third party notice shall be lodged in process with a certificate of execution thereon.

(*b*) The order granting leave to serve a third party notice may contain a warrant for arrestment to found jurisdiction, or for arrestment or inhibition on the dependence.

[2] (*c*) Upon the lodging of answers for a third party, a record shall be made up and adjusted in the same way as if the third party had been originally a defender to the action. The defender who has served the third party notice shall make up the record. Not later than 14 days after lodging of answers for the third party he shall deliver at least six copies of the Open Record to each of the solicitors for the other parties and shall at the same time lodge two copies in the General Department. The third party, if he so desires, may answer the averments of the pursuer in the same way as if the third party had been called as a defender; and the averments of one party against another may be adopted by any of the other parties to the action. Save as herein provided, the same procedure shall be followed, as between the defender and the third party, or as between the pursuer and the third party, as would have been followed in an ordinary action between those parties as pursuer and defender therein respectively.

(*d*) The court, if satisfied that no competent or relevant averments of a right of contribution, relief or indemnity, or connecting the third party with the subject matter of the action, have been stated against the third party, may, after hearing parties in the procedure roll, dismiss the case so far as directed against the third party.

(*e*) Where enquiry by way of proof or jury trial is necessary between the parties to the action, or any of them, the court may allow the case so far as directed against the third party to proceed to proof, or jury trial, along with the action between the pursuer and the defender, or separately therefrom, or may deal with the matter otherwise as in its discretion it thinks fit. In any case in which the merits of the pursuer's case are challenged by a third party, such third party shall be entitled to appear at the proof or trial of the pursuer's case, and to take part in the cause and lead evidence therein as if he were a defender; and such evidence, so far as competent and relevant, shall be evidence for or against the pursuer, or for or against the defender, and shall be available to all the parties in the cause.

(*f*) In any action in which a third party notice has been served, the court may after a proof or jury trial pronounce a decree in favour of the pursuer against the third party, or may assoilzie the third party from any liability to the pursuer in respect of the subject matter of the action, as if he had been a party to the original action, but without prejudice to any liability of the third party to the defender.

(*g*) Where a third party in his answers makes, as against any person who is not already a party to the action, a claim of the nature specified in this Rule, the provisions hereof shall apply *mutatis mutandis* to the claim between the third party and such other person.

(*h*) Subject to the provisions herein contained, the court shall have full power to pronounce a judgment or judgments or apply a verdict or verdicts in favour of or against any of the various parties to a cause in which a third party notice has been served and to deal with expenses as between them.

(*i*) Any judgment or verdict applied against a third party shall take effect and be extractable in the same way as a judgment or verdict against a defender.

[3] (2) This rule shall apply to a pursuer making a claim of the nature specified in paragraph (1) in respect of a counter-claim by a defender against any person who is not already a party to the action, as it applies to a defender.

NOTES

[1] As amended by S.I. 1980 No. 1144.

[2] As amended by S.I. 1976 No. 2197.

[3] Added by S.I. 1980 No. 1144.

Borrowing process

86. Upon entering appearance, the defender shall have right to borrow the principal summons and any productions which may have been lodged and he shall be bound to return the same not later than the last day on which defences may be lodged, or along with the defences if these are lodged earlier.

Borrowing process where several defenders

87.—(*a*) If appearance is separately entered by two or more defenders, they shall have right to borrow the principal summons and any productions which may have been lodged in the order in which they have entered appearance; and such order shall be recorded in the Office of Court, and as so recorded shall be final and conclusive.

(*b*) Subject to agreement among all the defenders who enter appearance, the defender who is first in order shall not be entitled to retain the principal summons and any productions which may have been lodged beyond the seventh day if there are two defenders and not more, or the fifth day, if there are three defenders and not more, after the day on which he entered appearance; and the defender who is next in order shall not be entitled to retain the principal summons and any productions which may have been lodged beyond the fourteenth day, if there are two defenders and not more, or the tenth day, if there are three defenders and not more, after the day on which he entered appearance: provided that in no case shall the principal summons and any productions which may have been lodged be retained by any defender beyond the fourteenth day after entering appearance, and that, if there are more than three defenders, any one of them who has not been permitted to borrow the principal summons and any productions which may have been lodged before his defences were due, may enrol a motion to be allowed to borrow the same and to lodge defences within such time as the court may fix; provided that, where two or more defenders have entered appearance through the same solicitor, they shall be deemed for the purposes of this paragraph to be one defender.

Caption on failure of defender to return summons, etc.

88. If a defender shall fail to return the principal summons and any productions which may have been lodged on or before any of the days above provided respectively, the clerk in charge of the process shall, if required, issue a caption for the same in common form.

[1] SECTION 2A—TIME TO PAY DIRECTIONS

NOTE

[1] Inserted by S.I. 1988 No. 2060.

Interpretation and application

88A.—(1) In this Section, "the Act of 1987" means the Debtors (Scotland) Act 1987.

(2) Words and expressions used in this Section which are also used in the Act of 1987 have the same meaning as in that Act.

Notice about time to pay directions

88B.—(1) In an action in which a defender may apply for a time to pay direction under section 1(1) of the Act of 1987, the pursuer shall serve on that defender a notice in Form 65 and an application in Form 66 at the same time as service of the summons or pleadings as amended by a minute of amendment calling him as a defender.

(2) Before serving a notice and an application under paragraph (1), the pursuer shall insert in Form 65 the date by which Form 66 must be returned to the court by the defender (being the date on which the *induciae* expire) and shall complete Part A of Form 66.

Applications for time to pay directions in undefended actions

88C.—(1) Where a defender does not enter appearance in an action and intends to apply for a time to pay direction and, where appropriate, recall or restriction of an arrestment, he shall complete and return the application in Form 66 to the court before the date stated in Form 65.

(2) Where the pursuer does not object to the application by a defender for a time to pay direction or the recall [or] restriction of an arrestment, he may enrol for decree in absence in terms of Rule 89 stating that he does not object to the application.

(3) Where the pursuer objects to the application by a defender for a time to pay direction or the recall or restriction of an arrestment, he shall intimate—

(*a*) the motion for decree in absence in terms of Rule 89; and

(*b*) the grounds of objection to the application by the defender,

in Form 67 to the defender on an *induciae* of seven days.

(4) On enrolling a motion for decree in absence, the pursuer shall lodge a copy of the Form 67 intimated to the defender.

(5) The defender need not appear at the hearing of the motion for decree in absence and may send to the Deputy Principal Clerk written representations in response to the note of objections of the pursuer.

(6) A motion for decree in absence to which paragraph (3) applies shall be starred.

Applications for time to pay directions where appearance entered but defences not lodged

88D.—(1) Where a defender, after entering appearance, does not lodge defences but intends to apply for a time to pay direction and where appropriate, recall or restriction of an arrestment, notwithstanding the date specified in Form 65 as the date by which Form 66 must be returned, he shall complete and return the application in Form 66 to the court not later than the day on which defences would have had to be lodged in process.

(2) Rules 88C(2) to (6) shall apply to an application under this rule as they apply to an application under that rule.

Applications for time to pay directions where defences lodged

88E. An application for a time to pay direction under section 1(1) of the Act of 1987 by—

(*a*) a defender in an action in which defences have been lodged by that defender; or

(*b*) a pursuer in a counterclaim or a third party,

shall be made by motion.

Applications for variation or recall of time to pay directions or arrestments

88F.—(1) An application by a creditor or debtor under section 3(1) of the Act of 1987 to vary or recall a time to pay direction or to recall or restrict an arrestment shall be made by motion.

(2) A motion under paragraph (1) shall—

(*a*) include a brief statement of the reason for the application; and

(*b*) be intimated to the debtor or creditor, as the case may be, on an *induciae* of 14 days by recorded delivery letter.

(3) On the enrolling of a motion under paragraph (1), there shall be lodged in process—

(*a*) a copy of the letter of intimation and the certificate of posting; and

(*b*) any document to be relied on at the hearing of the motion.

Appeals

88G.—(1) An application for leave to appeal under section 103(3) of the Act of 1987 shall be made within seven days of the date of the interlocutor to be appealed against.

(2) The decision of the Lord Ordinary or vacation judge granting or refusing such leave to appeal shall be final.

(3) Where such leave to appeal has been granted, an appeal under section 103(3) of the Act of 1987 shall be made by motion enrolled in the single bills before a division of the Inner House for review of the Lord Ordinary's interlocutor, within 14 days of the date on which leave was granted.

Notice for payment of interest on a decree

88H. Where a creditor wishes to recover interest (other than interest awarded as a specific sum) under a decree containing a time to pay direction, the notice to be served under section 1(7) of the Act of 1987 shall be served on the debtor by the creditor—

(*a*) in the case of a decree containing a time to pay direction for payment by instalments, not later than 14 days before the date on which the last instalment is due to be paid; and

(*b*) in the case of a decree containing a time to pay direction for payment by deferred lump sum, not later than 14 days before the date on which the lump sum is to be paid.

SECTION 3—DECREE IN ABSENCE

Decree in absence and recall thereof

[1] **89.** (*a*) If in any cause other than a cause in which it is incompetent to decern without proof a defender fails to enter appearance in terms of Rule 81, or if, having duly entered appearance he fails to lodge defences in terms of paragraph (*a*) of Rule 83, the pursuer may enrol for decree in absence; and the cause will then appear in the printed rolls, in the roll of undefended causes, on the first available day thereafter whether in session or vacation.

(*aa*) Subject to the following provisions of this Rule, where any action appears in the roll as an undefended cause, the court shall without the attendance of counsel or solicitor, grant decree in absence in terms of the conclusions of the summons, or subject to such restrictions as may be set out in a minute written on the summons by the solicitor for the pursuer; and the decree may be extracted on the expiry of 10 days from the date on which it was granted, but not before.

(*ab*) No reclaiming motion may be brought to recall a decree in absence granted under this Rule.

[3] (*ac*) The motion enrolled for decree in absence shall state the ground of jurisdiction of the court and, in a cause to which the Civil Jurisdiction and Judgments Act 1982 applies, the domicile of the defender (as determined by the provisions of that Act) in so far as it is known to the pursuer.

(*b*) In an undefended cause in which the summons has been served on a defender outside the United Kingdom under Rule 74B and he has no known solicitor in Scotland, the court shall, in the interlocutor granting decree in absence, supersede extract of the decree for such period beyond seven days as seems reasonable to the court to allow for the number of days required in the ordinary course of post for the sending of a letter from Edinburgh to the defender and the sending of an answer to Edinburgh.

(*c*) Where a copy of the summons has been served on a defender outside the United Kingdom under Rule 74B and decree in absence is pronounced against that defender because he has not entered appearance, intimation of a copy of the interlocutor granting decree shall be made within seven days of the date of decree to that defender in accordance with paragraph (1) of Rule 74B.

(*d*) Where a copy of the summons has been served on a defender outside the United Kingdom under Rule 74B and decree in absence has been pronounced against that defender because he has not entered appearance, the court may, on the motion of that defender, recall the decree and allow defences to be lodged if—

(i) the defender, without any fault on his part, did not have knowledge of the summons in sufficient time to defend;

(ii) the defender has disclosed a *prima facie* defence to the action on the merits;

(iii) the motion is made within a reasonable time after the defender had knowledge of the decree; and

(iv) the motion is not made after the expiry of one year from the date of the decree.

(*e*) *When defender resident or carrying on business in England or Northern Ireland, and without known solicitor in Scotland.* In any undefended cause in which decree is pronounced against a defender who is described as resident or carrying on business in England or Northern Ireland and has no known solicitor in Scotland, such defender may, at any time not later than the tenth day after the day on which such decree was pronounced, enrol for recall of such decree and for allowing defences to be received provided that should the said tenth day not be an enrolling day the motion may be enrolled on the next enrolling day thereafter; and the court shall recall the decree and allow defences to be received without any award

[THE NEXT PAGE IS C 31]

of expenses against the defender; and the cause shall thereupon be treated as if defences had been lodged in due time.

(*f*) Without prejudice to the other rules of this section, the defender may, not later than the tenth day from the date of a decree in absence, enrol for the recall of such decree and for allowing defences to be received, provided that should the said tenth day not be an enrolling day the motion may be enrolled on the next enrolling day thereafter; and on such enrolment, and on the defender paying £4·20 to the pursuer and exhibiting to the Clerk of Court a receipt therefor, the court shall recall the decree in absence and allow the defences to be received, and the cause shall thereafter proceed as if the defences had been lodged in due time.

(*g*), (*h*) [Revoked by S.I. 1990 No. 705.]

(*i*) Subject to paragraph (*d*), where, after personal service of a summons on a defender or after the entering of appearance for the defender, a decree in absence upon which a charge is competent has been granted, and—

(i) it has not been recalled,
(ii) it has been extracted,
(iii) a charge upon it has not been brought under review by suspension, and
(iv) 60 days have elapsed since the expiry of that charge,

then the decree shall have effect as a decree *in foro*.

(*j*) The recall of any decree under this Rule shall be without prejudice to the validity of anything already done or transacted, or of any contract made or obligation incurred, under and in virtue of the decree recalled, or of any appointment made or power granted therein or thereby.

NOTE

[1] As amended by the Decimal Currency Act 1969, s.10(1), S.I. 1984 No. 472, S.I. 1986 No. 1941 and S.I. 1987 Nos. 1206 and 2160.

[1] SECTION 3 (A)—INTERIM PAYMENTS

NOTE

[1] Added by S.I. 1974 No. 845.

Interim payment of damages

89A(1). (*a*) In any action of damages for personal injuries, the pursuer may at any time after defences have been lodged apply to the court for an order for interim payment of damages by the defender or defenders, or where there are two or more of them against any one of them.

(*b*) Such application shall be made by way of motion, on an *induciae* of fourteen days.

(*c*) If on hearing the application and any opposition thereto by the defender or defenders, the court is satisfied—

(i) that the defender or defenders have admitted liability in the pursuer's action, or
(ii) that, if the action proceeded to proof, the pursuer would succeed in the action on the question of liability without any substantial finding of contributory negligence on his part or on the part of any person in respect of whose injury or death the pursuer's claim arises, and would obtain decree for damages against the defender or defenders, or where there are two or more of them, against any one of them, the court may, if it thinks fit, order the defender, or where there are two or more of them any one or more of the defenders to make an interim payment to the pursuer of such amount as it thinks just, not exceeding a reasonable proportion of the damages which in the opinion of the court are likely to be recovered by the pursuer. Such payment may be ordered to be made in one sum or otherwise as the court thinks fit.

(*d*) No order shall be made against a defender under this Rule of Court unless it appears to the court that the defender concerned is either a person who is insured in respect of the pursuer's claim, or is a public authority, or is a person whose means and resources are such as to enable him to make the interim payment.

(*e*) Notwithstanding the making or refusal of an order for an interim payment, a second or subsequent application may be made upon cause shown by reason of a change of circumstances.

(*f*) Subject only to the provisions of Rules 131 to 134 hereof any interim payments shall be paid to the pursuer, unless the court otherwise directs.

(*g*) The provisions of this Rule shall apply *mutatis mutandis* to a counterclaim for damages for personal injury made by any defender.

(*h*) For the purposes of this Rule the words "personal injuries" shall include any disease and any impairment of a person's physical or mental condition.

Adjustment on final decree

89A (2). Where a defender has made an interim payment under Rule 89A (1), the court may make such order, when final decree is pronounced, with respect to the interim payment as may be necessary for giving effect to the defender's final liability to the pursuer and in particular may order—

(*a*) repayment by the pursuer of any sum by which the interim payment exceeds the amount which that defender is liable to pay the pursuer, or

(*b*) payment by any other defender or Third Party of any part of the interim payment which the defender who made it is entitled to recover from him by way of contribution or indemnity or in respect of any remedy or relief relating to or connected with the pursuer's claim.

[1] Section 3(B)—Summary Decree

NOTE

[1] Added by S.I. 1984 No. 499.

Summary decree

89B.—(1) This Rule applies to any cause commenced by summons other than—

(*a*) a consistorial action as defined by Rule 154;

(*b*) [Revoked by S.I. 1990 No. 705.]

(*c*) an action of multiplepoinding;

(*d*) an action of proving the tenor; and

(*e*) an action under the Presumption of Death (Scotland) Act 1977.

(2) Subject to paragraphs (3) to (6) of this Rule, in a cause to which this Rule applies, the pursuer may, at any time after a defender has lodged defences, apply by motion to the court for summary decree against that defender on the ground that there is no defence to the action or a part of it disclosed in the defences.

(3) In applying for summary decree the pursuer may move the court—

(*a*) to grant decree in terms of all or any of the conclusions of the summons;

(*b*) to pronounce an interlocutor sustaining or repelling a plea-in-law; or

(*c*) to dispose of the whole or a part of the subject matter of the action.

(4) Where a motion is to be made under this Rule—

(*a*) the motion shall be intimated by recorded delivery letter to all other parties to the action on an *induciae* of 14 days;

(*b*) there shall be lodged at the same time as enrolment—

(i) a copy of each letter of intimation; and

(ii) the Post Office receipt in respect of the posting of each letter of intimation.

(5) At the hearing of a motion under this Rule the court may—

(*a*) if satisfied that there is no defence to the action or to any part of it to which the motion relates, grant the motion for summary decree in whole or in part as the case may be; or

(*b*) order any party, or a partner, director, officer or office-bearer of, any party—

(i) to produce any document; or

(ii) to lodge an affidavit or affidavits in support of any assertion of fact made in the pleadings or at the bar.

(6) Notwithstanding the granting or refusal of a motion for summary decree, a second or subsequent motion may be made upon cause shown by reason of a change of circumstances.

(7) Where a defender has lodged a counterclaim—

(*a*) the defender may apply by motion to the court for summary decree against the pursuer on that counterclaim or part of it on the ground that the pursuer has no defence to the counterclaim;

(*b*) paragraphs (3) to (6) shall apply to a motion by a defender under this paragraph as they apply to a motion by a pursuer under paragraph (2); and

(*c*) this paragraph does not apply to a counterclaim which is a claim referred to in paragraph (1).

(8) Notwithstanding the provisions of paragraphs (*a*) and (*b*) of Rule 264, an interlocutor pronounced under this Rule may be reclaimed against only with leave of the Lord Ordinary or Vacation Judge, and on such conditions, if any, as he thinks fit, not later than seven days after the day on which the interlocutor was pronounced.

Section 4—Making-up and Closing Record: Amendment

Making up record

[1] **90.**—(1) The pursuer shall, not later than the fourteenth day after the day on which the time for lodging defences expired, or on which the defences were lodged and intimation made to the pursuer in terms of paragraph (*a*) of Rule 83 whichever is the earlier, deliver at least six copies of the Open Record to the solicitor for the defender, or to each of the solicitors for the defenders, if more than one, and shall at the same time lodge two copies in the General Department.

(2) If the pursuer shall fail to deliver and lodge the copies as aforesaid, the defender may enrol the cause and move for decree of dismissal.

(3) The parties shall adjust the pleadings.

(4) The case shall be put out in the Adjustment Roll as soon as may be.

(5) On the case first appearing before the court in the Adjustment Roll, the court shall pronounce an interlocutor continuing the case in the roll for a period of twelve weeks.

(6) [Revoked by S.I. 1987 No. 2160.]

(7) Where a case has been sisted any period of adjustment prior to the sist will be reckoned as part of the period of adjustment.

NOTE
[1] As amended by S.I. 1980 No. 1144.

Variation of adjustment period

[1] **90A.**—(1) The court may vary an interlocutor pronounced under Rule 90 by restricting or extending the period of 12 weeks in accordance with the provisions of this rule.

(2) At any time after the expiry of a period of at least four weeks from the date of that interlocutor the court may pronounce an interlocutor closing the record if, but only if,—

(*a*) any party—
(i) enrols a motion in that behalf; and
(ii) lodges in process a copy of the open record adjusted to the date of enrolment of the motion; and
(iii) shows cause; or

(*b*) before the expiry of a period of 10 weeks from that date, the parties of consent enrol a motion in that behalf.

(3) The court may pronounce an interlocutor continuing the case in the Adjustment Roll for such period or periods additional to the period of 12 weeks as it thinks fit if any party—

(*a*) enrols a motion in that behalf; and
(*b*) lodges in process a copy of the open record adjusted to the date of enrolment; and
(*c*) shows special cause.

NOTE
[1] Added by S.I. 1980 No. 1144.

Closing record

[1] **91.**—(1) The court shall, on the date on which the period allowed for adjustment expires, pronounce an interlocutor closing the record.

(2) The pursuer shall, not later than the fifth Wednesday after the date of the interlocutor closing the record:—

(*a*) deliver not less than six copies of the Closed Record to the other party or each of the other parties as the case may be; and
(*b*) lodge three copies thereof in the General Department, one of which shall be the process copy.

[THE NEXT PAGE IS C 33]

(3) The pursuer shall, on lodging copies of the Closed Record in accordance with paragraph (2), enrol a motion craving the court either:—

(*a*) of consent:—

(i) to appoint the cause to the Procedure Roll for consideration of all the preliminary pleas of parties or certain of them as specified, as the case may be;

(ii) to allow issues for the trial of the cause by jury;

(iii) to allow trial of the cause by jury without issues;

(iv) to allow a proof;

(v) to allow to parties a proof before answer of their respective averments under reservation of such preliminary plea or pleas as may be specified;

(vi) to allow to parties a preliminary proof upon specified matters or in respect of specified pleas;

(vii) to make some other specified order; or

(*b*) if parties have been unable to agree on further procedure, to appoint parties to be heard on the By Order (Adjustment) Roll.

(4) A motion of consent under paragraph (3)(*a*) shall not require the attendance of counsel.

(5) If the pursuer fails to comply with any of the requirements of paragraph (2), the court may, on the motion of the defenders, dismiss the action.

(6) The court may, on or after pronouncing an interlocutor ordering further procedure in terms of paragraph (3) in any action which is one of several actions arising from the same cause of action, on the motion of any party to any such cause after hearing parties to all such actions, appoint that action or any other of those actions to be the leading action and to sist the other actions pending the determination of that action.

NOTE

[1] Substituted by S.I. 1982 No. 1825.

Abandonment

[1] **91A.**—(1) In any action the pursuer may, at any time before the proof or trial has begun, abandon the action on paying full expenses to the defender, and may, if otherwise competent, bring a new action.

(2) In any action the pursuer may, at any time after the proof or trial has begun and before avizandum is made or the charge begun, move the Lord Ordinary for leave to abandon the action; and the Lord Ordinary may on being satisfied that it is just and proper in the circumstances to do so, grant leave subject to payment by the pursuer of the defender's expenses within such time as he may specify; and in the event of those expenses not being paid within that time, the defender shall be entitled to be assoilzied from the conclusions of the action with expenses.

NOTE

[1] Added by S.I. 1984 No. 472.

Report by judge

[1] **91B.**—(1) The Lord Ordinary may at any stage of an action, on intimation to the parties, report the action or any incidental matter which may arise in the course of the action, to the Inner House for a ruling; and on such a ruling being given shall give effect to it.

(2) In relation to any incidental matter reported to it under paragraph (1)—

(*a*) the Inner House may dispose of the matter summarily;

(*b*) any judgment or order made by the Inner House in respect of that matter shall be final;

(*c*) the Inner House may determine any question of expenses relating to the matter reported, or may reserve any such question.

NOTE
[1] Added by S.I. 1984 No. 472 and as amended by S.I. 1986 No. 1937.

Fixing and allocation of diets

[1] **91C.**—(1) As soon as convenient after the allowance of a proof (including a proof before answer) or the approval of issues, the keeper of the rolls shall publish in the rolls a list of causes in which diets are to be fixed or allocated.

(2) Within 28 days of the appearance of a cause in a list published under paragraph (1), each party shall ensure that Form 63 is completed and delivered to the keeper of the rolls.

(3) The keeper of the rolls may allocate a diet of proof or jury trial having regard to the information provided in Form 63.

(4) [Revoked by S.I. 1990 No. 2118.]

[2] (5) Where a party fails to comply with paragraph (2), the keeper of the rolls may arrange for the cause to be put out by order before a Lord Ordinary.

[2] (6) At a by order hearing under paragraph (5), the court shall—

(*a*) seek an explanation as to why Form 63 was not completed and delivered timeously;

(*b*) ascertain the information sought in Form 63; and

(*c*) make such order as to expenses as it may consider appropriate.

[2] (7) Where Form 63 is completed and delivered to the keeper of the rolls before the hearing of the cause by order under paragraph (5), the keeper of the rolls may cancel the by order hearing.

[2] (8) Where, at any time after Form 63 has been completed and delivered to the keeper of the rolls, a party's estimate of the likely length of the proof or jury trial alters materially, that party shall inform the keeper of the rolls of the new estimated length.

NOTES
[1] Added by S.I. 1987 No. 1206.
[2] As amended by S.I. 1990 No. 2118.

Amendment of pleadings: powers of the court

92.—(1) In any defended cause it shall be competent to the court at any time before final judgment:—

(*a*) To allow any amendment of the summons or other writ which may be necessary for the purpose of determining in the existing action the real question in controversy between the parties, notwithstanding that in consequence of such amendment the sum sued for is increased or restricted or a different remedy from that originally concluded for is thereby sought.

(*b*) To allow any amendment which may be necessary to correct or supplement the designation of any party to the action, or to enable any party who has sued or has been sued in his own right to sue or be sued in a representative capacity, or to enable any party who has sued or who has been sued in a representative capacity to sue or be sued in his own right or in a different representative capacity, or to add the name of an additional pursuer or of a person whose concurrence is necessary, or where the action has been commenced in the name of the wrong person as pursuer or where it is doubtful whether it has been commenced in the name of the right person, to allow any other person to be sisted as pursuer in substitution for, or in addition to, the original pursuer.

[1] (*c*) In any case in which it appears that all parties having an interest have not been called, or that the action has been directed against the wrong person, to allow any amendment inserting in the summons or other writ an additional or substitute defender and containing averments of fault directed against said defender and to order the record as so amended to be served on such additional or substitute defender along with a notice in

terms of Form 6 specifying the date by which defences or answers must be lodged; and thereafter a copy of the said notice shall be lodged in process with a certificate of execution thereon and the action as so amended shall proceed in every respect as if such defender had originally been made a party to the cause.

(*d*) To allow any amendment of the condescendence, defences, answers, or pleas-in-law which may be necessary for determining in the existing action the real question in controversy between the parties.

(2) In exercising the powers hereinbefore conferred, the court shall attach such conditions as may be just, and shall hold the party making the amendment liable in the expenses thereby occasioned unless it is made to appear that it is just and equitable that the expenses occasioned by the amendment should be otherwise dealt with.

(3) In any undefended action it shall be competent to the court to allow the like amendments to be made as are hereinbefore authorised in the case of defended actions: provided that unless the amendment is formal in character the court shall direct the summons or other writ as amended to be served upon the absent defender with liberty to him to lodge defences within such time as may be proper.

(4) Any amendment allowed under this Rule shall not have the effect of validating diligence used upon the dependence of the action so as to prejudice the rights of creditors of the defender interested in defeating such diligence, but shall be operative to the effect of obviating any objections to such diligence, when stated by the defender himself or by any person representing him by a title, or in right of a debt contracted by him subsequent to the execution of such diligence.

NOTE

[1] As amended by S.I. 1967 No. 1789.

SECTION 5—MOTIONS

Motions

[1] **93.**—(*a*) Motions on behalf of any party to a cause, other than motions

[THE NEXT PAGE IS C 35]

made at the Bar during any hearing of the cause, shall be enrolled and made by entry in the motion sheet.

(*b*) The entry shall specify the terms of the motion, and shall bear the date of the enrolment and a certificate that the motion has been intimated to the other party, and shall be signed by the solicitor making the enrolment or by his clerk on his behalf, who shall also hand to the Clerk of Court a slip containing the names of the parties and the counsel in the cause.

(*c*) All such enrolments shall be made at the Office of Court, and may be made at any time before 12.30 p.m., provided that written intimation of intention to make such enrolment, and of the terms of the motion, shall have been given to the solicitor or solicitors of the other party or parties to the cause so as to reach the said solicitor or solicitors at his or their office or offices not later than 12.30 p.m. on the day before enrolment except by consent.

(*d*) All such motions so enrolled shall appear, if in session, in the issue of the printed rolls issued on the day after the day of enrolment as for hearing in the motion roll or single bills on the second day after the enrolment. If the attendance of Counsel is required the motion shall be starred.

(*e*) If on the day after the day on which the enrolment is made as aforesaid, the solicitor or solicitors for the other party or parties or any of them or their clerks shall mark the motion as appearing in the motion sheet with the word "Opposed", the motion shall be heard in the motion roll or single bills on the second day after the day of enrolment, if in session; and, in that case, the cause shall be starred in the issue of the printed rolls issued on the day after the day of enrolment, as to be heard by counsel; provided that written intimation of the fact that a motion has been marked as "Opposed" shall be given to the solicitor or solicitors of the other party or parties to the cause so as to reach the offices of such solicitor or solicitors not later than 12.30 p.m. on the day on which the motion is marked as "Opposed".

(*f*) When a cause is called for hearing in the motion roll or single bills, and is dropped without any motion being made, the Auditor shall, in taxing any expenses found due (either as between party and party or as between solicitor and client) to the party on whose behalf the enrolment in the motion sheet was made, disallow the expenses occasioned by the said enrolment, unless he is satisfied that the cause was properly enrolled and properly dropped.

(*g*) Examples of the enrolment of a motion in the motion sheet, and of the marking of the same with the word "Opposed", will be found in Form 8.

NOTE

[1] As amended by S.I. 1980 No. 1144.

Powers of Depute Clerks of Session

[1] **93A.** A Depute Clerk of Session may, subject to any direction he may be given by a judge—

(*a*) write an interlocutor (other than a final interlocutor) in respect of a motion which is not starred;

(*b*) sign any such interlocutor as Clerk of Court on behalf of the judge, and any such interlocutor so written and signed shall be treated for all purposes as if it had been written and signed by the judge; and an extract of any such interlocutor, shall not, by reason only of it being so written and signed, be invalid.

NOTE

[1] Added by S.I. 1978 No. 799 and as amended by S.I. 1984 No. 472.

SECTION 6—PROCEDURE ROLL

Procedure Roll

94.—(*a*) Causes sent to Procedure Roll may be put out for hearing in the course of any week; provided that no such additional cause shall, except of consent of parties, be called earlier than the second day after the day on which it is so put out in the printed rolls.

(*b*) The calling of any cause put out for hearing in the Procedure Roll shall be peremptory in the same way as the calling of a cause in the summar or short roll of the Inner House.

[1] (*c*) If no counsel or solicitor who has a right of audience in the Court of Session attends on either side, the Lord Ordinary may pronounce an interlocutor dismissing the action, and finding neither party entitled to expenses, and the said interlocutor may be recalled only on being reclaimed to the Inner House, upon such conditions as to expenses or otherwise as may be imposed by the court.

[1] (*d*) When on such calling of a cause counsel or a solicitor who has a right of audience in the Court of Session shall appear on one side only, the Lord Ordinary, if the pursuer's counsel or a solicitor who has a right of audience in the Court of Session fails to attend, may pronounce an interlocutor dismissing the action and finding the pursuer liable in expenses; if the defender's counsel or solicitor who has a right of audience in the Court of Session fails to attend, the Lord Ordinary may pronounce an interlocutor granting decree by default with expenses; and the said interlocutors may be recalled only in the like manner and on the like conditions as are mentioned in paragraph (*c*) of this rule.

(*e*) It shall always be competent for parties having a cause standing in the Procedure Roll, in regard to which they have come to be agreed that it should be disposed of by a proof, or by a trial by jury, or otherwise, to enrol the cause in order that the matter may be brought before the court, which may allow a proof or jury trial, or may pronounce such other interlocutor as may be just and proper in the circumstances.

NOTE

[1] As amended by S.I. 1991 No. 2483, with effect from 25th November 1991.

SECTION 7—COMMISSIONS FOR RECOVERY OF DOCUMENTS FOR EXAMINATION OF WITNESSES, ETC.

Application for commission and diligence for recovery of documents

95.—[1] (*a*) Any application for commission and diligence for the recovery of documents made in a cause before calling shall be made by letter addressed to the Deputy Principal Clerk craving that the court should grant such commission and diligence and enclosing a copy of the specification. The letter shall at the same time be intimated along with a copy of the specification, to the other party and where necessary to the Lord Advocate, and the Deputy Principal Clerk, or a clerk instructed by him, shall forthwith bring the application before a Lord Ordinary in chambers, making intimation to the parties of place and hour. The clerk shall be accompanied by counsel or solicitor or both counsel and solicitor for the applicant and for any party who wishes to oppose the application and for the Lord Advocate if he wishes to oppose the application. The solicitor or counsel for the applicant shall produce to the Lord Ordinary the principal summons bearing the signet. After hearing parties' explanations, the Lord Ordinary may either grant or refuse the commission in whole or in part, or as amended by or before him. The Lord Ordinary's interlocutor shall be final.

(*b*) Any application for commission and diligence for the recovery of documents made after calling shall be made by motion. A detailed and articulate specification of the documents sought to be recovered shall be lodged in the General Department at the time of enrolling such motion as aforesaid, and a copy or copies of such specification shall be sent to the solicitor or solicitors of the other party or parties, or where necessary to the Lord Advocate, along with the intimation of the enrolment.

NOTE

[1] As amended by S.I. 1991 No. 2483, with effect from 25th November 1991.

Application for an order under section 1 of the Administration of Justice (Scotland) Act 1972

[1] **95A.**—(*a*) Any application for an order for the inspection, photographing, preservation, custody, and detention of documents and other property (including, where appropriate, land) or for the production, recovery or the taking of samples thereof or the carrying out of any experiment thereon made in a cause before calling shall be made by letter addressed to the Deputy Principal Clerk craving that the court should grant such an order and specifying the order sought. The letter shall at the same time be intimated to the other party, to any third party haver and where necessary to the Lord Advocate, and the Deputy Principal Clerk, or a clerk instructed by him, shall forthwith bring the application before a Lord Ordinary in chambers, making intimation to the parties of place and hour. The clerk shall be accompanied by counsel or solicitor or both counsel and solicitor for the applicant and for any party who wishes to oppose the application and for the Lord Advocate if he wishes to oppose the application. The solicitor or counsel for the applicant shall produce to the Lord Ordinary the principal summons bearing the signet. After hearing parties' explanations, the Lord Ordinary may either grant or refuse the order sought, in whole or in part, or as amended and may

[THE NEXT PAGE IS C 37]

order the applicant to find such caution as the Lord Ordinary thinks fit. The Lord Ordinary's interlocutor shall be final.

(*b*) Any application for such an order as is referred to in the immediately preceding paragraph made after calling shall be made by motion. A detailed and articulate specification of the documents and other property (including, where appropriate, land) sought to be inspected, photographed, preserved, taken into custody, detained, produced, recovered, sampled or experimented upon, shall be lodged in the General Department at the time of enrolling such motion as aforesaid, and a copy or copies of such specification shall be sent to the Solicitor or Solicitors of the other party or parties, to any third party haver and where necessary to the Lord Advocate, along with the intimation of the enrolment. In granting such an order the court may order the applicant to find such caution as it thinks fit.

(*c*) Any application for such an order as is referred to in paragraph (*a*) hereof, made where proceedings have not been commenced, by any person who appears to the court to be likely to be a party to or Minuter in proceedings which are likely to be brought, shall be made by Petition presented to the Outer House, and the provisions of Rules 191 to 198 shall apply thereto, provided, however that the court may make an order for such intimation to third party havers as it thinks fit and may order the Petitioner to find such caution as it thinks fit.

(*d*) An application for an order under section 1(1A) of the Administration of Justice (Scotland) Act 1972—

(i) in an existing process, shall be made by motion; and

(ii) in any other case, shall be made by petition presented to the Outer House, specifying the matters in respect of which information is sought of persons who might be witnesses or defenders.

NOTE

[1] Added by S.I. 1972 No. 2021 and as amended by S.I. 1986 No. 1955 and S.I. 1987 No. 1206, and (with effect from 25th November 1991) S.I. 1991 No. 2483.

Optional procedure before executing commission and diligence

96.—(*a*) Any party who has obtained a commission and diligence for the recovery of documents may, at any time before executing the same against another party or other parties to the cause, or against any third-party haver, serve upon such party, or parties, or haver, an order on the printed official form shewn in Form 9.

(*b*) Such order shall be served by registered or recorded delivery letter, and may be addressed to the care of the known solicitor or solicitors for the party or parties, or for the third-party haver, from whom the documents are sought to be recovered.

(*c*) Such order shall be obtempered by such party, or parties, or by such third-party haver, in the manner and within the time specified therein.

(*d*) Not later than the day after the day on which the order, certificate in terms of Form 9, and inventoried productions (if any) are received by the Deputy Principal Clerk, official intimation shall be given by him to the solicitors of the parties to the cause that the order has been served and obtempered; and it shall not be competent for any party, other than the party who served the order, to borrow any of the productions until after the expiry of seven days from the date of such official intimation.

(*e*) If the party who served the order is not satisfied that full production has been made under the specification, or that adequate reasons for non-production have been given, he may execute the commission and diligence as provided in Rule 97, notwithstanding his adoption in the first instance of the foregoing procedure by order.

(*f*) In the event of the production under such order as aforesaid of extracts from books, whether such extracts are certified or not, the court may, on motion enrolled, order that the party who served the order shall be at liberty to inspect and take copies of any entries in any books falling under the specification, subject, in the event of any question of confidentiality arising, to the inspection being made, and the copies being taken, at the sight of the commissioner appointed in the interlocutor granting the commission and diligence; and the court may, on cause shewn, order the production of any books (not being bankers' books or books of public record) falling under a specification, notwithstanding the production of certified extracts therefrom.

[1] (*g*) Any party who has obtained an order for inspection, photographing, preservation, custody or detention of documents or other property in terms of Rule of Court 95A shall serve by registered or recorded delivery letter a certified copy of the Interlocutor granting such order, upon any other party or parties to the cause, or, as appropriate, upon any haver of said documents or upon any party with an interest in said property, and such order shall be obtempered by the party or parties to whom it is directed in the manner and within the time specified therein.

NOTE

[1] Added by S.I. 1972 No. 2021.

Execution of commission and diligence for recovery of documents

97.—(*a*) The report of the execution of any commission and diligence, together with any documents recovered, and inventory thereof, shall be lodged by the commissioner in the hands of the Deputy Principal Clerk; and the report as so lodged shall have endorsed thereon a note of all fees and outlays incurred to or by the commissioner and his clerk.

(*b*) Not later than the day after the day on which the report with the relative documents (if any) and inventory are lodged as aforesaid, official intimation thereof shall be given by the said Deputy Principal Clerk to the solicitors of the parties to the cause.

(*c*) The intimation so given to the solicitor of the party who obtained the commission and diligence shall include a note of the fees and outlays of the commissioner and his clerk as endorsed on the report; and, upon delivery by the said solicitor to the said Deputy Principal Clerk of a written discharge of the amount of said fees and outlays such solicitor may lodge in process any of the productions he may wish so to lodge.

(*d*) If the solicitor for the party who obtained the commission and diligence shall fail to deliver a written discharge as provided in the immediately preceding paragraph of this rule within three days of the date of the official intimation referred to in paragraph (*b*) of this rule, the solicitor for the other party may, within four days thereafter, deliver such discharge, and uplift and lodge in process any of the productions he may wish so to lodge.

(*e*) It shall not be competent for any party, other than the party whose solicitor delivers the foresaid discharge to the said Deputy Principal Clerk, to borrow any of the productions until after the expiry of seven days from the date of such delivery.

Confidentiality

98. In any case in which, either under the optional procedure provided in Rule 96, or in the execution of a commission and diligence in manner provided by Rule 97, confidentiality is claimed for any of the documents produced, such documents shall be enclosed in a separate sealed packet, which shall not be opened or put in process except by authority of the court obtained on the motion of the party serving the order, or executing the commission and diligence, after opportunity has been given to the party, parties or third-party haver, making production, to be heard.

Demand for admission

99. Either party may by letter call upon the other party to admit without prejudice the date, signature, transmission, or receipt, of any relevant document, or the verbal accuracy of a copy thereof, within such time as the court may appoint; and in case of refusal or delay to admit any such matter within the time appointed, the expense of any proof rendered necessary by such refusal or delay shall be paid by the party refusing or delaying, whatever

[THE NEXT PAGE IS C 39]

the result of the cause may be, unless the court shall certify that the refusal or delay was reasonable: and no expense of proving any document shall be allowed unless the procedure authorised by this paragraph has been followed forth.

Commission for examination of witness

100.—(*a*) Any application for a commission to examine a witness in a cause before calling shall be made by letter addressed to the Deputy Principal Clerk containing a note of the names and addresses of the witnesses and the reason why it is considered necessary to have their evidence taken on commission. The letter shall be accompanied by the principal summons bearing the signet, and an interlocutor sheet, and the Deputy Principal Clerk shall forthwith bring the application before a Lord Ordinary in Chambers. The Lord Ordinary's interlocutor shall be final.

(*b*) Any application for a commission to examine a witness in a cause made after calling shall be made by motion.

(*c*) Where a commission is granted by the court for the examination of a witness, the court may, on the motion of any party to the cause, dispense with interrogatories in all cases where the commission falls to be executed within the United Kingdom, and may also dispense with interrogatories where the commission is to be executed abroad, on being satisfied that such a course is expedient in the interests of the parties to the cause and conducive to the administration of justice.

(*d*) The provisions of Rule 97 shall apply *mutatis mutandis* to the report of a commission for examination of witnesses, provided that the party obtaining the report shall lodge the same in process.

Evidence liable to be lost

101. Where there is reason to believe that the evidence of a witness may be lost, or delay and inconvenience occasioned in obtaining the evidence of such witness at a proof, it shall be competent at any time after service of the summons to apply to the court to have the evidence of such witness taken by a Lord Ordinary or by a commissioner appointed by the court: if the application is made before calling, it shall be made as directed in Rule 100 (*a*); if after calling, it shall be made by motion; provided that, in ship-collision cases, such application shall only be granted on condition that the applicant shall, at least twenty-four hours before the evidence is taken before the Lord Ordinary or the commissioner, lodge in the General Department a preliminary act, which the Lord Ordinary or commissioner shall be entitled to open before the witness is examined.

Letters of request

[1] **102.**—(1) This rule applies to applications to the court for a letter of request to a court or tribunal outside Scotland to obtain evidence of the kind specified in paragraph (2) of this rule, being evidence obtainable within the jurisdiction of that court or tribunal, for the purposes of civil proceedings commenced before the Court of Session.

(2) An application under paragraph (1) of this rule may be made in relation to a request—

(*a*) for the examination of witnesses;
(*b*) for the production of documents;
(*c*) for the inspection, photographing, preservation, custody or detention of any property;
(*d*) for the taking of samples of any property and the carrying out of any experiments on or with any property.

(3) An application to which this rule applies shall be made by way of a

minute lodged in process and framed in accordance with Form 10, to which is appended a proposed letter of request framed in accordance with Form 11.

(4) On consideration of the minute and proposed letter of request, and after allowing the other parties to lodge answers, and after hearing any objections, the application may be granted and a letter of request authorised to be issued.

(5) Unless the court or tribunal to which a letter of request is addressed under this rule, is a court or tribunal in a country or territory—

(*a*) where the official language or one of the official languages is English; or

(*b*) in relation to which the Deputy Principal Clerk certifies that no translation is required,

then the applicant shall, before the issue of the letter, lodge in process a translation of the letter and relative interrogatories, if any, into the language of that court or tribunal.

(6) It shall be a condition of granting any such letter of request that the solicitor for the applicant shall become personally liable for the whole expenses which may become due and payable in respect thereof to the court or tribunal obtaining the evidence and to any witnesses who may be examined for that purpose; and he shall consign such sums in respect of such expenses as the court shall think proper.

(7) The letter of request when duly issued shall together with any interrogatories adjusted according to the present practice and the relative translations, be forwarded forthwith by the Deputy Principal Clerk to such person and in such manner as the Lord President may direct.

NOTE

[1] Substituted by S.I. 1976 No. 283.

[1] **102A.**—(1) This rule applies to applications made to the Court of Session for an order for evidence to be obtained in Scotland in pursuance of a request issued—

(*a*) by or on behalf of a court or tribunal exercising jurisdiction outside Scotland, being evidence to be obtained for the purposes of civil proceedings commenced or contemplated before that court or tribunal; or

(*b*) by or on behalf of a court or tribunal exercising jurisdiction outside the United Kingdom, being evidence to be obtained by the examination of witnesses, either orally or in writing, or the production of documents, for the purpose of criminal proceedings commenced before that court or tribunal.

(2) An application to which this rule applies shall be made by way of Petition to the Inner House, and shall have a certificate appended—

(*a*) certifying that the application is made in pursuance of a request issued by or on behalf of a court or tribunal exercising jurisdiction outside Scotland, or where the request relates to criminal proceedings, outside the United Kingdom;

(*b*) certifying that the evidence to be obtained is for the purposes of civil proceedings commenced or contemplated, or criminal proceedings commenced, as the case may be, before that court or tribunal;

(*c*) in the case of criminal proceedings, certifying that the proceedings are not of a political nature; and

[2] (*d*) signed:—

(i) in the case of a court or tribunal in the United Kingdom which exercises jurisdiction outside Scotland, by a duly authorised officer of that court or tribunal;

(ii) in the case of a court or tribunal outside the United Kingdom, a duly authorised diplomatic or consular representative of the country or territory within which the court or tribunal exercises jurisdiction.

(3) (*a*) Where in pursuance of an order of the court granting the prayer of a Petition under this rule, a witness is cited to attend to give evidence, and he claims that he is not a compellable witness by virtue of the provisions of section 3 of the Evidence (Proceedings in Other Jurisdictions) Act 1975, the court, or a Commissioner appointed by the court to take the evidence of that witness, may, if the claim is not supported by a statement in the request issued by or on behalf of the foreign court or tribunal or is not conceded by the applicant, take his evidence and have it recorded in a separate document.

(*b*) If a Commissioner appointed to take evidence refuses to do so on the ground that the witness is not a compellable witness, the applicant may apply to the court to order him to do so.

(*c*) Where a Commissioner takes evidence under sub-paragraph (*a*) or (*b*) of this paragraph of this rule, he shall certify the claim and the grounds upon which it was made, and send the certificate to the court, which shall cause the certificate to be sent to the foreign court or tribunal with a request to them to determine the claim.

(*d*) On receipt of the determination of the foreign court or tribunal the court shall give notice of the determination to the person who made the claim and shall, in accordance with the determination, send the document in which that person's evidence is recorded to the foreign court or tribunal, or return it to that person, as the case may be.

[3] (4) Where, on an application under section 1 of the Evidence (Proceedings in Other Jurisdictions) Act 1975 as applied by section 92 of the Patents Act 1977, an order is made for the evidence of witnesses to be taken, the court may, on an application in that behalf made to it by way of motion before that evidence is taken, allow an officer of the European Patent Office to attend the hearing and examine the witnesses or to request the court or Commissioner before whom the hearing takes place to put specified questions to the witnesses.

[4](5) A person who is served with an order requiring him to give evidence, or is cited to attend to give evidence by virtue of such an order, may apply to the court by motion in the Single Bills to have the order varied or recalled.

NOTES

[1] Added by S.I. 1976 No. 283.
[2] Substituted by S.I. 1982 No. 1825.
[3] Added by S.I. 1978 No. 955.
[4] Inserted by S.I. 1990 No. 705.

Warrant for production of original documents from public records

103.—(*a*) Where any party to a cause desires to obtain from the Keeper of any public record production of the originals of any register or deed under his custody, he shall apply by motion to the court, in session or vacation, after two days' notice of such application given in writing to the Keeper in charge of the originals.

(*b*) If it shall appear to the court that it is necessary for the ends of justice that such application should be granted, authority shall be given to such Keeper, on production of a certified copy of the interlocutor, to exhibit the original registers or deeds to the court and that in the hands of an officer to be selected by the said Keeper.

(*c*) The expense attending the transmission and exhibition of such original registers or deeds shall be defrayed, in the first instance, by the party or parties on whose application they are exhibited.

(*d*) Where production or exhibition of such original registers or deeds is desired in any court outwith Scotland, the application for such production or exhibition shall be made by letter addressed to the Principal Clerk of Session, who shall forthwith bring the application before a Lord Ordinary in Chambers who may grant authority to the said Keeper to exhibit the original registers or deeds to the said court, and that in the hands of an officer to be selected by the said Keeper. Paragraph (*c*) of this rule shall apply to such applications.

Warrant for transmission of process from another court

104. When it is deemed necessary by any of the parties to a cause that any extracted or unextracted process in the custody of the Keeper of the Records of Scotland or any process depending, or that may have depended, in any inferior court in Scotland, should be lodged in process, it shall be competent for the party to apply to the court by motion duly intimated to the opposite party or to his solicitor, as required by Rule 93, for a warrant to authorise and direct the Keeper of the Records of Scotland or the clerk of any inferior court before which such process is depending, or may have depended, on production of a certified copy of the interlocutor, to deliver up the same to the Deputy Principal Clerk, in order that the same may be lodged in process, upon delivery of the warrant, and a proper receipt and obligation for redelivery after the disposal of the cause; and, provided that such application has been intimated to the Keeper of the Records of Scotland or such other custodier two days before such motion is enrolled, it shall be competent to the court, if it shall see cause, to grant such warrant, in such terms and under such conditions as may be deemed necessary.

Transmission on contingency

[1] **104A.**—(1) An application for transmission to the court of a cause depending before the sheriff on the ground of contingency with a Court of Session cause may be made—

(*a*) by motion at the instance of a party to the cause depending before the court;

(*b*) by minute at the instance of any other person having an interest (including a party to the cause depending before the sheriff).

(2) A copy of the process of the cause depending before the sheriff, certified by the sheriff clerk shall be lodged with any motion enrolled or any minute lodged under paragraph (1).

(3) A decision made on an application under paragraph (1) shall not be appealable, but an application that has been refused may, in the event of any change of circumstances, be renewed.

NOTE

[1] Added by S.I. 1984 No. 472.

Transmission to sheriff court

104B.—(1) Where a cause is remitted to the sheriff court under section 14 of the Law Reform (Miscellaneous Provisions) (Scotland) Act 1985, the deputy principal clerk shall, within four days after the interlocutor remitting the cause has been pronounced, transmit the process to the sheriff clerk of the sheriff court specified in the interlocutor.

(2) When transmitting a process under paragraph (1), the deputy principal clerk shall, at the same time—

(*a*) send written notice of the transmission to the parties to the cause; and

(*b*) certify on the interlocutor sheet that such written notice has been given.

(3) Failure of the deputy principal clerk to comply with paragraph (2) shall not affect the validity of the remit under paragraph (1).

NOTE

[1] Added by S.I. 1986 No. 1955 and as amended by S.I. 1987 No. 1206.

New procedure in place of minute of wakening

105. It shall not be necessary to waken a cause which, according to the existing law and practice, would be deemed to have fallen asleep by reason of the fact that no interlocutor had been pronounced therein within a year and a day of the date of the last interlocutor. Instead, any motion to be

[THE NEXT PAGE IS C 43]

made after the lapse of one year from the date of the last interlocutor shall be intimated to the opposite party not less than fourteen days prior to the date of enrolment thereof, provided that if the address of the opposite party is unknown and cannot be found the court may, on a statement to that effect made at the bar, dispense with intimation, and the interlocutor shall bear to be pronounced in respect of such statement.

Minute of transference

106. It shall be competent to any party having an interest to have the cause transferred against any party or parties to lodge a minute craving a transference of the cause against such party or parties; and the court may thereupon grant warrant for serving a copy of the summons or other original pleading upon the party or parties against whom such cause is sought to be transferred, and at the same time shall allow such party or parties to give in a minute of objections to such transference within a time to be specified in the interlocutor; such interlocutor shall also be intimated to any other parties in the cause; and if the court shall think fit to transfer the cause in terms of the said minute an interlocutor shall be pronounced holding the cause as transferred against the party or parties named in such minute; provided that nothing herein contained shall prevent the court from sisting any person upon his own application by minute as a party to the cause where such person is, according to the existing practice, entitled to be sisted as representative, trustee, or guardian, or in any other relation to any party who shall be already a party to the cause or who shall have died during the dependence thereof.

Warrant for citing witnesses

[1] **106A.** A certified copy of the interlocutor approving issues or allowing proof in any action shall be a sufficient warrant to any messenger-at-arms to cite witnesses and havers to the trial or proof in question, at the instance of any party to the action.

NOTE

[1] Added by S.I. 1984 No. 472.

Party litigants to find caution before instructing citation of witnesses

[1] **106B.**—(1) Where a party to a cause is a party litigant, he shall, before instructing a messenger-at-arms to cite a witness, find caution for such expenses as can reasonably be anticipated to be incurred by the witness in answering the citation.

(2) The party litigant shall, not later than three months before the diet of proof, apply to the court by motion to fix caution in such sum as the court shall consider reasonable according to the number of witnesses he proposes to cite and the period for which they may be required to attend at court.

NOTE

[1] Added by S.I. 1986 No. 1955.

SECTION 8—PROOFS

Lodging and returning productions for proofs

[1] **107.** In all causes in which a proof shall be allowed, all productions which are intended to be used or put in evidence at the proof, shall be lodged according to inventory on or before the twenty-eighth day prior to the day appointed for the proof, and notice of the lodging thereof shall at the same time be sent to the solicitor of the opposite party; and no other production shall be used or put in evidence at the proof, unless by consent of parties or by permission of the judge presiding thereat, on cause shewn to his satisfaction, and on such terms, as to expenses or otherwise, as to

him shall seem proper. All steps of process and productions borrowed shall be returned to process before noon on the day preceding the date of the proof.

NOTE

[1] As amended by S.I. 1972 No. 2022.

Separate parts of proof

108. Without prejudice to the existing law and practice with respect to preliminary proofs, in any action with pecuniary conclusions the court may separate the proof on the merits from proof on the question of the amount for which decree should be pronounced.

Conditions for receiving written statements in evidence without being spoken to by a witness

[1] **108A.**—(1) Any written statement (including an affidavit) or report, admissible under section 2(1)(*b*) of the Civil Evidence (Scotland) Act 1988 may be received in evidence in any category of civil proceedings without being spoken to by a witness subject to the provisions of this rule.

(2) The following provisions of this rule do not apply to any such written statement or report in respect of which express provision is made in these rules for its admissibility in evidence in relation to a particular category of civil proceedings.

(3) Application to the court to receive any such written statement or report in evidence without being spoken to by a witness shall be made by way of motion.

(4) Subject to paragraph (5), on enrolling any such motion, the applicant shall lodge—

(*a*) the written statement or report as a production;

(*b*) in any case where the other party or parties have not agreed to the written statement or report in question being received in evidence without being spoken to by a witness, an affidavit or affidavits in support of the motion stating—

(i) the name, designation, and qualifications (if any) of the author of the statement or report in question;

(ii) the circumstances in which it was written; and

(iii) the reasons for the application.

(5) Paragraph (4) does not apply to an application made in respect of a written statement or report in the form of an affidavit which includes the information specified in subparagraph (*b*) of paragraph (4).

(6) Any such motion which is unopposed may be granted by the court without a hearing.

(7) On the hearing of any such motion, the court may grant the motion, with or without conditions, or may refuse it, or may continue the motion to enable such further information to be obtained as it may require for the purpose of determining the application.

(8) Expressions used in this rule and in the Civil Evidence (Scotland) Act 1988 shall have the meaning they have in that Act.

NOTE

[1] Inserted by S.I. 1989 No. 435.

Admissions by parties

109.—(*a*) When the parties are agreed in admitting any facts alleged on record, or any matter of fact whether alleged therein or not, or the authenticity of writings or the sufficiency of copies or extracts as equivalent to the originals, a minute of the admissions, signed by the counsel for the party or parties making such admissions, shall be lodged in process.

(*b*) All admissions so made may be read and used in evidence at the trial, if otherwise competent.

(*c*) In taxing any account of expenses, the Auditor shall disallow the expense of any evidence led on matters covered by such admissions, unless special cause is shewn to him to the contrary.

Rulings by Lord Ordinary on matters of evidence

110. If, in the course of the proof, any of the parties is dissatisfied with a ruling by the Lord Ordinary admitting or rejecting any evidence or line of evidence, such party may request that the Lord Ordinary's ruling and such party's objections, which he stated at the time, be immediately recorded in the notes of evidence, and they shall be so recorded under the direction of the Lord Ordinary.

Rules as to witnesses at proofs

111.—(*a*) It shall be the duty of solicitors to see that all witnesses are enclosed under the charge of the macers of court in one of the witness-rooms provided for that purpose.

(*b*) Each solicitor, before the examination of his witnesses commences, shall give to the macer a numbered list of his witnesses in the order in which it is proposed to call them.

(*c*) No witness shall leave the witness-room except with the permission of the clerk of court until called by the macer to be in readiness for being examined. Witnesses shall not walk about the passages or enter any of the court-rooms until after examination, or until dismissed by the macer by order of the court.

(*d*) After a witness has been enclosed by the macer, no person other than the solicitor of the party citing the witness, shall have access to him, nor shall any person interfere with the macers in regard to such witness.

(*e*) The macers shall enforce the provisions of the foregoing paragraphs of this rule, and report to the court if any person, solicitor or other, shall transgress the same.

[1] (*f*) In all actions (whether the hearing is by proof or jury trial) witnesses shall be examined in the presence of parties or their counsel.

NOTE

[1] Added by S.I. 1984 No. 472.

Death, disability or retiral of judge

[1] **112.** In the event of the death, disability or retiral of a Lord Ordinary before whom a proof has been taken in whole or in part, it shall be competent for the court on an application by any party made by motion in the Inner House to direct:—(*a*) that the cause shall be continued before, and shall be disposed of by, another Lord Ordinary, (*b*) that the notes of evidence already taken, as certified by the shorthand writer, shall be evidence in the cause, and (*c*) that the original Lord Ordinary's notes shall be made available to the Lord Ordinary before whom the cause continues. An application by any party by motion under this rule shall be heard in the Single Bills and it shall not be necessary for any documents to be lodged in support of the application unless the court otherwise directs.

NOTE

[1] As amended by S.I. 1976 No. 137.

Recording of evidence in proofs

113.—(*a*) Unless otherwise provided in these Rules, evidence in all actions depending before the Court of Session whether taken in court or on Commission shall be recorded by a shorthand-writer, to whom the oath *de fideli administratione* in connection with Court of Session service generally shall have been administered. Notes of evidence provided for the use of the court shall be certified by the shorthand-writer or shorthand-writers (if more than one) as a faithful record of the evidence. The court may make such alterations on the notes of evidence as appear to be necessary, and where such alterations are made shall authenticate the notes as the notes used by the court as the record of evidence.

(*b*) Transcripts of Notes of Evidence will only be made on directions from the court, and the cost thereof in defended cases will in the first instance be payable by the solicitors for the parties in equal shares. Where an undefended case is continued, or where for other reasons the court considers it necessary that the notes should be extended for the use of the court and so directs, the cost will be borne by the pursuer's solicitor in the first instance. In any case where the Notes of Evidence have not been extended, but are required for a reclaiming motion, the solicitor for the reclaimer may request the shorthand-writer to extend the notes, and the transcript will thereupon be lodged in process, the cost being payable in the first instance by the reclaimer's solicitor.

(*c*) Notes of Evidence shall, except by leave of the court, only be borrowable for the purpose of enabling parties to consider the taking of a reclaiming motion.

[1] (*d*) *Carbon copies*. Where Notes of Evidence have been directed to be supplied for the use of the court, carbon copies may be made available to parties at a cost of 6p per sheet payable to the shorthand-writer by the solicitors for the parties obtaining the said copies.

NOTE

[1] As amended by the Decimal Currency Act 1969, s.10(1).

Section 9—Trial by Jury

Application for trial of the cause by jury on issues

[1] **114.**—(*a*) In a cause, being a cause appropriate for jury trial, where the court allows issues on a motion of consent of parties or after hearing

[THE NEXT PAGE IS C 45]

parties on the by order (adjustment) roll or the procedure roll, the pursuer shall within 14 days of the date of the interlocutor allowing issues, lodge a proposed issue for the trial of the cause by jury, with a copy for the court, and shall at the same time deliver a copy to the solicitor acting for the other party or parties.

(2) Notwithstanding that an interlocutor has been pronounced allowing issues, where a pursuer fails to lodge a proposed issue for the trial and to deliver a copy thereof in accordance with paragraph (1), he shall, unless on special cause shown the court otherwise determines, be held to have passed from his application for trial of the cause by jury, and any inquiry into the facts of the cause shall be taken by a proof unless a proposed issue is lodged by some other party under paragraph (3).

(3) In the event of the pursuer failing to lodge a proposed issue in terms of paragraph (1) the defender or any other party to the action may, if he or they maintain that the cause should be tried by jury with issues, within seven days after the expiry of the period of 14 days provided for in paragraph (1) lodge a proposed issue with a copy for the court and at the same time deliver a copy to the solicitor acting for the other party or parties.

(4) Where a proposed issue has been lodged in pursuance either of paragraph (1) or (3) the other party or parties to the cause may, within seven days after the day on which such proposed issue has been lodged, lodge a proposed counter-issue with a copy for the court and at the same time deliver a copy to the solicitor acting for the other party or parties.

(5) A proposed counter-issue lodged by a party or parties to the cause in pursuance of paragraph (4) may include any question of fact which is made the subject of specific averment on record or is relevant to his or their pleas, notwithstanding that it does not in terms meet the proposed issue or issues.

(6) The party lodging a proposed issue in pursuance of paragraph (1) or (3) shall, not later than seven days after the day on which any such proposed counter-issue or counter-issues have been lodged and intimated or, if no proposed counter-issue has been lodged, on the expiry of the period allowed for lodging a proposed counter-issue in paragraph (4), enrol a motion for approval of the proposed issue; and on intimation being made to him of that motion, any party who has lodged a proposed counter-issue under paragraph (4) shall, within seven days of such intimation, enrol a motion for approval of the proposed counter-issue, and any such motion may be marked as opposed in accordance with Rule 93.

(7) The Lord Ordinary may, either without hearing parties or after hearing parties in the motion roll, grant the motion or motions for approval of the proposed issue and any proposed counter-issue and authenticate by his signature the proposed issue or any proposed counter-issue either as lodged or as the same may have been adjusted, or in his discretion appoint the cause to procedure roll for the hearing of parties.

NOTE

[1] Substituted by S.I. 1982 No. 1825.

Application for trial of the cause by jury without issues

[1] **115.**—(1) If, on the lodging of the closed record, a motion is made in terms of Rule 91(3) to allow trial of the cause by jury without issues, or if any party at the hearing of the cause in the by order (adjustment) roll or the procedure roll moves the court for such an order, the Lord Ordinary may, in his discretion, either order the cause to be tried without issues or allow issues for the trial of the cause.

(2) If the Lord Ordinary allows issues Rule 114 shall apply to those issues as it applies to issues allowed under paragraph (1) of that rule.

NOTE

[1] Substituted by S.I. 1982 No. 1825.

Application for trial of the cause by jury, when parties at variance

[1] **116.**—(*a*) The court after hearing parties in Procedure Roll in pursuance of an order made under Rule 91 or Rule 114 shall dispose of the contentions and pleas of parties as shall seem just; and in the event of the cause being found, in whole or in part, relevant for enquiry, the court may either allow or dispense with issues, or if the court thinks that such enquiry or any part thereof should not be taken before a jury, the court may pronounce an interlocutor allowing a proof.

(*b*) In a cause tried by jury with an issue and counter-issue, the presiding judge may, after the evidence has been led, submit to the jury in writing along with the issue and counter-issue such further question or questions as may appear to him to be required by the circumstances of the case, but where he does so the powers exercisable under Rule 128 in relation to a special verdict shall not be exercisable by him.

NOTE

[1] Substituted by S.I. 1976 No. 137.

Objections to issues as adjusted

117.—(*a*) In any cause in which issues are adjusted in the Outer House for trial by jury, and in which any of the parties objects to the issues so adjusted, or desires to obtain a variation of such issues, or to have other issues added to, or substituted for, those which have been so adjusted, such party may, subject to the provisions of paragraph (*b*) of Rule 264, reclaim to the Inner House against the interlocutor adjusting such issues in manner directed in Rule 262; and generally the provisions of all the rules of Chapter V shall apply.

(*b*) Any party so reclaiming shall, at the same time as he enrols his motion for review lodge in process the issues or counter-issues proposed by him (shewing the deletion, variation, addition or substitution he desires) together with ten copies thereof; and shall also at the same time deliver to the other party or parties copies of the said issues or counter-issues.

Jury precept

[1] **117A.**—(1) Not less than 14 days before the diet for jury trial, the pursuer shall attend at the General Department and request the issue of a jury precept.

(2) Where a jury precept is issued, it shall be transmitted by a clerk of session to the sheriff clerk at Edinburgh who shall prepare in accordance with such precept a list of jurors composed of an equal number of men and women.

NOTE

[1] Inserted by S.I. 1990 No. 2118.

Procedure under the Sex Disqualification (Removal) Act 1919 with reference to jury trials

118.—(*a*) Any application by the parties or any of them under section 1(*b*) of the Sex Disqualification (Removal) Act 1919 shall be made by motion at the time when a date is appointed for the trial, or, if a new trial is ordered, at the time when a date is appointed for such new trial.

(*b*) In all cases in which a precept is issued for the preparation of a list of jurors, the precept shall state, in the event of any order having been made under section 1(*b*) of the said Act, either on the motion of any of the parties or in the discretion of the judge, that the list is to be composed of men only or of women only, as the case may be. In all such cases the sheriff-clerk shall make up a panel or list so that the same is composed of men only, or of women only, as the case may be.

(*e*) Where no order has been made under section 1(*b*) of the said Act, the list of jurors prepared in pursuance of such precept shall be composed of equal numbers of men and women jurors.

Exemption from jury service

119—(*a*) Any person summoned to serve on a jury may as soon as may be after receipt of the citation apply to the Deputy Principal Clerk of Session for exemption from service, and the Deputy Principal Clerk may, if he is satisfied that there are good and sufficient grounds for exemption, grant such application.

(*b*) Every citation upon a person to attend as a juror shall contain a notification as nearly as may be in the terms shewn in Form 12 in the Appendix.

(*c*) Nothing herein shall prejudice the right of the judge presiding at the trial at any time before the jury is empanelled to excuse any person summoned to attend as a juror from attendance.

View

120. Any party intending to apply for a view shall not later than the fourteenth day before the day fixed for the trial enrol a motion for a view.

Lodging and returning productions

121. Rule 107 shall apply, *mutatis mutandis*, in all causes appointed to be tried before a jury, and all steps of process and productions borrowed shall be returned two days before the trial.

Admissions by parties

122.—(*a*) When the parties are agreed in admitting any facts alleged on record, or any matter of fact whether alleged therein or not, or the authenticity of writings or the sufficiency of copies or extracts as equivalent to the

[THE NEXT PAGE IS C 47]

originals, a minute of the admissions, signed by the counsel for the party or parties making such admissions, shall be lodged in process.

(*b*) All admissions so made may be read and used in evidence at the trial, if otherwise competent.

(*c*) In taxing any account of expenses. the Auditor shall disallow the expense of any evidence led on matters covered by such admissions, unless special cause is shewn to him to the contrary.

Oaths and affirmations

[1] **122A.**—(1)(*a*) The clerk of court shall administer the oath collectively to the jury in accordance with the forms set out in part 1 of the Table below.

(*b*) In the case of any juror who elects to affirm the clerk shall administer the affirmation in accordance with the form set out in part 2 of the Table;

(2)(*a*) Where the judge administers the oath to a witness, he shall do so in accordance with the form set out in part 3 of the Table;

(*b*) In the case of a witness who elects to affirm the judge shall administer the affirmation in accordance with the form set out in part 4 of the Table.

TABLE

PART 1

Form of Oath for Jurors

The jurors to raise their right hands and the clerk of court to ask them: "Do you swear by Almighty God that you will well and truly try the issue and give a true verdict according to the evidence?" The jurors to reply: "I do".

PART 2

Form of Affirmation for Jurors

The jurors to repeat after the clerk of court: "I, [name], do solemnly, sincerely and truly declare and affirm that I will well and truly try the issue and give a true verdict according to the evidence".

PART 3

Form of Oath for Witnesses

The witness to raise his right hand and repeat after the judge: "I swear by Almighty God that I will tell the truth, the whole truth and nothing but the truth".

PART 4

Form of Affirmation for Witnesses

The witness to repeat after the judge: "I solemnly, sincerely and truly declare and affirm that I will tell the truth, the whole truth and nothing but the truth".

NOTE

[1] Added by S.I. 1984 No. 472.

Rulings by the presiding judge on matters of evidence

123. If, in the course of the trial, any of the parties is dissatisfied with a ruling by the presiding judge admitting or rejecting any evidence or line of evidence, such party may request that the judge's ruling and such party's objections, which he stated at the time, be immediately recorded in the notes of evidence, and they shall be so recorded under the direction of the presiding judge.

Exceptions to the judge's charge

124.—(*a*) If any of the parties desires to except to any direction by the judge in his charge to the jury on a point of law, or desires the judge to give a direction differing from or supplementary to the directions in the charge, he shall, immediately on the conclusion of the charge, intimate his desire to the presiding judge, who shall thereupon either direct the jury to retire and hear counsel for the parties in court, or direct the jury to remain in court and hear counsel in chambers.

(*b*) At such hearing, counsel for the party dissatisfied with the charge shall formulate in writing the particular exception taken by him, or the particular direction desired by him; and the exception or direction, together with the judge's determination thereon, shall be recorded in a note of exceptions under the direction of the judge and shall be certified by him.

(*c*) Thereafter the judge may give such further or other directions to the jury in open court as the circumstances may seem to him to require, before the jury are enclosed to consider their verdict.

Applying the verdict

125.—(*a*) After a verdict has been returned by the jury, it shall be engrossed on the issue, or on the closed record if the cause is tried without issues, and shall in either case be dated and signed by the Clerk of Court who attends the trial.

(*b*) It shall be competent for either party, at any time after the expiry of seven days after the day on which the verdict was engrossed and signed, to enrol a motion for application of the verdict, entering up of judgment and awarding of expenses, and such motion shall be disposed of by the court in the same way as other motions so enrolled.

[1] (*c*) Where in the course of a trial the presiding judge has directed the jury on any matter of law subject to the opinion of the Inner House on that direction, and the party against whom the verdict is returned applies to the Inner House to enter the verdict for him, it shall not be necessary for the purposes of that application to print the notes of evidence, but the notes of the presiding judge may be produced at any time if required.

NOTE

[1] Added by S.I. 1984 No. 472.

Motion for new trial

126.—(*a*) If any of the parties is dissatisfied with the verdict, either on the ground that it is contrary to the evidence, or on the ground of misdirection by the, judge, or on the ground of the undue admission or rejection of evidence, or on the ground of excess or inadequacy of damages, or of *res noviter veniens ad notitiam*, or for any other cause which is essential to the justice of the cause, he may before 1 p.m. on the eighth day after the day on which the verdict was engrossed and signed, enrol a motion for the granting by the Inner House of a new trial, specifying the ground or grounds of such motion; provided that when a special verdict has been returned and applied under Rule 128 any of the parties may enrol a motion for a new trial upon any of the grounds above specified not later than the twenty-first day after the day on which the special verdict was applied, and provided that a motion for a new trial on the ground of undue admission or rejection of evidence, or on the ground of misdirection by the judge, shall not be granted unless the admission or rejection of such evidence was objected to at the trial and recorded in the notes under direction of the judge or in the case of misdirection, unless the procedure prescribed in Rules 123 and 124 has been complied with.

(*b*) The provisions of Rules 262 and 263 shall apply to all such motions, and the procedure laid down therein shall be followed forth.

(*c*) All such motions shall be heard and disposed of by one or other Division of the Inner House or by such Division sitting along with the judge who presided at the trial, subject to the same procedure including production of the Notes of Evidence and other papers if any, and of any exception together with the presiding judge's determination thereon, as would apply in the case of a motion for review of an interlocutor pronounced in the Outer House enrolled and made by a party reclaiming against such interlocutor. If, after hearing parties upon such motion or upon an appeal under section 31(2) of the Sheriff Courts (Scotland) Act 1907, the court are unanimously of the opinion that the verdict under review is contrary to the evidence and, further, that they have before them all the evidence that could reasonably be expected to be obtained relevant to the cause, they shall be entitled to set aside the verdict and, in place of granting a new trial, to enter judgment for the party unsuccessful at the trial.

Failure to appear

127. If either party shall not appear at the trial of the cause, then if the party appearing is the pursuer in the issue or the party on whom the burden of proof lies, he shall be entitled to lead evidence, and go to the jury for a verdict; and, if the party appearing is the defender in the issue or the party on whom the burden of proof does not lie, he shall be entitled to obtain a verdict in his favour without leading evidence.

Special verdict

128.—(*a*) Where, in any case set down for trial by jury, it appears to the presiding judge that it is expedient that the jury should return a special verdict in the form hereinafter set forth, the presiding judge may so direct the jury.

(*b*) Such special verdict shall be returned in the form of answers to specific questions, which shall include a question relative to the amount at which the jury assesses damages, if any damages are awarded.

(*c*) Such specific questions shall be settled by the presiding judge who may hear the parties before finally settling the same. The presiding judge may so hear parties either in court or in chambers, and in the former case, either outwith or in the presence of the jury.

(*d*) Where a special verdict has been so returned the answers to the specific questions shall be read over to the jury and upon their assent thereto shall be recorded and signed by the clerk who officiated at the trial, and the jury shall thereupon be discharged but said answers shall not be held to constitute a verdict until their effect has been determined by the court. Thereafter, the presiding judge either at the same or at a subsequent diet, shall hear parties and apply the verdict.

Reclaiming against application of special verdict

129.—(*a*) If any of the parties is dissatisfied with the application of the verdict by the presiding judge as provided for by Rule 128 he may bring the interlocutor applying the verdict under review by a reclaiming motion in the mode prescribed by Rule 262, without leave, not later than the twenty-first day after the day on which the said interlocutor is pronounced.

(*b*) At the hearing of said reclaiming motion, whether alone, or along with a motion for a new trial under Rule 126, the court shall not enter the

[THE NEXT PAGE IS C 49]

verdict against any party in whose favour it has been applied by the presiding judge, without giving such party an opportunity of moving for a new trial, upon any ground or grounds upon which he might have desired to move for a new trial under Rule 126 if the verdict had not been applied in his favour by the presiding judge.

Recording evidence and judge's charge in jury trials

130. The provisions of Rule 113 relating to the recording of evidence in proofs shall apply *mutatis mutandis* to the recording of the evidence and judge's charge in jury trials.

SECTION 10—MINORS' AND PUPILS' DAMAGES

Factors for administration of sums of damages recovered by minors and pupils

131.—(*a*) In any action of reparation in which decree is granted for payment of a sum of damages to, or in which decree of absolvitor has been pronounced following upon an extra-judicial settlement in favour of, any

(i) pupil child, acting with the concurrence of a curator *ad litem*; or

(ii) minor *pubes* acting with or without the concurrence of his or her father or of a curator *ad litem*; or

(iii) parent acting on behalf of his or her pupil child,

it shall be competent for the court granting such decree, if it appears that there is no person available to give a full and valid discharge for the damages, or if the court is satisfied that the administration of the damages for the benefit of such minor or pupil cannot otherwise be reasonably secured, to appoint *de plano* some responsible person as factor in accordance with the provisions hereinafter contained.

(*b*) Every appointment of a factor under this rule shall be limited to take effect in so far only as regards the said damages.

(*c*) In appointing any such factor, the court may give him such powers of disbursing both the capital and the income of said damages to or for behoof of the minor or pupil, and such other powers as may be thought necessary or expedient in the interest of such minor or pupil, and may direct that the said damages (both capital and income) shall be paid to or for behoof of the minor or pupil in such amounts and at such times as the court may fix.

(*d*) Such factor shall be bound to find caution for his intromissions and shall be under the superintendence of the Accountant of Court by virtue of the Pupils Protection (Scotland) Act 1849, and the Judicial Factors (Scotland) Act 1889.

Procedure in application for factor

132.—(*a*) Application for the appointment of a factor under this section may be at the instance of any party to the action, and shall be made by motion relative to a minute lodged in process, at any time before extract; and the court may order such intimation of the minute as the circumstances of the case may require.

(*b*) The party lodging the minute shall at the time furnish a copy thereof to the Accountant of Court, and shall certify on the principal minute that each copy has been furnished.

(*c*) The minute may be incorporated in a minute of a judicial tender or acceptance thereof or in a joint minute for the parties, or may be in the form of a separate paper, and in any case shall set forth (i) the kind of factor to be appointed, and the name of the person or persons for whom he is to be appointed, (ii) the amount of the sum to be under his administration, and (iii) the name and designation of the person proposed as factor.

[1] (*d*) *Legally aided cases.* Where such a sum of money as is referred to in Rule 131 becomes payable to a person under legal disability to whom, or

on whose behalf, a legal aid certificate has at any time been issued in respect of such action of damages the provisions of Rule 6 of the Act of Sederunt (Legal Aid Rules) 1958 shall have effect, but it shall be open to the Law Society of Scotland to apply to the court for the appointment of a factor in terms of Rule 132 hereof.

NOTE
[1] Added by S.I. 1974 No. 845.

Extracts

[1] **133.** Where a factor has been appointed, the process shall forthwith be transmitted to the Accountant of Court in like manner as if the appointment had been made upon a separate petition; and upon the interlocutor sheet being marked to the effect that caution has been received, such marking shall be an authority for the issue of a certified copy interlocutor of the appointment.

NOTE
[1] As amended by S.I. 1967 No. 487.

Discharge, death or resignation of factor

134.—(*a*) Any factor appointed under this section may apply for discharge by letter addressed to the Deputy Principal Clerk of Session, who, with the concurrence of the Accountant of Court, may bring the application before a Lord Ordinary sitting in chambers; and such Lord Ordinary may grant the discharge and order delivery of the bond of caution.

(*b*) In the event of the death or resignation of a factor appointed under this section, any person interested, or the Accountant of Court, may apply for a new appointment by letter addressed to the Deputy Principal Clerk of Session, who may bring the application before a Lord Ordinary sitting in chambers, and such Lord Ordinary may make the appointment.

[1] Section 11—Provisional Damages

NOTE
[1] Added by S.I. 1984 No. 919.

Application and interpretation

134A.—(1) This section applies to an action for damages for personal injuries in which—

(*a*) there is proved or admitted to be a risk that at some definite or indefinite time in the future the injured person will, as a result of the act or omission which gave rise to the cause of action, develop some serious disease or suffer some serious deterioration in his physical or mental condition; and

(*b*) the responsible person was, at the time of the act or omission giving rise to the cause of action—

(i) a public authority or public corporation; or

(ii) insured or otherwise indemnified in respect of the claim.

(2) Unless the context otherwise requires, expressions used in this section and also used in the Administration of Justice Act 1982 shall have the meaning given to them in that Act.

(3) In this section—

(*a*) "award of provisional damages" means an award of damages for personal injuries assessed on the assumption that the injured person will not develop the disease or suffer the deterioration in his condition;

(*b*) "award of further damages" means an award of further damages if he develops the disease or suffers the deterioration.

Application for provisional damages

134B.—An application by an injured person for an award of provisional damages shall be made by concluding in the summons for such an award, and making averments supporting that conclusion, including averments relating to the matters mentioned in Rule 134A(1), together with an appropriate plea-in-law.

Application for further damages and procedure

134C.—(1) Subject to any period specified by the court in making an award of provisional damages, an application by an injured person for an award of further damages may be made at any time during his lifetime by minute concluding for such an award, and containing averments supporting that conclusion, together with an appropriate plea-in-law.

(2) The minute shall be intimated by the minuter to the other parties to the action and if they are insured or otherwise indemnified to their insurers or indemnifiers, if known, who may lodge answers.

(3) The court may allow the parties such time for adjustment of the minute and any answers as it thinks fit.

Appeal

134D.—For the purposes of appeal, an interlocutor disposing of the merits of an action to which this section applies and making an award of provisional damages, shall be treated as a final interlocutor.

[1] Section 12—Lodging of Documents Founded On

NOTE

[1] Inserted by S.I. 1990 No. 705.

Lodging of documents founded on

134E.—(1) Any deed, writing or other document founded on by a party in his pleadings shall, so far as in his possession or within his control, be lodged in process by that party—

(*a*) when founded on in the summons or condescendence annexed thereto, at the time of lodging the summons for calling;

(*b*) when founded on in defences, at the time of lodging the defences;

(*c*) when founded on in an adjustment to the pleadings, at the time when such an adjustment is intimated; and

(*d*) when founded on in any minute, answers thereto or adjustments on such a minute and answers, at the time of lodging the minute or answers or intimating the adjustments, as the case may be.

(2) Paragraph (1) shall be without prejudice to any power of the court to order production of any document or grant a commission and diligence for recovery of it.

(3) Where a party fails to lodge a deed, writing or other document in accordance with paragraph (1), he may be found liable in the expenses of any order for production or for commission and diligence for recovery of it obtained by another party to the action.

CHAPTER III

Special Actions

Section 1—Admiralty Causes

Definition of Admiralty causes

135. Admiralty causes include causes arising out of:—

(i) Claims for possession of a ship, or the earnings of a ship, or the protection of the interests of one or more co-owners as against the others to enable a ship to be employed, the examination of accounts between the co-owners, or the apportionment of the earnings of a ship after such examination;

(ii) Claims or disputes in regard to mortgages of ships or shares in a ship;

(iii) Contracts of bottomry and *respondentia*;

[THE NEXT PAGE IS C 51]

(iv) Claims under contracts of affreightment, charter-parties and bills of lading;
(v) (*a*) Loss of life or personal injury and (*b*) loss of or damage to property arising out of collisions at sea;
(vi) Claims by owners of cargo for damage occurring to cargo;
(vii) Claims for limitation of liability;
(viii) Pilotage;
(ix) Civil salvage;
(x) Claims for necessaries;
(xi) Towage;
(xii) Masters' and seamen's wages and disbursements;
(xiii) General average;
(xiv) Forfeiture of ships to the Crown;
(xv) Marine insurance;
(xvi) Maritime liens.

All such causes shall be initiated in the Outer House by summons on the official printed form, and shall conform to the provisions of Rule 70, except as otherwise provided by any of the Rules of this Chapter.

Forms of action

136.—(*a*) Action against the owners or parties interested in a ship or cargo may be brought (i) *in rem*, or (ii) *in personam*, or (iii) both *in rem* and *in personam*, according as the conclusions appended to the summons are directed (i) to recovery in respect of a lien against the ship or cargo or the proceeds thereof, as sold under order of court, or (ii) to a decree in common form against the defenders, or (iii) to both (i) and (ii).

(*b*) The nature of the cause, as being (i) *in rem*, or (ii) *in personam*, or (iii) both *in rem* and *in personam*, shall be distinguished on the official printed form of summons, and on the official backing thereof, by inserting immediately below the space for the letter and number of the cause the words "Admiralty Action *in rem*", or "Admiralty Action *in personam*", or "Admiralty Action *in rem* and *in personam*".

Actions in rem

137. In proceedings by action *in rem* directed against a ship or cargo the ship or cargo shall be arrested under an arrestment hereinafter referred to as an arrestment *in rem*. Such arrestment may be effected upon a warrant to arrest contained in the summons.

(*a*) If the owners of, and parties interested in, the ship or cargo, are known to the pursuer they shall be called by name; but if the names of the owners of the ship or cargo are unknown, it shall be competent to call those whose names are unknown as "the owners of, or parties interested in, the ship" (*name her and her port of registry, if known, and call the master if known as representing the owners thereof or of the cargo*). Specimens of the filling in of the official printed form of summons for the purposes of an action *in rem* are shown in Form 13, and of a suitable conclusion in Form 2.

(*b*) Any person who is an owner of, or a party interested in, the *res* may enter appearance at any time before final judgment in the cause, notwithstanding that the time for entering appearance has expired, and may enrol a motion for leave to lodge defences, or to take such steps in the process as he may be advised.

Actions in personam

138. In an action *in personam* directed against the owners of a ship or cargo, such owners shall, so far as their names are known to the pursuer, be called by name. In the case of a vessel not being a British ship, where the names of the owners of the ship or cargo are unknown to the pursuer, the master of the ship may be called as defender representing the owners of the ship or cargo. In such a case the warrant to arrest to found jurisdiction must be used against the master in his representative capacity. A specimen of the filling in of the official printed form of summons for the purposes of an action *in personam* directed against the master as representing the owners is shewn in Form 14.

Actions both in rem *and* in personam

139. In an action *in rem* and *in personam*, the form of summons will be a suitable combination and adaptation of Forms 13 and 14.

Execution of arrestments and intimation and advertisement of actions in rem

140.—(*a*) When the summons as signeted bears warrant for arrestment *in rem* (as provided for in Rule 74) the arrestment shall be executed by a messenger-at-arms affixing a schedule of arrestment to the mainmast or single mast of the vessel, or where there is no mast, in some prominent part. At the time of executing any such arrestment as aforesaid, the messenger-at-arms shall deliver to the master of the ship or other person on board and in charge thereof, or of the cargo, as representing the owners and parties interested, a copy of the schedule and execution. If no such person is on board, the execution of arrestment shall so state and the pursuer may then serve the arrestment on the Customs Officer at the port where the ship lies or apply by motion of the court for a direction. The court may order such other intimation or advertisement of the dependence of an action *in rem* as it may deem necessary.

(*b*) If any cargo has been landed or transhipped, or in course of being landed or transhipped, the arrestment of the cargo (but only in so far as it has not been delivered to the owner thereof, or to his agents) shall be effected by the messenger-at-arms placing the schedule of arrestment in the hands of the custodier for the time being of the cargo, or, when such cargo has been landed on to the quay, or into the shed of any port or harbour authority, by the messenger-at-arms delivering to the harbour-master a schedule of arrestment of the cargo.

(*c*) It shall not be necessary for the messenger-at-arms to serve separate schedules of arrestment to found jurisdiction on the dependence or *in rem*, but it shall be competent to combine one or other of such arrestments in one schedule of arrestment.

[1] (*d*) Where a *res* has been arrested under warrant contained in an action *in rem*, or where the pursuer has used arrestment on the dependence, and the defender or other person shewing an interest desires to have such arrestment recalled or to seek authority to move an arrested vessel before the calling of the summons, it shall be competent for him to apply to the court, by motion; and the Deputy Principal Clerk of Session shall, so soon thereafter as is practicable, intimate to the parties when and where the application will be disposed of by a Lord Ordinary in chambers, or in vacation or recess by the Vacation Judge. The Lord Ordinary or Vacation Judge shall be attended by the clerk and counsel, solicitor or both counsel and solicitor for each party. The pursuer's solicitor or counsel shall produce to the Lord Ordinary or Vacation Judge the principal summons and the certificate of the execution of the arrestment; and the Lord Ordinary or Vacation Judge may, on cause shewn, and on such terms as may be proper and expedient in the circumstances, recall the arrestment.

(*dd*) Rule 74(h) shall apply to an application for recall of an arrestment on the dependence of an action or for authority to move an arrested vessel made after calling in an action *in rem*.

(*e*) A commission fee paid to a person finding security for release of a ship from arrestment, whether in an action *in rem* or otherwise in security, may be recovered on taxation in a judicial account to an amount not exceeding one pound per cent. of the amount secured.

NOTE

[1] As amended by S.I. 1990 No. 705 and (with effect from 25th November 1991) S.I. 1991 No. 2483.

Inducia*e on summons*

141. In all summonses in Admiralty causes, the *induciae* shall be determined in accordance with the provisions of Rule 72.

Service on master and decree in personam

142. In all causes *in personam* in which the summons is served on the master of the ship as representing the owners or parties interested, it shall be competent to pronounce decree against the master in his representative capacity; provided that in any cause *in personam* or in any combined action *in rem* and *in personam* it shall be competent to pronounce a decree *in personam* against an owner or party interested only when such owner or party interested has been called or added as a defender.

Order for sale of ship or other arrested property

143. In an Admiralty action in which a finding is made by the court that the pursuer has a claim which falls to be satisfied out of the arrested *res*, it shall be competent for the pursuer to apply to the court by motion to order the sale of the ship or other arrested property at such upset price or reduced upset price as the court may fix. Where the sale of the ship or other arrested property is ordered by the court, the entire conduct of the sale, including advertisement, shall be under the direction of the Deputy Principal Clerk. The interlocutor directing the sale, if the *res* is a ship or a share therein, shall contain a declaration vesting in the Deputy Principal Clerk the right to transfer the ship or share, and the Deputy Principal Clerk shall thereupon be entitled to transfer the ship or share in the same manner and to the same extent as if he were the registered owner thereof. The price received shall be consigned in the court under deduction of all dues payable up to the date when the court adjudges the ship or other arrested property to belong to the purchaser to Her Majesty's Customs or to the dock or harbour authority within whose undertaking the said ship or other arrested property is then lying and in respect of which such dock or harbour authority has a statutory power to detain the ship or other arrested property. Upon such consignation being made, the interlocutor adjudging the ship or other arrested property shall declare the same to belong to the purchaser thereof, freed and disburdened of all bonds, mortgages, liens, rights of retention and other incumbrances affecting the same and shall order the said ship or other arrested property to be delivered to the purchaser on presentation of a certified copy of the said interlocutor; and the court shall order such advertisement and intimation for claims on the consigned fund as it shall think fit. The court shall, after such enquiry and hearing as it may consider necessary, deal with all questions of expenses and rank and prefer the other claimants in their order of preference to the balance of the said fund, or make such other order as may be just.

Ship collisions: preliminary acts: procedure

144. The provisions of this rule shall apply, subject to Rule 145, to all actions of damages arising out of collisions between vessels at sea.

(*a*) The summons shall be in a form as shewn in Forms 13 and 14 or a suitable combination and adaptation thereof, with the appropriate conclusion or conclusions and such warrants to arrest as may be considered necessary appended thereto. The summons shall not have annexed to it any condescendence or note of pleas-in-law.

(*b*) Within seven days after the day on which the summons is called the pursuer shall lodge in the process a sealed envelope containing (i) a document to be called the preliminary act for the pursuer in the form shewn in Form 15 with the particulars required duly filled in, and (ii) a short condescendence and note of pleas-in-law.

Intimation of the lodging of the said envelope shall be given by the pursuer to the defender or his solicitor. Except as provided in (*d*) below the sealed envelope shall only be opened on an order by the court.

(*c*) The defender shall lodge in the General Department not later than seven days after the day on which the preliminary act for the pursuer is lodged a sealed envelope containing a preliminary act for the defender in the form shewn in Form 15 with the particulars required duly filled in.

(*d*) When the preliminary act for the defender is lodged, the sealed envelopes for the pursuer and the defender shall be opened by the clerk of the process and the contents shall be marked as numbers of process. The solicitors for the parties shall exchange copies of the documents contained in their respective envelopes.

(*e*) Not later than seven days after the day upon which the said envelopes are opened the defender if so advised may lodge defences with a note of pleas-in-law and any counter-claim upon which he proposes to found with the appropriate conclusion or conclusions and with an articulate numbered statement of facts and note of pleas-in-law. If the defender lodges a counter-claim the pursuer may lodge answers thereto within seven days.

(*f*) Not later than seven days after the day on which defences are lodged or after the day on which the pursuer lodges answers to a counter-claim the pursuer's solicitor shall make up and deliver to the solicitor for the defender six copies of the open record in ordinary form with copies of the preliminary acts for the pursuer and the defender appended thereto. He shall also lodge two copies of the said record in the process.

(*g*) No amendment, adjustment or alteration may be made upon a preliminary act after it has been lodged except by order of the court. If it appears to the court that the statements required by the preliminary act are not fully set out the court may order the party concerned to make the necessary additions thereto. Statements made in a preliminary act shall have effect as formal admissions of fact.

(*h*) Save as provided in (*g*) above, parties may adjust the open record. When the record has been closed the case shall thereafter proceed as in an ordinary action.

(*j*) The court may on cause shewn extend or abridge the time for carrying out any of the aforesaid steps of process.

Application to dispense with preliminary acts

145.—(*a*) Any party may within seven days after the day on which the summons is called, apply to the court by written note for an order dispensing with procedure by way of preliminary acts.

(*b*) The note shall be intimated to the other party or parties who may, if so advised, lodge answers thereto within such time as the court may direct.

(*c*) The court, after hearing the party or parties, may if satisfied that procedure by way of preliminary act is not appropriate to the circumstances of the case, order that they may be dispensed with.

(*d*) If the court orders that preliminary acts shall be dispensed with the pursuer shall lodge a condescendence and note of pleas-in-law within such time as the court shall direct and the case shall thereafter proceed as in an ordinary action.

(*e*) If the court refuses the said note the pursuer shall, if he has not already done so, lodge a preliminary act and condescendence and note of pleas-in-law in terms of Rule 144 within such time as the court shall direct and the case shall thereafter proceed in accordance with the provisions of said Rule.

(*f*) It shall not be competent to reclaim against an interlocutor of the Lord Ordinary dispensing or refusing to dispense with preliminary acts.

Nautical assessors

146. In causes arising out of collisions at sea, where the court is assisted by a nautical assessor at the proof, it shall not be competent for any of the parties to lead expert evidence of nautical matters.

Lodging productions for proofs in ship-collision and salvage causes

147. Without prejudice to the provisions of Rule 107 the parties shall, in all ship-collision and salvage causes, within four days of the interlocutor allowing proof, or within four days before the taking of evidence on commission, or on or before such other date as the court, on special cause shewn, shall fix, lodge in process (i) the ship's log-books, including scrap log-books, of the ships concerned, (ii) all *de recenti* written reports in connection with the collision or salvage by the masters or mates of the vessels concerned to their owners, and (iii) any report of any survey of the vessel in respect of which damages or salvage is claimed.

International Oil Pollution Compensation Fund

[1] **147A.**—(1) In any action brought against an owner or guarantor in respect of liability under section 1 of the Merchant Shipping (Oil Pollution) Act 1971, notice of the action shall be given under section 6(2) of the said Act of 1974 to the Fund by the pursuer by intimation in accordance with the provisions of paragraph (2).

(2) Where intimation is proposed to be made to the Fund under this rule, the official printed form of summons shall be filled up so as to contain a warrant for intimation in the following terms—

> "Warrant to intimate to the International Oil Pollution Compensation Fund (*address*) as a person having an interest in this action";

and Rule 76 shall apply to the execution of a warrant under this rule as it applies to the execution of a warrant under that rule with the substitution for the reference to Form 5 of a reference to Form 5C.

(3) In any case where the Fund is not a party to an action to which this rule applies, a defender in the action may in accordance with the provisions of Rule 85 (third party notices) apply to the court for leave to serve a third party notice on the Fund, and the provisions of Rule 85 shall apply to any such application.

(4) Where in any proceedings under section 4 of the said Act of 1974 the court gives judgment against the Fund, the Clerk of Court shall within 14 days of the issue of the judgment send a copy thereof to the Fund.

NOTE

[1] Added by S.I. 1979 No. 670.

[1] Section 2—Commercial Causes

NOTE

[1] Substituted by S.I. 1988 No. 1521.

Application

148.—(1) In an action to which paragraph (2) applies, the pursuer may elect to adopt the procedure in this Section.

[1] (2) This Section applies to—

(*a*) an action relating to—

(i) the construction of a commercial or mercantile document;
(ii) the sale or hire purchase of goods;
(iii) the export or import of merchandise;
(iv) the carriage of goods by land, air or sea (other than an Admiralty action);
(v) a building, engineering or construction contract;
(vi) a commercial lease;
(vii) insurance;
(viii) banking;
(ix) the provision of financial services;
(x) mercantile agency;
(xi) mercantile usage or custom of trade; and

(*b*) an action not falling within sub-paragraph (*a*) but relating to a dispute of a business or commercial nature, and any such action in which an election has been made under paragraph (1) may be referred to as a commercial action.

(3) An election under paragraph (1) shall be made by signeting a summons with the words "Commercial Action" marked above the instance, and on the backing, of the summons.

(4) Subject to the provisions of this Section, the other provisions of the Rules of the Court of Session, so far as applicable, apply to the practice and procedure to which this Section applies.

NOTE

[1] Substituted by S.I. 1990 No. 2118.

Nominated judges

149. A commercial action shall be heard by a Lord Ordinary nominated by the Lord President or, in the absence of a nominated judge, by any other Lord Ordinary or by a vacation judge.

Commercial roll

150. A commercial action shall be assigned to the commercial roll.

Procedure following the lodging of defences

151.—(1) Within 14 days after defences have been lodged in process, a commercial action shall be put out by order on the commercial roll for hearing on a specified date.

(2) The appearance of a commercial action by order shall not affect the right of any party to apply to the court by motion.

(3) All motions that require the attendance of counsel or relate to matters mentioned in paragraph (4)(*b*) shall be heard when the commercial action is heard by order.

(4) At the first, or any subsequent hearing by order, the court—

(*a*) may make such further order as it thinks fit for the speedy determination of the question in dispute between the parties;

(*b*) may—

(i) allow a specified period of adjustment;

(ii) allow an amendment;

(iii) ordain a party to give further specification of his case in his pleadings;

(iv) allow a counter-claim to be lodged;

(v) grant warrant for service of a third party notice;

(vi) remit to a man of skill;

(vii) where it proposes to appoint an action to the procedure roll under sub-paragraph (*c*)(i), ordain a party to lodge a concise note of his proposed argument within such time as it considers appropriate;

(*c*) shall, where adjustment has not been allowed or the period of adjustment has expired—

(i) appoint the action to the procedure roll, or allow a proof, or a proof before answer, of the whole or such part of the action as the court shall think fit; or

(ii) make such other order as it thinks fit for the further progress of the action.

(5) Where the court makes an order under paragraph (4)(*c*)(i), it may order the pursuer to make up a closed record; and rule 91(2) and (3) (closing record) shall apply.

Withdrawal from commercial roll

151A.—(1) The court may, on its own motion or on the motion of any party, if it thinks it appropriate to do so, withdraw an action from the commercial roll.

(2) Where the court pronounces an interlocutor withdrawing an action from the commercial roll, the action shall proceed as an ordinary action.

(3) An interlocutor withdrawing or refusing to withdraw an action from the commercial roll shall be final.

Transfer to commercial roll

151B.—(1) In an action in which the pursuer has not elected to adopt the provisions of this Section, a party may apply by motion to have the action appointed to the commercial roll.

(2) A motion under paragraph (1) shall be heard by a judge mentioned in rule 149.

(3) An interlocutor appointing or refusing to appoint an action to the commercial roll under paragraph (1) shall be final.

Inspection and recovery of documents

151C.—(1) Within 28 days of an interlocutor allowing a proof or proof before answer, each party to a commercial action shall intimate to every other party a list of the documents relating to the matters at issue between them which are, or to the best of his knowledge have been, in his possession or control.

(2) A party who has received a list of documents intimated under paragraph (1) may inspect those documents which are in the possession or control of the party intimating the list within 28 days of the receipt of the list at a time and place to be mutually arranged between those parties.

(3) A party shall have the right to obtain a copy or copies of any document under paragraph (2) on payment of a copying fee of not more than that prescribed by item 2 in Chapter I of the Table of Fees in rule 347.

(4) Nothing in this rule shall affect—

(*a*) the law relating to, or the right of a party to object to, the inspection of a document on the ground of privilege or confidentiality; or

(*b*) the right of a party to apply for an order under rule 95 for a commission and diligence for recovery of documents or under rule 95A for an order under section 1 of the Administration of Justice (Scotland) Act 1972.

Exchange of lists of witnesses

151D.—(1) Within 28 days of an interlocutor allowing a proof or proof before answer, each party to a commercial action shall intimate to every other party a list containing the names and addresses of the witnesses whom he intends to call to give evidence.

(2) Where a party seeks to call as a witness a person not on his list intimated under paragraph (1), and any other party objects, he shall seek leave of the court to do so, which leave may be granted on such conditions, if any, as the court thinks fit.

Evidence generally

151E.—(1) Where possible, parties shall agree any statement or document not in dispute.

(2) A party may apply by motion for a specified statement or document to be admitted as evidence without calling as a witness the maker of the statement or document, and the court may make such order upon such conditions, if any, as it thinks fit.

Customs of trade

151F.—(1) This rule applies to a commercial action in which a custom of trade or commercial usage is pled.

(2) Where objection is taken at any hearing by order to the legality or validity of a custom of trade or commercial usage pled, the court shall appoint a hearing on such objection.

(3) At a hearing appointed under paragraph (2), the court—

(*a*) may sustain, repel or reserve the objection;

(*b*) where the objection is repelled or reserved, shall make a remit to which paragraph (5) shall apply and, where facts require to be ascertained to determine the legality of an alleged custom or usage, may include the determination of the dispute on the facts in the remit; and

(*c*) shall make such other order as it thinks fit for the further progress of the action.

(4) Where no objection is taken to the legality or validity of a custom or usage pled, at any hearing on the commercial roll, the court—

(*a*) may make a remit to which paragraph (5) shall apply; and

(*b*) shall, where it makes such a remit, make such other order as it thinks fit for the further progress of the action.

(5) Where a remit is made under paragraph (3)(*b*) or (4)(*a*), it shall be made to any person or persons engaged in the particular trade in question to report on the existence and scope of the custom or usage; and the report shall be conclusive of the existence and scope of the custom or usage.

[THE NEXT PAGE IS C 57]

(6) Where a remit is made under paragraph (3)(*b*) or (4)(*a*), the party who pleads the custom or usage shall instruct the reporter within 14 days of the date of the remit and be responsible, in the first instance, for payment of his fees.

(7) The reporter shall lodge the report, together with a copy for each party, with the Deputy Principal Clerk of Session.

(8) On receipt of a report, the Deputy Principal Clerk of Session shall—

(*a*) intimate the receipt of the report to each party;

(*b*) request the party responsible under paragraph (6) for payment of the fees for the report to produce to him a discharge in respect of those fees; and

(*c*) on sight of the discharge mentioned in sub-paragraph (*b*)—

(i) lodge the report in process; and

(ii) intimate to each party that this has been done.

PROVISIONS COMMON TO ADMIRALTY AND COMMERCIAL CAUSES

Evidence and admissions

152. In any Admiralty or commercial cause the court may accept as evidence affidavits. Where, in the opinion of the court, any affidavit produced is insufficient to enable the question at issue to be disposed of, the party lodging the same may be called upon to lodge a supplementary affidavit, or, where the circumstances reasonably permit, to prove the relevant facts by the ordinary rules of evidence.

Applicability of other rules to Admiralty and commercial causes

153. So far as not inconsistent with the rules in this section the rules dealing with ordinary actions shall apply *mutatis mutandis* to Admiralty and commercial causes.

[1] SECTION 2A—EXCHEQUER CAUSES

NOTE

[1] Added by S.I. 1984 No. 472.

Commencement

153A.—(1) An exchequer cause may be commenced by summons and when so commenced shall proceed as nearly as may be as an ordinary action.

(2) Subject to Rule 153D, all proceedings in exchequer causes shall be brought in the first instance before the Lord Ordinary in exchequer causes.

Suspension

153B. An application for the suspension of any decree, charge, threatened charge or diligence in an exchequer cause may be made to the Lord Ordinary in exchequer causes by the Crown, or any subject, in the same manner and to the same extent and effect as such an application is made in an ordinary action.

Review

153C. An interlocutor pronounced by the Lord Ordinary in exchequer causes shall, for the purposes of review of that interlocutor, have effect as an interlocutor pronounced in an ordinary action.

Appeal

153D. Any appeal by way of stated cases in an exchequer cause shall be brought before the Inner House.

Extracts

153E. The extractor shall give priority over all other business to extracts in exchequer causes.

[1] SECTION 3—CONSISTORIAL ACTIONS

NOTE

[1] Rules 154 to 170D substituted by S.I. 1976 No. 1994.

PRELIMINARY

Application and interpretation

[1] **154.**—[2] (1) Except in so far as otherwise expressly provided, the provisions of this section apply to all consistorial actions including actions of divorce, separation, declarator of nullity of marriage, declarator of marriage, declarator of legitimacy, declarator of bastardy, actions for financial provision after overseas divorce and actions of aliment.

(2) Subject to the provisions of this section, the provisions of these rules so far as applicable apply with any necessary modifications to the practice and procedure in consistorial actions.

[2] (3) In this section, unless the context otherwise requires—

"The Act of 1938" means the Divorce (Scotland) Act 1938;

"The Act of 1958" means the Matrimonial Proceedings (Children) Act 1958;

"The Act of 1973" means the Domicile and Matrimonial Proceedings Act 1973;

"The Act of 1976" means the Divorce (Scotland) Act 1976;

"The Act of 1985" means the Family Law (Scotland) Act 1985;

"improper association" means sodomy, incest or any homosexual relationship;

"mental disorder" means mental illness or mental deficiency however caused or manifested.

(4) Unless the context otherwise requires, a rule referred to by number, means the rule so numbered in this section, and a paragraph, sub-paragraph or head referred to by number or letter means a paragraph so numbered or lettered in that rule, a sub-paragraph so numbered or lettered in that paragraph and head so numbered or lettered in that sub-paragraph respectively.

(5) In this section, a form referred to by number means the form so numbered in the Appendix to these rules or a form substantially to the like effect, with such variations as the circumstances of the particular case may require.

NOTES

[1] Substituted by S.I. 1976 No. 1994.

[2] As amended by S.I. 1986 No. 1231.

SUMMONS

Warrants for intimation

[1] **155.**—(1) Subject to paragraph 2, in an action where the pursuer alleges that the defender has committed adultery with another person, warrant for intimation to that person shall be endorsed on the summons in the following terms:—

"Warrant to intimate to (name and address) as a person with whom the defender is alleged to have committed adultery", unless that person is not named in the summons and, if the adultery is relied on for the purposes of section 1(2)(*a*) of the Act of 1976, the summons contains an averment that his or her identity is not known to the pursuer.

(2) In an action where the pursuer alleges that the defender has been guilty of rape upon or incest with a named person, paragraph (1) shall not apply.

(3) In an action where—

(*a*) the defender's address is unknown; or

(*b*) the defender is a person who is suffering from a mental disorder, warrant for intimation to—

(i) every child of the marriage between the parties who has reached the age of 12 years in the case of a girl and 14 years in the case of a boy; and

(ii) one of the defender's next-of-kin who has reached the above age; and

(iii) the defender's *curator bonis*, if any,

shall, subject to paragraph (4), be endorsed on the summons in the following terms:—

"Warrant to intimate to (name and address) as the child of the marraige and (name and address) the (relationship to defender) and one of the next-of-kin of the defender and (name and address) *curator bonis* of the defender."

(4) Warrant for intimation to a person such as is mentioned in heads (i) to (iii) of paragraph (3), shall not be required under that paragraph if—

(*a*) the address of that person is unknown to the pursuer; and

(*b*) there is an averment to that effect in the summons.

(5) In any action relating to a marriage which was entered into under a law which permits polygamy in which one of the decrees specified in section 2(2) of the Matrimonial Proceedings (Polygamous Marriages) Act 1972 is sought, and either party to the marriage in question has any spouse additional to the other party, warrant for intimation to any such additional spouse shall be endorsed on the summons in the following terms:—

[THE NEXT PAGE IS C 59]

"Warrant to intimate to (name and address) as an additional spouse of the (pursuer) *or* (defender)."

[2] (6) In an action where the court may make an order mentioned in sub-paragraph (*a*) of paragraph (6) of Rule 170B, intimation shall be made in accordance with the provisions of that sub-paragraph.

[2] (7) In an action where an application is made under sub-paragraph (*a*) of paragraph (4) of Rule 170D, intimation shall be made in accordance with the provisions of sub-paragraph (*c*).

NOTES

[1] Substituted by S.I. 1976 No. 1994.

[2] Added by S.I. 1982 No. 1825.

Warrants for diligence on the dependence

[1] **155A.**—(1) An application for a warrant for inhibition, or arrestment, on the dependence of an action in which a claim to which section 19(1) of the Family Law (Scotland) Act 1985 applies is made shall not be endorsed on the summons but shall be made by motion.

(2) A motion under paragraph (1) of this rule enrolled before the calling of the summons shall not require to be intimated to any other party.

NOTE

[1] Inserted by S.I. 1991 No. 1157.

Conclusions

[1] **156.**—(1) The form of the conclusions of the summons shall be in accordance with the appropriate form set out in Form 2.

(2) It shall be competent in the conclusions to include a conclusion in the following terms:- "For such other order as the court may consider appropriate."

NOTE

[1] Substituted by S.I. 1976 No. 1994 and as amended by S.I. 1986 No. 1231.

Averments

[1] **157.**—(1) Where—

(*a*) the address of the defender is unknown, or

(*b*) the identity or address of any person mentioned in Rule 155 as a person in respect of whom a warrant for intimation requires to be endorsed on the summons is unknown,

there shall be included in the condescendence of the summons an averment of that fact, together with averments setting out the steps, if any, taken by the pursuer to ascertain that person's address, or as the case may be, that person's identity.

[2] (2) In any action of divorce or separation where the facts set out in section 1(2)(*d*) or (*e*) of the Act of 1976 are relied upon or in which the pursuer has reason to believe that the defender is undergoing treatment for mental disorder in a hospital, averments setting out the financial position of the pursuer and, so far as known to the pursuer after appropriate inquiry, the financial position of the defender and any child of the marriage who is dependent upon them and the financial arrangements proposed or sought on divorce or separation shall be included in the condescendence of the summons.

(3)(*a*) In every action of divorce, separation, declarator of marriage, or declarator of nullity of marriage, the condescendence of the summons shall include a statement of whether to the knowledge of the pursuer any proceedings are continuing in any country outside Scotland, which are in respect of the marriage to which the summons relates or are capable of affecting its validity or subsistence.

(*b*) Where such proceedings outside Scotland are continuing, the statement shall include the following particulars:—

(i) the court, tribunal or authority before which they have been commenced;

(ii) the date of their commencement;

(iii) the names of the parties;

(iv) the date, or expected date of any proof in the proceedings; and

(v) such other facts as may be relevant to the question of whether the proposed action in the Court of Session should be sisted under Schedule 3 to the Act of 1973.

(*c*) Where such proceedings outside Scotland are continuing and the Court of Session action is defended and either—

(i) the summons does not contain the statement; or

(ii) the particulars mentioned in sub-paragraph (*b*) are incomplete or erroneous,

the defences or minute lodged by any party to that action shall include the statement and, where appropriate, those particulars.

(*d*) The proceedings mentioned in paragraph (*a*) are continuing for the purposes of this paragraph at any time after they are commenced and before they are finally disposed of.

NOTES

[1] Substituted by S.I. 1976 No. 1994.

[2] As amended by S.I. 1980 No. 1144.

Service

Inducise

[1] **158.** The *induciae* for the citation of a defender or any person in respect of whom a warrant for intimation requires to be endorsed shall be in accordance with Rule 72.

NOTE

[1] Substituted by S.I. 1986 No. 1941.

Citation

[1] **159.**—(1) Subject to paragraph (2) and Rule 74B, citation in any action shall be executed either—

(*a*) personally; or

(*b*) if the person executing the citation after due inquiry has reasonable grounds for believing that the defender is residing at a particular dwelling place, by leaving the citation in the hands of a resident at, or depositing it in the dwelling place; or

(*c*) by post.

(2) Where the place where the defender resides cannot be ascertained or citation cannot be successfully effected in accordance with a method permitted under paragraph (1) of this Rule or Rule 74B(1), citation shall be made edictally on an *induciae* of 21 days.

(3) Citation executed by post shall, subject to the provision of paragraph (5) be by means of—

(*a*) a messenger-at-arms; or

[2] (*b*) a solicitor,

posting by registered or recorded delivery letter addressed to the defender and having on the face of the letter the notice set out in paragraph (4), a copy of the summons with citation in the terms set out in Form 3, and in an action to which Rule 161 applies, the notices referred to in that rule in relation to that action.

(4) The notice mentioned in paragraph (3) shall be in the following terms:—

"This letter contains a citation to or intimation from the Court of Session, Scotland. If delivery of the letter cannot be made it is to be returned immediately to the Deputy Principal Clerk of Session, 2 Parliament Square, Edinburgh."

(5) In any action where defender suffers or appears to suffer from mental disorder and is resident in a hospital or other similar institution, citation shall be executed by addressing the registered or recorded delivery letter to the medical officer in charge of that hospital or institution enclosing a certificate in the terms set out in Form 21 with a request in the terms set out in Form 20 that he either—

(*a*) deliver the copy of the summons personally to the defender together with any notice sent therewith in accordance with the provisions of Rule 161 and explain the contents to him; or

(*b*) certify on soul and conscience that such delivery or explanation would be dangerous to the health or mental condition of the defender,

and complete the certificate accordingly and return it to the pursuer's solicitor to be attached to the summons lodged for calling.

(6) Where the certificate returned under paragraph (5) bears that no delivery of the summons was made to the defender, it shall be competent for the court at any stage in the proceedings before decree to order such further medical enquiry and such further service as it may think fit.

[THE NEXT PAGE IS C 61]

(7) On the citation being executed by post, the messenger-at-arms or solicitor who executed it shall return the execution in terms of Form 3, together with the Post Office receipt for the letter.

(8) Citation executed by post is a valid citation unless and until the defender proves that the letter was not tendered or left at his address.

NOTES

[1] Substituted by S.I. 1976 No. 1994, and as amended by S.I. 1980 No. 1144, S.I. 1986 No. 1941 and S.I. 1987 No. 1206.

[2] As amended by S.I. 1991 No. 2483, with effect from 25th November 1991.

Intimation

[1] **160.**—[2] (1) A warrant for intimation to any person mentioned in Rule 155, 170B (6)(*a*), 170D(4)(*c*) and (9) and 188D (10) may be executed at the same time as or after, the citation of the defender, and Rule 159 (apart from paragraph (5)) shall apply to the execution of the warrant as it applies to the execution of a citation with the substitution for the reference to citation of a reference to intimation and for the reference to Form 3 of a reference to Form 16, 17, 18, 18A, 18B, 18C or 18D, as the case may be.

(2) Execution of a warrant for intimation shall be certified by attaching to the summons a copy of the intimation and a certificate of execution.

NOTES

[1] Substituted by S.I. 1976 No. 1994.

[2] Substituted by S.I. 1977 No. 1621, and as amended by S.I. 1982 No. 1381 and S.I. 1986 No. 1231.

Notice in divorces and separations

[1] **161.**—(1) Where the facts set out in section 1(2)(*d*) of the Act of 1976 (2 years non-cohabitation and the defender's consent to decree) are relied on in an action of divorce, a notice in the terms set out in Form 15A shall be sent with the copy of the summons served on the defender, together with a notice in the terms set out in Form 15E.

(2) Where the facts set out in section 1(2)(*d*) of the Act of 1976 (2 years non-cohabitation and the defender's consent to decree) are relied on in an action of separation, a notice in the terms set out in Form 15B shall be sent with the copy of the summons served on the defender, together with a notice in the terms set out in Form 15E.

(3) Where the facts set out in section 1(2)(*e*) of the Act of 1976 (5 years non-cohabitation) are relied upon in an action of divorce, a notice in the terms set out in Form 15C shall be sent with the copy of the summons served on the defender.

(4) Where the facts set out in section 1(2)(*e*) of the Act of 1976 (5 years non-cohabitation) are relied upon in an action of separation, a notice in the terms set out in Form 15D shall be sent with the copy of the summons served on the defender.

NOTE

[1] Substituted by S.I. 1976 No. 1994.

Intimation where improper association

[1] **162.**—(1) In an action where the pursuer alleges an improper association (other than adultery) between the defender and another named person, the pursuer shall immediately after the calling of the summons, enrol a motion for intimation to that person, and the Court at the hearing of the motion may make an order for intimation or an order dispensing with intimation to that person, as it thinks fit.

(2) Where the court makes an order for intimation under paragraph (1), Rule 160 shall apply to intimation to that person as it applies to intimation to a person mentioned in Rule 155, with the substitution for the reference to Forms 16, 17, 18, 18A and 18B of a reference to Form 19.

(3) Where the court makes an order dispensing with intimation to that

person under paragraph (1) it may also make an order that the name of that person be deleted from the condescendence of the summons.

NOTE

[1] Substituted by S.I. 1976 No. 1994.

163. [Revoked by S.I. 1978 No. 161.]

Procedure Before Proof Allowed

Power to order intimation

[1] **164.** The court may in any action order intimation to be made to such person as it thinks fit.

NOTE

[1] Substituted by S.I. 1976 No. 1994.

Third parties entering the process

[1] **165.** Any person upon whom intimation of an action has been made under this section may apply for leave to lodge defences or answers or minute, as the case may be, and the court may grant that application.

NOTE

[1] Substituted by S.I. 1976 No. 1994.

Consent to grant of decree

[1] **166.**—(1) Where, in an action of divorce or separation in which the facts set out in section 1(2)(*d*) of the Act of 1976 (two years non-cohabitation and the defender's consent to decree) are relied on, the defender wishes to indicate to the court that he consents to the grant of a decree, he shall do so by giving notice in writing to that effect to the Deputy Principal Clerk of Session.

(2) For the purposes of paragraph (1) a notice of consent in the terms set out in Form 15E containing a statement that the defender consents to the grant of a decree shall be treated as notice under that paragraph if it is signed by the defender, and the evidence of one witness shall be sufficient for the purposes of establishing that the signature on the notice of consent bearing to be that of the defender is in fact that of the defender.

(3) A defender in an action of divorce or separation where the summons includes, for the purposes of the said section 1(2)(*d*), an averment that he consents to the grant of a decree may give notice in writing to the court that he has not consented to a decree being granted or that he withdraws any consent which he has already given.

(4) In a case where the defender gives notice under paragraph (3), the Deputy Principal Clerk of Session shall intimate its terms to the solicitor representing the pursuer.

(5) On receiving intimation under paragraph (4) of a notice given under paragraph (3), the pursuer shall, if none of the other facts mentioned in section 1(2) of the Act of 1976 are averred in the summons, enrol a motion for the action to be sisted, and the court may grant that motion.

(6) If such a motion is granted and the sist is not recalled or renewed within a period of 6 months from the date of the interlocutor granting the sist, the pursuer shall be deemed to have abandoned the action.

NOTE

[1] Substituted by S.I. 1976 No. 1994.

Special applications

[1] **167.**—(1) For appointment of curator *ad litem*:

(*a*) In an action of divorce or separation where it appears to the court that the defender is a person who is suffering from mental disorder, the court shall, on the expiry of the period for lodging defences—
(i) appoint a curator *ad litem* to the defender; and
(ii) in the case of a divorce or separation under section 1 (2) (*d*) of the Act of 1976, make an order informing the Mental Welfare Commission for Scotland of the ground of the action and requesting them to provide a report indicating whether in their opinion the defender is capable of deciding whether or not to give consent to the granting of decree.

(*b*) The solicitor representing the pursuer shall as soon as reasonably practicable after the making of an order under head (i) of paragraph (*a*) appointing a curator *ad litem* to the defender, send to the curator the certified copy summons (which may be borrowed from process for this purpose) and defences, if any.

(*c*) The curator *ad litem* may, within 14 days of the Commission providing the report requested under head (ii) of paragraph (*a*), or in any case where no such report is requested, within 14 days of his appointment under head (i) of that paragraph lodge—
(i) defences to the action; or
(ii) a minute adopting defences already lodged; or
(iii) a minute stating that he does not intend to lodge defences and may appear in the action at any time to protect the interests of the defender.

(2) *Under the Act of 1973.* Any application for a sist, or the recall of a sist under Schedule 3 to the Act of 1973, shall be by way of motion.

NOTE
[1] Substituted by S.I. 1976 No. 1994.

Undefended actions

[1] **168.**—(1) The provisions of this rule—
(*a*) apply to all actions of divorce and of separation and aliment in which no defences have been lodged;
(*b*) do not apply to any such action where it appears to the court that the defender is a person who is suffering from mental disorder except in an action where the curator *ad litem* for the defender has lodged a minute intimating that he does not intend to defend the action;
(*c*) may apply to any action of divorce and of separation and aliment which proceeds at any stage as undefended if the court so directs;
(*d*) may apply to the merits of any such action as is mentioned in sub-paragraph (*c*) if the court so directs, notwithstanding that the action is defended on an ancillary matter;

and in this rule " action " means any action to which this rule so applies.

Evidence

(2) In all actions evidence submitted in the form of affidavits shall, subject to the provisions of this rule, be admissible in place of parole evidence.

(3) For the purposes of this rule—
(*a*) " affidavit " includes affirmation and statutory or other declaration;
(*b*) an affidavit shall be treated as admissible if it is duly emitted before a Notary Public, or any other competent authority.

(4) Proof in all actions shall, unless in any particular action the court otherwise directs, be by way of evidence submitted in the form of affidavits

and such evidence shall not be treated as being insufficient for the purposes of proof by reason only that it is not supported by parole evidence.

(5) In all actions in which there are children under 16 for whose custody maintenance and education the court has jurisdiction to make provision, evidence relative to the welfare of every such child shall, unless the court thinks fit to direct otherwise, be submitted in the form of affidavits, at least one of which shall be emitted by a person other than either of the parties to the action.

(6) In any action, evidence submitted in the form of a written statement bearing to be that of a duly qualified medical practitioner, which has been signed by him and lodged in process, shall be admissible in place of parole evidence.

Procedure

(7) In any action, if counsel on consideration of the available affidavits and supporting documents is satisfied that a motion for decree may properly be made, he may move the court by way of written minute in the process signed by him, to grant decree in terms of the conclusions of the summons or in such restricted terms as may be appropriate.

(8) The minute referred to in paragraph (7) shall be in the following terms:—

" AB for the pursuer having considered the evidence contained in the affidavits and the other documents all as specified in the Schedule hereto and being satisfied that upon this evidence a motion for decree [in terms of the conclusions of the summons] or [in such restricted terms as may be appropriate] may properly be made, moves the court accordingly.

In respect whereof,

(*Signature*)

Schedule

(No. and specify documents) ".

(9) The solicitor for the pursuer shall lodge—

(*a*) in process—

(i) the minute signed by counsel;

(ii) the productions specified in the Schedule to the minute;

(*b*) in the general office of the Court, the official form of application for the grant of decree duly completed by him.

(10) The court may at any time after those documents have been duly lodged, without requiring the appearance of counsel in court—

(*a*) grant decree in terms of the motion for decree contained in the minute; or

(*b*) put the case out by order for such further procedure, including proof by parole evidence, as the court thinks appropriate.

(11) Notice shall be given in the Rolls of Court of all actions where decree has been granted without requiring the appearance of counsel in court, and in all such actions the Extractor of Court may, not sooner than 21 days thereafter, issue to both parties extract and copy extract decrees.

NOTE

[1] Substituted by S.I. 1978 No. 106 and as amended by S.I. 1980 No. 1144.

Defended actions

[1] **168A.**—(1) Subject to the provisions of this rule, where defences are lodged, the parties may adjust their respective pleadings for a period of 6 weeks from the date on which they are lodged.

(2) No Open Record shall be made up except with the leave of the court on special cause shown.

(3) The court may, on a motion in that behalf and on special cause

shown, extend the six week adjustment period for such additional period or periods as it thinks fit.

(4) [Revoked by S.I. 1990 No. 705.]

[2] (5) Within 14 days of the expiry of the adjustment period the pursuer shall subject to Rule 188D (6)—

(*a*) make up a copy of the adjusted pleadings in the form of a Closed Record; and

(*b*) lodge three copies thereof in process; and

(*c*) deliver one copy thereof to the other party or parties and

(*d*) enrol a motion for the case to be sent to either—

(i) the Procedure Roll; or

(ii) if proof is likely to be of short duration, Roll 1; or

(iii) if any other case, Roll 2.

(6) Where the requirements of sub-paragraphs (*a*) to (*c*) of paragraph (5) have been complied with, the court may send the case to the Procedure Roll or to Roll 1 or Roll 2, as it thinks fit.

NOTES

[1] Added by S.I. 1980 No. 1144.

[2] As amended by S.I. 1982 No. 1381.

Procedure After Proof Allowed

Late appearance by defender

[1] **169.**—(1) The court may make an order with or without conditions, allowing a defender in any action—

(*a*) to appear and be heard at the diet of proof although he may not have lodged defences, but he shall not be allowed to lead evidence without the pursuer's consent;

(*b*) to lodge defences and to lead evidence at any time before decree has been pronounced;

(*c*) to reclaim within the reclaiming days although he was not present, or represented, at the proof.

(2) In a case where the court makes an order under paragraph (1)(*b*), the pursuer may lead further evidence by recalling witnesses already examined or otherwise, whether or not he closed his proof before the order was made.

NOTE

[1] Substituted by S.I. 1976 No. 1994.

Suspension incompetent in undefended action

[1] **170A.** It shall not be competent for the defender to bring a suspension of any decree of divorce pronounced in an undefended action.

NOTE

[1] Added by S.I. 1976 No. 1994.

Parental Rights, Care and Supervision Etc. of Children

[1] **170B.**—(1) *Interpretation.* In this rule—

(*a*) "parental rights" has the meaning assigned to it by section 8 of the Law Reform (Parent and Child) (Scotland) Act 1986;

(*b*) any reference to an action is a reference to an action for divorce, nullity of marriage or separation;

(*c*) any reference to child is, unless the context otherwise requires, a reference to—

(i) a child of the marriage between the parties to the action;

(ii) a child of one party to the marriage (including an illegitimate or an adopted child) who has been accepted as one of the family by the other party, being a child of under 16 years of age.

(2) [Revoked by S.I. 1986 No. 1946.]

(3) *Claim by defender.* The defender in an action may claim parental rights of a child by lodging defences containing, in addition to averments and pleas-in-law, a conclusion for parental rights of that child.

(4) *Opposition by defender.* In an action where the pursuer claims parental rights of a child and the defender does not want to claim parental rights himself but wishes to oppose the pursuer's claim, he may do so by lodging defences.

(5) *Joint minute.* The parties to an action may enter into a joint minute agreeing the parental rights of a child, and the court may interpone authority to that minute.

(6) *Intimation to third parties*—(*a*) In an action where the court may make an order—

(i) in respect of the parental rights of a child who is in the care of a local authority;

(ii) in respect of the parental rights of a child mentioned in head (ii) of paragraph (1)(*c*) who is liable to be maintained by a third party;

[1a](iii) in respect of the parental rights of a child in the *de facto* custody of a third party;

intimation of the action shall be made to the local authority or third party concerned by endorsing on the summons a warrant for intimation in the following terms: "Warrant to intimate to (name and address) as (the local authority having care of (name and address of child. *or* (a person who is liable to maintain (name and address of child. *or* (the person who in fact has parental rights of (name and address of child.", and Rule 160 shall apply to the execution of that warrant.

(*b*) In an action where the court—

(i) proposes to commit the care of a child to an individual other than one of the parties to the marriage or to a local authority under section 10 of the Act of 1958,

(ii) has made an order placing a child under the supervision of a local authority under section 12 of the Act of 1958,

the court shall order intimation to be made to the individual, or the local authority concerned of the matters specified in the order, and for the purposes of any such intimation Rule 160 shall apply to the order for intimation under this sub-paragraph as it applies to a warrant for intimation mentioned in that rule with the omission of any reference to a Form.

[2] (*c*) In an action where the court may make an order mentioned in sub-paragraph (*a*) in respect of the parental rights of a child and the defender has a conclusion for parental rights of that child in his defences—

(i) the defender shall enrol a motion for a warrant to intimate to the local authority or third party concerned; and

(ii) Rule 160 shall apply to the execution of any such warrant granted by the court.

(7) *Sisting of third parties*—(*a*) a person to whom intimation has been made under paragraph (6) may apply to be heard in the action by way of minute—

(i) in the case of a local authority or of a third party mentioned in paragraph (6)(*a*), craving leave to be sisted as a party to the action and making any relevant averments in relation to the care and maintenance of the child, or the maintenance of the child, as the case may be;

(ii) in the case of an individual or a local authority mentioned in head (i) of paragraph (6)(*b*), making any relevant averments in relation to the care, maintenance or education of the child.

(*b*) On the lodging of a minute under paragraph (*a*), either party to the marriage may lodge answers thereto within such period as the court may allow.

[2a] (8) *Applications after decree in relation to children.* An application made after decree for, or for the variation or recall of, an order—

(*a*) relating to the parental rights of a child;
(*b*) under Part II of the Act of 1958; or
(*c*) for aliment for a child under 18 years of age,

shall be made in the process of the original action.

[2a] (9) *Interim extract.* A final decree in an action in which an application may be made under paragraph (8) shall be capable only of interim extract.

[3] (10) *Variation of aliment and access*—(*a*) An application to the court for the variation or recall of an order for aliment or interim aliment or access shall, subject to sub-paragraph (*d*), be made by motion.

(*b*) A motion under this paragraph shall—

(i) include a brief statement of the reason for the variation or revocation sought; and
(ii) be intimated, subject to sub-paragraph (*c*), to the other party or to a solicitor known to be acting on his behalf on an *induciae* of 14 days.

(*c*) In the case of a motion relating to the variation or recall of an order for aliment, intimation shall be made by means of recorded delivery.

(*d*) On intimation of a motion relating to the variation or recall of an order for aliment under this paragraph, the party making intimation shall lodge in process—

(i) a copy of the letter of intimation,
(ii) the Post Office receipt in respect of the posting of the letter of intimation, and
(iii) written evidence of that party's earnings, or if he or she is not employed, written evidence to that effect,

(*e*) At the hearing of a motion relating to the variation or recall of an order for aliment or access under this paragraph, the court may, if the motion is opposed and if in the opinion of the court it is desirable to do so, order that the application be made by way of minute; and on the making of such an order the court may make such order as to the lodging of answers as it thinks fit.

(*f*) Where an application is made by minute under sub-paragraph (*e*), the minute shall contain supporting conclusions, averments and pleas-in-law.

[4] (11) *Averments of other proceedings relating to children.* A party under this section to a cause which includes an application for a custody order (as defined by section 1(1)(*b*) of the Family Law Act 1986) shall make averments in his pleadings giving particulars of any other proceedings known to him (whether in Scotland or elsewhere and whether concluded or not) which relate to the child in respect of whom the custody order is sought.

[4] (12) *Disclosure of information about child's whereabouts.* Where the court pronounces an interlocutor ordering a person to disclose information to the court as to a child's whereabouts under section 33(1) of the Family Law Act 1986, it may do so by ordaining that person to appear before it or to lodge an affidavit.

[4] (13) *Applications for interdict under the Family Law Act 1986.* An application by a person mentioned in section 35(4)(*b*) or (*c*) of the Family Law Act 1986 for interdict or interim interdict under section 35(3) of that Act shall be made by minute in the cause in which the application is to be made.

[5] (14) *Applications for custody to which Part II of the Children Act 1975 applies.*

(*a*) Where in an action a person ("the minuter") applies by minute for custody of a child, the court shall on granting leave to the minuter to be sisted as a party, order the minuter to give notice—

(i) at the same time to each known parent of the child in Form 68 together with, where the minuter is not a parent, tutor, curator, or guardian of the child, a consent form in Form 69; and

(ii) where the minuter is not a parent of the child and he resides in Scotland when the minute is presented, within seven days to the local authority within whose area the minuter resides in Form 70; or

(iii) where the minuter is not a parent of the child and he does not reside in Scotland when the minute is presented, in Form 70 within such time as the court shall determine to such local authority as the court shall specify.

(*b*) Where a parent, tutor, curator or guardian consents to the minuter being granted custody of a child, he shall—

(i) complete and sign a consent form in Form 69;

(ii) have his signature witnessed; and

(iii) return the form to the minuter.

(*c*) At any stage of the cause, where it appears to the court to be desirable in the circumstances of the case in order to safeguard the interests of a child, the court shall appoint a curator *ad litem*.

(*d*) A curator *ad litem* appointed under sub-paragraph (*c*) shall have the following duties:—

(i) to enquire into, so far as he considers necessary the matters averred in the minute and in any report by a local authority under sub-paragraph (*e*);

(ii) to enquire into any other matters which appear to him to be relevant;

(iii) to consider whether the granting of custody to the minuter is in the interests of the child;

(iv) to perform such other duties as appear to him to be necessary or as the court may require; and

(v) to prepare a report in relation to the exercise of the above duties.

(*e*) On completion of a report under section 49(2) of the Children Act 1975, the local authority shall—

(i) lodge three copies of the report in process; and

(ii) where a curator *ad litem* has been appointed, send a copy of the report to him.

(*f*) The curator *ad litem* shall, on completion of his report, lodge three copies of it in process.

(*g*) On receipt of the report of the local authority, and, where a curator *ad litem* has been appointed, the report of the curator *ad litem*, the General Department shall—

(i) inform the minuter that a report has been lodged; and

(ii) make available to the minuter, and to every other party, a copy of each report.

(*h*) This paragraph shall, with the necessary modifications apply to a pursuer or defender who is not a parent of a child in respect of whom custody is sought as it applies to a person who applies by minute.

[5] (15) *Referral to family conciliation service.* In any action where the custody of, or access to, a child is in dispute, the court may, at any stage of the action where it considers it appropriate to do so and the parties to the dispute agree, refer that dispute to a specified family conciliation service.

NOTES

[1] Added by S.I. 1976 No. 1994 and as amended by S.I. 1986 No. 1955.

[1a] As amended by S.I. 1990 No. 705.

[2] Added by S.I. 1984 No. 499.

[2a] Substituted by S.I. 1990 No. 705.

[3] Added by S.I. 1977 No. 1621.

[4] Added by S.I. 1988 No. 615.

[5] Added by S.I. 1990 No. 705.

Restriction on removal of child

[1] **170C.**—(1) An application under section 13 of the Act of 1958 for interim interdict prohibiting the removal of a child furth of Scotland or out of the control of the person in whose custody the child is, shall be made by motion.

(2) An application by virtue of section 51(1) of the Children Act 1975 by a person other than a party to the cause to remove a child from the custody of the person claiming custody in the cause, shall be made by minute.

NOTE

[1] Substituted by S.I. 1986 No. 515.

Financial Provision on Divorce

Applications for financial provision

[1] **170D.**—(1) *Application by pursuer for financial provision.* An application to the court under section 8(1) of the Act of 1985 by the pursuer in an action of divorce for one or more of the following orders:—

(*a*) an order for the payment of a capital sum or the transfer of property to him by the other party to the marriage;

(*b*) an order for the making of a periodical allowance to him by the other party to the marriage;

(*c*) an incidental order within the meaning of section 14(2) of the Act of 1985,

shall be made by including conclusions in the terms set out in Form 2 and supporting averments in the summons specifying the nature of the order the pursuer seeks.

[2] (2) *Application by defender for financial provision.* An application to the court by the defender in an action for divorce for an order mentioned in paragraph (1) shall be made in defences including in addition to supporting averments and pleas-in-law, a conclusion in the terms set out in Form 2 specifying the nature of the order the defender seeks; and, where a defender makes such a claim, he may apply by motion for a warrant to use any form of diligence which would be competent on the dependence had the claim been concluded for in a summons.

[3,4] (3) *Subsequent applications for and variation of periodical allowance.* An application to the court by either party in an action of divorce for an order under section 8(2), by virtue of section 13(1)(*b*) or (*c*), of the Act of 1985—

(*a*) for payment by the other party to the marriage of a periodical allowance;

(*b*) for an order for payment of periodical allowance to be varied or recalled,

shall be made by motion; and Rule 170B(10) shall apply to a motion under this paragraph for an order for payment of, or variation or recall of a periodical allowance, as it applies to a motion for variation or revocation of an order for aliment. Where an application under this paragraph is ordered to proceed by minute under Rule 170B(10), a party may apply to the court by motion for interim variation pending determination of the application.

[3] (4) *Applications for orders relating to avoidance transactions.* (*a*) An application to the court by either party in an action of divorce under section 18 of the Act of 1985, shall be made by including supporting conclusions, averments and pleas-in-law in the summons, defences, or minute, as the case may be.

(*b*) The applicant in an application for an order under section 18 of the

Act of 1985 shall, subject to the following provisions of this paragraph, intimate the summons, defences or minute by means of which he makes that application to any third party in whose favour the transfer of, or transfer involving, property is to be or was made and to any other person having an interest in the transfer of, or transfer involving, property, and any such third party or other person may lodge answers thereto within such period as the court may allow.

(*c*) Intimation of any summons to any person under sub-paragraph (*b*) shall be made by endorsing on the summons a warrant in the following terms: "Warrant to intimate to (name and address) as (the person in whose favour the transfer of [*or* transaction involving] property referred to in the condescendence of this summons was made (*or* is to be made)) *or* (a person having an interest in the transfer of [*or* transaction involving] property referred to in the condescendence of this summons)"; and Rule 160 shall apply to the execution of that warrant.

(*d*) Intimation of any defences or minute to any person under sub-paragraph (*b*) shall be made in accordance with an order of the court, being such order for intimation as the court thinks proper to make on the motion of the defender or minuter, as the case may be.

(5) *Opposition by defender to claim for financial provision or aliment.* Opposition by a defender to financial provision sought by the pursuer in an action of divorce shall be made in defences.

(6) *Warrant for execution on decree of interim aliment pending disposal of action.* (*a*) The Principal Clerk or the Deputy Principal Clerk or anyone authorised by either of them in that behalf may append to an official certified copy of an interlocutor granting decree for interim aliment a warrant for execution in the following terms:—"and the Lords of Council and Session grant warrant for all lawful execution upon the aforementioned decree for interim aliment."

(*b*) Rule 65 applies to that warrant as it applies to the warrant in an extract of a decree.

(7) *Subsequent applications for, or variation or recall of, certain orders for financial provision.* An application for an order—

(*a*) for variation or recall under section 14(4), of an incidental order under section 8(2), of the Act of 1985;

(*b*) setting aside or varying an agreement as to financial provision under section 16 of the Act of 1985; or

(*c*) relating to avoidance transactions under section 18 of the Act of 1985 after decree of divorce,

shall be made by minute in the process of the action of divorce.

(8) *Variation of date or method of payment of capital sum or date of transfer of property.* An application under section 12(4) of the Act of 1985 shall be made by motion in the process of the action of divorce; and Rule 170B(10) shall apply to a motion under this paragraph as it applies to a motion under Rule 170B(10).

(9) *Intimation to creditor.* Where property, in respect of which there is an application for an order for transfer under section 8(2) of the Act of 1985, is subject to a security, there shall be intimation in Form 18E, together with a copy of the pleadings in the application, to the creditor on a warrant for intimation—

(*a*) in the case of a summons, endorsed on the summons in the following terms:—"Warrant to intimate to (*name and address*) as a person who is believed to be a creditor of (*name of party*); or

(*b*) in any other case, granted by the court.

[THE NEXT PAGE IS C69]

(10) *Sisting of creditor.* (*a*) A creditor to whom intimation has been given under paragraph (9), may apply to be heard in the cause by way of minute craving leave to be sisted as a party to the cause and making any relevant averments.

(*b*) Where a creditor has lodged a minute under sub-paragraph (*a*), either party to the marriage may lodge answers thereto within such period as the court may allow.

(11) *Actions of declarator of nullity of marriage.* This rule applies to an action of declarator of nullity of marriage as it applies to an action of divorce.

[5] (12) *Subsequent applications for incidental orders*—An application for an incidental order (within the meaning of section 14(2) of the Act of 1985) after the grant or refusal of decree shall be made by motion; and rule 170B(10) shall apply to a motion under this paragraph as it applies to a motion under that paragraph.

NOTES

[1] Added by S.I. 1976 No. 1994 and as amended by S.I. 1986 No. 1231.
[2] As amended by S.I. 1990 No. 705 and 1991 No. 1157 (with effect from 27th May 1991).
[3] Substituted by S.I. 1977 No. 1621.
[4] As amended by S.I. 1987 No. 1206.
[5] Added by S.I. 1990 No. 705.

Simplified Procedure

Applications

[1] **170E.**—(1) The provisions of this rule and of the following rules of this section shall have effect in relation to applications for divorce to which this rule applies ("simplified divorce applications") for the purpose of providing a procedure for obtaining a decree of divorce other than procedure by way of summons.

(2) This rule applies to an application for divorce by a party to a marriage if, but only if—

(*a*) that party applies for divorce in reliance on the facts set out in section 1(2)(*d*) (2 years non cohabitation and the defender's consent to decree) or section 1(2)(*e*) (5 years non cohabitation) of the Act of 1976;

(*b*) in an application for divorce under the said section 1(2)(*d*), the other party consents to decree of divorce being granted;

(*c*) no other proceedings are pending in any court which could have the effect of bringing the marriage to an end;

(*d*) there are no children of the marriage under the age of 16 years;

(*e*) neither party applies for an order for financial provision on divorce;

(*f*) neither party suffers from mental disorder.

(3) If an application made under this rule ceases to be an application to which this rule applies at any time before it is finally disposed of, then the application shall cease to have effect and shall be treated as having been abandoned.

NOTE

[1] Added by S.I. 1982 No. 1679.

Form of application

[1] **170F.**—(1) A simplified divorce application relying on the facts set out in the said section 1(2)(*d*) shall be made in the terms set out in Form 19A.

(2) A simplified divorce application relying on the facts set out in the said section 1(2)(*e*) shall be made in the terms set out in Form 19B.

(3) An application made under paragraph (1) or paragraph (2) must be signed by the applicant, and in an application under paragraph (1) the form

of consent must also be signed by the party giving consent, otherwise the application shall not have effect.

NOTE
[1] Added by S.I. 1982 No. 1679.

Lodging applications

[1] **170G.** The applicant shall deliver the application or cause it to be delivered (by post or by hand) duly completed and signed to the Principal Clerk of Session at the Court together with—

(*a*) an extract or certified copy of the marriage certificate, and
(*b*) the fee specified in respect of a simplified divorce application in Rule 346.

NOTE
[1] Added by S.I. 1982 No. 1679.

Registration, etc.

[1] **170H.**—(1) The Principal Clerk shall give directions in relation to the administrative procedures to be followed on the lodging of simplified divorce applications, for the registration and service of applications, for having them brought before the court for consideration, and in the event of decree of divorce being granted, for intimation to the parties, and related matters, and such directions shall have effect subject to the provisions of these rules.

(2) A simplified divorce application shall have effect on registration in accordance with paragraph (1) and shall, subject to the following rules of this section, be treated for all purposes as a summons in an action of divorce that has commenced; without prejudice to this generality the following rules shall apply to such an application as they apply to a summons in an action of divorce, namely Rules 158 to 160, 164, and 170A.

NOTE
[1] Added by S.I. 1982 No. 1679.

Service

[1] **170I.**—(1) *Citation.* On registration of a simplified divorce application, the Principal Clerk or any officer authorised by him in that behalf shall grant warrant for citation or intimation as the case may be, in respect of that application, and citation or intimation may proceed on any such warrant signed by the Principal Clerk or, as the case may be, by any such officer.

(2) In the application of Rule 159 (citation) to the execution of a warrant for citation under paragraph (1),—

(*a*) for sub-paragraph (*b*) of paragraph (3) of that rule substitute—

"(*b*) the Principal Clerk of Session or an officer duly authorised by him, posting by registered or recorded delivery letter addressed to the other party and having on the face of the letter the notice set out in paragraph (4), a copy of the application with citation in the terms set out in Form 19C or 19D as the case may be";

(*b*) for the notice set out in paragraph (4) of that rule substitute—

"This letter contains a citation to or intimation from the Court of Session, Scotland. If delivery of the letter cannot be made within 7 days of the date of posting it is to be returned thereafter to the DSP section, Parliament House, Edinburgh EH1 1RQ."

(*c*) in paragraph (7) of that rule, for the word "Solicitor" substitute "the Principal Clerk or officer duly authorised by him", and after "Form 3" add the words "with any necessary modifications".

(3) *Intimation.* In any simplified divorce application where the facts set out in the said section 1(2)(*e*) are relied on and the address of the other party is not known and cannot reasonably be ascertained, warrant for intimation shall be made to—

(*a*) every child of the marriage between the parties, and

(*b*) one of the next-of-kin of the other party who has reached the age of 12 years in the case of a girl and 14 years in the case of a boy.

(4) If the address of any person mentioned in sub-paragraphs (*a*) or (*b*) of that paragraph is not known and cannot reasonably be ascertained by the applicant, intimation shall be made edictally by the transmission to the Extractor of such information as he may require.

(5) Rule 160 shall apply to the execution of any such warrant as it applies to the execution of a warrant on a summons, the reference in that rule to Rule 159 being a reference to Rule 159 as applied by this rule, and the references to Forms 16 to 18C being a reference to Form 19E.

NOTE

[1] Added by S.I. 1982 No. 1679 and as amended by S.I. 1987 No. 1206.

Third parties entering process

[1] **170J.** Any person upon whom intimation of an application for divorce has been made under Rule 170I may oppose the granting of decree of divorce by way of a letter to the court giving reasons for his opposition to the application.

NOTE

[1] Added by S.I. 1982 No. 1679.

Extract decree

[1] **170K.** On decree of divorce being granted in a simplified divorce application, an extract of the decree shall be granted immediately.

NOTE

[1] Added by S.I. 1982 No. 1679.

Applications after decree

[1] **170L.** For the purpose of a party to a simplified divorce application making an application to the court in respect of any matter after decree of divorce has been granted, the application shall be made by way of minute

in the form and in the matter in which it would have been made if the decree of divorce had been granted in an action of divorce commenced by summons, together with a process.

NOTE

[1] Added by S.I. 1982 No. 1679.

Financial Provision after Overseas Divorce or Annulment

Application for financial provision

[1] **170M.**—(1) An application under section 28 or 29A of the Matrimonial and Family Proceedings Act 1984 for financial provision after a divorce or annulment in an overseas country shall be made by summons.

(2) An application for—

(*a*) variation or recall of an order for periodical allowance; or

(*b*) variation of the date or method of payment of a capital sum or the date of transfer of property under section 12(4) of the Act of 1985,

shall be made by motion in the process of the action for financial provision under paragraph (1); and Rule 170B(10) shall apply to a motion under this paragraph as it applies to a motion made under Rule 170B(10).

(3) An application for variation or recall of an incidental order within the meaning of section 14(2) of the Act of 1985 shall be made by minute in the process of the action for financial provision under paragraph (1).

NOTE

[1] Added by S.I. 1986 No. 1231.

Applications Relating to Aliment

Undefended action of aliment

[1] **170N.**—(1) In an action of aliment or an application under Rule 170R, Rule 168 shall not apply and, subject to paragraph (2), Rule 89 (decree in absence) shall apply where the defender fails to enter appearance or fails to lodge defences.

(2) Where a motion for decree under paragraph (1) is enrolled, there shall be lodged all documentary evidence of the means of the parties available to the pursuer in support of the amount of aliment sought.

(3) Where the court requires an appearance, the cause shall be put out for hearing as a starred motion on the motion roll.

NOTE

[1] Added by S.I. 1986 No. 1231.

Variation or recall of decree of aliment

[1] **170P.**—An application to vary or recall a decree of aliment under section 5 of the Act of 1985 shall be made by motion in the process of the action for aliment; and Rule 170B(10) shall apply to a motion made under this rule as it applies to a motion made under Rule 170B(10).

NOTE

[1] Added by S.I. 1986 No. 1231.

Variation or termination of agreement on aliment

[1] **170R.**—(1) An application for variation or termination of an agreement on aliment under section 7(2) of the Act of 1985 shall be made by summons.

(2) In an application under this Rule a party may apply to the court by motion for interim variation pending determination of the action.

NOTE

[1] Added by S.I. 1986 No. 1231 and as amended by S.I. 1987 No. 1206.

SECTION 4—REDUCTIONS

Defences

171. It shall not be competent for a defender who objects on any ground to satisfy production to lodge only preliminary defences; but if he intends to defend the action, he shall lodge his defences on the merits along with his preliminary defences.

Where no objection to satisfy production

172. Where the defender does not state any objection against satisfying production, he shall, along with his defences, produce the writs or documents sought to be reduced so far as the same are in his possession or within his control.

Where production objected to

173. If in his defences (so far as preliminary), the defender objects to production on the ground that the action is incompetent, or irrelevant, or otherwise, and in the event of his defences (so far as preliminary) being repelled by the court, the defender shall satisfy production by lodging in process the writs or documents sought to be reduced, so far as in his possession or within his control, within seven days after the day on which the interlocutor repelling his defences (so far as preliminary) was pronounced; and, if he shall fail so to do, the pursuer may enrol the cause for decree by default; provided that, with consent of parties, the court may hold production satisfied by copies of the writs or documents sought to be reduced.

Challenge of deed or writing ope exceptionis

174. Where, in any cause, a deed or writing is founded on by either party, all objections thereto may be stated and maintained by way of exception without the necessity of bringing a reduction thereof, unless the court shall consider that the matter would be more conveniently tried in a separate action of reduction.

SECTION 5—MULTIPLEPOINDINGS

Pursuer and service

[1] **175.** —(1) A multiplepoinding may be raised by any person holding, or having an interest in or claim on, the fund *in medio*, in his own name.

(2) The summons shall be served on, as defenders, all persons so far as known to the pursuer as having an interest in the fund *in medio*, including the holder of the fund where the pursuer is not the holder of the fund.

NOTE

[1] Substituted by S.I. 1986 No. 1941.

Condescendence of the fund

[1] **176.**—(*a*) If the pursuer is the holder of the fund *in medio*, he shall condescend on the said fund, either in the condescendence annexed to the summons, or in a separate paper lodged along with the summons at calling.

(*b*) If the holder of the fund *in medio* is not the pursuer, then, not later than the fourteenth day after the day on which the summons is called, he shall either lodge a precise and articulate condescendence of the funds in his hands (stating any claim or lien which he may profess to have upon those funds), or, if he objects to the action on the ground of incompetency or otherwise, he may lodge defences to the action not later than said fourteenth day, and in any event disclose all persons so far as known to him as having an interest in the fund *in medio*.

NOTE
[1] As amended by S.I. 1986 No. 1941.

Defences; record on summons and defences

[1] **177.**—(*a*) If any of the parties to the action objects to the action on the ground of incompetency or otherwise, he or they may lodge defences not later than the fourteenth day after the day on which the summons is called.

(*b*) If defences are lodged either in terms of paragraph (*b*) of Rule 176, or in terms of paragraph (*a*) of this rule, a record shall be made up and closed, and the cause shall proceed for the purpose of determining the objections stated in the defences, all as in the case of an ordinary action.

NOTE
[1] As amended by S.I. 1986 No. 1941.

Advertisement for absent parties

[1] **178.** If no defences are lodged, or if (even when defences are lodged) it is for any reason considered advisable to intimate the dependence of the action by advertisement, the pursuer may enrol (not earlier in any case than the day after the last day for lodging defences) for an order for the advertisement of the dependence of the action in such newspapers, and for such number of insertions, as he may desire, in order that any party not otherwise cited may enter appearance on or before a date named; provided always that it shall be competent for the court at any time to order such advertisement, or to order intimation of the dependence of the action to any person not called as a defender to the action, *ex proprio motu*; and a copy of the advertisement or advertisements, together with a certificate signed by the solicitor of the party who obtained the order or on whom the order was made, that the advertisements have been duly made, and a return of the execution of any intimation so ordered, shall be lodged in process by such solicitor.

NOTE
[1] As amended by S.I. 1986 No. 1941.

Once and single payment: order and advertisement for claims

[1] **179.** When no advertisement for absent parties is moved for or ordered in terms of the immediately preceding rule, the pursuer may not earlier than the day after the last day for lodging defences enrol for a finding that he is liable only in once and single payment, and that the condescendence annexed to the summons shall be held as a condescendence of the fund *in medio*, and for an order for claims by a specified date, and for advertisement of such order; provided always that it shall be competent for the court at any time to make an order, or renewed order, for claims, and to appoint advertisement thereof, and to order intimation thereof to any person not called as a defender to the action, *ex proprio motu*; and a copy of the advertisement or advertisements, together with the solicitor's certificate, and a return of the execution of any intimation so ordered, shall be lodged in process.

NOTE
[1] As amended by S.I. 1986 No. 1941.

Form of claims

180. The claimants shall state their respective claims in the form of condescendences, claims, and pleas-in-law, and shall produce per inventory

[THE NEXT PAGE IS C 71]

therewith their grounds of debt and other writings for instructing their claims.

Claims not timeously lodged

181. A claimant who fails to lodge his claim on or before the date specified in the order for claims may enrol to have his claim received at a later date; and the court may allow the claim to be received on such terms as to expenses as to the court shall seem proper.

Record on condescendence of the fund and objections thereto

182.—(*a*) If a condescendence of the fund *in medio* shall have been lodged in terms of paragraph (*a*) or paragraph (*b*) of Rule 176, or if such a condescendence shall have been lodged at any time before the expiry of the period fixed for lodging claims, and if any of the parties desires to object to such condescendence, it shall be competent for him, or them, not earlier than the day after the expiry of the period for lodging claims, to enrol for an order appointing objections to be lodged by a certain date.

(*b*) If no condescendence of the fund *in medio* shall have been lodged before the expiry of the period for lodging claims, it shall be competent for any of the parties to the cause to enrol for an order on the party or claimant who is possessed of the funds to lodge such a condescendence, and appointing any objections thereto to be lodged by a certain date.

(*c*) A record shall be made up on such condescendence and objections and the cause shall proceed for the purpose of determining such objections as in the case of an ordinary action.

Where no competition: ranking for aught yet seen

183. If no objections shall have been lodged to the condescendence of the fund *in medio*, or if objections shall have been lodged after the condescendence shall have been approved by the court, and if it shall appear that there is no competition, the court may, for aught yet seen rank and prefer the parties who have lodged claims, and, in the event of the fund *in medio* not having been consigned, may grant decree for payment out of the fund *in medio* of the sums in respect of which the said parties have been respectively ranked, or may grant warrant to the bank to pay to the said parties the sums for which they have been so ranked, and warrant to the Accountant of court to endorse and deliver the consignation receipt to the bank in order that said payments may be made, either on an extract or on a certified copy of the interlocutor, as may be desired, provided that no decree for payment out of the fund *in medio* shall be made until the Certificates referred to in Rule 36 have been lodged in process.

Reclaiming by belated claimant against a ranking for aught yet seen

184. It shall be competent for a claimant who has failed to lodge a claim before such ranking for aught yet seen, to reclaim against the interlocutor making such ranking at any time while the action is still in dependence by enrolling a motion for review; and, on consideration of such motion, the Division before which it is brought may recall the interlocutor, and remit the cause to the Outer House to receive the claim on such terms as to expenses as may be just and proper.

Where there is competition: record on condescendences and claims

185. Where there is competition, a motion shall be enrolled for an order to print the record and thereafter a record shall be made upon the condescendences and claims as in an ordinary action, any of the claimants being allowed, at adjustment, to state at the close of his condescendence his objections to any other claim or claims, in the form of answers to a condescendence with a note of pleas-in-law; and the cause shall proceed as in the case of an ordinary action.

Section 6—Proving of the Tenor

Parties

186. In any action of proving of the tenor, all parties interested in the deed shall be called as defenders, and if the pursuer alone has an interest, it shall not be necessary to call the lieges as defenders.

Lodging of adminicles

187. All adminicles of the tenor of the deed to be proved, such as drafts, copies, letters, bills, and the like, so far as in the possession of the pursuer or within his control, shall be lodged along with the summons at calling.

Procedure

188. The cause shall proceed in all respects as in the case of an ordinary action; provided that, where no appearance has been entered or no defences lodged, the Lord Ordinary shall appoint a proof to be led, and dispose of the cause as accords.

[1] Section 7—References and Applications under the Defamation Act 1952

Procedure

[1] **188A.**—(*a*) Any reference to the court under section 4 (4) of the Defamation Act 1952 shall (i) where proceedings for libel or slander have been taken be made by minute lodged in the process and (ii) where no such proceedings have been taken be made by petition, stating in either instance the question to be determined by the court and the contentions of the minuter or petitioner thereon as the case may be, and having appended thereto a copy of the relative offer of amends and declaration. On such minute or petition being lodged the other party may lodge answers thereto within such period as the Lord Ordinary may allow.

(*b*) Any application to the court under section 4 (4) of the Defamation Act 1952 shall be made by petition and on such petition being lodged the other party may lodge answers thereto within such period as the Lord Ordinary may allow.

NOTE

[1] Added by S.I. 1966 No. 868.

[1] Section 8—Actions and Applications under the Presumption of Death (Scotland) Act 1977

[1] **188B.**—(1) In this rule—

(*a*) " the Act " means the above Act;

(*b*) " action " means an action of declarator under section 1 (1) of the Act;

(*c*) " application " means an application under section 4 (1) of the Act;

(*d*) " remitted action " means an action of declarator raised in the sheriff court and remitted to the Court of Session under section 1 (6) of the Act;

(*e*) " remitted application " means an application made in the sheriff court and remitted to the Court of Session under section 4 (4) of the Act.

(2) An application shall be made by way of minute in the original process.

(3) The pursuer in an action and the minuter in an application shall, subject to the provisions of this rule, intimate the summons or minute, as the case may be, to the following persons—

(*a*) the missing person's—
  (i) husband or wife, as the case may be, and
  (ii) children, including illegitimate or adopted children; or, if he has no children, his nearest known relative;

(*b*) any person, including any insurance company, who as far as the pursuer is aware, has any interest in the action;

(*c*) the Lord Advocate,

and any such person may lodge defences to an action or answers to a minute, as the case may be, within such period as the court may allow.

(4) Any summons intimated to any person under paragraph (3) shall contain a warrant in the following terms:—

" Warrant to intimate to (name and address) as (husband *or* wife *or* child *or* nearest relative) *or* (a person having an interest in the presumed death) of (name and last known address of the missing persons) and to the Lord Advocate ";

and Rule 76 shall apply to the execution of a warrant under this Rule as it applies to the execution of a warrant under that rule with the substitution for the reference to Form 5 of a reference to Form 5B.

(5) Intimation of a minute to any person under paragraph (3) shall be made in accordance with an order of the court, being such order for intimation as the court thinks proper to make on the motion of the minuter having regard to the provisions of that paragraph.

(6) The court may, on the motion of the pursuer in any action or the minute in an application, dispense with intimation under sub-paragraphs (3) (*a*) or (*b*);

(7) The solicitor for the pursuer in an action or for the minuter in an application (not being an application brought on the basis that the missing person's present whereabouts are known) shall, on the expiry of the period within which defences or answers require to be lodged and without any defences or answers having been lodged indicating knowledge of the present whereabouts of the missing person, enrol a motion for advertisement of the facts relating to the missing person which are set out in the summons or minute in such specified newspapers or other publications as appear to be appropriate in all the circumstances, and the court shall order such advertisement, in terms of the motion or otherwise, as it thinks fit.

(8) Any remitted action shall, notwithstanding that it has been remitted from the sheriff court, be proceeded with in the Outer House as if it were an action raised in the Court of Session.

(9) Any remitted application shall, notwithstanding that it has been remitted from the sheriff court, be proceeded with in the Outer House as if it were an application made in the Court of Session.

[2] (10) In an action under this rule, subject to provisos (*a*) and (*b*) in Rule 72, the *inducÌae* in the summons shall be 28 days after the date of the execution of service.

NOTE
[1] Added by S.I. 1978 No. 161.
[2] Added by S.I. 1978 No. 1804.

[1] SECTION 9—APPLICATIONS UNDER SECTION 85 OF THE FAIR TRADING ACT 1973

[1] **188C.** Any application by the Secretary of State to the court for an order under section 85 (7) of the Fair Trading Act 1973, or under any enactment by which the provisions of that section are applied, shall be by way of minute specifying the circumstances in which the order is sought; and the court may on a motion in that behalf make such order as it thinks fit.

NOTE
[1] Added by S.I. 1980 No. 892.

[1] SECTION 10—APPLICATIONS UNDER THE MATRIMONIAL HOMES (FAMILY PROTECTION) (SCOTLAND) ACT 1981

[1] **188D.** (1) In this rule—
(*a*) " the Act " means the above Act;
(*b*) a reference to a section by number is a reference to the section of that number in the Act;
(*c*) any expressions used in this rule and in the Act have the meaning assigned to them by the Act.

(2) Subject to paragraphs (3) and (4), an application to the court for an order under any provision of the Act shall be made by petition.

(3) An application to the court for an order under the following provisions of the Act and of those provisions as applied by section 18 shall be made by motion—
(*a*) section 3 (4) (interim order for regulation of rights of occupancy etc.);
(*b*) section 4 (6) (interim order suspending occupancy rights);
(*c*) section 5 (variation and recall of orders regulating occupancy rights and of exclusion orders);
(*d*) section 15 (1) (order attaching power of arrest), if made after the application for matrimonial interdict;
(*e*) section 15 (2) and (5) (variation and recall of matrimonial interdict and power of arrest);
(*f*) proviso to section 18 (1) (extension of period).

(4) An application to the court for an order under the provisions of the Act referred to in paragraphs (3) and (5) may be made in a consistorial action—
(*a*) in the case of a provision referred to in paragraph (3), by motion;
(*b*) in the case of a provision referred to in paragraph (5), by including supporting conclusions, averments and pleas-in-law in the summons or defences, or by minute.

(5) The provisions of the Act referred to in paragraph (4) are—
(*a*) sections 2 (1) (*e*) and 2 (4) (*a*) (authorisation of non-essential repairs);
(*b*) sections 2 (3), (4) (*b*) and (5) (*b*) (apportionment of expenditure);
(*c*) section 3 (1) (declaration, enforcement, restriction, regulation and protection of occupancy rights);
(*d*) section 3 (2) (use of furniture and plenishings);
(*e*) section 3 (7) (compensation for loss of use of occupancy, use of furniture etc.);
(*f*) section 4 (1), (4) and (5) (exclusion orders);
(*g*) section 7 (order dispensing with consent);
(*h*) section 13 (1) (transfer of tenancy order);
(*i*) section 13 (9) (vesting order).

(6) If an application is made by minute in a consistorial action under paragraph (4) and answers to that minute are lodged in the action, then whether or not the minute and answers are adjusted, they shall not be included with the other pleadings in the action in the form of a closed record, but shall be made up separately in the form of a closed record; and Rule 168A (5) shall apply to that record as it applies to the record made up from the adjusted pleadings.

(7) The applicant shall, subject to paragraph (8) intimate the writ or the terms of the motion by which the application is made—
(*a*) in any application under the Act, to the other spouse, and in any application under section 18 or to which section 18 applies, to the other partner;
(*b*) in an application by a third party under sections 7 and 8 (1), to both spouses;

(*c*) in an application under sections 2(1)(*e*), 2(4)(*a*), 4, 7, 13 and 18, if the entitled spouse or partner is a tenant or occupies the matrimonial home by the permission of a third party, to the landlord, or as the case may be, to the third party;

(*d*) to such other persons as the court may order;

and any such person may lodge answers or a minute, as the case may be, within such period as the court may allow, or if the application is by motion, may oppose the motion.

(8) The court may, having regard to circumstances of any such application and on cause shown, dispense with any intimation required under paragraph (7).

(9) Where an application is made to the court by motion under paragraph (3) or paragraph (4)(*a*), the terms of the motion shall be intimated to any person upon whom intimation requires to be made under paragraph (7) at least seven days before the motion is enrolled, unless the court on cause shown orders a lesser period.

(10) In any case where an application under the Act is made by summons in a consistorial action, intimation of the summons to any person under sub-paragraph (*c*) or (*d*) of paragraph (7) shall be made by endorsing on the summons a warrant in the following terms: "Warrant to intimate to (name and address) as a person with an interest in the order sought in the (number) conclusion of this summons"; and Rule 160 shall apply to the execution of that warrant.

(11) A sist under section 7(4) shall, in a consistorial action, apply only to such part of that action as relates to the enforcement of occupancy rights by a non-entitled spouse unless the court otherwise orders.

[2] (12) If, by virtue of section 15(1), a power of arrest is attached to an interdict, the applicant shall, as soon as possible after service of the interdict together with the attached power of arrest on the non-applicant spouse, ensure that there is delivered—

(*a*) to the chief constable of the police area in which the matrimonial home is situated; and

(*b*) if the applicant spouse (within the meaning of section 15(6)) resides in another police area, to the chief constable of that other police area,

a copy of the application for the interdict and of the interlocutor granting the interdict together with a certificate of service of the interdict, and, where the application to attach the power of arrest to the interdict was made after the interdict was granted, a copy of that application and of the interlocutor granting it and a certificate of service of the interdict together with the attached power of arrest, and in either case shall immediately thereafter lodge in process a certificate of execution of delivery.

(13) Where any matrimonial interdict to which there is attached a power of arrest, is varied or recalled or the power of arrest ceases to have effect by reason of decree of divorce or nullity being pronounced, the spouse who applied for the variation or recall or for divorce or nullity shall ensure that there is delivered as soon as possible—

(*a*) to the chief constable of the police area in which the matrimonial home is situated; and

(*b*) if the applicant spouse (within the meaning of section 15(6)) resides in another police area to the chief constable of that other police area,

a copy of the application for variation or recall and of the interlocutor granting the variation or recall, or as the case may be, a copy of the interlocutor granting decree, and shall immediately thereafter lodge in process a certificate of execution of delivery.

(14) The clerk of court shall notify the landlord of the making of an order granting an application under section 13(1) and section 13(9);

(15) For the purposes of proof in any application to the court for an order under any provision of the Act, evidence submitted in the form of affidavits shall be admissible in place of parole evidence; and such evidence

shall not be treated as being insufficient for the purposes of proof by reason only that it is not supported by parole evidence.

NOTES

[1] Added by S.I. 1982 No. 1381.

[2] As amended by S.I. 1991 No. 2483, with effect from 25th November 1991.

[1] SECTION 11—OPTIONAL PROCEDURE IN CERTAIN ACTIONS OF REPARATION

NOTE

[1] Added by S.I. 1985 No. 227.

Application and interpretation

188E.—(1) The provisions of this section apply to an action of reparation for personal injuries or for the death of a relative in which election has been made to adopt the procedure in this section.

(2) Subject to the provisions of this section, the other provisions of the Rules of Court, so far as applicable, apply to the practice and procedure to which this section applies.

(3) In this section, a form referred to by number means the form so numbered in the Appendix to the rules, or a form substantially to the like effect, with such variation as circumstances may require.

Summons

188F.—(1) A pursuer may elect to adopt the procedure in this section by serving a summons with condescendence and pleas-in-law annexed in Form 27A.

(2) A summons in Form 27A under this rule shall be on the official printed Form 1 together with the official printed backing.

(3) A summons served under this rule—

(*a*) shall constitute a waiver by the pursuer of his right to jury trial;

(*b*) shall not, subject to rule 188I, affect any right of a defender to apply for jury trial.

Induciae

188G.—(1) Subject to paragraph (2), the *induciae* of a summons served under Rule 188F shall be 28 days after the execution of service.

(2) Where the defender is domiciled outside Europe, the *induciae* of a summons served under Rule 188F shall be 42 days after the execution of service.

Defences

188H.—Defences shall be in the form of brief answers to the condescendence annexed to the summons, together with any necessary pleas-in-law.

Application by defender for jury trial

188I.—(1) If a defender intends to apply for jury trial, he shall, at the same time as lodging his defences, lodge a minute stating his intention to apply for jury trial.

(2) Where a defender does not lodge a minute under paragraph (1), he shall be held to have waived his right to jury trial.

(3) Where the defender lodges a minute under paragraph (1), the pursuer shall make up an open record in accordance with Rule 90(1) and the action shall proceed as an ordinary action.

Diet roll

188J.—(1) Within 14 days after defences have been lodged, the action shall be sent to the diet roll and put out for hearing on a specified date.

(2) Any hearing on the diet roll shall be heard before a Lord Ordinary.

(3) The appearance of the cause for hearing on a particular date on the diet roll shall not affect the right of any party to apply to the court by motion.

(4) When an action has been sent to the diet roll, all motions enrolled in the cause shall be heard on the diet roll.

(5) An open record shall not be made up unless so ordered by the court, and Rules 90 and 90A shall not apply to any such action.

(6) At the first or any subsequent hearing on the diet roll, the court may make such order or orders as it thinks fit for the further progress of the action, and in particular—

(*a*) may—

(i) on special cause shown, allow a specified period of adjustment on the motion of any party;

(ii) on special cause shown, allow an amendment on the motion of any party;

(iii) on special cause shown on the motion of any party, ordain another party to give further specification of his case in the pleadings;

(iv) on special cause shown, or of its own motion, because the difficulty or complexity of the case makes the action unsuitable for the procedure under this section, order that the action proceed as an ordinary action and appoint the cause to the adjustment roll;

(v) on cause shown, allow a party to bring in a third party to the action under Rule 85, provided that no allowance of a third party notice, except on special cause shown, may be given after the final appearance on the diet roll;

(vi) on special cause shown, appoint the action to be heard on the procedure roll; or

(vii) remit to a man of skill;

(*b*) must, where adjustment has not been allowed or the period for adjustment has expired, appoint the action to a proof or a proof before answer as appropriate—

(i) on the question of liability and quantum of damages; or

(ii) where liability is admitted, on the question of quantum of damages; or

(iii) where quantum of damages is agreed, on the question of liability; and

(iv) where there is an issue on a third party notice, on that issue at the same time or thereafter;

(*c*) where an action requires to be heard again on the diet roll, shall appoint the action to be heard on a specified date for further orders.

(7) On allowance of a hearing on the procedure roll or a proof or proof before answer, the court shall determine whether a closed record of the pleadings of the parties shall be made up.

[1] (8) Where the court orders a closed record to be made up in any action, the provisions of Rule 91 (except paragraph (6)) shall not apply to that action.

NOTE

[1] As amended by S.I. 1990 No. 2118.

Inspection and recovery of documents

188K.—(1) Without prejudice to Rule 188M, within 14 days of the interlocutor pronouncing an order for a proof or proof before answer, each party to the action shall intimate to any other party a list of the documents which are or have been in his possession or control relating to the matters in issue between them.

(2) A party who has received a list of documents from another party may inspect those documents, which are in the possession or control of the party intimating the list, within seven days at a time and place fixed by the party intimating the list which is reasonable to both parties.

(3) Nothing in this rule shall affect—

(*a*) the law relating, or the right of a party, to object to the inspection of a document on the ground of privilege or confidentiality; or (*b*) the right of a party to apply under Rule 95 for a commission and diligence for recovery of documents or under Rule 95A for an order under section 1 of the Administration of Justice (Scotland) Act 1972.

Exchange of list of witnesses

188L.—(1) Within 28 days after the interlocutor pronouncing an order for a proof or proof before answer, each party to the action shall intimate to any other party a list of witnesses whom he intends to call to give evidence.

(2) A party who seeks to call as a witness a person not on his list intimated under paragraph (1), and any other party objects, shall seek leave of the court to do so, which leave may be granted on such conditions, if any, as the court thinks fit.

Exchange of reports of skilled witnesses

188M.—(1) Not later than 28 days before a proof or a proof before answer, a party shall disclose the substance of any evidence of a skilled witness to the other parties in the form of a written report.

(2) Where a report is not agreed, a party may call as skilled witnesses those witnesses the substance of whose evidence has been disclosed in accordance with paragraph (1) of this rule.

(3) The number of skilled witnesses for any party shall be limited to one medical expert and one expert of any other kind, except on cause shown.

Evidence generally

188N.—(1) Where possible, parties shall agree photographs, sketch plans and any statement or document not in dispute.

(2) A party may apply by motion for certain specified evidence to be received by way of affidavit, and the court may make such order as it thinks fit.

(3) A party may apply by motion for a specified statement or document to be admitted as evidence without calling as a witness the maker of the statement or document, and the court may make such order and on such conditions, if any, as it thinks fit.

Reclaiming

188P.—Notwithstanding the provisions of paragraphs (*b*) and (*c*) of Rule 264, an interlocutor pronounced in the diet roll which does not dispose of, either by itself or taken with a previous interlocutor, the whole subject-matter of the action, may be reclaimed against only with leave of the Lord Ordinary or Vacation Judge not later than seven days after the date on which the interlocutor was pronounced.

CHAPTER IV

PETITIONS

Section 1—Petitions other than for Suspension, Suspension and Interdict and Suspension and Liberation

Outer House petitions

189.—[1] (*a*) All petitions initiated in the Court of Session and not falling within any of the classes mentioned in Rule 190, including (notwithstanding the generality of sub-head (*g*) of subsection (3) of section 6 of the Administration of Justice (Scotland) Act 1933) the following:—

(i) Petitions for the appointment of judicial factors, factors *loco tutoris* or *loco absentis*, factors pending litigation, or *curator bonis* to a minor or incapax;

(ii) Petitions, whether at common law or under statute, for the appointment of factors on the estates of partnerships or joint adventures;

[1a] (iii) Petitions, whether at common law, under statute or invoking the *nobile officium*, relating to the administration of trusts or the office of trustee, but excluding petitions for approval of a *cy près* scheme, variation of trust purposes under section 1 of the Trusts (Scotland) Act 1961 or in relation to endowments under sections 105, 106, 108 or 108A of the Education (Scotland) Act 1980;

[1b] (iv) Petitions for the appointment or removal of trustees;

[1a] (v) Petitions under the Companies Acts (including applications under section 245B of the Companies Act 1985) or the Insolvency Act 1986 except those mentioned in Rule 190(viii);

(vi) Petitions under the Entail Acts;

[1c] (vii) Petitions under the Bankruptcy (Scotland) Act 1985;

(viii) Petitions under the Conveyancing (Scotland) Act 1874;

(ix) [Revoked by S.I. 1978 No. 161.]

(x) Petitions under the Registration of Business Names Act 1916;

(xi) Petitions under the Lands Clauses Consolidation (Scotland) Act 1845;

(xii) Petitions for summary trial under section 10 of the Administration of Justice (Scotland) Act 1933;

(xiii) Petitions for appointment of curators under section 12 of the Administration of Justice (Scotland) Act 1933;

[2] (xiv) Petitions under section 9 of the Administration of Justice Act 1920, and the Foreign Judgments (Reciprocal Enforcement) Act 1933 and applications for registration under section 4 of, or section 18 of and Schedule 7 to, the Civil Jurisdiction and Judgments Act 1982;

[THE NEXT PAGE IS C 75]

(xv) Petitions for recall of arrestments and inhibitions which have been granted on a bill or a bill for letters;
(xvi) Petitions for suspension, suspension and interdict, and suspension and liberation;
[3] (xvii) Petitions under the Patents Act 1949, the Registered Designs Act 1949, and the Patents Act 1977;
(xviii) [Revoked by S.I. 1978 No. 161.]
(xix) Petitions under the Special Roads Act 1949, sections 13–15, Part IV of the First Schedule;
(xx) Petitions for the custody of children brought under any Act of Parliament or at common law;
(xxi) Petitions for admission as a solicitor;
(xxii) Any other petitions which, according to former practice, were presented in the Bill Chamber;
[4] (xxiii) All petitions under the Guardianship of Children (Scotland) Acts 1886 to 1973;
[5] (xxiv) Petitions under the Adoption (Scotland) Act 1978; and
[6] (xxv) Petitions and complaints in respect of breach of interdict;
[7] (xxvi) Petitions under the Matrimonial Homes (Family Protection) (Scotland) Act 1981;
[8] (xxvii) Petitions under article 24 of Schedule 1, or Schedule 4, to the Civil Jurisdiction and Judgments Act 1982;
[9] (xxviii) Petitions under section 75(2) of the Local Government (Scotland) Act 1973;
[9] (xxix) Applications under the Mortgaging of Aircraft Order 1972,
[10] (xxx) Applications under section 27 of the Civil Jurisdiction and Judgments Act 1982;
[10] (xxxi) Applications under section 8 of the Law Reform (Miscellaneous Provisions) (Scotland) Act 1985, which shall be by petition where rectification of a document is not to be sought with other remedies in a cause initiated by summons;
[10] (xxxii) Petitions for judicial review;
[10] (xxxiii) Petitions under the Child Abduction and Custody Act 1985;
[10] (xxxiv) Petitions under the Financial Services Act 1986;
[10] (xxxv) Petitions under section 6(3) of the Law Reform (Parent and Child) (Scotland) Act 1986;
[10] (xxxvi) Applications under section 48, 49 or 93 of the Banking Act 1987;
[11] (xxxvii) Applications under any enactment unless otherwise provided in these Rules or any other enactment,

shall be presented to the Outer House, and shall be lodged in the Petition Department.

[12] (*b*) An application for rectification of a deed under section 8 of the Law Reform (Miscellaneous Provisions) (Scotland) Act 1985 may be made by petition presented to the Outer House, or by summons, where ancillary to other conclusions.

NOTES

[1] As amended by S.I. 1970 No. 134.
[1a] Substituted by S.I. 1987 No. 1206. As amended by S.I. 1990 No. 2118.
[1b] As amended by S.I. 1987 No. 1206.
[1c] As amended by S.I. 1986 No. 514.
[2] As amended by S.I. 1986 No. 1941.
[3] As amended by S.I. 1978 No. 155.
[4] Added by S.I. 1974 No. 945.
[5] Substituted by S.I. 1987 No. 2160.
[6] Added by S.I. 1980 No. 1144.
[7] Added by S.I. 1982 No. 1381.
[8] Added by S.I. 1986 No. 1941.
[9] Added by S.I. 1987 No. 1206.

[10] Added by S.I. 1987 No. 2160.
[11] Added by S.I. 1990 No. 705.
[12] Added by S.I. 1986 No. 1955. S.I. 1991 No. 2483 revoked the original para. (*b*) and retitled the original para. (*c*), with effect from 25th November 1991.

Inner House petitions

[1] **190.** All petitions initiated in the Court of Session and falling within any of the classes following:—

(i) Petitions and Complaints other than in cases of breach of interdict;
(ii) Petitions for possession or specific performance;
(iii) Petitions in respect of failure to perform any public or official duty, which would according to the law and practice existing immediately prior to the commencement of the Administration of Justice (Scotland) Act 1933, be presented to the Inner House;
(iv) Petitions under the Acts relating to solicitors or notaries public (other than petitions for admission as a solicitor);
(v) Petitions incidental to a cause already before the Inner House;
(vi) Petitions to the court invoking the *nobile officium* except those mentioned in Rule 189 (*a*);
(vii) Petitions by trustees for directions;
(viii) Petitions under sections 136 or 425 of the Companies Act 1985;
(ix) Petitions under section 1 of the Trusts (Scotland) Act 1961;
(x) Petitions under sections 105, 106, 108 or 108A of the Education (Scotland) Act 1980;

shall be presented to the Inner House, marked "Inner House" on the backing thereof and shall be lodged in the Petition Department; provided that petitions incidental to a cause already before the Inner House shall be lodged either in the General Department, or in the Petition Department, according as the cause itself belongs to the one or the other of said Departments.

NOTE

[1] As amended by S.I. 1970 No. 134, S.I. 1976 No. 283, S.I. 1977 No. 1621, S.I. 1980 No. 1144 and S.I. 1987 No. 1206.

Form of petition

[1] **191.** All petitions shall be on the printed official form, which, with the official printed backing thereon (Form 28), shall be filled in and completed either in manuscript, typescript or print; provided that:—

(*a*) A narrative or statement of facts in articulate numbered paragraphs setting forth the facts and circumstances which form the grounds of the petition shall in all cases precede the prayer; and in all petitions presented under any statute or statutes authorising the petition or regulating the proceedings therein, the narrative shall expressly refer to the relevant section or sections of such statute or statutes.

(*aa*) The narrative of the petition shall include a paragraph stating—
   (i) the ground of jurisdiction of the court, unless jurisdiction would arise only if the respondent prorogated the jurisdiction of the court (without contesting jurisdiction);
   (ii) where appropriate, whether there is reason to believe that there exists an agreement prorogating the jurisdiction of a court in a particular country; and
   (iii) whether proceedings involving the same cause or matter are in subsistence between the parties in a country to which the Convention in Schedule 1 to the Civil Jurisdiction and Judgments Act 1982 applies, unless the court has exclusive jurisdiction.

(*b*) The prayer shall specially crave warrant for such intimation, service and advertisement as may be necessary, having regard to the nature of the petition, or as the petitioner may desire; and the names, designations, addresses and capacities of all persons on whom the petition is to be served, distinguishing any upon whom the petition is to be served edictally, shall be set forth in a Schedule annexed to the Petition and referred to in the prayer.

(*c*) If any dispensation with intimation or service is desired, it must be specially craved in the prayer, and the grounds of dispensation must be set forth in the narrative; and in petitions for appointment of a *curator bonis* to an incapax, if dispensation of service on the incapax is craved, two medical certificates stating reasons for such dispensation, in respect of the dangerous effects of service on the incapax or otherwise, shall be lodged along with the petition.

NOTE
[1] As amended by S.I. 1987 No. 1206.

Inducia *in petitions*

[1] **192.**—(1) The *induciae* in a petition shall be—

(*a*) in the case of service within Europe, 21 days after the date of execution of service;

(*b*) in the case of personal service outside Europe, 21 days after the date of execution of service; and

(*c*) in any other case of service outside Europe, 42 days after the date of execution of service.

(2) Where service is executed in Scotland by registered or recorded delivery letter, the *induciae* shall be reckoned from 24 hours after the date of posting.

(3) An application to shorten or extend the *induciae* shall be made by motion.

NOTE
[1] Substituted by S.I. 1986 No. 1941.

Signature of petitions

[1] **193.** Petitions for suspension, suspension and interdict, suspension and liberation and petitions under the Bankruptcy (Scotland) Act 1985 may be signed by the petitioner's solicitor, and a petitioner for sequestration of his own estates may sign the petition himself. All other petitions shall be signed by counsel or a solicitor who has a right of audience in the Court of Session and no further or other signature shall be required.

NOTE
[1] As amended by S.I. 1986 No. 514 and (with effect from 25th November 1991) S.I. 1991 No. 2483.

Papers to be marked

194. Each step of the process lodged along with the petition shall be marked on the backing thereof with the same letter and number as shall be given on lodging to the petition itself.

Lodging of documents founded on

[1] **194A.**—(1) Any deed, writing or other document founded on by a party in his pleadings shall so far as in his possession or within his control, be lodged by that party—

(*a*) when founded on in an adjustment to the pleadings, at the time when such an adjustment is intimated; or

(*b*) in any other case, when the paper in which the document is founded on is lodged.

(2) Paragraph (1) shall be without prejudice to any power of the court to order production of any document or grant a commission and diligence for recovery of it.

(3) Where a party fails to lodge a deed, writing or other document in accordance with paragraph (1), he may be found liable in the expenses of any order for production or for commission and diligence for recovery of it obtained by another party to the petition.

NOTE
[1] Inserted by S.I. 1990 No. 705.

Intimation and service including edictal service

195.—(*a*) All petitions shall, without enrolment, appear, if in session, in the printed rolls of court for the first available day after lodging, in the motion roll of the Outer House or in the single bills of the Inner House, as the case may be, for an order for such intimation, advertisement and service as may be necessary; and, if in vacation or recess, all such petitions shall, without enrolment, be brought before the Vacation Judge for a like order; provided that, in the case of proceedings under the Bankruptcy (Scotland) Act 1913, a petition for warrant to cite may, on being lodged, be brought forthwith by the Deputy Principal Clerk, or by a clerk instructed by him, before a Lord Ordinary in court or in chambers, who, notwithstanding that the petition has not appeared in the motion roll, may grant warrant.

[1] (*b*) Rules 74A, 74B and 75 shall apply to the intimation and service of a petition as they apply to the citation and service of a summons;

[2] (*c*) The citation and execution of service by post shall be as nearly as may be in the terms set forth in Form 30.

(*d*) All certificates of execution or intimation of a petition or note shall be written upon a certified copy of the petition or note lodged in process.

NOTE
[1] As amended by S.I. 1986 No. 1941.

Answers

196.—(*a*) Answers may be lodged at any time within the *induciae*, whether such *induciae* expire in session, vacation or recess; provided that the court may, on cause shewn, prorogate the time for lodging answers and allow the same to be received though not lodged within the *induciae*.

(*b*) All answers shall be in the form of articulate numbered answers to the narrative or statement of facts in the petition.

(*c*) The court may at any time, before disposal of the petition, allow the parties to adjust their pleadings; and replies and duplies shall not be lodged except by order of the court.

Unopposed petitions

[1] **197.** After the period of intimation and service in a petition has expired without answers being lodged, the petition shall, after such enquiry into, or verification of, the grounds of the petition (whether by evidence, remit, affidavit, or otherwise) as may be necessary, and subject to the provisions of Rule 198, be disposed of as accords; provided that:—

(*a*) Where a petition has been served on a respondent outside the United Kingdom under Rule 74B and the whole or a part of the prayer of the petition other than a procedural order has been granted without that respondent having lodged answers, intimation of a copy of the interlocutor granting the whole or a part of the prayer of the petition shall be made to that respondent in accordance with Rule 74B.

(*b*) Where a petition has been served on a respondent outside the United Kingdom under Rule 74B and an interlocutor has been pronounced granting the whole or a part of the prayer of the petition other than a procedural order without that respondent having lodged answers, the court may, on the motion of that respondent recall the interlocutor and allow answers to be lodged if—

(i) the respondent, without any fault on his part, did not have knowledge of the petition in sufficient time to lodge answers;

(ii) the respondent has disclosed a *prima facie* answer to the petition on the merits;

(iii) the motion is made within a reasonable time after the respondent had knowledge of the petition; and

(iv) the motion is not made after the expiry of one year from the date of the interlocutor sought to be recalled.

(*c*) The recall of any interlocutor under paragraph (*b*) shall be without prejudice to the validity of anything already done or transacted, or of any contract made or obligation incurred, under and in virtue of the interlocutor recalled, or of any appointment made or power granted therein or thereby.

(*d*) The provisions of this rule are without prejudice to the power of the court to make interim appointments or orders at any stage of the cause.

(*e*) A motion to grant the prayer of the petition shall state the ground of jurisdiction of the court and, in a cause to which the Civil Jurisdiction and Judgments Act 1982 applies, the domicile of the respondent (as determined by the provisions of that Act) in so far as it is known to the petitioner.

NOTE

[1] As amended by S.I. 1986 No. 1941 and S.I. 1987 Nos. 1206 and 2160.

Motions in opposed and unopposed petitions

[1] **198.** Save as herein otherwise provided, all motions, other than motions made at the Bar during any hearing of the cause, shall be enrolled and made by entry in the motion sheet; and the provisions of Rules 93 and 93A shall apply *mutatis mutandis* to all petitions.

NOTE

[1] As amended by S.I. 1978 No. 799.

Report by Judge

198A.—(1) The Lord Ordinary may at any stage of a cause commenced by petition, on intimation to the parties, report the petition, or any incidental matter which may arise in the course of the petition, to the Inner House for a ruling; and on such a ruling being given shall give effect to it.

(2) The Inner House may, after consideration of any such report, either—

(*a*) dispose of the petition or any incidental matter so reported; or

(*b*) give such instructions to the Lord Ordinary in respect thereof as it thinks fit.

(3) It shall not be competent to reclaim against an interlocutor pronounced by the Lord Ordinary in accordance with a ruling or instruction given by the Inner House under this Rule.

NOTE

[1] Substituted by S.I. 1986 No. 1937 and as amended by S.I. 1987 No. 1206.

[1] SECTION 2—JUDICIAL FACTORS

NOTE

[1] As amended by, and Rules 201A and 201B inserted by, S.I. 1986 No. 514.

PUPILS PROTECTION (SCOTLAND) ACT 1849; JUDICIAL FACTORS (SCOTLAND) ACT 1889; BANKRUPTCY (SCOTLAND) ACT 1985

Definition of judicial factors

199. The expression "judicial factor" includes *curator bonis*, factor *loco tutoris*, factor *loco absentis*, and factor on trust or other estates, and also includes guardians where caution is required.

Accountant of Court: caution, penal interest, etc.

200.—(*a*) *Copies of proceedings for Accountant of Court.* Copies of all petitions, answers, and other papers, relative to the appointment of any judicial factor, or to any judicial factory, shall, at the same time as they are

[THE NEXT PAGE IS C 79]

lodged in the Petition Department, be supplied to the Accountant of Court by the party or parties lodging the principal document, and copies of all interlocutors granting or refusing applications for special powers shall be supplied, within two days of issue, to the Accountant by the solicitor.

(*b*) *Transmission of processes to Accountant of Court.* The clerks of the Petition Department are authorised and directed to transmit to the Accountant of Court at all times, on his requisition, the proceedings, or such part thereof as he may require, in all processes of judicial factory, or other processes relative thereto, depending in the court, in so far as such proceedings may not at the time be required for the use of the court.

(*c*) *Time for finding caution.* When not otherwise expressed in the interlocutor appointing a judicial factor, the time for finding caution shall be limited to one calendar month from the date of the interlocutor: provided that on motion enrolled at any time before the expiry of that period the court may on cause shewn, prorogate the time for finding caution.

(*d*) *Bonds of caution received by Accountant of Court.* The Accountant of Court shall receive bonds of caution offered for judicial factors.

(*e*) *Procedure in finding caution.* On a judicial factor being appointed subject to caution being found, the process shall be forthwith transmitted to the Accountant of Court, in order that the matter of caution may be dealt with; and:—

[1] (i) The Accountant of Court shall, on the bond of caution being delivered to him, and on being satisfied as to its form and due execution, and as to the sufficiency of the cautioner, make a marking on the margin of the interlocutor sheet to the effect that caution has been received, stating the amount for which caution has been found, and adding his signature and the date; and such marking shall be an authority for the issue of a certified copy interlocutor of the appointment.

(ii) Where it is proposed that the caution be limited as authorised by section 27 of the Pupils Protection (Scotland) Act 1849, caution to the extent of not less than two-thirds of the value of the moveable and other easily realisable estate shall be found to the satisfaction of the Accountant of Court, who shall not report thereon to the court except in the event of his requiring larger caution than aforesaid and then only if the factor in writing shall require him so to report; and the court, in considering the said report, shall instruct the amount of caution to be found, being for not less than two thirds of the value of the said moveable and other easily realisable estate;

[2] (iii) During the subsistence of a factory, the Accountant of Court may at any time require the factor to increase the amount of the existing cautionary bond, or to find new or additional caution, or to procure a company bond in substitution for, or in addition to, that of an existing cautioner; and may also at any time authorise the factor to decrease the amount of the existing caution by a certain sum: provided always that, if the Accountant of Court should require caution to be found or increased to cover more than two-thirds of the value of the moveable and other easily realisable estate, the factor may require him in writing to report the matter to the court; and the court, on considering such report, shall instruct the amount of caution to be found as hereinbefore provided;

(iv) The Accountant of Court shall, in January yearly, prepare and submit a list of approved guarantee companies for the consideration and approval of the Lord President. In the event of a company not on the list being proposed as cautioner for a factor, the Accountant of Court may at any time submit the name of such company for the consideration of the Lord President, and such company, if approved by him, shall be included in the said list.

(*f*) *Premiums to guarantee companies and expenses of bond of caution.* The Accountant of Court shall allow as a charge against the factory estates (1) the premium paid by the factor where a company bond of caution has been accepted, or such part thereof as he deems proper, and (2) the expense of the necessary procedure in obtaining the approval of a bond of caution or the limitation, increase, or reduction of the amount.

(*g*) *Penal interest.* When the Accountant of Court is satisfied that the circumstances under which penal interest has been incurred under section 5 of the Pupil's Protection (Scotland) Act 1849, are such as to justify remission or modification of the penalty, he may, in his sole discretion, remit or modify it.

NOTES

[1] As amended by S.I. 1967 No. 487.

[2] As amended by S.I. 1985 No. 1600, which refers *per incuriam* to Rule 200 (*c*) (iii).

Applications by Judicial Factors to Accountant of Court

[1] **200A.**—(1) A judicial factor making an application under section 2(3) of the Trusts (Scotland) Act 1961 to the Accountant of Court for his consent to the doing of an act to which that section applies shall on the date on which he makes the application or as soon as possible thereafter notify the persons specified in paragraph (2) by notice sent by recorded delivery post of the following matters:—

(*a*) the date of the application;

(*b*) the act to which it relates;

(*c*) the right of that person to object to the doing of that act by notice sent by recorded delivery post to the Accountant of Court and to the judicial factor within a period of twenty eight days from the date on which the notice was posted;

(*d*) that in the absence of any such objection, the Accountant of Court may consent to the doing of that act.

(2) The persons referred to in paragraph (1) are:—

(*a*) the judicial factor's cautioner;

(*b*) the petitioner for the appointment of a judicial factor on the estate;

(*c*) the persons upon whom the petition for appointment was served, including the ward, if he was so served and there is no change in circumstances which would warrant service on him being dispensed with.

(3) The judicial factor shall, on serving a notice on any person under paragraph (1), send to the Accountant of Court a duly completed notice of execution of service.

NOTE

[1] Added by S.I. 1980 No. 1803. Applied to judicial factors appointed by the sheriff; see S.I. 1980 No. 1803.

Applications to encroach on capital

[1] **200B.**—(1) In any case where the income from the estate of a ward is insufficient for the maintenance of the ward, the judicial factor may apply to the Accountant of Court for his consent to encroach on the capital of the estate for the purpose of maintaining the ward.

(2) An application under paragraph (1) shall be made by letter and shall be supported by such information as the Accountant of Court may require.

(3) The Accountant of Court shall—

(*a*) appoint the judicial factor to intimate the making of the application in accordance with paragraphs (4) and (5); or

(*b*) require him to apply by note to the court for special powers.

(4) Where the Accountant of Court appoints intimation to be given under paragraph (3)(*a*), the judicial factor shall send by registered post or first class recorded delivery service to the persons specified in paragraph (5)—

(*a*) a copy of the letter of application; and
(*b*) a notice setting out—
(i) the right of the person receiving the notice to object to the proposed encroachment by lodging any objections in writing with the Accountant of Court, and intimating a copy thereof to the judicial factor, within 28 days of the date on which the notice was posted; and
(ii) that, in the absence of any such objection, the Accountant of Court may consent to the encroachment sought.

(5) The persons to whom notice is to be given under paragraph (4) are—
(*a*) the cautioner of the judicial factor;
(*b*) the petitioner for the appointment of the judicial factor;
(*c*) the ward, unless the circumstances of the ward are such that would warrant service on him of a petition for the appointment of his judicial factor being dispensed with;
(*d*) the persons upon whom the petition for appointment of the judicial factor was served and whose whereabouts are known to the judicial factor; and
(*e*) all other persons who have an interest in the estate and whose identity and whereabouts are known to the judicial factor.

(6) The judicial factor shall, on serving a notice on any person under paragraph (4), send to the Accountant of Court a duly completed execution of service with a copy of the notice sent appended to it.

(7) On the expiry of the period for lodging objections, where no objections have been lodged, the Accountant of Court may consent to the encroachment sought (subject to such conditions as he thinks fit) or require the judicial factor to apply to the court for special powers.

(8) On the expiry of the period for lodging objections where objections have been lodged, the judicial factor shall apply to the court for special powers.

NOTE
[1] Inserted by S.I. 1990 No. 705.

Factors on estate of deceased person
[2] **201.** This rule applies to judicial factors appointed under section 11A of the Judicial Factors (Scotland) Act 1889:—
(*a*) *Form of petition.* In the case of any petition presented to the court under the said section for appointment of a judicial factor on the estate of a person deceased, the official printed form of petition shall be filled in and completed as nearly as may be in the terms set forth in Form 29.
(*b*) *Intimation and service.* Besides intimation on the walls and in the

[THE NEXT PAGE IS C 81]

minute book in common form, of which certificates shall be produced, intimation shall be made in the *Edinburgh Gazette*, in the terms as nearly as may be of Form 31; and a full copy of the petition shall be served on such of the persons named in the petition as representatives of the deceased as are not parties thereto; and a copy of the *Edinburgh Gazette* containing the intimation and an execution of service of the petition shall be produced before the petition is disposed of. The citation and the execution of service shall be as nearly as may be in the terms set forth in Form 30.

(*c*) *Appointment of judicial factor.* The court shall not make the appointment of the judicial factor until the lapse of fourteen days, or such other time as the court may fix, after the publication of the foresaid notice in the *Edinburgh Gazette* and after the date of service (when such service is required) of the petition on the representatives of the deceased; provided always that the court, if in any case it shall see cause to do so, may make an interim appointment of such factor at an earlier date.

[1] (*d*) *Notice calling for claims.* In order to ascertain the claims upon the estate, the factor shall, within fourteen days of the issue to him of the first certified copy interlocutor of his appointment, cause to be inserted in the *Edinburgh Gazette* a notice in the form, as nearly as may be, set forth in Form 32, and shall lodge in process a copy of the *Edinburgh Gazette* containing the said notice and he shall also insert a similar notice in such newspapers as may appear to him to be proper.

(*e*) *Claims.* The factor shall examine the claims of the creditors in order to ascertain whether the debts are justly due from the estate of the deceased, and may call for further evidence in support of the claims, and may, if he sees fit, require the creditors to constitute the same by decree in a competent court in an action to which the factor shall be called as a defender. For the purpose of ranking and payment of creditors, the date of the factor's appointment shall be the date equivalent to the date of sequestration.

[1] (*f*) *Inventory of estate.* The factor shall, within six months at latest from the date of the issue to him of the first certified copy interlocutor of his appointment, lodge with the Accountant of Court a full inventory of the estate of the deceased, and shall produce therewith or exhibit all such writs and documents of importance belonging to the estate as may have been obtained by him, and shall, at the same time, or at such later time as the Accountant of Court may sanction, report a state of the debts appearing to be due by the deceased, distinguishing those for which claims have been lodged by creditors and the evidence upon which the same rest, and the claims made and lodged with him by persons interested in the succession of the deceased and the grounds thereof; and the said inventory, when adjusted and signed as after mentioned, with the state of debts, shall remain in the possession of the Accountant of Court; and all creditors and persons interested in the succession of the deceased, or their solicitors, shall have access to the same in the hands of the Accountant of Court, at his office.

(*g*) *State of funds and scheme of division.* The judicial factor shall prepare a state of funds and scheme of division amongst the creditors, and shall lay the same before the Accountant of Court, along with all writings and documents upon which it proceeds, and shall afford to the Accountant of Court all explanations thereon which may be required by him; and the Accountant of Court shall make a report in writing on the said state of funds and scheme of division, containing such observations thereon as he shall think fit and proper to be submitted to the court. Should there be no funds available for division after payment of the debts specified in paragraph (*n*) of this rule, the factor shall prepare and lay before the Accountant of Court a state of funds only, and the Accountant of Court shall report thereon. Should there be no creditors the factor shall immediately proceed to prepare a Report with regard to the disposal of the surplus estate in terms of paragraph (*o*) of this rule, without lodging any State of Funds.

(*h*) *Notice of scheme of division to creditors.* Immediately on the Accountant of Court's report being made, the factor shall lodge the same in court, and shall transmit to each person who has lodged with him a claim on the estate of the deceased a notice by post intimating that the state of funds and scheme of division (or state of funds only, as the case may be), and report thereon, have been lodged in court, and stating the amount for which the creditor has been ranked, and whether his claim is to be paid in full, or by a dividend, and the amount thereof, and in case of claims rejected, or for payment of which no funds are available, stating that fact; and a notice as nearly as may be in the terms of Form 33 shall also be inserted in the *Edinburgh Gazette*; and if any persons, other than those who have lodged claims with the factor shall be stated in the petition to the court, or in the books, deed of settlement, or other papers of the deceased, to be creditors of the estate or interested therein, or if the factor shall otherwise have reason to believe that other persons are either creditors of the estate or interested therein, he shall give notice by letter, through the post office, to such persons, that no dividend is allotted to them in the scheme of division.

(*j*) *Objections to scheme of division.* All creditors, and other persons interested in the succession of the deceased, shall be entitled to examine the state of funds and scheme of division lodged in court, and also the claims and the vouchers or evidence thereof lodged with the factor; and any creditor, or other person dissatisfied either with the state of funds or with the scheme of division, may lodge a notice of objections thereto, signed by counsel, in the Petition Department, within three weeks from the last date of such notices; and until the lapse of said period of three weeks the court shall not approve of the state of funds or scheme of division.

(*k*) *Objections to be disposed of by the court.* If objections are lodged to the state of funds or scheme of division, the court shall dispose of the same, after hearing counsel for the objectors and for the judicial factor and making all necessary investigations in regard to the same. If the objections be sustained to any extent, the necessary alterations shall be made on the said state or scheme.

(*l*) *Adjusted scheme of division.* When the scheme of division is adjusted, it shall be approved of by the court; and the factor shall pay, deliver, or convey to the parties therein set forth the sums or receipts allocated to them respectively in the said scheme of division.

(*m*) *Partial dividends on first scheme of division.* Where a partial division of funds among the creditors who have claimed may be made with safety to the interests of all concerned, the judicial factor may, with the approval of the Accountant of Court, prepare a state of the funds and first scheme of division as soon as may be after the time notified for lodging the claims of creditors; and, the same having been submitted to the Accountant of Court and reported on by him to the court, and notice having been given in terms of paragraph (*h*) of this rule to each creditor of such state of funds and first scheme of division having been lodged, the court may, on considering the same (but not earlier than six months after the death of the deceased), approve of that scheme of division, and the factor shall pay, deliver, or convey, in terms thereof; provided always that dividends corresponding to the amount of the claims of creditors whose debts have not at that period been admitted by the judicial factor, or whose debts are future or contingent, and also the full amount of such debts as are claimed as preferable, but the priority of which is not admitted by the factor, shall be retained and deposited in bank to meet such claims, if ultimately sustained, or when the same shall become payable or prestable.

(*n*) *Deathbed and funeral expenses, etc., of deceased.* Out of the first funds realised by him the factor shall reserve sufficient to defray the estimated cost of his administration (including the expenses connected with his appointment and of all necessary intimations to creditors); thereafter he shall be entitled, out of the said funds, and without waiting for the expiry of six months from the death of the deceased, to pay the deathbed and funeral expenses of the deceased, rent, taxes, and such servants' wages as are privileged debts, and interest becoming due or past due, to creditors having preferences over the estate.

(*o*) *Disposal of surplus of estate.* In the event of there being a residue after payment of the creditors, the judicial factor shall submit to the Accountant of Court a statement of the amount of the residue, the parties claiming the same, and their respective grounds of claim; and shall pay over the said residue to the party or parties found entitled thereto by the court on report by the Accountant of Court. Should it appear to the court that it is desirable that the factor should continue to administer the surplus estate, the court may direct accordingly. The factor shall report the surplus under this paragraph, notwithstanding that there may remain unpaid debts to secured creditors who do not desire immediate payment of their loans or debts, or whose securities cannot be realised owing to their immaturity or owing to statutory restrictions applicable to them. The parties claiming the estate shall be advised by the factor of the date on which his report, and the Accountant of Court's report, are being considered by the court, so that they may, if they so desire, lodge objections thereto.

(*p*) *Discharge of factor.* When applying to the court for his discharge the factor shall serve the petition on the representatives of the deceased and also upon the cautioner for the judicial factor, and insert a notice thereof in the *Edinburgh Gazette* in terms of Form 34, and the petition shall not be disposed of until fourteen days after such service and notice, and until a copy of the *Edinburgh Gazette* containing such notice, and an execution or acceptance of service of the petition and a certificate of intimation on the walls and in the minute book shall be lodged in process.

NOTES

[1] As amended by S.I. 1967 No. 487.

[2] As amended by S.I. 1986 No. 514, with saving for petitions brought under the Bankruptcy (Scotland) Act 1913, s.163, before 1st April 1986.

Forms prescribed under the Bankruptcy (Scotland) Act 1985

201A.—(1) The register of insolvencies kept by the Accountant in Bankruptcy under section 1(1)(*c*) of the said Act of 1985 shall be in the form set out in Form 34A of the Appendix.

(2) The memorandum to be sent by a permanent trustee to the keeper of the register of inhibitions and adjudications under section 14(4) of that Act shall be in the form set out in Form 34B of the Appendix.

(3) A notice by a trustee under a trust deed for creditors to be recorded in the register of inhibitions and adjudications under paragraph 2(1) of

Schedule 5 to that Act shall be in the form set out in Form 34C of the Appendix.

(4) A notice under paragraph 2(2) of the said Schedule 5 recalling a notice referred to in paragraph (3) shall be in the form set out in Form 34D of the Appendix.

Sederunt book held by Accountant in Bankruptcy under section 62 of the Bankruptcy (Scotland) Act 1985

201B. The Accountant in Bankruptcy shall hold the sederunt book for a period of at least six months from the date he receives it from the permanent trustee, and shall make it available for inspection during such reasonable office hours and may allow such extracts to be made of entries in the sederunt book by such persons as he thinks fit.

[1] Section 2A—Causes Under the Criminal Justice (Scotland) Act 1987

NOTE

[1] Inserted by S.I. 1990 No. 705.

Interpretation

201C.—(1) In this section, "the Act of 1987" means the Criminal Justice (Scotland) Act 1987.

(2) Words and expressions used in this section which are also used in the Act of 1987 have the same meaning as in that Act unless the context otherwise requires.

Remits from the High Court of Justiciary

201D.—(1) This rule applies where the High Court of Justiciary remits a case to the Court of Session under section 3(5) of the Act of 1987 for a decision on a question of fact or law as regards the assessment of the proceeds of drug trafficking.

(2) The Deputy Principal Clerk, on receiving a case remitted from the High Court of Justiciary, shall have the case put out on the By Order Roll before a Division of the Inner House at the earliest opportunity for an order for further procedure and shall intimate the diet to the prosecutor and the accused.

(3) Before the hearing on the By Order Roll, the prosecutor shall lodge in the Petition Department—

(*a*) a process (consisting of an inventory of process, and interlocutor sheet, a duplicate inventory of process, a motion sheet and a minute of proceedings);

(*b*) four copies of the relevant indictment; and

(*c*) four copies of all other documents to be used at that hearing.

(4) Not later than 48 hours before any subsequent hearing, parties shall lodge four copies of any further documents to be used at such a hearing.

(5) After the court has decided the question in the case remitted to it, the Deputy Principal Clerk shall transmit the decision of the court to the Deputy Principal Clerk of Justiciary.

Applications for restraint orders

201E.—(1) An application under section 8(1) of the Act of 1987 for a restraint order, shall be made by petition presented to the Outer House and shall not be intimated.

(2) Rules 191(*aa*), (*b*) and (*c*), 192 and 195 to 197 shall not apply to a petition to which this rule applies.

General provisions in relation to restraint orders

201F.—(1) The period within which an application other than an application by the Lord Advocate under section 8(2)(*b*) of the Act of 1987 to vary or recall a restraint order is to be made shall be 21 days of the applicant receiving notice of the restraint order.

(2) Where a restraint order is made, the Lord Advocate shall serve a copy of it and of the petition on all persons named in the interlocutor as restrained by the order and give notice of it to all persons affected by the restraint order.

(3) Rules 74A, 74B and 75 shall apply to the service of a copy of an order under paragraph (2) of this rule as they apply to citation and service of a summons.

Miscellaneous applications

201G.—(1) An application under section 8(2) (variation or recall of restraint order), 8(5) (recall of restraint order) or 11(1) or (5) (recall or restriction of arrestment or inhibition), of the Act of 1987 shall be made by motion in the process of the petition to which the application relates.

(2) A motion under paragraph (1) shall include a brief statement of the reasons for the application; and the court may, at the hearing of the motion, order that the application be made by note.

(3) A motion under paragraph (1) for an order under section 8(2)(*b*) of the Act of 1987 shall be intimated by recorded delivery letter on an *induciae* of 14 days and the applicant shall lodge in process a copy of the letter of intimation and the Post Office receipt of posting of the letter.

(4) A motion under paragraph (1) by the Lord Advocate in relation to an application to extend a restraint order under section 8(2) of the Act of 1987 shall not be intimated.

(5) An application under section 11(1) of the Act of 1987 (warrant for arrestment or inhibition) may be made in the prayer of the petition for a restraint order under section 8(1) of the Act of 1987 or, if made after presentation of the petition, by motion in that process and shall not be intimated.

(6) An application under section 12 of the Act of 1987 (interdict) may be made in the prayer of the petition for a restraint order under section 8(1) of the Act of 1987 or, if made after presentation of the petition, by note in that process; and rule 201F(2) and (3) shall apply to the service of an interdict as it applies to the service of a restraint order.

(7) An application under section 25(1) (variation of confiscation order) or 26(1) (compensation) of the Act of 1987 shall be made by petition presented to the Outer House.

(8) An application by the Lord Advocate under section 41 of the Act of 1987 (disclosure of information by Government departments) may be made—

(*a*) by petition presented to the Outer House;

(*b*) where there is a restraint order in force, by note in the process of the application for the restraint order; or

(*c*) where an administrator has been appointed, by note in that process.

Applications for appointment of administrators

201H.—(1) An application under section 13(1) of the Act of 1987 for the appointment of an administrator shall be made—

(*a*) where a restraint order has been made, by note in the process of the application for the restraint order; or

(*b*) in any other case, by petition presented to the Outer House.

(2) Rules 191(*aa*), (*b*) and (*c*), 192 and 195 to 197 shall not apply to a petition to which this rule applies.

Incidental applications in an administration

201J.—(1) An application under section 13(1) (which is not made in the petition for appointment of an administrator) or 13(4) (making or altering a requirement or removal of administrator), 13(5) (appointment of new administrator on death, resignation or removal of administrator), 14(1)(*n*) (directions as to functions of administrator), or 16 (directions for application of proceeds) of the Act of 1987 shall be made by note in the process of the petition for appointment of the administrator under section 13(1) of the Act of 1987.

(2) An application under section 14(1)(*o*) (special powers of administrator), 14(3) (vesting of property in administrator) or 24 (orders of realisation of property) of the Act of 1987 may be made in the prayer of the petition for appointment of an administrator under section 13(1) of the Act of 1987 or, if made after presentation of the petition, by note in that process.

General provisions in relation to an administration

201K.—(1) Notification by a clerk of court under section 13(3)(*a*) of the Act of 1987 to a person of a requirement to give possession of property to an administrator shall be made by intimation of a certified copy of the interlocutor making the requirement.

(2) Where the court considers making an order under section 24(1) of the Act of 1987 to facilitate the realisation of property, it shall fix a date for a hearing on the Motion Roll (in the first instance) and the petitioner or noter, as the case may be, shall serve a notice in Form 71 on any person who has an interest in that property that such person may appear and make representations to the court at that hearing.

Papers for Accountant of Court in an administration

201L.—(1) A copy of the petition, answers and any other paper or document relative to the appointment of an administrator appointed under section 13(1) of the Act of 1987 shall, at the same time as they are lodged in the Petition Department, be supplied to the Accountant of Court by the petitioner, and copies of all interlocutors granting or refusing applications for special powers or directions shall be supplied, within two days of issue, to the Accountant of Court by the party making the application.

(2) The clerks of the Petition Department shall transmit to the Accountant of Court, at any time at his request, the process or such part as he may require in an administration under Part I of the Act of 1987 which is in dependence before the court, in so far as such process may not be required at the time for the use of the court.

Caution for administrator

201M. A certified copy interlocutor of the appointment of an administrator appointed under section 13(1) of the Act of 1987 shall not be issued until the Accountant of Court has given written intimation to the Petition Department that he is satisfied with the caution found by the administrator.

Duties of administrator

201N.—(1) As soon as possible, but not later than three months, after the date of his appointment, the administrator shall lodge with the Accountant of Court—

(*a*) an inventory of the property in respect of which he has been appointed;

(*b*) all vouchers, securities and other documents which are in his possession; and

(*c*) a statement of that property which he has in his possession or intends to realise.

(2) An administrator shall maintain accounts of his intromissions with the property in his charge and shall—

(*a*) lodge an account of his intromissions with the Accountant of Court in such form as the Accountant of Court may require—

(i) six months after the date of his appointment; and
(ii) at six monthly intervals after the first account during the subsistence of his appointment,

unless the Accountant of Court agrees to waive the lodging of an account where the administrator certifies that there have been no intromissions during a particular accounting period; and

(*b*) lodge, with the account of his intromissions, all supporting vouchers and other documents as the Accountant of Court may require.

State of funds and scheme of division

201P.—(1) The administrator shall—

(*a*) where there are funds available for division, prepare a state of funds after application of sums in accordance with section 16(1) of the Act of 1987 and a scheme of division amongst those who held property which has been realised under that Act and lodge them with the Accountant of Court, along with all relevant documents; or

(*b*) where there are no funds available for division, prepare such a state of funds only and lodge it with the Accountant of Court; and

(*c*) give to the Accountant of Court all explanations which may be required by him.

(2) The Accountant of Court shall make a report in writing on the state of funds and scheme of division, containing such observations as he shall think fit and proper to be submitted to the court, and shall return the state of funds and scheme of division to the administrator together with a principal copy of his report.

(3) The administrator shall, on receiving the report of the Accountant of Court—

(*a*) lodge it in process together with the state of funds and scheme of division;

(*b*) send a copy of the report of the state of funds and scheme of division to the Lord Advocate; and

(*c*) send to each person who held property which has been realised under the Act of 1987 a notice by post intimating that the state of funds and scheme of division (or state of funds only, as the case may be), and the report of the Accountant of Court, have been lodged in court; stating the amount for which that person has been ranked, and whether he is to be paid in full, or by a dividend, and the amount thereof, or that no funds are available for payment.

Objections to scheme of division

201Q.—(1) A person wishing to be heard by the court in relation to the distribution of property under section 16(2) of the Act of 1987 shall lodge a note of objections signed by counsel in the process in which the scheme of division relates within 21 days of the date on which the notice under rule 201P(3)(c) was sent.

(2) After the period for lodging a notice of objections has expired and no notice has been lodged, the administrator may enrol a motion for approval of the scheme of division.

(3) After the period for lodging a notice of objections has expired and a notice of objections has been lodged, the court shall put the cause out for a hearing to approve, and if necessary adjust, the scheme of division.

Appeals against determination of outlays and remuneration

201R.—(1) An appeal under section 18(2) of the Act of 1987 against a determination by the Accountant of Court shall be by note in the process of the petition for appointment of the administrator.

(2) Where a note is lodged under paragraph (1), the appeal shall be put out by order by the Keeper of the Rolls for a hearing before a Lord Ordinary as soon as convenient.

[1] Section 2B—Causes under the Prevention of Terrorism (Temporary Provisions) Act 1989

NOTE
[1] Inserted by S.I. 1991 No. 1183, with effect from 3rd June 1991.

Interpretation

201S.—(1) In this Section, "the Act of 1989" means the Prevention of Terrorism (Temporary Provisions) Act 1989.

(2) Words and expressions used in this Section which are also used in the Act of 1989 have the same meaning as in that Act unless the context otherwise requires.

Applications for restraint orders

201T.—(1) An application under paragraph 13(1) of Schedule 4 to the Act of 1989 for a restraint order, shall be made by petition presented in the Outer House.

(2) Rules 191(*aa*), (*b*) and (*c*), 192, and 195 to 197 shall not apply to a petition to which this rule applies.

General provisions in relation to restraint orders

201U.—(1) Where a restraint order is made, the Lord Advocate shall serve a copy of it and of the petition on all persons named in the interlocutor as restrained by the order and give notice to all persons affected by the restraint order.

(2) Rule 74A, 74B and 75 shall apply to the service of a copy of an order under paragraph (1) as they apply to citation and service of a summons.

Miscellaneous applications

201V.—(1) An application under paragraph 13(4) (discharge of a restraint order), 14(2) (variation or recall of restraint order), 14(3) (recall of restraint order) or 16(2)(*a*) or (6)(*a*) (recall or restriction of arrestment or inhibition) of Schedule 4 to the Act of 1989 shall be made by motion in the process of the petition to which the application relates.

(2) A motion under paragraph (1) shall be intimated by first class recorded delivery letter on an *induciae* of seven days and the applicant shall lodge in process a copy of the letter of intimation and the Post Office receipt of posting of the letter.

(3) A motion under paragraph (1) shall include a brief statement of the reasons for the application; and the court may, at the hearing of the motion, order that the application be made by note.

(4) An application under paragraph 16(1) of Schedule 4 to the Act of 1989 (warrant for arrestment or inhibition) may be made in the prayer of the petition for a restraint order under paragraph 13(1) of Schedule 4 to the Act of 1989 or, if made after presentation of the petition, by motion in that process and shall not be intimated.

(5) An application under paragraph 17(1) of Schedule 4 to the Act of 1989 (compensation) shall be made by petition presented in the Outer House.

Powers and duties of administrator appointed under paragraph 11(1)(b) of Schedule 4 to the Act of 1989

201W.—(1) Subject to any condition or exception specified by the court, an administrator—

(*a*) shall be entitled to take possession of the property as regards which he has been appointed and of any document which both—
  (i) is in the possession or control of the person (in this Section referred to as "A") in whom the property is vested; and
  (ii) relates to the property;

(*b*) shall be entitled to have access to, and to copy, any document relating to the property and not in such possession or control as is mentioned in sub-paragraph (*a*) above;
(*c*) may bring, defend or continue any legal proceedings relating to the property;
(*d*) may borrow money in so far as it is necessary to do so to safeguard the property and may for the purposes of such borrowing create a security over any part of the property;
(*e*) may, if the administrator considers that to do so would be beneficial for the management and realisation of the property enter into any control, or execute any deed, as regards the property;
(*f*) may effect or maintain insurance policies as regards the property;
(*g*) may, where A has uncompleted title to any of the property, complete title thereto: provided that completion of title in A's name shall not validate by accretion any unperfected right in favour of any person other than the administrator;
(*h*) may sell (but not to himself or an associate of his), the property and redeem any obligation secured thereon;
(*i*) may discharge any of his functions through agents or employees: provided that the administrator shall be personally liable to meet the fees and expenses of any such agent or employee out of such remuneration as is payable to the administrator by virtue of paragraph 12(2) and (3) of Schedule 4 of the Act of 1989;
(*j*) may take such professional advice as he may consider requisite for the proper discharge of his functions;
(*k*) may at any time apply to the Court of Session for directions as regards the discharge of his functions;
(*l*) may exercise any power specifically conferred on him by the Court, whether such conferral was at the time of his appointment or on his subsequent application to the Court in that regard; and
(*m*) may do anything incidental to the above powers and duties.

(2) Subject to the proviso to sub-paragraph (*g*) of paragraph (1) above—
(*a*) a person dealing with an administrator in good faith and for value shall not require to determine whether the administrator is acting within the powers mentioned in that subsection; and
(*b*) the validity of any title shall not be challengeable by reason only of the administrator having acted outwith those powers.

(3) The exercise of a power mentioned in any of sub-paragraphs (*c*) to (*h*) of paragraph (1) above shall be in A's name.

Further duties of administrator

201X.—(1) As soon as possible, but not later than three months, after the date of his appointment, the administrator shall lodge with the Accountant of Court—
(*a*) an inventory of the property in respect of which he has been appointed;
(*b*) all land certificates, title deeds, vouchers, and other documents which relate to that property and are in his possession; and
(*c*) a statement of the property which he has in his possession or intends to realise.

(2) An administrator shall maintain accounts of his intromissions with the property in his charge and shall—
(*a*) lodge an account of his intromissions with the Accountant of Court in such form as the Accountant of Court may require—
(i) six months after the date of his appointment; and
(ii) at six monthly intervals after the first account during the subsistence of his appointment, unless the Accountant of Court agrees to waive the lodging of an account where the administrator certifies that there have been no intromissions during a particular accounting period; and

(*b*) lodge, with the account of his intromissions all such supporting vouchers and other documents as the Accountant of Court may require.

Money received by administrator

201Y.—(1) Subject to paragraph (2) below, all money received by an administrator in the exercise of his powers and duties shall be deposited by him in an appropriate bank or institution, in the name of A.

(2) The administrator may at any time retain in his hands a sum not exceeding £200.

(3) In paragraph (1) above, "appropriate bank or institution" means the Bank of England, an institution authorised under the Banking Act 1987 or a person for the time being specified in Schedule 2 to that Act.

[1] SECTION 2C—DISCHARGE OF FACTORS, TUTORS AND CURATORS

NOTE

[1] Rules 201Z–201FF inserted by S.I. 1991 No. 1915 with effect from 18th November 1991.

Interpretation and application

201Z.—(1) In this Section—

"judicial factor" includes tutor and curator;

"judicial factory" includes tutory and curatory.

(2) This Section shall apply only to a judicial factor appointed as a—

(*a*) curator or *curator bonis*;

(*b*) tutor;

(*c*) factor *loco tutoris* or *loco absentis*; or

(*d*) commissary factor.

Appliciations for certificate of discharge

201AA. Where a judicial factory is terminated by reason of its recall or the death or coming of age of the ward, or by reason of the exhaustion of the estate, the judicial factor or, where he has died after the termination of the judicial factory, his representatives may apply in writing to the Accountant of Court for a certificate of discharge.

Notices to cautioner and interested parties

201BB.—(1) The judicial factor shall give notice by post by the first class recorded delivery service of an application under rule 201AA to—

(*a*) the cautioner; and

(*b*) any person with an interest in the estate of the ward.

(2) Such a notice shall contain information about—

(*a*) the availability for inspection in the office of the Accountant of Court of the audited accounts of the judicial factor;

(*b*) the time within which any party may make representations under rule 201CC; and

(*c*) the effect of the issue of a certificate of discharge.

Representations to Accountant of Court

201CC. Any person to whom notice has been given under rule 201BB may make written representations relating to the application to the Accountant of Court within 21 days from the date of notice to him under that rule.

Determination of Accountant of Court

201DD. On the expiry of the period specified in rule 201CC, the Accountant of Court shall—

(*a*) consider the application and any representations made; and (*b*) intimate to the factor, to the Deputy Principal Clerk of Session and to any party who has made representations, a copy of his determination to issue or refuse to issue a certificate of discharge together with a note of his reasons for making that determination.

Certificates of discharge

201EE.—(1) The Accountant of Court—

(*a*) shall not sign a certificate of discharge until the time for lodging an appeal under rule 201FF has expired; and

(*b*) shall, on issuing a certificate of discharge, give notice that he has issued it to the Deputy Principal Clerk of Session.

(2) The issue of a certificate shall be sufficient authority for the judicial factor to uplift his bond of caution.

Appeals

201FF.—(1) The judicial factor, or any person who has made representations under rule 201CC, may, within 14 days of intimation under rule 201DD, appeal against the determination of the Accountant of Court to the Lord Ordinary.

(2) An appeal under paragraph (1) shall be—

(*a*) by letter to the Deputy Principal Clerk containing a statement of the grounds of appeal; and

(*b*) intimated to the Accountant of Court.

(3) On receipt of an appeal under paragraph (1) the Deputy Principal Clerk shall place the papers before a Lord Ordinary in chambers for determination of the appeal.

(4) On disposing of the appeal, the Lord Ordinary shall—

(*a*) direct the Accountant of Court to sign the certificate of discharge;

(*b*) appoint the factor to lodge a petition for discharge; or

(*c*) make such further order as he considers appropriate.

[1] SECTION 3—COMPANIES

NOTE

[1] Rules 202–218S substituted by S.I. 1986 No. 2298 in relation to proceedings commenced on or after 29th December 1986.

Interpretation

202.—(1) In this Section—

"the Act of 1986" means the Insolvency Act 1986;

"registered office" means:—

(*a*) the place specified, in the statement of the company delivered to the registrar of companies under section 10 of the Companies Act 1985, as the intended place of its registered office on incorporation; or

(*b*) where notice has been given by the company to the registrar of companies under section 287 of the Companies Act 1985 of a change of registered office, the place specified in the last such notice;

"the insolvency judge" means the Lord Ordinary nominated by the Lord President to deal with proceedings under the Act of 1986 or any rules made under that Act or under the Company Directors Disqualification Act 1986, or a Lord Ordinary acting in his place;

"the Insolvency Rules" means the Insolvency (Scotland) Rules 1986.

(2) Unless the context otherwise requires, words and expressions used in this Section which are also used in the Act of 1986 or the Insolvency Rules have the same meaning as in that Act or those Rules.

PART I

COMPANY VOLUNTARY ARRANGEMENTS

Lodging of nominee's report (Part 1, Chapter 2 of the Insolvency Rules)

203.—(1) This rule applies where the company is not being wound up, is not in liquidation and an administration order is not in force in respect of it.

(2) A report of a nominee, sent to the court under section 2(2) of the Act of 1986, shall be accompanied by a covering letter, lodged in the Petition Department and marked by a clerk of court with the date on which it is received.

(3) The report shall be placed before the insolvency judge for consideration of any direction which he may make under section 3(1) of the Act of 1986.

(4) An application by a nominee to extend the time within which he may lodge his report under section 2(2) of the Act of 1986 shall be made by letter addressed to the Deputy Principal Clerk, who shall cause it to be placed before the insolvency judge for determination.

[THE NEXT PAGE IS C 85]

(5) The letter of application under paragraph (4) and a copy of the reply by the court shall be placed by the clerk of court with the nominee's report when it is subsequently lodged.

(6) A person who states in writing that he is a creditor, member or director of the company may, by himself or his agent, on payment of the appropriate fee, inspect the nominee's report lodged under paragraph (2).

Lodging of nominee's report (Part 1, Chapter 4 of the Insolvency Rules)

204.—(1) This rules applies where the company is being wound up, is in liquidation or there is an administration order in force in respect of it.

(2) Where a report of a nominee is sent to the court under section 2(2) of the Act of 1986, it shall be lodged in the process of the petition to wind up the company or the petition for an administration order which is in force in respect of it, as the case may be.

(3) Where the nominee is not the liquidator or administrator, the report shall be placed before the insolvency judge for consideration of any direction which he may make under section 3(1) of the Act of 1986.

(4) An application by a nominee to extend the time within which he may lodge his report under section 2(2) of the Act of 1986 shall be made by letter addressed to the Deputy Principal Clerk who shall cause it to be placed before the insolvency judge for determination.

(5) The letter of application under paragraph (4) and a copy of the reply by the court shall be placed by the clerk of court in the process of the petition to wind up the company or the petition for an administration order which is in force in respect of it, as the case may be.

(6) A person who states in writing that he is a creditor, member or director of the company may, by himself or his agent, on payment of the appropriate fee, inspect the nominee's report lodged under paragraph (2).

Applications to replace nominee

205. An application under section 2(4) of the Act of 1986 to replace a nominee who has failed to lodge a report under section 2(2) of the Act of 1986, shall be made:—

(*a*) by petition where the company is not being wound up, is not in liquidation and an administration order is not in force in respect of it; or

(*b*) by note in the process of the petition to wind up the company or the petition for an administration order which is in force in respect of it, as the case may be,

and shall be intimated and served as the court shall direct.

Report of meetings to approve arrangement

206. The report of the result of a meeting to be sent to the court under section 4(6) of the Act of 1986 shall be sent to the Deputy Principal Clerk, who shall cause it to be lodged:—

(*a*) in a case to which rule 203 applies, with the nominee's report lodged under that rule; or

(*b*) in a case to which rule 204 applies, in the process of the petition to wind up the company or the petition for an administration order which is in force in respect of it, as the case may be.

Abstracts of supervisor's receipts and payments and notices of completion of arrangement

207. An abstract of receipts and payments prepared by a supervisor and sent to the court under rule 1.21(2) of the Insolvency Rules or a notice of completion of the arrangement (together with a copy of the supervisor's report) to be sent to the court under rule 1.23(3) of those rules shall be sent to the Deputy Principal Clerk, who shall cause it to be lodged—

(*a*) in a case to which rule 203 applies, with the nominee's report lodged under that rule; or
(*b*) in a case to which rule 204 applies, in the process of the petition to wind up the company or the petition for an administration order which is in force in respect of it, as the case may be.

Form of certain applications

208.—(1) This rules applies to applications under any of the following provisions of the Act of 1986 or the Insolvency Rules:—

(*a*) section 6 (to challenge a decision in relation to an arrangement);
(*b*) section 7(3) (to challenge actings of a supervisor);
(*c*) section 7(4)(*a*) (by supervisor for directions);
(*d*) section 7(5) (to appoint a supervisor);
(*e*) rule 1.21(5) (to dispense with sending abstracts or reports or to vary dates on which obligation to send abstracts or reports arises);
(*f*) rule 1.23(4) (by supervisor to extend period for sending notice of implementation of arrangement or report); and
(*g*) any other provision relating to company voluntary arrangements not specifically mentioned in this Part.

(2) An application shall be made—

(*a*) in a case to which rule 203 applies, by petition; or
(*b*) in a case to which rule 204 applies, by note in the process of the petition to wind up the company or the petition for an administration order which is in force in respect of it, as the case may be.

Part II

Administration Orders

Petitions for administration orders

209.—(1) A petition for an administration order under section 9 of the Act of 1986 shall be presented to the Outer House.

(2) Rules 191 to 198 shall apply to a petition presented under paragraph (1), subject to rule 210.

(3) A petition under paragraph (1) shall include averments in relation to:—

(*a*) the petitioner and the capacity in which he presents the petition, if other than the company;
(*b*) whether it is believed that the company is, or is likely to become, unable to pay its debts and the grounds of that belief;
(*c*) which of the purposes specified in section 8(3) of the Act of 1986 is expected to be achieved by the making of an administration order;
(*d*) the company's financial position, specifying (so far as known) assets and liabilities, including contingent and prospective liabilities;
(*e*) any security known or believed to be held by creditors of the company, whether in any case the security confers power on the holder to appoint a receiver, and whether a receiver has been appointed;
(*f*) so far as is known to the petitioner, whether any steps have been taken for the winding up of the company, giving details of them;
(*g*) other matters which, in the opinion of the petitioner, will assist the court in deciding whether to grant an administration order;
(*h*) whether a report has been prepared under the rule 2.1 of the Insolvency Rules (independent report on affairs of the company), and, if not, an explanation why not; and
(*i*) the person proposed to be appointed as administrator, giving his name and address and whether he is qualified to act as an insolvency practitioner in relation to the company.

(4) There shall be produced with the petition:—
(*a*) any document instructing the facts relied on, or otherwise founded on, by the petitioner; and
(*b*) where a report has been prepared under rule 2.1 of the Insolvency Rules, a copy of that report.

Notice of petition

210. Notice of the petition on the persons upon whom notice is to be given under rule 2.2 of the Insolvency Rules shall be in accordance with rule 195 of these rules unless the court otherwise directs.

Form of certain applications and appeals

211.—(1) An application or appeal under any of the following provisions of the Act of 1986 or the Insolvency Rules shall be made by note in the process of the petition for an administration order which is in force:—
(*a*) section 13(2) (application for appointment to fill a vacancy in office of administrator);
(*b*) section 14(3) (application by administrator for directions);
(*c*) section 15(2) (application by administrator for power to dispose of property subject to a security);
(*d*) section 18(1) (application by administrator for discharge or variation of administration order);
(*e*) section 19(1) (application for removal from office of administrator);
(*f*) section 22(5) (application for release from, or extension of time for, obligation to submit statement of affairs);
(*g*) section 27(1) (application for protection of interest of creditors and members);
(*h*) rule 2.6(2) (appeal against decision of administrator as to expenses of submitting statement of affairs);
(*i*) rule 2.16(3) (application by administrator for increase of remuneration); and
(*j*) any other application under a provision relating to administration orders not specifically mentioned in this Part.

(2) An application by an administrator to extend the period for sending an abstract of his receipts and payments under rule 2.17(2) of the Insolvency Rules shall be made by motion in the process of the petition.

[1] (3) Where a petition for an administration order has been presented or an administration order has been made, any person showing an interest who wishes to apply to the court for an order under section 175(2) of the Companies Act 1989 shall apply by note in the process of the petition for the administration order.

[1] (4) The court shall not make an order under section 175(2) of the Companies Act 1989 unless intimation has been made to such persons having an interest as the court considers necessary and any such person has had an opportunity to be heard.

NOTE

[1] Inserted by S.I. 1991 No. 1157, with effect from 27th May 1991.

Report of administrator's proposals

212.—(1) A report of the meeting to approve the administrator's proposals to be sent to the court under section 24(4) of the Act of 1986 shall be sent to the Deputy Principal Clerk, who shall cause it to be lodged in the process of the petition.

(2) Where the report lodged under paragraph (1) discloses that the meeting has declined to approve the administrator's proposals, the cause shall be put out "By Order" for determination by the insolvency judge of any order he may make under section 24(5) of the Act of 1986.

Abstracts of administrator's receipts and payments

213. An abstract of receipts and payments of an administrator to be sent to the court under rule 2.17(1) of the Insolvency Rules shall be sent to the Deputy Principal Clerk who shall cause it to be lodged in the process of the petition.

PART III

RECEIVERS

Applications to appoint a receiver

214.—(1) A petition under section 54(1) of the Act of 1986 to appoint a receiver shall be presented to the Outer House.

(2) Subject to rule 215, rules 191 to 198 apply to a petition presented under paragraph (1) of this rule.

(3) A petition under paragraph (1) shall include averments in relation to:—

(*a*) any floating charge and the property over which it is secured;

(*b*) so far as known to the petitioner, whether any petition for an administration order has been made in respect of the company, giving details of it;

(*c*) other matters which, in the opinion of the petitioners, will assist the court in deciding whether to appoint a receiver; and

(*d*) the person proposed to be appointed as receiver, giving his name and address and that he is qualified to act as a receiver.

(4) There shall be produced with the petition any document instructing the facts relied on, or otherwise founded on, by the petitioner.

Intimation, service and advertisement

215.—(1) Intimation, service and advertisement of the petition shall be made in accordance with rule 195 unless the court otherwise directs.

(2) Unless the court otherwise directs, there shall be included in the order for service, a requirement to serve:—

(*a*) upon the company; and

(*b*) where a petition for an administration order has been presented, on that petitioner and any respondent to that petition.

(3) Subject to paragraph (5), service of a petition on the company shall be effected at its registered office:—

(*a*) by registered or recorded delivery post addressed to the company; or

(*b*) by messenger-at-arms:—

(i) leaving the citation in the hands of a person who, after due inquiry, he has reasonable grounds for believing to be a director, other officer or responsible employee of the company or authorised to accept service on behalf of the company; or

(ii) if there is no such person as is mentioned in head (i) present, depositing it in the registered office in such a way that it is likely to come to the attention of such a person attending at that office.

(4) Where service is effected in accordance with paragraph (3)(*b*)(ii), the messenger-at-arms thereafter shall send a copy of the petition and citation by ordinary first class post to the registered office of the company.

(5) Where service cannot be effected at the registered office of the company or the company has no registered office:—

(*a*) service may be effected at the last known principal place of business of the company in Scotland or at some place in Scotland at which the company carries on business, by leaving the citation in the hands of such a person as is mentioned in paragraph (3)(*b*)(i) or by depositing it as specified in paragraph (3)(*b*)(ii); and

(*b*) where the citation is deposited as is specified in paragraph (3)(*b*)(ii), the messenger-at-arms thereafter shall send a copy of the petition and citation by ordinary first class post to such place mentioned in sub-paragraph (*a*) of this paragraph in which the citation was deposited.

(6) Unless the court otherwise directs, the petition shall be advertised forthwith:—

(*a*) once in the *Edinburgh Gazette*; and

(*b*) once in one or more newspapers as the court shall direct for ensuring that it comes to the notice of creditors of the company.

(7) An advertisement under paragraph (6) shall state:—

(*a*) the name and address of the petitioner;

(*b*) the name and address of the solicitor for the petitioner;

[THE NEXT PAGE IS C 89]

(*c*) the date on which the petition was presented;
(*d*) the precise order sought;
(*e*) the *induciae*; and
(*f*) that any person who intends to appear in the petition must lodge answers to the petition within the *induciae*.

(8) The *induciae* within which answers may be lodged and after which further consideration of the petition may proceed shall be 8 days after such intimation, service and advertisement as the court may have ordered.

Form of certain applications where receiver appointed

216.—(1) An application under any of the following sections of the Act of 1986 shall be made by petition or, where the receiver was appointed by the court, by note in the process of the petition for appointment of the receiver:—

(*a*) section 61(1) (by receiver for authority to dispose of interest in property);
(*b*) section 62 (for removal or resignation of receiver);
(*c*) section 63(1) (by receiver for directions);
(*d*) section 69(1) (to enforce receiver to make returns, etc.); and
(*e*) any other section relating to receivers not specifically mentioned in this Part.

(2) An application under any of the following provisions of the Act of 1986 or the Insolvency Rules shall be made by motion in the process of the petition:—

(*a*) section 67(1) or (2) (by receiver to extend time for sending report); and
(*b*) rule 3.9(2) (by receiver to extend time for sending abstract of receipts and payments).

PART IV

WINDING UP BY THE COURT OF COMPANIES REGISTERED UNDER THE COMPANIES ACTS AND OF UNREGISTERED COMPANIES

Petitions to wind up a company

217.—(1) A petition to wind up a company by the court under the Act of 1986 shall be presented to the Outer House.

(2) Rules 191 to 198 apply to a petition under paragraph (1), subject to the following provisions of this Part.

(3) A petition under paragraph (1) shall include:—

(*a*) particulars of the petitioner, if other than the company;
(*b*) in respect of the company:—
  (i) its registered name;
  (ii) the address of its registered office, and any change of that address within the last 6 months so far as known to the petitioner;
  (iii) a statement of its nature and objects, the amount of its capital (nominal and issued) and indicating what part is called up, paid up or credited as paid, and the amount of the assets of the company so far as known to the petitioner;
(*c*) a narrative of the facts on which the petitioner relies and any particulars required to instruct the title of the petitioner to present the petition;
(*d*) the name and address of the person to be appointed as interim liquidator and a statement that he is qualified to act as an insolvency practitioner in relation to the company; and
(*e*) a prayer setting out the orders applied for, including any intimation, service and advertisement and any appointment of an interim liquidator.

(4) There shall be lodged with the petition any document:—
(*a*) instructing the title of the petitioner; and
(*b*) instructing the facts relied on, or otherwise founded on, by the petitioner.

Intimation, service and advertisement

218.—(1) Subject to the following provisions of this rule, intimation, service and advertisement shall be in accordance with rule 195 unless the court:—
(*a*) summarily dismisses the petition; or
(*b*) otherwise directs.

(2) Unless the court otherwise directs, there shall be included in the order for service, a requirement:—
(*a*) to intimate on the walls of the court;
(*b*) where the petitioner is other than the company, to serve upon the company;
(*c*) where the company is being wound up voluntarily and a liquidator has been appointed, to serve upon the liquidator;
(*d*) where a receiver has been appointed for the company, to serve upon the receiver;
(*e*) where the company is:—
(i) a recognised bank or licensed institution within the meaning of the Banking Act 1979; or
(ii) an institution to which sections 16 and 18 of that Act apply as if it were licensed,

and the petitioner is not the Bank of England, to serve upon the Bank of England.

(3) Subject to paragraph (5), service of a petition on the company shall be effected at its registered office:—
(*a*) by registered or recorded delivery post addressed to the company; or
(*b*) by messenger-at-arms:—
(i) leaving the citation in the hands of a person who, after due inquiry, he has reasonable grounds for believing to be a director, other officer or responsible employee of the company or authorised to accept service on behalf of the company; or
(ii) if there is no such person as is mentioned in head (i) present, depositing it in the registered office in such a way that it is likely to come to the attention of such a person attending at that office.

(4) Where service is effected in accordance with paragraph (3)(*b*)(ii), the messenger-at-arms thereafter shall send a copy of the petition and citation by ordinary first class post to the registered office of the company.

(5) Where service cannot be effected at the registered office or the company has no registered office:—
(*a*) service may be executed at the last known principal place of business of the company in Scotland or at some place in Scotland at which the company carries on business by leaving the citation in the hands of such a person as is mentioned in paragraph (3)(*b*)(i) or by depositing it as specified in paragraph (3)(*b*)(ii); and
(*b*) where the citation is deposited as is specified in paragraph (3)(*b*)(ii), the messenger-at-arms thereafter shall send a copy of the petition and the citation by ordinary first class post to such place mentioned in sub-paragraph (*a*) of this paragraph in which the citation was deposited.

(6) Unless the court otherwise directs, the petition shall be advertised forthwith:—

(*a*) once in the Edinburgh Gazette; and
(*b*) once in one or more newspapers as the court shall direct for ensuring that it comes to the notice of creditors of the company.

(7) An advertisement under paragraph (6) shall state:—
(*a*) the name and address of the petitioner and, where the petitioner is the company, its registered office;
(*b*) the name and address of the solicitor for the petitioner;
(*c*) the date on which the petition was presented;
(*d*) the precise order sought;
(*e*) where a provisional liquidator has been appointed by the court, his name, address and the date of his appointment;
(*f*) the *induciae*; and
(*g*) that any person who intends to appear in the petition must lodge answers to the petition within the *induciae*.

(8) The *induciae* within which answers may be lodged and after which further consideration of the petition may proceed shall be 8 days after such intimation, service and advertisement as the court may have ordered.

Lodging of caveats

218A.—(1) A company, debenture holder, holder of a floating charge, receiver, shareholder of a company or other person claiming an interest, apprehensive that a petition to wind up that company may be presented and wishing to be heard by the court before an order for intimation, service and advertisement is pronounced, may lodge a caveat in the Petition Department.

(2) [Revoked by S.I. 1990 No. 2118.]

(3) Where a caveat has been lodged and has not expired, no order may be pronounced without the person lodging the caveat having been given an opportunity to be heard by the court.

Remits

218B.—(1) An application by virtue of section 120(3)(*a*)(i) of the Act of 1986 to remit a petition to a sheriff court shall be made by note in the process of the petition.

(2) An application by virtue of section 120(3)(*a*)(ii) of the Act of 1986 to remit a petition from a sheriff court to the Court of Session, or section 120(3)(*b*) of that Act to remit a petition from one sheriff court to another, shall be made by petition.

(3) A note under paragraph (1) or a petition under paragraph (2) shall include a statement of the grounds on which the remit is sought.

Substitution of creditor or contributory for petitioner

218C.—(1) This rule applies where a petitioner:—
(*a*) is subsequently found not entitled to present the petition;
(*b*) fails to make intimation, service and advertisement as directed by the court;
(*c*) consents to withdraw the petition or to allow it to be dismissed or refused;
(*d*) fails to appear when the petition is called for hearing; or
(*e*) appears, but does not move for an order in terms of the prayer of the petition.

(2) The court may, on such terms as it considers just, sist as petitioner in room of the original petitioner any creditor or contributory who, in the opinion of the court, is entitled to present a petition.

(3) An application by a creditor or contributory to be sisted under paragraph (2):—
(*a*) may be at any time before the petition is dismissed or refused; and
(*b*) shall be made by note in the process of the petition, and if necessary the court may continue the cause for a specified period to allow a note to be presented.

Advertisement of appointment of liquidator

218D. Where a liquidator is appointed by the court, the court may order that the liquidator shall advertise his appointment once in one or more newspapers as the court shall direct for ensuring that it comes to the notice of creditors of the company.

Provisional liquidators

218E.—(1) An application to appoint a provisional liquidator under section 135 of the Act of 1986 may be made:—

(*a*) by the petitioner, in the prayer of the petition or subsequently by note in the process of the petition; or

(*b*) by a creditor or contributory of the company, the company, the Secretary of State or a person entitled under any enactment to present a petition to wind up the company, in a note in the process of the petition.

(2) The petition or note, as the case may be, shall include averments in relation to:—

(*a*) the grounds on which it is proposed that a provisional liquidator should be appointed;

(*b*) the name and address of the person to be appointed as provisional liquidator and that he is qualified to act as an insolvency practitioner in relation to the company; and

(*c*) whether, to the knowledge of the applicant, there is a receiver for the company or a liquidator has been appointed for the voluntary winding up of the company.

(3) Where the court is satisfied that sufficient grounds exist for the appointment of a provisional liquidator, it shall, on making the appointment, specify the functions to be carried out by him in relation to the affairs of the company.

(4) The applicant shall send a certified copy of the interlocutor appointing a provisional liquidator forthwith to the person appointed.

(5) On receiving a certified copy of his appointment on an application by note, the provisional liquidator shall intimate his appointment forthwith:—

(*a*) once in the Edinburgh Gazette; and

(*b*) once in one or more newspapers as the court shall direct for ensuring that it comes to the notice of the creditors of the company.

(6) An application for discharge of a provisional liquidator shall be by note in the process of the petition.

Applications and appeals in relation to a statement of affairs

218F.—(1) An application under section 131(5) of the Act of 1986 for:—

(*a*) release from an obligation imposed under section 131(1) or (2) of the Act of 1986; or

(*b*) an extension of time for the submission of a statement of affairs,

shall be made by note in the process of the petition.

(2) A note under paragraph (1) shall be served on the liquidator or provisional liquidator, as the case may be.

(3) The liquidator or provisional liquidator may lodge answers to the note or lodge a report of any matters which he considers should be drawn to the attention of the court.

(4) Where the liquidator or provisional liquidator lodges a report under paragraph (3), he shall send a copy of it to the noter forthwith.

(5) Where the liquidator or provisional liquidator does not appear, a certified copy of the interlocutor pronounced by the court disposing of the note shall be sent by the noter forthwith to him.

(6) An appeal under rule 4.9(6) of the Insolvency Rules against a refusal by the liquidator of an allowance towards the expenses of preparing a statement of affairs shall be made by note in the process of the petition.

Appeals against adjudication of claims

218G.—(1) An appeal under section 49(6) of the Bankruptcy (Scotland) Act 1985 as applied by rule 4.16 of the Insolvency Rules, by a creditor or contributory of the company against a decision of the liquidator shall be made by note in the process of the petition.

(2) A note under paragraph (1) shall be served on the liquidator.

(3) On receipt of the note served on him under this rule, the liquidator forthwith shall send or deliver to the court the claim in question and a copy of his adjudication for lodging in process.

(4) After the note has been disposed of, the court shall return the claim and the adjudication to the liquidator together with a copy of the interlocutor.

Appointment of liquidator by the court

218H.—(1) An application to appoint a liquidator under section 139(4) of the Act of 1986 shall be made by note in the process of the petition.

(2) Where the court appoints a liquidator under section 138(5) of the Act of 1986, it shall send a certified copy of the interlocutor pronounced by the court to the liquidator forthwith.

Removal of liquidator

218J. An application by a creditor of the company for removal of a liquidator or provisional liquidator from office under section 172 of the Act of 1986 or for an order under section 171(3) of that Act directing a liquidator to summon a meeting of creditors for the purpose of removing him shall be made by note in the process of the petition.

Applications in relation to remuneration of liquidator

218K.—(1) An application by a liquidator under rule 4.34 of the Insolvency Rules shall be made by note in the process of the petition.

(2) An application by a creditor of the company under rule 4.35 of the Insolvency Rules shall be made by note in the process of the petition.

(3) A note under paragraph (2) shall be served on the liquidator.

Application to appoint a special manager

218L.—(1) An application under section 177 of the Act of 1986 by a liquidator or provisional liquidator for the appointment of a special manager shall be made by note in the process of the petition.

(2) The cautioner, for the caution to be found by the special manager within such time as the court shall direct, may be:—

(*a*) a private person, if approved by the court; or

(*b*) a guarantee company, chosen from a list of such companies prepared for this purpose annually by the Accountant of Court and approved by the Lord President.

(3) A bond of caution certified by the noter under rule 4.70(4) of the Insolvency Rules shall be delivered to the Petition Department by the noter, marked as received by a clerk of court and transmitted forthwith by him to the Accountant of Court.

(4) On receipt of the bond of caution, there shall be issued forthwith to the person appointed to be special manager a certified copy of the interlocutor appointing him.

(5) An application by a special manager to extend the time within which to find caution shall be made by motion.

Other applications

[1] **218M.** An application under the Act of 1986 or rules made under that Act, or under Part VII of the Companies Act 1989, in relation to a winding up by the court not specifically mentioned in this Part shall be made by note in the process of the petition.

NOTE

[1] As amended by S.I. 1991 No. 1157, with effect from 27th May 1991.

PART V

DISQUALIFICATION OF COMPANY DIRECTORS

Applications for disqualification orders

218N.—(1) This rule applies to the following applications:—

(*a*) applications under the following provisions of the Company Directors Disqualification Act 1986:—

(i) section 3(2) (for disqualification for persistent breaches of companies legislation);

(ii) section 6(1) (to disqualify unfit directors of insolvent companies);

(iii) section 8 (for disqualification of unfit director after investigation of company);

(iv) section 11(1) (for leave by undischarged bankrupt to be concerned in a company);

(*b*) an application for leave under that Act; and

(*c*) an application by the Secretary of State under rule 4(2) of the Insolvent Companies (Reports on Conduct of Directors) (No. 2) (Scotland) Rules 1986 (for direction to comply with requirement to furnish information, etc.).

(2) An application to which this rule applies shall be made by petition presented to the Outer House and shall be dealt with by the insolvency judge.

[1] (3) Rules 191 to 198 and 218 (except paragraphs (6) and (8)) shall apply to a petition under this rule; and the petition shall be intimated to the Secretary of State for Trade and Industry unless presented by him.

NOTE

[1] Substituted by S.I. 1990 No. 705.

PART VI

GENERAL PROVISIONS

Application

218P. This Part applies to Parts I to IV of this Section.

Applications by note and appeals

218Q.—(1) An application by note, or an appeal, to the court shall be intimated, served and, if necessary, advertised as the court shall direct.

(2) A petition, application by note, appeal or motion, to the court shall be dealt with by the insolvency judge.

Affidavits

218R. The court may accept as evidence an affidavit lodged in support of a petition or note.

Notices, reports and other documents sent to the court

218S. Where, under the Act of 1986 or rules made under that Act:—

(*a*) notice of a fact is to be given to the court;

(*b*) a report is to be made, or sent, to the court; or

(*c*) some other document is to be sent to the court,

it shall be sent or delivered to the Deputy Principal Clerk, who shall cause it to be lodged in the appropriate process.

[1] SECTION 4—ADOPTION OF CHILDREN

ADOPTION ACTS 1958 TO 1964 AND CHILDREN ACT 1975

NOTE

[1] Substituted by S.I. 1984 No. 997.

Interpretation

219.—(1) In this section, unless the context otherwise requires—

"the 1978 Act" means the Adoption (Scotland) Act 1978;

"adoption agency" means a local authority or an approved adoption society;

"Her Majesty's Forces" means the Royal Navy, the regular armed forces as defined by section 225 of the Army Act 1955, the regular air force as defined by section 223 of the Air Force Act 1955, the Queen Alexandra's Royal Naval Nursing Services and the Women's Royal Naval Service; and

"Registrar General" means the Registrar General of Births, Deaths and Marriages for Scotland.

(2) Expressions which are used in this section and are also used in the 1978 Act have the same meaning as in that Act.

(3) In this section, a form referred to by number means the form so numbered in the Appendix to the rules or a form substantially to the like effect, with such variation as circumstances may require.

Freeing for adoption

220.—(1) An application by an adoption agency for an order freeing a child for adoption under section 18(1) of the 1978 Act shall be made by petition in the Outer House.

(2) Rules 192 and 195 to 197 shall not apply to a petition under this rule, and the petition shall not be intimated on the walls or in the minute book or advertised.

(3) A petition under paragraph (1) shall include averments about, or refer to a report or other documents produced which deal with, the following matters—

(*a*) whether the petition is presented with the consent of a parent or guardian;

(*b*) whether the petitioner is applying for dispensation of the agreement of a parent or guardian under section 18(1)(*b*) of the 1978 Act and on what ground in section 16(2) of the 1978 Act dispensation is sought;

(*c*) how the needs of the child came to the notice of the petitioner;

(*d*) any relevant family circumstances of the child;

(*e*) a description of the physical and mental health of the child (including any special needs) and his emotional, behavioural and educational development;

(*f*) an account of the discussion by the petitioner with the parents or guardians of the child and, if appropriate, with the child about their wishes and the alternatives to adoption;

(*g*) the knowledge of the petitioner of the position of other relatives or persons likely to be involved;

(*h*) an account of the search by the petitioner for any parent or guardian who cannot be found;

(*i*) the likelihood of placement of the child for adoption and whether a petition for an adoption order is likely in the near future;

(*j*) the arrangements of the petitioner to care for the child after the granting of the prayer of the petition for an order freeing a child for adoption;

(*k*) whether the petitioner has given each parent or guardian who can be found an opportunity to make a declaration under section 18(6) of the 1978 Act that he prefers not to be involved in future questions concerning the adoption of the child;

(*l*) an account of the inquiries by the petitioner into the circumstances of any reputed father;

(*m*) the intentions of the petitioner about giving notice to a former parent or guardian under section 19(2) and (3) of the 1978 Act; and

(*n*) any other information which may be of assistance to the court.

(4) Where a petition is presented with the consent of a parent or guardian, there shall be appended to the petition a consent in Form 37 duly signed by that parent or guardian and witnessed.

(5) There shall be lodged in process with the petition—

(*a*) an extract of the entry, if any, in the Register of Births relating to the child; and

(*b*) any other document founded on by the petitioner for the purpose of vouching averments in the petition.

(6) On presentation of the petition, the court—

(*a*) shall appoint a reporting officer with the duties in Rule 224(1);

(*b*) shall appoint a curator *ad litem* with the duties in Rule 224(4) where it appears that a parent or guardian of the child is unwilling to agree to the making of an adoption order; and

(*c*) may appoint a curator *ad litem* with the duties in Rule 224(4) in any case where it appears to the court to be desirable in the circumstances of the case in order to safeguard the interests of the child.

(7) Where a curator *ad litem* is appointed, the court may order the petitioner, a local authority or the reporting officer to make available to the curator *ad litem* any report or information in relation to the child and the natural father and mother of the child.

(8) The reporting officer shall, on completion of his report, lodge three copies of it in process together with—

(*a*) any agreement under section 18(1)(*a*) of the 1978 Act in Form 37A;

(*b*) any consent under section 18(8) of the 1978 Act in Form 38; and

(*c*) any declaration under section 18(6) of the 1978 Act in Form 37A.

(9) The curator *ad litem* shall, on completion of his report, lodge three copies of it in process.

(10) On receipt of the report of the reporting officer and, where one has been appointed, the report of the curator *ad litem*, the petition department shall—

(*a*) inform the petitioner that the reports have been lodged and that a motion for a hearing to determine the application must be enrolled within seven days; and

(*b*) make available to the petitioner, and to any other party, a copy of the report.

(11) At the motion for a hearing to determine the application, the court shall consider—

(*a*) whether to require any person, whose agreement or consent is required to be given or dispensed with, to attend the hearing to determine the application;

(*b*) whether to require intimation of the date of the hearing to determine the application to any other person; and

(*c*) whether to require the reporting officer or a curator *ad litem* to perform any other duties.

(12) On a date being fixed for a hearing to determine the application, the petitioner shall intimate the date of the hearing in Form 39—

(*a*) to every person who can be found whose agreement or consent is required to be given or dispensed with;

(*b*) to the reporting officer and, where one has been appointed, to the curator *ad litem*; and

(*c*) to any person upon whom intimation has been ordered by the court under paragraph (11)(*b*).

(13) At the hearing to determine the application—

(*a*) the petitioner, the reporting officer and, where one has been appointed, the curator *ad litem* shall, if required by the court, appear and may be represented;

(*b*) any person required by the court to attend the hearing shall appear and may be represented; and

(*c*) any other person upon whom intimation was made under paragraph (12)(*a*) or (*c*) may appear or be represented.

(14) The court shall, where a declaration has been made under section 18(6) of the 1978 Act, record the fact of that declaration in the interlocutor making the order freeing a child for adoption.

Revocation of freeing for adoption order

221.—(1) An application by a former parent under section 20(1) of the

1978 Act for revocation of an order freeing a child for adoption shall be made by note in the process of the petition for that order.

(2) Rules 191 to 196 and 198 shall apply to a note under this Rule as they apply to a petition, except that a note under this Rule shall not be intimated on the walls or in the minute book or advertised.

(3) On presentation of the note, the court—

(*a*) shall make an order for service upon—

(i) the petitioner;

(ii) any person upon whom the petition was intimated, except a parent or guardian who has made a declaration under section 18(6) or 19(4) of the 1978 Act;

(iii) any adoption agency in which parental rights and duties relating to the child are vested by virtue of section 21 of the 1978 Act; and

(*b*) shall appoint a curator *ad litem* with the duties in Rule 224(5) where it appears to the court to be desirable in the circumstances of the case in order to safeguard the interests of the child.

(4) Where a curator *ad litem* is appointed, the court may order the adoption agency, a local authority or the reporting officer to make available to the curator *ad litem* any report or information in relation to the child and the natural father and mother of the child.

(5) The curator *ad litem* shall, on completion of his report, lodge three copies of it in process.

(6) On receipt of the report of the curator *ad litem*, where one has been appointed, the petition department shall—

(*a*) inform the noter that the report has been lodged and that a motion for a hearing to determine the application must be enrolled within seven days; and

(*b*) make available to the noter and to any other party, a copy of the report.

(7) At the motion for a hearing to determine the application, the court shall consider, in an application to which section 20(5) of the 1978 Act applies, whether to grant leave to allow the application to proceed.

(8) On a date being fixed for a hearing to determine the application, the noter shall intimate the date of the hearing in Form 39A to the adoption agency and, where one has been appointed, to the curator *ad litem*.

(9) At the hearing to determine the application, the noter, the adoption agency and, where one has been appointed, the curator *ad litem* shall appear and may be represented.

(10) An application, by an adoption agency having the parental rights and duties relating to a child, for leave under section 20(2) of the 1978 Act to place that child for adoption while the application under this Rule for revocation of an order freeing that child for adoption is pending, shall be made by motion in the process for revocation of that order.

Adoption orders

222.—(1) An application for an adoption order shall be made by petition in the Outer House by the proposed adopter in Form 36.

(2) Rules 191, 192 and 195 to 197 shall not apply to a petition under this Rule, and a petition shall not be intimated on the walls or in the minute book or advertised.

(3) Where a person, who proposes to present a petition for an adoption order, desires that his identity should not be disclosed to any person whose agreement is required under section 16(1) of the 1978 Act, he may apply in writing to the clerk of court before presenting the petition for a serial number to be assigned to him, and in such a case—

(*a*) the record of the serial number assigned and the person to whom it applies shall be confidential and open only to the court; and (*b*) an agreement under section 16(1) of the 1978 Act in Form 37B shall not name the petitioner but shall refer to him as the petitioner to whom that serial number has been assigned and shall specify the year in which that serial number was applied.

(4) There shall be lodged in process with the petition—

(*a*) an extract of the entry, if any, in the Register of Births relating to the birth of the child;

(*b*) an extract of the entry in the Register of Births relating to the birth of the petitioner;

(*c*) in the case of a petition by a married couple, an extract of the entry in the Register of Marriages relating to their marriage;

(*d*) where the child was not placed for adoption with the applicant by an adoption agency, three copies of a medical report showing the physical and mental health of the child (including any special needs) and his emotional, behavioural and educational development; and

(*e*) any other document founded on by the petitioner for the purpose of vouching averments in the petition.

(5) On presentation of the petition, the court—

(*a*) shall make an order requiring the petitioner to give notice in Form 39B—

(i) where the child has been placed for adoption, to the adoption agency which placed the child; or

(ii) where the child has not been placed for adoption, to the local authority within whose area the petitioner lives;

(*b*) shall appoint a reporting officer with the duties in Rule 224(2);

(*c*) shall appoint a curator *ad litem* with the duties in Rule 224(6) where the child is not free for adoption and it appears that a parent or guardian is unwilling to agree to the making of an adoption order; and

(*d*) may appoint a curator *ad litem* with the duties in Rule 224(6) where it appears to the court to be desirable in the circumstances of the case in order to safeguard the interests of the child.

(6) Where a curator *ad litem* is appointed, the court may order the adoption agency, a local authority or the reporting officer to make available to the curator *ad litem* any report or information in relation to the child and the natural father and mother of the child.

(7) A report by a local authority under section 22(2), or an adoption agency under section 23, of the 1978 Act shall include the following matters—

(*a*) information about how the needs of the child came to the notice of the agency;

(*b*) the family circumstances of the child;

(*c*) where the child was placed for adoption by an adoption agency, a description of the physical and mental health of the child (including any special needs) and his emotional, behavioural and educational development;

(*d*) an account of the discussion with the parents or guardians of the child and, if appropriate, with the child about their wishes and the alternatives to adoption;

(*e*) the position of other relatives or persons likely to be involved;

(*f*) an account of the search for a parent or guardian who cannot be found;

(*g*) information about the mutual suitability of the petitioner and the child for the relationship created by adoption and the ability of the petitioner to bring up the child including an assessment of the personality of the petitioner and, where appropriate, that of the child;

(*h*) particulars of all members of the household of the petitioner and their relationship to the petitioner;

(*i*) a description of the accommodation in the home of the petitioner;
(*j*) in a petition by one of two spouses, why the other spouse has not joined in the petition;
(*k*) whether the petitioner understands the nature and effect of an adoption order and in particular that the order, if made, will make the petitioner responsible for the maintenance and upbringing of the child;
(*l*) whether the means and standing of the petitioner are such as to enable him to maintain and bring up the child suitably, and what right or interest in property the child has;
(*m*) whether any payment or other reward in consideration of the adoption, other than an approved adoption allowance, has been received or agreed upon;
(*n*) what insurance has been offered on the life of the child;
(*o*) the religious persuasion of the petitioner;
(*p*) considerations arising from the difference in age between the petitioner and the child if this is more or less than the normal difference in age between parents and children;
(*q*) whether adoption is likely to safeguard and promote the welfare of the child throughout its childhood; and
(*r*) any other information which may be of assistance to the court.

(8) On completion of a report under section 22(2) or 23 of the 1978 Act, the local authority or adoption agency shall—
(*a*) lodge three copies of the report in process; and
(*b*) send a copy of the report to the reporting officer and, where one has been appointed, to the curator *ad litem*.

(9) The reporting officer shall, on completion of his report, lodge three copies of it in process together with—
(*a*) any agreement under section 16(1) of the 1978 Act in Form 37B; and
(*b*) any consent under section 12(8) of the 1978 Act in Form 38A.

(10) The curator *ad litem* shall, on completion of his report, lodge three copies of it in process.

(11) On receipt of the reports of the reporting officer, the local authority or adoption agency and, where one has been appointed, the report of the curator *ad litem*, the petition department shall—
(*a*) inform the petitioner that the reports have been lodged and that a motion for a hearing to determine the application must be enrolled within seven days; and
(*b*) make available to the petitioner, and to any other party, a copy of each report.

(12) At the motion for a hearing to determine the application, the court shall consider—
(*a*) whether to require any person, whose agreement or consent is required to be given or dispensed with, to attend the hearing to determine the application;
(*b*) whether to require intimation of the date of the hearing to determine the application to any other person; and
(*c*) whether to require the reporting officer or a curator *ad litem* to perform any other duties.

(13) On a date being fixed for a hearing to determine the application, the petitioner shall intimate the date of the hearing in Form 39C—
(*a*) to every person who can be found whose agreement or consent is required to be given or dispensed with;
(*b*) to the local authority or adoption agency which lodged the report under paragraph (8), the reporting officer and, where one has been appointed, to the curator *ad litem*; and
(*c*) to any person upon whom intimation has been ordered by the court under paragraph (12)(*b*).

(14) At the hearing to determine the application—

(*a*) the petitioner, the adoption agency, the reporting officer and, where one has been appointed, the curator *ad litem* shall, if required by the court, appear and may be represented;

(*b*) any person required by the court to attend the hearing shall appear and may be represented; and

(*c*) any other person upon whom intimation was made under paragraph (13)(*a*) or (*c*) may appear or be represented.

(15) Where the court has made an *interim* order, the petitioner shall, before the expiry of the period specified in the *interim* order, enrol the cause for a further hearing.

(16) Where, in relation to a child under 16, the court refuses to make an adoption order and considers—

(i) that the child should be placed under the supervision of a specified local authority; or

(ii) that the child should be committed to the care of a specified local authority,

the following provisions of this rule shall apply—

(*a*) the court shall appoint intimation to be made to the local authority and give the local authority an opportunity to make representations;

(*b*) any representations of a local authority shall be made by minute in the petition process;

(*c*) on a minute being lodged in process, the court shall order service of the minute upon the parties to the petition who may lodge answers within such period as the court may allow; and

(*d*) after the period for answers has expired, the court shall put the cause out by order for a hearing to determine the matter.

Adoption of children abroad

223.—(1) An application for an order under section 49(1) of the 1978 Act shall be made by petition in the Outer House.

(2) The provisions of Rule 222, except paragraph (5)(*b*), shall apply to an application under this Rule as they apply to an application under that Rule.

(3) On presentation of the petition, the court shall appoint a reporting officer with the duties in Rule 224(3).

Duties of reporting officer and curator ad litem

224.—(1) A reporting officer appointed under Rule 220(6) (freeing for adoption) shall have the following duties—

(*a*) to inquire into the facts and circumstances averred in the petition;

(*b*) to ascertain the whereabouts of each parent or guardian and, if practicable, to meet them;

(*c*) to witness any agreement by a parent or guardian who is within Scotland to the freeing for adoption under section 18(1) of the 1978 Act in Form 37A; and to ensure that the agreement is given freely, unconditionally and with full understanding of what is involved;

(*d*) where a parent or guardian is furth of Scotland, to confirm his views in writing and to ensure that any agreement under section 18(1) of the 1978 Act is witnessed in accordance with Rule 230(1).

(*e*) to witness any consent of a minor under section 18(8) of the 1978 Act in Form 38 and to ensure that he understands the consequences of that consent;

(*f*) where the agreement or consent of a parent or guardian or the consent of a minor is sought to be dispensed with, to consider whether the ground of dispensation has been made out;

(*g*) to consider whether the petitioner has made every reasonable effort to find every person whose agreement is required;

(*h*) to consider whether other persons with a relevant interest should be informed of the petition;

(*i*) to inquire whether the petitioner has considered the position of any reputed father;

(*j*) where the child is illegitimate, to consider the prospect of any application by a reputed father for a custody order and whether such an application would be likely to be refused;

(*k*) to discuss alternatives to adoption with each parent or guardian who can be found;

(*l*) to explain the implications of a freeing order to each parent or guardian who can be found;

(*m*) to ensure that each parent or guardian who can be found understands he may be able to apply under section 20 of the 1978 Act and Rule 221 for revocation of an order under section 18 of the 1978 Act, and the procedure for making such application;

(*n*) to ensure that each parent or guardian who can be found has been given an opportunity to make a declaration under section 18(6) of the 1978 Act that he prefers not to be involved in future questions concerning the adoption of the child;

(*o*) to consider whether the account by the petitioner of why the application is for a freeing order and not a full adoption order is satisfactory;

(*p*) to consider whether the account by the petitioner of the prospects of arranging adoption after a freeing order is correct;

(*q*) to consider whether any payment prohibited by section 51 of the 1978 Act has been made or received;

(*r*) to ensure that each parent or guardian who can be found is aware of the date of the hearing to determine the application if he wishes to appear;

(*s*) to draw to the attention of the court any matter which may be of assistance; and

(*t*) to prepare a report in relation to the exercise of the above duties.

(2) A reporting officer appointed under Rule 222(5) (adoption) shall have the following duties—

(*a*) to inquire into the facts and circumstances averred in the petition and the report of the adoption agency;

(*b*) to ascertain the whereabouts of each parent or guardian and, if practicable, to meet them;

(*c*) to witness any agreement by a parent or guardian who is within Scotland to the adoption under section 16(1) of the 1978 Act in Form 37B, and to ensure that the agreement is given freely, unconditionally and with full understanding of what is involved;

(*d*) where a parent or guardian is furth of Scotland, to confirm his views in writing and to ensure that any agreement under section 16(1) of the 1978 Act is witnessed in accordance with Rule 230(1);

(*e*) to witness any consent of a minor under section 12(8) of the 1978 Act in Form 38A and to ensure that he understands the consequences of that consent;

(*f*) to ensure that each parent or guardian whose agreement is required understands that in agreeing to the adoption he is giving up all future claims to the child and that all parental rights and duties will vest in the adopter;

(*g*) where the agreement of a parent or guardian or the consent of a minor is sought to be dispensed with, to consider whether the ground of dispensation has been made out;

(*h*) in the case of a child not free for adoption, to consider whether the adoption agency has made every reasonable effort to find every person whose agreement is required;

(*i*) to consider whether other persons with a relevant interest should be informed of the petition;
(*j*) in the case of a child not free for adoption, that the adoption agency has considered the position of any reputed father;
(*k*) where the child is illegitimate, to ascertain whether the father has a custody order and, if not, is not applying for one;
(*l*) to ascertain the wishes of the child, if practicable;
(*m*) to ascertain whether the requirements of section 13 of the 1978 Act have been complied with;
(*n*) to consider whether it is desirable for the welfare of the child that an interim order should be made or whether conditions should be imposed in any adoption order or whether an order for custody should be made;
(*o*) where a previous application for adoption has been refused to which section 24(1) of the 1978 Act applies, to report on whether there has been any change of circumstances or other reason which might lead the court to allow the application to proceed;
(*p*) in the case of a child not free for adoption, to consider whether there has been any payment or reward in consideration of the adoption;
(*q*) to ensure that each parent or guardian whose agreement is required or may be dispensed with is aware of the date of the hearing to determine the application if he wishes to appear;
(*r*) to draw to the attention of the court any matter which may be of assistance; and
(*s*) to prepare a report in relation to the exercise of the above duties.

(3) A reporting officer appointed under Rule 223(3) (adoption of children abroad) shall have the following duties—
(*a*) the duties in paragraph (2) of this rule; and
(*b*) to obtain a statement from a qualified person in the country in which the petitioner is intending to adopt the child whether there is any legal obstacle to the adoption taking place.

(4) A curator *ad litem* appointed under Rule 220(6) (freeing for adoption) shall have the following duties—
(*a*) to inquire into, so far as he considers necessary, the matters averred in the petition;
(*b*) to inquire into any other matters which appear to him to be relevant to the making of an order freeing the child for adoption;
(*c*) to consider whether, in his opinion, the child should be present at the hearing to determine the application;
(*d*) to perform such other duties as appear to him to be necessary or as the court may require; and
(*e*) to prepare a report in relation to the exercise of the above duties.

(5) A curator *ad litem* appointed under Rule 221(3) (revocation of freeing for adoption order) shall have the following duties—
(*a*) to inquire into the facts and circumstances averred in the note;
(*b*) to determine whether 12 months have elapsed between the making of the freeing order and the date of presentation of the note;
(*c*) where a previous application under section 20 of the 1978 Act was refused, to inquire whether there has been any change of circumstances or other reason which the court should know about when considering whether to allow the application to proceed;
(*d*) to inquire into any other matters which appear to him to be relevant to the revocation of the order freeing the child for adoption;
(*e*) to consider whether, in his opinion, the child should be present at the hearing to determine the application;
(*f*) to perform such other duties as appear to him to be necessary or as the court may require; and

(*g*) to prepare a report in relation to the exercise of the above duties.

(6) A curator *ad litem* appointed under Rule 222(5) (adoption) shall have the following duties—

(*a*) to inquire into, so far as he considers necessary, the matters averred in the petition and in any report under Rule 222(7);

(*b*) to inquire into any other matters which appear to him to be relevant to the making of an adoption order;

(*c*) to consider whether, in his opinion, the child should be present at the hearing;

(*d*) to perform such other duties as appear to him to be necessary or as the court may require; and

(*e*) to prepare a report in relation to the exercise of the above duties.

Special application for appointment of reporting officer

225.—(1) Where a person intends to present a petition under Rules 220, 222 or 223 and seeks the appointment of a reporting officer before that petition is presented, he may apply under this Rule for the appointment of a reporting officer.

(2) An application shall be made by letter addressed to the deputy principal clerk together with any necessary supporting documents and shall be dealt with by a Lord Ordinary in chambers.

(3) The interlocutor of the Lord Ordinary shall be written on an interlocutor sheet and shall be final.

(4) The letter of application and interlocutor sheet shall be kept in the petition department and subsequently added to the process in the petition.

Application for transfer of parental rights and duties between adoption agencies

226.—(1) An application for transfer of parental rights and duties between adoption agencies under section 21 of the 1978 Act shall be made by note in the process of the petition for an order freeing a child for adoption.

(2) Rules 191 to 198 shall apply to a note under this Rule as they apply to a petition except that a note under this Rule shall not be intimated on the walls or in the minute book or advertised.

Application for return, removal or prohibition of removal, of child

227.—(1) An application for an order to return a child to, or to ordain a person not to remove a child from, the custody of the applicant under section 29 of the 1978 Act shall be made—

(*a*) in relation to section 27(1) or 28(1) of the 1978 Act, by note in the process of the petition for an adoption order or of the petition for an order under section 49(1) of the 1978 Act;

(*b*) in relation to section 27(2) of the 1978 Act, by note in the process of the petition for an order freeing a child for adoption; and

(*c*) in relation to section 28(3) of the 1978 Act, by petition in the Outer House.

(2) An application for leave—

(*a*) to remove a child under section 27(1) or 28 of the 1978 Act, shall be made by note in the process of the petition for an adoption order or of the petition for an order under section 49(1) of the 1978 Act;

(*b*) to remove a child under section 27(2) of the 1978 Act, shall be made by note in the process of the petition for an order freeing a child for adoption;

(*c*) to give notice under section 30(2) of the 1978 Act (of intention under section 30(1)(*b*)), shall be by note in the process of the petition for an adoption order or of the petition for an order under section 49(1) of the 1978 Act.

(3) Rules 191 to 198 shall apply to a petition or note under this Rule as they apply to a petition except that a petition or note under this Rule shall not be intimated on the walls or in the minute book or advertised.

Application to amend or revoke a direction in, or revoke an, adoption order

228.—(1) An application—

(*a*) to amend, or to revoke a direction in, an adoption order under paragraph 4(1) of Schedule 1 to the 1978 Act; or

(*b*) to revoke an adoption order under section 46(1) of the 1978 Act,

shall be made by petition in the Outer House.

(2) Rules 191 to 198 shall apply to a petition under this Rule as they apply to a petition except that a petition under this Rule shall not be intimated on the walls or in the minute book or advertised.

Registration

229.—On the making of—

(*a*) an adoption order, an amendment to, or a revocation of, an adoption order; or

(*b*) an order under section 49(1) of the 1978 Act,

a certified copy of the order of the court shall be transmitted by the clerk of court to the Registrar General by personal delivery in a sealed envelope marked "confidential".

Miscellaneous provisions

230.—(1) An agreement under section 16(1) or 18(1) of the 1978 Act by a parent or guardian, or a consent under section 12(8) or 18(8) of the 1978 Act by a minor, who is furth of Scotland shall be witnessed—

(*a*) if the agreement or consent is executed in England and Wales or Northern Ireland, by a justice of the peace;

(*b*) if the agreement or consent is executed outside the United Kingdom—

(i) by a British consular officer;

(ii) by a notary public;

(iii) by a person authorised to administer an oath for any judicial or legal purpose in the country in which it is executed; or

(iv) where the person making the agreement or consent is serving in any of Her Majesty's Forces, by an officer holding a commission in any of those forces.

(2) Where a declaration is made by a former parent under section 19(4) of the 1978 Act to the adoption agency in whose favour an order has been made under section 18 of the 1978 Act—

(*a*) the adoption agency shall—

(i) lodge the declaration in process;

(ii) enrol a motion to have the declaration recorded; and

(*b*) the court shall record the declaration by pronouncing an interlocutor recording the fact of that declaration.

(3) An extract of an adoption order or an order under section 49(1) of the 1978 Act shall not be issued except by order of the court on application by petition in the Outer House setting forth the reasons for which the extract is required.

(4) After an order referred to in Rule 229 has been transmitted to the Registrar General or an extract has been issued under paragraph (3) of this rule, the clerk of court or the extractor, as the case may be, shall place the whole process in a sealed envelope marked "confidential" bearing only the name of the petitioner and the name and surname of the child to whom the order relates and the date of the order; and the envelope shall not be opened by or made accessible to any person within 100 years after the date of the adoption order or the order under section 49(1) of the 1978 Act except—

[1] (*a*) to an adopted child who has reached the age of 17 years and to whom the order refers or to a solicitor, local authority or adoption agency authorised in writing by the adopted person to obtain information from the process;

(*b*) by or to the deputy principal clerk of session or the extractor, as the case may be, on the written application to him by an adoption agency with the agreement of the adopted person for the purpose of ascertaining the name of the adoption agency, if any, responsible for placing that person for adoption and informing that person of the name of that adoption agency;

(*c*) by order of the court on application by petition in the Outer House by another court or authority (whether within the United Kingdom or not) having power to authorise an adoption which requests that information be made available from the process for the purpose of discharging its duties in considering an application for adoption;

(*d*) by order of the court on application by petition in the Outer House by a person setting forth the reasons for which access to the process is required; or

(*e*) to a person who is authorised in writing by the Secretary of State to obtain information from the process for the purpose of such research as is designed to improve the working of adoption law and practice.

(5) In any cause to which this section applies, the court may, before determining the application, order—

(*a*) production of further documents (including affidavits); or

(*b*) parole evidence.

(6) Unless the court otherwise directs, in any cause to which this section applies—

(*a*) all documents lodged in process, including a report by an adoption agency, a reporting officer or a curator *ad litem* shall be treated as confidential and open only to the court, the parties, the reporting officer and the curator *ad litem*; and

(*b*) a reporting officer or curator *ad litem* shall regard all information obtained by him in relation to the cause as confidential, and not to be divulged to any person except to a person to whom it may be necessary to do so for the proper execution of his duties.

(7) In any cause to which this section applies, the court may make such order as to liability for expenses, including the expenses of an adoption agency which prepared a report, a reporting officer, a curator *ad litem* and any other person who attends the hearing to determine the application, as it thinks fit and may—

(*a*) modify those expenses; or

(*b*) direct those expenses to be taxed on such scale as it may determine.

(8) Where a reporting officer or a curator *ad litem* is to be appointed by the court, such person shall be appointed from a panel established under the Curators *Ad Litem* and Reporting Officers (Panels) (Scotland) Regulations 1984 except where the court considers, in exceptional circumstances, that it would be appropriate to appoint a person who is not a member of a panel other than an employee of an adoption agency, which is a party to the proceedings, or who has been involved in making any arrangements for the adoption of the child.

NOTE

[1] As amended by S.I. 1987 No. 2160.

Section 4A—Convention Adoption Orders

(Adoption (Scotland) Act 1978)

Interpretation

[1] **230A.**—(1) In this section, unless the context otherwise requires—

(*a*) "the 1978 Act" means the Adoption (Scotland) Act 1978;

"Convention proceedings" means proceedings on an application for a Convention adoption order under section 17, and proceedings under section 47, of the 1978 Act;

"Registrar General" means the Registrar General of Births, Deaths and Marriages for Scotland;

(*b*) Expressions which are used in this section and are also used in the 1978 Act, have the same meaning as in that Act.

(2) Any reference in this section to any enactment shall be construed as a reference to that enactment as amended, extended or applied by any other enactment.

(3) Any reference in this section to the nationality of a person who is not solely a United Kingdom national means that person's nationality as determined in accordance with section 63 of the 1978 Act.

NOTE

[1] Added by S.I. 1978 No. 1373, and as amended by S.I. 1984 No. 997.

Extent and application

[1] **230B.**—(1) This section applies to Convention proceedings.

(2) Subject to paragraph (1), Rules 223, 224(2) and (6), 225, 227, 229 and 230 (except paragraph (2) of that Rule) apply to Convention proceedings as they apply to proceedings in applications under those rules.

NOTE

[1] Added by S.I. 1978 No. 1373, and as amended by S.I. 1984 No. 997.

Applications

[1] **230C.**—(1) All applications for a Convention Adoption Order shall be by way of petition to the Inner House, and shall, subject to the provisions of this rule, be in the form set out in Form 36 with the substitution for any reference to an Adoption Order of a reference to a Convention Adoption Order.

(2) A petitioner in a petition under paragraph (1) shall include averments stating—

(*a*) that he is applying for a Convention Adoption Order;

(*b*) the country of which he is a national;

(*c*) the country of which the child he proposes to adopt is a national;

(*d*) the place where he habitually resides and the country in which it is;

(*e*) the place where the child habitually resides and the country in which it is;

(*f*) whether any country mentioned is a Convention country;

(*g*) whether the child is, or has been, married;

(*h*) in a case where the petitioner is a national of a Convention country, or in a case where both petitioners are nationals of the same Convention country, whether there are specified provisions in respect of that country, and if there are, that the adoption is not prohibited by any such specified provision;

(*i*) in a case where the child is not a United Kingdom national, the provisions, if any, relating to consents and consultations of the internal law relating to adoption of the Convention country of which the child is a national.

(3) (*a*) Those averments shall be fully investigated by the curator *ad litem* and the results of his investigation shall be included in his report.

(*b*) Where in the course of these investigations the curator *ad litem* requires a report from any authority outside Great Britain, he shall request the local authority to request that other authority to provide that report.

(4) The prayer of the petition shall request the court to direct the Registrar-General—

(*a*) to insert the words "Convention Order" in the entry to be made by him in the Adopted Children Register regarding the adoption;

(*b*) to intimate the terms of the order to the authorities mentioned in Rule 230H or 230I, as the case may be.

NOTE
[1] Added by S.I. 1978 No. 1373.

Documentary evidence
[1] **230D.** For the purposes of proceedings in petitions brought under the provisions of this section, written statements (including affidavits) and reports are admissible in place of parole evidence, if the court, on the application of the party proposing to rely on such a statement or report, so directs.

NOTE
[1] Added by S.I. 1978 No. 1373.

Evidence of nationality
[1] **230E.**—(1) Any document which is to be used for the purpose of satisfying the court as to the nationality of a petitioner or of the child shall be lodged together with the petition, or as soon as possible thereafter.

(2) Where a petitioner claims that for the purposes of section 17(2)(*a*), (4)(*a*) or (5)(*a*) of the 1978 Act he or the child is a national of a Convention country, he shall lodge together with the petition or as soon as possible thereafter, a written statement by an expert in the law of that country as to the law of that country relating to the nationality applicable to that person.

NOTE
[1] Added by S.I. 1978 No. 1373, and as amended by S.I. 1984 No. 997.

Evidence of consents, etc.
[1] **230F.**—(1) This rule applies to Convention proceedings in which the child it is proposed to adopt is not a United Kingdom national.

(2) A petitioner shall lodge together with the petition, or as soon as possible thereafter, a written statement by an expert in the law of the country of which the child is a national setting out the consents and consultations (if any) required by that law for the purposes of an adoption, and whether and on what conditions they may be dispensed with, and in the case of consents, the form in which they may be given.

(3) Any document signifying the consent of a person to, or otherwise containing the opinion of a person with respect to the making of, the Convention Adoption Order shall be in a form which complies with the internal law relating to adoption of the Convention country of which the child is a national, but where the court is not satisfied that a person consents with full understanding of what is involved, it may call for further evidence.

(4) A document referred to in paragraph (3) shall, if sufficiently attested, be admissible as evidence of the consent or, as the case may be, of the opinion it contains without further proof of the signature of the person by whom it is executed.

(5) A petitioner in proceedings to which this rule applies, shall, in any case in which a hearing is ordered, serve a notice of hearing in terms of Form 38 upon—

(*a*) all persons whose consent to the making of the order is required and who are not petitioners;

(*b*) all persons who, in accordance with the internal law relating to adoption of the country of which the child is a national, have to be consulted about, but do not have to consent to, the adoption.

(6) For the purposes of section 17(7)(*a*) of the 1978 Act, the proper officer of the court to whom any person whose consent is required under or who is consulted in pursuance of the internal law relating to adoption of the Convention country of which the child is a national may communicate his

opinion on the adoption is the Deputy Principal Clerk of the Court of Session.

NOTE
[1] Added by S.I. 1978 No. 1373, and as amended by S.I. 1984 No. 997.

Dispensing power

[1] **230G.** Where under Rule 230F any consent or consultation is not duly signified to the court as having been given or undertaken, and the court is satisfied that under the internal law of the country concerned that consent or consultation could properly be dispensed with, the court may dispense with that consent or consultation in accordance with the provisions of that law.

NOTE
[1] Added by S.I. 1978 No. 1373.

Notice to Registrar General

[1] **230H.**—(1) The Deputy Principal Clerk shall send to the Registrar General—

(*a*) together with any Convention Adoption Order made under the provisions of this section, a notice specifying and requesting him to inform the authorities mentioned in paragraph 2 of the terms of the order;

(*b*) together with any order made under section 46(2) of the 1978 Act revoking a Convention Adoption Order, a notice specifying and requesting him to inform the authorities mentioned in paragraph 3 of the terms of the order.

(2) The authorities referred to in paragraph (1)(*a*) are the designated authorities of any Convention country—

(*a*) of which the child is a national;
(*b*) in which the child was born;
(*c*) in which a petitioner habitually resides;
(*d*) of which a petitioner is a national.

(3) The authorities referred to in paragraph (1)(*b*) are the designated authorities of any Convention country—

(*a*) of which the adopted person is a national;
(*b*) in which the adopted person was born.

NOTE
[1] Added by S.I. 1978 No. 1373, and as amended by S.I. 1984 No. 997.

Revocation, etc., of regulated adoptions

[1] **230I.**—(1) This rule applies to applications for an order under section 46(2) and 47 of the 1978 Act.

(2) An application shall be made by way of petition to the Inner House.

(3) An application under section 47(1) of the 1978 Act (annulment) shall not, except with the leave of the court, be made later than two years after the date of the regulated adoption to which it relates.

(4) Where the adopted person is under the age of 18 on the date of the presentation of a petition under this rule, the court shall appoint a curator *ad litem* and Rule 224(6) shall apply to the petition as it applies to a petition under that rule.

(5) (*a*) Where the court has ordered that a regulated adoption be annulled or revoked or that an overseas adoption or a determination shall cease to be valid in Great Britain, the Deputy Principal Clerk shall serve notice of the order on the Registrar General, and shall specify in the notice—

(i) the date of the adoption;
(ii) the name and address of the authority which granted the adoption;

(iii) the names of the adopter or adopters and of the adopted person as given in the petition;
(iv) the country in which the adoption was granted;
(v) the country of which the adopted person is a national;
(vi) the country in which the adopted person was born,

and where any country so specified is a Convention country shall request the Registrar General to inform the designated authorities of that country of the terms of the order.

NOTE
[1] Added by S.I. 1978 No. 1373, and as amended by S.I. 1984 No. 997.

Order
[1] **230J.** Where the applicant is a national or both applicants are nationals of a Convention country, the court shall take account of any specified provision (as defined in section 17(8) of the 1978 Act of the internal law of that country before any decision is made to postpone the determination of the application and to make an interim order.

NOTE
[1] Added by S.I. 1978 No. 1373, and as amended by S.I. 1984 No. 997.

Attestation
[1] **230K.** A document shall be sufficiently attested for the purpose of this section if it is attested by any of the following persons:—

(*a*) if it is executed in the United Kingdom—
(i) a justice of the peace; or
(ii) if it is executed in Scotland, a sheriff; or
(iii) if it is executed in England or Wales, an officer of a county court appointed for the purposes of section 87 of the County Courts Act 1959, or a justice's clerk within the meaning of section 21 of the Justices of the Peace Act 1949.

(*b*) if it is executed elsewhere, any person mentioned in Rule 230(1).

NOTE
[1] Added by S.I. 1978 No. 1373, and as amended by S.I. 1984 No. 997.

Translations
[1] **230L.** Where any document is served outside the United Kingdom in a country in which English is not an official language, the petitioner shall provide and send with the document a translation of it in the official language of the country in which service is to be effected or, if there is more

[THE NEXT PAGE IS C 103]

than one official language of the country, in any one of those languages which is appropriate to the place in that country where service is to be effected.

NOTE
[1] Added by S.I. 1978 No. 1373.

SECTION 5—SUMMARY TRIAL

(ADMINISTRATION OF JUSTICE (SCOTLAND) ACT 1933, SECTION 10)

Provision for summary trial of certain causes

231.—(*a*) The parties to any dispute or question desiring to proceed under the provisions of section 10 of the Administration of Justice (Scotland) Act 1933, shall proceed by means of petition presented to the Outer House. The petition shall set forth the dispute or question which has arisen between them, and shall contain a crave that the dispute or question shall be referred to a particular Lord Ordinary for his determination.

(*b*) The petition shall be presented by both the parties to the dispute or question or by all the parties, if more than two, and shall set forth shortly the facts or circumstances on which the dispute or question arises. Where the parties are agreed on the facts, the petition shall set forth concisely the questions which have arisen between them. Where the parties are not agreed on the facts, they shall specify the fact or facts on which they are in dispute and shall set forth or reserve any further questions which may arise when the dispute on fact has been determined.

[1] (*c*) The principal petition shall be signed on behalf of the parties by their respective counsel or a solicitor who has a right of audience in the Court of Session.

[1] (*d*) The petition shall then be put before the Lord Ordinary named in the petition on the earliest available day, but not later than the seventh day after the date of lodging. Where the seventh day expires in vacation or recess, without the petition having been brought before the Lord Ordinary, the petition shall be put before the Lord Ordinary concerned on the first sederunt day of the ensuing session.

[1] (*e*) If, when the petition is first brought before the Lord Ordinary, it appears from the petition that the parties are agreed on the facts, the Lord Ordinary shall direct the cause to be tried before him either in court or in Chambers, on a date not later than six weeks (excluding vacation and recess) from the date of such direction except on cause shown; and if it appears from the petition that the parties are at variance as to the facts, the Lord Ordinary shall appoint a proof to be taken before him either in court or in Chambers.

(*f*) Notwithstanding anything in the foregoing paragraphs it shall be competent for the Lord Ordinary to take any hearing or proof in vacation or recess, but this matter shall be entirely in his discretion.

(*g*) Any evidence led at a proof allowed under paragraph (*e*) of this rule shall not be taken down in shorthand and recorded, unless the parties so agree.

(*h*) If, in the course of the enquiry into a dispute or question, it appears that the determination of the dispute or question may affect the status of any party, the Lord Ordinary shall report the matter to the Lord President, who, if so advised, shall appoint the parties to shew cause, before one or other of the divisions of the court, why the petition should proceed under section 10 of the Act; and the court may, after hearing parties, either direct that the petition shall proceed (subject to such conditions as it may think just), or may dismiss the cause.

(*j*) Except as in this rule provided, the procedure under this rule shall be such as the parties may, with consent of the Lord Ordinary, agree upon; or, failing such agreement, as the Lord Ordinary may order.

(*k*) The Lord Ordinary shall have power to dispose of all questions of expenses; and he may pronounce any decree which he may deem necessary to enable his decision of a dispute or question under this section to be carried into effect. Any such decision by the Lord Ordinary in any proceedings under this rule shall be in the form of an interlocutor which shall be extractable in common form.

(*l*) Any decree or interlocutor of the Lord Ordinary in any proceedings under this rule shall be final and binding only on the parties thereto, and shall not be subject to review by reclaiming or otherwise.

(*m*) In the event of the unavailability, illness, retirement or death of the Lord Ordinary before a dispute or question has been determined, it shall be competent for the parties to apply by joint minute lodged in the process for the cause to be referred to another Lord Ordinary named in the said joint minute, and the cause shall thereupon be transferred to such Lord Ordinary, who shall take up the procedure at the point which had been reached by his predecessor; provided that the Lord Ordinary to whom the cause is so referred may rehear the evidence of all or any of the witnesses heard by his predecessor.

(*n*) It shall be competent to the parties to any cause in dependence in the Outer House not affecting the status of any person, at any stage prior to the hearing of the cause in Procedure Roll, or, where there is no such hearing, prior to the diet of proof or trial, to agree that the cause shall be heard, tried or determined by a particular Lord Ordinary in accordance with the provisions of section 10 of the Act. The agreement of parties to this effect shall be signified by a joint minute in the terms set forth in Form 40. Upon such joint minute being lodged in process, the Lord Ordinary shall pronounce an interlocutor directing that the cause shall proceed before the particular Lord Ordinary named in the joint minute as a cause under section 10 of the Act, and thereafter the provisions of paragraphs (*d*) to (*m*) of this rule shall apply to further procedure in the cause; provided that in paragraph (*d*), the date of such interlocutor shall be substituted for the date of lodging of the petition, and the word "petition" in paragraphs (*d*) and (*e*) shall mean the record or other document containing the pleadings of the parties.

(*o*) For the purposes of section 10 of the Act and the provisions of this rule a dispute or question affecting status shall include any dispute or question which would be the proper subject of, or might depend on, the decision in

[2] (i) an action of divorce, or of nullity of marriage, or of declarator of marriage, or of separation *a mensa et thoro*, or of adherence;
(ii) an action of putting to silence, or of declarator of legitimacy or bastardy;
(iii) an action of aliment not depending on contractual obligation;
(iv) an action for custody of children;
(v) an action of declarator of domicile; or
(vi) an action which raises questions of the capacity of an individual or corporation to act or contract.

NOTES

[11] As amended by S.I. 1991 No. 2483, with effect from 25th November 1991.

[1] Substituted by S.I. 1967 No. 387.

[2] As amended by S.I. 1978 No. 161.

SECTION 6—PETITION BY TRUSTEES FOR DIRECTIONS

(ADMINISTRATION OF JUSTICE (SCOTLAND) ACT 1933, SECTION 17(vi))

Scope of application

232. It shall be competent for the trustees under any trust deed, as defined by the Trusts (Scotland) Act 1921, or for a majority and quorum of them, to make application to the court for direction on questions relating to the investment, distribution, management, or administration of the trust estate under their charge, or as to the exercise of any power vested in, or as to the performances of any duty imposed on, them, notwithstanding that such direction may affect contingent interests in the trust estate whether of persons in existence at, or of persons who may be born after, the date of such direction.

Form of petition and procedure

233.—(*a*) Such application shall be made by petition signed by counsel and presented to the Inner House and lodged in the Petition Department. The petition, after such narrative as may be necessary, shall set forth clearly and succinctly the question or questions upon which the direction of the court is asked and may include in an appendix any relevant documents.

(*b*) The court may order intimation of the petition to creditors, beneficiaries, or other persons interested in the subject matter of the petition; and if any of such parties wish to appear, either in support of, or in opposition to, the petition, they may lodge a minute setting forth their position within such period as the court may direct.

(*c*) The petition shall be disposed of in the summar roll; but the court may order such enquiry by proof before a judge of the Inner House, or by remit to a reporter, or by affidavit, as may be considered necessary.

(*d*) The court shall dispose of all questions of expenses, and any direction pronounced by the court on the petition shall be in the form of an interlocutor which shall be extractable in common form.

(*e*) The provisions of sections 59 and 60 of the Court of Session Act 1868 shall apply to petitions under this section.

Section 7—Petitions for Suspension, Suspension and Interdict, and Suspension and Liberation

Form of petition: lodging of papers

234. The provisions of Rules 191 and 194 shall apply to all petitions for suspension, suspension and interdict, and suspension and liberation; provided that to the narrative or statement of facts there shall be appended a note of the petitioner's pleas-in-law. It shall not be necessary in any such petition as aforesaid to make offer of caution or consignation.

Signature of petition

235. All petitions as aforesaid shall be signed by the petitioner's counsel or solicitor, and no further or other signature shall be required.

Interim orders and intimation

[1] **236.**—(*a*) All petitions as aforesaid shall be presented to the Outer House and shall be brought forthwith by the Deputy Principal Clerk or a clerk instructed by him before a Lord Ordinary, sitting either in court or in Chambers. If any interim order is desired, such clerk shall be accompanied by the petitioner's counsel, or by his solicitor, or by both counsel and solicitor. The Lord Ordinary shall by interlocutor order intimation and answers on such *induciae* as he may fix; and, if moved for, may pronounce such interim orders as may be meet and convenient in the circumstances of the cause, either with or without caution, consignation or other condition, as the Lord Ordinary may see fit. Intimation shall be made by serving a full copy of the petition, along with a copy of the interlocutor, on the respondent.

(*b*) In cases in which any interim order is desired and in which a caveat has been lodged for the respondent, the Principal Clerk shall fix a hearing of parties before a Lord Ordinary so soon as is reasonably practicable and shall intimate the date of the hearing to the parties concerned.

(*c*) After hearing parties on the petition and answers (in the event of answers being lodged under the order referred to in paragraph (*a*) of this rule), or after the hearing, in the event of a caveat having been lodged for the respondent, the Lord Ordinary may make such interim order, or further interim order as may be meet and convenient in the circumstances, either with or without caution, consignation or other condition, or may vary or recall any interim order, as he may see fit.

(*d*) The time allowed for answering a petition shall not begin to run till the date of intimation of the order; and, if the interlocutor ordering intimation shall contain an interim sist of execution, or interim interdict or interim liberation on caution or consignation and caution or consignation shall not have been received by the Deputy Principal Clerk at said date, then the said time shall not begin to run till the date when caution or consignation shall be received; provided that (subject always to the power of the court to prorogate the time for finding caution or making consignation) the petition may be refused if caution shall not be found or consignation made within fourteen days.

(*e*) The Lord Ordinary may refuse the petition in whole or in part, or may declare any interim interdict already granted to be perpetual, or may appoint the cause to the adjustment roll.

(*f*) [Revoked by S.I. 1990 No. 2118.]

NOTE

[1] As amended by S.I. 1984 No. 499.

Petitions for suspension of inferior court decrees in absence under £50

237. All petitions for suspension of decrees pronounced by inferior courts in absence of defenders, in causes under £50 value, shall be remitted by the Lord Ordinary to the inferior court if it be competent, with any instructions which the Lord Ordinary may consider necessary.

Caution: general provisions

238.—(*a*) *Obligations of cautioners.* All bonds of caution in petitions or motions for suspension, suspension and interdict, or suspension and liberation and the like, shall oblige the cautioner, his heirs and executors, for payment of the sums or doing of the deeds for which he has become cautioner to the parties to whom he is bound, as validly and in the same manner as the parties for whom he is cautioner, their heirs and successors, are obliged themselves.

(*b*) *Form of bond of caution.* Every bond of caution, whether in cases of juratory or common caution in the Petition Department, shall be extended by or by direction of the Deputy Principal Clerk in the proper form, and shall contain the necessary clauses adapted to the regulations herein prescribed; and in cases of juratory caution along with the bond the said clerk shall give out a form of the oath to be taken and subscribed by the petitioner and a form of the inventory and enactment thereon.

(*c*) *Sufficiency of caution.* It shall be the duty of the Deputy Principal Clerk in the first instance to consider the sufficiency of the caution offered when the bond of caution is tendered, and for this purpose to request information if this appears to be called for.

(*d*) *Form of Objections.* If the party entitled to the benefit of the caution has objections to state, he shall do so in the form of a letter to the Deputy Principal Clerk specifying the objections.

(*e*) *Procedure in Disposal of Objections.* The Deputy Principal Clerk shall take said objections and any further information which he may have called for into consideration in coming to a decision as to the sufficiency of the caution; alternatively he may in his discretion refer the matter for decision by the court. Where the Deputy Principal Clerk makes a decision as to the sufficiency of the Bond of Caution, any party aggrieved by his decision may bring the matter before the court upon a motion.

[THE NEXT PAGE IS C 107]

(*f*) *Where cautioner insolvent.* In any case in which caution has been or may hereafter be found, it shall be competent to the party entitled to the benefit thereof, in case the cautioner shall have been sequestrated or become notour bankrupt, or have executed a trust disposition for behoof of his creditors, or have called a meeting of his creditors to consider the state of his affairs, or shall have died unrepresented, to present a note, the same being previously intimated in common form, stating the circumstances which have emerged, and praying the court to order new caution to be found; and the court shall pronounce such order thereon as the justice of the case shall require.

Caution in petitions or motions for suspension of decree or charge, suspension and interdict or suspension and liberation and the like

239. In petitions or motions for suspension caution shall be taken not only for obedience to the charge, but also for refunding to the charger such expenses as the court may modify at the discussing of the suspension, suspension and interdict, suspension and liberation and the like.

Juratory caution

240. In cases of petitions for suspension, or for suspension and interdict, or for suspension and liberation and the like being presented on juratory caution, the Lord Ordinary shall, when he appoints the petition to be answered, name a commissioner to take the petitioner's deposition; and the petitioner shall intimate to the opposite party, or his solicitor, to attend at the time and place fixed by the commissioner in order that they may have an opportunity of cross-interrogating him, if they see fit, whether he have any lands in property or liferent, or bonds, bills or contracts containing sums of money; and, in case he acknowledge the same, he shall condescend thereon, and depone that he has no other lands, bonds, bills or contracts containing sums of money belonging to him; and the petitioner shall also lodge with the Deputy Principal Clerk (i) the bond of caution; (ii) a full inventory of his subjects and effects of every kind; (iii) an enactment subjoined to the inventory, bearing that he will not dilapidate any of his property, and that he will not dispose of the same, or uplift any of the debts due to him, without consent of the respondent or his solicitor, or the authority of the judge (under pain of imprisonment, or being otherwise punished as being guilty of fraud), till the petition be discussed, and till there be an opportunity of doing diligence for any expenses that may ultimately be found due by him; and further, the petitioner shall lodge in the hands of the said clerk the vouchers of any debts due to him, and the title deeds of any heritable subject belonging to him, so far as the same be in his possession or within his power; and the petitioner shall also grant a special disposition to the respondent (if so required) of any heritable subject he may be possessed of, and an assignment of all debts or other rights due to him, for the respondent's further security; the said disposition and assignation to be made out at the expense of the respondent, and by his solicitor, and the same with the said vouchers and title deeds, if so deposited, to remain in the hands of the said clerk, subject to the directions of the court, till the petition be discussed; and until all lodgment shall be made it shall not be necessary for the opposite party to give in his answers.

Intimation of production of writs, and certificate of intimation

241. When any paper is lodged by a party prior to the pronouncement of an interlocutor appointing the cause to the adjustment roll or refusing the petition, his solicitor shall give notice in writing on the same day to the solicitor for the other party that such paper is in the clerk's hands; and a certificate of such intimation shall be lodged in the Petition Department, otherwise the said paper shall not be laid before the Lord Ordinary who is to advise the petition.

Petition for suspension of decree of inferior court

242.—(*a*) *Production of process.* In all cases in which the Lord Ordinary shall think it expedient, before appointing the cause to the adjustment roll or refusing a petition to which it is competent to appoint answers to be made, to order production of the proceedings in the inferior court brought under his review, the petitioner shall, within such time as the Lord Ordinary may direct, produce to the clerk of the inferior court a certified copy of the interlocutor ordering such production. Should the petitioner fail to do so, the petition shall be refused and expenses be found due. On production to the clerk of any inferior court of a copy duly certified by or under the direction of the Deputy Principal Clerk of an interlocutor of the Lord Ordinary ordering the process before such court to be produced, such clerk shall be bound to transmit the whole steps of process, conform to inventory, to the Deputy Principal Clerk.

(*b*) *Interlocutor refusing suspension after proof in inferior court.* The Lord Ordinary, when he refuses a petition for suspension of a judgment of an inferior court proceeding on a proof, shall, on reviewing such judgment, distinctly specify in his interlocutor the several facts material to the case which he finds to be established by the proof, and express how far his judgment proceeds on the matter of fact as found, or on the matter of law, and the several points of law which he means to decide.

When petition refused on failure to find caution, or to comply with conditions

243. When any petition for suspension, or for suspension and interdict, or for suspension and liberation, shall (during either session or vacation) be refused, in respect that caution has not been found, or consignation made, or upon any ground not on the merits; and likewise when any such petition shall by interlocutor have been appointed to the adjustment roll and a certificate of no caution or consignation, or of other failure to implement any condition of such interlocutor, has been issued, it shall be competent, on payment of previous expenses, to present a second petition, the procedure upon which shall be the same as is provided with regard to petitions for suspension, suspension and interdict, or suspension and liberation, as the case may be.

Certificate of refusal of petition

244. In all petitions for suspension and interdict or for suspension and liberation, when refused, the certificate of refusal shall not be issued till forty-eight hours after the entry of the refusal in the minute book.

When interlocutor appointing the cause to the adjustment roll

245.—(*a*) When a petition for suspension, suspension and interdict, or suspension and liberation, is appointed by interlocutor to the adjustment roll in cases in which caution is to be found or consignation to be made, or conditions to be implemented, such interlocutor shall not take effect until caution has been found or consignation made or the conditions implemented.

(*b*) When a petition for suspension, or for suspension and interdict, or for suspension and liberation, has been appointed to the adjustment roll on caution or consignation, or on any condition requiring to be implemented before the interlocutor takes effect, the opposite party shall not be entitled to a certificate of no caution or consignation, or other failure to implement such condition, without intimating to the party that he is to apply to the Deputy Principal Clerk for such certificate; and the Deputy Principal Clerk shall not give out the certificate until the expiry of twenty-four hours after such intimation.

Final judgment in certain cases

246. Where a petition for suspension, suspension and interdict, or suspension and liberation, has been lodged, and no appearance has been entered, and no answers have been lodged, the Lord Ordinary shall have power to pronounce a final judgment, in whole or in part, granting the prayer of the petition, suspending the charge, sisting execution or declaring the interim interdict to be perpetual, or the interim liberation to be final; and the Lord Ordinary shall have power to award expenses against the respondent and to decern for the taxed amount thereof.

Procedure after the cause has been appointed to the adjustment roll

247. Not later than seven days after the day on which (1) the Lord Ordinary's interlocutor appointing the cause to the adjustment roll has been pronounced and (2) caution or consignation, if ordered, has been found or made, or the conditions defined in such interlocutor have been implemented, the petitioner shall deliver at least six copies of the open record, consisting of the petition and answers, to the solicitor of the respondent or to each of the solicitors of the respondents, if more than one, and shall also lodge two copies in the office of the Petition Department; the case shall then appear in the adjustment roll as provided in paragraph (*c*) of Rule 90, and the proceedings shall thereafter be the same as in an ordinary action.

[1] SECTION 8—PETITIONS UNDER THE ADMINISTRATION OF JUSTICE ACT 1920, SECTIONS 9 AND 10, AND THE FOREIGN JUDGMENTS (RECIPROCAL ENFORCEMENT) ACT 1933 AND THE ARBITRATION (INTERNATIONAL INVESTMENT DISPUTES) ACT 1966

NOTE

[1] As amended by S.I. 1971 No. 1809.

Petitions under the Administration of Justice Act 1920, sections 9 and 10

[1] **248.**—(*a*) An application to the Court of Session under section 9 of the above-mentioned Act, for enforcement of judgments obtained in superior courts in any part of Her Majesty's Dominions outside the United Kingdom, to which Part II of the above-mentioned Act extends, shall be made by petition to the Outer House. The petition shall specify the full name, title, trade or business, and usual or last known place of abode of the judgment creditor and judgment debtor respectively. There shall be produced with the petition the judgment or a certified copy thereof.

(*b*) The Lord Ordinary, on being satisfied by affidavit or otherwise that the application falls within the requirements of the statute, and that the judgment which it is sought to be registered is not a judgment to which section 5 of the Protection of Trading Interests Act 1980 applies, may grant warrant for the registration of the judgment.

(*c*) The warrant for registration shall specify a date before which the judgment debtor is to be entitled to apply to the Lord Ordinary to set aside the registration. In fixing the said date regard shall be had to the place of residence of the judgment debtor.

[2] (*d*) Upon presentation by the petitioner of a certified copy of the warrant for registration to the Keeper of the Registers of Scotland, along with the judgment or certified copy judgment, the Keeper shall immediately register the same in the Register of Judgments in the Books of the Lords of Council and Session. Extract of the registered judgment shall be superseded until a certificate is granted by the Deputy Principal Clerk in terms of paragraph (*f*) of this rule.

[2] (*e*) Notice of the registration shall immediately be intimated by the petitioner to the judgment debtor in the following or similar terms:—

"I hereby give you notice that a judgment (*specifying name*) has been registered in the Register of Judgments in the Books of the Lords of Council and Session, and that if you intend to apply to have the registration set aside you must do so before (*specify date*),"

or in such other terms, and in such manner, as the court may direct.

The execution of such intimation shall be lodged in process.

(*f*) If no application is made within the specified time to have the registration set aside, or if such an application has been made and refused, the Deputy Principal Clerk shall grant a certificate to that effect. Extract of the registered judgment may thereafter be issued. The warrant for diligence shall be in common form, and shall be executed upon a charge of fifteen days, or such other period as the Lord Ordinary may fix.

(*g*) If the application to have the registration set aside is granted, a certificate to that effect by the Deputy Principal Clerk shall be a sufficient warrant to the Keeper of the Registers of Scotland to cancel the registration and return the judgment to the creditor or his solicitor.

(*h*) An application to the court under section 10 of the Act for a certified copy of a judgment obtained in the Court of Session for enforcement in some part of Her Majesty's Dominions outside the United Kingdom shall be made by petition to the Outer House. There shall be lodged with the petition an extract decree setting forth the judgment. The court, on being satisfied by affidavit or other proper evidence that the judgment debtor is resident in some part of Her Majesty's Dominions outside the United Kingdom to which Part II of the Act extends, shall pronounce an order ordaining the Deputy Principal Clerk to issue a certified copy of the judgment under the seal of the court.

The Certificate shall be in the following terms:—

"I certify that the foregoing extract decree is a true copy of a judgment obtained in the Court of Session, and this certificate is issued in accordance with section 10 of the Administration of Justice Act 1920, and in obedience to an order by Lord dated

(*Signed*) Deputy Principal Clerk of the Court of Session at Edinburgh."

NOTES

[1] As amended by S.I. 1980 No. 891.

[2] As amended by S.I. 1986 No. 1941.

Petitions under the Foreign Judgments (Reciprocal Enforcement) Act 1933

[1] **249.**—1. An application under section 2 of the Foreign Judgments (Reciprocal Enforcement) Act 1933 (hereinafter called "the Act"), to have a foreign judgment to which Part I of the Act applies registered in the Books of the Lords of Council and Session may be made by petition to the Outer House.

2. (1) An application for registration shall be supported by an affidavit of the facts—

(*a*) exhibiting a certified copy of the judgment issued by the original court and authenticated by its seal and a translation of the judgment certified by a Notary Public or authenticated by affidavit.

(*b*) stating to the best of the information and belief of the deponent—

(i) that the applicant is entitled to enforce the judgment;

(ii) as the case may require, either that at the date of the application the judgment has not been satisfied, or, if the judgment has been satisfied in part, what the amount is in respect of which it remains unsatisfied;

(iii) that at the date of the application the judgment can be enforced by execution in the country of the original court;

(iv) that if the judgment were registered, the registration would not be, or be liable to be, set aside under section 4 of the Act;

(v) that the judgment is not a judgment to which section 5 of the Protection of Trading Interests Act 1980 applies.

(*c*) specifying the amount of the interest, if any, which under the law of the country of the original court has become due under the judgment up to the time of registration;

and shall be accompanied by such other evidence with respect to the matters referred to in sub-paragraph (iii) of paragraph (*b*) or paragraph (*c*) above as may be required having regard to the provisions of the Order in Council extending the Act to the country of the original court.

(2) Where the sum payable under the judgment is expressed in a currency other than the currency of the United Kingdom, the affidavit shall also state the amount which that sum represents in the currency of the United Kingdom calculated at the rate of exchange prevailing at the date of the judgment.

(3) The affidavit shall also state the full name, title, trade or business and the usual or last known place of abode or of business of the judgment creditor and the judgment debtor respectively, so far as known to the deponent.

(4) Where a judgment is in respect of different matters, and some, but not all, of the provisions of the judgment are such that if those provisions had been contained in separate judgments, those judgments could properly have been registered, the affidavit shall state the provisions in respect of which it is sought to register the judgment.

3. Save as otherwise provided by any relevant Order in Council, the court may, in respect to an application for registration, order the judgment creditor to find security for the expenses of the application and of any proceedings which may thereafter be brought to set aside the registration.

4. The affidavit, if any, shall be intituled:—

"In the matter of the Foreign Judgments (Reciprocal Enforcement) Act 1933, and in the matter of a judgment of the (*describing the Court*) obtained in (*describing the cause or matter*) and dated the day of , 19 ."

5. (1) The court on being satisfied that the application falls within the requirements of the Act may grant warrant for the registration of the judgment.

(2) Every order granting warrant as aforesaid shall state the period within which after service of the notice of registration as aftermentioned an application may be made to set aside the registration.

(3) In fixing the period within which application may be made to set aside the registration, the court shall have regard in the case of a judgment debtor furth of Scotland to the periods for superseding extract of a decree in absence laid down in paragraph (*b*) of Rule 89.

(4) The court may, on an application made at any time while it remains competent for any party to apply to have the registration set aside, grant an extension of the period (either as originally fixed or as subsequently extended) during which an application to have the judgment set aside may be made.

6. There shall be kept in the Petition Department of the court by, or under the direction of, the Deputy Principal Clerk, a register of the judgments ordered to be registered under the Act.

[1] 7. Upon presentation by the petitioner of a certified copy of the warrant for registration to the Keeper of the Registers of Scotland, along with the judgment or certified copy judgment, the Keeper shall immediately register the same in the Register of Judgments in the Books of the Lords of Council and Session. Extract of the registered judgment shall be superseded until a certificate is granted by the Deputy Principal Clerk in terms of paragraph 11 of this Rule.

8. (1) Notice in writing of the registration of a judgment must be served by the petitioner on the judgment debtor—

(*a*) if within Scotland by personal service unless some other mode of service is ordered by the court;
(*b*) if furth of Scotland by edictal citation in accordance with Rule 75.

(2) The notice of registration shall state—

(*a*) full particulars of the judgment registered and the order for registration;
(*b*) the name and address of the judgment creditor or of his solicitor;
(*c*) the right of the judgment debtor to apply on the grounds provided in the Act to have the registration set aside; and
(*d*) in accordance with the terms of the order giving leave to register, within what time from the date of service of the notice an application to set aside may be made:

and subject to these requirements shall be as near as may be in the form laid down in paragraph (*e*) of Rule 248.

A certificate of execution of the notice of registration shall be lodged in process, and if a certificate is not so lodged, the judgment creditor shall not be at liberty to do diligence on the judgment without leave of the court.

9. (1) An application to set aside the registration of judgment shall be made by Petition to the Outer House in ordinary form supported by affidavit.

(2) On any such application the court may order such enquiry as may be necessary.

10. (1) A registered judgment shall not be extracted until after the expiration of the period which, in accordance with the provisions of paragraph 5(3) of this Rule, is specified in the order giving leave to register as the period within which an application may be made to set aside the registration or, if an order is made extending the period so specified, until after the expiration of the extended period.

(2) If an application is made to set aside the registration of a judgment, the judgment shall not be extracted until such application has been disposed of.

11. If no application is made within the specified time to have the registration set aside, or if such an application has been made and refused, the Deputy Principal Clerk shall grant a certificate to that effect. Extract of the registered judgment may thereafter be issued. The warrant for diligence shall be in common form, and shall be executed upon a charge of fifteen days or such other period as the Lord Ordinary may fix.

12. If any question arises whether a foreign judgment can be enforced by execution in the country of the original court, or what interest is payable under the foreign judgment under the law of that country, that question shall be determined in accordance with such provisions, if any, in that behalf, as are contained in the Order in Council extending the Act to that country.

13. (1) An application under section 10 of the Act for a certified copy of a judgment obtained in the Court of Session shall be made by petition to the Outer House. There shall be lodged with the Petition an extract decree setting forth the judgment. The court on being satisfied by affidavit or other evidence, that the requirements of the Act have been satisfied shall pronounce an order ordaining the Deputy Principal Clerk to issue a certified copy of the judgment. The certificate shall be under the seal of the Court and shall be in the following terms:—

"I certify that the foregoing extract decree is a true copy of a judgment obtained in the Court of Session and this certificate is issued in accordance with section 10 of the Foreign Judgments (Reciprocal Enforcement) Act 1933, and in obedience to an order by Lord
dated

"(Signed)
"Deputy Principal Clerk of the Court of Session at Edinburgh."

NOTE
[1] As amended by S.I. 1986 No. 1941.

(2) There shall be issued along with the foregoing certificate the following further certificate also under the seal of the court and certified by the Deputy Principal Clerk—

A certificate enumerating and identifying and having annexed to it copies of the summons or petition by which the proceedings were instituted, shewing the manner in which the summons or petition was served on the defender or respondent and whether the defender or respondent appeared thereto, and the objections made to the jurisdiction, if any, the pleadings, if any, in the proceedings, a copy of the opinions, if any, of the judge or judges who took part in the judgment, a statement that the time limit for appeal has expired and that no appeal has been taken, or that an appeal was taken but was refused, and such other particulars as it may be necessary to give to the foreign tribunal in which it is sought to obtain execution of the judgment. Copies of the foregoing documents shall be supplied where necessary by the solicitor of the person making the application.

14. These Rules shall, in relation to any judgment, have effect subject to any such provisions contained in the Order in Council extending the Act to the country of the original court as are declared by the Order in Council to be necessary for giving effect to the agreement made between Her Majesty and that country in relation to matters for which provision is made by these Rules.

NOTE

[1] As amended by S.I. 1980 No. 891.

Registration of Awards under the Arbitration (International Investment Disputes) Act 1966

[1] **249A.**—1. In this Rule—"The Act of 1966" means the Arbitration (International Investment Disputes) Act 1966; "award" means an award rendered pursuant to the Convention; "the Convention" means the Convention referred to in section 1(1) of the Act of 1966.

2. An application to have an award registered in the Books of the Lords of Council and Session shall be made by petition to the Outer House.

3. An application for registration shall be supported by an affidavit of the fact—

(*a*) exhibiting a copy of the award certified pursuant to the Convention;

(*b*) stating the full name, title, trade or business and the usual or (where appropriate) the last known place of abode or of business of the person seeking recognition of the award and of the other party to the investment dispute respectively, so far as known to the deponent; and

(*c*) stating to the best of the information and belief of the deponent—

(i) that the applicant is entitled to enforce the award;

(ii) as the case may require, either that at the date of the application the pecuniary obligations imposed by the award have not been satisfied, or, if the award has been satisfied in part, what the amount is in respect of which it remains unsatisfied;

(iii) whether at the date of the application the enforcement of the award has been sisted (provisionally or otherwise) pursuant to the Convention and whether any, and if so what, application has been made pursuant to the Convention which, if granted, might result in a sist of enforcement of the award.

4. Where the pecuniary obligations imposed by the award are expressed in a currency other than the currency of the United Kingdom, the affidavit shall also state the amount which that sum represents in the currency of the United Kingdom calculated at the rate of exchange prevailing at the date of the award.

[THE NEXT PAGE IS C 113]

5. The court on being satisfied that the application falls within the requirements of the Act of 1966 may grant warrant for the registration of the award.

6. There shall be kept in the Petition Department of the court, by or under the direction of the Deputy Principal Clerk, a register of the awards ordered to be registered under the Act of 1966.

7.—(1) Notice in writing of the registration of the award shall be served by the petitioner on the other party to the investment dispute—

(*a*) if within Scotland, by personal service unless some other mode of service is ordered by the court;

(*b*) if furth of Scotland, by edictal citation in accordance with Rule 75.

(2) The notice of registration shall state—

(*a*) full particulars of the award registered and the order for registration;

(*b*) the name and address of the person seeking recognition or enforcement of the award or of his solicitor.

(3) A certificate of execution of the notice of registration shall be lodged in process; and if a certificate is not so lodged, an extract of the registered award shall not be issued, and diligence on the award shall not be done, without leave of the court. The warrant for diligence shall be in common form, and shall be executed upon a charge of fifteen days or such other period as the Lord Ordinary may fix.

8. Where it appears to the court on granting leave to register an award, or on an application made by the other party to the investment dispute after an award has been registered—

(*a*) that the enforcement of the award has been sisted (whether provisionally or otherwise) pursuant to the Convention, or

(*b*) that an application has been made pursuant to the Convention which, if granted, might result in a sist of the enforcement of the award,

the court shall, or in the case referred to in sub-paragraph (*b*), may, sist execution of the award for such time as it considers appropriate in the circumstances.

9. An application under paragraph 8 of this Rule by the other party to the investment dispute shall be made by petition to the Outer House and supported by an affidavit of the facts.

NOTE

[1] Added by S.I. 1971 No. 1809.

[1] Section 8A

Registration of awards under the Multilateral Investment Guarantee Agency Act 1988

249AA. Paragraphs 2, 3 and 5 to 9 of rule 249A shall apply, with the necessary modifications, to an award rendered under Article 4 of Annexe II to the convention referred to in section 1(1) of the Multilateral Investment Guarantee Agency Act 1988 as they apply to an award rendered under the convention referred to in section 1(1) of the Arbitration (International Investment Disputes) Act 1966.

NOTE

[1] Inserted by S.I. 1990 No. 705.

[1] Section 8AA

Registration and Enforcement of Arbitral Awards Under Article 35 of the Model Law on International Commercial Arbitration

NOTE

[1] Inserted by S.I. 1991 No. 2213.

Application for registration

249AB.—(1) An application for registration in the Books of Council and Session for enforcement of an arbitral award under article 35 of Schedule 7 to the Law Reform (Miscellaneous Provisions) (Scotland) Act 1990 (in this Section referred to as "the Act of 1990") shall be made by petition presented in the Outer House.

(2) A petition under paragraph (1) shall set out the reasons for which registration for enforcement is sought.

(3) A motion to grant the prayer of a petition in which no answers have been lodged shall not require an appearance for the petitioner unless the court so requires.

(4) Where the court requires an appearance under paragraph (3), the hearing shall be in chambers.

Registration

249AC.—(1) The court, on being satisfied that the arbitral award may be registered, shall grant decree and warrant for registration in the Books of Council and Session.

(2) On decree being granted under paragraph (1), the Deputy Principal Clerk shall enter the decree in a register of arbitral awards to be registered under article 35 of Schedule 7 to the Act of 1990.

(3) Upon presentation by the petitioner to the Keeper of the Registers of—

(*a*) a certified copy interlocutor of the decree and warrant for registration; and

(*b*) a certified copy of the arbitral award to be registered, and, where the arbitral award is in a language other than English, a translation into English certified by a person qualified to do it, the same shall be registered in the Books of Council and Session in the Register of Judgments whereupon the Keeper of the Registers shall issue an extract of the registered recommendation, determination or award, as the case may be, with warrant for execution.

[1] SECTION 8B

REGISTRATION FOR ENFORCEMENT OF RECOMMENDATIONS, DETERMINATIONS AND AWARDS UNDER SECTION 9 OF THE MERCHANT SHIPPING (LINER CONFERENCES) ACT 1982

NOTE

[1] Inserted by S.I. 1986 No. 799.

Application for registration

249B.—(1) An application for registration for enforcement of a recommendation, determination or award under section 9 of the Merchant Shipping (Liner Conferences) Act 1982 (in this section referred to as "the Act of 1982") shall be made by petition presented to the Outer House.

(2) Rules 192 and 195 to 197 shall not apply to a petition under this section.

(3) A petition under paragraph (1) shall—

(*a*) set forth the reasons for which registration for enforcement is sought; and

(*b*) state, if it is the case, that the recommendation is not unenforceable under section 9(2) of the Act of 1982.

(4) In a petition for registration for enforcement of a recommendation, there shall be produced with the petition—

(*a*) a certified copy of the recommendation, the reasons therefor and the record of settlement;

(*b*) where the recommendation, the reasons or the record of settlement are in a language other than English, a translation into English certified by a person qualified to do it; and

(*c*) a copy of the acceptance of the recommendation by the parties upon whom it is binding.

(5) In a petition for registration for enforcement of a determination or award of costs, there shall be produced with the petition a certified copy of the determination or award.

(6) The motion to grant the prayer of the petition shall be dealt with in the Outer House by a Lord Ordinary and shall not require an appearance for the petitioner unless the court so requires.

(7) Where the court requires an appearance under paragraph (6), the hearing shall be in chambers.

Registration

249C.—(1) The court, on being satisfied that the recommendation, determination or award may be registered, shall grant decree and warrant for registration in the Books of Council and Session.

(2) On decree being granted under paragraph (1)—

(*a*) the deputy principal clerk shall enter the decree in a register of recommendations, determinations and awards to be registered under section 9 of the Act of 1982; and

(*b*) the petitioner shall intimate the decree and warrant for registration of the recommendation, determination or award to the party against whom it may be enforced.

(3) Upon presentation by the petitioner to the Keeper of the Registers of—

(*a*) a certified copy interlocutor of the decree and warrant for registration; and

(*b*) a certified copy of the recommendation, determination or award to be registered, and, where the recommendation, determination or award is in a language other than English, a translation into English certified by a person qualified to do it,

the same shall be registered in the Books of Council and Session in the Register of Judgments whereupon the Keeper of the Registers shall issue an extract of the registered recommendation, determination or award with warrant for execution.

[1] SECTION 8C

Recognition and Enforcement of Judgments under the Civil Jurisdiction and Judgments Act 1982

NOTE

[1] Added by S.I. 1986 No. 1941.

Interpretation

249D.—(1) In this section—

"the Act of 1982" means the Civil Jurisdiction and Judgments Act 1982;

"domicile" is to be determined in accordance with the provisions of sections 41 to 46 of, and articles 52 and 53 of Schedule 1 to, the Act of 1982;

"Keeper of the Registers" means the Keeper of the Registers of Scotland;

"protective measures" include arrestment, inhibition, poinding or interim interdict.

(2) Words and expressions which are used in this section and are used in the Act of 1982 have the same meaning as in that Act, unless the context otherwise requires.

(3) In this section a form referred to by number means the form so numbered in the Appendix to the Rules or a form substantially to the like effect, with such variation as circumstances may require.

Application for registration

249E.—(1) An application for registration of a judgment under section 4 of the Act of 1982 shall be—

(*a*) made *ex parte* in Form 53; and

(*b*) signed by—

(i) the applicant;

[1] (ii) a solicitor; or

(iii) an advocate.

(2) There shall be produced with the application—

(*a*) the following documents—

(i) a certified copy of the judgment to be registered;

(ii) a document which establishes that, according to the law of the country in which the judgment has been given, the judgment is enforceable and has been served;

(iii) where judgment has been given in absence (that is to say, in default of appearance), the original or a certified copy of the document which establishes that the party against whom judgment was given in absence was served with the document initiating the proceedings or with an equivalent document;

(iv) where appropriate, a document showing that the applicant is in receipt of legal aid in the country in which the judgment was given;

(v) where the judgment or any other document produced is in a language other than English, a translation into English certified by a person qualified as a translator;

(*b*) an affidavit stating—

(i) whether the judgment provides for the payment of a sum of money;

(ii) whether interest is recoverable on the judgment in accordance with the law of the country in which judgment was given, and if so, the rate of interest, the date from which interest is due and the date on which interest ceases to accrue; and

(iii) where appropriate, the sterling equivalent at the relevant rate of exchange of the amount of money expressed in a foreign currency which is recoverable by the applicant;

(iv) an address within the jurisdiction of the court for service on the applicant;

(v) so far as known to the deponent, the usual or last known address or place of business of the person against whom the judgment was given;

(vi) to the knowledge and belief of the deponent, the grounds on which the applicant is entitled to enforce the judgment; and

(vii) whether at the date of the application the judgment has not been satisfied or the part or amount in respect of which it is unsatisfied.

(3) Where the applicant does not produce the documents required under paragraph (2)(*a*), the court may—

(*a*) fix a time within which the documents are to be lodged in process;

(*b*) accept equivalent documents; or

(*c*) dispense with the requirement to produce the documents.

NOTE

[1] As amended by S.I. 1991 No. 2483, with effect from 25th November 1991.

Hearing of application

249F.—(1) The application shall be dealt with in the Outer House by a Lord Ordinary and shall not require an appearance for the applicant unless the court so requires.

(2) Where the court requires an appearance, the hearing shall be in chambers.

Warrant for registration

249G.—(1) The court shall, on being satisfied that the application meets the requirements of the Act of 1982, grant warrant for the registration of the judgment and—

(*a*) grant decree in terms of the judgment to be registered; or

(*b*) where necessary, grant decree in accordance with Scots law.

(2) The interlocutor granting decree and warrant under paragraph (1) shall—

(*a*) state the period within which the interlocutor may be appealed against; and

(*b*) give notice that the applicant may extract the decree and proceed to do diligence in execution, save that—

(i) no action of furthcoming following upon an arrestment;

(ii) no sale following upon a poinding; and

(iii) no adjudication following upon an inhibition,

shall be competent until the expiry of the period of lodging an appeal and any appeal has been disposed of.

(3) The applicant may apply to the court at any time in the process of the application under Rule 249E(1) for protective measures until the expiry of the period for lodging an appeal and any appeal has been disposed of.

(4) Any diligence in execution or other protective measures shall be of no effect unless intimation of the decree and warrant for registration under Rule 249J(1) is made within 21 days from the date or execution of the diligence or other protective measures.

Intimation to applicant

249H. The court shall, on granting or refusing the application to register a judgment under Rule 249E(1), intimate the decision to the applicant by sending him a copy of the interlocutor in a registered or recorded delivery letter to the address for service in Scotland of the applicant.

Registration

249I.—(1) Where the court grants decree and warrant for registration of a judgment, the deputy principal clerk shall enter the decree in a register of judgments to be registered under the Act of 1982.

(2) Upon presentation by the applicant to the Keeper of the Registers of—

(*a*) a certified copy of the decree and warrant for registration; and

(*b*) a certified copy of the judgment to be registered, and, where the judgment is in a language other than English, a translation into English certified by a person qualified as a translator,

the same shall be registered in the Books of Council and Session in a register called the Register of Judgments whereupon the Keeper of the Registers shall issue an extract of the registered judgment with warrant for execution.

Intimation of registration

249J.—(1) Intimation of the decree and warrant for registration of a judgment shall be made by the applicant to the person against whom judgment was given and decree and warrant for registration granted, by serving a notice in Form 54.

(2) Service of intimation under paragraph (1) shall be made in accordance with Rule 74A, 74B or 75 as the case may be.

Appeals

249K.—(1) An appeal under Article 37 of Schedule 1 to the Act of 1982 by a person against whom judgment was given and decree and warrant for registration granted shall be made to the Outer House in Form 42.

(2) An appeal under Article 40 of Schedule 1 to the Act of 1982 by an applicant against a refusal to grant decree and warrant for registration of a judgment shall be made to the Outer House in Form 42.

(3) Subject to paragraphs (4) and (5) of this rule, Rule 290 shall apply to an appeal under paragraph (1) or (2) of this rule as it applies to an appeal under that Rule.

(4) Where the respondent is domiciled furth of the United Kingdom—

(*a*) in relation to an appeal under paragraph (1) of this Rule, intimation required by paragraph (*f*) of Rule 290 shall be made to the address for service of the respondent in Scotland;

(*b*) in relation to an appeal under paragraph (2) of this rule, intimation required by paragraph (*f*) of Rule 290 shall be made in accordance with Rule 74B or 75 as the case may be.

(5) An appeal under paragraph (1) or (2) shall be made—

(*a*) in the case of an appeal under paragraph (1), within one month of intimation of the decree and warrant for registration of the judgment, or within two months of intimation of such decree and warrant where intimation was made on a person domiciled in another Contracting State;

(*b*) in the case of an appeal under paragraph (2), within one month of the interlocutor refusing the application under Rule 249E(1).

(6) Where an appeal under paragraph (1) is successful, the court shall, on the motion of the appellant, pronounce an interlocutor recalling any protective measure.

Reclaiming

249L.—(1) Any party dissatisfied with the interlocutor of the Lord Ordinary in an appeal under Rule 249K on a point of law may reclaim against that interlocutor by a motion for review by the Inner House in accordance with Rules 262 to 264.

(2) Where a reclaiming motion under paragraph (1) against the registration of a judgment is successful, the court shall, on the motion of the appellant, pronounce an interlocutor recalling any protective measure.

Application for recognition

249M.—(1) For the purposes of the second paragraph of Article 26 of Schedule 1 to the Act of 1982, the registration of a judgment under the foregoing rules of this section shall be a decision also that the judgment is recognised.

(2) Where an application is made for recognition of a judgment under Article 26 of Schedule 1 to the Act of 1982, the foregoing rules of this section shall apply to such an application as they apply to an application for registration under section 4 of the Act of 1982, except that—

(*a*) it shall not be necessary to produce any documents required by Rule 249E(2)(*a*)(ii) or (iv); and

(*b*) [Rule] 249I(2) shall not apply.

Enforcement of Court of Session decree or writ registered in the Books of Council and Session in another Contracting State

249N.—(1) Where a person seeks to enforce a decree or other interlocutor of the Court of Session under section 12 of the Act of 1982 in another Contracting State he shall apply in writing to the deputy principal clerk for—

(*a*) a certificate in Form 55;

(*b*) a certified copy interlocutor; and
(*c*) if required, a certified copy of the opinion of the court.

(2) A certificate shall not be issued under paragraph (1)(*a*) unless there is produced an execution of service of the decree or other interlocutor on the person upon whom it is sought to be enforced in accordance with Rule 74A, 74B or 75 as the case may be.

(3) Where a person seeks to enforce a writ registered for execution in the Books of Council and Session under article 50 of Schedule 1 to the Act of 1982 he shall apply in writing to the Keeper of the Registers for a certificate in Form 59 and produce—

(*a*) an extract of the writ in respect of which the certificate is sought; and
(*b*) an affidavit verifying that enforcement has not been suspended and that the time available for enforcement has not expired.

Enforcement of United Kingdom judgments in other parts of the United Kingdom (Money provisions)

249P.—(1) Where a person seeks to enforce a money provision in a judgment of the Court of Session under section 18 of, and Schedule 6 to, the Act of 1982, or in a writ registered in the Books of Council and Session under article 50 of Schedule 1 to the Act of 1982, in another part of the United Kingdom he shall apply in writing—

(i) in the case of a decree or other interlocutor, to the deputy principal clerk for a certificate in Form 56; or
(ii) in the case of a writ registered for execution in the Books of Council and Session, to the Keeper of the Registers for a certificate in Form 60 together with an extract of the writ for which a certificate is sought,

and produce an affidavit—

(*a*) in the case of an application to the deputy principal clerk, stating the sum or aggregate of the sums, including expenses, payable and unsatisfied;
(*b*) verifying that the time for enrolling a reclaiming motion or appeal has expired without a reclaiming motion or appeal having been enrolled, or, a reclaiming motion or appeal having been enrolled, that such motion or appeal has been finally disposed of; and that enforcement of the judgment has not been suspended and the time available for its enforcement has not expired; and
(*c*) stating the address of the party entitled to enforce, and the usual or last known address of the party liable to execution on, the judgment.

(2) An application for registration in the Court of Session of a certificate in relation to a money provision in a judgment from another part of the United Kingdom under section 18 of, and Schedule 6 to, the Act of 1982 shall be made within six months from the date of issue of the certificate by producing to the Keeper of the Registers a certificate in the appropriate form prescribed by the original court under paragraph 4(1) of Schedule 6 to the Act of 1982.

(3) Upon presentation by the applicant of the certificate under paragraph (2), the Keeper of the Registers shall—

(*a*) register the certificate in the Register of Judgments of the Books of Council and Session; and
(*b*) issue an extract of the certificate with warrant for execution.

(4) An application—

(*a*) under paragraph 9 of Schedule 6 to the Act of 1982 to sist proceedings for enforcement of a certificate registered under paragraph (3) of this rule; or
(*b*) under paragraph 10 of Schedule 6 to the Act of 1982 to reduce the registration of a certificate under paragraph (3) of this Rule.

shall be made by petition to the Outer House, and Rules 191 to 198 shall apply.

Enforcement of United Kingdom judgments in other parts of the United Kingdom (Non-money provisions)

249Q.—(1) Where a person seeks to enforce a non-money provision in a judgment of the Court of Session under section 18 of, and Schedule 7 to, the Act of 1982 in another part of the United Kingdom, he shall apply in writing—

(i) in the case of decree or interlocutor, to the deputy principal clerk for a certified copy interlocutor and, if necessary, a certified copy of the opinion of the court;

(ii) in the case of a writ registered for execution in the Books of Council and Session, to the Keeper of the Registers for a certificate in Form 61, together with an extract of the writ for which a certificate is sought,

and produce an affidavit—

(*a*) verifying that the time for enrolling a reclaiming motion or appeal has expired without a reclaiming motion or appeal having been enrolled, or, a reclaiming motion or appeal having been enrolled, that such motion or appeal has been finally disposed of; and that enforcement of the judgment has not been suspended and the time available for its enforcement has not expired; and

(*b*) stating the address of the party entitled to enforce, and the usual or last known address of the party liable to execution on, the judgment.

(2) The deputy principal clerk shall, on certifying the copy interlocutor, and, where required, the opinion of the court, attach the same to a certificate in Form 57.

(3) The Keeper of the Registers shall, on issuing a certificate in Form 61, attach the same to an extract of the document to be enforced.

(4) An application for registration in the Court of Session of non-money provisions in a judgment from another part of the United Kingdom under section 18 of, and Schedule 7 to, the Act of 1982 shall be made in Form 58.

(5) There shall be produced with the application under paragraph (4)—

(*a*) a certified copy of the judgment of the original court; and

(*b*) a certificate in the appropriate form prescribed by the original court under paragraph 4(1)(*b*) of Schedule 7 to the Act of 1982 issued not more than six months before the date of the application.

(6) The application under paragraph (4) shall be dealt with in the Outer House by a Lord Ordinary in chambers and shall not require an appearance for the applicant unless the court so requires.

(7) The court shall, in relation to an application under paragraph (4), on being satisfied that the application meets the requirement of section 18 of, and Schedule 7 to, the Act of 1982, grant warrant for the registration of the judgment and where necessary pronounce decree in accordance with Scots law.

(8) Where the court grants warrant for registration, Rule 249I shall apply to the registration of a judgment under paragraph (7) as it applies to registration of a judgment under section 4 of the Act of 1982.

(9) An application—

(*a*) under paragraph 8 of Schedule 7 to the Act of 1982 to sist proceedings for enforcement of a judgment registered under paragraph (8) of this rule; or

(*b*) under paragraph 9 of Schedule 7 to the Act of 1982 to reduce a judgment registered under paragraph (8) of this Rule,

shall be made by petition to the Outer House, and Rules 191 to 198 shall apply.

Cancellation of registration

249R. Where—

(*a*) warrant for registration under Rule 249G or registration under Rule 249I is ordered to be cancelled after an appeal or a reclaiming motion; or

(*b*) registration under Rule 249P(3) or 249Q(8) is reduced, a certificate to that effect by the deputy principal clerk shall be sufficient warrant to the Keeper of the Registers to cancel the registration and return the judgment, certificate or other documents to the person who applied for registration.

[1] SECTION 8D

Reciprocal Enforcement of Orders in Relation to Confiscation of Proceeds of Crime

NOTE

[1] Inserted by S.I. 1987 No. 12.
Heading substituted by S.I. 1990 No. 705.

Interpretation

249S.—[1] (1) In this Section—

"the Act of 1987" means the Criminal Justice (Scotland) Act 1987;

"the Act of 1988" means the Criminal Justice Act 1988;

"Keeper of the Registers" means the Keeper of the Registers of Scotland.

"the Act of 1989" means the Prevention of Terrorism (Temporary Provisions) Act 1989.

(2) [Revoked by S.I. 1991 No. 1157, with effect from 27th May 1991.]

NOTE

[1] As amended by S.I. 1990 No. 705 and (with effect from 3rd June 1991) S.I. 1991 No. 1183.

Applications for registration

249T.—[1] (1) An application to which this rule applies shall be made by petition presented in the Outer House.

[1, 2] (1A) This rule applies to an application under—

(*a*) section 28(1) of the Act of 1987 for registration of an order to which section 27 of that Act applies;

(*b*) section 30A(1) of the Act of 1987 for registration of an external confiscation order;

(*c*) section 91(1) of the Act of 1988 for registration of an order to which section 90 of that Act applies, and

(*d*) paragraph 19(2) of Schedule 4 to the Act of 1989 for registration of an England and Wales order, Northern Ireland order or Islands order.

(2) There shall be produced with a petition under paragraph (1) a certified copy of the order which is sought to be registered.

(3) Rules 192 and 195 to 197 shall not apply to a petition under this section.

(4) The motion to grant the prayer of a petition under paragraph (1) shall not require an appearance for the petitioner unless the court so requires.

(5) Where the court requires an appearance under paragraph (4), the hearing shall be in chambers.

NOTES

[1] As substituted for former para. (1) by S.I. 1991 No. 1157, with effect from 27th May 1991.

[2] As amended by S.I. 1991 No. 1183, with effect from 3rd June 1991.

Registration

249U.—[1] (1) The court, on being satisfied that the application meets the requirements of the Act of 1987 or the Act of 1988 or the Act of 1989, as the case may be, shall—

(*a*) grant decree and warrant for the registration of the order sought to be registered;

(*b*) where necessary, grant decree of the order sought to be registered in accordance with Scots law and grant decree and warrant for registration of that decree; and

(*c*) where warrant for execution is sought, grant decree and warrant for registration in the Books of Council and Session.

[1] (2) Where the court grants decree under paragraph (1), the deputy principal clerk shall enter the order in a register for the registration of orders under the Act of 1987 or the Act of 1988 or the Act of 1989, as the case may be.

(3) Where decree and warrant for execution has been granted under paragraph (1)(*c*), upon presentation by the petitioner to the Keeper of the Registers of—

(*a*) a certified copy of the interlocutor granting such decree and warrant for registration; and

(*b*) a certified copy of the order to be registered,

the same shall be registered in the Register of Judgments of the Books of Council and Session whereupon the Keeper of the Registers shall issue an extract of the registered order and decree with warrant for execution.

NOTE

[1] As amended by S.I. 1990 No. 705 and (with effect from 3rd June 1991) S.I. 1991 No. 1183.

Intimation of registration

249V.—[1] (1) Intimation of a decree and warrant for registration and of registration of an order under Rule 249U shall be made by the petitioner in Form 62 or 62A, as the case may be to the person against whom the decree and warrant for registration was granted.

(2) Service of the intimation under paragraph (1) shall be made in accordance with Rule 74A, 74B or 75, as the case may be, and an execution of service shall be lodged in process.

NOTE

[1] As amended by S.I. 1991 No. 1183, with effect from 3rd June 1991.

Suspension of enforcement

[1] **249W.** Where an order has been registered under Rule 249U, the court may on the application of the person against whom the order may be enforced by note in the process of the petition, if satisfied that it is sought to have the order set aside or quashed in the court which made the order—

(*a*) suspend enforcement of the registered order; and

(*b*) sist any proceedings for enforcement of the registered order.

NOTE

[1] As amended by S.I. 1990 No. 705.

Modification and cancellation of registration

[1] **249X.**—(1) An application to modify or cancel the registration of an order registered under Rule 249U shall be made—

(*a*) by the petitioner, by motion in the process of the petition; and

(*b*) by any other interested party, by note in the process of the petition.

(2) There shall be produced with the application a certified copy of any order which modifies or revokes the registered order or which causes that order to cease to have effect.

(3) The court shall, on being satisfied—

(*a*) that the registered order has been modified or revoked or has ceased to have effect; or

(*b*) that the registration of an external confiscation order should be cancelled in terms of section 30A(3) of the Act of 1987,

pronounce an interlocutor so modifying or cancelling the registration as the case may be.

(4) Where the court pronounces an interlocutor under paragraph (3), the deputy principal clerk shall modify or cancel the registration in the register kept under Rule 249U(2) in accordance with that interlocutor.

NOTE
[1] As amended by S.I. 1991 No. 1157.

Applications for inhibition and arrestment
249Y.—[1] (1) An application under section 11(1) of the Act of 1987 as applied by subsection (6) of that section or section 92(1) of the Act of 1988 or paragraph 16(1) of Schedule 4 to the Act of 1989 for warrant for inhibition or arrestment shall be made—
(*a*) by motion in the process of the petition for registration under Rule 249U where the prayer of the petition has previously been granted; or
(*b*) in the prayer of that petition.
(2) A motion under paragraph (1)(*a*) shall not require an appearance for the prosecutor unless the court so requires, in which case the hearing shall be in chambers.

NOTE
[1] As amended by S.I. 1990 No. 705 and S.I. 1991 No. 1183.

[1] SECTION 9—CAUSES RELATING TO PATENTS, DESIGNS, COPYRIGHT AND TRADE MARKS

NOTE
[1] Substituted for former Sections 9 and 9A by S.I. 1991 No. 1621.

Application and Interpretation
250.—(1) This Section applies to any proceedings—
(*a*) under the Act of 1938;
(*b*) under the Act of 1949;
(*c*) under the Registered Designs Act 1949;
(*d*) under the Act of 1977;
(*e*) under the Act of 1988;
(*f*) under the Defence Contracts Act 1958; or
(*g*) for the determination of a question relating to a patent under the inherent jurisdiction of the court.
(2) In this Section—
"the Act of 1938" means the Trade Marks Act 1938;
"the Act of 1949" means the Patents Act 1949;
"the Act of 1977" means the Patents Act 1977;
"the Act of 1988" means the Copyright, Designs and Patents Act 1988;
"the Comptroller" means the Comptroller-General of Patents, Designs and Trade Marks;
"existing patent" means a patent mentioned in section 127(2)(*a*) or (*c*) of the Act of 1977;
"the Journal" means the journal published in accordance with rules made under section 123(6) of the Act of 1977;
"patent" means an existing patent or a patent under the Act of 1977;
"patentee" has the meaning assigned to it in section 101(1) of the Act of 1949.

Patents judge
251. All proceedings in the Outer House in a cause to which this Section applies shall be brought before a judge of the court nominated by the Lord President as the patents judge or, where the patents judge is not available, any other judge of the court (including a vacation judge).

Pre-proof hearing

252.—(1) In a cause under the Act of 1949 or the Act of 1977, not later than six weeks after—

(*a*) in a cause initiated by summons, the closing of the record, or

(*b*) in a cause initiated by petition, the expiry of any period of adjustment allowed, there shall be a pre-proof hearing on such date as the Keeper of the Rolls shall, subject to paragraph (2), fix.

(2) The Keeper of the Rolls shall consult the patents judge and the parties before fixing a date for a pre-proof hearing under paragraph (1) and shall, unless parties otherwise agree, give 14 days' notice of such a date.

(3) Not less than seven days before the pre-proof hearing, each party shall lodge in process, and send to every other party a notice of any issue sought to be raised on a preliminary plea against any other party.

(4) At a pre-proof hearing, the court shall consider—

(*a*) whether to direct that any issue of law or fact (including validity, infringement, an application for amendment of a patent under section 75 of the 1977 Act, damages or other remedies sought) should be determined separately from any other issue;

(*b*) whether the cause should be appointed to the Procedure Roll for consideration of any preliminary plea, and may order—

(i) a party, whose plea is to be considered, to lodge in process a note of argument consisting of brief numbered paragraphs stating the grounds on which he proposes to submit that the preliminary plea should be sustained and to send a copy of it to every other party within a specified period; and

(ii) any other party to lodge in process a note of argument in reply and to send a copy of it to every other party, within a specified period thereafter; and

(*c*) whether—

(i) to remit to the Patent Office for a report and what the terms of the remit should be;

(ii) to order a party to make available to any other party a copy of any documents;

(iii) to appoint an assessor or assessors;

(iv) a meeting of experts should be held for the purpose of producing a joint report on the general state of the art;

(v) to order each party to make available to every other party a copy of any precognitions, or reports, of skilled witnesses on any matter which is not the subject of a joint report under head (iv) and the time by which they are to be made available;

(vi) to order the advisers of the parties to meet for the purpose of agreeing and preparing a single paginated inventory of productions, and if necessary to fix a date by which this is to be done;

(vii) to make an order regulating the making of any experiment, inspection, test or report;

(viii) to fix a date by which a notice under rule 253 shall be served; and

(ix) to fix the time within which, notwithstanding rule 107, any production shall be lodged or within which any other step may be taken.

(5) At a pre-proof hearing, the court may—

(*a*) continue the hearing to another date;

(*b*) without prejudice to paragraph (6), order a further pre-proof hearing on a specified date or a date to be afterwards fixed; or

(*c*) give such further directions as to the conduct of the cause as it considers appropriate.

(6) The court may order a further pre-proof hearing at any time of its own motion or on the motion of any party.

(7) Where a party intends to seek a particular order at a pre-proof hearing, he shall give written notice to the court and to every other party not less than seven days before the hearing, of the order sought and the reason for seeking it.

Notices to admit and notices of non-admission

253.—(1) In a cause under the Act of 1949 or the Act of 1977, at any time after defences or answers have been lodged but not later than such date as has been fixed by the court at a pre-proof hearing, a party may intimate on any other party to the cause a notice or notices calling on him to admit for the purposes of that cause only—

(*a*) such facts relating to an issue averred in the pleadings as may be specified in the notice;

(*b*) that a particular document lodged in process and specified in the notice is—

(i) an original document;

(ii) where it is not a copy authenticated by the person making the copy, a true copy of an original document;

(iii) correct in the particular respects specified in the notice.

(2) Where a party upon whom a notice has been served under paragraph (1)—

(*a*) does not admit any of the facts specified in the notice; or

(*b*) does not admit, or desires to challenge, the authenticity or correctness of any document specified in the notice,

he shall, within 28 days after the date on which the notice under paragraph (1) was intimated on him intimate to the party intimating the notice on him a notice of non-admission to that effect.

(3) A party who fails to serve a notice of non-admission under paragraph (2) shall be deemed to have admitted the matters specified in the notice intimated under paragraph (1) unless the court, on special cause shown, otherwise directs.

(4) A party who intimates a notice of non-admission under paragraph (2) shall, unless the court otherwise directs, be liable to the party intimating the notice under paragraph (1) for the expenses of proving the matters specified in that notice if those matters are held by the court as established in evidence.

(5) The party lodging a notice under paragraph (1) or a notice of non-admission under paragraph (2) shall lodge a copy of it in process.

(6) An admission, or a deemed admission under paragraph (3), shall not be used against the party by whom it was made or deemed to be made other than in the cause for the purpose of which it was made or deemed to be made or in favour of any person other than the party by whom the notice was given under paragraph (1).

(7) The court may, at any time, allow a party to amend or withdraw an admission made by him on such conditions, if any, as it considers appropriate.

Applications for leave to amend specifications

254.—(1) A patentee or the proprietor of a patent intending to apply to the court under section 30 of the Act of 1949 or section 75 of the Act of 1977 (which provide for leave to amend specification) shall give notice of his intention to the Comptroller and at the same time deliver to him a form of advertisement—

(*a*) identifying the proceedings depending before the court in which it is intended to apply for such leave;

(*b*) giving particulars of the amendment sought;

(*c*) stating the address of the applicant for service within the United Kingdom; and

[THE NEXT PAGE IS C 115]

(*d*) stating that any person intending to oppose the amendment who is not a party to the proceedings must, within 28 days after the appearance of the advertisement, give written notice of that intention to the applicant and to the Deputy Principal Clerk.

(2) On receipt of a form of advertisement under paragraph (1), the Comptroller shall cause the advertisement to be inserted once in the Journal.

(3) A person who gives notice of intention to oppose the amendment in accordance with the advertisement shall be entitled to be heard on the application subject to any order of the court as to expenses.

(4) Not later than 35 days after the appearance of the advertisement, the applicant shall make his application under section 30 of the Act of 1949 or section 75 of the Act of 1977, as the case may be, by motion intimated, together with a copy of the specification certified by the Comptroller and showing in coloured ink the amendment sought, to—

(*a*) the Comptroller;

(*b*) every other party; and

(*c*) any person who has intimated his intention to oppose the amendment.

(5) On enrolling a motion under paragraph (4), the applicant shall lodge in process—

(*a*) a copy of the Journal containing the advertisement referred to in paragraph (2); or

(*b*) a certificate of publication by the publisher stating the date of publication and the text of the advertisement.

(6) At the hearing of a motion under paragraph (4)—

(*a*) where there is no opposition to the amendment sought, the court may—

(i) grant the application; or

(ii) make such order for further procedure as it considers necessary; or

(*b*) where there is opposition to the amendment sought, the court shall ordain the applicant to lodge a minute setting forth the grounds of his application within such period as the court considers reasonable, and allow any party or person opposing the amendment to lodge answers to the minute in process within a specified period thereafter.

(7) Within seven days after the expiry of the time for lodging answers under paragraph (6)(*b*), the applicant shall enrol a motion for an order for further procedure.

(8) On a motion under paragraph (7), the court may—

(*a*) grant the application;

(*b*) determine whether the motion shall be heard at the same time as the hearing of the depending cause relating to the patent in question or at a different time;

(*c*) determine the manner in which evidence shall be given and, if the evidence is to be given by affidavits, the period within which the affidavits must be lodged; or

(*d*) make such other order for further procedure as it considers necessary.

(9) Where the court allows the specification to be amended, the applicant shall forthwith—

(*a*) lodge with the Comptroller a certified copy of the interlocutor; and

(*b*) if so required by the court or the Comptroller, leave at the Patent Office a new specification and drawings as amended, prepared in compliance with the Act of 1949 or the Act of 1977, as the case may be, and any rules made under either of those Acts.

(10) On receiving the certified copy interlocutor or under paragraph (9), the Comptroller shall cause it to be inserted at least once in the Journal.

Applications for revocation of patents

255.—(1) Subject to paragraph (2), an application under section 72 of the Act of 1977 (revocation of a patent) shall be made by petition presented in the Outer House.

(2) Where an action is depending before the court between the same parties in relation to the patent in question, such an application may be made by counterclaim in that action; and rule 84 shall apply to any such counterclaim.

Proceedings for infringement

256.—(1) In any cause where it is alleged that a patent has been infringed, the person alleging infringement must aver in the petition or summons, as the case may be, particulars of the infringement relied on, showing which of the claims in the specification of the patent are alleged to have been infringed and giving at least one instance of each type of infringement alleged.

(2) Where, as a defence to such an allegation, it is averred that at the time of the infringement there was in force a contract or licence relating to the patent—

(*a*) made by or with the consent of the person alleging the infringement, and

(*b*) containing a condition or term void by virtue of section 44 of the Act of 1977,

the person stating that defence must aver particulars of, the date of, and the parties to, each such contract or licence and particulars of each such condition or term.

Objections to validity of patent

257.—(1) A person who—

(*a*) presents a petition under section 32 of the Act of 1949 or makes an application under section 72 of the Act of 1977 for revocation of a patent, or

(*b*) being a party to an action relating to a patent—

(i) challenges the validity of the patent, or

(ii) applies by counterclaim in an action for revocatiton of the patent,

shall aver the grounds on which the validity of the patent is challenged.

(2) Where the grounds in respect of which averments are required under paragraph (1) include—

(*a*) want of novelty, or

(*b*) want of any inventive step,

the averments shall include the matters specified in paragraph (3).

(3) The matters referred to in paragraph (2) are—

(*a*) the manner, time and place of every prior publication or use relied on; and

(*b*) where prior use is alleged—

(i) specification of the name of every person alleged to have made such use;

(ii) an averment as to whether such use is alleged to have continued until the priority date of the claim in question or of the invention, as the case may be, and, if not, the earliest and latest date on which such use is alleged to have taken place;

(iii) a description accompanied, if necessary, by drawings sufficient to identify such use; and

(iv) if such use relates to machinery or apparatus, an averment as to whether the machinery or apparatus is in existence and where it can be inspected.

(4) Where, in the case of an existing patent—

(*a*) one of the grounds on which the validity of the patent is challenged is that the invention, so far as claimed in any claim of the complete specification, is not useful, and

(*b*) it is intended, in connection with that ground, to rely on the fact that an example of the invention which is the subject of any such claim cannot be made to work, either at all or as described in the specification,

the averments shall specify that fact and identify each such claim and shall include particulars of each such example, specifying the respects in which it is alleged that it does not work or does not work as described.

Determination of question or application where Comptroller declines to deal with it

257A. Where the Comptroller—

(*a*) declines to deal with a question under the following sections of the Act of 1977:—

(i) section 8 (entitlement to patents, etc.),

(ii) section 12 (entitlement to foreign and convention patents),

(iii) section 37 (right to patent after grant), or

(iv) section 61(3) (infringement of patent),

(*b*) declines to deal with an application under section 40 of that Act (compensation of employees for certain inventions), or

(*c*) issues a certificate under section 72(7)(*b*) of that Act (revocation of patent should be determined by the court),

any person entitled to do so may, within 28 days after the decision of the Comptroller, apply by petition presented in the Outer House to have the question or application, as the case may be, determined by the court.

Applications by employees for compensation under section 40 of the Act of 1977

257B.—(1) An application under section 40(1) or (2) of the Act of 1977 (compensation of employees for certain inventions) shall be made by summons commenced within the period which begins when the relevant patent is granted and which expires one year after it had ceased to have effect.

(2) Where a patent has ceased to have effect by reason of a failure to pay any renewal fee within the period prescribed for the payment of that fee and an application is made to the Comptroller under section 28 of the Act of 1977 (restoration of lapsed patent), the period within which the application by summons is to be made shall—

(*a*) if restoration is ordered, continue as if the patent has remained continuously in effect; or

(*b*) if restoration is refused, be treated as if expiring one year after the patent ceased to have effect or 6 months after the refusal, whichever is the later.

Proceedings for determination of certain disputes

257C. A reference or application under the following enactments shall be made by petition presented in the Outer House:—

(*a*) a reference under—

(i) section 48 of the Act of 1949 or section 58 of the Act of 1977 (which provide for disputes as to Crown use);

(ii) paragraph 3 of Schedule 1 to the Registered Design Act 1949 (disputes as to Crown use);

(iii) section 4 of the Defence Contracts Act 1958 (payments for use and determination of disputes); or

(iv) section 251(1) (design right matters), or section 252(1) (disputes as to Crown use), of the Act of 1988;

(*b*) an application under section 45(3) of the Act of 1977 (variation of certain contracts).

Applications for rectification of Register of Designs or Patents

257D.—(1) Subject to paragraph (2), an application under section 20(1) of the Registered Designs Act 1949 (rectification of Register of Designs) or section 34(1) of the Act of 1977 (rectification of Register of Patents) shall be made by petition in the Outer House.

(2) Where an action for infringement of a patent is depending before the court, such an application may be made by a counterclaim in that action.

(3) In an application under section 34(1) of the Act of 1977, the applicant shall intimate the application to the Comptroller, who may lodge answers in process and be heard on the application.

Counterclaim for rectification of Register of Designs

257E.—(1) Where, in any cause, an infringement of the copyright in a registered design is alleged, the party against whom the allegation is made may—

(*a*) put in issue the validity of the registration of that design;

(*b*) counterclaim for an order that the Register of Designs be rectified by cancelling or varying the registration; or

(*c*) put in issue such validity and make such a counterclaim.

(2) A party to any such cause who counterclaims for an order that the Register of Designs be rectified shall intimate to the Comptroller a copy of the counterclaim; and the Comptroller may, or (if ordered to do so by the court) shall, lodge answers in process and be heard in any such cause.

Appeals from Comptroller

257F.—(1) Subject to the following paragraphs of this rule, an appeal under the Act of 1949, the Act of 1977 or the Act of 1988 from a decision of the Comptroller shall be heard by the patents judge.

(2) Rule 290 shall apply to any such appeal as if it were an appeal under that rule, with the substitution for references to the Inner House of references to the Outer House and for references to the single bills of references to the Motion Roll.

(3) Subject to paragraph (4), an appeal shall be lodged in the General Department—

(*a*) in the case of a decision on a matter of procedure, within 14 days after the date of the decision; and

(*b*) in any other case, within six weeks after the date of the decision.

(4) Except with leave of the court, no appeal under this rule shall be entertained unless it has been lodged within the period specified in paragraph (3) or within such further period as the Comptroller may allow on an application made to him before the expiry of that period.

(5) Any determination by the Comptroller that a decision is on a matter of procedure shall be treated as being itself a decision on a matter of procedure.

(6) Intimation under rule 290(*e*) shall be ordered to be made to the Comptroller and to every other party to the proceedings before the Comptroller.

(7) On receiving intimation of the appeal, the Comptroller shall forthwith transmit to the Deputy Principal Clerk all the papers relating to the matter which is the subject of the appeal.

(8) A respondent who, not having appealed from the decision of the Comptroller, wishes to contend at the hearing of the appeal that the decision or the grounds of the decision should be varied shall—

(*a*) specify the grounds of that contention in his answers; and (*b*) intimate those answers to the Comptroller and to every other party to the proceedings before the Comptroller.

(9) Intimation of the date of the hearing of the appeal shall be made to the Comptroller by the appellant not less than seven days before that date, unless the court otherwise directs.

(10) An appeal under this rule shall be a re-hearing and the evidence led on apeal shall be the same as that led before the Comptroller; and, except with the leave of the court, no further evidence shall be led.

Intimation to Comptroller of reclaiming motion

257G. The marking of a reclaiming motion from a decision of the patent judge on an appeal from a decision of the Comptroller shall be intimated by the reclaimer to the Comptroller as well as to the other parties to the appeal.

Communication of information to European Patent Office

257H.—(1) The court may authorise the communication to the European Patent Office or the competent authority of any country which is a party to the European Patent Convention of any such information in the records of the court as the court considers appropriate.

(2) An application for such information shall be made by letter addressed to the Deputy Principal Clerk.

(3) Before complying with an application for the disclosure of information under paragraph (1), any person appearing to be affected by the application shall be given the opportunity of making representations to the patents judge in chambers on the question whether the information should be disclosed; and the decision of the patents judge shall be final and not subject to review.

(4) In this rule, "the European Patent Convention" has the meaning assigned in section 130(1) and (6) of the Act of 1977.

Applications under the Act of 1938 and the Act of 1988

257I.—(1) An application under section 99, 195 or 230 of the Act of 1988 (which provide for orders for delivery in respect of infringement of copyright, rights in performances and design rights) shall be made—

(*a*) in a cause depending before the court, by motion; or

(*b*) where there is no depending cause, by petition presented in the Outer House.

(2) An application under section 114, 204 or 231 or the Act of 1988 (which provide for orders for disposal in respect of infringement of copyright, rights in performances and design rights) shall be made—

(*a*) in a cause depending before the court, by motion; or

(*b*) where there is no depending cause, by petition presented in the Outer House; and

the applicant shall intimate the application to all persons, so far as known to the petitioner or reasonably ascertainable, having an interest in the copy, article, recording or other thing which is the suject of the application, including any person in whose favour an order could be made in respect of the copy, article, recording or other thing under any of the said sections of the Act of 1988 or section 58C of the Act of 1938 (order for disposal in respect of infringement of trade marks).

(3) An application under section 58C of the Act of 1938 shall be made by petition presented in the Outer House and the petitioner shall intimate the petition to all persons, so far as known to the petitioner or reasonably ascertainable, having an interest in the goods or material which are the subject of the application, including any person in whose favour an order could be made in respect of the goods or material under that section or section 114, 204 or 231 of the Act of 1988.

Applications for leave to proceed

257J.—(1) Where leave of the court is required under the Act of 1988 before an action may proceed, the pursuer shall apply by motion for leave to proceed before the summons is signeted.

(2) A motion under paragraph (1) shall be heard in chambers.

(3) Where such leave is granted, a copy of the interlocutor allowing leave shall be attached to the copy of the summons served on the defender.

Assessors

257K. In any proceedings before the patents judge, the number of assessors to be summoned, if any, shall be such as the court considers appropriate.

SECTION 10—APPEALS AND REFERENCES UNDER THE TELEGRAPH ACTS

Scope of petition and procedure

258.—(*a*) Applications for a re-hearing under section 4 of the Telegraph Act 1878 as amended by section 2 of the Railway and Canal Commission (Abolition) Act 1949, and References to the Court of Session under section 1 of the Telegraph (Arbitration) Act 1909, as amended by the said section 2 shall be made by petition presented to the Outer House and lodged in the Petition Department. The petition shall set forth shortly the question at issue and the facts which give rise to it and (in the case of a re-hearing) the determination of the sheriff.

(*b*) The petition shall be heard and determined by the judge designated from time to time by the Lord President.

(*c*) The procedure shall be summary and in the discretion of the designated judge, and the decision of the designated judge shall be final and not subject to review.

SECTION 11—APPLICATIONS FORMERLY DEALT WITH BY THE RAILWAY AND CANAL COMMISSION

Scope of petition and procedure

[1] **259.**—(*a*) Applications under any enactment which are referred to the Court of Session pursuant to subsection (1) of section 1 of the Railway and Canal Commission (Abolition) Act 1949 (other than those to which Rule 258 applies) shall be made by petition presented to the Outer House. Applications which are referred to the Court of Session pursuant to the provisions of the Mines (Working Facilities and Support) Act 1966 shall be lodged along with a petition presented to the Outer House. Any petition presented in terms of this Rule shall narrate the facts and crave the rights or relief to which the petitioner claims to be entitled.

(*b*) The petition shall be heard and determined by the judge designated for the purposes of Rule 258, and shall proceed as an Outer House petition subject to the ordinary rules as to reclaiming.

(*c*) Any person liable to make periodical or other payments under any order of the court of the Railway and Canal Commission extending to Scotland and made before the first day of April 1949, shall apply by petition under this Rule for directions regulating future payments under the said order.

NOTE

[1] As amended by S.I. 1966 No. 1283.

SECTION 12—PETITIONS UNDER THE TRUSTS (SCOTLAND) ACT 1961

Procedure, service and intimation

260.—(*a*) All applications for the variation of trust purposes under section 1 of the Trusts (Scotland) Act 1961, shall be made by petition presented to the Inner House.

(*b*) The provisions of Rules 191 to 198 shall apply, *mutatis mutandis*, to such petitions.

(*c*) The petition shall be served on the Keeper of the Records of Scotland, or on the sheriff clerk of the sheriffdom in which the deed is registered.

(*d*) In an application in which the petitioner craves the court to authorise an arrangement under subsection (4) of section 1 of the Act, it shall not be necessary to set forth in the petition the amount of the income of an alimentary beneficiary from all sources, or the details thereof.

(*e*) Where a truster or settlor or any other person who has contributed, or is liable to contribute, to the trust estate is alive at the date of the presentation of a petition for the variation of the trust purposes, then, in addition to such other intimation, service and advertisement as may be necessary having regard to the nature of the petition, the court may order intimation to be made to such person.

[1] SECTION 13—PETITIONS UNDER THE GUARDIANSHIP ACT 1973

Procedure, service and intimation

[1] **260A.**—(*a*) All applications under section 10(3) of the Guardianship Act 1973, shall be made by petition presented to the Outer House.

(*b*) The provisions of Rules 191 to 198 shall apply, *mutatis mutandis*, to such petitions.

(*c*) Any application under section 10(5) or 12(1) of the Act to vary or discharge any order made respectively under section 10(3) or section 11 thereof shall be made by way of minute in the process setting forth any relevant averments in support of said application. On such a minute being lodged answers thereto may be lodged, within such period as the court may allow, by any other person showing an interest.

(*d*) Where the court, in pursuance of section 11 of the Act, proposes to make an order committing the care of a child to a specified local authority, the court shall appoint intimation of the proposal to be made to the local authority, and any representations made by them under sections 11(4) of the Act shall be made by minute. On such a minute being lodged the parties to the proceedings may lodge answers thereto within such period as the court may allow.

NOTE
[1] Added by S.I. 1974 No. 945.

[1] SECTION 14—APPLICATION FOR JUDICIAL REVIEW

NOTE
[1] Added by S.I. 1985 No. 500, in relation to proceedings commenced on or after 30th April 1985.

260B.—(1) *Application.* An application to the supervisory jurisdiction of the court which immediately before the coming into operation of this rule would have been made by way of summons or petition, shall be made by way of an application for judicial review in accordance with the provisions of this rule.

(2) In paragraph (1), "petition" includes a summary petition under section 91 of the Court of Session Act 1868 (order for restoration of property or specific performance).

(3) Paragraph (1) does not apply to an application to the court made, or which could be made, by way of appeal or review under and by virtue of any enactment, including an application under—

(*a*) paragraph 15 of Schedule 1 to the Acquisition of Land (Authorisation Procedure) (Scotland) Act 1947 (validity of compulsory purchase order);

(*b*) sections 232 (validity of structure plans) and 233 (validity of other orders, decisions and directions) of the Town and Country Planning (Scotland) Act 1972;

(*c*) paragraph 2 of Schedule 2 to the Roads (Scotland) Act 1984 (validity of orders).

(4) *Powers of Court.* The court, in exercising its supervisory jurisdiction in respect of an application for judicial review, may—

(*a*) grant or refuse the application or any part of it, with or without conditions;

(*b*) make such order in relation to the decision in question as it thinks fit, whether or not such order was sought in the application, being an order that could be made if sought in any action or petition, including an order for reduction, declarator, suspension, interdict, implement, restitution, payment (whether of damages or otherwise), and any interim order;

(*c*) subject to the provisions of this rule, make such order in relation to procedure as it thinks appropriate in the circumstances.

[1] (5) *Form of application.* An application for judicial review shall be made by way of petition in the form set out in Form 39D in the Appendix or as nearly as may be in that form having regard to the circumstances, and signed by the applicant's counsel or solicitor.

(6) *Application to nominated judge.* An application for judicial review shall be heard by a judge nominated by the Lord President for the purposes of this rule, or by any other single judge, including the vacation judge.

NOTE
[1] As amended by S.I. 1990 No. 705.

Procedure on application

(7) *General*. Subject to the provisions of this rule, the ordinary rules relating to petitions to the Outer House shall apply to a petition under this rule.

(8) *Documents*. The applicant shall, on lodging the petition, also lodge all relevant documents in his possession and under his control and an inventory of those documents.

(9) If the applicant founds in the petition on any documents not in his possession or under his control, he shall append to the petition a schedule specifying the documents and the person or persons respectively in whose possession or under whose control they are.

(10) *Affidavits*. If the decision, act or omission in question and the basis on which it is complained of is not apparent from the documents lodged with the petition, an affidavit shall be lodged stating the terms of the decision, act or omission and the basis on which it is complained of.

(11) *First order*. On being lodged, the petition and documents shall be brought immediately by the Deputy Principal Clerk, or a person authorised by him, before a judge for—

(*a*) an order specifying—
- (i) a period for intimation and service;
- (ii) such advertisement as he thinks fit;
- (iii) such persons, if any, upon whom service is to be made in addition to the persons specified in the schedule for service;
- (iv) such documents, if any, as he thinks should be served on any such persons together with the petition and copy interlocutor;
- (v) a date for a hearing ("the first hearing"), being a date not earlier than seven days after the expiry of the period specified for intimation and service;

(*b*) any interim order,

and the judge may grant such an order although the petition has not appeared in the motion roll.

(12) The applicant shall immediately give effect to the requirements of the first order in respect of intimation, advertisement and service and shall intimate the date of that first hearing to those persons upon whom he requires to make service and lodge the relative certificates of execution of advertisement and service in process before the first hearing.

(13) A person to whom intimation of the first hearing has been made under paragraph (12) and who intends to appear—

(*a*) shall intimate his intention to do so to the applicant's solicitor and to the Keeper of the Rolls, not later than 48 hours before the date of the hearing;

[THE NEXT PAGE IS C 122/1]

(*b*) may lodge answers and any relative documents.

(14) Any person not specified in the first order as a person upon whom service requires to be made may enrol a motion for leave to enter the process; and if the motion is granted the provisions of this rule shall apply with any necessary modifications to that person as they apply to a person so specified.

(15) *First hearing*. The judge at the first hearing shall satisfy himself that the applicant has duly complied with the requirements of the first order, and may adjourn or continue the first hearing to another date on such terms and conditions (if any) as he may order, and may make such further order as he thinks fit, including an order for service upon a person not specified in the first order.

(16) Subject to paragraph (15), the judge shall hear the parties to the application for judicial review, and thereafter—

(*a*) he may determine the application, or

(*b*) if he does not determine the application, shall make such interim order or such order for further procedure as he thinks fit, and in particular he may—

(i) order answers to be lodged within such time as he may specify in the order;

(ii) order further specification in the petition or answers in relation to such matters as he may specify in the order;

(iii) order any facts founded on by a party at the hearing to be supported by evidence on affidavit to be lodged within such time as he may specify in the order;

(iv) order any party who appears to lodge such documents relative to the application within such period as he may specify in the order;

(v) appoint a reporter to report to him on such matters of fact as he may specify in the order;

(vi) order a hearing on such issues as he may specify in the order ("the second hearing").

(17) *Second hearing*. If the judge orders a second hearing under paragraph 16, the Keeper of the Rolls shall, in consultation with the judge and the parties or their solicitors, fix a date for the second hearing as soon as reasonably practicable.

(18) Subject to the terms of any order for further procedure made under paragraph (16), at least seven days before the date of the second hearing, the parties shall lodge all documents and affidavits to be founded on by them at the second hearing, together with a copy thereof for the use of the judge.

(19) At any time before the date of the second hearing, the judge may cause the application for judicial review to be put out for hearing on the by order roll for the purpose of obtaining such information from the parties as he may consider necessary for the proper disposal of the application at the hearing, and at any such by order roll hearing may make such order for that purpose as he considers necessary and appropriate having regard to all the circumstances, including an order that a commissioner appointed by him recovers such documents or takes such evidence of such witnesses as he may specify.

(20) At the second hearing, the judge may—

(*a*) adjourn the hearing;

(*b*) continue the hearing for such further procedure as he may order;

(*c*) determine the application.

(21) *Reclaiming*. No reclaiming motion may be made against an order made under this rule (other than an order under paragraph 16(*a*) or 20(*c*)) except with leave of the judge.

(22) Leave of the judge must be applied for by way of motion not later than seven days after the date on which the order in question was made.

[1] SECTION 15—PETITIONS FOR CUSTODY OF CHILDREN

NOTE
[1] Added by S.I. 1986 No. 515.

Application and interpretation

260C.—(1) This section applies to a petition for custody of a child.

(2) In this section, unless the context otherwise requires, "the Act of 1975" means the Children Act 1975.

(3) Words and expressions which are used in this section and are also used in the Act of 1975 have the same meaning as in that Act.

(4) In this section, a form referred to by number means the form so numbered in the Appendix or a form substantially to the like effect, with such variation as circumstances may require.

Procedure in petition for custody

260D.—(1) Subject to paragraph (2) of this Rule, Rules 191 to 198 apply to a petition under this section.

[1] (2) On making an order for intimation and service under Rule 195, the court shall make an order requiring the petitioner to give notice—

(*a*) at the same time to each known parent of the child in the form set out in Form 68 together with, where the petitioner is not a parent, tutor, curator or guardian of the child, a consent form as set out in Form 69; and

(*b*) where the petitioner is not a parent of the child and he resides in Scotland when the petition is presented, within seven days to the local authority within whose area the petitioner resides in Form 70; or

(*c*) where the petitioner is not a parent of the child and he does not reside in Scotland when the petition is presented, within such time as the court shall determine to such local authority as the court shall specify in Form 70.

[1] (3) Where a parent, tutor, curator or guardian consents to the petitioner being granted custody of a child, he shall—

(*a*) complete and sign a consent form as set out in Form 69;

(*b*) have his signature witnessed; and

(*c*) return the form to the petitioner.

(4) At any stage of the cause, where it appears to the court to be desirable in the circumstances of the case in order to safeguard the interests of a child, the court shall appoint a curator *ad litem*.

(5) A curator *ad litem* appointed under Rule 260D(4) shall have the following duties:—

(*a*) to enquire into, so far as he considers necessary, the matters averred in the petition and in any report by a local authority under Rule 260D(6);

(*b*) to enquire into any other matters which appear to him to be relevant;

(*c*) to consider whether the granting of custody to the petitioner is in the interests of the child;

(*d*) to perform such other duties as appear to him to be necessary or as the court may require; and

(*e*) to prepare a report in relation to the exercise of the above duties.

(6) On completion of a report under section 49(2) of the Act of 1975, the local authority shall—

(*a*) lodge three copies of the report in process; and

(*b*) where a curator *ad litem* has been appointed, send a copy of the report to him.

(7) The curator *ad litem* shall, on completion of his report, lodge three copies of it in process.

(8) On receipt of the report of the local authority, and, where a curator *ad litem* has been appointed, the report of the curator *ad litem*, the Petition Department shall—

(*a*) inform the petitioner that a report has been lodged; and

(*b*) make available to the petitioner, and to any other party, a copy of each report.

(9) After the Petition Department has informed the petitioner that all reports have been lodged, the petition shall proceed as an ordinary petition.

[2] (10) In a petition in which custody of, or access to, a child is in dispute, the court may, at any stage of the cause where it considers it appropriate and the parties to the dispute agree, refer that dispute to a specified Family Conciliation Service.

NOTES

[1] As amended by S.I. 1990 No. 705.

[2] Inserted by S.I. 1990 No. 705.

Applications to be made in the process of the petition

260E.—(1) An application, by a person concerned, to vary or discharge an interlocutor pronounced in a petition under this section shall—

(*a*) if made before a final interlocutor, be made by motion unless the court directs the application to be made by minute in the process of the petition; or

(*b*) if made after a final interlocutor, be made by minute in the process of the petition.

(2) An application to remove a child from the custody of the petitioner by virtue of section 51(1) of the Act of 1975 by a person other than a respondent who has lodged answers shall be made by minute in the process of the petition.

(3) An application under section 52(*b*) of the Act of 1975 by a person who is not a party to the petition shall be made by minute in the process of the petition.

Averments of other proceedings relating to children

[1] **260EA.** A party to a cause under this section for a custody order as defined by section 1(1)(*b*) of the Family Law Act 1986 shall make averments in his pleadings giving particulars of any other proceedings known to him (whether in Scotland or elsewhere and whether concluded or not) which relate to the child in respect of whom the custody order is sought.

NOTE

[1] Added by S.I. 1988 No. 615.

Disclosure of information about child's whereabouts

[1] **260EB.** Where the court pronounces an interlocutor ordering a person to disclose information to the court as to a child's whereabouts under section 33(1) of the Family Law Act 1986, it may do so by ordaining that person to appear before it or to lodge an affidavit.

NOTE

[1] Added by S.I. 1988 No. 615.

Applications for interdict under the Family Law Act 1986

[1] **260EC.** An application by a person mentioned in section 35(4)(*b*) or (*c*) of the Family Law Act 1986 for interdict or interim interdict under section 35(3) of that Act shall be made by minute in the cause in which the application is to be made.

NOTE

[1] Added by S.I. 1988 No. 615.

[1] Section 16—Petitions in Relation to Parentage

NOTE

[1] Added by S.I. 1986 No. 1955.

Applications to court for consent to take blood sample

260F. Where there is no cause in dependence before the court in which an application under section 6(3) of the Law Reform (Parent and Child) (Scotland) Act 1986 may be made by motion, the application shall be made by petition presented to the Outer House.

Consent by mother to petition

260G. Where, in a petition by the father of an illegitimate child to be appointed tutor or curator of his child, the mother of that child consents to the appointment, there shall be lodged with the petition a form of consent by the mother signed by her and witnessed.

[1] Section 17—Applications Under the Child Abduction and Custody Act 1985

NOTE

[1] Added by S.I. 1986 No. 1955.

Application and interpretation

260H.—(1) This section applies to applications under the Child Abduction and Custody Act 1985.

(2) In this section—

"the Act of 1985" means the Child Abduction and Custody Act 1985;

"the Hague Convention" means the convention defined in section 1(1) of the Act of 1985;

"the European Convention" means the convention defined in section 12(1) of the Act of 1985;

"relevant authority" means a sheriff court, a children's hearing within the meaning of Part III of the Social Work (Scotland) Act 1968, the High Court, a county court or magistrates' court in England and Wales, the High Court, a county court or a magistrates' court in Northern Ireland, or the Secretary of State.

(3) Words and expressions used in this section which are also used in the Act of 1985 have the same meaning as in that Act.

International child abduction (the Hague Convention)

[1] **260J.**—(1) An application for return of a child to which Part I of the Act of 1985 applies shall be made by petition presented to the Outer House, and—

(*a*) shall include averments about—

(i) the identity of the petitioner and the person alleged to have removed or retained the child;

(ii) the identity of the child and his date of birth;

(iii) the whereabouts or suspected whereabouts of the child;

(iv) the date on which the child is alleged to have been wrongfully removed or retained;

(v) the grounds on which the petition is based; and

(vi) any civil cause in dependence before any other court or authority in respect of the child, or any proceedings specified in section 9 of the Act of 1985 relating to the merits of the rights of custody of the child in or before a relevant authority;

(*b*) a certified or authorised copy of any relevant decision or agreement shall be produced with the petition.

(2) An application for access to a child to which Part I of the Act of 1985 applies shall be made by petition presented to the Outer House, and—

(*a*) shall include averments about—

(i) the identity of the petitioner;

(ii) the identity of the child and his date of birth;

(iii) the parents or guardians of the child;

(iv) the whereabouts of the child;

(v) the factual and legal grounds on which access is sought; and

(vi) any civil cause in dependence before any other court or authority in respect of the child, or any proceedings specified in section 9 of the Act of 1985 relating to the merits of the rights of custody of the child in or before a relevant authority;

(*b*) there shall be produced with the petition a certified copy of any relevant decision or agreement.

(3) An application for declarator that removal or retention of a child was wrongful under section 8 of the Act of 1985 shall be made by petition presented to the Outer House, and—

(*a*) shall include averments about—

(i) the identity of the pursuer and of the person who is alleged to have removed or retained the child;

(ii) the identity of the child and his date of birth;

(iii) the whereabouts or suspected whereabouts of the child;

(iv) the date on which the child is alleged to have been wrongfully removed or retained;

(v) the proceedings which gave custody to the pursuer; and

(vi) the proceedings under the Hague Convention in relation to which this action is necessary;

(*b*) there shall be produced with the summons any relevant document.

[THE NEXT PAGE IS C 122/5]

(4) The *induciae* in a petition under this rule shall be four days.

(5) The persons upon whom service shall be made in a petition under this rule shall be—

(*a*) the person alleged to have brought the child into the United Kingdom;

(*b*) the person with whom the child is presumed to be;

(*c*) any parent or guardian of the child if he or she is within the United Kingdom and not otherwise a party; and

(*d*) the Chief Executive of the local authority, and the reporter to the children's panel in the local authority area, in which the child resides; and

(*e*) any other person who may have an interest in the child.

(6) Where a document lodged is in a language other than English, there shall be lodged in process a translation into English certified by a person qualified as a translator.

(7) Where a petition is presented under paragraph (1) and there are proceedings specified in section 9 of the Act of 1985 relating to the merits of the rights of custody of the child in dependence in or before a relevant authority, the court shall give notice to the relevant authority of the petition, and in due course of the outcome of the petition.

(8) Where the court receives a notice equivalent to that under paragraph (7) from the High Court in England and Wales or Northern Ireland, all proceedings in any cause specified in section 9 of the Act of 1985 relating to the merits of the rights of custody of the child shall be sisted by the court until the dismissal of the proceedings in that other court under the Hague Convention; and the deputy principal clerk shall notify the parties to the cause of the sist and of any such dismissal.

(9) At any stage of a petition under paragraph (1), the court may, of its own motion or on the motion of any party, pronounce an interlocutor remitting the cause to the High Court in England and Wales or Northern Ireland.

(10) Where a cause is remitted under paragraph (9), the deputy principal clerk forthwith shall—

(*a*) transmit the process to the appropriate officer of the appropriate court;

(*b*) send written notice of the transmission to the parties to the cause; and

(*c*) certify on the interlocutor sheet that such written notice has been given.

(11) Where a cause is remitted under paragraph (9), the question of expenses shall not be determined by the court, but shall be at the discretion of the court to which the cause is transferred.

(12) Where a cause is remitted to the Court of Session from the High Court in England or Wales or Northern Ireland—

(*a*) the deputy principal clerk shall, upon receipt of the order transferring the cause and any process, notify the parties of the transfer;

(*b*) the cause shall be deemed to be a petition as if it has been raised in the Court of Session; and

(*c*) the cause shall be put out "by order" before a Lord Ordinary for further procedure within two court days of the transfer.

NOTE

[1] As amended by S.I. 1991 No. 1157, with effect from 27th May 1991.

Recognition and enforcement of custody decisions (the European Convention)

260K.—(1) An application under section 15 of the Act of 1985 to declare a decree for custody not to be recognised shall be made by petition presented to the Outer House.

(2) An application—

(*a*) for registration under section 16 of the Act of 1985;

(*b*) for registration under section 16, and enforcement under section 18, of the Act of 1985; or

(*c*) for enforcement under section 18 of the Act of 1985,
of a decision relating to the custody of a child, shall be made by petition presented to the Outer House.

(3) An application under section 17(4) of the Act of 1985 for variation or revocation of a registered decision by a person appearing to the court to have an interest in the matter, shall be made by note in the process of the petition for registration.

(4) An application by an interested person under section 23(2) of the Act of 1985 in any custody proceedings for declarator that the removal of a child was unlawful, shall be made—

(*a*) by minute in the process of a cause commenced by summons; or
(*b*) by note in the process of a cause commenced by petition.

(5) In a cause under this rule—

(*a*) there shall be included, averments about—
(i) the identity of the petitioner, pursuer, minuter or noter, as the case may be, and his interests in the cause;
(ii) the identity of the child and his date of birth;
(iii) the parents or guardians of the child;
(iv) the order which is required to be registered, enforced, declared unlawful declared not recognised, varied or revoked, as the case may be;
(v) the whereabouts or suspected whereabouts of the child; and
(vi) any civil cause in dependence before any other court or authority in respect of the child, or any proceedings specified in section 20(2) of the Act of 1985 in dependence in or before a relevant authority;

(*b*) there shall be produced with the process of the cause—
(i) a certified or authenticated copy of a decision to be registered or enforced;
(ii) where the decision to be registered was given in the absence of the person against whom the decision was made or in the absence of his legal representative, a document which establishes (subject to Article 9(1)(*a*) of the European Convention in Schedule 2 to the Act of 1985) that that person was duly served with the document which instituted the original proceedings;
(iii) a certificate or affidavit to the effect that the decision to be registered is enforceable in accordance with the law of the State in which the decision was made; and
(iv) any other relevant document.

(6) The *induciae* in a petition under this rule shall be four days.

(7) Where a minute or note is lodged under this rule, the court shall make such order as to the *induciae*, intimation, service and the lodging of answers as it thinks appropriate.

[1] (8) A cause under this rule shall be served on—

(*a*) the person alleged to have brought the child into the United Kingdom or removed the child from the United Kingdom, as the case may be;
(*b*) the person with whom the child is presumed to be in the United Kingdom;
(*c*) the mother and father of the child if he or she is within the United Kingdom and not otherwise a party; and
(*d*) the Chief Executive of the local authority, and the reporter to the children's panel in the local authority area, in which the child resides; and
(*e*) any other person who may have an interest in the child.

(9) Where a document lodged is in a language other than English, there shall be lodged in process a translation into English certified by a person qualified as a translator.

(10) Where a decision relating to custody is ordered to be registered under this rule, the deputy principal clerk shall enter the decree or other interlocutor in a register of decisions registered under the Act of 1985.

(11) Where a petition is presented under paragraph (2) of this rule and there are proceedings in dependence, or proceedings commence after the petition is presented or after a decision relating to custody has been registered, in or before a relevant authority which are proceedings specified in section 20(2) of the Act of 1985—

(*a*) the petitioner shall inform the court by including averments or lodging an affidavit, as the case may be, to that effect containing a concise statement of the nature of those proceedings; and

(*b*) the court shall give notice to the relevant authority of the petition, and in due course of the outcome of the petition.

(12) Where the court receives a notice equivalent to that under paragraph (11) from the High Court in England and Wales or Northern Ireland, the deputy principal clerk shall notify the parties to any cause which is one specified in section 20(2) of the Act of 1985.

(13) At any stage of a cause under this rule, the court may, of its own motion or on the motion of any party, pronounce an interlocutor remitting the cause to the High Court in England and Wales or Northern Ireland.

(14) Where a cause is remitted under paragraph (13), the deputy principal clerk forthwith shall—

(*a*) transmit the process to the appropriate officer of the appropriate court;

(*b*) send written notice of the transmission to the parties to the cause; and

(*c*) certify on the interlocutor sheet that such written notice has been given.

(15) Where a cause is remitted under paragraph (13), the question of expenses shall not be determined by the court, but shall be at the discretion of the court to which the case is transferred.

(16) Where a cause is remitted to the court from the High Court in England and Wales or Northern Ireland—

(*a*) the deputy principal clerk shall, upon receipt of the order transferring the cause and any process, notify the parties of the transfer;

(*b*) the cause shall be deemed to be an action or petition, as the case may be, as if it had been raised in the Court of Session; and

(*c*) the cause shall be put out "by order" before a Lord Ordinary for further procedure within two court days of the transfer.

(17) Where a decision registered under section 16 of the Act of 1985 is varied or revoked by an authority in the Contracting State in which the decision was made, the court shall—

(*a*) on cancelling the registration of a decision which it has been notified has been revoked, notify—

(i) the person appearing to the court to have actual custody of the child;

(ii) the person on whose behalf the petition for registration was made; or

(iii) any other party to that petition; or

(*b*) on being notified of the variation of a decision, notify—

(i) the person having actual custody of the child; and

(ii) any party to the petition for registration of the decision,

of the variation, and any such person may apply by note in the process of the petition for registration of the decision for the purpose of making representations before the registration is varied.

(18) A person appearing to the court to have an interest in the cancellation or variation of a decision registered under section 16 of the Act of 1985 may apply by note in the process of the petition for registration of the decision or lodge answers to a note presented under paragraph (17).

NOTE
[1] As amended by S.I. 1991 No. 1157, with effect from 27th May 1991.

General provisions

260L.—(1) An application for a certified copy or extract of a decree or other interlocutor relating to a child in respect of whom the applicant wishes to apply under the Hague Convention or the European Convention in another Contracting State, shall be made by letter to the deputy principal clerk; and the certified copy or extract shall be supplied free of charge.

(2) In cause under this section, the court may, where it has reason to believe that any person may have information about the child who is the subject of the cause, order that person to disclose such information by attending before it or by lodging an affidavit.

(3) Subject to the provisions of this section, Rules 191 to 198 shall apply to a petition under this section.

[1] SECTION 18—CAUSES UNDER THE FINANCIAL SERVICES ACT 1986

NOTE
[1] Added by S.I. 1987 No. 2160.

Interpretation

260M. In this section, "the Act of 1986" means the Financial Services Act 1986.

Causes under the Financial Services Act 1986

260N.—(1) An application by virtue of any of the following provisions of the Financial Services Act 1986 shall be made by petition presented to the Outer House:–

(*a*) sections 6, 61, 71(1), 91(4), 104(4), 131(8) and 184(8) (applications by the Secretary of State or a designated agency for interdict or restitution);

(*b*) sections 12, 20, 37(8) and 39(8) (applications by the Secretary of State or a designated agency for compliance orders);

(*c*) section 13(5) (applications by recognised organisation to have a direction set aside);

(*d*) section 93 (applications by the Secretary of State or a designated agency to remove, replace a manager or trustee or to wind up a unit trust scheme); and

(*e*) Schedule 11—

(i) paragraph 6(1) (applications by registrar of friendly societies for compliance orders);

(ii) paragraph 7(4) (applications by recognised self regulating organisations to set aside a direction);

(iii) paragraph 22 (applications by registrar of friendly societies for interdict or to remedy a contravention); and

(iv) paragraph 23(1) so far as it modifies section 61 as applied by section 71(1) (applications by registrar of friendly societies for interdict or restitutions).

(2) Certification by inspectors to the court by virtue of section 94(3) or under section 178(1) of the Act of 1986 shall be made by petition presented to the Outer House.

(3) No order shall be made under section 6, 61, 71, 91, 104, 131 or 184 of, or paragraph 22 of Schedule 11 to, the Act of 1986 against any person unless he is a party to the cause in which the order is to be pronounced.

(4) Where a question of the interpretation of any of the rules or regulations referred to in section 61(1)(*a*) of the Act of 1986 arises in a petition

under this rule, the Secretary of State, a designated agency or any person referred to in section 61(1)(*a*)(iv) of that Act and not already a party in the cause may make representations to the court by lodging answers to the petition.

[1] SECTION 19—REGISTRATION AND ENFORCEMENT OF CUSTODY ORDERS UNDER THE FAMILY LAW ACT 1986

NOTE
[1] Added by S.I. 1988 No. 615.

Interpretation
260P.—(1) In this section—
"the Act of 1986" means the Family Law Act 1986;

[THE NEXT PAGE IS C 122/9]

[1] "appropriate court" means the High Court in England and Wales or the High Court in Northern Ireland or, in relation to a specified dependent territory, the corresponding court in that territory, as the case may be;

[2] "corresponding court" in relation to a specified dependent territory means the corresponding court specified in relation to that territory in Schedule 3 to the Family Law Act 1986 (Dependent Territories) Order 1991;

"custody order" has the meaning assigned to it by sections 1, 32, 40, 42(5) and 42(6) of the Act of 1986;

"deputy principal clerk" means the deputy principal clerk of session or another officer authorised by him;

[1,3] "proper officer" means the Secretary of the principal registry of the Family Division of the High Court in England and Wales or the master (care and protection) of the High Court in Northern Ireland or, in relation to a specified dependent territory, the corresponding officer of the appropriate court in that territory, as the case may be;

"register" means the custody orders register kept under Rule 260Q; and

[2] "specified dependent territory" means a dependent territory specified in column 1 of Schedule 1 to the Family Law Act 1986 (Dependent Territories) Order 1991.

(2) An application for the purposes of Part I of the Act of 1986 in relation to orders under section 1(1)(*b*) of that Act means an application by summons, petition, defences, answers or minute.

NOTES

[1] As amended by S.I. 1990 No. 2118.

[2] Inserted by S.I. 1991 No. 2483, with effect from 25th November 1991.

[3] As amended by S.I. 1991 No. 2483, with effect from 25th November 1991.

Custody orders register

260Q.—(1) The deputy principal clerk shall maintain a register to be called the custody orders register.

[1] (2) In part I of the register there shall be recorded applications for registration of a custody order in another part of the United Kingdom or a specified dependent territory; and in part II of the register there shall be recorded custody orders registered for enforcement in Scotland.

NOTE

[1] As amended by S.I. 1991 No. 2483, with effect from 25th November 1991.

Applications for registration of custody orders in another court

260R.—[1] (1) An application under section 27 of the Act of 1986 to register a custody order made by the Court of Session in an appropriate court shall be made by letter to the deputy principal clerk.

(2) An application under paragraph (1) shall be accompanied by—

(*a*) a copy of the letter of application;

(*b*) an affidavit by the applicant;

(*c*) a copy of that affidavit;

(*d*) a certified copy interlocutor of the custody order;

(*e*) a certified copy interlocutor of any variation which is in force of the custody order; and

(*f*) any other document relevant to the application together with a copy of it.

(3) An affidavit required under this Rule should set out—

(*a*) the name and address of the applicant and his right under the custody order;

(*b*) the name and date of birth of the child in respect of whom the custody order was made, the present whereabouts or suspected whereabouts of the child and the name of any person with whom he is alleged to be;

(*c*) the name and address of any other person who has an interest in the custody order;

[2] (*d*) whether the custody order is to be registered in England and Wales, Northern Ireland or a specified dependent territory and the court in which it is to be registered;

(*e*) whether the custody order is in force;

(*f*) whether the custody order is already registered and, if so, where it is registered; and

(*g*) details of any order known to the applicant which affects the child and is in force in the jurisdiction in which the custody order is to be registered.

(4) Where the deputy principal clerk refuses to send an application under this Rule to the appropriate court on the ground that the custody order is no longer in force, he shall notify the applicant in writing; and the applicant shall have the right to have the application brought before the Lord Ordinary for determination.

(5) The deputy principal clerk shall retain the letter of application under this Rule together with any documents which accompanied it and which are not transmitted to the appropriate court under section 27(3) of the Act of 1986.

NOTES

[1] As amended by S.I. 1990 No. 2118.

[2] As substituted by S.I. 1991 No. 2483, with effect from 25th November 1991.

Transmission of application for registration

260S.—(1) Where the deputy principal clerk is satisfied that the custody order is in force, he shall send the documents mentioned in section 27(3) of the Act of 1986 to the proper officer of the court in which the custody order is to be registered.

(2) For the purposes of section 27(3)(*b*) of the Act of 1986 the prescribed particulars of any variation which is in force of a custody order shall be a certified copy interlocutor of any such variation.

(3) On sending an application under paragraph (1), the deputy principal clerk shall make an entry in part I of the register recording the date and particulars of the application and the custody order.

(4) On receiving notification from a proper officer of an appropriate court that the custody order has been registered in that court under section 27(4) of the Act of 1986, the deputy principal clerk shall record the date of registration in part I of the register.

Registration of custody orders from another court

260T.—(1) The prescribed officer under section 27(4) of the Act of 1986 shall be the deputy principal clerk.

[1] (2) Where the deputy principal clerk receives a certified copy of a custody order from a court for registration under section 27(4) of the Act of 1986, he shall enter the following particulars in part II of the register—

(*a*) the name and address of the applicant and his interest under the custody order;

(*b*) a brief description of the nature of the custody order, the date and the court which made it; and

(*c*) the name and whereabouts or suspected whereabouts of the child who is the subject of the custody order, his date of birth and the date on which he will attain the age of 16.

(3) On registering the custody order, the deputy principal clerk shall—

(*a*) retain the application and the documents which accompanied it; and

(*b*) give notice in writing—

(i) to the court from which he received the application; and

(ii) to the applicant who applied for registration,

that the custody order has been registered.

(4) Where the deputy principal clerk notifies an applicant under paragraph (3), he shall state the date when the registration of the custody order will automatically cease to have effect on the child attaining the age of 16.

NOTE

[1] As amended by S.I. 1990 No. 2118.

Cancellation or variation of registered custody orders

260U.—(1) Where the Court of Session revokes, recalls or varies a custody order which it has made, the deputy principal clerk, on being informed by the party who applied for the revocation, recall or variation that the custody order has been registered in an appropriate court, shall—

(*a*) send a certified copy interlocutor of the revocation, recall or variation to the proper officer of the court in which the custody order is registered;

(*b*) record the transmission of the certified copy in part I of the register; and

(*c*) record the revocation, recall or variation in part I of the register.

(2) On receiving notification from the proper office of the court in which the custody order is registered that he has amended his record, the deputy principal clerk shall record the fact that the amendment has been made in part II of the register.

[1] (3) Where the deputy principal clerk receives a certified copy of an order which revokes, recalls or varies a custody order registered in the Court of Session from a court, he shall—

(*a*) make an entry noting the change and the date of it in part II of the register; and

(*b*) give notice in writing—

(i) to the court from which he received the certified copy of an order which revokes, recalls or varies the custody order;

(ii) to the person who applied for registration of the custody order; and

(iii) if different, to the person who applied for the revocation, recall or variation of the custody order,

that he has amended the register.

(4) An application to the Court of Session under section 28(2) of the Act of 1986 to cancel all or a part of the registration of a custody order which it has registered shall be made by petition and shall be served on—

(*a*) the person who applied for registration, if he is not the petitioner; and

(*b*) any other interested person.

(5) Where, under section 28(2) of the Act of 1986, the court cancels all or a part of the registration of a custody order which it has registered, the deputy principal clerk shall—

(*a*) make an entry noting the cancellation and the date of it in part II of the register; and

(*b*) give notice in writing to—

(i) the court which made the custody order;

(ii) the person who applied for registration; and

(iii) if different, the person who applied for cancellation of the custody order.

NOTE

[1] As amended by S.I. 1990 No. 2118.

Enforcement of registered custody orders in Scotland

260V.—(1) Proceedings under section 29(1) of the Act of 1986 to enforce a custody order registered in the Court of Session shall be by petition presented to the Outer House.

(2) Where the petitioner in an application under section 29(1) of the Act of 1986 is not the person who applied for registration, the petition shall be served on that person.

(3) Subject to paragraph (4), Rules 191 and 193 to 198 apply to a petition under this rule.

(4) There shall be such intimation and service of a petition under this rule as the court may require.

Applications to sist or refuse enforcement proceedings

260W.—(1) An application under section 30(1) of the Act of 1986 to sist enforcement proceedings shall be made—

(*a*) by lodging answers at any time in the process of the petition for enforcement; or

(*b*) where answers have been lodged by the party making the application, by motion,

and served or intimated (as the case may be) on every other party and, if he is not a party, the applicant for registration of the custody order.

(2) An application under section 30(3) of the Act of 1986 to recall a sist of enforcement proceedings shall be made by motion.

(3) An application under section 31(1) of the Act of 1986 to dismiss a petition for enforcement shall be made—

(*a*) by lodging answers at any time in the process of the petition for enforcement;

(*b*) where answers have been lodged by the party making the application, by motion; or

(*c*) at a hearing assigned for that purpose,

and served or intimated (as the case may be) on every other party and, if he is not a party, the applicant for registration of the custody order.

(4) Where the court pronounces an interlocutor under section 30(2) or (3) or section 31(3) of the Act of 1986, the deputy principal clerk shall—

(*a*) make an entry noting the terms of the interlocutor and the date in part II of the register; and

(*b*) give notice in writing—

(i) to the person who applied for registration where he was not a party to the application under section 30(1) or section 31(1) or (2) of the Act of 1986; and

(ii) to the court from which the application for registration was received,

of the terms of the interlocutor.

Miscellaneous provisions

260X.—(1) Where the court pronounces an interlocutor ordering a person to disclose information to the court as to a child's whereabouts under section 33(1) of the Act of 1986, it may do so by ordaining that person to appear before it or to lodge an affidavit.

(2) An application by a person mentioned in section 35(4)(*b*) or (*c*) of the Act of 1986 for interdict or interim interdict under section 35(3) of that Act shall be made by minute in the cause in which the application is to be made.

(3) The register may be inspected by—

(*a*) the person who applied for registration; and

(*b*) any other person who satisfies the deputy principal clerk that he has an interest to do so.

[1] Section 20

Applications Under Section 8(1) of the Access to Health Records Act 1990

NOTE

[1] Inserted by S.I. 1991 No. 2652 (effective 16th December 1991).

Applications

260Y.—(1) This Section applies to applications under section 8(1) of the Access to Health Records Act 1990.

(2) In this Section—

"the Act of 1990" means the Access to Health Records Act 1990;

"the Regulations" means the Access to Health Records (Steps to Secure Compliance and Compliants Procedures) (Scotland) Regulations 1991;

"complaint" means a written notice of complaint under regulation 3 or 4 of the Regulations;

"report" means a report under regulation 6 of the Regulations.

(3) An application under section 8(1) of the Act of 1990 shall be made by petition presented to the Outer House.

(4) An application under section 8(1) of the Act of 1990 may not be made unless the petition is presented—

(*a*) where the applicant has received a report, within one year of the date of the report;

(*b*) where the applicant has not received a report, within 18 months of the date of the complaint;

(5) A petition under paragraph (3) shall state those steps prescribed in the Regulations which have been taken to secure compliance with the Act of 1990.

(6) Such a petition, when presented, shall be accompanied by—

(*a*) a copy of the application under section 3 of the Act of 1990 for access to the health record in question;

(*b*) a copy of the compliant;

(*c*) if applicable, a copy of the report.

CHAPTER V

Inner House

Section 1—Reclaiming

Scope of this section

[1] **261.** The provisions of this section of this chapter shall apply with regard to all interlocutors pronounced in the Outer House, or by the Vacation Judge, which it is desired to submit to the Inner House for review including any interlocutor pronounced by the nominated judge when disposing of appeals under Rule 292(*b*) hereof.

NOTE

[1] As amended by S.I. 1975 No. 89.

[THE NEXT PAGE IS C 122/13]

Mode of reclaiming

262.—(*a*) Any party to a cause who is dissatisfied with such an interlocutor may, subject to the provisions herein contained, reclaim against the same by a motion for the review of such interlocutor by the Inner House, such motion to be as nearly as may be in terms of Form 41.

(*b*) All such motions shall be enrolled, made, and intimated, in the same way as is directed in paragraphs (*a*), (*b*), and (*c*), of Rule 93.

(*c*) Every reclaiming motion whether enrolled before or after the whole cause has been decided in the Outer House, shall have the effect of submitting to the review of the Inner House the whole of the prior interlocutors of the Lord Ordinary of whatever date, not only at the instance of the party reclaiming, but also at the instance of all or any of the other parties who have appeared in the cause, to the effect of enabling the court to do complete justice, without hindrance from the terms of any interlocutor which may have been pronounced by the Lord Ordinary, and without the necessity of any counter reclaiming motion; and after a reclaiming motion has been presented, the reclaimer shall not be at liberty to withdraw it without the consent of the other parties as aforesaid; and if he shall not insist therein, any other party in the cause may do so, in the same way as if it had been presented at his own instance.

(*d*) When in any reclaiming motion or appeal the parties are agreed that on any separate branch of the case the interlocutor reclaimed or appealed against is not to be submitted for review, it shall not be necessary to reproduce the notes of evidence or documents relating to such separate branch.

Objections to competency

263.—(*a*) If before one o'clock on the first business day after the day on which the enrolment is made (on Saturdays before twelve o'clock) the motion is not marked with the word "Opposed as incompetent" (which marking, if made, shall bear its date, and shall be signed by the solicitor making the same or by his clerk on his behalf), the motion shall be brought on the earliest available sederunt day before one or other Division of the Inner House in Chambers; and such Division may, without hearing any party, either send the cause to the summar roll or direct the same to be heard in the single bills, and the cause shall be so heard.

(*b*) If before one o'clock on the day after the day on which the enrolment is made (on Saturdays before twelve o'clock) an objection to the motion shall be marked in manner foresaid, the cause shall be put out in the single bills on the earliest available sederunt day. The court may hear and dispose of the objections in the single bills or send the cause to the summar roll.

(*c*) When a cause is called in the single bills on account of an objection to competency of reclaiming, or when a cause is sent to the summar roll on an objection to competency which has been reserved in single bills, and the objection is not maintained, the court may find the objector liable in any expenses occasioned by the objection.

Reclaiming days, and leave to reclaim

264.—[0] (*a*) An interlocutor disposing either by itself, or taken along with a previous interlocutor or interlocutors of—

(i) the whole subject-matter of the cause; or

(ii) the whole merits of the cause but reserving, or not disposing of, the question of expenses,

pronounced in any cause initiated in the Outer House either by summons or by petition may be reclaimed against, without leave, not later than 21 days (whether in session or vacation) after the day on which the interlocutor was pronounced. In the case of such an interlocutor containing an award of custody, access or aliment, the marking of a reclaiming motion shall not excuse obedience to or implement of the award of custody, access or aliment unless by order of the Lord Ordinary or one of the Divisions of the Inner House or the Vacation Judge.

[1] (*b*) An interlocutor disposing of part of the merits of the cause, or

[THE NEXT PAGE IS C 123]

allowing or refusing proof or jury trial (but, in case of refusal, without disposing of the whole merits of the cause), or limiting the mode of proof, or adjusting issues for jury trial, or allowing jury trial without issues, or granting or refusing or recalling or refusing to recall interim interdict or interim liberation or in relation to an exclusion order under section 4 of the Matrimonial Homes (Family Protection) (Scotland) Act 1981, or granting or refusing or recalling a sist of execution or procedure, may be reclaimed against, without leave, not later than the fourteenth day after the day on which the said interlocutor is pronounced; provided that when such an interlocutor is pronounced in vacation or recess, or when the fourteenth day after the day on which the interlocutor is pronounced falls in vacation or recess, the reclaiming days shall be extended to 21.

(*c*) An interlocutor allowing or refusing in whole or in part a commission and diligence for the recovery of documents applied for after calling of the summons and any other interlocutor (not being a decree in absence nor a decree by default, nor one of the interlocutors dealt with in the immediately preceding paragraphs of this rule) may be reclaimed against, with leave of the Lord Ordinary who pronounced the same, or (in vacation or recess) with leave of the Vacation Judge, not later than the seventh day (whether in session, vacation or recess) after the day on which the said interlocutor is pronounced; provided that (i) it shall not be competent to ask or obtain leave except during the currency of the reclaiming days; (ii) it shall not be competent to reclaim against the grant or refusal of leave by the Lord Ordinary or the Vacation Judge; and (iii) such leave shall not, standing the interlocutor reclaimed against, excuse obedience to or implement of the interlocutor, unless by order of the Lord Ordinary, or one or other Division, or (in vacation) of the Vacation Judge.

(*d*) In any case of mistake or inadvertence, the court may, in its discretion, allow a motion for review to be received and proceed, though not enrolled within the reclaiming days defined in the preceding paragraphs of this rule, but only on such conditions as to expenses as the court may think proper.

(*e*) Notwithstanding the foregoing provisions, it shall be competent to reclaim, without leave, against a decree by default at any time before extract; and where the default has been in failing to lodge a paper the paper must be lodged on or before the enrolment of the motion for review; otherwise, the motion shall be refused. No decree by default shall be recalled except upon such conditions as to expenses or otherwise as the court may think proper.

(*f*) The deliverance of a Lord Ordinary that the stamp upon any document is sufficient, or that such document does not require a stamp, shall not be subject to review.

[2] (*g*) Paragraphs (*a*), (*b*) and (*c*) of this rule shall not apply to interlocutors pronounced in the winding up of a company and, subject to paragraphs (*d*) and (*e*) of this rule, and to the other rules of this section, section 277(3) of the Companies Act 1948, c. 38, shall continue to apply to all such interlocutors.

[3] (*h*) It shall not be competent for any party to a petition for suspension, suspension and interdict, or suspension and liberation, to reclaim against any interlocutor awarding expenses in respect of a certificate of no caution or consignation; and accordingly the fact that an interlocutor has been reclaimed against shall not prevent the issue of a certificate of refusal nor hinder the interlocutor submitted to review from being carried into effect unless the court shall, on cause shewn, stay proceedings.

NOTES

[0] Substituted by S.I. 1990 No. 705.

[1] As amended by S.I. 1977 No. 1621, S.I. 1980 No. 1144 and S.I. 1985 No. 1600.

[2] Substituted by S.I. 1967 No. 1090. Section 277(3) of the Companies Act 1948 is now s.162(4) of the Insolvency Act 1986.

[3] As amended by S.I. 1980 No. 1144.

Section 2—Special Cases

To be presented and heard in the Inner House

265.—(*a*) All special cases under section 63 of the Court of Session Act 1868,[(1)] shall be presented to the Inner House, and shall be lodged in the General Department.

(*b*) On being so lodged, any such special case shall, without passing through single bills, be heard in due course in the short roll of one or other Division of the Inner House.

[1] (*c*) The special case may be amended by consent of the parties.

NOTES

[(1)] Section 63 of the Court of Session Act 1868 is now s.27 of the Court of Session Act 1988.

[1] Added by S.I. 1984 No. 472.

Appointment of curator ad litem *to party* incapax

266.—(*a*) If any of the parties to a special case, as presented, is *incapax* in respect of non-age, insanity or otherwise, it shall be the duty of the other parties (which duty may be performed by any of them), on presentation of the special case, to enrol a motion for appointment of an advocate as curator *ad litem* to such *incapax*; and it shall be competent for the court to appoint such curator *ad litem*.

(*b*) Any such curator *ad litem* appointed as aforesaid shall be given all necessary facilities by the other parties; and, if he is satisfied that the special case is fully and accurately stated in reference to the interests of the *incapax*, may sign it (with or without the amendments consented to by him and the other parties) as curator *ad litem*. If he is not given all necessary facilities by the other parties, or is not satisfied that the special case is fully and accurately stated in reference to the interests of the *incapax*, it shall be his duty to report orally to the division by whom he was appointed; and such division may then recall his appointment and dispose of the special case as shall seem just.

(*c*) It shall not be competent to award expenses against such curator *ad litem* in any circumstances, but he shall be entitled to his expenses as may be directed by the court.

Section 3—Appeals from Inferior Courts Generally (Including Lyon Court, Sheriff Courts, etc.), Appeals under the Agricultural Holdings (Scotland) Act 1949, Section 75 and Schedule VI and Appeals under the Industrial Relations Act 1971

Scope of section

267. Subject always to the provisions contained in Rules 276 to 289 the rules contained in this section shall, notwithstanding any provision in any Act of Parliament to the contrary, apply with regard to all appeals from any interlocutor, judgment or determination (including decrees of removing) pronounced by any inferior court (other than the Land Court) which may competently be submitted for review to the Court of Session, or to a judge thereof.

Time and mode of appeal: transmission: intimations

[1] **268.**—[2] (1) Except as otherwise provided in any other enactment, an appeal from an inferior court shall be marked not later than 21 days after the date of the interlocutor, judgment or determination appealed against; and shall be by note of appeal written by the appellant or his solicitor on the interlocutor sheet, minute of court, or other written record containing the interlocutor, judgment or determination appealed against, or on a

separate sheet lodged with the clerk of the inferior court; and such note of appeal shall be as nearly as may be in the following terms:— "The (*pursuer, applicant, claimant, defender, respondent, or other party*) appeals to the Court of Session"; and shall be signed by the appellant or his solicitor, bear the date on which it is signed and specify the name and address of the solicitors who will be acting for the appellant in the appeal.

[1] (2) Where a person fails to mark an appeal within the time specified under paragraph (1) or any other enactment, as the case may be, that person shall include, in a note of appeal made in accordance with paragraph (1), an application for leave to appeal out of time; and a Division of the Inner House may, on the motion of that person in the single bills, grant leave to appeal out of time on such conditions, if any, as to expenses or otherwise as the court considers appropriate.

(3) Within four days after an appeal shall have been taken in manner foresaid, the clerk of the inferior court or tribunal shall transmit the process to the Deputy Principal Clerk who, on receipt of the same, shall subjoin to

[THE NEXT PAGE IS C 125]

the note of appeal a marking of the date on which it is received; provided that, in an appeal from any tribunal whose proceedings are minuted or recorded in official books, copies of such proceedings certified by the clerk to such tribunal shall be transmitted as aforesaid in lieu of the process above referred to, and shall as so transmitted and received be the equivalent of such process, and shall in all such cases be accompanied by a separate note of appeal in manner provided in paragraph (*a*) of this rule.

(4) Within the said four days, the clerk of the inferior court or tribunal shall send written notice of the appeal to the other party or parties, or to his or their solicitor or solicitors and certify on the interlocutor sheet that he has done so; provided that failure to give such notice shall not invalidate the appeal, but the court may give such remedy for any disadvantage or inconvenience thereby occasioned as may in the circumstances be considered proper and necessary.

NOTES

[1] As amended by S.I. 1990 No. 2118.

[2] As amended by S.I. 1991 No. 2483, with effect from 25th November 1991.

Entering appearance: lodging: failure to lodge: abandonment and sist

[1] **269.**—[2] (*a*) Within fourteen days of the receipt by the Deputy Principal Clerk of the process in appeal, the parties, or the solicitors for the parties, shall cause to be written on the interlocutor sheet, minute of court, or other written record containing the interlocutor, judgment or determination appealed against, or on the separate sheet referred to in paragraph (*a*) of Rule 268, their names and addresses, and (in the case of parties' solicitors) shall specify the parties for whom they respectively act.

(*b*) Within twenty-eight days of the receipt by the Deputy Principal Clerk of the process in an appeal, the appellant shall (whether in session or in vacation) make up and lodge in the General Department a process as prescribed in Rule 20, which shall include the inferior court process (detailed in the inventory and duplicate inventory of the Court of Session process), and he shall also lodge therewith a process copy of the record and ten further copies thereof containing any amendments allowed since the closing of the record, or other pleadings in the cause, interlocutors or other orders, and note of appeal, and deliver at least ten copies thereof to the solicitor of the respondent, or to each of the solicitors of the respondents (if more than one); and, if the appellant shall fail within the said period of twenty-eight days to lodge and deliver the papers required as aforesaid, he shall be held to have abandoned his appeal and shall not be entitled to insist therein except upon being reponed as hereinafter provided; provided however that, within fourteen days after receipt by the Deputy Principal Clerk of the process in an appeal, the appellant may enrol a motion for a sist of process, and if, on cause shewn, the court or Vacation Judge grants such sist, the running of the said twenty-eight days shall be postponed until the sist is recalled. An unopposed motion for the recall of such sist may, in vacation or recess, be disposed of by the Vacation Judge.

(*c*) At the time when the appellant lodges the process and other papers in terms of the immediately preceding paragraph of this rule, he shall enrol and intimate to the respondent a motion for an order for hearing.

NOTES

[1] As amended by S.I. 1974 No. 845.

[2] As amended by S.I. 1991 No. 2483, with effect from 25th November 1991. See Practice Note 13th November 1969, *infra*.

Objections to competency

270.—(*a*) If, on the day after the day on which the enrolment is made in terms of paragraph (*c*) of the immediately preceding rule, the respondent shall not mark the motion as appearing in the motion sheet, with the words "Opposed as incompetent" (which marking, if made, shall bear its date, and shall be signed by the solicitor making the same, or by his clerk on his behalf) the motion shall, on the earliest available sederunt day, be brought before one or other Division of the Inner House in Chambers; and such Division may, without hearing any party, either send the cause to the summar or short roll, or if the Division thinks proper, direct the same to be heard in single bills.

(*b*) If, on the day after the day on which the enrolment is made an objection to the motion shall be marked in manner aforesaid, the cause shall be put out for hearing in the single bills on the earliest available sederunt day.

Reponing

271. It shall be lawful for the appellant, within seven days after the appeal has been held to be abandoned in accordance with paragraph (*b*) of Rule 269, to enrol a motion to be reponed. Such motion shall then be put out in the single bills before one or other Division of the Inner House, or before the Vacation Judge (as the case may be), and shall only be granted upon cause shewn, and upon such conditions as to payment of expenses to the respondent, or otherwise, as shall seem just.

Respondent may proceed with abandoned appeal: retransmission of abandoned appeal

272.—(*a*) It shall be lawful for the respondent, within seven days after the appeal has been held to be abandoned in accordance with paragraph (*b*) of Rule 269, to lodge a copy of the record and others, as provided in said paragraph (*b*), and thereafter to insist in the appeal as if it had been taken by himself; in which case the appellant shall also be entitled to insist in the appeal; and the provisions regulating appeals by an appellant shall apply equally to appeals insisted in under this section by the respondent.

[1] (*b*) On the expiry of the said period of seven days after the appeal has been held to be abandoned as aforesaid, if the appellant shall not have been reponed and if the respondent does not insist in the appeal, or on receipt by the Deputy Principal Clerk of a letter signed by the solicitors for all parties stating that the appellant has abandoned the appeal, the judgment or judgments complained of shall become final, and shall be treated in all respects as if no appeal had been taken against the same; and the Deputy Principal Clerk shall cause the process to be retransmitted to the clerk of the inferior court; provided always that before retransmitting the process the Deputy Principal Clerk shall cause to be engrossed upon the interlocutor sheet, minute of court, or other written record containing the interlocutor, judgment or determination appealed against, or on the separate sheet referred to in paragraph (*a*) of Rule 268, a certificate in these terms:—"(*Date*) Retransmitted in respect of the abandonment of the appeal"—and, in respect of such certificate, the inferior court shall, on a motion being made to that effect, grant decree for payment to the respondent in the appeal of the expenses of the abandoned appeal which expenses are to be taxed by the Auditor of Court of the Court of Session.

NOTE

[1] As amended by the Decimal Currency Act 1969, s. 10(1), and S.I. 1985 No. 1600.

Appeals against interlocutor applying verdict

273.—(*a*) In appeals against interlocutors applying verdicts of juries in a sheriff court, it shall not be necessary to lodge copies of the notes of evidence unless an order appointing the same to be lodged shall be made by the court.

(*b*) If in any such appeal, the court shall order a new trial, it shall be the duty of the party wishing to proceed with the cause in the sheriff court to furnish the sheriff court with a certified copy of the interlocutor making such order, and also to borrow the sheriff court process and transmit the same to the sheriff court.

SECTION 4—CAUSES REMITTED FROM SHERIFF COURTS

Process on remit

[1] **274.** The Deputy Principal Clerk shall, on receiving the process in a case transmitted to him by a sheriff clerk, cause the date of receipt to be entered on the interlocutor sheet.

NOTE

[1] Substituted by S.I. 1980 No. 1801.

Procedure on remit

[1] **275.**—[2] (1) Within 14 days of receipt by the Deputy Principal Clerk of a process transmitted under Rule 274, the parties, or the solicitors for the parties, shall cause to be written on the interlocutor sheet, minute of court, or other written record of the remitted cause or on a separate sheet, their names and addresses, and (in the case of parties' solicitors) shall specify the parties for whom they respectively act.

(2) Within 28 days of receipt by the Deputy Principal Clerk of the process in the remitted cause:—

(*a*) the party on whose motion the remit was made, or

(*b*) in a cause remitted by the sheriff of his own accord, the pursuer or first pursuer,

shall (whether in session or in vacation) make up and lodge in the General Department a process as prescribed in Rule 20, which shall include the sheriff court process (detailed in the inventory and duplicate inventory of the Court of Session process) and shall also lodge therewith a process copy of the initial writ and defences or record or other pleadings as the case may be and three further copies thereof including any amendments allowed, interlocutors or other orders, and deliver at least six copies to the solicitor for the other party or to each of the solicitors of the other parties (if more than one).

(3) In a remitted cause:—

(*a*) the party on whose motion the remit was made, or

(*b*) in a cause remitted by the sheriff on his own accord, the pursuer or first pursuer,

shall, at the time of lodging the documents required under paragraph (2), apply in the single bills for further procedure and intimate the application to the other party or parties.

(4) Within 14 days after receipt by the Deputy Principal Clerk of the process in a remitted cause, a party in the cause may apply in the single bills for a sist of process and if, on cause shown, the court grants the sist the running of the 28-day period in paragraph (2) shall be postponed until the sist is recalled.

(5) If—

(*a*) the party on whose motion the remit was made, or

(*b*) in a cause remitted by the sheriff of his own accord, the pursuer or first pursuer

fails to comply with any requirement of this rule:—

(i) he may nevertheless, within the period of seven days following the period of 28 days in paragraph (2) apply in the single bills to be reponed on cause shown, in the same manner and subject to the same conditions as apply under Rule 271 to an appeal;

(ii) any other party to the action may, within the said period of seven days, proceed with the action in accordance with the provisions of Rule 272.

(6) If, in a case to which paragraph (5) applies, the period of seven days expires without any such action as is mentioned under heads (i) and

(ii) of that paragraph being taken, the remit shall be treated as abandoned, and the Deputy Principal Clerk shall cause:—

(*a*) the words "Re-transmitted in respect that the remit has been abandoned" to be entered on the interlocutor sheet; and

(*b*) the process to be transmitted back to the sheriff clerk.

(7) The Vacation Judge may deal by way of motion, with the following matters:—

(*a*) an application under paragraph (4) or (5); and

(*b*) an unopposed application for the recall of a sist granted under paragraph (4).

NOTES

[1] As substituted by S.I. 1982 No. 1825.

[2] As amended by S.I. 1991 No. 2483, with effect from 25th November 1991.

SECTION 5—APPEALS BY WAY OF STATED CASE, SPECIAL CASE, SUBMISSION AND REFERENCE UNDER CERTAIN STATUTES

Rules under which regulated

[1] **276.** All appeals by way of stated case, special case, case, reference or submission (hereinafter referred to as "the case") against the decision of any court, the Secretary of State, a Minister, a Department statutory tribunal, referee or authority (hereinafter referred to as "the tribunal") and all stated cases by an arbiter and all statutory proceedings for obtaining the opinion of the court on a question either prior to the issue of a decision by the tribunal or by way of appeal against a decision by the tribunal, shall subject to the provisions of the statute allowing such appeal or proceedings (hereinafter referred to as "the statute") and these Rules be regulated by Rules 277 to 280, provided that "the question" shall in the said Rules be construed as "the question of law" unless the statute allows an appeal on a question other than a question of law.

NOTE

[1] As amended by S.I. 1972 No. 2021.

Preparation of the case for presentation to the court

277. Where the court is authorised to make regulations by Act of Sederunt for obtaining, settling, stating and authenticating the case for presentation to the court, the following provisions shall have effect:

[1] (*a*) Any party desiring to have a case, application for which must be presented prior to the issue of the decision of the tribunal, may at any time prior thereto apply to the clerk of the tribunal for a case for the opinion of the Court of Session on any question, and any party desiring to have a case which may be presented following upon the issue of the decision of the tribunal or, in a case where a statement of the reasons for a decision was given later than the issue of the decision, on the issue of such a statement, may, within fourteen days after the issue thereof, similarly apply for such a case. Such applications shall be made by minute, and shall set forth the question on which the case is applied for.

(*b*) The clerk of the tribunal shall forthwith intimate such application and the question of law on which the case is applied for to the other party, who shall be entitled within seven days after the receipt thereof to lodge a minute setting forth any additional question proposed as the subject matter of the case, and the provisions of paragraphs (*c*) and (*d*) of this rule shall apply to any such application and to any such additional question.

(*c*) If the application is presented before the facts have been ascertained by the tribunal, and if the tribunal is of opinion that it is necessary or expedient that the facts should be ascertained before the application is disposed of, it may postpone further consideration of the application until the facts have been ascertained by it.

(*d*) On consideration of any such application, whether after the facts have been ascertained or at an earlier stage (should the tribunal think it necessary or expedient then to consider it), the tribunal may, if it is of opinion that the proposed question does not arise or that a decision upon it is unnecessary for the purpose of the appeal or is frivolous, refuse to state a case on such question; but in that event it shall intimate its decision to the parties and grant a certificate to the applicant, specifying the reason of refusal and bearing the date of the refusal; and if such refusal is made after the facts have been ascertained, such certificate shall be accompanied by a note of the proposed findings in which the facts which have been ascertained, and on which the tribunal proposes to base its decision, shall be set forth, and if such refusal is made before the facts have been ascertained the certificate shall be accompanied by a note of, or sufficient reference to, the averments of the parties in the appeal or their admissions therein on which the refusal is based.

(*e*) If and when the tribunal decides to state a case on any application it shall cause its decision to be intimated to the parties not later than the expiry of 28 days after the date on which the application was made, and within fourteen days after the despatch of such intimation it shall cause the case to be prepared and submitted in draft to the parties: within twenty-one days from the receipt of the draft case, each party shall return it to the clerk of the tribunal with a note of any additions, alterations, or amendments which he may desire to have made thereon.

(*f*) (i) Should the parties fail to agree as to the terms of the case, or should any of them fail to return the draft case, the tribunal shall adjust the terms of the case and in any event the terms of the case shall be subject to the approval of the tribunal.

(ii) When a draft case is being settled by the tribunal, it may add thereto such further or additional findings in fact and such additional questions as it may think necessary for the due disposal of the subject matter of the case.

(*g*) The case shall bear to be stated by the tribunal and shall be authenticated by the clerk thereof, who shall thereupon cause it to be delivered to the party, or the party who first applied for it.

(*h*) The party to whom the case has been so delivered—

(i) shall intimate in writing to the other party whether he intends to proceed with the case, and shall also send to him a copy of the case, within seven days (under the Finance Act 1960, thirty days) after the case has been delivered to him by the clerk of the tribunal.

(ii) if he intends to proceed with the case, he shall also within the said seven days (under the Finance Act 1960, thirty days) lodge the principal case with the Deputy Principal Clerk, together with a certificate under the hand of himself or his solicitor of the notice having been given to the other parties; and, in the event of his failing so to lodge the case, the respondent in the appeal shall be entitled to apply to the tribunal, who, upon a motion made before it to that effect and on being satisfied of such failure, shall dispose of the proceedings, and may, if one party only has applied for a stated case, find him liable in payment to the other party of the sum of £5·25 of expenses.

(*j*) The party to whom the case has been delivered, if he does not intend to proceed with it, shall immediately after the expiry of seven days from the date of the delivery of the case to him return the case to the clerk of the tribunal, who shall thereupon deliver it to the other party if that party had also applied for a case and that other party shall thereupon be entitled to proceed in the manner provided in paragraph (*h*)(ii) above.

[2] (*k*) (i) The party to whom the case has been delivered shall within 14 days after the principal case has been received by the said Deputy Principal Clerk, lodge the same in the General Department along with a process and copies of productions for the use of the court in terms of Rules 20 and 25(*b*), and shall at the same time intimate the lodging of the case to the opposite party or his solicitor, and deliver to him at least six copies of the case, and, if he shall fail within the said period to lodge the case as aforesaid, or to be reponed against his failure to do so by motion made to the court during session, or to the Vacation Judge during vacation, within the following seven days, he shall be held to have abandoned his appeal.

(ii) If the other party has also applied for a stated case and has had no opportunity of proceeding with his appeal, the party to whom the case was delivered shall forthwith intimate to the other party that he has abandoned his appeal; and the other party shall then be entitled to proceed in the manner provided in the immediately preceding sub-paragraph; provided that the days shall be reckoned from the intimation of the abandonment; and if such party fails so to proceed he shall in like manner be held to have abandoned his appeal.

[3] (iii) On the abandonment of the appeal by the only party, or by both parties, entitled to proceed, the Deputy Principal Clerk shall engross upon the case, which must be returned to him for that purpose, and sign a certificate in the following or similar terms; (*date*) "Retransmitted in respect of abandonment"—and retransmit the case accordingly; and in respect of said certificate the tribunal shall, upon a motion being made before it to that effect, dispose of the proceedings, and may, if one party only has applied for a stated case, find him liable for payment to the other party in the appeal of the sum of £5·25 of expenses.

NOTES

[1] As amended by S.I. 1982 No. 1825.

[2] As amended by S.I. 1984 No. 499.

[3] As amended by the Decimal Currency Act 1969, s.10(1).

Procedure for ordaining the tribunal to state a case

278. When the tribunal has refused to state and sign a case the party whose application has been refused may, within fourteen days from date of such refusal, apply by a written note to one of the divisions of the Inner House lodged in the General Department for an order upon the other party to shew cause why a case should not be stated. Such note shall state shortly the nature of the case, the facts and the question which the applicant desires to raise, and shall be accompanied by the above-mentioned certificate of refusal, and the Division shall, after intimation to the other parties, dispose of it summarily. If an order is pronounced requiring the tribunal to state a case, the case shall be stated as required by the statute or these Rules, and these Rules so far as applicable shall apply to the subsequent procedure. Intimation of the decision or order shall be made to the tribunal by the despatch by registered or recorded delivery letter of a certified copy thereof to the clerk to the tribunal by the applicant.

Form of stated case or special case, submission or reference

279.—(*a*) The case shall refer to the statute under which it is presented, and shall state in articulate numbered paragraphs the facts and circumstances out of which the case arises, as the same may be agreed, found, or referred (as the case may be), and shall set out the question for answer by the court.

(*b*) The form of the case shall, as nearly as may be, be as shewn in form 43.

Procedure in the Court of Session

280—(*a*) The party to whom a case has been delivered, on lodging a copy thereof in terms of Rule 277(*k*)(i) shall at the same time enrol and intimate to the opposite party a motion for an order for hearing. The said motion shall be brought before one or other Division of the Inner House in chambers and such Division may, without hearing any party, either send the case to the summer roll, or, if the Division thinks proper, direct the same to be heard in single bills.

(*b*) The court may, at any time before the final disposal of the case, allow the case to be amended with consent of the parties thereto, and may remit the case for re-statement, or further statement in whole or in part; and if, in order to the disposal of the case, any enquiry into matters of fact is competent and required, the Division before which the case depends may remit to a reporter or to a Lord Ordinary or to one of their own number to take evidence.

Revenue Appeals (other than appeals relating to penalties)

[1] **281.**—(1) This rule applies to appeals to the Court of Session as the

[THE NEXT PAGE IS C 131]

Court of Exchequer in Scotland under any enactment providing for appeal by way of stated case to the court from a determination of the General or Special Commissioners, not being an appeal to which Rule 282 applies, and in particular applies to the following enactments:—

(*a*) section 56 of the Taxes Management Act 1970;
(*b*) paragraph 10(4) of Schedule 4 to the Finance Act 1975;
(*c*) paragraph 14 of Schedule 2 to the Oil Taxation Act 1975;
[2] (*d*) regulation 10 of the Stamp Duty Reserve Tax Regulations 1986.

(2) On the case being stated and signed and sent to the party requiring it he shall within 30 days of the date on which it was sent to him, send notice in writing of the fact that the case has been stated on his application, together with a copy of the case, to the other party and shall intimate to the other party whether or not he intends to proceed with the case, and if he so intends, he shall within that period send the principal case to the Deputy Principal Clerk of Session who shall docquet it, and within 30 days after the date of so sending it, the appellant shall lodge the principal case in the General Department together with a process and ten copies of the case.

(3) On lodging the principal case the party lodging it shall:—

(*a*) enrol a motion for an order for hearing, and
(*b*) intimate to the other party or his solicitor that he has lodged the principal case and enrolled the motion, and
[3] (*c*) deliver to the other party or his solicitor such number of copies of the case, not exceeding six, as he may require.

(4) The motion shall be brought before either Division of the Inner House in chambers, and the Division may send the case to the Summar Roll, or, if the Division thinks proper, direct the case to be heard in the Single Bills.

(5) If the party requiring the case fails to comply with any time limit imposed by this rule he shall be held to have abandoned the case.

NOTES
[1] Substituted by S.I. 1976 No. 1849.
[2] Inserted by S.I. 1990 No. 705.
[3] As amended by S.I. 1984 No. 499.

Revenue Appeals relating to penalties

[1] **282.**—(1) This rule applies to appeals to the Court of Session as the Court of Exchequer in Scotland under any enactment providing for an appeal to the court from a determination of the General of Special Commissioners relating to the award, imposition or recovery of a penalty, and in particular applies to an appeal from the award of any penalty under the following enactments:—

(*a*) section 53(2) of the Taxes Management Act 1970;
[2] (*b*) section 100C(4) of the said Act;
(*c*) paragraph 1 of Schedule 2 to the Oil Taxation Act 1975.

(2) In an appeal to which this rule applies, the appellant shall within 30 days of the determination of the Commissioners intimate his appeal in writing to them and to the other party and the grounds of his appeal.

(3) The Commissioners shall on receiving intimation of an appeal under paragraph (2), state and sign a case for the opinion of the court, setting out the facts found by them and their determination thereon.

(4) For the purposes of further procedure under this rule, Rule 281 shall apply to an appeal under this rule as it applies to an appeal under that rule.

NOTES
[1] Substituted by S.I. 1976 No. 1849.
[2] As amended by S.I. 1990 No. 705.

Appeals against determinations of the Board relating to Capital Transfer Tax, Inheritance Tax or Stamp Duty Reserve Tax

[1] **283.**—[2] (1) This Rule applies to appeals under section 222(3) of the Inheritance Tax Act 1984 or regulation 8(3) of the Stamp Duty Reserve Tax Regulations 1986.

[2] (2) An application by an appellant for leave to appeal to the Court of Session against any determination of the Board specified in a notice given by the Board to the appellant under section 221 of the said Act or regulation 6 of the said Regulations shall be made in writing and lodged with the General Department within 30 days of the date on which the Board intimate to the appellant that they do not agree that the appeal be to the court.

[2] (3) An application under paragraph (2) shall set out the matters it is contended are to be decided on appeal and shall be accompanied by—

(*a*) a copy of the notice in writing and grounds of appeal given to the Board; and

(*b*) the reasons stating why the appeal should be to the court.

(4) On lodging his application the appellant shall lodge with it a certificate that a copy of the application has been sent to the Solicitor of Inland Revenue for Scotland on behalf of the Board with the date of posting thereof, and the Board may lodge answers thereto within 14 days of the said date of posting.

(5) On expiry of the said period of 14 days, the appellant shall—

(i) enrol a motion for an order for hearing, and

(ii) intimate the motion to the Solicitor of Inland Revenue for Scotland on behalf of the Board.

(6) The motion shall be brought before either Division of the Inner House in chambers, and the Division may send the case to the Summar Roll, or if the Division thinks proper, may direct the case to be heard in the Single Bills.

[2] (7) In a case where the court grants leave to appeal or, where it is agreed between the appellant and the Board that the appeal be to the court, the appellant shall lodge in the General Department within 14 days of the date on which leave to appeal is granted or, as the case may be, of the date on which the Board intimate their agreement to the appellant, a statement of facts and the grounds on which he contends the Board's determination is erroneous, and shall at the same time send a copy thereof to the Solicitor of Inland Revenue for Scotland on behalf of the Board.

(8) Within 14 days of the date of posting to them of the appellant's statement of facts and grounds of appeal, the Board may lodge answers thereto in the General Department and on so doing shall send a copy thereof to the appellant.

(9) In a case where the Board sends answers under paragraph (8), a record of the statement of facts and answers and of the respective contentions of the appellant and the Board shall be made up and ten copies thereof shall be lodged by the appellant in the application process, and may, on the motion of either party, be adjusted for such period as the court may determine.

(10) In a case where there are no answers by the Board the appellant shall lodge in the General Department, within 14 days of the expiry of the period mentioned in paragraph (8), ten copies of the statement of facts and grounds of appeal.

(11) Paragraph (3) of Rule 281 shall apply to an appellant under this rule as it applies to a party lodging a principal case under that rule, and paragraphs (4) and (5) of Rule 281 shall apply for the purposes of the hearing and disposal of an appeal under this rule as they apply to the hearing and disposal of an appeal under that rule.

(12) Where it appears to the court considering an appeal under this rule that any question as to the value of land in the United Kingdom requires to be determined, the court shall remit the case—

(*a*) if the land is in Scotland, to the Lands Tribunal for Scotland;

(*b*) if the land is in England or Wales, to the Lands Tribunal;

(*c*) if the land is in Northern Ireland, to the Lands Tribunal for Northern Ireland,

to determine that question and remit back to the court for further procedure.

[3] (13) Where an appellant fails to comply with a time limit under this rule he shall be held to have abandoned his appeal.

NOTES

[1] Substituted by S.I. 1976 No. 1849.

[2] As amended by S.I. 1990 No. 705.

[3] Inserted by S.I. 1990 No. 705.

Special cases under the Representation of the People Act 1948, section 70

[1] **284.** Special cases under the Representation of the People Act 1948, section 70, shall be subject to the following provisions supplementary to the provisions of Rules 277 to 280;

(*a*) Where several persons have lodged minutes with the sheriff clerk, and it appears to the sheriff that such minutes, or any two or more of them, raise the same question of law or questions of law, it shall be competent for the sheriff to consolidate the appeals in one special case; and, in that event, the sheriff shall state in the special case the circumstances in which he has consolidated the appeals, and shall moreover name therein such one of the appellants as he may in his discretion select as "the appellant". Such appellant shall supply copies of the special case as lodged to any other appellants, on their request and at their charges.

(*b*) On the special case being lodged in the General Department as aforesaid, the case shall be put out in the printed rolls of court for hearing before the Registration Appeal Court on the earliest available day.

(*c*) The court shall, in its decision, specify every alteration or correction, if any, to be made upon the register in pursuance of such decision; and a copy of such decision shall, within four days, be sent by the Deputy Principal Clerk to the registration officer.

NOTE

[1] As amended by S.I. 1980 No. 1144.

Applications for leave to appeal from a Pensions Appeal Tribunal

285.—(1) Applications to the Court of Session for leave to appeal from the decision of a Pensions Appeal Tribunal shall be disposed of by a single judge nominated for that purpose from time to time by the Lord President, and the decision of such judge on any such application shall be final.

(2) Such application shall only be made if leave to appeal has first been refused by the Pensions Appeal Tribunal, and shall be made within twenty-eight days of the date of the decision of the Tribunal refusing such leave.

(3) Such applications shall be made by lodging in the General Department a note as nearly as may be in terms of Form 45. A copy of said note shall at the same time be served upon the opposite party or his solicitor, who shall within fourteen days thereafter intimate in writing to the Deputy Principal Clerk whether he desires to be heard.

(4) On the expiry of the said period of fourteen days, the note shall be brought by the Deputy Principal Clerk before the nominated judge in chambers, and the subsequent procedure shall be summary and such as the said judge in his discretion may direct. Without prejudice to the aforesaid generality, it shall be competent for the said judge to grant the application without a hearing, or to dispose of it after a hearing in chambers or in open court, and at any such hearing to proceed in the absence of a party who has intimated that he does not desire to be heard; or to order written answers; or to remit to the chairman of the Tribunal for a report on any matter.

(5) A certified copy of the interlocutor granting or refusing any such application shall be sent by the Deputy Principal Clerk to the Pensions Appeal Office and to the parties or their solicitors.

(6) The applicant for a pension shall be entitled to the reasonable

expenses of successfully applying for leave to appeal, or of opposing, successfully or unsuccessfully, an application for such leave by the Minister of Pensions.

Stated cases under the Pensions Appeal Tribunals Act 1943, section 6

286.—(1) When leave to appeal has been granted by a Pensions Appeal Tribunal or under Rule 285, the chairman shall, within twenty-eight days of the date of the decision granting leave to appeal, prepare a draft stated case and shall within the said period send a copy thereof to the Minister of Pensions and to the claimant for a pension or, if he has so requested, to his solicitor.

(2) Within fourteen days thereafter the Minister and the claimant shall return the draft case to the chairman with any additions or alterations which they or either of them may desire to have made thereon.

(3) Should the parties fail to agree as to the terms of the case, or should either or both fail to return the draft case revised as above provided, the terms of the case shall be adjusted by the chairman, and in any event the terms of the case shall be subject to the approval of the chairman. The case shall then be signed by the chairman and shall be sent forthwith to the appellant, or his solicitor as the case may be, or where both parties are appellants, to the party who first applied for a stated case.

(4) Subject to the provisions of this rule, the provisions of these rules relative to appeals by way of stated case shall *mutatis mutandis* apply for the purpose of regulating further procedure; provided (i) that the claimant for a pension shall be entitled to his reasonable expenses in every such appeal irrespective of the result, and (ii) that, if the appellant fails duly to prosecute the appeal, the respondent may bring the matter before the court by written note to the Inner House lodged in the General Department, and in any such case the court shall pronounce such order as may seem to them just.

(5) On the final disposal of any appeal the Deputy Principal Clerk shall, in accordance with such directions as the court may give, transmit to the Pensions Appeal Office a certified copy of the interlocutor or interlocutors of the court.

(6) If, after application for leave to appeal has been made to the Pensions Appeal Tribunal, the parties agree as to the answers to the questions of law which would require to be stated by the chairman of the Tribunal, it shall be competent for the parties to lodge a joint note signed by counsel for both parties, setting forth the terms of an agreement come to by the parties as to the questions of law and the answers thereto, dispensing with the necessity for the chairman of the Tribunal preparing a draft stated case, and requesting the court to interpone authority to the terms of the agreement as set forth in said joint note. Any order then pronounced by the court shall have the same force and effect as an order pronounced under the Rules of Court affecting the disposal of appeals by way of stated cases. The court in making any such order shall have power to find the claimant (or appellant) entitled to his expenses in connection with the presentation of a joint note and incidental procedure connected therewith.

(7) When under this rule a document requires to be served on or sent to the Minister of Pensions, it should be delivered or sent to the Solicitor in Scotland for the Minister of Pensions for the time being.

Stated cases under section 103 of the Local Government (Scotland) Act 1973

[1] **287.** The procedure for stated cases in terms of section 103 of the Local Government (Scotland) Act 1973 shall be regulated by the provisions contained in Rules of Court 276 to 280 inclusive.

NOTE

[1] Substituted by S.I. 1974 No. 1946.

Social Security Acts

[1] **288.**—(1) This rule applies to the following references and appeals under the Social Security Acts—

(*a*) a reference to the court by the Secretary of State under section 94 or section 114(5) of the Social Security Act 1975;

(*b*) an appeal to the court by an aggrieved person under section 94 or section 114(5) of that Act;

(*c*) a reference to the court by the Occupational Pensions Board under section 86 of the Social Security Act 1973, as amended by the Social Security Pensions Act 1975; and

(*d*) an appeal to the court by an aggrieved person under the said section 86;

[2] (*e*) a reference or an appeal to the court under section 11(4) and (5) of the Social Security and Housing Benefits Act 1982.

(2) A reference or an appeal to which this rule applies, shall be by way of stated case.

[3] (3) An aggrieved person who is entitled to have, and who wishes, a case to be stated under this rule shall, within 28 days of receiving notice of the decision against which he wishes to appeal or within 28 days of being furnished by the Secretary of State with a statement of the grounds of the decision in accordance with the Social Security (Determination of Claims and Questions) Regulations 1975, by notice in writing addressed to the Secretary of State, or the Occupational Pensions Board, or the Reserve Pensions Board, as the case may be, require the Secretary of State or the Board to state a case.

(4) An aggrieved person sending a notice under paragraph (3) of this rule shall send a copy of the notice to any other party to the proceedings in which the decision appealed against was made.

(5) Where the Secretary of State or either Board—

(*a*) receives a notice under paragraph (3) of this rule;

(*b*) decides to make a reference to the court to which this Rule applies, the Secretary of State or the Board shall state a case specifying the facts found and the decision made as soon as possible, and send it by registered or recorded delivery post to the aggrieved person or as the case may be, the other party or parties to the case.

[3] (6) Subject to the provisions of this rule, Rules 277 to 280 shall apply to stated cases under this rule and for the purpose of the application of those rules a reference mentioned in paragraph (1) shall be treated as an application to which those rules apply, except that the time limit specified in rule 277(*e*) shall not apply to a reference from an Occupational Pensions Board mentioned in sub-paragraph (*c*) of paragraph (1).

NOTES

[1] Substituted by S.I. 1976 No. 779.

[2] Added by S.I. 1983 No. 397.

[3] As amended by S.I. 1983 No. 397.

Appeals under the Cinematograph Films Act 1927, section 9

289.—(*a*) Any person aggrieved by the refusal of the Board of Trade to register a film, or to register a film as a British film, or by a decision of the Board of Trade to correct the registration of a film and whose principal place of business is in Scotland, may, within twenty-one days of such refusal or decision, or within such further time as the court may hold (on consideration of any appeal presented under paragraph (*b*) of this rule) to have been reasonable in the circumstances, give to the Board of Trade notice in writing requiring the matter to be referred to the court, and the Board of Trade shall, within seven days of the receipt of the notice, (1) refer the matter to the court by sending the notice duly endorsed as "referred" to the Deputy Principal Clerk, and (2) give written notice to the person aggrieved that this has been done.

(*b*) Within fourteen days of the receipt by such person of the said written notice, or within such further time as the court may hold (on consideration of any appeal presented under this paragraph) to have been reasonable in the circumstances, the person aggrieved may present an appeal against such refusal or decision of the Board of Trade to the Inner House, and lodge the same in the General Department. The provisions of Rules 279 and 280 shall thereafter apply.

Appeals under section 50 of the Social Work (Scotland) Act 1968

[1] **289A.**—(1) Where within the period mentioned in section 50(2) of the Social Work (Scotland) Act 1968 an application is made to the sheriff to state a case under subsection (1) of that section, the sheriff shall, within fourteen days after the date on which the application is made, prepare a draft stated case and shall cause a copy thereof to be sent forthwith to the applicant and the other parties including the reporter in the case if he is not the applicant.

(2) Where on an application being made to him as aforesaid it appears to the sheriff that any report or statement lodged with the sheriff clerk by the reporter in accordance with section 49(2) or 49(3) of the said Act of 1968 in the appeal to the sheriff is relevant to any issue which is likely to arise in the proceedings upon the stated case and the report or statement has been returned to the reporter in accordance with Rule 16(3) of the Act of Sederunt (Social Work) (Sheriff Court Procedure) Rules 1971, the sheriff may require the reporter to lodge again the report or statement with the sheriff clerk.

(3) If the applicant or any of the other parties including the reporter in the case if he is not the applicant desires to have any adjustments made on the draft case he shall, within fourteen days after the date on which a copy of the draft was sent to him as aforesaid, return that copy to the sheriff showing thereon the said adjustments.

(4) As soon as possible after the return of the said copies of the draft case or, in the event of default in the return thereof, upon the expiry of the period of fourteen days mentioned in the last foregoing paragraph, the sheriff shall state and sign the case for the opinion of the court and the sheriff clerk shall deliver the case to the party who applied for it or, as the case may be, who first applied for it and at the same time shall return to the reporter any report or statement lodged with him under paragraph (2) above.

[2] (5) Subject to the next following paragraphs the provisions of paragraphs (*h*), (*j*) and (*k*) of Rule 277 shall apply to the procedure thereafter as if any reference in those paragraphs to a party included a reference to the reporter and as if in paragraphs (*h*)(ii) and (*k*)(iii) there were omitted the words "and it may, if one party only has applied for a stated case, find him liable for payment to the other party of the sum of £5·25 of expenses" and with any other necessary modifications.

(6) The reporter shall, within seven days after the date on which the case is, in accordance with Rule 277(*k*), lodged in the general department, deliver to the Deputy Principal Clerk, the principal and ten copies of every report or statement which he was required by the sheriff to lodge again with the sheriff clerk under paragraph (2) above but no copy of any such report or statement shall be made available to any of the other parties except on the order of the court.

(7) The report may direct that all or any of the proceedings upon the stated case shall be heard in chambers.

(8) Subject to any order in that behalf made by the court, any reports or statements delivered to the Deputy Principal Clerk under paragraph

(6) of this Rule shall remain in his custody until the appeal is determined or abandoned and thereupon he shall return the said copies to the reporter.

(9) No expenses shall be awarded to or against any party in respect of any of the proceedings upon the stated case.

NOTES

[1] Added by S.I. 1971 No. 203.
[2] As amended by the Decimal Currency Act 1969, s.10(1).

Section 6—Other Statutory Appeals

Form of appeal

[1] **290.**—[2] (*a*) Subject to the supplementary provisions contained in Rules 291 to 294, all statutory appeals (which shall include applications for leave to appeal) and applications of the nature of appeals to the court (other than the appeals and proceedings referred to in Rule 276) against a decision of the Secretary of State, a Minister, a department, statutory tribunal including a value added tax tribunal, referee or authority shall be taken within such time as may be prescribed by the particular statute under which the appeal is presented, or, if no time is prescribed, not later than 42 days after the date on which the decision, order, scheme, determination, refusal, or other act of the authority or person complained of, was intimated to the appellant; and shall (notwithstanding anything in any Act of Parliament to the contrary) be by written appeal presented to the Inner House and lodged in the General Department. Any such appeal shall refer to the particular statute and section under which the appeal is brought, and shall specify the decision, order, scheme, determination, refusal, or other act complained of as aforesaid, and shall identify the same by the date on which it was made or done and on which it was intimated to the appellant, and by any other necessary particulars.

(*b*) Wherever possible, the decision, order, scheme, determination, refusal, or other act appealed against shall be set forth in the appeal; and if the appeal is against only a part of such decision, order, scheme, determination, refusal, or other act, the part appealed against shall be specified or distinguished.

(*c*) The appeal shall state in brief numbered propositions the grounds of appeal, and shall be accompanied by any documents founded on by the appellant so far as in his possession or within his control.

(*d*) The form of such appeal shall, as nearly as may be, be as shewn in Form 42.

(*e*) All such appeals shall, on the first available day after lodging, appear, without enrolment, in the printed rolls of court in the single bills for an order for intimation of the appeal to the respondent, and to such other person or persons as the court may think proper, and appointing him or them to lodge answers, if so advised, within such *induciae* as the court may fix. In vacation the order for intimation may be made by the Vacation Judge.

(*f*) The intimation shall be made by registered or recorded delivery letter enclosing a copy of the appeal and of the interlocutor of the court, and a notice that the *induciae* commence to run only on the day after the day on which the said letter was posted.

(*g*) Answers may be lodged not later than the last day of the *induciae* in concise and articulate form, together with any documents founded on therein and the cause shall forthwith be enrolled for further procedure.

(*h*) Rules 270 to 272 shall *mutatis mutandis* apply to such appeals.

[3] (*i*) Where intimation of a statement of the reasons for a decision was given later than the decision, the period of 21 days within which an appeal

must be presented under paragraph (*a*) shall be calculated from the date of intimation of the statement of reasons.

NOTES

[1] As amended by S.I. 1973 No. 540.

[2] As amended by S.I. 1984 No. 499 and S.I. 1986 No. 1955.

[3] Added by S.I. 1982 No. 1825.

[1] *Stated cases under the Tribunals and Inquiries Act 1971, section 13(2)*

[1] **291.**—(1) Stated cases under the Tribunals and Inquiries Act 1971, section 13(2), which have been stated upon the application of a party to proceedings depending before a tribunal, shall be subject to the provisions of Rules 277 to 280.

(2) It shall be competent for a Tribunal, of its own motion, to state a case for the opinion of the Court of Session on any question arising in the course of proceedings before it, in which event the following provisions shall have effect:—

(*a*) When the Tribunal decides to state a case it shall cause its decision to be intimated to the parties and within fourteen days after the despatch of such intimation it shall cause the case to be prepared and submitted in draft to the parties; within twenty-one days from the receipt of the draft case each party shall return it to the Clerk of the Tribunal with a note of any additions, alterations or amendments which he may desire to have made thereon and thereafter the Tribunal shall finally adjust the case.

(*b*) The case shall bear to be stated by the Tribunal and shall be authenticated by the Clerk thereof who shall thereupon:—

(i) send a copy of the case to each party to the proceedings, and

(ii) transmit the principal case to the Deputy Principal Clerk of Session together with a certificate under the hand of himself or his solicitor certifying that a copy thereof has been sent to each party to the proceedings.

(*c*) The Clerk to the Tribunal shall within fourteen days after the principal case has been received by the said Deputy Principal Clerk lodge in the General Department a copy of the case along with a Process and copies of productions for the use of the court in terms of Rules 20 and 26(*b*) and shall at the same time intimate the lodging of the case to each party to the proceedings and shall deliver to each party five copies of the case.

(*d*) Rules 279 and 280 shall apply to stated cases under this Rule.

NOTE

[1] As amended by S.I. 1971 No. 265, S.I. 1972 No. 1835, S.I. 1974 No. 1603, S.I. 1975 No. 89 and S.I. 1985 No. 1600.

Appeals under the Tribunals and Inquiries Act 1971, section 13(1)

[1] **292.**—(*a*) Where such appeals appear in the printed rolls of court in the single bills for an order for intimation (in terms of Rule 290(*e*)) such intimation shall be not only to the persons mentioned in Rule 290(*e*) but also to any other party to the proceedings before the Tribunal and to the Chairman of the Tribunal.

(*b*) Subject to the foregoing paragraphs Rule 290 shall apply to such appeals, save only that in respect of such appeals as are referred to in the foregoing paragraph the provisions of Rule 290 (*a*) to (*g*) only shall apply and that these appeals when lodged shall forthwith be placed before the nominated judge for such an order as is specified in Rule 290 (*c*).

NOTE

[1] As amended by S.I. 1972 No. 1835, S.I. 1974 No. 1603, S.I. 1975 No. 89, and S.I. 1985 No. 1600.

Appeals under the Tribunals and Inquiries Act 1971, section 13 (5)

[1] **293.**—(*a*) Where such appeals from a decision of the Minister of Transport and Civil Aviation appear in the printed rolls of court in the single bills for an order for intimation (in terms of Rule 290 (*e*)) such intimation shall be to the Minister and to every person who had or if aggrieved would have had a right to appeal to the Minister, whether or not he has exercised that right.

(*b*) The Minister shall be entitled to take such part in the proceedings as he may think fit.

(*c*) If the court is of opinion that the decision of the Minister was erroneous in point of law, it shall not set aside or vary the order of the Minister but may remit the matter to him for determination in accordance with the decision of the court on the point of law.

[THE NEXT PAGE IS C 139]

(*d*) Subject to the foregoing paragraph Rule 290 shall apply to such appeals.

NOTE

[1] As amended by S.I. 1972 No. 1835.

[1] **293A.**—(*a*) Where under Rule 290 an appeal under section 41 of the Consumer Credit Act 1974 by a company registered in Scotland or by any other person whose principal or prospective principal place of business in the United Kingdom is in Scotland against a decision of the Secretary of State from a determination of the Director General of Fair Trading appears in the printed rolls of court in the single bills for an order for intimation, such intimation shall be to the Secretary of State and, where the appeal is by a licensee under a group licence against compulsory variation, suspension or revocation of that licence, to the original applicant, if any, and to such other person as the court may order.

(*b*) The court may remit the matter to the Secretary of State for the purpose of enabling him to provide the court with such further information as the court may require.

(*c*) If the court is of the opinion that the decision appealed against was erroneous in point of law, it shall not set aside or vary that decision but shall remit the matter to the Secretary of State with the opinion of the court for hearing and determination by him.

NOTE

[1] Added by S.I. 1976 No. 847.

Appeals from Social Security Commissioners

[1] **293B.**—(1) Subject to the provisions of this Rule, Rule 290 shall apply to an appeal against a decision of a Commissioner under section 14 of the Social Security Act 1980.

(2) In a case where a Commissioner has granted leave to appeal against such a decision and has specified the Court of Session as the appropriate court under that section, the period within which the appeal has to be lodged under paragraph (*a*) of Rule 290 shall be six weeks commencing on the date on which the appellant was given the decision of the Commissioner granting leave.

(3) In a case where a Commissioner has refused leave to appeal against such a decision and has specified the Court of Session as the appropriate court under that section, an application to the court for leave to appeal against that decision shall be made—

(*a*) within a period of six weeks commencing on the date on which the applicant was given the decision refusing leave to appeal;

(*b*) by lodging in the General Department of the court an application to the Inner House in the form of a Note stating briefly the nature of and reasons for the application and attaching six copies of the decision against which leave to appeal is sought and six copies of the decision refusing leave to appeal.

and the Division before whom the application comes shall, after intimation in accordance with paragraph (5), dispose of the application summarily.

(4) Where the court grants an application for leave to appeal under paragraph (3), the period within which the appeal has to be lodged under paragraph (*a*) of Rule 290 shall be six weeks commencing on the date on which the court pronounces the interlocutor granting leave.

(5) Where an appeal against a decision of a Commissioner under the said section 14 appears in the single bills for an order for intimation under paragraph (*e*) of Rule 290, the court shall, in addition to any order for intimation it may make under that paragraph, order intimation to be made

on the Secretary of State for Social Services, and if it appears that a person has been appointed by him to pursue a claim for benefit to which the appeal relates, on that person.

(6) In this rule, " Commissioner " and " the appropriate court " have the same meaning as in the said section 14.

NOTE

[1] Added by S.I. 1980 No. 1754.

Appeals under the Finance Act 1894, section 10

294.—(*a*) *Preliminary procedure.* The appellant shall, within one month from the date of the notification to him or his solicitor of the decision or claim of the commissioners, deliver to them a written appeal containing a statement of the grounds of such appeal. The statement shall specify explicitly the several grounds upon which the appellant contends that the decision or claim of the commissioners is erroneous; and, if he contends that the value put upon any property by the commissioners is excessive, he shall therein identify such property, and state the value which he contends should be put upon the same.

(*b*) *Notice by commissioners of withdrawal of decision.* The commissioners shall, within one month from the delivery to them of the said written appeal notify to the appellant or his solicitor whether they have withdrawn the decision or claim appealed against, or have determined to maintain the same, either in whole or in part.

(*c*) *Methods of Appeal.* The appellant may, within one month from the date of the notification by the commissioners of their determination to maintain their decision or claim either in whole or in part, or (in the event of an application being made under paragraph (*e*) of this rule) within ten days from the date of the interlocutor disposing of such application, proceed either (i) by lodging his appeal in the General Department for disposal in the Inner House; or (ii) where the value as alleged by the commissioners of the property in respect of which the dispute arises does not exceed £10,000, by presenting a petition in the sheriff court for the county within which the appellant resides or the property is situated. The provisions of Rule 290 of this Chapter shall apply in the cases of an appeal to the Court of Session. In the case of a petition in a sheriff court, the sheriff shall order the petition to be served on the commissioners or on the Solicitor of Inland Revenue for Scotland on their behalf, and may, if he thinks fit, appoint answers to such petition to be lodged, or parties to be heard thereon with or without answers, and may thereafter give decree granting or refusing the prayer of the petition or may take such other course with regard thereto as to him may seem proper.

(*d*) *Statements in appeal or petition.* The appellant shall not in his appeal as lodged, or in his petition, state any grounds of appeal not specifically set forth in the statement of the grounds of appeal delivered by him, along with the appeal, to the commissioners; provided always, that the court or sheriff may at any time, before or at the hearing, allow the appellant to amend his appeal or petition upon such terms as the court or sheriff may think right.

(*e*) *Leave to appeal without paying duty.* Where the appellant desires to apply for leave to bring an appeal without payment, or on part payment only, of the duty (under the provisions of subsection (4) of section 10 of the Act) he shall, within fourteen days from the date of the notification given by the commissioners, in terms of paragraph (*c*) of this rule, present a note to the Inner House or the sheriff craving for such leave; and shall specify therein the grounds on which his application is made; on presentation of the Note the appellant shall enrol a motion for an order for intimation thereof to the Lord Advocate who may, if so advised, lodge Answers thereto within fourteen days after receipt of said intimation.

(*f*) *Abandonment of appeal.* If the appellant shall not proceed with his appeal as provided in paragraph (*c*) of this rule, he shall be held to have abandoned the same, and shall not be entitled to proceed thereafter with it.

(*g*) *Procedure in Court of Session and in any sheriff court.* Except in so far as inconsistent with the provisions of this rule, or of the said Act, the Court of Exchequer (Scotland) Act 1856 shall apply to all such appeals originating in the Court of Session; and the Sheriff Courts (Scotland) Acts 1907 to 1939 shall apply to all such petitions originating in any sheriff court.

SECTION 6A—APPENDICES

Lodging of Appendix

[1] **294A.**—(*a*) In any cause depending before the Inner House in which, in accordance with present practice it is requisite that an Appendix should be lodged, the prints of such Appendix shall be lodged not later than three months from the date of the interlocutor appointing the cause to the Summar Roll or Short Roll provided that within seven days of the date of such interlocutor the appellant may enrol for a sist of process and if, on cause shown, the court or Vacation Judge grants such sist the running of said period of three months shall be postponed until the sist is recalled. An unopposed motion for the recall of such sist may in vacation be disposed of by the Vacation Judge.

(*b*) If the prints of the Appendix are not lodged within the said period of three months or before the expiry of any prorogation of that period allowed by the court, the appeal shall be held to have been abandoned and the appellant shall not be entitled to insist therein except upon being reponed as hereinafter provided.

(*c*) At any time before the date on which said prints of the Appendix are due to be lodged the party due to lodge the same may enrol for prorogation of the time for lodging said prints. Such motion shall be put out in the Single Bills before one or other Division of the Inner House, or before the Vacation Judge (as the case may be), and shall only be granted upon cause shown and upon such conditions as shall seem just to the court.

(*d*) It shall be lawful for the appellant within seven days after the appeal has been held to be abandoned in accordance with paragraph (*b*) of this Rule to enrol a motion to be reponed. Such motion shall be put out in the Single Bills before one or other Division of the Inner House, or before the Vacation Judge (as the case may be) and shall only be granted on cause shewn, and upon such conditions as to payment of expenses to the respondent or otherwise, as shall seem just.

(*e*) It shall be lawful for the respondent within seven days after the appeal has been held to be abandoned in accordance with paragraph (*b*) hereof to enrol a motion for leave to insist upon the appeal and the court, when granting such motion, shall direct the respondent to lodge prints of the Appendix within such period as the court thinks fit; in which case the appellant shall also be entitled to insist in the appeal; and the provisions regulating appeals by an appellant shall apply equally to appeals insisted in under this paragraph by the respondent.

(*f*) On the expiry of the period of seven days after the appeal has been held to be abandoned as aforesaid, if the appellant shall not have been reponed, and if the respondent does not insist in the appeal, or on receipt by the Deputy Principal Clerk of a letter signed by the solicitors for all parties stating that the appellant has abandoned the appeal, the judgment or judgments complained of shall become final, and shall be treated in all respects as if no appeal had been taken against the same. In the case of appeals from the Outer House any party to the cause may enrol in the Single Bills to have the cause remitted back to the Outer House to proceed as accords; and in the case of other appeals the provisions of Rule of Court 272 (*b*) shall apply.

(*g*) For the purposes only of this Rule the expression "Appeal" shall mean any proceedings in the Inner House for which it is requisite that an

Appendix should be lodged, and the expression "Appellant" shall include reclaimer.

NOTE
[1] Added by S.I. 1972 No. 2022.

[1] Section 6B

Notices of Grounds of Appeal

NOTE
[1] Inserted by S.I. 1987 No. 1206.

Grounds of appeal

294B.—(1) Where a reclaiming motion has been enrolled or an appeal from an inferior court has been lodged in the general department, the cause shall appear in the single bills at the earliest convenient date for an order under paragraph (2) and, unless opposition has been marked, the attendance of counsel will not be required.

[1] (2) On appearance in the single bills under paragraph (1), in the absence of any opposition, or where any opposition is unsuccessful, the court shall appoint—

(*a*) the reclaimer or appellant; and

(*b*) any respondent wishing to bring any interlocutor under review or challenge the grounds on which the Lord Ordinary or court below has pronounced the interlocutor under review,

to lodge grounds of appeal within 28 days.

(3) Grounds of appeal shall consist of brief specific numbered propositions stating the grounds upon which it is proposed to submit that the reclaiming motion or appeal should be allowed or as the case may be.

(4) Where a reclaimer or appellant fails to lodge grounds of appeal, a respondent may enrol to have the reclaiming motion or appeal dismissed or refused.

(5) A party lodging grounds of appeal shall—

(*a*) intimate a copy to any other party; and

(*b*) enrol for an order for hearing.

(6) A party who has lodged grounds of appeal may, on cause shown, apply for leave to amend his grounds of appeal at any time.

NOTE
[1] As amended with effect from 27th May 1991 by S.I. 1991 No. 1157, which refers in error to rule 294(2)(*b*).

[1] Section 6C

Allocation of Diets

NOTE
[1] Inserted by S.I. 1987 No. 1206.

Fixing and allocation of diets

294C.—(1) Within 28 days of a cause depending before the Inner House being appointed to the summar roll for hearing, each party shall ensure that Form 63 is completed and delivered to the keeper of the rolls.

(2) The keeper of the rolls may fix or allocate a diet for the hearing, having regard to the information provided in Form 63.

(3) Where a party fails to comply with paragraph (1), the keeper of the rolls may arrange for the cause to be put out by order before a Division.

(4) At a by order hearing under paragraph (3) the court shall—

(*a*) seek an explanation as to why Form 63 was not completed and delivered timeously;

(*b*) ascertain the information sought in Form 63; and

(*c*) make such order as to expenses as it considers appropriate.

(5) Where Form 63 is completed and delivered to the keeper of the rolls

before the hearing of the cause by order under paragraph (3), the keeper of the rolls may cancel the by order hearing.

(6) Where, at any time after Form 63 has been completed and delivered to the keeper of the rolls, a party's estimate of the likely length of the hearing alters materially, that party shall inform the keeper of the rolls of the new estimated length.

(7) Not later than five weeks before the hearing of the cause on the summar roll, the keeper of the rolls shall arrange for the cause to be put out by order.

(8) At a by order hearing under paragraph (7), parties shall—

(*a*) advise the court whether or not the summar roll hearing is to proceed; and

(*b*) where such hearing is to proceed, provide the court with a re-assessment of the likely duration of the hearing.

SECTION 7—INNER HOUSE INTERLOCUTORS

Adjustment and signing

295.—(*a*) An interlocutor disposing without the hearing of parties of an unopposed motion under Rule 93 or Rule 263 shall be adjusted and signed by the judge presiding at the time when the motion is brought before the Division.

(*b*) Any other interlocutor shall be adjusted and signed by the judge who presided in the Division when the matter to be dealt with in the interlocutor was determined, or, in the event of the death, absence or disability of such judge, by the senior remaining judge of the Division which determined the matter. Such interlocutors shall be adjusted and signed as soon as reasonably practicable after the matter has been so determined, and after such consultation, if any, with the remaining memubers or member of that Division as the presiding judge or senior remaining judge may deem necessary.

(*c*) The judge signing an Inner House interlocutor shall be authorised to append the letters I.P.D. to his signature as conclusive evidence that the requirements of the foregoing paragraphs have been complied with.

SECTION 8—INNER HOUSE JUDGMENTS

Vacation or recess

296.—(*a*) It shall be competent for judgment to be given in vacation or recess disposing in whole or in part, so far as appropriate without a further hearing of counsel, of any cause depending before the Inner House by the issue of an interlocutor adjusted and signed as after mentioned together with the opinions of the judges who determined the matter.

(*b*) Any such interlocutor shall be adjusted and signed by the judge who presided in the Division when the case was heard, after such consultation, if any, with the remaining members of that Division as he may deem necessary, and such judge shall be authorised to append the letters I.P.D. to his signature as conclusive evidence that the requirements of this Rule have been complied with.

[1] CHAPTER V A

EUROPEAN COURT

NOTE

[1] Added by S.I. 1972 No. 1981.

Interpretation

[1] **296A.** In this Chapter:

(i) any expression defined in Schedule 1 to the European Communities Act 1972 has the meaning there given to it.

(ii) "reference" means a reference to the European Court for a

[THE NEXT PAGE IS C 143]

preliminary ruling under Article 177 of the E.E.C. Treaty, Article 150 of the Euratom Treaty or Article 41 of the E.C.S.C. Treaty or a ruling on the interpretation of the Conventions (as defined by section 1(1) of the Civil Jurisdiction and Judgments Act 1982) under Article 3 of Schedule 2 to that Act.

(iii) "pursuer" shall include petitioner, reclaimer or appellant.

(iv) "appeal" shall include reclaiming motion.

NOTE

[1] Added by S.I. 1972 No. 1981, and as amended by S.I. 1986 No. 1941.

Form of Reference

[1] **296B.** A reference shall be made by the court in the form of a Case, as nearly as may be in terms of Form 52, having annexed thereto a certified copy of the interlocutor making the reference. When the court decides that a preliminary ruling should be sought the court shall give directions to the parties as to the manner in which the case is to be stated, drafted and adjusted.

NOTE

[1] Added by S.I. 1972 No. 1981.

Sist of Proceedings

[1] **296C.** If the court makes a reference the proceedings shall, unless the court when making such a reference otherwise orders, be sisted until the European Court has given a preliminary ruling on the question or questions referred to it.

NOTE

[1] Added by S.I. 1972 No. 1981.

Transmission of reference to the European Court

[1] **296D.**—(*a*) When a reference has been drafted and adjusted at the sight of the court, the court shall then by interlocutor order the reference to be made and the pursuer shall prepare and lodge in process one copy thereof for each of the parties to the proceedings, one copy for transmission to the European Court and one process copy.

(*b*) The Principal Clerk shall send a copy of the reference to the Registrar of the European Court but, unless the court otherwise directs, a copy thereof shall not be sent to the Registrar so long as an appeal or further appeal against the interlocutor making the reference is pending, and for this purpose an appeal or further appeal shall be treated as pending (where one is competent but has not been brought) until the expiration of the time for bringing that appeal.

NOTE

[1] Added by S.I. 1972 No. 1981.

[1] **296E.** Save in the case of Summary Trial an interlocutor making a reference may be appealed against, without leave, not later than the fourteenth day whether in Session, vacation or recess, after the day on which the said interlocutor is pronounced.

NOTE

[1] Added by S.I. 1972 No. 1982.

[1] CHAPTER V B

EUROPEAN COMMUNITY JUDGMENTS

NOTE

[1] Added by S.I. 1972 No. 1982.

Interpretation

[1] **296F.**—In this Chapter:

(i) "Community judgment" means any decision, judgment or order which is enforceable under or in accordance with Articles 187 or 192 of the E.E.C. Treaty, Articles 18, 159 or 164 of the Euratom Treaty, or Articles 44 or 92 of the E.C.S.C. Treaty.

(ii) "Euratom inspection order" means an order made by or in the exercise of the functions of the President of the European Court or by the Commission of the European Communities under Article 81 of the Euratom Treaty.

(iii) "Order for enforcement" means an order by or under the authority of the Secretary of State that the Community judgment to which it is appended is to be registered for enforcement in the United Kingdom.

NOTE

[1] Added by S.I. 1972 No. 1982.

Register

[1] **296G.** A register shall be kept by the Deputy Principal Clerk of Session for the purpose of registering any Community judgment to which the Secretary of State has appended an order for enforcement or any Euratom inspection order or any of the European Court that enforcement of a registered Community judgment shall be suspended.

NOTE

[1] Added by S.I. 1972 No. 1982.

Registration

[1] **296H.**—(i) An application for registration of a Community judgment or Euratom inspection order shall be made by Petition to the Outer House at the instance of the person or persons entitled to enforce it, and the court shall direct that any Euratom inspection order or any Community judgment to which the Secretary of State has appended an order for enforcement shall be registered in the Register referred to in the immediately preceding Rule of Court.

(ii) An application for registration of any such order or Community judgment shall be accompanied by the Community judgment and the order for its enforcement or the Euratom inspection order, or a copy thereof, and, where the Community judgment or Euratom inspection order is not in the English language, a translation thereof in that language certified by a notary public.

(iii) Where the application is for registration of a Community judgment under which a sum of money is payable, the Petition shall also set forth:—

(*a*) the name, trade or business and the usual or last known place of abode or business of the judgment debtor, so far as known to the Petitioner;

(*b*) to the best of the information and belief of the petitioner, as the case may require, either that, at the date of the application the judgment has not been satisfied, or the amount in respect of which it remains unsatisfied; and

(*c*) where the sum payable under the judgment is not expressed in the currency of the United Kingdom, the amount which that sum represents in the currency of the United Kingdom calculated at the rate of exchange prevailing at the date when the judgment was originally given.

(iv) Upon registration of any such order or Community judgment the fact of registration shall forthwith be intimated by the person or persons who have made registration to the person or persons against whom the judgment or order was given or made; and together with such intimation there shall be sent a copy of the registered community judgment and the order for its enforcement or the Euratom inspection order, and there shall be intimated the name and address of the person on whose application the judgment or order was registered or of his solicitor or agent on whom, and at which, service may be effected.

(v) Where such intimation relates to a Community judgment under which a sum of money is payable, it shall also state that the debtor may apply within 28 days of the date of the intimation or thereafter with the leave of the court, for the variation or cancellation of the registration on the ground that the judgment was partly or wholly satisfied at the date of registration.

(vi) There shall be no execution without the leave of the court on a Community judgment under which a sum of money is payable until 28 days after the date of the intimation under this rule, or any application made within that period for the variation or cancellation of the registration is determined.

(vii) Where it appears that a Community judgment under which a sum of money is payable has been partly satisfied at the date of the application for its registration, the judgment shall be registered only in respect of the balance remaining payable at that date.

(viii) Upon registration of a Euratom inspection order, the court may make such order as it thinks fit against any person for the purpose of ensuring that effect is given to the Euratom inspection order.

NOTE
[1] Added by S.I. 1972 No. 1982.

Variation or Cancellation of Registration

[1] **296J.** An application seeking the variation or cancellation of any registration shall be made by Minute in the process in which said registration was ordered, and the Minuter shall enrol for an Order for intimation and service of the Minute upon the Petitioner and any other person or persons having an interest; and the court, if satisfied, shall direct that the Register shall be varied as sought by the Minuter.

NOTE
[1] Added by S.I. 1972 No. 1982.

Suspension of enforcement of Community judgments

[1] **296K.** An order of the European Court that enforcement of a registered Community judgment be suspended shall, on production of the order to the Court of Session and on application made by Minute in the process be registered forthwith and shall be of the same effect as if the order had been an order made by the Court of Session on the date of its registration suspending the execution of the judgment for the same period and on the same conditions as are stated in the order of the European Court; and no steps to enforce the judgment shall be taken while such an order remains in force.

NOTE
[1] Added by S.I. 1972 No. 1982.

CHAPTER VI

Special Courts

SECTION 1—ELECTION PETITIONS

Presentation of petition

297.—[1] (*a*) The presentation of a parliamentary or European Assembly election petition shall be made by lodging it in the Petition Department together with a process and fifteen full copies of the petition.

(*b*) On receipt of said Petition a copy thereof shall be sent by the Deputy Principal Clerk of Session to the returning officer of the constituency to which the said petition relates.

NOTE
[1] As amended by S.I. 1979 No. 516.

Form of petition

298.—[1] (*a*) A parliamentary or European Assembly election petition shall be as nearly as possible in the form shown in Form 46 and shall be signed by the petitioner, or all the petitioners if more than one.

[1,2] (*b*) A parliamentary or European Assembly election petition shall specify the names and designations of the petitioner or petitioners and of the person or persons referred to as, or deemed to be, the respondent or respondents in terms of section 121(2) of the Representation of the People Act 1983, in this section called "the Act", and shall set forth articulately in numbered paragraphs:—

(i) the right of the petitioners within section 121(1) of the Act;
(ii) the proceedings at and the result of the election; and
(iii) the facts relied on in support of the prayer of the petition.

NOTES
[1] As amended by S.I. 1979 No. 516.
[2] As amended by S.I. 1985 No. 1426.

Notice of solicitor's name and address for notices

299.—[1] (*a*) Along with the petition there shall be lodged in the Petition Department a writing signed by or on behalf of the petitioner giving the name of an enrolled solicitor whom he authorises to act on his behalf, or stating that he acts for himself, as the case may be.

(*b*) The Deputy Principal Clerk shall keep a book at his office, in which he shall enter all addresses and the names of solicitors given under the preceding paragraph of this Rule.

NOTE
[1] As amended by S.I. 1991 No. 2483, with effect from 25th November 1991.

Fixing of security for expenses

[1] **299A.** On presentation of a parliamentary election petition, a motion shall be enrolled for the fixing of the amount of security for expenses.

NOTE
[1] Inserted by S.I. 1985 No. 1426.

Caution for expenses

[1] **300.** In the event of the security to be given by the petitioners in terms of section 136 of the Act being in whole or in part by bond of caution, the bond of caution as required by the Act shall be as nearly as may be in the form shewn in Form 48 and shall, within three days of presentation of the petition, be lodged with the Deputy Principal Clerk.

NOTE
[1] As amended by S.I. 1985 No. 1426.

Consignation in security

301. In the event of the required security being in whole or in part by a consignation of money, such money shall be consigned with one of the joint stock banks in Scotland in name of the Accountant of Court, and the consignation receipt therefor shall, within three days of presentation of the petition, be lodged in process and shall be retained as a security for the purpose for which security is required by the Act.

Sufficiency of caution

302. When security is tendered in the form of a bond of caution lodged as aforesaid, the sufficiency thereof shall be attested to the satisfaction of the Deputy Principal Clerk.

Service of petition

[1] **303.** The petitioner, if he acts for himself, or the solicitor for the petitioner shall within five days of the presentation of the petition serve on the respondent and the Lord Advocate a notice of the presentation of the petition, a notice of the nature and amount of the proposed security, and a copy of the petition and shall within five days thereafter lodge in process a copy of the petition with execution of service thereon in the form as nearly as may be *mutatis mutandis* of the form of execution of service of a summons, and with a copy of the notice of the presentation of the petition and of the nature and amount of the proposed security appended thereto.

NOTE

[1] As amended by S.I. 1985 No. 1426.

Objection to security

[1] **304.**—(*a*) The time within which the respondent may object to any bond of caution in terms of section 136(4) of the Act shall be 14 days after service of the notice of the proposed security.

(*b*) The objection shall be lodged in the Petition Department, and shall set forth in writing the specific ground or grounds thereof.

(*c*) When the petitioner has named a solicitor or given an address in terms of Rule 299, the respondent shall deliver a copy of the objection to the solicitor or send the same by post to the address given, so that it shall be received by the solicitor or delivered at the address on or before the date of lodging the objection.

NOTE

[1] As amended by S.I. 1985 No. 1426.

Diet for hearing on objection to security

305. As soon as possible after the lodging of the objection, the Deputy Principal Clerk shall fix a diet for the hearing thereof and shall give notice of the time and place of the diet to the parties or their solicitors.

Hearing on objection

306.—(*a*) At the diet for the hearing on the objection the Deputy Principal Clerk shall hear the submissions of any parties who shall be present or represented by counsel or solicitors and shall forthwith allow or disallow the objection.

(*b*) If the objection shall be allowed, the Deputy Principal Clerk shall, in his deliverance to that effect, state the amount of consignation or additional consignation required to make the security sufficient.

(*c*) The time within which the petitioner may remove the objection by a consignation of money shall be five days from the date of the deliverance of the Deputy Principal Clerk; provided that within the said time the petitioner may mark an appeal to one of the judges on the rota for the trial of parliamentary election petitions, or to the vacation judge, in which case the said period shall run from the date of the deliverance of that judge.

List of election petitions

307.—[1,2] (*a*) In preparing the list of parliamentary or European Assembly election petitions in terms of section 138(1) of the Act, the Deputy Principal Clerk shall insert the names of the solicitors (if any) acting for the petitioners and respondents, and the addresses (if any) to which notices may be sent.

[1] (*b*) The list of parliamentary or European Assembly election petitions may be inspected at the Petition Department at any time during office hours.

NOTES

[1] As amended by S.I. 1979 No. 516.
[2] As amended by S.I. 1985 No. 1426.

Time and place of trial

308.—[1] (*a*) The time and place of the trial of a preliminary or European Assembly election petition shall be fixed by one of the judges on the rota for the trial of parliamentary election petitions or the Vacation Judge, and the Deputy Principal Clerk shall intimate the diet of trial by post to the parties, Lord Advocate and to the returning officer, at least fifteen days before the day appointed for the trial; and the returning officer shall forthwith publish the same in the county, or burgh or burghs to which it relates.

NOTE

[1] As amended by S.I. 1979 No. 516 and S.I. 1985 No. 1426.

Interlocutory matters

309. All interlocutory questions and matters, except as otherwise provided in the Act or by these Rules, shall be made upon motion and intimated to the other party or parties.

Procedure where seat claimed

310.—[1] (*a*) When a petitioner claims the seat for an unsuccessful candidate, alleging that he had a majority of lawful votes, the party complaining of and the party defending the election or return shall, at least six days before the day appointed for the trial, respectively lodge in process a list of the voters intended to be objected to, and of the objections to each such voter, and shall send a copy of that list to the other party or parties and to the Lord Advocate to the petition [*sic*].

(*b*) No evidence shall be allowed to be given against any vote or in support of any objection which is not specified in the list, except by leave of the election court or, on motion heard before the date of the trial, of any of the judges, upon such terms as to amendment of the list, postponement of the enquiry, and payment of expenses as may be ordered.

NOTE

[1] As amended by S.I. 1985 No. 1426.

[1] *Evidence of undue return under section 139(5) of the Act*

311.—[1] (*a*) On the trial of a petition complaining of an undue return, and claiming the seat for some person, when a respondent intends to give evidence to prove that the election of such person was undue, under authority of section 139(5) of the Act, such respondent shall, at least six days before the day appointed for the trial, lodge in process a list of the objections to the election upon which he intends to rely, and shall send a copy of that list to the other party or parties to the petition and to the Lord Advocate.

(*b*) No evidence shall be allowed to be given by or for a respondent in support of any objection to the election not specified in the list, except by leave of the election court or, on motion heard before the date of the trial, of any of the judges, upon such terms as to amendment of the list, postponement of the enquiry, and payment of expenses, as may be ordered.

NOTE
[1] As amended by S.I. 1985 No. 1426.

Postponement of trial

312.—(*a*) It shall be competent for the election court or any of the judges on the rota for the trial of parliamentary election petitions, on special cause shown by a party to the petition or *ex proprio motu*, to postpone the trial of a petition to such day as he may name.

(*b*) Notice of such postponement shall be sent by the Deputy Principal Clerk to the returning officer who shall forthwith publish the same within the constituency.

Statement of matters

[1] **313.** Any party to the petition may, at least six days before the day appointed for the trial, lodge in process a statement of the matters upon which he intends to lead evidence; provided that a copy of such statement shall first have been sent to the other party or parties to the petition and to the Lord Advocate.

NOTE
[1] As amended by S.I. 1985 No. 1426.

Evidence at trial

314. No evidence shall be received at the trial except as to matters contained in the lists referred to in Rules 310 and 311 and the statements referred to in Rule 313, if any, and tending to support or rebut the same, or matters which have already been sufficiently set forth in the petition, except by leave of the court or one of the judges, and upon such conditions as to postponement of the trial, payment of expenses, and otherwise, as may be ordered; provided that the admissibility of any evidence sought to be led on the above matters shall be within the discretion of the election court.

Warrant to cite witnesses

315. The warrant for the citation of witnesses to the trial of any election petition shall be issued on the motion of any party to the trial, and shall be as nearly as may be, in the form shewn in Form 49.

Expenses of witnesses

316. The reasonable expenses of any witness shall be ascertained by the Clerk of Court, and upon a certificate under his hand allowing the same, the said expenses shall, in the first instance, be paid by the party adducing such witness.

Clerk of Court at trial

[1] **317.** At any election court held for the trial of a parliamentary or European Assembly election petition an officer to be named by the Principal Clerk of Session with the sanction of the Court shall attend and discharge the duties of Clerk of Court.

NOTE
[1] As amended by S.I. 1979 No. 516.

Application to state special case

318.—[1] (*a*) An application to state a special case, as provided in section 146(1) of the Act, shall be made by motion to either Division of the Inner House, or to the Vacation Judge.

(*b*) Parties shall be given an opportunity to be heard on the said motion, and the application shall be disposed of either by allowing adjustment of a special case or by refusal of the application.

NOTE

[1] As amended by S.I. 1985 No. 1426.

Opinion of court under section 146(4) of the Act

[1] **319.** If it shall appear to the election court to be expedient that the opinion of the court should be obtained, as provided for by section 146(4) of the Act, the question or questions to be submitted to the court shall be set forth in a case adjusted by the election court.

NOTE

[1] As amended by S.I. 1985 No. 1426.

Notice of application for leave to withdraw

[1] **320.**—(*a*) A notice of intention to withdraw an election petition in terms of section 147 of the Act shall be, as nearly as may be, in the form shewn in Form 51.

(*b*) A copy of the notice shall be sent by the petitioner to the respondent, the Lord Advocate, and to the returning officer who shall publish it in the county, or burgh or burghs to which it relates, and the petitioner shall advertise the notice in at least one newspaper circulating in the constituency.

NOTE

[1] As amended by S.I. 1985 No. 1426.

Leave to withdraw petition

321. An application for leave to withdraw a petition shall be, as nearly as may be, in the form shewn in Form 50, shall state the ground on which the application for withdrawal is intended to be supported, shall be signed by the person making the application and by the consenters, if any, or by their respective solicitors, and shall be lodged in process.

Application to be substituted as petitioner on withdrawal

322. Any person who might have been petitioner in respect of the election to which the petition relates may, within five days after notice of intention to withdraw is published by the returning officer, give notice in writing, signed by him or on his behalf, to the Deputy Principal Clerk of his intention to apply at the hearing to be substituted for the petitioner; provided that any informality in such notice shall not defeat such application if in fact made at the hearing, subject to such order as to postponement of the hearing and as to expenses as the court shall think just.

Security of substituted petitioner

323.—(*a*) The time within which security shall be given on behalf of a substituted petitioner before he proceeds with his petition shall be five days after the order of substitution.

(*b*) The substituted petitioner shall lodge the writing referred to in Rule 299 (*a*) within five days after the order of substitution.

Hearing of application for leave to withdraw

324. The time and place for hearing the application shall be fixed by one of the judges, or by the Vacation Judge, who shall hear and determine the same, unless he shall deem it expedient that the same shall be heard and determined by one of the Divisions of the Inner House; provided that the time fixed for the hearing shall be not less than a week after any, notice of intention to apply shall have been given to the Deputy Principal Clerk in terms of Rule 320, and in the event of such notice having been given the Deputy Principal Clerk shall inform the applicant to be substituted as petitioner, or his solicitor, of the time and place of the hearing.

Death of petitioner

[1] **325.** In the event of the death of the petitioner or the surviving petitioner, notice thereof under section 152(3) of the Act shall be given and advertised by the solicitor (if any) formerly acting for the petitioner, or by the respondent or returning officer or other person interested to whose knowledge the death of the petitioner shall come, in like manner *mutatis mutandis* as notice of intention to withdraw a petition, and shall be published in the manner provided in rule 320.

NOTE

[1] As amended by S.I. 1985 No. 1426.

Application to be substituted on death of petitioner

[1]**326.** Any application to be substituted as a petitioner in the event of the death of the petitioner or the surviving petitioner shall be made within one calendar month of the notice given in terms of the last foregoing rule, and shall be made by motion.

Notice that respondent does not oppose

[1] **327.** A respondent other than a returning officer may give notice that he does not intend to oppose the petition in terms of section 153(1)(*a*) of the Act by lodging in process not less than six days before the day appointed for the trial, a notice thereof signed by that respondent: and upon lodging such notice he shall forthwith send a copy thereof by post to the petitioner or his solicitor, the Lord Advocate, and to the returning officer, who shall cause the same to be published in the county, or burgh or burghs to which it relates, and the trial of the petition shall thereupon be postponed.

NOTE

[1] As amended by S.I. 1985 No. 1426.

Death of respondent

[1] **328.** If the respondent dies; or in the case of a parliamentary election is summoned to Parliament as a peer of Great Britain, or if the House of Commons have resolved that his seat is vacant, any person entitled to be a petitioner under the Act in respect of the election to which the petition relates, may, under section 153 of the Act, give notice of the fact in the county, or burgh or burghs to which it relates, by causing such notice to be published in at least one newspaper circulating therein, and by sending a copy of such notice, signed by him or on his behalf, to the returning officer and a like copy to the Deputy Principal Clerk.

NOTE

[1] As amended by S.I. 1979 No. 516 and S.I. 1985 No. 1426.

Application to be admitted as respondent

[1] **329.** The time within which a person may apply to be admitted as a respondent in terms of section 153 of the Act shall be ten days after notice is given under Rule 328, or such further time as the court may allow.

NOTE

[1] As amended by S.I. 1985 No. 1426.

Expenses in proceedings under the Act

330. When any expenses are awarded in the course of proceedings under the Act, the award of the same shall be deemed equivalent to a finding of expenses in the Court of Session; and the account thereof, when lodged, shall be taxed by the Auditor of the Court and the taxed amount shall be decerned for by the election court or one of the judges.

Proceedings not vitiated by objection of form

331. No proceedings under the Act shall be affected or defeated by any objection of mere form.

SECTION 2—APPEALS FROM THE DECISIONS OF REFEREES UNDER THE FINANCE (1909–10) ACT 1910, AND THE MINING INDUSTRY ACT 1926

Constitution of court

332. The judges of the Court of Session named for the purpose of hearing appeals under the Valuation of Lands (Scotland) Acts, when they sit to hear appeals under section 33 of the Finance (1909–10) Act, 1910, in this section called "the Act", shall sit with the same powers and under the same rules as if they were appointed to sit as an Extra Division of the Inner House to hear and dispose of such appeals; provided always, that in appeals from the sheriff under said Act it shall not be necessary for the court to specify in any interlocutor any findings of fact or in law upon which the judgment of the court is founded.

Time for appeal

333. Applications to a referee to state and sign a case under the Act shall be made within twenty-one days after the receipt by the appellant of the referee's determination, and such application shall set forth the questions of law on which the opinion of the said judges is sought.

Procedure in appeal

334.—(*a*) Any case stated under the Act shall refer to the particular statute under which it is presented and shall state in articulate numbered paragraphs the facts and circumstances out of which the case arises, as the same may be agreed, found, or referred, and shall set forth the question or questions for answer by the court. The form of the case shall be, as nearly as may be, as shewn in Form 43.

(*b*) The party who has obtained a case shall within seven days after the receipt thereof transmit the same to the Deputy Principal Clerk and at the same time transmit a copy thereof to the opposite party or his solicitor. Within fourteen days after the case has been transmitted, the party obtaining same shall lodge in the General Department the said case, along with a process and copies of productions for the use of the court in terms of Rules 20 and 26 (*b*), and shall at the same time intimate the lodging of the case to the opposite party or his solicitor and deliver to him at least ten copies thereof.

Rolls

335. All such appeals shall be published in the printed rolls of the Court of Session under the heading "Lands Valuation Appeal Court"; provided always that the single bills of the court shall be called before one of said judges sitting alone, with power always to him to refer any matter to a sitting of the full court.

Extracts

336. The Extractor of the Court of Session shall grant extract of the judgments of the court in common form.

Minute-Book

337. Judgments of the court shall be read in the minute-book of the Court of Session in common form.

Payment of duty

338. Subject to the provisions of subsection (4) of section 10 of the Finance Act 1894, the appellant shall not be entitled to appeal against the decision of the referee except on payment of, or giving security for, the duty claimed by the Commissioners, or such portion of it as is then payable by him.

Leave to appeal without payment

339. Where the appellant desires to apply for leave to bring an appeal without payment, or on part payment only of the duty under the provisions of subsection (4) of section 10 of the Finance Act 1894, he shall, within fourteen days from the date of the decision of the referee, present a note to the court craving such leave, and shall specify therein the grounds on which his application is made; on presentation of the note the appellant shall enrol a motion for an order for intimation thereof to the Lord Advocate who may, if so advised, lodge answers thereto within fourteen days after receipt of said intimation.

CHAPTER VII

Section 1.—Fee-fund Dues

[Revoked]

. . . .

Section 2.—Table of Fees of Solicitors in the Court of Session

[Rules 347–350]

. . . .

[See Division A—Fees, Stamps and Capital Taxes]

[THE NEXT PAGE IS C 153]

CHAPTER VIII

ADVOCATES

Admission as advocate

[1] **351. The Faculty of Advocates at a duly constituted meeting of the Members of Faculty may, subject to the approval of the court, make such Rules and Regulations regarding the terms and conditions of admission to the Faculty as they may from time to time consider necessary.**

NOTE

[1] Substituted by S.I. 1968 No. 1016.

APPENDIX

FORMS

[1] FORM 1

[2] Summons and Backing

NOTES

[1] As amended by S.I. 1974 No. 845, and (with effect from 25th November 1991) S.I. 1991 No. 2483.

[2] N.B. This is the official printed form which, along with the official printed backing (see *infra*), must be used for all summonses.

(This space will contain the letter and number assigned to the Summons on being lodged for calling.)

In the Court of Session
A.B. (*designation and address*) Pursuer;
against
C.D. (*designation and address*) Defender.

Elizabeth II, by the Grace of God, of the United Kingdom of Great Britain and Northern Ireland and of Her other Realms and Territories, Queen, Head of the Commonwealth, Defender of the Faith, To the said C.D.

Whereas by this Summons, the pursuer craves the Lords of our Council and Session to pronounce a decree against you in terms of the conclusions appended hereto. We therefore charge you that, if you have any good reason why such decree should not be pronounced, you cause appearance to be entered on your behalf in the Office of the Court, 2 Parliament Square, Edinburgh, on the calling of the Summons in Court, which calling will be not earlier than the (*fourteenth*) day from the date of service upon you of this Summons; and take warning that, if appearance is not so entered on your behalf, the Pursuer may proceed to obtain decree against you in your absence.

This summons is warrant for *arrestment to found jurisdiction, arrestment or inhibition on the dependence, or to dismantle a specified ship, as may be required. (See also Rule 76, paragraphs (b) and (c) of Rule 155, and paragraph (c) of Rule 170.)*

Given under our Signet at Edinburgh

(*Signed*) (*Name and address of pursuer's Solicitor.*)

(*Here follow the Conclusions in the short form or forms shewn in Form 2, followed by the Condescendence and Note of Pleas-in-Law.*)

Backing of Summons

	(This space will contain the letter and number assigned to the Summons on being lodged for calling.)

Summons

A.B. Pursuer;

against

C.D. Defender.

Action of (*Here state nature of action as in the headings of the forms of conclusion shewn in Form 2.*)

(*Name of pursuer's Edinburgh Solicitor.*)

[1] FORM 2

[2] Forms of Conclusion

NOTES

[1] As amended by S.I. 1969 No. 1819.

[2] A conclusion for interest and expenses is given as an illustration in Example (1). In other cases where conclusions for interest or expenses are appropriate these will be varied as required.

---

(1) *Action for payment.* For payment to the pursuer by the defender (*jointly and severally, or severally, or otherwise as may be appropriate*) of the sum of with interest thereon at the rate of per centum per annum from the day of , until payment and expenses of the action.

(2) *Action of damages.* For payment to the pursuer by the defender of the sum of .

(3) *Action of reduction.* For production and reduction of (*specify deed to be set aside*).

(4) *Action of declarator.* For declarator (*state declarator asked as in present practice*).

(5) *Action of count, reckoning and payment.* For count and reckoning with the pursuer for the defender's intromissions with (*describe fund or estate*) and for payment to the pursuer by the defender of the balance found due to him, or otherwise of the sum of

(6) *Action of proving the tenor.* For declarator that (*the lost deed*) was of the tenor following (*set out the terms of the lost deed*), and that the decree to be pronounced herein shall be equivalent to the original deed.

(7) *Action of multiplepoinding and exoneration.* For distribution of (*describe the fund in medio*) among the claimants found entitled thereto, and exoneration (*of the holder of the fund*).

(8) *Action of furthcoming.* For payment to the pursuer by the arrestee of £ or of such sum as may be owing by the arrestee to (*the common debtor*) and arrested in his hands by the pursuer, or at least of so much thereof as shall satisfy the pursuer in (1) the payment of the expenses of and incidental to the sale and (2) the principal sum of £ and interest thereon at the rate of per centum per annum from the date of citation until payment as shall satisfy the pursuer in the principal sum of

or

For delivery to the pursuer or to such person as the Court may appoint of the moveables belonging to or owing by the arrestee to (*the common debtor*) and arrested in his hands by the pursuer; and for warrant for the sale of such moveables under such conditions as may be directed; and for furthcoming and payment to the pursuer of the proceeds thereof, or at least of so much thereof as shall satisfy the pursuer (*as above*).

(9) *Admiralty action in rem.* For declarator that the pursuer has a lien over the .... (*the ship*) for the sum of £ in respect of (*state the basis of the lien, as e.g. the collision—giving date*); and for declarator that the pursuer's said lien to the extent of the said sum of £ with interest thereon at from to is preferable to the right of all others having or pretending to have rights in the said ship; and for warrant to sell the said .... (*ship*) on said lien being declared, and to apply the proceeds in satisfaction of the said lien in or towards payment of the said sum of £ and interest.

(10) *Action of Declarator of Marriage.* For declarator that the pursuer and defender were lawfully married to one another by (*here specify mode in which marriage was contracted, as e.g.* (1) *interchange of consent de praesenti (time and place*), *or* (2) *cohabitation habit and repute* (*time and place*), *or* (3) *promise* (*time*) *subsequente copula at* (*time and place*)).

(11) *Action of Declarator of Nullity of Marriage.* For declarator that a pretended marriage between the pursuer and defender at (*place*) on (*date*) is null by reason of (*here specify ground of nullity as e.g.* (1) *the pursuer's or defender's impotency, or* (2) *the parties being within the forbidden degrees or* (3) *the defender being married to* *or* (4) *non-age of one of the parties or* (5) *insanity of one of the parties at the date of the marriage or* (6) *non-residence in Scotland of both the parties prior to the marriage*).

(12) *Action of Declarator of Legitimacy.* For declarator that (*name and designation*) is (*or was*) the lawful son (*or daughter*) of (*name and designation*).

(13) *Action of Declarator of legitimation per subsequens matrimonium.* For declarator that , who was born on (*date*) is (*or was*) the child of (*name and designation*) and (*name and designation*) and was legitimated by the subsequent marriage of the said and on (*date*). (*Add conclusion for aliment, if appropriate.*)

[1] (14) (*a*) *Action of declarator of illegitimacy.* For declarator that (*name and designation*) is illegitimate and is not the lawful child of (*name and designation*).

(*b*) *Action of declarator of parentage or non-parentage.* For declarator that (*name and designation*) is [*or* was] [not] the parent [or child] of (*name and designation*).

[2] (15) *Action of separation.* For separation of the defender from the pursuer on the ground (of the defender's behaviour *or* of the defender's adultery *or* of the defender's desertion for a period of two years or more *or* of non-cohabitation for a period of two years or more and the defender's consent to the granting of decree of separation *or* of non-cohabitation for a period of five years or more.) (Add conclusion for aliment if appropriate.)

NOTES

[1] Substituted by S.I. 1986 No. 1955.
[2] Substituted by S.I. 1976 No. 1994.

---

[1] (16) *Action of divorce.* For divorce of the defender from the pursuer in respect that the marriage has broken down irretrievably by reason of (the defender's adultery *or* the defender's behaviour *or* the defender's desertion of the pursuer for a period of two years or more *or* non-cohabitation for two years or more and the defender's consent to decree of divorce *or* non-cohabitation for five years or more).

NOTE

[1] Substituted by S.I. 1976 No. 1994.

---

[1] (17) *Conclusion for periodical allowance and capital sum.* For payment by the defender to the pursuer of (1) a capital sum of £ with interest thereon at the rate of per centum per annum from the date of decree to follow hereon until payment; and (2) a periodical allowance of £ per week (month) payable until the remarriage or death of the pursuer.

NOTE

[1] Substituted by S.I. 1976 No. 1994.

---

(18) *Action of Adherence.* For decree ordaining the defender to adhere to the pursuer and cohabit with her as his wife (*or* with him as her husband).

(19) *Action of Putting to silence.* For decree ordaining the defender to desist from asserting that he (*or* she) is the husband (*or* wife *or* child *or other relative*) of the pursuer, and putting her (*or* him) to silence thereanent.

[1] (20) *Conclusion for custody of children.* For custody of and , the children of the marriage under the age of sixteen years and payment by the defender to the pursuer of (*specify the rate of aliment*) as aliment for each child while in the custody of the pursuer and unable to earn a livelihood; and for leave to any party claiming an interest to apply to the Court thereanent until (*insert the date when youngest child will attain sixteen years of age*).

NOTE

[1] As amended by S.I. 1976 No. 1994.

---

(21) *Action for salvage.* For payment to the pursuer by the defender of the sum of £ for salvage services performed by the pursuer to the vessel on the day of or for such an amount of salvage as to the Court may seem just or (*in the case of a summons for apportionment*) for payment to the pursuer of an equitable proportion of the above award of £ . (*Here refer to the agreement under which the total amount of the salvage award was fixed.*)

(22) *Action of Implement.* For decree ordaining the defender (*state the order craved and add such alternative conclusions as may be appropriate*).

(23) *Adjudication for debt.* [1] (*a*) For adjudication of the heritable property of the defender, that is to say, All and Whole (describe subjects by reference or otherwise) from the defender to the pursuer; and that for payment to the pursuer of the principal sum, interest and expenses of process and of extract (or as the case may be) contained in a decree (detail particulars of decree in pursuer's favour); According as the same shall extend when accumulated at the date of decree to follow hereon and of the interest of the said accumulated sum at the rate of *per centum per annum* during the non-redemption of the said heritable property, and the expenses of the infeftment to follow on the said decree of adjudication with interest thereon at the rate of *per centum per annum* from the date of disbursing the same during the non-redemption.

(*b*) *Heritable securities.* For adjudication of a bond and disposition in security (*describe the bond*) and of the subjects contained in the said bond, viz. All and Whole (*describe the subjects by reference or otherwise*) from the defender to the pursuer for payment of (*describe debts*), during the non-redemption of the said lands and others.

NOTE

[1] Substituted by S.I. 1977 No. 1621.

---

(24) *Adjudication in implement.* For adjudication from the defender of All and Whole (*describe subjects by reference or otherwise*) and all rights of the defender therein and the rents thereof from and after the term of (*date of entry under missives*) in implement of missives of sale (*dated*) between the defender and the pursuer and for declarator that the said lands and others belong to the pursuer and his heirs and assignees; and for decree ordaining the defender to free and relieve the said lands and others of all burdens and incumbrances affecting the same, of all feuduties, cess, minister's stipend, and public and parochial burdens affecting the said lands at and preceding the pursuer's said term of entry, or otherwise for payment of the sum of (*state amount*) or such sum as may be required for that purpose.

(25) *Declarator and division or sale.* For declarator that the pursuer is entitled to insist in an action of division or sale of All and Whole (*describe subjects by reference or otherwise*); and for division of the said subjects between the pursuer and the defender, or if the division of the said subjects is found to be impracticable or inexpedient for declarator that the same should be sold and the proceeds divided between the pursuer and the defender, and for warrant to sell accordingly; and for allocation of the expenses of the sale and of this process between the pursuer and the defender.

(26) *Maills and Duties under Heritable Securities Act 1894.* For declarator that the pursuer has right to the rents, maills, and duties of the subjects and others specified in the bond and disposition in security for , granted by in favour of dated and recorded in the register or at least so much of the said rents, maills, and duties as will satisfy and pay the pursuer the principal sum of £ , with interest thereon at the rate of per centum per annum from the day of liquidate penalty and termly failures, all as specified and contained in the said bond and disposition in security dated and recorded as aforesaid.

(*Intimation to tenants in form of Schedule B of 1894 Act.*)

(27) *Poinding of the Ground.* (*a*) *Against debtor in possession.* For warrant to poind and distrain all moveable goods and effects poindable or distrainable belonging to the defender which are or shall happen to be upon the ground of the lands and others described and contained in the bond and disposition in security (*or where the action proceeds on a real burden, the disposition or other writ by which it is constituted*) aftermentioned, vizt. All and Whole (*describe subjects by reference or otherwise*): And for payment thereof to the pursuer of the amount of the principal sum of £ liquidate penalty and termly failures, with interest on said principal sum from the term of and in all time coming during the not redemption conform to bond and disposition in security dated and recorded in the Division of the General Register of Sasines applicable to the county of the both days of granted by the defender in favour of the pursuer (*or where the pursuer is not the original bondholder*, in favour of and to which the pursuer has now right in virtue of (*describe title*)).

(*b*) *Against debtor and tenants.* For warrant to poind and distrain all moveable goods and effects poindable or distrainable of the defender principal debtor, and of the defenders and his tenants or possessors of the lands and others aftermentioned which are or shall happen to be upon the grounds of the said lands and other described and contained in the bond and disposition in security aftermentioned, vizt. All and Whole (*give description of subjects sufficient to identify them*) but in so far as relates to the said tenants and possessors to the amount only of the respective rents due or that may become due by them and for payment thereof to the pursuer to the amount of the principal sum of £ liquidate penalty and termly failures specified and contained in the bond and disposition in security dated and recorded in the Division of the General Register of Sasines applicable to the county of the both days of granted by the defender A.B. in favour of the pursuer, with interest from the term of and in all time coming during the not redemption.

[1] FORM 3

Form of Citation and Execution when service is by registered or recorded delivery letter

Citation

In Her Majesty's name and authority, the summons of which the foregoing is a full copy is hereby served upon you (*name, designation and address of defender*) by me (*name, designation and address*), solicitor for the pursuer.

The number of days on the expiry of which, in terms of the said summons you are charged to cause notice of appearance to be entered on your behalf is reckoned from twenty-four hours after the date of posting hereof.

Dated this day of .

(*Signed*) (*Solicitor for the pursuer*).

Execution

This summons executed by me (*name, designation and address*), solicitor for the pursuer, against the defender(s) by posting, on (*date*) between the hours of and at the post office, a copy of the same to him or them, with citation subjoined, in a registered or recorded delivery letter addressed as follows (*address*) and the post office receipt for the said letter accompanies this execution.

(*Signed*) (*Solicitor for the pursuer*).

NOTE

[1] As amended by S.I. 1991 No. 2483, with effect from 25th November 1991.

[1] FORM 4

Form of Citation when service is edictal

Citation

In Her Majesty's name and authority, the summons of which the foregoing is a full copy is hereby served edictally upon you the said by me (*name, designation and address*), solicitor for the pursuer.

Dated this day of

(*Signed*) (*Solicitor for the pursuer*).

NOTE

[1] As amended by S.I. 1991 No. 2483, with effect from 25th November 1991.

Rule 75(3) [1] FORM 4A

Citation by advertisement

IN THE COURT OF SESSION

in causa

[A.B.] (*address*)

Pursuer

against

[C.D.]

Defender

An action has been raised in the Court of Session, Parliament Square, Edinburgh, [Scotland,] by A.B., pursuer. The pursuer calls as a defender, C.D., whose last known address was

If C.D. wishes to challenge the jurisdiction of the court or to defend the action he should immediately contact the Deputy Principal Clerk of Session, Court of Session, Parliament Square, Edinburgh (Telephone 031-225 2595).

(*Signed*)
[Solicitor for pursuer]
(*Address*)

NOTE

[1] Added by S.I. 1986 No. 1941.

FORM 5

Form of Intimation to Heritable Creditor of Defender in action relating to heritage

Take notice that an action, a copy of the summons in which is pre-fixed hereto, has been raised against the defender as owner of land over which you are believed to hold a heritable security; and that you may if you so desire apply to the Court for leave to state defences to the action within fourteen days after the expiry of days from the date of service hereof (*or if the warrant is executed contemporaneously with citation of the defender* within fourteen days after the calling of the summons in Court which will not be earlier than days from the date of service hereof).

The date of service hereof is reckoned as commencing on the expiry of twenty-four hours after the date of posting hereof.

Dated this day of

(*Signed*) (*Solicitor for the pursuer*).

[1] FORM 5A

Form of intimation to executor or relative in an action for damages

Take notice that an action has been raised at the instance of (name and address) against (name and address) being a person you are believed to have a title to sue in an action based on the injuries from which the late (name and former address) died or on his death: and that you are entitled to be added as an additional pursuer in this action and accordingly you may if you so desire apply to the court to be so added within 14 days after the expiry of days from the date of service hereof (*or if the warrant is executed at the same time as the citation of the defender* within 14 days after the calling of the summons in court which will not be earlier than days from the date of service hereof), and in the event of you making such an application you are required to serve notice thereof on all the parties to this action.

A copy of the summons (*or* open record *or* closed record) in the action is attached.

[It is proposed to apply to the court for authority to dispense with intimation to the persons mentioned in paragraph 1 of the summons whose whereabouts are said to be unknown. If you know the whereabouts of any of those persons, you are requested to inform the Deputy Principal Clerk of Session, Court of Session, Edinburgh.]

The date of service hereof is reckoned as commencing on the expiry of 24 hours after the date of posting hereof.

Dated this day of

(*Solicitor for Pursuer*)

NOTE

[1] Added by S.I. 1976 No. 2020 and substituted by S.I. 1984 No. 920.

---

[1] FORM 5B

Form of Intimation in an Action of Declarator of Death

To (*name and address as in warrant*)

Take notice that an action, a copy of the summons in which is prefixed hereto, has been brought to have it declared that (name and last known address of missing person) is dead, and that you may if you so desire apply to the Court for leave to state defences to the action within fourteen days after the calling of the summons in Court which will not be earlier than days from the date of service hereof. The date of intimation hereof is reckoned as commencing on the expiry of 24 hours after the date of posting hereof.

Dated this (insert date of posting).

(Address) (*Signed*) A.B.
(*Solicitor for Pursuer*)

NOTE

[1] Added by S.I. 1978 No. 161.

---

[1] FORM 5C

Form of Intimation to the International Oil Pollution Compensation Fund

To the International Oil Pollution Compensation Fund (*address*) take Notice that an action, a copy of the summons in which is prefixed hereto, has been raised by (*name and designation*) against (*name and designation*) in which the Court may make an order which is binding upon you, and that you may if you so desire apply to the Court for leave to appear as a party to the action within 14 days after the calling of the summons in Court which will not be earlier than days from the date of service hereof.

The date of service hereof is reckoned as commencing on the expiry of 24 hours after the date of posting hereof.

Dated this (*insert date of posting*)
(*Address*)

(*Signed*)
(*Solicitor for Pursuer*)

NOTE
[1] Added by S.I. 1969 No. 670.

Form 6

Form of Notice to additional or substituted defender

To (*designation and address*)

Take notice that in the action in which is the pursuer and is the defender, copies of the summons and defences (or the record in which as now amended) are herewith enclosed, your name has, by order of the Court dated , been added (*or substituted*) as a defender to the said action; and the conclusions of the action, originally directed against the said are now (*also*) directed against you. If you desire to defend the said action you are charged to lodge defences thereto in the office of the Court of Session, 2 Parliament Square, Edinburgh, within days from the date of service hereof, under certification that, if you fail to do so, the said may proceed and obtain decree against you in absence.

Dated this day of
(*Signed*) (*Solicitor for the pursuer*).

Form 7

Third Party Notice in the cause between

A.B. *Pursuer*
and
C.D. *Defender*
and
E.F. *Third Party*

To E.F.

This Notice is served upon you by the above named C.D. by virtue of an order granted by Lord , in the action in which the above named A.B. is the pursuer and C.D. the defender. In the action the pursuer claims against the defender £ as damages in respect of (*or otherwise as the case may be*) as more fully appears in the copy summons and condescendence (*or* copy record in the action) enclosed herewith.

The defender admits (*or* denies) liability to the pursuer but claims that (if he is liable to the pursuer) you are liable to relieve him wholly (*or* partially) of his liability in respect of (*set forth contract or other right of contribution, relief, or indemnity*) as more fully appears from his defences lodged in the above action and enclosed herewith,

or

The defender denies any liability for the injury said to have been suffered by the pursuer and maintains that the liability, if any, to the pursuer rests solely on you (*or* on you along with) as more fully appears from his defences lodged in the above action and enclosed herewith.

or

The defender denies any liability for the injury said to have been suffered by the pursuer but maintains that if there is any liability he shares that liability with you, as more fully appears from his defences lodged in the above action and enclosed herewith.

or

The defender admits liability in part for the injury suffered by the pursuer but disputes the amount of damages and maintains that his liability falls to be shared with you, as more fully appears from his defences lodged in the above action and enclosed herewith.

or

The defender admits liability in part for the injury suffered by the pursuer and for the damages claimed but maintains that his liability falls to be shared with you, as more fully appears from his defences lodged in the above action and enclosed herewith.

or

(*otherwise as the case may be*)

And take notice that if you wish to appear in the action and resist either the claim of the pursuer against the defender, or the claim of the defender against you, you must lodge answers in the action not later than , otherwise the Court may pronounce such judgment in the matter of the claim by the defender against you as it thinks fit.

Dated this day of
(*Signed*) (*Solicitor for the defender*).

[1] FORM 8

Example of enrolment in Motion Sheet, and of marking therein

(*Date*).

On behalf of the pursuer—for commission and diligence for recovery of documents conform to specification No. of Process—Intimated to defender—p. W.X. (*pursuer's Counsel or solicitor who has a right of audience in the Court of Session*).

(*Signed*) (*Signature of pursuer's solicitor, or of his clerk*). (*Date*).

On behalf of the defender—pursuer's motion opposed—intimated to pursuer—p. (*defender's Counsel or solicitor who has a right of audience in the Court of Session*).

(*Signed*) (*Signature of defender's solicitor, or of his clerk*).

NOTE

[1] As amended by S.I. 1991 No. 2483, with effect from 25th November 1991.

FORM 9

Form of Order of Court and Certificate in Optional Procedure for recovery of documents

Order by the Court of Session at Edinburgh.
In the Cause (*year and Serial Number*)
in which
A.B. (*designed*) is Pursuer
and
C.D. (*designed*) is Defender

To (*name and designation of party or parties or third-party haver, from whom the documents are sought to be recovered*).

Take notice that you are hereby required to produce to the Deputy Principal Clerk of Session, 2 Parliament Square, Edinburgh, within seven days of the service upon you of this Order,

(1) This Order itself which must be produced intact;
(2) A Certificate, sworn, in terms of the form appended hereto, and
(3) All documents in your possession falling within the specification enclosed herewith, together with a list or inventory of such documents signed by you as relative to this Order and your Certificate.

Production may be made either by lodging the above at the said office of the Court of Session, or by registered or recorded delivery letter or registered postal packet enclosing the same, and addressed to the said Deputy Principal Clerk at said office.

(*Signature and business address of the solicitor of the party in whose favour Commission and Diligence has been granted.*)

(*Date*)

NOTE.—If you claim confidentiality for any of the documents produced by you, such documents must nevertheless be produced, but may be placed in a special sealed enclosure by themselves, marked "Confidential".

Certificate

(*Date*)

I hereby Certify with reference to the order of the Court of Session in the cause (*year and serial number*) and relative specification of documents, served upon me and marked respectively X and Y,

(1) that the documents which are produced and which are enumerated in the inventory signed by me and marked Z, are the whole documents in my possession falling under the Specification

or

that I have no documents in my possession falling within the Specification.

(2) that, to the best of my knowledge and belief, there are in existence other documents falling within the Specification, but not in my possession, namely (*describe them by reference to one or more of the descriptions of documents in the Specification*), which were last seen by me on or about (*date*), at (*place*), in the hands of (*name and address of the person*)

or

that I know of the existence of no documents in the possession of any person, other than myself, which fall within the Specification.

(*Signed*)

[1] Form 10

Form of Minute for Letters of Request

Minute for A.B. (design)

[*Counsel or solicitor who has a right of audience in the Court of Session*] for the Minuter states that the evidence specified in the Schedule is required for the purpose of these proceedings and prays the Court to issue a letter of request to (*specify the Court or tribunal having powers to obtain the evidence*) to obtain the evidence so specified.

(*signed by Counsel*).

NOTE

[1] Substituted by S.I. 1976 No. 283. As amended by S.I. 1991 No. 2483, with effect from 25th November 1991.

Form 11

Form of Letter of Request

(Items to be included in all Letters of Request.)

1. Sender	.... (identity and address).............. ....
2. Central authority of the requested State	.... (identity and address) ....
3. Person to whom the executed request is to be returned	.... (identity and address) ....
4. The undersigned applicant has the honour to submit the following request:	
5. a. Requesting judicial authority	.... (identity and address) ....
b. To the competent authority	.... (the requested State) ....
6. Names and addresses of the parties and their representatives	
a. Pursuer	....
b. Defender	....
c. Other parties	....
7. Nature and purpose of the proceedings and summary of the facts	....
8. Evidence to be obtained or other judicial act to be performed	....

(Items to be completed where applicable)

9. Identity and address of any person to be examined	....
10. Questions to be put to the persons to be examined or statement of the subject-matter about which they are to be examined	.... (or see attached list) ....
11. Documents or other property to be inspected	(specify whether it is to be produced, copied, valued, etc.) ....

12. Any requirement that the evidence be given on oath or affirmation and any special form to be used	.... (in the event that the evidence cannot be taken in the manner requested, specify whether it is to be taken in such manner as provided by local law for the formal taking of evidence) ....
13. Special methods or procedure to be followed	....
14. Request for notification of the time and place for the execution of the request and identity and address of any person to be notified	....
15. Request for attendance or participation of judicial personnel of the requesting authority at the execution of the letter of request	....
16. Specification of privilege or duty to refuse to give evidence under the law of the State of origin	....
17. The fees and costs incurred will be borne by	.... (identity and address) ....

(Items to be included in all Letters of Request.)

18. Date of request	....
19. Signature and seal of the requesting authority	....

NOTE
[1] Substituted by S.I. 1983 No. 656.

Form 12

Notice to be endorsed on the Citation served on a person summoned to serve as a juror

Notice

The person on whom this citation is served may apply to the Deputy Principal Clerk of Session, 2 Parliament Square, Edinburgh, 1, to be exempted from service under it for medical or other reasons, as soon as possible after receipt of this citation.

Form 13

Specimen of filling-in of the Official Printed Form of Summons in an Admiralty Action in rem

In the Court of Session,
Admiralty Action *in rem*.
A.B. (*designation and address*) Pursuer;
against
The Owners of the S.S. Q.R. Defenders.

Elizabeth II, by the Grace of God, of the United Kingdom of Great Britain and Northern

Ireland, and of Her other Realms and Territories, Queen, Head of the Commonwealth, Defender of the Faith, to E.F. (*name and address*) only known owner or party interested in S.S. Q.R. of the port of L. and others, the owners and parties interested in the said S.S. Q.R. Defenders *or* to G.H. Master of and representing the owners of the S.S. Q.R. of the port of L. Defender. (*Vary as required if the action is directed against owners of cargo.*)

Whereas, etc. (*as in Form 1*)

or

(*Where the Pursuer is not in a position to call as defenders the owners of or parties interested or the master.*)

In the Court of Session.
Admiralty Action *in rem.*
A.B. (*designation and address*) Pursuer;
against

The S.S. Q.R. and the owners thereof and other parties interested therein, Defenders.

Elizabeth II, by the Grace of God, of the United Kingdom of Great Britain and Northern Ireland and of Her other Realms and Territories, Queen, Head of the Commonwealth, Defender of the Faith, to the owners of the S.S. Q.R. of the port of L. and others interested therein, Defenders. (*Vary as required.*)

Whereas, etc. (*as in Form 1*).

Form 14

Specimen of filling-in of the Official Printed Form of Summons in an Admiralty Action in personam

In the Court of Session
Admiralty Action *in personam*
A.B. (*designation and address*) Pursuer;
against
E.F. the Master of the S.S. Q.R. Defender.

Elizabeth II, by the Grace of God, of the United Kingdom of Great Britain and Northern Ireland, and of Her other Realms and Territories, Queen, Head of the Commonwealth, Defender of the Faith, to E.F. (*designation and address*) Master of the S.S. Q.R. of the port of L. presently at M. as representing the owners thereof against whom arrestments have been used *ad fundandam jurisdictionem*, Defender. (*Vary as required if the action is directed against owners of cargo.*)

Whereas, etc. (*as in Form 1*).

[THE NEXT PAGE IS C 163]

[1] Form 15

Form of Preliminary Act in Ship-Collision Cases

In the action which in are Pursuers;
and
are Defenders.

Preliminary Act
for
Pursuer (*or* Defender)

(*a*) The names of the vessels which came into collision, their ports of registry, and the names of their masters.

(*b*) The date and time of the collision.

(*c*) The place of the collision.

(*d*) The direction and force of the wind.

(*e*) The state of the weather.

(*f*) The state, direction and force of the tidal or other current.

(*g*) The magnetic course steered and speed through the water of the vessel when the other vessel was first seen or immediately before any measures were taken with reference to her presence, whichever was the earlier.

(*h*) The lights (if any) carried by the vessel.

(*i*) The distance and bearing of the other vessel if and when her echo was first observed by radar.

(*j*) The distance, bearing and approximate heading of the other vessel when first seen.

(*k*) What light or combination of lights (if any) of the other vessel was first seen.

(*l*) What other lights or combinations of lights (if any) of the other vessel were subsequently seen, before the collision, and when.

(*m*) What alterations (if any) were made to the course and speed of the vessel after the earlier of the two times referred to in article (*g*) up to the time of the collision, and when, and what measures (if any), other than alterations of course and speed, were taken to avoid the collision, and when.

(*n*) The parts of each vessel which first came into contact and the approximate angle between the two vessels at the moment of contact.

(*o*) What sound signals (if any) were given, and when.

(*p*) What sound signals (if any) were heard from the other vessel and when.

(*Signed by Counsel or solicitor who has a right of audience in the Court of Session*)

(*Dated*)

NOTE

[1] As amended by S.I. 1991 No. 2483, with effect from 25th November 1991.

---

[1] Form 15A

Form of Notice to defender where it is stated he consents to the granting of decree of divorce
(Rule 161(1))

Take Notice that the copy summons served on you together with this Notice states that you consent to the grant of decree of divorce.

1. If you do so consent the consequences to you are that—

(*a*) provided the pursuer establishes the fact that there has been no cohabitation between the parties to the marriage at any time during a continuous period of two years after the date of the marriage and immediately preceding the bringing of this action and that you consent, a decree will be granted;

(*b*) on the grant of a decree of divorce you may lose your rights of succession to the pursuer's estate;

(*c*) decree of divorce will end the marriage thereby affecting any right to such pension as may depend upon the marriage continuing or upon your being left a widow; the State widow's pension will not be payable to you when the pursuer dies;

(*d*) apart from these consequences there may be others applicable to you depending upon your particular circumstances.

2. If you do consent to the grant of decree you are still entitled to apply to the Court in this action—

(*a*) to make financial provision for you under the Divorce (Scotland) Act 1976 by making an order—

(i) for the payment by the pursuer to you of a periodical allowance;

(ii) for the payment by the pursuer to you of a capital sum;
(iii) varying the terms of any marriage settlement.
(*b*) to make an order providing for the custody, maintenance and education of any child of the marriage, or any child accepted as such, who is under 16 years of age.

3. In order to make such an application to the Court you require to lodge defences in this action. If you wish to make such an application you should consult a solicitor.

4. If after considering the foregoing you wish to consent to decree you should complete and sign the attached Form of Notice of Consent, and send it to the Deputy Principal Clerk of Session, 2 Parliament Square, Edinburgh, within 14 days of the receipt of this Notice.

5. If after consenting you wish to withdraw your consent you must immediately inform the Deputy Principal Clerk of Session at the above address in writing that you withdraw your consent to decree being granted against you in the action at the instance of (insert name and address of your husband or wife as the case may be).

NOTE
[1] Added by S.I. 1976 No. 1994.

[1] FORM 15B

Form of Notice to defender where it is stated he consents to the granting of decree of separation (Rule 161(2))

Take Notice that the copy summons served on you together with this Notice states that you consent to the grant of decree of separation—

1. If you do so consent the consequences to you are that—
   (*a*) provided the pursuer establishes the fact that there has been no cohabitation between the parties to the marriage at any time during a continuous period of two years after the date of the marriage and immediately preceding the bringing of this action and that you consent, a decree of separation will be granted;
   (*b*) on the grant of decree of separation you will be obliged to live apart from the pursuer but the marriage will continue to subsist. A husband will continue to have a legal obligation to support his wife and children;
   (*c*) apart from these consequences there may be others applicable to you depending upon your particular circumstances.

2. If you do consent to the grant of decree you are still entitled to apply to the Court in this action—
   (*a*) if you are the wife, for payment by the pursuer to you of aliment; and
   (*b*) for an order providing for the custody, maintenance and education of any child of the marriage, or any child accepted as such, who is under 16 years of age.

3. In order to make such an application to the Court you require to lodge defences to this action. If you wish to make such an application you should consult a solicitor.

4. If after considering the foregoing you wish to consent to decree you should complete and sign the attached Form of Notice of Consent and send it to the Deputy Principal Clerk of Session, 2 Parliament Square, Edinburgh, within 14 days of the receipt of this Notice.

5. If after consenting you wish to withdraw your consent you must immediately inform the Deputy Principal Clerk of Session at the above address, in writing, that you withdraw your consent to decree being granted against you in the action at the instance of (insert name and address of your husband or wife as the case may be).

NOTE
[1] Added by S.I. 1976 No. 1994.

[1] FORM 15C

Form of Notice to defender in an action of divorce where it is stated there has been 5 years non-cohabitation (Rule 161(3))

1. Take Notice that the copy summons served on you together with this Notice states that there has been no cohabitation between you and the pursuer at any time during a continuous period of 5 years after the date of the marriage and immediately preceding the commencement of this action and that if the pursuer establishes this as a fact and the Court is satisfied that the marriage has broken down irretrievably a decree will be granted, unless in the opinion of the Court the grant of decree would result in grave financial hardship to you.

2. Decree of divorce will end the marriage thereby affecting any right to such pension as

may depend upon the marriage continuing or upon your being left a widow; the State widow's pension will not be payable to you when the pursuer dies. You may also lose your rights of succession to the pursuer's estate.

3. You are entitled, whether or not you dispute that there has been no such cohabitation during such a period, to apply to the Court in this action—

(*a*) to make financial provision for you under the Divorce (Scotland) Act 1976 by making an order—

(i) for the payment by the pursuer to you of a periodical allowance;

(ii) for the payment by the pursuer to you of a capital sum;

(iii) varying the terms of any marriage settlement;

(*b*) to make an order providing for the custody, maintenance and education of any child of the marriage or of any child accepted as such, who is under 16 years of age.

4. In order to make such an application to the Court you require to lodge defences to this action.

5. If you wish to make any such application to the Court in this action you should consult a solicitor.

NOTE

[1] Added by S.I. 1976 No. 1994.

---

[1] Form 15D

Form of Notice to defender in an action of separation where it is stated there has been 5 years non-cohabitation (Rule 161(4))

1. Take Notice that the copy summons served on you together with this Notice states that there has been no cohabitation between you and the pursuer at any time during a continuous period of 5 years after the date of the marriage and immediately preceding the commencement of this action and that if the pursuer establishes this as a fact and the Court is satisfied that there are grounds justifying decree of separation a decree will be granted, unless in the opinion of the Court the grant of decree would result in grave financial hardship to you.

2. On the grant of decree of separation you will be obliged to live apart from the pursuer but the marriage will continue to subsist. A husband will continue to have a legal obligation to support his wife and children.

3. You are entitled, whether or not you dispute that there has been no such cohabitation during such a period, to apply to the Court in this action—

(*a*) if you are the wife, for payment by the pursuer to you of aliment; and

(*b*) for an order providing for the custody, maintenance and education of any child of the marriage, or any child accepted as such, who is under 16 years of age.

4. In order to make such an application to the Court you require to lodge defences to this action.

5. If you wish to make any such application to the Court in this action you should consult a solicitor.

NOTE

[1] Added by S.I. 1976 No. 1994 and as amended by S.I. 1980 No. 1144.

---

[1] Form 15E

Form of Notice of Consent in actions of divorce and separation under section 1(2)(d) of the Divorce (Scotland) Act 1976

I (full name and address of the defender to be inserted by the pursuer's solicitor before sending Notice) have received a copy of the summons in the action against me at the instance of (full name and address of pursuer to be inserted by pursuer's solicitor before sending Notice).

I understand that it states that I consent to the grant of decree of divorce/separation* in this action.

I have considered the consequences to me mentioned in the Notice sent together with this Notice.

I consent to the grant of decree of divorce/separation* in this action.
(*Signed*)
(*Dated*) Defender
* delete whichever does not apply.

NOTE
[1] Added by S.I. 1976 No. 1994 and as amended by S.I. 1980 No. 1144.

[1] Form 15F

Form of Request for proof before answer in undefended actions

1. Ground of Action
2. Full name of pursuer
3. Full name of defender
4. Name of Counsel or solicitor who has a right of audience in the Court of Session
5. Name of Solicitor(s) (If pursuer is an Assisted Person, please give individual partner's name)
6. Date of Calling
7. Date when proof before answer allowed
8. Is there a cross-action and if so what stage has it reached?
9. Date of last interlocutor if any, subsequent to date of allowance of proof before answer
10. Estimated duration of proof (if likely to exceed normal time for an undefended proof)
11. If requesting accelerated diet state reason and also state date of diet of proof if already fixed

Date allocated for proof

NOTE
[1] Added by S.I. 1976 No. 1994. As amended by S.I. 1991 No. 2483, with effect from 25th November 1991.

[1] Form 16

Form of Intimation to alleged adulterer in action of divorce or separation

To (*name and address as in warrant*).

Take notice that in an action a copy of the summons in which is prefixed hereto you are alleged to have committed adultery with the defender on the occasions therein specified and that if so advised you may within fourteen days after the expiry of days from the date of service hereof [*or if the warrant is executed contemporaneously with citation of the defender* within fourteen days after the calling of the summons in Court which will not be earlier than days from the date of service hereof] apply to the Court for leave to appear as a party in order to dispute the truth of the averments made against you.

The date of service hereof is reckoned as commencing on the expiry of 24 hours after the date of posting hereof.

Dated this (*insert date of posting*).

(*Signed*) A.B.,
(*Address*) (Solicitor for the Pursuer).

NOTE
[1] As amended by S.I. 1976 No. 1994.

[1] Form 17

Form of Intimation to children and next of kin in consistorial causes where the defender's address is unknown

To (*name and address as in warrant*).

Take notice that an action, a copy of the summons in which is prefixed hereto, has been raised against your (*father, mother, brother, or other relative as the case may be*) and that if you know of his (*or* her) present address you are requested to forward the same to the Deputy Principal Clerk of Session, 2 Parliament Square, Edinburgh, forthwith; and that in any event you may if you so desire apply to the Court for leave to state defences to the action within fourteen days after the expiry of days from the date of service hereof (*or if the warrant is executed contemporaneously with citation of the defender* within fourteen days after the calling of the summons in Court which will not be earlier than days from the date of service hereof).

The date of service hereof is reckoned as commencing on the expiry of 24 hours after the date of posting hereof.

Dated this (*insert date of posting*).

(*Signed*) A.B.,
(*Address*) (Solicitor for Pursuer).

NOTE

[1] As amended by S.I. 1976 No. 1994.

---

[1] FORM 18

Form of Intimation to children and next of kin in action of divorce where defender suffers from mental disorder

To (*name and address as in warrant*).

Take notice that an action, a copy of the summons in which is prefixed hereto, has been raised against (*name and designation*) your (*father, mother, brother, sister or other relative as the case may be*) and that you may if you so desire apply to the Court for leave to state defences to the action within fourteen days after the calling of the summons in Court which will not be earlier than days from the date of service hereof.

The date of service hereof is reckoned as commencing on the expiry of 24 hours after the date of posting hereof.

Dated this (*insert date of posting*).

(*Signed*) A.B.,
(*Address*) (Solicitor for Pursuer).

NOTE

[1] As amended by S.I. 1976 No. 1994.

---

[1] FORM 18A

Form of Intimation to additional spouse of either party in proceedings relating to polygamous marriage

To (*name and address as in warrant*).

Take notice that an action, a copy of the summons in which is prefixed hereto, has been raised by (*name and designation*) against (*name and designation*) the said (*name of party concerned*) being your spouse, and that you may if you so desire apply to the Court for leave to appear as a party to the action within fourteen days after the calling of the summons in Court which will not be earlier than days from the date of service hereof.

The date of service hereof is reckoned as commencing on the expiry of 24 hours after the date of posting hereof.

Dated this (*insert date of posting*).

(*Signed*) A.B.,
(*Address*) (Solicitor for Pursuer).

NOTE

[1] Added by S.I. 1976 No. 1994.

---

[1] FORM 18B

Form of Intimation to local authority or third party who may be liable to maintain child

To (*name and address as in warrant*).

Take notice that an action, a copy of the summons in which is prefixed hereto, has been raised by (*name and designation*) against (*name and designation*) in which the Court may make an order in respect of the custody of (*name and designation*), a child (in your care) *or* (liable to be maintained by you), and that you may if you so desire apply to the Court for leave to appear as a party to the action within fourteen days after the calling of the summons in Court which will not be earlier than days from the date of service hereof.

The date of service hereof is reckoned as commencing on the expiry of 24 hours after the date of posting hereof.

Dated this (*insert date of posting*).

(*Signed*) A.B.,
(*Address*) (Solicitor for Pursuer).

NOTE
[1] Added by S.I. 1976 No. 1994.

[1] FORM 18C

Form of Intimation to third party or other person having an interest in a settlement

To (*name and address as in warrant*).

Take notice that an action, a copy of the summons in which is prefixed hereto, has been raised by (*name and designation*) against (*name and designation*) in which the Court may make an order (reducing or varying a settlement (or disposition)) made by the said (*name*) in your favour (in which you have an interest) *or* (interdicting the making of a settlement (or disposition)) by the said (*name*) in your favour (in which you will have an interest), and that you may if you so desire apply to the Court for leave to appear as a party to the action within fourteen days after the calling of the summons in Court which will not be earlier than days from the date of service hereof.

The date of service hereof is reckoned as commencing on the expiry of 24 hours after the date of posting hereof.

Dated this (*insert date of posting*).

(*Signed*) A.B.,
(*Address*) (Solicitor for Pursuer).

NOTE
[1] Added by S.I. 1977 No. 1621.

[1] FORM 18D

Form of Intimation to third party or other person having an interest in an application under the Matrimonial Homes (Family Protection) (Scotland) Act 1981

To (*name and address as in warrant*).

Take notice that proceedings, a copy of the writ in which is attached have been raised by (*name and designation*) against (*name and designation*) in which the court may make an order affecting rights in a house (*or* in property) mentioned therein in which you have an interest, and that you may if you so desire apply to the court for leave to appear as a party to the proceedings within fourteen days after the expiry of days from the date of service hereof. The date of service hereof is reckoned as commencing on the expiry of 24 hours after the date of posting hereof.

Dated this (*insert date of posting*).

(*Signed*) A.B.,
(*Address*) (Solicitor for Pursuer).

NOTE
[1] Added by S.I. 1982 No. 1381.

Rule 170D(9) [1] FORM 18E

Form of intimation to a person having an interest as a creditor in the transfer of property subject to a security

IN THE COURT OF SESSION

in causa

A B (*address*)

Pursuer

against

C D (*address*)

Defender

To (*name and address*)
TAKE NOTICE

1. That in an action in the Court of Session, Parliament Square, Edinburgh, of which a copy of the summons [*or* defences *or* record *as the case may be*] is attached to this notice of intimation, the pursuer [*or* defender] seeks an order for the transfer of certain property to him [*or* her] under section 8(2) of the Family Law (Scotland) Act 1985.

2. That you may have an interest, in the property for which an order for transfer is sought, as a person having a right in security over that property being (*state property subject to the security*).

3. That the court may not make an order under section 8(2) of the Family Law (Scotland) Act 1985 without the consent of the creditor having a security over the property unless he has been given an opportunity of being heard by the court. Paragraph 4 of this notice of intimation informs you how you may apply to be heard by the court.

4. That you may, if you so desire, apply to the court to be sisted as a party to the action under rule 170D(10)(*a*) of the Rules of the Court of Session in respect of your interest as a creditor, within days after the calling of the summons which will not be earlier than days [*or* after the expiry of days] from the date of service of this notice of intimation. To do this you must lodge a minute in the process of the action in the Court of Session seeking leave to be sisted as a party and stating the grounds on which you wish to be heard.

Dated this day of 19

(Signed)
[Solicitor for Pursuer *or*
Defender],
(*Address*).

YOU ARE ADVISED TO CONSULT A SOLICITOR ABOUT THIS MATTER IMMEDIATELY.

NOTE
[1] Added by S.I. 1986 No. 1231.

---

[1] FORM 19

Form of Intimation to Person with whom an improper association is alleged to have occurred

Take notice that in an action, a copy of the summons in which is prefixed hereto, the defender is alleged to have had an improper association with you and that if so advised you may within fourteen days after the expiry of days from the date of service hereof (*or if the*

[THE NEXT PAGE IS 168/1]

PARTIES TO AN ACTION - LITIGANTS

- sh. ct. can entertain action at instance of any person eg foreigners can raise actions
- action can be raised against any person in sh. ct.

2 Tests: - 1) is the action competent 2) does ct. have).

- Complications arise with part. litigants:-

① BANKRUPTS - once sequestrated trustee is appointed + ingathers sums owed + settles debts due
- generally B. cannot sue or be sued in respect of his entitlements BUT - can still sue/be sued in actions of a PERSONAL NATURE eg divorce
- sue for damages for personal injury - solatium, patrimonial loss, loss of wages - only solatium can be kept rest goes to trustee
- if action already underway when B is sequestrated it may be SISTED - trustee can decide whether to proceed. If fails trustee personally liable for ALL expenses of case from START of the action, even before he was involved. OK if sufficient funds in B's estate to meet this - if not trustee must pay from his own pocket
- if trustee doesn't wish to proceed, B may be entitled to pursue action in his own name for patrimonial loss - only if trustee + creditors have abandoned claim. If successful money goes to trustee + creditors ;- - GRUNDIE v JOHN MITCHELL, GRANGEMOUTH (1984)

② CHILDREN :-

1) PUPILS - girls <12, boys <14
- generally cannot sue alone - pupils tutors + administrator in law should be involved. They are father + mother if child is legitimate or mother only if illegitimate
- rights of mother + father are equal - can be raised by 1 without consent of other
- suing a child - if know identity of 1 of tutors then raise action against them. Tutor AD LITEM may be appointed for purposes of case - this may be a relative of child or independent solicitor
- if don't know identity of parents raise action in name of child + ask ct. to find out parents identity or appoint tutor ad litem

GO TO C 169

warrant is executed contemporaneously with citation of the defender) within fourteen days after the calling of the summons in Court which will not be earlier than days from the date of service hereof) apply to the Court for leave to appear as a party in order to dispute the truth of the averments made against you.

The date of service hereof is reckoned as commencing on the expiry of 24 hours after the date of posting hereof.

Dated this (*insert date of posting*).

(*Address*) (*Signed*) A.B.,

(Solicitor for Pursuer).

NOTE

[1] As amended by S.I. 1976 No. 1994.

---

[1] FORM 19A

Under the Divorce (Scotland) Act 1976, Section 1(2)(*d*) Simplified Procedure

Court of Session
Divorce Section (SP)
Parliament House
Edinburgh EH1 1RQ

Tel: 031–225 2595 Ext 316

APPLICATION FOR DIVORCE (WITH CONSENT OF OTHER PARTY TO THE MARRIAGE) HUSBAND AND WIFE HAVING LIVED APART FOR AT LEAST 2 YEARS

Before completing this form, you should have read the leaflet entitled "Do it yourself divorce", which explains the circumstances in which a divorce may be sought by that method. If the simplified procedure appears to suit your circumstances, you may use this form to apply for divorce.

Below you will find directions designed to assist you with your application. Please follow them carefully. In the event of difficulty, you may contact the Court's Divorce Section at the above address, or any Sheriff Clerk's Office or Citizens Advice Bureau.

Directions for making Application

WRITE IN INK, USING BLOCK CAPITALS

Application (Part 1)

1. Complete and sign Part 1 of the form (pages 3–7), paying particular attention to the notes opposite each section.

Consent of Husband/Wife (Part 2)

2. When you have filled in Part 1 of the form, attach the (blue) Instruction Sheet SP3 to it and send both documents to your husband/wife for completion of the consent at Part 2 (page 9).

   NOTE: If your husband/wife does NOT complete and sign the form of consent, your application cannot proceed further under the simplified procedure. In that event, if you still wish to obtain a divorce, you should consult a solicitor.

Affidavit (Part 3)

3. When the application has been returned to you with the Consent (Part 2) duly completed and signed, you should then take the form to a Justice of the Peace, Notary Public, Commissioner for Oaths or other duly authorised person so that your affidavit in Part 3 (page 10) can be completed and sworn.

Returning completed Application Form to Court

4. When directions 1–3 above have all been carried out, your application is now ready to be sent to the Court. With it you must enclose:

   (i) Your marriage certificate (the document headed "Extract of an entry in a Register of Marriages"), which will be returned to you in due course, and

   (ii) Either a cheque or postal order for the sum of £40 in respect of the Court fee, crossed and made payable to "Court of Session",

   or a completed form SP15, claiming exemption from the Court fee.

5. **Receipt of your application will be promptly acknowledged. Should you wish to withdraw the application for any reason, please contact the Court immediately.**

PART 1

WRITE IN INK, USING BLOCK CAPITALS

1.
NAME AND ADDRESS OF APPLICANT

Surname .... Other name(s) in full ....

Present Address ....

.... Daytime Telephone Number (if any) ....

....

2.
NAME AND ADDRESS OF HUSBAND/WIFE

Surname .... Other name(s) in full ....

Present Address ....

.... Daytime Telephone Number (if any) ....

....

3.
JURISDICTION

Please indicate with a tick (✓) in the appropriate box or boxes which of the following apply:

(i) I consider myself to be domiciled in Scotland ☐

or

(ii) I have lived in Scotland for a period of at least 12 months immediately before the date of signing this application ☐

or

(iii) My husband/wife considers himself/herself to be domiciled in Scotland ☐

or

(iv) My husband/wife has lived in Scotland for a period of at least 12 months immediately before the date of signing this application. ☐

4.
DETAILS OF PRESENT MARRIAGE

Place of Marriage .... (Registration District)

Date of Marriage: Day .... month .... year ....

5.
PERIOD OF SEPARATION

(i) Please state the date on which you ceased to live with your husband/wife. (If more than 2½ years, just give the month and year) Day . . . Month . . . Year . . .

(ii) Have you lived with your husband/wife since that date? (*Tick box which applies*) ☐ YES NO ☐

(iii) If yes, for how long in total did you live together before finally separating again? .... months

---

6.
RECONCILIATION

Is there any reasonable prospect of reconciliation with your husband/wife? (*Tick box which applies*) ☐ YES NO ☐

Do you consider that the marriage has broken down irretrievably? (*Tick box which applies*) ☐ YES NO ☐

7.
CONSENT

Does your husband/wife consent to a divorce being granted? (*Tick box which applies*) ☐ YES NO ☐

8.
MENTAL DISABILITY

Is your husband/wife incapable of managing his/her affairs because of a mental disorder (whether illness or deficiency?) (*Tick box which applies*) ☐ YES NO ☐

(If yes, give details)

9.
CHILDREN

Are there any children of the marriage under the age of 16? (*Tick box which applies*) ☐ YES NO ☐

10.
OTHER COURT ACTIONS

Are you aware of any Court actions currently proceeding in any country (including Scotland) which may affect your marriage? (*Tick box which applies*) ☐ YES NO ☐

(If yes, give details)

11.
REQUEST FOR DIVORCE AND DISCLAIMER OF FINANCIAL PROVISION

I confirm that the facts stated in Sections 1–10 above apply to my marriage.

I do NOT ask the Court to make any financial awards in connection with this application.

I request the Court to grant decree of divorce from my husband/wife.

....
(Date) (Signature)

IMPORTANT—Part 1 MUST be completed, signed and dated before sending the application form to your husband/wife.

PART 2

CONSENT BY APPLICANT'S HUSBAND/WIFE TO DIVORCE

NOTE: **Before completing this Part of the form, please read Part 1 and the notes opposite (page 8).**

I, ...
(Full names, in BLOCK letters, of Applicant's husband/wife)

residing at

....
(Address, also in BLOCK letters)

....

....

HEREBY STATE THAT

a. I have read Part 1 of this application;
b. The Applicant has lived apart from me for a continuous period of 2 years immediately preceding the date of the application (Section 11 of Part 1);
c. I do not ask the Court to make any order for payment to me by the Applicant of a periodical allowance (i.e. a regular payment of money weekly or monthly, etc for maintenance);
d. I do not ask the Court to make any order for payment to me by the Applicant of a capital sum (i.e. a lump sum payment);
e. I understand that divorce may result in the loss to me of property rights; and
f. I CONSENT TO DECREE OF DIVORCE BEING GRANTED IN RESPECT OF THIS APPLICATION.

....
(Date) (Signature)

NOTE: You may withdraw your consent, even after giving it, at any time before divorce is granted by the Court. Should you wish to do so, you must immediately advise:

The Court of Session
Divorce Section (SP)
Parliament House
Edinburgh EH1 1RQ

PART 3

APPLICANT'S AFFIDAVIT

To be completed only after Parts 1 and 2 have been signed and dated.

I, (*insert Applicant's full name*) ....

residing at (*insert Applicant's present home address*) ....

....

Town .... Country ....

SWEAR that to the best of my knowledge and belief:

(1) the facts stated in Part 1 of this Application are true; and

(2) the signature in Part 2 of this Application is that of my *husband/wife.

Signature of Applicant ....

To be completed by Justice of Peace, Notary Public or Commissioner for Oaths

SWORN at (Place) ....

this .... day of .... 19.........

before me (full name) ....

(full address) ....

....

....

Signature ....

*Justice of Peace/*Notary Public/*Commissioner for Oaths

*Delete as appropriate

NOTE
[1] Added by S.I. 1982 No. 1679 and substituted by S.I. 1983 No. 1210.

[1] FORM 19B

Under the Divorce (Scotland) Act 1976, Section 1(2)(*e*) Simplified Procedure

Court of Session
Divorce Section (SP)
Parliament House
Edinburgh EH1 1RQ
Tel: 031–225 2595 Ext 316

APPLICATION FOR DIVORCE
HUSBAND AND WIFE HAVING LIVED APART FOR AT LEAST 5 YEARS

Before completing this form, you should have read the leaflet entitled "Do it yourself divorce" which explains the circumstances in which a divorce may be sought by that method. If the simplified procedure appears to suit your circumstances, you may use this form to apply for divorce.

Below you will find directions designed to assist with your application. Please follow them carefully. In the event of difficulty, you may contact the Court's Divorce Section at the above address, or any Sheriff Clerk's Office or Citizens Advice Bureau.

Directions for making Application.

WRITE IN INK, USING BLOCK CAPITALS

Application (Part 1)

1. Complete and sign Part 1 of the form (pages 3–7), paying particular attention to the notes opposite each section.

Affidavit Part 2

2. When you have completed Part 1, you should take the form to a Justice of the Peace, Notary Public, Commissioner for Oaths or other duly authorised person so that your affidavit in Part 2 (page 8) can be completed and sworn.

Returning completed Application Form to Court

3. When directions 1 and 2 above have all been carried out, your application is now ready to be sent to the Court. With it you must enclose:
   (i) Your marriage certificate (the document headed "Extract of an entry in a Register of Marriages")—check the notes on page 2 to see if you need an up-to-date one (the certificate will be returned to you in due course), and
   (ii) Either a cheque or postal order for the sum of £40 in respect of the Court fee, crossed and made payable to "Court of Session",
   or a completed form SP15, claiming exemption from the Court fee.

4. Receipt of your application will be promptly acknowledged. Should you wish to withdraw the application for any reason, please contact the Court immediately.

PART 1

WRITE IN INK, USING BLOCK CAPITALS

1.
NAME AND ADDRESS OF APPLICANT

Surname .... Other name(s) in full ....

Present Address ....

.... Daytime Telephone Number (if any) ....

....

2.
NAME OF HUSBAND/WIFE

Surname .... Other name(s) in full ....

....

3.
ADDRESS OF HUSBAND/WIFE

(if the address of your husband/wife is not known and cannot reasonably be ascertained, please enter "not known" in this section; you must take all reasonable steps to find out where your husband/wife is living and state here what steps you have taken, and then proceed to section 4)

Present Address ....

.... Daytime Telephone Number (if any) ....

....

4.
Only complete this section if you do not know the present address of your husband/wife

NEXT-OF-KIN

Name .... Address ....

Relationship to your husband/wife ....

....

CHILDREN OF THE MARRIAGE

Names and dates of birth	Addresses
....	....
	....
....	....
	....
....	....
	....

If insufficient space is available here to list all the children of the marriage, please continue on a separate sheet and attach to this form.

5.
JURISDICTION

Please indicate with a tick (√) in the appropriate box or boxes which of the following apply:

(i) I consider myself to be domiciled in Scotland ☐

or

(ii) I have lived in Scotland for a period of at least 12 months immediately before the date of signing this application ☐

or

(iii) My husband/wife considers himself/herself to be domiciled in Scotland ☐

or

(iv) My husband/wife has lived in Scotland for a period of at least 12 months immediately before the date of signing this application ☐

6.
DETAILS OF PRESENT MARRIAGE

Place of marriage .... (Registration District)

Date of Marriage (Day) .... (Month) .... (Year) ....

7.
PERIOD OF SEPARATION

(i) Please state the date on which you ceased to live with your husband/wife. (If more than $5\frac{1}{2}$ years, just give the month and year) Day...... Month...... Year....

(ii) Have you lived with your husband/wife since that date? (*Tick box which applies*) ☐ YES NO ☐

(iii) If yes, for how long in total did you live together before finally separating again? .... months

8.
RECONCILIATION

Is there any reasonable prospect of reconciliation with your husband/wife? (*Tick box which applies*) ☐ YES NO ☐

Do you consider that the marriage has broken down irretrievably? (*Tick box which applies*) ☐ YES NO ☐

9.
MENTAL DISABILITY

As far as you are aware is you husband/wife incapable of managing his/her affairs because of a mental disorder (whether illness or deficiency?) (*Tick box which applies*)

☐ YES NO ☐
(If yes, give details)

10.
CHILDREN

Are there any children of the marriage under the age of 16? (*Tick box which applies*)

☐ YES NO ☐

11.
OTHER COURT ACTIONS

Are you aware of any Court actions currently proceeding in any counry (including Scotland) whioch may affect your marriage? (*Tick box which applies*)

☐ YES NO ☐
(If yes, give details)

12.
DECLARATION AND REQUEST FOR DIVORCE

I confirm that the facts stated in sections 1–11 above apply to my marriage.

I do not ask the Court to make any financial awards in connection with this application.

I believe that no grave financial hardship will be caused to my husband/wife as a result of the granting of this application.

I request the Court to grant decree of divorce from my husband/wife.

....
(Date) (Signature of Applicant)

PART 2

APPLICANT'S AFFIDAVIT

To be completed only after Part 1 has been signed and dated.

I, (*insert Applicant's full name*) ....

residing at (*insert Applicant's present home address*) ....

....

Town .... Country ....

Swear that to the best of my knowledge and belief the facts stated in Part 1 of this Application are true.

Signature of Applicant ....

To be completed by Justice of Peace, Notary Public or Commissioner for Oaths

SWORN at (Place) ....

this .... day of .... 19..........

before me (full name) ....

(full address) ....

....

....

....

Signature ....

*Justice of Peace/*Notary Public/*Commissioner for Oaths

*Delete as appropriate

NOTE

[1] Added by S.I. 1982 No. 1679, substituted by S.I. 1983 No. 1210 and as amended by S.I. 1987 No. 1206.

---

[1] FORM 19C

CITATION IN SECTION 1(2)(*d*) CASES

Under the Divorce (Scotland) Act 1976, Section 1(2)(*d*) Simplified Procedure

M ....

....

.... Edinburgh 19

APPLICATION FOR DIVORCE (WITH CONSENT OF OTHER PARTY TO THE MARRIAGE) HUSBAND AND WIFE HAVING LIVED APART FOR AT LEAST 2 YEARS.

You are hereby served with an application by your husband/wife which asks the Court to grant a decree of divorce.

If you wish to oppose the granting of such decree, you should put your reasons in writing and send your letter to the address shown below. Your letter must reach the Court before

Assistant Clerk of Session/
Messenger-at-Arms

IMPORTANT NOTE:
If you wish to exercise your right to claim a financial award you should immediately advise the Court that you oppose the application for that reason, and thereafter consult a solicitor.

Court of Session
Divorce Section (SP)
Parliament House
Edinburgh EH1 1RQ
Tel: 031–225 2595 Ext 316

NOTE
[1] Added by S.I. 1982 No. 1679 and substituted by S.I. 1983 No. 1210.

---

[1] FORM 19D

CITATION IN SECTION 1(2)(*e*) CASES

Under the Divorce (Scotland) Act 1976, Section 1(2)(*e*) Simplified Procedure

M ....

....

.... Edinburgh 19

APPLICATION FOR DIVORCE
HUSBAND AND WIFE HAVING LIVED APART FOR AT LEAST 5 YEARS

Your husband/wife has applied to the Court for divorce on the ground that the marriage has broken down irretrievably *because you and (s)he have lived apart for a period of at least 5 years.*

A copy of the application is hereby served upon you.

1. Please note:
   (a) that the Court may not make financial awards under this procedure and that your husband/wife is making no claim against you for payment of a periodical allowance (i.e. regular payment of money weekly, monthly etc. for his/her maintenance) or a capital sum (i.e. lump sum).
   (b) that your husband/wife states that you will not suffer grave financial hardship in the event of decree of divorce being granted.
2. Divorce may result in the loss to you of property rights (e.g. the right to succeed to the Applicant's estate on his/her death) or the right, where appropriate, to a widow's pension.
3. If you wish to oppose the granting of a divorce, you should put your reasons in writing and send your letter to the address shown below. Your letter must reach the Court before

4. In the event of the divorce being granted, you will be sent a copy of the extract decree. (Should you change your address before receiving the copy extract decree, please notify the Court immediately.)

Assistant Clerk of Session/
Messenger-at-Arms

IMPORTANT NOTE:
If you wish to exercise your right to claim a financial award you should immediately advise the Court that you oppose the application for that reason, and thereafter consult a solicitor.

Court of Session
Divorce Section (SP)
Parliament House
Edinburgh EH1 1RQ
Tel: 031–225 2595 Ext 316

NOTE
[1] Added by S.I. 1982 No. 1679 and substituted by S.I. 1983 No. 1210.

[1] FORM 19E

INTIMATION TO CHILDREN/NEXT OF KIN IN SIMPLIFIED DIVORCE APPLICATION

Under the Divorce (Scotland) Act 1976, Section 1(2)(*e*) Simplified Procedure

M ....

....

.... Edinburgh 19

APPLICATION FOR DIVORCE HUSBAND AND WIFE HAVING LIVED APART FOR AT LEAST 5 YEARS

.... (Applicant) v. .... (Respondent)

1. In the above application, a copy of which is enclosed, the Applicant has indicated that you are the of whose present address is unknown to the Applicant.
2. Should you know the present address of your or how he/she may be contacted, you are requested to give this information at once to:
   Court of Session
   Divorce Section (SP)
   Parliament House
   Edinburgh EH1 1RQ
   Tel: 031–225–2595 Ext 316

This will enable the Court to inform the Respondent that the Application has been made.

3. If you are unable to provide the above information, and/or you desire for your own interest to oppose the application for divorce, you should write to the above address not later than stating the reason for your opposition.

Assistant Clerk of Session/Messenger-at-Arms.

NOTE
[1] Added by S.I. 1982 No. 1679 and substituted by S.I. 1983 No. 1210.

[1] FORM 20

Form for Transmission to Medical Officer of Hospital or similar Institution

To (*insert name and address*)

In accordance with the Rules of the Court a copy of a summons at the instance of (*name and*

[THE NEXT PAGE IS C 169]

2) MINORS - girls 12-18, boys 14-18
- curators are now both parents - Guardianship Act 1973
- minor IS litigant [can sue alone] BUT ought to sue / be sued with consent + concurrence of curator
- if NO curators, minor can sue in own name + ct. can be asked to appoint a CURATOR AD LITEM (looks after only ct action of curator bonis)

③ MENTAL INCAPACITY - if ceases to be of full mental capacity normal for ct. to appoint CURATOR BONIS to look after financial affairs of incapax.
- CB as approp. person to sue / be sued - not incapax himself
- CB may be appointed by Sh. Ct. or Ct. of S who have concurrent J.
- CB must be an ind. - incompetent to appoint a co. - BROGAN CASE (1986)
- if defender becomes insane during course of litigation must be sisted so that a CB can be appointed.

④ ASSIGNEES - 3rd parties may take over an action
- intimation must be given of right to sue
- if sue as assignee normally sues in own name
- NOTE - must ensure that assignation has been validly granted as at date of the action
- BENTLEY V. MACFARLANE (1964) - A assigned to B his right of action against D. Defence said that right had been assigned. B reassigned to A the right of action
HELD - in deciding A's title to sue, should be determined at time of RAISING action + so was incompetent + couldn't be cured by a subsequent assignation
- CAUTIONARY OBLIGATIONS - a GUARANTEE - where 1 party undertakes an obligation to a 3rd party eg A→B, C might act as cautioner to A. so if A doesn't pay B then he can seek money from C. Creditor can sue EITHER principal obligator OR cautioner OR BOTH

⑤ FIRMS - have separate legal persona - can be sued / sue in their own name BUT ind. partners are still personally liable for debts of their firm. liability is unlimited - RULE 14(1)
- if decree is against ind. can enforce decree against inds. assets even though ind. is not mentioned in decree. Enforced against all assets, not just assets of that part. business
- GOOD PRACTICE - better to know real names behind the business BECAUSE if decree is merely against business in its trading name may have problems enforcing it against ind. partners [as don't know who they are]

GO TO C175

aadress) against (*name and address*) is sent herewith and you are requested to deliver it personally to the said and to explain the contents or purport thereof to him (*or her*) unless you are satisfied that such delivery or explanation would be dangerous to his (*or her*) health or mental condition. You are further requested to complete and return to me in the enclosed stamped and addressed envelope the certificate appended hereto, striking out what is not applicable.

(*Address and date*) (Solicitor for Pursuer).

NOTE

[1] As amended by S.I. 1976 No. 1994.

---

[1] FORM 21

Form of Certificate by Medical Officer of Hospital or similar Institution

I (*name and designation*) certify on soul and conscience that, having had transmitted to me a copy summons of divorce at the instance of (*name and designation*) Pursuer, against (*name and designation*) Defender, (*a*) I have on the day of personally delivered a copy thereof to the said defender who is under my care at (*address*) and I have explained the contents or purport thereof to him (*or her*).

or

(*b*) I have not delivered a copy thereof to the said defender who is under my care at (*address*) and I have not explained the contents or purport thereof to him (*or her*) and that for the following reasons (*state reasons*).

(*Signature and designation*)

(*Address and date*)

NOTE

[1] As amended by S.I. 1976 No. 1994.

---

[1] FORM 22

Form of Letter of Request (Consistorial Causes)

The Principal Clerk of Session,
Parliament House,
Edinburgh.

I (We) request that search be made in the records of Court for information as to the granting of a decree of divorce in the action at the instance of (*name, designation and address*) Pursuer against (*name, designation and address*) Defender, granted on (*date or approximate date*).

Should the above decree of divorce be traced I (we) desire a certificate evidencing that it was granted and I (we) enclose fee of 75p.

(*Signed*) A.B.
(*Address and date*)

NOTE

[1] As amended by S.I. 1969 No. 475 and the Decimal Currency Act 1969, s. 10 (1).

---

[1] FORM 23

Form of Certificate of Divorce

Court of Session,
Parliament House,
Edinburgh.
(*date*)

To A.B. (*name and address of the writer of the Letter of Request*).

I hereby certify that on the day of 19 , the Court of Session in Scotland pronounced decree of divorce in an action in which C.D. (*designation and address*) was pursuer and E.F. (*designation and address*) was defender.

(*Signed*)

Principal Clerk of Session.

NOTE

[1] Substituted by S.I. 1968 No. 1759.

---

[1] Form 24

Form of Letter of Request for Certificate of Nullity of Marriage

The Principal Clerk of Session,

Parliament Square,

Edinburgh.

I (We) request that search be made in the Records of Court as to the granting of a decree of nullity of marriage in the action at the instance of (*name, designation and address*) Pursuer against (*name, designation and address*) Defender, granted on (*date or approximate date*).

Should the above decree of nullity be traced I (we) desire a certificate that it was granted and I (we) enclose fee of 75p.

(*Signed*) A.B.

(*Address and date*)

NOTE

[1] As amended by S.I. 1969 No. 475 and the Decimal Currency Act 1969, s. 10 (1).

Form 25

Form of Certificate of Nullity of Marriage

Court of Session,

Parliament House,

Edinburgh.

(*date*)

To A.B. (*name and address of the writer of the Letter of Request*).

I hereby certify that on the day of 19 , the Court of Session in Scotland pronounced a decree of nullity of the marriage of A.B. (*designation and address*) and C.D. (*designation and address*) in an action in which the said A.B. was Pursuer and the said C.D. was Defender.

(*Signed*)

Principal Clerk of Session.

[1] Form 26

Form of Letter of Request for Certificate of Dissolution of Marriage

The Principal Clerk of Session,

Parliament House,

Edinburgh.

I (We) request that search be made in the records of Court for information as to the granting of a decree of dissolution of marriage in the Petition in which (*name, designation and address*) was Petitioner and (*name, designation and address*) was Respondent, granted on (*date or approximate date*).

Should the above decree of dissolution of marriage be traced I (we) desire a certificate evidencing that it was granted and I (we) enclose fee of 75p.

(*Signed*) A.B.

(*Address and date*)

NOTE

[1] As amended by S.I. 1969 No. 475 and the Decimal Currency Act 1969, s. 10 (1).

FORM 27

Form of Certificate of Dissolution of Marriage

Court of Session,
Parliament House,
Edinburgh.
(*date*)

To A.B. (*name and address of the writer of the Letter of Request*).

I hereby certify that on the day of 19 , the Court of Session in Scotland pronounced a decree dissolving the marriage of A.B. (*designation and address*) and C.D. (*designation and address*) in a Petition in which the said A.B. was Petitioner and the said C.D. was Respondent.

(*Signed*)
Principal Clerk of Session.

Rule 188F [1] FORM 27A

Form of summons, condescendence and pleas-in-law in an action for reparation (optional procedure)

IN THE COURT OF SESSION

SUMMONS

(Action for Reparation (Optional Procedure))

AB (*designation and address*), Pursuer

against

CD (*designation and address*), Defender

[*Address, Charge and Warrants as in Form 1*]

[*Back of first page*]

CONCLUSIONS

FIRST. For payment by the defender to the puruser of the sum of (£) STERLING, or such other greater or smaller sum as to the court shall seem proper, with interest, at the rate of interest in rule of court 66 applicable at the date of decree, from the date of decree to follow hereon until payment.

SECOND. For the expenses of the action.

[*Next page*]

CONDESCENDENCE

I. The pursuer is (*state date of birth; in an action for personal injuries, state occupation and relation to defender; or, in an action for the death of a relative, state relation to the deceased*). The defender is (*state occupation*).

[II. *In the case of an action for the death of a relative*, The deceased was (*state dates of birth, marriage and death, occupation and relation to defender*)].

III. (*In numbered articles, each new part of the averments in a separate article, state briefly the facts relied on as causing the accident or death*).

[[IV.] *In the case of fault at common law*. The accident [*or* death of the deceased] was caused by the fault and negligence of the defender at common law. The defender was in breach of his duty to take reasonable care for the safety of the pursuer [*or* the deceased] *or as may be (no other specification of particular duties or breaches is normally required)*].

[[V.] *In the case of breach of statutory duty*. Further and in any event the [*or* The] accident [*or* death of the deceased] was caused by the breach by the defender of a statutory duty. The defender was in breach of the duty imposed upon him by (*state provision of enactment; no other specification of the duty or breach is normally required*).]

[IV.] As a result of the accident [*or* the death of the deceased] the pursuer suffered loss, injury and damage. (*State briefly, in an action for personal injuries, the injuries sustained and consequent damage suffered, loss of past and/or future earnings, any other relevant loss and whether credit is to be given for any National Insurance benefits received; or, in an action for death of a relative, the loss of society, loss of support and earnings of the deceased*).

[V.] The defender has been called upon to make reparation to the pursuer but delays or refuses to do so.

PLEAS-IN-LAW

1. The pursuer having suffered loss, injury and damage through the fault and negligence [and] [*or* breach of statutory duty] of the defender is entitled to reparation therefor from him.
2. The sum sued for being a reasonable estimate of the loss, injury and damage sustained by the pursuer, decree therefor should be pronounced in that sum.

IN RESPECT WHEREOF
(*Signed*)
(*Address*)
Solicitor for Pursuer.

NOTE

[1] Inserted by S.I. 1985 No. 227.

---

[1] FORM 28

Form of Petition and Backing

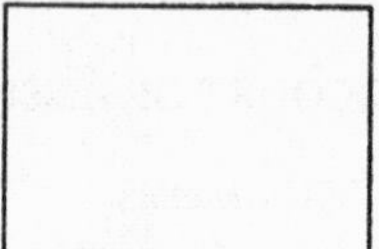

(*This space will contain the letter and number assigned to the appeal on being lodged.*)

Unto the Right Honourable the Lords of Council and Session,

The Petition of A.B. (*name, designation, and address of petitioner*). Humbly sheweth

That (*here set forth in numbered paragraphs the facts and circumstances which form the grounds of the petition*).

May it therefore please your Lordships to (*add prayer as in present practice*)

According to Justice, etc.

(*Signature of Counsel or solicitor who has a right of audience in the Court of Session.*)

Backing of Petition

(*This space will contain the letter and number assigned to the petition on being lodged.*)

The Petition
of
A.B.
for
(*here describe shortly the nature or object of the petition*).
R.S. (*name of petitioner's solicitor*).

NOTE

[1] As amended by S.I. 1991 No. 2483, with effect from 25th November 1991.

---

[1] FORM 29

Specimen of Form 28 filled in for petition under section 11A of the Judicial Factors (Scotland) Act 1889

Unto the Right Honourable the Lords of Council and Session,

The Petition of (*here state the names and designations of the petitioners, and whether they apply in the character of creditors or of persons having interest in the succession of the party deceased*). Humbly sheweth

1. (*Name and design the party deceased*) died on the day of and left no settlement appointing trustees or other parties to manage his estate, or part thereof (or that the trustees or other parties appointed by him to manage his estate have not accepted or acted).

2. The petitioner (*or* petitioners) (*here state, if creditors, the nature and amount of the debt*

due to them by the deceased, and how constituted, vouched or established, and referring to the evidence of the existence of the debt, as produced with the petition, or, if persons having an interest in the succession, the nature of their interest in the succession).

3. The estate of the said deceased , so far as known to the petitioner (*or* petitioners), consists of (*here state the nature of the estate, whether heritable or moveable, stock in trade, interest in a partnership, professional business, or whatever else it may be. State any other facts which may appear to be of importance to the particular case*).

4. The following persons are, to the best of the petitioner's knowledge and belief, the legal representatives of the deceased, or have an interest in his estate (*here state the names and designations of those persons, their degree of relationship, or the nature of their interest in the succession*).

5. The following persons are, to the best of the petitioner's knowledge and belief, all the creditors of the deceased (*name and design them*).

6. The petitioner is (*or* petitioners are) entitled, under section 11A of the Judicial Factors (Scotland) Act 1889, to make the present application for the appointment of a judicial factor on the estate of the said deceased, with the powers therein conferred and respectfully suggest (*name and designation*) as a fit and proper person for the office.

May it therefore please your Lordships to appoint intimation of this petition to be made on the walls and in the minute-book, in common form, and in the *Edinburgh Gazette*, and to be served upon the parties named and designed in the Schedule annexed hereto and to ordain and all parties claiming interest to lodge answers hereto if so advised within fourteen days after such intimation and service; and thereafter, on resuming consideration of the same, to appoint the said or such fit person as to your Lordships shall seem proper to be judicial factor on the estate of the said deceased , and that with all the powers of the statute, he always finding caution before extract, and to find the petitioner entitled to the expenses of this application and the procedure following thereon out of the factory estate, and to decern; or to do otherwise in the premises as to your Lordships shall seem proper.

According to Justice, etc.

(*Signed by Counsel or solicitor who has a right of audience in the Court of Session.*)

NOTE

[1] As amended by S.I. 1986 No. 514 and (with effect from 25th November 1991) S.I. 1991 No. 2483.

Form 30

Form of Citation and Execution of Service

I, , Enrolled Solicitor, by virtue of a Deliverance dated the day of , pronounced by Lord upon the Petition given in and presented for and in name of the therein named and designed do hereby, in Her Majesty's name and authority, and in name and authority of the said Lord , lawfully serve the foregoing copy of said Petition and Deliverance upon you (*name and designation*) that you may not pretend ignorance of the same, and desire and require you to lodge answers to said Petition, if so advised, within days from the date of this my service in terms of said Deliverance.

This I do upon the day of , being the date of the posting of this service and requisition. The period within which you are required to lodge answers, if so advised, is reckoned from 24 hours after posting hereof.

(*Signed*)

(*Address*)

Form of Execution of Service

This Petition with Deliverance annexed executed by me Enrolled Solicitor, upon the within designed by posting on the day of , 19 , between the hours of and o'clock at the Post Office, Edinburgh, a copy of the same, with citation subjoined, to him (or them) in a registered or recorded delivery letter (or letters) addressed to his (*or* their) last known address as follows:—

and also edictally on the said by posting on the said date between the said hours at the said Post Office a copy of the same for him (*or* them) with citation subjoined in a registered or recorded delivery letter (*or* letters) addressed as follows:—The

Extractor of the Court of Session, 2 Parliament Square, Edinburgh, and the post office receipts for said letters accompany this execution.

(*Signed*)

(*Address*)

[1] FORM 31

Form of Intimation to be inserted in the "Edinburgh Gazette" under paragraph (b) of Rule 201

To the creditors and other persons interested in the succession of the deceased (*naming and designing him*).

[THE NEXT PAGE IS C 173]

A Petition has been presented to the Court of Session by , a creditor (*or* creditors), to the amount required (or by having an interest in the succession of the said deceased , the said deceased having left no settlement appointing trustees, or other parties having power to manage his estate (*or as the case may be*, the trustees under the deceased's settlement, not accepting or acting), praying, under section 11A of the Judicial Factors (Scotland) Act 1889, for the appointment of a judicial factor on said estate; and which Petition will be again moved in Court, on or after the day of , of all which notice is hereby given.

(*Signature and address of petitioner's solicitor.*)

(*Date*)

NOTE

[1] As amended by S.I. 1986 No. 514.

[1] FORM 32

Form of Intimation to be inserted in the "Edinburgh Gazette" under paragraph (d) of Rule 201

To the creditors and other persons interested in the succession of the deceased (*designing him*).

A.B. (*naming and designing him*), having been appointed by the Court of Session judicial factor on the estate of the said deceased under section 11A of the Judicial Factors (Scotland) Act 1889, requires all the lawful creditors of the said and other persons interested in his estate, to lodge with the judicial factor, within four months after the date of this notice, a statement of their claims as creditors of the deceased, or as otherwise interested in his estate; with such vouchers or other written evidence as they may have to found upon in support of their claims; in order to the same being considered and reported upon by the judicial factor.

(*Signature and address of judicial factor.*)

(*Date*)

NOTE

[1] As amended by S.I. 1986 No. 514.

FORM 33

Form of Intimation to be inserted in the "Edinburgh Gazette" under paragraph (h) of Rule 201

To the creditors and other persons interested in the succession of the deceased (*designing him*).

A.B., , judicial factor on the estate of the said deceased , hereby intimates that he has prepared and lodged in Court a state of funds and scheme of division of the said estate, to be considered and approved of by the Court, of which all concerned are hereby required to take notice.

(*Signature and address of judicial factor.*)

(*Date*)

FORM 34

Form of Intimation to be inserted in the "Edinburgh Gazette" under paragraph (p) of Rule 201

To the creditors and other persons interested in the succession of the deceased (*designing him*).

A.B., , judicial factor on the estate of the deceased. , has presented a petition to the Court of Session, for his discharge of the office of judicial factor, of which notice is hereby given, and that the petition will be again moved in Court on or after the day of

(*Signature and address of judicial factor.*)

(*Date*)

FORM 34A

Rule 201A(1) Form of register of insolvencies

A. Sequestrations

Name of debtor	
Debtor's residence and his principal place of business (if any) at date of sequestration or date of death	
Date of death in case of deceased debtor	
Occupation of debtor	
Name and address of petitioner for sequestration	
Court by which sequestration awarded	
Sheriff court to which sequestration remitted (where applicable)	
Date of first order	
Date of award of sequestration	
Date of recall of sequestration (where applicable)	
Name and address of interim trustee and date of appointment	
Name and address of permanent trustee and date of confirmation of appointment	
Date of debtor's discharge and whether on composition or by operation of law	
Date of interim trustee's discharge	
Date of permanent trustee's discharge	

B. Protected Trust Deeds for Creditors

Name and address of granter of trust deed	
Name and address of trustee under the deed	
Date (or dates) of execution of deed	
Date on which copy deed and certificate of accession were registered	

Date of registration of statement indicating how the estate was realised and distributed and certificate to the effect that the distribution was in accordance with the trust deed	
Date of trustee's discharge	
Date of registration of copy of order of court that non acceding creditor is not bound by trustee's discharge	

NOTE
[1] Inserted by S.I. 1986 No. 514.

Rule 201A(2) [1] FORM 34B

Form of memorandum by permanent trustee to be recorded in the register of inhibitions and adjudications under section 14(4) of the Bankruptcy (Scotland) Act 1985

From: A.B. *(name and address)* trustee in the sequestration of
C.D. *(name and address)*
To: Keeper of the register of inhibitions and adjudications

A certified copy of the order of the court awarding sequestration on *(date)* in respect of C.D. is recorded in your Register on *(date)*.

Record this memorandum to renew the effect of that recording for a further period of 3 years.

(Date) *(Signed)* A.B. [*or* to EF., solicitor for A.B.]

NOTE
[1] Inserted by S.I. 1986 No. 514.

Rule 201A(3) [1] FORM 34C

Form of notice of inhibition by trustee under trust deed to be recorded in the register of inhibitions and adjudications under paragraph 2(1) of Schedule 5 to the Bankruptcy (Scotland) Act 1985

A trust deed within the meaning of the Bankruptcy (Scotland) Act 1985 has been granted by C.D. *(name and address)* and delivered to A.B. *(name and address)* as trustee acting under the trust deed.

Under the trust deed the estate of C.D. has been conveyed to A.B. as trustee for the benefit of the creditors generally of C.D.

(Date) *(Signed)* A.B. [*or* E.F., solicitor for A.B.]

NOTE
[1] Inserted by S.I. 1986 No. 514.

Rule 201A(4) [1] FORM 34D

Form of notice of recall of inhibition under paragraph 2(2) of Schedule 5 to the Bankruptcy (Scotland) Act 1985 to be recorded in the register of inhibitions and adjudications

The notice by A.B. *(name and address)* as trustee under the trust deed for creditors of C.D. *(name and address)* recorded on *(date)* is now recalled.

(Date) *(Signed)* A.B. [*or* E.F., solicitor for A.B.]

NOTE
[1] Inserted by S.I. 1986 No. 514.

FORM 35

Form of Statement by Liquidator of a Company under section 342 of the Companies Act 1948[1]

Form No. 92 (Scot.)

No. of Company . . . .

THE COMPANIES ACT 1948

Liquidator's Statement of Account under Section 342 and relative Rules of Court.
Name of Company Limited.
Nature of winding up:—
(*a*) Members' Voluntary
(*b*) Creditors' Voluntary
(*c*) By the Court
(*d*) Under the supervision of the Court.
Date of commencement of winding-up
Date to which last statement, if any, made up
Date to which this statement is made up
Name and address of liquidator
LIQUIDATOR'S STATEMENT OF ACCOUNTS for the period from
to

NOTES

(1) Where practicable, receipts and payments should be individually listed, but trading and certain other recurring transactions may be suitably grouped or collated if these are numerous.

(2) Contra items such as cash lodged in bank on current account or on deposit receipt or withdrawn therefrom should be excluded from the receipts and payments shown below.

(3) No balance should be shown on this Account. The balance and its analysis should be entered on the back of this form.

(4) Where there have been no receipts or payments since the last Account, the Liquidator shall give a certificate below to that effect.

RECEIPTS	Amount		PAYMENTS	Amount	
Nature of Receipts	£	p	*Nature of Payments*	£	p
Total receipts from last account			Total payments from last account		
Total receipts carried forward			Total payments carried forward		

at 19

	£	p
Total Receipts, per Account		
Total Payments, per Account		
Balance		
Made up as follows:—		
1. Cash in hands of Liquidator		
2. Balances at Bank:		
On Current Account		
On Deposit Receipt		
3. Investments made by Liquidator		
Balance as above		

PROGRESS REPORT

	£
A. Amount of the total estimated assets and liabilities at the date of the commencement of the winding up per Statement of Affairs	
Assets— *less:* Secured Creditors Debenture Holders	
less: Preferential claims & services	
Available for Unsecured Creditors	
Unsecured Creditors	

NOTE

[1] See now the Companies Act 1985, s. 641.

[THE NEXT PAGE IS C 175]

- sometimes important to sue inds. eg where firm has dissolved

BUT - should always be possible to find out who is trading as a business -

- Business Names Act 1985 s.1-5 - ind, group or unlimited co. must disclose names of partners on their note paper + at place of business.

- limited cos. - can check with the Register of Companies

(6) Local Authorities, Health Boards, Harbour Boards etc - set up under statute. Statute will give proper name + authorise how to sue body

(7) Crown - sue the Lord Advocate

(8) Clubs, Societies + Associations - if wish to sue them, look at their constitution. Competent to sue club in its name only -

- BORLAND v LOCH WYNOCH GOLF CLUB (1986)

NOTE - R.14(1) - doesn't apply to clubs + associations [not unlimited liability]

- decree against club is not warrant for diligence against ind. members

(9) VEXATIOUS LITIGANTS - can sue as much as you like

BUT - may be declared a vexatious litigant under VEXATIOUS ACTIONS ACT 1898

- if person feels he has been victim of excessive litigation he can apply to LA who gets order from Ct. of S. saying no applications can be raised in Ct. of S/Sh. Ct. without leave of Ct. of S. Leave will only be granted if action is not vexatious [without substance]

- ct. must be satisfied that person has habitually + persistently instituted vexatious legal proceedings without any reasonable grounds; eg

- LORD ADVOCATE v HENDERSON (1983) - H raised 6 actions against public bodies relating to his dismissal

(10) FOREIGNERS - where party to action doesn't reside or carry on business in Scotland + has no assets in Scotland, ct. can be asked to have foreign litigant 'SIST A MANDATORY' ie introduce a mandatory

- Scottish litigant entitled to have someone in Scotland responsible to ct. for conduct of the action + for expenses

- whether or not ordered is within discretion of the sh.

- apply at early stage - if delay may be taken to have waived your right by implication

- normally required for P. outwith Scotland. Foreign D. may also be asked to sist a mandatory

- mandatory must be solvent, not a co-litigant. Must be normally resident in Scot. BUT may reside elsewhere in UK as Scottish decree readily enforceable in rest of UK - GO TO C179

B. Total amount of the capital paid up at the commencement of the winding up
C. General description and estimated value of:
(i) any material alterations to the amounts shown in (A) above
(ii) outstanding unrealised assets
D. Causes which delay the termination of the winding up
E. Period within which the Liquidator expects to complete the winding up
F. Date of payment and amount of last premium of Liquidator's bond of caution (state also amount of bond and renewal date)

Signature of Liquidator Date

This form should be completed and sent to the Registrar, Companies Registration Office, Exchequer Chambers, 102 George Street, Edinburgh, 2, within thirty days after twelve months from the date of commencement of winding up, and at six-monthly intervals thereafter. The final return should be sent immediately the assets have been fully realised and distributed, notwithstanding that six months may not have elapsed since the last return.

Rule 222(1) [1] FORM 36

Petition for adoption order or an order under section 49(1) of the Adoption (Scotland) Act 1978 as filled in on official printed Form 28

UNTO THE RIGHT HONOURABLE THE LORDS OF COUNCIL AND SESSION,
PETITION
of

A.B. (*name designation and address*) [*or serial number where one has been assigned on application*]

for

An Adoption Order

under the Adoption (Scotland) Act 1978

[*or* an Order under section 49(1) of the Adoption (Scotland) Act 1978]
in respect of

E.F. (*name as in birth certificate, or name by which child is ordinarily known, and address*).

HUMBLY SHEWETH—

1. That the petitioner is desirous of adopting the child, E.F., under the provisions of the Adoption (Scotland) Act 1978.

2. That the petitioner is domiciled in
and resides at

3. That the occupation of the petitioner is

4. That the petitioner is married [*or* unmarried], a widow [*or* a widower] (*if married, state whether spouse resides with or apart from, the petitioner*).

5. That the petitioner is years of age.

6. That the petitioner has resident with him the following persons namely,

7. That the petitioner [and his spouse] is [*or* are respectively] related to the child as follows:— [*or* that the petitioner [and his spouse] is not [*or* are not, nor is either of them] related to the child].

8. That the child is—
(*a*) of the sex;

(*b*) unmarried;

(*c*) a child of (*name of mother*) and (*name of father, if known*);

(*d*) of British [*or*] nationality;

(*e*) years of age, having been born on the day of 19 ; at in the county of ;

(*f*) was received into the care and possession of the petitioner on ;

(*g*) has been continuously in his care and possession since ;

(*h*) has the following tutors, curators or guardians (*names and addresses*), ; and

(*i*) entitled to the following property, namely,

[9. *Where the child was not placed for adoption.* That a medical report on the health of the child is produced herewith.]

[10. That the child is free for adoption under section 18 of the 1978 Act. A certified copy interlocutor of the (*name of court*) dated the day of 19 , is produced. The interlocutor freeing the child for adoption has not been revoked under section 20 of the 1978 Act. In terms of that interlocutor the parental rights and duties relating to the child were vested in (*name of adoption agency*). [The parental rights and duties relating to the child were transferred to (*name of adoption agency*) by interlocutor of (*name of court*) under section 21 of the 1978 Act on day of 19 . A certified copy of that interlocutor is produced.].]

[11. That the child is in the care of who has [*or* have] the rights and duties of a parent or guardian [*or* the parental rights and duties] in respect of the child.]

[12. That (*name*) of (*address*) is liable to pay aliment to the child by interlocutor of the (*name of court*) [*or* by an agreement of (*names of parties to agreement*)] dated the day of 19 .]

[13. That the petitioner believes and avers that (*names(s)*) is [*or* are] willing to agree to the making of an adoption order [*or* an order under section 49 of the 1978 Act] in favour of the petitioner.]

[14. That the petitioner desires the court to dispense with the agreement of (*names(s)*) on the ground that .]

[15. That the petitioner believes and avers that the child, being a minor, consents to the making of an adoption order [*or* an order under section 49(1) of the 1978 Act] in favour of the petitioner. [*Or* That the petitioners desires the court to dispense with the consent of the child on the ground that he is incapable of giving his consent because (*state reason*) .]]

16. That the child has lived with the petitioner continuously since the day of 19 . [He has accordingly had his home with the petitioner during the preceding five years.]

[17. That on the day of 19 the child was placed with the petitioner for adoption by (*name of adoption agency*) [*or* received into the custody of the petitioner in the following circumstances].]

[18. That the petitioner notified the (*name of local authority*) on the day of 19 of his intention to petition for an adoption order [*or* an order under section 49 of the 1978 Act] in respect of the child.]

[19. That the child has not been the subject of an adoption order or of a petition for an adoption order [save that (*state order and petition if any*)].]

[20. That the petitioner is prepared to undertake, if an adoption order [*or* an order under section 49 of the 1978 Act] is made in this petition, to make the following provision for the child .]

[21. That the petitioner has not received or agreed to receive and no person has made or agreed to make or give to the petitioner any payment or reward in consideration of the adoption of the child [except as follows].]

[22. That the petitioner intends to adopt the child under the law of [*or* within] (*state country*) which is the country of the domicile of the petitioner. [The petitioner wishes to remove the child from Great Britain for the purpose of adoption.]]

23. That this petition is presented under the provisions of the Adoption (Scotland) Act 1978, and Rule of Court 222 [*or* 223].

MAY IT THEREFORE please your Lordships to dispense with intimation and to order notice of this petition to be served by registered or recorded delivery letter post or otherwise on such person or persons as your Lordships may think proper; and to appoint a reporting officer, and, if necessary, a curator *ad litem* to the child sought to be adopted, and direct him [*or* them] to report; and thereafter, on resuming consideration hereof, together with the report by the reporting officer, and that of the curator *ad litem* if one is appointed, pronounce an interlocutor authorising the petitioner to adopt the child [*or* vesting in the petitioner the parental rights and duties relating to the child under section 49 of the Adoption (Scotland) Act 1978], E.F., in terms of the Adoption (Scotland) Act 1978, on such terms and conditions, if any, as your Lordships may think fit; and to direct the Registrar General for Scotland to make an entry regarding the adoption [*or* order under section 49 of the 1978 Act] in the Adopted Children Register in the form prescribed by him, giving the name as the Christian and as the surname of the child in that form; and, further, upon proof to the satisfaction of your Lordships in the course of the proceedings to follow hereon, to find that the child was born on the day of in the year and is identical with the child to whom an entry numbered and made on the day of in the year in the register of births for the registration district of in the county of relates; and to direct the Registrar General to cause such birth entry to be marked with the word "Adopted" [*or* "Proposed Foreign Adoption"] [and (*inserted only where the child was born in Scotland*) to include the above-mentioned date of birth in the entry recording the adoption in the manner indicated in that form]; and to pronounce such other or further orders or directions upon such matters, including the expenses of this petition, as your Lordships may think fit.

ACCORDING TO JUSTICE, etc.

(*Signed*)
[Counsel (*or* solicitor who has a right of audience in the Court of Session) for Petitioner]

NOTE

[1] Substituted by S.I. 1984 No. 997. As amended by S.I. 1991 No. 2483, with effect from 25th November 1991.

Rule 220(4) [1] FORM 37

Consent of a parent or guardian to petition for an order freeing a child for adoption under section 18 of the Adoption (Scotland) Act 1978

UNTO THE RIGHT HONOURABLE THE LORDS OF COUNCIL AND SESSION
in
PETITION
of
A.B. (*address*)
for
An order freeing the child E.F. for adoption
under section 18 of the Adoption (Scotland) Act 1978

I, , of (*address*) being a parent [*or* guardian] of the child, E.F., hereby state—

(1) That I consent to the petition of A.B., an adoption agency, for an order freeing the child for adoption.

(2) That I understand that the petitioner cannot apply to the court for an order freeing the child for adoption without the consent of a parent or guardian, unless the petitioner is applying for dispensation of the agreement of each parent or guardian of the child and the child is in the care of the petitioner.

(*Signed by parent or guardian*)

This consent was signed by before me at on the day of 19 .

(*Signed*)

(*Designation*)

(*Address*)

NOTE
[1] Inserted by S.I. 1984 No. 997.

Rule 220(8)(a) [1] FORM 37A

Agreement of a parent or guardian to an adoption order in a petition for an order freeing a child for adoption under section 18 of the Adoption (Scotland) Act 1978

[*Heading as in Form 37*]

I, , of (*address*) being a parent [*or* guardian] of the child, E.F., hereby state—

(1) That I understand that the effect of an adoption order would be to deprive me permanently of the parental rights and duties relating to the child and to vest them in the adopters; and that if and when an adoption order is made, I shall have no right to see or get in touch with the child or to have him [*or* her] returned to me.

(2) That I understand that the court cannot make an order freeing a child for adoption without the agreement of each parent or guardian of the child to the making of an adoption order, unless the court dispenses with that agreement on the ground that the person concerned—

(*a*) cannot be found or is incapable of giving agreement, or

(*b*) is withholding his agreement unreasonably, or

(*c*) has persistently failed without reasonable cause to discharge the parental duties in relation to the child, or

(*d*) has abandoned or neglected the child, or

(*e*) has persistently ill-treated the child, or

(*f*) has seriously ill-treated the child and the rehabilitation of the child within the household of the parent or guardian is unlikely.

(3) That I also understand that, when the hearing on the petition to determine the application for an order freeing the child for adoption is heard, this document may be used as evidence of my agreement to the making of an adoption order unless I inform the court that I no longer agree.

(4) That I freely, and with full understanding of what is involved, agree unconditionally to the making of an adoption order.

(5) [That I have been given an opportunity of making a declaration that I prefer not to be involved in future questions concerning the adoption of the child. I understand that if I make such a declaration I will not be told when the child has been adopted or whether he has been placed for adoption. I also understand that I will not be able to apply for a revocation of the order freeing the child for adoption if I make such a declaration. I hereby declare freely, and with full understanding of what is involved, that I do not wish to be involved in future questions concerning the adoption of the child.] [*or* That I have been given an opportunity of making a declaration that I prefer not to be involved in future questions concerning the adoption of the child, and the effect of making such a declaration has been explained to me. I do not wish to make such delaration.]

[(6) That I have not received or given any payment or reward for, or in consideration of, the adoption of the child, for any agreement to the making of an adoption or consent to the making of an application for an order freeing the child for adoption, for placing the child for adoption with any person or making any arrangements for adoption of the child, other than a payment to an adoption agency for their expense incurred in connection with the adoption.]

(*Signed by parent or guardian*)

This agreement was signed by before me at on the day of 19 .

(*Signed*)

(*Designation*)

(*Address*)

NOTE
[1] Inserted by S.I. 1984 No. 997.

Rule 229(9)(a) or 223(2) [1] FORM 37B

Agreement of a parent or guardian to an adoption order or an order under section 49 of the Adoption (Scotland) Act 1978

[*Heading as in Form 36*]

I, , of (*address*) being a parent [*or* guardian] of the child, E.F., hereby state—

(1) That I understand that the effect of an adoption order [*or* an order under section 49 of the Adoption (Scotland) Act 1978] will be to deprive me permanently of the parental rights and duties relating to the child and to vest them in the petitioner; and in particular I understand that, if an order is made, I shall have no right to see or get in touch with the child or to have him [*or* her] returned to me.

(2) That I understand that the court cannot make an adoption order [*or* an order under section 49 of the 1978 Act] in relation to the child, unless the child is free for adoption, without the agreement of each parent or guardian of the child unless the court dispenses with an agreement on the ground that the person concerned—

(*a*) cannot be found or is incapable or giving agreement, or

(*b*) is witholding his agreement unreasonably, or

(*c*) has persistently failed without reasonable cause to disch rge the parental duties in relation to the child; or

(*d*) has abandoned or neglected the child, or

(*e*) has persistently ill-treated the child, or

(*f*) has seriously ill-treated the child and the rehabilitation of the child within the household of the parent or guardian is unlikely.

(3) That I also understand that when the hearing on the petition to determine the application for an adoption order [*or* an order under section 49 of the 1978 Act] in relation to the child is heard, this document may be used as evidence of my agreement to the making of the order unless I inform the court that I no longer agree.

(4) That I hereby freely, and with full understanding of what is involved, agree unconditionally to the making of an adoption order [*or* an order under section 49 of the 1978 Act] in relation to the child in this petition.

[(5) That I have not received or given any payment or reward for, or in consideration of, the adoption of the child, for any agreement to the making of an adoption order or placing the child for adoption with any person or making any arrangements for the adoption of the child, other than a payment to an adoption agency for their expenses incurred in connection with the adoption.]

(*Signed by parent or guardian*)

This agreement was signed by before me at on the day of 19 .

(*Signed*)

(*Designation*)

(*Address*)

NOTE
[1] Substituted for former Form 37 by S.I. 1984 No. 997.

Rule 220(8)(b)

[1] FORM 38

Consent of a minor to an order freeing him for adoption under section 18 of the Adoption (Scotland) Act 1978

[*Heading as in Form 37*]

I, , of (*address*) being a minor and the child in respect of whom the petition for an order freeing me for adoption is presented, hereby state—

(1) That I understand that an order freeing me for adoption cannot be made without my consent. The effect of my consent has been explained to me.

(2) That I also understand that, when the hearing on the petition to determine the application for an order freeing me for adopting is heard, this document may be used as evidence of my consent to the making of an order freeing me for adoption unless I inform the court that I no longer consent.

(3) That I, with full understanding of what it involves, consent to the making of an order freeing me for adoption.

(4) That I understand, if an order is made freeing me for adoption and a petition for my adoption is subsequently presented to the court, that my consent to any order for my adoption will still be required to be obtained.

(*Signed by minor*)

This consent was signed by before me at on the day of 19 .

(*Signed*)

(*Designation*)

(*Address*)

NOTE
[1] Inserted by S.I. 1984 No. 997.

Rule 222(9)(b) or 223(2) [1] Form 38A

Consent of a minor to an order for his adoption or to an order under section 49 of the Adoption (Scotland) Act 1978

[*Heading as in Form 36*]

I, , of (*address*) being a minor and the child in respect of whom the petition for an order for my adoption [*or* an order under section 49 of the Adoption (Scotland) Act 1978] is presented, hereby state—

(1) That I understand that an order for my adoption [*or* an order under section 49 of the 1978 Act] cannot be made without my consent. The effect of my consent has been explained to me.

(2) That I also understand that, when the hearing on the petition to determine the application for an adoption order [*or* an order under section 49 of the 1978 Act] is heard this document may be used as evidence of my consent to the making of an order for my adoption [*or* an order under section 49 of the 1978 Act] by the petitioner unless I inform the court that I no longer consent.

(3) That I, with full understanding of what it involves, consent to the making of an order for my adoption [*or* an order under section 49 of the 1978 Act] by the petitioner.

(*Signed by the minor*)

This consent was signed by before me at on the day of 19 .

(*Signed*)

(*Designation*)

(*Address*)

NOTE
[1] Inserted by S.I. 1984 No. 997.

Rule 220(12) [1] Form 39

Notice of hearing to determine application for an order freeing a child for adoption

In the Court of Session

in

Petition

of

A.B. (*address*)

for

An order freeing the child E.F for adoption under section 18 of the Adoption (Scotland) Act 1978

To (*name and address*)

Take notice

1. That the hearing in this petition to determine the application for an order freeing the child, E.F. for adoption will come before the Lord Ordinary in the Court of Session, Parliament Square, Edinburgh on the day of 19 , at o'clock and that you

may then appear and be heard personally or by counsel on the question whether an order freeing the child for adoption should be made.

2. That you are [not] obliged to attend the hearing [unless you wish to do so].

3. That while the petition is pending a parent or guardian of the child who did not consent to the making of the application must not, except with the leave of the court, remove the child from the actual custody of the person with whom the child has his home against the will of that person.

[4. That the court has been requested to dispense with your agreement to the making of an adoption order on the ground[s] that .]

Dated the day of 19 .

(*Signed*)

[Solicitor for Petitioner]

(*Address*)

NOTE
[1] Inserted by S.I. 1984 No. 997.

Rule 221(8) [1] FORM 39A

Notice of hearing of an application for the revocation of an order freeing a child for adoption

IN THE COURT OF SESSION

in

NOTE

by

C.D. (*address*)

for

Revocation of an order freeing the child E.F. for adoption

To (*name and address*)

TAKE NOTICE

1. That the hearing in this Note to determine the application for revocation of an order freeing the child for adoption will come before the Lord Ordinary in the Court of Session, Parliament House, Edinburgh on the day of 19 , at o'clock and that you may then appear and be heard personally or by counsel on the question whether the order freeing the child for adoption should be revoked.

2. That you are [not] obliged to attend the hearing [unless you wish to do so].

Dated the day of 19 .

(*Signed*)

[Solicitor for Noter]

(*Address*)

NOTE
[1] Inserted by S.I. 1984 No. 997.

Rule 222(5)(a) or 223(2) [1] FORM 39B

Notice to adoption agency or local authority of presenting a petition for an adoption order or for an order under section 49 of the Adoption (Scotland) Act 1978

IN THE COURT OF SESSION

in

PETITION

of

A.B. (*address*)

for

An adoption order [*or* an order under section 49 of the Adoption (Scotland) Act 1978] in respect of the child E.F.

To (*name and address*)

Take notice

1. That the petitioner has presented a petition to the Court of Session for an adoption order [*or* an order under section 49 of the Adoption (Scotland) Act 1978] in respect of the child E.F.

2. That the petition relates to a child who was placed for adoption by you on the day of 19 [*or* was not placed for adoption].

3. That you are required under section 23 [*or where notice has been given under section 22(1)*, you were notified on the day of 19 that you were required [*or where notice has not been given under section 22(1)*, you are required] under section 22(1)] of the 1978 Act to submit to the court a report including the matters mentioned in Rule 222(7) of the Rules of the Court of Session.

4. That on completion of your report you are required under Rule 222(8) of the Rules of the Court of Session to lodge three copies of the report in process in the Petition Department, Court of Session, Parliament Square, Edinburgh and to send a copy to (*name and address*), the reporting officer [and a copy to (*name and address*), the curator *ad litem* to the child E.F.] in this petition.

Dated the day of 19 .

(*Signed*)

[Solicitor for Petitioner]

(*Address*)

NOTE
[1] Inserted by S.I. 1984 No. 997.

Rule 222(13) or 223(2)

[1] FORM 39C

Notice of hearing of application for an adoption order or an order under section 49 of the Adoption (Scotland) Act 1978

IN THE COURT OF SESSION

in

PETITION

of

A.B. (*address*)

for

An adoption order [*or* an order under section 49 of the Adoption (Scotland) Act 1978] in respect of the child E.F.

To (*name and address*)

Take notice

1. That the hearing in this petition to determine the application for an adoption order [*or* an order under section 49 of the Adoption (Scotland) Act 1978] will come before the Lord Ordinary in the Court of Session, Parliament House, Edinburgh on the day of 19 , at o'clock and that you may then appear and be heard personally or by counsel on the question whether an adoption order [*or* an order under section 49 of the 1978 Act] should be made.

2. That you are [not] obliged to attend the hearing [unless you wish to do so].

3. That while the petition is pending a parent or guardian of the child who has agreed to the making of an order must not, except with the leave of the court, remove the child from the actual custody of the petitioner.

[4. That the petition states that the child has had his home with the petitioner for the five years preceding the presentation of the petition and accordingly, if that is correct, no person is entitled, against the will of the petitioner, to remove the child from the actual custody of the petitioner except with the leave of the court or under authority conferred by any enactment or on the arrest of the child.]

[5. That the court has been requested to dispense with your agreement to the making of an order on the ground[s] that .]

Dated the day of 19

(*Signed*)

[Solicitor for Petitioner]

(*Address*)

NOTE

[1] Substituted for former Form 38 by S.I. 1984 No. 997.

Rule 260B(5) [1] Form 39D

Form of Petition in application for Judicial Review

UNTO THE RIGHT HONOURABLE
THE LORDS OF COUNCIL AND SESSION

Petition

of

[AB] (*address*)

for

Judicial review of (*state briefly matter sought to be reviewed*) by [CD]

Humbly Sheweth

1. That the petitioner is (*state designation, title and interest of petitioner*). The respondent is (*state designation and relation of respondent to matter to be reviewed*). [The following persons may have an interest].

2. That on (*date*) the respondent (*specify act, decision or omission to be reviewed*).

3. That the petitioner seeks (*state remedies sought (final and interim) including damages or restitution*). The petitioner craves the court to pronounce such further order, decrees or orders as may seem to the court to be just and reasonable in all the circumstances of the case.

4. That the petitioner challenges the decision [*or* act *or* omission] of the respondent on the following ground(s).

5. (*State shortly (in numbered paragraphs) facts in support of the ground(s) of challenge*).

[6]. (*State briefly (in numbered paragraphs) the legal argument with reference to enactments or judicial authority on which it is intended to rely*).

Plea(s)-in-Law

(*Specify pleas-in-law relating to each ground of challenge and remedy sought*)

According to Justice etc.
(*signed by counsel or solicitor*)

Schedule for Service

Respondent(s) upon whom service is sought in common form
Respondent(s) upon whom service is sought edictally
Interested parties upon whom service is sought in common form
Interested parties upon whom service is sought edictally

Schedule of Documents

(*Specify documents founded on (Rule 260B(9))*)

NOTE
[1] Inserted by S.I. 1985 No. 500. Renumbered by S.I. 1990 No. 705.

[1] FORM 40

Form of Joint Minute consenting to Summary Trial

Parties concur in craving that the cause shall be remitted to Lord for determination by him under section 10 of the Administration of Justice (Scotland) Act 1933.

(*To be signed by Counsel or solicitor who has a right of audience in the Court of Session for each party.*)

NOTE

[1] As amended by S.I. 1991 No. 2483, with effect from 25th November 1991.

---

[1] FORM 41

Forms of (a) reclaiming, and (b) objection to competency

(*Date*)

(*a*) On behalf of the defender—for review by the Inner House of the Lord Ordinary's interlocutor of (*Date*)—Intimated to pursuer, p. Y.Z. (*defender's Counsel or solicitor who has a right of audience in the Court of Session*).

(*Signed*) O.P. (*Signature of defender's Solicitor, or of his Clerk.*)

(*Date*)

(*b*) On behalf of the pursuer—defender's motion opposed as incompetent—Intimated to defender—p. W.X. (*pursuer's Counsel or solicitor who has a right of audience in the Court of Session*).

(*Signed*) M.N. (*Signature of pursuer's Solicitor, or of his Clerk.*)

NOTE

[1] As amended by S.I. 1991 No. 2483, with effect from 25th November 1991.

FORM 42

Form of Appeal (or application in the nature of appeal) under particular statutes

(*This space will contain the letter and number assigned to the appeal on being lodged.*)

Appeal
to
The Court of Session
Under (*quote the particular statute and section thereof*)
By
(*name, designation and address of appellant*)
Against

An (*order, determination, or as the case may be*) of (*name the authority or tribunal*) dated (*give date*), and communicated to the appellant on (*date*), in the following terms:—(*quote the order or determination*).

The appellant appeals against the foregoing (*order, determination, etc.*) on the following grounds.

Grounds of Appeal.

(*State the grounds articulately in numbered paragraphs.*)

(*Signed*) M.N. (*Signature of appellant's solicitor.*)

(*Date*)

FORM 43

Form of Case (stated, special or referred) under certain statutes

(*This space will contain the letter and number assigned to the case on being lodged.*)

Case
for
The Court of Session
Under (*quote the particular statute and section thereof*)
(*names, designations, and addresses of parties or party*)

(*Narrate the facts and circumstances out of which the case arises, articulately and in numbered paragraphs, and set out the question(s) for answer by the Court.*)

(*Signed*) M.N. (*Signature of person stating or referring case.*)

(*Date*)

Form 44

Execution of Charge

Upon the day of in the year I, Messenger-at-Arms (*or other officer of Court entitled to execute diligence*), by virtue of the within Extract and Warrant at the instance of the within named and designed A. against the also within named and designed B., passed, and in Her Majesty's name and authority lawfully charged the said B. to make payment of the within mentioned sum or sums of money, principal, interest and expenses (*or* to implement and perform the obligations within mentioned, *or both to pay and perform as the Extract and Warrant may require*) (*add* "so far as incumbent upon him" *if there be other*

[THE NEXT PAGE IS C 179]

INITIAL WRIT – commences all ordinary actions. Statutory form in 1907 Act D4/5

1) HEADING – contains sheriffdom + name of ct.

2) INSTANCE – includes details of the parties identities
- particulars should include – party's FULL NAME – still desirable to give maiden name of women in divorce actions
- designation used to be given but not needed now
- address of parties – if residential, prefix it with 'residing at'
- statutory bodies – refer to statutes
- special capacities have to be set out eg suing as exor. – must be stated in writ with the identity of deceased
- designation in instance must be clear cut! –
- KAY v MORRISONS REPRESENTATIVES (1984) – D.'s designed as reps. of the late J. Morrison whose whereabouts are unknown to the P. HELD – incompetent but time given to amend

3) CRAVE – "the pursuer craves the ct." + set forth the specific decree/warrant asked for. ie P. sets out the remedy he's seeking. Critically important as can only get what he asks for

(A) Crave in an Action for payment of money
- normally crave for payment in Sterling – don't have to spell out amount in words
- may be approp. to crave for payment in foreign currency
eg COMMERZBANK v LARGE (1977) – HELD – competent to crave decree in a foreign currency in a Scottish action provided foreign currency was true currency of P.'s loss
BUT – NORTH SCOTTISH HELICOPTERS v UNITED TECHNOLOGIES CORP (1988)
- P.'s paid for repairs to helicopter in US dollars. They were Scottish based co. + didn't have a trading a/c in US dollars so NOT entitled to decree in US dollars. Entitled to decree in sterling of amount required to purchase dollars to pay their repair a/c
- may sue in foreign currency but conversion has to be done if intend to enforce decree in UK – done at latest possible opportunity

INTEREST – P. will normally crave interest in addition to principal sum sued for.
Rate of
(I) Interest – Act of Sederunt states that rate at moment is 15% if there is no other rate ~~to~~ available to you

GO TO C195

debtors or obligants in the Extract) and that to the said A. within days next after the date of my said charge under the pain of (poinding *or* imprisonment).

This I did by delivery to (*or* leaving for *as the case may be*) the said B. personally a full copy of the within Extract, before and in presence of C. witness to the premises.

(*Officer's signature.*)

(*Witness' signature.*)

FORM 45

Form of Application for Leave to Appeal

Pensions Appeal Tribunals Act 1943
Note
by
A.B. (name and design the applicant) or the Minister of Pensions
for
Leave to Appeal

1. On the Pensions Appeal Tribunal refused the applicant's (*or* the Minister's) application for leave to appeal against their decision dated refusing a pension to the applicant (*or* finding that the applicant was entitled to a pension on the grounds of attributability, *or as the case may be*).

2. A copy of the Statement of the Case is produced herewith. (*N.B. a copy is obtainable from the Pensions Appeal Office.*)

3. The reasons given by the Tribunal for their decision on the merits were as follows:—

(*Quote*)

4. The reasons given by the Tribunal for refusing leave to appeal were as follows:—

(*Quote*)

5. The grounds of this application are—(state briefly in propositional form and without reproducing evidence the point or points of law on which it is maintained that the Tribunal erred).

In respect whereof

[1] FORM 46

Form of Parliamentary or European Assembly Election Petition

Representation of the People Act 1983

Election for (*state place*) held on the day of 19

Petition
of

A. (*name and designation*) or A., B., and C. (*names and designations*) whose name (*or* names are) subscribed hereto,

against

D. (*name and designation*), as the member whose election or return is complained of, (and

E. as the returning officer, *as the case may be*), Respondent(s).

Humbly sheweth:—

1. That the first named petitioner voted (*or* had a right to vote, *as the case may be*) as an elector at the above election (*or* claims to have had a right to be elected or returned at the above election, *or* was a candidate at the above election, *as the case may be*). The second named petitioner (*here state in like manner the right of each petitioner*).

2. That the said election was held on the day of , 19 , when A.B. and C.D. (*name them*) were candidates, and the Returning Officer has returned A.B. (*name*) as being duly elected.

3. That (*state the facts on which the petitioners rely*).

May it therefore please the Court to determine that the said A.B. was not duly elected or returned, and that the election was void (*or* that the said C.D. was duly elected, and ought to have been returned *as the case may be*).

According to Justice, etc.

NOTE

[1] As amended by S.I. 1979 No. 516 and S.I. 1985 No. 1426.

[1] FORM 47

Form of Notice of the presentation of an Election Petition and of the nature of the proposed security

Representation of the People Act 1983

Take notice that under the Representation of the People Act 1983, and the Rules of Court, a Petition has been presented to the Petition Department of the Court of Session touching the election of a member of Parliament [*or* representative to the Assembly of the European Communities] for the (*place*), of which Petition the foregoing is a full copy, and that you are named therein as a respondent: and Take notice that the security which has been given in terms of section [136] of the above Act is in the form of a bond of caution to the amount of £ granted by A.B. and C.D. (*names and designations*) *or* by consignation of £ in the Bank of . If you desire to object to the above bond of caution in terms of section 136(4) of the above Act, you may do so within 14 days of the date hereof by lodging the objection in writing in the Petition Department of the Court of Session and sending or delivering a full copy of the same to me at the following address (*address within three miles of the General Post Office, Edinburgh*). (*Delete the last foregoing sentence if the consignation is wholly of money.*)

NOTE

[1] As amended by S.I. 1979 No. 516 and S.I. 1985 No. 1426.

[1] FORM 48

Form of Bond of Caution in Election Petition

Representation of the People Act 1983

We, A.B. and C.D. (*names and designations*), considering that a Petition has been presented by E.F., complaining of an undue return (*or* undue election *as the case may be*) of G.H. as a member to serve in Parliament for the county of (*or* burgh of) (*or* district of burghs) (*or* representative to the Assembly of the European Communities for (*name of constituency*)) upon the day of , 19 , and that by section 136 of the Representation of the People Act 1983, it is provided that security for the payment of all costs, charges, and expenses that may become payable by the petitioner in terms of the said Act, shall, on presentation of such Petition, be given on behalf of the petitioners, to the amount of £ ; and that by the Rules of the Court of Session for the trial of Election Petitions, under the said Act, it is prescribed that the security so to be given on behalf of the petitioners may be by lodging a bond of caution, in terms of the said Act; and seeing that we, the said parties, are willing to grant such bond, therefore we, the said parties, as cautioners, sureties, and full debtors for and with the said E.F., petitioner, do hereby bind and oblige ourselves conjunctly and severally, and our respective heirs, executors, and successors whomsoever, that the said E.F., petitioner shall make payment of all costs, charges, and expenses that may become payable by him to any person or persons, by virtue of any decree to be pronounced in the said Petition; and that to the amount of £ sterling, with one-fifth part more of liquidate penalty in case of failure; and we consent to the registration hereof for execution. In witness whereof, etc.

NOTE

[1] As amended by S.I. 1979 No. 516 and S.I. 1985 No. 1426.

FORM 49

Form of Warrant to cite witnesses in Election Petition

Representation of the People Act 1983

(*place and date*)

Having considered the motion for the petitioner (or respondent), grants warrant to all officers of the law for citing (*name them*) to attend the Court, for the trial of the

Election Petition to be held at within (*name court-house*) on the day of , 19 , at o'clock forenoon (or forthwith, *as the case may be*), to be severally examined as witnesses in the manner of the said Petition, and to attend the said Court until their examination shall have been completed.

(Signed)

Judge of the said Court.

NOTE

[1] As amended by S.I. 1985 No. 1426.

---

[1] FORM 50

Form of Application for leave to withdraw Election Petition

Representation of the People Act 1983

County (*or* burgh *or* district of burghs *or* European Assembly constituency) of

Petition of presented on the day of , 19 .

The petitioners (or the petitioner A.B. (*name*) with the consent of the petitioners C.D. and E.F. (*names*) (*or as the case may be*)) apply for leave to withdraw their Petition on the following grounds: (*state grounds*), and pray that a day may be appointed for hearing their application.

Dated the day of , 19 .

(*To be signed by the applicants and consenters, if any, or their respective Solicitors, who shall each append to their signature a statement of whether they sign as or on behalf of an applicant or a consenter.*)

NOTE

[1] As amended by S.I. 1979 No. 516 and S.I. 1985 No. 1426.

---

[1] FORM 51

Form of Notice of proposed withdrawal of Election Petition

Representation of the People Act 1983

In the Election Petition for in which is petitioner and is respondent.

Notice is hereby given that the above petitioner has, on the day of , 19 , lodged at the office of the Deputy Principal Clerk of Session notice of application to withdraw his Petition, of which the following is a copy:—(Set it out).

And take notice, that by the Act and Rules of Court, any person who might have been a petitioner, in respect of the said election, may, within five days after publication of this Notice give notice in writing, signed by him or on his behalf, to the said Deputy Principal Clerk of Session, 2 Parliament Square, Edinburgh, of his intention to apply at the hearing to be substituted for the petitioner.

Dated the day of , 19 .

(Signed by the Petitioner or his Solicitor)

NOTE

[1] As amended by S.I. 1985 No. 1426.

---

[1] FORM 52

Case for the European Court

[Here set out a statement of the case for the European Court, giving brief particulars of the case and the issues between the parties, any relevant facts found by the Court, any relevant

rules and provisions of Scots Law, and the relevant Treaty provisions, acts, instruments or rules of Community law giving rise to the reference.]

The preliminary ruling of the Court of Justice of the European Communities is accordingly sought on the following questions—1., 2. etc. [insert the questions on which the ruling is sought.]

Dated the day of , 19 .

NOTE

[1] Added by S.I. 1972 No. 1981.

Rule 249E(1) [1] FORM 53

Application for registration of a judgment under section 4 of the Civil Jurisdiction and Judgments Act 1982

IN THE COURT OF SESSION

in causa

APPLICATION

of

[A.B.] (*address*)

under the Civil Jurisdiction and Judgments Act 1982

for registration of

a judgment of the (*name of court*)

dated the day of 19

1. That this application is made by (*name of applicant*) to register a judgment [*or decision or other order*] of the (*name of court*) of (*date of judgment*).

2. That in the cause in which the judgment [*or decision or other order*] was pronounced, A.B. was pursuer [*or* defender *or as the case may be*] and C.D. was defender [*or* pursuer *or as the case may be*].

3. The applicant is a party having an interest to enforce the judgment [*or decision or other order*] because (*state reasons*).

4. That this application is supported by the affidavit of (*name of deponent*) and the documents produced therewith.

5. That the applicant seeks warrant to register the judgment [and for decree in terms thereof] [and for decree to be pronounced in the following or such other terms as to the court may seem proper:— (*state terms in which decree is to be pronounced in accordance with Scots law*)].

6. That the applicant seeks the authority of the court to execute the protective measure[s] of (*state measures*), for the following reasons (*state reasons*).

7. That this application is made under section 4 of the Civil Jurisdiction and Judgments Act 1982 and Rule 249E of the Rules of the Court of Session.

IN RESPECT WHEREOF

(*Signed*)
Applicant [or Solicitor for Applicant *or* Counsel]
[*Address of solicitor*]

NOTE
[1] Added by S.I. 1986 No. 1941.

Rule 249J(1) [1] FORM 54

Intimation of decree and warrant for registration of a judgment under section 4 of the Civil Jurisdiction and Judgments Act 1982

IN THE COURT OF SESSION

in causa

APPLICATION

of

[A.B.] (*address*)

under section 4 of the Civil Jurisdiction and Judgments Act 1982

for registration of

a judgment of the (*name of court*)

dated the day of 19

To (*name of person against whom judgment was given and decree and warrant for registration granted*).

TAKE NOTICE that an interlocutor dated the day of 19 , a certified copy of which is attached, was pronounced in the Court of Session granting decree and warrant for registration of the (*judgment, decision or other order*) of the (*name of court*) dated the day of 19 , for (*state briefly the terms of the judgment*).

You have the right to appeal to a Lord Ordinary in the Outer House of the Court of Session, Parliament Square, Edinburgh against the interlocutor granting decree and warrant for registration within one month [*or* two months *as the case may be*] from the date of service of this notice upon you. Where service has been executed by post, service shall be reckoned from 24 hours after the date of posting.

An appeal shall be in Form 42 of the Appendix to the Rules of the Court of Session.

The registered judgment and decree of the Court of Session may not be enforced in Scotland until the expiry of the period within which you may appeal and any appeal has been disposed of.

The applicant may, however, take certain steps of diligence in execution of the registered judgment and decree of the Court of Session as a protective measure, **without actual enforcement**, until the expiry of the period within which you may appeal and any appeal has been disposed of.

[The applicant applied to the court for other protective measures until the expiry of the period of lodging an appeal and any appeal has been disposed of. The following other protective measures were granted by the court:—

.]

Diligence in execution or other protective measures shall be of no effect unless service of this notice has been made within 21 days from the date of execution of the diligence or other protective measure.

Intimation of an appeal should be made to the applicant, A.B., at the following address for service in Scotland:—

Dated this day of 19 .

(*Signed*)
Applicant [*or* Solicitor or Applicant, Messenger-at-Arms or other officer]
(*Address*)

NOTE

[1] Added by S.I. 1986 No. 1941.

Rule 249N(1)

[1] FORM 55

Certificate under section 12 of the Civil Jurisdiction and Judgments Act 1982

IN THE COURT OF SESSION

CERTIFICATE

under the Civil Jurisdiction and Judgments Acts 1982

in causa

[*or* in petition of]

[A.B.] (*address*)

Pursuer [*or* Petitioner]

against

[C.D.] (*address*)

Defender [*or* Respondent]

I, , a Deputy Principal Clerk of the Court of Session, do hereby certify—

1. That the summons [*or* petition], raised [*or* presented] by the pursuer [*or* petitioner] A.B. was executed by citation of the defender C.D. served on him [*or* was served on the respondent C.D.] on the day of 19 by (*state method of service*).

2. That in the summons [*or* petition] the pursuer, sought [payment of the sum of £ in respect of (*state briefly the nature of the claim*)] [and (*state other conclusions of the summons or orders sought in the prayer of petition*]).

3. [That the defender C.D. entered appearance on the day of 19] [and lodged defences on the day of 19]
[*or* That the defender C.D. did not enter appearance].

4. That the pursuer [*or* petitioner] obtained decree [*or other order*] against the defender [*or* respondent] in the Court of Session for [payment of the sum of £] [or *state briefly the terms of the interlocutor or opinion of the court*] [and *state briefly other conclusions of the summons or orders sought in the prayer of the petition granted*] together with the expenses of the cause in the sum of £ , all in terms of the certified copy interlocutor attached hereto.

5. That [no] objection to the jurisdiction of the court has been made [on the grounds that].

6. That the decree includes interest at the rate of *per centum per annum* on the total of the sum of £ and expenses of £ from the day of 19 until payment.

7. That the interlocutor containing the decree [*or other order*] has been served on the defender.

8. That the time for reclaiming (appealing) against the interlocutor has expired [and no reclaiming motion (appeal) has been enrolled within that time] [*or* and a reclaiming motion (appeal) having been enrolled within that time, has [not] been finally disposed of].

9. That enforcement of the decree has not for the time being been suspended and the time available for its enforcement has not expired.

10. That the whole pleadings of the parties are contained in the Closed Record [*or* summons *or* petition], a copy of which is attached.

11. That this certificate is issued under section 12 of the Civil Jurisdiction and Judgments Acts 1982 and rule 249N of the Rules of the Court of Session.

Dated the day of 19 .

(*Signed*)
Deputy Principal Clerk of Session.

NOTE
[1] Added by S.I. 1986 No. 1941.

Rule 249P(1)(l) [1] FORM 56

Certificate of money provisions in an interlocutor for registration under Schedule 6 to the Civil Jurisdiction and Judgments Act 1982

IN THE COURT OF SESSION

CERTIFICATE

under the Civil Jurisdiction and Judgments Acts 1982

in causa

[*or* in petition of]

[A.B.] (*address*)
Pursuer [*or* Petitioner]

against

[C.D.] (*address*)
Defender [*or* Respondent]

I, , a Deputy Principal Clerk of the Court of Session, do hereby certify—

1. That the pursuer A.B. obtained decree [*or other order*] against the defender C.D. on the- day of 19 in the Court of Session for payment of the sum of £ in respect of (*state briefly the nature of the claim and terms of the interlocutor*) together with the sum of £ as expenses.

2. That the interlocutor granting decree [*or other order*] was obtained on the grounds (*state grounds briefly*).

3. That the decree [*or other order*] carries interest at the rate of *per centum per annum* on the total of the sum of £ and expenses of £ from the day of 19 until payment.

4. That the time for reclaiming (appealing) against the interlocutor has expired [and no reclaiming motion (appeal) has been enrolled within that time] [and a reclaiming motion (appeal) having been enrolled within that time, has been finally disposed of].

5. That enforcement of the decree [*or other order*] has not for the time being been suspended and that the time available for its enforcement has not expired.

[THE NEXT PAGE IS C 189]

6. That this certificate is issued under section 18 of, and paragraph 4(1) of Schedule 6 to, the Civil Jurisdiction and Judgments Act 1982 and rule 249P(1) of the Rules of the Court of Session.

Dated the day of 19 .

(*Signed*)
Deputy Principal Clerk of Session.

NOTE
[1] Added by S.I. 1986 No. 1941.

Rule 249Q(2) [1] FORM 57

Certificate of non-money provisions in an interlocutor for registration under Schedule 7 of the Civil Jurisdiction and Judgments Act 1982

IN THE COURT OF SESSION

CERTIFICATE

under the Civil Jurisdiction and Judgments Acts 1982

in causa

[*or* in petition of]

[A.B.] (*address*)
Pursuer [*or* Petitioner]

against

[C.D.] (*address*)
Defender [*or* Respondent]

I, , a Deputy Principal Clerk of the Court of Session, do hereby certify—

1. That the copy of the interlocutor attached hereto is a true copy of the decree [*or other order*] obtained in the Court of Session [and that the copy of the opinion of the court attached hereto is a true copy thereof] and is issued in accordance with section 18 of the Civil Jurisdiction and Judgments Act 1982.

2. That the time for reclaiming (appealing) against the interlocutor has expired [and no reclaiming motion (appeal) has been enrolled within that time] [and a reclaiming motion (appeal) having been enrolled within that time has been finally disposed of].

3. That enforcement of the decree [*or other order*] has not for the time being been suspended and that the time available for its enforcement has not expired.

4. That this certificate is issued under section 18 of, and paragraph 4(1)(*b*) of Schedule 7 of the Civil Jurisdiction and Judgments Act 1982 and rule 249Q(2) of the Rules of the Court of Session.

Dated the day of 19 .

(*Signed*)
Deputy Principal Clerk of Session.

NOTE
[1] Added by S.I. 1986 No. 1941.

Rule 249Q(4) [1] FORM 58

Application for registration of a judgment under section 18 of, and Schedule 7 to, the Civil Jurisdiction and Judgments Act 1982

IN THE COURT OF SESSION

in causa

APPLICATION

of

[A.B.] (*address*)

under the Civil Jurisdiction and Judgments Act 1982

for registration of

a judgment of the (*name of court*)

dated the day of 19

1. That this application is made by (*name of applicant*) to register a judgment [or *decision or other order*] of the (*name of court*) of (*date of judgment*).

2. That in the cause in which the judgment [*or decision or other order*] was pronounced A.B. was plaintiff [*or* defendant *or as the case may be*] and C.D. was defendant [*or* plaintiff *or as the case may be*].

3. The applicant is a party having an interest to enforce the judgment [*or decision or other order*] because (*state reasons*).

4. That the applicant believes and avers that the usual [*or* last known] address of the (*state party liable in execution*) is (*state address*).

5. That the applicant seeks warrant to register the judgment [and for decree in terms thereof] [and for decree to be pronounced in the following or such other terms as to the court may seem proper:— (*state terms in which decree is to be pronounced in accordance with Scots law*)].

6. That this application is made under section 18 of, and paragraph 5(1) of Schedule 7 to, the Civil Jurisdiction and Judgments Act 1982 and rule 249Q(4) of the Rules of the Court of Session.

IN RESPECT WHEREOF

(*Signed*)
Applicant [*or* Solicitor for Applicant]
(*Address*)

NOTE
[1] Added by S.I. 1986 No. 1941.

Rule 249N(3) [1] FORM 59

Certificate by Keeper of the Registers of writ registered for execution in the Books of Council and Session for registration under Article 50 of Schedule 1 to the Civil Jurisdiction and Judgments Act 1982

REGISTERS OF SCOTLAND

CERTIFICATE
Under the Civil Jurisdiction and Judgments Act 1982

of

Deed [*or other writ*]

between
[A.B.] (*address*)

and

[C.D.] (*address*)

registered for execution in the Books of Council and Session

I, , the Keeper of the Registers of Scotland, and as such, Keeper of the Register of Deeds, Bonds, Protests and other writs registered for execution in the Books of Council and Session, do hereby certify—

1. That A.B. registered in the Books of Council and Session on the day of 19 for execution against C.D. a (*describe writ and state terms of writ for which enforcement is to be sought*).

2. That the extract of the deed [*or other writ*] attached hereto is a true copy of the deed [*or other writ*] registered for execution by A.B.

[3. That the deed [*or other writ*] carries interest at the rate of *per centum per annum from the day of* *19 until payment.*]

[4. That enforcement of the deed] [*or other writ*] has not for the time being been suspended and that the time available for its enforcement has not expired.

5. That this certificate is issued under article 50 of Schedule 1 to the Civil Jurisdiction and Judgments Act 1982 and rule 249N(3) of the Rules of the Court of Session.

Dated the day of 19 .

(*Signed*)
Keeper of the Registers of Scotland.

NOTE
[1] Added by S.I. 1986 No. 1941.

Rule 249P(1)(ii) [1] FORM 60

Certificate by Keeper of the Registers of money provisions in a writ registered for execution in the Books of Council and Session for registration under Schedule 6 to the Civil Jurisdiction and Judgments Act 1982

REGISTERS OF SCOTLAND

CERTIFICATE
Under the Civil Jurisdiction and Judgments Act 1982

of

Deed [*or other writ*]

between

[A.B.] (*address*)

and

[C.D.] (*address*)

registered for execution in the Books of Council and Session

I, , the Keeper of the Registers of Scotland, and as such, Keeper of the Register of Deeds, Bonds, Protests and other writs registered for execution in the Books of Council and Session, do hereby certify—

1. That A.B. registered in the Books of Council and Session on the day of 19 for execution against C.D. a (*describe writ and state terms of money provision in writ for which enforcement is to be sought*).

2. That the money provision in the deed [*or other writ*] carries interest at the rate of *per centum per annum* from the day of 19 until payment.

3. That enforcement of the deed [*or other writ*] has not for the time being been suspended and that the time available for its enforcement has not expired.

4. That this certificate is issued under section 18 of, and paragraph 4(1) of Schedule 6 to, the Civil Jurisdiction and Judgments Act 1982 and rule 249P(1) of the Rules of the Court of Session.

Dated the day of 19 .

(*Signed*)
Keeper of the Registers of Scotland.

NOTE
[1] Added by S.I. 1986 No. 1941.

Rule 249Q(1)(ii) [1] FORM 61

Certificate by Keeper of the Registers of non-money provisions in a writ registered for execution in the Books of Council and Session for registration under Schedule 7 to the Civil Jurisdiction and Judgments Act 1982

REGISTERS OF SCOTLAND

CERTIFICATE
Under the Civil Jurisdiction and Judgments Act 1982

of

Deed [*or other writ*]

between

[A.B.] (*address*)

and

[C.D.] (*address*)

registered for execution in the Books of Council and Session

I, , the Keeper of the Registers of Scotland, and as such, Keeper of the Register of Deeds, Bonds, Protests and other writs registered for execution in the Books of Council and Session, do hereby certify—

1. That the extract of the deed [*or other writ*] attached hereto is a true copy of the deed [*or other writ*] registered for execution by A.B. and is issued in accordance with section 18 of the Civil Jurisdiction and Judgments Act 1982.

2. That enforcement of the deed [*or other writ*] has not for the time being been suspended and that the time available for its enforcement has not expired.

3. That this certificate is issued under section 18 of, and paragraph 4(1)(*b*) of Schedule 7 to the Civil Jurisdiction and Judgments Act 1982 and rule 249Q(1) of the Rules of the Court of Session.

Dated the day of 19 .

(*Signed*)
Keeper of the Registers of Scotland.

NOTE
[1] Added by S.I. 1986 No. 1941.

Rule 249V(1)

[1] Form 62

Intimation of decree and warrant for registration of an order under the Criminal Justice (Scotland) Act 1987 or the Criminal Justice Act 1988

IN THE COURT OF SESSION

in

PETITION

of

[A.B.] (*address*)

under section 28 [or 30A] of the Criminal

Justice (Scotland) Act 1987

[*or* 91 of the Criminal

Justice Act 1988]

for

registration of an order of

(*name of court*)

Dated the .... day of .... 19......

To (*name of person against whom the order was made and decree and warrant for registration granted*).
Take notice that an interlocutor dated the .... day of 19......, a certified copy of which is attached, was pronounced in the Court of Session granting decree and warrant for registration in the Court of Session [and for registration in the Register of Judgments of the Books of Council and Session] of the order of the (*name of court*) dated the .... day of .... 19...... that (*briefly describe order*).
The order was registered in the Court of Session on (*date*).
[The order was registered in the Register of Judgments of the Books of Council and Session on (*date*) and an extract of the registered order and decree with warrant for execution has been issued by the Keeper of the Registers. Diligence in execution of the order may now be taken against you to enforce the order.]

Dated this .... day of .... 19......

(*Signed*)
Petitioner [or Solicitor for petitioner].
(*Address*)

NOTE

[1] Added by S.I. 1987 No. 12 and as amended by S.I. 1990 No. 705 and (with effect from 27th May 1991) 1991 No. 1157.

Rule 249V(1) [1] FORM 62A

Intimation of decree and warrant for registration of an order of the Court in England and Wales, Northern Ireland or elsewhere in the British Islands under the Prevention of Terrorism (Temporary Provisions) Act 1989

IN THE COURT OF SESSION

in

PETITION

of

[A.B.] (*Address*)

under paragraph 19(2) of Schedule 4 to the Prevention of Terrorism (Temporary Provisions) Act 1989

for

registration of an order of the (*specify court*)

Dated the .... day of .... 19......

To (*name of person against whom the order was made and decree and warrant for registration granted*).

Take notice that an interlocutor dated the .... day of 19...... a certified copy of which is attached, was pronounced in the Court of Session granting decree and warrant for registration in the Court of Session [and for registration in the Register of Judgments of the Books of Council and Session] of the order of the (*specify the court*) dated the .... day of .... 19...... that (*briefly describe order*).

The order was registered in the Court of Session on (*date*).

[The order was registered in the Register of Judgments of the Books of Council and Session on (*date*) and an extract of the registered order and decree with warrant for execution has been issued by the Keeper of the Registers. Diligence in execution of the order may now be taken against you to enforce the order.]

Dated this .... day of .... 19......

(*Signed*)
Petitioner [*or* Solicitor for Petitioner].
(*Address*)

NOTE

[1] Added by S.I. 1991 No. 1183.

Rules 91C2 and 294C(1) [1] FORM 63

Form for information for fixing and allocation of diet for hearing

Part I—Estimated length of hearing

(To be signed by counsel or a solicitor who has a right of audience in the Court of Session)

Name of case .... v. ....

....

For pursuer/defender/other ....

Nature of hearing (e.g. proof, reclaiming motion) ....

[THE NEXT PAGE IS C 195]

- if there is an agreement between parties stipulating a different rate of interest this other rate will prevail

  - BANK OF SCOTLAND v DAVIS (1982) – can obtain interest at a rate in terms of the agreement irrespective of the 'legal rate'

- if want interest at more than legal rate have to justify this in Iw

  - Petroleum Industry Training Board v Jenkins (1982) – legal rate – 11%. Actions undefended. P. craved 17% but didn't say why he wanted it so Sh granted decree at 11% only

  - Royal Bank of Scotland v Biggs (1982) – contract provided for 16% but had no justifications. Sh. said he had no right to refuse interest payments so granted decree with interest at 16%

- contract may stipulate for fluctuating lending rate eg interest payable at 5% above banks base lending rate

(II) Date from which interest is to be craved:-

(a) if there is a contract stipulating a date that contractual date may be inserted

(b) Other cases, with exception of damages, normally only crave from date of citation ie date when Iw is served on D.

BUT – may be able to crave from an earlier date:-

- HUNTER v LIVINGSTON DEVELOPMENT CORP. (1984)

(c) Interest on damages – dealt with by statute

- Interest on Damages (S) Act 1958 as amended S.1(1) – B44 + 95

  - from date when right of action arose – normally date when loss occurred

NOTE – Ct. can always award interest for a SHORTER period than you ask but cannot award more

- S.1(1A) – Ct. in certain circumstances must award interest – puts onus on Ct. where damages relate to personal injuries to award interest on the damage for personal injury unless there are special circumstances not to (WHOLE award sought doesn't have to relate to personal injuries)

PREDOMINANT VIEW – crave interest from date of accident. May be unnecessary to claim interest in this way:-

GO TO (40)

I estimate that the hearing will last .... (days)

Dated .... (signed)

.... (name)

Part II—Supplementary information

(To be completed by solicitor only if information is available and can be disclosed: such information will be treated *in confidence by court officials*)

A. Proof or jury trial

Total number of witnesses ....

Expert witnesses (state number and nature of evidence, e.g. medical) ....

....

Witnesses from abroad or having to travel long distances to court (provide appropriate details) ....

....

B. All cases

Any other relevant information ....

....

....

Part III—Notice of allocation of diet

(To be completed by solicitor)

Allocation of a diet at short notice is/is not* acceptable. The minimum notice required is .... weeks.

*(Delete as necessary)

Dated .... (signed)

.... (name of firm)

N.B. There is an obligation on a party to intimate to the keeper of the rolls any alteration to the estimate in Part I of this Form (see Rules 91C(8) and 294C(6)).

NOTE

[1] Added by S.I. 1987 No. 1206. As amended by S.I. 1991 No. 2483, with effect from 25th November 1991.

FORM 64

[Added by S.I. 1987 No. 1206. Revoked by S.I. 1990 No. 2118.]

Rule 88B(1) [1] FORM 65

Form of notice to debtor under the Debtors (Scotland) Act 1987 about time to pay directions

(Court Ref No.)

IN THE COURT OF SESSION

in causa

[A.B.] *(address)*
Pursuer

against

[C.D.] *(address)*
Defender

To (*insert name of defender to whom notice is directed*)

YOUR RIGHTS UNDER THE DEBTORS (SCOTLAND) ACT 1987

The purpose of this notice is to advise you of your rights under the Debtors (Scotland) Act 1987.

The Act gives you a right to apply to the court for a "time to pay direction" directing that any sum of money you are ordered to pay to the pursuer (which may include interest and court expenses) shall be by way of instalments or deferred lump sum (that is by way of one total payment by a specified date).

In addition, when making a time to pay direction the court may recall or restrict an arrestment made in connection with the action or debt (e.g. your bank account may have been arrested freezing the money in it).

If you admit that the sum claimed by the pursuer is due but you wish to apply for a time to pay direction you should read on. If you do not admit the sum claimed by the pursuer is due you should NOT complete the attached application but should consult a solicitor IMMEDIATELY about defending the action.

HOW TO APPLY FOR A TIME TO PAY DIRECTION WHEN CLAIM ADMITTED AND YOU DO NOT WANT TO DEFEND THE ACTION

1. Attached to this notice is an application for a time to pay direction and for recall or restriction of an arrestment, if appropriate. If you want to make an application you should complete and lodge the completed application with the court on or before the date given below. *No court fee is payable when lodging the application.*

2. Before completing the application please read carefully the notes attached to this notice. In the event of difficulty you may contact the General Department in the Office of Court of the Court of Session, 2 Parliament Square, Edinburgh. (Telephone 031–225 2595.)

3. The date by which you must return the application form is

HOW TO COMPLETE THE APPLICATION

PLEASE WRITE IN INK USING BLOCK CAPITALS.

PART A of the application will have been completed in advance by the pursuer and gives details of the pursuer **and you** as the **defender**.

PART B—if you wish to offer instalments enter the amount and tick the appropriate box at B3(1).

If you wish to offer to pay the full sum due in one deferred payment enter the date at which you offer to pay at B3(2).

PART C—You should give full details of your financial position in the appropriate boxes.

PART D—If you wish the court, when making the time to pay direction, to recall or restrict an arrestment made in connection with the action then enter the appropriate details about what has been arrested and the place and date of the arrestment at D5, and attach the Schedule of Arrestment (i.e. the formal document which told you of the arrestment of your assets) or a copy of it. You should then complete D6 by deleting the words which do not apply.

Sign the application where indicated and send to the court. Retain the copy summons and pages 1 and 2 of this notice as you may need them at a later stage. You should ensure that your application arrives at the court **before** the date specified in paragraph 3 of Form 65.

WHAT WILL HAPPEN NEXT

If the pursuer does **not** accept your offer a hearing will be fixed and the pursuer will advise you in writing of the date and time.

If the pursuer **accepts** your offer, then a copy of the court order for payment (called an extract decree) will be served on you by the pursuer advising when payment of instalments should commence or by what date payment is to be made and to whom payments should be sent.

IF YOU ARE NOT SURE WHAT TO DO YOU SHOULD CONSULT A SOLICITOR OR A CITIZENS ADVICE BUREAU IMMEDIATELY

NOTE

[1] Added by S.I. 1988 No. 2060.

Rules 88B(1), 88C(1) and 88D(1) [1] FORM 66

Form of application for a time to pay direction

(Court Ref. No.)

IN THE COURT OF SESSION

APPLICATION FOR A TIME TO PAY DIRECTION

Under The Debtors (Scotland) Act 1987

by

PART A* ....
....
....
.... **Defender**

*This section must be completed by pursuer before service

In an action raised by

....
....
....
.... **Pursuer(s)**

This application must be sent to the court on or before

PART B

1. I am the defender in the action brought by the above named pursuer[s].
2. I admit the claim and apply to the court for a time to pay direction.
3. I offer †(1) To pay by instalments of £ ....

*Tick one box only
†Delete whichever is not applicable
‡Insert date

EACH ... WEEK ☐ * FORTNIGHT ☐ * MONTH ☐ *

†(2) To pay the sum ordered in one payment by ‡......... 19.....

PART C

4. My financial position is as follows:—

*Tick one box only

My outgoings are:	Weekly* ☐	Fortnightly* ☐	Monthly* ☐	My income is:	Weekly* ☐	Fortnightly* ☐	Monthly* ☐

Outgoings		Income	
Rent/House purchase loan	£	Wages/Pensions	£
Heating	£	Social Security	£
Food	£	Other(*specify*)	£
HP, etc	£		
Other	£		
Total	£	Total	£

Here list all capital, if any (e.g. value of house, amount in bank/building society accounts, shares or other investments):

Here list any outstanding debts:

PART D

*Delete if not applicable

5. *I seek to have recalled or restricted an arrestment of which the details are as follows (*Please state, and attach Schedule of Arrestment or a copy*):–

6. This application is made under the Debtors (Scotland) Act 1987. Therefore I ask the court:–

(a) to make a time to pay direction; and
*(b) to recall the above arrestment; or
*(c) to restrict the above arrestment:–†

*Delete if not applicable
†State the restriction wanted

Signed ....
Defender

Date .... 19.....

This application should be sent to the Deputy Principal Clerk of Session, Court of Session, 2 Parliament Square, Edinburgh.

NOTE
[1] Added by S.I. 1988 No. 2060.

Rule 88C(3) and (4) [1] FORM 67

Form of notice of application for decree and objection to application made by defender on Form 66

(Court Ref. No.)

IN THE COURT OF SESSION

in causa

[A.B.] (*address*)
Pursuer

against

[C.D.] (*address*)
Defender

To (*insert name of defender to whom notice is directed*)

This notice tells you that the pursuer—
(a) intends to apply for decree against you; and
(b) objects to all or part of the application which you made on Form 66.

I, , the solicitor for the pursuer, give you notice:—

(1) That on (*date of proposed enrolment*) I shall enrol the following motion in the above action against you and that this will come before the court on (*date and time*):—

(*insert terms of motion*)

(2) That the pursuer objects to the application which you have made for—
(i) a time to pay direction,*
(ii) recall or restriction of an arrestment made against you,*
and will ask the court not to grant your application for the following reasons—

(*set forth reasons in numbered paragraphs*).

You have the right to attend the hearing on (*insert date motion will come before the court*) and make any further points in answer to the pursuer's objections.

If you do not wish to attend court, you may reply to the pursuer's objections to your application in a letter addressed to the Deputy Principal Clerk of Session, 2 Parliament Square, Edinburgh. This letter must reach him by (*insert the date before the day on which the motion will come before the court*). The court will consider this letter at the hearing of the pursuer's motion and objection.

If you do not attend court and you wish to know the outcome of the hearing before you receive formal notice of the decree you should contact the General Department of the Court of Session, 2 Parliament Square, Edinburgh. (Telephone: 031–225 2595).

IF YOU ARE NOT SURE WHAT TO DO YOU SHOULD CONSULT A SOLICITOR OR A CITIZENS ADVICE BUREAU IMMEDIATELY.

(*signed*)
Solicitor for pursuer

Date 19

*Delete if not applicable.

NOTE
[1] Added by S.I. 1988 No. 2060.

Rule 260D(2)(*a*) [1] FORM 68

Notice to parent of presentation of petition for custody of a child

IN THE COURT OF SESSION

in

PETITION

of

A.B. *(address)*

for

Custody of the child E.F.

To *(name and address)*

TAKE NOTICE

1. That the petitioner has presented a petition to the Court of Session for custody of the child E.F. A copy of the petition is attached to this notice.

2. That the petitioner, being a relative [*or* step-parent] of the child, has the consent of [*or* seeks the consent of] *(name of parent, tutor, curator or guardian)* who is a parent [*or* guardian] of the child, and has had care and possession of the child for the three months preceding the presentation of this petition on *(date)*.

or

2. That the petitioner has the consent of [*or* seeks the consent of] *(name of a parent, tutor, curator or guardian)* who is a parent [*or* guardian] of the child and has had care and possession of the child for a period or periods before presentation of this petition which amounted to at least 12 months including the three months preceding the presentation of this petition on *(date)*.

or

2. That the petitioner has had care and possession of the child for a period or periods before the presentation of this petition which amounted to at least three years including the three months preceding the presentation of this petition on *(date)*.

or

2. That the petitioner intends to establish the following as showing cause why the petitioner should be granted custody of the child *(state briefly the grounds on which custody is sought or refer to the relevant paragraphs of the petition)*.

*[3. That if you wish to consent to the petitioner being granted custody of the child if the court approves, you should complete the form which is enclosed.

or

*3. That *(name of parent, tutor, curator or guardian)* has consented to the petitioner being granted custody of the child if the court approves.]

4. That if you wish to oppose this petition, and oppose the granting of custody of the child to the petitioner, you must lodge answers to the petition. If you propose to lodge answers, you are required to do so within days from the date of this notice. The period within which you are required to lodge answers begins to run 24 hours after the date of this notice.

[5. That the petition states that the child has been in the care and possession of the petitioner for a period or periods which amount to three years and accordingly, if that is correct, it is an offence to remove the child from the custody of the petitioner against the will of the petitioner except with the authority of the court or under the authority of any enactment or on the lawful arrest of the child].

Dated the day of 19

(Signed)
(Address)

[Solicitor for petitioner]

YOU ARE ADVISED TO CONSULT A SOLICITOR ABOUT THIS MATTER IMMEDIATELY.

Note
*Both alternative paragraphs 3 should be struck out if the petitioner is a parent or guardian.

NOTE
[1] Added by S.I. 1986 No. 515. Renumbered and amended by S.I. 1990 No. 705.

Rule 260D(2)(*b*) and (*c*) [1] FORM 69

Consent of a parent, tutor, curator or guardian to the granting of custody of a child to the petitioner

UNTO THE RIGHT HONOURABLE
THE LORDS OF COUNCIL AND SESSION

in

PETITION

of

A.B. *(address)*

for

Custody of the child E.F.

I, , of *(address)*, being a parent [*or* tutor, curator, guardian *as the case may be*] of the child E.F., hereby state—

(1) That I understand that if I consent to the granting of custody to the petitioner, the care, possession and control of the child may be granted by the court to the petitioner.

(2) That I consent to the petitioner being granted custody of the child, if the court approves.

(Signed by parent or guardian)

Dated the day of 19.

(Signed by witness)	*(Signed by witness)*
Full name of witness	Full name of witness ....
Designation	Designation ....
Address	Address ....
....	....

This form, if completed, should be returned to [the solicitor for the petitioner,] (*name and address*).

NOTE
[1] Added by S.I. 1986 No. 515. Renumbered and amended by S.I. 1990 No. 705. As amended by S.I. 1990 No. 2118.

Rule 260D(2)(*b*) and (*c*) [1] FORM 70

Notice to local authority of presentation of petition for custody of a child under section 49(1) of the Children Act 1975

IN THE COURT OF SESSION

in

PETITION

of

A.B. *(address)*

for

Custody of the child E.F.

To *(name and address)*

TAKE NOTICE

1. That the petitioner has presented a petition to the Court of Session for custody of the child E.F. A copy of the petition is attached.

2. That you are required under section 49(2) of the Children Act 1975 to submit to the court a report on all the circumstances of the child and on the proposed arrangements for the care and upbringing of the child.

3. That you are required to prepare the report without delay.

4. That on completion of your report you are required under Rule 260D(6) of the Rules of the Court of Session to lodge three copies of the report in process in the Petition Department, Court of Session, Parliament Square, Edinburgh [and to send a copy of the report to *(name and address)*, the curator *ad litem* to the child].

Dated the day of 19 .

(Signed)
(Address)

[Solicitor for Petitioner]

NOTE
[1] Added by S.I. 1986 No. 515. Renumbered by S.I. 1990 No. 705.

Rule 201K(2) [1] FORM 71

Notice to person with interest in property subject to an application for an order under section 24 of the Criminal Justice (Scotland) Act 1987

(Court Ref No.)

IN THE COURT OF SESSION

in

Petition [*or* Note]

of

[AB] *(address)*

for an order under sections 13 and 24
[*or* section 24] of the Criminal Justice
(Scotland) Act 1987

in respect of the estate of
[CD] *(address)*

To: *(insert name and address of person to whom notice is to be given)*

This Notice—
- (*a*) gives you warning that an application has been made to the Court of Session for an order which may affect your interest in property;
- (*b*) informs you that you have an opportunity to appear and make representations to the court before the application is determined.

TAKE NOTICE

1. That on (*insert date*) in the High Court of Justiciary at (*insert place*) a confiscation order was made under section 1 of the Criminal Justice (Scotland) Act 1987 in respect of [CD] (*insert address*).

2. That on (*insert date*) the administrator appointed under section 13(1)(a) of the said Act of 1987 on (*insert date*) was empowered to realise property belonging to the said [CD].

or

2. That on (*insert date*) the administrator was appointed under section 13(1)(b) of the said Act of 1987 on (*insert date*) to realise property belonging to the said [CD].

3. That application has been made by petition [*or* note] for an order under section 24 of the said Act of 1987 (*here set out briefly the nature of the order sought*). A copy of the petition [*or* note] is attached.

4. That you have the right to appear before the court (in person or by counsel or by a solicitor who has a right of audience in the Court of Session) and make such representations as you may have in respect of the order applied for. The court has fixed (*insert day and date fixed for hearing the application*) at 10 am within the Court of Session, Parliament Square, Edinburgh as the time when you should appear to do this.

5. That if you do not appear or are not represented by counsel or by a solicitor who has a right of audience in the Court of Session on the above date, the order applied for may be made in your absence.

(*signed*)
Solicitor for Petitioner [*or* Noter]

(*address*)

IF YOU ARE NOT SURE WHAT TO DO, YOU SHOULD CONSULT A SOLICITOR OR A CITIZENS ADVICE BUREAU IMMEDIATELY

NOTE

[1] Inserted by S.I. 1990 No. 705. As amended by S.I. 1991 No. 2483, with effect from 25th November 1991.

Rule 68I(1)

[1] FORM 72

FORM OF CAVEAT

CAVEAT

for

[A.B.] (*design**)

Should any application be made to the court for (*here specify the nature of the application(s) to which this caveat is to apply*) against .... [*or* by C.D. (*design*)], it is requested that intimation be made to the undernoted before any order is pronounced.

(*Signed*)
[A.B.] [or Solicitor for [A.B.]]

Caveator's telephone number

(only when caveat not lodged by a solicitor) ....

Solicitor

Name ....

Address ....

Tel No ....

Reference ....

Out of hours contacts

Name and telephone number 1..
2..

*State whether the caveat is lodged in an individual capacity, a specified representative capacity (e.g. as trustee of a named trust) or both such capacities.

*Where appropriate, state also the nature of the caveator's interest (e.g. shareholder; debenture holder).

NOTE
[1] Added by S.I. 1990 No. 2118.

[THE NEXT PAGE IS C 401]

- ORR v METCALF (1953) – pursuer failed to claim interest from date of accident but ct. held this was unnecessary

(B) Crave of Expenses – if get a decree in absence will only get award of exps. if you have asked for them
- if action is defended then will probably get them at end of day

(C) Seeking warrant to arrest on the dependence – a form of anticipatory diligence

(4) <u>CONDESCENDENCE</u> – state in numbered paras. the facts which form the ground of the action

Article 1 of condescendence – usually contains details of).
- ct. has to be satisfied it has). so must set out requirements as imposed by Rule 3 – parties can prorogate) ie can agree which ct. will hear the case
- 3(3) – IW will refer to proceedings pending against a party in another ct. – say there are no proceedings if there are none
- 3(4) – ground of) of ct. must be stated

- THEN – facts of P.'s case is set out.

<u>NOTE</u> – will only be allowed to lead evidence on facts stated in your condescendence (although amendments may be allowed during case). What need to aver depends on what your case is about

(5) PLEAS-IN-LAW – state in numbered sentences the basic proposition of law
- IW is to be signed by P. or his sol. after his pleas-in-law

GO TO D23

Other Acts of Sederunt

Accountant of Court

(C.A.S., G, III)

(S.R. & O. 1913 No. 638)

Form of Consignation Books

1. The books directed by section 4 of the Court of Session Consignation (Scotland) Act 1895, to be kept by the Accountant of Court shall be in the following form, viz.:—

REGISTER OF CONSIGNATIONS UNDER SECTION 4 OF THE COURT OF SESSION CONSIGNATIONS (SCOTLAND) ACT 1895

No.	Date of Consignation.	By whom and Cause in which Consignation made.	Office mark.	Bank.	Date of Lodging in Bank.	Sum consigned.	Deposits withdrawn from Bank.				Signature of Persons receiving Payment.	Date of Warrant.
							Principal.	Interest.	Total.	Date of Payment.		

The Entail Acts

[21st November 1922]

The Lords of Council and Session, in pursuance of the power vested in them by section 51 of the Entail Amendment Act 1848, and by section 2 of the Entail (Scotland) Act 1882, and considering that it is expedient to make further regulation as to the disentailing and acquisition in fee-simple of the price of entailed estates sold by virtue of the Act last mentioned, and consigned in bank, or invested, in terms of section 23 thereof, enact and declare as follows, viz.:—

That in any petition for authority to acquire in fee-simple the price of such entailed estates sold as aforesaid where such price has been consigned as aforesaid, or the investments representing said price, and made as aforesaid, or any part of said price or investments, it shall be sufficient without executing or recording any instrument of disentail to make summary application to the court in manner provided by section 26 of the first-mentioned Act for warrant and authority for payment to the petitioner of such price, or any part thereof, or for transfer to the petitioner of such investments, or any part thereof, all as belonging to himself in fee-simple.

Re-allocation of Deficiency of Stipend caused by Surrenders

(S.R. & O. 1925 No. 1060)

[15th July 1925]

Whereas it is provided by the Church of Scotland (Property and Endowments) Act 1925, section 41, that section 106 of the Court of Session (Scotland) Act 1868, (which relates to Acts of Sederunt), shall, for the purposes of Acts of Sederunt relating to the Court of Teinds, have effect as if references to that Act in the section included reference to the Church of Scotland (Property and Endowments) Act 1925, and whereas it is, *inter alia*, enacted by the said Court of Session (Scotland) Act 1868, section 106, that the Court of Session may from time to time make such regulations by Act of Sederunt for altering the course of proceeding thereinbefore prescribed in respect to the matters to which that Act relates, and whereas it is provided in paragraph 8 of the Sixth Schedule of the said Church of Scotland (Property and Endowments) Act 1925, that in certain cases the deficiency of stipend caused by a surrender shall be re-allocated among the heritors in the parish (if any) who have unexhausted teinds not yet allocated for stipend, the Lords of Council and Session hereby enact and declare that:—

1. Any claim under said paragraph 8 of the Sixth Schedule to have a deficiency of stipend re-allocated among those heritors in the parish (if any) who have unexhausted teinds not yet allocated for stipend shall be disposed of either in a depending process of locality relative to the said parish or in the proceedings for adjustment of the teind roll thereof.

2. The notification which the Clerk of Teinds is required by said paragraph 8 to make to the common agent of the heritors shall be given in such depending process or in the proceedings for adjustment of the teind roll, as the case may be.

3. In the application of paragraph 8 to the case of a depending process of locality it shall not be necessary for the Clerk of Teinds to issue any certificate specifying the amounts of stipend payable by the heritors whose teinds are affected by the re-allocation. Said re-allocation shall be made in the interim or final locality, as the case may be.

Procedure under Section 10 of the Church of Scotland (Property and Endowments) Act 1925, and the Fourth Schedule to the said Act, and for other Purposes

(S.R. & O. 1925 No. 1062)

[17th July 1925]

The Lords of Council and Session, in pursuance of the powers vested in them by the Church of Scotland (Property and Endowments) Act 1925, do hereby repeal Book H, Chapter ii, of the codifying Act of Sederunt without prejudice to any application for augmentation competently made before the passing of the said Act, or to anything following on such application or done therein, and enact and declare as follows:—

Sittings of Teind Court.—1. That the Court of the Commissioners for Teinds shall meet once a fortnight on Friday during the sitting of the Court of Session at such hours as shall be convenient.

AUGMENTATION, MODIFICATION, AND LOCALITY

Applications under section 10, the Church of Scotland (Property and Endowments) Act 1925

1. Applications under section 10 may be made by way of summons to the Court of Teinds. The pursuer shall state in the summons as accurately as he can the date when the last application for an augmentation was made, the number of chalders modified in stipend by the court, the value of same (including any allowance for furnishing communion elements), calculated in accordance with the provisions of the Fourth Schedule of the statute, and the surplus teinds which the pursuer believes to be available to allow of augmentation in terms of the statute, and may be in the form of Schedule A hereto annexed.

Citation and Notice

2.—(*a*) As soon as a summons of modification and locality is raised and signeted, it shall be competent to the pursuer to cite the titulars and tacksmen of the teinds, heritors, and liferenters, and all others having, or pretending to have, interest in the teinds of the parish, by a notice in writing affixed to the most patent door of the church, by the clerk of the kirk session or a police constable stating that the minister of the parish has raised a summons of modification and locality of his stipend which will be called in court on , being the day of next to come, not being less than six weeks after the date of the notice; and such clerk or constable shall return a certificate, subscribed by himself and two witnesses, that such notice has been affixed by him.

(*b*) The pursuer shall also cause notice to be inserted two several days in the *Scotsman* newspaper, and in a newspaper circulating in the county in which the parish referred to in such notice is situated, that he has raised a summons of modification and locality which will be called in court on , being the day of , not being less than six weeks from the date of the first advertisement.

(*c*) The mode of citation and the *induciae* above mentioned shall be deemed sufficient although one or more of the defenders shall be a pupil or minor out of the kingdom at the time such citation shall be given.

Citation of Crown

3. When it is necessary to call the Lord Advocate on behalf of His Majesty or of the Crown, or any public department, he shall be cited upon the *induciae* of six weeks.

Certificates and Executions of Citation

4. Such certificate by the clerk or constable, with the notices in the newspapers above mentioned or certificate by the pursuer's agents of the due appearance in the requisite newspapers of such notices, and execution of citation to the Lord Advocate, shall be held as sufficient citation to all parties.

Death of a Defender

5. When any of the defenders die during the dependence of the process, his heir may be called by a diligence in the manner and upon the *induciae* hitherto used; but such diligence may be executed either by a messenger-at-arms or a constable or under the provision of the Citation Amendment (Scotland) Act 1882.

Wakening of Process

6. When it is necessary to waken a process, it must be done by a summons or by a minute of wakening, in which all parties having interest must be called in the same manner, and on the same *induciae* as in the original process.

Note of Stipend and Rental to be Lodged

7. The pursuer of every process of modification and locality shall, as soon as the summons is signeted, lodge with the clerk of court a note, stating the amount of the stipend, distinguishing how much is paid in money, and how much in victual, and in what species of victual, and the measure by which it is paid; and also stating the amount of the communion elements. The pursuer must also, at the same time, produce a rental of the parish, distinguishing the rent of each heritor.

First Enrolment

8. As soon as the summons is called in court the pursuer may enrol it in the Teind Motion Roll of the Lord Ordinary; and all concerned will be allowed to see the summons and writings therewith produced in the clerk's hands for fourteen days.

Second Enrolment

9. After the elapse of the time for seeing, the pursuer may enrol the cause for a remit to the clerk to report whether there are any surplus teinds in the parish.

Third Enrolment

10. When the clerk's report is prepared, the pursuer may enrol the cause to consider same and thereupon—

(*a*) If the clerk has reported that there appear to be no surplus teinds in the parish the Lord Ordinary may either pronounce a decree accordingly, or ordain the pursuer to lodge a condescendence giving detailed particulars of the surplus teinds in the parish alleged in the summons to be available for an augmentation in terms of the statute.

(*b*) If it shall appear that there are surplus teinds in the parish the Lord Ordinary shall find in general terms accordingly, and, at the same time, shall ordain the heritors or their agents to meet for the purpose of naming a person to be suggested to the Lord Ordinary as common agent for conducting the locality, and a short notice of this interlocutor shall be inserted in the *Scotsman* newspaper, and in a newspaper circulating in the county in which the parish referred to in said notice is situated, the expense thereof to be paid by the common agent out of the general fund (unless in any case the appointment of a common agent shall be dispensed with by the Lord Ordinary); and shall further ordain the heritors to produce their rights to their teinds, if they any have, in the hands of the clerk within a time to be specified in the interlocutor, not being less than three months from the date thereof; with certification that after the elapse of that time, a remit shall be made to the clerk to prepare a scheme of locality either according to the rental lodged by the pursuer in case no rights are produced, or according to the State of Teinds lodged by the common agent (or by the heritors, as the case may be) as to the rights and interests which are produced by the heritors.

(*c*) The Lord Ordinary may pronounce such other or further order as shall seem to him to be necessary or expedient.

Agent for Party may not be Common Agent

11. No person who is agent for the minister or titular, or for any heritor in the parish, shall be appointed common agent.

Common Agent to prepare State of Teinds

12. The common agent, after his nomination has been confirmed by the court (or the heritors, as the case may be), on the expiry of the time specified within which the heritors shall produce their rights to their teinds, shall prepare and lodge a State of Teinds.

Preparation of Locality before the Lord Ordinary

13. After the elapse of the time for the heritors producing their rights to their teinds, a remit shall be made to the clerk to prepare a scheme of locality, either according to the rental lodged by the pursuer, in case no rights are produced, or according to the State of Teinds lodged by the common agent (or by the heritors, as the case may be), in terms of section 10 of the statute; and this scheme so prepared shall immediately be approved by the Lord Ordinary as an interim scheme, according to which the minister's stipend shall be paid, until a final·locality shall be settled, and the minister furnished by the common agent (or by the heritors, as the case may be) with an extracted decree, at the expense of the heritors, and for which he is entitled to take credit in his account.

Preparation and Approval of Rectified Locality

14. If it shall appear, at any period or periods, that, under an interim locality, prepared and approved of in terms of the foresaid provisions, the minister is unable through surrender of teinds or other causes affecting its efficacy to operate payment to any considerable extent of the stipend awarded to him, then and in that case it shall be competent to the Lord Ordinary, on the motion of the minister or other party interested, to appoint a new interim scheme of locality to be prepared, and also a state of arrears remaining due from the causes before specified, to be made up; and when the said rectified locality and state of arrears shall be approved of, the Lord Ordinary shall give decreet for the arrears, and the rectified locality shall subsist as a new interim rule of payment of the stipend then current, and until it be set aside by any other rule which may afterwards be granted, on cause shewn.

Heritors' Motion for Rectified Locality

15. Under the reservation after provided as to expenses, it shall be competent to any heritor or heritors, the state of whose teinds has been materially altered by decreets of valuation, or by other circumstances, which may have occurred subsequent to the approval of an interim scheme, to apply for a rectification of the locality, giving effect to the new or corrected State of Teinds; and when the rectified locality shall be approved of by the Lord Ordinary as a new rule of payment, he shall, at the same time, appoint a state of arrears to be prepared, if the state of the process and the interests of the parties render this necessary, with power to give him decreet for the same.

New Interim Scheme on Account of Surrenders

16. Where any new interim scheme or schemes shall be rendered necessary by surrenders, or by production of rights made by heritors, or by any other unexpected emergency occurring subsequent to the previous interim scheme or schemes, it shall be competent to the Lord Ordinary to lay the expense of the new interim scheme and state of arrears, or such part thereof as may appear proper, on the party whose surrender, or productions or proceedings as aforesaid, shall make such new interim scheme necessary, unless such heritor or heritors shall be able to instruct a reasonable cause to the contrary to the satisfaction of the Lord Ordinary; in which last case the expense shall be defrayed by the common agent (if any).

Preparation of Final Locality

17. That as soon as proceedings with regard to the interim locality are concluded, a scheme of a final locality shall be forthwith prepared, and the common agent shall distribute copies of this state and scheme among the agents for the heritors, as soon as may be after such state and scheme are prepared; and no new scheme shall thereafter be received, except upon payment of such expenses as may be occasioned by such new production, to be modified by the Lord Ordinary.

Disposal of Objections to Final Locality

18. After the foresaid state and scheme shall have been distributed among the heritors, the Lord Ordinary shall ordain objections thereto to be given in by any of the heritors who think themselves aggrieved by the proposed mode of allocation; and the Lord Ordinary may either hear parties *viva voce* upon such objections, and the answers that may be made thereto at the bar; or he may, if he shall see cause, allow all concerned to give in written answers to such objections within such time as he shall think proper to appoint, and shall thereafter proceed, in so far as regards any application for prorogating the time for giving in papers, in the manner directed by section 12 of the Court of Session Act 1825.

Review of Lord Ordinary's Judgment

19. When the Lord Ordinary has pronounced a judgment, other than a finding or decree as to surplus teinds, it may be reviewed by the Division to which the cause belongs by giving in a note, which must be lodged within twenty-one days after the date of the judgment complained of, and the procedure on that note shall be the same as in reviewing judgments of a Lord Ordinary in the Court of Session.

Form of Extract of Decreets of Locality and Warrants of Charge

20. Decreets of locality and warrants of charge shall be issued, in the form and to the effect of the schedules B and C respectively hereto annexed, as nearly as the circumstances of each case may admit of: Reserving always right to parties so advised, to take full extracts, according to the ancient form, when they require the same, in terms of the statute; Provided also, that the dues of extract in whatever form the same may be given out, shall be charged in precise conformity with the statute.

SCHEDULES REFERRED TO

SCHEDULE A

[1] *Summons of Modification and Locality*

GEORGE THE FIFTH, ETC.—Whereas it is humbly meant and shewn to us by our lovite(s), The Reverend (*name*), the present Minister of the Parish of in the Presbytery of and County of ,—*Pursuer*; That the last application for an augmentation of the stipend of this parish was made on (*being the date of the signeting of the summons*): That the augmentation then granted was chalders in addition to the then old stipend and allowance for furnishing the communion elements, making the amount of the present stipend, as last modified by the Court of Teinds, chalders, with £ for furnishing the communion elements (*or as the case may be*), which modified stipend was found, in the Decree of Locality following upon said modification to be equivalent to (B F P L) of meal, (B F P L) of barley and £ of money sterling, inclusive of the allowance for communion elements (*state precisely the totals of the different kinds of victual and of the money*): That the value thereof, converted into money according to the provisions of the Fourth Schedule of the [Church of Scotland (Property and Endowments) Act 1925] [2] is £ : That after deducting the said sum of £ there are, according to the State of Teinds in the last locality process (*or otherwise as the pursuer may specifically condescend*), surplus teinds in the parish amounting to £ or thereby available for an augmentation of the pursuer's stipend: That the following are the whole parties whom it is necessary to call as defenders in the present action, *videlicet*:—(*Here insert the names and designations of the defenders, specifying the characters in which they are called*): THEREFORE the Lords of our Council and Session, Commissioners appointed for Plantation of Kirks and Valuation of Teinds, per the Lord Ordinary in Teind causes, OUGHT and SHOULD find that there are surplus teinds in the parish available for an augmentation of the pursuer's stipend in accordance with the provisions of section 10 of the last-mentioned Act, and OUGHT and SHOULD modify, settle and appoint a constant local stipend, with the allowance for furnishing communion elements, to the pursuer and his successors in right of the emoluments of the cure of said parish, and establish and proportion a locality of the same; and DECERN for payment thereof to the pursuer and his successors in right of the emoluments of the cure of said parish against the heritors, titulars, tacksmen, and others, intromitters with the rents and teinds of the said parish, and that at the terms following, *videlicet*:—the money stipend and allowance for furnishing the communion elements at Whitsunday and Martinmas yearly, by equal portions, and the value of the victual money according to the highest fiars' prices of the same in the county of between Yule and Candlemas yearly, after the separation of the crop from the ground, or as soon thereafter as the said fiars' prices shall have been struck, beginning the first payment thereof at Whitsunday (*next*) for one-half of the said money, and the other half at Martinmas thereafter, and the value of the victual betwixt Yule and Candlemas (*next*) or as soon thereafter as the said fiars' prices shall have been struck for crop and year ; and so forth, yearly and termly thereafter, in all time coming; and for the greater expedition the pursuer is willing to refer the verity of the rental of the parish herewith produced to the heritors' oaths *simpliciter*, instead of all further probation; and in case of any of the said defenders appearing and occasioning unnecessary expense to the pursuer in the process to follow hereon, such defender or defenders OUGHT and SHOULD be DECERNED and ORDAINED, by decree foresaid, to make payment to the pursuer of the sum of £100 sterling, or of such other sum as our said Lords shall modify, as the expenses of the process to follow hereon, besides the dues of extract, conform to the [2] [Acts of Parliament thereanent] of Parliament, writs libelled, laws, and daily practice of Scotland, used and observed in the like cases, as is alleged.—OUR WILL IS HEREFORE, and we charge you that on sight hereof ye pass, and in our name and authority lawfully SUMMON, WARN, AND CHARGE the defenders, personally or at their respective dwelling-places, if within Scotland upon six days' warning, and if in Orkney or Shetland upon forty days' warning, and if furth of Scotland by delivering a copy hereof at the office of the Keeper of the Record of Edictal Citations at Edinburgh, in terms of the statute and Act of Sederunt thereanent, and that upon sixty days' warning; and the tutors and curators or other guardians of such of the defenders as are minors, if they any have, for their interest, also at the said office of the Keeper of the Record of Edictal Citations at Edinburgh, on the same *induciæ* as the minors themselves, or by the notices and in the forms prescribed by the Statute 15 & 16 Geo. 5, c. 33, and relative Acts of Sederunt, and that upon six weeks' warning; and all others having or pretending to have interest in the said matter, to compear before our said Lords Commissioners for Plantation of Kirks and

Valuation of Teinds, at Edinburgh, or where they may then happen to be for the time, the day of Nineteen hundred and in the hour of cause, with continuation of days, to answer at the instance of the pursuer in the matter libelled: That is to say, the defenders to hear and see the premises verified and proven, and decree and sentence pronounced, conform to the conclusions above written, in all points, or else to allege a reasonable cause in the contrary, with certification as effeirs.—According to Justice, as ye shall answer to us thereupon: Which to do we commit to you and each of you full power by these our letters, delivering them by you duly executed and endorsed again to the bearer.—Given under our signet at Edinburgh, the day of in the year of our reign, 19 .

(*To be signed by the Clerk of Teinds.*)

NOTES

[1] N.B. When the Church of Scotland General Trustees are the Pursuers or the Pursuer's stipend has been standardised, this form may be applied *mutatis mutandis*.

[2] Substituted by S.I. 1925 No. 1063.

SCHEDULE B

[1] *Form of Extract Decreet of Modification and Locality*

At Edinburgh, the day of Sitting in judgment, the Lords of Council and Session, Commissioners appointed for Plantation of Kirks and Valuation of Teinds, in the process of Modification and Locality raised and pursued at the instance of the Reverend Minister of the Gospel, of the Parish of against the Officers of State, as representing His Majesty, for the interest of the Crown, and also against the whole Heritors, Titulars, Tacksmen, Liferenters, and others, intromitters with the Rents and Teinds of the said Parish, modified, decerned, and ordained, and hereby modify, decern, and ordain the constant Stipend and Provision of the Kirk and Parish of to have been for crop, and year Nineteen hundred and yearly, since and in time coming, such a quantity of Victual, half Meal, half Barley, in Imperial Weight and Measure, as shall be equal to Chalders of the late Standard Weight and Measure of Scotland, payable in Money, according to the highest fiars' prices of the County annually, with chalders of augmentation payable in money according to the Standard Value in terms of the Church of Scotland (Property and Endowments) Act 1925 (or with the sum of £ sterling of augmentation in terms of the Church of Scotland (Property and Endowments) Act 1925, being the amount of the surplus teinds in the parish available to meet *pro tanto* the statutory augmentation of chalders), and that for Stipend, with Sterling for furnishing the Communion Elements, payable the money stipend and allowance for communion elements at Whitsunday and Martinmas yearly by equal portions, and the victual betwixt Yule and Candlemas yearly after the separation of the crop from the ground or as soon thereafter as the Fiars' Prices of the County of shall be struck. Which Modified Stipend, and Modification for furnishing the Communion Elements, the said Lords decern and ordain to be yearly paid to the said Kirk and Parish, by the Titulars and Tacksmen of the Teinds, Heritors, and Possessors of the Lands and others, intromitters with the Rents and Teinds of the said Parish, out of the first and readiest of the Teinds, parsonage and vicarage, of the same, conform to the Division and Locality following, viz. (*the Locality to be taken in here in figures and then say*), beginning the first term's payment thereof, for the said crop and year Nineteen hundred and , as at the term of Whitsunday, Nineteen hundred and as regards the money stipend and communion elements, and as regards the victual stipend betwixt Yule and Candlemas, after the separation of the crop from the ground, or as soon thereafter as the fiars' prices of the County are struck; and so forth yearly and termly in all time coming. The said Lords, as Commissioners foresaid, also decerned and ordained, and hereby decern and ordain, the whole Heritors of the said Parish, to make payment to Common Agent in the process of their respective shares of the sum of £ sterling, being the amount of the account of the taxed expenses incurred by him in obtaining the Decreet of Locality; As also of their respective shares of the sum of £ sterling, being the expense of Extracting this Decreet and proportioning the Expenses among the Heritors, including therein Two pounds sterling, of fee-fund dues; making in whole £ sterling, and that in proportion to their several Teind Rentals in Process, and Scheme of Division made up and certified by the Clerk as relative hereto. And the said Lords of Council and Session, Commissioners foresaid, Grant Warrant to Messengers-at-Arms, in His Majesty's Name and Authority, to charge the Titulars and Tacksmen of the Teinds, Heritors, Feuars, Farmorers, Wadsetters, Liferenters, Factors, Chamberlains, Tenants, Occupiers, and Possessors of the Lands and others, intromitters with the Rents and Teinds of the said Parish of Defenders, personally, or at their respective dwelling-places, if within Scotland, and if furth thereof, by delivery of a Copy of Charge at the Office of the Keeper of Edictal Citations at Edinburgh, to make payment of the foresaid Stipend and Communion Element Money, each of them for his or her own part and portion thereof, conform to the Division and Locality above set down, and that at the terms of payment above expressed,—in terms and to the effect contained in the Decreet of Locality and Extract above written, and here held as repeated *brevitatis causa*: as also of their respective proportions of the foresaid sums of Expenses and Dues of Extract, conform to the Scheme of Division above referred to; and that to the Reverend , Pursuer, and his successors in right of the emoluments of the cure of said parish, and to the said Common Agent, respectively, within ten days if within Scotland, and if furth thereof, within sixty days after they are respectively charged to that effect, under the pain of Poinding, the terms of payment of said Stipend being always first come and bygone; And also Grant Warrant to Arrest the foresaid Defenders' readiest Goods, Gear, Debts, and sums of Money, in payment and satisfaction of their respective portions of Stipend and Communion Element Money, and also of their respective proportions of the Expenses foresaid, and Dues of Extract; And if the said Defenders fail to obey the said Charge, then after the said Charge is elapsed, to Poind their readiest Goods, Gear, Debts, and other effects; and if needful for effecting the said Poinding Grant Warrant to Open all shut and lockfast places, in form as effeirs.

NOTE

[1] N.B. When the Church of Scotland General Trustees are the Pursuers or the Pursuer's stipend has been standardised, this form may be applied *mutatis mutandis*.

SCHEDULE C

Form of Warrant of Charge in terms of the Debtors (Scotland) Act 1838, ss. 1 and 8

And the said Lords, as Commissioners foresaid, Grant Warrant to Messengers-at-Arms, in His Majesty's name and authority, to charge the foresaid titulars and tacksmen of Teinds, Heritors, Feuars, Farmorers, Wadsetters, Liferenters, Factors, Chamberlains, Tenants, Occupiers, and Possessors of the Lands and other intromitters with the Rents and Teinds of the said Parish of personally, or at their respective dwelling-places, if within Scotland, or if furth thereof, by delivering a Copy of Charge at the Office of the Keeper of the Record of Edictal Citations at Edinburgh, to make payment of the foresaid Stipend and Communion Element Money, each of them for his or her own part and portion thereof, conform to the Division and Locality inserted in the great decerniture of the foregoing Decreet, and that at the terms of payment therein the victual betwixt Yule and Candlemas yearly after the separation of the crop above written, and here referred to, and held as repeated *brevitatis causa*; and that to the Reverend now Minister of the Parish of within ten days, if within Scotland, and if furth thereof, within sixty days after they are respectively charged to that effect, under pain of Poinding, the terms of payment being always first come and bygone; And also Grant Warrant to Arrest the foresaid Defenders' readiest Goods, Gear, Debts, and sums of Money, in payment and satisfaction of their respective portions of the aforesaid Stipend and Communion Element Money; and if the said Defenders fail to obey the said Charge, then after the said Charge is elapsed, to Poind their readiest Goods, Gear, and other effects; and if needful for effecting the said Poinding, Grant Warrant to Open all shut and lockfast places, in form as effeirs.—Given at Edinburgh, the day of One thousand nine hundred and

Procedure relating to the Preparation, Issuing, Adjustment, and Custody of Teind Rolls under the Church of Scotland (Property and Endowments) Act 1925

(S.R. & O. 1925 No. 1063)

[28th October 1925]

The Lords of Council and Session, in pursuance of the powers vested in them by the Church of Scotland (Property and Endowments) Act 1925, enact and declare as follows, viz.:—

1. A teind roll of a parish shall be prepared on application to the Court of Teinds by Petition at the instance of the Church of Scotland General Trustees.

2. The Petition may be presented at any time after the date of standardisation of the stipend of the parish provided that:

(*a*) a final decree of locality following upon any application for an augmentation of stipend under section 10 of the foresaid Act has been pronounced; or

(*b*) the time within which proceedings under section 10 (2) of the foresaid Act may be taken has expired; or

(*c*) the General Trustees state in the Petition that it is not intended to make any application under section 10 of the foresaid Act.

3. The Petition may be in the form of the Schedule hereto annexed.

4. All petitions shall be enrolled in the Teind Motion Roll of the Lord Ordinary for an order for intimation. It shall be sufficient intimation to all parties concerned that a copy of the Petition be affixed to the most patent door of the church of the parish to which the application applies on two successive Sundays before the diet of public worship on each of these days, and a notice intimating the Petition be inserted in the *Scotsman* newspaper, and in a newspaper circulating in the county in which the parish referred to in said notice is situated, once a week for two successive weeks in each of such newspapers, provided always that the Lord Ordinary may make such other or further order regarding intimation as he may consider to be necessary or expedient in the circumstances of the case.

5. After the period of intimation ordered by the Lord Ordinary has expired, the Petition may be enrolled for an order as follows, viz.:—

(*a*) *If a state of teinds has been lodged with the Clerk of Teinds by the titulars or heritors*, for a remit to the Clerk to prepare a teind roll.

(*b*) *If no state of teinds has been so lodged* (and unless an application under paragraph 6 hereof shall be granted), for an order on the heritors to meet and choose a common agent, and to lodge a state of teinds within a time to be specified in such order, and upon such state of teinds being lodged for a remit to the Clerk to prepare a teind roll.

6. On enrolment under paragraph 5 hereof, the petitioners or any heritor or titular may apply by motion to dispense with the appointment of a common agent and also (if the circumstances justify that course) with the preparation and lodging by the heritors of a state of teinds.

7. In any case in which application is made to dispense with the appointment by the heritors of a common agent the Lord Ordinary may by interlocutor make such orders with regard to the conduct of the process as he may think just and expedient, and may require as a condition of granting the application that the party applying shall make such provision as to the court may appear just and sufficient for the payment of the fee fund dues, including the expense of preparing the teind roll.

8. In any case in which the preparation and lodging of a state of teinds by the heritors is dispensed with, the Lord Ordinary shall remit to the Clerk of Teinds to prepare and lodge a teind roll according to the state of the teinds as disclosed in the last locality process.

9. The procedure for the appointment of a common agent shall be the same *mutatis mutandis* as for the appointment of a common agent in a process of locality.

10. After the teind roll has been prepared the clerk shall print and report the same to the Lord Ordinary, who shall take the roll into consideration and shall make such order as he shall think fit with respect to intimation of the roll by advertisement or on the church door or otherwise (including where necessary an order on the heritors for the appointment of a common agent in the event of such appointment having been formerly dispensed with).

11. The teind roll shall be retained in the hands of the clerk subject to inspection by any party interested, and shall not be lent or given out to any person whatsoever. But after the Lord Ordinary has made an order for intimation printed copies may be supplied to the common agent for distribution among the heritors, and where there is no common agent to any heritor who applies.

12. The Lord Ordinary shall either hear parties *viva voce* upon such objections as may be lodged within eighteen months after the order for intimation of the teind roll, and upon any answers that may be made thereto at the Bar; or he may, if he shall see cause, allow all concerned to give in written answers to such objections within such time as he shall think proper to appoint, and shall thereafter proceed, in so far as regards any application for prorogating the time for giving in papers, in the manner directed by section 12 of the Court of Session Act 1825.

13. After (*a*) the objections (if any) to the teind roll have been disposed of by the Court, and (*b*) any extrajudicial surrenders of teind made before the passing of the said Church of Scotland (Property and Endowments) Act 1925, have been intimated, and evidence thereof produced, to the clerk (which shall be done before the expiry of six months after the date of the order for intimation of the teind roll), and (*c*) any surrenders of teind made in accordance with the provisions of the Sixth Schedule of the said Church of Scotland (Property and Endowments) Act 1925, have become effectual, and (*d*) intimation has been received by the clerk claiming that the deficiency of stipend caused by such surrenders shall be reallocated among the heritors in the parish who have unexhausted teinds not yet allocated for stipend, and (*e*) objections, if any, of any heritor to such reallocation have been disposed of by the Lord Ordinary, a remit shall be made to the clerk to amend the roll, and if, in virtue of the amendments, the Lord Ordinary shall deem it necessary, he may order the clerk to reprint the roll as amended before declaring the roll to be final.

14. After the Lord Ordinary has by interlocutor declared the roll to be final he shall, where a common agent has been appointed, direct that an account of the expenses incurred to the common agent be lodged in process, and when lodged remit the same to the auditor to tax and report; and after approving of such report, shall grant decree against the heritors in favour of the common agent for the taxed amount of the expenses as approved, and for the expense of extracting the decree and proportioning the same in accordance with a scheme of apportionment thereof prepared by the clerk in terms of the provisions of section 11 (3) of the said Church of Scotland (Property and Endowments) Act 1925.

15. Except in the cases specified in the said Church of Scotland (Property and Endowments) Act 1925, in which the finding or judgment of the Lord Ordinary is declared to be final, any judgment of the Lord Ordinary may be submitted to review by the Division to which the cause belongs by giving in a Note, which must be lodged within twenty-one days after the date of the finding or judgment complained of, and the procedure on that Note shall be the same as in reviewing judgments of a Lord Ordinary in the Court of Session.

16. The clerk shall, on receiving notice of any change of ownership of the lands contained in one entry in the teind roll in respect of which lands a standard charge has been constituted in accordance with the provisions of section 12 of the said Church of Scotland (Property and Endowments) Act 1925, insert in the teind roll the name of the new proprietor as stated in said notice; such notice may be in the form of Schedule A annexed to the Conveyancing (Scotland) Act 1874, provided always that notice of change of ownership of part only of an entry in the teind roll shall be given effect to by the clerk only where the provisions of section 13 of the said Church of Scotland (Property and Endowments) Act 1925, are complied with in said notice.

17. Where a standard charge has been constituted on the lands of any heritor in terms of the provisions of section 12 of the said Church of Scotland (Property and Endowments) Act 1925, and the same has been redeemed in accordance with the provisions of that section, or where a stipend exigible from the teinds of any lands of a heritor has been redeemed in accordance with the provisions of section 14 of the last-mentioned Act, the clerk shall, on receiving notice in writing of such redemption signed on behalf of the General Trustees and the owner of the lands the standard charge on which has been redeemed, or of the lands the stipend in respect whereof has been redeemed, make an entry to that effect in the teind roll.

18. An excerpt from a teind roll of any entry or entries therein certified by the Clerk of Teinds shall be received in any Court of Law as sufficient evidence of such entry or entries.

SCHEDULE REFERRED TO

UNTO THE RIGHT HONOURABLE

THE LORDS OF COUNCIL AND SESSION,
COMMISSIONERS FOR THE PLANTATION OF KIRKS AND VALUATION OF TEINDS,

THE
PETITION
OF
THE CHURCH OF SCOTLAND GENERAL TRUSTEES, incorporated by the Church of Scotland (General Trustees) Order 1921;

Humbly sheweth,—

THAT by the Church of Scotland (Property and Endowments) Act 1925, section 11, it is provided, *inter alia*, that " There shall be prepared by the Clerk of Teinds for every parish in Scotland a Teind Roll specifying in sterling money (*a*) the total teind of that parish; and (*b*) the amount of that total applicable to the lands of each heritor; and (*c*) the value of the whole stipend payable to the minister, so far as payable out of teinds, including vicarage teinds payable as stipend and surrendered teinds so payable; and (*d*) the proportion of that value payable by each heritor in the parish."

That the stipend[s] of the Minister[s] of the [United] Parish[es] of [ ] in the Presbytery of [ ] and County [or Counties] of [ ], became standardised within the meaning of the foresaid Act as at the term of Martinmas 19[ ], in consequence of the [death, resignation or translation of the Minister, or intimation in terms of section 4 of the said Act by the Minister to the petitioners of his election, or notification in terms of section 5 of said Act by the petitioners to the Minister and other parties mentioned in the said section—*the particulars and dates should be shortly stated*].

That the final augmentation in terms of section 10 of said Act has been localled upon the heritors conform to Decree of Locality made final on [*give date*]: *or* That no proceedings are to be taken to obtain an augmentation under section 10 of said Act: *or* That the Lord Ordinary has pronounced a finding that there is no surplus teind in the parish available for an augmentation under section 10 of said Act: *or* That the time within which proceedings under section 10 (2) of the foresaid Act may be taken has expired.

That in these circumstances the preparation of a Teind Roll of the Parish[es] of [ ] should now be proceeded with in terms of section 11 of the said Act.

May it therefore please your Lordships to appoint this Petition to be intimated to all parties concerned by affixing a copy thereof to the most patent door of the church of the said parish[es] on two successive Sundays before the diet of public worship on each of these days, and by inserting a short notice thereof in the Scotsman newspaper and in [another newspaper circulating in the county in which the said parish[es] [are] situated] *once a week for two successive weeks, or in such other or further form and manner as to your Lordships may seem proper; to appoint the heritors of the said parish[es] of to meet and choose a common agent; to appoint said heritors to lodge a State of Teinds; to remit to the Clerk of Teinds to prepare a Teind Roll in terms of said Act 15 & 16 Geo. 5, c. 33, and upon the Teind Roll being reported to your Lordships, and after considering the same with any Objections and any Answers thereto and along with any Surrenders of Teinds that may be duly made, to adjust and complete said Roll, and to declare the same to be a Final Teind Roll.*

According to Justice, etc.

Intimation of Decrees registered in the Books of Council and Session pursuant to the Indian and Colonial Divorce Jurisdiction Act 1926

(S.R. & O. 1927 No. 1054)

[1st November 1927]

The Lords of Council and Session, considering that by section 1, subsection 3 of the Indian and Colonial Divorce Act, it is enacted that:—

> On production of a Certificate purporting to be signed by the proper officer of the High Court in India by which Decree of Divorce is made, the decree shall, if the parties to the marriage are domiciled in Scotland, be registered in the Books of Council and Session and upon such registration shall as from the date of registration, have the same force and effect, and proceedings may be taken thereunder as if it had been a decree made by the Court of Session on that date on which it was made by the High Court in India

do hereby enact and declare that it shall be the duty of the Keeper of the Register of Deeds in the Books of Council and Session on the registration of any such Decree to supply an Extract of same to the Registrar General and that without fee.

Amending the Four Acts of Sederunt dated 10th July 1811, and the Act of Sederunt dated 18th February 1916, anent the Various Public Registers of Scotland, and making Further Regulations thereanent

(S.R. & O. 1934 No. 97)

[2nd February 1934]

The Lords of Council and Session considering that by four Acts of Sederunt of date 10th July 1811, it was *inter alia* provided that the various Minute Books and Registers therein referred to should be written in books issued and marked to the Keepers of the said Minute Books and Registers by the Lord Clerk Register or the Deputy Clerk Register, and that by the Lord Clerk Register (Scotland) Act 1879, s.6, it was provided that the Deputy Clerk Register should have the whole rights, authorities, privileges and duties in regard to the Public Registers, Records or Rolls of Scotland theretofore vested in the Lord Clerk Register. And considering that the foresaid Acts of Sederunt contained certain regulations and directions regarding the quality of paper, the number of lines and the numbers of words to be written on each page of the books to be issued and marked as aforesaid and that by an Act of Sederunt of date 18th February 1916 it was *inter alia* provided that the Deputy Clerk Register should have power to vary these regulations and directions from time to time as might be necessary, and that after the date of the passing of that Act the regulations and directions to be observed by the Keepers of the various Registers should be such as might from time to time be set forth on the title page of the volumes to be marked and issued to them as aforesaid. And considering that it was further declared that if at any time thereafter it should be necessary, in order to facilitate new methods of framing all or any of the various Registers, the books to be marked and issued as aforesaid might be so marked and issued in an unbound form or otherwise as the Deputy Clerk Register might direct. And further considering that by the Reorganisation of Offices (Scotland) Act 1928, s. 5 (1), it was provided that the whole powers and duties of the Deputy Clerk Register should be transferred to and vested in the Keeper of the Registers and Records of Scotland.

And now seeing that it is expedient that a photographic process of copying writs should be substituted for typing in the Department of the Registers and Records of Scotland and that this process does not permit of the issuing of marked volumes in conformity with the practice enjoined by the foresaid Acts of Sederunt, the Lords hereby enact and enjoin that after the date of the passing of this Act a photographic process of copying writs may be introduced in substitution for typing under such conditions and subject to such regulations and at such time or times as the Keeper of the Registers and Records may deem expedient, and that thereafter it shall not be necessary to issue marked volumes in conformity with the said practice, except to the Town Clerks of those Burghs in which the Burgh Registers have not been discontinued, and to Sheriff Clerks for the Register of Deeds in the Sheriff Court Books.

And the Lords do further declare that if, after the introduction of a photographic process, any writ presented for registration be found unsuitable for the process, owing to its illegibility or inconvenient size or for any other reason, the Keeper of the Registers and Records may cause such writ to be typed in the manner heretofore in use, and the copy of the writ so typed shall form part of the Record in the same way as a copy of a writ reproduced by the photographic process.

And the Lords do further enact that the photographic record of the various Registers, along with the record of any writ or writs typed as aforesaid, shall be made up into bound volumes of such a size and form as may be found convenient, which volumes shall be authenticated on the first and last pages thereof by the signature of the Keeper of the Registers and Records, and shall be open to the lieges at such times and under such conditions as are at present applicable to the Public Records as hitherto framed and preserved in H.M. General Register House, or at such other times and under such other conditions as may be prescribed.

And the Lords further enact that if at any time difficulties emerge which, in the opinion of the Keeper of the Registers and Records, might constitute a danger to the safety or accessibility of the Public Registers, it shall be the duty of the said Keeper to report the same to the Lords of Council and Session.

[THE NEXT PAGE IS C 418]

Edictal Citations, Commissary Petitions and Petitions of Service

(S.I. 1971 No. 1165)

[16th July 1971]

The Lords of Council and Session, by virtue of the powers conferred upon them by sections 16 and 34 of the Administration of Justice (Scotland) Act 1933 and section 22 of the Succession (Scotland) Act 1964 and of all other powers competent to them in that behalf, do hereby enact and declare as follows:—

1.—(1) The provisions of section 51 and 52 of the Court of Session Act 1825, in so far as they prescribe procedure for and in connection with edictal citations, charges, publications, citations and services sometime made at the Market Cross of Edinburgh, pier and shore of Leith, as against persons furth of Scotland, shall no longer apply.

(2) All such edictal citations, charges, publications, citations and services shall be done and performed by service of a copy thereof at the office of the Keeper of Edictal Citations of the Court of Session, in the manner now practised in cases of citation or charge at the dwelling house of a party not personally apprehended; and the Keeper of Edictal Citations or his clerk shall record on each such copy delivered to him the date of receipt by his office.

(3) Each such copy as is referred to in the last foregoing sub-paragraph shall be preserved for three years from the date of the receipt recorded thereon, and it shall at all times be available for inspection at the office of the Keeper of Edictal Citations during that period.

2.—(1) The provisions of section 4 of the Confirmation and Probate Act 1858, in so far as they prescribe procedure in petitions for the appointment of an executor, shall no longer apply.

(2) Every petition for the appointment of an executor shall be intimated by the Sheriff Clerk affixing a full copy of the petition on the door of the Sheriff Court house or in some conspicuous place of the Court or of the office of the Sheriff Clerk, in such manner as the Sheriff shall direct.

3.—(1) The provisions of section 30 of the Titles to Land Consolidation (Scotland) Act 1868, as saved by section 37 of the Succession (Scotland) Act 1964, in so far as they prescribe procedure in petitions of service, shall no longer apply.

(2) A petition presented to the Sheriff of Chancery for general service, where the domicile of the deceased is known and was within Scotland, shall not proceed until the Sheriff Clerk of Chancery shall have received official notice from the sheriff clerk of the county of the domicile of the person deceased that publication has been made in such county, and such publication shall be effected by affixing an abstract of the petition on the door of the sheriff court house or in some conspicuous place of the court or of the office of the sheriff clerk, in such manner as the sheriff of the county shall direct.

(3) A petition presented to the Sheriff of Chancery for Special Service or a petition presented to the Sheriff of Chancery under section 10 of the Conveyancing (Scotland) Act 1874, shall not proceed until the Sheriff Clerk of Chancery shall have received official notice (i) from the sheriff clerk of the county or of each of the counties in which the lands are situated that publication has been made in such county or in each such county as the case may be, and either (ii) where the domicile of the deceased is known and was within Scotland, from the sheriff clerk of the county of the domicile of the person deceased that publication has been made in such county, or (iii) where the domicile of the deceased is furth of Scotland or is unknown, from the sheriff clerk of the Lothians and Peebles at Edinburgh that publication has been made at Edinburgh; and each such publication shall be effected by affixing an abstract of the petition on the door of the sheriff court house or in some conspicuous place of the court or of the office of the sheriff clerk, in such manner as the sheriff of the county or counties shall direct.

(4) A petition presented to the Sheriff of Chancery for General Service, where the domicile of the deceased was furth of Scotland or where such domicile is unknown and the person deceased died more than ten years prior to the presentation of the petition, shall not proceed until the Sheriff Clerk of Chancery shall have received official notice from the Sheriff Clerk of the Lothians and Peebles at Edinburgh that publication has been made at Edinburgh, and such publication shall be effected by affixing an abstract of the petition on the door of the sheriff court house or in some conspicuous place of the court or of the office of the sheriff clerk, in such manner as the Sheriff of the Lothians and Peebles shall direct.

(5) In each such petition as aforesaid, no further publication shall be necessary.

4. This Act of Sederunt may be cited as the Act of Sederunt (Edictal Citations, Commissary Petitions and Petitions of Service) 1971, and shall come into operation on 16th August 1971.

Expenses of Party Litigants

(S.I. 1976 No. 1606)

[28th September 1976]

The Lords of Council and Session, under and by virtue of the powers conferred upon them by section 16 of the Administration of Justice (Scotland) Act 1933, section 32 of the Sheriff Courts (Scotland) Act 1971, and section 1 of the Litigants in Person (Costs and Expenses) Act 1975, and of all other powers competent to them in that behalf, do hereby enact and declare:—

Citation, commencement and interpretation

1.—(1) This Act of Sederunt may be cited as the Act of Sederunt (Expenses of Party Litigants) 1976 and shall come into operation on 1st October 1976.

(2) The Interpretation Act 1889 shall apply for the interpretation of this Act of Sederunt as it applies for the interpretation of an Act of Parliament.

Expenses allowable to party litigants

[1] **2.**—(1) Where in any proceedings in the Court of Session or the sheriff court, any expenses of a party litigant are ordered to be paid by any other party to the proceedings or in any other way, the auditor may, subject to the following provisions of this Rule, allow as expenses such sums as appear to the auditor to be reasonable having regard to all the circumstances in respect of—

(*a*) work done which was reasonably required in connection with the cause, up to the maximum of two-thirds of the sum allowable to a solicitor for that work under the table of fees for solicitors in judicial proceedings; and

(*b*) outlays reasonably incurred for the proper conduct of the cause.

(2) Without prejudice to the generality of paragraph (1) above, the circumstances to which the auditor shall have regard in determining what sum, if any, to allow in respect of any work done, shall include—

(*a*) the nature of the work;

(*b*) the time taken and the time reasonably required to do the work;

(*c*) the amount of time spent in respect of which there is no loss of earnings;

(*d*) the amount of any earnings lost during the time required to do the work;

(*e*) the importance of the cause to the party litigant;

(*f*) the complexity of the issues involved in the cause.

(3) In this Rule—

(*a*) the word "auditor" includes any person taxing or otherwise determining a claim for expenses incurred in any proceedings in the Court of Session or in the sheriff court;

(*b*) the expression "remunerative time" in relation to a litigant, means time when he is earning or would have been earning but for work done in or in connection with proceedings in court;

(*c*) the expression "leisure time" in relation to a litigant, means time other than remunerative time.

(*d*) the expression "table of fees for solicitors in judicial proceedings" means—

(i) in relation to a cause in the Court of Session, the table of fees in Rule 347 of the Rules of Court in force at the time the work is done; and

(ii) in relation to an ordinary action in the Sheriff Court, the table of fees in Schedule 2 to the Act of Sederunt (Alteration of Sheriff Court Fees) 1971 in force at the time the work is done.

NOTE

[1] As amended by S.I. 1983 No. 1438.

Messengers-at-Arms and Sheriff Officers Rules 1991

(S.I. 1991 No. 1397)

[15th July 1991]

ARRANGEMENT OF RULES

The Lords of Council and Session, under and by virtue of the powers conferred on them by section 75 of the Debtors (Scotland) Act 1987 and of all other powers enabling them in that behalf, do hereby enact and declare:—

PART I

INTRODUCTORY

Citation, commencement and revocation

1.—(1) This Act of Sederunt may be cited as the Act of Sederunt (Messengers-at-Arms and Sheriff Officers Rules) 1991 and shall come into force on 15th July 1991.

(2) The Act of Sederunt (Messengers-at-Arms and Sheriff Officers Rules) 1988 is hereby revoked.

(3) This Act of Sederunt shall be inserted in the Books of Sederunt.

Interpretation

2.—(1) In this Act of Sederunt unless the context otherwise requires

"the Act of 1987" means the Debtors (Scotland) Act 1987;

"committee of examiners" means the committee appointed under rule 6(1) below;

"Lyon Clerk" means the Lyon Clerk and Keeper of the Records;

"Lord Lyon" means the Lord Lyon King of Arms;

"Lord President" means the Lord President of the Court of Session;

"Policy" means, except in Schedule 2, the single document referred to in rule 9(2) below;

"regional sheriff clerk" means a sheriff clerk appointed by the Secretary of State to be a regional sheriff clerk;

"sheriff clerk" means the sheriff clerk of the sheriff court in which the application for a commission as a sheriff officer was granted; and

"the Society" means the Society of Messengers-at-Arms and Sheriff Officers.

(2) A reference to a specified form in this Act of Sederunt means the forms so specified in Schedule 1 to this Act of Sederunt or a form substantially to the same effect with such variation as circumstances may require.

PART II

QUALIFICATIONS, TRAINING AND EXAMINATIONS

Qualification as officer of court

3.—(1) Subject to paragraph (3) below, a person may not be an officer of court unless—

(*a*) he has attained the age of 20 years;

(*b*) he is not over the age of 70 years.

(*c*) subject to rule 5(2) below, he has undergone a period of training for three years with a person who is in practice as an officer of court;

(*d*) the officer of court with whom he has undergone a period of training has issued a certificate stating that the period of training has been completed satisfactorily;

(*e*) within five years before applying for a commission as a sheriff officer, he has passed all such examinations as may be required by the committee of examiners; and

(*f*) he has attained the educational standard determined by the committee of examiners.

(2) An officer of court shall retire from practice as an officer of court on attaining the age of 70 years.

(3) Paragraph (1) of this rule shall not apply to a person who was in practice as an officer of court on 30th November 1988.

(4) Paragraph (2) of this rule shall not apply to a person who was—

(*a*) in practice as an officer of court, and

(*b*) aged 70 years or over,

on 30th November 1988.

Qualification as messenger-at-arms

4.—(1) A sheriff officer may not become a messenger-at-arms unless—

(*a*) subject to paragraph (2) below, he has been in practice as a sheriff officer for a period of not less than two years; and

(*b*) within five years before applying to the Court of Session for recommendation for appointment as a messenger-at-arms, he has passed all such examinations as may be required by the committee of examiners.

(2) The Court of Session may, in an application to which rule 7 below applies, on special cause shown, reduce the period of practice required under paragraph (1)(*a*) above.

Training

5.—(1) An officer of court shall be responsible for the training required by rule 3(1)(c) above of any person whom he employs for the purpose of becoming an officer of court.

(2) The sheriff principal of the sheriffdom to whom an application for a first commission as a sheriff officer under rule 8(1) below is made may, having regard to the previous experience of the applicant, on the written application of that person, reduce the period of training to a period of not less than one year.

Examinations

6.—(1) The Society shall appoint a committee of examiners to examine any person who seeks to apply to become an officer of court.

(2) The committee of examiners shall consist of not more than five persons of whom—

(*a*) not more than three shall be members of the Society nominated by the Society;

(*b*) one shall be a solicitor nominated by the Law Society of Scotland; and

(*c*) one shall not be a member of the Society but shall be nominated by the Society, in consultation with the sheriffs principal and approved by the Lord President.

(3) The committee of examiners, in consultation with the Society, shall be responsible for—

(*a*) determining the educational standard required of candidates;

(*b*) setting examination papers; and

(*c*) regulating and fixing fees for examinations.

Part III

Applications for Commission

Applications for recommendation for commission as messenger-at-arms

7.—(1) An application by a sheriff officer for recommendation for a commission as a messenger-at-arms under section 77(1) of the Act of 1987 shall be by petition presented to the Outer House of the Court of Session in Form 1 and signed by the petitioner or his solicitor.

(2) There shall be lodged with a petition under paragraph (1) above—

(*a*) an inventory of productions;

(*b*) a copy of the entry in the Register of Births relating to the petitioner;

(*c*) a certificate from the Society that the petitioner has passed such examinations as may be required by the committee of examiners; and

(*d*) a certificate from another officer of court stating the period that the petitioner has been in practice as a sheriff officer.

(3) A petition under paragraph (1) above shall not require a process and shall not be intimated on the walls of court, served or advertised.

(4) Where the court grants the prayer of such a petition, the clerk of the Petition Department of the Court of Session shall send a copy of the petition, with interlocutor granting the prayer written on it, to the Lyon Clerk.

(5) Subject to rule 11(10) below, the Lord Lyon shall not issue a commission to a sheriff officer as a messenger-at-arms until the sheriff officer has lodged with the Lyon Clerk—

(*a*) a copy letter of receipt of a premium receipt issued by a regional sheriff clerk in terms of rule 10(3) below; and

(*b*) such further evidence as the Lord Lyon may require that the Policy in respect of which the premium receipt was issued is in force and applies to the commission of the sheriff officer as a messenger-at-arms.

(6) When the Lord Lyon issues a sheriff officer with a commission as a messenger-at-arms under section 77(1) of the Act of 1987, he shall administer to him the oath or declaration of allegiance to the Sovereign and the oath or declaration *de fideli administratione officii*.

(7) A commission as a messenger-at-arms shall cease to have effect when the holder of it attains the age of 70 years.

(8) Paragraph (7) of this rule shall not apply to a person who was—

(*a*) in practice as a messenger-at-arms, and

(*b*) aged 70 years or over,

on 30th November 1988.

Application for commission as sheriff officer

8.—(1) An application by a person for a commission as a sheriff officer in a particular sheriffdom or a particular district of a sheriffdom shall be by initial writ in a summary application in Form 2 to the sheriff principal in such sheriff court as the sheriff principal shall direct and shall be signed by the applicant or his solicitor.

(2) There shall be lodged with an initial writ under paragraph (1) of this rule—

(*a*) an inventory of productions;

(*b*) a copy of the entry in the Register of Births relating to the applicant;

(*c*) the certificate required by rule 3(1)(*d*) above;

(*d*) a certificate from the Society to the effect that the applicant has passed such examinations as may be required by the committee of examiners; and

(*e*) two references of good character.

(3) An application under paragraph (1) above shall not be served but shall be ordered to be—

(*a*) intimated on the walls of every sheriff court in the sheriffdom or district of the sheriffdom for which appointment as a sheriff officer is sought; and

(*b*) advertised once in Form 3 in such newspapers circulating in the sheriffdom as the sheriff principal shall require.

(4) A person who intends to object to such an application shall lodge answers to the application with the sheriff clerk within 30 days from the date of such intimation and advertisement.

(5) Where the sheriff principal is satisfied that the applicant is suitably qualified, and is a fit and proper person, to be a sheriff officer, he may grant to the applicant a commission as sheriff officer in his sheriffdom or a district within that sheriffdom.

(6) Subject to paragraph (7) and rule 11(11) below the sheriff principal shall not issue a commission to a sheriff officer until the sheriff officer has sent to the sheriff principal—

(*a*) the Policy required under rule 9 below; or

(*b*) evidence satisfactory to the sheriff principal that the sheriff officer is covered by an existing Policy,

together with such further evidence as the sheriff principal may require that the Policy is in force and applies to the sheriff officer.

(7) In the application of paragraph (6) above in a case where the sheriff officer already holds a commission as a sheriff officer, it shall be sufficient for the sheriff officer to send to the sheriff principal—

(*a*) a copy letter of receipt of a premium receipt, issued by the regional sheriff clerk under rule 10(3) below; and

(*b*) such further evidence as the sheriff principal may require that the Policy in respect of which the premium was issued is in force and applies to the commission of the sheriff officer in his sheriffdom.

(8) When the sheriff principal issues a commission to a sheriff officer he, or a sheriff, shall administer to the sheriff officer the oath or declaration *de fideli administratione officii*.

(9) Where a person intends to apply to be a sheriff officer in more than one sheriffdom, he shall make a summary application under paragraph (1) of this rule in each sheriffdom in which he seeks to be appointed as sheriff officer.

(10) Where a sheriff officer is issued with a further commission as a sheriff officer in a sheriffdom other than the sheriffdom in which he first obtained a commission, he shall intimate a copy of his subsequent commission, certified by the sheriff clerk, to the sheriff principal of each sheriffdom in which he already holds a commission as a sheriff officer.

(11) Where a messenger-at-arms is issued with a further commission as a sheriff officer he shall intimate a copy of that commission, certified by the sheriff clerk, to the Lord Lyon.

(12) A commission as a sheriff officer shall cease to have effect when the holder of it attains the age of 70 years.

(13) Paragraph (12) of this rule shall not apply to a person who was—

(*a*) in practice as a sheriff officer, and

(*b*) aged 70 years or over,

on 30th November 1988.

PART IV

THE POLICY

Caution and professional indemnity insurance

9.—(1) An officer of court and any partnership of officers of court shall be covered by—

(*a*) a bond of caution to the value of not less than £50,000 in respect of each claim covering each commission held by each officer of court to whom the bond of caution applies as sheriff officer and, where applicable, as a messenger-at-arms, and

(*b*) a policy of professional indemnity insurance for not less than £100,000 in respect of each claim—

(i) in the case of an officer of court, covering each commission held by him as a sheriff officer and, where applicable, as a messenger-at-arms, and any employee of the officer of court; and

(ii) in the case of a partnership of officers of court, covering the firm, any partner of the firm in respect of each commission held by him as a sheriff officer and, where applicable, as a messenger-at-arms, and any employee of the firm.

(2) The bond of caution and policy of professional indemnity insurance required under paragraph (1) above shall be incorporated in a single document and shall be—

(*a*) in such terms as may be approved by the sheriffs principal and the Lord Lyon;

(*b*) obtained from a company on the list of guarantee companies approved by the Lord President under rule 200 (*e*)(iv) of the Rules of the Court of Session; and

(*c*) renewed annually.

Renewals of policy

10.—(1) Each year every officer of court shall, within 30 days after the expiry of the current Policy, lodge, in accordance with the following paragraphs of this rule, a premium receipt from a company approved under rule 9(2)(b) above stating that he is covered by a Policy in accordance with rule 9 above.

(2) There shall be sent to the sheriff principal of the sheriffdom in which the first current commission of the officer of court as a sheriff was granted—

(*a*) the premium receipt referred to in paragraph (1) above; and
(*b*) such further evidence as the sheriff principal may require that the Policy in respect of which the premium receipt was issued is in force and applies to the sheriff officer.

(3) On being satisfied as to the premium receipt and any further evidence sent to him under paragraph (2) above, the sheriff principal shall cause the premium receipt to be lodged with the regional sheriff clerk who shall issue to the officer of court a letter of receipt of such premium receipt and such copy letters of receipt as may reasonably be required by the officer of court.

(4) Where an officer of court holds a commission as a sheriff officer in more than one sheriffdom, he shall send to the sheriff principal of every sheriffdom in which he holds a commission (other than the first current commission)—
(*a*) a copy letter of receipt of such a premium receipt issued by the regional sheriff clerk; and
(*b*) such further evidence as the sheriff principal may require that the Policy in respect of which the premium receipt was issued is in force and applies to the commission of the sheriff officer in his sheriffdom.

(5) Where an officer of court is also a messenger-at-arms, he shall send to the Lyon Clerk—
(*a*) a copy letter of receipt of such a premium receipt issued by the regional sheriff clerk in respect of his commission as a sheriff officer; and
(*b*) such further evidence as the Lord Lyon may require that the Policy in respect of which the premium receipt was issued is in force and applies to the commission of the officer of court as a messenger-at-arms.

(6) Where an officer of court fails to lodge a premium receipt under paragraph (1) above—
(*a*) in respect of any commission as a sheriff officer, the sheriff principal may suspend the officer of court from practice as a sheriff officer; and
(*b*) where applicable, in respect of his commission as a messenger-at-arms, a Lord Ordinary may, following a report sent to the Deputy Principal Clerk of Session by the Lyon Clerk, suspend the officer of court from practice as a messenger-at-arms.

(7) Where an officer of court has been suspended under paragraph (6) above, and subsequently lodges a premium receipt under paragraph (1) above, the sheriff principal and, where applicable, in respect of his commission as a messenger-at-arms a Lord Ordinary may recall his suspension.

Transitional provisions

11.—(1) This rule applies to officers of court who are in practice on the date on which this Act of Sederunt comes into force.

(2) In this rule—
(*a*) "the operative date" means the date on which this Act of Sederunt comes into force;
(*b*) "the compliance date" in respect of an officer of court means whichever shall first occur of—
(i) the date on which the bond of caution in respect of that officer of court current on the operative date expires;
(ii) where more than one bond of caution is current in respect of that officer of court on the operative date, the date on which the first such bond expires;
(iii) the date on which the policy of professional indemnity insurance current in respect of that officer of court on the operative date expires; and

(iv) where more than one such policy of professional indemnity insurance is current in respect of that officer of court on the operative date, the date on which the first such policy expires; and

(*c*) "the prescribed documents" means—

(i) a copy letter of receipt issued by a regional sheriff clerk in respect of the bond of caution required under paragraph 1 of Schedule 2; and

(ii) a copy letter of receipt issued by a regional sheriff clerk in respect of a copy premium receipt from an insurance company for the policy of professional indemnity insurance required under paragraph 2 of Schedule 2.

(3) Within 30 days of the compliance date an officer of court shall send a Policy, together with such further evidence as the sheriff principal may require that the Policy is in force and applies to the officer of court, to the sheriff principal of the sheriffdom in which his first current commission as a sheriff officer was granted.

(4) On being satisfied as to the Policy and any further evidence furnished under paragraph (3) above, the sheriff principal shall cause the Policy and any such further evidence to be transmitted to the regional sheriff clerk who shall issue to the officer of court a letter of receipt of the Policy and such copy letters of receipt as may reasonably be required by the officer of court.

(5) Where an officer of court holds a commission as a sheriff officer in more than one sheriffdom, he shall send to the sheriff principal of every sheriffdom in which he holds a commission (other than the first current commission)—

(*a*) a copy letter of receipt of the Policy issued by the regional sheriff clerk under paragraph (4) above; and

(*b*) such further evidence as the sheriff principal may require that the Policy is in force and applies to the commission of the sheriff officer in his sheriffdom.

(6) Where an officer of court is also a messenger-at-arms, he shall send to the Lyon Clerk—

(*a*) a copy letter of receipt of the Policy issued by the regional sheriff clerk in respect of his commission as a sheriff officer; and

(*b*) such further evidence as the Lord Lyon may require that the Policy is in force and applies to the commission of the officer of court as a messenger-at-arms.

(7) Where an officer of court fails to lodge a Policy under paragraph (3) above—

(*a*) in respect of any commission as a sheriff officer, the sheriff principal may suspend the officer of court from practice as a sheriff officer; and

(*b*) where applicable, in respect of his commission as a messenger-at-arms, a Lord Ordinary may, following a report sent to the Deputy Principal Clerk of Session by the Lyon Clerk, suspend the officer of court from practice as a messenger-at-arms.

(8) Where an officer of court has been suspended under paragraph (7) above and subsequently lodges a Policy under paragraph (3) above the sheriff principal and, where applicable, in respect of his commission as a messenger-at-arms, a Lord Ordinary may recall his suspension.

(9) Until the compliance date, an officer of court shall comply with Schedule 2 to this Act of Sederunt.

(10) Where an officer of court—

(*a*) applies for recommendation for a commission as a messenger-at-arms; and

(*b*) the prayer of the petition under rule 7(1) above is granted before the compliance date in respect of that officer of court, notwithstanding rule 7(5) above, the Lord Lyon shall not issue a commission to that officer of court as a messenger-at-arms until that officer of court has lodged with the Lyon Clerk

(i) the prescribed documents; or

(ii) the copy letter of receipt and further evidence referred to in rule 7(5) above.

(11) Where an officer of court—

(*a*) applies for a commission as a sheriff officer in a particular sheriffdom or a particular district of a sheriffdom, and

(*b*) his application' is granted before the compliance date in respect of that officer of court,

notwithstanding rules 8(6) and 8(7) above, the sheriff principal shall not issue a commission to the officer of court in respect of that sheriffdom or district until the officer of court has sent to the sheriff principal

(i) the prescribed documents; or

(ii) the copy letter of receipt and further evidence referred to in rule 8(7) above.

PART V

ACCOUNTS

Officers of court to keep accounts

12. Every officer of court shall keep—

(*a*) written books and accounts, separately in respect of each client creditor, to show all monies collected by him from the creditor's debtor; and

(*b*) a separate bank account in respect of client creditors.

Accountant's certificate

13.—(1) Every officer of court shall deliver annually to every sheriff principal from whom he holds a commission and, if he is a messenger-at-arms, to the Lyon Clerk a certificate by an accountant within six months of the end of his accounting year in respect of that year.

(2) Such a certificate shall state that in the opinion of the accountant satisfactory accounts have been kept in accordance with rule 12 above.

(3) In order to enable an accountant to grant such a certificate, every officer of court shall make available to the accountant such books and accounts as the accountant may reasonably require.

(4) If, after making the examination referred to in paragraph (3) above, it appears to the accountant that he is not able to sign such a certificate, he shall prepare a report giving his reasons.

(5) Where an accountant prepares a report under paragraph (4) above, he shall send a copy of it—

(*a*) in the case of a sheriff officer, to every sheriff principal who has granted a commission to the sheriff officer;

(*b*) in the case of a messenger-at-arms, to the Lyon Clerk; and

(*c*) to the officer of court concerned.

(6) In this rule, "an accountant" means an accountant in public practice as a professional accountant who is a member of one of more of the following bodies:—

(*a*) the Institute of Chartered Accountants of Scotland;

(*b*) the Institute of Chartered Accountants in England and Wales;

(*c*) the Institute of Chartered Accountants in Ireland; and

(*d*) the Chartered Association of Certified Accountants.

(7) Where an officer of court fails to deliver to the sheriff principal or the Lyon Clerk a certificate by an accountant under paragraph (1) above—

(*a*) in respect of his commission as a sheriff officer, the sheriff principal may suspend the officer of court from practice as a sheriff officer; and

(*b*) where applicable, in respect of his commission as a messenger-at-arms, a Lord Ordinary may, following a report sent to the Deputy Principal Clerk of Session by the Lyon Clerk, suspend the officer of court from practice as a messenger-at-arms.

(8) Where an officer of court has been suspended under paragraph (7) above and subsequently lodges a certificate by an accountant under paragraph (1) above, the sheriff principal and, where applicable, in respect of his commission as a messenger-at-arms, a Lord Ordinary may recall his suspension.

Part VI

Official Functions and Extra-Official Activities

Official functions

14.—(1) Without prejudice to rule 16 in the First Schedule to the Sheriff Courts (Scotland) Act 1907, rule 11 of the Act of Sederunt (Summary Cause Rules, Sheriff Court) 1976, section 91(2) of the Act of 1987, and any functions under any other enactment, an officer of court may exercise the following official functions—

(*a*) subject to paragraph (2) below, collect any debt constituted by decree or recoverable by summary warrant;

(*b*) execute diligence; or

(*c*) execute a citation or serve any document required under any legal process, in any place in respect of which he holds a commission as an officer of court.

(2) A debt constituted by decree or recoverable by summary warrant may be collected—

(*a*) in the case of a decree or summary warrant of the sheriff court, by a sheriff officer; or

(*b*) in the case of a decree or summary warrant of the Court of Session, by a messenger-at-arms.

(3) Without prejudice to rule 16 in the Fist Schedule to the Sheriff Courts (Scotland) Act 1907, rule 11 of the Act of Sederunt (Summary Cause Rules, Sheriff Court) 1976, section 91(2) of the Act of 1987, and any functions under any other enactment, a person who holds a commission as a sheriff officer may practise as a sheriff officer only in the sheriffdom or district of a sheriffdom in respect of which he has been granted a commission under rule 8(5) above.

(4) An officer of court may refuse to execute a citation, serve any document required under any legal process or execute diligence where—

(*a*) the prescribed, or reasonable, expenses have not been tendered to him or secured by or on behalf of the person instructing him; or

(*b*) it is not reasonably practicable for him to carry out his instructions and this has been intimated forthwith on receipt of the instructions to the person instructing him.

(5) An officer of court may not—

(*a*) form a company within the meaning of section 735(1) of the Companies Act 1985 for the purpose of exercising any of his official functions; or

(*b*) exercise any of his official functions as an employee of a company within the meaning of section 735(1) of the Companies Act 1985.

Extra-official activities

15.—(1) Subject to paragraph (2) below, the extra-official activities of an officer of court may include—

(*a*) collection for remuneration of any debt not constituted by decree where authorised to do so under rule 16 below; or

(*b*) in the absence of any statutory provision to the contrary, service on a person for remuneration of any notice which is required to be served under any enactment.

(2) An officer of court who performs an extra-official activity under paragraph (1) above shall not state or imply that he is acting in his capacity as an officer of court.

(3) An officer of court may not be—

(*a*) an auctioneer with his own auction room;

(*b*) an elected or appointed member of a public or local authority;

(*c*) a house factor;

(*d*) a member of the Faculty of Advocates;

(*e*) a member of the Law Society of Scotland;

(*f*) a member of the United Kingdom, or European, Parliament;

(*g*) a money lender; or

(*h*) a police officer.

Applications for authorisation to collect debts not constituted by decree

16.—(1) A sheriff principal may, on the application of a sheriff officer who has his principal place of business in the sheriffdom and holds a commission from the sheriff principal, authorise that sheriff officer for remuneration to collect or be engaged in the collection of debts not constituted by decree on such conditions as the sheriff principal may consider appropriate.

(2) An application by a sheriff officer under paragraph (1) above shall be made in writing and shall disclose any material interest held by the sheriff officer, a member of his family or a business associate in any organisation on behalf of which he seeks authority to collect debts.

(3) Where a sheriff officer, a member of his family or a business associate acquires an interest mentioned in paragraph (2) above, after authorisation under paragraph (1), above, and intends to collect debts not constituted by decree on behalf of that organisation, the sheriff officer shall make a further application to the sheriff principal under paragraph (1) above.

Part VII

Registers of Officers of Court

Keeping of registers

17. There shall be kept—

(i) by the regional sheriff clerk in respect of every sheriff officer who holds a commission in the sheriffdom; and

(ii) by the Lyon Clerk in respect of every messenger-at-arms,

a record book in which there shall be registered in respect of each officer of court—

(*a*) the address of his principal, and any other, place of business or employment, his private address and any change of such address;

(*b*) every commission held by him as an officer of court;

(*c*) any extra-official activities carried on by him for remuneration, and any authorisation by a sheriff principal in respect of any such activity;

(*d*) any interest disclosed by him under rule 16(2) or (3) above;

(*e*) any suspension or deprivation of office and any recall of suspension or deprivation of office;

(*f*) the date on which he ceased to practise where notice to that effect has been given;
(*g*) the dates of his accounting year; and
(*h*) the renewal date in each year of the Policy currently in force in respect of each commission held by him as an officer of court.

Intimation of information by officers of court for registers

18.—(1) An officer of court shall intimate any change of his employment, business or private address within 21 days of such change—
(*a*) to the regional sheriff clerk of each sheriffdom in which he holds a commission as a sheriff officer; and
(*b*) in the case of a messenger-at-arms, to the Lyon Clerk.

(2) An officer of court who engages in extra-official activities (whether an activity under rule 15(1) above or otherwise) shall intimate such activities and any authorisation and interests disclosed by him under rule 16(2) or (3) above—
(*a*) to the regional sheriff clerk of each sheriffdom in which he holds a commission as a sheriff officer; and
(*b*) in the case of a messenger-at-arms, to the Lyon Clerk.

(3) An officer of court who intends to cease to practise as a sheriff officer shall, before the date on which he ceases to practise, give notice of the date on which he will cease to practise—
(*a*) in the case of a sheriff officer, to the sheriff principal of each sheriffdom in which he holds a commission as a sheriff officer; and
(*b*) in the case of a messenger-at-arms, to the Lyon Clerk.

(4) An officer of court shall give notice of the dates of his accounting year and of the renewal date in each year of the Policy currently in force in respect of each commission held by him as an officer of court—
(*a*) in the case of a sheriff officer, to the regional sheriff clerk of each sheriffdom in which he holds a commission as a sheriff officer; and
(*b*) in the case of a messenger-at-arms, to the Lyon Clerk.

Part VIII

Reports and Investigations of Conduct of Officers of Court

Reports and complaints

19.—(1) A copy of a report prepared under section 78(3) of the Act of 1987 in respect of a messenger-at-arms shall be sent to the Deputy Principal Clerk of Session who shall put the copy report before a judge nominated by the Lord President.

(2) Where a judge of the Court of Session or a sheriff principal has reason to believe that an officer of court may have been guilty of misconduct as provided in section 79(1)(*c*) of the Act of 1987, he shall put the allegation in writing.

(3) A report or complaint under section 79(1)(*b*)(i) of the Act of 1987 in respect of a messenger-at-arms shall be sent to the Deputy Principal Clerk of Session who shall put the report or complaint, as the case may be, before the judge nominated under section 79(2) of that Act.

Opportunity to officer of court to reply to allegation of misconduct

20. Where a report or complaint under section 79(1)(*a*) or (*b*), or a complaint under section 79(1)(*c*), of the Act of 1987 has been made, the judge nominated under section 79(2) of that Act or the sheriff principal, as the case may be, shall cause a copy of the report or complaint to be sent to the officer of court about whom an allegation of misconduct has been made together with a letter requesting him to reply within 14 days admitting, denying or giving an explanation of the alleged misconduct.

Part IX

Disciplinary Proceedings

Disciplinary proceedings against messengers-at-arms

21.—(1) Disciplinary proceedings under section 79(3)(*a*) of the Act of 1987 against a messenger-at-arms shall be by petition presented to the Outer House of the Court of Session in which the messenger-at-arms complained against shall be made the respondent.

(2) Subject to the following provisions of this rule, rules 191 to 198 of the Rules of the Court of Session shall apply to a petition under this rule.

(3) A petition under paragraph (1) above shall include—

(*a*) averments specifying—

(i) the alleged misconduct;

(ii) the facts established by the investigation under section 79(2) of the Act of 1987 alleged to be the probable cause of misconduct; and

(*b*) a prayer praying the Lords of Council and Session to order—

(i) service of the petition on the respondent;

(ii) the respondent to lodge answers within 21 days from the date of service;

(iii) intimation of the petition to the Lord Advocate;

(iv) a date for a hearing for further procedure; and

(v) in the event of the respondent being found guilty of misconduct, such order under section 80(5) of the Act of 1987, if any, as the court considers appropriate.

(4) When making the first order for service and intimation, the Lord Ordinary shall fix a date for a hearing for further procedure; and the petitioner shall intimate that date to the respondent and the Lord Advocate.

Procedure in proceedings against messengers-at-arms

22.—(1) this rule applies to a petition under rule 21 above.

(2) Subject to the following provisions of this rule, the Lord Ordinary shall determine the procedure to be followed in such a petition.

(3) Where the respondent fails to appear or be represented at the hearing for further procedure, the Lord Ordinary may grant the prayer of the petition.

(4) Where a further hearing or a proof is ordered, the petitioner shall fix a date with the Keeper of the Rolls of the Court of Session, and the Keeper of the Rolls shall fix an early date.

(5) Where a proof is fixed—

(*a*) the interlocutor allowing the proof shall be sufficient warrant for the citation of witnesses on not less than seven days' notice; and

(*b*) the parties may agree to dispense with the services of a shorthand writer.

(6) After a hearing on the question whether there was misconduct by the respondent, the Lord Ordinary may give his decision orally or make avizandum and issue his decision in writing at a later date.

(7) Where the Lord Ordinary pronounces an interlocutor under paragraph (3) or (6) above, or issues his decision in writing under paragraph (6), the clerk of court shall send a copy of the interlocutor or a copy of the decision, as the case may be, to the respondent.

(8) Where the respondent is found guilty of misconduct after a hearing to determine that matter, the court shall make no order under section 80(5) of the Act of 1987 without first giving the respondent an opportunity to be heard, or to make representations in writing, in mitigation.

(9) A hearing of a petition under section 79(3)(*a*) of the Act of 1987 shall be held in public unless—

(*a*) the respondent requests that it be held in private; or
(*b*) the judge considers that it would be prejudicial to the interests of justice if the hearing were not held, in whole or in part, in private.

(10) Where—
(*a*) a fine is imposed on the respondent, the clerk of court shall intimate details of the fine to the Lord Advocate;
(*b*) an order is made for repayment under section 80(5)(*d*) of the Act of 1987, the clerk of court shall intimate the order to the person to whom repayment is to be made; and
(*c*) an order is made under section 80(1), (4) or (8)(*b*) of the Act of 1987, the clerk of court shall intimate the order to the company from which the Policy currently in force in respect of the respondent was obtained.

(11) The warrant attached to an extract of a decree for payment of a fine shall be in the following terms:—"and the Lords grant warrant for all lawful execution hereon".

Disciplinary proceedings against sheriff officers

23.—(1) Disciplinary proceedings under section 79(3)(*a*) of the Act of 1987 against a sheriff officer shall be by initial writ in a summary application, to the sheriff principal who appointed the solicitor under section 79(2) of the Act of 1987 to investigate, in which the sheriff officer complained against shall be made the respondent.

(2) An application under paragraph (1) above shall include—
(*a*) averments specifying—
(i) the alleged misconduct;
(ii) the facts established by the investigation under section 79(2) of the Act of 1987 alleged to be the probable cause of misconduct; and
(*b*) a crave seeking the sheriff principal to order—
(i) service of the application on the respondent;
(ii) the respondent to lodge defences within 14 days from the date of service;
(iii) intimation of the application to the Lord Advocate;
(iv) a date for a hearing for further procedure; and
(v) in the event of the respondent being found guilty of misconduct, such order under section 80(7) of the Act of 1987, if any, as the court considers appropriate.

(3) When making the first order for service and intimation, the sheriff principal shall fix a date for a hearing for further procedure; and the applicant shall intimate that date to the respondent and the Lord Advocate.

Procedure in proceedings against sheriff officers

24.—(1) This rule applies to an application under rule 23 above.

(2) Subject to the following provisions of this rule, the sheriff principal shall determine the procedure to be followed in such an application.

(3) Where the respondent fails to appear or to be represented at the hearing for further procedure, the sheriff principal may grant the crave of the application.

(4) Where a proof is fixed—
(*a*) the interlocutor allowing the proof shall be sufficient warrant for the citation of witnesses on not less than seven days' notice; and
(*b*) the parties may agree to dispense with the services of a shorthand writer.

(5) After a hearing on the question whether there was misconduct by the respondent, the sheriff principal may give his decision orally or make avizandum and issue his decision in writing at a later date.

(6) Where the sheriff principal pronounces an interlocutor under paragraph (3) or (5) above, or issues his decision in writing under paragraph (5), the clerk of court shall send a copy of the interlocutor or a copy of the decision, as the case may be, to the respondent.

(7) Where the respondent is found guilty of misconduct after a hearing to determine that matter, the court shall make no order under section 80(7) of the Act of 1987 without first giving the respondent an opportunity to be heard, or to make representations in writing, in mitigation.

(8) A hearing of an application under section 79(3)(*a*) of the Act of 1987 shall be held in public unless—

(*a*) the respondent requests that it be held in private; or

(*b*) the sheriff principal considers that it would be prejudicial to the interests of justice if the hearing were not held, in whole or in part, in private.

(9) Where—

(*a*) a fine is imposed on the respondent, the sheriff clerk shall intimate details of the fine to the Lord Advocate;

(*b*) an order is made for repayment under section 80(7)(*b*) of the Act of 1987, the clerk of court shall intimate the order to the person to whom repayment is to be made; and

(*c*) an order is made under section 80(2), (6) or (8)(*b*) or 81(3) of the Act of 1987, the clerk of court shall intimate the order to the company from which the Policy currently in force in respect of the respondent was obtained.

(10) The warrant attached to an extract of a decree for payment of a fine shall be in the following terms:—"and the Sheriff Principal grants warrant for all lawful execution hereon".

Remits of disciplinary proceedings

25. Where it is considered appropriate in the circumstances of a particular case, disciplinary proceedings may be remitted—

(*a*) by the Court of Session, to a sheriff principal to report; or

(*b*) by a sheriff principal, to another sheriff principal.

Opportunity to officer of court to make representations where order considered under section 80(1) and (2) of the Act of 1987

26. Where the Court of Session under section 80(1), or a sheriff principal under section 80(2), of the Act of 1987 considers making an order under one of these subsections, the Court of Session or the sheriff principal, as the case may be—

(*a*) shall give the officer of court an opportunity to make representations orally or in writing; and

(*b*) may ordain the officer of court to appear,

before making such an order.

Appeals

27.—(1) An appeal from Lord Ordinary or sheriff principal to the Inner House of the Court of Session under section 82 of the Act of 1987 shall be made within 21 days of the date of the decision appealed against.

(2) Subject to paragraph (1) above, rule 290 of the Rules of the Court of Session shall apply to an appeal under section 82 of the Act of 1987.

Suspension under particular rules

28.—(1) Where the sheriff principal suspends an officer of court from practice as a sheriff officer under rule 10(6)(*a*), 11(7)(*a*) or 13(7)(*a*) above, he shall cause intimation to be made—

(*a*) to every other sheriff principal from whom the sheriff officer holds a commission as a sheriff officer; and (*b*) where the sheriff officer is also a messenger-at-arms, to the Deputy Principal Clerk of Session and the Lord Lyon.

(2) Where the Court of Session suspends an officer of court from practice as a messenger-at-arms under rule 10(6)(*b*), 11(7)(*b*) or 13(7)(*b*) above, it shall cause intimation to be made to the Lord Lyon, who shall cause intimation thereof to be made to every sheriff principal from whom the officer of court holds commission as a sheriff officer.

(3) Where a sheriff principal receives intimation under paragraph (1)(*a*) or (2) above, he may suspend the officer of court from practice as a sheriff officer.

(4) Where the Deputy Principal Clerk of Session receives intimation under paragraph (1)(*b*) above, he shall place the intimation before a Lord Ordinary, who may suspend the officer of court form practice as a messenger-at-arms.

(5) Where, after an officer of court has been suspended under rule 10(6), 11(7) or 13(7) above, that officer of court subsequently lodges the premium receipt, Policy or certificate, as the case may be, the regional sheriff clerk of the sheriffdom in which the officer of court's first current commission as a sheriff officer was granted shall intimate that fact to—

(*a*) every other sheriff principal from whom the officer of court holds a commission as a sheriff officer; and

(*b*) where the sheriff officer is also a messenger-at-arms, to the Deputy Principle Clerk of Session and the Lord Lyon,

and each sheriff principal and, where applicable, respect of his commission as a messenger-at-arms, a Lord Ordinary, may recall his suspension.

PART X

MISCELLANEOUS

Mandate to recover debt in diligence

29. Instructions to an officer of court to execute diligence in execution shall, unless the contrary intention is expressed, include a mandate to recover payment for, or on account of, any debt in respect of which the diligence is executed.

Dealings in goods poinded or sold by virtue of diligence

30. An officer of court shall not—

(*a*) himself or through an agent, purchase any goods poinded or sold by virtue of a diligence in which he has acted in course of one of his official functions;

(*b*) share with the creditor any goods of a debtor or the proceeds of sale of such goods adjudged to the creditor of the debtor by virtue of diligence in which the officer of court has acted in course of one of his official functions; or

(*c*) share with the purchaser any profit made by the purchaser in re-selling any goods bought at a sale carried out by virtue of diligence in which the officer of court has acted in course of one of his official functions.

Official identity card

31. An officer of court shall forthwith upon ceasing to practise as an officer of court deliver the official identity card issued to him under section 86 of the Act of 1987 to the person from whom he holds his commission.

SCHEDULE 1

FORMS

Rule 7(1) FORM 1

Form of petition to the Court of Session for recommendation for a commission as a messenger-at-arms

UNTO THE RIGHT HONOURABLE
THE LORDS OF COUNCIL AND SESSION

PETITION

[AB] (*address*)

for

Recommendation for a commission as a messenger-at-arms

HUMBLY SHEWETH

1. That the petitioner was born on and is a sheriff officer.
2. That the first current [or only] commission of the petitioner as a sheriff officer was granted by the sheriff principal of (*name of sheriffdom*) at (*name of court*) on (*insert date*).
3. That the petitioner has been in practice as a sheriff officer for a period of years. [The petitioner seeks to have the period of practice required under rule 4(1)(*a*) of the Messengers-at-Arms and Sheriff Officers Rules 1991 reduced from two years to (*state period*). He does so on the following grounds, namely (*state grounds*).]
4. That the petitioner holds a certificate from the Society of Messengers-at-Arms and Sheriff Officers that he has passed the examinations of that Society.
5. That the petitioner has not been convicted of any offence [except (*state any convictions which are not spent convictions by virtue of the Rehabilitation of Offenders Act 1974*)].
6. That the petitioner is a fit and proper person to be granted a commission as a messenger-at-arms and makes this application for a recommendation to the Lord Lyon King of Arms for a commission as a messenger-at-arms.
7. That this petition is presented under section 77(1) of the Debtors (Scotland) Act 1987 and rule 7 [or rules 4(2) and 7] of the Messengers-at-Arms and Sheriff Officers Rules 1991.

MAY IT THEREFORE please your Lordships [to reduce the period of practice required under rule 4(1)(a) of the Messengers-at-Arms and Sheriff Officers Rules 1991 from two years to (*insert period*) and] to recommend the petitioner to the Lord Lyon King of Arms for a commission as a messenger-at-arms; or to do otherwise in the premises as to your Lordships shall seem proper.

ACCORDING TO JUSTICE, &c

Rule 8(1) FORM 2

Form of initial writ in summary application to the sheriff principal for a commission as a sheriff officer

SHERIFFDOM OF AT

INITIAL WRIT

in causa

[AB] (*address*)

Applicant

for

A commission as a sheriff officer

The applicant craves the court to grant to him a commission as a sheriff officer in the [(*name of district(s)*) district of the] sheriffdom of (*name of sheriffdom*).

CONDESCENDENCE

1. The applicant was born on
2. The applicant has [or proposes to have] a principal place of business [or is to be employed] at (*insert address*). [He has (an)other place(s) of business at (*insert address(es)*).] [The applicant holds a commission as a sheriff officer in the following sheriffdom(s) [or districts of sheriffdoms]]. [He holds a commission as a messenger-at-arms.
3. The applicant has undergone a period of training with [CD], sheriff officer, (*insert business address*) for a period of years. [The period of training was reduced to year(s) by the sheriff principal on (date). A [certified] copy of the relevant interlocutor is produced].
4. The applicant holds a certificate of completion of training issued by [CD]. He also holds a certificate from the Society of Messengers-at-Arms and Sheriff Officers that he has passed the examination of that Society.
5. The applicant is of good character as endorsed by the two character references produced. The applicant has not been convicted of any offence [except (state any convictions which are not spent convictions by virtue of the Rehabilitation of Offenders Act 1974)].
6. The applicant is a fit and proper person to hold a commission as a sheriff officer in the sheriffdom [of (*insert name of district*) district of the sheriffdom] and makes this application for a commission.
7. This application is made under rule 8 of the Messengers-at-Arms and Sheriff Officers Rules 1991.

PLEA-IN-LAW

The applicant being a fit and proper person to hold a commission as a sheriff officer, the application should be granted as craved.

IN RESPECT WHEREOF

Applicant [or EF]
(*insert business address*)
Solicitor for applicant]

Rule 8(3)(b) FORM 3

Notice of advertisement in newspaper of application for commission as a sheriff officer

APPLICATION by [AB]

for

COMMISSION AS A SHERIFF OFFICER

NOTICE is hereby given that application has been made to the sheriff principal of (*name of sheriffdom*) at (*name of court*) by [AB] (*address or business address*) for a commission as a sheriff officer in (*name of sheriffdom or district of sheriffdom*). The sheriff principal, by interlocutor (*insert date*), ordered any person who wishes to object to the application of [AB] to lodge answers to the application with the sheriff clerk at (*name and address of court*) within 30 days from the date of this notice.

(*name and address of solicitor*)
Solicitor for applicant

SCHEDULE 2

TRANSITIONAL PROVISIONS

Bonds of caution

1.—(1) An officer of court shall be covered by a bond of caution in the form set out in sub-paragraph (2) of this paragraph to the value of £50,000 from a company on the list of guarantee companies approved by the Lord President under rule 200(*e*)(iv) of the Rules of the Court of Session in respect of any commission held by him as—

(*a*) a sheriff officer; and

(*b*) where applicable, a messenger-at-arms,

and the bond of caution shall be renewed annually.

(2) The form referred to in sub-paragraph (1) of this paragraph is as follows—

BOND OF CAUTION

We, (*name of cautioner*), having a registered office at (*insert address*), hereby BIND and OBLIGE ourselves and our whole funds and property as cautioner and surety for the period from to ; for (*name and address of officer of court*) as OFFICER OF COURT that he shall faithfully, truly and honestly use and exercise the duties of the office of OFFICER OF COURT to ALL and SUNDRY without fear and favour upon payment of his reasonable expenses and if he fails to execute these duties, we shall incur whatsoever damages, interest and expenses any person shall happen to sustain through the dishonest, illegal or fraudulent actions or omissions of (*name of officer of court*). I, (*name of officer of court*), as principal, do hereby BIND and OBLIGE myself, my heirs, executors and successors and we, (*name of cautioner*), as cautioner, do hereby BIND and OBLIGE ourselves jointly and severally to pay and make good the same to any person interested and wronged by declaring that the obligation on us, the cautioner, is (in accordance with [paragraph 1 of Schedule 2 [rule 9] of the Messengers-at-Arms and Sheriff Officers Rules [1991] [1988]) restricted to, and shall not exceed the sum of, £50,000.

We, (*name of cautioner*) accordingly, hereby BIND and OBLIGE ourselves, within the aforementioned limits of the cautionary obligation, for the damages, interest and expenses any such person shall sustain hereby:

And we consent to the registration hereof for preservation and execution: IN WITNESS WHEREOF.

Policies of professional indemnity insurance

2.—(1) An officer and any partnership of officers of court shall be covered by a policy of professional indemnity insurance from an insurance company to a minimum limit of £100,000 in respect of—

(*a*) the officer of court in respect of any commission as—
   (i) a sheriff officer; and
   (ii) where applicable, a messenger-at-arms;
(*b*) the partnership of officers of court in respect of the firm; and
(*c*) the partnership of officers of court in respect of its employees.

and the policy shall be renewed annually.

(2) Every policy of professional indemnity insurance shall be in such terms as may be approved by the sheriffs principal and the Lord Lyon.

[THE NEXT PAGE IS C 481]

Service of Documents Abroad

Guidance on Procedures in the Court of Session and the Sheriff Court

This guidance is additional to the information contained in the *Practical Handbook on the Operation of the Hague Convention of 15 November 1965 on the Service Abroad of Judicial and Extra-Judicial Documents in Civil or Commercial Matters* [see Appendix VII]. While every effort has been made to ensure the accuracy of this guidance, circumstances do vary and it is advisable to check the position in cases of doubt.

Scottish Courts Administration,
Div. II Branch I,
26–27 Royal Terrace,
Edinburgh, EH7 5AH.

Tel. 031–556 0755.

March 1991.

CONTENTS

INTRODUCTION

This guidance note is intended to aid the practical application of the Scottish rules of court on service of documents abroad but it must be stressed that the position regarding any particular country may change.

Since the coming into force of the Civil Jurisdiction and Judgments Act 1982 [see Division B] on 1st January 1987, service of documents abroad is governed by the appropriate rules of the Court of Session and the sheriff courts.

In the Court of Session the relevant rule is rule 74B; this is applied to consistorial actions by rule 159(1) and to petitions by rule 195(*b*) [see Division C].

In the sheriff court, ordinary cause rules 12 and 139 govern service of documents abroad and for summary causes and small claims rule 9 of the summary cause rules applies [see Division D].

However in addition to compliance with these Scottish court rules, for service to be effective compliance is necessary either with the requirements of service set out in international Conventions or in the internal law of the country where service is to be made.

Sheriff court rules provide that where service in terms of either the Hague or Brussels Conventions (see below for details of the two Conventions) is applicable, decree shall not be given until it is established that service or delivery of the writ under the Convention was effected in sufficient time to enable the defender to defend himself. (Article 15 of the Hague Convention on the Service Abroad of Judicial and Extra Judicial Documents in Civil or Commercial Matters, dated 15th November 1965, and article 27(2) of the 1968 European Convention on Jurisdiction and the Enforcement of Judgments in Civil and Commercial Matters apply.)

Service outwith the United Kingdom

There are four broad categories of countries in which service is to be effected:—

Non-Convention states—Where service is to be effected in a state which has no Convention between itself and the United Kingdom.

A non-Convention state, as the term implies, is a state which is not party to the Hague or Brussels Conventions and does not have a bilateral Convention with the UK. For example, UK dependent territories will not normally have a Convention with the United Kingdom on service and most Commonwealth states also fall within this category. A list of the United Kingdom's dependent territories can be found in Appendix I.

Hague Convention states—Where service is to be effected in a state which is a party to the Hague Convention on the Service Abroad of Judicial and Extra Judicial Documents in Civil or Commercial Matters, dated 15th November 1965 (Cmnd. 3986 (1969)).

The text of the Convention is printed in full in Appendix 3 of Professor A. E. Anton's book *Civil Jurisdiction in Scotland* (published by W. Green & Son Ltd. (1984) with supplement by A. E. Anton and P. R. Beaumont (1987)). A list of the Hague Convention countries can be found in Appendix II.

Brussels Convention states—Where service is to be effected in a state which is a party to the European Convention on Jurisdiction and the Enforcement of Judgments in Civil and Commercial Matters of 1968.

The text of the Convention is set out in Schedule 1 to the Civil Jurisdi-cAppendix III.

Bilateral Convention states—Where service is to be effected in a state which has a Convention with the United Kingdom on the service of writs other than the Hague or Brussels Conventions.

The bilateral Convention states are listed in Appendix IV.

SERVICE IN A NON-CONVENTION STATE

Service in a non-Convention state of a document relating to an action raised in a Scottish court has to be by a method permitted both under the domestic law of the foreign state and in accordance with the Scottish rules of court on service.

Court of Session actions

Rule 74B(1) identifies five methods of service:—

by post;

through the central or other appropriate authority of the country in which the defender is to be found, at the request of the Foreign Office;

through a British Consular officer in the country in which the defender is to be found at the request of the Foreign and Commonwealth Office;

by an *huissier* or other judicial officer or competent official in the country in which the defender is to be found at the request of a messenger at arms; and

personal citation by the pursuer or his agent.

Sheriff court actions

For ordinary causes rule 12(1)(*a*) provides that service may be effected in either of two ways:—

in accordance with the rules for personal service under the domestic law of the place in which service is to be effected; or

by posting in Scotland a copy of the document in question in a registered or recorded delivery letter or the nearest equivalent which the available postal services permit, addressed to the defender at his residence or place of business.

Ordinary cause rule 139 and summary cause rule 9 have similar provisions. The rules require that if service is effected outside the United Kingdom, Channel Islands or Isle of Man the pursuer must lodge a certificate to the effect that the form of service employed was in accordance with the law of the place where service was effected.

Acceptable methods

Detailed advice and guidance on service in a non-Convention state should be sought from a person with knowledge of the local legal requirements.

The Foreign and Commonwealth Office, Nationality and Treaty Department, Clive House, Petty France, London, SW1H 9HD (tel. 071–270 4086 or 4087) holds lists of local solicitors in many Commonwealth states and UK dependent territories and may also be able to advise generally on permitted methods of service in non-Convention states. It may be that an approach to the Embassy or the High Commission of the country where service is to be effected should be considered; *Whitaker's Almanack* is a useful source of addresses and telephone numbers. Service by post from Scotland or by a local lawyer in the foreign state is understood to be acceptable in many Commonwealth states.

Sometimes service by Consular officer may be possible although it is understood to be refused in respect of all Commonwealth or former Commonwealth states.

Postal service is not permitted in Switzerland and is understood not to be acceptable in Liechtenstein.

SERVICE IN A HAGUE CONVENTION STATE

As with service in a non-Convention state, service in a Hague Convention state has to be by a method permitted by Scottish rules of court and the foreign state. Further information is available in the *Practical Handbook on the Operation of the Hague Convention of 15 November 1965 on the Service Abroad of Judicial and Extra-Judicial Documents in Civil and Commercial Matters* (published by Maarten Kluwers (1983), with supplements, distributed in the United Kingdom by Butterworths). The *Practical Handbook* contains details on acceptable methods of service in Hague Convention countries, and while this information may now be obsolescent the handbook should be consulted where possible.

Methods of service

The methods of service provided for by the Hague Convention are:—

(a) Service by or through a central authority in the state addressed on the request of an authority in the state of origin. In the United Kingdom the central authority is the Foreign and Commonwealth Office (articles 3 to 7).
(b) Service by post (unless the state of destination objects) (article 10).
(c) Service directly by the judicial officers, officials or other competent persons of the state of origin directly through similar persons in the state of destination (article 10b).
(d) Service by any interested person directly through the judicial officers, officials or other competent persons of the state of destination (article 10c).
(e) Service through consular or diplomatic channels to designated authorities (article 9).
(f) Service through diplomatic or consular agents (subject to restriction arising from the right of states to oppose this method as respects nationals other than those of the state of origin of the document) (article 8).
(g) Service according to bilateral agreements specifying other methods such as direct transmission between authorities (article 11).

For the list of states party to the Hague Convention and for which the methods of service outlined above are applicable see Appendix II. The Hague Convention does not apply to cases arising in the United Kingdom where documents are for service in United Kingdom dependent territories. The method outlined for service in a non-Convention state may be appropriate for service in dependent territories. However there are no British consular officers in the dependent territories. The usual practice is for Scottish solicitors to instruct agents in the territory concerned.

Where possible the *Practical Handbook* should be consulted for the detail as to the acceptable methods in the state of destination. Thereafter a comparison of the arrangements for service permitted in the state of destination with the range of options set out in rule 74B(1) for Court of Session documents, and with rules 12(1)(*b*)(i)–(v) and 139(1)(*b*)(i)–(v) of the ordinary cause rules and rule 9(1)(*b*)(i)–(v) of the summary cause rules for sheriff court actions, will determine the competent methods of service available. If a selection of methods is available then the particular circumstances of the case will assist in determining the most appropriate method for service. Appendix V provides examples which may be of some assistance.

Postal service

Most countries which are parties to the Hague Convention permit postal service from Scotland. However Czechoslovakia, Egypt, the Federal Republic of Germany, Israel, Norway and Turkey are believed to have objected to postal service. Botswana accepts postal service in principle but has made reservations in respect of High Court and magistrates court proceedings.

The arrangements for personal service are more complicated and the *Practical Handbook* should be consulted in respect of each country.

SERVICE IN A BRUSSELS CONVENTION STATE

Although the Brussels Convention does not itself make provision for the service of documents, article IV of the Annexed Protocol, which may be found in Schedule 1 to the Civil Jurisdiction and Judgments Act 1982, provides that: "Judicial and extrajudicial documents drawn up in one Contracting State which have to be served on persons in another Contracting State shall be transmitted in accordance with the procedures laid down in the conventions and agreements concluded between the Contracting States." Documents may also be sent by the appropriate public officers of the state in which the document has been drawn up directly to the appropriate public officers of the state in which the addressee is to be found. This applies unless the state of destination objects to such service. The Federal Republic of Germany objects to the direct transmission of documents to process servers in Germany. Subject to this exception it is understood that no Community state has objected to article IV. The document will then be forwarded in accordance with the law of the state of destination and the certificate recording this will be sent directly to the officer of the state of origin.

The Brussels Convention's provisions on service apply only between the contracting states to the Brussels Convention. The provisions of article IV of the Annexed Protocol were intended simply to add an extra method of transmission of documents for service on top of the arrangements provided for under the Hague Convention.

SERVICE IN A BILATERAL CONVENTION STATE

As with service in Hague Convention and Brussels Convention States, service in a state with which the United Kingdom has a bilateral Convention on the service of documents has to be by a method permitted by the Scottish rules of court and in terms of the particular Convention. The states with which the United Kingdom has a bilateral Convention are listed in Appendix IV. If service is to be effected in one of these states then the Foreign and Commonwealth Office, Nationality and Treaty Department (tel. 071–270 4086 or 4087) can advise on permitted methods.

MISCELLANEOUS

1. Practical steps

Once the category of the state for service has been established, the Rules of Court should be consulted to determine the particular documents to be served, and the number of copies of the writ and translations necessary. For details of the court's certification requirements that the method of service adopted is permitted in the state of service see below. The following may be required:—

(a) copy summons with warrant for service;
(b) letter requesting service;
(c) translation of all documents into local official language;

(d) certificate of accuracy of translation with designation and qualification of translator;

where service is under article 3 of the Hague Convention (i.e. service by a central authority) the following are also required:—

(e) a completed typed formal request for service in accordance with the annex to the Hague Convention (see Appendix VI);
(f) summary of the document to be served (as per Appendix VI);
(g) duplicates of all documents.

Service by post

Where service is effected by posting in Scotland, items (a), (c) and (d) if appropriate should suffice.

Service through another agency

Where service is effected through another agency, whether through sheriff officers or messengers at arms to *huissiers* or local lawyers abroad or through a Consular officer abroad, items (a), (b), (c) and (d) will be required.

Service through the Foreign and Commonwealth Office

Where service is effected through the Foreign and Commonwealth Office items (a), (b), (c) and (d) together with the appropriate Foreign and Commonwealth Office fee.

Service under article 3 of the Hague Convention

Where service is to be effected by a foreign central authority through the Foreign and Commonwealth Office under article 3 of the Hague Convention, all the items listed at (a)–(g) will be required together with the appropriate fee. The Foreign and Commonwealth Office (tel. 071–270 4086 or 4087) should be consulted for details of the current fee.

A translation may not always be needed if service is to be effected personally on a British national by a Consular officer abroad, although in such cases in relation to Court of Session actions an application to the court to dispense with the provisions of rule 74B(7)(*a*) would be required. Where a translation is needed this may be by a person with sufficient knowledge in the language, whether qualified translator, teacher or another person of recognised competence in the language, unless in relation to service in a Hague Convention State the *Practical Handbook* indicates otherwise.

2. Certification that method of service is permitted

Court of Session practice

Court of Session practice requires certification that the method of service used satisfies rule 74B(1); i.e. that it is permitted either under a Convention or by the laws of the state of destination.

Where service has been effected in a non-Convention country, the certificate should be given by a person who is conversant with the laws of that country and who is either a person practising or entitled to practise as an advocate or solicitor in that country or a duly accredited representative of the government of that country. No such certificate is required, however, in respect of service effected in the Channel Islands or the Isle of Man.

Where service has been effected in a Convention state (whether a Hague, Brussels or bilateral Convention state) by a method specified in the Convention, the Scottish solicitor in the case may certify that the method used is permitted under the Convention.

If service under a Convention or in a Convention state has been effected in accordance with the law of the state of destination, the certificate should be provided by a person who is conversant with the laws of the country in which service has been effected and who is either a person practising or entitled to practise as an advocate or solicitor in that country or a duly accredited representative of the government of that country.

While in most cases the appropriate certificate will be sufficient, it remains open to the court to require such further evidence as it thinks necessary in any particular case.

Sheriff court practice

Where service is to be effected under the Hague Convention by:—

(a) a method prescribed by the internal law of that country (ordinary cause rule 12(*b*)(i)); or

(b) a central authority (ordinary cause rule 12(*b*)(ii)); or

(c) a British consular authority (ordinary cause rule 12(*b*)(iii)); or

(d) an *huissier*, judicial officer or competent official of the country where service is to be made (ordinary cause rule 12(*b*)(v)),

a certificate of execution of service must be lodged in process as provided for in ordinary cause rules 12(4)(*b*) or 12(6), as appropriate.

Where service is effected on a person outwith Scotland (other than in another part of the United Kingdom, the Channel Islands or the Isle of Man) in a non-Convention state (ordinary cause rule 12(*a*)(i)) and the service is made in accordance with the rules for personal service under the domestic law of that country, the pursuer must lodge a certificate as provided in ordinary cause rule 12(6).

3. Role of the Foreign and Commonwealth Office

The Foreign and Commonwealth Office has a role in serving documents abroad under the Hague Convention, bilateral Conventions and in non-Convention countries. Although the Foreign and Commonwealth Office can advise on locally permitted methods of service of documents abroad, service through the Foreign and Commonwealth Office should ideally be a measure of last resort when other methods have been tried unsuccessfully or are not permitted in the state of destination.

Limited Foreign and Commonwealth Office resources and a reduced consular network throughout the world has meant that there are greater costs in serving documents in remoter parts in previous years. Also Commonwealth states exclude service through consular channels and in other states such service may also be excluded.

The costs of serving through the Foreign and Commonwealth Office will be related to the actual costs of service and in certain areas this could be considerably more than the current minimum fee of £30 (fee with effect from April 1989).

Any documents for service through the Foreign and Commonwealth Office should be sent to the Foreign and Commonwealth Office, Nationality and Treaty Department, Clive House, Petty France, London, SW1H 9HD (tel. 071–270 4086 or 4087).

APPENDIX I

UNITED KINGDOM DEPENDENT TERRITORIES

Anguilla
Bermuda
British Antarctic Territory
British Indian Ocean Territory
Cayman Islands
Falkland Islands
Gibraltar
Hong Kong
Montserrat

Pitcairn, Henderson, Ducie and Oeno Islands
St Helena and Dependencies
South Georgia and the South Sandwich Islands
The Sovereign Base Area of Akrotiri and Dhekelia
Turks and Caicos Islands
Virgin Islands

APPENDIX II

HAGUE CONVENTION STATES

Antigua and Barbuda
Barbados
Belgium
Botswana**
Canada
Cyprus
Czechoslovakia*
Denmark
Egypt*
Finland
France
Federal Republic of Germany*
Greece
Israel
Italy
Japan
Luxembourg
Malawi
Netherlands (including Aruba)
Norway*
Pakistan
Portugal
Spain
United States (with extensions to dependent territories)
United Kingdom (with extensions to dependent territories)
Seychelles
Sweden
Turkey*

*Denotes countries which have objected to postal service.

**The *Practical Handbook* should be consulted for advice on the use of postal service in Botswana.

APPENDIX III

BRUSSELS CONVENTION STATES

Belgium
Denmark
France
Germany
Greece**
Ireland*
Italy
Luxembourg
Netherlands
Portugal***
Spain***
United Kingdom

*Ireland is the only member of the European Community which is not also a party to the 1965 Hague Convention.

**The United Kingdom has now ratified the Greek Accession to the Brussels Convention and on 1st October 1989 the Civil Jurisdiction and Judgments Act 1982 (Amendment) Order 1989 (S.I. 1989 No. 1346) came into force with the effect in the UK of extending the 1968 Brussels Judgments Convention to Greece.

***The Spanish and Portuguese Accession Treaty to the Brussels Convention was signed at San Sebastian, Spain on 26th May 1989. This Accession Treaty will require to be ratified by the UK in accordance with section 14 of the Civil Jurisdiction and Judgments Act 1982.

APPENDIX IV

BILATERAL CONVENTION STATES

Austria*
Belgium
Czechoslovakia
Denmark
Finland
France
German Democratic Republic*
Federal Republic of Germany
(including West Berlin)
Greece
Hungary*
Iraq*
Israel
Italy
Laos*
Lebanon*
Netherlands
Norway
Poland*
Portugal
Romania*
Spain
Sweden
Syria*
Turkey
Yugoslavia*

*Denotes countries which are non-Hague or non-Brussels Convention States.

APPENDIX V

PRACTICAL EXAMPLES

A. Court of Session action
Service of an ordinary action in the Federal Republic of Germany.

Steps undertaken

1. Consult rule 74B.
2. Study *Practical Handbook* and ascertain that Germany is a member of the Hague Convention. Study the *Practical Handbook* under Federal Republic of Germany in conjunction with paragraph (1) of rule 74B for acceptable methods and unacceptable methods of service there.
3. Conclude that central authority method is appropriate.
4. Consider rule 74B for further guidance; for example:
   (a) Paragraph (1)(*b*) and (4) providing for service through a central authority via the Foreign and Commonwealth Office.
   (b) Paragraph (7) requiring translation into German of all papers.
   (c) Paragraph (8) requiring the translation to be certified as a correct translation by the person making it and containing his name, address and qualifications.
5. Type out appropriate Hague Convention form as per *Practical Handbook* (see Appendix VI for ease of reference).
6. Send the relevant documents to the Foreign and Commonwealth Office for service in the Federal Republic of Germany, together with a duplicate of those documents.

B. Service in a simplified divorce case in Federal Republic of Germany

Steps undertaken

1. Consult sheriff court ordinary cause rule 139—persons abroad (Federal Republic of Germany).
2. Study *Practical Handbook* and learn that Germany is a member of the Hague Convention on Service. Therefore look at rule 139(1)(*b*) for options.
3. Study the *Practical Handbook* under Federal Republic of Germany for acceptable methods and unacceptable methods of service there.
4. Conclude that central authority method is appropriate.
5. Study the sheriff court rules for further guidance, for example:
   (a) Rule 139(1)(b)(ii) providing for service through a central authority via the Foreign and Commonwealth Office.
   (b) Rule 139(2) and rule 138 setting out the requirements for the form of citation.

(c) Rule 139(4)—the sheriff clerk to send a copy of the application with citation attached with a request for service addressed to the Foreign and Commonwealth Office, and lodging in process a certificate of execution by the serving authority in due course.
(d) Rule 139(6) requiring translation into German of all papers and the notice on the envelope.
(e) Rule 139(7) requiring the translation to be certified as a correct translation by the person making it and containing his name, address and qualifications for lodging in process.

APPENDIX VI

ANNEX TO THE HAGUE CONVENTION - FORMS

REQUEST

FOR SERVICE ABROAD OF JUDICIAL OR EXTRAJUDICIAL DOCUMENTS

Convention on the service abroad of judicial and extrajudicial documents in civil or commercial matters, signed at The Hague, 15 November 1965.

Identity and address of the applicant	Address of receiving authority

The undersigned applicant has the honour to transmit - in duplicate - the documents listed below and, in conformity with article 5 of the above-mentioned Convention, requests prompt service of one copy thereof on the addressee, ie.,

(identity and address) ____________________

____

(a) In accordance with the provisions of sub-paragraph (a) of the first paragraph of article 5 of the Convention *.
(b) In accordance with the following particular method (sub-paragraph (b) of the first paragraph of article 5) *:

____

____

____

(c) by delivery to the addressee, if he accepts it voluntarily (second paragraph of article 5) *.

The authority is requested to return or to have returned to the applicant a copy of the documents - and of the annexes * - with a certificate as provided on the reverse side.

List of Documents

____

____

____

____

____

____

____

____________________ **Done at**

____________________ **Date**

____________________ **Signature and/or stamp**

** Delete if inappropriate*

Reverse of the request

CERTIFICATE

The undersigned authority has the honour to certify, in conformity with article 6 of the Convention,

1) that the document has been served *

- **the (date)** ____________

- **at (place, street, number)** ____________

____

- **in one of the following methods authorised by article 5 -**

(a) in accordance with the provisions of sub-paragraph (a) of the first paragraph of article 5 of the Convention *.

(b) in accordance with the following particular method *: ____________

____

(c) by delivery to the addressee, who accepted it voluntarily *.

The documents referred to in the request have been delivered to :

- **(identity and description of person)** ____________

____

- **relationship to the addressee (family, business or other) :** ____________

____

2) that the document has not been served, by reason of the following facts *:

____

____

____

In conformity with the second paragraph of article 12 of the Convention, the applicant is requested to pay or reimburse the expenses detailed in the attached statement *.

Annexes

Documents returned : ____________

____

____

Done at

In appropriate cases, documents establishing the service : **Date**

____________ **Signature and/or stamp**

____

____

**** Delete if inappropriate***

SUMMARY OF THE DOCUMENT TO BE SERVED

Convention on the service abroad of judicial and extrajudicial documents in civil or commercial matters, signed at The Hague, 15 November 1965.

(article 5, fourth paragraph)

Name and address of the requesting authority : ______________________________

____

____

Particulars of the parties *: ______________________________

____

____

JUDICIAL DOCUMENT **

Nature and purpose of the document : ______________________________

____

____

Nature and purpose of the proceedings and, where appropriate, the amount in dispute : ______________________________

____

____

Date and place for entering appearance **: ______________________________

____

Court which has given judgment **: ______________________________

____

Date of judgment **: ______________________________

Time limits stated in the document **: ______________________________

EXTRAJUDICIAL DOCUMENT **

Nature and purpose of the document : ______________________________

____

____

Time limits stated in the document **: ______________________________

____

____

* *If appropriate, identity and address of the person interested in the transmission of the document.*

** *Delete if inappropriate*

APPENDIX VII

SOURCES OF FURTHER INFORMATION

1. *The Practical Handbook on the Operation of the Hague Convention of 15 November 1965 on the Service Abroad of Judicial and Extra-Judicial Documents in Civil and Commercial Matters*—published by Maarten Kluwers and distributed in the UK by Butterworths. First supplement March 1985. (Each of the departments of the Central Office of the Court of Session has a copy of the handbook available for inspection.)

2. *Civil Jurisdiction in Scotland* by A. E. Anton—published by W. Green & Son (1984), with supplement by A. E. Anton and P. R. Beaumont (1987). This contains the text of the Civil Jurisdiction and Judgments Act 1982 and the Hague Convention.

3. The Foreign and Commonwealth Office,
Nationality and Treaty Department,
Clive House,
Petty France,
London, SW1H 9HD.
(Tel. 071-270 4086 or 4087.)

4. Scottish Courts Administration,
Division II Branch 1,
26/27 Royal Terrace,
Edinburgh, EH7 5AH.
(Tel. 031-556 0755.)

[THE NEXT PAGE IS C 501]

OFFICERS OF THE CT.

① Sheriff Principal - 6 Sheriffdoms each with full-time SP
- responsible for administration of cts. in his sheriffdom
- don't sit as judge at 1st instance but there is right of appeal to him from sh.
- Qualifications - 10 years as an advocate or solicitor

② Sheriff - Qualifications - same as for S.P.
- Appointed to part. sheriffdom + has power to act as sheriff only in that sheriffdom. In practice they are delegated to sit in a part. sheriff ct. or cts.
- JURISDICTION - cases normally raised at a part ct. in the J. (sheriffdom) BUT competent to raise action at different ct. in that sheriffdom
- SIMPSON V BRUCE (1984) - D. raised in Linlithgow. Urgent action for interdict sought on a holiday in Linlithgow so P. raised action in Edinburgh. Competency challenged but held competent

③ "Floating Sheriffs" - introduced by Sheriff Ct. (S) Act 1971 s.10 - allows S.of S to allow a SP or sheriff to sit in any sheriffdom so can go anywhere when need arises

④ Temporary Sheriff - advocate / sol. in private practice with 5 years experience

⑤ Honorary Sheriff - not paid. Usually appointed by SP. Doesn't need legal qualifications. Person of standing in community. Deals usually with urgent cases, handy in remote areas

⑥ Sheriff - Clerk - appointed by S.of S. - usually full time civil servant. Not qualified solicitors.
- Experts on matters of procedure
- normally has a staff of deputes with same powers as Sh. Cl.
- Regional Sheriff - Clerk - power throughout sheriffdom.
- responsible for administration rather than procedure

⑦ Auditor of Court - appointed by SP + is frequently the sh. cl.
- function - takes account of expenses ie vets accounts

⑧ Procurator Fiscal - has limited function in civil cases
- Fatal Accident enquiries - coordinated by PF under 1976 FA Enquiries Act
- Quasi Criminal matters - although in civil ct. some things can give rise to criminal consequences

GO TO C601

Court of Session Practice Notes

23rd July 1952

Cases have been occurring in which Divorce Summonses have designed the defender as " at present a prisoner in " a named prison. This designation enters the Minute Book and if, as frequently happens after a long interval, a certificate or extract is required of the decree of divorce, the designation will re-appear. It is suggested to solicitors that, subject to suitable arrangements being made to secure that service is duly made, it is undesirable that the instance of the Summons should needlessly place on permanent record the fact that the defender was at the time temporarily in custody.

16th April 1953

A case having occurred in which two decrees of declarator of marriage were pronounced relating to the same irregular marriage, the parties having lost touch with each other, arrangements have been made that in all such cases the Registrar General will be prepared on application to state whether a previous declarator has been granted and recorded in his Registers, and a letter from him certifying the result of his search should be lodged in process before the proof.

28th January 1955

Jury Trials

In copying Issues and Counter Issues for the use of the court at the trial of the cause it is not necessary for parties to reproduce the docquet of authentication.

28th September 1956

It has been arranged that photostatic copies of entries in the Register of Births will be treated by the court as equivalent to the principals. In Scotland, applications for such photostatic copies should be made to the Registrar General of Births, Deaths and Marriages for Scotland, who holds duplicate originals of all entries, but in England where the system is different, applications should be made to the local Registrars.

11th January 1957

On and after 31st January all motions enrolled on Thursday for Saturday will appear in the motion roll for the following Tuesday with the exception of matters of especial urgency which in the discretion of the Deputy Principal Clerk may be put out for hearing on the Saturday.

15th November 1957

The attention of all members of the legal profession is drawn to complaints which have been received from hospital boards regarding the condition in which hospital reports and X-ray plates, produced for use in the courts, have been returned to hospitals on the termination of proceedings. It is reported that X-ray plates in particular have been returned so folded and cracked that their value has been most seriously affected when the condition of the patient has required further examination of the plates.

It is hoped that in future the greatest care will be used in dealing with such productions, especially in guarding them from damage during transmission.

7th May 1959

Appeals to the House of Lords

Notice has been given of certain changes in the Standing Orders of the House of Lords and in the directions as to procedure in relation to appeals with effect from 1st April 1959. In particular with reference to judgments of the courts below, it is provided that—

> " If the cause has been reported in a Report which is ordinarily received in court, copies of the Report may be lodged in lieu of the reproduction in the Appendix of the judgments of the courts below *in extenso*."

In this connection, solicitors acting for appellants are invited to inform the Editor of Session Cases, in writing, *immediately* it has been decided to appeal a case to the House of Lords. If such intimation is made, the report of the case in Session Cases will be expedited so that it may be available for lodging with the appellant's case and Appendix.

16th November 1961

On and after 21st November 1961, it shall be sufficient compliance with any requirement for the walling of an application to the Court of Session that a typed slip shall be lodged for walling specifying (a) the nature of the application (*e.g.*, Petition, Note, etc.), (b) the name and address of the applicant, (c) the general purposes of the application (*e.g.*, for reduction of capital, custody, etc.) and (d) the name of the solicitor for the applicant.

After said date a full copy of the application shall no longer be lodged for walling.

20th March 1962

Where, in the opinion of one party to an action in the Court of Session, there is unnecessary delay on the part of another party in lodging his account of expenses for taxation, it shall be competent for the first-mentioned party to enrol a motion with a view to moving the court to ordain the other party to lodge his account for taxation within such period as the court may deem reasonable.

26th October 1962

As from this date, in every action in which the record is closed, the solicitor for the pursuer shall lodge in process three copies of the closed record. One copy will be the process copy, the second will be for the use of the Clerk of Court and the third will be transmitted by the Petition or General Department to the Principal Clerk and used by him for the preparation of lists of proofs, etc., for fixing diets.

28th June 1963

Notwithstanding that a case has been sent to the " By Order (Adjustment) " Roll at the closing of the Record, issues and counter issues must still be lodged in terms of the Rules of Court.

26th November 1963

Where a case is closed and sent to the By Order (Adjustment) Roll and the prints of the Closed Record are brought in late but in time for the By Order Appearance, no motion will normally be required.

A motion would be necessary if, for example, a counter issue were due to be lodged and not enough time would elapse by the By Order appearance. Each case will be dealt with on its merits.

15th July 1964

Copies of productions for the use of the court shall be made available at least 48 hours before the diet of proof or jury trial.

10th March 1966

A summons of divorce or declarator of marriage where the address of the defender is unknown and the marriage has been celebrated in Scotland must be rejected out of hand if no up-to-date marriage certificate is produced when the summons is lodged.

1st June 1967

At the appearance in the By Order (Adjustment) Roll on and after 23rd June 1967, counsel for the parties will be expected to state to the Court whether they have agreed as to the future procedure in the cause and with what result.

If not agreement has been reached counsel for each of the parties will be expected to state to the Court the considered attitude to be adopted by the party for whom he appears with regard to the future procedure in the cause, and in particular without prejudice to the right of any party to make at that stage any appropriate motion with regard to that future procedure whether that party is to contend

(1) that any preliminary plea should be sustained or repelled without inquiry into the facts, or
(2) that certain of the averments should not be remitted to probation, in which event a specific plea directed to this matter shall be stated on record, or
(3) that any preliminary plea should be reserved until after inquiry into the facts, or
(4) that any inquiry should be by way of proof rather than trial upon an issue, or
(5) that any proof allowed should be in any way restricted and if so to what extent.

The interlocutor pronounced by the Court in the By Order (Adjustment) Roll shall specify what the Lord Ordinary has decided as regards these contentions or any of them.

The Court may take into account in determining any question of expenses at any subsequent stage of the cause the submission made by the parties in the By Order (Adjustment) Roll.

6th June 1968

It shall no longer be necessary, in connection with any action pending before the Court of Session, that a Medical Certificate should bear the words " on soul and conscience."

6th June 1968

An Officer who has furnished a Report to the Court under subsection (1) of section 11 of the Matrimonial Proceedings (Children) Act 1958 shall not be cited as a witness unless, in terms of subsection (4) of said section, the Court, on consideration of such a Report, either *ex proprio motu* or on the application of any person interested requires the person who furnished the Report to appear and be examined on oath regarding any matter dealt with in the Report, and such person may be examined or cross-examined accordingly.

18th July 1968

The attention of solicitors is called to the Act of Sederunt dated 11th July 1968 which prescribes the form of an extract decree of divorce. In cases where the prescribed form is applicable it shall no longer be necessary to prepare a Note to the Extractor. In all other cases the Note to the Extractor will continue to be required.

All amendments to the Instance and Conclusions of the Summons must have been given effect to before the Extract is ordered.

16th December 1968

The operation of Rules of Court 90 (c) and 91 (a) to (c), in so far as they regulate the procedure relating to the Adjustment Roll, will continue to be suspended, and in room thereof the following procedure will apply:

1. At the first appearance of a cause in the Adjustment Roll a continuation of 12 weeks, excluding vacations, will be given in every case, without the attendance of Counsel, provided that (1) not earlier than four weeks after the date of the Interlocutor continuing the cause for adjustment it shall be competent to any party to the cause to enrol that the Record be closed, and the Court in considering such motion, shall have regard to the state of the pleadings as adjusted, as at the date of the enrolment; (2) it shall be competent for any party to the cause to enrol for an extension of the 12-week period of adjustment, which shall only be granted on special cause shown. The party enrolling in either of these two instances shall lodge in process a copy of the Open Record showing all adjustments as at the date of the enrolment and the dates on which such adjustments were made, and (3) it will be open to parties to enrol of consent, at any time not later than 14 days before the expiry of the said 12-week period of adjustment, to close the Record and for proof or allowance of issues or to appoint the cause to the By Order (Adjustment) Roll.

2. When a cause has been sisted any period of adjustment prior to the sist will be reckoned as part of the period of adjustment.

3. Not later than 1 p.m. on the Monday preceding the termination of said twelve-week period of adjustment it will be open to parties to enrol of consent for proof or allowance of issues. The appropriate interlocutor, bearing the date of the appearance of the cause in the Continued Adjustment Roll will thereafter be written. In all causes in which no such enrolment is made an interlocutor will be written on said date appointing the cause to the By Order (Adjustment) Roll. No appearance of Counsel will be required in either of these cases. The By Order (Adjustment) Roll is intended to apply only to causes where there is some dispute as to what the future of the cause should be. Notwithstanding that a cause has been sent to the By Order (Adjustment) Roll issues and counter issues must still be lodged in terms of Rule 114.

4. After the Record has been closed any alteration to the pleadings which, if the Record had not been closed would have been made by adjustment, shall be made by Minute of Amendment and Answers, and in deciding the conditions as regards expenses on which such alterations may be allowed the Court shall take into account the nature of the adjustments made by the parties during the period of adjustment and the dates on which such adjustments were intimated. To enable the Court to determine the question of expenses the party craving leave to amend shall lodge prior to the hearing a copy of the Open Record showing all adjustments to date and the dates when such adjustments were made.

[1] 5. All causes appointed to the By Order (Adjustment) Roll will appear therein on the fifth Friday after the closing of the Record and where the fifth Friday falls in vacation or recess the cause will appear on the first Friday of the ensuing session, provided that not later than 1 p.m. on the Wednesday of the third week after the date of the closing of the Record it will be open to parties to enrol of consent for proof or allowance of issues or to appoint the cause to the Procedure Roll; and on such motion being granted the cause shall be deleted from the By Order (Adjustment) Roll.

NOTE

[1] See Practice Note, 23rd November 1973, *infra*.

6. Any offer of a proof before answer during the period between the closing of the Record and the disposal of the cause in the By Order (Adjustment) Roll shall be intimated in writing by the solicitor making such offer to the opposite party or parties not later than forty-eight hours before the appearance of the cause in the By Order (Adjustment) Roll.

18th July 1969

With effect from 1st August 1969, the amount of the Fee Fund Dues which are payable when lodging an Account of Expenses in process should not be included as an outlay in the Account. The sum paid for these Fee Fund Dues will be added to the total amount of the Account by the Auditor.

[1] **13th November 1969**

1. All motions for interim custody and for interim aliment, or for a variation thereof, shall as from this date be on a seven day intimation, except in the case of special urgency, when the normal 48 hours intimation will apply.

2. Appeals and Remits from Inferior Courts. Notwithstanding the terms of Rule of Court 269 (*a*) as from this date it shall be sufficient compliance therewith if the Edinburgh solicitors for the parties within the prescribed period intimate appearance by recorded delivery letter to the Deputy Principal Clerk. The receipt of the appeal or remit will thereafter be intimated by the Deputy Principal Clerk to the solicitors concerned.

3. Remits to Reporters in Consistorial Causes. As from this date the party moving the court for a remit, or the pursuer or minuter where the remit is made by the court *ex proprio motu*, shall in the first instance be responsible for the Reporter's fees and outlays, including the cost of both copies of the Report and the fee to the Reporter's Clerk. Where the remit is made by the court *ex proprio motu* it shall be the duty of the solicitor for the pursuer or minuter to instruct the Reporter, by submitting to him a copy of the Interlocutor containing the remit, a copy of the summons, and any relevant productions. In all other cases this duty shall devolve upon the party moving the court for a remit. The provisions of Rule of Court 97 shall apply *mutatis mutandis* to such remits.

NOTE

[1] See Practice Note, 9th July 1974, *infra*.

3rd December 1969

When a petition under the Trusts (Scotland) Act 1961 is ready for hearing it is requested that the solicitor for the Petitioner should attend upon the Principal Clerk in order that a date may be fixed for the disposal of the petition.

16th January 1970

Modification of Expenses Awarded against Assisted Persons

In future, in all actions in which expenses are awarded against an assisted person, it shall not be necessary for the Court, unless it thinks fit to order otherwise, to remit the account of expenses of the party in whose favour the award is made, to the Auditor of Court for taxation, but the court may, on the motion of any party to the cause, proceed forthwith to determine to what extent the liability of the assisted person for such expenses shall be modified.

20th February 1970

Because of unavoidable deletions from and additions to the By Order (Adjustment) Roll after its publication in the week's Roll, it is suggested that solicitors should await the second publication of the Roll on the following Wednesday, when the numbering of each case is finally determined, before instructing Counsel.

31st March 1970

Vacation Court

1. All motions which would require the appearance of counsel in session will require the appearance of counsel or solicitor in vacation.
2. At the time when a motion is enrolled for the vacation court the enrolling solicitor shall be informed whether or not appearance is required. This intimation shall not subsequently be revoked or altered.
3. The vacation court will commence at 10.30 a.m. Arrangements have been made for bail appeals and sentences to be taken on a day other than the day of the vacation court.
4. All unopposed motions in which appearance is required shall be heard before opposed motions and shall be called in alphabetical order. No distinction should be made between petition department and general department motions.
5. Thereafter opposed motions will be taken. A list of such motions in alphabetical order will be affixed to the notice board as soon as practicable after 2.15 p.m. on the day preceding the vacation court. The opposed motions will be called in the order in the list and no distinction should be made between petition department and general department motions. Counsel will be expected to inform the judge if any motion is expected to be complicated or to take a long time, in which event the judge may order it to be taken at the end of the opposed motions list.

14th May 1970

As from this date a Bond of Caution can be uplifted from the Accountant of Court on exhibition to him of the Interlocutor granting discharge. For this purpose the process should be transmitted to the Accountant by the solicitor.

This Note is issued to confirm the practice that it is in the discretion of the Lord Ordinary to grant a right of reply to the defender's speech made at the conclusion of a proof.

2nd March 1972

In conformity with the existing practice in criminal proceedings, where, in a civil action, objection is taken to the competency or relevancy of a question, the shorthand writer will record the submissions of Counsel.

5th May 1972

In order to facilitate more expeditious disposal of cases in Procedure Roll, the court will, from and after 19th May 1972, in any case where it is moved that a cause be sent to Procedure Roll, ask to be supplied by Counsel with the best estimate that can be made of the duration of the debate. One of the effects of this, it is hoped, will be to enable the Principal Clerk to group together, for hearing on any particular day, a number of cases of short duration. Although intimation of diets of Procedure Roll will continue to be peremptory, the Principal Clerk will, if requested, provide a fixed diet for any case which might occupy a full day or longer.

14th December 1972

Medical records required for the purposes of a court action should at all times be available to a party's medical attendant.[1] With effect from this date it will be the duty of the solicitor concerned immediately on receipt by him of such records to furnish the medical attendant with a copy thereof. If medical records are received by the court marked " confidential " it will be the duty of the solicitor concerned immediately to enrol a motion to have the envelope containing such records opened up and, if the court admits the same, to transmit a copy thereof without delay to the medical attendant.

NOTE

[1] " Medical attendant " means " general practitioner." The practice note does not refer to hospital records.

[1] 4th January 1973

With effect from Thursday, 26th April 1973 and for an experimental period, the following provisions will apply herewith notwithstanding any Rule of Court inconsistent.

(1) In a consistorial cause an open record shall only be made up with leave of the court on special cause shown.

(2) Where any action, such as is referred to in Rule 165 (*a*) is defended only on the amount of the capital sum, periodical allowance or aliment, the defender or his *curator ad litem* shall not lodge a minute in terms of said Rule but shall lodge defences. All references in Rule 165 (*a*) to answers being lodged by the other party, and the whole of Rule 165 (*b*) shall during the operation of this practice note be suspended.

(3) In all cases to which Rule 167 (*d*) relates a defender shall in the circumstances therein specified lodge defences, and no answers shall be required of the pursuer.

(4) In any consistorial cause in which defences or a minute in terms of Rule 161 have been lodged, the parties to all consistorial actions signetted on and after said date may adjust their respective pleadings, subject to paragraph (5) hereof, for a period, excluding vacations, not exceeding six weeks from the date of the lodging of the defences or minute.

(5) If any party to the cause wishes an extension of said adjustment period he may enrol at any time before the expiry of said period for such an extension, which shall only be granted by the court on special cause shown.

(6) Within 14 days from the expiry of the said six week adjustment period, or any extension thereof, the pursuer shall:—

(*a*) make up a copy of the adjusted pleadings in a form equivalent to that of a Closed Record;

(*b*) lodge three copies thereof in process, which copies may be in typescript;

(*c*) supply one copy to each other party to the cause; and

(*d*) enrol a motion craving the court to send the cause to the appropriate Roll for proof or to the Procedure Roll.

(7) There will be two Rolls of defended consistorial causes in which proof has been allowed. Roll number 1 will consist of those cases the proof in which is likely to be of short duration. Such cases will normally be those in which the defences relate solely to access, aliment, periodical allowance, or capital sum, but may include certain cases in which custody of children is in issue between the parties and which might be suitable for inclusion in this Roll. Roll number 2 will consist of all other cases.

NOTE

[1] See Practice Note, 1976 no. 5, *infra*.

14th April 1973

Office of Auditor of Court of Session: Value added tax; Taxation of expenses in (1) Civil proceedings; (2) Criminal proceedings and (3) General business.

The Act of Sederunt (Rules of Court Amendment No. 2) 1973 which came into operation on 2nd April 1973, authorises solicitors to make an addition to fees, where appropriate, of such amount as is equivalent to the rate of value added tax at the date of its first introduction on 1st April 1973, or from time to time. (Note: the reference to Chapter VI in the above Act is intended for Chapter V.)

Value added tax was introduced by the Finance Act 1972. Every taxable person as defined by the Act must be registered and in general terms (and subject to the exceptions set out in the Act) whenever a taxable person supplies goods or services in the United Kingdom in the course of business a liability to tax arises.

Responsibility for making a charge for VAT in a proper case and for accounting to Customs and Excise for the proper amount of VAT is solely that of the registered person concerned.

The following directions will apply to all accounts lodged for taxation which include any charge for work done or services rendered on or after 1st April 1973, namely:—

1. *Registered Number*

The registered number allocated by Customs and Excise to every person registered under the Act must appear in a prominent place at the head of every Account of Expenses, Business Accounts, Note of Fee, account or voucher on which VAT is claimed or chargeable.

2. *Action before Taxation*

(a) If there is a possibility of a dispute as to whether any person claiming expenses is a taxable person or whether any service in respect of which a charge is proposed to be made in the account is zero rated or exempt, reference should be made to Customs and Excise, and wherever possible, a statement produced on taxation.

(b) Where VAT is claimed by a person who is engaged in business and the expenses of the proceedings to be submitted for taxation are chargeable as an expense of that business, then (unless the paying party agrees the basis on which VAT is claimed) a certificate must be produced on taxation that the receiving party is not entitled to recover, or is only entitled to recover a stated proportion of, the VAT claimed on such expenses as input tax in his VAT account with Customs and Excise. A form of certificate to be given by the Solicitor or accountant for the party receiving expenses is set out in the schedule hereto.

3. *Form of Accounts*

The form of accounts in practice will require amendment as follows:—

(a) *Apportionment*

The account must be divided into separate parts so as to show the work done on a day to day basis before and from 1st April 1973. Wherever a lump sum charge has been made for work, only part of which was performed by 31st March 1973, the lump sum or scale fee must also be apportioned.

(b) *Disbursements*

(i) VAT attributable to any disbursement must be shown stating it has been paid. This will consist of the VAT which has been paid at the time when the account is drawn and an amount in respect of any unpaid disbursement. These amounts may be shown in the disbursement column immediately below the disbursement to which it relates.

(ii) Posts and incidents should be charged with VAT even though they bear no tax when the Solicitor incurs them.

It is otherwise where the disbursement is normally charged as a specific disbursement to the client, *e.g.* the cost of travel by public transport on a specific journey for a particular client. Taxi fares, however, are subject to VAT.

The end of the account must show the total for VAT including the VAT on the fees and posts.

The fee fund dues on Auditor's fee will be calculated on the total of profit fees and disbursements as lodged without the VAT thereon.

(c) *Legal Aid*

In legal aid cases the account must be drawn so as to show the total VAT on counsel's fees as a separate item from the VAT on profit costs and other disbursements and must take account of the fact that VAT will only be payable on 90 per cent. of the solicitor profit fees and counsel's fees (see para. 7 below).

4. *Tax Invoice in Judicial Proceedings*

The taxed account is always retained in process so that where a Solicitor waives his Solicitor and own client expenses and accepts the taxed expenses payable by the unsuccessful party in settlement it will be necessary for a short statement as to the amount of the taxed expenses and the VAT thereon to be prepared for use as the tax invoice.

5. *Vouchers*

Where receipted accounts for disbursement made by the solicitor or his client are retained as tax invoices a photostat copy of any such receipted account may be produced and will be accepted as sufficient evidence of payment when disbursements are vouched.

6. *Rate of VAT*

The rate of VAT which will be applied on taxation will be the rate at that date, save in respect of disbursements which have been paid when the rate will be the rate at the date of payment. Should there be a change in the rate applied on taxation between the date of taxation and the signing of the report of taxation, any interested party may apply for the taxation to be varied so as to take account of any increase or reduction in the amount of tax payable. Once the report of taxation has been signed no variation will be possible.

7. *Calculation of VAT Recoverable by a Legally Aided Party*

VAT will not be recoverable on the 10 per cent. of the solicitor's fees and counsel's fees which is retained by the legal aid fund. Accordingly, the recoverable VAT must be calculated on 90 per cent. of the Solicitor's fees and 90 per cent. of counsel's fees. This will not apply to other disbursements, which are paid in full by the legal aid fund.

8. *Auditor's Reports*

In non legal aid cases the total VAT allowed will be shown as a separate item. In legal aid cases the VAT on counsel's fees will be shown separately from the remaining VAT.

9. *Posts and Incidents*

Posts and incidents must be shown separately at the different rates in operation before and after 1st April 1973. Posts and incidents are not chargeable on the 10 per cent. increase in fees for VAT.

10. *Fee Fund Dues and Auditor's Fees*

The sums payable as fee fund dues on an account of expenses or as Auditor's fees should not be added to the account. The appropriate sum will be added to the account by the Auditor. When it is impossible to ascertain the correct sum payable as fee fund dues when lodging an account in process (*e.g.* where an additional fee is allowed under the Rules of Court 347 (*d*)) arrangements may be made for the fee fund stamps to be affixed to the account after taxation.

11. *Witnesses Expenses*

In cases where it is impossible, because of the incidence of VAT for witnesses to incur accounts for subsistence at or below the levels prescribed by the Act of Sederunt (Rules of Court Amendment No. 5) 1970, such higher sums may be allowed as the Auditor may determine as having been reasonably incurred.

SCHEDULE

FORM OF CERTIFICATE

Address:
Date:

To: The Auditor of the Court of Session

A. *v.* B.C. Ltd.

With reference to the pending taxation of the defender's (or as the case may be) fees and disbursements herein which are payable by the pursuer, or (as the case may be) we the undersigned as (solicitors to) (the auditors of) the above-named defender (or as the case may be) company, hereby certify that the defender (or as the case may be) company on the basis of its last completed VAT return would (not be entitled to recover) (be entitled to recover only per cent. of the) value added tax on such fees and disbursements, as input tax pursuant to s. 3 of the Finance Act 1972.

(Signed) ....
Solicitor/Auditor, to/or (Defender)
....
Registered No. ....

23rd November 1973

By Order (Adjustment) Roll

Paragraph 5 of the Practice Note dated 16th December 1968 [*supra*] is amended as from this date to the effect that a motion enrolled of consent for proof or allowance of issues or to appoint the cause to the Procedure Roll will no longer require the written concurrence of the opposite party but such a motion will require to be intimated in the usual way.

Paragraph 5 is further amended, to the effect that from and after 5th December 1973, all causes appointed to the By Order (Adjustment) Roll will appear on the fifth *Wednesday* after the closing of the Record and where the fifth Wednesday fallvs in vacation or recess the cause will appear on the first Wednesday of the ensuing session.

Should any case remain in the published By Order (Adjustment) Roll after a motion has been enrolled, the disposal of which would result in the case being removed from that Roll, no appearance of counsel in the By Order Roll will be necessary.

9th July 1974

Fees and Expenses of Reporters in Matters Affecting Children

The payment of fees and expenses to Reporters is governed by the Practice Note dated 13th November 1969. Recent experience has shown, however, that in many instances payments to Reporters of their fees and reimbursement of their necessary expenses are being delayed for unacceptably long periods after their Reports have been lodged with the Deputy Principal Clerk of Session. It appears therefore that the terms of the Practice Note are not in all cases being observed. Attention is accordingly drawn once again to that Practice Note which is in the following terms:—

> "Remits to Reporters in Consistorial Causes. As from this date the party moving the Court for a remit, or the pursuer or minuter where the remit is made by the Court *ex proprio motu*, shall in the first instance be responsible for the Reporter's fees and outlays, including the cost of both copies of the Report and the fee to the Reporter's Clerk. Where the remit is made by the Court *ex proprio motu* it shall be the duty of the solicitor for the pursuer or minuter to instruct the Reporter, by submitting to him a copy of the Interlocutor containing the remit, a copy of the summons, and any relevant productions. In all other cases this duty shall devolve upon the party moving the Court for a remit. The provisions of Rule of Court 97 shall apply *mutatis mutandis* to such remits."

Solicitors are reminded that in Legal Aid cases arrangements already exist under which, on receipt of intimation of a note of the Reporter's fee and outlays, an application to the Legal Aid Central Committee for the necessary advance will normally be granted immediately.

21st November 1974

Fixing of Undefended Proofs

As from Tuesday, 7th January, 1975, the attendance of solicitors for the purpose of fixing diets of undefended proofs will no longer be required. The new procedure will be as follows:—

1. On a proof before answer being allowed the solicitor for the pursuer will complete a Form in the terms annexed hereto. Solicitors will require to reproduce their own copies of the Form and will either post or deliver the same to the Assistant to the Principal Clerk, Room 25, Parliament House, Edinburgh.

2. On receipt of said completed Form the Assistant to the Principal Clerk will allocate a date for the proof and return the Form to the solicitor bearing thereon the date allocated. The completed Form will take the place of the old proof slip and should be presented by the Solicitor without delay, to the Process Department for completion of the Interlocutor allowing the proof before answer.

3. There will be no change in the existing practice of fixing continued proofs.

Request for Diet of Undefended Proof

1. Full name of pursuer ....
2. Full name of defender ....
3. Name of Counsel ....
4. Ground of action ....
5. Date of Calling ....
6. Date when proof before answer allowed ....
7. Date of last Interlocutor, if any, subsequent to date of allowance of p.b.a. ....
8. Estimated ruation of proof (if likely to exceed the normal time for an undefended proof) ....
9. If requesting accelerated diet, state reason, and also state date of diet of proof if already fixed ....
10. Date allocated for proof (to be filled in by the Assistant to the Principal Clerk) ....

17th December 1974

A case arose recently where a copy Summons was posted to a member of Her Majesty's Forces whose address was a private billet in Northern Ireland. The envelope containing the copy Summons revealed his name, rank and number. In future, such information should be excluded from the address on the envelope, and the recipient should be addressed as if he were a private citizen. Where the address of the barracks to which the recipient is attached is known, any document should be sent there rather than to his private billet.

20th December 1974

[Revoked by No. 2 of 1987: 30th July 1987.]

29th May 1975

Solicitors who attend Parliament House frequently are reminded that they may collect completed Proof forms in Folders provided in Cabinet at entrance to General Department. Completed forms for those Solicitors who only occasionally attend will be returned by post.

Diets of Proof and Hearing

1. Without prejudice to the procedure set out in the Practice Note of 20th December 1974, an application for the allocation of a special diet may, of consent of all parties concerned and if made before a diet has been fixed, be submitted to the Principal Clerk. Such an application will only be granted on cause shown.

Where such an application is refused and parties express to the Principal Clerk dissatisfaction with his decision he will bring the matter to the notice of the Lord President. Thereafter it will be disposed of in chambers at the earliest convenient time, either by the Lord President or by a judge nominated by him.

2. It will be appreciated that in planning the major work of the court, accurate forecasts of the probable duration of proofs, trials and hearings are essential if inconvenience to litigants and practitioners is to be minimised and the best use of judicial time secured. Solicitors are again reminded of the importance of giving the most accurate possible forecast of the time likely to be required in cases for which diets are to be fixed. If at any time after such an initial forecast has been intimated it becomes clear that the time allotted for a particular case is likely to be materially longer or shorter than the case will require, solicitors are urged to inform the Keeper of the Rolls at the earliest possible moment.

1976 No. 1

1. In an attempt to reduce delays at the public counter of the sections of the General Department it is proposed, with the approval of the Lord President and the concurrence of the Joint Committee, to introduce for an experimental period a system whereby in the majority of consistorial actions the court will allow proof before answer without the necessity for the enrolment of a motion to that effect. It is also hoped to save time and trouble both to practitioners and departmental staff by eliminating the necessity for the attendance of practitioners at the General Department for the purpose of copying the interlocutor allowing proof before answer.

2. The following procedure therefore will apply from the 2nd February 1976.

(1) In all consistorial actions, in which either no defences are lodged or in which no motion has already been enrolled, a proof before answer will be allowed without the enrolment of a motion as soon after the lapse of seven days from the date of calling as may be practicable. Separate motions will still be required in all cases in which procedure other than a straightforward proof before answer is necessary.

(2) Lists of cases which have been dealt with under this procedure will be published in the daily rolls during session and from time to time during vacation giving the following information:—(i) The names of the parties, (ii) the name of the solicitor for the pursuer, (iii) the name of the judge who has allowed proof before answer, and (iv) the date of the relevant interlocutor.

(3) As soon as publication has taken place under the foregoing provisions practitioners will be free to request a diet of proof in conformity with existing practice. It will be the duty of practitioners to draw to the attention of the General Department any case in which action under sub-paragraph (1) appears to have been overlooked.

(4) Practitioners will not be expected to copy interlocutors allowing proof before answer unless they wish them to be officially certified.

1976 No. 2

Petition for sanction of schemes of arrangement under section 206 of the Companies Act 1948:—solicitors are advised that when they enrol a motion for a first order in such a petition they may at the same time enrol a separate motion of the same date for the appointment by the court of a reporter for the process. The person so appointed will be the same person to whom the court will ultimately remit the petition for report.

1976 No. 3

1. For the following reasons it has been decided that it would be desirable to combine the process of signeting a summons with that of registration of the cause in the offices of the Court of Session:

(a) Having regard to the restricted hours within which a summons normally can be signeted, the signeting of over 13,000 summonses a year causes inconvenience to practitioners. One consequence has been that summonses are not, and cannot be, examined as critically as is desirable. Thus errors which a detailed scrutiny would have disclosed are not detected, and time and trouble are subsequently required to rectify matters. It would clearly be advantageous to all if a critical scrutiny were to be effected by an appropriate authority prior to the summons passing the signet, and one way in which this could be achieved would be to have the responsibilities for signeting assumed by suitable officers on the staff of the Court.

(b) At present there is no means by which a service copy summons served by post and returned to the court as undelivered under the provisions of the Citation Amendment Acts can be swiftly and effectively related to the relevant process. Because of the importance to the court of the provisions for service, the accurate processing of returned citations makes a substantial demand on administrative time. Registration before service, by allowing returned citations to be immediately married to the process, would not only save staff time but, by reducing the margin of error, would render the litigation procedure more efficient.

(c) Similarly, the many letters presently addressed to the court by recipients of a service copy summons which cannot be related to an action already registered present a problem whose solution is prodigal of staff time. For instance, it is often difficult to discover whether or not the inquirer is writing about an action already lodged, one about to be lodged, or one merely being contemplated. In addition, letters arrive from next-of-kin giving new addresses of defenders, but the court staff can, under present procedure, take no action to pass on this information because they are unaware of the identity of the solicitor for the pursuer until a summons is lodged for calling. Registration prior to service again presents a simple and effective solution to these difficulties.

(d) The restricted hours of attendance at the Signet Office presently place some constraint on the freedom of action of practitioners. It would be advantageous if a summons for signeting could be lodged at any time during the general hours of the offices of court and be collected, after scrutiny, by subsequent arrangement (with exceptional facilities being provided outwith normal hours for cases of urgency).

(e) Delays at the public counter of the sections of the general department place unjustifiable demands on the time of practitioners and their employees. These delays could be considerably reduced if the scrutiny, registration and signeting were a single procedure capable of being carried out in the absence of practitioners at a time when officers of the general department were not subject to other urgent pressures. For example, a summons for signeting, along with a process and, in consistorial actions, the relevant productions, might normally be handed over the counter one day and collected the next. During the intervening period the summons would be examined for errors capable of rectification before signeting with a view to reducing, if not obviating, subsequent motions for amendment of the summons. The numbering of the steps of process and the inclusion of the serial number might be the responsibility of the general department staff and not, as at present, that of the presenter of the summons; this should again save time and trouble to practitioners and their staffs.

(f) Delays are also caused by attendance at the sections in the general department at the stage of lodging for calling. These could largely be eliminated by the introduction of a system of prior registration and scrutiny. It is envisaged that, after service, the summons, with a calling slip, would be returned to the general department and left to be examined. If found to be in order the summons would be called; if not the solicitor would be informed. To allow time for checking the executions of service, the summons would require to be returned two days before the day on which it was to be called, and it is thought that such an extended period ought not to prove objectionable. It happens at present during vacation and the proposed procedure should again restrict, if not eliminate, delay at the counter.

2. It has for these reasons been agreed by the Keeper of the Signet that he will grant a commission to the Principal Clerk of Session and Justiciary to signet summonses and letters and in future that all summonses, and letters of inhibition, etc., shall be signeted by a court official acting under authority from the Principal Clerk.

3. Commencing on 3rd May 1976 the following procedure will apply:

(i) Summonses for signeting will be presented to the general department within the prescribed hours of that office. At the time of presentation solicitors will also lodge a complete process, including the productions in consistorial cases, and will pay both the fee exigible under the present table for signeting and that prescribed in respect of lodging for calling. (In due course it is hoped that a unified fee for both processes will be authorised.) Once a fiat has been obtained, letters of inhibition, etc., may be presented for signeting and immediate return during office hours.

(ii) All summonses lodged before 4.00 p.m., if found to be in order, will be registered, signeted and available for collection by 10.30 a.m. the following day.

(iii) Before service, solicitors must endorse on each service copy the appropriate registration number assigned to the summons and process.

(iv) In an emergency a summons may be registered and signeted outwith the prescribed hours of the general department. For this purpose an officer of the Court of Session will be available to attend at Parliament House on request, and the name and telephone number of the appropriate duty officer will be published weekly in the rolls and posted on the walls of the court.

(v) Should a summons require to be re-signeted this will be done without extra charge.

(vi) Summonses shall be lodged for calling in the general department not later than 1 p.m. on the second day preceding any calling day and to that extent Rule 78 (*a*) is meantime suspended.

1976 No. 4

Fee fund dues

As solicitors will be aware, the Court of Session (Scotland) (Fees) Order 1976, made on 10th February 1976, enacted that as from 1st April 1976 all fees payable to the Court of Session will cease to be collected in stamps. It is recognised that the payment of many individual fees, whether by cheques or by cash, would present some inconvenience to practitioners and that even the physical transmission of funds would create security difficulties. It has accordingly been decided that the general interest would best be served by the introduction of a credit system, and the following arrangements will therefore apply as from 1st April 1976.

1. There will be a central cashier's office for the Court of Session which will in the meantime be situated in room J15.

2. No cash will be handed over in either the general or petition departments in respect of any fee which is payable there. Instead, any fee due to be paid in either of these departments by any solicitor will be debited by the cashier to the account of the appropriate firm. This will include fees due in respect of requests for certified copy interlocutors.

3. A statement of account will thereafter be rendered to the appropriate firm weekly. This statement will show both the details of the individual items and the total due, and will be for immediate settlement which may be made by a single payment at the office of the cashier during business hours.

4. It is an essential feature of the scheme that all accounts be settled promptly and it is hoped that solicitors will co-operate with the departments in this respect.

5. The credit scheme will not in the meantime apply to payments falling to be made in the office of the extractor, in the opinions room, and in the teinds and the justiciary offices.

6. During the period from 1st April to 2nd May (when on the latter date the Court of Session will assume the duties of the signeting office) signeting dues will be payable in cash.

1976 No. 5

1. In an attempt to minimise the difficulties being experienced in the disposal of the constantly increasing volume of business on the motion roll, the following modifications to the existing procedure applicable to the lodgment, publication and disposal of motions are proposed as from 6th January 1977.

2. The latest time for lodging or marking opposition to a motion will be advanced by thirty minutes from 1.00 p.m. to 12.30 p.m., and to that extent Rules 93 (*c*), 198 and 262 are till further notice to be regarded as modified.

3. The existing practice of allocating daily to individual judges a substantial roll of both starred and unstarred motions will be discontinued. Only starred motions will be allocated to named judges. Lists of such motions will continue to be published in the rolls as at present.

4. A single comprehensive list of unstarred motions will also be published in the rolls daily. These motions will not be assigned to an individual judge, but will be dealt with by the court in accordance with existing practice under administrative arrangements decided upon as being from day to day most convenient.

5. Inquiries in relation to starred motions should therefore continue to be addressed to the appropriate Depute Clerk of Session. Any queries as to the allocation of unstarred motions should in the first instance be directed to the Assistant Keeper of the Rolls who will be able to indicate to which depute responsibility for disposal has been delegated.

6. Practitioners are asked to help the court to avoid delay in the disposal of starred motions by giving to the Keeper of the Rolls prior notice of any motion which may involve substantial discussion and thus be liable to

pre-empt judicial time for more than 30 minutes. Where possible, ad hoc arrangements will be made for the hearing of such a case and the co-operation of all concerned in complying with this request will be much appreciated.

7. The principles set out in this practice note have been discussed with representatives of Faculty and the joint committee.

1976 No. 6

Defended Consistorial Causes—4th January 1973

The object of this practice note which is published [*supra*] was to bring such actions into a state of readiness to be sent to the appropriate rolls for disposal on a shorter pleading timetable than is prescribed by the rules of court. Late lodging of records has been defeating this object in a significant number of instances, and practitioners are accordingly reminded of the importance of complying strictly in all such actions with the requirements of paragraph 6 of the practice note.

1977 No. 1

1. In order to ensure as smooth a transition as possible between arrangements for the despatch of business under the old and new consistorial procedures, it would be desirable to minimise the backlog of outstanding cases falling to be dealt with under the former grounds of jurisdiction. To this end, it is proposed to make available during the current term sufficient diets of undefended proof as to enable arrears substantially to be overcome and it is hoped that practitioners will co-operate in this respect by making arrangements to fix diets of proof in all possible outstanding undefended cases. The profession is advised that after the end of the current term difficulty may be experienced in the assignment of diets of undefended proof in any case brought under the former procedure.

2. It is unlikely that except in very special situations diets of proof for cases raised under the new procedure will be available before the commencement of the summer term.

3. Solicitors are therefore requested:—

(a) To apply as soon as possible for diets of proof in undefended actions signeted prior to 1st January 1977 and in which proof has been allowed.

(b) To inform the General Department of all actions signeted before 1st January 1977 in which further proceedings are *not* now contemplated.

(c) When submitting proof application forms in respect of actions signeted *after* 1st January 1977 to indicate the grounds of actions as follows:—

Irretrievable breakdown—behaviour/desertion/adultery/non-cohabitation two years/non-cohabitation five years.

1977 No. 2

Agents are reminded of the necessity in making applications for undefended proofs in consistorial actions signeted after 1st January 1977 to ensure that the words " Irretrievable Breakdown " are given in answer to question 1 on Form 15.

1977 No. 3

March 11, 1977

1. The attention of practitioners is drawn to the provisions of section 2 of the Divorce (Scotland) Act 1976, and to the long title.

2. The provisions of section 2 are designed to facilitate and encourage the reconciliation of estranged spouses who are, or may become, involved in

a consistorial action. By enacting those provisions, Parliament has emphasised the importance of exploring the possibility of effecting a reconciliation between the parties to a marriage which has not broken down irretrievably. Central and local government agencies have likewise sanctioned this policy by giving assistance in cash or in kind to voluntary organisations concerned with marriage counselling.

3. Experience shows that once an action has been raised, it is usually too late for the parties to attempt to effect a reconciliation, and it is not expected that the court will be frequently requested, or be in a position, to exercise the powers conferred on it by section 2 (1) of the Act (power to continue an action to enable attempts to be made to effect a reconciliation). In these circumstances, in order to promote the success of the legislative policy, legal practitioners who are consulted about marital problems with a view to consistorial proceedings should try to identify, at as early a stage as possible, those cases in which the parties might benefit from the expert advice and guidance of a marriage counsellor, and in those cases should encourage the parties to seek such advice and guidance.

4. There are a number of voluntary organisations, some of them denominational, concerned with marriage counselling who have branch offices in Scotland. Direct liaison or referral by a solicitor will often not present any difficulty, but advice concerning the appropriate organisation may usually be obtained from the local citizens' advice bureau or social work department.

1977 No. 4, Office of Auditor of Court of Session

Value added tax; Taxation of expenses in (1) *Civil proceedings;* (2) *Criminal proceedings; and* (3) *General business.*

The auditor refers to the above practice note:[1] Accounts are being lodged for taxation which do not conform to the directions or to the act of sederunt dated 28th February 1973. Solicitors are therefore requested to comply in order to save unnecessary time both in the auditor's office and at taxations.

For the guidance of solicitors it is explained that where the recoverable expenses of a legally aided party are paid by the Law Society of Scotland out of the legal aid fund without taxation, value added tax is not recoverable on the 10 per cent. of solicitors' fees and counsel's fees which is retained by the legal aid fund. Attention is directed to paragraph 3 (*c*) (forms of accounts) and paragraph 7 (calculation of VAT) in the above practice note.

An example of an abstract where a dual taxation has been carried out by the auditor in any of the circumstances likely to be encountered is appended for reference.

NOTE

[1] See Practice Note of 14th April 1973.

Abstract Party & Party, Legal Aid Fund—Pre- and Post-Legal Aid

TAXED OFF		LEGAL AID FUND			PARTY & PARTY		
P. & P.	L.A.	VAT	Disbs.	Fees and Posts	VAT	Disbs.	Fees and Posts
	PRE LEGAL AID—POST VAT						
£10.00	£00.00 Taxed Off				£0.80	£30.00	£60.00 10.00
							50.00
	Add 30% to 1/9/76						15.00
							65.00
	Add VAT on Solicitors' Fees and Posts						5.20
							70.20
	Add Disbursements						30.00
							£100.20
	Add VAT on Disbursements						80
							101.00
	Add Fee Fund Dues						2.00
							£103.00

	LEGAL AID–POST VAT						
£10.00	£15.00	£0.72	£20.00	£35.00	£4.04	£65.00	£140.00
	Taxed Off			15.00			10.00
				20.00			130.00
	Add VAT on 90% Solicitors' Fees and Posts			1.44			9.36
				21.44			139.36
	Add disbursements			20.00			65.00
				41.44			204.36
	Add VAT on Disbursements			0.72			4.04
				42.16			208.40
	Add Fee Fund Dues			1.00			4.00
	TOTAL			£43.16			£212.40

LEGAL AID ABSTRACT	
Solicitors' Fees and Posts	£150.00
VAT on 90%	10.80
Counsel's Fees	55.00
VAT on 90%	3.96
Disbursements	35.00
VAT on 100%	0.80
TOTAL	£255.56

11th April 1978

Notes by the Dean of the Faculty of Advocates and the President of the Law Society of Scotland for the Guidance of Members of the Faculty and of the Society in regard to Affidavit Evidence in Undefended Divorce Actions

1. It has been suggested to us by the Lord President that we might give guidance to the profession regarding the procedure to be followed in connection with the Act of Sederunt which comes into operation on 25th April 1978. In the hope that it might be helpful, we now do so on entirely general lines. Decisions in regard to particular situations will fall to be made by the legal advisers of the party concerned, and these notes do not claim to be in any way exhaustive.

2. Precognitions of parties and witnesses should be as ample and as relevant as it is possible to make them, bearing in mind that, except for the very small proportion of cases defended on the merits of the case, they will eventually become the basis of affidavits. The procedure at the initiating stage of the action will follow the same pattern as at present. Precognitions will be taken from the pursuer and witnesses and will be provided to counsel, who will draft the summons in the ordinary way. The one exception is that, where matters relating to children are involved, a precognition should be taken from the witnesses referred to in rule 2 (5) of the Act of Sederunt.

3. Once it has been ascertained that the action is not to be defended, it will be imperative that all the productions are uplifted from the process and passed to the solicitor concerned with the taking of the affidavits.

4. We do not feel it possible to provide a style of affidavit, but suggest that the affidavits of parties and witnesses should follow step by step the averments in the summons. The drafter of an affidavit should provide himself, before drawing it, with a copy of the summons, a copy of the appropriate precognition, and the relative productions. The affidavit to be taken from a witness should follow the averments in the summons to the extent that these are within the knowledge of that particular witness. The drafter must take care that an affidavit contains only matters of fact to which the party or the witness in question can testify, and that it is correct at the date at which it is sworn.

5. On the matter of the qualifications of the person before whom the affidavit is taken, the Rules provide that the affidavit is admissible if it is duly emitted before a notary public or other competent authority. This means a notary public, justice of the peace, commissioner of oaths or other statutory authority within the meaning of the Statutory Declarations Act 1835. In the examples given hereafter, we shall assume that the affidavit is in fact taken before a solicitor who is a notary public, and therefore we refer to the party before whom the affidavit is sworn as " the notary." The solicitor acting in the action may well be called on also to act in a notarial capacity, when the affidavit is subsequently sworn. We consider that he is in no way disqualified from doing so merely because of his interest in the action. In acting in a notarial capacity he must, however, as a competent authority, observe all the normal rules in this connection, and must satisfy himself as to the capacity of the witness to make the statement, and ensure that the witness understands that it constitutes his or her evidence in the case.

6. The pursuer or the witness must appreciate the importance of the affidavit. The affidavit should be typed on substantial paper, should be backed up longways, and should be stitched or stapled. It must commence with the words " At , the day of 19 , in the presence of , Compeared who being solemnly sworn, Depones as follows ." The full name, age, address and occupation

must be given, and it must thereafter proceed in the first person and should take the form of numbered paragraphs. The witness must be placed on oath, or must affirm, and each page will require to be signed by both the witness and the notary. We do not think it essential that it should be sealed by the notary, but it is of importance that the document should be of a shape and size convenient to be lodged as part of the process. The affidavit should end with the words " All of which is truth as the Deponent shall answer to God," or " All of which is affirmed to be true," as appropriate.

7. On the matter of productions, those required, when an affidavit is being taken, may already have been lodged in process, but there may be some productions (such as photographs) which are produced by the witness to the notary when the affidavit is sworn, and which may not by that time have been lodged in process.

8. As earlier indicated, productions already lodged in process must be borrowed up, and put to the party or the witness in the appropriate part of the affidavit. Each production will require to be referred to in the affidavit by its number of process and must be docqueted and signed by the party or witness and the notary. If a production has not yet been lodged when the affidavit is being taken, it will require to be identified by the witness in his evidence in the affidavit, and will then be docqueted with regard to the affidavit and signed by the party or witness and the notary. It will then be lodged as a production. Obviously, certain productions will be docqueted with regard to more than one affidavit.

9. In adultery cases, under the old procedure, a photograph of the defender was usually required, but a photograph of the pursuer was often unnecessary because the pursuer required to appear in court. Under the new procedure, in such cases, photographs of both the pursuer and the defender will require to be produced, put to the appropriate party or witnesses in the affidavit, and signed and docqueted with reference thereto in the manner already described. In certain circumstances, a photograph may have to be identified and docqueted by more than one person, as in the case of the photograph of a party requiring to be spoken to by the pursuer and two inquiry agents.

10. All affidavits lodged must be of as recent a date as is possible in the circumstances. The aim should be to submit these to counsel immediately after they are taken, because once counsel has signed the minute, they will be brought before a judge very quickly. This factor is particularly important in (1) cases involving children, (2) those in which financial conclusions are involved, or (3) in any other circumstances where the evidence of a party or witness is liable to change through the passage of time. The notary will require to ensure, therefore, that an affidavit represents the deponent's evidence on such matters at the time the affidavit is sworn.

11. In cases involving custody and welfare of children, the terms of rule 2 (5) relating to an independent witness should be borne in mind. The evidence of that witness must present the court with a full picture of the position regarding the child or children. It is, however, clear that such independent evidence in no way relieves the pursuer from testifying fully the position regarding the children in his or her own affidavit, so far as within his or her knowledge. Whatever else the affidavits of the pursuer and the independent witness contain, their evidence should certainly include the following:

(*a*) the qualifications of the witness, if not a parent, to speak about the child; how often, for example, and in what circumstances, does the witness normally see the child;

(*b*) a description of the home conditions in which the child lives;

(*c*) observations upon the child's general appearance, interests, state of health and well-being;

(*d*) information, where relevant, about the school the child attends; whether and to what extent he has contact with other children and relatives;

(*e*) observations on the relationship between the child and the person in whose care he or she lives, on the child's attitude towards each of the parents and on the extent of contact with the parent or parents with whom the child is not living.

12. Where financial conclusions are involved, it is even more important that the evidence is full, accurate and up to date. In the past, the evidence of the pursuer and the witnesses on these matters has often required to be supplemented at the proof by questions from the Bench or from counsel. This will no longer be possible, and the affidavits must be so framed as to exclude the necessity for supplementary questions. Failure to do so might result in the case being sent to the by order roll. If, after an affidavit has been taken, and the solicitor concerned has parted with it, a material change of circumstances occurs, it is essential that counsel be immediately informed, and, where necessary, that a further affidavit be sworn.

13. Where the pursuer in an action is speaking in the affidavit of the financial position of the defender, it is essential that the affidavit should state the date, as precisely as possible, at which that information was valid. Otherwise it may be assumed by the court that the pursuer is speaking to the defender's position at the date of the affidavit. The court must be provided with as up-to-date information as possible about the defender's ability to pay the sums the pursuer is seeking, and these sums should be such as that evidence justifies. The pursuer must, of course, speak also to his or her own financial position, at the date of the affidavit. Where the pursuer cannot obtain recent information as to the defender's means, we would suggest that, if the pursuer's advisers approve, assessment should be left to the judge, and in such cases it may be that counsel and solicitors would be willing to incorporate in the terms of the minute, after the words "in terms of the conclusions of the Summons" the words "or such other sum (or sums) as the Court may think proper".

14. Where the pursuer does not seek a capital allowance, or a periodical allowance, or aliment for the child or children, it is essential that the reasons for this are fully narrated in the affidavit. Where these reasons are capable of corroboration by witnesses, they should be dealt with in the witnesses' affidavits. Similarly, where a wife pursuer does not seek an award of expenses against the defender, she must give reasons for this in her affidavit, especially where she has a legal aid certificate.

15. We take the view that the minute must be signed by the counsel who has examined the affidavit evidence and no one else. This should be the case, whether or not the counsel who examined the affidavit evidence also drew the summons.

16. In consent cases, the defender's written consent form will also have to be borrowed up, put to the pursuer in his or her affidavit, and docqueted and identified in the same way as other productions.

17. In our view, the new procedure will not prevent the parties to the

action agreeing the financial or other ancillary conclusions by joint minute. For so long as these ancillary conclusions are opposed, the affidavit procedure cannot be used for matters covered thereby, but it can be used for the merits of the action. If and when the ancillary conclusions are successfully negotiated, a joint minute may then be lodged and the case brought under the rules by Rule 2 (*c*). If a joint minute is signed before an affidavit or supplementary affidavit is emitted by the pursuer, that affidavit should refer to the arrangements in the joint minute.

18. As far as those members of the profession who are called upon to advise defenders are concerned, the new procedure does not alter the rules the defences in this type of action may be lodged at any time before the granting of decree, or that the decree may be reclaimed against within twenty-one days. Advisers are, however, reminded that the whole procedure from start to finish may well take a much shorter time than at present, and defenders who wish to contest any of the conclusions in whole or in part should be advised to enter the process without delay, and if appropriate, steps should be taken to sist the proceedings to enable the defender to apply for legal aid.

19. These notes have the general approval of the Lord President.

1978, Allocation of diets

[Revoked by No. 2 of 1987: 30th July 1987.]

3rd January 1980

In order to clarify the position regarding inclusive fees elected to be charged in undefended actions of divorce where proof is taken by affidavit evidence, the following provisions will apply as from 7th January 1980: (1) *In actions where decree was granted on or before 27th November 1979.* Solicitors may elect to charge an inclusive fee in terms of the now revoked Rule of Court 347 Chapter V, together with outlays as taxed by the auditor of court. (2) *In actions where decree is granted between 28th November 1979 and 6th January 1980.* Solicitors may elect to charge an inclusive fee in terms of Rule of Court 347 Chapter III Part III as introduced by Act of Sederunt (Rules of Court Amendment No. 6) (Solicitors' Fees) 1979 together with outlays as taxed by the auditor of court. (3) In actions where a Minute craving decree is lodged on or after 7th January 1980, but where the summons was signeted *prior* to that date, solicitors may elect to charge an inclusive fee as specified in para. (2) above, together with outlays not exceeding the sum of £85 inclusive of VAT, or, if exceeding the aforementioned figure, as the same shall be taxed by the auditor of court. (4) In actions where a Minute craving decree is lodged after 7th January 1980, and where the summons was signeted *on or after* that date, solicitors may elect to charge an inclusive fee in terms of Rule of Court 347 Chapter III Part III (as amended by Act of Sederunt (Rules of Court Amendment No. 7) (Solicitors' Fees No. 2) 1979) together with outlays as specified in para. (3) above.

Where solicitors elect to charge an inclusive fee when lodging the Minute craving decree they should annex a minute to the principal summons showing the fee elected and also add the following wording to the Minute craving decree: "and in addition to find the pursuer entitled to the fees stated in the Minute of Election annexed to the Summons and for outlays not exceeding £85, or, if exceeding this figure, as the same shall be taxed by the Auditor of Court." In these cases, before ordering extract of the interlocutor granting the inclusive fee, the solicitor should lodge in process either (a) a note of outlays not exceeding £85, inclusive of VAT, or (b) a taxed account of outlays.

9th July 1980

Extracts Department Regulations

Section A

All decrees other than those regulated by Section B

1. Acts and Decrees other than Decrees in absence may be transmitted to the Extractor on the eighth day after the date of the interlocutor. Decrees in absence may be transmitted on the eleventh day after the date of the interlocutor. The Lord Ordinary may on cause shown authorise immediate extract. All amendments which have been allowed to the instance and/or conclusions of a Summons and all amendments which have been allowed to a Petition must be given effect to on the principal Writ concerned prior to ordering extract.

Once a process has been transmitted for extract in conformity with the above provisions, extract will be prepared and issued unless interdicted by the court or unless the clerk to the process intimates that a party to the cause desires to enrol a reclaiming motion.

2. In the case of a final extract all steps of process must be returned and all productions borrowed before transmission. This should be attended to by all the parties prior to the date when extract is competent (see Reg. 1).

3. Along with each process transmitted for extract there must be lodged a Note to the Extractor specifying:—

(*a*) The leading names and addresses of the parties.

(*b*) A copy of the interlocutor or interlocutors of which extract is desired.

The note to the Extractor must be signed by the solicitor ordering extract, who should state the party for whom he acts, and should be typewritten (double line spacing) on ordinary foolscap paper and folded shortwise.

4. No extract will be issued until the fee fund dues shall have been paid.

5. When adjudications for debt are transmitted for extract there must be lodged at the same time a STATE of the ACCUMULATED SUM certified by the solicitor.

5A. In actions for payment in a foreign currency there must be lodged along with the Note to the Extractor a certified statement of the rate of exchange prevailing at the date of the extract sought and of the sterling equivalent, at that rate, of the principal sum and interest.

Section B

Decrees of Divorce, Nullity of Marriage and Dissolution of Marriage

Decrees pronounced on or after 23rd September 1975

6. In cases where the decree is pronounced on or after 23rd September 1975 an Extract thereof will be available to the solicitor for the pursuer or petitioner after the expiry of twenty-one days at the Extractor's office provided no reclaiming motion has been made.

7. At the same time a copy of the extract will be sent to the defender or respondent where his or her address is known.

[1] **8.** Additional official extracts of all such decrees may be obtained from the extracts office on payment of a fee of £8·00 per extract.

NOTE

[1] See S.I. 1991 No. 332.

Decrees pronounced prior to 23rd September 1975

9. Subject to regulation 10 in cases where the decree has been pronounced prior to 23rd September 1975, the process must be transmitted to the extracts office by an Edinburgh agent who will be sent a fee notice when the extract is ready to be uplifted.

10. In cases where a decree has been extracted prior to 1st July 1968, an extract from the Register may be obtained from the Keeper of the Records of Scotland.

NOTES

An extract should be carefully examined. After the Record Copy has been transmitted to the Keeper of the Records, which transmission is made in the early months of each year, alteration in the extract cannot be made except by authority of the court.

In view of the fact that the process can be transmitted for extract on the eighth day after the date of the interlocutor and while the reclaiming days are still running, the losing party, if he is not to acquiesce, ought to advise the other party of his intention to reclaim.

Extracts issued in terms of *Section B* show the ground of the decree, findings as to custody, access, reservation date, interdict, orders under the Matrimonial Homes (Family Protection) (Scotland) Act 1981 and any pecuniary provisions including expenses. Should an extract be required showing any other matter solicitors must proceed in terms of *Section A*.

30th October 1980

Remits to local authorities in consistorial causes

As from this date, when a local authority is appointed to report to the court in terms of section 11 of the Matrimonial Proceedings (Children) Act 1958, the party moving the court for a remit, or where the remit is made by the court *ex proprio motu* the pursuer or minuter, shall in the first instance be responsible for the settlement of any claim which may be made by the local authority in terms of section 11(5) of that Act for expenses incurred in connection with the preparation of such a report. Where the remit is made by the court *ex proprio motu* it shall be the duty of the solicitor for the pursuer or minuter to instruct the reporting authority by submitting to the chief executive thereof a copy of the interlocutor containing the remit, a copy of the summons, and any relevant productions. In all other cases this duty shall devolve upon the party moving the court for a remit. The provisions of Rule of Court 97 shall apply *mutatis mutandis* to such remits.

26th March 1981

From time to time the result of the allowance of substantial amendment of pleadings in the course of reclaiming motions is that matters which have become of material importance in the action have not been the subject of consideration by the Lord Ordinary. Practitioners are reminded that in such circumstances the Inner House may think it desirable to require the case to be remitted to the Lord Ordinary for further hearing. In order that this possible course of action may be explored before reclaiming motions are put out for hearing any party enrolling a motion for a record to be amended in terms of a minute of amendment and any answers thereto should at the same time enrol for a direction as to further procedure.

10th February 1983

In consistorial actions where a curator *ad litem* is appointed to the defender and the said curator subsequently lodges a minute in terms of Rule of Court 167(*c*)(iii) stating that he does not intend to lodge defences, the court, when allowing a proof by way of affidavit evidence shall also pronounce an order directing that the fee of and the expenses incurred by the curator *ad litem* be payable by the pursuer.

15th September 1983

The attention of solicitors is drawn to the fact that considerable delays are occurring in the returning of medical records to health boards. The lack of records can seriously impede the continuing treatment of a patient. It is therefore the duty of solicitors who have recovered medical records from health boards to borrow from process and return all medical records to the lending authority as soon as it is known that the documents are no longer required or as soon as a cause is concluded. Records should also be made available to a hospital immediately on request if they are required at any stage for the treatment of the individual concerned.

21st March 1985

The attention of solicitors is drawn to the fact that as the result of the recent extension of word processing facilities in the Court of Session now available to the Extracts Department, the form of extract in decrees of divorce will include (a) the divorce, (b) decrees for custody, access, aliment, periodical allowance, capital sum and expenses and (c) decrees for interdict and orders under the Matrimonial Homes (Family Protection) (Scotland) Act 1981.

21st February 1986

Notwithstanding the terms of Rule of Court 189(*b*), as from 1st March 1986 all applications for fiats shall be lodged in the signeting office in the general department.

21st February 1986

[Revoked by No. 1 of 1989: 12th January 1989.]

27th March 1986

The attention of practitioners is drawn to the terms of para. 1(2) of the practice note of 16th December 1968 (*Parliament House Book*, p. C504) which deals with the requirement to lodge a copy of the open record as adjusted when a party enrols for an extension of the 12-week period of adjustment of the adjustment roll.

27th March 1986

1. In order to facilitate the implementation of s.13 of the Bankruptcy (Scotland) Act 1985 which comes into force on 1st April 1986, solicitors may include in a petition for sequestration the nomination of an appointee to the office of interim trustee, selected from the official list of interim trustees held by the accountant of court, without prejudice to the court's power to appoint such person as it sees fit to said office.

2. The petition should also state whether or not the net unsecured assets of the debtor exceed £150,000, as, where the assets exceed such sum, special arrangements will be required of the finding in caution.

27th March 1986

1. *Application.* This note regulates the procedure in an action or petition following an interlocutor allowing a minute of amendment to be received and answers to be lodged by introducing time limits with a view to preventing undue delay, and takes effect on 28th April 1986.

2. *Adjustment of minute and answers*. Parties may adjust the minute and answers for a period of 28 days from the date on which answers are lodged, or in a case where more than one set of answers are lodged, from the date on which the last set is lodged.

3. *Continuation*. The period of adjustment under para. 2 may be extended for such further period as the court may allow on cause shown.

4. *Motion*. The party who has lodged the minute shall (a) within 14 days of the expiry of that period; or (b) if no answers are lodged, within 14 days after the last date for lodging answers, enrol a motion to amend the record in terms of the minute and answers, or the minute as the case may be.

5. *By order*. If a party fails to enrol a motion within the 14–day period, the court shall put the cause out for hearing in the by order roll, and thereafter may make such order, including an order as to expenses, as it thinks fit.

6th November 1986

Applications to the court for leave to appeal against a decision of the Employment Appeal Tribunal where the tribunal has refused leave to appeal

. With effect from 10th November 1986, where an application for leave to appeal against a decision of the Employment Appeal Tribunal is made, there shall be produced along with the opinion of the tribunal (and where appropriate the opinion of the industrial tribunal):

(i) a certificate by the tribunal refusing leave to appeal;
(ii) a note of the grounds of appeal submitted to the tribunal;
(iii) a note by the chairman of the tribunal setting out the reasons for refusal; and
(iv) the applicant's proposed grounds of appeal to be submitted to the court should the application for leave by granted.

4th December 1986

[Revoked by No. 2 of 1987: 30th July 1987.]

10th December 1986

1. Notwithstanding the provisions of Rule of Court 93, as from 29th December 1986 and for an experimental period, all unopposed motions enrolled for hearing in the Outer House, other than those referred to in paragraph 9 hereof, shall *not*, in the first instance, require the appearance of counsel.

Categories of unopposed motions

2. (1) Those motions which are according to present practice unstarred shall continue to be enrolled in the same manner as hitherto. (2) Those motions of a procedural nature, which have hitherto required the appearance of counsel, shall be dealt with by the clerk of court. (3) Those motions which have hitherto required the appearance of counsel and which will require to receive judicial consideration shall be dealt with by the judge in chambers.

Information to be supplied to the court

3. (1) Written reasons or explanations shall be incorporated in or produced as a paper apart along with motions categorised in paras. 2(2) and 2(3) and any relevant documentary evidence produced therewith where appropriate. (2) Details of the motions in the category referred to in para. 2(2), and illustrations of the information required, are set forth in

appendix I to this practice note. (3) Similar details in respect of para. 2(3) are set forth in appendix II to this practice note. Details in this appendix are not exhaustive but practitioners should apply the principles illustrated therein to any motion which is not covered thereby.

Procedure in respect of disposal of motions

4. In regard to motions referred to in paras. 2(1) and 2(2) the following procedures shall apply: (1) Where the clerk of court is satisfied that any such motion may be granted he shall prepare and sign the appropriate interlocutor (subject to the provisions of Rule of Court 93A). (2) Where the clerk of court is not satisfied with the motion as enrolled, he shall either (a) where there is a defect of a technical nature (e.g. specification for the recovery of documents for which there is no call on record) which cannot be remedied immediately, drop the motion; or (b) consult with the practitioner to obtain any additional information which would allow the motion to be granted in full or in such restricted terms as may be agreed. (3) Where the clerk of court after such consultation is still not so satisfied, he shall either (a) of consent, drop the motion; or (b) arrange that the motion be put out starred in order that counsel may be heard thereon.

5. In regard to motions referred to in para. 2(3), the following procedures shall apply: (1) On receipt of such a motion, the terms thereof and any documentation relative thereto shall be examined by the clerk of court for any obvious errors or omissions. (2) Where any such error or omission is discovered, the clerk of court shall consult with the practitioner to obtain further information. (3) Where the clerk of court, with or without such consultation, is satisfied with the terms of and any documentation relative to such a motion, he shall present the papers to the Lord Ordinary in chambers. (4) After consideration of such papers the Lord Ordinary shall either (a) grant the motion in full; (b) grant the motion in such restricted terms as may be agreed after further consultation between the clerk of court and the practitioner; (c) of consent drop the motion; or (d) direct that the motion be put out starred in order that counsel may be heard thereon.

6. Where the Lord Ordinary has directed that a motion is to be put out starred in terms of paras. 4(3)(b) or 5(4)(d), the clerk of court, in consultation with the practitioner, shall arrange for such appearance in the motion roll on a mutually convenient date.

7. To facilitate consultation referred to in paras. 4 and 5 hereof, all motions shall include the name of the individual practitioner with whom contact should be made by the clerk of court.

8. Where, by 12.30 p.m. on the day the motion appears on the rolls, either (a) the clerk of court has been unable to consult with the practitioner through the absence of the individual or someone authorised to deputise for him; or (b) such additional information as has been sought is not available to the clerk of court, the clerk of court may drop the motion.

9. The present practice in regard to the appearance of counsel in (i) motions before calling; (ii) orders before service of a petition (which do not appear in the motion roll); and (iii) motions for interim orders under the Matrimonial Homes (Family Protection) (Scotland) Act 1981, shall continue to apply in the meantime.

N.B.

1. Practitioners who encounter problems in regard to the new procedure are requested to communicate with either of the deputy principal clerks, Mr V. A. Woods or Mr H. S. Foley, who will be monitoring the procedure.

2. In an effort to ensure that motions are properly enrolled, the following are published as examples of motions and relative information which would be acceptable to the court. (1) "On behalf of the pursuer to allow a further continuation of the period of adjustment for four weeks in respect

that extensive adjustments were received from the defenders two days ago and further advice now has to be obtained from pursuer's expert witness."
(2) "On behalf of the pursuer for interim custody of the child . . . and for interim aliment for said child at the rate of . . . in respect of (1) the averments contained in articles 4 and 5 of the condescendence and (2) [where appropriate] the other factors narrated in paper apart 'A' annexed hereto."

Appendix I

Column 1	*Column 2*
Dispensation with service or intimation (or further service any document).	Reason for dispensation to be stated. Any previous executions of service or intimation to be lodged with this motion.
Second sist for legal aid.	Reason for application to be stated.
Late documents.	Reason for the delay on lodging the document to be stated.
Commission to take evidence.	Reason for the taking of the evidence on commission to be stated. Where appropriate any supporting documents such as medical or birth certificates to be lodged.
Application for authority to print a record on minute and answers or on petition and answers (as adjusted where appropriate) which is not made of consent.	Adjustments should be shown on principal documents to enable clerk of court to decide whether the expense of printing a record is necessary.
Continuation of adjustment period or restoration of cause to adjustment roll.	Reason for further continuation of adjustment or resoration to the roll to be stated. Any adjustments made to date should be shown on either an adjusted copy of the open record or, in the case of minute and answers, on the principal documents.
Lost step in process.	Explanation of the likely fate of the lost step of process and efforts made to try and trace same to be stated.
To allow a parole consistorial proof (other than nullity).	Reason why affidavit procedure inappropriate to be stated.
To discharge diet of proof or jury trial.	Reason for discharge to be stated, with provision for expenses.
Recall of arrestment/inhibition (by party who has arrested/inhibited).	Reason for recall to be stated. (As a party is entitled to recall any diligence no reason is really necessary other than why it requires to be done by motion as opposed to extra-judicially.)
Prorogation of time for lodging documents outwith time ordered by interlocutor or imposed by Rule of Court.	Reason why time limit cannot be complied with to be stated.
Prorogation of time for finding caution.	Reason why time limit cannot be complied with to be stated.
First order in judicial review (not accompanied by a motion for an interim order therein).	(As the only matter in contention at this stage is the date of the first hearing—which can be arranged between keeper and clerk, as is indeed the practice—there would seem to be no necessity for agents to supply further information.)

Appendix II

Column 1	*Column 2*
Interim custody and aliment (and variation thereof).	Up to date information on custody arrangements and the financial circumstances of the parties to be submitted along with the motion. Where information regarding the financial position of the other party is not available or cannot be obtained an appropriate explanation should be made in the motion sheet and the most recent information should be produced. (To enable the court to excercise its discretion in respect of any award of aliment the motion should include the phrase "or such other lesser sum as to the court shall seem proper".)
Interim access (and variation thereof).	Details of the arrangements for access should be provided with the motion sheet.
Assessment of liability for expenses under s. 2 (6) (*e*) of Legal Aid (Scotland) Act 1967.	Motion to be accompanied by statement of parties' income and expenditure (either wage certificates or a certificate of earnings) and a statement of estimated expenses.
Recall of arrestment/inhibition (by party other than party who arrested/inhibited).	Copy letter of intimation confirming that the other party has received intimation of the motion to be produced, with provision for expenses.
To open "confidential" envelope recovered under specification.	Reason as to why contents are relevant to be stated. Copy letter of intimation to havers to be produced.
Appointment ad interim of curator/factor after service of petition.	Reason for application to be stated.
Appointment of provisional/official liquidator.	Statement of assets of the company to be included.
Of new for appointment of curator/factor.	Reason why caution not found timeously to be included.
For award of sequestration	Name of proposed interim trustee to be included.
For appointment of a curator ad litem.	Reason for the appointment to be included. Where necessary, relevant medical certificate to be produced.

Note. The last four items in this appendix could well be added to appendix I were it not for the fact that the interlocutors would still require the signature of the judge.

27th March 1987

Publication of adjustment rolls

As from the commencement of the summer session of the court the practice whereby causes due to call in the adjustment roll and continued adjustment roll are published in the rolls of court on the preceding Friday and Monday will cease, and the following practice will be introduced in place thereof:—

1. A list of causes calling in the adjustment roll on any Wednesday will be published on that day with a note of the date to which the adjustment of record has been continued prefixed thereto.
2. A list of causes due to call in the continued adjustment roll on any Wednesday will be published on the preceding Friday.

To facilitate identification of causes in each of the aforementioned lists the names of the solicitors for parties will be shown.

No. 1 of 1987: 16th July 1987

Bankruptcy procedure

With effect from Monday, 20th July 1987, a new procedure will commence in accordance with s.12(2) of the Bankruptcy (Scotland) Act 1985 for the citation of debtors in sequestration proceedings at the instance of a creditor or a trustee acting under a trust deed. The procedure for ordering a respondent to enter appearance in a sequestration process will no longer apply and the court will now fix a date for the debtor to appear when issuing the first deliverance in the sequestration.

After presentation of the petition, the court on granting a first deliverance citing the debtor shall fix a hearing for a date more than 14 days from the date of the first deliverance. Any request for an earlier diet should be made within 24 hours of the presentation of the petition.

One day a week will be fixed for the hearing of orders for sequestration (not the first deliverance which can be dealt with on any date) and that will be on a Thursday of each week. Counsel will be required to appear at that hearing to move for the sequestration order in anticipation of an appearance by a debtor. The new procedure will also require the petitioner's counsel to make a motion at the bar for sequestration as no motion will now be enrolled in the motion sheet for an award of sequestration.

No. 2 of 1987: 30th July 1987

Fixing and allocation of diets of proof or jury trial, or hearings in the Inner House in reclaiming motions or appeals from inferior courts

1. Rules of Court 91C and 294C, inserted by Act of Sederunt (Rule of Court Amendment No. 4) (Miscellaneous) 1987 (S.I. 1987 No. 1206), which come into force on 3rd August 1987, make new provision for (a) the fixing and allocation of diets of proof (including proof before answer) or jury trial and (b) the allocation of diets for hearings in reclaiming motions and appeals from inferior courts in the Inner House.

2. Rules of Court 91C and 294C will apply only to those causes in which a proof is allowed or issues are approved or which is appointed to the summar roll on or after 3rd August 1987, except that (a) Rule 91C(4) and (5), (6), (7) and (8) as appropriate will also apply to those causes in which a proof or jury trial has been fixed or allocated for a date on or after 17th November 1987; and (b) Rule 294C(7) and (8) will apply to those causes in which a hearing on the summar roll has been fixed for a date on or after 22nd September 1987.

3. Copies of Forms 63 and 64, required under Rule 91C or 294C to be completed and delivered to the keeper of the rolls by solicitors for all parties in a cause sent to proof or jury trial, or hearings in the Inner House, may be obtained from the assistant keeper of the rolls.

4. Where there is an estimate that the length of a proof, jury trial or hearing will be not more than four days, the keeper of the rolls will normally allocate a diet of the length sought. Where there is an estimate that the length of proof, jury trial or hearing will be more than four days or there is a substantial variation in the estimates given by the parties to the cause, the keeper of the rolls will communicate with parties with a view to ascertaining a better estimate and fixing a diet.

5. When a diet of proof, jury trial or hearing has been fixed or allocated, the keeper of the rolls will (a) give written notice of the diet allocated to the solicitor for each party or the party litigant; and (b) be responsible for inserting the date(s) fixed or allocated in the interlocutor allowing proof or jury trial.

6. The following practice notes are hereby revoked: practice note 20th December 1974; practice note 1978 (allocation of diets); notice 4th December 1986.

No. 3 of 1987: 30th July 1987

Fixing and allocation of diets of procedure roll hearings

Where a cause is appointed to the procedure roll, to enable a diet of hearing to be fixed or allocated the pursuer's solicitor will require to supply upon the backing of one of the copies of the closed record lodged in process the names of counsel for the parties and the estimated duration of the hearing.

Notice: 3rd December 1987

Following representations from interested individuals and bodies a working group examined and reported on the proposal that judges' opinions should be prepared and published to a common style. One of the recommendations, since approved by the Lord President, was that the names of local correspondents be included on the backing of the opinion and thereafter published with the report of the case. This information is only available if Edinburgh solicitors include the details on the backing of the record. Practitioners are requested to provide these details with immediate effect, as agreed at the recent meeting of the Joint Committee of Legal Societies in Edinburgh and Midlothian.

Notice: 11th December 1987

With a view to improving communication between court staff and solicitors in a cause, solicitors are requested to provide their reference on the backing of their principal writ. It would also be of considerable assistance in this regard if the respective references of solicitors were shown on any closed record lodged in process.

No. 4 of 1987: 11th December 1987

1. From 5th January 1988, where particulars of any cause set down for hearing are published in the rolls of court, the name(s) of counsel in the cause will not be shown.

2. With regard to the motion roll, notwithstanding the provision in Rule of Court 93(*b*), the solicitor or his representative shall, when enrolling a motion in any cause, hand to the clerk a slip containing the names of the parties and the title of his firm abbreviated to the first two names thereof, where appropriate.

3. In consequence of the foregoing, and in order to facilitate communication between counsel in a cause solicitors, when instructing counsel for any proof, jury trials or debate, should provide him/her where possible with the name of counsel for the other party or parties.

No. 1 of 1988: 1st March 1988

Children: supervision of access arrangements by social work department

1. From time to time social work departments are ordered by the court to supervise access arrangements by a party to children. Often the views of the particular department have not been sought before the order is made and this has been causing some difficulty. In future the following rule will apply.

2. Where the court, either *ex proprio motu* or at the request of a party, indicates its intention to make an award of access subject to supervision by a social work department of a local authority, the court will: (a) appoint intimation of the motion for access (and such indication that the social work department supervise access) to the chief executive of the local authority by the party moving the motion for access; and (b) put the case out by order within such time as the court considers appropriate to enable the local authority to make any representations (through counsel or in writing) at the hearing.

No. 2 of 1988: 2nd March 1988

Solicitors are reminded that, in addition to the provisions of Rule of Court 200, a copy of any petition presented to the Outer House should be lodged, at the same time as the principal petition, for the use of the Advocates' Library.

No. 3 of 1988: 26th May 1988

Fee fund dues

1. The Court of Session etc. Fees Amendment Order 1988 which comes into force on 1st June 1988 increases most existing fees and introduces certain new fees. Solicitors are requested to note the practice to be followed in respect of the following paragraphs of the said order.

(1) Paragraph B5—Notwithstanding the terms of this paragraph, the fee for defences, answers or other writ or enrolment etc. by which a party other than the originating party first makes appearance in an action of divorce shall be £40.

(2) Paragraphs B5 and C4—Joint minute. Where a defender's/respondent's first appearance is by way of a joint minute the appropriate fee will be payable by the defender/respondent. In such circumstances, where the pursuer/petitioner lodges the joint minute and the defender/respondent is represented, the fee therefor will be debited to the defender's/respondent's solicitors' account. In the event that the defender/respondent is representing himself, or his solicitor does not operate a credit account, the pursuer's/petitioner's solicitor will require either to be liable for payment of the fee due or to arrange for the defender/respondent, or his solicitor as the case may be, to lodge the joint minute and pay the appropriate fee.

(3) Paragraph C11—Closed record. When a closed record is lodged the account of each solicitor acting in the cause will be debited for the appropriate fee. Where a defender is representing himself, or his solicitor does not operate a credit account, a note of the fee due will be rendered for payment within 14 days.

Accounting arrangements

2. The current accounting arrangements are being reviewed in the light of the additional fees introduced by the Fees Order and a further practice note will be issued in this regard on completion of that review.

No. 4 of 1988: 30th June 1988

Fee fund dues

From 1st July 1988, a Kalamazoo System of receipting/debiting will be introduced in all offices of the Court of Session and High Court of Justiciary. Solicitors will be issued with an individual receipt/debit slip for every first paper or document lodged, or for enrolment or opposition to a motion by which a party, other than the originating party, first makes appearance in a cause or proceeding.

Paragraph B11 makes provision for charging to each party of a fee in respect of the lodging of a closed record. In addition to the receipt/debit slip issued to the party lodging the closed record, a receipt/debit slip will also be issued to each other party to the cause. This will be deposited in the appropriate solicitors' box outside the General Department. Where no box is available it will be mailed directly to the party concerned or their representative.

The credit system introduced on 1st April 1976 and detailed in Practice Note No. 4 of 1976, will continue to operate as before. Please note that payments falling to be made in the office of the Extractor, and in the Teinds and Justiciary offices will continue to be excluded from the credit scheme.

Notice: 1st July 1988

Further to Practice Note No. 4 of 1988 a list of standard abbreviations for use with the Kalamazoo System has been devised. These abbreviations will be contained on the receipt/debit slip issued and also on the principal credit account rendered for payment by the cashier each month.

A/C EXPS	Accounts of Expenses
ANS	Answers
CAV	Caveat
CCI	Certified Copy Interlocutor
CERT FEE	Certification Fee
C/R	Closed Record
DEFS	Defences
EXT	Extract Abbreviate
FIAT	Fiat
FIRST APP	First Appearance into process, other than by originating party
HOL	Certification of proceedings for Appeal to House of Lords
J/M	Joint Minute
J/P	Jury Precept
LOR	Letter of Request
LVA	Lands Valuation Appeal
MAD	Minute after Decree
M/E	Minute of Election
NOTE	Note
OBJ	Objections
OHF	Out of hours fee
OP	Opinion
PH	Photocopying
PROT	Protestation
R/M	Reclaiming Motion
SCA	Sheriff Court Appeal
SP/C	Special Case
ST/C	Stated Case
S/S	Signet and Summons
TEIND	Teind

No. 6 of 1988: 8th September 1988

Post Office industrial dispute: alternative arrangements for intimation
[Spent.]

Notice: 22nd September 1988

[In a notice outlining recent improvements in average waiting times for disposal of different kinds of actions, the Court of Session published the following table showing the current availability of earlier than average dates for hearings. Practitioners are urged to make use of this facility wherever practicable.]

*Availability of earlier than average dates for hearings**

		Hearing dates available within (working months)
(a) Jury trials (from date record closed)—where estimated duration does not exceed 2 days		3
(b) Ordinary proofs (from date record closed)—where estimated duration does not exceed	(i) 1 day	As early as required
	(ii) 2 days	3
(c) Optional procedure proofs (from date last diet roll/allowance of proof)—where estimated duration does not exceed	(i) 1 day	As early as required
	(ii) 2 days	2
(d) Defended consistorial proofs (from date record lodged)—where estimated duration does not exceed	(i) 1 day	As early as required
	(ii) 2 days	3

* In cases of demonstrable urgency (e.g. concerning custody of children) very early diets are arranged as a matter of course.

No. 7 of 1988: 8th December 1988

Registration and enforcement of money judgments under s.4 of the Civil Jurisdiction and Judgments Act 1982

1. In order to facilitate the enforcement of money judgments expressed in a currency other than sterling and registered under s.4 of the Civil Jurisdiction and Judgments Act 1982, a certificate of conversion, obtained in accordance with this Practice Note, shall be appended to the extract issued by the Keeper of the Registers under rule 249I(2).

2. Before seeking registration by the Keeper in accordance with R.C.S. r. 249I(2), the applicant shall present to the Petition Department of the office of Court—

(i) a typed copy of the decree and warrant for registration for certification for the purposes of rule 249I(2)(*a*);

(ii) a banker's certificate of the rate of exchange prevailing *at the date of the extract sought* and of the sterling equivalent at that rate of the principal sum, interest and expenses contained in the judgment; and

(iii) a prepared certificate of currency conversion in the following form:

"IN THE COURT OF SESSION

Certificate of Currency Conversion

in causa

Application of

(*Designation of applicant(s)*)

under the Civil Jurisdiction and Judgments Act 1982 for registration of a judgment of the (*name of court*) of (*date of judgment*) in the cause of (*name of pursuer*) against (*name of defender*).

In terms of a certificate dated at (*place*) on (*date*) the sterling equivalent of (a) the principal sum is (£ p); (b) the interest thereon is (£ p); and (c) the expenses is (£ p) at the rate of exchange prevailing at that date.

Date
Clerk of Session"

3. The certificate of conversion issued by the Petition Department shall be presented to the Keeper of the Registers along with the documents listed in rule 249I(2).

4. Any request for an extract shall be presented to the Keeper of the Registers no later than the first working day after issue of the certificate of currency conversion.

No. 1 of 1989: 12th January 1989

Enrolment of motions

With a view to relieving congestion in the public offices of the Court during the forenoon hours of business, notwithstanding the terms of Rule of Court 93(*c*), from 16th January 1989, for an experimental period, motions may be enrolled at any time between the hours of 10 a.m. and 1 p.m. and 2 p.m. and 4 p.m., and the provisions set out in the following table shall apply:

Latest time of enrolment	*Latest time for opposition*	*Day of publication in rolls*	*Court hearing*
Monday 4 p.m.	Tuesday 12.30 p.m.	Tuesday	Wednesday
Tuesday 4 p.m.	Wednesday 12.30 p.m.	Wednesday	Thursday
Wednesday 4 p.m.	Thursday 12.30 p.m.	Thursday	Friday
Thursday 4 p.m.	Monday 12.30 p.m.	Monday	Tuesday
Friday 4 p.m.	Monday 12.30 p.m.	Monday	Tuesday

This Practice Note supersedes the Practice Note dated 21st February 1986.

No. 2 of 1989: 18th May 1989

Appendix in reclaiming motions and appeals from sheriff court

1. While Rule of Court 294A deals with the lodging of an Appendix in any cause in which "in accordance with present practice it is requisite that an Appendix should be lodged", there appears to be some doubt as to when an Appendix is required to be lodged.

2. In order to clarify matters in that regard the following provisions will apply from this date:

(1) In every cause in which a reclaiming motion is enrolled or an appeal from the sheriff court is lodged, the record shall include, where available, a copy of the opinion of the Lord Ordinary or judgment of the sheriff principal/sheriff, as the case may be.

(2) An Appendix shall require to be lodged, in accordance with Rule of Court 294A where—

(*a*) such opinion or judgment is not available for inclusion in the record; and/or

(*b*) it is required to produce notes of evidence and/or any documents necessary for the determination of the cause.

No. 1 of 1990: 22nd March 1990

Fixing and Allocation of Diets—Form 64

Notwithstanding the terms of Rule of Court 91C(4)–(8) as from this date practitioners will not be required to lodge Form 64 in relation to any action or petition before the court.

Notice: 22nd March 1990

Commissions to take evidence and/or recover documents—Attendance of shorthand writers

Practitioners will wish to note that, with effect from 1st April 1990, Scottish Courts Administration will no longer pay for the attendance of shorthand writers at civil commissions. From that date, fees payable will be in the first instance the responsibility of the party instructing attendance.

No. 2 of 1990: 31st May 1990

Ex tempore judgments

For the avoidance of doubt it is confirmed that where the court issues an *ex tempore* judgment the interlocutor resulting therefrom will be signed and dated on the day that judgment is delivered and not at the date of the issue of the opinion. The reclaiming days will commence on the date of issue of the interlocutor and not on the date of issue of the opinion.

Notice: 7th March 1990

Agents are reminded of the importance of notifying the keeper's office of any motion likely to take longer than 20 minutes. There have been a number of recent instances where either no prior notification has been given to this office or the estimate given is so wildly at variance with the eventual duration as to imply that no thought was given to the original estimate. On a number of occasions this has caused unacceptable delays in the commencement of proofs where, had proper notification been given, the matter could have been dealt with by another judge at a later stage in the morning.

No. 2 of 1991: 21st February 1991

Pre-proof by order hearings in long causes

1. For an experimental period from 1st March 1991, in any cause, other than those under the optional procedure, in which a diet of proof or proof before answer of five days or more has been fixed, the cause will be put out by order before a Lord Ordinary approximately six weeks before that diet.

2. At the by order hearing, the court will expect to be informed about—

(*a*) the outstanding issues in dispute between the parties and the steps (if any) which have been or are being taken to resolve them before the diet;

(*b*) the prospects of settlement before the diet;

(*c*) the extent to which agreement has been or can be reached on any photographs, sketch plans, statements, documents or other evidence;

(*d*) the appropriateness of intimation by each party to the cause to the other parties of (i) a list of witnesses whom he intends to call to give evidence, and (ii) any written report of a skilled witness; and

(*e*) whether the proof is likely to require the number of days allotted to it, or whether it is likely to require additional days.

3. The court may recommend that, before the diet, parties should:–

(*a*) exchange lists of witnesses whom they intend to call to give evidence;

(*b*) exchange written reports of skilled witnesses;

(*c*) lodge a joint minute agreeing any evidence;

(*d*) take such other steps as may appear appropriate with a view to the expeditious resolution of the proceedings.

4. Any such recommendation will be recorded in the minute of proceedings. The response of the parties to such recommendations may be taken into account by the court in any subsequent award of expenses.

No. 3 of 1991: 26th April 1991

Procedure roll

1. In order to reduce the number of causes being appointed to the procedure roll unnecessarily (80 per cent. of cases appointed to that roll are taken off the roll before any hearing), the court expects that—

(*a*) on the closing of the record, discussions will take place between parties about the future procedure in the cause with particular regard to the resolution of points at issue without recourse to a hearing on the procedure roll; and

(*b*) where a cause is appointed to the procedure roll, the party whose plea is to be argued will inform his opponent of the nature of his proposed argument at the earliest opportunity.

2. The court may, in determining any question of expenses arising out of a hearing on the procedure roll, take into account the extent to which parties have complied with paragraph 1 above.

No. 4 of 1991: 1st May 1991

Advance copies of opinions

Practitioners are reminded that the only purpose of the informal practice under which advance copies of opinions are provided to them, is to allow them to prepare, in consultation with counsel, motions for expenses, leave to reclaim, etc, with a view to minimising the Court time required for the advising of the opinion.

It is a condition of this practice that neither the opinion itself nor any indication of the contents thereof should be revealed to any other person, including any party to the action involved, in advance of the date of the advising.

There have been a number of instances where this requirement of confidentiality has been breached. Any further breaches may lead to this practice being withdrawn and a return to the system by which opinions were issued only on the day on which they were to be advised.

No. 7 of 1991: 20th June 1991

Reclaiming motions

1. Practitioners are reminded that, when enrolling a reclaiming motion in a case in respect of which no opinion has been issued, they should advise the depute clerk

(*a*) that a reclaiming motion has been enrolled, and

(*b*) that an opinion is required.

2. Further, and as from this date, when enrolling a reclaiming motion where a matter likely to be at issue at the hearing of the reclaiming motion is not covered by an opinion already in process (*e.g.* the disposal of expenses following upon the appearance of judgment) practitioners will require

(*a*) to indicate in the motion sheet the particular matter which is not so covered, and

(*b*) advise the depute clerk that an opinion is required thereon.

No. 8 of 1991: 30th September 1991

Transaction of business by post and facsimile transmission

1. In the interests of providing a more comprehensive service to practitioners, as from 14 October 1991 and for an experimental period, a party may

(1) lodge a step of process or production or other document by post; and
(2) in addition to the provisions of Rule of Court 93, and subject to the terms of paragraph 10 of this Practice Note, enrol a motion or opposition to a motion by post or FAX

Subject to the provisions of this Practice Note, the provisions of the Rules of Court and existing Practice Notes shall apply to the practice and procedure to which this Practice Note applies.

Fees

2.—(1) Where any item of business transacted by post requires payment of a fee, a solicitor's cheque for the appropriate fee must be enclosed with the item, unless the solicitor holds a Court of Session account.

(2) No item of business which requires payment of a fee may be transacted by FAX unless the solicitor holds a Court of Session account.

Signature of steps of process

3. In order to facilitate the introduciton of this Practice Note, the following steps of process will not require signature.

(*a*) minute of amendment;
(*b*) answers to a minute of amendment;
(*c*) minute of sist;
(*d*) minute of transference;
(*e*) minute of objection to a minute of transference; and
(*f*) note of objections to Auditor's Report.

Signet

4.—(1) A summons, accompanied by the process, or bill and letters for inhibition, accompanied by relevant supporting documents, may be lodged for signet by post.

(2) If in order,

(*a*) the summons; or
(*b*) the letters of inhibition, together with the relevant supporting documents

duly signeted will be returned by post.

(3) If there is a defect of a kind which cannot be remedied by a telephone call from the Signet Officer

(*a*) the summons and process; or
(*b*) the bill and letters for inhibition, together with the relevant supporting documents

will be returned by post with a letter stating the reasons for their return.

Calling of summons

5.—(1) Where a summons is lodged for calling by post, there shall be enclosed along with the summons (which shall have the execution of service attached) a typewritten calling slip detailing the names and addresses of parties and the counsel and solicitor for the pursuer.

(2) If the summons is accepted for calling, the Assistant Clerk shall advise the solicitor of the calling date by letter;

(3) If there is a defect of a kind which may be dealt with by telephone the Assistant Clerk shall telephone the solicitor for the pursuer. If the defect cannot be remedied by telephone the summons will be returned to the solicitor by post with a letter stating the reasons.

Entering appearance by post or FAX

6. Where appearance is entered on behalf of a defender to an action by post or by FAX, details of the process number, parties to the action and date of calling along with the names of Counsel and solicitor(s) represent-

ing the defender, (and in multi-defender cases which defender they represent) must be received in the General Department not later than 4p.m. on the last day for entering appearance.

Petitions and notes—warrant for intimation and service

7.—(1) Where a petition or note is lodged by post, it shall be accompanied, where applicable, by a motion enrolled in terms of paragraph 10 of this Practice Note.

(2) Where an interlocutor pronounced following the procedure set forth in paragraph (1) above contains a warrant for intimation and service of the petition or note, a copy of the interlocutor will be transmitted by post to the solicitor who lodged the petition or note.

Walling of petitions and notes

8. Where a petition or note requires to be intimated on the walls of court, a copy of the first page of the petition or note may be transmitted by post or by FAX to the Petition Department which will arrange for the petition or note to be walled.

Lodging of steps of process and productions by post

9.—(1) As from 14 October 1991 productions lodged in the General and Petition Departments shall be numbered as sub-numbers of the number of process assigned to the inventory of productions (*e.g.* inventory of productions—No. 15 of process; production 1—No. 15/1 of process; production 2—No. 15/2 of process; etc.).

(2) A step of process or inventory of productions sent by post, must

(*a*) be received in the Office of Court not later than the last day for lodging it; and

(*b*) if intimated, be marked accordingly.

(3) Where a solicitor proposes to lodge an Inventory of Productions and accompanying productions by post, he must

(*a*) contact the appropriate section of the General Department or the Petition Department, as the case may be, to ascertain from the Assistant Clerk the relevant number of process; and

(*b*) cause the relevant number of process and the case number to be marked on the Inventory of Productions and each production.

(4) Where a motion is required to be enrolled in respect of the lodgment of any document by post, the motion shall be sent with the document in accordance with paragraph 10.

Enrolment of motions by post or FAX

10.—(1) All motions and all oppositions to motions may be enrolled by post.

(2) All motions and all oppositions to motions, other than those accompanied by

(*a*) a signed step of process;

(*b*) an Open or Closed Record or Appeal Print or Appendix; or

(*c*) any other document of more than four pages (including backing sheet) in length,

may be enrolled by FAX.

(3) A motion or opposition in terms of paragraphs 10(1) or 10(2) above shall be enrolled by completing the pro-forma which forms Appendix A or Appendix B, as the case may be, and having due regard, so far as the effective date of enrolment is concerned, to the terms of Practice Note No. 1 of 1989, by transmitting to the appropriate department of court, together with

(*a*) any paper apart required under paragraph 3 of the Practice Note of 10 December 1986, and

(*b*) any relevant document or step of process which may be transmitted with it in terms of this Practice Note.

(4) A motion or opposition enrolled in terms of the foregoing may be transmitted at any time of the day but must be received in the Office of Court at such time as shall comply with the latest times for enrolment and opposition set out in the table to Practice Note No. 1 of 1989.

(5) Where a motion referred to in column 1 of Appendix C is enrolled by FAX, a document lodged as a production solely in support of the motion may also be transmitted by FAX (with an Inventory of Productions), provided that the original of the document shall be lodged as a production—

(*a*) in the event of opposition to the motion, or

(*b*) at the request of the Court.

Enrolment of motions at public counter

11. A motion or opposition enrolled at the public counter shall be enrolled by completing Part II and, where applicable, Part III of the *pro forma* which forms Appendix A or Appendix B as the case may be.

Appendix A

Form of Motion

PART I Sheet 1 of .... sheets

Name of pursuer/petitioner* ....

Name of first defender/respondent* ....

Name and nature of Petition (eg John Smith's Curatory) ....

....

Court case number .... Date of last interlocutor ....

Is case due in court during the next seven days? Yes/No*

(If Yes, state reason)

Name of firm enrolling motion

PART II

Solicitor for .... Ref No. ....

Rutland Exchange No. .... Town ....

Tel No. .... FAX No. ....

Date of enrolment of motion ....

Has motion been intimated? Yes/No* If yes, give date ....

State terms of motion

* delete as appropriate

PART III

MOTION SLIP—General Department only

Name of case# .... v ....

Name of firm ....

eg (John Smith &c v John Brown &c).

APPENDIX B

FORM OF OPPOSITION

PART I Sheet 1 of .... sheets

Name of pursuer/petitioner* ....

Name of first defender/respondent* ....

Name and nature of petition (eg John Smith's Curatory) ....

....

Name of firm enrolling opposition ....

PART II

Solicitor for .... Ref No. ....

Rutland Exchange No. .... Town ....

Tel No. .... FAX No. ....

Date of enrolment of opposition ....

Date opposition intimated

Nature and effective date of enrolment of motion to be opposed ....

* delete as appropriate

PART III

OPPOSITION SLIP—General Department only

Name of case# .... v ....

Name of firm ....

eg (John Smith &c v John Brown &c).

APPENDIX C

Column 1 *Motion*	Column 2 *Supporting document*
1. Assessment of liability for expenses under provisions of Legal Aid legislation	—Minute for Assessment
2. Commission to take evidence	—Medical Certificate
3. Interim custody, aliment	—Wages Certificate &c.
4. Open Confidential Envelope	—Copy letter of intimation to haver
5. Motion for recall of arrestment/inhibition under Rule of Court 74(*g*)	—Copy letter of intimation

Notice: 30th September 1991

Transaction of business by post and FAX

1. As from 14 October 1991, and in terms of Practice Note No. 8 of 1991 issued on 30 September 1991, certain classes of business transacted in the Court of Session may be conducted by post or by FAX.

2. Practitioners availing themselves of this service must ensure that they are conversant with the Rules of Court and the procedures and time limits in those rules. Failure to observe these may cause delay, inconvenience and unnecessary expense and could have serious implications for the conduct of the case. Practitioners are responsible for ensuring that the Rules of Court are observed and in particular for ensuring that documents transmitted by post or by FAX are received timeously and, where applicable, are fully and accurately completed. In particular and, in regard to motions or oppositions enrolled in petitions, practitioners should ensure that sufficient information is provided in Appendix A or Appendix B of the said Practice Note which will facilitate the identification of the petition.

3. Where a fee is chargeable in relation to any item of business, that item will be accepted by post only (a) from solicitors with a Court of Session account or (b) when accompanied by a solicitor's cheque for the appropriate fee and by FAX only from solicitors with a Court of Session account. Practitioners who wish to open a Court of Session account should apply to the Cashier, Court of Session, 2 Parliament Square, Edinburgh. Practitioners who do not wish to open such an account should be aware of the up to date fees applicable. The fees are reviewed annually with any changes normally taking effect from 1 April.

4. Practitioners should ascertain from the General or Petition Department the case number of existing cases before enrolling a motion or lodging a document therein. The case number for new cases is shown at the top of the summons returned for service in terms of paragraph 4(2) or the copy interlocutor transmitted in terms of paragraph 7(2) of said Practice Note and should be noted for future use.

5. Practitioners who intend to conduct business by means of FAX are reminded that FAX machines can receive messages outwith the hours during which business is normally conducted in the Court of Session. It follows therefore that there may be advantage in transmitting a message in the evening for the following day rather than waiting until the following day when the line may be busier.

6. Practitioners who intend to conduct business by means of FAX should ensure that appropriate arrangements are made to deal expeditiously with FAX transmissions from the Court of Session (*e.g.* returned motions).

7. It is unnecessary to send a hard copy of any FAX message sent in terms of the Practice Note.

8. The following are the FAX numbers to be used for transacting business under the said Practice Note:—

(*a*) General Department 031–225 5496; and

(*b*) Petition Department 031–225 7233.

9. Any enquiry in regard to the above service should be directed to Mr Gordon Ellis, 031–225 2595, Ext. 245.

No. 1 of 1992: 9th January 1992

Judicial review of decision of adjudicator appointed under section 12 of the Immigration Act 1971

1. Practitioners are advised that, where a decision of an adjudicator appointed under section 12 of the Immigration Act 1971 is subject to an application for judicial review in terms of Rule of Court 260B, the adjudicator should not be called as a respondent in the petition but he should receive intimation thereof as a person who may have an interest.

2. In any such petition, the Home Secretary should be called as respondent.

[THE NEXT PAGE IS C 601]

(9) <u>Sheriff Officer</u> - appointed + removed by SP
- they enforce orders of the ct. by diligence
- not full-time civil servants but independent self-employed persons who are instructed by ind. litigants to enforce a decree [by diligence]
- Messenger-at-Arms - enforces orders of Ct. of S. - often firms practice as both S.O. + M at A.
- must have no personal interest in decree he's asked to enforce
  - LAURENCE JACK COLLECTIONS v HAMILTON (1976)
    - P.'s L/C were debt collection agency. Partners were also sheriff officers. Employee of sheriff officers firm asked to carry out diligence for a debt. <u>HELD</u> - diligence incompetent as S.O. had an interest in recovery
  - BRITISH RELAY v KAY (1976) - S.O. could not act as a debt collector + also a SO in same case

(10) <u>Solicitors</u> - conduct most sh. ct. litigation BUT always possible for ind. to conduct case by himself
- if wishes to be represented must be by a sol. or advocate. MINOR EXCEPTIONS - summary causes - at initial stages litigant may be represented by someone not legally qualified.
- may appear before any sh. ct. in Scotland
- must always act within terms of his mandate ie on instructions by his client
  BUT - not for every procedural matter when he has discretion in incidental aspects of case. BUT in any critical matter must have clients mandate

Digest of Practice

The Digest of Practice is a brief guide to the statutory provisions, Rules of Court, Acts of Sederunt and Practice Notes, mostly contained in *The Parliament House Book*, which regulate aspects of Court of Session procedure.

ABBREVIATIONS

1868 Act .... Court of Session Act 1868
1907 Act .... Sheriff Courts (Scotland) Act 1907
1971 Act .... Sheriff Courts (Scotland) Act 1971
1980 Act .... Law Reform (Miscellaneous Provisions) (Scotland) Act 1980
1985 Act .... Law Reform (Miscellaneous Provisions) (Scotland) Act 1985
1988 Act .... Court of Session Act 1988
A.S. .... Act of Sederunt
C.A.S. .... Codifying Act of Sederunt 1913
P.N. .... Practice Note
R.C. .... Rules of Court 1965, as amended

Abandonment of Action

After record closed.—A.S., 11th July 1828, para. 115.
Counter-claim, effect of.—R.C., 84(*d*).
Proof or jury trial, before begun.—R.C., 91A(1).
Proof or jury trial, in course of.—R.C., 91A(2).

Abandonment of Appeal

Finance Act 1894.—R.C., 294.
Finance (1909–10) Act 1910.—R.C., 332.
Inferior courts.—1907 Act, rule 96; R.C., 269, 271 and 272.
Solicitors (Scotland) Acts.—R.C., 5 and 7.

Absence

Decree in.—See DECREE IN ABSENCE.
Of counsel in procedure roll.—R.C., 94(*c*) and (*d*).

Accountant in Bankruptcy—R.C., 201A–201B.

Accountant of Court

Applications by judicial factors.—R.C., 200A.
Applications to encroach on capital.—R.C., 200B.
Caution.—R.C., 200(*c*)–(*f*).
Copies of proceedings for, in factory petitions.—R.C. 200(*a*).
Drug trafficking, duties in relation to proceedings concerning, R.C. 201L–201R.
Fee-fund dues.—S.I. 1984 No. 256, Division A.
Payment of government duties.—R.C., 36.
Transmission of processes to.—R.C., 200(*b*).

Act of Sederunt

Power to regulate procedure by.—1988 Act, ss.5, 6.

Adjustment of Record—See RECORD.

Procedure.—R.C., 267–273.
Remit to sheriff court.—1988 Act, s.32(2).
Time.—1907 Act, rule 91.

Appeal to House of Lords.—See also DIRECTIONS AS TO PROCEDURE AND STANDING ORDERS, Division B.
Appeal dismissed for want of prosecution.—1988 Act, s.43.
Appealable interlocutors.—1988 Act, s.40.
Cause appealed from sheriff court.—1988 Act, s.32(5).
Exchequer cause.—1988 Act, ss.24, 52(3).
Interest, order for payment of.—1988 Act, ss.42, 43.
Interim orders.—1988 Act, s.41.
Special case.—1988 Act, s.27(5).

Appeals under Particular Statutes—R.C., 276–289.
See also under the particular statutes and ABANDONMENT OF APPEAL.
Form.—R.C., 279; App. 43.
Ordaining tribunal to state case.—R.C., 278.
Preparation of case.—R.C., 277.
Procedure in Court of Session.—R.C., 280.

Appearance
Appeal.—R.C., 269(*a*).
Ordinary action.—R.C., 81.

Appendices
Lodging.—R.C., 294A; P.N., 18th May 1989.

Arbiters
Judges' power to act as.—1980 Act, s.17.

Arbitration
Arbitration (International Investment Disputes) Act 1966.—R.C., 249A.
International commercial arbitration, registration and enforcement of awards.—R.C., 249AB–249AC.
Stated case in.—R.C., 276–280.

Arrestment
Admiralty cause.—1988 Act, s.6(iii); R.C., 74, 140.
Counter-claim.—R.C., 84(*c*).
On dependence.—R.C., 74, 84(*c*), 155A, 170D(2).
Recall of.—R.C., 88F(2).
Ship.—1988 Act, s.6(iii); R.C., 74, 140.
To found jurisdiction.—1988 Act, s.6(vii); R.C., 74.
Warrant.—R.C., 70(2).

Assessors
Nautical.—Nautical Assessors (Scotland) Act 1894, amended by Administration of Justice (Scotland) Act 1933; R.C., 37, 39–46.

Other causes.—1988 Act, s.5(*i*); R.C., 38, 39, 41–45.
Patents, designs, etc.—Patents Act 1977, s.98(2); R.C., 37, 39–45, 252(4)(*c*), 257K.

Auditor of Court
Fees.—S.I. 1984 No. 256, Division A.
Report and objections.—R.C., 349.
Transmissions.—R.C., 348.
Vacation.—R.C., 1(*a*)(v).

Augmentations, Modifications, etc.—See CHURCH OF SCOTLAND.

Bankruptcy.—See also ACCOUNTANT IN BANKRUPTCY; JUDICIAL FACTOR.
Interim trustee, appointment of.—P.N., 27th March 1986.
Petition for sequestration.—Bankruptcy (Scotland) Act 1985, ss.5–11; R.C., 189(*a*)(vii) and 191–198; P.N., 16th July 1987 (No. 1).

Borrowing
Process.—R.C., 32.
Process, on entering appearance.—R.C., 86.
Process, where several defenders.—R.C., 87.
Productions after execution of commission.—R.C., 97.
Return before jury trial.—R.C., 121.
Return before proof.—R.C., 107.
Return, failure to.—R.C., 88.
Writs not borrowable.—R.C., 31.

By Order (Adjustment) Roll.—R.C., 91(*c*); P.N., 1st June 1967.

Calling of Summons.—R.C., 78.

Capital Transfer Tax, Appeals—R.C., 283.

Caption—R.C., 88.

Caution
Bonds of, lodging with Accountant of Court.—R.C., 13(*d*), 200(*d*), 206(*d*).
Guarantee companies.—R.C., 200(*e*)(iv) and (*f*), and 206(*b*), (*c*) and (*e*).
Judicial factor.—R.C., 200.
Juratory.—R.C., 240.
Liquidator.—R.C., 206.
Minor's or pupil's damages.—R.C., 131.
Suspension.—R.C., 234–247.

Caveat
Form.—R.C., 68I; App. 72.
Lodging.—R.C., 68I.

Orders against which caveats may be lodged.—R.C., 68H.
Renewal.—R.C., 68I.
Suspension.—R.C., 236.
Winding-up petition.—R.C., 218A.

Central Office—R.C., 12.

Certificate of Execution
Divorce or Separation.—R.C., 155(*d*), 160(*b*); App. 3.
Petitions.—R.C., 195; App. 30.
Summons.—R.C., 74(*a*), 74A(3), (7), 77; App. 3.

Children—See also CONSISTORIAL ACTIONS; CUSTODY OF CHILDREN.
Curators, discharge of.—R.C., 201Z–201FF.
Guardians, appointment of.—Law Reform (Parent and Child) (Scotland) Act 1986, ss.3 and 4; Age of Legal Capacity (Scotland) Act 1991, s.5.
Parentage, proceedings in relation to.—R.C., 189(*a*)(xxxv), 260F–260G.
Parental rights, orders concerning.—1988 Act, s.20; R.C., 170B.
Pupils protection.—R.C., 200(g).
Tutors, discharge of.—R.C., 201Z–201FF.

Church of Scotland
Augmentation, etc.—A.S., 17th July 1925.
Preparation, etc., of teind rolls.—S.R. & O. 1925 No. 1098.
Re-allocation of deficiency of stipend caused by surrenders.—S.R. & O. 1925 No. 1060.

Cinematograph Films Act 1927—R.C., 289.

Citation
Admiralty cause.—R.C., 141 and 142.
Advertisement, by.—R.C., 75; App. 4A.
Company.—See COMPANY.
Consistorial actions.—See CONSISTORIAL ACTIONS.
Delict, actions founded on.—R.C., 75A.
Edictal.—R.C., 74A(2), 75 and 195(*b*)(ii); App. 4.
Execution, Certificate of.—See CERTIFICATE OF EXECUTION.
Foreign countries, service in.—R.C., 74B; and see Scottish Courts Administration Guidance pp. **C** 481 *et seq*.
Inducia.—See INDUCIAE.
Modes.—Citation Amendment (Scotland) Act 1882; Execution of Diligence (Scotland) Act 1926; R.C., 68A, 74A, 160.
Objection after appearance.—R.C., 82.
Warrant, petition.—R.C., 195(*a*).
Warrant, summons.—R.C., 74.

Civil Jurisdiction and Judgments Act 1982—R.C., 249D–249R; App. 53–61; P.N., 8th December 1988.

Commercial Actions

Affidavits.—R.C., 152.
Commercial roll.—1988 Act, s.6(i); R.C., 150.
Customs of trade.—R.C., 151F.
Definition.—R.C., 148(2).
Evidence.—R.C. 151C–151F.
Judges.—R.C., 149.
Procedure.—R.C., 151, 151C.
Transfer to roll.—R.C., 151B.
Withdrawal from roll.—R.C., 151A.

Commission to Recover Documents

Application for Commission.—R.C., 95.
Attendance of shorthand writers.—Notice, 22nd March 1990.
Certified copy interlocutor as warrant.—1988 Act, s.50.
Commercial action.—R.C., 151C.
Confidentiality.—R.C., 98.
Documents founded on by party.—R.C., 134E.
Execution of commission.—R.C., 97.
Expenses.—R.C., 134E(3).
Power to regulate procedure.—1988 Act, s.5(*d*).
Recovery by order.—R.C., 96; App. 9.
Reparation, optional procedure.—R.C., 188K, 188M.

Commission to Take Evidence

Application for commission.—1988 Act, ss.10, 25(3), 38; R.C., 100.
Attendance of shorthand writers.—Notice, 22nd March 1990.
Certified copy interlocutor as warrant.—1988 Act, s.50.
Evidence in other jurisdictions.—Evidence (Proceedings in Other Jurisdictions) Act 1975; R.C., 190(vi).
Evidence liable to be lost, etc.—R.C., 101.
Execution of commission.—R.C., 97, 100(*d*).
Inspection, photographing, etc., Order for.—Administration of Justice (Scotland) Act 1972, s.1; R.C. 95A.
Interrogatories, dispensing with.—R.C., 100 (*c*).
Letters of request.—R.C., 102; App. 10 and 11.

Company

Administration orders.—R.C., 209.
Appeal from liquidator.—R.C., 218F(6), 218G(1).
Caveat.—R.C., 218A.
Disqualification of directors.—R.C., 218N.
Intimation of petition.—R.C., 209(2), 215, 218, 218N(3), 218Q(1).
Liquidator.—R.C., 217(3)(*e*), 218D, 218F–218K; Form 35.
Provisional liquidator.—R.C., 218E.
Receivers.—Insolvency Act 1986, s.54; R.C., 214–216.
Reclaiming.—R.C., 264(*g*).
Remit to or from sheriff court.—R.C., 218B.
Service.—Companies Act 1985, s.725; R.C., 215(3), (5), 218(3), (5).
Special manager.—R.C., 218L.
Voluntary arrangements.—R.C., 203–208.
Winding up procedure.—R.C., 217–218M.

Conclusion, Forms of.—R.C., App. 2.

Consigned Money

Election petitions.—R.C., 301.
Generally.—Court of Session Consignations (Scotland) Act 1895; C.A.S., G, iii; R.C., 36.
Government duties.—R.C., 36.
Price of ship or other arrested property in Admiralty cause.—R.C., 143.
Receipts, to be lodged with Accountant of Court.—R.C., 13 (*d*).

Consistorial Actions

Access, variation of.—R.C., 170B (10).
Access, supervision of.—P.N., 1st March 1988.
Aliment, application for.—R.C., 170D (5), 170L, 170N.
Aliment, variation of.—R.C., 170B (10), 170P, 170R.
Arrestment on dependence.—R.C., 155A.
Capital sum and periodical allowance, application for.—Family Law (Scotland) Act 1985, ss.8–14; R.C., 170D.
Capital sum and periodical allowances, defence only on amount of.—R.C., 165.
Citation.—R.C., 159, 170 I(1), (2).
Consent to decree.—R.C., 166.
Consistorial roll.—1988 Act, s.6(i).
Curator ad litem appointed to defender.—P.N., 10th February 1983.
Custody claimed by defender.—R.C., 170B (3).
Custody, other proceedings relating to.—R.C., 170B(11).
Custody, variation of order for.—R.C., 170B (2)(8).
Decree for interim aliment, warrant for execution.—R.C., 170D (6).
Decree, record and certificate of.—App. 22–27.
Defended action.—R.C., 168A.
Definition.—Conjugal Rights (Scotland) Amendment Act 1861, s.19; R.C., 154.
Fee-fund dues, remission of.—R.C., 343.
Fees in undefended actions of divorce.—P.N., 3rd January 1980.
Financial provision, application for.—R.C., 170D, 170M.
Improper association.—R.C., 162.
Incidental orders, after decree granted.—R.C., 170D(12).
Induciae.—R.C., 158.
Inhibition on dependence.—R.C., 155A.
Insanity.—R.C., 167; App. 20, 21.
Interdict prohibiting removal of child.—R.C., 170C.
Interdict under Family Law Act 1986.—R.C., 170B(13).
Intimation, forms.—App. 15–19.
Intimation, to children and next of kin.—R.C., 155(3), 160, 170 I(3).
Intimation, to paramour.—R.C., 155(1).
Intimation, to third parties.—R.C., 170B (6).
Intimation, where defender insane.—R.C., 155(5), 167.
Intimation, where improper association.—R.C., 162.
Irretrievable breakdown.—Divorce (Scotland) Act 1976; P.N., 1977 No. 2.
Jurisdiction respecting children.—Matrimonial Proceedings (Children) Act 1958, ss.7–15.
Nullity of marriage, financial provision on.—Family Law (Scotland) Act 1985, s.17.
Parental rights, orders concerning.—1988 Act, s.20.
Periodical allowance, capital sum or variation of settlement.—R.C., 170D.
Presumption of death and dissolution of marriage.—Divorce (Scotland) Act 1938, s.5; R.C., 163; 189 (*a*)(xviii).

Proceedings outside Scotland.—Domicile and Matrimonial Proceedings Act 1973, Scheds. 2 and 3; R.C., 157(3), 170B(11), 170M.
Property, order for transfer of.—Family Law (Scotland) Act 1985, ss.8, 12, 14, 15.
Remits to local authorities.—P.N., 30th October 1980.
Remits to reporters.—P.N., 13th November 1969.
Removal of child.—R.C., 170C.
Simplified procedure.—R.C., 170E–170L; App. 19A–19E.
Sist of parties.—R.C., 170B (7).
Summons.—R.C., 155; App. 1 and 2.
Undefended action.—R.C., 168; P.N., 11th April 1978.

Consumer Credit Act 1974, s.41.—R.C., 293A.

Convention Adoption Orders.—Children Act 1975; Adoption Act 1976.
Applications.—R.C., 230C.
Attestation of documents.—R.C., 230K.
Dispensing power.—R.C., 230G.
Evidence.—R.C., 230D–F.
Notice to Registrar-General.—R.C., 230H.
Order.—R.C., 230J.
Revocation of regulated adoptions.—R.C., 230I.
Translations.—R.C., 230L.

Conveyancing (Scotland) Act 1874, Petition under.—R.C., 189 (*a*)(viii).

Copyright, Designs and Patents Act 1988.—R.C., 189 (*a*)(xvii), 250–257K.

Counsel.—See ADVOCATE.

Counter-claim
Ordinary action.—1988 Act, s.6(v); R.C., 84.
Ship collision cases.—R.C., 144 (*e*) (*f*).

Counter-Issue.—R.C., 91 (*c*), 114 (*c*) (*d*), 116 (*a*).

Criminal Justice (Scotland) Act 1987.—R.C., 201C–201R, 249S–249Y.

Curator ad litem
Adoption.—R.C., 220(6), (7), (9), 221(3)–(5), 222(5), (10), 224(4)–(6), 230(6), (8).
Consistorial Actions.—P.N., 10th February 1983.
Damages.—R.C., 131.
Incurable insanity.—R.C., 170.
Special case under 1988 Act.—R.C., 266.

Curator bonis, Petition for.—R.C., 189 (*a*) (i).

Curators, Discharge of.—R.C., 201Z–201FF.

Custody of Children
Child Abduction and Custody Act 1985.—R.C., 260H–260L.
Children Act 1975, Pt. II.—R.C., 170B(14); App. 68–70.
Family Conciliation Service, referral to.—R.C., 170B(15), 260D(10).
Family Law Act 1986, proceedings under.—R.C., 170B(11)–(13), 260EA–260EC.
Family Law Act 1986, registration and enforcement of orders.—R.C., 260P–260X.
Parental rights, applications concerning.—R.C., 170B(8).
Parental rights, orders concerning.—1988 Act, s. 20.
Petition for.—R.C., 189(*a*)(xx), (xxxiii), 260C–260EC; App. 68–70.

Customs of Trade.—R.C., 151F.

Damages
Interim payments.—R.C., 89A.
Minors and pupils.—R.C., 131–134.
Provisional damages.—R.C., 134A–134D.

Damages (Scotland) Act 1976.—R.C., 75A.

Debtors (Scotland) Act 1987.—R.C., 88A–88H; App. 65–67.

Defamation Act 1952.—R.C., 188A.

Decree by Default
Failure to lodge closed record.—R.C., 91(*f*).
Failure to satisfy production in reduction.—R.C., 173.
Procedure Roll, absence from.—R.C., 94(*d*).
Reclaiming against.—R.C., 264(*c*)(*e*).

Decree in Absence
Expenses, Taxation of.—R.C., 89(*g*), (*h*).
Procedure.—R.C., 88C(3), 89.
Recall.—R.C., 89.
Reclaiming against.—R.C., 264.
Suspension of.—1988 Act, s.34.

Defamation Act 1952.—R.C., 188A.

Defence Contracts Act 1958.—R.C., 250–257.

Defences.—R.C., 83.

Defenders

Adding new.—R.C., 92; App. 6.
Borrowing process.—R.C., 86, 87.
Furth of Scotland: designation.—R.C., 71.
Furth of Scotland: intimation.—R.C., 75, 75A, 89.
Roll of.—R.C., 78 (*c*).

Diets, Fixing—R.C., 17; 91C, 294C; App. 63; P.N., Nos. 2 and 3 of 1987: 30th July 1987; P.N., 22nd March 1990.

Directions, Petition by Trustees for.—R.C., 190(ix), 232 and 233.

Discipline Tribunal

Solicitors (Scotland) Act 1980, ss.50–54.—R.C., 7, 8.

Divorce.—See CONSISTORIAL ACTIONS

Documents.—See COMMISSION; INVENTORY; LODGING PAPERS; PAPERS.

Drug Trafficking, Proceedings in connection with.—R.C. 201C–201R, 249S–249Y; App. 62, 71.

Duplicate Inventory of Process.—R.C., 20 and 24.

Edictal Citation.—See CITATION.

Election Petitions.—1988 Act, s.44; R.C., 297–331; App. 46–51.

Electoral Registration Appeals.—R.C., 284.

Employment Appeal Tribunal

Leave to appeal from.—P.N., 6th November 1986.

English Judgment.—See FOREIGN JUDGMENTS.

Enrolling.—See APPEAL AND MOTIONS.

Entail Petition.—R.C., 189(*a*)(vi).

Euratom Inspection Order.—R.C., 296 H.

European Assembly Election Petition.—R.C., 297.

European Community Judgments

Civil Jurisdiction and Judgments Act 1982, recognition and enforcement under.—R.C., 249D-N, 249R; App. 53–54, 59.
Registration under E.E.C. Treaties.—R.C., 296 F–H.

European Court

References to.—R.C., 296 A–E; App. 52.

Evidence.—See also COMMISSION TO RECOVER DOCUMENTS; COMMISSION TO TAKE EVIDENCE.
Commercial actions.—R.C., 151C–151F.
Power to regulate admission.—1988 Act, s.5(*e*).
Recording of.—R.C., 113, 130.
Reparation, optional procedure.—R.C., 188N.
Rulings as to.—R.C., 110, 123.
Written statements.—Civil Evidence (Scotland) Act 1988, s.2; R.C., 108A.

Ex Tempore Judgments

Issue of interlocutor.—P.N., 31st May 1990.

Exchequer Causes

Appeal.—R.C., 153D.
Appeal to House of Lords.—1988 Act, ss.24, 52(3).
Commencement.—R.C., 153A.
Extracts.—R.C., 153E.
Judge.—1988 Act, s.3.
Precedence of.—1988 Act, s.23.
Review.—R.C., 153C.
Sittings of court.—R.C., 68F.
Suspension.—R.C., 153B.

Execution of Charge.—App., 44.

Execution of Summons.—Citation Amendment (Scotland) Act 1882, s.4(3); R.C., 77.

Expenses

Auditor's report, approval of and objections to.—R.C., 349, Division A.
Charging order.—Solicitors (Scotland) Act 1980, s.62.
Commission and diligence.—R.C., 134E(2).
Extract.—R.C., 63A.
Fees, power to regulate.—1988 Act, s.5(*g*).
Fees, Table of Solicitors'.—R.C., 347, Division A.
Power to regulate.—1988 Act, s.5(*h*).
Procedure roll.—R.C., 94(*c*), (*d*).

Public Records.—R.C., 103(*c*).
Summary taxation of solicitor's account.—R.C., 350.
Taxation, regulations for.—R.C., 347–350.
Transmission to Auditor.—R.C., 348.

Extractor
Edictal citations.—R.C., 75(*a*).
Reference to Principal or his Office.—R.C., 12(*c*).
Transmission of process from.—R.C., 32A, 104.

Extracts
Authentication of.—R.C., 63.
Decrees of divorce.—P.N., 21st March 1985.
Decrees where further application may be made in respect of children.—R.C., 170(B)(9).
Department Regulations.—P.N., 9th July 1980.
Execution on.—R.C., 67, 68; App. 44.
Expenses.—R.C., 63A.
Form.—R.C., 63–65.
Interest under.—R.C., 66.
Interim decree.—1988 Act, s.47(3).
Not bar to review.—R.C., 63B.

Facsimile transmission.—See FAX, TRANSACTION OF BUSINESS BY.

Factor.—See JUDICIAL FACTOR.

Fair Trading Act 1973.—R.C., 188C.

Fax, Transaction of Business by.—P.N., 30th September 1991; Notice, 30th September 1991.

Fee Fund Dues.—S.I. 1984 No. 256, Division A; P.N., 26th May 1988; 30th June 1988.

Fees, Solicitors'.—See EXPENSES.

Fiat, Application for.—R.C., 189(*b*); P.N., 21st February 1986.

Finance Act 1894, Appeals.—R.C., 294, 338–339.

Finance (1909–10) Act 1910, Appeals.—R.C., 332–339.

Financial Services Act 1986.—R.C., 189(*a*)(xxxiv), 260M–260N.

Foreign Courts

Letter of request to.—R.C., 102.
Production of original documents in.—R.C., 103(*d*).

Foreign Judgments

Civil Jurisdiction and Judgments Act 1982, recognition and enforcement under.—R.C., 249D-N, 249R; App. 53–54, 59; P.N., 8th December 1988.
"Dominions," etc.—Administration of Justice Act 1920; R.C., 189(*a*)(xiv), 248; Foreign Judgments (Reciprocal Enforcement) Act 1933, s.7.
Drug Trafficking Offences Act 1986, registration and enforcement under.—R.C., 249S–249Y; App. 62.
England and Northern Ireland.—Judgments Extension Act 1868; C.A.S., B, vi, 5; R.C., 189(*a*)(xiv), 249P-R: App. 56–58, 60–61.
Money judgments.—P.N., 8th December 1988.
Rest of World.—Foreign Judgments (Reciprocal Enforcement) Act 1933; R.C., 189(*a*)(xiv), 249.

Foreign Law Ascertainment

"Dominions."—British Law Ascertainment Act 1859; R.C., 190(vi).
Rest of World.—R.C., 190(vi).

Foreign Tribunals Evidence Act 1856.—R.C., 190(vi).

Foreign Witness.—See COMMISSION TO TAKE EVIDENCE; LETTERS OF REQUEST.

Government Duties

Funds in manibus curiae.—R.C., 36.

Guarantee Companies, List of.—R.C., 200(*e*)(iv) and 206(*c*).

Guardianship of Children (Scotland) Acts 1886 to 1973.

Petition under.—R.C., 189(*a*)(xxiii), 260A.

Health Records, Access to.—R.C., 260Y.

House of Lords, Appeal to.—See APPEAL TO HOUSE OF LORDS.

Immigration

Adjudicator's decision, petition for judicial review of.—P.N., 9th January 1992.

Induciae

Admiralty causes.—R.C., 141.
Arrestment, recall of.—R.C., 88F(2).
Consistorial action.—R.C., 159, 170(*c*).
Decree in absence, motion for.—R.C., 88C(3).
Delict, actions founded on.—R.C., 75A(1).
Ordinary action.—R.C., 72, 74(*b*).
Petition.—R.C., 192, 195(*b*).
Receiver, petition for appointment.—R.C., 215(8).
Reparation, optional procedure.—R.C., 188G.
Shortening or extending.—R.C., 72(*b*).

Time to pay direction, recall of.—R.C., 88F(2).
Winding up, petition for.—R.C., 218(8).

Inheritance Tax, Appeals.—R.C., 283.

Inhibition
Counterclaim.—R.C., 84(*c*).
On dependence.—R.C., 74, 84(*c*), 155A, 170D(2).
Registration.—R.C., 74(*e*).
Subscription of bill.—1988 Act, s.49.
Third Party Notice.—R.C., 85(*b*).
Warrant.—R.C., 70(2).

Insolvency Act 1986.—See RECEIVERS.

Interdict
Interim orders.—1988 Act, s.47; R.C., 79(1), 236.
Interim: breach of.—1988 Act, s.47(1).
Interim: removal of child.—R.C., 157, 170C.
Petition.—R.C., 234, 235.
Specific relief.—1988 Act, s.46.

Interest
Appeal to House of Lords.—1988 Act, ss.42, 43.
Judicial rate.—R.C., 66.
Time to pay direction in force.—R.C., 88H; App. 65–67.

Interim Orders.—1988 Act, ss.35(1), 41, 47; R.C., 79, 236.

Interim Payments.—R.C., 89A.

Interlocutor
Appeal from sheriff court.—1988 Act, s.32(4).
Appealable to House of Lords.—1988 Act, s.40.
Certified copy, as warrant.—1988 Act, s.50.
Correction.—R.C., 30.
Inner House.—R.C., 295, 296.
Issue of shares at a discount.—R.C., 218.
Powers of Depute Clerks of Session.—R.C., 93A.
Prefixing.—R.C., 27.
Sheet.—R.C., 20, 23, 133, 200(*e*)(i).
Signing.—R.C., 30.

International Oil Pollution Compensation Fund.—R.C., 147A; App. 5B.

Interrogatories.—See COMMISSION TO TAKE EVIDENCE.

Intimation

Admiralty Causes.—R.C., 144(*b*), 145(*b*).
Appeal.—R.C., 268(*c*).
Auditor's report.—R.C., 349.
Commission, application for.—R.C., 95(*a*), 97(*b*).
Company, petitions concerning.—R.C., 209(2), 215, 218, 218N(3), 218Q(1).
Consistorial Action.—See CONSISTORIAL ACTIONS.
Defences, early lodging of.—R.C., 83(*a*).
Edictal citation, on.—R.C., 75(*c*), 195(*b*).
Heritable creditors, to.—R.C., 76; App. 5, 18E.
Issues.—R.C., 114(*a*).
Lodging step of process.—R.C., 21.
Motion.—R.C., 93(*c*)(*e*).
Petition procedure.—R.C., 195.
Productions, lodging of.—R.C., 107, 121.
Reclaiming.—R.C., 262.
Recorded delivery.—R.C., 68A.
Remitted Cause.—R.C., 274(*b*).
Statutory appeal.—R.C., 276–280.
Summary procedure, consent to.—R.C., 148(*b*).
Suspension.—R.C., 236(*a*).

Inventory

Duplicate of process.—R.C., 20, 24.
Process.—R.C., 20.
Productions.—R.C., 134E.
Productions at calling.—R.C., 20, 78(*d*).
Productions before jury trial.—R.C., 121; P.N., 15th July 1964.
Productions before proof.—R.C., 107; P.N., 15th July 1964.

Judges

Composition of court.—1988 Act, s.2.
Death, disability or retiral.—R.C., 112.
Exchequer causes.—1988 Act, s.3.
Number.—1988 Act, s.1.
Power to act in cases relating to rates and taxes.—1988 Act, s.4.
Re-employment of retired.—1985 Act, s.22.
Vacation powers.—1988 Act, s.5(*k*); R.C., 1.

Judgments

Advance copies.—P.N., 1st May 1991.
Finality of.—1988 Act, ss.18, 39.

Judgments Extension Act 1868.—See FOREIGN JUDGMENTS.

Judicial Factor

Bankruptcy Act.—R.C., 201–201B; App. 29–34D.
Caution.—R.C., 200(*c*) to (*f*).
Definition.—R.C., 199.
Discharge of.—R.C., 201Z–201FF.
Documents for Accountant.—R.C., 200(*a*).
Penal interest.—Judicial Factors Act 1849, s.5; R.C., 200(*g*).

Transmission of process to Accountant.—R.C., 200(*b*).

Judicial Review.—R.C., 260B; App. 39D.
Immigration adjudicator.—P.N., 9th January 1992.

Jurisdiction
Averments to found.—R.C., 70(1)(*c*).
Contesting by defender.—R.C., 83(*e*).

Jury Trial
Abandonment.—R.C., 127.
Actions appropriate.—1988 Act, ss.9, 11.
Admissions.—R.C., 122.
Application by defender under optional procedure.—R.C., 188I.
Application for and adjustment of issues.—R.C., 114–116.
Application for consent to Accountant.—R.C., 200A; Trusts (Scotland) Act 1961, s.2(3).
Applying verdict.—R.C., 125.
Approval of issues.—R.C., 114(*d*).
Exceptions.—R.C., 124.
Expenses.—See EXPENSES.
Fee-fund dues.—S.I. 1984 No. 256, Division A.

Fixing of diet.—P.N., 30th July 1987 (No. 2).
Illness of juror.—1988 Act, s.15.
Jurors.—1868 Act, s.45; R.C., 118, 119; App. 12; 1980 Act, ss.1, 2 and Sched. 1; 1988 Act, ss.12, 13, 15.
Lodging Productions.—R.C., 121.
Motion for New Trial.—1988 Act, ss.29, 30; R.C., 126.
Non-attendance.—1980 Act, s.2.
Offences.—1980 Act, s.3.
Precept.—R.C., 117A.
Reclaiming on issues.—R.C., 117, 264(*b*).
Special verdict.—R.C., 128, 129.
Third party procedure.—R.C., 85(*e*).
Trial without issues.—R.C., 115, 116(*b*).
Verdict.—1988 Act, ss.16, 17, 31, and see *Special verdict.*
Verdict by majority.—1988 Act, s.17(2).
View.—1988 Act, s.14; R.C., 120.

Lands Clauses Consolidation (Scotland) Act 1845, Petition under.—R.C., 189(*a*)(xi).

Law Reporters
Copies of papers for.—R.C., 26(*b*).

Letters of Request.
Witness in Scotland.—R.C., 102A.
Witness outside Scotland.—R.C., 102; App. 10, 11.

Letters of Request (Husband and Wife).—R.C., 169; App. 22, 24 and 26.

Letters Passing the Signet.—R.C., 73(*b*).

Libraries
Copies of papers for.—R.C., 26(*b*).

Liquidator.—See COMPANY.

Local Government (Scotland) Act 1973, s.103.—R.C., 287.

Lodging Papers.—R.C., 134E, 194A.
Closed Record.—R.C., 91(*e*)(*f*).
Copies for use of the Court.—R.C., 26, 114, 275(*a*)(ii).
Fax, by.—P.N., 30th September 1991; Notice, 30th September 1991.
Intimation.—See INTIMATION.
Marking date.—R.C., 29.
Marking serial letter and number.—R.C., 25, 194.
Open record.—R.C., 90.
Post, by.—P.N., 30th September 1991; Notice, 30th September 1991.
Productions before proof or trial.—R.C., 107, 121.

Lord Advocate

Consistorial causes.—1907 Act, s.38B; 1988 Act, s.19.
Exchequer causes.—1988 Act, ss.22, 23.

Lord President

Exercise of powers by Lord Justice-Clerk.—R.C., 68G.

Lyon Court, Appeals from.—R.C., 267–272.

Maintenance Orders (Reciprocal Enforcement).—See Division K.

Maritime Lien.—1988 Act, s.6(iii); R.C., 74, 140.

Matrimonial Homes (Family Protection) (Scotland) Act 1981.—R.C., 188D; App. 18D.

Matrimonial Proceedings (Children) Act 1958.—See Consistorial Causes.

Merchant Shipping (Liner Conferences) Act 1982.—R.C., 249B–249C.

Messengers-at-Arms.—A.S., 15th July 1991 (S.I. 1991 No. 1397).

Mines (Working Facilities and Support) Act 1966.—R.C., 259.

Mining Industry Act 1926.—R.C., 332–339.

Minors' and Pupils' Damages.—1988 Act, s.5(*f*); R.C., 131–134.

Minute Book.—R.C., 18, 80.

Motion

Enrolment.—R.C., 93, App. 8; P.N., 11th January 1957; P.N., 1976 No. 5; P.N., 10th December 1986, 11th December 1987 (No. 4), 12th January 1989, 30th September 1991; Notice, 30th September 1991.
Interim orders.—R.C., 79.
Notification of time required.—Notice, 7th March 1991.
Ordinary action.—R.C., 93.
Petition.—R.C., 198.
Powers of Depute Clerks of Session.—R.C., 93A.
Sheet.—R.C., 20, 93.
Unopposed.—P.N., 10th December 1986.
Vacation.—R.C., 1(*a*).

Multilateral Investment Guarantee Agency Act 1988.—R.C., 249AA.

Multiplepoinding

Defences.—R.C., 176(*b*), 177.
Government duties.—R.C., 36.
Procedure.—R.C., 175–185; App. 2(7).

Nautical Assessors.—See Assessors.

New Trial.—See Jury Trial.

Notaries Public.—R.C., 4, 11, 190(iv).

Oaths and Affirmations.—R.C., 122A.

Oil, International Pollution Compensation Fund.—R.C., 147A; App. 5B.

Oil Taxation Act 1975
Appeals.—R.C., 281.
Appeals relating to penalties.—R.C., 282.

Papers.—See also LODGING PAPERS.
Form of.—R.C., 19.
Petition.—R.C., 191, 194.
Printing optional.—R.C., 19, 26, 70, 191.
Sheet for signature.—R.C., 22.
Size.—R.C., 26.
Summons.—R.C., 70, 78(*d*).

Parliamentary Election Petition.—R.C., 297–331.

Patents.—R.C., 189(*a*)(xvii), 250–257K.
Assessors.—R.C., 37, 39–45, 252(4)(*c*), 257K.

Pensions Appeal Tribunal.—R.C., 285, 286; App. 45.

Petition
Answers.—R.C., 196.
Citation.—R.C., 195; App. 30.
Copy of.—R.C., 200; P.N., 2nd March 1988.
Department.—R.C., 12, 13.
Directions.—R.C., 190(ix), 232, 233.
Disposal of.—1988 Act, s.25.
Form.—R.C., 191; App. 28, 29.
Induciae.—R.C., 192.
Information on.—P.N., 11th December 1987.
Inner House.—R.C., 190.
Lodging of documents founded on.—R.C., 194A.
Marking of papers.—R.C., 194.
Motions.—R.C., 198; P.N., 21st February 1986.
Outer House.—1988 Act, s.25; R.C., 189.
Reclaiming.—R.C., 261–264.
Signature.—R.C., 193.
Unopposed.—R.C., 197.

Post, Transaction of business by.—P.N., 30th September 1991; Notice, 30th September 1991.

Practice Notes.—See pp. **C** 501 *et seq.* Practice notes dealing with specific matters are noted under the relevant headings.

Presumption of Death (Scotland) Act 1977.—R.C., 188B.

Procedure Roll
Abandonment of preliminary pleas.—R.C., 94(*e*).
Calling peremptory.—R.C., 94(*b*)(*c*)(*d*).
Discussions prior to hearing.—P.N., 26th April 1991.
Putting out cases.—R.C., 16, 94(*a*); P.N., No. 3 of 1987: 30th July 1987.
Sending to Roll.—R.C., 91(*c*)(iii), 114(*f*).

Process
Borrowing and returning.—R.C., 32, 107, 121.
Borrowing on entering appearance.—R.C., 86, 87.
Caption.—R.C., 88.
Fees.—R.C., 35.
Index.—R.C., 33.
Papers.—See PAPERS.
Steps.—R.C., 20.
Transmission.—R.C., 34, 104.

Productions.—See also INVENTORY; LODGING.
Medical records, return to health boards.—P.N. 15th September 1983.

Proof.—See also EVIDENCE.
Additional in appeal.—1988 Act, ss.32(3), 37.
Allowance.—1988 Act, s.9; R.C., 91(*c*).
Evidence.—R.C., 113.
Fixing diet.—R.C., 17; P.N., 9th May 1975, No. 2 of 1987: 30th July 1987.
In Inner House.—1988 Act, ss.32(3), 37.
Lodging productions.—R.C., 107.
Pre-proof by order hearings.—P.N., 21st February 1991.
Separate parts.—R.C., 108.

Protestation.—R.C., 80.

Proving the tenor.—R.C., 186–188; App., Form 2(6).

Public Records.—R.C., 103.

Railway and Canal Commission.—R.C., 259.

Receivers.—Insolvency Act 1986, s.54; R.C., 214–216.

Reclaiming
Against application of special verdict.—R.C., 129.
Appendix.—R.C., 294A; P.N., 18th May 1989.
Copies of papers for judges.—R.C., 26(*b*).
Default, decree by.—R.C., 264(*e*).
Effect.—R.C., 262(*c*).
Entitlement.—1988 Act, s.28.
Grounds, notice of.—R.C., 294B.

Information in cases pending.—R.C., 294C; App. 63; P.N., No. 2 of 1987: 30th July 1987.
Issues.—R.C., 117.
Late motion.—R.C., 264(*d*).
Leave.—R.C., 264(*c*).
Liquidation.—R.C., 264(*g*).
Method.—R.C., 262; App. 41.
Objection to competency.—R.C., 263.
Opinion, obtaining of.—P.N., 20th June 1991.
Reclaiming days.—R.C., 117, 264.
Rehearing before larger court.—1988 Act, s.36.
Reparation, optional procedure.—R.C., 188P.
Substantial amendment of pleadings.—P.N., 26th March 1981.
Suspension.—R.C., 264(*h*).

Record
Adjustment.—R.C., 90A; P.N., 27th March 1986.
Amendment.—R.C., 92; P.N., 27th March 1986.
Closing.—R.C., 91.
Information on.—P.N., 3rd December 1987, 11th December 1987.
Lodging closed.—R.C., 91(5).
Lodging open.—R.C., 90(1).

Recovery of Documents.—See COMMISSION.

Reduction
Conclusions.—R.C., 70(*a*); App. 2(3).
Counter-claim.—R.C., 84(*j*).
Defences.—R.C., 171.
Ope exceptionis.—R.C., 174.
Production of writs.—R.C., 172.

Registered Designs Acts 1949 to 1961; Copyright, Designs and Patents Act 1988.—R.C., 189(*a*)(xvii), 250–257, 257I–257J.

Registration Appeal Court.—R.C., 284.

Remit to Sheriff Court
Action.—1985 Act, s.14; 1907 Act, rule 20A.
Petition for winding up.—R.C., 218B(1).

Remit to Person of Skill
Power to regulate fees.—1988 Act, s.7.

Remitted Cause from Sheriff Court.—1971 Act, s.37; 1907 Act, rule 20; R.C., 85, 274, 275. See also R.C., 104A.
Petition for winding up.—R.C., 218B(2).

Reparation
Optional procedure.—R.C., 188E–188P.

Reponing
Appeal.—R.C., 271.
Decree in absence.—R.C., 89(*f*).
Ranking for aught yet seen.—R.C., 183.
Remitted causes.—R.C., 275(*b*).

Report to Inner House.—R.C. 91B.

Restoration of Possession, Order for.—1988 Act, s.45(*a*).

Restrictive Trade Practices Act 1956.—S.I. 1957 No. 147.

Revenue Appeals.—R.C., 281–283.

Roll of Defenders.—R.C., 78(*c*).

Rolls.—R.C., 14–18.

Rules Council
Composition.—1988 Act, s.8.
Members.—See Courts and Offices Division.
Powers.—1988 Act, s.8.

Sequestration, Petition for.—See Bankruptcy.

Service.—See Citation.

Sessions of Court.—1988 Act, s.5(*j*); R.C., 68B–68D.

Sex Disqualification (Removal) Act 1919.—R.C., 118.

Sheriff Court, Appeal from. See Appeal from Sheriff Court.

Sheriff Court, Causes Remitted from.—See Remitted Cause from Sheriff Court.

Sheriff Court, Remit of Action to.—See Remit of Action to Sheriff Court.

Sheriff Officers.—A.S., 15th July 1991 (S.I. 1991 No. 1397).

Ship.—See Admiralty Cause.

Shorthand Writer
Duties.—R.C., 113(*a*), 130.
Fees.—R.C., 347, Chap. IV, Division A.

Signature
Defences, Answers, etc.—R.C., 28.
Interlocutor.—R.C., 22.
Petition, ordinary.—R.C., 193.
for summary trial.—R.C., 231(*c*).
for suspension.—R.C., 193, 235.
Signet, Letters passing the.—R.C., 73(*b*).
Summons.—R.C., 73(*a*).
in consistorial actions.—R.C., 155(*e*).

Signet, Letters passing the.—R.C., 73(*b*).

Social Security Acts.—R.C., 288.

Social Work (Scotland) Act 1968, s.50.—R.C., 289A.

Solicitor
Admission.—See DIVISION F; R.C., 2, 3.
Discipline, etc.—See DIVISION F; R.C., 5–10.
Fees.—See EXPENSES.
Right of audience.—1988 Act, s.48.

Special Case
1988 Act.—1988 Act, s.27; R.C., 265, 266.
Other statutes.—R.C., 276–289. See particular statutes.

Special Verdict.—R.C., 128, 129.

Specific Performance
Statutory duty.—1988 Act, s.45(*b*).

Specification of Documents.—See COMMISSION.

Stamp Duty Reserve Tax, Appeals.—R.C., 283.

Stated Case.—R.C., 276–289. See particular statutes.

Statutory Appeals.—R.C., 290.

Summary Decree.—R.C., 89B.

Summary Trial.—1988 Act, s.26; R.C., 189(*a*)(xii), 231; App. 40.

Summons

Calling.—R.C., 78.
Conclusions.—R.C., 70(*a*); App. 2.
Form.—R.C., 70, 188F; App. 1, 27A.
Information on.—P.N., 11th December 1987.
Initiation of proceedings.—R.C., 69.
Signature.—R.C., 73(*a*).
Signeting.—R.C., 73(*b*), 74.

Suspensions

Breach of interim interdict.—1988 Act, s.47(1).
Caution.—R.C., 238–240, 243.
Of decree in absence.—1988 Act, s.34.
Of decree in consistorial action.—R.C., 163(*d*).
Of decree in inferior court.—1988 Act, s.35; R.C., 242.
Petition.—R.C., 189(*a*)(xvi), 234, 235, 237.
Procedure.—R.C., 236, 241, 245–247.
Reclaiming.—R.C., 262, 264(*h*).
Refusal of petition, certificate of.—R.C., 244.

Taxation.—See EXPENSES.

Taxes Management Act 1970

Appeals.—R.C., 281.
Appeals relating to penalties.—R.C., 282.

Taxes upon Funds in Manibus Curiae.—R.C., 36.

Teind Office.—R.C., 12 and 13(*c*).

Telegraph Acts.—R.C., 258.

Third Party Notices.—R.C., 85; App. 7.

Time to Pay Directions.—R.C., 88A–88H; App. 65–67.

Trade Marks.—R.C., 250–257K.

Transference of Cause.—R.C., 106.

Transmission of Process

Appeal against interlocutor applying verdict.—R.C., 273(*b*).
Appeal from inferior court.—R.C., 268(*b*).
Factory process to Accountant.—R.C., 200(*b*).
On contingency.—1988 Act, s.33; R.C., 104A.
Warrant for, from another court.—R.C., 104.

Transmission of Records.—R.C., 32A.

Tribunals and Inquiries Act 1971
Appeals under s.13(1).—R.C., 292.
Appeals under s.13(5).—R.C., 293.
Special Cases under s.13(2).—R.C., 291.

Trustees' Petition for Directions.—1988 Act, s.6(vi); R.C., 190(viii), 232 and 233.

Trusts (Scotland) Act 1921.—R.C., 232.

Trusts (Scotland) Act 1961.—R.C., 189(*a*)(iii), 190(x) and 260.

Tutors, Discharge of.—R.C., 201Z–201FF.

Undefended Cause.—See DECREE IN ABSENCE.

Vacation
Admiralty causes.—R.C., 140(*d*).
Adoption of children.—R.C., 229.
Appeals by way of stated case, etc.—R.C., 277(*k*).
Appeals from inferior Courts.—R.C., 269(*b*) and 271.
Applications to prohibit removal of child.—R.C., 157.
Court.—R.C., 68E; P.N., 31st March 1970.
Inner House judgments.—R.C., 296.
Interlocutors, signing of.—R.C., 30(3).
Petitions.—R.C., 195(*a*).
Reclaiming days.—R.C., 264(*a*), (*b*) and (*c*).
Remitted causes.—R.C., 275(*b*).
Statutory appeals.—R.C., 290(*e*).
Summons, calling of.—R.C., 78(*b*).
Vacation Judge, powers of.—1988 Act, s.5(*k*); R.C., 1.

Value Added Tax.—P.N., 14th April 1973; P.N., 1977 No. 4.

Verdict.—See JURY TRIAL.

Wakening of Cause, procedure in place of.—R.C., 105.

Winding-up.—See COMPANY.

Witness
At proof.—R.C., 111.
Caution for expenses by party litigant.—R.C., 106B.
Citation.—Citation Amendment (Scotland) Act 1882.

Commissions for Examination.—R.C., 100.
English or Irish.—Attendance of Witnesses Act 1854. See LETTERS OF REQUEST.
Experts, Certification of.—R.C., 347—Chapter II, note 5.
Experts, Number of, where assessor.—R.C., 42 and 146.
Fees and Expenses.—R.C., 347—Chapter II.
Foreign.—See LETTERS OF REQUEST.
Presence in Court.—Evidence (Scotland) Act 1840, s.3.
Reparation, optional procedure.—R.C., 188L, 188M.
Warrant to Cite.—R.C., 106A.

DIVISION D

Courts, Lower

Statutes

Acts of Sederunt, etc.

Acts of Court and Practice Notes

Notes for Guidance

[THE NEXT PAGE IS D 7]

[1] Notice of Accidents Act 1894

(57 & 58 Vict. c. 28)

An Act to provide for notice of and inquiry into accidents occurring in certain employments and industries. [20th July 1894]

NOTE

[1] Notification of accidents in mines, quarries, factories, workshops: see the Notice of Accidents Act 1906. Certain powers of the Board of Trade now transferred to the Minister of Transport by the Ministry of Transport Act 1919, s.2, S.I. 1970 No. 1681, S.I. 1976 No. 1773 and S.I. 1979 No. 751. See also S.I. 1970 No. 1537. Restricted by the Road and Rail Traffic Act 1933, s.43(2).

Notice to Board of Trade of accidents in certain employments

[1] **1.**—(1) Where there occurs in any employment to which this section applies any accident which causes to any person employed therein either loss of life or such bodily injury as to cause him to be absent throughout at least one whole day from his ordinary work, his employer shall, as soon as possible and, in case of an accident not resulting in death, not later than six days after the occurrence of the accident, send to the Board of Trade notice in writing of the accident, specifying the time and place of its occurrence, its probable cause, the name and residence of any person killed or injured, the work on which any such person was employed at the time of the accident, and, in the case of an injury, the nature of the injury.

[2] (2) If any person wilfully makes default in complying with the requirements of this section he shall be liable on summary conviction to a fine not exceeding level 1 on the standard scale.

(3) [Repealed by the Notice of Accidents Act 1906, Sched.]

NOTES

[1] As amended by the Notice of Accidents Act 1906, s.6.

[2] As amended by virtue of the Criminal Procedure (Scotland) Act 1975, ss.289C and 289G.

Application of provisions as to notice

2.—(1) Section 1 of this Act shall apply to the employments specified in the Schedule to this Act.

(2) If the Board of Trade are of opinion that any other employment in which twenty persons or more, not being domestic servants, are employed by the same employer, is specially dangerous to life or limb, the Board may, by order, direct that section 1 of this Act shall apply to that employment, and thereupon, while the order is in force, that section shall apply accordingly.

(3) The Board of Trade may, by order, revoke or modify any order made under the foregoing powers, and modify or limit the application of section 1 of this Act to the employments specified in the Schedule to this Act.

(4) The Board of Trade may also, by order, require any further particulars to be specified in the notice to be sent in pursuance of section 1 of this Act.

(5) Every order made under this section shall be notified in the *London Gazette* and in such other manner as may appear to the Board of Trade sufficient for giving publicity thereto, and shall be laid before both Houses of Parliament as soon as may be after it is made.

Power to hold formal investigation in case of serious accidents

3. Where it appears to the Board of Trade that any accident involving loss of life or bodily injury is of sufficient importance to require a formal investigation of the accident, and of its causes and circumstances, the Board may by order direct such investigation to be held, and with respect to any such investigation the following provisions shall have effect:—

(1) The Board may appoint a competent person to hold the investigation, and may appoint any person possessing legal, medical, or special knowledge to act as assessor in holding the investigation, and may assign to any such person such remuneration as the Board, with the approval of the Treasury, determine:

(2) The person appointed to hold the investigation (hereinafter called the court) shall hold the same in open court in such manner and under such conditions as the court may think most effectual for ascertaining the causes and circumstances of the accident, and enabling the court to make the report in this section mentioned:

(3) The court shall have for the purpose of the investigation all the powers of a court of summary jurisdiction when acting as a court in the exercise of its ordinary jurisdiction, and all the powers of an inspector under the Railway Regulation Acts 1840 to 1889, and in addition the following powers; namely—

(*a*) Power to enter and inspect, or to authorise any person to enter and inspect, any place or building the entry or inspection whereof appears to the court requisite for the said purpose;

(*b*) Power, by summons signed by the court, to require the attendance of all such persons as it thinks fit to call before it and examine for the said purpose, and for that purpose to require answers or returns to such inquiries as it thinks fit to make;

(*c*) Power to require the production of all books, papers, and documents which it considers important for the said purpose;

(*d*) Power to administer an oath and require any person examined to make and sign a declaration of the truth of the statements made by him in his examination:

(4) Every person attending as a witness before the court, and not being the employer of the person killed or injured, or in the employment of that employer, shall be allowed such expenses as would be allowed to a witness attending before a court of record, and in case of dispute as to the amount to be allowed the same shall be referred by the court to a master of the Supreme Court, who on request signed by the court shall ascertain and certify the proper amount of the expenses:

(5) The court holding an investigation under this section shall make a report to the Board of Trade, stating the causes of the accident and its circumstances, and adding any observations which the court thinks right to make, and the Board may cause any such report to be made public in such manner as the Board think fit:

(6) The court may order any costs and expenses incurred in and about an investigation under this section (including any remuneration payable to any person appointed to hold the investigation or to act as assessor) to be paid by any person summoned before it, if it finds that the accident was due to the act or default or negligence of that person; and any such order shall, on the application of any person entitled to the benefit thereof, be enforced by any court of summary jurisdiction as if the costs and expenses were a penalty imposed by the court: but subject to any such order such costs and expenses

shall be deemed to be part of the expenses of the Board of Trade in the execution of this Act:

[1] (7) If any person without reasonable excuse (proof whereof shall lie on him) either fails, after having had the expenses (if any) to which he is entitled tendered to him, to comply with any summons or requisition of a court holding an investigation under this section, or prevents or impedes the court in the execution of its duty, he shall for every such offence be liable, on summary conviction, to a fine not exceeding level 1 on the standard scale, and in the case of a failure to comply with a requisition for making any return or producing any document shall be liable, on summary conviction, to a fine not exceeding £10 for every day that such failure continues.

NOTE

[1] As amended by the Criminal Procedure (Scotland) Act 1975, s.289C (4), (5), (8), and by virtue of *ibid.*, s.289G.

Expenses of Board of Trade

4. The expenses of the Board of Trade in the execution of this Act shall be defrayed out of moneys to be provided by Parliament.

Application to Government departments

5. This Act shall apply in the case of accidents occurring to persons employed by a department of the Government, and in such cases the notice to be given by the employer shall be given by such person as the department by general rule direct.

Savings

6. Nothing in this Act shall apply to any employment which is for the time being regulated by any Act of Parliament administered by the Secretary of State or by inspectors appointed by him, or shall require notice to be given of any accident of which notice is required by any other Act to be given to the Board of Trade.

Application to Scotland

7. In the application of this Act to Scotland—

The expression "court of summary jurisdiction" shall mean the sheriff[1]:

The expression "master of the Supreme Court" shall mean the auditor of the Court of Session.

Every order made under this Act and required to be notified in the *London Gazette*, shall, if it relates to Scotland, be notified in the *Edinburgh Gazette*.

NOTE

[1] For the interpretation of the term "sheriff," see now the Sheriff Courts (Scotland) Act 1971, s.4 and the Interpretation Act 1978, Sched. 1.

. . . . . .

Short title

9. This Act may be cited as the Notice of Accidents Act 1894.

SCHEDULE

[1] 1. Construction or repair of any railway, tramroad, tramway.

2. [Repealed by the Factory and Workshop Act 1895.]

3. Use or working of any traction engine or other engine or machine worked by steam in the open air.

NOTE

[1] As amended by the Factories Act 1937, s.159, Sched. 4.

[1] Sheriff Courts (Scotland) Act 1907

(7 Edw. 7 c. 51)

An Act to regulate and amend the laws and practice relating to the civil procedure in sheriff courts in Scotland, and for other purposes. [28th August 1907]

NOTE

[1] As amended by the Sheriff Courts (Scotland) Act 1913.

For the interpretation of the terms "sheriff" and "sheriff-substitute" throughout this Act, see now the Sheriff Courts (Scotland) Act 1971, s.4, and the Interpretation Act 1978, Sched. 1.

Preliminary

Short title

1. This Act may be cited for all purposes as the Sheriff Courts (Scotland) Act 1907.

2. [Repealed by the Statute Law Revision Act 1927.]

Interpretation

3. In construing this Act (unless where the context is repugnant to such construction)—

(*a*) "Sheriff" includes sheriff-substitute;
(*b*) "Tenant" includes sub-tenant;
(*c*) "Lease" includes sub-lease;
(*d*) "Action" or "cause" includes every civil proceeding competent in the ordinary sheriff court;
(*e*) "Person" includes company, corporation, or association and firm of any description nominate or descriptive, or any Board corporate or unincorporate;
(*f*) "Sheriff-clerk" includes sheriff-clerk depute;
(*g*) "Agent" means a law-agent enrolled in terms of the Law Agents (Scotland) Act 1873;
(*h*) "Final judgment" means an interlocutor which, by itself, or taken along with previous interlocutors, disposes of the subject-matter of the cause, notwithstanding that judgment may not have been pronounced on every question raised, and that the expenses found due may not have been modified, taxed or decerned for;
(*i*) [Repealed by the Sheriff Courts (Scotland) Act 1971, Sched. 2.]
(*j*) "Small Debt Acts" means and includes the Small Debt (Scotland) Acts 1887 to 1889, and Acts explaining or amending the same;
(*k*) "Initial writ" means the statement of claim, petition, note of appeal, or other document by which the action is initiated;
(*l*) "Procurator-Fiscal" means procurator-fiscal in the sheriff court;
(*m*) [Repealed by the Statute Law (Repeals) Act 1989, Sched. 1, Pt. I.]
(*n*) "Pursuer" means and includes any person making a claim or demand, or seeking any warrant or order competent in the sheriff court;
(*o*) "Defender" means and includes any person who is required to be called in any action;
(*p*) "Summary application" means and includes all applications of a summary nature brought under the common law jurisdiction of the sheriff, and all applications, whether by appeal or otherwise, brought under any Act of Parliament which provides, or, according to any

practice in the sheriff court, which allows that the same shall be disposed of in a summary manner, but which does not more particularly define in what form the same shall be heard, tried, and determined;

(*q*) [Repealed by the Law Reform (Miscellaneous Provisions) (Scotland) Act 1980, Sched. 3.]

JURISDICTION

Jurisdiction

[1] **4.** The jurisdiction of the sheriffs, within their respective sheriffdoms, shall extend to and include all navigable rivers, ports, harbours, creeks, shores, and anchoring grounds in or adjoining such sheriffdoms. And the powers and jurisdictions formerly competent to the High Court of Admiralty in Scotland in all maritime causes and proceedings, civil and criminal, including such as may apply to persons furth of Scotland, shall be competent to the sheriffs, provided the defender shall upon any legal ground of jurisdiction be amenable to the jurisdiction of the sheriff before whom such cause or proceeding may be raised, and provided also that it shall not be competent to the sheriff to try any crime committed on the seas which it would not be competent for him to try if the crime had been committed on land: Provided always that where sheriffdoms are separated by a river, firth, or estuary, the sheriffs on either side shall have concurrent jurisdictions over the intervening space occupied by water.

NOTE

[1] Repealed, so far as relating to criminal proceedings, by the Criminal Procedure (Scotland) Act 1975, Sched. 10.

Extension of jurisdiction

[1] **5.** Nothing herein contained shall derogate from any jurisdiction, powers, or authority presently possessed or in use to be exercised by the sheriffs of Scotland, and such jurisdiction shall extend to and include—

[2] (1) Actions of declarator (except declarators of marriage or nullity of marriage);

(1A) [Repealed by the Law Reform (Parent and Child) (Scotland) Act 1986, Sched. 2.]

[3] (2) Actions for aliment or separation (other than any action mentioned in subsection (2A) below):

[4] (2A) Actions, arising out of an application under section 31(1) of the Maintenance Orders (Reciprocal Enforcement) Act 1972, for the recovery of maintenance:

[5] (2B) Actions for divorce:

[6] (2C) Applications for orders relating to parental rights under section 3 of the Law Reform (Parent and Child) (Scotland) Act 1986.

(3) Actions of division of commonty and of division or division and sale of common property, in which cases the Act of 1695 concerning the division of commonties shall be read and construed as if it conferred jurisdiction upon the sheriff court in the same manner as upon the Court of Session:

(4) Actions relating to questions of heritable right or title (except actions of adjudication save in so far as now competent and actions of reduction) including all actions of declarator of irritancy and removing, whether at the instance of a superior against a vassal or of a landlord against a tenant:

(5) Suspension of charges or threatened charges upon the decrees of court granted by the sheriff or upon decrees of registration proceeding upon bonds, bills, contracts or other obligations registered in the books of the sheriff court, the books of council and session, or any others competent.

NOTES

[1] Explained (legal aid): see S.I. 1958 No. 1872, r. 2(2). Excluded by the Land Registration (Scotland) Act 1979, ss. 21(6) and 22(7). As amended by the Law Reform (Miscellaneous Provisions) (Scotland) Act 1980, s. 15(*a*) and Sched. 3, and the Civil Jurisdiction and Judgments Act 1982, Sched. 14.

[2] As amended by the Law Reform (Parent and Child) (Scotland) Act 1986, Sched. 2.

[3] Substituted by the Family Law (Scotland) Act 1985, Sched. 1, para. 1. As amended by the Law Reform (Parent and Child) (Scotland) Act 1986, Sched. 2. See the Domicile and Matrimonial Proceedings Act 1973, Sched. 2.

[4] Inserted by the Domestic Proceedings and Magistrates' Courts Act 1978, Sched. 2.

[5] Inserted by the Divorce Jurisdiction, Court Fees and Legal Aid (Scotland) Act 1983, s. 1.

[6] Inserted by the Law Reform (Parent and Child) (Scotland) Act 1986, Sched. 1, para. 3.

Power of sheriff to order sheriff clerk to execute deeds relating to heritage

[1] **5A.**—(1) This section applies where—

(*a*) an action relating to heritable property is before the sheriff; or

(*b*) it appears to the sheriff that an order under this section is necessary to implement a decree of a sheriff relating to heritable property.

(2) Where the grantor of any deed relating to the heritable property cannot be found or refuses or is unable or otherwise fails to execute the deed, the sheriff may—

(*a*) where subsection (1)(*a*) above applies, on application;

(*b*) where subsection (1)(*b*) above applies, on summary application,

by the grantee, make an order dispensing with the execution of the deed by the grantor and directing the sheriff clerk to execute the deed.

(3) Where in pursuance of an order under this section a deed is executed by the sheriff clerk, it shall have the like force and effect as if it had been executed by the grantor.

(4) In this section—

"grantor" means a person who is under an obligation to execute the deed; and

"grantee" means the person to whom that obligation is owed.

NOTE

[1] Inserted by the Law Reform (Miscellaneous Provisions) (Scotland) Act 1985, s.17.

Action competent in sheriff court

[1] **6.** Subject to section 8 of the Domicile and Matrimonial Proceedings Act 1973 and Chapter III of Part I of the Family Law Act 1986 any action competent in the sheriff court may be brought within the jurisdiction of the sheriff—

(*a*) Where the defender (or when there are several defenders over each of whom a sheriff court has jurisdiction in terms of this Act, where one of them) resides within the jurisdiction, or having resided there for at least forty days has ceased to reside there for less than forty days and has no known residence in Scotland:

(*b*) Where a defender carries on business, and has a place of business within the jurisdiction, and is cited either personally or at such place of business:

(*c*) Where the defender is a person not otherwise subject to the jurisdiction of the courts of Scotland, and a ship or vessel of which he is the owner or part owner or master, or goods, debts, money, or other moveable property belonging to him, have been arrested within the jurisdiction:

(*d*) Where the defender is the owner or part owner or tenant or joint tenant, whether individually or as a trustee of heritable property within the jurisdiction, and the action relates to such property or to his interest therein:

(*e*) Where the action is for interdict against an alleged wrong being committed or threatened to be committed within the jurisdiction:

(*f*) Where the action relates to a contract the place of execution or performance of which is within the jurisdiction, and the defender is personally cited there:

(*g*) Where in an action of furthcoming or multiplepoinding the fund or subject *in medio* is situated within the jurisdiction; or the arrestee or holder of the fund is subject to the jurisdiction of the court:

(*h*) Where the party sued is the pursuer in any action pending within the jurisdiction against the party suing:

[2] (*i*) Where the action is founded on delict, and the delict forming the cause of action was committed within the jurisdiction:

(*j*) Where the defender prorogates the jurisdiction of the court.

NOTES

[1] Excluded by the Civil Jurisdiction and Judgments Act 1982, s. 20(3). This section ceases to have effect in relation to actions to which s. 45 of the Administration of Justice Act 1956 applies; *ibid.* s. 45(6).

As amended by the Domicile and Matrimonial Proceedings Act 1973, Sched. 4 and by the Family Law Act 1986, Sched. 1, para. 3.

[2] Substituted by the Law Reform (Jurisdiction in Delict) (Scotland) Act 1971, s. 1(2).

Privative jurisdiction in causes under fifteen hundred pounds value

[1] **7.** All causes not exceeding £1,500 in value exclusive of interest and

[THE NEXT PAGE IS D 13]

PROTESTATION - where P. fails to take a case this procedure is available to D. who can force P. to go ahead with his action or drop it altogether

D. has to have service copy of writ + produce it at the time

Agent says "The D. craves protestation for not insisting" Sh. has discretion + may grant Protestation. A token amount of expenses may be granted against P. - R36

- P. has 7 days from granting of protestation to change mind or protestation shall be extracted + instance falls. P. must still pay protestation money

---

REPONING - R28 - a decree which becomes final is not one which can be reponed

Reponing is a procedure whereby D. who has had decree in absence granted against him can have decree recalled + can defend action

- Alternatives to reponing - P's sol. may agree to notice of intention to defend being lodged late if good reason which would satisfy ct. on reponing. Sol. endorses docquet on notice of intention to defend consenting to late lodging. Case will proceed as if notice lodged on time
  - even if P.'s sol. does not consent D. can ask ct. to serve notice of intention to defend + intimate motion to P's sol.

    SEE R.28

- Proposed defence is as important as explanation for failure to lodge notice of intention to defend on time. Sh. doesn't hear evidence BUT must be satisfied proposed defence, if proved, would be a valid defence
  Sh. must also be satisfied with D.'s explanation for failure to appear! - NORTH SEA LTD v SCOTT (1986) RAYMOND v JACK (1988)
  Sh. may RESTRICT grounds on which D. can defend action eg D. disputes quantum of liability for accident but admits liability - sh. may grant reponing that action defended on quantum only.
- If failure to lodge due to negligence of D's sol. sh. may not grant reponing notice as D. will have remedy against sol.

DEFENDED CAUSES - GO TO D29

expenses competent in the sheriff court shall be brought and followed forth in the sheriff court only, and shall not be subject to review by the Court of Session: Provided that nothing herein contained shall affect any right of appeal competent under any Act of Parliament in force for the time being.

NOTE

[1] As amended by the Sheriff Courts (Scotland) Act 1971, Sched. 2, S.I. 1976 No. 900, the Law Reform (Miscellaneous Provisions) Act 1980, Sched. 3, and S.I. 1988 No. 1993.

8. [Repealed by the Sheriff Courts (Scotland) Act 1971, Sched. 2.]

9. [Repealed by the Sheriff Courts (Scotland) Act 1913, s.1.]

Privilege not to exempt from jurisdiction

10. No person shall be exempt from the jurisdiction of the sheriff court on account of privilege by reason of being a member of the College of Justice.

SHERIFFS

Appointment of sheriffs and salaried sheriffs-substitute

11. The right of appointing to the salaried offices of sheriff and salaried sheriff-substitute shall be vested in His Majesty, and shall be exercised on the recommendation of the Secretary for Scotland.

12, 13. [Repealed by the Sheriff Courts (Scotland) Act 1971, Sched. 2.]

Salaries of sheriffs and sheriffs-substitute

[1] **14.** It shall be lawful to grant to any sheriff or sheriff-substitute such salary as to the Treasury may seem meet, and every such salary shall be paid quarterly or otherwise in every year as the Treasury may determine, and shall be charged upon and be payable out of the Consolidated Fund.

NOTE

[1] As amended by the Sheriffs' Pensions (Scotland) Act 1961, Sched. 1.

15, 16. [Repealed by the Sheriff Courts (Scotland) Act 1971, Sched. 2.]

Honorary sheriff-substitute

17. The sheriff may by writing under his hand appoint such persons as he thinks proper to hold the office of honorary sheriff-substitute within his sheriffdom during his pleasure, and for whom he shall be answerable. An honorary sheriff-substitute, during the subsistence of his commission, shall be entitled to exercise the powers and duties appertaining to the office of sheriff-substitute. An honorary sheriff-substitute shall hold office, notwithstanding the death, resignation, or removal of the sheriff, until his commission shall be recalled by a succeeding sheriff. In this section "sheriff" does not include sheriff-substitute.

18, 19. [Repealed by the Sheriff Courts (Scotland) Act 1971, Sched. 2.]

20. [Repealed by the Sheriffs' Pensions (Scotland) Act 1961, Sched. 2.]

21. [Repealed by the Sheriff Courts (Scotland) Act 1971, Sched. 2.]

22–24. [Repealed by the Sheriff Courts and Legal Officers (Scotland) Act 1927, Sched.]

25, 26. [Repealed by the Sheriff Courts (Scotland) Act 1971, Sched. 2.]

APPEALS

Appeal to sheriff

[1] **27.** Subject to the provisions of this Act an appeal to the sheriff shall be competent against all final judgments of the sheriff-substitute and also against interlocutors—

(*a*) Granting or refusing interdict, interim or final;

(*b*) Granting interim decree for payment of money other than a decree for expenses, or making an order *ad factum praestandum*;

(*c*) Sisting an action;

(*d*) Allowing or refusing or limiting the mode of proof;

(*e*) Refusing a reponing note; or

(*f*) Against which the sheriff-substitute either *ex proprio motu* or on the motion of any party grants leave to appeal;

Provided always that notwithstanding the death, resignation, or removal of a sheriff, appeals may be taken from the judgment of the sheriff-substitute, which appeals shall be heard by the succeeding sheriff when he shall enter upon office. It shall be competent for the sheriff, when the action is before him on appeal on any point, to open the record *ex proprio motu* if the record shall appear to him not to have been properly made up, or to allow further proof.

NOTE

[1] As amended by the Law Reform (Miscellaneous Provisions) (Scotland) Act 1980, Sched. 3.

Appeal to the Court of Session

[1] **28.**—(1) Subject to the provisions of this Act, it shall be competent to appeal to the Court of Session against a judgment either of a sheriff or of a sheriff-substitute if the interlocutor appealed against is a final judgment; or is an interlocutor—

(*a*) Granting interim decree for payment of money other than a decree for expenses; or

(*b*) Sisting an action; or

(*c*) Refusing a reponing note; or

(*d*) Against which the sheriff or sheriff-substitute, either *ex proprio motu* or on the motion of any party, grants leave to appeal.

(2) Nothing in this section nor in section 27 of this Act contained shall affect any right of appeal or exclusion of such right provided by any Act of Parliament in force for the time being.

NOTE

[1] See S.I. 1949 No. 2062. As amended by the Sheriff Courts (Scotland) Act 1971, Sched. 2.

Effect of appeal

29. An appeal shall be effectual to submit to review the whole of the interlocutors pronounced in the cause, and shall be available to and may be insisted in by all other parties in the cause notwithstanding they may not have noted separate appeals. An appeal shall not prevent immediate execution of a warrant of sequestration for rent, or of warrants to take inventories, or place effects in custody *ad interim*, or warrants for interim preservation, and an interim interdict, although appealed against, shall be binding till recalled.

30. [Repealed by the Law Reform (Miscellaneous Provisions) (Scotland) Act 1980, Sched. 3.]

31. [Repealed by the Law Reform (Miscellaneous Provisions) (Scotland) Act 1980, s. 11 and Sched. 3.]

32. [Repealed by the Sheriff Courts (Scotland) Act 1913, s. 1.]

33. [Repealed by the Juries Act 1949, Sched. 3.]

[1] REMOVINGS

NOTE

[1] The provisions of this Act relating to removings are, in the case of an agricultural holding, subject to the Agricultural Holdings (Scotland) Act 1991, s. 21: see subs. (4).

Removings

[1] **34.** Where lands exceeding two acres in extent are held under a probative lease specifying a term of endurance, and whether such lease contains an obligation upon the tenant to remove without warning or not, such lease, or an extract thereof from the books of any court of record shall have the same force and effect as an extract decree of removing obtained in an ordinary action at the instance of the lessor, or any one in his right, against the lessee or any party in possession, and such lease or extract shall along with authority in writing signed by the lessor or any one in his right or by his factor or law agent be sufficient warrant to any sheriff-officer or messenger-at-arms of the sheriffdom within which such lands or heritages are situated to eject such party in possession, his family, sub-tenants, cottars, and dependants, with their goods, gear, and effects, at the expiry of the term or terms of endurance of the lease: Provided that previous notice in writing to remove shall have been given—

(*a*) When the lease is for three years and upwards not less than one year and not more than two years before the termination of the lease; and

(*b*) In the case of leases from year to year (including lands occupied by tacit relocation) or for any other period less than three years, not less than six months before the termination of the lease (or where there is a separate ish as regards land and houses or otherwise before that ish which is first in date):

Provided that if such written notice as aforesaid shall not be given the lease shall be held to be renewed by tacit relocation for another year, and thereafter from year to year: Provided further that nothing contained in this section shall affect the right of the landlord to remove a tenant who has been sequestrated under the Bankruptcy (Scotland) Act 1913, or against whom a decree of cessio has been pronounced under the Debtors (Scotland) Act 1880, or who by failure to pay rent has incurred any irritancy of his lease or other liability to removal: Provided further that removal or ejectment in virtue of this section shall not be competent after six weeks from the date of the ish last in date: Provided further that nothing herein contained shall be construed to prevent proceedings under any lease in common form; and that the foregoing provisions as to notice shall not apply to any stipulations in a lease entitling the landlord to resume land for building, planting, feuing, or other purposes or to subjects let for any period less than a year.

NOTE

[1] Reference to the Bankruptcy (Scotland) Act 1913 inserted by virtue of the Interpretation Act 1889, s. 38 (1).

Letter of removal

35. Where any tenant in possession of any lands exceeding two acres in extent (whether with or without a written lease) shall, either at the date of entering upon the lease or at any other time, have granted a letter of removal, either holograph or attested by one witness, such letter of removal shall have the same force and effect as an extract decree of removing, and shall be a sufficient warrant for ejection to the like effect as is provided in regard to a lease or extract thereof, and shall be operative against the granter of such letter of removal or any party in his right within the same time and in the same manner after the like previous notice to remove: Provided always that where such letter is dated and signed within twelve months before the date of removal or before the first ish, if there be more than one ish, it shall not be necessary that any notice of any kind shall be given by either party to the other.

Notice to remove

36. Where lands exceeding two acres in extent are occupied by a tenant without any written lease, and the tenant has given to the proprietor or his agent no letter of removal, the lease shall terminate on written notice being given to the tenant by or on behalf of the proprietor, or to the proprietor by or on behalf of the tenant not less than six months before the determination of the tenancy, and such notice shall entitle the proprietor, in the event of the tenant failing to remove, to apply for and obtain a summary warrant of ejection against the tenant and every one deriving right from him.

Notice of termination of tenancy

37. In all cases where houses, with or without land attached, not exceeding two acres in extent, lands not exceeding two acres in extent let without houses, mills, fishings, shootings, and all other heritable subjects (excepting land exceeding two acres in extent) are let for a year or more, notice of termination of tenancy shall be given in writing to the tenant by or on behalf of the proprietor or to the proprietor by or on behalf of the tenant: Provided always that notice under this section shall not warrant summary ejection from the subjects let to a tenant, but such notice, whether given to or by or on behalf of the tenant, shall entitle the proprietor to apply to the sheriff for a warrant for summary ejection in common form against the tenant and every one deriving right from him: Provided further that the notice provided for by this section shall be given at least forty days before the fifteenth day of May when the termination of the tenancy is the term of Whitsunday, and at least forty days before the eleventh day of November when the termination of the tenancy is the term of Martinmas.

SUMMARY REMOVINGS

Summary removing

[1] **38.** Where houses or other heritable subjects are let for a shorter period than a year, any person by law authorised may present to the sheriff a summary application for removing, and a decree pronounced in such summary cause shall have the full force and effect of a decree of removing and warrant of ejection. Where such a let is for a period not exceeding four months, notice of removal therefrom shall, in the absence of express stipulation, be given as many days before the ish as shall be equivalent to at least one-third of the full period of the duration of the let; and where the let exceeds four months, notice of removal shall, in the absence of express stipulation, be given at least forty days before the expiry of the said period. Provided that in no case shall notice of removal be given less than twenty-eight days before the date on which it is to take effect.

NOTE

[1] Proviso added by the Rent (Scotland) Act 1971, Sched. 18.

Notice of termination in respect of dwelling-houses

[1] **38A.** Any notice of termination of tenancy or notice of removal given under sections 37 and 38 above in respect of a dwelling-house, on or after the date of the coming into operation of section 123 of the Housing Act

1974, shall be in writing and shall contain such information as may be prescribed by virtue of section 131 of the Rent (Scotland) Act 1971, and Rule 112 of Schedule 1 to this Act shall no longer apply to any such notice under section 37 above.

NOTE

[1] Added by the Housing Act 1974, Sched. 13, para. 1.

Lord Advocate as party to action for divorce

[1] **38B.**—(1) The Lord Advocate may enter appearance as a party in any action for divorce, and he may lead such proof and maintain such pleas as he thinks fit, and the sheriff shall, whenever he considers it necessary for the proper disposal of any such action, direct that the action shall be brought to the notice of the Lord Advocate in order that he may determine whether he should enter appearance therein.

(2) No expenses shall be claimable by or against the Lord Advocate in any action in which he has entered appearance under this section.

NOTE

[1] Inserted by the Court of Session Act 1988, Sched. 1, para. 2.

Orders with respect to children

[1] **38C.**—(1) In any action for divorce or separation, the sheriff may make, with respect to any child of the marriage to which the action relates, such order (including an interim order) as he thinks fit relating to parental rights, and may vary or recall such order.

(2) In this section—

(*a*) "child" and "parental rights" have the same meaning as in section 8 of the Law Reform (Parent and Child) (Scotland) Act 1986;

(*b*) "child of the marriage" includes any child who—

(i) is the child of both parties to the marriage, or

(ii) is the child of one party to the marriage and has been accepted as a child of the family by the other party.

NOTE

[1] Inserted by the Court of Session Act 1988, Sched. 1, para. 2.

Procedure Rules

Procedure rules

39. Subject to the provisions of any Act of Parliament in force after the passing of this Act, the procedure in all civil causes shall be conform to the rules of procedure set forth in Schedule 1 hereto annexed. Such rules shall be construed and have effect as part of this Act.

Court of Session to regulate fees, etc.

[1] **40.** The Court of Session may from time to time, by act of sederunt, make such regulations for regulating the fees of agents (other than such of the fees of agents as the Secretary of State may regulate under or by virtue of section 14A of the Legal Aid (Scotland) Act 1967), officers, shorthand writers, and others: Provided that every such act of sederunt shall, within one week from the date thereof, be transmitted by the Lord President of the Court of Session to the Secretary of State, in order that it may be laid before the Houses of Parliament; and, if either of the Houses of Parliament shall within 36 days after it has been laid before them resolve that the whole or any part of such act of sederunt ought not to continue in force, the whole or such part thereof as shall be included in such resolution shall from and after the date of the passing of such resolution cease to be binding.

NOTE

[1] As amended by the Secretaries of State Act 1926, s.1(3), the Administration of Justice (Scotland) Act 1933, Sched., by the Divorce Jurisdiction, Court Fees and Legal Aid (Scotland) Act 1983, Sched. 1, para. 7 and Sched. 2 and (*prosp.*) by the Law Reform (Miscellaneous Provisions) (Scotland) Act 1990, Sched. 9. See the Statutory Instruments Act 1946, s.5(2).

41. [Repealed by the Administration of Justice (Scotland) Act 1933, Sched.]

Small Debts Acts

42–48. [Repealed by the Sheriff Courts (Scotland) Act 1971, Sched. 2.]

Postal Charge

49. [Repealed by the Execution of Diligence (Scotland) Act 1926, s.7.]

Summary Applications

Summary applications

[1] **50.** In summary applications (where a hearing is necessary) the sheriff shall appoint the application to be heard at a diet to be fixed by him, and at that or any subsequent diet (without record of evidence unless the sheriff shall order a record) shall summarily dispose of the matter and give his judgment in writing: Provided that wherever in any Act of Parliament an application is directed to be heard, tried, and determined summarily or in the manner provided by section 52 of the Sheriff Courts (Scotland) Act 1876, such direction shall be read and construed as if it referred to this section of this Act: Provided also that nothing contained in this Act shall affect any right of appeal provided by any Act of Parliament under which a summary application is brought.

NOTES

[1] "Rules 1, 3, 4, 5(3), 10 to 12 and 14 to 19 of the Ordinary Cause Rules shall apply to a summary application in so far as they are not inconsistent with section 50 of the Act of 1907": S.I. 1983 No. 747, reg. 5, as amended by S.I. 1988 No. 1978.

The Poor's Roll

51. [Repealed by the Statute Law (Repeals) Act 1973.]

Repeal

52. [Repealed by the Statute Law Revision Act 1927.]

SCHEDULES

[1] FIRST SCHEDULE

NOTE

[1] As substituted by S.I. 1983 No. 747, affecting any action or proceedings commenced on or after 1st September 1983.

Arrangement of Ordinary Cause Rules

Introduction

Initial Procedure

Commencement of Cause

Period of Notice

Citation and Service

Undefended Causes

[THE NEXT PAGE IS D 19]

RE-SERVICE – of no significance in ordinary actions, R.17 only relevant in summary application where a precise date is given when D. has to come to ct. to say whether he will defend action – difficulties if you post C. today + it is returned – hearing now 19 days ahead + so too late to reserve by S.O. because less than 21 days notice. SOLUTION – wait until case calls in ct. + say unable to grant because of return + ask sh. to grant W. to reserve

---

FROM D22/1

- HENDERSON v NOBLE (1987) – P. raised action + served IW + checked at end of period for notice. Sh. Ct. said no notice + P. obtained decree in absence. Turned out had been period of notice – sh. ct. made a mistake. D. could raise action for reduction in Ct. of S. – granted without difficulty
  Qu. of expenses – ct. decided that D. should get expenses against P. because P. should have checked process to see whether notice had been lodged
  BUT – only get a process in defended actions + not even at this stage in proceedings. Ct. getting confused with Ct. of S. procedure as opposed to Sh. Ct. procedure.

UNDEFENDED ACTIONS – 22 + 23 – special procedures. Otherwise P. can obtain a decree automatically if undefended. Basic procedure in R.21 – see R.21
- P's sol. can restrict minute to ask for less than is craved
  eg D. may have made a payment to account

RULE 24 – P. will normally be entitled to expenses from D. if action is undefended
- All expenses set out in Act of Sederunt
- Auditor of Ct. normally taxes the amount in undefended actions
- Act provides for certain inclusive fees for all work involved up to stage of obtaining decree. Also charge outlays, warrant dues + cost of services eg recorded delivery costs. Principal IW then returned to ct.
- when Sh. Ct. gets IW back it is checked over + he will normally present it to Sh. who may state decree in chambers
- JURISDICTION – 21(a) + (b)

- Time to pay directions in undefended actions – 21B
- Extract – R.25
- Amendment – R.27
- Tabling + Process – 35 – 42
  - PROCEDURE – sol. goes to ct. on day case enrols for tabling. Sh. Ct. reads through list of cases which enrol for tabling. P's sol. says; 'pursuers case tables'. D's sol. will normally make a motion to ct. Either;–
  1) Normally order for defences will be made + case continued
  2) Case could be sisted eg if D. wants chance to apply for legal aid
  3) Parties may think case can be settled out of ct. so on JOINT MOTION may ask for a continuation eg of 4 weeks
  Case doesn't have to be continued with an order for defences – 35(3)
- P's sol. may fail to turn up + so not tabled – see 35(2)

GO TO D13

Proof

Evidence

67 Reference to oath.
68 Objection to documents.
69 Remit to person of skill.
70 Evidence to lie *in retentis*.
71 Evidence taken on commission.
72 Affidavit evidence.
72A Conditions for receiving written statements in evidence without being spoken to by a witness.
73 Recording of evidence.

Witnesses and Havers

74 Citation.
75 Form of citation.
76 Second diligence against witness.
77 Warrant to arrest.

Productions

78 Production and recovery of documents.
79 Lodging productions for proofs.
80 Ordering of production of documents by sheriff.
81 Optional procedure before executing commission and diligence.
82 Confidentiality.
83 Warrant for production of original documents from public records.
84 Orders for inspection.

Procedure at Proof

85 Proof to be taken continuously.
86 Objections.
87 Incidental appeal against rulings on confidentiality of evidence and production of documents.
88 Parties to be heard at close of proof.

Procedure after Judgment

Judgment

89 Judgment.

Extract

90 Extract.
90A Extract decree of divorce.

Appeal

91 Time-limit for appeal.
92 Application for leave to appeal and appeal therefrom.
93 Form of appeal and giving of notice to parties.
94 Reclaiming petition or oral hearing may be ordered or dispensed with.
95 Interim possession may be regulated pending appeal.
96 Abandonment of appeal.

Expenses

97 Decree for expenses may be extracted in solicitor's name.
98 Objection to auditor's report.

Particular Procedures

Sequestration for Rent

99 Actions craving payment of rent.
100 Warrant to inventory and secure.

DAMAGES

Damages (Scotland) Act 1976

Interim payment of damages

Provisional damages

RULES FOR REGULATING THE PROCEDURE OF THE ORDINARY CAUSE

INTRODUCTION

Dispensing power of sheriff

1. The sheriff may in his discretion relieve any party from the consequences of any failure to comply with the provisions of these Rules which is shown to be due to mistake, oversight or other cause, not being wilful non-observance of the same, on such terms and conditions as seem just; and in any such case the sheriff may make such order as seems just by way of extension of time, lodging or amendment of papers or otherwise so as to enable the cause to proceed as if such failure had not happened.

Representation

[1] 2.—(1) Subject to paragraph (2) of this rule, a party to any proceedings arising solely under the provisions of the Debtors (Scotland) Act 1987 shall be entitled to be represented by a person other than a solicitor or an advocate provided that the sheriff is satisfied that such person is a suitable representative and is duly authorised to represent the party.

(2) Paragraph (1) shall not apply to appeals to the sheriff principal.

(3) Where a party to any cause is represented by a solicitor, any reference in the rules to that party shall, where appropriate, be construed as a reference to the solicitor representing that party.

NOTE

[1] Substituted by S.I. 1988 No. 1978.

INITIAL PROCEDURE

COMMENCEMENT OF CAUSE

The initial writ

[1] 3.—(1) All ordinary causes shall be commenced by initial writ as nearly as may be in accordance with Form A as set out in the Appendix to this Schedule.

(2) The initial writ shall contain averments about any agreement which the pursuer has reason to believe may exist prorogating jurisdiction over the subject matter of the cause to another court.

(3) The initial writ shall contain averments about any proceedings which the pursuer has reason to believe may be pending before another court involving the same cause of action and between the same parties as those named in the initial writ.

[2] (4) An article of condescendence shall be included in the initial writ stating the ground of jurisdiction of the court.

(5) In an action of divorce or of separation the initial writ shall contain an article of condescendence specifying whether to the knowledge of the pursuer any proceedings are continuing in Scotland or in any other country which are in respect of the marriage to which the initial writ relates or are capable of affecting its validity or subsistence, and, if such proceedings are continuing, shall further specify—

(*a*) the court, tribunal or authority before which they have been commenced;
(*b*) the date of commencement;
(*c*) the names of the parties;
(*d*) whether any proof or other hearing has been appointed, and, if so, the date; and
(*e*) any other relevant facts in connection with such proceedings which might assist the sheriff to determine whether the action before him should be sisted in terms of his powers under Schedule 3 to the Domicile and Matrimonial Proceedings Act 1973 (sisting of consistorial actions).

(6) For the purposes of paragraph (5), proceedings shall be treated as continuing where proceedings, in respect of that marriage or capable of affecting its validity, have been instituted before a court, tribunal or other authority and such proceedings have not been finally disposed of.

(7) The information required by paragraph (5) shall, in all actions of divorce or of separation, be inserted in any defences or minute lodged by any party in such action, insofar as that information is additional to or contradictory of any such particulars provided by the pursuer in the action, or in any case in which the pursuer has provided no such statement.

[THE NEXT PAGE IS D 23]

Warrant of Citation - pursuers solicitor delivers writ to sh. cl. + pays a fee. Sh.Cl. then checks it over to make sure it is ex facie in order. Vets it generally for J. + competence. May do it there + then or may have to be completed a few days later. If satisfied he grants a W of C which is the auth. of the ct. to proceed with the action

Sh. Cl. decides which warrant is appropriate - R.5

He attaches W. to initial writ + return it to you

BUT - Sh. Cl. may not be happy with initial writ + refuse to sign it

so - if he refuses to sign W it should be sent to sheriff for his consideration - 8(3)

OR writ may contain order shortening/extending the period of notice or ordering D. not to do something eg interim interdict - must be signed by sheriff

TIME LIMITS - personal bar - problems in cases where there are T.L. eg 3 years T.L. for raising an action for personal injuries. Prescriptive period is stopped by valid SERVICE - getting W. doesn't stop time bar running however

- if we near to a T.L. always use S.O. + not post. Ensure S.O. knows of T.L. Extra expense involved is worthwhile

- if no form of C, no copy of citation etc - defective service - if no TL no problem BUT crucial where TL has expired + no re-service can be effective

NOW - added provision for ct. to override TL in personal injuries actions where equitable to do so. Case law on what is equitable - P+L (S) Act 1973

CASE - P.'s sol. raised action just before expiry of TL BUT incorrect postal citation a week before expiry (before days of eq. power). So no formal citation + no appearance entered to cure defect. P. served again by S.O. but time barred so P's sol. had to pay off prof. negl.

THOMPSON v WIGGIS LTD (1981) - C. messed up just before TL - copy of P's legal aid memorandum sent instead of IW - not a valid C. D's sol. entered appearance + argued it was time barred - R18 applied + defect cured

- D's argued no C. at all so defect could not be cured. Sh. thought C. was to bring to notice of D. that action was being raised against him so was a C.

JOHN G. KINNAID + CO v TAGGART (1974) - C. failed to specify date of posting - crucial as triggers of date of notice. D. chose not to appear as cure defects in C.

- Don't lodge notice of intention to defend but don't do nothing as may have decree in absentia against you - write to Sh.Cl. pointing out there has been a defective C. + suggest that R.17 applies. If appears to Sh. that defective service then may not grant decree in absence as it appears no valid C. ∴ reservice is necessary (17)

- If Sh. grants decree must raise action of reduction for decree AND actions of C.

- If no notice of intention to defend is lodged then decree in absence may be obtained

- At end of period of notice P's sol. should check to see whether such notice has been lodged - duty of sol. to check

- Sometimes D's sol. will intimate notice to P's agent

GO TO D18/1

(8) Any application made by any party in an action of divorce or separation for an order in terms of Schedule 2 (ancillary and collateral orders), or for a sist of such an action or the recall of a sist in terms of Schedule 3, to the Domicile and Matrimonial Proceedings Act 1973, shall be made by written motion.

(9) Unless the sheriff on cause shown otherwise directs, in an action of divorce a warrant for citation shall not be granted without there being produced with the initial writ—

(*a*) an extract of the relevant entry in the register of marriages; and

(*b*) where appropriate, an extract of the relevant entry in the register of births.

(10) In an action relating to the custody of a child by a person by virtue of section 47 of the Children Act 1975—

(*a*) the parents of the child shall be named and designed in the initial writ as defenders in the cause; and

(*b*) if their address is known, citation of and service upon them shall proceed in accordance with rules 8 to 10, 12, and 15 to 17.

(11) In an action for custody of a child in which consent of the parent, tutor, curator or guardian of the child is required by section 47 of the Children Act 1975, a form of consent as nearly as may be in accordance with Form T1 as set out in the Appendix to this Schedule shall be lodged in process.

NOTE

[1] As amended by S.I. 1984 No. 255, 1986 Nos. 513, 1230, 1946 and 1966 and 1988 No. 1978.

Signature and backing of initial writ

4. The initial writ shall be signed by the pursuer or his solicitor and the name and address of that solicitor, if any, shall be stated upon the back of every service copy.

Warrant of citation

[1] 5.—(1) The warrant of citation in any ordinary cause other than an action of divorce and of separation or an action in which a time to pay direction under the Debtors (Scotland) Act 1987 may be applied for by the defender shall be framed as nearly as may be in accordance with Form B as set out in the Appendix to this Schedule.

(2) In an action of divorce or of separation the warrant of citation shall be framed as nearly as may be in accordance with Form B1 as set out in the Appendix to this Schedule.

(3) In a summary application, where citation is necessary, the warrant of citation shall be framed as nearly as may be, subject to paragraph (4), in accordance with Form B2 as set out in the Appendix to this Schedule.

(4) In a summary application in which a time to pay direction under the Debtors (Scotland) Act 1987 may be applied for by the defender, the warrant of citation shall be framed as nearly as may be in accordance with Form B3 as set out in the Appendix to this Schedule.

(5) In an ordinary cause in which a time to pay direction under the Debtors (Scotland) Act 1987 may be applied for by the defender, the warrant of citation shall be framed as nearly as may be in accordance with Form B4 as set out in the Appendix to this Schedule.

(6) In any cause in which warrant for citation in accordance with Forms B3 or B4, as the case may be, is appropriate, there shall be served on the defender (along with the initial writ and warrant) a notice in accordance with Form B5 (ordinary action) or B6 (summary application), as the case may be, as set out in the Appendix to this Schedule.

NOTE

[1] As amended by S.I. 1984 No. 255, 1986 No. 1230 and 1988 No. 1978.

Application for a warrant for arrestment to found jurisdiction

6.—(1) Application for a warrant for arrestment to found jurisdiction may be made in the crave of the initial writ.

(2) Averments to justify the granting of a warrant for arrestment to found jurisdiction shall be included in the condescendence.

Period of Notice

Period of notice after citation

[1] 7.—(1) Subject to Rule 11(2)(*a*) and to paragraph (2) of this rule causes shall proceed after the following periods of notice have been given to the defender—

(*a*) 21 days where the defender is resident or has a place of business within Europe;

(*b*) 42 days when the defender is resident or has a place of business outside Europe.

(2) The sheriff may, on cause shown, shorten or extend the period of notice on such conditions as to the form or manner of service as the sheriff may direct, but in any case where the period of notice is reduced at least two days notice shall be given.

(3) Where a period of notice expires on a Saturday, Sunday, public or court holiday the period of notice shall be deemed to expire on the first following day on which the sheriff clerk's office is open for civil court business.

NOTE

[1] As amended by S.I. 1988 No. 1978.

Citation and Service

Signature of warrants

8.—(1) Warrants for citation or for arrestment on the dependence may be signed by the sheriff or the sheriff clerk.

(2) Warrants containing an order shortening or extending the period of notice or any other order may only be signed by the sheriff.

(3) If for any reason the sheriff clerk refuses to sign a warrant, the writ may be presented to the sheriff for his consideration and signature if appropriate.

Form of citation and certificate

[1] 9.—(1) Subject to rule 11, citation in any ordinary cause other than an action of divorce or of separation or an action in which a time to pay direction under the Debtors (Scotland) Act 1987 may be applied for by the defender shall be given as nearly as may be in accordance with Form C as set out in the Appendix to this Schedule which shall be prefixed to a copy of the initial writ and warrant of citation.

(2) In an action of divorce or of separation citation shall be given as nearly as may be in accordance with Form C1 as set out in the Appendix to this Schedule which shall be prefixed to a copy of the initial writ and warrant of citation.

(2A) In any ordinary cause in which a time to pay direction under the Debtors (Scotland) Act 1987 may be applied for by the defender, citation shall be given as nearly as may be in accordance with Form C2 as set out in the Appendix to this Schedule which shall be prefixed to a copy of the initial writ and warrant of citation.

(2B) In a summary application in which a time to pay direction under the Debtors (Scotland) Act 1987 may be applied for by the respondent, citation shall be given as nearly as may be in accordance with Form C3 set out in the Appendix to this Schedule and in any other summary application shall be given as nearly as may be in accordance with Form C4 set out in the Appendix to this Schedule.

(3) The certificate of citation shall be as nearly as may be in accordance with Form D as set out in the Appendix to this Schedule which shall be annexed to the initial writ.

(4) When citation is by an officer of court, one witness shall be sufficient for the execution of citation.

(5) The certificate of citation shall be signed by the officer and the witness and shall specify whether the citation was personal, or, if otherwise, the mode of citation and the name of any person to whom the citation was delivered.

(6) When citation is effected in terms of paragraph (2) of Rule 10 the certificate shall also contain a statement of the mode of service previously attempted, the circumstances which prevented such service being effected and a statement that a copy was sent in accordance with the provisions of paragraph (3) of that rule.

NOTE

[1] As amended by S.I. 1984 No. 255, 1986 No. 1230, 1988 No. 1978 and 1992 No. 249 (effective 4th May 1992).

Service within Scotland by officer of court

10.—(1) Any initial writ, decree, charge, warrant or other order or writ following upon such initial writ or decree may be served by an officer of court on any person:—

(*a*) personally, or

(*b*) by being left in the hands of an inmate of or employee at the person's dwelling place or place of business.

(2) Where an officer of court has been unsuccessful in effecting service in accordance with either sub-paragraphs (*a*) or (*b*) of paragraph (1), he may, after making diligent inquiries, serve the document in question either—

(*a*) by depositing it in that person's dwelling place or place of business by means of a letterbox or by other lawful means, or

(*b*) by affixing it to the door of that person's dwelling place or place of business.

[1] (3) Except where rule 111 applies and has been complied with, if service is effected under paragraph (2) the officer shall as soon as possible after such service send by ordinary post to the address at which he thinks it most likely that the person may be found a letter containing a copy of the document.

NOTE

[1] As amended by S.I. 1992 No. 249 (effective 4th May 1992).

Citation of persons whose address is unknown

[1] 11.—(1) Without prejudice to the provisions of Rule 11A, where a defender's address is unknown to the pursuer, the sheriff shall grant warrant to cite the defender—

(*a*) by the publication in a newspaper circulating in the area of the defender's last known address of an advertisement as nearly as may be in accordance with Form E as set out in the Appendix to this Schedule: or

CITATION OF WARRANT – what do you send to D.?
R9 – must get a full copy of IW + warrant + a photocopy of warrant granted by Sh. Cl. + a citation. Form of citation – R9/O24
with time for payment – as well as C. must also send approp. form, usually B5 telling D. he has right to apply for time to pay + how to go about it. There is a form provided to be filled in + sent back to ct. with details with his income

[THE NEXT PAGE IS D 25]

RULE 11 – important that D. is told that proceedings are to be initiated. 2 ways of doing this – 11(1)(a) + (b)

(*b*) by displaying on the walls of court a copy of the instance and crave of the initial writ, warrant of citation and notice as nearly as may be in accordance with Form E1 as set out in the Appendix to this Schedule,

and the period of notice, which shall be fixed by the sheriff, shall run from the date of publication of the advertisement or display on the walls of court, as the case may be.

(2) Where citation requires to be effected under paragraph (1), the pursuer shall lodge a service copy of the initial writ and a copy of the warrant of citation with the sheriff clerk from whom they may be uplifted by the defender.

(3) If a defender has been cited in accordance with paragraph (1), and after the cause has commenced his address becomes known, the sheriff may allow the initial writ to be amended subject to such condition as to re-service, intimation, expenses, or transfer of the cause as seems just.

(4) Where advertisement in a newspaper is required for the purpose of citation under this rule, a copy of the newspaper containing said advertisement shall be lodged with the sheriff clerk.

(5) Where display on the walls of court is required under paragraph (1)(*b*), the pursuer shall supply to the sheriff clerk for that purpose a certified copy of the instance and crave of the initial writ and the warrant of citation.

NOTE

[1] As amended by S.I. 1986 No. 1230.

Intimation to persons in actions of divorce or of separation where defender is suffering from mental disorder or his whereabouts are unknown

[1] 11A.—(1) In an action of divorce or an action of separation, where the defender's address is unknown or the defender is a person suffering from a mental disorder within the meaning of the Mental Health (Scotland) Act 1984, warrant for citation shall, subject to paragraph (2), include an order for intimation of the initial writ to—

(*a*) every child of the marriage between the parties who has reached the age of 12 years in the case of a girl and 14 years in the case of a boy;

(*b*) one of the defender's next-of-kin who has reached the above age; and

(*c*) the curator *bonis* to the defender, if any.

(2) Intimation to a person mentioned in sub-paragraphs (*a*) to (*c*) of paragraph (1) shall not be required under that paragraph if—

(*a*) the address of that person is unknown to the pursuer; and

(*b*) there is an averment to that effect in the initial writ.

(3) Intimation to a person mentioned in sub-paragraphs (*a*) to (*c*) of paragraph (1) shall be as nearly as may be in accordance with Form V1 (where the defender is suffering from mental disorder) or Form V2 (where the defender's address is unknown) as set out in the Appendix to this Schedule.

(4) In any action to which this rule applies, where the defender suffers or appears to suffer from a mental disorder and is resident in a hospital or other similar institution, citation shall be executed by addressing the registered or recorded delivery letter to the medical officer in charge of that hospital or institution enclosing a certificate in accordance with Form V with a request set out in Form W that he either—

(*a*) deliver the copy of the initial writ with warrant thereon personally to the defender together with any notice sent therewith in accordance with the provisions of rule 131 and explain the contents to him: or

(*b*) certify that such delivery or explanation would be dangerous to the health or mental condition of the defender,

and complete the certificate accordingly and return it to the solicitor to the pursuer to be attached to the initial writ lodged for calling.

(5) Where the certificate returned under paragraph (4) bears that no delivery of the initial writ was made to the defender, it shall be competent for the sheriff at any stage in the proceedings before decree to order such further medical enquiry and such further service as he may think fit.

(6) A person receiving intimation under paragraph (1) may apply within the period of notice by minute craving to be sisted as a party and for leave to lodge defences or answers as the case may be.

NOTE

[1] Inserted by S.I. 1984 No. 255 as amended by S.I. 1986 No. 1230.

Citation of or service on persons outwith Scotland

[1] 12.—(1) Subject to the following provisions of this rule, an initial writ or decree, or any other writ or order following upon such initial writ or decree or any charge or warrant, may be served outwith Scotland on any person—

(*a*) at a known residence or place of business in England, Wales, Northern Ireland, the Isle of Man, the Channel Islands or any country with which the United Kingdom does not have a convention providing for service of writs in that country—

(i) in accordance with the rules for personal service under the domestic law of the place in which service is to be effected; or

(ii) by posting in Scotland a copy of the document in question in a registered or recorded delivery letter or the nearest equivalent which the available postal service permit addressed to the person at his residence or place of business;

(*b*) in a country which is a party to the Hague Convention on the Service Abroad of Judicial and Extra-Judicial Documents in Civil or Commercial Matters dated 15th November 1965 or the European Convention on Jurisdiction and the Enforcement of Judgments in Civil and Commercial Matters as set out in Schedule 1 to the Civil Jurisdiction and Judgments Act 1982—

(i) by a method prescribed by the internal law of the country where service is to be effected for the service of documents in domestic actions upon persons who are within its territory;

(ii) by or through a central authority in the country where service is to be effected at the request of the Foreign Office;

(iii) by or through a British Consular authority at the request of the Foreign Office;

(iv) where the law of the country in which the person resides permits, by posting in Scotland a copy of the document in a registered or recorded delivery letter or the nearest equivalent which the available postal services permit addressed to the person at his residence; or

(v) where the law of the country in which service is to be effected permits, service by an *huissier*, other judicial officer or competent official of the country where service is to be made;

(*c*) in a country with whom the United Kingdom has a convention on the service of writs in that country other than the conventions mentioned in sub-paragraph (*b*), by one of the methods approved in the relevant convention.

(2) Any document which requires to be posted in Scotland for the purposes of this rule shall be posted by a solicitor or an officer of court, and the forms for citation and certificate of citation in Rule 9 shall apply to a postal citation under this rule as they apply to a citation under that rule.

(3) On the face of the envelope used for postal service under this rule, there shall be written or printed a notice in the same or similar terms as that required in the case of ordinary service under Rule 15(3).

(4) Where service is effected by a method specified in paragraph (1)(*b*)(ii) or (iii), the pursuer shall—

(*a*) send a copy of the writ and warrant for service with citation attached, or other document, with a request for service to be effected by the method indicated in the request to the Secretary of State for Foreign and Commonwealth Affairs; and

(*b*) lodge in process a certificate of execution of service signed by the authority which has effected service.

(5) Where service is effected by the method specified in paragraph (1)(*b*)(v) the pursuer, his solicitor or the officer of court, shall—

(*a*) send to the official in the country in which service is to be effected a copy of the writ and warrant for service with citation attached, or other document, with a request for service to be affected by delivery to the defender or his residence; and

(*b*) the pursuer shall lodge in process a certificate of execution of service by the official who has effected service.

(6) Where service is effected in accordance with paragraph (1)(*a*)(i) or (1)(*b*)(i), the pursuer shall lodge a certificate by a person who is conversant with the law of the country concerned and who practices or has practised as an advocate or solicitor in that country or is a duly accredited representative of the Government of that country, stating that the form of service employed is in accordance with the law of the place where the service was effected. It of shall not be necessary to lodge a certificate where service has taken place in another part of the United Kingdom, the Channel Isles or the Isle of Man.

(7) Every writ or document and every citation and notice on the face of the envelope referred to in paragraph (3) shall be accompanied by a translation in an official language of the country in which service is to be executed unless English is an official language of that country.

(8) A translation referred to in paragraph (7) shall be certified as a correct translation by the person making it and the certificate shall contain the full name, address and qualifications of the translator and be lodged along with the execution of citation or certificate of execution.

NOTE

[1] Substituted by S.I. 1986 No. 1946.

Days of charge

[1] 13.—(1) The period for payment specified in any charge following on a decree for payment granted in an ordinary cause shall be 14 days if the person on whom it is served is within the United Kingdom and 28 days if he is outside the United Kingdom or his whereabouts are unknown.

(2) The period in respect of any other form of charge in respect of an ordinary cause decree shall be 14 days.

NOTE

[1] Substituted by S.I. 1988 No. 1978.

Service of charge where defender's address is unknown

[1] 13A.—(1) Where a defender's address is unknown to the pursuer, a charge shall be deemed to have been served on the defender if it is served on the sheriff clerk of the sheriff court district where the defender's last known address is located and is displayed by the sheriff clerk on the walls of that court for the period of the charge.

(2) On receipt of such a charge the sheriff clerk shall display it on the walls of court.

(3) The period specified in the charge shall run from the first date on which it was displayed on the walls of court and it shall remain displayed for the period of charge.

(4) On the expiry of the period of charge the sheriff clerk shall endorse a certificate on the charge certifying that it has been displayed in accordance with this rule and shall thereafter return it to the officer of court by whom service was effected.

NOTE

[1] Added by S.I. 1990 No. 661.

Persons carrying on business under a trading or descriptive name

14.—(1) Any person or persons carrying on a business under a trading or descriptive name, may sue or be sued in such trading or descriptive name alone, and any extract of a decree pronounced in the sheriff court, or of a decree proceeding upon any deed, decree arbitral bond, protest of a bill, promissory note or banker's note, or upon any other obligation or document on which execution may competently proceed, recorded in the sheriff court books against such person or persons, under such trading or descriptive name, shall be a valid warrant for diligence against such person or persons.

(2) Any initial writ or decree, or any other writ or order following upon such initial writ or decree or any charge or warrant issued in any cause to which this rule applies may be served at any place of business or office at which such business is carried on within the sheriffdom of the sheriff court in which the cause is brought or, in the event of there being no place of business within that sheriffdom, service may be effected at any place where such business is carried on (including the place of business or office of the clerk or secretary of any company, corporation or association or firm).

[THE NEXT PAGE IS D 27]

METHOD OF CITATION – 1) BY POST 2) BY SHERIFF OFFICER

Postal citation can be done by a sol. or sh. officer. R.16 – any I.W or subsequent writ may be served anywhere in Scotland without having to be endorsed by Sh. Cl. Postal citation most frequently used as 1st attempt to serve I.W.

R15 – has to be recorded delivery 1st class service. Always approp. unless sheriff requires personal service in interim interdict actions

R.15(2) – period of notice shall start to run on day after posting

If postal citation used, R15(3) gives provisions for what has to go onto the envelope – PO must know that ct. document is in envelope. Wording states envelope contains a ct. citation + if delivery is ineffective must be returned to approp. sh. ct. – a returned C. Normally returned with note saying why delivery ineffective

CERT. OF C. – signed by sol. who has effected service certifying he has done so. Statutory form – R9(3) – Form D.
Cert. of C. must be signed by same sol. who signed C.

2) If postal citation unsuccessful must resort under R.10 to citation by officer of ct. These methods cannot be used by a sol. only by sh. officer. S.O. needs principal IW – ask him to serve it on D. + give a reason why postal service was ineffective. S.O. + 1 witness must take the documents to D's house. Method of service depends on what he finds

(i) Personal service – 10(1)(a) – if gets an answer may hand it to him
If D. refuses to accept documents ct. will still see this as citation. S.O. reports to ct. exactly what happened

(ii) Where person answering door is not D, S.O. can serve documents on person who happens to be there – C. can be served in hands of employee at persons place of business (not place of employment) or inmate at dwelling place

(iii) if gets no answer keyhole citation may be available – R. 10(2)
– diligent enquiries – must satisfy himself that D. actually resides/have place of business there. Make enquiries with neighbours etc.

If used 'keyhole' method follow 10(3) – his diligent enquiries may have thrown up new info. on likely address. Must then prepare a cert. of C.

Under 9(4) 1 witness sufficient for execution of C.

9(5) – cert. must be signed by both S.O. + witness – should specify mode of citation + name of any person on whom it was delivered

9(6) – where keyhole method used cert. shall state mode of service previously attempted + that copy of documents have been sent in accordance with

Postal citation

15.—(1) In any case in which it is competent to serve or intimate any document or to cite any person by recorded delivery, such service, intimation or citation, when made by recorded delivery, shall only be competent if it is made by recorded delivery first class service.

[1] (2) Notwithstanding the terms of section 4(2) of the Citation Amendment (Scotland) Act 1882, where service is by post the period of notice shall run from the beginning of the day next following the date of posting.

(3) On the face of the envelope used for postal service under this rule there shall be written or printed the following notice or a notice to the like effect—

> "This letter contains a citation to or intimation from [*specify the Court*]. If delivery of the letter cannot be made at the address shown it is to be returned immediately to [*give the official name and office or place of business of the Clerk of Court*]".

(4) The certificate of citation in the case of postal service shall have annexed to it any relevant postal receipts.

NOTE

[1] As amended by S.I. 1992 No. 249 (effective 4th May 1992).

Endorsation unnecessary

16. Any initial writ or decree, or any other writ or order following upon such initial writ or decree or any charge or warrant may be served, enforced or otherwise lawfully executed anywhere in Scotland without endorsation by a sheriff clerk and, if executed by an officer, may be so executed by an officer of the court which granted it or by an officer of the sheriff court district within which it is to be executed.

Re-service

17. If it appears to the sheriff that there has been any failure or irregularity in service upon a defender, the sheriff may authorise the pursuer to re-serve the initial writ upon such conditions as seem just.

Personal bar

18.—(1) A party who appears may not state any objection to the regularity of the service upon himself, and his appearance shall remedy any defect in the service.

(2) Nothing in this rule shall preclude a party from pleading that the court has no jurisdiction.

Transfer of Causes

Transfer to another sheriff court

19.—(1)(*a*) Subject to paragraph (*c*), where a cause in which there are two or more defenders has been brought in the sheriff court of the residence or place of business of one of them, the sheriff may transfer the cause to any other sheriff court which has jurisdiction over any of the defenders.

(*b*) Subject to paragraph (*c*), where a plea of no jurisdiction is sustained the sheriff may transfer the cause to the sheriff court before which it appears to him it ought to have been brought.

(*c*) The sheriff shall not transfer a cause to another sheriff court under paragraphs (*a*) and (*b*) above except on the motion of one or more of the parties and unless he considers it expedient to do so having regard to the convenience of the parties and their witnesses;

(*d*) The sheriff may upon sufficient cause remit any cause to another sheriff court.

(2) On making an order under paragraph (1) transferring a cause to another sheriff court the sheriff—

(*a*) shall state his reasons for doing so in the interlocutor;

(*b*) may make the order subject to such conditions as to expenses or otherwise as he thinks fit.

(3) The sheriff court to which a cause is transferred under paragraph (1) shall accept the cause.

(4) A transferred cause shall proceed in all respects as if it had been originally brought in the court to which it is transferred.

(5) An interlocutor transferring a cause shall, with leave of the sheriff, be subject to review by the sheriff principal but shall not be further subject to review.

Remit of cause to the Court of Session

20.—(1) The sheriff clerk shall, within the period of four days after the sheriff has pronounced an interlocutor remitting a cause to the Court of Session, transmit the process to the deputy principal clerk of session.

(2) The sheriff clerk shall within that period send written notice of the remit to the party or parties and certify on the interlocutor sheet that he has done so, but failure to do so shall not affect the validity of the remit.

Remit of cause from the Court of Session

[1] 20A.—(1) On receipt of the process in an action which has been remitted from the Court of Session, the sheriff clerk shall—

(*a*) record the date of such receipt on the interlocutor sheet;

(*b*) enrol the cause for further procedure on the first court day occurring not earlier than 14 days after the date of receipt of the process; and

(*c*) forthwith send written notice of the date of calling of the action to the parties.

(2) The action shall thereafter proceed on the existing process unless the sheriff otherwise directs.

NOTE

[1] Inserted by S.I. 1986 No. 1966.

UNDEFENDED CAUSES

Minute for granting of decree without attendance

[1] 21.—(1)(*a*) Subject to paragraph (2) of this rule and Rule 21A, if the defender does not lodge a notice of intention to defend or a minute under Rule 34 or an application for a time to pay direction under the Debtors (Scotland) Act 1987 or if the defender has lodged such application and the pursuer does not object thereto or to any recall or restriction of an arrestment sought therein, the sheriff may on the pursuer endorsing a minute in that behalf on the initial writ at any time after the expiry of the period for lodging that notice or minute grant decree or other order in terms of the minute so endorsed without requiring the attendance of the pursuer in court: provided that the sheriff shall not grant decree in the cause unless it appears *ex facie* of the initial writ that a ground of jurisdiction exists under the Civil Jurisdiction and Judgments Act 1982.

(*b*) In the case of a defender domiciled in another part of the United Kingdom or in another Contracting State, the sheriff shall not grant decree in absence until it has been shown that the defender has been able to receive the initial writ in sufficient time to arrange for his defence or that all necessary steps have been taken to that end; and for the purposes of this sub-paragraph—

(i) the question as to whether a person is domiciled in another part of the United Kingdom shall be determined in accordance with sections 41 and 42 of the Civil Jurisdiction and Judgments Act 1982;

(ii) the question as to whether a person is domiciled in another Contracting State shall be determined in accordance with Article 52 of Schedule 1 to that Act; and

(iii) the term "Contracting State" has the meaning assigned to it by section 1 of that Act.

(2) Paragraph (1) does not apply to actions—

(*a*) of divorce or of separation;

(*b*) relating to tutory, curatory, custody or access or any right or authority relating to the welfare or upbringing of a child conferred on a parent by any rule of law;

(*c*) for declarator of parentage, non-parentage, legitimacy, legitimation or illegitimacy.

NOTE

[1] As amended by S.I. 1984 No. 255, 1986 Nos. 1230, 1946 and 1966 and 1988 No. 1978.

Decree in causes to which the Hague Convention applies

21A. Where in any civil proceedings (including proceedings for divorce, separation and aliment and actions for custody of children), the initial writ has been served in a country to which the Hague Convention on the Service Abroad of Judicial and Extra-Judicial Documents in Civil or Commercial Matters dated 15th November 1965 applies, decree shall not be granted until it is established to the satisfaction of the sheriff that the requirements of Article 15 of that Convention have been complied with.

Applications for time to pay directions in undefended causes

[1] 21B.—(1) This rule applies to ordinary causes in which a time to pay direction may be applied for under the Debtors (Scotland) Act 1987.

(2) A defender in a cause which is otherwise undefended, who wishes to apply for a time to pay direction, and where appropriate, to have an arrestment recalled or restricted, may complete and lodge with the sheriff clerk the relevant part of form B5 before the expiry of the period of notice.

(3) Where the pursuer does not object to the defender's application, he shall minute accordingly and for decree in accordance with Rule 21; and the sheriff may grant decree or other order in terms of the application and minute.

(4) Where the pursuer objects to the defender's application he shall minute accordingly and for decree in terms of Rule 21; and the sheriff clerk shall thereafter enrol the cause for hearing of the defender's application and intimate the hearing to the defender and pursuer.

(5) The sheriff shall consider the application on the date fixed for hearing or at any continuation thereof and may then or after further consideration grant or refuse it as may seem to him appropriate whether or not any of the parties appear and grant decree accordingly.

NOTE

[1] Inserted by S.I. 1988 No. 1978.

Applications for time to pay directions in summary applications

[1] 21C.—(1) This rule applies in summary applications in which a time to pay direction may be applied for under the Debtors (Scotland) Act 1987.

(2) A defender may apply for a time to pay direction and, where appropriate, for recall or restriction of an arrestment—

(*a*) by appearing and making the appropriate motion at the diet fixed;

(*b*) except where the period of notice has been shortened in accordance with Rule 7(2), by completing and returning to the sheriff clerk at least seven days before the diet fixed for hearing the appropriate portion of Form B6; or

(*c*) by application to the court at any stage in the proceedings prior to final decree being granted.

NOTE

[1] Inserted by S.I. 1988 No. 1978.

Procedure in undefended actions relating to parental rights

[1] 22.—(1) If no notice of intention to defend has been lodged in an action relating to tutory, curatory, custody or access or any right or authority relating to the welfare or upbringing of a child conferred on a parent by any rule of law and the pursuer has returned the initial writ to the sheriff clerk the action shall be called in court.

(2) In any such action decree may be granted after such inquiry as the sheriff thinks necessary.

NOTE

[1] As amended by S.I. 1986 Nos. 1230 and 1966.

Procedure where actions of divorce or separation or actions affecting parentage are undefended

[1] 23.—(1) This rule—

(*a*) applies to all actions of divorce, actions of separation and actions for declarator of parentage, non-parentage, legitimacy, legitimation or illegitimacy in which no notice of intention to defend has been lodged;

(*b*) may apply to any such action which proceeds at any stage as undefended if the court so directs;

(*c*) may apply to the merits of any such action as is mentioned in sub-paragraph (*b*) if the court so directs, notwithstanding that the action is defended on an ancillary matter.

(2) Proof in all such actions, unless in any particular action the sheriff otherwise directs, shall be by way of evidence submitted in the form of affidavits and such evidence shall not be treated as being insufficient for the purposes of proof by reason only that it is not supported by parole evidence.

(3) The sheriff may, at any time after the endorsation of the minute referred to in Rule 72(5), without requiring the appearance of parties before him—

(*a*) grant decree in terms of the motion for decree; or

(*b*) remit the cause of such other procedure, including proof by parole evidence, as the sheriff may deem appropriate.

(4) The sheriff clerk shall, on the expiry of 14 days after the granting of decree in terms of paragraph (3), issue to each party to the action an extract of the decree of divorce.

NOTE

[1] Substituted by S.I. 1984 No. 255 and as amended by S.I. 1986 Nos. 1230 and 1966.

Decree for expenses

24. At the same time as granting a decree in absence or thereafter the sheriff may grant a decree for expenses.

Granting of decree is normally administrative.

Issue of extract decree Extract will be given to P's sol.

25.—(1) On the expiry of 14 days following the granting of a decree in absence the sheriff clerk may issue an extract of the decree.

(2) The sheriff may on cause shown order the extract to be issued at an earlier date.

Extract decree will set out details of ct, parties, date of decree, form of decree + w of Ct. for approp. diligence/enforcement.

May be approp. to amend I/W before extract eg may be error in name/address of party. Procedure for amendment in R.27

[THE NEXT PAGE IS D 29]

Finality of decree in absence

26. Subject to section 9(7) of the Land Tenure Reform (Scotland) Act 1974, a decree in absence which has not been recalled or brought under review by suspension or by reduction shall become final, and be entitled to all the privileges of a decree *in foro*—

(*a*) on the expiry of six months from its date or from the date of the charge under it, where the service of the initial writ or of the charge has been personal;

(*b*) in any event, on the expiry of 20 years from its date.

Amendment of initial writ

27.—(1) In an undefended action the sheriff may—

(*a*) allow the pursuer to amend the initial writ in any way permitted by Rule 64;

(*b*) order the amended initial writ to be re-served on the defender on such a period of notice as he thinks fit.

(2) The defender shall not be liable for the expense occasioned by any such amendment unless the sheriff otherwise directs.

(3) No such amendment shall have the effect of validating diligence used on the dependence of the action so as to prejudice creditors of the defender, but it shall have the effect of obviating objections to such diligence when stated by the defender himself or by any person representing him by a title, or in right of a debt contracted by him subsequent to the using of such diligence; and any diligence which was competent on the original initial writ shall be competent on the amended initial writ.

Reponing

Reponing

[1] 28.—(1) In any action (other than an action of divorce or of separation), the defender may apply to be reponed by lodging with the sheriff clerk, before implement in full of a decree in absence, a note setting forth his proposed defence and explaining his failure to appear.

(2) A copy of the note lodged under paragraph (1) shall be served on the pursuer.

(3) The sheriff may, following consideration of the note, recall the decree so far as not implemented subject to such order as to expenses as seems to him just; and the cause shall thereafter proceed in all respects as if the defender had appeared.

(4) A reponing note, when duly lodged and served upon the pursuer, shall have effect to sist diligence.

(5) Any interlocutor or order recalling, or incidental to the recall of, a decree in absence shall be final and not subject to review.

NOTE

[1] As substituted by S.I. 1990 No. 2105.

29–32. [Revoked by S.I. 1990 No. 2105.]

Defended Causes to Proof

Intention to Defend

Notice of intention to defend

[1] 33. If a defender intends to challenge the jurisdiction of the court or to state a defence he shall before the expiry of the appropriate period of notice exhibit to the sheriff clerk the service copy of the initial writ and lodge with him a notice of intention to defend as nearly as may be in terms of Form F as set out in the Appendix to this Schedule and shall at the same time intimate the lodging of that notice to the pursuer. The lodging of such notice of intention to defend shall not imply acceptance of the jurisdiction of the court.

NOTE

[1] As amended by S.I. 1986 No. 1946 and 1992 No. 249 (effective 4th May 1992).

Minute relating to aliment, periodical allowance, capital payment or transfer of property

[1] 34.—(1) In an action of separation, affiliation and aliment or for custody of a child, a defender who intends only to dispute the amount of aliment may, in place of lodging a notice of intention to defend, lodge a minute to that effect condescending on the relevant facts.

(2) In an action of divorce, a defender who intends only to dispute liability for, or the amount of, or raise other matters relating to, aliment, periodical allowance, capital payment or transfer of property may, in place of lodging a notice of intention to defend, lodge a minute condescending on the relevant facts.

(3) In an action of divorce or of separation, a defender may, without lodging a notice of intention to defend, apply to the court by minute craving an order for aliment, periodical allowance, capital payment or transfer of property and such minute shall crave the order which he claims the sheriff should make, and condescend on the relevant facts.

(4) On the lodging of a minute under paragraph (1), (2) or (3)—

(*a*) the sheriff clerk shall enrol the cause for a hearing, and the defender shall send a copy of the minute and intimate the date of the hearing to the pursuer; and

(*b*) the pursuer shall return the initial writ to the sheriff clerk at or before the hearing, but shall not, unless the sheriff otherwise directs, require to lodge a process.

(5) At the hearing, the sheriff may resolve the matter or continue the cause for such further procedure as he considers appropriate.

(6) In an action referred to in this rule, the sheriff may grant decree in terms of a joint minute dealing with aliment, periodical allowance, capital payment or transfer of property whether or not these have been craved in the initial writ or minute.

NOTE

[1] Substituted by S.I. 1986 No. 1230.

Tabling

35.—(1) Where a notice of intention to defend has been lodged, the sheriff clerk shall enrol the cause for tabling on the first court day occurring after the expiry of the appropriate period of notice.

(2) A cause which has not been tabled, and in which protestation has not been craved, shall drop from the roll, but within three months the sheriff may direct it to be again enrolled for tabling under such conditions as to notice, or reservice, or expenses, or otherwise as seem just.

(3) At tabling, the sheriff may, on the motion of either party, continue the cause without ordering defences to be lodged.

Protestation

36.—(1) On any occasion on which the cause is enrolled for tabling and not tabled, the defender or his agent, upon producing the service copy of the writ, may crave protestation for not insisting, which the sheriff may grant, and shall fix the amount of protestation money payable to the defender.

(2) Protestation shall not be extracted before the expiry of seven clear days from the date of its granting, except where arrestments have been used, in which case it may be extracted after the expiry of 48 hours from that date.

(3) Upon protestation being extracted, the instance shall fall.

(4) Before extract, protestation may be recalled, and the sheriff may allow the pursuer to proceed with the cause upon making payment to the defender of the amount of protestation money, and upon such other conditions as the sheriff thinks fit.

The Process

Lodging of process by pursuer

37. In a cause in which a notice of intention to defend has been lodged, the pursuer shall at or before tabling lodge with the sheriff clerk the principal initial writ and a copy initial writ with warrant thereon certified by the pursuer, principal and duplicate interlocutor sheets, and principal and borrowing inventory of process, and the sheriff clerk shall endorse on all documents lodged in process the date of lodging.

Custody of process

38.—(1) The principal initial writ, the principal interlocutor sheets and borrowing inventory of process shall remain in the custody of the sheriff clerk.

(2) The sheriff may make a special order to the contrary in respect of the principal initial writ.

Borrowing of process

39.—(1) A process may be borrowed only by a solicitor or by his authorised clerk for whom he shall be responsible.

(2) All remedies competent to enforce the return of a borrowed process may proceed on the warrant of the court from whose custody the process was obtained, whether the borrower is or is not within its jurisdiction.

(3) A party litigant shall not borrow a process except by leave of the sheriff and subject to such conditions as the sheriff may impose but may inspect a process and obtain copies, where practicable, from the sheriff clerk.

(4) All numbers of process borrowed shall be returned to the sheriff clerk not later than two days before the date of the proof.

Failure to return process

40.—(1) When a solicitor or party litigant has borrowed a process, or any part of a process, and fails to return it for any diet at which it is required, the sheriff may impose upon such solicitor or party litigant a fine not exceeding £50, which shall be payable to the sheriff clerk; but an order imposing a fine may, on cause shown, be recalled by the sheriff who granted it.

(2) Orders made under this rule shall not be subject to appeal.

Replacement of lost documents

41. When any part of process is lost or destroyed, a copy thereof, authenticated in such manner as the sheriff may require, may be substituted and shall, for the purposes of the action to which the process relates, be treated as having the same force and effect as the original.

Borrowing of certified copy initial writ for purposes of arrestment and issue of precepts of arrestment

42.—(1) The Certified copy initial writ with warrant thereon may be borrowed by any party to the action and shall be sufficient warrant to arrest on the dependence if it is otherwise competent to do so.

(2) Separate precepts of arrestment may be issues by the sheriff clerk on production to him of an initial writ, containing claims for payment of money, on which a warrant of citation has been granted, or of a liquid document of debt.

Defences and Adjustment

Defences

43.—(1) Where defences have not been lodged at tabling, the sheriff, in the interlocutor pronounced at tabling or otherwise, shall appoint a period within which defences shall be lodged.

(2) On lodging defences the defender shall send a copy to the pursuer.

Form of defences

44. Defences shall be in the form of answers in paragraphs corresponding to the paragraphs of the condescendence, and shall have appended a note of the defender's pleas-in-law.

Implied admissions

45. Every statement of fact made by one party shall be answered by the other party, and if a statement made by one party of a fact within the knowledge of the other party is not denied by that other party, the latter shall be held as admitting the fact so stated.

Adjustment of pleadings

46. Subject to the provisions of Rules 47 and 48 all adjustments of the pleadings shall be made by parties only on the certified copy of the initial writ, the defences or answers, as the case may be, and shall be immediately intimated in writing to all other parties.

Open record

47.—(1) The sheriff may at any time before the closing of the record, on the application of a party to the action or *ex proprio motu*, order the pursuer to lodge in process a record of the pleadings as adjusted to the date of the order and to intimate a copy of all other parties.

(2) Any adjustments made after that date shall be made on that record and intimated to all other parties.

Alteration of sum sued for

48.—(1) In a cause in which all other parties have lodged defences or answers the pursuer may, prior to the closing of the record and without leave of the sheriff, alter any sum sued for by amending the crave of the initial writ, the certified copy of the initial writ and any record.

(2) The pursuer shall immediately intimate any such amendment in writing to all other parties.

Adjustment period

49.—(1) In the interlocutor pronounced at tabling or otherwise the sheriff shall appoint the date on which the cause shall appear on the adjustment roll.

(2) No continuation of the adjustment after the first shall be allowed except on cause shown.

(3) Cause shall not be shown under paragraph (2) by reason only that parties agrees to a continuation.

(4) In considering whether cause has been shown under paragraph (2) the sheriff shall take into account any additional time which may have been available for adjustment owing to a court vacation occurring (in whole or in part) after the lodging of defences.

Third Party Procedure

Third party notice

50.—(1) Where in any cause, a defender claims that he has any right of contribution, relief, or indemnity against any person who is not already a party to the cause, or that a person whom the pursuer is not bound to call as a defender should be made a party to the cause along with the defender in respect that such person is either solely liable or jointly and severally liable with the defender to the pursuer in respect of the subject matter of the cause, the defender may set forth in his defences or in a separate statement of facts the grounds upon which he maintains that any such person (hereinafter called a third party) is liable to him by way of contribution, relief, or indemnity, or should be made a party to the cause and the defences or statement of facts shall also contain appropriate pleas-in-law directed against such third party.

(2) Thereafter the defender may lodge a motion for the purpose of obtaining an order for the service of a third party notice upon such third party upon such period of notice as is referred to in Rule 7, and if the motion is granted, the third party shall be a party to the cause and may lodge answers on or before a date appointed by the sheriff for the regulation of further procedure.

(3) Averments directed against a third party shall be made prior to the closing of the record, or, at the discretion of the sheriff and subject to such conditions as to the sheriff seem just, at a later stage, but in no event later than the commencement of the hearing of the cause on its merits.

(4) A third party notice shall be as nearly as may be in terms of Form G as set out in the Appendix to this Schedule and the answers by a third party shall be headed "Answers for E.F. Third Party in the action at the instance of A.B. Pursuer against C.D. Defender": and the following provisions of this rule shall apply to the procedure under the notice.

(5) A third party notice shall be served on the third party in any manner and on such period of notice in which an initial writ may competently be served on a defender and shall be accompanied by a copy of the initial writ and defences, or the record, if any.

(6) A copy of the third party notice with a certificate of execution thereon shall be lodged in process.

(7) The order granting leave to serve a third party notice may contain a warrant for arrestment to found jurisdiction, or for arrestment on the dependence.

(8) Averments to justify the granting of a warrant for arrestment to found jurisdiction shall be included in the defences or the separate statement of facts referred to in paragraph (1) of this rule.

(9) On the date appointed by the sheriff for the regulation of further procedure or at any time thereafter the sheriff may grant such decree, interlocutor or order as seems just.

(10) Any decree, interlocutor, or order against the third party shall take effect and be extractable in the same way as a decree, interlocutor or order against the defender.

(11) This rule also applies to a claim—

(*a*) by a third party; or

(*b*) by a pursuer in respect of a counter-claim by a defender, as it applies to a claim by a defender.

[1] PARTY MINUTER PROCEDURE

NOTE

[1] Inserted by S.I. 1992 No. 249 (effective 4th May 1992).

Party minuter

50A.—(1) Any person who has not been called as a defender or third party may apply by minute to the sheriff for leave to enter a process as a party minuter and to lodge defences.

(2) An application under this rule shall specify—

(*a*) the applicant's title and interest to enter the process; and

(*b*) the grounds of the defence which he proposes to state.

(3) On the lodging of a minute under this rule, the sheriff shall appoint a date for hearing the minute; and the applicant shall forthwith serve a copy of the minute and of the order for a hearing on the parties to the cause.

(4) After hearing the applicant and any party to the cause, the sheriff may, if he is satisfied that the applicant has shown title and interest to enter the process, grant the applicant leave to enter the process as a party minuter and to lodge defences and may make such order as to expenses or otherwise as he considers appropriate.

(5) Where an application under this rule is made after the closing of the record, the sheriff—

(*a*) shall only grant leave under paragraph (4) if he is satisfied as to the reason why earlier application was not made; and

(*b*) may make such further order as to expenses or otherwise as he considers appropriate.

COUNTER-CLAIM PROCEDURE

Counter-claim

51. The defender may make a counter-claim against the pursuer by lodging in process a separate document headed "Counter-claim for the Defender" a copy of which shall be sent to the pursuer.

Form of counter-claim

52. The counter-claim shall contain a crave or craves in a form which if the counter-claim had been enforced by way of a separate cause would have been appropriate in that cause; it shall also contain a statement of facts setting out in numbered paragraphs the facts on which the counter-claim is founded and shall have appended a note of the pleas-in-law which are necessary to support the counter-claim.

Warrants of counter-claim

53.—(1) The defender may apply for warrant to use any form of diligence by way of arrestment which could be used on the dependence of a separate cause brought to enforce the matter of the counter-claim.

(2) Such application shall be made by appending to the crave of the counter-claim the words "warrant for arrestment on the dependence applied for", and shall be granted by the sheriff clerk who receives the counter-claim adding the words "Grants warrant as craved", and adhibiting his signature together with the date below those words.

(3) Any such warrant shall have the like effect as it would have in an initial writ.

Disposal of counter-claim

54. The sheriff may—

(*a*) deal with the counter-claim as if it had been stated in a substantive cause;

(*b*) regulate procedure as he thinks fit; and

(*c*) grant decree for the counter-claim in whole or in part, or for the difference between it and the sum claimed.

Abandonment where counter-claim

55.—(1) A pursuer shall not be prevented from abandoning a cause by reason only of a counter-claim by the defender.

(2) The abandoning of any cause by the pursuer shall not affect a counter-claim made in respect of that cause; and the counter-claim shall continue as a separate cause.

(3) Any expenses payable by the pursuer as a condition of, or in consequence of abandoning the cause shall not include the expenses of the counter-claim.

(4) A defender who has counter-claimed may abandon his counter-claim by lodging in process a minute to that effect, and thereafter the sheriff may, on payment by the defender of the expenses incurred by the pursuer in connection with the counter-claim, dismiss the counter-claim.

(5) If the defender fails, within 14 days of the date of taxation, to pay those expenses, the pursuer shall be entitled to decree of absolvitor with expenses in the counter-claim.

Counter-claim for custody, access or maintenance

56.—[1] (1) In any cause in which custody of, access to, or maintenance for, a child is sought or could competently be sought the defender may make any claim relating to such matters of a kind which a pursuer may make in such a cause; and Rules 51 to 55 shall apply to any such claim as they apply to a counter-claim.

[2] (2) Where a defender makes a counter-claim under paragraph (1), he may, where it would otherwise be competent, incorporate a crave for an order for aliment, periodical allowance, capital payment or transfer of property rather than proceed by way of separate minute under rule 34.

[2] (3) In a cause referred to in this rule, the sheriff may grant decree in terms of a joint minute dealing with custody of, access to, or maintenance for, a child, aliment, periodical allowance, capital payment or transfer of property whether or not those have been craved in the initial writ or counter-claim.

NOTES

[1] As amended by S.I. 1984 No. 255 and 1986 No. 1230.

[2] Added by S.I. 1986 No. 1230.

INCIDENTAL PROCEDURE

Motions

57. Any motion endorsed as unopposed may be granted by the sheriff in chambers without hearing the parties.

Applications for time to pay directions and for recall or restriction of arrestments in defended causes

[1] 57A. In any defended cause in which it is competent to do so, the sheriff may, on a motion by the defender at any time before decree is granted, grant a time to pay direction and, where appropriate, an order recalling or restricting an arrestment.

NOTE

[1] Inserted by S.I. 1988 No. 1978.

Abandonment of cause

58.—(1) A pursuer may at any stage of a cause before an interlocutor granting absolvitor or dismissing the cause has been pronounced offer to abandon the cause by lodging in

[THE NEXT PAGE IS D 31]

process a minute to that effect and thereafter the sheriff may, on payment to the defender of his expenses, dismiss the cause.

(2) If the pursuer fails, within 14 days of the date of taxation, to pay the defender's expenses, the defender shall be entitled to decree of absolvitor, with expenses.

Decree by default

[1] 59.—(1) In a defended cause other than an action of divorce or of separation, if any production or step of process has not been lodged or an order has not been implemented within the time required by any enactment or order of the sheriff, or if one party fails to appear or be represented at a diet, the sheriff may grant decree as craved or decree of absolvitor, or may dismiss the cause, with expenses.

(2) If none of the parties appears the sheriff may dismiss the cause.

(3) In any action the sheriff may, on cause shown, prorogate the time for lodging any production or step of process or for implementing any order.

NOTE

[1] As amended by S.I. 1984 No. 255 and 1986 No. 1230.

Summary decree

[1] 59A.—(1) This rule applies to any cause other than—

(*a*) a consistorial action;

(*b*) an action of multiplepoinding; or

(*c*) an action under the Presumption of Death (Scotland) Act 1977.

(2) A pursuer may, at any time after the defender has lodged defences, apply by written motion to the court—

(*a*) to grant decree in terms of all or any of the craves of the initial writ;

(*b*) to pronounce an interlocutor sustaining or repelling a plea-in-law; or

(*c*) to dispose of the whole or part of the subject matter of the action,

on the ground that there is no defence to the action or a part of it disclosed in the defences.

(3) A motion under this rule shall be intimated to all other parties to the cause on a period of notice of 14 days.

(4) After hearing a motion under this rule, the sheriff may, if he is satisfied that there is no defence to the action or to any part of it to which the motion relates—

(*a*) grant summary decree against the defender in terms of the motion in whole or in part; or

(*b*) order any party or a partner, director, officer or office bearer of any party—

(i) to produce any document or article; or

(ii) to lodge an affidavit or affidavits in support of any averment of fact made in the pleadings or at the hearing of the motion.

(5) Notwithstanding the grant or refusal of a motion under this rule a further motion under this rule may be made by the pursuer on cause shown by reason of a change of circumstances.

(6) Where—

(*a*) a defender has lodged a counterclaim; or

(*b*) a defender or third party has made a claim against another defender or against a third party, who has lodged defences or answers,

he may apply by motion in accordance with this rule for summary decree on that counterclaim or claim or part of it, on the ground that the other party has no defence to it; and the terms of paragraphs (1) to (5) of this rule shall apply to a motion by a defender or third party as they apply to a motion by a pursuer.

NOTE

[1] Inserted by S.I. 1992 No. 249 (effective 4th May 1992).

Late appearance by defender in actions of divorce and of separation

[1] 59B.—(1) The sheriff may make an order, with or without conditions, allowing a defender in an action of divorce or of separation who has not lodged a notice of intention to defend or defences—

(*a*) to appear and be heard at a diet of proof;

(*b*) to lodge defences and to lead evidence at any time before decree of divorce or of separation has been pronounced; or

(*c*) to appeal within 14 days of the decree of divorce or of separation.

(2) Where an order is made under paragraph (1)(*a*), a defender may not lead evidence without the consent of the pursuer.

(3) Where an order is made under paragraph (1)(*b*), the pursuer may lead further evidence, by recalling witnesses already examined or otherwise, whether or not he closed his proof before the order was made.

NOTE

[1] Substituted by S.I. 1986 No. 1230. Renumbered by S.I. 1992 No. 249 (effective 4th May 1992).

Transfer of cause on death of party

60.—(1) Where any depending case cannot proceed owing to the death of any party and that party's representatives do not sist themselves in his place, any other party may lodge a minute craving transfer of the cause against those representatives.

(2) The sheriff may on the lodging of any such minute, grant warrant for serving a copy of the initial writ upon those representatives, and if he does so, shall at the same time allow them to lodge a minute of objections to such transference within such time as may be specified in the interlocutor, and shall order intimation of his interlocutor to be made to any other parties to the cause.

(3) The sheriff may, after considering any objections to the minute, pronounce an interlocutor transferring the cause against their representatives.

Effect of absence of interlocutors

61. A cause shall not be held to have fallen asleep by reason only that no interlocutor has been pronounced therein within a year and a day of the date of the last interlocutor.

Closing of Record to Proof

Closing of the record

62.—(1) When the pleadings have been adjusted the sheriff shall close the record and make such further order as he thinks fit.

(2) Not later than 14 days after the closing of the record the pursuer shall lodge in process a certified copy of the closed record.

Preliminary pleas

63.—(1) At the time of the closing of the record the parties shall state the preliminary pleas, if any, on which they insist and the sheriff shall fix a date for a debate on any such plea that is insisted in except where, upon a motion by the parties to reserve their pleas, he allows a proof before answer.

(2) The sheriff shall repel any such plea that is not insisted in.

Amendment of pleadings: powers of the sheriff

[1] 64.—(1) In any defended cause the sheriff may at any time before final judgment—

(*a*) allow any amendment of the initial writ or other writ which may be necessary for the purpose of determining in the existing cause the real question in controversy between the parties, notwithstanding that in consequence of such amendment a different remedy from that originally craved is thereby sought, or, after the closing of the record, that the sum sued for is increased or restricted;

(*b*) allow any amendment which may be necessary to correct or supplement the designation of any party to the cause, or to enable any party who has sued or has been sued in his own right to sue or be sued in a representative capacity, or to enable any party who has sued or who has been sued in a representative capacity to sue or to be sued in his own right or in a different representative capacity, or to add the name of an additional pursuer or of a person whose concurrence is necessary, or where the cause has been commenced in the name of the wrong person as pursuer or where it is doubtful whether it has been commenced in the name of the right person, to allow any other person to be sisted as pursuer in substitution for, or in addition to, the original pursuer;

(*c*) in any case in which it appears that all parties having an interest have not been called, or that the cause has been directed against the wrong person, allow any amendment inserting in the initial writ or writ an additional or substitute defender and containing averments directed against said defender and to order the record as so amended to be served on such additional or substitute defender along with a notice in terms of Form H as set out in the Appendix to this Schedule specifying the date by which defences or answers must be lodged; provided that in any case in which a time to pay direction under the Debtors (Scotland) Act 1987 may be applied for by the defender a notice in terms of Form HH as set out in the Appendix to this Schedule together with Form B5 shall be served on such additional or substitute defender in place of Form H; and thereafter a copy of the said notice shall be lodged in process with a certificate of execution thereon and the cause as so amended shall proceed in every respect as if such defender had originally been made a party to the cause;

(*d*) allow any amendment of the condescendence, defences, answers or pleas-in-law which may be necessary for determining in the existing cause the real question in controversy between the parties.

(2) In allowing an amendment under paragraph (1), the sheriff may attach such conditions as seem just, and shall find the party making the amendment liable in the expenses thereby occasioned unless it is just and equitable that the expenses occasioned by the amendment should be otherwise dealt with.

(3) No amendment allowed under paragraph (1) shall prejudice the rights of creditors of the defender by giving validity to diligence used on the dependence of the cause; but no objections to such diligence shall have effect when stated by the defender himself or by any person representing him by a title, or in right of a debt contracted by him, subsequent to the execution of such diligence.

NOTE

[1] As amended by S.I. 1988 No. 1978.

Renouncing of probation

65. If at any time on or after closing the record the parties wish to renounce probation they may do so by lodging with the sheriff clerk a joint minute to that effect with or without a statement of admitted facts and productions, and on the lodging of the joint minute the sheriff may order the cause to be debated.

Ordering of proof

66. If proof is necessary, the sheriff shall fix a date for taking the proof, and may limit the mode of proof.

Reference to oath

67.—(1) Where any party desires to refer any matter to his opponent's oath he shall lodge with the sheriff clerk a minute to that effect.

(2) If the party to whose oath reference has been made fails to appear at the diet for taking his deposition the sheriff may hold him as confessed and grant decree accordingly.

Objections to documents

68.—(1) When a deed or writing is founded on by any party in a cause, all objections to the deed or writing may be stated and maintained by way of exception, without reducing it.

(2) The sheriff may, where an objection is stated under paragraph (1) and where an action of reduction would be competent, order the objector to find caution, or to make consignation as he shall direct.

Remit to person of skill

69.—(1) Where all compearing parties to the cause concur the sheriff may remit to any person of skill or other person to report on any matter of fact and the report of such person shall be final and conclusive with respect to the matter of the remit.

(2) Before the sheriff so remits, the parties shall lodge in process a joint minute setting out the matters which are to be the subject of the remit.

(3) The expense of the execution of the remit shall in the first instance be paid by the parties equally unless the sheriff otherwise directs.

(4) In undefended causes the sheriff may on the motion of the pursuer remit to a man of skill or other person.

PROOF

EVIDENCE

eg witness about to die or go abroad

Evidence to lie in retentis

70. Evidence in danger of being lost may be taken to lie *in retentis* and, if satisfied that it is desirable so to do, the sheriff may, upon the motion of any party at any time, either take such evidence himself, or grant authority to a commissioner to take it.

DEFENDED ACTION – if more than 1 D. + notice relates only to some then specify in heading party to whom notice relates

– notice signed by D's sol. On lodging must exhibit service copy of IW to ascertain date of service + i.e. when period of notice started running

43(1) – period for lodging defences in Aberdeen – usually 12 days, in urgency 6 days
May be extended if good reason to do so

44 – if more than 1 D. state if for 1st D, 2nd etc.
Numbered paras. corresponding to condescendence – 3 possible answers to averments of fact :- 1) Admitted 2) Denied
3) Not Known + not admitted – only appropriate wrt facts not within knowledge of D.

[THE NEXT PAGE IS D 33]

45 – Implied admissions

– PRACTICE OF ANSWERS – must go through IW with D + decide what is admitted + denied
– best to make specific admissions repeating wording given in IW
– group together admissions, denials + NKNA – ADD QUOAD ULTRA DENIED
– a blanket denial of everything else
– don't use quoad ultra admitted because dangerous as – adjustment of pleadings AFTER defences lodged + pursuer could slip in further averments of fact – then you are caught with your general admission
– EXPLAINED + AVERRED – opportunity for D. to give his version of facts
– At eventual proof party CANNOT lead evidence of facts not averred
– continue cause to adjustment roll for few weeks to allow adjustment

ADJUSTMENT – R46 – basic procedure for adjustment – an informal process which takes place outwith ct.
– if case call on adj roll – merely for sh. to find out if ready to go to ct.
– may write or type adj.
– Adj. may simply be sent by letter to other party
– own copy of pleadings must have Adj. marked up as well
– IW may look very untidy

R.47 – open record compulsory in Ct of S – deals with Sh. Ct. version

GO TO D35

Evidence taken on commission

71. The evidence of any witness or haver resident beyond the jurisdiction of the court, or who although resident within the jurisdiction resides at some place remote from the court, or who is by reason of illness, age or infirmity, or other sufficient cause, unable to attend the diet of proof may be taken by commission in like manner as evidence to lie *in retentis*.

Affidavit evidence

[1] 72.—(1) The provisions of this rule—

(*a*) apply to all parts of actions of divorce, of separation and of declarator of parentage, non-parentage, legitimacy, legitimation or illegitimacy which proceed as undefended and to opposed interim orders under the Matrimonial Homes (Family Protection) (Scotland) Act 1981;

(*b*) do not apply to any action of divorce, of separation or of declarator of parentage, non-parentage, legitimacy, legitimation or illegitimacy where it appears to the sheriff that a defender is a person who is suffering from a mental disorder within the meaning of the Mental Health (Scotland) Act 1984 except where the curator *ad litem* for the defender has lodged a minute intimating that he does not intend to defend the action.

(2) Evidence submitted in the form of affidavits shall, subject to the provisions of this rule, be admissible in place of parole evidence.

(3) For the purpose of this rule—

(*a*) "affidavit" includes affirmation and statutory or other declaration;

(*b*) an affidavit shall be treated as admissible if it is duly emitted before a notary public or any other competent authority.

(4) Evidence submitted in the form of a written statement bearing to be that of a duly qualified medical practitioner, which has been signed by him and lodged in process, shall be admissible in place of parole evidence.

(5) Where it is intended to submit evidence only by means of affidavits the sheriff, at any time after the expiry of the period within which a notice of intention to defend or a minute under Rule 34 must be lodged, the pursuer having lodged the necessary evidence on affidavit and having endorsed a minute in accordance with Form X on the initial writ, may grant decree or other order in terms of that minute, without requiring the attendance of the pursuer in court.

NOTE

[1] As amended by S.I. 1984 No. 255 and 1986 Nos. 1230 and 1966.

Conditions for receiving written statements in evidence without being spoken to by a witness

[1] 72A.—(1) Any written statement (including an affidavit) or report, admissible under section 2(1)(*b*) of the Civil Evidence (Scotland) Act 1988 may be received in evidence in any ordinary cause without being spoken to by a witness subject to the provisions of this rule.

(2) The following provisions of this rule do not apply to any such written statement or report in respect of which express provision is made in these rules for its admissibility in evidence in relation to a particular category of ordinary cause.

(3) Application to the sheriff to receive any such written statement or report in evidence without being spoken to by a witness shall be made by way of motion.

(4) Subject to paragraph (5), on enrolling any such motion, the applicant shall lodge—

(*a*) the written statement or report as a production;

(*b*) in any case where the other party or parties have not agreed to the written statement or report in question being received in evidence without being spoken to by a witness, an affidavit or affidavits in support of the motion stating—

(i) the name, designation, and qualifications (if any) of the author of the statement or report in question;

(ii) the circumstances in which it was written; and

(iii) the reasons for the application.

(5) Paragraph (4) does not apply to an application made in respect of a written statement or report in the form of an affidavit which includes the information specified in sub-paragraph (*b*) of paragraph (4).

(6) On the hearing of any such motion, the sheriff may grant the motion, with or without conditions, or may refuse it, or may continue the motion to enable such further information to be obtained as he may require for the purpose of determining the application.

(7) For the purpose of this rule—
- (*a*) expressions used in this rule and in the Civil Evidence (Scotland) Act 1988 shall have the meaning they have in that Act;
- (*b*) "affidavit" includes affirmation and statutory or other declaration;
- (*c*) an affidavit shall be treated as admissible if it is duly emitted before a notary public or any other competent authority.

NOTE

[1] Inserted by S.I. 1989 No. 436.

Recording of evidence

73.—(1) In every defended cause the evidence shall be recorded by a shorthand writer, approved by the sheriff, unless the parties shall by agreement and with the consent of the sheriff dispense with the recording of such evidence. The responsibility for instructing a shorthand writer for a proof shall lie with the pursuer.

(2) Evidence adduced before a commissioner may be recorded by a shorthand writer or clerk approved by the commissioner. The responsibility for instructing a shorthand writer shall lie with the party moving for the commission.

(3) Where evidence is recorded by a shorthand writer or clerk the sheriff or commissioner shall administer the oath *de fideli administratione* to the shorthand writer or clerk who shall record the evidence by question and answer. The extended notes of evidence certified by such shorthand writer shall be the notes of the oral evidence in the case.

(4) It shall be unnecessary to record evidence in an undefended proof.

(5) If the correctness of the notes of evidence or of a deposition is questioned, the sheriff may satisfy himself in regard thereto by the examination of witnesses or otherwise, and may amend the record of evidence or a deposition.

(6) When a shorthand writer is so employed to record evidence, he shall in the first instance be paid, as regards commissions by the party moving for the commission, and as regards proofs by the parties equally. The solicitors of parties shall be personally liable for the shorthand writer's fees and the sheriff may make an order directing payment to be made.

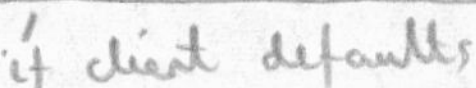

WITNESSES AND HAVERS

Citation

74.—(1) A copy of an interlocutor certified by the sheriff clerk allowing a proof or fixing a diet for the trial of any cause or for the examination of witnesses or havers shall be sufficient warrant for citation of witnesses or havers.

(2) If any witnesses or haver duly cited on a period of notice of at least seven days and after having been paid his travelling expenses if the same shall have been demanded, fails to attend a diet, either before the sheriff or before his commissioner, such witness or haver may be ordained by the sheriff to forfeit and pay a penalty not exceeding £250, unless a reasonable excuse be offered and sustained, and the sheriff may grant decree for said penalty in favour of the party on whose behalf said witness or haver was cited.

Form of citation

75.—(1) Witnesses and havers may be cited as nearly as may be in terms of Form I as set out in the Appendix to this Schedule and the certificate of citation shall be as nearly as may be in terms of Form J as set out in the Appendix to this Schedule.

(2) A solicitor who cites a witness or haver shall be personally liable for his fees and expenses.

(3) In the event of a solicitor who has cited a witness or haver intimating to him that his citation is cancelled, the solicitor shall advise him that said cancellation is not to affect any other citation which he may have received from another party in that cause.

Second diligence against witness

76.—(1) The sherifff may grant second diligence to compel the attendance of a witness or haver under pain of arrest and imprisonment until caution can be found as the sheriff may require for his due attendance.

(2) The warrant for a second diligence shall be effective in any sheriffdom without endorsation and the expenses thereof may be decerned for against the witness or haver.

Warrant to arrest

77. Where any witness or haver fails to answer a citation after having been duly cited the sheriff may, upon production of a relevant certificate of citation, grant warrant for the apprehension of the witness or haver and for bringing him to the court, and the expenses thereof may be deemed for against the witness or haver.

Productions

Production and recovery of documents

78.—(1) Each party shall, along with his pleadings, or at least before the closing of the record, if required by any other party in the cause or by the sheriff, lodge any documents founded upon in the pleadings, so far as the same are within his custody or power.

(2) Where such documents are not produced by any party to the cause or are in the hands of third parties, the sheriff may, on the motion of any party, grant commission and diligence for their recovery and may on that account delay closing the record.

(3) At any time after tabling, the sheriff, on the motion of either party, may grant commission and diligence for the recovery of such documents contained in a specification as he shall deem relevant to the cause.

Lodging productions for proofs

79. In all causes in which a proof has been allowed, all documents, plans, maps, models and other productions which are intended to be used or put in evidence at the proof, shall be lodged along with an inventory with the sheriff clerk on or before the fourteenth day prior to the day appointed for the proof, and notice of the lodging thereof shall at the same time be sent to the other party or parties; and no other production shall be used or put in evidence at the proof unless by consent of parties or by permission of the sheriff presiding thereat, on cause shown to his satisfaction, and on such terms as to expenses or otherwise as seems just.

Ordering of production of documents by sheriff

80. The sheriff may order production of documents at any stage of the cause, and the sheriff may allow a party, at any time before judgment, to produce any document which he has failed to produce timeously, on such conditions as to payment of expenses and allowing further proof as to the sheriff shall seem just.

Optional procedure before executing commission and diligence

81.—(1) Any party who has obtained a commission and diligence for the recovery of documents may, at any time, before executing the same against another party or other parties to the cause, or against any haver, serve upon such party, or parties, or haver, an order with certificate attached in terms of Form K as set out in the Appendix to this Schedule.

(2) Such order shall be served by registered or recorded delivery letter, and may be addressed to the care of the known solicitor or solicitors for the party or parties, or for the haver, from whom the documents are sought to be recovered.

(3) Such order shall be obtempered by such party, or parties, or by such haver, in the manner and within the time specified therein.

[THE NEXT PAGE IS D 35]

R.48 - used to be that amendment proc. under 64 had to be used involving a provision of the ct. 48 allows alteration of sum without consent of ct.

-only applies to sum sued for - any other alterations to crave must be done by way of R.64

- Still open to cross-examine party at proof on deleted adjustments

TIME PROVISION - 49 - fairly strict in theory

- 62 - sheriff shall close record + no further adjustments without leave of sh.

SKELETON DEFENCES - occur where a party not in a position to lodge defences

- to comply with ct. order party can lodge S.D. ie extremely brief + contain DENIALS of the condescendance. THEN during adjustment period more info. can be put in to flesh out the S.D. ie delete denials in answers + put in further answers

- sometimes D. gets to delay case by putting in S.D. - buys time

- Used to be thought that nothing wrong with practice of lodging S.D. + gains all the way with them eg FORBES v DOUGLAS (1974)

NOW - judicial position moved towards view that D. must frankly admit those defences which it can openly admit

- DON'T resort to SD unless a stop gap is necessary

PROPRIETY OF DEFENCE - sol. must be satisfied that it is a stateable case as a matter of law

- STEWART v MACDONALD (1987) - July 1986 case sisted to allow defence to apply for legal aid (appeared defence only stalling). In Oct. case came before ct. again - sh. recalled sist + case continued for 14 days + to be called on an adjustment roll. On adjustment still hadn't been lodged - still in skeleton form. Sh. refused to allow defences to be received + granted decree by default

Appeal to Sh. Pin. - defences still in skeleton form + appeal refused

- Sol. who resorts to S.D. may put himself in a position where he is personally liable for P.'s expenses in action

COUNTER CLAIMS - D. may feel that he has claim against P.

SEE 51 - 56

- only certain claims can be set off - LIQUID CLAIMS

eg X borrows money from Y - Y supplies goods to X

- both liquid claims + so can be set off against each other - Y sues for 10K, X can counter-claim for 6K + ct. can grant 4K

- if 1 of claims is illiquid - cannot be set off against a liquid one unless they both arise from the same contract

- in sh. ct. counter-claims are only competent as regards money claims

- in Ct. of S - McLEAN v MARR (1976) - action for declarator of servitude. Counterclaimed for interdict - proper in Ct. of S. - GO TO D36/1

(4) When the order, certificate in terms thereof and inventoried documents (if any) are received by the sheriff clerk, official intimation shall be given by him forthwith to the solicitor or solicitors of the party or parties to the cause that the order has been served and obtempered; and it shall not be competent for any party, other than the party who served the order, to borrow any of the documents until after the expiry of seven days from the date of such official intimation.

(5) If the party who served the order is not satisfied that full production has been made under the specification, or that adequate reasons for non-production have been given, he may execute the commission and diligence in normal form, notwithstanding his adoption in the first instance of the foregoing procedure by order.

(6) In the event of the production under such order as aforesaid of extracts from books whether such extracts are certified or not, the sheriff may, on cause shown, order that the party who served the order shall be at liberty to inspect and take copies of any entries in any books falling under the specification, subject, in the event of any question of confidentiality arising, to the inspection being made, and the copies being taken, at the sight of the commissioner appointed in the interlocutor granting the commission and diligence; and the sheriff may, on cause shown, order the production of any books (not being bankers' books or books of public record) falling under a specification, notwithstanding the production of certified extracts therefrom.

Confidentiality

82. In any cause in which, either under the optional procedure provided in Rule 81 or in the execution of a commission and diligence in normal form, confidentiality is claimed for any of the documents produced, such documents shall be enclosed in a separate packet, which shall not be opened or put in process except by authority of the sheriff obtained on the application of the party serving the order, or executing the commission and diligence, after opportunity has been given to the party, parties or haver, making production, to be heard.

Warrant for production of original documents from public records

83.—(1) Where any party to a cause desires to obtain from the Keeper of the Registers of Scotland or the Keeper of the Records of Scotland production of the originals of any register or deed under his custody, he shall apply by motion to the sheriff before whom the cause depends, after seven days' notice of such application given in writing to the Keeper in charge of the originals.

(2) Upon such application the sheriff may by interlocutor, certify that it is necessary for the ends of justice that the application should be granted, and the party may make application by letter (enclosing a copy of the interlocutor duly certified by the sheriff clerk or one of his deputes) addressed to the principal clerk of session, for an order from the Lords of Council and Session authorising the Keeper to exhibit the original of any register or deeds to the sheriff, and that in the hands of an officer to be selected by the said Keeper.

(3) The principal clerk of session shall submit the same to a Lord Ordinary in Chambers, who, if satisfied, shall grant a warrant on behalf of the Lords of Council and Session. A certified copy of said warrant shall be served upon the Keeper.

(4) The expense attending the transmission and exhibition of such original registers or deeds shall be defrayed in the first instance by the party or parties on whose application they are exhibited.

Orders for inspection

84.—(1) Any application to the sheriff for an order for the inspection, photographing, preservation, custody or detention of documents or other property (including, where appropriate, land) or for the production, recovery or the taking of samples thereof or the carrying out of any experiment thereon or therewith made in any civil proceedings which have been commenced before that sheriff shall be made by minute craving that the sheriff should grant such an order and specifying the order sought.

(2) Upon such minute being lodged, the sheriff shall forthwith appoint—

(*a*) the application to be heard at a diet to be fixed by him, and

(*b*) appoint intimation to other parties to the proceedings and to such other persons as appear to him to have an interest relevant to the application.

(3) After hearing parties, the sheriff may either grant or refuse the order sought, in whole or in part, or as amended, and may order the applicant to find such caution for any loss, damage or expenses which may be incurred as a result of the application as to the sheriff seems just.

(4) Any application to the sheriff for such an order as is referred to in paragraph (1),

made where proceedings have not been commenced, by any person who appears to the sheriff to be likely to be a party to or minuter in proceedings which are likely to be brought, shall be made by initial writ served upon all persons who are likely to be parties to such proceedings when commenced; and such application shall be and shall be dealt with as a summary application, provided that the sheriff may make an order for such intimation to such other persons as appear to him to have an interest relevant to the application, and may order the applicant to find such caution for any loss, damage or expense which may be incurred as a result of the application as to the sheriff seems just.

(5) Any party who has obtained an order under this rule shall serve by registered or recorded delivery letter a certified copy of the interlocutor granting such order upon:—

(*a*) (i) in the case of an order made under paragraph (3), any other party or parties to the cause;

(ii) in the case of an order made under paragraph (4), any person upon whom service has been made; and

(*b*) such other persons to whom the sheriff has appointed intimation of the application to be made;

but it shall not be necessary to serve such certified copy on any person who was present or represented when the application was heard; and such order shall be obtempered by the party or parties to whom it is directed in the manner and within the time specified therein.

Orders to disclose identity of persons

[1] 84A.—(1) An application for an order under section 1(1A) of the Administration of Justice (Scotland) Act 1972 requiring a person to disclose such information as he has as to the identity of any person who might be a witness in a cause in dependence before that sheriff court shall be made by minute in the process of that cause craving such an order and specifying the order sought.

(2) On a minute being lodged under paragraph (1), the sheriff shall appoint forthwith—

(*a*) the application to be heard at a diet to be fixed by him; and

(*b*) intimation to be made to any other party to the cause and to such other person as appears to him to have an interest in the application.

(3) After hearing parties, the sheriff may either grant or refuse the order sought in whole or in part, or as amended, and subject to such conditions, including caution, as he thinks fit.

(4) An application for an order under section 1(1A) of the Administration of Justice (Scotland) Act 1972 requiring a person to disclose such information as he has as to the identity of any person who might be a witness or defender in any civil proceedings which are likely to be brought, shall be made by summary application.

(5) A summary application under paragraph (4) shall crave the order which is sought and shall specify the nature of the proposed proceedings and the information required.

(6) On presentation of a summary application under paragraph (4), the sheriff may make an order for intimation to such persons as appear to him to have an interest in the application.

(7) After the hearing of the summary application, the sheriff may grant the order sought in whole or in part, or as amended, subject to such conditions, including caution, as he thinks fit.

(8) Subject to paragraph (9), a certified copy interlocutor granting an order made under this rule shall—

(*a*) be served upon the person to whom it is directed; and

(*b*) be intimated to any other person to whom intimation of the minute or application, as the case may be, has been made,

by the party in whose favour it has been granted.

(9) An interlocutor granting an order under this rule shall not be served upon, or intimated to, a person who was present or represented when the application under this rule was determined.

(10) An interlocutor of the court under this rule shall be obtempered by the person to whom it is directed in the manner and within the time specified.

NOTE

[1] Inserted by S.I. 1986 No. 1966.

Procedure at Proof

Proof to be taken continuously

85. The proof shall be taken so far as possible continuously, but the sheriff may adjourn the diet from time to time.

Objections

86.—(1) All objections to the admissibility of oral or documentary evidence or to the production of documents, the submissions of parties in relation thereto and the decision of the sheriff or commissioner thereon shall be recorded by the shorthand writer and be extended with the notes of evidence; provided that the sheriff or commissioner may also, if he considers it necessary or desirable to do so, dictate to the shorthand writer a short note of the objection and decision.

(2) The sheriff or commissioner if he considers an objection of sufficient importance may direct that the evidence to which the objection relates should be recorded separately from the remainder of the evidence or report of proceedings.

(3) Where the recording of evidence has been dispensed with in terms of Rule 73, the sheriff, if called upon to do so, shall—

(i) in the case of objections to the admissibility of evidence on the ground of confidentiality or to producing a document on any ground, record in a note the terms of such objections and his decision thereon; and

(ii) in all other cases record, in the note to his interlocutor disposing of the merits of the cause the terms of any objections and his decision thereon.

Incidental appeal against rulings on confidentiality of evidence and production of documents

87.—(1) Where a party to the cause or other person objects to the admissibility of oral or documentary evidence on the ground of confidentiality or to producing a document on any ground, any party or person may, if dissatisfied with the ruling of the sheriff respecting the objection, express immediately his formal dissatisfaction and, with leave of the sheriff, appeal to the sheriff principal, who shall dispose of the appeal with the least possible delay; but otherwise it shall not be competent during a proof to submit to review any decision of the sheriff as to the admissibility of evidence or the production of documents.

(2) The incidental appeal referred to in paragraph (1) shall not remove the cause from the sheriff who may proceed with the cause as regards points not necessarily dependent upon the ruling appealed against.

Parties to be heard at close of proof

88. At the close of the proof, or at an adjourned diet it for any reason the sheriff shall have seen fit to postpone the hearing, the sheriff shall hear parties and thereafter shall pronounce judgment with the least possible delay.

From D35

COUNTER CLAIMS FOR CUSTODY –

- G v H (1976) – action for delivery of child. D. counter-claimed for custody of child. P's sol. argued it was incompetent for a counter-claim. Sh. disagreed

BUT – ORR v ORR (1978) – Same point – sh. agreed with P's solicitor.

- Counter claim should normally be lodged at as early an opportunity as possible
- Usual for P. to ask ct. for right to lodge answers to counter-claim – set out in numbered paras. with admissions, denials, NK + NA

THIRD PARTY PROCEDURE – D37

[THE NEXT PAGE IS D 37]

THIRD PARTY PROCEDURE – eg road accident case – Passenger A in car with B, accident with car C. A sues C. C might say it was B's fault + want to sue him

– Prior to 1983 – A could bring in B but C (defender) couldn't force him to do this. All C could do was defend + if found liable would have to raise separate action against B

R.50(1) – circumstances where available – see 50(1)

'contribution, relief or indemnity' – can arise by common law or contract

– J+S obligants have a right against one another – up to creditor to decide who he will sue. Although 1 might have full amount he can then go against other D. to reclaim

– Contractual obligations – common to find an indemnity clause in contract of a sub-contractor

– Pursuer may be convened as 3rd party in exceptional circumstances:-

– BUCHAN v THOMPSON (1976)

– Employers Liability (Defective Equipment) Act 1969

– employer made vicariously liable for negligence on a contractor making equipment. Employee simply sues employer.

– Employer has right of relief against manufacturer

– YULE v OAKS-SIMPSON (1984)

– A sues C but finds that was B's fault – can bring in B as an additional defender OR abandon action against C + go against B

– Nothing to prevent D. from bringing in 3rd party who has previously been sued by P. for same matter PROVIDED that action against other party was not proceeded with to a conclusion.

– J+S liability – with J+S liability P. alleging he could have sued 3rd party but didn't want to. J+S only gives rights to D. not P. If both parties found at fault no problem eg C5%, B 95% – ct. issue decree for 100% against C [person P. took action against], followed by decree for 95% from B to C.

– if ct. decides all B's fault A gets no decree because didn't bring him in as Defender. B is brought in only for C's benefit

– if P. thinks any chance that D. may escape liability then should bring in 3rd party defender

CLOSED RECORD 039

PROCEDURE AFTER JUDGMENT

JUDGMENT

Judgment

89.—[1] (1) The sheriff shall append to all interlocutors, except those of a formal nature, a note setting out the grounds upon which he has proceeded and in his final interlocutor on the merits he shall set out his findings in fact and in law separately: Provided always that this paragraph shall not apply to decrees in actions of divorce and of separation and aliment which have proceeded as undefended.

(2) Where an interlocutor with note appended thereto is pronounced by the sheriff otherwise than in the presence of the parties, the sheriff clerk shall forthwith provide the parties with a copy of such interlocutor and note free of charge.

(3) The sheriff may produce or sign any interlocutor when furth of his sheriffdom, but the date of every interlocutor shall be deemed to be the date upon which it is entered in the books of the court.

(4) At any time before extract, or before the transmission of a process in which an appeal has been taken the sheriff may correct any clerical or incidental error in his interlocutor or note.

NOTE

[1] As amended by S.I. 1984 No. 255.

EXTRACT

Extract

90.—(1) Subject to the provisions of paragraph (3) hereof, any decree, interlocutor or order pronounced in a defended cause may be extracted at any time at which it is not possible for any party to mark or pursue an appeal or apply for leave to appeal.

(2) Where, following the pronouncing of any decree, interlocutor or other order the sheriff has reserved any question of expenses, extract may be issued only after the expiry of 14 days from the date of the interlocutor disposing of such expenses, unless the sheriff directs otherwise.

(3) The sheriff on cause shown may grant a motion to allow extract to be applied for and issued earlier than is provided for in paragraphs (1) and (2) provided the motion is made either in the presence of parties or the sheriff is satisfied that proper intimation of the terms of the motion has been made in writing to all other parties.

(4) Nothing in this rule shall affect the power of the sheriff to supersede extract.

Extract decree of divorce

[1] 90A. Every extract decree of divorce shall be as nearly as may be in accordance with Form Z as set out in the Appendix to this Schedule.

NOTE

[1] Inserted by S.I. 1984 No. 255.

APPEAL

Time-limit for appeal

91. Any appealable interlocutor may be appealed within 14 days of the date of that interlocutor if not sooner extracted following a motion for early extract.

Application for leave to appeal and appeal therefrom

[1] 92.—(1) Application for leave to appeal against an interlocutor of a sheriff shall only be competent if made within seven days of the date of the interlocutor against which it is desired to appeal, but such application shall not be competent if the interlocutor has been extracted following a motion for early extract.

(2) Where leave to appeal has been granted, an appeal shall be made—

(*a*) where the appeal relates to a time to pay direction or any order connected therewith, within 14 days; or

(*b*) in any other case, within seven days,

of the granting of leave.

(3) An application for leave to appeal relating to a time to pay direction or the recall or restriction of an arrestment shall specify the question of law upon which the appeal is to proceed.

NOTE

[1] As amended by S.I. 1988 No. 1978.

Form of appeal and giving of notice to parties

93.—(1) An appeal shall be taken by note of appeal which shall be written by the appellant on the interlocutor sheet, or other written record containing the interlocutor appealed against, or on a separate sheet lodged with the sheriff clerk; and such note of appeal shall be as nearly as may be in the following terms:—

"The (pursuer, applicant, claimant, defender, respondent or other party) appeals to the sheriff principal/or/to the Court of Session".

and such note of appeal shall be signed by the appellant, and shall bear the date on which it is signed.

(2) Where the appeal is an appeal to the Court of Session the note of appeal shall specify the name and address of the solicitors in Edinburgh who will be acting for the appellant in the appeal.

(3) On an appeal being taken to the sheriff principal the sheriff clerk shall transmit the process within four days to the sheriff principal, and on an appeal to the Court of Session he shall transmit the process within four days to the deputy principal clerk of session.

(4) Within the period of four days the sheriff clerk shall send written notice of the appeal to the other party or parties and certify on the interlocutor sheet that he has done so; but failure to give such notice shall not invalidate the appeal.

Reclaiming petition or oral hearing may be ordered or dispensed with

94. The sheriff principal may order a reclaiming petition and answers, or may hear parties orally or may, on the motion of all parties and if to the sheriff principal it seems just, dispose of the appeal without ordering either a reclaiming petition and answers or an oral hearing.

Interim possession may be regulated pending appeal

95. Notwithstanding an appeal, the sheriff or sheriff principal from whose decision appeal has been taken shall have power to regulate all matters relating to interim possession, to make any order for the preservation of any property to which the action relates or for its sale if perishable, or for the preservation of evidence, or to make in his discretion any interim order which a due regard to the interests of the parties may require. Such orders shall not be subject to review except by the Appellate Court at the hearing of the appeal.

Abandonment of appeal

96. After an appeal to the sheriff principal has been noted the appellant shall not be entitled to abandon it unless of consent of all parties, or by leave of the sheriff principal.

EXPENSES

Decree for expenses may be extracted in solicitor's name

97. Expenses allowed in any cause, whether in absence or *in foro*, unless modified at a fixed amount, shall be taxed before decree is granted for them, and the sheriff may allow a decree for expenses to be extracted in the name of the solicitor who conducted the cause.

Objection to auditor's report

98.—[1] (1) Where an account of expenses awarded in any cause is lodged for taxation, the account and process shall be transmitted by the sheriff clerk to the auditor of court, and the auditor shall assign a diet of taxation not earlier than seven days from the date he receives the account and intimate that diet forthwith to the party who lodged the account.

(2) The party who lodged the account of expenses shall then, forthwith, send a copy thereof and intimate the date, time and place of the diet of taxation to each of the other parties and when the account has been taxed the auditor shall re-transmit the process with the account and his report to the sheriff clerk.

(3) Where the auditor has reserved consideration of the account at the date of the taxation he shall inform the parties who attended the taxation of his decision.

(4) A party may lodge a note of objections to an account as taxed only where he attended the diet of taxation, and the note of objections shall be lodged within seven days from the date of the taxation of the account, and the sheriff shall dispose of such objection in a summary manner, with or without answers.

(5) If no note of objections is lodged within said period the sheriff may grant decree for the expenses as taxed.

NOTE

[1] As amended by S.I. 1992 No. 249 (effective 4th May 1992).

Particular Procedures

Sequestration for Rent

Actions craving payment of rent

[1] 99.—(1) In actions for sequestration and sale in respect of non-payment of rent, for recovery, or in security of rent, whether brought before or after the term of payment, payment of rent may be craved and decree for payment of such rent or part thereof when due and payable, may be pronounced and extracted in common form.

(2) There shall be served on the defender in such actions, along with the initial writ, warrant and citation, a notice in accordance with Form H8 as set out in the Appendix to this Schedule.

NOTE

[1] As amended by S.I. 1988 No. 1978.

Warrant to inventory and secure

100.—(1) In the first deliverance on an initial writ for sequestration for rent the sheriff may sequestrate the effects of the tenant, and grant warrant to inventory and secure them.

(2) All warrants to sequestrate, inventory, sell, eject or relet shall include authority to open shut and lockfast places for the purpose of carrying such warrant into execution.

Sale of effects

101.—(1) The sheriff may order the sequestrated effects to be sold at the sight of an officer of court or other named person.

[THE NEXT PAGE IS D 39]

CLOSING OF RECORD - sh. will decide when pleadings are adjusted + will then make any further order as he thinks fit - looks to parties sol. for guidance

- PRELIMINARY PLEA IN LAW - can be decided without inquiry into merits / facts of case as a plea that action is:-

  - incompetent / that P. has no title to sue / that action is time-barred / that ct. has no J.

  - may be a factual dispute eg plea to J. SO LIMITED evidence may have to be led.

  - PP may be to relevancy of case - 2 meanings:-

    1) Ordinary meaning - pleadings have nothing to do with case

    2) Pleadings, to be relevant, must justify the granting of the crave when the law as set out in the plea in law is applied to them

- Same rules apply to defences - D. must be able to have defences which have possibility of succeeding

- Relevancy may apply to whole case or smaller part of case

- Party entitled to FAIR NOTICE of opponents case ∴ averments must be sufficiently specific - opponent should be in a position to check accuracy of averments being made. If not possible averments may be struck out of case by sh.

SEE R.63

- if no PP are insisted on a PROOF is fixed where issue is one of fact - whoever proves their facts will win.

- at DEBATE - matters which arise are purely of LAW. If PP is well-founded + is directed at whole action the action will be DISMISSED, [as opposed to ABSOLVITOR where can't be raised again, dismissed forever] so will always be open to P. to raise another action

  BUT - before sh. can dismiss case has to be sure that P. cannot / will not succeed even if he proves everything he claims he can. If he is unsure what will happen he will set a PROOF BEFORE ANSWER ie doesn't give a judgement on PP [ie dismiss or go on] until he has heard proof.

63(1) - PBA may be sought by parties themselves

- if act for P. + D. has PP on relevancy - record is closed + D. insists on plea so a debate can be fixed. P. may be happy enough with a PBA - so he can ask sh. ct. to note that he is offering PBA - case will go to debate + P. can recover his expenses for the debate from the D.

- PRELIMINARY PROOF - may be approp. where there are matters of fact which must be established before PP can be decided

GO TO P40

(2) When a sale follows it shall be reported within 14 days and the pursuer shall lodge with the sheriff clerk the roup rolls or certified copies thereof and a state of debt.

(3) In the interlocutor approving the report of sale, or by separate interlocutor, the sheriff may grant decree against the defender for any balance remaining due.

Care of effects

102. The sheriff may at any stage appoint a fit person to take charge of the sequestrated effects, or may require the tenant to find caution that they shall be made available.

Removing

Action of removing where fixed term of removal

[1] 103.—(1) Subject to section 24 of the Agricultural Holdings (Scotland) Act 1949, an action of removing may be raised at any time, provided the tenant has bound himself to remove by writing, dated and signed within 12 months of the term of removal, or, where there is more than one ish, of the ish first in date to remove.

(2) Subject to the said section 24, when the tenant has not so bound himself an action of removing may be raised at any time, but—

(*a*) in the case of a lease of lands exceeding two acres in extent for three years and upwards, an interval of not less than one year nor more than two years shall elapse between the date of notice of removal and the term of removal first in date;

(*b*) in the case of a lease of lands exceeding two acres in extent, whether written or verbal, held from year to year or under tacit relocation, or for any other period less than three years, an interval of not less than six months shall elapse between the date of notice of removal and the term of removal first in date; and

(*c*) in the case of houses let with or without land attached not exceeding two acres in extent, as also of land not exceeding two acres in extent without houses, as also of mills, fishings, shootings, and all other heritable subjects excepting land exceeding two acres in extent, and let for a year or more, 40 days at least shall elapse between the date of notice of removal and the term of removal first in date.

(3) In any defended action of removing the sheriff may order the defender to find caution for violent profits.

(4) In actions of declarator of irritancy and removing by a superior against a vassal, the pursuer shall call as parties the last entered vassal and such heritable creditors and holders of postponed ground burdens as are disclosed by a search for 20 years prior to the raising of the action and the expense of the search shall form part of the pursuer's expenses of process.

NOTE

[1] As amended by S.I. 1983 No. 1546.

Form of notice of removal

[1] 104. Notices under sections 34, 35 and 36 of the Act of 1907 shall be as nearly as may be in terms of Form L as set out in the Appendix to this Schedule, and a letter of removal may be in terms of Form M as set out in the Appendix to this Schedule.

NOTE

[1] As amended by S.I. 1983 No. 1546.

Form of notice under section 37

[1] 105. Notices under section 37 of the Act of 1907 shall be as nearly as may be in terms of Form N as set out in the Appendix to this Schedule, and such form may be used also for notices to the proprietor by or on behalf of the tenant.

NOTE

[1] As amended by S.I. 1983 No. 1546.

Removal notices

[1] 106. Removal notices under sections 34, 35, 36, 37 and 38 of the Act of 1907 may be given by a messenger-at-arms or sheriff officer, or by registered letter signed by the person entitled to give such notice, or by the law agent or factor of such person, posted at any post office within the United Kingdom in time to admit of its being delivered at the address thereon on or prior to the last date upon which by law such notice must be given, addressed to the person entitled to receive such notice, and bearing the particular address of such person at the time if the same be known, or, if the same be not known, then to the last known address of such person.

NOTE

[1] As amended by S.I. 1983 No. 1546.

Evidence of notice to remove

107.—(1) A certificate of notice under Rule 104 dated and endorsed upon the lease or extract, or upon the letter of removal, and signed by the sheriff officer, messenger-at-arms, or by the person giving the notice, or his law agent, or factor, or an acknowledgement of notice endorsed on the lease or extract or letter of removal by the party in possession or his agent shall be sufficient evidence that notice has been given.

(2) Where there is no lease, a certificate endorsed upon a copy of the notice or letter,

Closed record must then be prepared – SEE 62(2)

AMMENDMENT OF CLOSED RECORD – possible to amend C.R.

NOTE – adjustment not possible after record closed [Adjustment of instance or crave is NOT possible even before closing record – amendment only way to change these – EXCEPT amount craved – see D35.]

– Ammendment can alter any part of C.R.

RULE 64 – wide powers of discretion given to sh. Applies only to defended causes. Applies at any time before final judgement.

(a) deals with changing remedy or altering sum sued for after closing of record – no clear auth. whether can change radically incompetent action to one which is competent eg Actions of reduction in Sh. Ct. is complete nullity – cannot amend such an action because it is incompetent BUT – action for damages + reduction would be allowed by deleting action for reduction part of crave

(b) Altering P. or any details of P. – can alter/correct designation of parties eg party has changed his address during the action

– can add a P. – eg action with minor child might need a curator added

– if action raised under name of wrong pursuer can amend to make it right P. – prior to 1983 had to start new action

GO TO D40/2

certified to be correct, by the person, sheriff officer, messenger-at-arms, law agent, or factor sending the same, which certificate shall be signed by such party sending the notice or letter, shall also be sufficient evidence that notice has been given.

(3) A certificate of notice under Rule 105 dated and endorsed upon a copy of the notice or letter signed by the party sending the notice, shall be sufficient evidence that such notice has been given.

Applications under Part II of the Conveyancing and Feudal Reform (Scotland) Act 1970

[1] 107A.—(1) An application or counter-application to the sheriff under Part II of the Conveyancing and Feudal Reform (Scotland) Act 1970 shall be brought—

(*a*) as an ordinary cause, where any other remedy is craved; or

(*b*) as a summary application, where no other remedy is craved.

(2) An interlocutor of the sheriff disposing of an application or counter-application under paragraph (1) shall be final and not subject to appeal except as to a question of title or as to any other remedy granted.

NOTE

[1] Added by S.I. 1990 No. 661.

SUMMARY SUSPENSION

Summary application for suspension of charge

108. Where a charge has been given on a decree of court granted by the sheriff or a decree of registration proceeding upon a bond, bill, contract, or other form of obligation registered in any sheriff court books, or in the Books of Council and Session, or any others competent or on letters of horning following on such decree, for payment of any sum of money the person so charged may apply in the sheriff court having jurisdiction over him for suspension of such charge and diligence.

Sist of diligence

109. On sufficient caution being found in the hands of the sheriff clerk for the sum charged for with interest thereon, and expenses, and a further sum to be fixed by the sheriff in respect of expenses to be incurred in the suspension process, the sheriff may sist diligence, order intimation and answers, and proceed to dispose of the cause in a summary manner.

Objections

110. If objections are taken to the competency or regularity of suspension proceedings, the judgment of the sheriff, on such objections, may be appealed to the sheriff principal whose judgment thereon shall be final.

ARRESTMENT

Service of schedule of arrestment

111. If a schedule of arrestment has not been personally served upon an arrestee, the arrestment shall only have effect if a copy of the schedule is also sent in a registered or recorded delivery letter to the last known place of residence of the arrestee, or, if such place of residence is unknown, or if the arrestee is a firm or corporation, to the arrestee's principal place of business if known, or, if not known, to any known place of business of the arrestee, and the officer shall in his execution certify that this has been done and specify the address in question.

Report of arrestment

112.—(1) An arrestment on the dependence of a cause used prior to service shall fall unless the cause shall have been served within 20 days from the date of arrestment and

(*a*) in the case of defended causes, has been tabled within 20 days of the first ordinary court day occurring subsequent to the expiry of the period of notice, or

(*b*) in the case of undefended causes, decree in absence has been taken within 20 days of the expiry of the period of notice.

(2) When such an arrestment has been executed the party using it or his agent shall forthwith report the execution to the sheriff clerk.

Multiplepoinding

Action of multiplepoinding

113. An action of multiplepoinding may be raised by any party holding, or having an interest in or claim on, the fund *in medio*.

Service of initial writ

114. The pursuer shall serve the initial writ on all persons so far as known to him having an interest in the fund *in medio*, including the holder of the fund where the pursuer is not the holder.

Order of advertisement

115. The sheriff may make an order for advertisement of the action in such newspapers as he considers necessary.

(c) Alterations to D. by adding an additional or substitute D.
Prior to 1983 could add a D. by amendment but couldn't delete wrong D.

(d) Amendment of anything which is real source of dispute - catch all provision
- Amendment may be needed in many circumstances
eg party changing address / change in factual circumstances
- may become necessary after debate if it is averred that P.'s pleadings are lacking in specification - if accept this will amend

LIMITATIONS TO AMENDMENT -
- introduction by way of amendment of matters/parties which are new AFTER expiry of T.L. - MAY NOT BE ALLOWED

[THE NEXT PAGE IS D 41]

eg A sues B more than 3 years after accident. Seeks leave to sue C as new D. Clearly if action against C time barred ∴ amendment to this effect would also be time barred.
- curing a radical defect outside T.L. or changing basis of case
eg case irrelevant after 3 years. P. seeks to amend to make it relevant - CANNOT do unless Ct. exercises discretion
- prejudice to opponent must not occur by way of amendment
- if don't get amendment right 1st time unlikely Ct. will allow another

Expenses of amendment - 64(2) - E of A. may be found to be expenses of the cause
- possible for sh. to find that person making amendment liable for all expenses to date

Cases on amendment - careful with pre '83 cases - Rules changed to bring into line with Ct. of S.

PROCEDURE FOR AMENDMENT - depends generally on nature of amendment
- very simple amendments - may be altered at bar in course of amendment
- minor matters - can move his Lordship to delete part of action or amend it
- most amendments - require to be put in form of minute of amendment
- opponent may not object OR may lodge answers

One view - duty to prepare amended C.R. is P.'s despite D. having made the amendment

GO TO D44/1

Condescendence on the fund

116. If the pursuer is the holder of the fund *in medio* he shall condescend in detail on the said fund in the condescendence of the initial writ.

Lodging of notice of appearance

117. If any party intends to lodge defences to the competency of the action, objections to the condescendence of the fund *in medio* or a claim on the fund *in medio*, he shall, before expiry of the appropriate period of notice lodge a notice of appearance, which shall be as nearly as possible in terms of Form O as set out in the Appendix to this Schedule, and shall specify therein the purpose of his intended appearance.

Lodging of process

118. Where a notice of appearance has been lodged, the cause shall table, and the pursuer shall lodge a process in accordance with Rule 37.

Lodging of defences, objections and claims where the holder is the pursuer

119.—(1) Where the holder of the fund *in medio* is the pursuer, the sheriff at tabling shall appoint a period within which any defences, objections or claims shall be lodged, and appoint a date on which the cause shall appear on the procedure roll.

(2) Defences, objections and claims shall be lodged with the sheriff clerk in a single document under separate headings.

(3) Each claimant shall lodge with his claim any documents founded on in his claim, so far as the same are within his custody or power.

Condescendence on the fund by holder who is not pursuer

120. Where the holder of the fund *in medio* is not the pursuer, the sheriff, at tabling shall appoint a period within which he is to lodge in process a detailed condescendence of the fund in his hands together with a list of all persons, so far as known to him, having an interest in the said fund, and shall appoint a date on which the cause shall appear on the procedure roll; and the procedure for the lodging of defences, objections and claims specified in Rule 119 shall be followed.

Disposal of defences

121.—(1) At the hearing on the procedure roll, where defences have been lodged, the sheriff may order the initial writ and defences to be adjusted in accordance with Rule 122 and thereafter shall close the record thereon and regulate further procedure.

(2) Unless the sheriff otherwise directs, defences shall be disposed of before any further procedure in the action.

Objections to fund in medio

122.—(1) Where objections to the fund *in medio* have been lodged the sheriff may, after disposal of any defences, order the condescendence of the fund and objections to be adjusted and thereafter shall close the record thereon and regulate further procedure.

(2) If no objections to the fund *in medio* have been lodged, or if objections have been lodged and disposed of, the sheriff, without order for intimation to any party, may on the motion of the holder of the fund approve the condescendence on the fund and find the holder liable only in once and single payment.

Consignation of the fund

[1] 123.—(1) At any time after the condescendence of the fund *in medio* has been approved, the sheriff may order it to be consigned or deposited in the hands of the sheriff clerk, or may order the whole or any part of the fund to be sold and the proceeds of sale to be consigned as aforesaid.

(2) After such consignation or deposit, it shall be competent for the holder of the fund *in medio* to apply for his exoneration and discharge.

NOTE

[1] As amended by S.I. 1983 No. 1546.

Expenses

124. The sheriff may allow the holder of the fund *in medio*, on his exoneration and discharge, his expenses out of the said fund as a first charge thereon.

Further service or advertisement

125. The sheriff may, on the motion of any party or *ex proprio motu*, at any time order further advertisement or service on any person.

Ranking of claims

126.—(1) After disposal of any defences, and after approval on the condescendence of the fund *in medio*, the sheriff, where there is no competition on the fund, may rank and prefer the claimants and grant decree in terms of said ranking.

(2) Where there is competition the sheriff may order claims to be adjusted in accordance with Rule 122 and thereafter shall close the record thereon and regulate further procedure.

Remit to Reporter

127.—(1) Where several claims have been lodged the sheriff may remit to a Reporter to prepare a scheme of division and report.

(2) The expenses of such remit, when approved by the sheriff, shall be made a charge upon the fund to be deducted before division.

Disposal of Money Payable to Persons Under Legal Disability

Disposal of money payable to persons under legal disability

128.—(1) Where in any action of damages by or on behalf of a person under legal disability, arising out of injury sustained by such person, or out of the death of some other person in respect of whose death the person under legal disability is entitled to damages, a sum of money becomes payable to such person, such sum shall unless otherwise ordered, be paid into court and shall be invested, applied, or otherwise dealt with and administered by the court for the benefit of the person entitled thereto, and the receipt of the sheriff clerk shall be a sufficient discharge in respect of the amount paid in.

(2) The sheriff clerk of any sheriff court is also authorised at the request of any competent court to accept custody of any sum of money paid into such court in any action of damages by or for behoof of a person under legal disability provided always that such person is then resident within the jurisdiction of such sheriff court and such sum shall be invested or otherwise dealt with as in this rule.

(3) Where any money is paid into court under this rule it shall thereafter be paid out by the sheriff clerk or otherwise applied for the benefit of the person entitled thereto after such intimation and service and such inquiry as the sheriff may direct.

(4) On payment into court under this rule of money which has become payable to a person under legal disability, the sheriff clerk shall:—

(*a*) issue to the person making the payment a receipt in or as nearly as may be in terms of Form P as set out in the Appendix to this Schedule to which receipt these shall be added a form in terms of Form Q as set out in the Appendix to this Schedule;

(*b*) transmit forthwith to the Secretary of State a copy of the said receipt, having appended thereto the additional particulars specified in Form R as set out in the Appendix to this Schedule and the person making the payment shall forthwith compiete and transmit to the Secretary of State Form Q intimating the payment into court.

(5) Any sum which in terms of this rule is ordered to be invested, shall be invested in any manner in which trustees are authorised to invest by virtue of the Trustee Investments Act 1961 and no such sum shall be invested otherwise than in accordance with this rule.

Miscellaneous

Recall or variation of decrees for aliment or orders for financial provision and of decrees regarding the custody of and access to children

[1] 129.—(1) Subject to paragraph (4), applications to which paragraph (2) applies shall be made by minute lodged in the original process in which decree was pronounced or an order granted.

(2) This rule applies to applications for—

(*a*) the recall or variation of a sheriff court decree for payment of aliment whether pronounced in favour of a spouse, a parent, or any other person or pronounced in respect of a legitimate or illegitimate child; or

(*b*) recall or variation of a periodical allowance;

(*c*) variation of the date or method of payment of a capital sum;
(*d*) variation of the date of transfer of property;
(*e*) the recall or variation of any decree regulating the custody of or access to legitimate or illegitimate children; or
(*f*) the recall or variation of an incidental order as defined in section 14(2) of the Family Law (Scotland) Act 1985 made before, on, or after, the date of the decree of divorce.

(3) The sheriff shall order the minute to be served on any other party and appoint answers to be lodged within a specified time and shall thereafter without closing the record, and after such proof or other procedure as to the sheriff seems necessary, dispose of the application.

(4) In an action of divorce or of separation, a party may, without making application under paragraph (1), crave an order relating to custody, aliment of or access to the children of the marriage, or aliment of one of the parties, notwithstanding that an order to the same or different effect has been made in a previous sheriff court process whether in the same or another sheriff court and the sheriff may make such new order thereanent as the circumstances at the date of the order require, whereupon the previous order shall cease to apply.

NOTE
[1] Substituted by S.I. 1986 No. 1230.

Intimation

[1] 130.—(1)(*a*) In an action where—
(i) adultery is averred by the pursuer or defender;
(ii) the name of the person with whom adultery is alleged to have been committed is disclosed in the action; and
(iii) such person is not a party to the action,
the sheriff shall not allow inquiry until a copy of the initial writ and a form of intimation as nearly as may be in accordance with Form H1 as set out in the Appendix to this Schedule have been intimated to such person or until the sheriff is satisfied that the address of such person is unknown.

(*b*) An order for such intimation may be contained in the original warrant of citation or intimation may be appointed to be made at a later stage.

(*c*) The requirement to intimate under this paragraph shall not apply where the pursuer alleges rape upon, or incest with, a named person by the defender.

(2)(*a*) In an action in which the pursuer alleges sodomy or any homosexual relationship between the defender and a named person, the pursuer shall, immediately after the expiry of the period of notice, enrol a motion for intimation to that person, and the sheriff, at the hearing of the motion, may make such order for intimation or for dispensing with intimation to that person as seems just.

(*b*) Where intimation is ordered under this paragraph, a form of intimation as nearly as may be in accordance with Form H2 as set out in the Appendix to this Schedule and a copy of the initial writ shall be intimated to the named person.

(3) Where the sheriff makes an order dispensing with intimation under paragraph (2), he may also make an order that the name of that person be deleted from the condescendence in the initial writ.

(4) In an action in which the sheriff may make an order in respect of the custody of a child—
(*a*) who is in the care of a local authority; or
(*b*) who is a child of one spouse (including an illegitimate or an adopted child), being a child under the age of 16 years and who is liable to be maintained by a third party,
the pursuer shall intimate a copy of the initial writ and form of intimation as nearly as may be in accordance with Form H3 as set out in the Appendix to this Schedule to the local authority or third party concerned.

(5) In an action relating to a marriage which was entered into under a law which permits polygamy and in which a decree of separation or a decree of divorce is sought, and either party to the marriage in question has any spouse additional to the other party, the warrant of citation shall include an order for intimation of the action to such additional spouse and the pursuer shall intimate a copy of the initial writ and form of intimation as nearly as may be in accordance with Form H4 as set out in the Appendix to this Schedule to such additional spouse.

(6) In an action in which the sheriff may make an order in respect of the custody of a child who is in *de facto* custody of a third party, the pursuer shall intimate a copy of the initial writ and form of intimation as nearly as may be in accordance with Form H5 as set out in the Appendix to this Schedule to the third party concerned.

(7) In an action in which the sheriff—

(*a*) proposes to commit the care of a child to an individual other than one of the parties to the marriage or to a local authority under section 10 of the Matrimonial Proceedings (Children) Act 1958 or section 11(1)(*a*) of the Guardianship Act 1973; the pursuer shall intimate a copy of the initial writ and form of intimation as nearly as may be in accordance with Form H6 as set out in the Appendix to this Schedule to the individual or local authority concerned; or

(*b*) has made an order placing a child under the supervision of a local authority under section 12 of the Matrimonial Proceedings (Children) Act 1958 or section 11(1)(*b*) of the Guardianship Act 1973; the sheriff clerk shall send a form of intimation thereof as nearly as may be in accordance with Form H6A as set out in the Appendix to this Schedule to the local authority concerned.

[2] (8) In an action for custody of a child by a person by virtue of section 47 of the Children Act 1975, that person shall give notice to—

(*a*) the local authority within whose area that person resides within seven days of lodging the action; or

(*b*) in any other case, such local authority as the court may direct under section 49(1) of the Children Act 1975,

by intimating to the local authority a copy of the initial writ together with a notice as nearly as may be in accordance with Form T2 as set out in the Appendix to this Schedule.

(9) In an action in which an order is sought by a pursuer or defender under section 8(1) of the Family Law (Scotland) Act 1985 for the transfer of property subject to security in which the consent of the creditor has not been obtained, the party seeking the order shall intimate a copy of the initial writ and form of intimation as nearly as may be in accordance with Form H7 as set out in the Appendix to this Schedule, to the creditor.

(10) Intimation under paragraph (4) or (5) may be dispensed with if the sheriff is satisfied that the address of the person to whom intimation is to be made is unknown.

[3] (11)(*a*) Intimation under this rule shall be on a period of notice of 21 days unless the sheriff shall consider it appropriate in the circumstances to appoint another period; provided that in no circumstances shall the period of notice be less than 48 hours.

(*b*) All warrants for intimation except those under paragraph (2), or where the period of notice is varied, may be signed by the sheriff clerk in conjunction with a warrant of citation under Rule 8(1).

(12) A person receiving intimation under paragraph (1), (2), (4), (5), (6), (7)(*a*) or (9) may apply within the period of notice by minute craving to be sisted as a party and for leave to lodge defences or answers as the case may be.

(13)(*a*) A minute lodged under paragraph (12) shall be accompanied by the service copy of the intimation.

(*b*) On receiving such a minute, the sheriff clerk shall assign a diet in the cause for a date after the expiry of the period of notice and the sheriff shall, at the diet, regulate the further procedure in the cause.

(*c*) The sheriff may authorise proof by affidavit evidence in respect of any matter not in dispute between the parties.

NOTES

[1] Substituted by S.I. 1986 No. 1230.

[2] As amended by S.I. 1986 No. 1966.

[3] As amended by S.I. 1988 No. 1978.

[THE NEXT PAGE IS D 43]

Notices in action of divorce and separation

[1] 131.—(1) Where the facts set out in section 1(2)(*d*) (two years' non-cohabitation and the defender's consent to decree) of the Divorce (Scotland) Act 1976, are relied on in an action of separation, a notice as nearly as may be in terms of Form S as set out in the Appendix to this Schedule shall be sent with the copy of the initial writ served on the defender, together with a notice as nearly as may be in terms of Form T as set out in the Appendix to this Schedule.

(2) Where the facts set out in section 1(2)(*d*) of the Divorce (Scotland) Act 1976 (two years' non-cohabitation and the defender's consent to decree) are relied upon in an action of divorce, a notice as nearly as may be in terms of Form S1 as set out in the Appendix to this Schedule shall be sent with the copy of the initial writ served on the defender together with a notice as nearly as may be in terms of Form T as set out in the Appendix to this Schedule.

(3) Where the facts set out in section 1(2)(*e*) of the Divorce (Scotland) Act 1976 (five years' non-cohabitation) are relied upon in an action of separation, a notice as nearly as may be in terms of Form S2 as set out in the Appendix to this Schedule shall be sent with the copy of the initial writ served on the defender.

(4) Where the facts set out in section 1(2)(*e*) of the Divorce (Scotland) Act 1976 (five years' non-cohabitation) are relied upon in an action of divorce, a notice as nearly as may be in terms of Form S3 as set out in the Appendix to this Schedule shall be sent with the copy of the initial writ served on the defender.

NOTE

[1] As amended by S.I. 1984 No. 255 and 1986 No. 1230.

Consent to grant of decree

132.—[1] (1) Where in an action of divorce or an action of separation in which the facts set out in section 1(2)(*d*) of the Divorce (Scotland) Act 1976, (two years' non-cohabitation and the defender's consent to decree) are relied on, the defender wishes to indicate to the court that he consents to the grant of a decree, he shall do so by giving notice in writing to that effect to the sheriff clerk at the sheriff court referred to in the initial writ who shall, on receipt of such notice, lodge it in process.

(2) For the purposes of paragraph (1) a notice of consent in the form set out in Form T containing a statement that the defender consents to the grant of a decree shall be treated as notice under that paragraph if it is signed by the defender; and the evidence of one witness shall be sufficient for establishing that the signature on the notice of consent bearing to be that of the defender is in fact that of the defender.

[1] (3) Where in an action of divorce or an action of separation the initial writ contains an averment for the purposes of the said section 1(2)(*d*) that the defender consents to the grant of a decree, he may give notice in writing to the court that he has not consented to a decree being granted or that he withdraws any consent which he has already given.

(4) In a case where the defender gives notice under paragraph (3) the sheriff clerk shall intimate its terms to the pursuer.

(5) On receiving intimation under paragraph (4) of a notice given under paragraph (3) the pursuer shall if none of the other facts mentioned in section 1(2) of the Divorce (Scotland) Act 1976, are averred in the initial writ, lodge a motion for the action to be sisted, and the sheriff may grant that motion.

(6) If such a motion is granted and the sist is not recalled or renewed within a period of six months from the date of the interlocutor granting the sist, the pursuer shall be deemed to have abandoned the action.

NOTE

[1] As amended by S.I. 1984 No. 255 and 1986 No. 1230.

Applications under the Family Law (Scotland) Act 1985

[1] 132A.—(1) Where, in an action in which an alimentary crave is or may be made, a party seeks an order under section 7(2) of the Family Law (Scotland) Act 1985 ("the 1985 Act") (variation or termination of agreement on aliment) he shall do so either in the initial writ or by separate minute in the process.

(2) Where an order referred to in paragraph (1) is sought in any other circumstances, application for the order shall be by way of summary application.

(3) Where a party seeks an order under section 16(1)(*a*) of the 1985 Act (order setting aside or varying term of agreement relating to a periodical allowance), application for the order shall be by way of summary application.

(4) Where a party in an action of divorce seeks an order under section 16(1)(*b*) of the 1985 Act (agreement or financial provision not fair and reasonable), he shall do so either in the initial writ or by separate minute in the process or, if appropriate, by way of counter-claim.

NOTE

[1] Inserted by S.I. 1986 No. 1230.

Applications to declare removal of a child unlawful

[1] 132B. Where, in any proceedings for custody of a child, an interested party wishes to make an application under section 23(2) of the Child Abduction and Custody Act 1985 for declarator that the removal of the child from the United Kingdom was unlawful, he shall make such application in the initial writ or counter-claim, or by separate minute in the process, as the case may be.

NOTE

[1] Inserted by S.I. 1986 No. 1966.

FAMILY LAW ACT 1986

Averments of other proceedings relating to children

[1] 132C. A party to any cause which includes an application for a custody order (as defined by section 1(1)(*b*) of the Family Law Act 1986), shall make averments in his pleadings giving particulars of any other proceedings known to him (whether in Scotland or elsewhere and whether concluded or not) which relate to the child in respect of whom the custody order is sought.

NOTE

[1] Inserted by S.I. 1988 No. 614.

Disclosure of information

[1] 132D. Where the court pronounces an interlocutor ordering a person to disclose information to the court as to a child's whereabouts under section 33(1) of the Family Law Act 1986, it may do so by ordaining that person to appear before it or to lodge an affidavit.

NOTE

[1] Inserted by S.I. 1988 No. 614.

Applications for interdict or interim interdict

[1] 132E. An application by a person mentioned in section 35(4)(*b*) or (*c*) of the Family Law Act 1986 for interdict or interim interdict under section 35(3) of that Act shall be made by minute in the cause in which the application is to be made.

NOTE

[1] Inserted by S.I. 1988 No. 614.

Referral to Family Conciliation Service

[1] 132F. In any cause where the custody of, or access to, a child is in dispute the sheriff may, at any stage in the proceedings where he considers it appropriate to do so, refer the parties to a specified Family Conciliation Service.

NOTE

[1] Added by S.I. 1990 No. 661.

Specification of prior maintenance orders

[1] 132G. In any proceedings in which an order for aliment or periodical allowance is sought, or is sought to be varied or recalled, by any party, the pleadings of that party shall contain an averment specifying whether and, if so, when and by whom, a maintenance order (within the meaning of section 106 of the Debtors (Scotland) Act 1987 (c. 18)) has been granted in favour of or against that party or of any other person in respect of whom the order is sought.

NOTE

[1] Added by S.I. 1990 No. 2238.

APPOINTMENT OF CURATOR *ad litem*

Special application for appointment of a curator ad litem

133.—[1] (1) In an action of divorce or an action of separation where it appears to the sheriff that the defender is suffering from mental disorder within the meaning of the Mental Health (Scotland) Act 1984, the sheriff shall:—

(*a*) appoint a curator *ad litem* to the defender; and

(*b*) in an action of divorce or an action of separation and aliment under section 1(2)(*d*) of the Divorce (Scotland) Act 1976, make an order informing the Mental Welfare Commission for Scotland of the ground of the action and requesting them to provide a report indicating whether in their opinion the defender is capable of deciding whether or not to give consent to the granting of decree.

(2) The pursuer shall within seven days of the making of an order under head (*a*) of paragraph (1) appointing a curator *ad litem* to the defender, send to the curator a certified copy initial writ and defences, if any.

(3) The curator *ad litem* may, within 14 days of the Commission providing the report under head (*b*) of paragraph (1), or in any other case in which no such report is requested, within 21 days of his appointment under head (*a*) of that paragraph lodge:—

(i) a notice of appearance;

(ii) defences to the action;

(iii) a minute adopting defences already lodged; or

(iv) a minute stating that he does not intend to lodge defences;

and may appear in the action at any time to protect the interests of the defender.

NOTE

[1] As amended by S.I. 1984 No. 255 and 1986 No. 1230.

[THE NEXT PAGE IS D 44/1]

MOTIONS - every time case calls in ct. the parties can move for something
- any major step in procedure usually requires a written notice
- motion normally runs in name of solicitors
eg Mason for the P. respectfully craves the ct. to receive + allow the motion of amendment for the P.
- when written motion presented to ct. a copy should be sent to all parties
- opponent should be allowed sufficient time to deal with it. No actual minimum T.L.
- if motion called on a busy roll good idea to continue to end of roll

R57 - introduced procedure for dealing with unopposed motions in chambers without parties being present

R.61 - Sisting of Actions

PREPARATIONS FOR PROOF - when record has been closed, debate IF NECESSARY, then proof
- R65 - probation simply means proof. Renouncing of probation suitable where all facts are agreed + matter can be decided by legal argument
R66 - Limiting mode of proof to eg writ or oath - matter for law of evidence
- should ask for limiting of mode when proof is fixed NOT after
- diff. cts have diff. procedures - some have list before sh. ct. Some sh. ct. will want case adjourned to a diet roll - allows sh. ct. to find out how long case will take + adjust date accordingly
R67 - Reference to Oath

REMIT TO PERSON OF SKILL - different from Judicial Reference
1) JUDICIAL REFERENCE - means of disposing of an action by arbitration within the ct. process. Dispute determined by some other expert - substitution of arbiter for sh.
- In arbitration - arbiter has no power to compel attendance of witness/documents
- Powers which ct. has can be invoked by J.R. - if party fails to attend he can be cited + brought
- Procedure only available by agreement of ALL PARTIES - competent at any stage PRIOR to hearing proof/case on its merits
- Parties normally lodge joint minute agreeing upon name of judicial referee - then up to him to decide case - only return to ct. to get witnesses etc. Decision is put in form of decree of ct.
- Referee decides whole matter + his award cannot be reviewed other than on grounds that arbiters decision can be appealed
- whether or not expenses are to be determined by referee or ct. will depend on the joint minute
- Approp. where sole issues are matters of fact in an area of technical complexity - GO TO 44/4/2

EUROPEAN COURT

European Court

134.—(1) Interpretation:

In this Rule—

(*a*) any expression defined in Schedule 1 to the European Communities Act 1972, has the meaning there given to it;

(*b*) "The European Court" means the Court of Justice of the European Communities;

[1] (*c*) "reference" means a reference to the European Court for a preliminary ruling under Article 177 of the European Economic Community Treaty, Article 150 of the European Atomic Energy Community Treaty or Article 41 of the European Coal and Steel Community Treaty or a ruling on the interpretation of the Conventions, as defined in section 1(1) of the Civil Jurisdiction and Judgments Act 1982, under Article 3 of Schedule 2 to that Act;

(*d*) "appeal" shall include an application for leave to appeal.

(2) A reference may be made by the sheriff *ex proprio motu* or on the motion of any party to the proceedings in the sheriff court.

(3) A reference shall be made in the form of a request for a preliminary ruling of the European Court as nearly as may be in terms of Form U as set out in the Appendix to this Schedule.

(4)(*a*) When the sheriff decides that a reference be made, he shall continue the cause simpliciter for the purpose and within four weeks thereafter draft a reference.

(*b*) On the reference being drafted, the sheriff clerk shall forthwith send a copy to each of the parties.

(*c*) Within four weeks from the date when copies of the draft have been sent to parties, each party may lodge in the hands of the sheriff clerk and send to each of the other parties in the proceedings a note of any adjustments he desires to have made in the draft reference.

(*d*) Within 14 days after the latest date on which any such note shall be lodged the sheriff, after considering any such adjustments, shall make and sign the reference.

(*e*) The sheriff clerk shall forthwith intimate the making of the reference to the parties in the proceedings.

(5) On a reference being made the proceedings shall, unless the sheriff when making such a reference otherwise orders be sisted until the European Court has given a preliminary ruling on the question or questions referred to it, provided that the sheriff shall have power to recall such sist for the purpose of making an interim order which a due regard to the interests of the parties may require.

(6) A copy of the reference certified by the sheriff clerk shall be transmitted by the sheriff clerk to the Registrar of the European Court, but unless the sheriff otherwise directs, such copy shall not be sent to the Registrar so long as an appeal or further appeal against the making of the reference is pending, and for this purpose an appeal or further appeal shall be treated as pending (where one is competent but has not been brought) until the expiration of the time for bringing that appeal.

NOTE

[1] As amended by S.I. 1986 No. 1946.

---

[1] SIMPLIFIED DIVORCE PROCEDURE

NOTE

[1] Added by S.I. 1984 No. 255.

Simplified procedure

135.—(1) The provisions of this rule and of the following rules of this section shall have effect in relation to applications for divorce other than by initial writ which are hereinafter referred to as "simplified divorce applications", and—

(*a*) the following rules of this section shall apply to simplified divorce applications;
(*b*) "the Act of 1976" means the Divorce (Scotland) Act 1976.

(2) This rule applies to an application for divorce by a party to a marriage if, but only if—

(*a*) that party applies for divorce in reliance on the facts set out in section 1(2)(*d*) (two years' non-cohabitation and the defender's consent to decree), or section 1(2)(*e*) (five years' non-cohabitation) of the Act of 1976;
(*b*) in an application for divorce under section 1(2)(*d*) of the Act of 1976, the other party consents to decree of divorce being granted;
(*c*) no other proceedings are pending in any court which could have the effect of bringing the marriage to an end;
(*d*) there are no children of the marriage under the age of 16 years;
(*e*) neither party applies for an order for financial provision on divorce; and
(*f*) neither party suffers from mental disorder within the meaning of the Mental Health (Scotland) Act 1984.

(3) If an application made under this rule ceases to be an application to which this rule applies at any time before it is finally disposed of, that application shall cease to have effect and shall be dismissed.

Form of application

136.—(1) A simplified divorce application relying on the facts set out in section 1(2)(*d*) of the Act of 1976 shall be made in accordance with Form SDA1 as set out in the Appendix to this Schedule.

(2) A simplified divorce application relying on the facts set out in section 1(2)(*e*) of the Act of 1976 shall be made in accordance with Form SDA2 as set out in the Appendix to this Schedule.

(3) An application made under paragraph (1) or (2) shall be signed by the applicant, and the form of consent in accordance with Form SDA3 as set out in the Appendix to this Schedule in an application under paragraph (1) shall be signed by the party giving consent, failing which the application shall not have effect.

Lodging applications

137. The applicant shall deliver the application or cause it to be delivered (by post or by hand) duly completed and signed to the sheriff clerk together with—

(*a*) an extract or certified copy of his marriage certificate; and
(*b*) the fee specified in respect of a simplified divorce application.

Citation

138.—(1) It shall be the duty of the sheriff clerk to cite any person or intimate any document in connection with a simplified divorce application. The form of citation in an application under Rule 136(2) shall be in accordance with Form SDA4 as set out in the Appendix to this Schedule.

[1] (2) The sheriff clerk may arrange for citation or intimation required in paragraph (1) to be made by registered or recorded delivery post or, on payment to the sheriff clerk of the specified additional fee, by sheriff officer or, if appropriate, by any other method provided for by Rule 139.

(3) Any citation of or intimation to a person by sheriff officer in terms of this rule shall be effected either by personal service or by being left in the hands of an inmate of, or employee at, the dwelling place or place of business of that person.

(4) On the face of the envelope used for postal service under this rule there shall be written or printed a notice as nearly as may be in the following form—

"This letter contains a citation to or intimation from the Sheriff Court (*specify court*). If delivery of the letter cannot be made within seven days of the date of posting it is to be returned immediately thereafter to the sheriff clerk (*specify court and address*)."

[1a] (5) Notwithstanding the terms of section 4(2) of the Citation Amendment (Scotland) Act 1882, where service is by post the period of notice shall run from the beginning of the day next following the date of posting.

[2] (6) The following periods of notice shall apply to any citation or intimation under this rule—

(*a*) 21 days when the defender is resident or has a place of business within Europe;
(*b*) 42 days when the addressee is resident or has a place of business outside Europe.

(7) The sheriff may, on cause shown, shorten or extend the period of notice on such conditions as to the form or manner of service as the sheriff may direct, but in any case where the period of notice is reduced at least two days' notice shall be given.

(8) Where a period of notice expires on a Saturday, Sunday, public or court holiday the period of notice shall be deemed to expire on the first following day on which the sheriff clerk's office is open for civil court business.

[2,3] (9) Where, in an application, the facts in section 1(2)(*e*) of the Act of 1976 are relied on and the address of the respondent is unknown—

(*a*) citation of the respondent shall be effected by displaying a copy of the application and notice as nearly as may be in accordance with Form SDA6 as set out in the Appendix to this Schedule on the walls of court and the period of notice shall be 21 days; and

(*b*) intimation shall be made to—

(i) every child of the marriage between the parties and

(ii) one of the next of kin of the respondent who has reached the age of 12 years in the case of a girl and 14 years in the case of a boy.

[3] (10) Intimation to a person referred to in sub-paragraph (9)(*b*)(i) and (ii) shall be effected by intimating a copy of the application and form of intimation as nearly as may be in accordance with Form SDA7 as set out in the Appendix to this Schedule.

[3] (11) Intimation to a person referred to in sub-paragraph (9)(*b*)(i) and (ii) shall not be required under paragraph 10 if the address of that person is unknown to the applicant.

NOTES

[1] As amended by S.I. 1986 No. 1946.

[1a] As substituted by S.I. 1992 No. 249 (effective 4th May 1992).

[2] As amended by S.I. 1988 No. 1978.

[3] As substituted by S.I. 1986 No. 1230.

Citation of or service on persons outwith Scotland

[1] 139.—(1) Subject to the following provisions of this rule, any simplified divorce application may be served outwith Scotland on any person—

(*a*) at a known residence or place of business in England and Wales, Northern Ireland, the Isle of Man, the Channel Islands or any country with which the United Kingdom does not have a convention providing for service of writs in that country—

(i) in accordance with the rules for personal service under the domestic law of the place in which service is to be effected; or

(ii) by posting in Scotland a copy of the application in a registered or recorded delivery letter or the nearest equivalent which the available postal services permit addressed to the person at his residence or place of business;

(*b*) in a country which is a party to the Hague Convention on the Service Abroad of Judicial and Extra-Judicial Documents in Civil or Commercial Matters dated 15th November 1965—

(i) by a method prescribed by the internal law of the country where service is to be effected for the service of documents in domestic actions upon persons who are within its territory;

(ii) by or through a central authority in the country where service is to be effected at the request of the Foreign Office;

(iii) by or through a British Consular authority at the request of the Foreign Office;

(iv) where the law of the country in which the person resides permits, by posting in Scotland a copy of the application in a registered or recorded delivery letter or the nearest equivalent which the available postal services permit addressed to the person at his residence; or

(v) where the law of the country in which the person resides permits, service by an *huissier*, other judicial officer or competent official of the country where service is to be made;

(*c*) in a country with which the United Kingdom has a convention on the service of writs in that country other than the convention in sub-paragraph (*b*), by one of the methods approved in the relevant convention.

(2) An application which requires to be posted in Scotland for the purposes of this rule shall be posted by the sheriff clerk and the form for citation in Rule 138 shall apply to a postal citation under this rule as they apply to a citation under that rule.

(3) On the face of the envelope used for postal service under this rule there shall be written

or printed a notice in the same or similar terms as that required in the case of ordinary service under Rule 138.

(4) Where service is effected by a method specified in paragraph (1)(*b*)(ii) or (iii), the sheriff clerk shall—

(*a*) send a copy of the application with citation attached with a request for service to be effected by delivery to the defender or his residence to the Secretary of State for Foreign and Commonwealth Affairs; and

(*b*) lodge in process a certificate of execution of service signed by the authority which has effected service.

(5) Where service is effected by the method specified in paragraph (1)(*b*)(v), the sheriff clerk shall—

(*a*) send to the official in the country in which service is to be effected a copy of the application with citation attached with a request for service to be effected by delivery to the defender or his residence; and

(*b*) lodge in process a certificate of execution of service by the official who has effected service.

(6) Every writ or document and every citation and notice on the face of the envelope under paragraph (3) shall be accompanied by a translation in an official language of the country in which service is to be executed unless English is an official language of that country.

(7) A translation under paragraph (6) shall be certified as a correct translation by the person making it and the certificate shall contain the full name, address and qualifications of the translator and be lodged along with the execution of citation or certificate of execution.

NOTE

[1] Substituted by S.I. 1986 No. 1946.

Opposition to applications

[1] 140.—(1) Any person who has been cited or to whom intimation has been made in connection with a simplified divorce application may challenge the jurisdiction of the court or oppose the granting of decree of divorce by letter to the court giving reasons for his opposition to the application.

(2) If opposition to a simplified divorce application is made in terms of paragraph (1) the sheriff shall dismiss the application unless he is satisfied that the reasons given for the opposition are frivolous.

(3) The sheriff clerk shall intimate the decision of the sheriff in respect of any opposition to the application to all parties concerned with the application.

(4) The lodging of a letter under paragraph (1) shall not imply acceptance of the jurisdiction of the court.

NOTE

[1] As amended by S.I. 1986 No. 1946.

Decree

141.—[1] (1) The sheriff may grant decree in terms of the simplified divorce application on the expiry of the period of notice if such application has been properly served: provided that, when the application has been served in a country to which the Hague Convention on the Service Abroad of Judicial and Extra-Judicial Documents in Civil or Commercial Matters dated 15th November 1965 applies, decree shall not be granted until it is established to the satisfaction of the sheriff that the requirements of Article 15 of that Convention have been complied with.

(2) The sheriff clerk shall, not sooner than 14 days after the granting of decree in terms of paragraph (1), issue to each party to the application an extract of the decree of divorce as nearly as may be in accordance with Form SDA5 as set out in the Appendix to this Schedule.

NOTE

[1] As amended by S.I. 1986 No. 1946.

Appeal

[1] 142.—A respondent may, within 14 days of the date of an interlocutor granting decree of divorce, appeal against that interlocutor by addressing a letter to the court giving reasons for his appeal.

NOTE

[1] As amended by S.I. 1986 No. 1230.

Subsequent applications

143.—(1) After the granting of decree of divorce, a party to a simplified divorce application may, in the event of a material change in the circumstances of one or other or both of the parties, make a subsequent application to the sheriff in respect of any matter.

(2) A subsequent application shall be made by minute in the original process of the simplified divorce application and such minute shall specify that there has been a material change in the circumstances of one or other or both of the parties since the granting of decree of divorce and shall specify the nature of such change of circumstances.

[1] DAMAGES

NOTE

[1] Added by S.I. 1984 No. 921. Rules 144–146 apply to actions raised on or after 1st September 1984; Rules 147–149 apply to all actions whether raised before or after that date.

DAMAGES (SCOTLAND) ACT 1976

Action for damages under the Damages (Scotland) Act 1976

144.—(1) This Rule and Rules 145 and 146 apply to any action in which, following the death of any person from personal injuries, damages are claimed either by the executor of the deceased in respect of the relevant injuries, or by any relative of the deceased in respect of the death of the deceased.

(2) The term "relative" shall have the meaning assigned to it by section 10 of and Schedule 1 to the Damages (Scotland) Act 1976.

Intimation to persons having title to sue under Schedule 1 to the Damages (Scotland) Act 1976

145.—(1) In an action to which Rule 144 applies the pursuer shall specify in the initial writ—

(*a*) that he is the only person with a title to sue the defender in respect of the injuries or death, or

(*b*) that there are other persons having a title to sue the defender in respect of the injuries or death and shall name and design such persons, or

(*c*) that there are other persons having a title to sue the defender but whose names or whereabouts are to the pursuer unknown and cannot reasonably be ascertained.

(2) The sheriff shall grant warrant for intimation of the action to any person named and designed in the initial writ in terms of sub-paragraph (*b*) of paragraph (1) hereof and the pursuer shall intimate the action to every such person as nearly as may be in accordance with Form CC as set out in the Appendix to this Schedule.

(3) The sheriff may, on the motion of a party to the action, or *ex proprio motu* order such advertisement of the action or intimation of it to be made to such persons as he deems appropriate.

Applications to sist as additional pursuer

146.—(1) A person to whom intimation has been made in accordance with Rule 145 may apply to the sheriff to be sisted as an additional pursuer in the action and such person shall give notice of his application to all parties to the action.

(2) Where a person to whom intimation has been made in accordance with Rule 145 does not apply to be sisted as an additional pursuer in the existing action but subsequently raises a further action against the same defender in respect of the same injuries or death, that person shall not, except on cause shown, be awarded the expenses of the subsequent action.

INTERIM PAYMENT OF DAMAGES

Applications for interim payment of damages

[1] 147.—(1) In any action of damages for personal injuries, the pursuer may at any time after the lodging of defences apply to the sheriff for an order that the defender or, where there are two or more defenders, any one or more of the defenders, make an interim payment of damages.

(2) An application in terms of paragraph (1) shall be made by motion which shall be served on the defender or defenders on a period of notice of 21 days.

(3) If after hearing the parties on the motion the sheriff is satisfied either—

(*a*) that the defender or defenders have admitted liability in the pursuer's action, or

(*b*) that, if the action proceeded to proof, the pursuer would succeed in the action on the question of liability without any substantial finding of contributory negligence on his part or on the part of any person in respect of whose injury or death the pursuer's claim arises, and would obtain decree for damages against the defender or, where there are two or more defenders, against any one or more of them,

the sheriff may, if he thinks fit, order the defender or, where there are two or more defenders, any one or more of them, to make an interim payment to the pursuer of such amount, not exceeding such reasonable proportion of the damages which in the opinion of the sheriff is likely to be recovered by the pursuer, as he deems appropriate.

(2) REMIT TO A PERSON OF SKILL – R.69 – involves part of decision making process being taken from ct. – only available for matters of fact
Person of skill does not decide the case, merely makes finding of fact [unlike J.R. where referee decides case]
– Approp. where – contract is clear + dispute about whether goods comply
– dispute over contract

R.70 – evidence in retentis
R.71 – evidence on commission

[THE NEXT PAGE IS D 44/5]

R.72 – affadavit evidence
R.72A – detailed procedures which apply where party wishes to submit written statements in evidence. Approp. where non-contentious matters
– necessary by way of motion to ask sh. to allow evidence

GO TO D 44/7

(4) A payment ordered to be made in terms of paragraph (3) may be ordered to be made in a lump sum or otherwise as the sheriff may deem appropriate.

(5) The sheriff shall not make an order under this rule unless he is satisfied that the defender concerned is either—

(*a*) a person who is insured in respect of the pursuer's claim, or
(*b*) a public authority, or
(*c*) a person whose means and resources are such as to enable him to make an interim payment.

(6) Notwithstanding the making or refusal of an order for interim payment, a second or subsequent application may be made upon cause shown by reason of a change of circumstances.

(7) Subject to the terms of Rule 128 or otherwise as the sheriff in his discretion may determine, any interim payment shall be made to the pursuer.

(8) The provisions of this rule shall apply *mutatis mutandis* to a counterclaim for damages for personal injury made by a defender.

(9) For the purposes of this rule the term "personal injuries" shall include any disease or any impairment of a person's physical or mental condition.

NOTE

[1] As amended by S.I. 1988 No. 1978.

Final orders where interim payment made

148. Where a defender has made an interim payment in terms of Rule 147 the sheriff may, when granting final decree, make such order with respect to the interim payment as he deems necessary to give effect to the defender's final liability to the pursuer, and in particular may order—

(*a*) that the pursuer repay to the defender any sum by which the interim payment exceeds the amount which that defender is liable to pay to the pursuer, or
(*b*) that any other defender or third party make payment of any part of the interim payment which the defender who made it is entitled to recover from that other defender or third party by way of contribution or indemnity or in respect of any remedy or relief relating to or connected with the pursuer's claim.

PROVISIONAL DAMAGES

Applications for further awards of damages

149. An application for a further award of damages in terms of section 12 of the Administration of Justice Act 1982 (award of provisional damages for personal injuries) shall be made by minute in the original process.

APPENDIX

FORMS

FORM A

Rule 3

Initial writ

SHERIFFDOM OF AT

A.B. [*design him; if he sues in any special capacity set that forth*], Pursuer,

Against

C.D. [*design him; if sued in any special capacity set that forth*], Defender.

The Pursuer craves the Court [*here set forth the specific decree, warrant or order asked*].

Condescendence,

[*State in numbered paragraphs the facts which form the ground of action*].

Pleas-in-Law

[*State in numbered sentences*]

[*To be signed*] A.B., Pursuer;

or

X.Y. [*add designation and business address*]
Solicitor for Pursuer.

[1] FORM B

Rule 5(1)

Warrant of citation

[*Place and date*] Grants warrant to cite the defender by serving a copy of the writ and warrant upon a period of notice of days, and appoints him, if he intends to defend, to lodge a

notice of intention to defend with the sheriff clerk at
within the said period of notice after such service (and grants warrant to arrest on the dependence). (Meantime grants interim interdict, or warrant to arrest on the dependence, or sequestrates and grants warrant to inventory; or otherwise, as the case may be and to arrest to found jurisdiction.)

NOTE
[1] As amended by S.I. 1984 No. 255.

---

[1] FORM B1 Rule 5(2)

Warrant of citation

Consistorial action
19

Grants warrant to cite the defender by serving a copy of the writ and warrant upon a period of notice of days, and appoints him if he intends to defend, or to dispute any claim made or make any claim to lodge the appropriate document with the Sheriff Clerk at (Meantime grants interim interdict, or warrant to arrest on the dependence as the case may be.)

NOTE
[1] Inserted by S.I. 1984 No. 255.

---

[1] FORM B2 Rule 5(3)

Warrant of citation summary application

[*Place and date*] Grants warrant to cite the defender [*or* respondent] by serving a copy of the writ and warrant upon a period of notice of days, and appoints him to answer within the Sheriff Court House at [in Room No, *or* in Chambers, *or as the case may be*], on the day of at o'clock noon. [*Where necessary add* (meantime sequestrates and grants warrant to inventory and secure); *or* (grants warrant to arrest on the dependence); *or otherwise as the case may be*].

NOTE
[1] As amended by S.I. 1992 No. 249 (effective 4th May 1992).

---

[1] FORM B3 Rule 5(4)

Warrant of citation—summary application where time to pay direction may be applied for

(*Place and date*) Grants warrant to cite the defender by serving
a copy of the writ and warrant, together with Form B6 as set out in the Appendix to the First Schedule to the Sheriff Courts (Scotland) Act 1907, upon a period of notice of days, and appoints him to answer within the Sheriff Court House at (in Room No. , *or* in Chambers, *or as the case may be*), on the day of at o'clock noon; Appoints the defender if he admits the claim and intends to apply for a time to pay direction (and where appropriate for recall or restriction of an arrestment) either to appear at that diet and make such application or to lodge the appropriate part of Form B6 duly completed with the sheriff clerk at (*place*) at least seven days before the diet; [*where appropriate add* meantime sequestrates and grants warrant to inventory and secure *or* grants warrant to arrest on the dependence *or otherwise as the case may be*].

NOTE
[1] Inserted by S.I. 1988 No. 1978.

---

[1] FORM B4 Rule 5(5)

Warrant of citation where time to pay direction may be applied for

(*Place and date*) Grants warrant to cite the defender by serving a copy of the writ and warrant, together with Form B5 as set out in the Appendix to the First Schedule to the Sheriff Courts (Scotland) Act 1907, upon a period of notice of days and appoints him (a) if he intends to defend to lodge a notice of intention to defend or (b) if he does not intend to defend but admits the claim and intends to apply for a time to pay direction (and where appropriate for recall or restriction of an arrestment) to lodge the appropriate part of Form B5 duly completed, with the sheriff clerk at within the period of notice after such service [and grants warrant to arrest on the dependence]. [*Where appropriate add* meantime grants interim interdict *or* warrant to arrest on the dependence *or* sequestrates and grants warrant to inventory *or otherwise, as the case may be* [and to arrest to found jurisdiction.]]

NOTE

[1] Inserted by S.I. 1988 No. 1978.

---

[1] FORM B5 Rule 5(6)

Notice to be served on defender in ordinary action where time to pay direction may be applied for

ACTION RAISED BY

....	....
....	....
....	....
.... PURSUER	.... DEFENDER

AT ....SHERIFF COURT
Including Address

COURT REF. NUMBER		DATE OF EXPIRY OF PERIOD OF NOTICE
	....	
	....	
.........../.........	....	....

THIS SECTION MUST BE COMPLETED BY PURSUER BEFORE SERVICE

Under the Debtors (Scotland) Act 1987

The Act gives you a right to apply to the court for a "time to pay direction" which is an order saying that you can pay any sum of money you are ordered to pay to the pursuer (which may include interest and court expenses) either by way of instalments or deferred lump sum. A deferred lump means that you must pay all the amount at one time within a specified period set by the court.

In addition when making a "time to pay direction" the court may recall or restrict an arrestment made on your property by the pursuer in connection with the action or debt (for example your bank account may have been frozen).

HOW TO APPLY FOR A TIME TO PAY DIRECTION WHEN CLAIM ADMITTED AND YOU DO NOT WANT TO DEFEND THE ACTION

1. Attached to this Notice at pages 3 and 4 is an application for a "time to pay direction" and recall or restriction of an arrestment, if appropriate. If you want to make an application

you should lodge the completed application with the court **before** the expiry of the period of notice—the date of which is given above. No court fee is payable when lodging the application.

2. Before completing the application please read carefully the notes overleaf on page 2. In the event of difficulty you may contact the court's Civil Department at the address above or any Sheriff Clerk's Office, Citizens Advice Bureau or a solicitor.

Note

Where this form is being served on a defender along with Form HH (notice to additional defender) the reference to "date of expiry of period of notice" should be amended to "date for lodging of defences or an application for a time to pay direction" and the references to "before the expiry of the period of notice" should be amended to "on or before the date for lodging of defences or an application for a time to pay direction".

HOW TO COMPLETE THE APPLICATION

PLEASE WRITE IN INK USING BLOCK CAPITALS

PART A of the application will have been completed in advance by the pursuer and gives details of the pursuer **and you as the defender.**

PART B—If you wish to apply to pay by instalments enter the amount and tick the appropriate box at B3(1). If you wish to apply to pay the full sum due in one deferred payment enter the period of deferment you propose at B3(2).

PART C—You should give full details of your financial position in the appropriate boxes.

PART D—If you wish the court when making the "time to pay direction" to recall or restrict an arrestment made in connection with the action then enter the appropriate details about what has been arrested and the place and date of the arrestment at 5, and attach schedule of arrestment or copy.

Sign the application where indicated and detach pages 3 and 4. Retain the copy initial writ and pages 1 and 2 of this form as you may need them at a later state. You should ensure that your application arrives at the court before the expiry of the period of notice.

WHAT WILL HAPPEN NEXT

If the pursuer objects to your application a hearing will be fixed and the court will advise you in writing of the date and time.

If the pursuer does not object to your application, then a copy of the court order for payment (called an extract decree) will be served on you by the pursuer's solicitor advising when payment should commence or be made.

COURT ....(Ref. No. ....) ......19....

APPLICATION FOR A TIME TO PAY DIRECTION

Under the Debtors (Scotland) Act 1987

PART A* **By** ....
....
....
.... **DEFENDER**

*(This section must be completed by pursuer before service)

IN AN ACTION RAISED BY
....
....
....
.... **PURSUER**

PART B

1. The applicant is a defender in the action brought by the above named pursuer.
2. The defender admits the claim and applies to the court for a "time to pay direction".
3. The defender applies (1) To pay by instalments of £..........

(Tick one box only) EACH.... WEEK ☐ FORTNIGHT ☐ MONTH ☐

OR

(2) To pay the sum ordered in one payment within .... WEEKS/MONTHS

PART C

4. The Defender's financial position is:—
(Tick one box only)

	Weekly	Fortnightly	Monthly		Weekly	Fortnightly	Monthly
My outgoings are:	☐	☐	☐	My income is:	☐	☐	☐

Rent/Mortgage	£	Wages/Pensions	£
Heating	£	Social Security	£
Food	£	Other	£
HP	£		
Other	£		
Total	£	Total	£

Dependants: Children—how many ☐ Dependent relatives—how many ☐

Here list all capital (if any), e.g. value of house; amount in bank/building society account, shares or other investments:

Here list any outstanding debts:

PART D

5. The defender seeks to recall or restrict an arrestment of which the details are as follows (please state, and attach schedule of arrestment or copy):—

6. This application is made under sections 1(1) and 2(3) of the Debtors (Scotland) Act 1987. Therefore the defender asks the court

*Delete what does not apply

*a. to make a "time to pay direction".
*b. to recall the above arrestment.
*c. to restrict the above arrestment (in which case state restriction wanted):—

(*signed*)
Defender

Date:—

NOTE
[1] Inserted by S.I. 1988 No. 1978.

---

[1] FORM B6 Rule 5(6)

Notice to be served on defender in summary application where time to pay direction may be applied for

IN SUMMARY APPLICATION BY

....	....
....	....
....	....
.... PURSUER	.... DEFENDER

AT ....SHERIFF COURT
Including Address

COURT REF. NUMBER		DATE OF HEARING
	....	
	....	....
.........../.........	....	

THIS SECTION MUST BE COMPLETED BY PURSUER BEFORE SERVICE

Under the Debtors (Scotland) Act 1987

The Act gives you a right to apply to the court for a "time to pay direction" which is an order saying that you can pay any sum of money you are ordered to pay to the pursuer (which may include interest and court expenses) either by way of instalments **or** deferred lump sum. A deferred lump sum means that you must pay all the amount at one time within a specified period set by the court.

In addition when making a "time to pay direction" the court may recall or restrict an arrestment made on your property by the pursuer in connection with the action or debt (for example your bank account may have been frozen).

HOW TO APPLY FOR A TIME TO PAY DIRECTION WHEN CLAIM ADMITTED AND YOU DO NOT WANT TO DEFEND THE ACTION

1. You may apply for a "time to pay direction" (and where appropriate for recall or restriction of an arrestment) by either

(*a*) appearing at the hearing—the date of which is given above and asking the court to make a "time to pay direction" (and where appropriate to recall or restrict an arrestment). If you prefer you may ask a solicitor or someone else to appear for you.

OR

(*b*) Completing and returning to the court at least seven days before the hearing, the application form at pages 3 and 4 of this notice. The address of the court is given above. No court fee is payable when lodging the application.

2. Before completing the application please read carefully the notes overleaf on page 2. In the event of difficulty you may contact the court's Civil Department at the address above or any Sheriff Clerk's Office, Citizens Advice Bureau or a Solicitor.

HOW TO COMPLETE THE APPLICATION

PLEASE WRITE IN INK USING BLOCK CAPITALS

PART A of the application will have been completed in advance by the pursuer and gives details of the pursuer **and you** as the **defender**.

PART B—If you wish to apply to pay by instalments enter the amount and tick the appropriate box at B3(1). If you wish to apply to pay the full sum due in one deferred payment enter the period of deferment you propose at B3(2).

PART C—You should give full details of your financial position in the appropriate boxes.

PART D—If you wish the court when making the "time to pay direction" to recall or restrict an arrestment made in connection with the action then enter the appropriate details about what has been arrested and the place and date of the arrestment at Part D5, and attach schedule of arrestment or copy.

Sign the application where indicated and detach pages 3 and 4. Retain the copy initial writ and pages 1 and 2 of this form as you may need them at a later stage. You should ensure that your application arrives at the court at least seven days before the hearing.

WHAT WILL HAPPEN NEXT

If the court makes a "time to pay direction" a copy of the court order for payment (called an extract decree) will be served on you by the pursuer's solicitor advising when payment should commence or be made.

If the court does not make a "time to pay direction" and makes an order for payment against you an order to pay (called a charge) may be served on you.

COURT ....(Ref. No. ....) ......19....

APPLICATION FOR A TIME TO PAY DIRECTION

Under the Debtors (Scotland) Act 1987

PART A*

By ....
....
....
.... **DEFENDER**

*(This section must be completed by pursuer before service)

IN A SUMMARY APPLICATION BY
....
....
....
.... **PURSUER**

PART B

1. The applicant is a defender in the action brought by the above named pursuer.
2. The defender admits the claim and applies to the court for a "time to pay direction".
3. The defender applies (1) to pay by instalments of £.........

(Tick one box only) EACH.... WEEK ☐ FORTNIGHT ☐ MONTH ☐

OR

(2) To pay the sum ordered in one payment within ....
WEEKS/MONTHS

PART C

4. The defender's financial position is:—
(Tick one box only)

	Weekly	Fortnightly	Monthly		Weekly	Fortnightly	Monthly
My outgoings are:	☐	☐	☐	My income is:	☐	☐	☐
Rent/Mortgage	£			Wages/Pensions	£		
Heating	£			Social Security	£		
Food	£			Other	£		
HP	£						
Other	£						
Total	£			Total	£		

Dependants: Children—how many ☐ Dependent relatives—how many ☐

Here list all capital (if any), e.g. value of house; amount in bank/building society account; shares or other investments:

Here list any outstanding debts:

PART D

5. The defender seeks to recall or restrict an arrestment of which the details are as follows (please state, and attach schedule of arrestment or copy):—

6. This application is made under sections 1(1) and 2(3) of the Debtors (Scotland) Act 1987.
Therefore the defender asks the court

*Delete what does not apply

*a. to make a "time to pay direction".
*b. to recall the above arrestment.
*c. to restrict the above arrestment (in which case state restriction wanted):—

(*signed*)
Defender

Date:—

NOTE
[1] Inserted by S.I. 1988 No. 1978.

FORM C

Rule 9

Citation

A.B., Pursuer against C.D., Defender Court Ref No

[*Place and date*] C.D., defender. You are hereby served with this copy writ and warrant, and required to answer thereto, conform to the said warrant.

IF YOU WISH TO DEFEND THIS ACTION you must lodge a notice of intention to defend with the Sheriff Clerk at within days after this date and at the same time present this copy initial writ.

IF YOU DO NOTHING IN ANSWER TO THIS DOCUMENT the court may regard you as admitting the claim made against you and the pursuer may obtain decree against you in your absence.

(*To be signed*)

P.Q., Sheriff Officer,
or
X.Y. [*add designation and business address*]
Solicitor for Pursuer

[1] FORM CC

Rule 145(2)

Intimation to persons having a title to sue

[*Place, date*]
Take notice that an action has been raised in Sheriff Court [*address*] by [*name and design*] against [*name and design*]. It is believed that you may have a title or interest to sue the said [*name*] in an action based upon [(the injuries from which the late [*name and design*] died) or (the death of the late [*name and design*]]. You may therefore be entitled to enter this action as an additional pursuer. If you wish to do so, you may apply to the Sheriff at the above-mentioned Sheriff Court to be sisted as an additional pursuer within 21 days after the expiry of days from the date of service hereof. In the event of your making such an application you are required to serve notice of it on all of the parties to the action.
The date of service hereof is reckoned as commencing on the day of posting.

Solicitor for Pursuer

NOTE

[1] Inserted by S.I. 1984 No. 921 and as amended by S.I. 1988 No. 1978.

[1] FORM C1

Rule 9

Consistorial Action

Court Ref No.

A.B., Pursuer against C.D., Defender

[*Place and date*] You are hereby served with this writ and warrant, and required to answer thereto conform to the said warrant.
IF YOU WISH TO DEFEND THIS ACTION or IF YOU WISH TO MAKE ANY CLAIM you should consult a solicitor with a view to lodging the appropriate document with the Sheriff Clerk at within 21 days after this date and at the same time present this copy initial writ.

IF YOU DO NOTHING IN ANSWER TO THIS DOCUMENT the court may regard you as admitting the claim made against you and the pursuer may obtain decree against you in your absence.

(*To be signed*)

E.F., Sheriff Officer,
or
G.H. [*add designation and business address*]
Solicitor for Pursuer

NOTE
[1] Inserted by S.I. 1984 No. 255 and as amended by S.I. 1988 No. 1978.

---

[1] FORM C2 Rule 9(2A)

Citation where time to pay direction may be applied for

[A.B.], Pursuer against [C.D.], Defender Court Ref No

(*Place and date*) [C.D.], defender. You are hereby served with this copy writ and warrant, together with Form B5 and required to answer thereto, conform to the warrant. Form B5 is served on you because it is considered that you may be entitled to apply for a "time to pay direction" (and for the recall or restriction of an arrestment used on the dependence of the action or in security of the debt referred to in the copy writ).

IF YOU WISH TO DEFEND THIS ACTION you must lodge a notice of intention to defend with the sheriff clerk at within the period of notice being days after this date and at the same time present this copy initial writ.

IF YOU ADMIT THE CLAIM AND WISH TO AVOID A COURT ORDER AGAINST YOU, the whole sum claimed including interest and any expenses due should be paid to the pursuer or his solicitor in good time before the expiry of the period of notice.

IF YOU ADMIT THE CLAIM AND WISH TO APPLY FOR A TIME TO PAY DIRECTION, you must complete the enclosed Form B5 and return it to the sheriff clerk within the period of notice.

IF YOU DO NOTHING IN ANSWER TO THIS DOCUMENT the court may regard you as admitting the claim made against you and the pursuer may obtain decree against you in your absence.

(*Signed*)
[P.Q.], Sheriff Officer,

[*or* [X.Y.] (*add designation and business address*)

Solicitor for Pursuer]

Date:—

NOTE
[1] Inserted by S.I. 1988 No. 1978.

---

[1] FORM C3 Rule 9(2B)

Citation where time to pay direction may be applied for in Summary Application

[A.B.], Applicant against [C.D.], Respondent Court Ref. No.

[*Place and date*] [C.D.], respondent. You are hereby served with this copy writ and warrant, together with Form B6 and required to reply conform to the warrant. Form B6 is served on you because it is considered that you may be entitled to apply for a "time to pay direction" (and for the recall or restriction of an arrestment used on the dependence of the application or in security of the debt referred to in the copy writ).

(*Signed*)
[P.Q.], Sheriff Officer,

[*or* [X.Y.] (*add designation and business address*)
Solicitor for Applicant]

NOTE
[1] Inserted by S.I. 1992 No. 249 (effective 4th May 1992).

[1] FORM C4 Rule 9(2B)

Citation for summary application

[A.B.], Applicant against [C.D.], Respondent Court Ref. No.

[*Place and date*] [C.D.] respondent. You are hereby served with this copy writ and warrant, and required to answer thereto, conform to the warrant.

(*Signed*)
[P.Q.], Sheriff Officer,

[*or* [X.Y.] (*add designation and business address*)
Solicitor for Applicant]

NOTE
[1] Inserted by S.I. 1992 No. 249 (effective 4th May 1992).

[1] FORM D Rule 9(2)

Certificate of citation

[*Place and date*] I, hereby certify that upon the day of I duly cited C.D., the defender, to answer to the foregoing writ. This I did by [*set forth mode of service, if by officer and not by post, add* in presence of L.M. (*design him*), witness hereto with me subscribing (*in actions in which a time to pay direction may be applied for set forth any form sent in accordance with Rule 5 and in actions of divorce and separation also set forth any forms sent in accordance with Rule 131*)].

[*To be signed*]

P.Q., Sheriff Officer,
L.M., Witness;
or
X.Y. [*add designation and business address*]
Solicitor for Pursuer

NOTE
[1] As amended by S.I. 1986 No. 1230 and 1988 No. 1978.

---

[1] FORM E Rule 11

Advertisement
Notice to [C.D.]

Court Ref. No.

An action has been raised in Sheriff Court by A.B. pursuer calling as a defender C.D. whose last known address was

If the said C.D. wishes to defend the action or to make any claim therein he/she should immediately contact the Sheriff Clerk [*address*] from whom he/she may obtain the service copy initial writ.

X.Y. [*add designation and business address*]
Solicitor for Pursuer
or
P.Q., Sheriff Officer

NOTE
[1] As amended by S.I. 1986 No. 1230 and 1992 No. 249 (effective 4th May 1992).

---

[1] FORM E1 Rule 11(1)(*b*)

Display on the walls of court

Court Ref. No.

An action has been raised in Sheriff Court by A.B. pursuer calling as a defender C.D. whose last known address was

If C.D. wishes to defend the action or to make any claim therein he/she should immediately contact the Sheriff Clerk [*address*] from whom he/she may obtain the service copy initial writ.

Tel No:—

(*Signed*) Sheriff Clerk
Date:—(*insert date*)

NOTE
[1] Inserted by S.I. 1986 No. 1230.

FORM F Rule 33

Notice of intention to defend

[*Place and date*]—C.D. [*design him*] Defender, intends to defend the action against him (and others) at the instance of A.B. [*design him*].

C.D. Defender
or
X.Y. [*add address*]
Defender's Solicitor

FORM G Rule 50(4)

Third party notice

Third Party Notice in the Cause between
A.B., Pursuer
and,
C.D., Defender
E.F., Third Party
to E.F.

This Notice is served upon you by the above named C.D. by virtue of an order granted by Sheriff in the action in which the above-named A.B. is the pursuer and C.D. the defender. In the action the pursuer claims against defender £ in respect of [*or otherwise as the case may be*] as more fully appears in the copy initial writ and defences [*or copy record in the action*] enclosed herewith.

The defender denies any liability but maintains that if there is any liability he shares that liability with you, as more fully appears from his defences lodged in the above action and enclosed herewith.

[THE NEXT PAGE IS D 44/7]

CITATION OF WITNESSES - 74-77 - to give evidence at a proof

- R.74 - basic auth. is interlocutor of ct. allowing proof or trial
  - time limits for citing witnesses - if not cited 7 days before proof then witness may not be subject to penalties if he fails to attend
  - witness entitled to have travelling expenses paid if he asks for them
  - In practice - best to give as much notice to the witness as possible
  - method of service same as for IW

R.75 - Form of Citation

R.76 - witnesses who do not turn up or refuse to attend

R.77 - Warrant for arrest

- HAVERS - people in possession of documents

- PRODUCTIONS - things or documents which party wishes to rely upon to prove his case

R.79 - ① - inventory of productions - merely a list of productions with numbers
  - good practice if when lodge an inventory you lodge a separate inventory + copies for sh. which he may refer to at proof

Notice ② Party always ought to send to opponent photocopies of all productions to date - be selective in photocopying - only copy the relevant parts

③ no other production shall be put in evidence if not lodged before T.L. If both sides consent then late productions may be allowed. Sh. might penalise in expenses a party who puts in late productions

- Production might not be lodged because you do not have them
  - necessary to seek commission + diligence to recover these documents

- R.78 - commission + diligence is at discretion of sh. Various procedural requirements follow :- ct. will appoint a Commissioner who will have auth. of ct. to recover documents
  - may cite havers to be questioned on oath + to bring with him any documents which fall within the specification
  - useful procedure where you think opponent has documents which he wants to delay production of.

- R.81 - OPTIONAL PROCEDURE - basically formal procedure used as a first attempt
  - FORM K is sent to haver of documents together with ct. order granting commission + diligence + list of specification

GO TO D44/9

or
[*otherwise as the case may be*]

And take notice that if you wish to resist either the claim of the pursuer against the defender, or the claim of the defender against you, you must lodge answers in the action not later than being the date appointed by the Court for the regulation of further procedure and must appear or be represented in court on that date, otherwise the Court may pronounce such decree against you as it thinks fit.

Dated this day of 19
[*Signed*] Solicitor for the Defender.

FORM H

Rule 64(1)

Notice to additional defender

To [*designation and address*] Court Ref No

Take notice that in the action in which A.B. is the Pursuer and C.D. is the Defender, in copies of the [*initial writ and defences*] [*closed record*] which are herewith enclosed, your name has, by order of the Court dated , been added/substituted as a Defender to the said action; and the action, originally directed against the said C.D. is directed against you.

IF YOU WISH TO DEFEND THIS ACTION you must lodge defences thereto with the Sheriff Clerk at within days from the date of service hereof.

IF YOU DO NOTHING IN ANSWER TO THIS DOCUMENT the Court may regard you as admitting the claim made against you and the Pursuer may proceed and obtain decree against you in your absence.

[*Date*] [*Signed*] P.Q., Sheriff Officer;
or
X.Y. [*add designation and business address*]
Solicitor for Pursuer [*or Defender*]

[1] FORM HH

Rule 64(1)(*c*)

Notice to additional defender where a time to pay direction may be applied for

To (*designation and address*) Court Ref. No.

Take notice that in the action in which [AB] is the pursuer and [CD] is the Defender, your name has, by order of the court dated been added/substituted as a defender to the action; and the action, originally directed against [CD] is directed against you. Copies of the initial writ and defences [*or* closed record] are [*or* is] enclosed. You are also served with Form B5.

Form B5 is served on you because it is considered that you may be entitled to apply for time to pay direction (and for the recall or restriction of an arrestment).

IF YOU WISH TO DEFEND THIS ACTION you must lodge defences thereto with the sheriff clerk at within days from the date of service hereof.

IF YOU ADMIT THE CLAIM AND WISH TO APPLY FOR A TIME TO PAY DIRECTION you must complete the enclosed Form B5 and return it to the sheriff clerk at within days from the date of service hereof.

IF YOU DO NOTHING IN ANSWER TO THIS DOCUMENT the court may regard you as admitting the claim made against you and the pursuer may proceed and obtain decree against you in your absence.

(*Signed*)
[P.Q.], Sheriff Officer,

[*or* [X.Y.] (*add designation and business address*)

[Solicitor for Pursuer] [*or* Defender]

Date:—

NOTE
[1] Inserted by S.I. 1988 No. 1978.

---

[1] FORM H1 Rule 130(1)(*a*)

Form of Intimation to alleged adulterer in action of divorce or separation

To [*name and address as in the warrant*]

Take note that in an action number ['*A' number*], you are alleged to have committed adultery. A copy of the initial writ is attached. If you wish to dispute the truth of the allegation made against you, you may lodge a minute with the Sheriff Clerk [*insert full address of Sheriff Clerk*] for leave to appear as a party. Your minute must be lodged within [21] days from [*insert date*], the date of posting of this intimation.

Date:— [*insert date*]

[*Signed*] A.B.
[Solicitor for Pursuer]

Note:
The minute to be lodged with the Sheriff Clerk must be in proper form. You should crave to be sisted as a party to the action and seek leave to lodge defences or answers. The minute must be accompanied by the appropriate fee of (£).
It may be in your best interests to consult a solicitor who, if necessary, will advise you on the availability of legal aid.

NOTE
[1] Inserted by S.I. 1986 No. 1230 and as amended by S.I. 1988 No. 1978.

---

[1] FORM H2 Rule 130(2)(*b*)

Form of intimation to person with whom an improper association is alleged to have occurred

To [*name and address as in the warrant*]

Take note that in an action number ['*A' number*], the defender is alleged to have had an improper association with you. A copy of the initial writ is attached. If you wish to dispute the truth of the allegation made against you, you may lodge a minute with the Sheriff Clerk [*insert full address of Sheriff Clerk*] for leave to appear as a party. Your minute must be lodged within [21] days from [*insert date*], the date of posting of this intimation.

Date:— [*insert date*]

[*Signed*] A.B.
[Solicitor for Pursuer]

Note:
The minute to be lodged with the Sheriff Clerk must be in proper form. You should crave to be sisted as a party to the action and seek leave to lodge defences or answers. The minute must be accompanied by the appropriate fee of (£).
It may be in your best interests to consult a solicitor who, if necessary, will advise you on the availability of legal aid.

NOTE
[1] Inserted by S.I. 1986 No. 1230 and as amended by S.I. 1988 No. 1978.

---

[1] FORM H3

Rule 130(4)

Form of intimation to a local authority or third party who may be liable to maintain a child

To [*name and address as in the warrant*]

Take note that in an action number [*'A' number*], the Court may make an order in respect of the custody of [*name and address*] a child in your care [*or* liable to be maintained by you]. A copy of the initial writ is attached. If you wish to appear as a party, you may lodge a minute with the Sheriff Clerk [*insert full address of Sheriff Clerk*], for leave to do so. Your minute must be lodged within [21] days from [*insert date*], the date of posting of this intimation.

Date:— [*insert date*]

[*Signed*] A.B.
[Solicitor for Pursuer]

Note:
The minute to be lodged with the Sheriff Clerk must be in proper form. You should crave to be sisted as a party to the action and seek leave to lodge defences or answers. The minute must be accompanied by the appropriate fee of (£).
It may be in your best interests to consult a solicitor who, if necessary, will advise you on the availability of legal aid.

NOTE
[1] Inserted by S.I. 1986 No. 1230 and as amended by S.I. 1988 No. 1978.

---

[1] FORM H4

Rule 130(5)

Form of Intimation to additional spouse of either party in proceedings relating to a polygamous marriage

To (*name and address as in the Warrant*)

Take note that an action for divorce [*or* separation] number (*'A' number*), involves (*name and designation*) your spouse. A copy of the Initial Writ is attached. If you wish to appear as a party, you may lodge a minute with the Sheriff Clerk (*insert full address of Sheriff Clerk*), for leave to do so. Your minute must be lodged within [21] days from (*insert date*), the date of posting of this intimation.

Date:— [*insert date*]

[*Signed*] A.B.
[Solicitor for Pursuer]

Note:
The minute to be lodged with the Sheriff Clerk must be in proper form. You should crave to be sisted as a party to the action and seek leave to lodge defences or answers. The minute must be accompanied by the appropriate fee of (£).
It may be in your best interests to consult a solicitor who, if necessary, will advise you on the availability of legal aid.

NOTE
[1] Inserted by S.I. 1986 No. 1230 and as amended by S.I. 1988 No. 1978.

---

[1] FORM H5 Rule 130(6)

Form of Intimation to person having *de facto* custody of children

To [*name and address as in the warrant*]

Take note that in an action number [*'A' number*], the court may make an order in respect of the custody of [*name and address*] a child/children at present in your custody. A copy of the initial writ is attached. If you wish to appear as a party, you may lodge a minute with the Sheriff Clerk [*insert full address of Sheriff Clerk*], for leave to do so. Your minute must be lodged within [21] days from [*insert date*], the date of posting of this intimation.

Date:— [*insert date*]

[*Signed*] A.B.
[Solicitor for Pursuer]

Note:
The minute to be lodged with the Sheriff Clerk must be in proper form. You should crave to be sisted as a party to the action and seek leave to lodge defences or answers. The minute must be accompanied by the appropriate fee of (£).
It may be in your best interests to consult a solicitor who, if necessary, will advise you on the availability of legal aid.

NOTE
[1] Inserted by S.I. 1986 No. 1230 and as amended by S.I. 1988 No. 1978.

[1] FORM H6 Rule 130(7)(*a*)

Form of intimation to local authority or third party to whom care of a child is to be given

To [*name and address as in the warrant*]

Take note that in an action number [*'A' number*], the court proposes to commit to your care the child [*name and address*]. A copy of the initial writ is attached. If you wish to appear as a party, you may lodge a minute with the Sheriff Clerk [*insert full address of Sheriff Clerk*], for leave to do so. Your minute must be lodged within [21] days from [*insert date*], the date of posting of this intimation.

Date:— [*insert date*]

[*Signed*] A.B.
[Solicitor for Pursuer]

Note:
The minute to be lodged with the Sheriff Clerk must be in proper form. You should crave to be sisted as a party to the action and seek leave to lodge defences or answers. The minute must be accompanied by the appropriate fee of (£).
It may be in your best interests to consult a solicitor who, if necessary, will advise you on the availability of legal aid.

NOTE
[1] Inserted by S.I. 1986 No. 1230 and as amended by S.I. 1988 No. 1978.

[1] FORM H6A Rule 130(7)(*b*)

Form of intimation to local authority of supervision order

Initial Writ

in

A.B. [*Address*] Pursuer(s)

against

C.D. [*Address*] Defender(s)

To [*name and address of local authority*]

TAKE NOTICE

That on [*date*] in the Sheriff Court at [*place*] the Sheriff made a supervision order under *section 12 of the Matrimonial Proceedings (Children) Act 1958/*section 11(1)(*b*) of the Guardianship Act 1973, placing the child [*name and address*] under your supervision. A certified copy of the sheriff's interlocutor is attached hereto.

Date:— [*insert date*]

[*Signed*] A.B.
Sheriff Clerk

*Delete as appropriate

NOTE

[1] Inserted by S.I. 1986 No. 1230.

---

[1] FORM H7 Rule 130(9)

Form of intimation to creditor in application for order for the transfer of property under section 8 of the Family Law (Scotland) Act 1985

To [*name and address as in the warrant*]

Take note that in an action number [*'A' number*] an order is sought for the transfer of property [*specify the order*], over which you hold a security. A copy of the initial writ is attached. If you wish to appear as a party, you may lodge a minute with the Sheriff Clerk [*insert full address of Sheriff Clerk*], for leave to do so. Your minute must be lodged within [21] days from [*insert date*], the date of posting of this intimation.

Date:— [*insert date*]

[*Signed*] A.B.
[Solicitor for Pursuer]

Note:
The minute to be lodged with the Sheriff Clerk must be in proper form. You should crave to be sisted as a party to the action and seek leave to lodge defences or answers. The minute must be accompanied by the appropriate fee of (£).
It may be in your best interests to consult a solicitor who, if necessary, will advise you on the availability of legal aid.

NOTE

[1] Inserted by S.I. 1986 No. 1230 and as amended by S.I. 1988 No. 1978.

---

[1] FORM H8 Rule 99(2)

Sequestration for rent—Notice informing defender of right to apply for certain orders under the Debtors (Scotland) Act 1987

Where articles are sequestrated for rent you have the right to apply to the sheriff for certain orders under the Debtors (Scotland) Act 1987.

1. You may apply to the sheriff within 14 days from the date articles are sequestrated for an order releasing any article on the ground that—

(*a*) it is exempt from sequestration for rent. (Articles which are exempt are listed in section 16 of the Debtors (Scotland) Act 1987.); or

(*b*) its inclusion in the sequestration for rent or its subsequent sale is unduly harsh.

2. Where a mobile home, such as a caravan, is your only or principal residence and it has been sequestrated for rent you may apply to the sheriff before a warrant to sell is granted for an order that for a specified period no further steps shall be taken in the sequestration.

Any enquiry relating to the above rights should be made to a solicitor, Citizens Advice Bureau or other local advice centre or to the sheriff clerk at (*address*).

NOTE

[1] Inserted by S.I. 1988 No. 1978.

FORM I Rule 75(1)

Citation

K.L. [*design him*], you are required to attend at Sheriff Court on 19 at as a witness for the in the action at the instance of A.B. [*design him*], against C.D. [*design him*] (and to bring with you [*specify documents*]). If you fail to attend without reasonable excuse having demanded and been paid your travelling expenses you may be ordered to pay a penalty not exceeding £250 and warrant may be granted for your arrest.

[*Date*] [*Signed*] P.Q., Sheriff Officer;
or
X.Y. [*add designation and business address*]
Solicitor for Pursuer [*or Defender*]

Note:

Within certain specified limits claims for necessary outlays and loss of earnings will be met. Claims should be made to the person who has cited you to attend court and proof of any loss of earnings should be given to that person. If you wish your travelling expenses to be paid prior to your attendance you should apply to the person who has cited you.

FORM J Rule 75(1)

Certificate of citation

I certify that on 19 I duly cited K.L. [*design him*] to attend at Sheriff Court on 19 at as a witness for the in the action at the instance of A.B. [*design him*] against E.F. [*design him*] (and I require him to bring with him [*specify documents*]). This I did [*set forth mode of citation*].

[Date] [*Signed*] P.Q., Sheriff Officer;
or
X.Y. [*add designation and business address*]
Solicitor for Pursuer [*or Defender*]

FORM K

Rule 81(1)

Notice in optional procedure for commission and diligence

Order by the Sheriff Court at ....

In the cause [*reference No.*]
in which
A.B. [*design*] is Pursuer
and
C.D. [*design*] is Defender

To [*name and designation of party or parties or haver, from whom the documents are sought to be recovered*]

Take notice that you are hereby required to produce to the sheriff clerk at within seven days of the service upon you of this order—

(1) this order itself which must be produced intact;

(2) a certificate signed and completed in terms of the form appended hereto; and

(3) all documents in your possession falling within the specification enclosed herewith, together with a list or inventory of such documents signed by you as relative to this order and your certificate.

Production may be made either by lodging the above at the said office of the sheriff clerk, or by registered or recorded delivery letter or registered postal packet enclosing the same, and addressed to the said sheriff clerk at said office.

[*Signature and business address of the solicitor of the party in whose favour commission and diligence has been granted*]
[*Date*]

Note:

If you claim confidentiality for any of the documents produced by you, such documents must nevertheless be produced, but may be placed in a special sealed enclosure by themselves, marked "confidential".

CERTIFICATE

I hereby certify with reference to the order of the sheriff court at in the cause [*reference No.*] and the relative specification of documents, served upon me and marked respectively X.Y.—

(1) that the documents which are produced and which are enumerated in the inventory signed by me and marked Z, are the whole documents in my possession falling under the specification

or

that I have no documents in my possession falling within the specification.

(2) that, to the best of my knowledge and belief, there are in existence other documents falling within the specification, but not in my possession, namely [*describe them by reference to one or more of the descriptions of documents in the specification*], which were last seen by me on or about [*date*], at [*place*], in the hands of [*name and address of the person*]

or

[THE NEXT PAGE IS D 44/9]

R.82 – party claiming confidentiality can produce them in a sealed package
Only opened with auth. of sh. if he is satisfied that documents are not confidential

– Mere fact that documents are recovered + in hands of sh. ct. then still not evidence for a party. Must be lodged as productions with inventory. Recovery by commission + diligence does not automatically make documents productions

R.84 – INSPECTION – eg of piece of machinery that you wish to have inspected if there has been an accident at work

– must lodge minute asking sh. to grant order + what order sought is
– once minute lodged ct. sets date for hearing + must be intimated to parties having an interest
– potential litigant may wish to carry out inspection to find out whether proceedings should be brought – IW in form of summary application is needed. Sh. has discretion to grant order
– if order granted then certified copy of interlocutor granting the order has to be served to any interested party

84A
– disclosure of info. as to ID of persons who may be potential witnesses or defenders [– ADMINISTRATION OF JUSTICE (S) ACT 1972]
– proceed by way of minute in an action which is already in ct. or by way of IW in form of summary application if no case already in ct.

PROOF ITSELF –

R.73 – RECORDING OF EVIDENCE [– recorded by shorthand writer. SW's are independent contractors. 2 main firms in Edinburgh. Fees laid down by Act of Sederunt]
– if likely to be long proof + spread over a few days then sheriff will be unlikely to dispense with SW
– grave disadvantage in dispensing with SW – very difficult to appeal on any matter of fact or sufficiency of evidence
(1) – responsibility for instructing SW is pursuers sol. – good idea when instructing her to send copy of closed record so she will know roughly what case is about
(3) SW is put on oath. Shall record evidence by qu. + answer – verbatim a/c. Extended notes of SW certified by SW are true transcript of evidence
(5) sh. may examine witnesses
(6) expenses

If undefended actions need not have S.W. GO TO D44/15

that I know of the existence of no documents in the possession of any person, other than myself, which fall within the specification.

[*Signed*]

FORM L Rule 104

Notice of removal

To [*name, designation, and address of party in possession*].

You are required to remove from [*describe subjects*] at the term of [*or if different terms, state them and the subjects to which they apply*], in terms of lease [*describe it*] or [*in terms of your letter of removal of date*] or [*otherwise as case may be*].

FORM M Rule 104

Letter of removal

To [*name and designation of addressee*].

[*Place and date*] I am to remove from [*state subjects by usual name of short description sufficient for identification*] at the term of

K.L. [*add designation and address*].

If not holograph to be attested thus—

M.N. [*add designation and address*], witness.

FORM N Rule 105

Notice of removal under s.37 of 1907 Act

To K.L. [*designation and address*].

You are required to remove from [ ] that portion of ground [*describe it*]; or the mill of [*describe it*]; or the shootings of the lands and estate of [*describe them*]; or [*other subjects to which this notice is applicable*], at the term of Whitsunday [*insert year*] [*or Martinmas, as the case may be, inserting after the year the words, being the 15th day of May, or the 11th day of November, or the 28th day of May, or the 28th day of November, as the case may be*].

NOTE

[1] As amended by S.I. 1983 No. 1546.

FORM O Rule 117

Notice of appearance

A.B., Pursuer against C.D., E.F., and G. H., Defenders

Court Ref No.

[*Place and date*]—C.D. [*design him*], defender, intends to appear in the above action and lodge *defences to the competency of the action.

*objections to the condescendence of the fund *in medio*

*a claim on the fund *in medio*.

[*Signed*] C.D., Defender

or

X.Y. [*add designation and business address*]
Solicitor for Defender

*delete as appropriate.

[1] FORM P Rule 128(4)

Receipt

In the Sheriff Court of at
Receipt for a Payment into Court

In the cause, matter or proceeding [*state names of parties or other appropriate description*]

[*Place and Date*]
A.B. [*design him*] has this day paid into Court the sum of £ being a payment into Court in terms of Rule 128 of of money which in an action of damages, has become payable to a person under legal disability.

(Note) If the payment is made under Rule 128(2) add "the custody of which money has been accepted at the request of (name of Court making request)."

[*Signed*] Sheriff Clerk
N.B. The person paying the money into Court is required to complete and transmit the subjoined Form Q to the Secretary of State, forthwith.

TO BE PERFORATED

NOTE
[1] As amended by S.I. 1986 No. 1230.

FORM Q Rule 128(4)

Letter intimating payment

[*Address*]
[*Date*]

To
The Secretary of State

Sir,
I/We paid into the Sheriff Court at on 19 , the sum of in the [*State name of cause, matter or proceeding*].

Yours faithfully
[*Signature*]

FORM R Rule 128(4)

Additional particulars for receipt

The above-mentioned payment into Court was:—
(*a*) Lodged on Deposit Receipt No. with the [*state name of Bank*] pending the Orders of the Court.
(*b*) Deposited in the National Savings Bank, Account No
(*c*) [*Otherwise as the case may be, stating similar particulars*].

Name and address of Solicitor [*or Insurance Company*] representing the person who made the payment into Court:—

[*Date*]
[*Signed*]

Sheriff Clerk

[1] FORM S Rule 131

Form of Notice to defender where it is stated he consents to the granting of decree of separation.

TAKE NOTICE that the copy initial writ served on you together with this Notice states that you consent to the grant of decree of separation—

1. If you do so consent the consequences to you are that—
   (*a*) provided the pursuer establishes the fact tnat there has been no cohabitation between the parties to the marriage at any time during a continuous period of two years after the date of the marriage and immediately preceding the bringing of this action and that you consent, a decree of separation will be granted;
   (*b*) on the grant of decree of separation you will be obliged to live apart from the pursuer but the marriage will continue to subsist; a husband will continue to have a legal obligation to support his wife and children;
   (*c*) apart from these consequences there may be others applicable to you depending upon your particular circumstances.

2. If you do consent to the grant of decree you may apply to the Court in this action—
   (*a*) for payment by the pursuer to you of aliment; and
   (*b*) for an order providing for access to or the custody, maintenance and education of any child of the marriage, or any child accepted as such, who is under 16 years of age.

3. In order to make such an application to the Court you require to give notice in the appropriate form to the Court. If you wish to make such an application you should consult a solicitor.

4. If after considering the foregoing, you wish to consent to decree, you should complete and sign the attached Form of Notice of Consent and send it to the Sheriff Clerk at the Sheriff Court referred to in the initial writ within 21 days of the date of this Notice.

5. If after consenting you wish to withdraw your consent you must immediately inform the Sheriff Clerk at the Sheriff Court referred to in the initial writ in writing that you withdraw your consent to decree being granted against you in the action at the instance of [*insert name and address of your husband or wife as the case may be*].

[*Date*] [*Signed*]
[*Signature of Pursuer or his Agent*]

NOTE

[1] As amended by S.I. 1984 No. 255, 1986 No. 1230 and 1988 No. 1978.

[1] FORM S1 Rule 131

Form of Notice to defender where it is stated he consents to the granting of decree of divorce.

TAKE NOTICE that the copy initial writ served on you together with the Notice states that you consent to grant of decree of divorce.

1. If you do so consent the consequences to you are that—
   (*a*) provided the pursuer establishes the fact that there has been no cohabitation between the parties to the marriage at any time during a continuous period of two years after the date of the marriage and immediately preceding the bringing of this action and that you consent, a decree will be granted;
   (*b*) on the grant of a decree of divorce you may lose your rights of succession to the pursuer's estate;
   (*c*) decree of divorce will end the marriage thereby affecting any right to such pension as may depend upon marriage continuing or upon your being left a widow; the State widow's pension will not be payable to you when the pursuer dies;
   (*d*) apart from these consequences there may be others applicable to you depending upon your particular circumstances.

2. If you do consent to the grant of decree you are still entitled to apply to the Sheriff in this action—

(*a*) to make financial provision for you under the Divorce (Scotland) Act 1976 by making an order—
   (i) for the payment by the pursuer to you of a periodical allowance;
   (ii) for the payment by the pursuer to you of a capital sum;
   (iii) varying the terms of any marriage settlement.
(*b*) to make an order providing for the custody, maintenance and education of any child of the marriage, or any child accepted as such, who is under 16 years of age.

3. In order to make such an application to the Sheriff you require to give notice in the appropriate form to the Court. If you wish to make such an application you should consult a solicitor.

4. If after considering the foregoing you wish to consent to decree you should complete and sign the attached Form of Notice of Consent, and send it to the Sheriff Clerk at the Sheriff Court referred to in the initial writ, within 21 days of the receipt of this Notice.

5. If after consenting you wish to withdraw your consent you must immediately inform the Sheriff Clerk at the Sheriff Court referred to in the initial writ in writing that you withdraw your consent to decree being granted against you in the action at the instance of [*insert name and address of your husband or wife as the case may be*].

NOTE
[1] Inserted by S.I. 1984 No. 255 and as amended by S.I. 1988 No. 1978.

---

[1] FORM S2 Rule 131

Form of Notice to defender in an action of separation where it is stated there has been five years' non-cohabitation

1. TAKE NOTICE that the copy initial writ served on you together with this Notice states that there has been no cohabitation between you and the pursuer at any time during a continuous period of five years after the date of the marriage and immediately preceding the commencement of this action and that if the pursuer establishes this as a fact and the Court is satisfied that there are grounds justifying decree of separation a decree will be granted, unless in the opinion of the Court the grant of decree would result in grave financial hardship to you.

2. On the grant of decree of separation you will be obliged to live apart from the pursuer but the marriage will continue to subsist. A husband will continue to have legal obligation to support his wife and children.

3. You are entitled, whether or not you dispute that there has been no such cohabitation during such a period, to apply to the Sheriff in this action—
(*a*) if you are the wife, for payment by the pursuer to you of aliment; and
(*b*) for an order providing for the custody, maintenance and education of any child of the marriage, or any child accepted as such, who is under 16 years of age.

4. In order to make such an application you require to give notice in the appropriate form to the Court. If you wish to make such an application you should consult a solicitor.

NOTE
[1] Inserted by S.I. 1984 No. 255 and amended by S.I. 1986 No. 1230.

---

[1] FORM S3 Rule 131

Form of Notice to defender in an action of divorce where it is stated there has been five years' non-cohabitation

1. TAKE NOTICE that the copy initial writ served on you together with this Notice states

that there has been no cohabitation between you and the pursuer at any time during a continuous period of five years after the date of the marrriage and immediately preceding the commencement of this action and that if the pursuer establishes this as a fact and the Court is satisfied that the marriage has broken down irretrievably a decree will be granted, unless in the opinion of the Court the grant of decree would result in grave financial hardship to you.

2. Decree of divorce will end the marriage thereby affecting any right to such pension as may depend upon the marriage continuing or upon your being left a widow, the State widow's pension will not be payable to you when the pursuer dies. You may also lose your rights of succession to the pursuer's estate.

3. You are entitled, whether or not you dispute that there has been no such cohabitation during such a period, to apply to the Sheriff in this action—

(*a*) to make financial provision for you under the Divorce (Scotland) Act 1976 by making an order—
  (i) for the payment by the pursuer to you of a periodical allowance;
  (ii) for the payment by the pursuer to you of a capital sum;
  (iii) varying the terms of any marriage settlement;

(*b*) to make an order providing for the custody, maintenance and education of any child of the marriage or of any child accepted as such, who is under 16 years of age.

4. In order to make such an application you require to give notice in the appropriate form to the Court. If you wish to make such an application you should consult a solicitor.

NOTE

[1] Inserted by S.I. 1984 No. 255.

---

[1] FORM T — Rule 131

Form of Notice of Consent in actions of divorce and of separation under section 1(2)(*d*) of the Divorce (Scotland) Act 1976.

I [*full name and address of the defender to be inserted by the pursuer or the pursuer's solicitor before sending Notice*] have received a copy of the initial writ in the action against me at the instance of [*full name and address of pursuer to be inserted by him or his solicitor before sending Notice*].

I understand that it states that I consent to the grant of decree (of divorce or of separation) in this action.

I have considered the consequences to me mentioned in the Notice sent together with this Notice.

I consent to the grant of decree (of divorce or of separation) in this action.

[*Dated*] [*Signed*]

Defender

NOTE

[1] As amended by S.I. 1984 No. 255 and 1986 No. 1230.

---

[1] FORM T1 — Rule 3(8)

Form of consent of parent, tutor, curator or guardian in proceedings for custody of children under section 47 of the Children Act 1975

In

.... Pursuer(s)

.... Defender(s)

I, [*name and address*] ....

....

confirm that I am the mother/father/guardian/tutor/curator* of the child [*insert full name of the child as it is given on the birth certificate, and the child's present address*] ....
....

I understand that if I consent to the granting of custody to the pursuer(s), the care, possession and control of the child may be granted to the pursuer(s) by the court.

I hereby consent to the making of a custody order in relation to the child [*name of child*] ...

in favour of [*name and address of pursuer(s)*] ....
....

Date at [*place*] .... the ....day of
.... 19

Signature of person consenting ....
Signature of Witness ....
Full Name ....
Designation ....
Address ....
....
Signature of Witness ....
Full Name ....
Designation ....
Address ....
....

*delete whichever is inappropriate.

NOTE
[1] Inserted by S.I. 1986 No. 513 and as amended by S.I. 1986 No. 1966.

[1] FORM T2 Rule 130(8)

Notice to local authority under section 49(1) of the Children Act 1975 of presentation of an initial writ for custody of a child under section 47 of that Act.

Initial Writ

in

A.B. [*address*] Pursuer(s)

for

Custody of the child E.F.

To [*name and address*]

TAKE NOTICE

1. That the pursuer has presented an initial writ to the Sheriff Court at [*address*] for the custody of the child E.F. A copy of the writ is attached to this notice.

2. That you are required under section 49(2) of the Children Act 1975 to submit to the court a report on all the circumstances of the child and on the proposed arrangements for the care and upbringing of the child.

Dated the day of 19

[*Signed*]
[*Address*]

[Solicitor for the pursuer]

NOTE
[1] Inserted by S.I. 1986 No. 513.

FORM U — Rule 134(3)

Request for preliminary ruling of the Court of Justice of the European Communities

[*Here set out a statement of the case for the European Court, giving brief particulars of the case and issues between the parties, and relevant facts found by the Court, any relevant rules and provisions of Scots law, and the relevant Treaty provisions, acts, instruments or rules of Community Law giving rise to the reference.*]

The preliminary ruling of the Court of Justice of the European Communities is accordingly sought on the following questions—1, 2, etc. [*Insert the questions on which the ruling is sought*].

Dated the day of 19

[1] FORM V — Rule 11A

Form of Certificate by medical officer of hospital or similar institution

I [*name and designation*] certify that, having had transmitted to me a copy initial writ in an action of divorce or of separation at the instance of [*name and designation*] Pursuer, against [*name and designation*] Defender,

(*a*) I have on the day of personally delivered a copy thereof to the said defender who is under my care at [*address*] and I have explained the contents or purport thereof to him (or her).

or

(*b*) I have no delivered a copy thereof to the said defender who is under my care at [*address*] and I have not explained the contents or purport thereof to him (or her) and that for the following reasons [*state reasons*].

[*Address and date*] [Signature and designation]

NOTE
[1] Added by S.I. 1984 No. 255.

---

[1] FORM V1 — Rule 11A(3)

Form of Intimation to children, next of kin and *curator bonis* in an action of divorce or separation where the defender suffers from a mental disorder

To [*name and address as in the warrant*]

Take note that an action of divorce [*or* separation] number [*'A' number*] has been raised against [*name, and designation*] your (father, mother, brother or other relative, or ward, as the case may be). A copy of the initial writ is attached. If you wish to appear as a party, you may lodge a minute with the Sheriff Clerk [*insert full address of Sheriff Clerk*], for leave to do so. Your minute must be lodged within [21] days from [*insert date*], the date of posting of this intimation.

Date:— [*insert date*] [*Signed*] A.B.
[Solicitor for Pursuer]

Note:
The minute to be lodged with the Sheriff Clerk must be in proper form. You should crave to be sisted as a party to the action and seek leave to lodge defences or answers. The minute must be accompanied by the appropriate fee of (£).
It may be in your best interests to consult a solicitor who, if necessary, will advise you on the availability of legal aid.

NOTE
[1] Inserted by S.I. 1986 No. 1230 and as amended by S.I. 1988 No. 1978.

---

[1] FORM V2 Rule 11A(3)

Form of Intimation to children and next of kin in an action of divorce or separation where the defender's address is unknown

To [*name and address as in the warrant*]

Take note that an action of divorce [*or* separation] number [*'A' number*], has been raised against [*name*] your [father, mother, brother or other relative *as the case may be*]. If you know of his/her present address, you are requested to forward the same to the Sheriff Clerk [*insert full address of Sheriff Clerk*] forthwith. You may also if you wish to appear as a party lodge a minute with the Sheriff Clerk for leave to do so. Your minute must be lodged within [21] days from [*insert date*], the date of posting of this intimation.

Date:— [*insert date*] [*Signed*] A.B.
[Solicitor for Pursuer]

Note:
The minute to be lodged with the Sheriff Clerk must be in proper form. You should crave to be sisted as a party to the action and seek leave to lodge defences or answers. The minute must be accompanied by the appropriate fee of (£).
It may be in your best interests to consult a solicitor who, if necessary, will advise you on the availability of legal aid.

NOTE
[1] Inserted by S.I. 1986 No. 1230 and as amended by S.I. 1988 No. 1978.

---

[1] FORM W Rule 11A

Form of Transmission to medical officer of hospital or similar institution

To [*insert name and address*]

In accordance with the Sheriff Courts (Scotland) Act 1907 a copy of the initial writ at the instance of [*name and address*] against [*name and address*] is sent herewith and you are requested to deliver it personally to the said and to explain the contents or purport thereof to him (or her) unless you are satisfied that such delivery or explanation would be dangerous to his (or her) health or mental condition. You are further requested to complete

and return to me in the enclosed stamped and addressed envelope the certificate appended hereto, striking out what is not applicable.

[*Address and date*] [*Solicitor for Pursuer*]

NOTE
[1] Added by S.I. 1984 No. 255.

[THE NEXT PAGE IS D 44/15]

R85 –

R86 – objections to evidence in course of proof where no record

R87 – Incidental appeals in confidentiality – party may object to giving evidence on grounds of confidentiality

- if sh. orders disclosure matter ceases to be confidential
- if sh. was wrong then of no assistance to party who has disclosed details

- Right of incidental appeal – party dissatisfied with ruling of sh. must express immediately his dissatisfaction + apply for appeal to S.P. who will deal with it without delay

(2) Sh. may proceed with proof on matters not dependent on the confidential info.

PROCEDURE – P. leads evidence 1st unless ct. ordains otherwise

- Each witness put on oath + examined, cross-examined + re-examined
- D. leads his witnesses
- At end sh. will ask parties if they wish to have shorthand notes extended – need not do so for sh. to give a decision
- Many cases – sh. will hear parties on evidence at close of proof if he requires it. At hearing sh. will hear parties
  - if PBA then matters of law which have been reserved will also fall to be heard.
- expenses can be reserved until after sh. has given decision

R.89 – JUDGEMENT

R.90 – EXTRACT OF DECREES – possibility of appeal:-

- interlocutor which can be appealed without leave must be appealed within 14days
- leave to appeal may be required – leave must be applied for within 7 days having elapsed from date of interlocutor

APPEALS – Sh. Ct. (S) Act 1907 s. 27 + 28

- s. 27 – appeals to S.P.
- s. 28 – appeals to Ct. of S

SEE RULES 91–96

- APPEAL BEFORE S.P. – procedural rules are part of lawyers rules to administer justice. In civil cases there can be an appeal directly from sh.'s decision to IH of Ct. of S.

BUT – most people will not do this because of the expense + delay – they can go to SP instead

GO TO D45

[1] FORM X

Rule 72(5)

A.B. for the pursuer having considered the evidence contained in the affidavits and the other documents all as specified in the Schedule hereto and being satisfied that upon the evidence a motion for decree (in terms of the crave of the initial writ) *or* (in such restricted terms as may be appropriate) may properly be made, moves the court accordingly,

In respect whereof
[*Signed*]
[*Designation*]

SCHEDULE

[*Number and specify documents considered*]

NOTE

[1] Added by S.I. 1984 No. 255.

---

[1] FORM Z

Rule 90A

Extract
Decree of
Divorce

SHERIFF COURT,

AT , the day of
Nineteen hundred and

in an action of Divorce
in the Sheriff Court of
at at the instance of

Pursuer

who were married at [*place*] on [*date*] Defender

The sheriff pronounced Decree:
(1) divorcing the Defender from the Pursuer
(2) awarding custody to the Pursuer/Defender of the following child children:
(3) ordaining payment:
(*a*) by the to the of £ per as aliment for each of said child/children until sixteen years of age:
(*b*) by the Defender to the Pursuer of a periodical allowance of £ per payable until her death or remarriage:
(*c*) by the Defender to the Pursuer of a capital sum of £
(*d*) by the to the of £ of expenses:

(4) finding the Defender liable to the Pursuer in expenses as the same may be subsequently taxed and decerned for:

(5) granting leave to any party showing interest to apply to the Court for any order required anent custody and aliment until 19 :

And the said Sheriff Grants Warrant for all lawful execution hereon:
Extracted at this
day of 19 by me
Sheriff Clerk of

Sheriff Clerk

NOTE
[1] Added by S.I. 1984 No. 255.

---

[1] FORM SDA1 Rule 136(1)

Under the Divorce (Scotland) Act 1976, Section 1(2)(*d*) Simplified Procedure

Sheriff Clerk
Sheriff Court House
....
....
(Tel.)..............................

APPLICATION FOR DIVORCE (WITH CONSENT OF OTHER PARTY TO THE MARRIAGE) HUSBAND AND WIFE HAVING LIVED APART FOR AT LEAST TWO YEARS

Before completing this form, you should have read the leaflet entitled "Do it yourself Divorce", which explains the circumstances in which a divorce may be sought by that method. If simplified procedure appears to suit your circumstances, you may use this form to apply for divorce.

Below you will find directions designed to assist you with your application. Please follow them carefully. In the event of difficulty, you may contact any Sheriff Clerk's Office or Citizens Advice Bureau or the Court of Session Divorce Section, Edinburgh

Directions for making application

WRITE IN INK, USING BLOCK CAPITALS

Application (Part 1) — 1. Complete and sign Part 1 of the form (pages 3–7), paying particular attention to the notes opposite each section.

Consent of Husband/Wife (Part 2) — 2. When you have filled in Part 1 of the form, attach the (blue) Instruction Sheet SP3 to it and send both documents to your husband/wife for completion of the consent at Part 2 (page 9).

NOTE: If your husband/wife does NOT complete and sign the form of consent, your application cannot proceed further under the simplified procedure. In that event, if you still wish to obtain a divorce, you should consult a solicitor.

Affidavit (Part 3) — 3. When the application has been returned to you with the Consent (Part 2) duly completed and signed, you should then take the form to a Justice of the Peace, Notary Public, Commissioner for Oaths or other duly authorised person so that your affidavit in Part 3 (page 10) can be completed and sworn.

Returning completed Application Form to Court

4. When directions 1–3 above have been carried out, your application is now ready to be sent to the Court at the above address. With it you must enclose:
   (i) Your marriage certificate (the document headed "Extract of an entry in a Register of Marriages", which will be returned to you in due course), and
   (ii) Either a cheque or postal order in respect of the Court fee, crossed and made payable to "the Sheriff Clerk",
   or a completed form SP15, claiming exemption from the Court fee.
5. Receipt of your application will be promptly acknowledged. Should you wish to withdraw the application for any reason, please contact the Sheriff Clerk immediately.

PART 1

WRITE IN INK, USING BLOCK CAPITALS

1.
NAME AND ADDRESS OF APPLICANT

Surname .... Other name(s) in full ....

Present Address ....

.... Daytime Telephone Number if any ....

....

2.
NAME AND ADDRESS OF HUSBAND/WIFE

Surname .... Other name(s) in full ....

Present Address ....

.... Daytime Telephone Number if any ....

....

3.
JURISDICTION

Please indicate with a tick (✓) in the appropriate box or boxes which of the following apply:

PART A
   (i) I consider myself to be domiciled in Scotland ☐
   (ii) I have lived in Scotland for a period of at least 12 months immediately before the date of signing this application ☐
   (iii) My husband/wife considers himself/herself to be domiciled in Scotland ☐
   (iv) My husband/wife has lived in Scotland for a period of at least 12 months immediately before the date of signing this application. ☐

PART B

(v) I have lived at the address shown in Section 1 for at least 40 days immediately before the date I signed this application. ☐

(vi) My husband/wife has lived at the address shown in Section 2 for at least 40 days immediately before the date I signed this application ☐

4.
DETAILS OF PRESENT MARRIAGE

Place of Marriage .... (Registration District)

Date of Marriage: Day .... month .... year ....

5.
PERIOD OF SEPARATION

(i) Please state the date on which you ceased to live with your husband/wife. (If more than 2½ years, just give the month and year) Day . . . Month . . . Year . . .

(ii) Have you lived with your husband/wife since that date? · (*Tick (√) box which applies*) ☐ YES NO ☐

(iii) If yes, for how long in total did you live together before finally separating again?

.................months

6.
RECONCILIATION

Is there any reasonable prospect of reconciliation with your husband/wife? (*Tick (√) box which applies*) ☐ YES NO ☐

Do you consider that the marriage has broken down irretrievably? (*Tick (√) box which applies*) ☐ YES NO ☐

7.
CONSENT

Does your husband/wife consent to a divorce being granted? (*Tick (√) box which applies*) ☐ YES NO ☐

8.
MENTAL DISABILITY

As far as you are aware is your husband/wife incapable of managing his/her affairs because of a mental disorder (whether illness or deficiency)? (*Tick box which applies*) ☐ YES NO ☐
(if yes, give details)

9.
CHILDREN

Are there any children of the marriage under the age of 16?
(*Tick (√) box which applies*) ☐ YES NO ☐

10.
OTHER COURT ACTIONS

Are you aware of any court actions currently proceeding in any country (including Scotland) which may affect your marriage?
(*Tick √ box which applies*) ☐ YES NO ☐
(if yes, give details)

11.
REQUEST FOR DIVORCE AND DISCLAIMER OF FINANCIAL PROVISION

I confirm that the facts stated in Sections 1–10 above apply to my marriage.

I do NOT ask the Court to make any financial awards in connection with this application.

I request the Court to grant decree of divorce from my husband/wife.

....
(Date) (Signature)

IMPORTANT—Part 1 MUST be completed, signed and dated before sending the application form to your husband/wife.

PART 2

CONSENT BY APPLICANT'S HUSBAND/WIFE TO DIVORCE

NOTE: Before completing this Part of the form,
please read the notes opposite

I, ...
(Full names, in BLOCK letters, of Applicant's husband/wife)

residing at

....
(Address, also in BLOCK letters)

....

....

HEREBY STATE THAT

a. I have read Part 1 of this application;
b. The Applicant has lived apart from me for a continuous period of two years immediately preceding the date of the application (Section 11 of Part 1);
c. I do not ask the Court to make any order for payment to me by the Applicant of a periodical allowance (i.e. a regular payment of money weekly or monthly, etc for maintenance);
d. I do not ask the Court to make any order for payment to me by the Applicant of a capital sum (i.e. a lump sum payment);

e. I understand that divorce may result in the loss to me of property rights; and

f. I CONSENT TO DECREE OF DIVORCE BEING GRANTED IN RESPECT OF THIS APPLICATION.

....
(Date) (Signature)

NOTE: You may withdraw your consent, even after giving it, at any time before divorce is granted by the Court. Should you wish to do so, you must immediately advise:

Address of Court
(Tel.)

PART 3

APPLICANT'S AFFIDAVIT

To be completed only after Parts 1 and 2 have been signed and dated.

I, (*insert Applicant's full name*) ....

residing at (*insert Applicant's present home address*) ....

....

Town .... Country ....

SWEAR that to the best of my knowledge and belief:

(1) the facts stated in Part 1 of this Application are true; and

(2) the signature in Part 2 of this Application is that of my *husband/wife.

Signature of Applicant ....

To be completed by Justice of the Peace, Notary Public or Commissioner for Oaths

SWORN at (Place) ....

this .... day of .... 19.........

before me (full name) ....

(full address) ....

....

....

Signature ....

*Justice of the Peace/*Notary Public/*Commissioner for Oaths
*Delete as appropriate

NOTE
[1] Added by S.I. 1984 No. 255.

[1] FORM SDA2 Rule 136(2)

Under the Divorce (Scotland) Act 1976, section 1(2)(*e*)
Simplified Procedure

Sheriff Clerk
Sheriff Court House
....
....
(Tel.)..............................

APPLICATION FOR DIVORCE
HUSBAND AND WIFE HAVING LIVED APART FOR AT LEAST FIVE YEARS

Before completing this form, you should have read the leaflet entitled "Do it yourself Divorce", which explains the circumstances in which a divorce may be sought by that method. If the simplified procedure appears to suit your circumstances, you may use this form to apply for divorce.

Below you will find directions designed to assist you with your application. Please follow them carefully. In the event of difficulty, you may contact the Sheriff Clerk's Office or Citizens Advice Bureau or the Court of Session Divorce Section, Edinburgh.

Directions for making application

WRITE IN INK, USING BLOCK CAPITALS

Application (Part 1)
1. Complete and sign Part 1 of the form (pages 3–7), paying particular attention to the notes opposite each section.

Affidavits (Part 2)
2. When you have completed Part 1, you should take the form to a Justice of the Peace, Notary Public, Commissioner for Oaths or other duly authorised person so that your affidavit in Part 2 (page 8) can be completed and sworn.

Returning completed Application Form to Court
3. When directions 1 and 2 above have all been carried out, your application is now ready to be sent to the Sheriff Clerk at the above address. With it you must enclose:
   (i) Your marriage certificate (the document headed "Extract of an entry in a Register of Marriages" the certificate will be returned to you in due course)—check the notes on page 2 to see if you need to obtain a letter from the General Register Office stating that there is no record of your husband/wife having divorced you, and
   (ii) Either a cheque or postal order in respect of the Court fee, crossed and made payable to "the Sheriff Clerk",
   or a completed form SP15, claiming exemption from the Court fee.

4. Receipt of your application will be promptly acknowledged. Should you wish to withdraw the application for any reason, please contact the Sheriff Clerk immediately.

WRITE IN INK, USING BLOCK CAPITALS PART 1

1.
NAME AND ADDRESS OF APPLICANT

Surname	....	Other name(s) in full	....
Present Address	....		....
	....	Daytime Telephone Number	
	....	if any	....

2.
NAME OF HUSBAND/WIFE

Surname .... Other name(s) in full ....

....

3.
ADDRESS OF HUSBAND/WIFE (if the address of your husband/wife is not known, please enter "not known" in this section and proceed to section 4)

Present Address .... Daytime Telephone Number if any ....

....

....

4.
Only complete this section if you do not know the present address of your husband/wife

NEXT-OF-KIN

Name .... Address ....

....

....

Relationship to your husband/wife ....

CHILDREN OF THE MARRIAGE
Names and dates of birth Addresses

....

....

....

....

....

....

If insufficient space is available to list all the children of the marriage, please continue on a separate sheet and attach to this form.

5.
JURISDICTION

Please indicate with a tick (√) in the appropriate box or boxes which of the following apply:

PART A

(i) I consider myself to be domiciled in Scotland ☐

(ii) I have lived in Scotland for a period of at least 12 months immediately before the date of signing this application ☐

(iii) My husband/wife considers himself/herself to be domiciled in Scotland ☐

(iv) My husband/wife has lived in Scotland for a period of at least 12 months immediately before the date of signing this application ☐

PART B

(v) I have lived at the address shown in Section 1 for at least 40 days immediately before the date I signed this application ☐

(vi) My husband/wife has lived at the address shown in Section 2 for at least 40 days immediately before I signed this application ☐

6.
DETAILS OF PRESENT MARRIAGE

Place of marriage .... (Registration District)

Date of Marriage (Day) .... (Month) .... (Year) ....

7.
PERIOD OF SEPARATION

(i) Please state the date on which you ceased to live with your husband/wife. (If more than 5½ years, just give the month and year) Day..... Month..... Year.....

(ii) Have you lived with your husband/wife since that date? ☐ YES NO ☐
(*Tick (√) box which applies*)

(iii) If yes, for how long in total did you live together before finally separating again?
..........months

8.
RECONCILIATION

Is there any reasonable prospect of reconciliation with your husband/wife? ☐ YES NO ☐
(*Tick (√) box which applies*)

Do you consider that the marriage has broken down irretrievably? ☐ YES NO ☐
(*Tick (√) box which applies*)

9.
MENTAL DISABILITY

Is your husband/wife incapable of managing his/her affairs because of a mental disorder (whether illness or deficiency?) ☐ YES NO ☐
(*Tick (√) box which applies*)
(if yes, give details)

10.
CHILDREN

Are there any children of the marriage under the age of 16? ☐ YES NO ☐
(*Tick (✓) box which applies*)

11.
OTHER COURT ACTIONS

Are you aware of any court actions currently proceeding in any country (including Scotland) which may affect your marriage? ☐ YES NO ☐
(*Tick (✓) box which applies*) (if yes, give details)

12.
DECLARATION AND REQUEST FOR DIVORCE

I confirm that the facts stated in sections 1–11 above apply to my marriage.

I do not ask the Court to make any financial awards in connection with this application.

I believe that no grave financial hardship will be caused to my husband/wife as a result of the granting of this application.

I request the Court to grant decree of divorce from my husband/wife.

....
(Date) (Signature of Applicant)

PART 2

APPLICANT'S AFFIDAVIT

(To be completed only after Part 1 has been signed and dated.)

I, (*insert Applicant's full name*) ....

residing at (*insert Applicant's present home address*) ....

....

Town .... Country ....

SWEAR that to the best of my knowledge and belief the facts stated in Part 1 of this Application are true.

Signature of Applicant ....

To be completed by Justice of the Peace, Notary Public or Commissioner for Oaths

SWORN at (Place) ....

this .... day of .... 19 ....

before me (full name) ....

(full address) ....

....

....

....

Signature ....

*Justice of the Peace/*Notary Public/*Commissioner for Oaths

*Delete as appropriate

NOTE

[1] Added by S.I. 1984 No. 000.

---

[1] FORM SDA3 Rule 136(3)

Under the Divorce (Scotland) Act 1976, section 1(2)(*d*)
Simplified Procedure

M ....

CONSENT TO APPLICATION FOR DIVORCE
HUSBAND AND WIFE HAVING LIVED APART FOR AT LEAST TWO YEARS.

In Part 1 of the enclosed form your husband/wife is applying for divorce on the ground that the marriage has broken down irretrievably because you and (s)he have lived apart for at least two years AND you consent to the divorce being granted.

Such consent must be given formally in writing at Part 2 of the application form. BEFORE completing that part, you are requested to read it over carefully so that you understand the effects of consenting to divorce. Thereafter—

If you wish to consent

(*a*) Check the details given by the applicant at Part 1 of the form to ensure that they are correct to the best of your knowledge;

(*b*) Complete Part 2 (Form of Consent) by entering your name and address at the appropriate place and adding your signature and the date; and

(*c*) Return the whole application form to your husband/wife at the address given in Part 1.

Once your husband/wife has completed the remainder of the form and has submitted it to the Court, a copy of the whole application (including your consent) will later be served upon you formally by the Court.

In the event of the divorce being granted, you will automatically be sent a copy of the extract decree. (Should you change your address before receiving the copy extract decree, please notify the Court immediately.)

If you do NOT wish to consent

Please return the application form, with Part 2 uncompleted, to your husband/wife and advise him/her of your decision.

The Court will NOT grant a divorce under this application if Part 2 of the form is not completed by you.

Sheriff Clerk
Sheriff Court

NOTE
[1] Added by S.I. 1984 No. 000.

---

[1] FORM SDA4 Rule 138(1)

CITATION IN SECTION 1(2)(*e*) CASES

Under the Divorce (Scotland) Act 1976, section 1(2)(*e*)
Simplified Procedure

M ....

....

.... 19

APPLICATION FOR DIVORCE
HUSBAND AND WIFE HAVING LIVED APART FOR AT LEAST FIVE YEARS

Your husband/wife has applied to the Court for divorce on the ground that the marriage has broken down irretrievably *because you and (s)he have lived apart for a period of at least five years.*

A copy of the application is hereby served upon you.

1. Please note:
   (*a*) that the Court may not make financial awards under this procedure and that your husband/wife is making no claim against you for payment of a periodical allowance (i.e. regular payment of money weekly, monthly etc. for his/her maintenance) or a capital sum (i.e. lump sum).
   (*b*) that your husband/wife states that you will not suffer grave financial hardship in the event of decree of divorce being granted.

2. Divorce may result in the loss to you of property rights (e.g. the right to succeed to the Applicant's estate on his/her death) or the right, where appropriate, to a widow's pension.
3. If you wish to oppose the granting of a divorce, you should put your reasons in writing and send your letter to the address shown below. Your letter must reach the Court before
4. In the event of the divorce being granted, you will be sent a copy of the extract decree. (Should you change your address before receiving the copy extract decree, please notify the Court immediately.)

Sheriff Clerk/
Sheriff Officer

Sheriff Clerk
Sheriff Court House
....
....
....
(Tel.)..................

EXPLANATORY NOTE: If you wish to exercise your right to claim a financial award you should immediately advise the Court that you oppose the application for that reason, and thereafter consult a solicitor.

NOTE
[1] Added by S.I. 1984 No. 255.

---

[1] FORM SDA5 Rule 141(1)

SHERIFF COURT

At the
day of Nineteen hundred and
in an action in the Sheriff Court of

at at the instance of

Applicant

Respondent

who were married at (place) on (date)

the Sheriff pronounced decree divorcing the Respondent from the Applicant

Extracted at the day of
Nineteen Hundred and by me Sheriff Clerk of

Sheriff Clerk

NOTE
[1] Inserted by S.I. 1984 No. 255.

---

[1] FORM SDA6 Rule 138(9)

Form of Intimation for display on walls of court

Court Ref. No.:

An application for divorce has been made in Sheriff Court by A.B. calling as defender C.D.

If C.D. wishes to oppose the granting of decree of divorce he/she should immediately contact the Sheriff Clerk from whom he/she may obtain a copy of the application.

Tel No:

[*Signed*] Sheriff Clerk

Date: [*insert date*]

NOTE

[1] Inserted by S.I. 1986 No. 1230.

---

[1] FORM SDA7 Rule 138(10)

Form of Intimation to children and next of kin in simplified divorce application

To [*name and address*]

TAKE NOTICE that an application for divorce [*number of application*] has been made against [*name of respondent*] your [father, mother, brother or other relative *as the case may be*]. A copy of the application is attached. If you know of his/her present address, you are requested to forward it to the Sheriff Clerk [*insert full address of Sheriff Clerk*] forthwith. You may also, if you wish, oppose the granting of decree of divorce by sending a letter to the court giving your reasons for your opposition to the application. Your letter must be sent to the Sheriff Clerk within [21] days from [*insert date*], the date of posting of this intimation.

Date: [*insert date*]

[*Signed*] A.B.
Sheriff Clerk

Note:
It may be in your best interests to consult a solicitor, who if necessary, will advise you on the availability of legal aid.

NOTE

[1] Inserted by S.I. 1986 No. 1230 and as amended by S.I. 1988 No. 1978.

[THE NEXT PAGE IS D 45]

[1] Reserve and Auxiliary Forces (Protection of Civil Interests) Act 1951

(14 & 15 Geo. 6, c. 65)

An Act to provide for protecting the interests of persons called up or volunteering for certain naval, military or air force service, or doing work or training under the National Service Act 1948, by virtue of being conditionally registered under that Act as conscientious objectors, and of other persons consequentially affected, in respect of civil rights and liabilities of theirs.

[1st August 1951]

NOTE

[1] As amended by the Agriculture Act 1958. Extended by the Post Office Act 1969, Sched. 4, para. 93(1). See the Merchant Shipping Act 1988, s.29(4).

FORM OF APPEAL - differs according to whether ordinary or summary procedure. Ordinary dealt with under s.27 of 1907 Act

- leave of sh. must be asked to appeal in some cases where there are interlocutory judgements
- R.91 - no leave required - 14 days
- R.92 - leave required - 7 days
- If dissatisfied with the decision of SP - may appeal decision to Ct of S under s.28 of 1907 Act
- SUMMARY CAUSE APPEAL - object to make summary cause go faster with a greater degree of certainty. Appellant much more restricted than in an ordinary action. No shorthand writer only sh. taking notes
- sh. finds facts which are held to be established by evidence + put these into stated case for appellant
- parties can ask sh. to adjust stated case if sh. has missed out a fact
- grounds in law in which to proceed are also stated eg a contract in law between parties for sale of car. If D. in breach of contract re delivery + P. entitled to damages
- Appeal to Ct. of S. from S.P. only if he certifies it is suitable for Ct. of S.
- Procedure for appeal in Small Claims roughly same as for summary cause - can appeal to S.P. but NOT Ct. of S.
- Don't appeal unless there is some reason for it - system comes to a halt + other party cannot the judgement

PART I

PROTECTION AGAINST CERTAIN LEGAL REMEDIES

. . . .

Provisions as to Scotland

Application of sections 8 to 12

7. The five next following sections shall apply to Scotland only.

General restrictions on execution and other remedies

8.—(1) In the cases mentioned in the next following section no person shall be entitled, subject to the provisions of this Part of this Act, to enforce, except with the leave of the appropriate court, a decree of any court (whether pronounced before or after the commencement of this Act) for the payment of a sum of money or for the recovery of possession of land:

Provided that nothing in this subsection shall apply to—

(*a*) any decree for damages in respect of loss or damage arising from any wrongful act or omission;

(*b*) any decree based upon a contract made after the relevant date;

(*c*) any decree for expenses;

1 (*d*) any decree for aliment or any decree or order enforceable by virtue of any enactment in like manner as a decree for aliment, or any order for payment under subsection (2) of section 3, or subsection (4) of section 5, of the Guardianship of Infants Act 1925 or under subsection (3) of section 11 of the Guardianship Act 1973; or

(*e*) any order made in criminal proceedings, or an order for the recovery of a penalty due in respect of a contravention of, or failure to comply with, any Act.

(2) In the cases mentioned in the next following section no person shall be entitled, subject to the provisions of this Part of this Act, except with the leave of the appropriate court—

(*a*) to do any diligence (not being diligence used only on the dependence of an action or *ad fundandam jurisdictionem*);

(*b*) to enforce any irritancy, legal or conventional;

(*c*) to realise any security or forfeit any deposits;

(*d*) to exercise any power of sale conferred by a heritable security;

(*e*) to institute an action of maills and duties; or

(*f*) to take or resume possession of any property by reason of any default by any person in the payment of money or the performance of any obligation:

Provided that this subsection shall not apply to any remedy or proceedings available in consequence of any default in the payment of a debt arising by virtue of a contract made after the relevant date or the performance of an obligation so arising, and nothing in this subsection shall affect—

(i) any right or power of pawnbrokers to deal with pledges; or

(ii) any remedy competent to a heritable creditor in possession of the security subjects at the relevant date;

(iii) any right or power of a person to sell goods in his custody arising by reason of default in the payment of a debt.

(3) If on any application for such leave as is required under this section for the enforcement of any decree or the exercise of any right or remedy mentioned in the foregoing provisions of this section, the appropriate court is of opinion that the person liable to implement such decree or perform the obligation in respect of which such right or remedy arises, is unable immediately to do so by reason of circumstances directly or indirectly attributable to his or someone else's performing or having performed a period of relevant

service, the court may, subject to the provisions of this Part of this Act, refuse leave to enforce the decree or to exercise the right or remedy or give leave therefor subject to such restrictions and conditions as the court thinks proper.

Any order pronounced under this subsection may be suspended, rescinded or varied by a subsequent order.

(4) The appropriate court, in determining for the purpose of the last foregoing subsection whether a person is unable immediately to implement the decree or perform the obligation in question by reason of any such circumstances as are mentioned in that subsection, or in determining the restrictions and conditions (if any) subject to which leave is to be given under that subsection, may take account of other liabilities, whether present or future, of that person.

(5) Where—

(*a*) a petition for sequestration has been presented against any debtor, and it is shown to the satisfaction of the court before which such petition depends that his inability to pay his debts is due to circumstances directly or indirectly attributable to his or someone else's performing or having performed a period of relevant service; or

(*b*) a winding-up petition has been presented against an exempt private company on the ground that it is unable to pay its debts, and it is shown to the satisfaction of the court before which such petition depends that its inability to pay its debts is due to circumstances directly or indirectly attributable to any person's performing or having performed a period of relevant service;

the court may sist the proceedings in the petition for such time and subject to such conditions as the court thinks fit.

In this subsection the expression " an exempt private company " shall be construed in accordance with subsection (4) of section 129 of the Companies Act 1948.

NOTE

[1] As amended by the Guardianship Act 1973, Sched. 5.

Scope of protection

9.—(1) Subject to the following provisions of this section, the provisions of subsection (1) or (2) of the last foregoing section shall apply to the exercise of any right or remedy in the following cases and in the following cases only, that is to say:—

(*a*) they shall apply (by virtue of this paragraph) where the person liable to implement the decree or to perform the obligation in question is for the time being performing a period of relevant service;

(*b*) they shall apply (by virtue of this paragraph but subject to any order of the appropriate court directing that they shall not so apply or shall cease so to apply) where the person liable as aforesaid has been performing a period of relevant service and while he was so doing an application was made to the appropriate court for leave under the last foregoing section to exercise the right or remedy;

(*c*) they shall apply in any case where—

(i) the appropriate court by order so directs, on the application of the person liable as aforesaid and on being satisfied that he is unable immediately to implement the decree or to perform the obligation in question by reason of circumstances directly or indirectly attributable to his or someone else's performing or having performed a period of relevant service; or

(ii) the person liable as aforesaid has made to the appropriate court an application for an order under this paragraph, and the application has not been disposed of, or not having made such an application has given to the proper person written notice of his intention to do so.

(2) A notice given for the purpose of paragraph (*c*) of the foregoing subsection shall expire at the expiration of fourteen days (or, if given in a class of case as to which a longer period is prescribed for the purposes of this subsection, at the expiration of that period) from the date on which it was given, and where the person giving a notice for that purpose has given a previous notice to the like effect the later notice shall have no operation unless the previous notice was withdrawn with the consent of the proper person before it expired.

(3) For the purpose of the foregoing subsections, the expression " the proper person " means the person seeking to exercise the right or remedy in question, but a notice shall be deemed to be given to the proper person if given to any person (whether the proper person or his agent or not) proceeding to enforce that right or remedy.

(4) Where the appropriate court makes an order under paragraph (*c*) of subsection (1) of this section with respect to the exercise of any right or remedy the powers of the court under the last foregoing section shall thereupon be exercisable as if an application for leave to exercise the right or remedy in question had been made under that section.

(5) The appropriate court, in determining for the purpose of the said paragraph (*c*) whether the applicant is unable immediately to implement the decree or to perform the obligation in question by reason of any such circumstances as are mentioned in that paragraph, may take account of other liabilities, whether present or future, of his.

(6) Any reference in subsection (3) of the last foregoing section or subsection (1) of this section to the person liable to implement the decree or to perform the obligation in question shall in a case where it is sought to exercise a right or remedy against one such person separately from any others who are also so liable, be construed as referring to him only and not including any such other person but, in a case where it is sought to exercise it against two or more such persons jointly, shall be construed as referring to all or any of the persons against whom it is sought to exercise the right or remedy; and in this subsection references to exercising a right or a remedy against a person shall include references to exercising it against property in which he has an interest or of which he is in possession.

(7) For the purposes of the last foregoing section, a person in right of a decree who presents a petition for sequestration or a winding up petition founded on the non-payment of money due under the decree shall be deemed to be enforcing the decree.

(8) For the purposes of the last foregoing section, the expression " the relevant date " means the date on which the service man in question began to perform the period of relevant service:

Provided that—

(*a*) For the purposes of any reference in that section to a contract made after the relevant date where a service man performs two or more periods of relevant service the said expression means the date on which he began the later or latest of those periods of service; and

(*b*) for the purposes of the proviso to subsection (2) of that section—

(i) where the said date was before the commencement of this Act, then subject to sub-paragraph (ii) of this paragraph the said expression means the date of that commencement; and

(ii) in a case to which the last foregoing section applies by virtue of paragraph (*c*) of subsection (1) of this section, the said expression means the date on which that section began so to apply.

Property in goods subject to hire-purchase agreement

[1] **10.**—(1) Where the appropriate court refuses leave under section 8 (3) of this Act to take or resume possession of goods subject to a hire-purchase agreement or a conditional sale agreement or to do diligence on any decree for the delivery of such goods, or gives leave subject to restrictions and conditions, and the person to whom they are hired, or, as the case may be, the buyer before possession is taken or resumed or diligence is done, pays the total price, the creditors' title to the goods shall, notwithstanding any failure to pay the total price at the time required by the agreement, vest in that person.

(2) Where the creditor under a hire-purchase agreement or a conditional sale agreement has taken possession of the goods hired or agreed to be sold under it, the appropriate court on an application under section 9 (1) (*c*) of this Act may, if it thinks fit, deal with the case as if the creditor were proceeding to take possession of the goods and, if it makes an order under that paragraph, may direct accordingly that the goods be restored to the person to whom they were hired or, as the case may be, the buyer: and if, after the creditor has taken possession of the goods, notice is given under that paragraph with respect to them, he shall not, so long as the notice is in force or any application in pursuance of the notice is undisposed of, deal with the goods in such a way as to prejudice the powers of the appropriate court under this subsection.

NOTE

[1] As substituted by the Consumer Credit Act 1974, Sched. 4.

Appropriate courts and procedure

[1] **11.**—(1) The appropriate court for the purposes of any of the provisions of this Part of this Act applying to Scotland shall be such court as the Court of Session may by Act of Sederunt designate, and different courts may be designated in relation to different classes of proceedings.

(2) The Court of Session may by Act of Sederunt make provision for requiring, or dispensing with, service of notice of any application under this Part of this Act upon persons who may be affected, whether by virtue of subsection (4) of section 8 or subsection (5) of section 9 of this Act or otherwise, and for enabling any such persons to be heard at the hearing, and may also make provision for the making of applications *ex parte* in such cases as may be prescribed by the Act of Sederunt.

(3) [Repealed by the Law Reform (Miscellaneous Provisions) (Scotland) Act 1966, Sched. Part I.]

NOTE

[1] See S.I. 1952 No. 117.

Interpretation of sections 8 to 11

12. For the purposes of sections 8 to 11 of this Act the expression " heritable security " includes a security constituted by *ex facie* absolute disposition.

Effect of failure to observe restrictions under Part I

Effect of failure to observe restrictions under Part I

[1] **13.**—(1) Omission to obtain leave required under section [8] of this Act, failure to observe a restriction or condition subject to which leave so required was given, or contravention of the prohibition in subsection [(2)] of section [10] of this Act against dealing with goods, shall not render invalid, or alter the effect of—

(*a*) anything which would have operated as a transfer of the title to any property or of the possession of any property if leave had not been required or the restriction, condition or prohibition had not been imposed;

(*b*) any payment, receipt, appointment or other transaction; or

(*c*) any legal proceedings.

(2) In any action for damages for conversion or other proceedings which lie by virtue of any such omission, failure or contravention, the court may take account of the conduct of the [defender] with a view, if the court thinks fit, to awarding exemplary damages in respect of the wrong sustained by the [pursuer].

(3) If in any action or proceedings which lie by virtue of any such omission, failure or contravention the court is satisfied that the [defender] acted honestly and reasonably, and ought fairly to be excused for it, the court may relieve the [defender] from liability in respect thereof.

(4) In so far as it appears to the appropriate court to be practicable to remedy the results of any such omission, failure or contravention as aforesaid specifically without prejudice to the interests of third parties, the court may give any such directions for restoration of property, repayment of money or other measures as may appear to the court to be requisite for that purpose.

In this subsection the expression " third parties " means persons other than—

(*a*) in the case of such an omission or failure in connection with the enforcement of a judgment, [decree] or order or the exercise of a remedy, the person proceeding thereto and any person acting in relation thereto on his behalf;

. . . . . .

(*c*) in the case of a contravention of the prohibition in subsection [(2)] of section [10] of this Act, the owner of the goods; and

(*d*) in any of the cases aforesaid, any person taking a transfer of the title to or possession of any property under a transaction in connection with which the omission, failure or contravention took place, if he took with knowledge of the circumstances which rendered what was done such an omission, failure or contravention.

(5) In relation to an action or other proceedings tried by a judge and jury—

(*a*) the references to the court in subsections (2) and (3) of this section shall be construed as references to the jury, but without prejudice to the power of the judge to give to the jury directions whether there is any evidence of facts justifying an award of exemplary damages on the one hand or the granting of relief on the other hand, or to give them advice as to the making of such an award or grant;

(*b*) the references to the court in subsection (4) of this section shall be construed as references to the judge alone.

NOTE

[1] As applicable to Scotland.

[1] Part II

NOTE
[1] For the application of Part II to Scotland, see s.24.

Protection against Insecurity of Tenure of Place of Residence

Protection during service other than short period of training

Period of residence protection, and scope of three succeeding sections (protection of tenure under lettings at a rent)

[1] **14.**—(1) The three next succeeding sections shall have effect, subject to subsection (2) of this section, in the case of a service man who performs a period of relevant service, other than a short period of training, either wholly after the commencement of this Act or partly theretofore and partly thereafter, for giving, during that period of service, or the residue of it if it began before the commencement of this Act, and four months from the date of the ending of it (in this Part of this Act referred to, in relation to such a service man, as his "period of residence protection"), security of tenure of premises which at any time during the period of protection are a rented family residence of his.

For the purposes of the operation of this Part of this Act at any time during a service man's period of residence protection—

(*a*) the expression "rented family residence" means premises in which (or in part of which) the service man was living immediately before the beginning of his period of service with a dependant or dependants of his in right of a tenancy at a rent of those premises being a tenancy vested in him or in that dependant or any of those dependants, and in which (or in part of which) at the time in question during the period of protection a dependant or dependants of his is or are living, whether with or without him, in right of such a tenancy of those premises being a tenancy vested in him or in that dependant or any of those dependants; and

(*b*) the expression "tenancy qualifying for protection" means the tenancy of a rented family residence of the service man in right of which a dependant or dependants of his is or are living therein or in part thereof at the time in question.

(2) The three next succeeding sections shall not have effect if and so long as the rented family residence—

(*a*) is a dwelling-house which consists of or comprises premises licensed for the sale of exciseable liquor on the premises; or

(*b*) is bona fide let at a rent which includes payments in respect of board.

NOTE
[1] As amended by the Rent (Scotland) Act 1971, Sched. 18.

Protection of tenure of furnished, and certain other, rented premises, by extension of the Furnished Houses (Rent Control) Act

[1] **15.**—[1a] (1) Subject to subsection (2) of the last preceding section where at any time during a service man's period of residence protection—

(*a*) the rented family residence is let under the tenancy qualifying for protection either on such terms as are mentioned in section 63(1) of the Rent (Scotland) Act 1984 (which relates to premises let in consideration of a rent which includes payment for the use of furniture or for services) or on terms of sharing with the lessor, and

(*b*) a notice to quit has been served by the lessor on the lessee (whether after or before the beginning of the period of protection) and the notice has not expired, but (*c*) the condition specified in subsection (1)(*b*) of section 72 of the Rent (Scotland) Act 1984 is not fulfilled,

the said section 72 shall apply in relation to the notice to quit as if that condition had been fulfilled as to the contract under which that tenancy subsists.

[2] (1A) This section does not apply in relation to any tenancy entered into on or after 1st December 1980.

(2) The reference in paragraph (*a*) of the preceding subsection to a letting on terms of sharing with the lessor is a reference to a letting under which—

(*a*) the lessee has the exclusive occupation of some accommodation (in this subsection referred to as "the separate accommodation");

(*b*) he has the use of other accommodation in common with the lessor or with the lessor and other persons; and

(*c*) the accommodation mentioned in the last preceding paragraph is or includes accommodation of such a nature that the circumstance specified in that paragraph is sufficient to prevent the separate accommodation from being a dwelling-house to which the Rent Restrictions Acts apply, whether apart from that circumstance it would be such a dwelling-house or not.

[3] (3) The subsistence of a Crown interest in premises shall not affect the operation of this section if the interest of the immediate landlord of the tenant under the tenancy in question is not a Crown interest; but nothing in this subsection shall be construed as excluding the operation of this Part of this Act in cases where there subsists a Crown interest not being the interest of the immediate landlord of the tenant under the tenancy in question.

[4] (4) References in the said section 72 to that section shall be construed as including references to the preceding provisions of this section and to the said section 72 as extended by those provisions.

(5) [Repealed by the Rent (Scotland) Act 1971, Sched. 20.]

NOTES

[1] As amended by the Rent (Scotland) Act 1971, Sched. 18 and (with effect from 31st January 1985) the Rent (Scotland) Act 1984, Sched. 8, Pt. II.

[1a] As amended by the Rent (Scotland) Act 1984, Sched. 8, Pt. II, with effect from 31st January 1985.

[2] Added by the Tenants' Rights, Etc. (Scotland) Act 1980, s.39(2), and as amended by the Rent (Scotland) Act 1984, Sched. 8, Pt. II, with effect from 31st January 1985.

[3] As substituted by the Rent (Scotland) Act 1971, Sched. 18.

[4] As amended by the Rent (Scotland) Act 1971, Sched. 18, the Tenants' Rights, Etc. (Scotland) Act 1980, Sched. 5, and (with effect from 31st January 1985) by the Rent (Scotland) Act 1984, Sched. 8, Pt. II.

Protection of tenure of certain rented premises by extension of Housing (Scotland) Act 1988

[1] **16.**—(1) Subject to subsection (2) of section 14 of this Act and subsection (3) below, if at any time during a service man's period of residence protection—

(*a*) a tenancy qualifying for protection ends without being continued or renewed by agreement (whether on the same or different terms and conditions), and

(*b*) by reason only of such circumstances as are mentioned in subsection (4) below, on the ending of that tenancy no statutory tenancy of the rented family residence would arise, apart from the provisions of this section,

sections 12 to 31 of the Housing (Scotland) Act 1988 shall, during the remainder of the period of protection, apply in relation to the rented family residence as if those circumstances did not exist and had not existed immediately before the ending of that tenancy and, accordingly, as if on the ending of that tenancy there arose a statutory assured tenancy during the remainder of that period.

(2) Subject to subsection (2) of section 14 of this Act and subsection (3) below, if at any time during a service man's period of residence protection—

(*a*) a tenancy qualifying for protection would come to an end, apart from the provisions of this section,

(*b*) by reason only of such circumstances as are mentioned in subsection (4) below that tenancy is not an assured tenancy, and

(*c*) if that tenancy had been an assured tenancy, it would not have come to an end at that time,

sections 12 to 31 of the Housing (Scotland) Act 1988 shall, during the remainder of the period of protection, apply in relation to the rented family residence as if those circumstances did not exist and, accordingly, as if the tenancy had become an assured tenancy immediately before it would otherwise have come to an end.

(3) Neither subsection (1) nor subsection (2) above applies if, on the ending of the tenancy qualifying for protection, a statutory tenancy arises.

(4) The circumstances referred to in subsections (1) and (2) above are one or more of the following, that is to say—

(*a*) that the circumstances mentioned in paragraph 2 of Schedule 4 to the Housing (Scotland) Act 1988 applied with respect to the tenancy qualifying for protection;

(*b*) that the circumstances mentioned in paragraph 5 of that Schedule applied with respect to the tenancy qualifying for protection; and

(*c*) that the reversion immediately expectant on the tenancy qualifying for protection belongs to any of the bodies specified in paragraph 11 of that Schedule.

NOTE

[1] Substituted by the Housing Act 1988, Sched. 17, para. 3. Amended (*prosp.*) by the Housing (Scotland) Act 1988, Sched. 10.

Provisions supplementary to section 16 in case of rented premises which include accommodation shared otherwise than with the landlord

[1] **17.**—(1) Where at any time during a service man's period of residence protection a tenancy qualifying for protection ends as mentioned in paragraph (*a*) of subsection (1) of the last preceding section, and immediately before the ending of the tenancy—

(*a*) the tenant under the terms of the tenancy had the exclusive occupation of some accommodation (in this section referred to as "the separate accommodation") and had the use of other accommodation in common with another person or other persons, not being or including the landlord, but

(*b*) by reason only of such circumstances as are mentioned in section 16(4) above, subsection (1) of section 14 of the Housing (Scotland) Act 1988 did not have effect as respects the separate accommodation,

then subject to the next succeeding subsection the said section 97 shall during the remainder of the period of protection apply in relation to the separate accommodation as if the circumstances referred to in paragraph (*b*) of this subsection did not exist, and had not existed immediately before the ending of the tenancy.

[2] (2) Where, at any time during a service man's period of residence protection—

(*a*) a tenancy qualifying for protection would come to an end, apart from the provisions of this section and section 16 above, and

(*b*) paragraphs (*a*) and (*b*) of subsection (1) above apply,

section 14 of the Housing (Scotland) Act 1988 shall, during the remainder of the period of protection, apply in relation to the separate accommodation as if the circumstances in subsection (1)(*b*) above did not exist and, accordingly, as if the tenancy had become an assured tenancy immediately before it would otherwise come to an end.

[2] (3) Neither subsection (1) nor subsection (2) above applies if, on the ending of the tenancy qualifying for protection, a statutory tenancy arises.

NOTES

[1] As amended by the Rent (Scotland) Act 1971, Sched. 18, the Tenants' Rights, Etc. (Scotland) Act 1980, s.39, and Sched. 5, the Rent (Scotland) Act 1984, Sched. 8, Pt. II and the Housing Act 1988, Sched. 17, para. 5.

[2] As substituted by the Housing Act 1988, Sched. 17, para. 5.

Protection of tenure, in connection with employment, under a licence or a rent-free letting, by extension of the Rent Acts

[1] **18.**—[2] (1) Where—

(*a*) a service man begins a period of relevant service, other than a short period of training, after the commencement of this Act, and immediately before beginning it he was living, together with a dependant or dependants of his, in any premises by virtue of a licence in that behalf granted to him by his employer in consequence of his employment, or by virtue of a tenancy so granted otherwise than at a rent (in this section referred to as a "rent-free tenancy"), or

(*b*) a service man is performing a period of relevant service, other than a short period of training, at the commencement of this Act, and immediately before beginning it he was living as aforesaid, and a dependant or dependants of his is or are living in the premises or in part thereof, otherwise than in right of a tenancy at a rent, at the commencement of this Act,

then during the service man's period of residence protection as defined in section 14 of this Act sections 12 to 31 of the Housing (Scotland) Act 1988 shall, subject to the provisions of this section, apply in relation to those premises as if instead of the licence, or of the rent-free tenancy, as the case may be, there had been granted to the service man a tenancy at a rent—

(i) a term of years certain expiring at the beginning of the period of service, or at the commencement of this Act if the period of service began theretofore, and

(ii) in other respects on the same terms and conditions (excluding any terms or conditions relating to the employment) as those on which the licence, or the rent-free tenancy, as the case may be, was granted;

and those premises shall be deemed to be during the period of protection a dwelling-house let on a statutory assured tenancy if apart from this section they would not have been so.

(2) [Repealed by the Housing Act 1988, Sched. 17, para. 6(3).]

(3) Subsection (1) of this section shall not have effect—

(*a*) where the licence, or the rent-free tenancy, as the case may be, was granted in connection with the management of premises licensed for the sale of intoxicating liquor for consumption thereon, or

(*b*) where the licence, or the rent-free tenancy, as the case may be, was granted pursuant to a contract which imposed on the grantor thereof an obligation to provide board for the service man and the dependant or dependants.

(4) As regards the assumption of the granting of a tenancy which is to be made for the purposes of subsection (1) of this section in a case where the grant in question was of a licence, if the granting of such a tenancy would have been a subletting of the premises it shall not be treated for any purpose as constituting a breach of any covenant or agreement prohibiting or restricting subletting.

(5) The subsistence of a Crown interest in the premises shall not affect the application of this section if the interest of the grantor of the licence, or the rent-free tenancy, as the case may be, is not a Crown interest.

(6) In relation to a policeman service man this section shall have effect with the substitution of a reference to a grant to him, either by the relevant police authority or by another person under arrangements made by that authority with that person, in consequence of the service man's membership of the relevant police force, for the reference in subsection (1) to a grant to a service man by his employer in consequence of his employment.

NOTES

[1] As amended by the Rent (Scotland) Act 1971, Sched. 18, and the Tenants' Rights, Etc. (Scotland) Act 1980, s.39 and Sched. 5.

[2] As amended by the Housing Act 1988, Sched. 17, para. 6.

Limitation on application of Housing (Scotland) Act 1988 by virtue of sections 16 to 18

[1] **19.** Where by virtue of sections 16 to 18 above, the operation of sections 12 to 31 of the Housing (Scotland) Act 1988 in relation to any premises is extended or modified, the extension or modification shall not affect—

(*a*) any tenancy of those premises other than the statutory assured tenancy which is deemed to arise or, as the case may be, the tenancy which is for any period deemed to be an assured tenancy by virtue of any of those provisions; or

(*b*) any rent payable in respect of a period beginning before the time when that statutory assured tenancy was deemed to arise or, as the case may be, before that tenancy became deemed to be an assured tenancy; or

(*c*) anything done or omitted to be done before the time referred to in paragraph (*b*) above.

NOTE

[1] As substituted by the Housing Act 1988, Sched. 17, para. 8.

Modifications of Rent Acts as respects occupation by employees

[1] **20.**—(1) Where the carrying out of duties connected with an employment which a service man had before beginning a period of relevant service (or, in the case of a policeman service man, the carrying out of his police duties) constitutes an obligation of a tenancy, and his performing that service prevents his carrying out those duties, the fact that he does not carry them out shall not be treated for the purposes of Case 1 in Schedule 2 to the Rent (Scotland) Act 1984 or Ground 13 in Schedule 5 to the Housing (Scotland) Act 1988 (which relates to recovery of possession where an obligation of a tenancy has been broken or not performed) as a breach or non-performance of the obligation.

(2) Case 7 in the said Schedule 2 or, as the case may be, Ground 17 in the said Schedule 5 (which relates to recovery of possession, without proof of suitable alternative accommodation, in circumstances connected with occupation by employees) shall not apply for the purposes of the proceedings on an application for possession of premises made at any time during a service man's period of residence protection (as defined in section 14 of this Act) if either—

(*a*) the premises are a rented family residence of his as defined in that section; or

(*b*) sections 12 to 31 of the Housing (Scotland) Act 1988 apply in relation to the premises as mentioned in section 18(1) of this Act and a dependant or dependants of the service man is or are living in the premises or in part thereof in right of the statutory assured tenancy or assured tenancy referred to in paragraph (*a*) of section 19 of this Act.

(3) Where the last preceding subsection has effect as to an application for possession, the circumstances specified in the Cases in Part I of the said Schedule 2 or, as the case may be, Grounds 10 to 17 in Part II of the said Schedule 5 in which the court has power to make or give an order or judgment for the recovery of possession without proof of suitable alternative accommodation shall include the circumstances specified in either of the following paragraphs, that is to say—

(*a*) that the landlord is a body who are statutory undertakers or a local authority or development corporation having public utility functions, and that the premises are required by that body in the public interest for occupation as a residence for some person who is engaged in their whole-time employment in connection with their public utility functions or with whom, conditional on housing accommodation being provided, a contract for such employment has been entered into;

(*b*) where the last preceding subsection has effect by virtue of paragraph (*b*) thereof and the service man in question is a policeman service man, that the premises are required by the relevant police authority for occupation as a residence by a member of the police force in question:

Provided that, where the court is satisfied that circumstances exist such as are specified in paragraph (*a*) of this subsection, the matters relevant for the court in determining under section 11(1) of the Rent (Scotland) Act 1984 or, as the case may be, section 18(4) of the Housing (Scotland) Act 1988 whether it is reasonable to make or give such an order or judgment shall (without prejudice to the generality of that subsection) include the question whether the body seeking the order or judgment have at their disposal any vacant accommodation which would be suitable alternative accommodation for the tenant, or will have such accommodation at their disposal at or before the time when it is proposed that the order or judgment should take effect.

(4) In the last preceding subsection the expressions "statutory undertakers" and "local authority" have the same meanings as in the Town and Country Planning Act 1947, the expression "development corporation" has the same meaning as in the New Towns Act 1946, and the expression "public utility functions" means powers or duties conferred or imposed by or under any enactment, being powers or duties to carry on a statutory undertaking (as defined in the said Act of 1947) or to provide public sewers or provide for the disposal of sewage, or being powers or duties of a river board or other drainage authority (as defined respectively in the River Boards Act 1948, and the Land Drainage Act 1930).

NOTE
[1] As amended by the Rent (Scotland) Act 1971, Sched. 18, the Rent (Scotland) Act 1984, Sched. 8, Pt. II and the Housing Act 1988, Sched. 17, para. 10.

Modifications of Agricultural Holdings Act 1948, where a tenant is a service man

21.—(1) The three next succeeding subsections shall have effect where the tenant of an agricultural holding to which this section applies performs a period of relevant service, other than a short period of training, either wholly after the commencement of this Act or partly theretofore and partly thereafter, and after the commencement of this Act, at a time during his period of residence protection, there is given to him notice to quit the holding, or notice to quit a part of the holding, being a part to which this section applies.

This section applies to any agricultural holding which comprises such a dwelling-house as is mentioned in paragraph 1 of Schedule 7 to the Agricultural Holdings Act 1948, and applies to any part of an agricultural holding being a part which consists of or comprises such a dwelling-house.

[1] (2) Subsection (1) of section 24 of the said Act of 1948 (which restricts the operation of notices to quit) shall apply notwithstanding the existence of any such circumstances as are mentioned in subsection (2) of that section; but where the Land Court is satisfied that such circumstances exist then (subject to the next succeeding subsection) the Land Court shall not be required to withhold its consent to the operation of the notice to quit by reason only that it is not satisfied that circumstances exist such as are mentioned in paragraphs (*a*) to (*e*) of subsection (1) of section 25 of that Act.

[2] (3) In determining whether to give or withhold its consent under the said section 24 the Land Court—

(*a*) if satisfied that circumstances exist such as are mentioned in subsection (2) of the said section 24 or in subsection (1) of the said section 25, shall consider to what extent (if at all) the existence of those circumstances is directly or indirectly attributable to the service man's performing or having performed the period of service in question, and

(*b*) in any case, shall consider to what extent (if at all) the giving of such consent at a time during the period of protection would cause special hardship in view of circumstances directly or indirectly attributable to the service man's performing or having performed that period of service;

and the Land Court shall withhold its consent to the operation of the notice to quit unless in all the circumstances it considers it reasonable to give its consent thereto.

(4) [Repealed by the Agriculture Act 1958, Sched. 2, Pt. II.]

(5) Where the tenant of an agricultural holding to which this section applies performs such a period of service as is mentioned in subsection (1) of this section and—

(*a*) a notice to quit the holding or a part thereof to which this section applies was given to him before the commencement of this Act or is given to him thereafter but before the beginning of his period of residence protection, and

(*b*) the tenant duly serves or has served a counter-notice under subsection (1) of the said section 24, and

[2] (*c*) the Scottish Land Court has not before the beginning of his period of residence protection decided whether to give or withhold consent to the operation of the notice to quit,

the two last preceding subsections shall (with the necessary modifications) apply in relation to the giving or withholding of consent to the operation of the notice to quit as they apply in relation to the giving or withholding of consent to the operation of a notice to quit given in the circumstances mentioned in subsection (1) of this section.

[3] (6) Section 27 of the said Scottish Act of 1949 (which authorises the Minister to make regulations as to matters arising out of sections 24 and 25 of that Act) shall apply in relation to the provisions of those sections as modified by the preceding provisions of this section as it applies in relation to the provisions of those sections apart from this section.

(7) [Repealed by the Agriculture Act 1958, Sched. 2, Pt. II.]

[4] (8) In this section the expression "agricultural holding" has the same meaning as in the said Act of 1948.

NOTES

[1] As amended by the Agriculture Act 1958, Sched. 1, Pt. II and Sched. 3.

[2] Substituted by the Agriculture Act 1958, Sched. 1, Pt. II.

[3] See S.I. 1952 No. 1338. "In subsection (6) the reference to section 27 of the Scottish Act of 1949 shall be construed as a reference to that section as originally enacted and not as amended by this Act": the Agriculture Act 1958, Sched. 1, Pt. II, para. 45(*d*).

[4] As amended by the Agriculture Act 1958, Sched. 2, Pt. II.

Facilities for action on behalf of men serving abroad in proceedings as to tenancies

[1] **22.**—[2] (1) Where in the course of any proceedings brought under the Rent (Scotland) Act 1984 or under Part II of the Housing (Scotland) Act 1988 or of any proceedings consequential upon the making of a reference or application to a rent assessment committee under Part VII of the said Act of 1984 or under Part II of the Housing (Scotland) Act 1988, or under this Part of this Act, it appears to the court or committee—

(*a*) that the proceedings relate to a tenancy or licence vested in a service man;

(*b*) that a person other than the service man desires to take a step in the proceedings on behalf of the service man at a time when he is serving abroad, or had purported to take a step in the proceedings on his behalf at a time when he was so serving; and

(*c*) that the said person, in seeking or purporting to take that step, is or was acting in good faith in the interests of the service man, and is or was a fit person to take that step on his behalf, but is or was not duly authorised to do so,

the court or committee may direct that the said person shall be deemed to be, or to have been, duly authorised to take that step on behalf of the service man.

(2) The provisions of the preceding subsection apply in relation to the institution of proceedings before a court as they apply in relation to the taking of a step in such proceedings, and apply in relation to the making of a reference or application to a rent tribunal as they apply in relation to the taking of a step in proceedings consequential upon the making of such a reference or application; and references in that subsection to proceedings brought or a reference or application made as therein mentioned include references to proceedings which purport to be so brought or to a reference or application which purports to be so made, as the case may be.

(3) Where in the course of any proceedings a court or tribunal gives a direction under subsection (1) of this section, the person to whom the direction relates shall have the like right of audience in those proceedings as the service man himself would have.

[3] (3A) In relation to any proceedings before a rent officer or rent assessment committee, within the meaning of the Rent (Scotland) Act 1984, subsections (1) to (3) of this section shall have effect as if the references to the court or tribunal included references to a rent officer or rent assessment committee.

(4) The Minister of Agriculture and Fisheries may make regulations—

(*a*) for enabling a counter-notice under subsection (1) of section 24 of the Agricultural Holdings Act 1948, to be served on behalf of a service man at a time when he is serving abroad, in a case where a notice to quit is given to him as mentioned in subsection (1) of section 21 of this Act; and

(*b*) for enabling any act or proceedings consequential upon the service of a counter-notice under subsection (1) of the said section 24 to be performed or conducted on behalf of a service man at a time when he is serving abroad, either in such a case as is mentioned in the preceding paragraph or in a case where subsection (5) of section 21 of this Act applies in relation to the service man.

(5) Regulations made under the last preceding subsection may contain such incidental and consequential provisions as may appear to the said Minister to be necessary or expedient for the purposes of the regulations.

(6) The power to make regulations under subsection (4) of this section shall be exercisable by statutory instrument, which shall be subject to annulment in pursuance of a resolution of either House of Parliament.

(7) References in this section to a time when a service man is serving abroad are references to a time when he is performing a period of relevant service and is outside the United Kingdom.

NOTES

[1] As amended by the Rent (Scotland) Act 1971, Sched. 18.

[2] As amended by the Housing Act 1988, Sched. 17, para. 12.

[3] Added by the Rent (Scotland) Act 1971, Sched. 18, and as amended by the Rent (Scotland) Act 1984, Sched. 8, Pt. II, with effect from 31st January 1985.

Interpretation of Part II

[1] **23.**—(1) In this Part of this Act, unless the context otherwise requires, the following expressions have the meanings hereby assigned to them respectively, that is to say:—

"agricultural land" has the same meaning as in section 115(1) of the Rent (Scotland) Act 1984;

"assured tenancy" and "statutory assured tenancy" have the same meaning as in Part II of the Housing (Scotland) Act 1988;

"Crown interest" means an interest belonging to His Majesty in right of the Crown or of the Duchy of Lancaster, or to the Duchy of Cornwall, or to a Government department, or held on behalf of His Majesty for the purposes of a Government department;

"dependant", in relation to a service man, means—

(*a*) his wife, and

(*b*) any other member of his family who was wholly or mainly maintained by him immediately before the beginning of the period of service in question;

in relation to a statutory tenancy or to a provision of the Rent (Scotland) Act 1984 "landlord" and "tenant" have the same meaning as in that Act but, subject to that, those expressions have the same meaning as in Part II of the Housing (Scotland) Act 1988;

"policeman service man" means a service man who, immediately before beginning the period of relevant service in question, was a member of a police force;

"relevant police authority" means, in relation to a police force, the police authority responsible for the maintenance of that force;

"statutory tenancy" means a right to retain possession of premises after the ending of a tenancy thereof, being a right arising on the ending of that tenancy from the operation of the Rent (Scotland) Act 1984 (or of the Rent (Scotland) Act 1984 as extended by this Part of this Act) in relation to a person as being, or being the widow of or otherwise related to, the former owner of the tenancy, or a right to retain possession of premises arising by virtue of subsection (1) of section 18 of this Act;

"tenancy" includes a statutory tenancy, and, apart from a statutory tenancy, means a tenancy created either immediately or derivatively out of the freehold, whether by a lease or underlease, by an agreement for a lease or underlease or by a tenancy agreement, but does not include any relationship between a mortgagor and a mortgagee as such.

(1A) Any reference in this Part of this Act to sections 12 to 31 of the Housing (Scotland) Act 1988 includes a reference to sections 47 to 55 of that Act so far as applicable to those sections.

(2) In this Part of this Act—

(*a*) references to the ending of a tenancy are references to the coming to an end thereof however brought about, whether by effluxion of time, notice to quit or otherwise, and in particular, as respects a statutory tenancy, include references to the coming to an end thereof as between the tenant and a landlord who is himself a tenant by reason of the ending of the tenancy of the landlord;

(*b*) references to a tenancy vested in any person include references to a tenancy vested in trustees, or held as part of the estate of a deceased person, where the first-mentioned person has a right or permission to occupy the premises arising by reason of a beneficial interest (whether direct or derivative) under the trusts or, as the case may be, in the estate of the deceased person or under trusts of which the deceased person was trustee.

(3) In this Part of this Act, and in the Rent (Scotland) Act 1984 or sections 12 to 31 of the Housing (Scotland) Act 1988 as applied by any provision thereof, references to rent shall be construed as including references to any sum in the nature of rent payable in respect of such a licence as is mentioned in section 18 of this Act.

NOTE

[1] As amended by the Police (Scotland) Act 1967, Sched. 5, the Rent (Scotland) Act 1971, Sched. 18, and the Rent (Scotland) Act 1984, Sched. 8, Pt. II and the Housing Act 1988, Sched. 17, para. 14.

Application of Part II to Scotland

24. In the application of the preceding sections of this Part of this Act to Scotland—

(*a*) for any reference to the Minister of Local Government and Planning or to the Minister of Agriculture and Fisheries there shall be substituted a reference to the Secretary of State; and for any reference to the county court there shall be substituted a reference to the sheriff[1];

[2] (*b*) and for any reference to such a dwelling-house as is mentioned in paragraph 1 of Schedule 7 to the Agricultural Holdings Act 1948, there shall be substituted a reference to a dwelling-house comprised in an agricultural holding and occupied by the person responsible for the control (whether as tenant or as servant or agent of the tenant) of the farming of the holding;

(*c*) [Repealed by the Agriculture Act 1958, Sched. 2, Pt. II.]

(*d*) for any reference to the Town and Country Planning Act 1947, there shall be substituted a reference to the Town and Country Planning (Scotland) Act 1947, and for references to the Furnished Houses (Rent Control) Act 1946, and to section 8 thereof, there shall be respectively substituted references to the Rent of Furnished Houses Control (Scotland) Act 1943, and to section 6 thereof;

(*e*) for any reference to a valuation list there shall be substituted a reference to a valuation roll; for any reference to a hereditament there shall be substituted a reference to lands and heritages; and for any reference to intoxicating liquor there shall be substituted a reference to exciseable liquor;

(*f*) the expression "licence" means a right or permission derived otherwise than under a lease; and any reference to the reversion immediately expectant on a tenancy shall be construed as a reference to the interest of the immediate landlord of the tenant under the tenancy;

(*g*) [Repealed by the Police (Scotland) Act 1967, Sched. 5]

(*h*) section 16 of this Act shall have effect as if for subsection (8) there were substituted the following subsection—

"(8) A notice for the purposes of this section may be served in like manner as a notice under section 349 of the Local Government (Scotland) Act 1947."

[3] (*j*) any reference to the Rent Restrictions Acts there shall be substituted a reference to the Rent (Scotland) Act 1971; and for any reference, however expressed, to a dwelling-house to which the Rent Restrictions Acts apply there shall be substituted a reference to a dwelling-house subject to a statutory tenancy within the meaning of the Rent (Scotland) Act 1971.

NOTES

[1] For the interpretation of the term "sheriff", see now the Sheriff Courts (Scotland) Act 1971, s.4, and the Interpretation Act 1978, Sched. 1.

[2] As amended by the Agriculture Act 1958, Sched. 2, Pt. II and the Agricultural Holdings (Scotland) Act 1991, Sched. 13.

[3] Added by the Rent (Scotland) Act 1971, Sched. 18.

Protection during short period of training

Protection during short period of training

25.—(1) Where a service man who has been living with a dependant or dependants of his in any premises in right of a tenancy, or of a licence in that behalf granted by his employer in consequence of his employment, performs a short period of training, then, for so long during that period and within fourteen days from the ending of it as the dependant or dependants and the service man or any of them is or are still living in the premises or any part thereof, no person shall be entitled, except with the leave of the appropriate court, to proceed—

(*a*) to execution on, or otherwise to the enforcement of, any judgment or order given or made against any of them for the recovery of possession of any part of the premises in which any of them is or are living, or

(*b*) to exercise against any of them any right to take possession of or to re-enter upon, any such part thereof.

(2) If, on any application for such leave as is required by the preceding subsection, the court is of opinion that, by reason of circumstances directly or indirectly attributable to the service man's performing or having performed the period of service in question, the judgment, order or right ought not to be immediately executed, enforced, or exercised, the court may refuse leave or give leave subject to such restrictions and conditions as the court thinks proper.

(3) References in this section to a judgment or order for the recovery of possession of premises include references to any judgment or order the effect of which is to enable a person to obtain possession of the premises, and in particular includes, in relation to a mortgagee, a judgment or order for the delivery of possession of the premises.

(4) For the purposes of this section a person shall be deemed to be proceeding to execution on, or otherwise to the enforcement of, a judgment or order in the circumstances in which, by virtue of subsection (9) of section 3 of this Act, he would be deemed to be so proceeding for the purposes of section 2 of this Act, and, where a person has, in a case for which leave was not required under this section, taken out any judicial process with a view to, or in the course of, the enforcement of a judgment or order or proceeded to the exercise of a right to take possession of or to re-enter upon premises, he shall be deemed to be proceeding to the enforcement of the judgment or order or to the exercise of the right when any step is taken by him or on his behalf towards its completion.

(5) The references in section 5 and subsection (1) of section 11 of this Act to the provisions of Part I of this Act shall include references to the provisions of this section, and the provisions of section 13 of this Act which relate to omission to obtain leave required under section 2 of this Act shall have effect in relation to omission to obtain leave required under this section.

(6) In this section the expression "dependant", in relation to a service man, means—

(*a*) his wife, and

(*b*) any other member of his family wholly or mainly maintained by him.

(7) In the application of this section to Scotland—

(*a*) the expression "licence" has the meaning assigned to it by paragraph (*f*) of section 24 of this Act;

(*b*) a reference to proceeding to execution on or otherwise to the enforcement of a judgment or order shall be construed as a reference to the enforcement of a decree, and any reference to a mortgagee shall be omitted;

(*c*) for the references to section 2 and to subsection (9) of section 3 of this Act there shall be respectively substituted references to section 8 and to subsection (7) of section 9 of this Act.

. . . . . .

Part III

Protection Against Insecurity of Tenure of Business and Professional Premises

Provisions as to Scotland

Application of sections 38 to 40

37. The three next following sections shall apply to Scotland only.

Application by service man for renewal of tenancy of business premises

38.—(1) Where—

(*a*) immediately before beginning (whether before or after the commencement of this Act) a period of relevant service other than a short period of training, a service man was the working proprietor of a business or a professional practice carried on in the premises or part of the premises comprised in a tenancy vested in him, and

(*b*) the landlord gives or has given to the service man notice of termination of tenancy taking effect after the commencement of this Act, and before the date of the ending of that period of service or before the expiration of two months from that date, and (*c*) at the time when an application for renewal of the tenancy is made in pursuance of the provisions hereinafter contained the service man is still the proprietor of the business or practice and the business or practice is still being carried on in the premises comprised in the tenancy,

the service man may, at any time before the notice of termination of tenancy takes effect and not later than the expiry of twenty-one days after the service of the notice or after the commencement of this Act, whichever is the later, apply to the sheriff for a renewal of his tenancy.

(2) For the purposes of paragraph (*a*) of the last preceding subsection a service man shall be deemed to have been at any time the working proprietor of a business or professional practice carried on as mentioned in that paragraph if, and only if, he was the proprietor of the business or practice during the whole of the period of one year immediately preceding that time and, during more than one-half of that period, either—

(*a*) he worked whole-time in the actual management or conduct of that business or practice, or

(*b*) he worked whole-time in the actual management or conduct of a business or professional practice of which that business or practice was a branch and was mainly engaged in the management or conduct of that branch.

(3) In the preceding provisions of this section the expression " proprietor " means, in the case of a business or practice carried on by a firm, a partner in the firm on terms and conditions entitling him to not less than one-half of the profits of the firm and, in the case of a business or practice carried on by a company, a person holding shares in the company amounting in nominal value to not less than one-half of the issued share capital of the company; and, in relation to a business or practice carried on by a partnership firm or by a company, references in those provisions to the proprietor of the business or practice include references to a person being one of two such partners in the firm or, as the case may be, being one of two persons each holding such shares in the company, and references to the working proprietor of the business or practice shall be construed accordingly.

(4) In relation to a business or practice carried on by a firm or by a company, references in the preceding provisions of this section to a tenancy vested in the service man include references to a tenancy vested in one or more partners in the firm, or vested in the company, as the case may be; and for the purposes of those provisions and of this subsection a tenancy shall be treated as having been vested at any time in a person if it was then vested in trustees, or held as part of the estate of a deceased person, and the first-mentioned person then had a right or permission to occupy the premises comprised in the tenancy, or the part of those premises in which the business or practice was being carried on, being a right or permission arising by reason of a beneficial interest (whether direct or derivative) under the trusts or, as the case may be, in the estate of the deceased person or under trusts of which the deceased person was trustee.

(5) In this section—

(*a*) the expression " profits " in relation to a firm means such profits of the firm as are from time to time distributable among the partners therein;

(*b*) the expression " company " has the same meaning as in the Companies Act 1948;

(*c*) the expression " share " includes stock and the expression " share capital " shall be construed accordingly;

and for the purposes of this section shares held by a person's wife, or held by him jointly with his wife, shall be treated as shares held by that person.

(6) The foregoing provisions of this section shall not have effect if at the

time when an application for renewal of the tenancy might otherwise be made—

(*a*) the premises comprised in the tenancy—

(i) are an agricultural holding within the meaning of the Agricultural Holdings (Scotland) Act 1949, or

(ii) consist of or comprise premises (other than premises excepted from this provision) licensed for the sale of exciseable liquor for consumption on the premises, or

(*b*) the tenancy of the premises was granted in pursuance of subsection (2) of section 4 of the War Damaged Sites Act 1949.

In this subsection the reference to premises excepted from the provision as to premises licensed for the sale of exciseable liquor is a reference to premises in respect of which—

(i) the excise licence for the time being in force is a licence the duty in respect of which is the reduced duty payable under section 45 of the Finance (1909–10) Act 1910, or a licence granted in pursuance of regulations under subsection (5) of the said section 45 (which relates to the granting of licences on the provisional payment of reduced duty); or

(ii) the Commissioners of Customs and Excise certify that no application under the said section 45 has been made in respect of the period for which the excise licence for the time being in force was granted, but that if such an application had been made such a licence could properly have been granted as is mentioned in the preceding paragraph.

Power of sheriff to grant new tenancy

[1] **39.**—(1) On any application under subsection (1) of the last foregoing section the sheriff may, subject as hereinafter provided, determine that the tenancy shall be renewed for such period, at such rent, and on such terms and conditions as he shall, in all the circumstances, think reasonable, and thereafter the parties shall be deemed to have entered into a new lease of the premises for that period, at that rent and on those terms and conditions.

(2) The period for which a tenancy may be renewed under the last foregoing subsection shall not extend beyond the expiry of four months from the end of the period of service in consequence of which the application was made.

(3) Notwithstanding anything in subsection (1) of this section, the sheriff may, if in all the circumstances he thinks it reasonable to do so, dismiss any application under subsection (1) of the last foregoing section, and shall not determine that a tenancy shall be renewed, if he is satisfied—

(*a*) that the tenant is in breach of any condition of his tenancy which in the opinion of the sheriff is material; or

(*b*) that the tenant is notour bankrupt or is divested of his estate by virtue of a trust deed for behoof of creditors, or, being a company, is unable to pay its debts; or

(*c*) that the landlord has offered to sell the premises to the tenant at such price as may, failing agreement, be fixed by a single arbiter agreed on by the parties or appointed, failing such agreement, by the sheriff; or

(*d*) that the landlord has offered to afford to the tenant, on terms and conditions which in the opinion of the sheriff are reasonable, alternative accommodation which, in the opinion of the sheriff is suitable for the purposes of the business carried on by the tenant in the premises; or

(*e*) that the tenant has given notice of termination of tenancy and in consequence of that notice the landlord has contracted to sell or let the premises or has taken any other steps as a result of which he would in the opinion of the sheriff be seriously prejudiced if he could not obtain possession of the premises; or

(*f*) that, having regard to all the circumstances of the case, greater hardship would be caused by determining that the tenancy shall be renewed than by refusing so to do.

(4) Where a tenancy has been renewed under subsection (1) of this section, the tenant shall have the like right to apply for further renewals as if the tenancy had been renewed by agreement between the landlord and the tenant, and accordingly the foregoing provisions of this section and the immediately preceding section shall, with any necessary modifications, apply to a tenancy which has been renewed under the said subsection (1) or under this subsection.

(5) If on any application under this section the sheriff is satisfied that it will not be possible to dispose finally of the application before the notice of termination of tenancy takes effect, he may make an interim order authorising the tenant to continue in occupation of the premises at such rent, for such period (which shall not exceed three months) and on such terms and conditions as the sheriff may think fit.

(6) Applications under subsection (1) of the last foregoing section shall be conducted and disposed of in the summary manner in which proceedings are conducted and disposed of under the Small Debt (Scotland) Acts 1837 to 1889, and the decision of the sheriff in any such application shall be final and not subject to review.

NOTE

[1] For the interpretation of the term "sheriff," see now the Sheriff Courts (Scotland) Act 1971, s.4, and the Interpretation Act 1978, Sched. 1.

Application to Crown property

40.—(1) The last two foregoing sections shall apply to any such premises as are mentioned therein in which the interest of the immediate landlord of the tenant belongs to His Majesty in right of the Crown or to a Government department or is held on behalf of His Majesty for the purposes of a Government department, in like manner as the said section applies to any other such premises.

(2) Where the Minister or Board in charge of any Government department is satisfied that for reasons of national security it is necessary that the use or occupation of any such premises in which the interest aforesaid belongs to a Government department or is held on behalf of His Majesty for the purposes of a Government department should be discontinued or changed, the Minister or Board may certify that this subsection applies to the premises; and where such a certificate is given the sheriff shall not determine that the tenancy shall be renewed.

. . . . . .

PART VII

MISCELLANEOUS AND GENERAL

Evidence as to performance of relevant service

[1] **60.**—(1) A certificate stating that a person has performed or is performing or is to perform a period of relevant service or of relevant service of any particular description, or the duration or the date of the beginning or ending of such a period, or whether such a period which has been or is being or is to be performed by any person is or is not a short period of training, being a certificate which is signed by a person authorised in that behalf—

(*a*) by the Defence Council

shall in all legal proceedings be sufficient evidence of the facts stated therein for the purposes of this Act except to any extent to which it is shown to be incorrect.

(2) A certificate signed by a person authorised in that behalf by the Defence Council stating that a person is not performing, and has not within a specified previous time performed, a period of relevant service in a specified force or forces (being a force or forces in respect of which the Defence Council keep records), shall in all legal proceedings be sufficient evidence of the facts stated therein for the purposes of this Act except to any extent to which it is shown to be incorrect.

(3) A certificate signed by a person authorised in that behalf by the Defence Council referring to an inquiry as to a person therein described and being to the effect that no person answering to that description is identifiable in the relevant records kept by the authority on whose behalf the certificate is signed, shall be sufficient evidence for the purposes of this Act that no such person is so identifiable.

(4) A certificate signed as aforesaid stating any matter as a matter appearing from records shall be treated for the purposes of subsection (1), and of subsection (2), of this section as stating it as a fact.

(5) A document purporting to be a certificate signed as aforesaid shall be deemed to be such unless the contrary is proved.

(6) The Defence Council shall be under obligation to secure that, on inquiry made to them for the purposes of this Act as to a person therein described, if the information appearing from records kept by them is such as to enable a certificate falling within subsection (1) or subsection (2) of this section to be given as to a person appearing to answer that description, or is such as to justify the giving of a certificate falling within subsection (3) of this section, such a certificate shall be given:

Provided that no certificate the giving of which would in the opinion of the authority to whom the inquiry is made be against the interests of national security shall be given.

NOTE

[1] As amended by S.I. 1964 No. 488, and the Statute Law (Repeals) Act 1977, Sched. 1, Pt. I. Functions of the Minister of Labour and National Service now exercisable by the Secretary of State for Employment: S.I. 1959 No. 1769, S.I. 1968 No. 729 and S.I. 1970 No. 1537.

. . . . .

Interpretation

[1] **64.**—(1) In this Act, unless the context otherwise requires, the following expressions have the meaning hereby assigned to them respectively, that is to say,—

[2] "conditional sale agreement" means an agreement for the sale of goods under which the purchase price or part of it is payable by instalments, and the property in the goods is to remain in the seller (notwithstanding that the buyer is to be in possession of the goods) until such conditions as to the payment of instalments or otherwise as may be specified in the agreement are fulfilled;

[2] "creditor" means the person by whom the goods are bailed or (in Scotland) hired under a hire-purchase agreement or, as the case may be, the seller under a conditional sale agreement, or the person to whom his rights and duties have passed by assignment or operation of the law;

[2] "hire-purchase agreement" means an agreement, other than a conditional sale agreement, under which—

(*a*) goods are bailed or (in Scotland) hired in return for periodical payments by the person to whom they are bailed or hired, and

(*b*) the property in the goods will pass to that person if the terms of the agreement are complied with and one or more of the following occurs—

(i) the exercise of an option to purchase by that person,

(ii) the doing of any other specified act by any party to the agreement,

(iii) the happening of any other specified event;

[3] "local authority" has the same meaning as in paragraph 6(1) of Schedule 3 to the Pensions (Increase) Act 1971 and any reference in this Act to a local authority shall apply also to the bodies mentioned in paragraph 6(2) of that Schedule;

[3] "local Act scheme" means the superannuation scheme administered by a local authority maintaining a superannuation fund under a local Act;

"relevant service" means service after the 15th day of July 1950 of a description specified in the First Schedule to this Act;

"service" means the discharge of naval, military or air force duties, and includes training for the discharge of such duties;

"service man" means a man who performs a period of relevant service;

"short period of training" means a period of relevant service of a description specified in paragraph 2 of the First Schedule to this Act to which a maximum period of fifteen days is attached, of a description specified in paragraph 6 thereof, or of a description specified in paragraph 7 thereof performed under an obligation or voluntary arrangements under which its continuous duration is limited to less than three months.

[2] "total price" means the total sum payable by the person to whom goods are bailed or hired under a hire-purchase agreement or, as the case may be, the buyer under a conditional sale agreement including any sum payable on the exercise of an option to purchase but excluding any sum payable as a penalty or as compensation or damages for a breach of the agreement.

(2) [Repealed by the Armed Forces Act 1981, Sched. 5.]

(3) [Repealed by the Statute Law (Repeals) Act 1977, Sched. 1, Pt. I.]

(4) In this Act, unless the context otherwise requires, references to any enactment shall be construed as references to that enactment as amended by or under any other enactment.

NOTES

[1] As amended by the Rent (Scotland) Act 1971, Sched. 20, and the Statute Law (Repeals) Act 1977, Sched. 1, Pt. I.

[2] Added by the Consumer Credit Act 1974, Sched. 4, para. 14.

[3] As substituted by the Superannuation Act 1972, Sched. 6.

SCHEDULES

FIRST SCHEDULE

SERVICE RELEVANT FOR THE PURPOSES OF THIS ACT

Sections 41 to 44 and sections 52, 63, 64

1. [1] (i) Service in pursuance of any notice or directions given under any enactment which provides for the calling out on permanent service, or the calling into actual service, or the embodiment, of any reserve or auxiliary force, or members thereof, or for the recall of service pensioners within the meaning of section 1(1) of the Reserve Forces (Safeguard of Employment) Act 1985.

(ii) Service, other than for the purposes of training only, in pursuance of any obligation or undertaking, whether legally enforceable or not, to serve when called upon as a commissioned officer, not being an obligation or undertaking to accept a permanent or short-service commission.

(iii), (iv) [Repealed by the Statute Law (Repeals) Act 1977, Sched. 1, Pt. I.]

(v) [Repealed by the Armed Forces Act 1981, Sched. 5.]

(vi)–(viii) [Repealed by the Statute Law (Repeals) Act 1977, Sched. 1, Pt. I.]

NOTE

[1] As amended by the Reserve Forces (Safeguard of Employment) Act 1985, Sched. 4, para. 1, with effect from 9th August 1985.

2. [Repealed by the Statute Law (Repeals) Act 1977, Sched. 1, Pt. I.]

3. [Repealed by the Statute Law (Repeals) Act 1977, Sched. 1., Pt. I.]

4. Service for a period of eighteen months for which an officer of any reserve force of the Royal Navy or of the Royal Marines, or an officer of reserve to, or on the retired or emergency list of, or holding a temporary commission in, the Royal Navy or the Royal Marines, volunteers.

5, 6. [Repealed by the Statute Law (Repeals) Act 1977, Sched. 1, Pt. I.]

7. Service, for the purposes of training only, for a continuous period of seven days or longer performed, whether under an obligation or under voluntary arrangements, by—

(*a*) an officer or man of any reserve force of the Royal Navy or of the Royal Marines, or an officer of reserve to, or on the retired or emergency list of, or holding a temporary commission in, the Royal Navy or the Royal Marines;

(*b*) an officer of any army reserve of officers, a man of any army reserve force, an officer or man of the Territorial Army, or an officer of the Territorial Army Reserve of Officers;

(*c*) an officer of the Royal Air Force Volunteer Reserve or of any air force reserve of officers or on the retired list of the Royal Air Force, a man of any air force reserve force, or an officer or man of the Royal Auxiliary Air Force or the Royal Auxiliary Air Force Reserve;

(*d*) a member of any reserve of the Women's Royal Naval Service or a member of the Naval Voluntary Aid Detachment Reserve.

not being service of a description specified in any of the preceding paragraphs of this Schedule.

Sheriff Courts (Civil Jurisdiction and Procedure) (Scotland) Act 1963

(1963 c. 22)

An Act to increase the amount by reference to which actions are classified as summary causes in the sheriff court in Scotland; to increase the amount by reference to which the small debt jurisdiction of the sheriff is limited; to amend the law with regard to the bringing of actions between spouses for interim aliment of small amounts in the sheriff's small debt court and with regard to the jurisdiction of the sheriff in such actions brought as aforesaid; and for purposes connected with the matters aforesaid. [10th July 1963]

1, 2. [Repealed by the Sheriff Courts (Scotland) Act 1971, Sched. 2.]

Actions for aliment of small amounts

[1] **3.**—(1) An action under section 2 of the Family Law (Scotland) Act 1985 for aliment only (whether or not expenses are also sought) may be brought before the sheriff as a summary cause if the aliment claimed in the action does not exceed—

(*a*) in respect of a child under the age of 18 years, the sum of £35 per week; and

(*b*) in any other case, the sum of £70 per week;

and any provision in any enactment limiting the jurisdiction of the sheriff in a summary cause by reference to any amount, or limiting the period for which a decree granted by him shall have effect, shall not apply in relation to such an action.

(2) [Repealed by the Civil Jurisdiction and Judgments Act 1982, Sched. 14.]

(3) The Lord Advocate may by order vary the amounts prescribed in paragraphs (*a*) and (*b*) of subsection (1) above.

(4) The power to make an order under subsection (3) above shall be exercisable by statutory instrument subject to annulment in pursuance of a

resolution of either House of Parliament and shall include power to vary or revoke any order made thereunder.

NOTE
[1] Substituted by the Family Law (Scotland) Act 1985, s. 23.

Citation, construction and commencement

4.—(1) This Act may be cited as the Sheriff Courts (Civil Jurisdiction and Procedure) (Scotland) Act 1963.

(2) In this Act the expression "the principal Act" means the Sheriff Courts (Scotland) Act 1907, as amended by any other enactment, and the principal Act and this Act shall be construed together as one.

(3) This Act shall come into operation on 1st October 1963.

Law Reform (Miscellaneous Provisions) (Scotland) Act 1966

(1966 c. 19)

An Act to exempt from arrestment on the dependence of an action sums falling to be paid by way of wages, salary or other earnings or by way of pension, to abolish the exemption from arrestment in execution of certain earnings payable by the Crown, and to provide for the variation from time to time of the amount of wages excepted from arrestment under the Wages Arrestment Limitation (Scotland) Act 1870; to amend section 5 of the Adoption Act 1958, and to provide in Scotland for the succession of an adopted person to the estate of his natural parent in certain circumstances; to amend section 5 of the Trusts (Scotland) Act 1961; to provide for the admission in evidence of certain documents in civil proceedings; to confer jurisdiction on the sheriff court to vary or recall certain orders of the Court of Session in respect of maintenance, custody and welfare of children, and to provide for the extension of certain time limits in appeals under the Summary Jurisdiction (Scotland) Act 1954; and to provide that acts of adjournal and acts of sederunt shall be statutory instruments. [3rd August 1966]

Wages, pensions, etc., to be exempt from arrestment on the dependence of an action

1.—(1) After the passing of this Act it shall not be competent to arrest on the dependence of an action any earnings or any pension.

(2)(*a*) For the purposes of this and of the next following section "earnings" means any sums payable by way of wages or salary (including any fees, bonus, commission, overtime pay or other emoluments payable in addition to wages or salary by the person paying the wages or salary or payable under a contract of service);

(*b*) in this section "pension" includes—

(i) any annuity in respect of past services, whether or not the services were rendered to the person paying the annuity, and any periodical payments by way of compensation for the loss, abolition or relinquishment, or any diminution in the emoluments, of any office or employment;

(ii) any pension or allowance payable in respect of disablement or disability.

2, 3. [Repealed by the Debtors (Scotland) Act 1987, Sched. 8.]

4. [Repealed by the Children Act 1975, Sched. 4, Pt. IV.]

5, 6. [See Division M.]

7. [Repealed by the Civil Evidence (Scotland) Act 1988, Sched.]

Variation and recall by the sheriff of certain orders made by the Court of Session in respect of maintenance, custody, etc., and amendment of section 2 of the Divorce (Scotland) Act 1938

[1] **8.**—(1) The provisions of this section shall apply to the following orders made by the Court of Session, that is to say—

(*a*) an award of aliment,

(*b*) an order for an annual or periodical allowance made under section 2 of the Divorce (Scotland) Act 1938, whether under that section as originally enacted or as amended by any subsequent enactment including this Act,

[2] (*c*) an order for a periodical allowance made under subsection (2) or (3) of section 26 of the Succession (Scotland) Act 1964 or under section 5 of the Divorce (Scotland) Act 1976 or section 29 of the Matrimonial and Family Proceedings Act 1984 or section 8 of the Family Law (Scotland) Act 1985,

[3] (*d*) an order made by virtue of section 9 of the Conjugal Rights (Scotland) (Amendment) Act 1861, or under Part II of the Matrimonial Proceedings (Children) Act 1958, or by virtue of Part II of the Guardianship Act 1973, and

(*e*) an order varying any such order as aforesaid.

[3a] (2) Where any person has a right to make application for the variation or recall of any order to which the provisions of this section apply, he may make an application in that behalf to the sheriff, and, subject to the provisions of the next following subsection, the sheriff shall have the like powers in relation to the application as the Court of Session.

(3) Where in any application under this section any other party to the action, not later than the first calling of the application in court, requests that it be remitted to the Court of Session, the sheriff shall so remit, and the Court of Session shall deal with it accordingly.

(4) Notwithstanding anything in Part I of the Public Records (Scotland) Act 1937 (transmission of court records to and from the Keeper of the Records of Scotland, etc.), the powers of the Court of Session, conferred by sections 16 and 34 respectively of the Administration of Justice (Scotland) Act 1933, to regulate its own procedure and that of the sheriff court,

shall include power to provide for the transmission to and from the sheriff court of any process in the action to which an application under this section relates[4]; and for the purposes of the said Act of 1937 and of this section any record of such an application shall be deemed to be a record of the Court of Session.

(5) [Repealed by the Divorce (Scotland) Act 1976.]

[5] (6) In this section—

"order" includes a provision in a final decree, but does not, include an interim order,

"party" means any person having a right to make application for the variation or recall of the order in question, and

"sheriff" means

(*a*) in relation to an order under subsection (1)(*a*), (*b*) or (*c*) above or an order varying any such order the sheriff having jurisdiction over any party on whom the application has to be served, on any of the grounds mentioned in paragraph (*a*), (*b*) or (*j*) of section 6 of the Sheriff Courts (Scotland) Act 1907;

(*b*) in relation to an order mentioned in subsection (1)(*d*) above or an order varying any such order, the sheriff having jurisdiction under section 9, 10 or 12 of the Family Law Act 1986.

NOTES

[1] See the Domicile and Matrimonial Proceedings Act 1973, s.10(2)(*b*).

[2] As amended by the Divorce (Scotland) Act 1976, Sched. 1, the Matrimonial and Family Proceedings Act 1984, Sched. 1, para. 7 and the Family Law (Scotland) Act 1985, Sched. 1, para. 5.

[3] As amended by the Guardianship Act 1973, Sched. 5.

[3a] As amended by the Family Law Act 1986, Sched. 2.

[4] See S.I. 1984 No. 667, *infra*.

[5] As amended by the Family Law Act 1986, Sched. 1, para. 8.

9. [Repealed by the Criminal Procedure (Scotland) Act 1975, Sched. 10.]

Acts of adjournal and acts of sederunt to be statutory instruments

10. Where any Act passed after the commencement of the Statutory Instruments Act 1946, whether before or after the commencement of this Act, confers power on the High Court of Justiciary to make provision in respect of any matter by act of adjournal, or on the Court of Session to make such provision by act of sederunt, any document by which that power is exercised shall, unless the Act conferring the power otherwise provides, be a statutory instrument, and the provisions of the said Act of 1946 shall apply to it as they apply to a statutory instrument made by a Minister of the Crown.

Interpretation, repeals, citation and extent

11.—(1) Any reference in this Act to an enactment shall be construed as a reference to that enactment as amended by any other enactment including this Act.

(2) [Repealed by the Statute Law (Repeals) Act 1974.]

(3) This Act may be cited as the Law Reform (Miscellaneous Provisions) (Scotland) Act 1966, and shall extend to Scotland only.

Sheriff Courts (Scotland) Act 1971

(1971 c. 58)

An Act to amend the law with respect to sheriff courts in Scotland, and for purposes connected therewith. [27th July 1971]

Part I

Constitution, Organisation and Administration

General duty of the Secretary of State

Secretary of State to be responsible for organisation and administration of sheriff courts

1. Subject to the provisions of this Act, the Secretary of State shall be under a duty to secure the efficient organisation and administration of the sheriff courts, and for the purpose of carrying out that duty shall have, in addition to any functions conferred on him by or under any other enactment, the functions conferred on him by the following provisions of this Act.

Sheriffdoms

Power of Secretary of State to alter sheriffdoms

2.—(1) The Secretary of State may by order alter the boundaries of sheriffdoms, form new sheriffdoms, or provide for the abolition of sheriffdoms existing at the time of the making of the order.

(2) An order under subsection (1) above may contain all such provisions as appear to the Secretary of State to be necessary or expedient for rendering the order of full effect and any incidental, supplemental or consequential provisions which appear to him to be necessary or expedient for the purposes of the order, including, but without prejudice to the generality of the foregoing words—

(*a*) provision for the abolition of any office,

(*b*) provisions amending, repealing or revoking any enactment (whether passed or made before or after the commencement of this Act, and including any enactment contained in or made under this Act).

(3) Where an order under subsection (1) above includes, by virtue of subsection (2)(*a*) above, provision for the abolition of any office, then—

(*a*) that provision shall have effect notwithstanding the provisions of any enactment (including any enactment contained in this Act), or of any instrument in terms of which any person holds that office;

(*b*) the Secretary of State may, with the concurrence of the Minister for the Civil Service, pay to or in respect of any person who suffers loss of employment, or loss or diminution of emoluments, which is attributable to the said provision such amount by way of compensation as may appear to the Secretary of State to be reasonable in all the circumstances.

(4) The power to make orders under subsection (1) above shall be exercisable by statutory instrument, but no order shall be made under that subsection unless a draft of the order has been laid before Parliament and approved by a resolution of each House of Parliament.

Sheriff court districts and places where sheriff courts are to be held

Sheriff court districts and places where sheriff courts are to be held

3.—(1) Subject to any alterations made by an order under section 2(1) of this Act or under subsection (2) below—

(*a*) the sheriff court districts existing immediately before the commencement of this Act shall continue to exist after such commencement, and

(*b*) sheriff courts shall, after such commencement, continue to be held at the places at which they were in use to be held immediately before such commencement.

(2) The Secretary of State may by order—

(*a*) alter the boundaries of sheriff court districts, form new districts, or provide for the abolition of districts existing at the time of the making of the order;

(*b*) provide that sheriff courts shall be held, or shall cease to be held, at any place.

(3) An order under subsection (2) above may contain all such provisions as appear to the Secretary of State to be necessary or expedient for

rendering the order of full effect and any incidental, supplemental or consequential provisions which appear to him to be necessary or expedient for the purposes of the order, including, but without prejudice to the generality of the foregoing words, provisions amending, repealing or revoking any enactment (whether passed or made before or after the commencement of this Act, and including any enactment contained in or made under this Act).

(4) The Secretary of State may, with the concurrence of the Minister for the Civil Service, pay to or in respect of any person who suffers loss of employment, or loss or diminution of emoluments, which is attributable to an order under subsection (2) above such amount by way of compensation as may appear to the Secretary of State to be reasonable in all the circumstances.

(5) The power to make orders under subsection (2) above shall be exercisable by statutory instrument.

(6) Without prejudice to subsection (1) above, any enactment or other instrument in force immediately before the commencement of this Act shall, to the extent that it fixes sheriff court districts or the places at which sheriff courts are to be held, cease to have effect.

Sheriffs principal and sheriffs

Offices of sheriff principal and sheriff

4.—(1) The office of sheriff (that is to say, the office known formerly as the office of sheriff depute, but known immediately before the commencement of this Act as the office of sheriff) shall be known as the office of sheriff principal, the office of sheriff substitute shall be known as the office of sheriff, and the office of honorary sheriff substitute shall be known as the office of honorary sheriff.

(2) Accordingly, any enactment or other document in force or having effect at the commencement of this Act which refers whether expressly or by implication, or which falls to be construed as referring, or as including a reference, to the office of sheriff (as defined in subsection (1) above), or to the office of sheriff substitute, or to the holder of any of the said offices, shall be construed in accordance with subsection (1) above.

[1] (3) Section 28 of the Interpretation Act 1889, shall not apply for the interpretation of this Act.

NOTE

[1] As amended by the Interpretation Act 1978, Sched. 3.

Qualification for offices of sheriff principal and sheriff

5.—(1) A person shall not be appointed to the office of sheriff principal or sheriff unless he is, and has been for at least ten years, legally qualified.

For the purposes of this subsection, a person shall be legally qualified if he is an advocate or a solicitor.

(2) Without prejudice to section 11(3) of this Act, in this section "sheriff principal" does not include a temporary sheriff principal and "sheriff" does not include a temporary sheriff or an honorary sheriff.

Disqualification of sheriffs principal and sheriffs

6.—(1) A sheriff principal to whom this subsection applies, or a sheriff, shall not, so long as he holds office as such—

(*a*) engage, whether directly or indirectly, in any private practice or business, or be in partnership with or employed by, or act as agent for, any person so engaged;

(*b*) [Repealed by the Law Reform (Miscellaneous Provisions) (Scotland) Act 1985, s. 20 and Sched. 4, with effect from 30th December 1985.].

(2) Subsection (1) above shall apply to any person holding the office of sheriff principal who is appointed to that office after the commencement of this Act and on whose appointment the Secretary of State directs that that subsection shall apply to him.

(3) The sheriff principal of any sheriffdom, not being either a sheriff principal who is restricted by the terms of his appointment from engaging in private practice or a sheriff principal to whom subsection (1) above applies, shall not, so long as he holds office as such, advise, or act as an advocate in any court, in any cause civil or criminal arising within or coming from that sheriffdom.

(4) Any reference in any enactment passed before the commencement of this Act to a sheriff principal who is restricted by the terms of his appointment from engaging in private practice shall be construed as including a reference to a sheriff principal to whom subsection (1) above applies.

(5) Without prejudice to the giving of any direction under section 11 (5) of this Act, in this section " sheriff principal " does not include a temporary sheriff principal and " sheriff " does not include a temporary sheriff or an honorary sheriff.

Jurisdiction of sheriff

7. For removal of doubt it is hereby declared that a sheriff by virtue of his appointment as such, has and is entitled to exercise the jurisdiction and powers attaching to the office of sheriff in all parts of the sheriffdom for which he is appointed.

Sheriff may be appointed to assist Secretary of State

8. Notwithstanding anything in section 6 of this Act, a person holding the office of sheriff principal or sheriff may, without relinquishing that office, be appointed by the Secretary of State to assist him to discharge the functions vested in him in relation to the organisation and administration of the sheriff courts, but a person so appointed shall not perform his duties as the holder of the office of sheriff principal or sheriff, as the case may be, while he retains that appointment.

Functions of Secretary of State in relation to sheriffs principal, sheriffs, etc.

Power of Secretary of State to give administrative directions

9. For the purpose of securing the efficient organisation and administration of the sheriff courts and, in particular, the speedy and efficient disposal of business in those courts, the Secretary of State may give such directions of an administrative nature as appear to him to be necessary or expedient, and any sheriff principal or sheriff, and any officer or servant engaged in the administration of the sheriff courts, to whom a direction is given under this section shall, subject to the provisions of this Act, give effect to that direction.

Secretary of State may authorise sheriff principal or direct sheriff to act in another sheriffdom

10.—[1] (1) Where a vacancy occurs in the office of sheriff principal of any sheriffdom the Secretary of State may, if it appears to him expedient so to do in order to avoid delay in the administration of justice in that sheriffdom, authorise the sheriff principal of any other sheriffdom to perform the duties of sheriff principal in the first-mentioned sheriffdom (in addition to his own duties) until the Secretary of State otherwise decides.

[1] (1A) Where the sheriff principal of any sheriffdom is unable to perform, or rules that he is precluded from performing, all of, or some part of, his duties as sheriff principal the Secretary of State may authorise the sheriff principal of any other sheriffdom to perform the duties of sheriff principal,

or as the case may be that part of those duties, in the first-mentioned sheriffdom (in addition to his own duties) until the Secretary of State otherwise decides.

(2) Where as regards any sheriffdom—

(*a*) a sheriff is by reason of illness or otherwise unable to perform his duties as sheriff, or

(*b*) a vacancy occurs in the office of sheriff, or

(*c*) for any other reason it appears to the Secretary of State expedient so to do in order to avoid delay in the administration of justice in that sheriffdom,

the Secretary of State may direct a sheriff appointed for any other sheriffdom to perform, in accordance with the terms of the direction, the duties of sheriff in the first-mentioned sheriffdom (in addition to or in place of his own duties) until otherwise directed by the Secretary of State, and any sheriff to whom a direction is given under this subsection shall give effect to that direction.

(3) A sheriff principal authorised, or a sheriff directed, under this section to perform duties in any sheriffdom shall for that purpose, without the necessity of his receiving a commission in that behalf, have and be entitled to exercise the jurisdiction and powers attaching to the office of sheriff principal or, as the case may be, sheriff in that sheriffdom.

(4) The Secretary of State may, with the approval of the Treasury, pay to a sheriff principal or a sheriff, in respect of any duties performed by that sheriff principal or sheriff (in addition to his own duties) in pursuance of an authority or direction under this section, such remuneration and allowances as may appear to the Secretary of State to be reasonable in all the circumstances.

(5) In this section " sheriff " does not include an honorary sheriff.

NOTE

[1] Subss. (1) and (1A) substituted for subs. (1) by the Law Reform (Miscellaneous Provisions) (Scotland) Act 1980, s. 10 (*a*).

Secretary of State may appoint temporary sheriffs principal and sheriffs

11.—[1] (1) Where a vacancy occurs in the office of sheriff principal of any sheriffdom the Secretary of State may, if it appears to him expedient so to do in order to avoid delay in the administration of justice in that sheriffdom, appoint a person to act as sheriff principal of the sheriffdom.

[1] (1A) Where the sheriff principal of any sheriffdom is unable to perform, or rules that he is precluded from performing, all of, or some part of, his duties as sheriff principal the Secretary of State may appoint a person to act as sheriff principal of the sheriffdom, or as the case may be to perform that part of the duties of the sheriff principal.

[1] (1B) A person appointed under subsection (1) or (1A) above shall be known as a temporary sheriff principal.

(2) Where as regards any sheriffdom—

(*a*) a sheriff is by reason of illness or otherwise unable to perform his duties as sheriff, or

(*b*) a vacancy occurs in the office of sheriff, or

(*c*) for any other reason it appears to the Secretary of State expedient so to do in order to avoid delay in the administration of justice in that sheriffdom,

the Secretary of State may appoint a person (to be known as a temporary sheriff) to act as a sheriff for the sheriffdom.

(3) A person shall not be appointed to be a temporary sheriff principal or a temporary sheriff unless he is legally qualified and has been so qualified—

(*a*) in the case of an appointment as a temporary sheriff principal, for at least ten years;

(*b*) in the case of an appointment as a temporary sheriff, for at least five years.

For the purposes of this subsection, a person shall be legally qualified if he is an advocate or a solicitor.

(4) The appointment of a temporary sheriff principal or of a temporary sheriff shall subsist until recalled by the Secretary of State.

(5) If the Secretary of State, on appointing any person to be a temporary sheriff principal or a temporary sheriff, so directs, the provisions of section 6 (1) of this Act shall apply in relation to that person as they apply in relation to a person holding the office of sheriff.

(6) A person appointed to be temporary sheriff principal of, or a temporary sheriff for, any sheriffdom shall for the purposes of his appointment, without the necessity of his receiving a commission in that behalf, have and be entitled to exercise the jurisdiction and powers attaching to the office of sheriff principal or, as the case may be, sheriff in that sheriffdom.

(7) The appointment of any person holding the office of sheriff to be a temporary sheriff principal shall not affect the commission held by that person as sheriff, but he shall not, while his appointment as a temporary sheriff principal subsists, perform any duties by virtue of the said commission.

(8) The Secretary of State may pay to any person appointed to be a temporary sheriff principal or a temporary sheriff such remuneration and allowances as the Treasury, on the recommendation of the Secretary of State, may determine.

NOTE

[1] Subss. (1), (1A) and (1B) substituted for subs. (1) by the Law Reform (Miscellaneous Provisions) Act 1980, s. 10 (*b*).

Removal from office, and suspension, of sheriff principal or sheriff

[1] **12.**—(1) The Lord President of the Court of Session and the Lord Justice Clerk may of their own accord and shall, if they are requested so to do by the Secretary of State, undertake jointly an investigation into the fitness for office of any sheriff principal or sheriff and, as soon as practicable after completing that investigation, shall report in writing to the Secretary of State either—

(*a*) that the sheriff principal or sheriff is fit for office, or

(*b*) that the sheriff principal or sheriff is unfit for office by reason of inability, neglect of duty or misbehaviour,

and shall in either case include in their report a statement of their reasons for so reporting.

(2) The Secretary of State may, if a report is made to him under subsection (1) above to the effect that any sheriff principal or sheriff is unfit for office by reason of inability, neglect of duty or misbehaviour, make an order removing that sheriff principal or sheriff from office.

(3) An order under subsection (2) above—

(*a*) shall be made by statutory instrument, which shall be subject to annulment in pursuance of a resolution of either House of Parliament,

(*b*) shall not be made so as to come into operation before the expiry, in relation to the order, of the period of forty days mentioned in section 5 (1) of the Statutory Instruments Act 1946.

(4) The Lord President of the Court of Session and the Lord Justice Clerk may, on undertaking an investigation under subsection (1) above or at any time during the course of such an investigation, if they think it proper so to do, recommend in writing to the Secretary of State that the sheriff principal or sheriff who is the subject of the investigation be suspended from office, and the Secretary of State may, on receiving such a recommendation as aforesaid, suspend that sheriff principal or sheriff from office.

(5) A sheriff principal or a sheriff suspended from office under subsection (4) above shall remain so suspended until the Secretary of State otherwise directs.

(6) The suspension from office of a sheriff principal or a sheriff under subsection (4) above shall not affect the payment to him of his salary in respect of the period of his suspension.

(7) In this section " sheriff principal " does not include a temporary sheriff principal and " sheriff " does not include a temporary sheriff or an honorary sheriff.

NOTE

[1] Extended by the District Courts (Scotland) Act 1975, s. 5 (8).

Functions of Secretary of State with respect to residence and leave of absence of sheriffs principal

13.—(1) The Secretary of State may require any sheriff principal (being a sheriff principal who is restricted by the terms of his appointment from engaging in private practice or to whom section 6 (1) of this Act applies) to reside ordinarily at such place as the Secretary of State may specify.

(2) The Secretary of State may approve such leave of absence for any sheriff principal (being a sheriff principal who is restricted by the terms of his appointment from engaging in private practice or to whom section 6 (1) of this Act applies) as appears to the Secretary of State to be proper, but the amount of leave so approved (other than leave granted on account of ill-health) shall not, unless the Secretary of State for special reasons otherwise permits, exceed seven weeks in any year.

Functions of Secretary of State with respect to number, residence and place of duties of sheriffs

14.—(1) The Secretary of State may, with the approval of the Treasury, by order prescribe the number of sheriffs to be appointed for each sheriffdom.

(2) The Secretary of State may require any sheriff to reside ordinarily at such place as the Secretary of State may specify.

(3) The Secretary of State—

(*a*) shall, on the appointment of a person to hold the office of sheriff for any sheriffdom,

(*b*) may, at any subsequent time while the said person holds that office,

give to that person a direction designating the sheriff court district or districts in which he is to perform his duties as sheriff:

Provided that a direction given to a sheriff under this subsection shall be subject to any instruction given to that sheriff under section 15 of this Act by the sheriff principal of the sheriffdom, being an instruction given for the purpose of giving effect to any special provision made by the sheriff principal under section 16 (1) (*b*) of this Act.

(4) If for the purpose of securing the efficient organisation and administration of the sheriff courts, and after consultation with the Lord President of the Court of Session the Secretary of State by order so directs, a person holding the office of sheriff for any sheriffdom shall, on such date as may be specified in the order, cease to hold that office and shall, on and after that date, without the necessity of his receiving a commission in that behalf, hold instead the office of sheriff for such other sheriffdom as may be so specified; and on making an order under this subsection with respect to any person the Secretary of State shall give to that person a direction under subsection (3) above designating the sheriff court district or districts in which he is to perform his duties as sheriff.

(5) In this section " sheriff " does not include an honorary sheriff, and in subsections (1) and (4) above does not include a temporary sheriff.

Functions of the sheriff principal in relation to sheriffs, etc.

General functions of sheriff principal

15.—(1) Subject generally to the provisions of this Act, and in particular to the provisions of this or any other Act conferring functions on the Secretary of State or anything done under any such provision, the sheriff principal of each sheriffdom shall be under a duty to secure the speedy and efficient disposal of business in the sheriff courts of that sheriffdom, and for the purpose of carrying out that duty shall have, in addition to any functions conferred on him by or under any other enactment, the functions conferred on him by the following provisions of this Act.

(2) For the purpose of securing the effective discharge of any of the said functions the sheriff principal of any sheriffdom may give such instructions of an administrative nature as appear to him to be necessary or expedient, and any sheriff appointed for that sheriffdom, and any officer or servant engaged in the administration of the sheriff courts in the sheriffdom, to whom an instruction is given under this section shall, subject to the provisions of this Act, give effect to that instruction.

Functions of sheriff principal with respect to duties and leave of absence of sheriffs

16.—(1) The sheriff principal of each sheriffdom shall make such arrangements as appear to him necessary or expedient for the purpose of securing the speedy and efficient disposal of business in the sheriff courts of that sheriffdom and in particular, but without prejudice to the generality of the foregoing words, may—

(*a*) subject to any direction given by the Secretary of State under section 9 of this Act, provide for the division of such business as aforesaid between the sheriff principal and the sheriffs appointed for the sheriffdom, and for the distribution of the business (so far as allocated to the sheriffs) amongst those sheriffs;

(*b*) where any of those sheriffs is by reason of illness or otherwise unable to perform his duties as sheriff, or a vacancy occurs in the office of sheriff in the sheriffdom, or for any other reason it appears to the sheriff principal expedient so to do in order to avoid delay in the administration of justice in the sheriffdom, make special provision of a temporary nature for the disposal of any part of the said business either by the sheriff principal or by any of the sheriffs appointed for the sheriffdom, in addition to or in place of the sheriff principal's or, as the case may be, that sheriff's own duties;

so, however, that nothing done under this subsection shall enable a sheriff to dispose of business which he does not otherwise have power to dispose of.

(2) The sheriff principal of any sheriffdom may approve such leave of absence for any sheriff appointed for that sheriffdom as appears to the sheriff principal to be proper, but the amount of leave so approved (other than leave granted on account of ill-health) shall not, unless the Secretary of State for special reasons otherwise permits, exceed seven weeks in any year.

(3) In subsection (2) above " sheriff " shall not include an honorary sheriff.

Sheriff principal may fix sittings and business of sheriff courts in sheriffdom, and sessions for civil business

17.—(1) The sheriff principal of each sheriffdom may by order prescribe—

(*a*) the number of sheriff courts to be held at each of the places within that sheriffdom at which a court is required under or by virtue of this Act to be held,

[1] (*b*) subject to section 25 (2) of this Act, the days on which and the times at which those courts are to be held,

(*c*) the descriptions of business to be disposed of at those courts.

(2) The sheriff principal of each sheriffdom shall by order prescribe the dates of the sessions to be held in the sheriff courts of that sheriffdom for the disposal of civil business, and may prescribe different dates in relation to different courts, so however that—

(*a*) there shall be held in the courts of each sheriffdom three sessions in each year for the disposal of civil business, that is to say, a winter session, a spring session and a summer session;

(*b*) the dates of the sessions prescribed under this subsection shall not be such as to allow, in any court, a vacation of longer than two weeks at Christmas time, four weeks in the spring and eight weeks in the summer.

(3) The sheriff principal of each sheriffdom shall, before the end of the spring session in each year, fix in respect of each sheriff court in that sheriffdom at least one day during the vacation immediately following that session for the disposal of civil business in that court, and shall, before the end of the summer session in each year, fix in respect of each court at least two days during the vacation immediately following that session for the said purpose; but civil proceedings in the sheriff courts may proceed during vacation as during session, and interlocutors may competently be pronounced during vacation in any such proceedings.

(4) A sheriff principal shall give notice of any matter prescribed or fixed by him under the foregoing provisions of this section in such manner as he may think sufficient for bringing that matter to the attention of all persons having an interest therein.

(5) Subject to anything done under subsection (1) above, or by an order under section 2 (1) or section 3 (2) of this Act, after the commencement of this Act—

(*a*) there shall be held at each of the places at which a sheriff court was in use to be held immediately before such commencement the same number of courts as was in use to be held there immediately before such commencement;

(*b*) the court days and times in use to be observed in any sheriff court immediately before such commencement (whether in pursuance of any enactment or other instrument or otherwise) shall continue to be observed in that court;

(*c*) the descriptions of business in use to be dealt with on court days in any sheriff court immediately before such commencement shall continue to be dealt with on those days.

(6) Without prejudice to subsection (5) above, any enactment or other instrument in force immediately before the commencement of this Act shall, to the extent that it contains provisions with respect to any matter which the sheriff principal has power to prescribe under subsection (1) above, cease to have effect.

NOTE

[1] See the Bail etc. (Scotland) Act 1980, s. 10 (2).

Secretary of State may exercise certain functions of sheriff principal in certain circumstances

18. If in any case the Secretary of State considers—

(*a*) that the exercise by the sheriff principal of any sheriffdom of any of the functions conferred on him by sections 15 to 17 of this Act, or

(*b*) that the failure of the sheriff principal of any sheriffdom to exercise any of the said functions,

is prejudicial to the speedy and efficient disposal of business in the sheriff courts of that sheriffdom or to the efficient organisation or administration of the sheriff courts generally, or is otherwise against the interests of the public, the Secretary of State may—

(i) (in the circumstances mentioned in paragraph (*a*) above) rescind that exercise of that function by the sheriff principal and, if he thinks fit, himself exercise that function in that case;

(ii) (in the circumstances mentioned in paragraph (*b*) above) himself exercise that function in that case,

and the exercise of any function of a sheriff principal by the Secretary of State under this section shall have effect as if it were an exercise of that function by the sheriff principal.

Miscellaneous

Travelling allowances for sheriffs principal

19. The Secretary of State may pay to any sheriff principal, in addition to the salary of that sheriff principal, such allowances as the Secretary of State, with the concurrence of the Treasury, may determine in respect of the travelling expenses incurred by the sheriff principal in the performance of the duties of his office.

Extension of purposes for which Lord Advocate may give instructions to procurators fiscal

20. The purposes for which the Lord Advocate may issue instructions to procurators fiscal under section 8(1) of the Sheriff Courts and Legal Officers (Scotland) Act 1927 shall include, in addition to the purpose mentioned in the said section 8(1), the speedy and efficient disposal of business in the sheriff courts.

21. [Repealed by the House of Commons Disqualification Act 1975, Sched. 3.]

Saving for existing functions

22. Nothing in the foregoing provisions of this Act shall affect the discharge by any person of any function lawfully held by him immediately before the commencement of this Act, except in so far as the discharge of that function is or would be inconsistent with any of those provisions or anything done thereunder.

. . . . . .

PART III

CIVIL JURISDICTION, PROCEDURE AND APPEALS

Civil Jurisdiction

Upper limit to privative jurisdiction of sheriff court to be £500

[1] **31.** Section 7 of the Sheriff Courts (Scotland) Act 1907 (which provides that all causes not exceeding £50 in value which are competent in the sheriff court are to be brought in that court only, and are not to be subject to review by the Court of Session) shall have effect as if for the words "£50" there were substituted the words "£1,500".

NOTE

[1] As amended by S.I. 1976 No. 900 and by S.I. 1988 No. 1993, in relation to proceedings commenced on or after 30th November 1988.

Regulation of procedure in civil proceedings

Power of Court of Session to regulate civil procedure in sheriff court

[1] **32.**—[2] (1) Subject to the provisions of this section, the Court of Session may by act of sederunt regulate and prescribe the procedure and practice to

be followed in any civil proceedings in the sheriff court (including any matters incidental or relating to any such procedure or practice), and, without prejudice to the generality of the foregoing words, the power conferred on the Court of Session by this section shall extend to—

(*a*) regulating the procedure to be followed in connection with execution or diligence following on any civil proceedings;

(*b*) prescribing the manner in which, the time within which, and the conditions on which, an appeal may be taken to the sheriff principal from an interlocutor of a sheriff, or to the Court of Session from an interlocutor of a sheriff principal or a sheriff (including an interlocutor applying the verdict of a jury), or any application may be made to the sheriff court, or anything required or authorised to be done in relation to any civil proceedings shall or may be done;

(*c*) prescribing the form of any document to be used in, or for the purposes of, any civil proceedings or any execution or diligence following thereon, and the person by whom, and the manner in which, any such document as aforesaid is to be authenticated;

(*d*) regulating the procedure to be followed in connection with the production and recovery of documents;

[3] (*e*) providing in respect of any category of civil proceedings for written statements (including affidavits) and reports, admissible under section 2(1)(*b*) of the Civil Evidence (Scotland) Act 1988, to be received in evidence, on such conditions as may be prescribed, without being spoken to by a witness;

(*f*) making such provision as may appear to the Court of Session to be necessary or expedient with respect to the payment, investment or application of any sum of money awarded to or in respect of a person under legal disability in any action in the sheriff court;

(*g*) regulating the summoning, remuneration and duties of assessors;

(*h*) making such provision as may appear to the Court of Session to be necessary or expedient for carrying out the provisions of this Act or of any enactment conferring powers or imposing duties on sheriffs principal or sheriffs or relating to proceedings in the sheriff courts;

(*i*) regulating the expenses which may be awarded by the sheriff to parties in proceedings before him:

Provided that nothing contained in an act of sederunt made under this section shall derogate from—

(i) the provisions of sections 35 to 38 of this Act (as amended by the Law Reform (Miscellaneous Provisions) (Scotland) Act 1985) with respect to summary causes, or

(ii) the provisions of subsection (8) of section 20 of the Race Relations Act 1968 with respect to the remuneration to be paid to assessors appointed under subsection (7) of that section.

(2) An act of sederunt under this section may contain such incidental, supplemental or consequential provisions as appear to the Court of Session to be necessary or expedient for the purposes of that act, including, but without prejudice to the generality of the foregoing words, provisions amending, repealing or revoking any enactment (whether passed or made before or after the commencement of this Act) relating to matters with respect to which an act of sederunt may be made under this section.

(3) Before making an act of sederunt under this section with respect to any matter the Court of Session shall (unless that act embodies, with or without modifications, draft rules submitted to them by the Sheriff Court Rules Council under section 34 of this Act) consult the said Council, and shall take into consideration any views expressed by the Council with respect to that matter.

(4) Section 34 of the Administration of Justice (Scotland) Act 1933 (power of Court of Session to regulate civil procedure in sheriff court) shall cease to have effect, but any act of sederunt made under or having effect by virtue of that section shall, if and so far as it is in force immediately before the

commencement of this Act, continue in force and shall have effect, and be treated, as if it had been made under this section.

NOTES

[1] See also the Maintenance Orders (Reciprocal Enforcement) Act 1972, ss. 19 and 31(3). Extended: see the Children Act 1975, ss. 66, 78, the Banking Act 1979, s. 31(7)(*b*), and the Debtors (Scotland) Act 1987, s.97. Applied: see the Children Act 1975, s. 78. See also the Presumption of Death (Scotland) Act 1977, s. 15(1).

[2] As amended by the Law Reform (Miscellaneous Provisions) (Scotland) Act 1985, Sched. 2, para. 12.

[3] Substituted by the Civil Evidence (Scotland) Act 1988, s. 2(4).

Sheriff Court Rules Council

[0] **33.**—(1) There shall be established a body (to be known as the Sheriff Court Rules Council, and hereafter in this section and section 34 called "the Council") which shall have the functions conferred on it by section 34, and which shall consist of—

(*a*) two sheriffs principal, three sheriffs, one advocate, five solicitors and two whole-time sheriff clerks, all appointed by the Lord President of the Court of Session, after consultation with such persons as appear to him to be appropriate;

(*b*) two persons appointed by the Lord President after consultation with the Secretary of State, being persons appearing to the Lord President to have—

(i) a knowledge of the working procedures and practices of the civil courts;

(ii) a knowledge of consumer affairs; and

(iii) an awareness of the interests of litigants in the civil courts; and

(*c*) one person appointed by the Secretary of State, being a person appearing to the Secretary of State to be qualified for such appointment.

(2) The members of the Council shall, so long as they retain the respective qualifications mentioned in subsection (1) above, hold office for three years and be eligible for re-appointment.

(3) Any vacancy in the membership of the Council occurring by reason of death, resignation or other cause before the expiry of the period for which the member whose place is so vacated was appointed shall be filled—

(*a*) if the member was appointed by the Lord President of the Court of Session, by the appointment by the Lord President, after such consultation as is mentioned in paragraph (*a*) or, as the case may be, (*b*) of subsection (1) above, of a person having the same qualifications as that member,

(*b*) if the member was appointed by the Secretary of State, by the appointment by the Secretary of State of another person appearing to the Secretary of State to have qualifications suitable for such appointment,

and a person so appointed to fill a vacancy shall hold office only until the expiry of the said period.

[1] (4) The Lord President of the Court of Session shall appoint one of the two sheriffs principal who are members of the Council as chairman thereof, and the Secretary of State shall appoint a [whole-time sheriff clerk as] secretary to the Council.

(5) The Council shall have power to regulate the summoning of meetings of the Council and the procedure at such meetings, so however that—

(*a*) the Council shall meet within one month of its being established and thereafter at intervals of not more than six months, and shall meet at any time on a requisition in that behalf made by the chairman of the Council or any three members thereof, and

(*b*) at any meeting of the Council six members shall be a quorum.

(6) The Rules Council for the sheriff court established under section 35 of the Administration of Justice (Scotland) Act 1933 is hereby dissolved, and the said section 35 shall cease to have effect.

NOTES

[0] As amended by the Law Reform (Miscellaneous Provisions) (Scotland) Act 1990, Sched. 8, para. 26.

[1] Words in square brackets repealed by the Law Reform (Miscellaneous Provisions) (Scotland) Act 1985, Sched. 4, with effect from 30th December 1985, but repealed (*prosp.*) by *ibid.*, Sched. 2, para. 13: see s.60(3).

Functions of Sheriff Court Rules Council

34.—(1) As soon as practicable after it has been established the Council shall review generally the procedure and practice followed in civil proceedings in the sheriff court (including any matters incidental or relating to that procedure or practice) and, in the light of that review and of the provisions of this Act, shall prepare and submit to the Court of Session draft rules, being rules which—

(*a*) are designed to regulate and prescribe that procedure and practice (including any such matters as aforesaid), and

(*b*) are such as the Court of Session have power to make by act of sederunt under section 32 of this Act,

and the Court of Session shall make an act of sederunt under the said section 32 embodying those rules with such modifications, if any, as they think expedient.

(2) After submitting draft rules to the Court of Session under subsection (1) above the Council shall keep under review the procedure and practice followed in civil proceedings in the sheriff court (including any matters incidental or relating to that procedure or practice), and the Council may prepare and submit to the Court of Session draft rules designed to deal with any of the matters relating to the sheriff court which the Court of Session have power under section 32 of this Act to regulate or prescribe by act of sederunt, and the Court of Session shall consider any draft rules so submitted and shall, if they approve the rules, make an act of sederunt under the said section 32 embodying those rules with such modifications if any, as they think expedient.

(3) For the purpose of assisting it in the discharge of its functions under the foregoing provisions of this section the Council may make representations on any aspect of the procedure or practice in civil proceedings in the sheriff court (including any matters incidental or relating to that procedure or practice), and shall consider any such representations received by it, whether in response to such an invitation as aforesaid or otherwise.

Summary causes

Summary causes

35.—(1) The definition of "summary cause" contained in paragraph (*i*) of section 3 of the Sheriff Courts (Scotland) Act 1907 shall cease to have effect, and for the purposes of the procedure and practice in civil proceedings in the sheriff court there shall be a form of process, to be known as a "summary cause", which shall be used for the purposes of all civil proceedings brought in that court, being proceedings of one or other of the following descriptions, namely—

[1] (*a*) actions for payment of money not exceeding £1,500[1a] in amount (exclusive of interest and expenses);

[1] (*b*) actions of multiplepoinding, actions of furthcoming and actions of sequestration for rent, where the value of the fund *in medio*, or the value of the arrested fund or subject, or the rent in respect of which sequestration is asked, as the case may be, does not exceed £1,500[1a] (exclusive of interest and expenses);

[2] (*c*) actions *ad factum praestandum* and actions for the recovery of possession of heritable or moveable property, other than actions in which there is claimed in addition, or as an alternative, to a decree *ad factum praestandum* or for such recovery, as the case may be, a decree for payment of money exceeding £1,500[1a] in amount (exclusive of interest and expenses);

(*d*) proceedings which, according to the law and practice existing immediately before the commencement of this Act, might competently be brought in the sheriff's small debt court or where required to be conducted and disposed of in the summary manner in which proceedings were conducted and disposed of under the Small Debt Acts;

and any reference in the following provisions of this Act, or in any other enactment (whether passed or made before or after the commencement of this Act) relating to civil procedure in the sheriff court, to a summary cause shall be construed as a reference to a summary cause within the meaning of this subsection.

[3] (1A) For the avoidance of doubt it is hereby declared that nothing in subsection (1) above shall prevent the Court of Session from making different rules of procedure and practice in relation to different descriptions of summary cause proceedings.

[4] (2) There shall be a form of summary cause process, to be known as a "small claim", which shall be used for the purposes of such descriptions of summary cause proceedings as are prescribed by the Lord Advocate by order.

[4] (3) No enactment or rule of law relating to admissibility or corroboration of evidence before a court of law shall be binding in a small claim.

[4] (4) An order under subsection (2) above shall be by statutory instrument but shall not be made unless a draft of it has been approved by a resolution of each House of Parliament.

NOTES

[1] As amended by S.I. 1976 No. 900 and S.I. 1981 No. 842.

[1a] As amended by S.I. 1988 No. 1993, in relation to proceedings commenced on or after 30th November 1988.

[2] As amended by S.I. 1976 No. 900 and S.I. 1981 No. 842. Excluded by the Land Tenure Reform (Scotland) Act 1974, s. 9(6).

[3] Inserted by the Law Reform (Miscellaneous Provisions) (Scotland) Act 1985, Sched. 2, para. 14, with effect from 30th December 1985.

[4] New subss. (2)–(4) substituted for subs. (2) by the Law Reform (Miscellaneous Provisions) (Scotland) Act 1985, s. 18(1).

Procedure in summary causes

36.—(1) In relation to summary causes the power conferred on the Court of Session by section 32 of this Act shall extend to the making of rules permitting a party to such a cause, in such circumstances as may be specified in the rules, to be represented by a person who is neither an advocate nor a solicitor.

(2) A summary cause shall be commenced by a summons in, or as nearly as is practicable in, such form as may be prescribed by rules under the said section 32.

[1] (3) The evidence, if any, given in a summary cause shall not be recorded.

(4) [Repealed by the Debtors (Scotland) Act 1987, Sched. 8.]

NOTE

[1] Excluded by the Maintenance Orders (Reciprocal Enforcement) Act 1972, s. 4(4)(*b*).

[THE NEXT PAGE IS D 87]

EXPENSES - judicial expenses not extrajudicial exp. Judicial Exp. are exp. of ct. action

- will ALWAYS be a judgement on exp. at end of case BUT may be an interim award of exp.
  eg an amendment is made - exp. probably made against amendee
- caution for exp. may be required
  eg if feel your opponent won't be able to pay your exp. if you win then should ask for caution
- expenses generally follow success - sometimes there is divided success - sh. has discretion how to award exps.
- where action relates to construction of will exps. generally paid out of estate BUT :-
  - JASSALS EXECUTRIX v JASSAL (1987) - executrix found personally liable to expenses due to lack of diligence in a claim.
- payment of exps. may be made a condition precedent of the action - may happen where ct. disapproves of way a party has conducted his defence.
  - BLYTH v WATSON (1987) - P's sol. found personally liable for D's exps. Case had been settled but further injury arose out of same matter later. Generally settlement is once + for all. P's sol. raised another action out of same accident - weren't allowed to do this + so had to pay the exps.

3 kinds of exps :- 1) Party + Party exps - recoverable from 1 party to another
2) Sol/Client exps. - those which a sol. can recover from his client
3) In actions of divorce - sol./client exps.

Counsel [Advocate]
Limits on what can be recovered
- cannot recover anything unless ct. has sanctioned employment of counsel
  If both sides have counsel then likely to get sanction
- even once sanctioned doesn't mean that you can recover all counsel's fees - 1 consultation in course of case except when an appeal before SP when allowed 1 further consultation
- Probably only worth employing counsel where action for large sum
- Sol. will prepare accounts, or send them to law accountants for taxation. Good practice to send a copy of account to opponent + adjust account informally without taxation.

98 Account sent to auditor of ct. + asked to fix a diet of taxation

GO TO D89

Further provisions as to small claims

[1] **36A.** Where the pursuer in a small claim is not—

(*a*) a partnership or a body corporate; or

(*b*) acting in a representative capacity,

he may require the sheriff clerk to effect service of the summons on his behalf.

NOTE

[1] Inserted by the Law Reform (Miscellaneous Provisions) (Scotland) Act 1985, s. 18(2).

Expenses in small claims

[1] **36B.**—(1) No award of expenses shall be made in a small claim in which the value of the claim does not exceed such sum as the Lord Advocate shall prescribe by order.

(2) Any expenses which the sheriff may award in any other small claim shall not exceed such sum as the Lord Advocate shall prescribe by order.

(3) Subsections (1) and (2) above do not apply to a party to a small claim—

(*a*) who being a defender—

(i) has not stated a defence; or

(ii) having stated a defence, has not proceeded with it; or

(iii) having stated and proceeded with a defence, has not acted in good faith as to its merits; or

(*b*) on whose part there has been unreasonable conduct in relation to the proceedings or the claim;

nor do they apply in relation to an appeal to the sheriff principal.

(4) An order under this section shall be by statutory instrument but shall not be made unless a draft of it has been approved by a resolution of each House of Parliament.

NOTE

[1] Inserted by the Law Reform (Miscellaneous Provisions) (Scotland) Act 1985, s. 18(2).

Remits

37.—[1] (1) In the case of any ordinary cause brought in the sheriff court the sheriff

(*a*) shall at any stage, on the joint motion of the parties to the cause, direct that the cause be treated as a summary cause, and in that case the cause shall be treated for all purposes (including appeal) as a summary cause and shall proceed accordingly;

(*b*) may, subject to section 7 of the Sheriff Courts (Scotland) Act 1907, on the motion of any of the parties to the cause, if he is of the opinion that the importance or difficulty of the cause make it appropriate to do so, remit the cause to the Court of Session.

(2) In the case of any summary cause, the sheriff at any stage—

(*a*) shall, on the joint motion of the parties to the cause, and

(*b*) may, on the motion of any of the parties to the cause, if he is of the opinion that the importance or difficulty of the cause makes it appropriate to do so,

direct that the cause be treated as an ordinary cause, and in that case the cause shall be treated for all purposes (including appeal) as an ordinary cause and shall proceed accordingly:

Provided that a direction under this subsection may, in the case of an action for the recovery of possession of heritable or moveable property, be given by the sheriff of his own accord.

[2] (2A) In the case of any action in the sheriff court, being an action for divorce or an action in relation to the custody, guardianship or adoption of a child the sheriff may, of his own accord, at any stage remit the action to the Court of Session.

[4] (2B) In the case of any small claim the sheriff at any stage—

(*a*) may, if he is of the opinion that a difficult question of law or a question of fact of exceptional complexity is involved, of his own accord or on the motion of any party to the small claim;

(*b*) shall, on the joint motion of the parties to the small claim,

direct that the small claim be treated as a summary cause (not being a small claim) or ordinary cause, and in that case the small claim shall be treated for all purposes (including appeal) as a summary cause (not being a small claim) or ordinary cause as the case may be.

[4] (2C) In the case of any cause which is not a small claim by reason only of any monetary limit applicable to a small claim or to summary causes, the sheriff at any stage shall, on the joint motion of the parties to the cause, direct that the cause be treated as a small claim and in that case the cause shall be treated for all purposes (including appeal) as a small claim and shall proceed accordingly.

[3] (3) A decision—

(*a*) to remit, or not to remit, under subsection (2A), (2B) or (2C) above; or

(*b*) to make, or not to make, a direction by virtue of paragraph (*b*) of, or the proviso to, subsection (2) above,

shall not be subject to review; but from a decision to remit, or not to remit, under subsection (1)(*b*) above an appeal shall lie to the Court of Session.

(4) In this section "sheriff" includes a sheriff principal.

NOTES

[1] As amended by the Law Reform (Miscellaneous Provisions) (Scotland) Act 1980, s. 16(*a*). See the Land Tenure Reform (Scotland) Act 1974, s. 9(6).

[2] Added by the Law Reform (Miscellaneous Provisions) (Scotland) Act 1980, s. 16(*b*). As amended by the Divorce Jurisdiction, Court Fees and Legal Aid (Scotland) Act 1983, Sched. 1, para. 12, the Law Reform (Parent and Child) (Scotland) Act 1986, Sched. 1, para. 11, and the Age of Legal Capacity (Scotland) Act 1991, Sched. 1, para. 35.

[3] As substituted by the Law Reform (Miscellaneous Provisions) (Scotland) Act 1980, s. 16(*c*). As amended by the Law Reform (Miscellaneous Provisions) (Scotland) Act 1985, s. 18(3)(*b*).

[4] Added by the Law Reform (Miscellaneous Provisions) (Scotland) Act 1988, s. 18(3).

Appeal in summary causes

[1] **38.** In the case of—

(*a*) any summary cause an appeal shall lie to the sheriff principal on any point of law from the final judgment of the sheriff; and

(*b*) any summary cause other than a small claim an appeal shall lie to the Court of Session on any point of law from the final judgment of the sheriff principal, if the sheriff principal certifies the cause as suitable for such an appeal,

but save as aforesaid an interlocutor of the sheriff or the sheriff principal in any such cause shall not be subject to review.

NOTE

[1] As amended by the Law Reform (Miscellaneous Provisions) (Scotland) Act 1985, s. 18(4). Excluded by the Debtors (Scotland) Act 1987, s.103(1).

Miscellaneous and supplemental

39, 40. [Repealed by the Law Reform (Miscellaneous Provisions) (Scotland) Act 1980, Sched. 3.]

Power of Her Majesty to vary limit to privative jurisdiction of sheriff court, etc.

[1] **41.**—(1) If it appears to Her Majesty in Council that the sum of £250 specified in any provisions of this Act mentioned in subsection (2) below (or such other sum as may be specified in that provision by virtue of an Order in Council under this section) should be varied, Her Majesty may by Order in Council, specifying the provision and the sum in question, direct

that the provision shall be amended so as to substitute for that sum such other sum as may be specified in the Order.

(2) The provisions referred to in subsection (1) above are—
section 31,
paragraphs (*a*), (*b*) and (*c*) of section 35.

(3) An Order in Council under this section may contain such incidental, supplemental or consequential provisions as appear to Her Majesty in Council to be necessary or expedient for the purposes of the Order.

(4) Any Order in Council made under this section may be revoked by a subsequent Order in Council under this section which substitutes another sum for the sum specified in the Order which is thereby revoked.

(5) No recommendation shall be made to Her Majesty in Council to make an Order under this section unless a draft of the Order has been laid before Parliament and approved by resolution of each House of Parliament.

NOTE

[1] As amended by the Law Reform (Miscellaneous Provisions) (Scotland) Act 1980, Sched. 3.

Application of provisions regarding jurisdiction and summary causes

42. The following provisions of this Act, namely—
section 31,
sections 35 to 40,

[THE NEXT PAGE IS D 89]

DIET – an informal procedure usually in auditors office. Will go through a/c + he may ask for further evidence

R.97 – decree for exps. may be extracted in sols. name – may arise to avoid possibility of 'set off' being pled by opponent
- if D has decree of exps. against him + D. has another liquid claim against P. then he can set this off
- decree may be extracted in name of sol. who did cause + P.'s sol. entitled to the money

TENDERS – frequently happens that D. wants to settle matter by negotiation + offer may be made. If offer accepted + discharge signed then claim contractually ENDED
- Proper way to make these tender is by separate minute of tender
  - not good practice to put it in the defences. May influence sh's. decision because he sees offer
- Minute of tender must meet P.'s crave. Need not be for same amount. However must cover every element in P.'s claim
- Tender must include offer of exps. up to date of tender but need not include exps. where it merely reiterates sum offered.
- if not offering exps. good practice to state why not
  - CAMPBELL v ROSSI (1975) – Small debt procedure where sum sued for was £50 or less. Sum sued for was £149 + raised by summary cause. D. tendered £40 + accepted. Were summary cause exps. allowable or small debt proc.
    HELD – highest exps were due unless expressly stated that lower exps. should be granted.
  - PERRY v CONNAL (1981) – Ordinary action for 550. Settled by tender + accepted 275. Should exps. be on ordinary scale or summary scale. HELD – entitled to summary scale only
- Tender normally stated to be without prejudice – cannot be referred to or founded upon by P.
- when lodged it is put into a sealed envelope by sh. cl. + kept separate from process to avoid influencing sh.
- Once tender lodged it normally remains unless superceded by higher figure. Tender can be formally withdrawn at any time. Even if not formally withdrawn, rendered inoperative by ever material change of circumstance:–
  - SOMMERVILLE v NCB (1963)

GO TO D93

section 46 (2) so far as relating to the enactments mentioned in Part II of Schedule 2,

Schedule 1 (except paragraph 1),

shall not apply in relation to any proceedings commenced before the commencement of this Act.

PART IV

MISCELLANEOUS AND GENERAL

Orders, etc.

43.—(1) Any power conferred by this Act to make an order shall include a power exercisable in the like manner and subject to the like conditions (if any) to vary or revoke the order by a subsequent order.

(2) It is hereby declared that any power conferred by this Act to include incidental, consequential or supplemental provisions in any instrument made under this Act includes a power to include transitional provisions in that instrument.

Expenses

44.—(1) There shall be paid out of moneys provided by Parliament any sums payable by the Secretary of State in consequence of the provisions of this Act.

(2) Any sums payable under or by virtue of this Act to the Secretary of State shall be paid into the Consolidated Fund.

(3) In the application of section 4 (1) of the Local Government (Scotland) Act 1966 (variation of rate support grant orders) to a rate support grant order made before the transfer date appointed under section 30 of this Act for a grant period ending after that date, the Secretary of State shall take into account any relief obtained, or likely to be obtained, by local authorities—

(*a*) which is attributable to the coming into operation of Part II of this Act, and

(*b*) which was not taken into account in making the rate support grant order the variation of which is in question.

The provisions of this subsection are without prejudice to section 4 (4) of the said Act of 1966 (under which an order under that section may vary the matters prescribed by a rate support grant order).

Interpretation

45.—(1) In this Act, unless the contrary intention appears—

(*a*) references to a sheriff principal include reference to a temporary sheriff principal, and references to the office of sheriff principal include references to an appointment as a temporary sheriff principal;

(*b*) references to a sheriff include references to a temporary sheriff and an honorary sheriff, and references to the office of sheriff include references to an appointment as a temporary sheriff and to the office of honorary sheriff;

(*c*) references to an honorary sheriff are references to a person holding the office of honorary sheriff in his capacity as such.

(2) In this Act—

(*a*) " enactment " includes an order, regulation, rule or other instrument having effect by virtue of an Act;

(*b*) any references to any enactment shall, unless the contrary intention appears, be construed as a reference to that enactment as amended or extended, and as including a reference thereto as applied, by or under any other enactment (including this Act).

(3) Subject to the foregoing provisions of this section and to any other express provision of this Act, expressions used in this Act and in the Sheriff Courts (Scotland) Act 1907 shall have the same meanings in this Act as in that Act.

Amendment and repeal of enactments

46.—(1) Schedule 1 to this Act (which contains certain minor and consequential amendments of enactments) shall have effect.

(2) The enactments mentioned in Schedule 2 to this Act are hereby repealed to the extent specified in relation thereto in column 3 of that Schedule.

Short title, commencement and extent

47.—(1) This Act may be cited as the Sheriff Courts (Scotland) Act 1971.

[1] (2) This Act shall come into operation on such date as the Secretary of State may appoint by order made by statutory instrument, and different dates may be appointed for different provisions of this Act, or for different purposes.

Any reference in any provision of this Act to the commencement of this Act shall, unless otherwise provided by any such order, be construed as a reference to the date on which that provision comes into operation.

[2] (3) This Act, except section 4 (offices of sheriff principal and sheriff), shall extend to Scotland only.

NOTES

[1] See S.I. 1971 No. 1582; S.I. 1973 No. 276 and S.I. 1976 No. 236. Power fully exercised.

[2] As amended by the House of Commons Disqualification Act 1975, Sched. 3.

SCHEDULES

SCHEDULE 1

Minor and Consequential Amendment of Enactments

General

1. In any enactment passed or made before the commencement of this Act, for any reference to a county, where it appears in relation to a sheriff or a sheriff substitute or in any similar context, there shall, unless the contrary intention appears, be substituted a reference to a sheriffdom.

NOTE

The remaining amendments are shown in the prints in *The Parliament House Book* of the Acts amended.

SCHEDULE 2

Repeal of Enactments

. . . . . .

NOTE

Repeals of provisions of Acts printed in *The Parliament House Book* are shown in the prints of those Acts.

District Courts (Scotland) Act 1975

(1975 c. 20)

An Act to make provision as respects district courts . . . in Scotland . . . and for connected purposes. [27th March 1975]

PART I

DISTRICT COURTS

Abolition of existing inferior courts and establishment of district courts

1.—(1) On 16th May 1975 the inferior courts in Scotland existing immediately before that date (in this Act referred to as "the existing courts") shall cease to exist, and on that date there shall be established, in accordance with the provisions of this Act, a district court for each commission area except in the case of a commission area in respect of which the Secretary of State otherwise directs, having regard to the likely lack of business for such a court.

In this subsection, "inferior courts" means all justice of the peace courts, quarter sessions, burgh courts, police courts, and the court of the bailie of the river and firth of Clyde.

(2) On and after that date, all functions of burgh magistrates, not otherwise provided for, shall be exercisable by a justice of the peace.

(3) Where proceedings were instituted before that date in any existing court and those proceedings have not been completed by that date, then, for the purpose of enabling those proceedings to be continued on and after that date, and for preserving in other respects the continuity of the administration of justice—

(*a*) the district court having jurisdiction in the area where the proceedings were instituted shall be treated as succeeding to, and being the same court as, the existing court concerned, and any verdict, sentence, order, complaint, notice, citation, warrant, bail bond or other proceedings or document shall have effect accordingly; and

(*b*) the clerk and the prosecutor of the existing court shall transfer all records, productions and documents relating to those proceedings to the clerk or, as the case may be, the prosecutor of the district court concerned.

(4) Where proceedings were instituted after 14th May 1969 in any existing court and were completed on or before 15th May 1975, the clerk of that court shall transfer all complaints, minutes and other records relating thereto to the clerk of the district court concerned.

(5) In the case of any other record or document relating to proceedings in the existing courts, the person having custody of it shall, on request by or on behalf of a district court, release it to that court for the purpose of proceedings in that court, and any record or document so released shall be returned to the person who released it as soon as may be after it has ceased to be required for the said purposes.

Further provision as to establishment and disestablishment of district courts

[1] **1A.**—(1) Where it appears to the Secretary of State that—

(*a*) there is insufficient business for the district court in a particular commission area; and

(*b*) such insufficiency of business is likely to continue,

he may by order provide that the district court for that area cease to exist on a specified date.

(2) Where it appears to the Secretary of State that, in a commission area in which there is no district court, there is likely to be sufficient business to

justify the establishment of such a court, he may by order provide for the establishment of such a court in that area on a specified date.

(3) An order under subsection (1) or (2) above may contain all such provisions as appear to the Secretary of State to be necessary or expedient for rendering the order of full effect and any incidental, supplemental or consequential provisions which appear to him to be necessary or expedient for the purposes of the order, including, but without prejudice to the generality of the foregoing words, provisions amending, repealing or revoking any enactment (whether passed or made before or after the commencement of this enactment).

(4) Before making an order under subsection (1) or (2) above, the Secretary of State shall consult the district or islands council for the area concerned, and such other persons as appear to him to have an interest in the proposed order.

(5) Orders under subsection (1) or (2) above shall be made by statutory instrument, which shall be subject to annulment in pursuance of a resolution of either House of Parliament.

NOTE

[1] Inserted by the Law Reform (Miscellaneous Provisions) (Scotland) Act 1985, s. 33, with effect from 30th December 1985.

District of, and exercise of jurisdiction by, district court

2.—[1] (1) Each commission area shall be the district of a district court, and the places at which a district court sits, and subject to section 10 of the Bail etc. (Scotland) Act 1980 (sittings of sheriff and district courts) the days and times when it sits at any given place, shall be determined by the local authority concerned.

(2) The jurisdiction and powers of the district court shall be exercisable by a stipendiary magistrate or by one or more justices, and no decision of the court shall be questioned on the ground that it was not constituted as required by this subsection unless objection was taken on that ground by or on behalf of a party to the proceedings not later than the time when the proceedings or the alleged irregularity began.

NOTE

[1] As amended by the Bail etc. (Scotland) Act 1980, Sched. 1: excluded by *ibid.* s. 10(3).

Jurisdiction and powers of district court

3.—(1) A district court shall have all the jurisdiction and powers of the existing courts (other than those of the justice of the peace small debt court and of quarter sessions) and also those hitherto exercisable by a burgh magistrate, judge of police, or justice of the peace when acting as a court of summary jurisdiction.

(2) A district court when constituted by a stipendiary magistrate shall, in addition to the jurisdiction and powers mentioned in subsection (1) above, have the summary criminal jurisdiction and powers of a sheriff.

(3) [Repealed by the Criminal Law Act 1977, Sched. 13.]

(4) Where several offences, which if committed in one commission area could be tried under one complaint, are alleged to have been committed in different commission areas, proceedings may be taken for all or any of those offences under one complaint before the district court of any one of such commission areas, and any such offence may be dealt with, heard, tried, determined, adjudged and punished as if the offence had been wholly committed within the jurisdiction of that court.

Procedure and practice in the district court

4.—(1) Subject to the provisions of this section, the rules of procedure and practice which immediately before 16th May 1975 applied to the existing courts shall, with any necessary modifications, apply on and after that date to the district court.

(2) The powers of the High Court under section 76(1)(*b*) of the Summary Jurisdiction (Scotland) Act 1954 to regulate procedure under that Act by acts of adjournal shall include power to regulate and prescribe by acts of adjournal the procedure and practice to be followed in any proceedings in the district court.

(3) An act of adjournal made under the said section 76(1)(*b*) in the exercise of the powers conferred by subsection (2) above may contain such incidental, supplemental, or consequential provisions as appear to the High Court to be necessary or expedient for the purposes of that act, including provisions amending, repealing or revoking any enactment (whether passed or made before or after the commencement of this Act) relating to matters with respect to which an act of adjournal may be made by virtue of those powers.

Stipendiary magistrates

5.—(1) Subject to subsections (2) and (3) below, a local authority may appoint a stipendiary magistrate to sit in a district court, and the terms and conditions of such an appointment, including superannuation and other benefits, shall be those applicable to service in local government.

(2) A person shall not be appointed to be a stipendiary magistrate unless he is, and has been for at least five years, legally qualified, and for the purposes of this subsection a person shall be legally qualified if he is an advocate or a solicitor.

(3) A person shall not be appointed to be a stipendiary magistrate until the Secretary of State approves—

(*a*) the establishment of the office of stipendiary magistrate in the district court concerned;

(*b*) the salary which it is proposed should pertain to that office; and

(*c*) the appointment of the person proposed for that office.

[THE NEXT PAGE IS D 93]

- personal injuries at work + future loss of earnings claim. On basis as pled D's lodged a tender. P. then died. As far future loss of earnings was concerned such as tendered was totally inappropriate to claim. Death of P. rendered tender inoperative

- Once tender lodged + intimated, P. can decide to accept it or not
  - minute of acceptance of tender is lodged in process. Decree in his favour
    - some D's don't like decrees against them eg companies + may prefer to settle extrajudicially with decree of absolvitor

- If case proceeds then tender may have a material effect on exps. at end of day - useful for D.
  - eg P. had a tender of £5000 + ct. awarded him 4750. In that situation P. by failure to accept a reasonable tender, has incurred some exp. + he should have to pay any extra exps. incurred.

- May be difficulties wrt accrual of interest from date of tender + date of award.
  - P. not entitled to an award of interest over + above the amount of the tender by Interest on Damages (S) Act 1958 as amended by 1971 Act s.1 + 1B

- If tender not accepted the interest element complicates the issue - interest will be accruing from date of tender. So when considering final award must deduct the interest which has accrued on the tender to see whether tender was more or less

- where tender not accepted within reasonable time of being made P. may still suffer adversely wrt exps. eg exps. incurred 14 days after tender is lodged + thereafter will be incurred by P.

- 'WILLIAMSON TENDER' - WILLIAMSON V McPHERSON (1957)
  - where there are 2 or more D's the qu. may arise as to proportion each is liable to P. By 1940 LR (MP)(S) Act blame can be apportioned by sh. 2D.p. may decide to offer that he has portion of liability. If not accepted + offer was more than what was eventually decided then ct. can award the exps. against the D. who refused the Williamson tender from the date when the tender should have been accepted

GO TO D97

(4) Where it appears to the Secretary of State that it is expedient so to do in order to avoid delays in the administration of justice in any district court, he may direct the local authority concerned to appoint a person qualified to be so appointed to act as stipendiary magistrate in that court during such period as the Secretary of State thinks fit.

(5) Any person who immediately before 16th May 1975 holds office as stipendiary magistrate for any area shall, on that date, become stipendiary magistrate in the district court having jurisdiction in that area and shall be deemed in all respects to have been appointed by virtue of this section.

(6) The salary of any such stipendiary magistrate as is mentioned in subsection (5) above shall not be less than that payable to him immediately before 16th May 1975.

(7) Every stipendiary magistrate shall, by virtue of his office, be a justice of the peace for the commission area in which he is appointed.

(8) Section 12 of the Sheriff Courts (Scotland) Act 1971 (removal from office of sheriff) shall apply in relation to a stipendiary magistrate as it applies in relation to a sheriff.

District prosecutor

6.—(1) Until the Lord Advocate directs that all prosecutions in a commission area shall proceed at the instance of a procurator fiscal appointed by him, every local authority shall appoint a district prosecutor for the district court and pay to him such reasonable salary as they may determine.

(2) A procurator fiscal appointed by the Lord Advocate or a district prosecutor may institute and carry on proceedings in the district court, and a procurator fiscal so appointed shall have all the powers and privileges of a district prosecutor.

(3) Within the district of the district court the district prosecutor shall have all the powers and privileges of a prosecutor in the existing courts and those pertaining by law to a procurator fiscal.

(4) The Lord Advocate may issue directions to a district prosecutor regarding the prosecution of offences in the district court, and the district prosecutor shall comply with any such direction.

(5) A district prosecutor shall report to the Lord Advocate on any matter concerning the discharge of his functions as and when called upon to do so by or on behalf of the Lord Advocate.

(6) A complaint at the instance of the district prosecutor for any district may, in the event of his dying or ceasing to be entitled to discharge the duties of district prosecutor for that district, be taken up and proceeded with by any other person entitled to discharge such duties.

(7) The offices of clerk to the district court and district prosecutor shall not be held by the same person or by persons who stand in relation to one another as partners or as employer and employee.

(8) A district prosecutor shall not be removed or suspended from office or have his salary diminished by a local authority without the consent of the Lord Advocate.

(9) The prosecutions authorised by virtue of this Act under complaint by the procurator fiscal or district prosecutor shall be without prejudice to complaints at the instance of any other person entitled to make the same.

Clerk of district court

7.—(1) It shall be the duty of each local authority to appoint and employ, whether on a full-time or part-time basis, an officer to act as clerk of the district court for their area, who shall also act as legal assessor in that court, and any person so appointed shall be an advocate or a solicitor.

(2) There shall be transferred to the clerks of the district courts all functions hitherto exercisable by clerks of the existing courts.

(3) Where under an agreement an officer of a regional council is placed at the disposal of a district council for the purposes of this section, that officer may perform the duties of clerk of the district court for the area concerned.

Court houses for district court

8.—(1) Every local authority shall provide suitable and sufficient premises and facilities for the purposes of the district court.

(2) Without prejudice to subsection (1) above, every regional, islands, or district council having control of premises used to any extent for the purposes of the existing courts as at 15th May 1975 shall make those premises available for the purposes of the district court, and, where those premises include accommodation used by the prosecutor in the existing courts or in the district courts, that accommodation shall be made available to any procurator fiscal appointed by the Lord Advocate to serve in the district court for such period and at such times as the fiscal may require.

. . . .

General

Amendments and repeals

24. . . .

(3) The Secretary of State may by order amend, repeal or revoke any provision of an Act passed or an instrument under an Act made before 16th May 1975 if it appears to him that that provision is inconsistent with any provision of this Act or requires modification in consequence of this Act.

(4) Where any local enactment provides for any matter which is also provided for by any provision of this Act or of any order made thereunder, the provision of this Act, or, as the case may be, of that order, shall have effect in substitution for the local enactment, which shall cease to have effect.

(5) Any order made under this section shall be made by statutory instrument, which shall be subject to annulment in pursuance of a resolution of either House of Parliament.

Expenses

25. There shall be defrayed out of moneys provided by Parliament—

(*a*) any expenses incurred by the Secretary of State under this Act; and

(*b*) any increase attributable to the provisions of this Act in the sums payable out of moneys so provided under any other enactment.

Interpretation

26.—(1) In this Act, unless the context otherwise requires—

" clerk of the district court " includes such depute clerk as may be required for the purposes of any district court;

" commission area " means a district or islands area within the meaning of the Local Government (Scotland) Act 1973;

" district prosecutor " includes such depute or assistant district prosecutor as may be required for the purposes of any district court;

" justice " or " justice of the peace " means a justice of the peace appointed under section 9 of this Act or deemed to have been so appointed;

" licensing court " and " court of appeal " have the same meanings as in the Licensing (Scotland) Act 1959;

" local authority " means a district council or an islands council;

" prescribed " means prescribed by regulations made by the Secretary of State.

(2) Any power conferred by this Act to make an order shall include power, exercisable in like manner and subject to the same conditions, to vary or revoke the order by a subsequent order.

(3) Unless the context otherwise requires, any reference in this Act to any other enactment is a reference thereto as amended, extended or applied by or under any other enactment, including this Act.

Short title, extent and commencement

27.—(1) This Act may be cited as the District Courts (Scotland) Act 1975, and, except section 24(1) and subsection (2) below and the entries in Schedule 1 to this Act relating to section 18(1) of the Police (Scotland) Act 1967, extends to Scotland only.

(2) This Act, except sections 8, 10, 11, 14, 16, 17, 20, 23, 26 and this section, shall come into force on 16th May 1975.

[1] Fatal Accidents and Sudden Deaths Inquiry (Scotland) Act 1976

(1976 c. 14)

An Act to make provision for Scotland for the holding of public inquiries in respect of fatal accidents, deaths of persons in legal custody, sudden, suspicious and unexplained deaths and deaths occurring in circumstances giving rise to serious public concern. [13th April 1976.]

NOTE

[1] See the Anatomy Act 1984, s.4(6).

Investigation of death and application for public inquiry

1.—(1) Subject to the provisions of any enactment specified in Schedule 1 to this Act and subsection (2) below, where—

(*a*) in the case of a death to which this paragraph applies—

(i) it appears that the death has resulted from an accident occurring in Scotland while the person who has died, being an employee, was in the course of his employment or, being an employer or self-employed person, was engaged in his occupation as such; or

(ii) the person who has died was, at the time of his death, in legal custody; or

(*b*) it appears to the Lord Advocate to be expedient in the public interest in the case of a death to which this paragraph applies that an inquiry under this Act should be held into the circumstances of the death on the ground that it was sudden, suspicious or unexplained, or has occurred in circumstances such as to give rise to serious public concern,

the procurator fiscal for the district with which the circumstances of the death appear to be most closely connected shall investigate those circumstances and apply to the sheriff for the holding of an inquiry under this Act into those circumstances.

(2) Paragraph (*a*) of subsection (1) above applies to a death occurring in Scotland after the commencement of this Act (other than such a death in a case where criminal proceedings have been concluded against any person in respect of the death or any accident from which the death resulted, and the Lord Advocate is satisfied that the circumstances of the death have been sufficiently established in the course of such proceedings), and paragraph (*b*) of that subsection applies to a death occurring there at any time after the date three years before such commencement.

(3) An application under subsection (1) above—

(*a*) shall be made to the sheriff with whose sheriffdom the circumstances of the death appear to be most closely connected;

(*b*) shall narrate briefly the circumstances of the death so far as known to the procurator fiscal;

(*c*) may, if it appears that more deaths than one have occurred as a result of the same accident or in the same or similar circumstances, relate to both or all such deaths.

(4) For the purposes of subsection (1)(*a*)(ii) above, a person is in legal custody if—

(*a*) he is detained in, or is subject to detention in, a prison, remand centre, detention centre, borstal institution, or young offenders institution, all within the meaning of the Prisons (Scotland) Act 1952; or

(*b*) he is detained in a police station, police cell, or other similar place; or

(*c*) he is being taken—

(i) to any of the places specified in paragraphs (*a*) and (*b*) of this subsection to be detained therein; or

(ii) from any such place in which immediately before such taking he was detained.

Citation of witnesses for precognition

2.—(1) The procurator fiscal may, for the purpose of carrying out his investigation under section 1(1) of this Act, cite witnesses for precognition by him, and this section shall be sufficient warrant for such citation.

(2) If any witness cited under subsection (1) above—

(*a*) fails without reasonable excuse and after receiving reasonable notice to attend for precognition by the procurator fiscal at the time and place mentioned in the citation served on him; or

(*b*) refuses when so cited to give information within his knowledge regarding any matter relevant to the investigation in relation to which such precognition is taken,

the procurator fiscal may apply to the sheriff for an order requiring the witness to attend for such precognition or to give such information at a time and place specified in the order; and the sheriff shall, if he considers it expedient to do so, make such an order.

[1] (3) If the witness fails to comply with the order of the sheriff under subsection (2) above, he shall be liable to be summarily punished forthwith by a fine not exceeding level 3 on the standard scale or by imprisonment for any period not exceeding 20 days.

NOTE

[1] As amended by the Criminal Justice Act 1982, Sched. 7.

Holding of public inquiry

3.—(1) On an application under section 1 of this Act being made to him, the sheriff shall make an order—

(*a*) fixing a time and place for the holding by him of an inquiry under this Act (hereafter in this Act referred to as "the inquiry"), which shall be as soon thereafter as is reasonably practicable in such courthouse or other premises as appear to him to be appropriate, having regard to the apparent circumstances of the death; and

(*b*) granting warrant to cite witnesses and havers to attend at the inquiry at the instance of the procurator fiscal or of any person who may be entitled by virtue of this Act to appear at the inquiry.

(2) On the making of an order under subsection (1) above, the procurator fiscal shall—

(*a*) intimate the holding of the inquiry and the time and place fixed for it to the wife or husband or the nearest known relative and, in a case where the inquiry is being held in respect of such a death as is referred to in section 1(1)(*a*)(i) of this Act, to the employer, if any, of the person whose death is the subject of the inquiry, and to such other person or class of persons as may be prescribed in rules made under section 7 (1) (*g*) of this Act; and

(*b*) give public notice of the holding of the inquiry and of the time and place fixed for it.

[THE NEXT PAGE IS D 97]

EXTRA JUDICIAL SETTLEMENT - parties settle out of ct. Parties enter a joint minute whereby there is a narration outlining that the matter has been settled out of ct. D. has a decree of absolvitor
- sh. is asked to interpose auth. to the joint minute + grant decree in terms thereof with no expps. due to or by either party
- joint minute must dispose of all the craves. Can put in at end of joint minute - 'Quoad ultra to dismiss the cause'

DEFAULT - failure of party / sol. to do something - R.59

ABANDONMENT - common law abandonment still possible
- R58

R.20 - remit to Ct. of S. - in cases of importance or complexity
1980 Act s.16
- Ct. of S. can remit to sh. ct. by LR(MP)(S) Act 1985
R. 20A regulates procedure

R.19 - transfer between sh. cts.

R.99-102 - actions for sequestration of rent - action by landlord exercising hypothec - attaches moveable property within the subjects + can have them sold to pay for rent

R.108-110 - summary suspension

R.111-112 - arrestment

R.113-127 - multiple poinding

R.144-146 - damages arising out of death of a relative

R.147-148 - interim damages

(3) Where an application under section 1 of this Act relates to more than one death, the order made under subsection (1) above shall so relate; and in this Act references to a death shall include references to both or all deaths or to each death as the case may require, and in subsection (2) (*a*) above the reference to the person whose death is the subject of the inquiry shall include a reference to each person whose death is the subject of the inquiry.

Conduct of public inquiry

4.—(1) At the inquiry, it shall be the duty of the procurator fiscal to adduce evidence with regard to the circumstances of the death which is the subject of the inquiry.

(2) The wife or husband, or the nearest known relative, and, in a case where the inquiry is being held in respect of such a death as is referred to in section 1 (1) (*a*) (i) of this Act, the employer, if any, of the person whose death is the subject of the inquiry, an inspector appointed under section 19 of the Health and Safety at Work etc. Act 1974 and any other person who the sheriff is satisfied has an interest in the inquiry may appear and adduce evidence at the inquiry.

(3) Subject to subsection (4) below, the inquiry shall be open to the public.

(4) Where a person under the age of 17 is in any way involved in the inquiry, the sheriff may, at his own instance or on an application made to him by any party to the inquiry, make an order providing that—

(*a*) no report of the inquiry which is made in a newspaper or other publication or a sound or television broadcast shall reveal the name, address or school, or include any particulars calculated to lead to the identification of that person;

(*b*) no picture relating to the inquiry which is or includes a picture of that person shall be published in any newspaper or other publication or televised broadcast.

[1] (5) Any person who contravenes an order made under subsection (4) above shall be guilty of an offence and shall be liable on summary conviction to a fine not exceeding level 4 on the standard scale in respect of each offence.

(6) The sheriff may, either at his own instance or at the request of the procurator fiscal or of any party who may be entitled by virtue of this Act to appear at the inquiry, summon any person having special knowledge and being willing to do so, to act as an assessor at the inquiry.

(7) Subject to the provisions of this Act and any rules made under section 7 of this Act, the rules of evidence, the procedure and the powers of the sheriff to deal with contempt of court and to enforce the attendance of witnesses at the inquiry shall be as nearly as possible those applicable in an ordinary civil cause brought before the sheriff sitting alone.

NOTE

[1] As amended by virtue of the Criminal Procedure (Scotland) Act 1975, ss. 289F and 289G.

Criminal proceedings and compellability of witnesses

5.—(1) The examination of a witness or haver at the inquiry shall not be a bar to criminal proceedings being taken against him.

(2) No witness at the inquiry shall be compellable to answer any question tending to show that he is guilty of any crime or offence.

Sheriff's determination, etc.

6.—(1) At the conclusion of the evidence and any submissions thereon, or as soon as possible thereafter, the sheriff shall make a determination setting out the following circumstances of the death so far as they have been established to his satisfaction—

(*a*) where and when the death and any accident resulting in the death took place;

(*b*) the cause or causes of such death and any accident resulting in the death;
(*c*) the reasonable precautions, if any, whereby the death and any accident resulting in the death might have been avoided;
(*d*) the defects, if any, in any system of working which contributed to the death or any accident resulting in the death; and
(*e*) any other facts which are relevant to the circumstances of the death.

(2) The sheriff shall be entitled to be satisfied that any circumstances referred to in subsection (1) above have been established by evidence, notwithstanding that that evidence is not corroborated.

(3) The determination of the sheriff shall not be admissible in evidence or be founded on in any judicial proceedings, of whatever nature, arising out of the death or out of any accident from which the death resulted.

(4) On the conclusion of the inquiry
(*a*) the sheriff clerk shall send to the Lord Advocate a copy of the determination of the sheriff and, on a request being made to him, send to any Minister or Government Department or to the Health and Safety Commission, a copy of
(i) the application made under section 1 of this Act;
(ii) the transcript of the evidence;
(iii) any report or documentary production used in the inquiry;
(iv) the determination of the sheriff, and
(*b*) the procurator fiscal shall send to the Registrar General of Births, Deaths and Marriages for Scotland the name and last known address of the person who has died and the date, place and cause of his death.

(5) Upon payment of such fee as may be prescribed in rules made under paragraph (i) of section 7 (1) of this Act, any person—
(*a*) may obtain a copy of the determination of the sheriff;
(*b*) who has an interest in the inquiry may, within such period as may be prescribed in rules made under paragraph (*j*) of the said section 7 (1), obtain a copy of the transcript of the evidence,

from the sheriff clerk.

Rules

7.—(1) The Lord Advocate may, by rules, provide in relation to inquiries under this Act—
(*a*) as to the form of any document to be used in or for the purposes of such inquiries;
(*b*) for the representation, on such conditions as may be specified in the rules, of any person who is entitled by virtue of this Act to appear at the inquiry;
(*c*) for the authorisation by the sheriff of the taking and holding in safe custody of anything which it may be considered necessary to produce;
(*d*) for the inspection by the sheriff or any person authorised by him of any land, premises, article, or other thing;
(*e*) that written statements and reports may, on such conditions as may be specified in the rules, be admissible in lieu of parole evidence;
(*f*) as to the duties, remuneration and other conditions of appointment of any assessor summoned under section 4 of this Act, and for keeping of lists of persons willing to act as such;
(*g*) as to intimation of the holding of the inquiry;
(*h*) as to the payment of fees to solicitors and expenses to witnesses and havers;
(*i*) as to the payment of a fee by a person obtaining a copy of the determination of the sheriff or a copy of the transcript of the evidence;

(*j*) as to the period within which a person entitled may obtain a copy of the transcript of the evidence at the inquiry;

(*k*) as to such other matters relating to procedure as the Lord Advocate thinks appropriate.

(2) The power to make rules conferred by any provision of this Act shall be exercisable by statutory instrument.

(3) Rules made by the Lord Advocate under this Act may contain such incidental, consequential and supplemental provisions as appear to him to be necessary or proper for bringing the rules into operation and giving full effect thereto.

Minor and consequential amendments and repeals

8. . . .

Application to continental shelf

[1] **9.** For the purposes of this Act a death or any accident from which death has resulted which has occurred—

(*a*) in connection with any activity falling within subsection (2) of section 23 of the Oil and Gas (Enterprise) Act 1982; and

(*b*) in that area, or any part of that area, in respect of which it is provided by Order in Council under subsection (1) of that section that questions arising out of acts or omissions taking place therein shall be determined in accordance with the law in force in Scotland,

shall be taken to have occurred in Scotland.

NOTE

[1] As amended by the Oil and Gas (Enterprise) Act 1982, Sched. 3, para. 34.

Interpretation, transitional, citation, commencement and extent

[1] **10.**—(1) Any reference in this Act to any other enactment shall be construed as a reference to that enactment as amended by or under any other enactment including this Act.

(2)–(3) [Repealed by the Statute Law (Repeals) Act 1989, Sched. 1, Pt. I.]

(4) This Act may be cited as the Fatal Accidents and Sudden Deaths Inquiry (Scotland) Act 1976.

(5) [Repealed by the Statute Law (Repeals) Act 1989, Sched. 1, Pt. I.]

(6) This Act, other than subsections (4) and (5) of section 4 and section 9 of this Act, extends to Scotland only.

NOTE

[1] The Act was brought into force on 1st March 1977 by S.I. 1977 No. 190.

. . . .

[1] Law Reform (Miscellaneous Provisions) (Scotland) Act 1985

(1985 c. 73)

An Act to amend the law of Scotland in respect of . . . certain courts and their powers; evidence and procedure; . . . and to make, as respects Scotland, certain other miscellaneous reforms of the law. [30th October 1985]

NOTE

[1] Of the provisions noted here, ss. 16 and 17 came into force on 30th December 1985, Sched. 2, para. 12 on 8th December 1986 and s. 18 on 30th November 1988.

. . . .

Provisions relating to civil jurisdiction and procedure

. . . .

Power of sheriff to interdict removal of child

16. [Repealed by the Family Law Act 1986, Sched. 2.]

Power of sheriff to order sheriff clerk to execute deeds relating to heritage

17. [New s. 5A of the Sheriff Courts (Scotland) Act 1907 is included in the print of that Act, *supra*.]

Small claims

18. [Amendments to ss. 35–38 of the Sheriff Courts (Scotland) Act 1971 are incorporated in the print of that Act, *supra.*]

. . . .

SCHEDULE 2

AMENDMENT OF ENACTMENTS

. . . .

Sheriff Courts (Scotland) Act 1971 (c. 58)

12. [Amendments to s.32 of the 1971 Act are incorporated in the print of that Act, *supra.*]

. . . .

[THE NEXT PAGE IS D 201]

Acts of Sederunt

Codifying Act of Sederunt

(C.A.S.)

(S. R. & O. 1913 No. 638)

(4th June 1913)

BOOK L—SHERIFF COURTS

CHAPTER I—NAUTICAL ASSESSORS IN SHERIFF COURT

(C.A.S. L, I)

Procedure and number of assessors

1. In any action or proceeding in the sheriff court to which the Nautical Assessors Act 1894 applies, the number of assessors to be summoned to the assistance of the court at any particular stage of the cause, whether on the initiative of the court or on the application of any party, shall be one in the case of a proof, and one or more than one in the case of a hearing on appeal, as the court shall think fit, provided always (*a*) that intimation of the name or names of the person or persons proposed to be summoned shall be given to the parties by the sheriff clerk at least *eight* days before the proof or the hearing for which the summons is to be issued; (*b*) that if any party intends to object to the person or persons proposed to be summoned he shall state his objection, with the grounds of it, by minute lodged in process within *two* days after receipt of the intimation; (*c*) that the objections, if any, shall be disposed of by the court at least *three* days before the proof or the hearing; (*d*) that if the objection is sustained, the like procedure shall be followed for securing another assessor, and the court shall, if necessary for that purpose, adjourn the proof of the hearing; and (*e*) that it shall be the duty of the sheriff-clerk, if no minute is lodged as aforesaid, or when any objection has been taken and repelled, to arrange for the attendance at the proof or hearing of the person or persons named in the foresaid intimation.

Remuneration of assessor

[1] **2.** The remuneration of every person attending as a nautical assessor under the aforesaid Act of Parliament shall be £3·15 a day for each day on which he so attends, and also for any Sunday over which he is necessarily detained at the seat of court, besides maintenance and travelling expenses. In the case of an assessor resident out of Scotland, he shall be entitled to charge a day for coming and a day for going at the above rate, but other assessors shall not be entitled to a fee for travelling days unless, owing to the distance from the seat of the court at which they reside, it is impossible, with reasonable convenience, to travel on the day or days on which they are required to sit in court.

NOTE

[1] As amended by the Decimal Currency Act 1969, s. 10 (1).

Consignation to meet expense

3. When, on the motion of a party to the cause, an assessor or assessors is or are to be summoned under the provisions of the foresaid Act of Parliament, the motion shall only be granted on condition that the party making it shall consign with the sheriff clerk such sum to meet the fees and expenses above provided as the court may determine; and when an assessor or assessors is or are to be summoned *ex proprio motu* of the court, such consignation shall be made by the pursuer of the action, unless the court shall otherwise direct.

CHAPTER II—LETTERS OF REQUEST—(FOREIGN WITNESSES)

(C.A.S. L,II)

Form of minute

1. Where the evidence of any witness resident abroad is material for the determination of a cause depending before a sheriff court, the party desiring to obtain such evidence may apply to the sheriff, by a minute in the form hereto appended (Schedule A), for a letter of request addressed to the judge or judges of the foreign tribunal within whose jurisdiction the witness is residing.

Form of letters

2. On considering such minute and hearing the objections thereto, if any, the sheriff may grant the same, and authorise a letter of request to be issued, which letter of request shall be in the terms hereto appended (Schedule B), and shall be signed by the sheriff. The said letter of request shall be prepared by the party moving for the same, and shall be lodged with the sheriff clerk along with the minute mentioned in the preceding section.

Agent bound in expense

3. It shall be a condition of granting any such letter of request that the agent for the party moving therefor shall, before the letter of request is issued, become personally bound for the whole expenses which may become due and payable in respect thereof to the court before which the evidence is taken, as well as to the witnesses examined, and make consignation of such sum to meet said expenses as the sheriff shall determine.

Translations of Letter and Interrogatories

4. There shall be lodged by the party obtaining a letter of request a translation into the language of the court to which the letter is directed, of the letter and of the relative interrogatories.

Transmission of Letter to Foreign Office

5. The letter of request, when issued and signed as aforesaid, shall, along with interrogatories adjusted according to the present practice, and the relative translations, be forthwith forwarded by the sheriff clerk to His Majesty's Secretary of State for Foreign Affairs, requesting that the evidence taken under the same shall, when received, be forwarded to him, under seal to abide the orders of court.

Definition of " sheriff "

6. In this section " sheriff " shall be held to include salaried sheriff substitute.

SCHEDULE A

Minute for A.B., pursuer [or C.D., defender], in the action presently depending in the Sheriff Court of at , at the instance of A.B. against C.D. for the pursuer [or defender] stated that the following persons, viz. [*state names and designations, including place of residence of proposed witnesses*], are material witnesses for the pursuer [or defender] in support of the claim [or defence] in this action, and he prayed the court to issue a letter of request, addressed to [*state the judge or tribunal within whose jurisdiction the witnesses are resident*], to take the evidence of said witnesses.

[*Signed by the parties' agent.*]

SCHEDULE B

Whereas an action is now pending in the Sheriff Court of at Scotland, in which A.B. is pursuer and C.D. is defender: And whereas it has been represented to the said court that it is necessary, for the purposes of justice and for the due determination of the matters in dispute between the parties, that the following persons should be examined as witnesses upon oath, that is to say:—

E.F., of
G.H., of
and I.J., of

And it appearing that such witnesses are resident within the jurisdiction of your honourable court:—

Now, I , *Sheriff* [or Sheriff-Substitute] of , have the honour to request and do hereby request, that for the reasons aforesaid, and for the assistance of the said court, you, as the president and judges of the said , or some one or more of you, will be pleased to summon the said witnesses to attend at such time and place as you shall appoint, before some one or more of you, or such other person as according to the procedure of your court is competent to take the examination of witnesses, and that you will cause such witnesses to be examined upon the interrogatories which accompany this letter of request, in the presence of the agents of the pursuer and defender, or such of them as shall, on due notice given, attend such examination.

And I further have the honour to request that you will be pleased to cause the answers of the said witnesses to be reduced into writing, and all books, letters, papers, and documents produced upon such examination to be duly marked for identification; and that you will be further pleased to authenticate such examination by the seal of your tribunal, or in such other way as in accordance with your procedure, and to return the same through His Majesty's Secretary of State for Foreign Affairs for transmission to me:

[*Signed by the Sheriff or Sheriff-Substitute.*]

[*Address to the Foreign Court.*]

CHAPTER VII-WINDING UP UNDER THE BUILDING SOCIETIES ACT 1874

(C.A.S., L, VII)

Form of application for winding up

1. All applications presented to the court for the winding up of a society registered under the Building Societies Act 1874, either voluntarily under the supervision of the sheriff court, or by the court, shall be by petition in form as nearly as may be of initial writs under the Act 7 Edw. VII. c. 51 (Sheriff Courts Act 1907), and the court shall order service and advertisement thereof in the *Edinburgh Gazette*, and such further advertisement, if any, as the court may consider necessary, and shall appoint the said petition to be heard on such early day as may be suitable.

Petition to be printed

2. The said petition shall be printed, and every shareholder and creditor of the company shall be entitled to receive from the solicitor of the petitioner a copy thereof on demand at his office.

Procedure on Petition

3. The court on the day appointed may hear the petitioner's proof in support of the petition, and may also hear any parties interested in support thereof or in opposition thereto, and also any application which may follow thereon in the course of the winding up, either in open court or in chambers, and may order such answers as may be deemed necessary, and may adjourn the hearing; and after such inquiry, by proof or otherwise, as may be deemed necessary, the court may order the society to be wound up, or may dismiss the petition, or may make such other order as may be just.

Procedure in winding up

4. The court may, as to all matters relating to the winding up, have regard to the wishes of the creditors or members, as proved by sufficient evidence; and may direct meetings of the creditors or members to be summoned, held, and conducted in such manner as may be directed, for the purpose of ascertaining their wishes, and may appoint a person to act as chairman of any such meeting, and to report the result of such meeting to the court. In the case of creditors regard is to be had to the value of the debt due to each creditor; and in the case of members, to the number of votes conferred on each member by the regulations of the society, or failing such regulations, to the number of shares held by each member.

Liquidator's appointment

5. For the purpose of winding up a society, a liquidator shall be appointed. The shareholders may nominate a liquidator at any meeting held by them, and called in terms of section 32 of the said Building Societies Act, for the purpose of resolving to wind up the society under supervision of the court, and of presenting a petition to the court to that effect; and the court shall confirm the nomination so made, unless sufficient cause to the contrary be shown. If the court do not confirm the nomination, or if no such nomination has been made before the presenting of the petition, the court shall, at the hearing of the said petition, or at any subsequent time, nominate a liquidator, either provisionally or otherwise. In the case of winding up by the court, the liquidator shall be nominated by the court. The court may also determine whether any and what security shall be given by the liquidator; and every appointment of a liquidator shall be advertised in such manner as the court may appoint.

Liquidator's tenure of office and remuneration

6. Any liquidator may resign, or may be removed by the court on due cause shown; and any vacancy in the office of a liquidator shall be filled up by the court. There shall be paid to the liquidator such salary or remuneration by way of percentage or otherwise as the court may direct.

Special powers

7. When in course of winding up the society it shall be necessary to carry on the business thereof for a time, or to make up titles to heritable property, or to compromise claims with contributories, these powers shall only be exercised with the sanction of the court, obtained upon a note presented to the court setting forth the grounds upon which the powers are asked for. The court may, on the presentation of such notes, order such intimation thereof as shall be deemed suitable and expedient in the circumstances. And further, it shall be competent to the liquidator to apply to the court for instruction and direction in regard to any matter wherein, in his judgment, such instruction and direction are necessary.

Law agents and factors

8. The liquidator shall have power to appoint a law agent to assist him in the performance of his duties, and also, with sanction of the court, to appoint a factor for taking charge of or managing any of the properties of the society.

General meetings of members in voluntary liquidation

9. Where a society is being wound up voluntarily under the supervision of the court, the liquidator may from time to time during the continuance of such winding up call general meetings of the members of the society; and in the event of the winding up continuing for more than one year, the liquidator shall call a general meeting of the members at the end of the first year, and of each succeeding year from the commencement of the winding up, or as soon thereafter as may be convenient, and shall lay before such meeting an account showing his acts and dealings, and the manner in which the winding up has been conducted during the preceding year.

State of liabilities and assets, etc., and objections thereto

10. The liquidator shall, as soon as may be after an order is made for winding up a society, make up and lodge in process a state showing—

(*a*) The liabilities and assets of the society in detail.

(*b*) The number of members, and the amounts standing to their credit in the books of the society.

(*c*) The liabilities of members of the society in terms of sections 13 and 14 of the Building Societies Act and of the rules of the society.

(*d*) The claims of depositors and other creditors, and the provision to be made for their payment.

(*e*) The sums to be repaid to the members, if any, after payment of the debts due by the society.

And such state may be objected to by any person having interest, and may be amended from time to time.

And the court may, after such notice or advertisement as may be thought proper, and after hearing any party or parties, sanction and approve of such state, or disapprove thereof; and if the same be sanctioned and approved of, the court may authorise the funds to be distributed in terms of such state; and thereafter, on being satisfied that payment has been made to the creditors of the society and depositors so far as possible, and to the members of the society in terms of the said state, or when any sum or sums payable to any member or members of the society have not been claimed, that such consignation thereof has been made by the liquidator as the court may direct, the court shall declare the winding up of the said society to be at an end and the society dissolved, discharge the liquidator of his whole actings and intromissions, and appoint his bond of caution, if any, to be delivered up.

Audit of liquidator's accounts

11. The accounts of the liquidator shall be audited annually. The audit shall be made by such person as the court may select, whether he be an auditor of court or not, and the auditor shall report to the court the audit so made. If it shall appear to the auditor that any payment by the liquidator should be disallowed, or that any charge has been incurred, as against the estate, which was unnecessary, or that any sum ought to have been, but is not, brought into account, he shall in his report bring the same under the notice of the court, setting forth the grounds of his opinion, and the court shall pronounce judgment upon the matter so reported upon as may seem just.

Expenses of winding up

12. The court may, in the event of the assets being insufficient to satisfy the liabilities, make an order as to the payment out of the estate of the society of the costs, charges, and expenses incurred in winding up the society in such order of priority as may be considered just.

Liquidator to deposit moneys in bank

13. The liquidator shall lodge all money received by him on account of the society in one of the banks in Scotland established by Act of Parliament or Royal Charter, in a separate account or on deposit, in his name as such liquidator, within seven days after the receipt thereof, unless the court has otherwise directed. If the liquidator shall keep in his hands more than £50 of money belonging to the society for more than seven days he shall be charged in his account with a sum at the rate of 20 per cent. per annum on the excess of the said sum of £50 for such time as it shall be in his hands beyond the said seven days, and the court may, in respect of any such retention, disallow the salary or remuneration of such liquidator, or may remove him from his office.

CHAPTER IX—INFERIOR COURTS JUDGMENTS EXTENSION ACT 1882

(C.A.S., L, IX)

Register of English and Irish judgments

1. In each county in Scotland, and at each place in such county at which the ordinary courts of the sheriffs-substitute are held, there shall be kept by the sheriff clerk a book, to be called " The Register of English and Irish Judgments ", in which shall be registered *in extenso* all certificates issued in terms of the said Act, from any of the inferior courts of England and Ireland, with the note of presentation appended to such certificate required by said Act.

Attestation of registration

2. After registration as aforesaid, the sheriff clerk shall append to such certificate and note of presentation an attestation, signed by himself, of the registration of the same, in the terms set forth in the annexed Schedule A, which registered certificate, with the attestation thereon by the sheriff clerk, shall be sufficient warrant to officers of court to charge the debtor in the judgment debt to make payment of the whole sums recoverable under such judgment, with the costs of obtaining and registering such certificate, within fifteen days after the date of such charge, and to use any further diligence that may be competent.

Fees

3. For granting any certificate issued in terms of said Act, and for registering any such certificate, with note of presentation as aforesaid, and attesting that such registration has been made, the sheriff clerk shall be entitled to charge the fees set forth in the Schedule B hereto annexed and for preparing and presenting any note of presentation required by said Act and obtaining the registration of any certificate, and the attestation of such registration, law agents shall be entitled to charge the fees also set forth in said Schedule B.

Sheriff clerk

4. The words " sheriff clerk " shall include sheriff clerk depute.

SCHEDULE A

[*Place and date.*]

I hereby declare that the foregoing certificate and note of presentation have been duly registered by me in the " Register of English and Irish Judgments " kept at this place, in terms of the Act 45 & 46 Vict. c. 31 and relative Act of Sederunt, Book L, Chapter IX.

A.B., sheriff clerk (or sheriff clerk depute) of

[1] SCHEDULE B

2. *Law Agents' Fees*

1. For preparing and presenting any note of presentation as required by said Act, and obtaining registration of certificate issued in terms of said Act, with such note of presentation together with attestation of such registration.

In cases where the debt or sum decerned for does not exceed £12	7p
In cases where the debt or sum decerned for exceeds £12 and does not exceed £50 ...	13p
In cases where the debt or sum decerned for exceeds £50 and does not exceed £200 .	17p
In all other cases	25p

NOTE
[1] As amended by the Decimal Currency Act 1969, s. 10 (2).

[1] *CHAPTER X—PROCEEDINGS UNDER THE REPRESENTATION OF THE PEOPLE ACT 1983*

(C.A.S., L, X)

NOTE
[1] As amended by S.I. 1985 No. 1427.

Initiation of proceedings

1. An election petition shall be in the form of an initial writ under the Sheriff Courts Act 1907. It shall be lodged with the sheriff clerk, who shall without delay transmit it to the sheriff, and the sheriff shall forthwith pronounce a deliverance fixing the amount of the security to be given by the petitioner, and, if he thinks it right, appointing answers within a specified time after service. Service shall be made of a notice of the presentation of the petition, a notice of the nature and amount of the security and a copy of the petition upon the respondent and the Lord Advocate either personally or by a registered letter sent to his known address and posted in time to admit of its being delivered in ordinary course of post within five days after the presentation of the petition.

Security for expenses

2.—(*a*) If the security proposed be in whole or in part by bond of caution, it shall be given by lodging with the sheriff clerk a bond for the amount specified in the sheriff's deliverance, which bond shall recite the nature of the petition, and shall bind and oblige the cautioner or cautioners and the petitioner conjunctly and severally, and their respective heirs, executors, and successors whomsoever, that the petitioner shall make payment of all costs, charges, and expenses that may be payable by him to any person or persons by virtue of any order or decree pronounced in the petition. The sufficiency of the cautioner or cautioners must be attested to the satisfaction of the sheriff clerk, as in the case of judicial bonds of caution.

(*b*) Objections to a bond of caution shall be lodged within 14 days from service of the notice of the nature and amount of the security with, and heard and disposed of by, the sheriff clerk, and, if any objection is allowed, it may be removed by a deposit of such sum of money as the sheriff clerk shall determine, made in manner aftermentioned and within five days after the date of the sheriff clerk's deliverance allowing the objection.

(*c*) If security be tendered in whole or in part by way of deposit of money, the deposit shall be made in such bank as the sheriff clerk may select, and the deposit receipt, which shall be taken in the joint names of the petitioner and the sheriff clerk, shall be handed to the sheriff clerk, and shall be held by him subject to the orders of the court in the petition.

Amendment of pleadings

3. The sheriff principal shall have power at any stage to allow the petition to be amended upon such conditions as to expenses or otherwise as he shall think just, provided always that no amendment altering the ground upon which the election was questioned in the petition as presented shall be competent, except to the extent sanctioned by section 129 (6) of the Representation of the People Act 1983.

Notice of date and place of trial

4. A notice of the time and place fixed by the sheriff principal for the trial shall, as soon as the interlocutor of the sheriff principal fixing these is received, be affixed by the sheriff clerk to the notice board at his principal office, and the sheriff clerk shall, not less than seven days before the day appointed for the trial, send by post one copy of such notice to the petitioner, another to the respondent, another to the Lord Advocate, and another to the returning officer, and the returning officer shall forthwith publish the same in the area for which the election questioned was held. The affixing of the notice of trial to the notice board at the sheriff clerk's office shall be deemed and taken to be notice in the prescribed manner within the meaning of the Act, and such notice shall not be vitiated by any miscarriage of or relating to all or any of the copies thereof herein directed to be sent by post, provided always that at any time before the trial it shall be competent to any party interested to bring the matter before the sheriff principal, who shall deal therewith as he may consider just.

Clerk of court

5. The sheriff clerk shall attend and act as clerk of court at the trial of the petition.

Shorthand writer's charges

6. The shorthand writer's charges, as fixed by the sheriff principal, shall be defrayed in the first instance by the petitioner.

Appeals

7. The application to state a special case referred to in section 146 (1) of the Representation of the People Act 1983 shall be made by minute in the petition proceedings.

List of votes objected to, and of objections

8. When a petitioner claims the seat for an unsuccessful candidate, alleging that such candidate had a majority of lawful votes, he and the respondent shall, five days before the day fixed for the trial, respectively deliver to the sheriff clerk, and send through the post to the other party and the Lord Advocate, a list of the votes intended to be objected to, and of the objections to each such vote, and the sheriff clerk shall allow inspection of such list to all parties concerned; and no evidence shall be allowed to be given against any vote or in support of any objection not specified in the list, except by leave of the sheriff principal granted upon such terms as to the amendment of the list, postponement of the trial, and payment of costs as to him may seem just.

Petition against undue return

9. When on the trial of a petition complaining of an undue return and claiming the office for some person the respondent intends to give evidence to prove that that person was not duly elected, such respondent shall, five days before the day appointed for the trial, deliver to the sheriff clerk, and send through the post to the petitioner and the Lord Advocate, a list of the objections to the election upon which he intends to rely; and no evidence shall be allowed to be given by a respondent in support of any objection to the election not specified in the said list, except by leave of the sheriff principal granted upon such terms as to the amendment of the list, postponement of the trial, and payment of costs as to him may seem just.

Witnesses' charges

10. The sum to be paid to a witness for attendance at the trial shall be certified by the sheriff clerk, and shall, in the first instance, be paid by the party adducing the witness. The sheriff clerk shall also be the proper officer to grant the certificate referred to in section 155 (2) of the Representation of the People Act 1983.

Leave to abandon

11. Application for leave to withdraw a petition shall be made by minute addressed to the court and as nearly as may be in the form of Schedule A hereto annexed, and shall be preceded by written notice of the intention to make it sent through the post to the respondent, to the Lord Advocate, and to the returning officer; and the returning officer shall publish the fact of his having received such a notice in the area for which the election questioned was held. The sheriff principal, upon the application being laid before him, shall, by interlocutor, fix the time—not being earlier than eight days after the date of the interlocutor—and place for hearing it, and the petitioner shall, at least six days before the day fixed for the hearing, publish in a newspaper circulating in the district named in the interlocutor a notice as nearly as may be in the form of Schedule B hereto annexed.

Decease of petitioner

12. In the event of the death of the sole petitioner, or of the survivor of several petitioners, the sheriff clerk shall, upon the fact being brought to his knowledge, insert in a newspaper circulating in the district a notice as nearly as may be in the form of Schedule C hereto annexed, and the time within which any person who might have been a petitioner in respect of the election may apply to the court to be substituted as a petitioner shall be 21 days from the publication of such notice.

Notice by respondent that he does not oppose petition

13. The manner and time of a respondent's giving notice that he does not intend to oppose a petition shall be by leaving a written notice to that effect at the office of the sheriff clerk at least six days (exclusive of the day of leaving such notice) before the day fixed for the trial; and upon such notice being left with the sheriff clerk, or upon its being brought to his knowledge that a respondent other than a returning officer has died, resigned, or otherwise ceased to hold the office to which the petition relates, he shall forthwith advertise the fact once in a newspaper circulating in the district, and shall also send intimation thereof by post to the petitioner, to the Lord Advocate, and to the returning officer, who shall publish the fact in the district. The advertisement to be made by the sheriff clerk shall state the last day on which, under these rules, application to be admitted as a respondent to oppose the petition can be made.

Application to be admitted as respondent

14. Application to be admitted as a respondent to oppose a petition on the occurrence of any of the events mentioned in section 153 (1) of the Representation of the People Act 1983 must be made within 10 days after the publication of the advertisement mentioned in the preceding rule, unless the sheriff principal on cause shewn sees fit to extend the time.

Public notice of abandonment

15. If notice of the petitioner's intention to apply for leave to withdraw, or of the respondent's intention not to oppose, or of the abatement of the petition by death, or of the occurrence of any of the events mentioned in section 153 (1) of the Representation of the People Act 1983, be received after the notice of trial has been published, the sheriff clerk shall give public notice that the trial will not proceed on the day fixed, and that by advertisement inserted once in a newspaper circulating in the district.

Notice to party's agent sufficient

16. When a petitioner or a respondent has left with the sheriff clerk a writing signed by him giving the name and address of some person entitled to practise as an agent before the court, whom he authorises to act as his agent in connection with the petition, a notice sent to such person at the address given shall be held to be notice to the petitioner or respondent as the case may be.

Cost of publication

[1] **17.** The cost of publishing any matter required by those rules to be published by the returning officer or by the sheriff clerk shall be paid in the first instance by the person moving in the matter, and shall form part of the general costs of the petition. The sheriff clerk shall be allowed, as part of the general costs of the petition, a fee of 10p for each copy of a notice or intimation sent, and for drawing each newspaper advertisement published by him under the authority of these rules.

NOTE

[1] As amended by the Decimal Currency Act 1969, s. 10 (2).

Expenses

18. The expenses of petitions and other proceedings under the Act shall be taxed by the auditor of the sheriff court.

19. [Revoked by S.I. 1985 No. 1427.]

Sheriff clerk

20. In these rules the term "sheriff clerk" means the sheriff clerk of the county within which the election questioned has taken place, and includes sheriff clerk depute.

SCHEDULE A

Representation of the People Act 1983

In the petition questioning the election for the of , in which is petitioner and is respondent.

The petitioner desires to withdraw his petition on the following grounds [*state grounds*], and humbly craves that a diet may be appointed for hearing his application. He has, in compliance with the general rules made by the Court of Session, given written notice of his intention to present this application to the respondent, to the Lord Advocate, and to the returning officer.

[*To be signed by the petitioner or his agent.*]

SCHEDULE B

Representation of the People Act 1983

In the petition questioning the election for the of , in which is petitioner and is respondent.

Notice is hereby given that the above petitioner has applied for leave to withdraw his petition, and that the sheriff principal has, by interlocutor dated the day of , assigned the day of at o'clock noon within the as a diet for hearing the application.

Notice is further given that under the Act any person who might have been a petitioner in respect of the said election may at the above diet apply to the sheriff principal to be substituted as a petitioner.

[*To be signed by the petitioner or his agent.*]

SCHEDULE C

Representation of the People Act 1983

In the petition questioning the election for the of , in which was the petitioner [*or* last surviving petitioner] and is the respondent.

Notice is hereby given that the above petition stands abated by the death of the petitioner [*or* last surviving petitioner], and that any person who might have been a petitioner in respect of the said election and who desires to be substituted as a petitioner must, within 21 days from this date, lodge with the undersigned, sheriff clerk of [*name county*], a minute craving to be so substituted.

Dated the day of 19

[*To be signed by the sheriff clerk.*]

CHAPTER XI—APPEALS TO THE COURT UNDER THE PILOTAGE ACT 1913

[1] (C.A.S., L, XI)

NOTE

[1] As amended by S. R. & O. 1919 No. 1615.

Procedure by initial writ

1. Appeals to the sheriff under section 28 of the Pilotage Act 1913, shall be by initial writ under the Sheriff Courts (Scotland) Acts 1907 and 1913 and the proceedings thereon shall be as laid down in those statutes.

Time for Appeal

2. Such initial writ shall be presented to the sheriff within twenty-one days from the date of the decision appealed from, and there shall be produced along with it two copies of the decision, one of which shall be certified to be a true copy by the clerk or secretary of the pilotage authority.

Citation of pilotage authority

3. On the initial writ being presented the sheriff clerk shall grant warrant to cite the pilotage authority, which citation shall be made by serving a copy of the writ and of the warrant of citation upon the clerk or secretary of the pilotage authority.

Expenses and fees

4. The expenses and court fees connected with the appeal shall be the same as prescribed for civil causes in the sheriff courts.

Nautical assessor

5. The provisions of the Nautical Assessors (Scotland) Act 1894, and relative provisions in Book L, Chapter I hereof, shall apply to the assessor of nautical and pilotage experience provided for by the said section of the Pilotage Act.

CHAPTER XV—REMOVINGS

(C.A.S., L, XV)

(Statute 1555, anent Warnings of Tenants)

1. Where a tenant is bound by his tack to remove without warning at the issue or determination of his tack, it shall be lawful to the heritor or other setter of the tack, upon such obligation, to obtain letters of horning, and thereupon to charge the tenant with horning forty days preceding the term of Whitsunday in the year in which his tack is to determine, or forty days preceding any other term of Whitsunday thereafter: And upon production of such tack and horning duly executed to the sheriff or sheriff-substitute of the shire where the lands lie, they are hereby authorised and required, within six days after the term of removal appointed by the tack, to eject such tenant, and to deliver the possession void to the setter, or those having right from him.

2. Where the tenant hath not obliged himself to remove without warning, in such case it shall be lawful to the heritor or other setter of the tack in his option, either to use the order prescribed by the Act of Parliament made in the year 1555, intituled "Act anent the Warning of Tenants", and thereupon pursue a warning and ejection, or to bring his action of removing against the tenant before the Judge Ordinary: And such action being called before the Judge Ordinary at least forty days before the term of Whitsunday, shall be held as equal to a warning execute in terms of the foresaid Act: And the Judge shall thereupon proceed to determine in the removing in the terms of that Act, in the same manner as if a warning had been executed in terms of the foresaid Act of Parliament.

3. Where a tack is assigned and the assignation not intimated by an instrument, or where the lands are sublet in whole or in part to sub-tenants, such horning execute as aforesaid, or where process of removing and decreet is obtained, or where warning in terms of the Act 1555 is used against the principal or original tacksman, the same shall be effectual against the assignees or sub-tenants, one or more, and the action of removing against the principal or original tacksman, and decreet of removing following thereon, shall be effectual against such assignees and sub-tenants as aforesaid, and shall be sufficient ground of ejecting them, anything in the former practice to the contrary notwithstanding.

4. Where a tenant has irritated his tack by suffering two years' rent to be in arrear, it shall be lawful to the setter or heritor to declare the irritancy before the Judge Ordinary, and to insist in a summar removing before him: and it shall be lawful to the sheriff or sheriff-substitute to find the irritancy incurred, and to decern in the removing, any practice to the contrary notwithstanding.

5. Where a tenant shall run in arrear of one full year's rent, or shall desert his possession and leave it unlaboured at the usual time of labouring, in these, or either of these cases, it shall be lawful to the heritor or other setter of the lands to bring his action against the tenant before the Judge Ordinary, who is hereby empowered and required to decern and ordain the tenant to find caution for the arrears, and for payment of the rent for the five crops following or during the currency of the tack, if the tack is of shorter endurance than five years, within a certain time to be limited by the judge, and failing thereof, to decern the tenant summarily to remove, and to eject him in the same manner as if the tack were determined and the tenant had been legally warned in terms of the foresaid Act 1555.

6. Upon passing of any bill of suspension of a decreet or process of removing, or at least within ten days after the date of the deliverance thereon, the complainer shall be bound to find sufficient caution, not only for implement of what shall be decerned on the suspension upon discussion thereof, but also for damage and expense in case the same shall be found due; and upon the complainers failing to find caution as aforesaid, such bill of suspension shall be held to be refused, and it shall be lawful for the other party to proceed in his action of removing, or in the execution of his decreet, as if no such bill of suspension had been presented or passed.

7. In all removings, whether originally brought before this court, or by suspension, they will proceed and determine the same summarily without abridging the course of any roll.

[1] Certain Forms of Procedure in the Sheriff's Ordinary and Small Debt Courts and for the Confirmation of Executors, and anent the Registers or Records to be Kept by Sheriff Clerks of Consignations, Sequestrations for Rent, Reports of Arrestment, and Reports of Poinding and Sale 1933

(S. R. & O. 1933 No. 48)

[3rd February 1933]

NOTE

[1] As amended by S. R. & O. 1936 No. 1410.

The Lords of Council and Session, in virtue of the powers conferred on them by section 2 of the Courts of Law Fees (Scotland) Act 1895, and by section 16 of the Sheriff Courts and Legal Officers (Scotland) Act 1927 with the concurrence of the Treasury, enact and declare as follows:

1. Schedule A annexed hereto is hereby substituted for Schedules A and B annexed to C.A.S., Book L, Chapter IV.

2. It shall not be necessary to keep, as a separate book, the "Register of Sequestrations for Rent" prescribed by section 7 of the Hypothec Amendment (Scotland) Act 1867. The particulars specified in the Schedule to that Act may be recorded in the Act Book of Court or other suitable register kept by the sheriff clerk.

[THE NEXT PAGE IS D 223]

3. The record kept by the sheriff clerk of warrants for arrestment on the dependence, reports thereof, loosings of arrestment, reports of poindings, reports of sales under poindings, and reports of sales following upon sequestrations for rent may be made in the appropriate A or B Register or other suitable register approved by the sheriff.

. . . . . .

7. In Summary Applications for removing under section 38 of the Sheriff Courts (Scotland) Act 1907, the Book of Causes, containing entries of the sheriff's deliverances, interlocutors, decrees and warrants, with the dates thereof, shall be signed each court day by the sheriff; and the forms contained in Schedule F annexed hereto shall be substituted for Form L annexed to Schedule I of the said Act, shall be signed by the sheriff clerk, shall have the force and effect of extracts, and may be written on the principal complaint, on the copy thereof, or, with necessary modifications separately.

. . . . . .

9. This Act of Sederunt shall come into operation on the 1st day of March 1933.

SCHEDULE A

Register of Sheriff Court Consignations

Date of Consignation.	Parties by whom Consignation is made—Cause and Court.	Sum Consigned.	Bank in which Money Lodged.	Date of Lodging in Bank.	Date of Payment.	Deposits withdrawn from Bank.			To Whom Paid and Receipts.	Sum Paid.
						Principal Sums.	Interest Thereon.	Total.		

SCHEDULE F

FORMS OF EXTRACTS OF DECREES IN SUMMARY REMOVING PETITION OR COMPLAINT

(1) EXTRACT OF DECREE AND WARRANT OF EJECTION

At the day of 19 , the Sheriff of Decerned and hereby Decerns, Granted and hereby Grants Warrant for Ejecting the said Defender, and others mentioned in the Complaint, from the subjects therein specified, such Ejection not being sooner than 19 at Twelve o'clock noon, Found and hereby Finds the said Defender liable to the Pursuer in the sum of of Expenses, and Decerns and Ordains instant Execution by Arrestment, and also Execution to pass hereon by Poinding and Sale for said Expenses, after a of Ten free days.

Sheriff Clerk.

(2) EXTRACT OF DECREE OF ABSOLVITOR

At the day of 19 the Sheriff of Assoilzied and hereby Assoilzies the within designed Defender from the foregoing Complaint, and Found and hereby Finds the within designed Pursuer, liable to the Defender in the sum of of Expenses, and Decerns and Ordains instant Execution by Arrestment, and also Execution to pass hereon by Poinding and Sale, after a of Ten free days.

Sheriff Clerk

(3) EXTRACT OF DECREE OF DISMISSAL

At the day of 19 the Sheriff of Dismissed and hereby Dismisses the foregoing Complaint, Found and hereby Finds the within designed Pursuer, liable to the Defender in the sum of of Expenses; and Decerns and Ordains instant execution by Arrestment, and also execution to pass hereon by Poinding and Sale after a of Ten free days.

Sheriff Clerk.

Appeals under the Betting and Lotteries Act 1934, 1935

(S. R. & O. 1935 No. 1312)

[19th December 1935]

The Lords of Council and Session, in terms of section 16 (2) and section 31 (5) of the Betting and Lotteries Act 1934 (hereinafter called " the Act ") do hereby enact and declare as follows:—

The holder of a licence which has been revoked under section 16 of the Act may appeal against such revocation, at any time within fourteen days after receipt by him of the notice of revocation, by initial writ under the Sheriff Courts (Scotland) Acts 1907 and 1913 and such appeal shall be disposed of as a summary application as defined in the said Acts.

Appeals under the Pharmacy and Poisons Act 1933, 1935

(S. R. & O. 1935 No. 1313)

[19th December 1935]

The Lords of Council and Session, in terms of section 21 (2) and section 30 (i) of the Pharmacy and Poisons Act 1933 (hereinafter called " the Act "), do hereby enact and declare as follows:—

Any person who is aggrieved by the refusal of the local authority to enter his name in the list of persons which, in terms of section 21 (1) of the Act, the local authority is required to keep, or by the removal of his name therefrom, may at any time within fourteen days after the receipt by him of the notice of refusal or removal, appeal against such refusal or removal by initial writ under the Sheriff Courts (Scotland) Acts 1907 and 1913, and such appeal shall be disposed of as a summary application as defined in the said Acts.

[1] Amend the Sheriff Courts (Scotland) Act 1907 and Codifying Act of Sederunt of 4th June 1913, 1936

(S. R. & O. 1936 No. 780)

[16th July 1936]

NOTE

[1] The amendments made by this Act of Sederunt to the Sheriff Courts (Scotland) Act 1907 have been incorporated in the print of that Act.

The Lords of Council and Session, under and by virtue of the provisions of the Administration of Justice (Scotland) Act 1933 and of the powers thereby confirmed on them do hereby enact and declare:—

. . . . . .

3. That section 1 of Chapter III of Book L of the Codifying Act of Sederunt of 4th June 1913 (C.A.S., L, III, 1) is hereby repealed and the following provision substituted therefor:—

(1) *Certificate by Officer of Inland Revenue.*

(1) No decree, warrant, or order for payment of any consigned money; and (2) no decree, warrant or order for transfer or conveyance to any person of any stocks, shares, or other property, heritable or moveable, in any process for the distribution of the estate of any deceased, pending in the sheriff court, shall issue until there is lodged with the sheriff clerk a certificate by the proper officer in the Department of Inland Revenue that all income tax, estate duty, legacy duty, succession duty, and any other duty payable to the Commissioners of Inland Revenue, have been paid and satisfied to the Department in respect of any such money, stocks, shares, or other property or any part thereof so to be paid, transferred, or conveyed as aforesaid.

4. That this Act of Sederunt shall come into force on 1st October 1936.

Appeals to the Sheriff under the Methylated Spirits (Sale by Retail) (Scotland) Act 1937, 1937

(S. R. & O. 1937 No. 1016)

[5th November 1937]

The Lords of Council and Session, under and by virtue of the powers conferred upon them by section 2(3) of the Methylated Spirits (Sale by Retail) (Scotland) Act 1937 (hereinafter called "the Act"), do hereby enact and declare as follows, viz.:

Any person who is aggrieved by the refusal of the local authority to enter his name in the list of persons which, in terms of section 2(1) of the Act, the local authority is required to keep, or by removal of his name therefrom, may, at any time within fourteen days after the receipt by him of the notice of refusal or removal, appeal against such refusal or removal by initial writ under the Sheriff Courts (Scotland) Acts 1907 and 1913, and such appeal shall be disposed of as a summary application as defined in the said Acts.

Introduction of a Photographic Process for copying Deeds and other Writings presented for Registration in the Sheriff Court Books and the Commissary Court Books 1944

(S. R. & O. 1944 No. 859)

[18th July 1944]

The Lords of Council and Session, under and by virtue of the provisions of section 16 of the Sheriff Courts and Legal Officers (Scotland) Act 1927 and of all other powers competent to them in that behalf, considering that by the Act of Sederunt of date 15th July 1937 it was *inter alia* ordained that sheriff clerks should use for the registration of deeds and other writings presented for preservation or preservation and execution only books or unbound volumes issued and marked by the Keeper of the Registers and Records of Scotland.

And now seeing that it may be expedient that the photographic process of copying authorised in the Department of the Registers and Records of Scotland by Act of Sederunt of date 2nd February 1934 should be used for the framing of the Register of Deeds and Probative Writs in the sheriff court and for the Commissary Court Books, the Lords do hereby enact and declare that, after the date of the passing of this Act, deeds and other writings presented for registration in those books may be reproduced by the photographic process and made up into bound volumes of such a size and form as may be found convenient and that in such sheriffdom or sheriff court districts as may be arranged with the respective sheriffs in consultation with the said keeper and under such directions as to compilation and authentication as the said keeper may deem expedient; that such bound volumes shall be open to the lieges at such times and under such conditions as are at present applicable to the Registers of Deeds and Probative Writs in the sheriff court and to the Commissary Court Books; and that thereafter it shall not be necessary to issue marked volumes in conformity with the practice heretofore to such sheriffdoms or sheriff court districts in which the photographic process is introduced.

And the Lords do further enact that the record of said registers shall be made up in manner provided by said Act of Sederunt of 1934 and that all deeds and other writings to be registered may be transmitted to the said keeper either by messenger or registered post.

Reserve and Auxiliary Forces (Protection of Civil Interests) 1952

(S.I. 1952 No. 117)

[22nd January 1952]

The Lords of Council and Session in exercise of the powers conferred upon them by section 11 of the Reserve and Auxiliary Forces (Protection of Civil Interests) Act 1951 and of all other powers enabling them in that behalf, do hereby enact and declare as follows:

Citation and commencement

1. This Act of Sederunt may be cited as the Act of Sederunt (Reserve and Auxiliary Forces (Protection of Civil Interests) 1952, and shall come into operation on the first day of March 1952.

Interpretation

2.—(1) In this Act of Sederunt, unless the context otherwise requires, the following expressions have the meanings hereby assigned to them that is to say:

"the Act" means the Reserve and Auxiliary Forces (Protection of Civil Interests) Act 1951;

"declaratory order" means an order under paragraph (*c*) of subsection (1) of section 9 of the Act;

"leave" means leave of the appropriate court under the Act.

(2) Any reference in this Act of Sederunt to a numbered form shall be construed as a reference to the form of that number in the Schedule to this Act of Sederunt or a form to the like effect.

(3) The Interpretation Act 1889 shall apply to the interpretation of this Act of Sederunt as it applies to the interpretation of an Act of Parliament.

Appropriate court

3.—(1) The appropriate court in relation to an application for leave to enforce, or for a declaratory order relating to, a decree, shall be:

(*a*) the court which pronounced the decree; or

(*b*) if the judgment has been obtained in a court outside Scotland and is registered in a court in Scotland for the purpose of enforcement, the court in which the judgment is registered.

(2) The appropriate court in relation to an application for leave to exercise any right or remedy mentioned in subsection (2) of section 8 or in paragraph (*b*) of subsection (1) of section 25 of the Act, or for a declaratory order relating to the exercise of any such right or remedy, shall be any court which according to present practice has jurisdiction to deal with causes or matters of the nature and value involved in the application.

(3) The appropriate court for the giving of directions for restoration of property, repayment of money or other measures under subsection (4) of section 13 of the Act shall be:

(*a*) where there has been an omission to obtain leave required under section 8 or section 25 of the Act, the court having jurisdiction to give such leave;

(*b*) where there has been a failure to observe a restriction subject to which leave so required was given, the court which imposed the restriction or condition; and

(*c*) where there has been a contravention of the prohibition in subsection (2) of section 10 of the Act against dealing with the goods, the court having jurisdiction to make a declaratory order in respect of the taking possession of the goods:

Provided that where any proceedings which lie by virtue of any such omission, failure or contravention have been instituted in any court, that court shall have jurisdiction to give such directions as aforesaid.

Form of, and procedure on, applications

4.—(1) Subject as hereinafter provided an application under the Act shall be initiated by a document (hereinafter referred to as an "application") in the forms, as nearly as may be:

(*a*) in the case of an application for leave to enforce a decree, or to present a petition for sequestration or a winding up petition founded on the non-payment of money due under a decree, of Form 1;

(*b*) in the case of an application for a declaratory order relating to a decree, of Form 2;

(*c*) in the case of an application for leave to exercise any right or remedy mentioned in subsection (2) of section 8 or in paragraph (*b*) of subsection (1) of section 25 of the Act, of Form 3; and

(*d*) in the case of an application for a declaratory order relating to the exercise of any such right or remedy as aforesaid, of Form 4.

(2) An application under the foregoing sub-paragraph shall be lodged in the case of an application to the Court of Session, in the Petition Department and, in the case of an application to the sheriff court, with the sheriff clerk. Every such application so lodged shall have attached to it a blank sheet of process paper.

(3) Upon the lodging of any application as aforesaid the clerk in charge of the Petition Department, or the sheriff clerk, as the case may be, shall appoint a diet for appearance and shall grant a warrant for intimation in Form 5, and a copy of the application, of the warrant for intimation and (except in the case of an application for a declaratory order) of the note set forth in Form 6 or Form 7, as the case may require, shall, not later than two days after the granting of the said warrant, be served upon the person liable to implement the decree or perform the obligation in question, or upon the proper person as defined in subsection (3) of section nine of the Act, as the case may be.

(4) A certificate of service in Form 8 shall be endorsed by or on behalf of the applicant on the process copy of the application before the date appointed in the warrant for intimation for the diet for appearance.

(5) At the diet for appearance appointed in the warrant for intimation the appropriate court shall dispose of the application, or appoint such further procedure as it may deem necessary.

Application for leave to enforce a decree made at the same time as motion for decree

5. An application for leave to enforce a decree may be made by verbal motion at the time when the motion for decree is made, and the appropriate court may, then, if it thinks fit, dispose of the application if:

(*a*) in the case of a defended action, the court is satisfied that due intimation of the intention so to apply has been made to the defender;

(*b*) in the case of an undefended action in the Court of Session or an ordinary cause in the sheriff court in which no notice of appearance has been lodged or in which the defender does not answer, a notice as nearly as may be in the form of Form 9 has been sent to the defender at least six clear days before the application is made; and

(*c*) in the case of a summary cause or small debt action in the sheriff court, there has been sent to the defender, either along with the initial writ or summons or at least six clear days before the application is made, a notice as nearly as may be in the form of Form 10.

Intimation to persons affected in certain cases

6. In the case of an application for leave to enforce a decree or for leave to exercise any right or remedy mentioned in subsection (2) of section 8 or in paragraph (*b*) of subsection (1) of section 25 of the Act the appropriate court, before considering the application, may order intimation thereof to any person whom the court considers to be interested therein, including the spouse of the person liable to implement the decree or perform the obligation in question, and may give to any person to whom intimation is so made an opportunity to be heard.

Service of application or notice on representative of service man

7. Where any person upon whom an application or notice is to be served under this Act of Sederunt (in this paragraph referred to as " the respondent ") is for the time being performing a period of relevant service, the appropriate court may, if, in view of any special circumstances, it considers it expedient to do so, authorise the application or notice to be served instead on any person (including the spouse of the respondent) who appears to the court to have been entrusted with the management of the respondent's affairs in general or of the premises or property to which the application or notice relates.

Application by representative on behalf of service man

8. Where a person who would be entitled to apply for a declaratory order is for the time being performing a period of relevant service, the appropriate court may, if, in view of any special circumstances, it considers it expedient to do so, treat as an application made by him for a declaratory order an application for that purpose made on his behalf by his spouse or by any other person acting in good faith in his interest.

Appearance of representative of service man

9.—(1) Where an application or notice is served in the manner provided by paragraph 7 of this Act of Sederunt or an application is made in the manner provided by the last foregoing paragraph of this Act of Sederunt, the person on whom the application or notice is served or by whom the application is made, as the case may be (in this paragraph referred to as " the representative "), shall be entitled to attend and be heard at that hearing of the application as if he were the respondent, or the person on whose behalf the application is made, as the case may be.

(2) If the appropriate court is of opinion that the representative has acted unreasonably in opposing, making or presenting the application, the appropriate court may make an order for payment by him of the expenses of any other party, but save as aforesaid the representative shall not be personally liable for any such expenses.

Recall or variation of orders

10. Any order made on any application referred to in this Act of Sederunt may, should subsequent circumstances render it just so to do, be recalled, suspended, discharged, or otherwise varied or altered on a motion to the court which made such order, after written intimation to all parties interested of the intention to make such motion.

Application may be heard and disposed of in Chambers

11. Any application under this Act of Sederunt to the Court of Session or to the sheriff court may be heard and disposed of by a judge or by the sheriff, as the case may be, either in court or in Chambers, whether during session, vacation or recess and any such application may be heard *in camera* if a judge or the sheriff so orders.

Postal services

12. Where the service of any document is required by this Act of Sederunt to be made, and the service is made by post, the date of making it shall be reckoned as the day after that on which the document was posted.

Fee fund dues

13. No fee fund dues or court fees shall be payable in proceedings on any application referred to in this Act of Sederunt.

Expenses

14. The expenses of proceedings on any application referred to in this Act of Sederunt shall be in the discretion of the appropriate court; and the appropriate court, if it thinks fit, may award no expenses or modify the amount thereof.

SCHEDULE

Form 1

Reserve and Auxiliary Forces (Protection of Civil Interests) Act 1951

Unto [specify Court]

Application
for
A.B. [designation]

A.B. applies to the court for leave to enforce a decree of the court dated [date] against the therein designed C.D., a copy of which decree is appended hereto [or otherwise competently produced and referred to] *or* [as the case may be] to present a petition for sequestration of the estate of C.D. [designation] or for the winding up of [specify company].

[Signature of applicant or solicitor or counsel.]

[Place and date.]

Form 2

Reserve and Auxiliary Forces (Protection of Civil Interests) Act 1951

Unto [specify court]

Application
for
A.B. [designation]

A.B. applies to the court for an order under paragraph (*c*) of subsection (1) of section 9 of the said Act directing that subsection (1) of section 8 of the said Act shall apply in relation to a decree by the court dated [date] against him in favour of the therein designed C.D., a copy of which decree is appended hereto [or otherwise competently produced and referred to].

[Signature of applicant or solicitor or counsel.]

[Place and date.]

FORM 3

RESERVE AND AUXILIARY FORCES (PROTECTION OF CIVIL INTERESTS) ACT 1951

Unto [specify Court]

Application
for
A.B. [designation]

A.B. applies to the court for leave to exercise the following right [or remedy] that is to say [specify right or remedy by reference to subsection (2) of section 8 or to paragraph (*b*) of subsection (1) of section 25 of the Act] against C.D. [designation] who is under the following obligation to the said A.B. [give brief particulars of obligation in question].

[Signature of applicant or solicitor or counsel.]

[Place and date.]

FORM 4

RESERVE AND AUXILIARY FORCES (PROTECTION OF CIVIL INTERESTS) ACT 1951

Unto [specify Court]

Application
for
A.B. [designation]

A.B. applies to the court for an order under paragraph (*c*) of subsection (1) of section 9 of the said Act directing that subsection (2) of section 8 of the said Act shall apply in relation to the following obligation which the said A.B. is alleged to be liable to perform in favour of C.D. [designation] that is to say [give brief particulars of obligation].

[Signature of applicant or solicitor or counsel.]

[Place and date.]

FORM 5

RESERVE AND AUXILIARY FORCES (PROTECTION OF CIVIL INTERESTS) ACT 1951

[Place and date.]

The court grants warrant for intimation and appoints parties to appear on the day of at o'clock in [place].

[Signature of clerk of court.]

NOTE.—The clerk in fixing the *induciae* shall have regard to the period necessary to enable the respondent to appear and shall, if necessary, consult the court.

FORM 6

NOTE ON THE EFFECT OF THE RESERVE AND AUXILIARY FORCES (PROTECTION OF CIVIL INTERESTS) ACT 1951

(For use with an application for leave to enforce a decree.)

The Reserve and Auxiliary Forces (Protection of Civil Interests) Act 1951, prevents the enforcement of the decree to which the application herewith applies if the court is of opinion that you are unable immediately to obey the order of the court contained in the decree by reason of circumstances directly or indirectly attributable to service to which the Act applies. If you desire to take advantage of the Act you should attend the court by yourself or by your solicitor (or, in the Court of Session, your counsel) on the date specified in the warrant for intimation, and satisfy the court that your inability to obey the order contained in the decree is due to the circumstances aforesaid. If the application has been served on your wife or other person entrusted with the management of your affairs or of the property to which the decree relates, the court will hear such person on your behalf.

FORM 7

NOTE ON THE EFFECT OF THE RESERVE AND AUXILIARY FORCES (PROTECTION OF CIVIL INTERESTS) ACT 1951

(For use with application for leave to exercise any right or remedy of the kind mentioned in subsection (2) of section 8 or in paragraph (*b*) of subsection (1) of section 25 of the Act.)

The Reserve and Auxiliary Forces (Protection of Civil Interests) Act 1951, prevents the exercise of certain rights including the right specified in the application herewith if the court is of opinion that by reason of circumstances directly or indirectly attributable to service to which the Act applies you are unable to perform the obligation in respect of which the aforesaid right arises. If you desire to take advantage of the Act you should attend the court by yourself or by your solicitor (or, in the Court of Session, your counsel) on the date specified in the warrant of intimation, and satisfy the court that your inability to perform your obligation is due to the circumstances aforesaid. If the application has been served on your wife or other person having the management of your affairs in general or of the property to which the right relates, the court will hear such person on your behalf.

FORM 8

CERTIFICATE OF SERVICE

I, [name, designation and address], solicitor for the applicant hereby certify that I have intimated the foregoing application, in terms of the foregoing warrant for intimation, to [name and designate persons upon whom service has been made] by posting on [date] between the hours of and at the Post Office a copy of the same to him *or* [them], together with a copy of a note in the terms of Form 6 (or, as the case may require, Form 7), in a registered letter [1] addressed as follows [address] and the post office receipt for the said registered letter accompanies this certificate.

[Signature of solicitor for applicant.]

[Date.]

NOTE

[1] See S.I. 1962 No. 1593.

FORM 9

RESERVE AND AUXILIARY FORCES (PROTECTION OF CIVIL INTERESTS) ACT 1951

In the Court of Session *or* [Sheriff Court of at .]

.... Pursuer

v.

.... Defender

To Defender above designed.

Take note that when decree is granted in the above cause [which will be enrolled in the undefended roll before Hon. Lord for the day of at 10 a.m. within the Parliament House, Edinburgh]

or

[in the Sheriff Court at before Sheriff on the day of at] the pursuer will make application to the court for leave to enforce the decree immediately in conformity with the above recited Acts and relative Act of Sederunt dated , 1952.

[Signature of applicant or officer of court or solicitor.]

[Place and date.]

NOTE.—The Reserve and Auxiliary Forces (Protection of Civil Interests) Act 1951, prevents the enforcement of the decree if the court is of opinion that you are unable immediately to obey the order of the court contained in the decree by reason of circumstances directly or indirectly attributable to service to which the Act applies. If you desire to take advantage of the Act you should attend the court by yourself or by your solicitor (or, in the Court of Session, your counsel) on the date when the motion for decree will be moved, and satisfy the court that your inability to obey the order of the court contained in the decree is due to the circumstances aforesaid. If the notice has been served on your wife or other person entrusted with the management of your affairs in general or of the property to which the action relates, the court will hear such person on your behalf.

FORM 10

RESERVE AND AUXILIARY FORCES (PROTECTION OF CIVIL INTERESTS) ACT 1951

Sheriff Court of at .

. . . . Pursuer

v.

. . . . Defender

To Defender above designed.

Take notice that when the above cause is called at the time and place specified in the [Initial Writ] *or* [summons] served herewith *or* [already served on you] application will be made, in the event of decree being granted, for leave to enforce the decree immediately in conformity with the above recited Acts and relative Act of Sederunt dated , 1952.

[Signature of applicant or officer of court or solicitor.]

[Place and date.]

NOTE.—The Reserve and Auxiliary Forces (Protection of Civil Interests) Act 1951, prevents the enforcement of the decree if the court is of opinion that you are unable immediately to obey the order of the court contained in the decree by reason of circumstances directly or indirectly attributable to service to which the Act applies. If you desire to take advantage of the Act you should attend the court by yourself or by your solicitor on the date when the motion for decree will be moved, and satisfy the court that your inability to obey the order of the court contained in the decree is due to the circumstances aforesaid. If the notice has been served on your wife or other person entrusted with the management of your affairs in general or of the property to which the action relates, the court will hear such person on your behalf.

Caravan Sites Appeals 1961

(S.I. 1961 No. 1018)

[9th May 1961]

The Lords of Council and Session, under and by virtue of the powers conferred upon them by section 32 of the Caravan Sites and Control of Development Act 1960 (hereinafter called "the Act"), do hereby enact and declare as follows:—

1. Appeals to the sheriff under sections 7(1) and 8(2) of the Act as modified by section 32 thereof, shall be by initial writ under the Sheriff Courts (Scotland) Acts 1907 and 1913, and shall be disposed of as summary applications as defined in the said Acts.

2. In any such application the sheriff may find either party liable in expenses.

3. This Act of Sederunt may be cited as the Act of Sederunt (Caravan Sites Appeals) 1961, and shall come into operation on 9th May 1961.

Enforcement Abroad of Sheriff Court Judgments 1962

(S.I. 1962 No. 1517)

[17th July 1962]

The Lords of Council and Session, under and by virtue of the powers conferred upon them by section 34(1) of the Administration of Justice (Scotland) Act 1933 and of all other powers competent to them in that behalf, do hereby enact as follows:—

Interpretation

1. In this Act of Sederunt—

"sheriff" includes sheriff-substitute;

"sheriff clerk" includes sheriff clerk depute;

"initial writ" means the statement of claim, petition, note of appeal, or other document by which the action is initiated.

[1] **2.** An application for a certified copy of a judgment obtained in a sheriff court, made for the purpose of the enforcement of the judgment in a country other than a country to which Parts I and II of the Civil Jurisdiction and Judgments Act 1982 applies, shall be made in that sheriff court by minute lodged in the process in which the judgment was obtained. There shall be lodged with the minute either an extract decree setting forth the judgment or a copy of the judgment. The sheriff, on being satisfied, by affidavit or by other proper evidence, as to the purpose for which the application is being made, shall pronounce an order ordaining the sheriff clerk to issue a certified copy of the judgment. The certificate shall be in the following terms:—

"I certify that the foregoing is a true copy of a judgment obtained in the Sheriff Court and that this certificate is issued for the purpose of the enforcement of the judgment in a country other than a country to which Parts I and II of the Civil Jurisdiction and Judgments Act 1982 applies and in obedience to an order by the Sheriff of dated

(Signed)
Sheriff Clerk."

NOTE
[1] As amended by S.I. 1986 No. 1947.

3. There shall be issued along with the foregoing certificate the following further certificate also certified by the sheriff clerk—

A certificate, enumerating and identifying and having annexed to it; (1) a copy of the initial writ by which the proceedings were initiated, showing the manner in which the initial writ was served on the defender or respondent and whether the defender or respondent appeared thereto, and the objections made to the jurisdiction if any; (2) a copy of the pleadings, if any, in the proceedings; (3) a copy of the opinion or note, if any, of the sheriff, and (4) a statement of such other particulars as it may be necessary to give to the foreign tribunal in which it is sought to obtain execution of the judgment. Copies of the foregoing documents shall be supplied where necessary by the person making the application.

4. This Act of Sederunt may be cited as the Act of Sederunt (Enforcement Abroad of Sheriff Court Judgments) 1962, and shall come into operation on 17th July 1962.

Building Appeals 1964

(S.I. 1964 No. 817)

[3rd June 1964]

The Lords of Council and Session, under and by virtue of the powers conferred upon them by section 16 of the Building (Scotland) Act 1959, do hereby enact and declare as follows:—

1. Appeals to the sheriff under section 16 of the Building (Scotland) Act 1959, shall be by initial writ under the Sheriff Courts (Scotland) Acts 1907 and 1913, and shall be disposed of as summary applications as defined in the Sheriff Courts (Scotland) Acts.

2. The sheriff may, before considering any such appeal, require the appellant to deposit in court such sum not exceeding £20 sterling as shall seem proper, to cover the expenses of the appeal.

3.—(1) In any such application as is referred to in paragraph 1 hereof the sheriff may, either *ex proprio motu* or on the motion of either party, nominate a technical assessor to sit with him at the hearing of the application.

(2) The remuneration (if any) to be paid to an assessor nominated under this section shall be determined by the auditor and shall be paid as part of the expenses of the application.

4. In any such application as is referred to in paragraph 1 hereof the sheriff may find either party liable in expenses.

5. This Act of Sederunt may be cited as the Act of Sederunt (Building Appeals) 1964, and shall come into operation on 15th June 1964.

Betting, Gaming and Lotteries Act Appeals 1965

(S.I. 1965 No. 1168)

[20th May 1965]

The Lords of Council and Session, under and by virtue of the powers conferred upon them by paragraph 24 of Schedule 1, paragraph 7 of Schedule 2, paragraph 13 of Schedule 3, paragraph 7 of Schedule 6, and paragraph 6 of Schedule 7 to the Betting, Gaming and Lotteries Act 1963, do hereby enact as follows:—

1–3. [Repealed by S.I. 1969 No. 1537.]

4. Any person who is aggrieved by the refusal of a registering authority to register him as a pools promoter, or by the revocation by a registering authority of his registration as a pools promoter, or by the revocation by a licensing authority of a licence in respect of a track for betting, or by the refusal of a local authority to grant or renew a permit for the provision of amusements with prizes, may at any time within 14 days after the receipt by him of the notice of refusal or revocation, appeal against such refusal or revocation by initial writ under the Sheriff Courts (Scotland) Acts 1907 and 1913, and such appeal shall be disposed of as a summary application as defined in the said Acts.

5. Any society which is aggrieved by the refusal or revocation by a local authority of the registration of the society for the purposes of section 45 of the Betting, Gaming and Lotteries Act 1963, may at any time within 14 days after the receipt by the society of the notice of refusal or revocation, appeal against such refusal or revocation by initial writ under the Sheriff Courts (Scotland) Acts 1907 and 1913, and such appeal shall be disposed of as a summary application as defined in the said Acts.

6. This Act of Sederunt may be cited as the Act of Sederunt (Betting, Gaming and Lotteries Act Appeals) 1965, and shall come into operation on 20th May 1965.

Housing Appeals 1966

(S.I. 1966 No. 845)

[12th July 1966]

The Lords of Council and Session, under and by virtue of the powers conferred upon them by section 166 of the Housing (Scotland) Act 1950 and of all other powers competent to them in that behalf, do hereby enact and declare as follows:—

1. Appeals to the sheriff under the Housing (Scotland) Act 1950, and under any enactment to which the provisions of subsections (1), (2) and (5) of section 166 of that Act have been applied, shall be by initial writ under the Sheriff Courts (Scotland) Acts 1907 and 1913 (c. 28), and shall be disposed of as summary applications as defined in the Sheriff Courts (Scotland) Acts.

2. The sheriff may, before considering any appeal under the Housing (Scotland) Act 1950 or under any enactment to which the provisions of subsection (4) of section 166 of that Act have been applied, require the appellant to deposit in court such sum not exceeding £20 sterling as shall seem proper, to cover the expenses of the appeal.

3. This Act of Sederunt may be cited as the Act of Sederunt (Housing Appeals) 1966, and shall come into operation on 1st October 1966.

Computer Evidence in the Sheriff Court 1969

(S.I. 1969 No. 1643)

[18th November 1969]

The Lords of Council and Session, by virtue of the powers conferred upon them by section 34 of the Administration of Justice (Scotland) Act 1933 and section 15 (6) of the Law Reform (Miscellaneous Provisions) (Scotland) Act 1968, do hereby enact and declare as follows:—

1. A party to any civil proceedings who wishes to rely on a statement contained in a document produced by a computer shall, not later than the date of closing the record, send to every other party to the proceedings a copy of the statement together with a notice in writing—

(*a*) intimating that the party intends to rely on the statement;

(*b*) stating that the statement is contained in a document produced by a computer; and

[1] (*c*) informing the party to whom it is addressed that he may give a counter-notice in terms of paragraph 3 hereof;

and the party so giving notice may within fourteen days thereafter lodge in process a certificate in terms of section 13 (4) of the Law Reform (Miscellaneous Provisions) (Scotland) Act 1968 relating to the document.

NOTE

[1] Substituted by S.I. 1970 No. 456.

2. When a certificate in terms of section 13 (4) of the Law Reform (Miscellaneous Provisions) (Scotland) Act 1968 shall have been lodged in process, a copy thereof shall be sent to every other party to the proceedings within fourteen days after the date of the notice referred to in paragraph 1 hereof.

3. Any party who receives such a notice as is mentioned in paragraph 1 hereof may, within twenty-one days thereafter, by counter-notice in writing addressed to the party who served the notice, require him, within twenty-one days, to furnish him in writing with all or any of the following information—

(*a*) any such information as might have been the subject of a certificate under section 13 (4) of the Law Reform (Miscellaneous Provisions)

(Scotland) Act 1968, except in so far as such information is the subject of a certificate lodged in process as aforesaid;

(*b*) the name, occupation, business address and place of residence of a person occupying at the material time a responsible position in relation to each of (i) the operation of the device involved in the production of the document, (ii) the management of the activities for the purposes of which the computer was used to store or process information, (iii) the supply of information to the computer, (iv) the operation of the computer, and (v) the operation of any equipment by means of which the document containing the statement was produced by the computer; and

(*c*) the name, occupation, business address and place of residence of the person who signed any certificate lodged in process in terms of section 13 (4) of the Law Reform (Miscellaneous Provisions) (Scotland) Act 1968.

4. Subject to the provisions of section 15 (8) of the Law Reform (Miscellaneous Provisions) (Scotland) Act 1968, a party upon whom a counter-notice has been served in terms of paragraph 3 hereof shall not be entitled to rely upon the statement in the document to which the notice under paragraph 1 hereof related, unless the counter-notice shall have been withdrawn by the party who gave it or unless the court shall be satisfied that the counter-notice was complied with so far as was reasonably possible.

5. Any party to whom information is furnished under a counter-notice by virtue of paragraph 3 hereof may, not later than twenty-eight days before the date of the proof or trial, by notice in writing require that the party wishing to rely on the statement in the document produced by a computer should call as a witness any person of whom particulars were furnished under sub-paragraph (*b*) or (*c*) of paragraph 3 hereof.

6. (i) Subject to the provisions of section 15 (8) of the Law Reform (Miscellaneous Provisions) (Scotland) Act 1968 a party who has been required to call any person as a witness in terms of paragraph 5 hereof shall not be entitled to rely upon the statement in the document to which the notice under paragraph 1 hereof related unless the notice requiring that person to be called as a witness shall have been withdrawn by the party who gave it, or unless that person shall be adduced as a witness, or unless the court shall be satisfied that such person is dead, or beyond the seas, or unfit by reason of his bodily or mental condition to attend as a witness, or cannot with reasonable diligence be identified or found, or cannot reasonably be expected (having regard to the passage of time and to all the circumstances) to have any recollection of matters relevant to the accuracy or otherwise of the statement in the document.

(ii) In the event that such person is not to be adduced as a witness for any reason aforesaid, the party wishing to rely on the statement in the document produced by a computer shall give notice in writing to every other party to the proceedings that such witness is not to be adduced and the reason therefor.

(iii) The notice referred to in sub-paragraph (ii) hereof shall be given not later than fourteen days after the date of the notice under paragraph 5 hereof or, if such reason could not reasonably have become known to him within that period, immediately such reason shall become known.

7. This Act of Sederunt shall apply to all civil proceedings in the Sheriff Court.

8. This Act of Sederunt may be cited as the Act of Sederunt (Computer Evidence in the Sheriff Court) 1969, and shall come into operation on 1st December 1969.

Sheriff Court Procedure under Part IV of the Housing (Scotland) Act 1969, 1970

(S.I. 1970 No. 1508)

[7th October 1970]

The Lords of Council and Session, under and by virtue of the powers conferred upon them by section 17 (1) of the Increase of Rent and Mortgage Interest (Restriction) Act 1920 as read with section 18 of the said Act and as extended by section 56 (2) of the Housing (Scotland) Act 1969 and of all other powers competent to them in that behalf, do hereby enact and declare as follows:—

1. (1) An appeal made under section 50 (1) of the Housing (Scotland) Act 1969 against the decision of a local authority refusing to issue a qualification certificate shall be made within twenty-eight days of the service on the applicant for the qualification certificate of the notice of refusal, or such longer period as the sheriff may allow, by initial writ under the Sheriff Courts (Scotland) Acts 1907 and 1913 and shall be disposed of as a summary application as defined in the said Acts.

(2) The persons upon whom warrant for citation on any initial writ lodged in terms of this paragraph shall be granted are (i) the clerk to the local authority which refused to issue the qualification certificate and (ii) the tenant of the dwelling in respect of which the application for a qualification certificate was made.

2. (1) An appeal under section 50 (2) of the Housing (Scotland) Act 1969 against the issue by a local authority of a qualification certificate shall be made within twenty-eight days of the service on the tenant of a copy of the qualification certificate, or such longer period as the sheriff may allow, by initial writ under the Sheriff Courts (Scotland) Acts 1907 and 1913, and shall be disposed of as a summary application as defined in the said Acts.

(2) The persons upon whom warrant for citation on any initial writ lodged in terms of this paragraph shall be granted are (i) the clerk to the local authority which issued the qualification certificate and (ii) the landlord of the dwelling in respect of which the qualification certificate was issued.

(3) Where a qualification certificate is quashed by an order under section 50 (2) of the Housing (Scotland) Act 1969, the sheriff clerk shall forthwith intimate the order to the rent officer for the area in which the dwelling to which the qualification certificate related is situated.

3. (1) An application to the sheriff under section 55 (2) of the Housing (Scotland) Act 1969 for an order empowering a landlord to enter a dwelling and carry out work, shall be made by initial writ under the Sheriff Courts (Scotland) Acts 1907 and 1913, and shall be disposed of as a summary application as defined in the said Acts.

(2) Warrant for citation on any initial writ lodged in terms of this paragraph shall be granted upon the tenant or tenants against whom the order is sought.

(3) Upon the motion of any tenant against whom an order is sought under section 55 (2) of the Housing (Scotland) Act 1969, the sheriff may order that the hearing of the application, or any part thereof, shall be in chambers.

4. This Act of Sederunt may be cited as the Act of Sederunt (Sheriff Court Procedure under Part IV of the Housing (Scotland) Act 1969) 1970 and shall come into operation on 23rd November 1970.

Firearms Appeals 1970

(S.I. 1970 No. 1984)

[16th December 1970]

The Lords of Council and Session, under and by virtue of the powers conferred upon them by section 21 (6) and section 44 (1) of the Firearms Act 1968 do hereby enact and declare as follows:—

1. An application to the sheriff under section 21 (6) of the Firearms Act 1968 shall be made by initial writ under the Sheriff Courts (Scotland) Acts 1907 and 1913 and shall be disposed of as a summary application as defined in the said Acts.

2. An appeal to the sheriff under section 44 of the Firearms Act 1968 shall be made by initial writ under the Sheriff Courts (Scotland) Acts 1907 and 1913, and shall be disposed of as a summary application as defined in the said Acts.

3. This Act of Sederunt may be cited as the Act of Sederunt (Firearms Appeals) 1970, and shall come into operation on 16th January 1971.

Social Work (Sheriff Court Procedure Rules) 1971

[See now Division K.]

Appeals against Poinding 1973

(S.I. 1973 No. 1860)

[Edinburgh, 7th November 1973]

The Lords of Council and Session, under and by virtue of the powers conferred on them by section 32 of the Sheriff Courts (Scotland) Act 1971 and of all other powers enabling them in that behalf, and after consultation with the Sheriff Court Rules Council, do whereby enact and declare as follows:—

1. This Act of Sederunt may be cited as the Act of Sederunt (Appeals against Poinding) 1973 and shall come into operation on 1st January 1974.

2.—(1) In this Act of Sederunt, unless the context otherwise requires— "the Act" means the Law Reform (Diligence) (Scotland) Act 1973[1]; "appeal" means an appeal under section 1 (4) of the Act; "sheriff clerk" includes sheriff clerk depute.

(2) The Interpretation Act 1889 shall apply to the interpretation of this Act of Sederunt as it applies to the interpretation of an Act of Parliament.

NOTE

[1] See Division B.

3. On the execution of a poinding in a dwellinghouse the poinding sheriff officer or messenger-at-arms shall deliver to the possessor of the poinded effects a notice in the Form A in the Schedule hereto.

4. Appeals shall be made by lodging with the sheriff clerk a form in, or as nearly as is practicable in, the Form B in the Schedule hereto.

5. On the lodging of an appeal the sheriff shall grant warrant for intimation and shall fix a date for hearing the appeal not sooner than the seventh day after such intimation, which warrant may be in the Form C in the Schedule hereto.

6. On the granting of a warrant for intimation the sheriff clerk shall forthwith intimate the appeal to the respondent and to the poinding sheriff officer or messenger-at-arms by transmitting a copy of the appeal and warrant, duly certified by him, by registered post or by recorded delivery first class service to each of the said respondent and sheriff officer or messenger-at arms at the address or addresses stated in the appeal. A certificate of execution of intimation may be in the Form D in the Schedule hereto.

7. All appeals shall be entered in a book to be kept for the purpose and such entries shall set forth the names and designations of the appellant, respondent, and poinding officer, the date of the poinding, the articles in respect of which the appeal is taken and the several deliverances and the dates thereof, which book shall be signed by the sheriff. The determinations and deliverances of the sheriff may be written on the principal appeal or separately, shall be signed by the sheriff clerk and shall have the force and effect of extract.

SCHEDULE

Form A.

Notice to the possessor of poinded effects.

The Law Reform (Diligence) (Scotland) Act 1973 provides that an article shall not be liable to be poinded at the instance of a creditor in respect of a debt due to him by a debtor if it is an article to which the Act applies and, being at the time of the poinding in a dwellinghouse in which the debtor is residing, it is reasonably necessary to enable him and any other person living in family with him in that dwellinghouse to continue to reside there without undue hardship. The Act at present applies to beds or bedding material, chairs, tables, furniture or plenishings providing facilities for cooking, eating or storing food, and furniture or plenishings providing facilities for heating.

Where any article is poinded in respect of a debt, then, without prejudice to any other remedy available to him, a debtor may within seven days from the date of the poinding appeal to the Sheriff on the ground that, by virtue of the provisions of the Act, the said article is not liable to be poinded.

Any enquiry relating to the making of such an appeal may be directed to the Sheriff Clerk's Office at

Form B.

In the Sheriff Court at Appeal under section 1(4) of the Law Reform (Diligence) (Scotland) Act 1973.

Appeal by

Applicant

in the poinding at the instance of

Respondent

1. The Appellant is the defender in an action at the instance of the respondent in (court) in which decree was granted on (date) against the Appellant for payment of (or as the case may be)

[THE NEXT PAGE IS D 253]

2. (name), Sheriff Officer, (address), on the instructions of the respondent executed a poinding of the appellant's effects on (date) at the dwellinghouse at (address)
Included amongst the effects poinded were the following articles:—

(a)
(b)

3. These articles are reasonably necessary to enable the appellant and the persons living in family with him in that dwellinghouse to continue to reside there without undue hardship.
4. This appeal is made under section 1(4) of the Law Reform (Diligence) (Scotland) Act 1973.

THEREFORE the Appellant craves the Court—

(a) To find that the articles referred to are articles to which section 1 of the Law Reform (Diligence) (Scotland) Act 1973 applies and are not liable to be poinded.
(b) To order that said articles be released from the poinding.
(c) To deal with the expenses of this Appeal as the Court may think fit.
(d) To sist meantime all further execution in respect of said articles.

Appellant
or
Appellant's Solicitors.

Form C.

Grants Warrant to intimate the foregoing Appeal and this warrant to the respondent and the therein designed Sheriff Officer/Messenger-at-Arms and Appoints them, if they intend to oppose the Appeal, to answer within the Sheriff Court at on the day of at o'clock noon. Further Appoints the said Sheriff Officer/Messenger-at-Arms to lodge a copy of the schedule of poinded effects in the hands of the clerk of court. Meantime, Grants interim sist of execution as craved.

Form D.

I, , Sheriff Clerk (Depute), did lawfully intimate the foregoing Appeal to the respondent and to the poinding Sheriff Officer/Messenger-at-Arms by posting a certified copy of the Appeal and warrant in a registered letter (or through the recorded delivery service) to each of them. The Post Office receipt for the said registered (or recorded delivery) letters are attached hereto.

Signed Sheriff Clerk or Sheriff Clerk Depute.

Interest in Sheriff Court Decrees or Extracts 1975

(S.I. 1975 No. 948)

[4th June 1975]

The Lords of Council and Session, under and by virtue of the powers conferred upon them by section 4 of the Administration of Justice (Scotland) Act 1972 and of all other powers competent to them in that behalf, do hereby enact and declare as follows:—

[1]**1.** In the case of any decree or extract in an action commenced on or after 1st July 1975 the provisions of section 9 of the Sheriff Courts (Scotland) Extracts Act 1892 as amended by the Act of Sederunt (Interest in Sheriff Court Decrees or Extracts) 1972 shall not apply. Instead there shall be substituted a new section 9 as follows:—

"where interest is included in a decree or extract, it shall be deemed to be at the rate of fifteen *per centum per annum*, unless otherwise stated".

NOTE

[1] Twelve per cent. substituted for eleven per cent., with effect from 5th April 1983, by S.I. 1983 No. 409.

Fifteen per cent. substituted for twelve per cent., with effect from 16th August 1985, by S.I. 1985 No. 1179.

2. This Act of Sederunt may be cited as the Act of Sederunt (Interest in Sheriff Court Decrees or Extracts) 1975, and shall come into operation on 2nd July 1975.

Proceedings under Sex Discrimination Act 1975, 1976

(S.I. 1976 No. 374)

[5th March 1976]

The Lords of Council and Session, under and by virtue of the powers conferred upon them by section 32 of the Sheriff Courts (Scotland) Act 1971 and section 75 of the Sex Discrimination Act 1975 and of all other powers competent to them in that behalf do hereby enact and declare:—

Citation, commencement and interpretation

1. This Act of Sederunt may be cited as the Act of Sederunt (Proceedings under Sex Discrimination Act 1975) 1976 and shall come into operation on 1st April 1976.

2.—(1) In this Act of Sederunt "the Act" means the Sex Discrimination Act 1975, and "the Commission" means the Equal Opportunities Commission established under section 53 of the Act.

(2) The Interpretation Act 1889 shall apply for the interpretation of this Act of Sederunt as it applies for the interpretation of an Act of Parliament.

Procedure

3. The following proceedings under the Act shall be commenced by Initial Writ under the Sheriff Courts (Scotland) Acts 1907 and 1913 and shall be disposed of as summary applications as defined in those Acts, namely:—

(*a*) an application by the Commission under section 59(4) for an order requiring a person to comply with a notice served on him under section 59(1);

(*b*) an appeal by a person under section 68(1) against a requirement of a non-discrimination notice served on him under section 67;

(*c*) an application by the Commission under section 71(1) for an order restraining a person from doing any of the acts referred to in that section;

(*d*) an application by the Commission under section 72(2) for a decision whether an alleged contravention of section 38, 39 or 40 has occurred;

(*e*) an application by the Commission under section 72(4) for an order restraining a person from doing any of the acts referred to in that section; and

(*f*) an application by a person under section 77(5) for an order removing or modifying any term of a contract made unenforceable by section 77(2).

Taxation

4. The expenses incurred by the Commission within the meaning and for the purposes of section 75(3) of the Act, shall be taxed or assessed by the auditor of the sheriff court in which proceedings under the Act were taken or would have been taken but for any compromise or settlement, as if they were outlays incurred by a solicitor on behalf of the applicant.

Summary Cause Rules, Sheriff Court 1976

(S.I. 1976 No. 476)

[24th March 1976]

ARRANGEMENT OF RULES

PART I

GENERAL RULES

Part II

Special Rules

Action for Payment of Money

Action of Furthcoming

Action of Court Reckoning and Payment

Recovery of Possession of Heritable Property

Action for Delivery

Action of Sequestration for Rent

The Lords of Council and Session, under and by virtue of the powers conferred on them by section 32 of the Sheriff Courts (Scotland) Act 1971 and of all other powers competent to them in that behalf do hereby enact and declare:—

Citation and commencement

1. This Act of Sederunt may be cited as the Act of Sederunt (Summary Cause Rules, Sheriff Court) 1976 and shall come into operation on 1st September 1976.

Interpretation

2.—[1] (1) In this Act of Sederunt unless the context otherwise requires— "the Act of 1907" means the Sheriff Courts (Scotland) Act 1907 as amended; "the Act of 1971" means the Sheriff Courts (Scotland) Act 1971; "the Act of 1975" means the Litigants in Person (Costs and Expenses) Act 1975; "authorised lay representative" means a person to whom section 32(1) of the Solicitors (Scotland) Act 1980 (offence to prepare writs) does not apply by virtue of section 32(2)(*a*) of that Act; and "summary cause" means the summary cause defined in section 35(1) of the Act of 1971.

(2) Other expressions used in this Act of Sederunt to which meanings have been assigned by the Act of 1907 shall, unless the context otherwise requires, have the same meaning in this Act of Sederunt as in that Act.

(3) References in the Schedule to this Act of Sederunt to a rule shall, unless the context otherwise requires, be construed as a reference to a rule contained in that Schedule and any reference in a rule contained in that Schedule to a paragraph shall be construed as a reference to a paragraph of that rule.

(4) A form referred to by letter means the form so lettered in the Schedule to this Act of Sederunt and any provision requiring the use of such a form shall be construed as a requirement to use that form subject to such combination with other forms or to such variation as the particular circumstances require.

(5) In this Act of Sederunt any reference to an enactment shall be construed as a reference to that enactment as amended or extended by or under any other enactment.

(6) The Interpretation Act 1889 shall apply for the interpretation of this Act of Sederunt as it applies for the interpretation of an Act of Parliament.

NOTE

[1] As amended by S.I. 1991 No. 821.

Procedure in summary causes

3.—[1] (1) The rules for regulating the procedure in a summary cause other than a small claim shall be the rules set out in the Schedule to this Act of Sederunt.

[2] (2) Rules 13A, 14, 20A, 27, 60, 72A, 84, 84A, 85, 87, 89(4), 103 to 107, 111, 128, 130(1) and 134 of the rules contained in Schedule I to the Act of 1907 shall apply to a summary cause in so far as they are not inconsistent with the rules set out in the Schedule to this Act of Sederunt. The remaining provisions of the said Schedule I shall not apply to a summary cause.

NOTES

[1] As amended by S.I. 1988 No. 1976.

[2] Substituted by S.I. 1983 No. 747 and as amended by S.I. 1986 No. 1966, S.I. 1989 No. 436 and S.I. 1990 No. 661.

Intimation

4. Except where the context otherwise requires any provision in the Schedule to this Act of Sederunt requiring papers to be sent to or any intimation to be made to any party, applicant or claimant shall be construed as if the reference to the party, applicant or claimant included a reference to the solicitor representing that party, applicant or claimant.

Dispensing power of sheriff

5. The sheriff may in his discretion relieve any party from the consequences of any failure to comply with the provisions of the rules set out in the Schedule to this Act of Sederunt which failure is shown to be due to mistake, oversight or other cause, not being wilful non-observance of the said rules on such terms and conditions as appear to be just; and in any such case the sheriff may make such order as may be just by way of extension of time, lodging or amendment of papers or otherwise, so as to enable the cause to proceed as if such failure had not happened.

Transitional

6. It shall not be competent to raise an action in the sheriff's small debt court or commence proceedings in a summary cause within the meaning of the Act of 1907 as originally enacted, after the date of the coming into operation of this Act of Sederunt, but where before that date such action has been raised or such proceedings have been commenced such action or proceedings shall proceed according to the law and practice in force immediately before the coming into operation of this Act of Sederunt.

PART I

GENERAL RULES

Form of summons

[1] **1.** A summons may be in one of the forms Aa to I.

NOTE

[1] As amended by S.I. 1992 No. 249 (effective 4th May 1992).

Statement of claim

[1] **2.**—[2] (1) There shall be annexed to the summons a statement of claim which shall give the defender fair notice of the claim and shall, in particular, include—

(*a*) details of the basis of the claim including any relevant dates;
(*b*) where the claim arises from the supply of goods or services, a description of the goods or services and the date or dates on or between which they were supplied and, where relevant, ordered;
(*c*) reference to any agreement which the pursuer has reason to believe may exist giving jurisdiction over the subject matter of the claim to another court; and
(*d*) reference to any proceedings which the pursuer has reason to believe may be pending before another court involving the same cause of action and between the same parties.

(2) The statement of claim shall contain averments about any agreement which the pursuer has reason to believe may exist prorogating jurisdiction over the subject matter of the cause to another court.

(3) The statement of claim shall contain averments about any proceedings which the pursuer has reason to believe may be pending before another court involving the same cause of action and between the same parties as those named in the initial writ.

NOTES

[1] As amended by S.I. 1986 No. 1946 and 1988 No. 1978.

[2] As substituted by S.I. 1992 No. 249 (effective 4th May 1992).

Signature and effect of summons

3.—(1) The summons shall be signed by the sheriff clerk:

Provided that—

(*a*) when the normal period of notice specified in rule 4 has been altered it shall be signed by the sheriff, and
(*b*) when the sheriff clerk has for any reason refused to sign the summons it may be signed by the sheriff.

[THE NEXT PAGE IS D 257]

(2) The signed summons shall be warrant for service on the defender and when the necessary provisions are included in the summons it shall be warrant (*a*) for arrestment on the dependence of the action, and (*b*) for arrestment to found jurisdiction.

Information on summons

[1] **3A.** The name and address of the pursuer's solicitor (if any) shall be entered by the solicitor on the principal summons, and the service document or service copy.

NOTE

[1] Added by S.I. 1980 No. 455.

Period of notice after citation

[1] **4.**—(1) Actions shall proceed after the appropriate period of notice of the summons has been given to the defender, namely

(*a*) 21 days when the defender is resident or has a place of business within Europe;

(*b*) 42 days when the defender is resident or has a place of business outwith Europe.

(2) The sheriff may, on cause shown, shorten or extend the period of notice on such conditions as to the form of service as he may direct, but in any case where the period of notice is reduced at least two days' notice shall be given.

(3) Where a period of notice expires on a Saturday, Sunday, public or local holiday the period of notice shall be deemed to expire on the first following day on which the sheriff clerk's office is open for civil court business.

NOTE

[1] As substituted by S.I. 1980 No. 455 and as amended by S.I. 1988 No. 1978.

Form of citation and certificate thereof

[1] **5.** Citation shall be given in form J and the certificate of citation shall be in form K and the said forms shall be annexed or attached to the summons or a copy thereof. When citation is by an officer of court, the certificate of citation shall be signed by him and shall specify whether the citation was personal or, if otherwise, the mode of citation and the name of any person to whom the citation was delivered. When citation is effected in accordance with paragraph (2) of rule 6 the certificate shall also contain a statement of the mode of service previously attempted and the circumstances which prevented such service from being effected.

NOTE

[1] As amended by S.I. 1980 No. 455.

Citation and service within Scotland by officer of court

[1] **6.**—(1) Any summons, decree, charge, warrant or other order or writ following upon such summons or decree issued in a summary cause may be validly served by an officer of court on any person,

(*a*) by being served personally, or

(*b*) by being left in the hands of an inmate at the person's dwelling place or of an employee at the person's place of business.

(2) Where an officer of court has been unsuccessful in effecting service in accordance with paragraph (1), he may, after making diligent inquiries, serve the said summons, decree, charge, warrant or other order or writ,

(*a*) by depositing it in the person's dwelling place or place of business by means of a letter box or by other lawful means, or (*b*) by affixing it to the door of the person's dwelling place or place of business.

Subject to the requirements of rule 111 of the rules contained in Schedule 1 to the Act of 1907, if [service is effected] in accordance with this paragraph, the officer shall thereafter send by ordinary post to the address at which he thinks it most likely that the person may be found, a letter containing a copy of any summons, decree, charge, warrant or other order or writ.

(3) In proceedings in or following on a summary cause it shall be necessary for any officer of court to be accompanied by a witness except where service, citation or intimation is to be made by post.

(4) In this rule "officer of court" includes a sheriff officer but not a messenger-at-arms.

NOTE

[1] As substituted by S.I. 1980 No. 455 and as amended by S.I. 1992 No. 249 (effective 4th May 1992). The words in square brackets are strictly speaking repealed by the latter instrument.

7. [Revoked by S.I. 1980 No. 455.]

Citation of or service on persons whose address is unknown

[1] **8.**—(1) When a defender's address is unknown to the pursuer, the sheriff may grant a warrant to cite the defender by the publication in a newspaper circulating in the area of the defender's last known address of an advertisement in form L and such citation shall be deemed to be good and sufficient for every purpose of law.

(2) When citation is to be effected in accordance with paragraph (1)—

(*a*) the period of notice shall be fixed by the sheriff and shall run from the date of publication; and

(*b*) a service copy summons or service document shall be lodged by the pursuer with the sheriff clerk from whom it may be uplifted by the defender.

(3) Where the address of the defender who has been cited in accordance with paragraph (1) becomes known after the cause has commenced, the sheriff may allow the summons to be amended subject to such conditions as to re-service, intimation, expenses, or transfer of the cause as he thinks fit.

(4) In every case where advertisement in a newspaper is required for the purpose of citation or service a copy of the newspaper containing said advertisement shall be lodged with the sheriff clerk.

NOTE

[1] As substituted by S.I. 1980 No. 455.

Citation of or service on persons outwith Scotland

[1] **9.**—(1) Subject to the following provisions of this rule, any summons or decree, or any other writ or order following upon such summons or decree, or any charge or warrant, may be served outwith Scotland on any person—

(*a*) at a known residence or place of business in England and Wales, Northern Ireland, the Isle of Man, the Channel Islands or any country with which the United Kingdom does not have a convention providing for service of writs in that country—

(i) in accordance with the rules for personal service under the domestic law of the place in which service is to be effected; or

(ii) by posting in Scotland a copy of the document in question in a registered or recorded delivery letter or the nearest equivalent which the available postal services permit addressed to the person at his residence or place of business;

(*b*) in a country which is a party to the Hague Convention on the Service Abroad of Judicial and Extra-Judicial Documents in Civil or Commercial Matters dated 15th November 1965 or the European Convention on Jurisdiction and Enforcement of Judgments in Civil and Commercial Matters as set out in Schedule 1 to the Civil Jurisdiction and Judgments Act 1982—

(i) by a method prescribed by the internal law of the country where service is to be effected for the service of documents in domestic actions upon persons who are within its territory;

(ii) by or through a central authority in the country where service is to be effected at the request of the Foreign Office;

(iii) by or through a British Consular authority at the request of the Foreign Office;

(iv) where the law of the country in which the person resides permits, by posting in Scotland a copy of the document in a registered or recorded delivery letter or the nearest equivalent which the available postal services permit addressed to the person at his residence; or

(v) where the law of the country in which service is to be effected permits, service by an *huissier*, other judicial officer or competent official of the country where service is to be made;

(*c*) in a country with which the United Kingdom has a convention on the service of writs in that country other than the conventions in subparagraph (*b*), by one of the methods approved in the relevant convention.

(2) A document which requires to be posted in Scotland for the purposes of this rule shall be posted by a solicitor or an officer of court, and the forms for citation and certificate of citation in rule 5 shall apply to a postal citation under this rule as they apply to a citation under that rule.

(3) On the face of the envelope used for postal service under this rule there shall be written or printed a notice in the same or similar terms as that required in the case of ordinary service under rule 10.

(4) Where service is effected by a method specified in paragraph (1)(*b*)(ii) or (iii), the pursuer shall—

(*a*) send a copy of the summons and warrant for service with citation attached, or other document, with a request for service to be effected by the method indicated in the request to the Secretary of State for Foreign and Commonwealth Affairs; and

(*b*) lodge in process a certificate of execution of service signed by the authority which has effected service.

(5) Where service is effected by the method specified in paragraph (1)(*b*)(v) the pursuer, his solicitor or the officer of court, shall—

(*a*) send to the official in the country in which service is to be effected a copy of the summons and warrant for service, with citation attached, or other document, with a request for service to be effected by delivery to the defender or his residence; and

(*b*) the pursuer shall lodge in process a certificate of execution of service by the official who has effected service.

(6) Where service is effected in accordance with paragraph (1)(*a*)(i) or (1)(*b*)(i), the pursuer shall lodge a certificate by a person who is conversant with the law of the country concerned and who practises or has practised as an advocate or solicitor in that country or is a duly accredited representative of the Government of that country, stating that the form of service employed is in accordance with the law of the place where the service was effected. It shall not be necessary to lodge such a certificate where service has taken place in another part of the United Kingdom, the Channel Isles or the Isle of Man.

(7) Every summons or document and every citation and notice on the face of the envelope referred to in paragraph (3) shall be accompanied by a translation in an official language of the country in which service is to be executed unless English is an official language of that country.

(8) A translation referred to in paragraph (7) shall be certified as a correct translation by the person making it and the certificate shall contain full name, address and qualifications of the translator and be lodged along with the execution of such citation or certificate of execution.

NOTE

[1] As substituted by S.I. 1986 No. 1946.

Postal citation

[1] **10.**—(1) In any case in which it is competent to serve or intimate any document or to cite any person by recorded delivery, such service, intimation or citation, when made by recorded delivery shall only be competent if it is made by recorded delivery first class service.

[2] (2) Notwithstanding the terms of section 4(2) of the Citation Amendment (Scotland) Act 1882, where service is by post the period of notice shall run from the beginning of the day next following the date of posting.

(3) On the face of the envelope used for postal service under this rule there shall be written or printed a notice in form Ka or in like form.

(4) The certificate of citation in the case of postal service shall have annexed to it any relevant postal receipts.

NOTES

[1] As amended by S.I. 1980 No. 455.

[2] As substituted by S.I. 1992 No. 249 (effective 4th May 1992).

Endorsation of summons by sheriff clerk of defender's residence not necessary

[1] **11.** Any summons, charge, warrant, arrestment or any order or writ following upon a summons or decree may be served, enforced or otherwise lawfully executed in Scotland without endorsation by a sheriff clerk and, if executed by an officer, may be so executed by an officer of the court which granted the summons, or by an officer of the sheriff court district in which it is to be executed.

NOTE

[1] As substituted by S.I. 1980 No. 455.

Re-service

[1] **12.**—(1) If it appears to the court that there has been any failure or irregularity in service upon a defender, the court may prior to or at the first calling and upon such conditions as seem just authorise the pursuer to re-serve the summons.

(2) Where re-service has been ordered in accordance with paragraph (1) or rule 8 the cause shall proceed thereafter as if it were a new cause.

NOTE

[1] As amended by S.I. 1978 No. 1805.

Defender appearing barred from objecting to citation

13. Except where jurisdiction has been constituted by arrestment to found jurisdiction a party who appears or is represented may not object to the regularity of the service and the appearance shall be deemed to remedy any defect in the service.

14. [Revoked by S.I. 1980 No. 455.]

Return of summons

[1] **15.**—(1) In an action for payment of money to which rules 50 to 55 apply the summons, together with the relevant certificate of citation shall be returned to the sheriff clerk on or before the return day referred to in rule 51.

(2) In all other actions, the summons together with the relevant certificate of citation shall be returned to the sheriff clerk at least 24 hours before the date of the first calling as defined in rule 18(1).

(3) Failure to comply with either paragraph (1) or (2) may result in the dismissal of the cause.

NOTE

[1] As substituted by S.I. 1980 No. 455 and as amended by S.I. 1988 No. 1978.

Book of Summary Causes

[1] **16.**—(1) The sheriff clerk shall keep a book to be known as the Book of Summary Causes in which shall be entered a note of all summary causes

and minutes under rules 19(1) and 92(1), setting forth the following particulars where appropriate—

(*a*) the names and designations of the parties,
(*b*) whether they are present or absent at the calling of the cause, and the names of their representatives,
(*c*) the nature of the cause,
(*d*) the amount of any claim,
(*e*) the date of issue of the summons,
(*f*) the mode of citation,
(*g*) the date of the return day,
(*h*) whether a notice of intention to appear has been lodged,
(*i*) any minute by the pursuer under rule 54 or 55(1),
(*j*) any interlocutors issued, and
(*k*) the final decree with the date thereof

which Book shall be signed in respect of each court day by the sheriff.

(2) The Book of Summary Causes may be made up of separate rolls each roll relating solely to proceedings of a particular description of summary cause.

(3) The Book of Summary Causes kept by the sheriff clerk shall be open for inspection during office hours to all concerned without fee.

NOTE
[1] As amended by S.I. 1980 No. 455.

Representation

[1] **17.**—(1) A party may be represented by an advocate, solicitor or, subject to the following provisions of this rule, an authorised lay representative.

(2) Subject to the following provisions of this rule, an authorised lay representative may, in representing a party, do all such things for the preparation and conduct of a cause as may be done by an individual conducting his own case.

(3) An authorised lay representative shall not appear in court on behalf of a party except at the first calling of a summary cause and, unless the sheriff otherwise directs, at any subsequent calling where the cause is not defended on the merits or on the amount of the sum due.

(4) An authorised lay representative shall cease to represent a party if the sheriff finds either that the authorised lay representative is not a suitable person to represent the party or that he is not authorised to do so.

(5) A party may be represented by a person other than an advocate or solicitor at any stage of any proceedings under the Debtors (Scotland) Act 1987, other than appeals to the sheriff principal, if the sheriff is satisfied that that person is a suitable person to represent the party at that stage and is authorised to do so.

NOTE
[1] As substituted by S.I. 1991 No. 821.

Applications for time to pay directions

[1] **17A.**—(1) This rule applies to summary causes, other than causes regulated by rules 50 to 55, in which a time to pay direction (including, where appropriate, an application for recall or restriction of an arrestment) under the Debtors (Scotland) Act 1987 may be applied for.

(2) Where a time to pay direction may be applied for by a defender, the pursuer shall serve on the defender a notice in accordance with Form Bb together with the summons.

(3) A defender may apply for a time to pay direction, and, where appropriate, for an order recalling or restricting an arrestment, by—

(*a*) appearing at the first calling of the cause and making the appropriate motion;
(*b*) except when the period of notice has been reduced under rule 4(2), completing and returning to the sheriff clerk to arrive at least

seven days before the first calling the appropriate portion of Form Bb; or

(*c*) written or oral application to the court at any other stage prior to final decree being granted.

NOTE

[1] Inserted by S.I. 1988 No. 1978.

First calling

[1] **18.**—(1) The date of the first calling of a summary cause is the date stated in the summons when the defender, if he wishes to defend the action or, where competent, to apply for a time to pay direction, is required to appear. The first calling and any continuation thereof may be before the sheriff clerk.

[2] (2) Where the first calling or any continuation of it is before the sheriff clerk, he—

(*a*) shall—

(i) on the motion of any party;

(ii) where there has been an application for a time to pay direction which has been objected to; or

(iii) where a motion is made for an order under section 48(2) of the Housing (Scotland) Act 1987; or

(*b*) may, of his own accord,

order that it be called before the sheriff on that or a subsequent day; and, for the purposes of paragraph (3), such calling before the sheriff shall not be treated as a continuation.

(3) No continuation of the first calling shall be granted except—

(*a*) on the joint motion of the parties, or

(*b*) on the motion of any party where the court in terms of rule 21 has granted leave to the defender to serve a counter claim within seven days of the first calling, or

(*c*) where a time to pay direction has been applied for by the defender; or

(*d*) if the court in all the circumstances considers it necessary,

when the court may continue the first calling on one occasion only to a roll not later than the first roll occurring after the expiry of 28 days.

(4) If it appears to the sheriff that the cause is clearly incompetent or that there is a patent defect of jurisdiction he may grant decree of dismissal with expenses.

(5) If the pursuer does not appear or is not represented at the first calling or at any continuation thereof at which the defender is present or represented and no defence has been stated the court shall grant decree of absolvitor with expenses.

(6) If the defender does not appear or is not represented at the first calling or at any continuation thereof and has not stated a defence or if the court is satisfied that he does not intend to defend the cause on the merits or on the amount of the sum due the court may grant decree with expenses against him: provided that the sheriff shall not grant decree in the cause unless it appears *ex facie* of the summons that a ground of jurisdiction exists under the Civil Jurisdiction and Judgments Act 1982.

(7) Where a defence is stated at the first calling or at any continuation thereof the court shall, subject to the provisions of paragraph (4), fix a diet of proof which proof shall be deemed to be a proof *habili modo* and the parties shall not be heard on any question of law other than questions relating to admissibility of evidence until the facts have been ascertained by proof or by the admission of parties or by a combination of these.

(8) In the case of a defender domiciled in another part of the United Kingdom or in another Contracting State, the sheriff shall not grant decree in absence until it has been shown that the defender has been able to receive the summons in sufficient time to arrange for his defence or that all necessary steps have been taken to that end; and for the purposes of this paragraph—

(*a*) the question as to whether a person is domiciled in another part of the United Kingdom shall be determined in accordance with sections 41 and 42 of the Civil Jurisdiction and Judgments Act 1982;

(*b*) the question as to whether a person is domiciled in another Contracting State shall be determined in accordance with Article 52 of Schedule 1 to that Act; and

(*c*) the term "Contracting State" has the meaning assigned to it by section 1 of that Act.

[3] (9) Where the sheriff is satisfied that the facts of the cause are sufficiently admitted, he may decide the cause on the merits at the first calling and, if appropriate, may make an award of expenses.

[3] (10) Where, at the first calling or at any subsequent stage of the proceedings, an issue in dispute is the quality or condition of an object the sheriff may inspect the object in the presence of the parties or their representatives in court or, if it is not practicable to bring the object to court, at the place where the object is located.

[3] (11) The sheriff may, if he considers it appropriate at the first calling or at any later stage of the proceedings, inspect any place material to a disputed issue in the cause, in the presence of the parties or their representatives.

NOTES

[1] As amended by S.I. 1986 No. 1946 and 1988 No. 1978.

[2] As substituted by S.I. 1991 No. 821.

[3] Inserted by S.I. 1992 No. 249 (effective 4th May 1992).

Decree in causes to which the Hague Convention applies

[1] **18A.** Where, in any civil proceedings (including proceedings for aliment), the summons has been served in a country to which the Hague Convention on the Service Abroad of Judicial and Extra-Judicial Documents in Civil or Commercial Matters dated 15th November 1965 applies, decree shall not be granted until it is established to the satisfaction of the sheriff that the requirements of Article 15 of that Convention have been complied with.

NOTE

[1] Added by S.I. 1986 No. 1946.

Recall of decree

[1] **19.**—(1)

(*a*) The pursuer, at any time within 21 days of the grant of decree of absolvitor in terms of rule 18(5), or

(*b*) the defender, at any time not later than 14 days after the execution of the charge or execution of arrestment, whichever first occurs, following on the grants of decree in terms of rule 18(6),

may apply for the recall of such decree by lodging with the sheriff clerk a minute in form M. Each party may apply for recall of a decree in the case on one occasion only.

(2) On the lodging of a minute, the sheriff clerk shall fix a date, time and place for a hearing. Not less than seven days before the hearing the minuter shall serve upon the other party a copy of the minute and intimate to him the date, time and place of the hearing.

(3) At the hearing the court shall recall the decree so far as not implemented whereupon the cause shall proceed in all respects as if the hearing were a first calling.

(4) [Revoked by S.I. 1990 No. 2105.]

(5) The sheriff may make such order as to expenses as he thinks fit.

(6) A minute to recall a decree granted in terms of rule 18(6) when duly lodged and intimated in accordance with the foregoing paragraphs shall operate as a sist of diligence. In actions to which rule 68A applies the lodging and intimating of such a minute shall not operate as a sist of diligence unless the sheriff directs otherwise.

(7) On intimation of the said minute the party in possession of the summons shall return it to the sheriff clerk.

NOTE

[1] As amended by S.I. 1980 No. 455 and 1990 No. 2105.

Defence

20. At the first calling or at any continuation thereof the defender shall state his defence which shall at that time be noted on the summons by the court:

Provided that the court may on cause shown grant leave to the defender in addition to lodge within 14 days of such leave being granted a supplementary note of his defence.

Counter claim

[1] **21.**—(1) Where a defender intends to plead any counter claim he shall lodge the same at the first calling or any continuation thereof, or, with leave of the court granted at the first calling on cause shown within seven days thereafter, failing which the counter claim, except with the pursuer's consent, shall not be pleaded as such.

(2) Where a pursuer intends to oppose the counter claim he shall lodge answers within seven days of the lodging of the counter claim.

(3) Any party lodging a counter claim or answers thereto shall at the same time intimate a copy thereof to any other party.

[2] (4) The defender may apply for warrant to use any form of diligence by way of arrestment which could be used on the dependence of a separate cause brought to enforce the matter of the counter claim.

[2] (5) An application under paragraph (4) shall be made by appending to the counter claim the words "warrant for arrestment on the dependence applied for" and shall be granted by the sheriff clerk who receives the counter claim by adding the words "Grants warrant as craved" and by adding his signature and the date below those words.

[2] (6) Any such warrant shall have the like effect as it would have in any summary cause summons.

NOTES

[1] As substituted by S.I. 1980 No. 455.

[2] Inserted by S.I. 1992 No. 249 (effective 4th May 1992).

Party minuter

[1] **21A.**—(1) Any person who has not been called as a defender may apply by incidental application to the sheriff for leave to enter a cause as a party minuter, and to state a defence.

(2) An application under this rule shall specify—

(*a*) the applicant's title and interest to enter the cause; and

(*b*) the grounds of the defence which he purposes to state.

(3) On the lodging of an application under this rule, the sheriff shall appoint a date for hearing the application; and the applicant shall forthwith serve a copy of the application and of the order for a hearing on the parties to the cause.

(4) After hearing the applicant and any party to the cause the sheriff may, if he is satisfied that the applicant has shown title and interest to enter the cause, grant the application and may make such an order as to expenses as he thinks fit.

(5) Where an application is granted the party minuter shall be treated as a defender and the cause shall proceed against him as if the hearing were a first calling.

NOTE

[1] Inserted by S.I. 1992 No. 249 (effective 4th May 1992).

Transfer to another court

22. A cause may be transferred to any other court, whether in the same sheriffdom or not, if the sheriff considers that it is expedient that this be done and a cause so transferred shall proceed in all respects as if it had originally been brought in that court.

Remit between summary and ordinary rolls

23.—(1) Where a direction has been made that an ordinary cause be treated as a summary cause the initial writ shall be deemed to be a summary cause summons and the cause shall be remitted to a summary cause roll occurring not more than seven days after the date of the direction:

Provided that if no appropriate summary cause roll occurs within that period the remit shall be to the roll first occurring.

(2) Where a direction has been made that a summary cause be treated as an ordinary cause the cause shall be remitted to the ordinary cause roll first occurring not sooner than seven days after the date of the direction.

Lodging of productions

[1] **24.**—(1) All productions which are intended to be used or put in evidence at a proof shall be lodged together with an inventory thereof with the sheriff clerk not later than seven days before the diet of proof and notice of the lodging thereof shall at the same time be sent to any other party.

(2) No productions other than those timeously lodged shall be used or put in evidence at the proof unless by consent of parties or by permission of

[THE NEXT PAGE IS D 263]

the presiding sheriff on cause shown to his satisfaction and on such terms as to expenses or otherwise as to him seem proper.

NOTE

[1] As substituted by S.I. 1980 No. 455.

Borrowing of productions

[1] **24A.**—(1) Any productions borrowed, receipts for which shall be entered in the inventory of productions, which inventory shall be retained by the sheriff clerk, shall be returned not later than noon on the day preceding the date of the proof.

(2) Productions may be borrowed only by a solicitor or by his duly authrised clerk for whom he shall be responsible.

[2] (3) A party litigant or authorised lay representative shall not borrow productions except by leave of the sheriff and subject to such conditions as the sheriff may impose, but may inspect them and obtain copies, where practicable, from the sheriff clerk.

NOTES

[1] Added by S.I. 1980 No. 455.

[2] As amended by S.I. 1991 No. 821.

Penalty for failure to return borrowed productions

25. When a solicitor has borrowed a production and fails to return it for any diet at which it is required the sheriff may impose upon such solicitor a fine not exceeding £5 which shall be payable to the sheriff clerk for behoof of the Crown and shall be recoverable by civil diligence. An order imposing a fine under this rule shall not be subject to review except that the sheriff who granted it may on cause shown recall it.

Documents lost or destroyed

26. When any summons, statement of claim, counter claim or note of defence, any book or document recording interlocutors or deliverances of the court or any document lodged with the sheriff clerk in connection with a summary cause is lost or destroyed, a copy thereof, authenticated in such manner as the sheriff may require, may be substituted and shall, for the purposes of the cause, including the use of diligence, be equivalent to the original.

Alteration of summons, etc.

27. At any time not later than seven days before the date fixed for the diet of proof in any cause, or at such time thereafter as he in special circumstances may allow, the sheriff may, on the motion of any party to permit alteration of the summons, statement of claim, counter claim or note of defence, grant that motion:

Provided that—

(*a*) if all parties are present or represented when the motion is made he is satisfied that reasonable notice of the motion has been given to the other parties, and

(*b*) if any of the parties is not present or represented when the motion is made, he may require such re-service or intimation or make such provision as to expenses as seems proper.

Decree by default and dismissal

[1] **28.**—(1) If in a summary cause after a defence has been stated a party has failed—

(*a*) to appear or be represented at any diet, or

(*b*) to implement an order of court

the cause shall be continued to a diet on the first appropriate summary cause roll occurring not earlier than 14 days from such failure to enable intimation to be given to any such party.

(2) Such intimation of the date of the continued diet shall be made by the sheriff clerk to the party concerned and shall include—

(*a*) a note of the reasons for the continuation, and

(*b*) a note that decree by default or of absolvitor may be granted in any of the following circumstances—

(i) if the party concerned fails to appear to be represented at the said continued diet, or

(ii) if at the said continued diet good cause is not shown for non-appearance at any prior diet, or

(iii) if any prior order of,court has not been implemented by the date of the said continued diet.

(3) In any of the circumstances described in paragraph (2) above, or if the party concerned fails to appear or be represented at any further diet, decree by default as craved or decree of absolvitor may be granted.

(4) If all parties fail to appear or be represented at any diet the sheriff, unless sufficient reason appears to the contrary, shall dismiss the cause.

NOTE

[1] As substituted by S.I. 1980 No. 455.

Citation of witnesses

29. The summons or the copy served on the defender shall be sufficient warrant for the citation of witnesses and havers, the period of notice required to be given to such witnesses or havers being not less than seven days.

Form of citation and execution thereof

30. The citation of a witness or haver shall be in form N and the certificate thereof shall be in form O and a solicitor who cites a witness or haver shall be personally liable for the fees of the witness or haver.

Failure to answer citation

[1] **31.** A witness or haver who fails to answer a citation after having been properly cited and offered his travelling expenses if he has asked for them may be ordered by the sheriff to pay a penalty not exceeding £250 unless a reasonable excuse is offered and sustained. The sheriff may grant decree for payment of the said penalty in favour of the party on whose behalf the witness or haver was cited.

NOTE

[1] As amended by S.I. 1992 No. 429 (effective 4th May 1992).

Witnesses failing to attend

[1] **32.** The sheriff may grant warrant to compel the attendance of a witness or haver under pain of arrest and imprisonment until caution can be found as the sheriff may require for his due attendance. The warrant shall be effective in any sheriffdom without endorsation and the expenses thereof may be awarded against the witness or haver.

NOTE

[1] As substituted by S.I. 1980 No. 455.

Procedure for restricted proof and reference to oath

33.—(1) Where any party desires to plead that proof be restricted to the writ or oath of any person that party shall lodge a minute to that effect signed by himself or his solicitor and shall also give notice in writing signed by himself or his solicitor to his opponent at least 14 days before the diet of proof:

Provided that the sheriff at the proof may on cause shown dispense with such notice.

(2) Where any party desires to refer any matter to his opponent's oath he shall lodge a minute to that effect signed by himself or his solicitor. If the party to whose oath reference has been made fails to appear at the diet for taking his deposition the sheriff may hold him as confessed and grant decree accordingly.

Preservation, and obtaining, of evidence

34.—(1) Evidence in danger of being lost may be taken to lie *in retentis* and, if satisfied that it is desirable so to do, the sheriff may, upon the motion of any party at any time, either take it himself, or grant authority to a commissioner to take it.

(2) The evidence of any witness or haver resident beyond the sheriffdom, or who although resident within the sheriffdom resides at some place remote from the court in which the diet of proof is to be held, or who is by reason of illness, age, infirmity or other sufficient cause unable to attend the diet of proof, may be taken in the same manner as is provided in paragraph (1).

(3) Evidence referred to in paragraphs (1) and (2) whether before the sheriff or a commissioner may be taken down by the sheriff or the commissioner or by a clerk or shorthand writer nominated by the sheriff or commissioner to whom the oath *de fideli administratione* shall be administered and such evidence may be recorded in narrative form or by question and answer as the sheriff or commissioner shall direct and the extended notes of such evidence certified by such clerk or shorthand writer shall be the notes of such oral evidence.

Remit to person of skill

35. The sheriff may remit to any person of skill, or other person, to report on any matter of fact; and, when such remit is made of consent of both parties the report of such person shall be final and conclusive with respect to the matter of the remit. When such a remit is made upon the motion of either party, the expense attending its execution shall in the first instance be paid by the party moving for it. When the remit is on joint motion, or by the sheriff of his own accord, the expense shall in the first instance be paid by the parties equally, unless the sheriff otherwise orders.

Abandonment of cause

[1] **36.** A pursuer may at any diet, before an order granting absolvitor or dismissing the cause has been pronounced, offer to abandon the cause, in which case the sheriff clerk, subject to the approval of the sheriff shall thereupon fix the amount to be paid by the pursuer of the defender's expenses and the cause shall be continued to the first appropriate summary cause roll occurring not sooner than 14 days thereafter. Where the pursuer makes payment to the defender of that amount before the continued diet the sheriff shall dismiss the cause unless the pursuer consents to absolvitor. Where the pursuer fails to pay that amount the defender shall be entitled to decree of absolvitor with expenses.

NOTE

[1] As amended by S.I. 1980 No. 455.

Diligence for recovery of documents

[1] **37.** At any time after a summons has been served the sheriff, on application being made to him by any party, may grant commission and diligence for the recovery of such documents referred to in a specification lodged by the party as the sheriff deems relevant to the cause.

NOTE

[1] As amended by S.I. 1992 No. 429 (effective 4th May 1992).

Optional procedure before executing commission and diligence

38.—(1) Any party who has obtained a commission and diligence for the recovery of documents may, at any time, before executing the same against another party or other parties to the cause, or against any haver, serve upon such party, or parties, or haver, an order with certificate attached in form P.

(2) Such order shall be served by registered or recorded delivery letter, and may be addressed to the care of the known solicitor or solicitors for the party or parties, or for the haver, from whom the documents are sought to be recovered.

(3) Such order shall be obtempered by such party, or parties, or by such haver, in the manner and within the time specified therein.

(4) When the order, certificate in terms thereof and inventoried documents (if any) are received by the sheriff clerk, official intimation shall be given by him forthwith to the solicitors of the parties to the cause that the order has been served and obtempered; and it shall not be competent for any party, other than the party who served the order, to borrow any of the documents until after the expiry of seven days from the date of such official intimation.

(5) If the party who served the order is not satisfied that full production has been made under the specification, or that adequate reasons for non-production have been given, he may execute the commission and diligence in normal form, notwithstanding his adoption in the first instance of the foregoing procedure by order.

(6) In the event of the production under such order as aforesaid of extracts from books whether such extracts are certified or not, the sheriff may, on cause shown, order that the party who served the order shall be at liberty to inspect and take copies of any entries in any books falling under the specification, subject, in the event of any question of confidentiality arising, to the inspection being made, and the copies being taken, at the sight of the commissioner appointed in the interlocutor granting the commission and diligence; and the sheriff may, on cause shown, order the production of any books (not being bankers' books or books of public record) falling under a specification, notwithstanding the production of certified extracts therefrom.

Confidentiality

[1] **39.** In any cause in which, either under the optional procedure provided in rule 38 or in the execution of a commission and diligence in normal form, confidentiality is claimed for any of the documents produced or where an order having been made under rule 68 (*c*) (i) in the Schedule to the Act of 1907 confidentiality is claimed for any of the documents or other property produced, such documents or property shall be enclosed in a separate sealed packet, which shall not be opened or put in process except by authority of the sheriff obtained on the application of the party serving the order, or executing the commission and diligence, after opportunity has been given to the party, parties or haver, making production, to be heard.

NOTE

[1] As substituted by S.I. 1980 No. 455.

Warrant for production of original documents from public records

40.—(1) Where any party to a cause desires to obtain from the Keeper of the Registers of Scotland or from the Keeper of the Records of Scotland production of the originals of any register or deed in his custody, he shall apply by written motion to the sheriff before whom the cause depends, after seven days notice of the intention to make such application has been given in writing to the Keeper in charge of the originals.

(2) Upon such application the sheriff may, by interlocutor, certify that it is necessary for the ends of justice that the application should be granted, and the party may make application by letter (enclosing a copy of the

interlocutor duly certified by the sheriff clerk) addressed to the Principal Clerk of Session for an order from the Lords of Council and Session authorising the Keeper to exhibit the original of any register or deed to the sheriff, and that in the hands of an officer to be selected by the said Keeper.

(3) The Principal Clerk of Session shall submit the same to a Lord Ordinary in Chambers, who, if satisfied, shall grant a warrant on behalf of the Lords of Council and Session. A certified copy of said warrant shall be served upon the Keeper.

(4) The expense attending the transmission and exhibition of such original register or deed shall be defrayed in the first instance by the party or parties on whose application they are exhibited.

Challenge of documents

41.—(1) When a deed or writing is founded on by any party in a cause all objections thereto may be stated and maintained without the necessity of bringing a reduction thereof.

(2) The sheriff may, where an objection is so stated and where an action of reduction would be competent, order the objector to find caution, or to make consignation as he directs.

Conduct of proof or hearing

42. The pursuer shall lead in the proof unless the sheriff on the motion of any of the parties which has been intimated to the other parties not less than seven days before the diet of proof directs otherwise.

Noting of evidence, etc.

[1] **43.**—(1) The sheriff who presides at the proof may make a note of the facts upon which parties are agreed or the parties or their solicitors may, and shall if required by the sheriff, lodge a joint minute of admissions signed by them, of the facts upon which they have reached agreement.

(2) The sheriff shall make for his own use notes of the evidence led at the proof, including any evidence the admissibility of which is objected to, and of the nature of any such objection and he shall retain these notes until after the expiry of the period during which an appeal is competent.

NOTE

[1] As amended by S.I. 1980 No. 455.

Objections to admissibility of evidence

44. Where in the course of a proof an objection is made to the admissibility of any evidence and that line of evidence is not abandoned by the party pursuing it, the sheriff shall, except where he is of the opinion that the evidence is clearly irrelevant or scandalous, note the terms of the objection and allow the evidence to be led reserving the question of its admissibility to be decided by him at the close of the proof.

Documents, etc., referred to during proof

45. Documents or other productions referred to during a proof, the record of any evidence taken in accordance with rule 34, any joint minute of admissions and the report of any person of skill to whom a matter has been remitted shall be retained in the custody of the sheriff clerk until after the expiry of the period during which an appeal is competent.

Parties to be heard at close of proof

[1] **46.**—(1) The sheriff shall hear the parties or their solicitors on all matters connected with the cause including liability for expenses at the close of the proof or at a subsequent diet if for any reason the sheriff continues the cause to such a diet:

Provided that if any party moves that the question of expenses be heard after the sheriff has given his decision the sheriff shall grant that motion.

(2) At the conclusion of that hearing the sheriff may either pronounce his decision or reserve judgment in which latter case he shall within 28 days thereof give his decision in writing and the sheriff clerk shall forthwith intimate it to the parties.

NOTE
[1] As amended by S.I. 1980 No. 455.

Arrestment
47. An arrestment to found jurisdiction or an arrestment on the dependence of an action used prior to service shall fall, unless the summons shall have been served within 42 days from the date of execution of the arrestment. When such an arrestment has been executed, the party using it or his solicitor shall forthwith report the execution to the sheriff clerk the certificate of execution being on the same paper as the summons.

Recall and restriction of arrestment
[1] **48.**—(1) A party may have an arrestment on the dependence of a cause loosed on paying into court, or finding caution to the satisfaction of the sheriff clerk in respect of, the sum claimed together with the sum of £50 in respect of expenses.

(2) On payment into court or the finding of caution to his satisfaction in accordance with paragraph (1), the sheriff clerk shall issue to the party a certificate which shall operate as a warrant for the release of any sum or property arrested and shall send a copy of the certificate to the party who instructed the arrestment.

(3) A party may at any time apply to the sheriff, duly intimated to the party who instructed the arrestment to recall or restrict an arrestment on the dependence of a cause, with or without consignation or caution.

(4) Where an application under paragraph (3) is granted, the sheriff clerk shall, when any condition imposed by the sheriff has been complied with, issue to the applicant a certificate which shall operate as a warrant for the release of any sum or property arrested to the extent ordered by the sheriff.

NOTE
[1] As substituted by S.I. 1992 No. 249 (effective 4th May 1992).

Part II

Special Rules

General
49. The provisions of Part I of these rules shall apply to the summary causes for which special rules are provided in this Part, except in so far as these provisions are inconsistent with the special rules.

Action for Payment of Money

General
[1] **50.**—(1) All actions for payment of money (as defined by section 35(1)(*a*) of the Act of 1971) in which a time to pay direction under the Debtors (Scotland) Act 1987 may be applied for shall, subject to rule 56, be proceeded with in accordance with rules 51 to 55.

(2) All actions for payment of money (as defined by section 35(1)(*a*) of the Act of 1971) in which a time to pay direction may not be applied for shall, subject to rule 56, be proceeded with in accordance with rules 51, 53 and 55.

[2] (3) A summary cause for payment of money shall proceed on a summons in form Aa.

[2] (4) A service copy summons—

(*a*) in form Ab in an action to which paragraph (1) applies; or
(*b*) in form Ac in an action to which paragraph (2) applies,
shall be served on the defender.

NOTES

[1] As substituted for rules 50 and 50A by S.I. 1988 No. 1978.

[2] As substituted for former paras. (3)–(5) by S.I. 1992 No. 249 (effective 4th May 1992).

Notice of intention to appear

[1] **51.**—(1) Where a defender intends—

(*a*) to challenge the jurisdiction of the court;
(*b*) to defend the action;
(*c*) to dispute the amount of the claim; or
(*d*) where he admits the claim, to make an oral application for a time to pay direction (including, where appropriate, an application for recall or restriction of an arrestment),

he shall intimate his intention to appear by completing the appropriate part of the response form attached to the service copy summons and shall lodge it with the sheriff clerk on or before the return day.

(2) A defender who intends to defend a summary cause and has lodged a notice in accordance with paragraph (1) may, at any time prior to the date of the first calling, lodge a written note of the defence which he proposes to state at the first calling.

(3) Where a defender lodges a written note of defence he shall at the same time send a copy to the pursuer.

NOTE

[1] As substituted by S.I. 1988 No. 1978 and as amended by S.I. 1992 No. 249 (effective 4th May 1992).

Applications in writing for time to pay directions etc.

[1] **52.** Where a defender admits the claim and does not intend to appear, he may make an application for a time to pay direction (including, where appropriate, an application for recall or restriction of an arrestment) by completing the appropriate part of the response form attached to the service copy summons and lodging it with the sheriff clerk on or before the return day.

NOTE

[1] As substituted by S.I. 1988 No. 1978 and as amended by S.I. 1992 No. 249 (effective 4th May 1992).

First calling

[1] **53.**—(1) The date of the first calling shall be seven days after the date specified for the return day.

(2) A first calling of a cause shall be held only where a notice of intention to appear has been lodged or an application for a time to pay direction (including, where appropriate, an application for recall or restriction of an arrestment) has been lodged and the pursuer has not minuted in terms of rule 54.

(3) The procedure at the first calling under paragraph (2) and any subsequent procedure shall be in accordance with Part I of these rules.

(4) At the first calling or at any continuation thereof the court shall consider any application for a time to pay direction (including, where appropriate, an application for recall or restriction of an arrestment) whether or not the defender is present or represented.

(5) In any defended cause in which it is competent to do so, the sheriff may, on a written or oral application by the defender at any time before decree is granted, grant a time to pay direction and, where appropriate, an order recalling or restricting an arrestment.

NOTE

[1] As amended by S.I. 1988 No. 1978.

Consent to proposals for payment

[1] **54.** Where an application for a time to pay direction (including, where appropriate, an application for recall or restriction of an arrestment) has been lodged in accordance with rule 52, the cause shall not be called in court if before the date specified in the summons for the first calling the pursuer enters a minute in the Book of Summary Causes intimating that he does not object to the application; and thereafter the court may grant decree accordingly.

NOTE

[1] As substituted by S.I. 1988 No. 1978.

No notice by defender

[1] **55.**—(1) Subject to paragraph (5), where neither a notice of intention to appear nor an application for a time to pay direction (including, where appropriate, an application for recall or restriction of an arrestment) has been lodged in accordance with rules 51 and 52, the cause shall not be called in court and, if before noon on the day prior to the date specified in the summons for the first calling the pursuer, his solicitor, or his solicitor's authorised clerk for whom the solicitor shall be responsible, enters a minute in the Book of Summary Causes or lodges a minute in form V, decree or other order in terms of that minute may be granted on the date so specified. A minute requesting an order for a continuation shall specify the reason why the continuation is necessary.

(2) If the pursuer does not enter a minute in the Book of Summary Causes or lodge a minute in form V in accordance with paragraph (1) the court shall dismiss the cause.

(3) Where a continuation is granted in accordance with paragraph (1) the cause shall call in court on the continued date.

(4) A decree granted in terms of paragraph (1) shall be subject to recall in accordance with the provisions of rule 19.

(5) The sheriff shall not grant decree in the cause unless it appears *ex facie* of the summons that a ground of jurisdiction exists under the Civil Jurisdiction and Judgments Act 1982.

(6) In the case of a defender domiciled in another part of the United Kingdom or in another Contracting State, the sheriff shall not grant decree in absence until it has been shown that the defender has been able to receive the summons in sufficient time to arrange for his defence or that all necessary steps have been taken to that end; and for the purposes of this paragraph—

(*a*) the question as to whether a person is domiciled in another part of the United Kingdom shall be determined in accordance with sections 41 and 42 of the Civil Jurisdiction and Judgments Act 1982;

(*b*) the question as to whether a person is domiciled in another Contracting State shall be determined in accordance with Article 52 of Schedule 1 to that Act; and

(*c*) the term "Contracting State" has the meaning assigned to it by section 1 of that Act.

NOTE

[1] As substituted by S.I. 1978 No. 1805 and amended by S.I. 1986 No. 1946 and 1988 No. 1978.

Shortened period of notice

56. The provisions of rules 51 to 55 shall not apply to the actions referred to in rule 50 where the sheriff has reduced the period of notice in accordance with the proviso to rule 4.

ACTION OF MULTIPLEPOINDING

Pursuer in multiplepoinding

57. A summary cause of multiplepoinding may be raised by any party holding or having an interest in or claim on the fund or subject *in medio* and the sheriff may allow the pursuer his expenses preferably out of the fund *in medio*.

Service of summons

[1] **58.** The summons shall be served on the defenders and claimants so far as known to the pursuer and also on the holder of the fund or subject *in medio* where the pursuer is not the holder.

NOTE

[1] As amended by S.I. 1980 No. 455.

[THE NEXT PAGE IS D 271]

First calling

59. If no defence or objection to the extent of the fund or subject *in medio* has been stated or if any defence stated has been repelled or objection to the extent of the fund or subject *in medio* dealt with the court shall order claims in form S to be lodged within 14 days and shall continue the cause to a claims diet at which all parties may appear or be represented.

Claims diet

60.—(1) At the claims diet if there is no competition between the claimants who appear, the sheriff may ordain the holder of the fund or subject *in medio* to make it over to the claimants in terms of their claims or otherwise and subject to such provisions as to expenses as he directs.

(2) If there is competition between the claimants who appear at the claims diet the sheriff shall fix a diet of proof and shall state the order in which the claimants shall lead at the proof.

Diet of proof

61. At the conclusion of a diet of proof fixed under the provisions of rule 60(2) the sheriff shall dispose of the cause and may order the holder of the fund or subject *in medio* or the sheriff clerk to make it over to such claimants, and in such quantity or amount as he may determine or otherwise as may be appropriate, and shall deal with all questions of expenses.

Advertisement

62. At any stage in the multiplepoinding if it appears to the sheriff that there may be other potential claimants who are not parties to the cause he may order such advertisement or intimation of the order for claims as he thinks proper.

Consignation

63. At any stage in a cause of multiplepoinding the sheriff may order that the fund or subject *in medio* be consigned in the hands of the sheriff clerk or order that any subject *in medio* be sold and the proceeds of sale consigned in the hands of the sheriff clerk.

ACTION OF FURTHCOMING

Expenses included in claim

64. The expenses of bringing a summary cause for furthcoming including the expenses of the arrestment shall be deemed to be part of the arrestor's claim which may be made good out of the arrested fund or subject.

ACTION OF COUNT RECKONING AND PAYMENT

First calling and defences

65.—(1) If at the first calling in an action of count reckoning and payment a defence is stated and is not repelled on the grounds that it is clearly incompetent, a proof on the questions raised by the defence shall be fixed.

(2) If at the first calling liability to account is admitted, or at any diet the defence stated has been repelled, the court shall order accounts to be lodged within 14 days and continue the cause to an accounting diet at which parties must appear or be represented.

Accounting diet

66. At the accounting diet, if there be any objection to the accounts which cannot be disposed of by argument at that diet, the sheriff shall fix a proof.

Diet of proof

67. At the conclusion of a proof fixed under the provisions of rule 66 the sheriff shall dispose of the cause and deal with all questions of expenses as he thinks fit.

Recovery of Possession of Heritable Property

Action raised under section 38 of the Act of 1907

68. A summary cause for the recovery of possession of heritable property raised under section 38 of the Act of 1907 may be at the instance of a proprietor or his factor or any other person by law authorised to pursue a process of removing.

Actions against persons in possession of heritable property without right or title

[1] **68A.** In an action for recovery of possession of heritable property against a person in possession *vi clam aut precario* and without right or title to possess or occupy that property, the sheriff may in his discretion and subject to rule 81A, shorten or dispense with any period of time provided anywhere in these rules. An application by a party under this rule to shorten or dispense with any such period may be made verbally and the provisions in rule 93(1) and (2) shall not apply, but the sheriff clerk shall enter details of any such application in the Book of Incidental Applications.

NOTE

[1] Added by S.I. 1980 No. 455.

Effect of decree

69. When decree for the recovery of possession is granted it shall have the same force and effect as a decree of removing, or a decree of ejection, or a summary warrant of ejection, or a warrant for summary ejection in common form, or a decree pronounced in a summary application for removing, in terms of sections 36, 37 and 38 respectively of the Act of 1907.

Preservation of defender's goods and effects

70. When decree is pronounced and the defender is neither present nor represented, the sheriff may give such directions as he deems proper for the preservation of the defender's goods and effects.

Action for Delivery

Diligence of decree

71. In an action for delivery the court may, when granting decree, grant warrant to search for and take possession of goods and to open shut and lockfast places. This warrant shall only apply to premises occupied by the defender and may only be executed after the expiry of a charge following upon the decree for delivery.

Action of Sequestration for Rent

General

72. Actions of sequestration for rent or in security of rent may be brought as summary causes whether they be brought after the term of payment or *currente termino*.

Appraisal, inventory and execution of citation

[1] **73.**—(1) The officer when he executes the warrant for sequestration shall have the effects appraised by one person who may also be a witness to the sequestration.

(2) An inventory or list of the sequestrated effects with the appraisal and a notice in accordance with form W shall be given to or left for the tenant who shall be cited thereafter in accordance with rule 5.

(3) The certificate of citation and sequestration with the appraisal shall be returned to the sheriff clerk within seven days of such citation.

NOTE

[1] As amended by S.I. 1988 No. 1978.

Procedure after calling

74.—(1) After hearing the cause the sheriff shall dispose of it as he thinks fit and may either recall the sequestration in whole or in part, or grant decree for the rent found due and grant warrant for the sale of the sequestrated effects.

(2) Where warrant for sale of the sequestrated effects has been granted the sale shall be carried out by an officer of court or by such other person as the sheriff may direct by public roup at such place as the sheriff may direct and after advertisement in a newspaper circulating in the district.

(3) Any proceeds of the sale surplus to the sum decerned for, the expenses awarded and the expenses of the sale, shall be returned to the owner, or if he cannot be found, consigned in the hands of the sheriff clerk.

(4) If the effects are not sold, they shall be delivered to the creditor at the appraised value to the amount of the sum decerned for and expenses, and the expenses of the sequestration and sale.

Sale to be reported within 14 days

75. A report of the proceedings in the sequestration and sale of proceeds, or of delivery of the effects, shall be made by the officer to the sheriff clerk within 14 days of the date of sale or delivery.

Recall of sequestration

76. If the tenant either pays to the landlord the rent due, with the expenses of raising the summons and sequestrating, or consigns the rent due, with a sum determined by the sheriff clerk to cover expenses, in the hands of

[THE NEXT PAGE IS D 273]

the sheriff clerk the sheriff clerk shall recall the sequestration by appropriately endorsing the summons or the defender's copy thereof.

Warrant to eject and re-let where premises displenished

77. If the officer who has executed a warrant for sale, or who was instructed to execute such a warrant, reports to the court that the premises are displenished the landlord may apply to the court to obtain a warrant to cite the defender to a fixed diet at which the sheriff may make such order as to ejection, re-letting, security, expenses or otherwise as he considers appropriate. Where a warrant to re-let is granted the rent accruing thereafter shall only be exigible for such period as the tenant continues to occupy the premises.

Warrant to sequestrate, etc.

78. All warrants to sequestrate, inventory, sell, eject or re-let shall be deemed to include authority, if need be, to open shut and lockfast places for the purpose of carrying such warrants into execution.

Action for Interim Aliment

Recall or variation of decree for aliment

[1] **79.**—(1) Applications for the recall or variation of any decree for payment of aliment pronounced in the small debt court under the Small Debt Acts or in a summary cause under the Act of 1971 shall be made by summons.

(2) The court may make such interim orders in relation to such applications or in relation to actions brought under section 3 of the Sheriff Courts (Civil Jurisdiction and Procedure) (Scotland) Act 1963 as it thinks fit.

NOTE

[1] As substituted by S.I. 1980 No. 455.

Moneylenders Action

Application of Act of Sederunt

80. The provisions of the Act of Sederunt to regulate procedure in actions in the Sheriff Court brought by persons registered under the Moneylenders Acts 1900–1927 shall apply *mutatis mutandis* to all summary causes brought by persons registered under the Moneylenders Acts 1900–1927 for the recovery of sums lent by such persons as if all references to a small debt action were references to a summary cause.

Part III

Appeals

Appeal to the sheriff principal

[1] **81.**—(1) To appeal to the sheriff principal the appellant shall lodge with the sheriff clerk not later than 14 days after the date of the final decree, a note of appeal specifying the ground upon which the appeal is to proceed and requesting a stated case and at the same time he shall intimate to the other parties the lodging of this note of appeal.

(2) Within 14 days of the lodging of the note of appeal the sheriff shall prepare and issue a draft stated case containing his findings in fact and law and where necessary a narrative of the proceedings before him, and a note stating the reasons for his decisions in law, and when questions of admissibility or sufficiency of evidence have arisen, a description of the evidence led at the proof to which these questions relate. A copy of the draft stated case shall be sent forthwith by the sheriff clerk to each of the parties.

(3) (*a*) Within 14 days of the issue of the draft stated case each of the parties shall lodge with the sheriff clerk a note of the questions of law which he wishes to raise during the appeal, and a note of any adjustments he desires to have made on the draft stated case. At the same time he shall send a copy of the note of questions of law and of the note of adjustments, if any, to the other parties.

(*b*) The questions of law may relate to matters which were not raised during the proof or at the hearing thereafter.

(*c*) The sheriff may on the motion of any party or of his own accord, and shall, where he proposes to reject any proposed adjustments, allow a hearing on adjustments, and may provide for further procedure prior to the hearing of the appeal as he thinks fit.

(4) Except on cause shown and subject to such conditions by way of expenses or otherwise as the sheriff principal thinks fit, a party shall during the hearing of the appeal be allowed to raise only questions of law of which notice has been given.

(5) Within 14 days after the latest date on which any notes of questions of law or of adjustments (if any) are lodged or in the event of a hearing on adjustments within 14 days of the date of that hearing, the sheriff, after considering these notes and any points made at the hearing, shall state and sign the case which shall include the questions of law stated by each of the parties and such other questions as the sheriff considers appropriate.

(5A) Where the sheriff is temporarily absent from duty for any reason, the sheriff principal may extend any period specified in paragraphs (2) or (5) for such period or periods as he considers reasonable.

(6) The sheriff clerk shall put before the sheriff principal all the documents and productions in the case, and the stated case, send to the parties a copy of the stated case and inform them in writing of the date, time and place of the hearing of the appeal by the sheriff principal.

NOTE

[1] As substituted by S.I. 1980 No. 455 and as amended by S.I. 1992 No. 249 (effective 4th May 1992).

Provisions for appeal in actions for recovery of heritable property to which rule 68A applies

[1] **81A.**—(1) In an action to which rule 68A applies it shall not be competent to shorten or dispense with the period for appeal specified in rule 81 (1); and in such an action notwithstanding the early issue of an extract decree it shall be competent to appeal within that period for appeal.

(2) In such an action the lodging of a note of appeal shall not operate as a sist of diligence unless the sheriff directs otherwise.

NOTE

[1] Added by S.I. 1980 No. 455.

Effect of and abandonment of appeal

82. When a note of appeal has been lodged it shall be available to and may be insisted on by all other parties in the cause notwithstanding that they may not have lodged separate appeals. After a note of appeal has been lodged, the appellant shall not be at liberty to withdraw it without the consent of the other parties which may be incorporated in a joint minute or by leave of the sheriff principal and on such terms as to expenses or otherwise as to him seems proper.

Hearing of appeal

[1] **83.**—(1) The sheriff principal shall hear the parties or their solicitors orally on all matters connected with the appeal including liability for expenses: but if any party moves that the question of liability for expenses be heard after the sheriff principal has given his decision the sheriff principal may grant that motion.

(2) The sheriff principal may permit a party to amend any question of law or to add any new question in accordance with rule 81 (4).

(3) The sheriff principal may—

(*a*) adhere to or vary the decree appealed against; or

(*b*) recall the decree appealed against and substitute another therefor; or

(*c*) remit, if he considers it desirable, to the sheriff, for any reason other than to have further evidence led.

(4) At the conclusion of the hearing the sheriff principal may either pronounce his decision or reserve judgment in which latter case he shall within 28 days thereof give his decision in writing and the sheriff clerk shall forthwith intimate it to the parties.

NOTE

[1] As substituted by S.I. 1980 No. 455.

Appeal to the Court of Session

[1] **84.**—(1) To obtain a certificate that a cause is suitable for appeal to the Court of Session an application for a certificate of suitability by the sheriff principal in form T shall be lodged with the sheriff clerk within 14 days of the date of the final decree.

(2) The sheriff clerk shall put the application for a certificate of suitability before the sheriff principal who without any further hearing of the parties or their solicitors shall grant or refuse the certificate.

(3) The sheriff clerk shall inform the parties in writing of the sheriff principal's decision and if the certificate is granted the applicant if he wishes to pursue the appeal shall not later than 21 days after the granting of the certificate, lodge with the sheriff clerk a note of appeal, written and signed by him or his solicitor on a separate sheet, and bearing the date on which it is signed, as nearly as may be in the following terms:—"The (pursuer, defender or other party) appeals to the Court of Session": all in terms of rule 268 (a) of the Act of Sederunt (Rules of Court, consolidation and amendment) 1965 as amended (hereinafter referred to as the Rules of Court).

(4) Within four days after the lodging of a note of appeal to the Court of Session the sheriff clerk shall transmit to the deputy principal clerk the note of appeal together with the documents put before the sheriff principal in terms of rule 81 (6), and a certified copy of the sheriff principal's final decree and of any written statement of the grounds of his decision made in terms of rule 86, all of which, for the purposes of rule 268 (b) of the Rules of Court, shall be deemed to be the process.

(5) The certificate of the intimation made by the sheriff clerk in terms of rule 268 (c) of the Rules of Court shall be sub-joined to the note of appeal.

NOTE

[1] As amended by S.I. 1980 No. 455.

Sheriff to regulate interim possession

85. Notwithstanding an appeal the sheriff shall have power to regulate all matters relating to interim possession, to make any order for the preservation of any property to which the action relates or for its sale, if perishable, or for the preservation of evidence, or to make in his discretion any interim order which a due regard for the interests of the parties may require. Such orders shall not be subject to review except by the appellate court at the hearing of the appeal.

Appeal in relation to a time to pay direction

[1] **85A.**—(1) This rule applies to appeals to the sheriff principal or to the Court of Session which relate solely to any application in connection with a time to pay direction.

(2) Rules 81, 81A, 82, 83(2) and 84 shall not apply to appeals under this rule.

(3) An application for leave to appeal against a decision in an application for a time to pay direction or any order connected therewith shall be made in writing, within seven days of that decision, to the sheriff who made the decision and shall specify the question of law upon which the appeal is to proceed.

(4) Where leave to appeal is granted, the appeal shall be lodged and intimated by the appellant to the other party within 14 days of the order granting leave and the sheriff shall state in writing his reasons for his original decision.

(5) An appeal to the sheriff principal shall proceed in accordance with paragraphs (1), (3) and (4) [of] rule 83.

(6) In an appeal to the Court of Session from the sheriff or the sheriff principal—

(*a*) there shall be specified in the appeal the name and address of the solicitor in Edinburgh who will be acting for the appellant; and

(*b*) the sheriff clerk shall transmit within four days to the Deputy Principal Clerk of Session—

(i) all documents and productions in the case;

(ii) a certified copy of the final decree;

(iii) the application for leave to appeal and the decision thereon;

(iv) the note of appeal;

(v) the sheriff's statement of reasons and, where appropriate, the sheriff principal's decision,

all of which shall be deemed to be the sheriff court process.

(7) Within the period of four days mentioned in paragraph (6)(*b*), the sheriff clerk shall send written notice of the appeal to the other party and a certificate of intimation of written notice of the appeal shall be appended by him to the note of appeal.

NOTE

[1] Inserted by S.I. 1988 No. 1978.

PART IV

DECREE

Pronouncement of decision

86. The sheriff principal if he pronounces his decision at the conclusion of the hearing of the appeal and the sheriff if he pronounces his decision at the conclusion of the hearing referred to in rule 46 shall state briefly the grounds of his decision including the reason for his decision on any questions of law or of admissibility of evidence. If the decision is pronounced after reserving judgment he shall give to the sheriff clerk a statement of his decision along with a brief note of the foregoing matters a copy of which shall be sent by the sheriff clerk to each of the parties along with the copy of the decision.

Final decree

[1] **87.** The final decree of the sheriff principal or the sheriff shall be pronounced, where expenses are awarded, only after expenses have been dealt with in accordance with rule 88.

NOTE

[1] As substituted by S.I. 1980 No. 455.

Expenses

[1] **88.**—[2] (1) Subject to paragraphs (2), (2A) and (2B) of this rule, the sheriff clerk shall, with the approval of the sheriff, assess the amount of expenses including the fees and outlays of witnesses awarded in any cause, in accordance with the statutory table of fees of solicitors appropriate to the summary cause.

(2) A party litigant, who is not represented and who would have been entitled to expenses if he had been represented by a solicitor or an advocate, may be awarded any outlays or expenses to which he might be found entitled by virtue of the Act of 1975 or any enactment under that Act.

(2A) A party who—

(*a*) is or has been represented by an authorised lay representative;

(*b*) but for that representation, would have been regarded as a party litigant; and

(*c*) would have been found entitled to expenses if he had been represented by a solicitor or an advocate,

may be awarded any outlays or expenses to which a party litigant might be found entitled by virtue of the Act of 1975 or any enactment made under that Act.

(2B) A party who is not an individual, and—

(i) is or has been represented by an authorised lay representative;

(ii) if unrepresented, could not represent itself; and

(iii) would have been found entitled to expenses if it had been represented by a solicitor or an advocate,

may be awarded any outlays to which a party litigant might be found entitled under the Act of 1975 or any enactment made under that Act.

(3) In every cause including an appeal where expenses are awarded the sheriff clerk shall in open court or in private hear the parties or their solicitors on the claims for expenses including fees, if any, and outlays.

(4) Except where the sheriff principal or the sheriff has reserved judgment or where he orders otherwise, the hearing on the claim for expenses shall take place immediately he pronounces his decision. When this hearing is not held immediately the sheriff clerk shall fix the date, time and place when he shall hear the parties or their solicitors in private thereon. The successful party's account of expenses shall be sent to the sheriff clerk and to each of the other parties at least seven days before this hearing.

(5) The sheriff clerk shall fix the amount of these expenses and shall report his decision to the sheriff principal or the sheriff in open court for his approval at a diet which the sheriff clerk has intimated to the parties. The sheriff principal or the sheriff, after hearing parties or their solicitors if objections are stated, shall pronouce final decree including decree for payment of expenses as approved by him. In an appeal the sheriff may pronounce this decree on behalf of the sheriff principal.

(6) Failure by any party to comply with any of the foregoing provisions of this rule or failure of the successful party or parties to appear at the hearing on expenses shall be reported by the sheriff clerk to the sheriff principal or the sheriff in open court at a diet which the sheriff clerk has intimated to the parties, and the sheriff principal or sheriff shall, unless sufficient cause be shown pronounce decree on the merits of the cause and find no expenses due to or by any party. Such decree shall be held to be the final decree for the purposes of these rules.

(7) The sheriff principal or sheriff may, if he thinks fit, on the application of the solicitor of any party to whom expenses may be awarded, made at or before the time of the final decree being pronounced grant decree in favour of that solicitor for the expenses of the cause.

NOTES

[1] As amended by S.I. 1980 No. 455 and 1991 No. 821.

[2] As substituted by S.I. 1992 No. 429 (effective 4th May 1992).

Extract of decree

[1] **89.**—(1) Extract of a decree signed by the sheriff clerk may be issued only after the lapse of 14 days from the granting of the decree: Provided that in actions other than actions to which rule 68A applies if an appeal has been lodged the extract may not be issued until the appeal has been disposed of.

(2) The extract decree which may be written on the summons or on a separate paper may be in one of the forms U1 to U14 and shall be warrant for all lawful diligence proceeding thereon.

NOTE

[1] As amended by S.I. 1980 No. 455.

PART V

MISCELLANEOUS

Poindings

90. The references in sections 23 and 25 of the Debtors (Scotland) Act 1838 to "2 valuators" and "witnesses" shall for the purpose of any poinding following on a summary cause be substituted by references to "1 valuator" and "witness."

Charge

[1] **91.**—(1) The period for payment specified in any charge following on a decree for payment granted in summary cause shall be—

(*a*) 14 days if the person on whom it is served is within the United Kingdom; and

(*b*) 28 days if he is outside the United Kingdom or his whereabouts are unknown.

(2) The period in respect of any other form of charge on a summary cause decree shall be 14 days.

NOTE

[1] As substituted by S.I. 1988 No. 1978.

Applications in same cause for variation, etc., of decree

[1] **92.**—(1) Where by virtue of any enactment the sheriff, without a new summary cause being initiated, may order—

(*a*) a decree granted in a summary cause to be varied, discharged or rescinded, or

(*b*) the execution of that decree in so far as it has not already been executed to be sisted or suspended

the party requesting the court to make such an order shall do so by lodging a minute to that effect.

(2) On the lodging of such a minute by the pursuer in a summary cause the sheriff clerk shall grant warrant to cite the defender:

Provided that the pursuer has returned the summons and extract decree in the summary cause.

(3) On the lodging of such a minute by the defender in the summary cause the sheriff clerk shall grant warrant to cite the pursuer ordaining him to return the summons and extract decree in the summary cause and may, where appropriate, grant interim sist of execution of the decree.

(4) The minute shall be heard in court only when seven days' notice of the minute and warrant has been given;

Provided that the sheriff may on cause shewn, alter the said period subject to there being a minimum period of two days.

(5) This rule shall not apply to any proceedings under the Debtors (Scotland) Act 1987 or to proceedings which may be subject to the provisions of that Act.

NOTE
[1] As amended by S.I. 1988 No. 1978.

Incidental applications

93.—(1) Except where otherwise provided, any application incidental to a pending summary cause shall be in writing and shall only be heard after two days' notice has been given to the other party or parties.

(2) The sheriff clerk shall keep a book to be known as the Book of Incidental Applications in which shall be entered all applications incidental to a pending summary cause, with the exception of minutes presented under the provisions of rules 19 (1) and 92 (1) and minutes entered in the Book of Summary Causes under the provisions of rules 54 and 55 (1). There shall be set forth in the said book the following particulars where appropriate—

(*a*) the names of the parties together with a clear reference to the entry in the Book of Summary Causes relating to the Summons;
(*b*) whether parties are present or absent at the hearing of the application, and the names of their representatives;
(*c*) the nature of the application, and
(*d*) any interlocutor issued or order made.

The said Book shall be signed by the sheriff on each day on which Incidental Applications are heard.

(3) The Book of Incidental Applications kept by the sheriff clerk shall be open for inspection during office hours to all concerned without fee.

[THE NEXT PAGE IS D 279]

[1]FORM Aa

SUMMARY CAUSE SUMMONS
CLAIM FOR PAYMENT
OF MONEY

Official Use Only
Summons No.
Return day
Calling date

Sheriff Court (name, address and tel. no.) **1**

Name and address of person making the claim (PURSUER) **2**

Name and address of person from whom money is claimed (DEFENDER) **3**

4 **CLAIM**
The Pursuer claims from the defender the sum of £ ... with interest on that sum at the rate of % annually from the date of service and expenses.

5

RETURN DAY	19		
CALLING DATE	19	at	am

*Sheriff Clerk to delete as appropriate

The pursuer is authorised to serve a service copy summons in *Form Ab/Form Ac on the defender not less than 21 days before the Return Day shown in the box above. The summons is warrant for arrestment on the dependence.

Sheriff Clerk Depute Date

Name, full address and tel. no. of pursuer's solicitor (if any)

6

NOTE:

The pursuer should complete boxes 1, 2, 3, 4 and 6 on this page, and the statement of claim on page 2.
The Sheriff Clerk will complete box 5.

STATE CLAIM HERE OR ATTACH A STATEMENT OF CLAIM
(to be completed by the pursuer)

1. The defender has refused or delayed to pay the sum claimed.
2. The details of the claim are*

*If necessary attach a separate sheet.

FOR OFFICIAL USE ONLY

DEFENCE OR STATEMENT OF DEFENCE

NOTE
[1] Forms Aa–Ac as substituted for former forms A and Aa by S.I. 1992 No. 249 (effective 4th May 1992).

---

[1]Form Ab

SUMMARY CAUSE SUMMONS
DEFENDER'S COPY
CLAIM FOR PAYMENT
OF MONEY WHERE TIME TO
PAY DIRECTION MAY BE
APPLIED FOR

Official Use Only
Summons No.

Sheriff Court (name, address and tel. no.)	**1**	
Name and address of person making the claim (PURSUER)	**2**	
Name and address of person from whom money is claimed (DEFENDER)	**3**	

4

CLAIM

1. The pursuer claims from you the sum of £ . . . (you will find details of the claim on page 2).

and

2. The pursuer claims interest on that sum at the rate of % annually from the date on which this summons was served on you.

and

3. The pursuer also claims from you the Court expenses.

5

RETURN DAY	19		
CALLING DATE	19	at	am

CITATION OF DEFENDER

Place Date

, defender,

you are served with this summons. The pursuer has been authorised by the Court to serve it on you.

SOLICITOR/SHERIFF OFFICER

Name, full address and tel. no. of pursuer's solicitor (if any)

6

NOTE:
The pursuer should complete boxes 1, 2, 3, 4 and 6 on this page, the statement of claim on page 2, and Section A on page 4 before service on the defender. The person serving the summons will complete box 5.

[*Page 2*]

STATEMENT OF CLAIM

1. The defender has refused or delayed to pay the sum claimed.

2. The details of the claim are*

*If necessary attach a separate sheet.

WHAT CAN I DO ABOUT THIS SUMMONS?

Decide whether you admit owing the money or not and what you want to do about it. Then look at the section on this page which covers your decision and follow the instructions in that section. You will find the RETURN DAY and the CALLING DATE on page 1. A leaflet "Guide to Summary Cause Procedure in the Sheriff Court" can be obtained from the sheriff clerk. If you wish further advice contact any Citizens Advice Bureau, Consumer Advice Centre or Trading Standards or Consumer Protection Department or a solicitor.

DO NOTHING

If you do nothing about this summons the court may order you to pay the pursuer the sum claimed including interest and expenses.

ADMIT THE CLAIM—and pay in full
If you want to avoid a court order against you, the whole sum claimed including interest and any expenses due should be paid **to the pursuer or his solicitor** in good time **before the return day**.

ADMIT THE CLAIM—and make written application to pay by instalments or by deferred lump sum
Complete and sign box 1 opposite on page 3 and section B on page 4, and return pages 3 and 4 to the court to arrive **on or before the return day.** If the pursuer does not accept your offer, the court will decide how the amount claimed is to be paid.

ADMIT THE CLAIM—and attend court to make application to pay by instalments or deferred lump sum
Complete and sign box 2 on page 3. Return pages 3 and 4 to the court to arrive **on or before the return day. You must attend or be represented at court on the calling date.** Your representative may be a solicitor or someone else having your authority. It may help you or your representative to bring pages 1 and 2 to the court. If you fail to return pages 3 and 4 as directed or if having returned them, you fail to attend or be represented, the court may decide the claim in your absence.

DENY THE CLAIM—and attend court to dispute the sum claimed or state a defence or challenge the jurisdiction of the court
Complete and sign box 3 on page 3. Return pages 3 and 4 to the court to arrive **on or before the return day. You must attend or be represented at court on the calling date.** Your representative may be a solicitor or someone else having your authority. It may help you or your representative to bring pages 1 and 2 to the court. **If you fail to return pages 3 and 4 as directed or if having returned them, you fail to attend or be represented, the court may decide the claim in your absence.**

WRITTEN NOTE OF PROPOSED DEFENCE—You may also send to the court a written note of the defence you propose to state at the calling date. You can send this note at any time **before the date of the calling date.** However you must still attend or be represented at court on the calling date.
If you decide to send a note you must send a copy of it to the pursuer.

KEEP PAGES 1 AND 2—YOU MAY NEED THEM AT A LATER STAGE

[*Page 3*]

YOUR RESPONSE TO THE SUMMONS

CLAIM ADMITTED—Under the Debtors (Scotland) Act 1987

The Act gives you the right to apply to the court for a "time to pay direction" which is an order saying that you can pay any sum you are ordered to pay to the pursuer either in instalments or by deferred lump sum. A deferred lump sum means that you must pay all the amount at one time within a specified period set by the court.

In addition when making a "time to pay direction" the court may recall or restrict an arrestment made on your property by the pursuer in connection with the action or debt (for example your bank account may have been frozen).

If the court makes a "time to pay direction" a copy of the court order (called an extract decree) will be served on you by the pursuer telling you when payment should start or when it is you have to pay the lump sum.

If the court does not make a "time to pay direction" and makes an order for immediate payment against you, an order to pay (called a charge) may be served on you if you do not pay.

Box 1

ADMIT THE CLAIM—and make written application to pay by instalments or deferred lump sum

I do not intend to defend the case but admit the claim and wish to make a WRITTEN APPLICATION about payment.

I have completed the application form in section B on page 4.

Signature ....

Box 2

ADMIT THE CLAIM—INTENTION TO APPEAR

I admit the claim and INTEND TO APPEAR OR BE REPRESENTED IN COURT.

Signature ....

Box 3

DENY THE CLAIM—INTENTION TO APPEAR

I do not admit the claim. I intend to appear or be represented in court to state my defence.

*I intend to challenge the jurisdiction of the court.
*I attach a note of my proposed defence which has been copied to the pursuer.

Signature .... *Delete as necessary

PLEASE REMEMBER

Send pages 3 and 4 to the court to arrive **on or before the return day** if you have signed any of the responses above. If you have admitted the claim do not send any payment to the court.

[*Page 4*]

SHERIFF COURT (including address)

SECTION A
This section must be completed before service

Summons No. ________
Return day________
Calling date ________

COURT STAMP
(OFFICIAL USE ONLY)

Pursuer's full name and address

Defender's full name and address

SECTION B

APPLICATION IN WRITING FOR A TIME TO PAY DIRECTION UNDER THE DEBTORS (SCOTLAND) ACT 1987 (payment by instalments or deferred lump sum)

CLAIM ADMITTED—I admit the claim and make application
(1) To pay by instalments of £..........

(Tick one box only)

EACH.... WEEK ☐ FORTNIGHT ☐ MONTH ☐

OR

(2) To pay the sum ordered in one payment within .... WEEKS/MONTHS

Signature ....

To help the Court please provide details of your financial position in the boxes below.

If necessary attach a separate sheet

My outgoings are:	Weekly ☐	Fortnightly ☐	Monthly ☐
Rent/Mortgage	£		
Heating	£		
Food	£		
HP	£		
Other	£		
Total	£		

My income is:	Weekly ☐	Fortnightly ☐	Monthly ☐
Wages/Pensions	£		
Social Security	£		
Other	£		
Total	£		

Dependent children—how many ☐ Dependent relatives—how many ☐

Here list all capital (if any) for example value of house; amount in bank/ building society account, shares or other investments:

APPLICATION FOR RECALL OR RESTRICTION OF AN ARRESTMENT

I seek the recall or restriction of the arrestment of which the details are as follows:—

Signature.. Date ....

NOTE

[1] Forms Aa–Ac as substituted for former forms A and Aa by S.I. 1992 No. 249 (effective 4th May 1992).

[1]FORM AC

SUMMARY CAUSE SUMMONS
DEFENDER'S COPY
CLAIM FOR PAYMENT OF MONEY

Official Use Only
Summons No.

Sheriff Court (name, address and tel. no.) **1**

Name and address of person making the claim (PURSUER) **2**

Name and address of person from whom money is claimed (DEFENDER) **3**

4 **CLAIM**

1. The pursuer claims from you the sum of £ . . . (you will find details of the claim on page 2).

and

2. The pursuer claims interest on that sum at the rate of % annually from the date on which this summons was served on you.

and

3. The pursuer also claims from you the Court expenses.

5

RETURN DAY	19		
CALLING DATE	19	at	am

CITATION OF DEFENDER

Place Date

, defender,

you are served with this summons. The pursuer has been authorised by the Court to serve it on you.

SOLICITOR/SHERIFF OFFICER

Name, full address and tel. no. of pursuer's solicitor (if any)

6

NOTE:

The pursuer should complete boxes 1, 2, 3, 4 and 6 on this page, the statement of claim on page 2, and Section A on page 3 before service on the defender. The person serving the summons will complete box 5.

[*Page 2*]

STATEMENT OF CLAIM

1. The defender has refused or delayed to pay the sum claimed.

2. The details of the claim are*

*If necessary attach a separate sheet.

WHAT CAN I DO ABOUT THIS SUMMONS?

Decide whether you admit owing the money or not and what you want to do about it. Then look at the section on this page which covers your decision and follow the instructions in that section. You will find the RETURN DAY and the CALLING DATE on page 1. A leaflet "Guide to Summary Cause Procedure in the Sheriff Court" can be obtained from the sheriff clerk. If you wish further advice contact any Citizens Advice Bureau, Consumer Advice Centre, Trading Standards or Consumer Protection Department or a solicitor.

DO NOTHING
If you do nothing about this summons the court may order you to pay the pursuer the sum claimed including interest and expenses.

ADMIT THE CLAIM—and pay in full
If you want to avoid a court order against you, the whole sum claimed including interest and any expenses due should be paid **to the pursuer or his solicitor** in good time **before the return day**.

DENY THE CLAIM—and attend court to dispute the sum claimed or state a defence or challenge the jurisdiction of the court
Complete and sign section B on page 3. Return pages 3 and 4 [*sic*] to the court to arrive **on or before the return day. You must attend or be represented at court on the calling date.** Your representative may be a solicitor or someone else having your authority. It may help you or your representative to bring pages 1 and 2 to the court. **If you fail to return pages 3 and 4** [*sic*] **as directed or if having returned them, you fail to attend or be represented, the court may decide the claim in your absence.**

WRITTEN NOTE OF PROPOSED DEFENCE—You may also send to the court a written note of the defence you propose to state at the calling date. You can send this note at any time **before the date of the calling date.** However you must still attend or be represented at court on the calling date.
If you decide to send a note you must send a copy of it to the pursuer.

KEEP PAGES 1 AND 2—YOU MAY NEED THEM AT A LATER STAGE

[*Page 3*]

SHERIFF COURT (including address)

SECTION A
This section must be completed before service

Summons No. ________
Return day________
Calling date ________

COURT STAMP
(OFFICIAL USE ONLY)

Pursuer's full name and address

Defender's full name and address

YOUR RESPONSE TO THE SUMMONS

SECTION B

DENY THE CLAIM—INTENTION TO APPEAR

I do not admit the claim.
I INTEND TO APPEAR OR BE REPRESENTED IN COURT TO STATE MY DEFENCE.

*I intend to challenge the jurisdiction of the court.
*I attach a note of my proposed defence which has been copied to the pursuer.

Signature .... * delete as necessary

PLEASE REMEMBER

Send this page to the court to arrive **on or before the return day** if you have signed Section B above.

If you have admitted the claim do not send any payment to the court.

NOTE
[1] Forms Aa–Ac as substituted for former forms A and Aa by S.I. 1992 No. 249 (effective 4th May 1992).

[THE NEXT PAGE IS D 281]

[1] FORM B

(Summons for payment of money—shortened period of notice only)

SHERIFF COURT ....

SUMMONS
in the case of

A.B.		Pursuer
	against	
X.Y.		Defender

To the said X.Y.:—

The pursuer claims that in the circumstances described in the statement of claim herewith you should be ordered to pay him the sum of £.................... and asks the court to grant a decree against you ordering you to pay that sum to the pursuer with interest at the rate of ....% annually from .... until payment, and to pay the expenses of this action.

You are therefore required to appear at the place, date and time mentioned below to answer the above claim and take warning that if you do not so appear the pursuer may obtain decree against you in your absence.

The pursuer is hereby authorised to serve a copy of this summons (*insert as appropriate*—together with form Bb) on you not less than .... days before the date on which you are required to appear. If the court requires to hear evidence a date shall be fixed for this purpose and the parties are hereby authorised to cite witnesses to attend on that date to give evidence. This summons is warrant for arrestment on the dependence of the action (and for arrestment to found jurisdiction).

Sheriff Court at (address) ....

On (day and date) ....

At (time) ....

NOTE

[1] As amended by S.I. 1988 No. 1978.

Rule 17A [1] FORM Bb

(Form of Notice to be Served on Defender where Time to Pay Direction may be Applied for under the Debtors (Scotland) Act 1987)

1. The Act gives you the right to apply to the court for a "time to pay direction" which is an order saying that you can pay any sum you are ordered to pay to the pursuer either in instalments or by deferred lump sum. A deferred lump sum means that you must pay all the amount at one time within a specified period set by the court.

2. In addition, when making a "time to pay direction" the court may recall or restrict an arrestment made on your property by the pursuer in connection with the action or debt (for example your bank account may have been frozen).

HOW TO APPLY FOR A TIME TO PAY DIRECTION WHEN CLAIM ADMITTED AND YOU DO NOT WANT TO DEFEND THE ACTION

1. You may apply for a "time to pay direction" by EITHER

(*a*) attending court on the CALLING DATE and asking the court to make a "time to pay direction". If you prefer you may ask a solicitor or someone else to appear for you;

OR

(*b*) completing page 4 of this form and returning it to the sheriff clerk to arrive at least seven days before the CALLING DATE.

The CALLING DATE is .... at .... am.

2. No court fee is payable when making an application for a "time to pay direction" whether you apply by appearing in court or by written application.

3. The court will decide what order is to be made and if a "time to pay direction" is made a copy of the court order (called an extract decree) will be served on you by the pursuer telling you when payment should start or when it is you have to pay the lump sum.

If the Court does not make a "time to pay direction" and makes an order for immediate payment against you, an order to pay (called a charge) may be served on you if you do not pay.

HOW TO COMPLETE THE APPLICATION

1. Section A has been completed already. You should complete section B.

2. (*a*) If you wish to apply to pay by instalments put in the amount you are proposing and tick the appropriate box.
   (*b*) If you wish to apply to pay the full sum due in one deferred payment enter the period of deferment you propose.

3. You should give full details of your financial position in the appropriate boxes.

4. If an arrestment has been made in connection with this action and you wish the court when making a "time to pay direction" to recall or restrict the arrestment enter the appropriate details about what has been arrested and the place and date and attach a schedule of arrestment or a copy.

5. Sign the application where indicated. Keep pages 1 and 2. Return pages 3 and 4 to the court to arrive at least seven days before the CALLING DATE.

SECTION A This section must be completed before service	Sheriff Court (including address)	Summons No. .... calling date ....
Pursuer's full name and address		Defender's full name and address

SECTION B

APPLICATION IN WRITING FOR A TIME TO PAY DIRECTION UNDER THE DEBTORS (SCOTLAND) ACT 1987

CLAIM ADMITTED—I admit the claim and make application
(1) To pay by instalments of £..........

(Tick one box only)

EACH.... WEEK ☐ FORTNIGHT ☐ MONTH ☐

OR

(2) To pay the sum ordered in one payment within ....
WEEKS/MONTHS

Signature ....

TO HELP THE COURT PLEASE PROVIDE DETAILS OF YOUR FINANCIAL POSITION IN THE BOXES BELOW

IF NECESSARY ATTACH A SEPARATE SHEET

My outgoings are:	Weekly ☐	Fortnightly ☐	Monthly ☐
Rent/Mortgage	£		
Heating	£		
Food	£		
HP	£		
Other	£		
Total	£		

My income is:	Weekly ☐	Fortnightly ☐	Monthly ☐
Wages/Pensions	£		
Social Security	£		
Other	£		
Total	£		

Dependants: Children—how many ☐ Dependent relatives—how many ☐

Here list all capital (if any) for example value of house; amount in bank/building society account, shares or other investments:

APPLICATION FOR RECALL OR RESTRICTION OF AN ARRESTMENT

I seek the recall or restriction of the arrestment of which the details are as follows:—

Signature ....

NOTE
[1] Inserted by S.I. 1988 No. 1978.

FORM C

(Summons for Recovery of Possession of Heritable Property)

SHERIFF COURT ....

SUMMONS
in the case of

A.B. Pursuer

against

X.Y. Defender

To the said X.Y.:—

The pursuer claims that in the circumstances described in the statement of claim herewith he is entitled to recover possession of the property at .... and that you refuse or delay to remove therefrom and asks the court to grant decree for removing you, your family, sub-tenants and dependants with your goods and possessions from the said property and for payment by you of the expenses of this action.

You are therefore required to appear at the place, date and time mentioned below to answer the above claim and take warning that if you do not so appear the pursuer may obtain decree against you in your absence.

The pursuer is hereby authorised to serve a copy of this summons on you not less than .... days before the date on which you are required to appear. If the court requires to hear evidence a date shall be fixed for this purpose and the parties are hereby authorised to cite witnesses to attend on that date to give evidence.

Sheriff Court at (address) ....

On (day and date) ....

At (time) ....

FORM D

(Summons of Sequestration for Rent)

SHERIFF COURT ....

SUMMONS
in the case of

A.B. Pursuer

against

X.Y. Defender

To the said X.Y.:—

The pursuer claims that in the circumstances described in the statement of claim herewith you owe [and/or will owe] him the sum of £ .... as rent for the premises at .... and that you refuse or delay to make payment and asks the court to grant warrant to list, value, sequestrate, and if need be secure the goods and effects within the said premises; to grant a decree ordering you to pay the said sum to the pursuer and the expenses of this action; and to grant warrant to sell the said goods and effects in payment of the said rent and expenses.

You are therefore required to appear at the place, date and time mentioned below to answer the above claim and take warning that if you do not so appear the pursuer may obtain decree against you in your absence. The pursuer is hereby authorised to sequestrate inventory and appraise your effects and thereafter to serve a copy of this summons on you not less than .... days before the date on which you are required to appear. If the court requires to hear evidence a date shall be fixed for this purpose and the parties are hereby authorised to cite witnesses for both parties to attend to give evidence on that date.

Sheriff Court at (address) ....
On (day and date) ....
At (time) ....

FORM E

(Summons of Multiplepoinding)

SHERIFF COURT ....

SUMMONS
in the case of

A.B. Pursuer

against

C.D.
E.F.
G.H.
and I.J. Defenders and/or Claimants

To the said C.D., E.F., G.H. and I.J.:—

The pursuer claims that in the circumstances described in the statement of claim herewith (pursuer/first named defender) is the holder of a fund or subject valued at £.......... on which competing claims are being made by the said C.D., E.F., G.H. and I.J.; the pursuer asks the court to grant a decree finding the holder of the fund or subject liable to make a single payment or delivery of the fund or subject, under deduction of the expenses of the action, to whomsoever shall be found by the court to be entitled thereto. You are therefore all required to appear at the place, date and time mentioned below to put forward your interest and take warning that if you do not so appear the case may proceed without your interest being considered.

The pursuer is hereby authorised to serve a copy of this summons on you not less than .... days before the date on which you are required to appear. If the court requires to hear evidence a date shall be fixed for this purpose and the parties are hereby authorised to cite witnesses to attend to give evidence on that date.

Sheriff Court at (address) ....
On (day and date) ....
At (time) ....

[THE NEXT PAGE IS D 283]

FORM F

(Summons of Furthcoming)

SHERIFF COURT ....

SUMMONS
in the case of

A.B.		Pursuer
	against	
X.Y.		Arrestee
	and	
C.D.		Common Debtor

To the said X.Y. and C.D.:—

The pursuer claims that in the circumstances described in the statement of claim herewith you the said C.D. are due to him the sum of £ .... and that he lawfully arrested in the hands of you the said X.Y. the goods or money described overleaf to the value of £.......... which ought to be made forthcoming to him; and asks the court to order you the said X.Y. and you the said C.D. for your interest to make forthcoming, pay and deliver to the pursuer the money, goods and effects arrested or so much thereof as will pay the sum of £.......... owing to the pursuer, together with the expenses of this action. In the event of the arrested funds being insufficient to meet the expenses of this action, the pursuer claims these expenses from you, the said C.D.

You are both therefore required to appear at the place, date and time mentioned below to answer the above claim and take warning that if you do not so appear the pursuer may obtain decree against you in your absence.

The pursuer is hereby authorised to serve a copy of this summons on you not less than .... days before the date on which you are required to appear. If the court requires to hear evidence a date shall be fixed for this purpose and the parties are hereby authorised to cite witnesses to attend to give evidence on that date.

Sheriff Court at (address) ....

On (day and date) ....

At (time) ....

[1] FORM G

(Summons for Delivery)

SHERIFF COURT ....

SUMMONS
in the case of

A.B.		Pursuer
	against	
X.Y.		Defender

To the said X.Y.:—

The pursuer claims that in the circumstances described in the statement of claim herewith he has right to possession of the article(s) there listed and asks the court to grant decree ordering you to deliver the said article(s) to the pursuer (or, alternatively, in the event of non-delivery ordering you to pay to the pursuer the sum of £.......... with interest at the rate of ....% per annum from .... until payment) and to pay the expenses of this action. You are therefore required to appear at the place, date and time mentioned below to answer the above claim and take warning that if you do not so appear the pursuer may obtain decree against you in your absence.

The pursuer is hereby authorised to serve a copy of this summons (*insert as appropriate*—together with form Bb) on you not less than .... days before the date on which

you are required to appear. If the court requires to hear evidence a date shall be fixed for this purpose and the parties are hereby authorised to cite witnesses to attend to give evidence on that date. This summons is warrant for arrestment on the dependence of the action (and for arrestment to found jurisdiction).
Sheriff Court at (address) ....
On (day and date) ....
At (time) ....

NOTE
[1] As amended by S.I. 1988 No. 1978.

---

[1] FORM H

(Summons for Implement)

SHERIFF COURT ....

SUMMONS
in the case of

A.B. Pursuer

against

X.Y. Defender

To the said X.Y.:—

The pursuer claims that in the circumstances described in the statement of claim herewith you are obliged to ....
....
and asks the court to grant decree against you ordering you to implement the said obligation (or, alternatively, ordering you to pay the sum of £ .... to the pursuer with interest at the rate of ....% annually from the date of decree until payment) and to pay the expenses of this action.

You are therefore required to appear at the place, date and time mentioned below to answer the above claim and take warning that if you do not so appear the pursuer may obtain decree against you in your absence. The pursuer is hereby authorised to serve a copy of this summons (*insert as appropriate*—together with form Bb) on you not less than .... days before the date on which you are required to appear. If the court requires to hear evidence a date shall be fixed for this purpose and the parties are hereby authorised to cite witnesses to attend to give evidence on that date. This summons is warrant for arrestment on the dependence of the action (and for arrestment to found jurisdiction).
Sheriff Court at (address) ....
On (day and date) ....
At (time) ....

NOTE
[1] As amended by S.I. 1988 No. 1978.

[1] FORM I

(Summons for Count, Reckoning and Payment)

SHERIFF COURT ....

SUMMONS
in the case of

A.B. Pursuer

against

X.Y. Defender

To the said X.Y.:—

The pursuer claims that in the circumstances described in the statement of claim herewith you have intromitted with (describe the fund or estate) in which the pursuer has an interest and asks the court to grant decree for count and reckoning with him for your said intromissions and for payment to the pursuer by you of the balance found due to him (or otherwise of the sum of £..........) with interest at the rate of ....% annually from the date of decree until payment and for payment by you of the expenses of this action.

You are therefore required to appear at the place, date and time mentioned below to answer the above claim and to lodge accounts of your said intromissions, or to show cause why you should not do so, and take warning that if you do not so appear decree may be pronounced in your absence.

The pursuer is hereby authorised to serve a copy of this summons (*insert as appropriate*—together with form Bb) on you not less than .... days before the date on which you are required to appear. If the court requires to hear evidence a date shall be fixed for this purpose and the parties are hereby authorised to cite witnesses to attend to give evidence on that date. This summons is warrant for arrestment on the dependence of the action (and for arrestment to found jurisdiction).

Sheriff Court at (address) ....
On (day and date) ....
At (time) ....

NOTE

[1] As amended by S.I. 1988 No. 1978.

---

[1] FORM J

X.Y. defender, you are hereby served with a copy of the above (or attached) summons.

To be signed by pursuer's solicitor
or officer of court.

NOTE

[1] As amended by S.I. 1988 No. 1978.

FORM K

(Place and date) I .... hereby certify that upon the .... day of .... I duly cited X.Y. the defender to answer to the foregoing summons. This I did by (set forth the mode of service).

To be signed by pursuer's solicitor
or officer of court.

[1] FORM Ka

This letter contains a citation to or intimation from .... Sheriff Court, if delivery of the letter cannot be made it is to be returned immediately to the Sheriff Clerk at ....
(insert address)

NOTE
[1] Added by S.I. 1980 No. 455.

FORM L

A summary cause has been raised in .... Sheriff Court by A.B. pursuer against C.D. defender, whose last known address was
....
(The cause will be called in court on .... at ....). If the said C.D. wishes to defend the cause he should immediately contact the sheriff clerk .... Tel. No: ....

To be signed by pursuer's solicitor
or officer of court.

[1] FORM M

Sheriff Court ....
No. of Case ....
.... against ....

The (pursuer or defender) moves the court to recall the decree pronounced on .... 19 .... in this case, [and in which execution of the charge/arrestment was effected on .... 19....].

To be signed by party or
his solicitor or authorised lay representative (if any).

NOTE
[1] As amended by S.I. 1991 No. 821.

---

[1] FORM N

A.B. (design) you are required to attend at .... Sheriff Court on .... 19.... at .... as a witness for the .... in the action at the instance of C.D. (design) against E.F. (design) (and to bring with you ....) and if you fail to attend you may be ordered to pay a penalty not exceeding £250.

To be signed by pursuer's solicitor
or officer of court (full name, address and
telephone number).

Note:
Within certain specified limits claims for necessary outlays and loss of earnings will be met. Claims should be made to the person who has cited you to attend court and proof of any loss of earnings should be given to that person.

NOTE
[1] As amended by S.I. 1980 No. 455 and S.I. 1992 No. 249 (effective 4th May 1992).

FORM O

I certify that on .... 19...., I duly cited A.B. (design) to attend at .... Sheriff Court on .... 19.... at .... as a witness for the .... in the action at the instance of C.D. (design) against E.F. (design) (and I required him to bring with him ....). This I did by ....

To be signed by pursuer's solicitor
or officer of court.

FORM P

(Order of Court and Certificate in
Optional Procedure for Recovery of Documents)
Order by the Sheriff Court at ....
In the cause (reference No.)
in which
A.B. (design) is Pursuer
and
C.D. (design) is Defender

To (name and designation of party or parties or haver, from whom the documents are sought to be recovered)

Take notice that you are hereby required to produce to the sheriff clerk at .... within 7 days of the service upon you of this order—

(1) this order itself which must be produced intact;
(2) a certificate signed and completed in terms of the form appended hereto; and
(3) all documents in your possession falling within the specification enclosed herewith, together with a list or inventory of such documents signed by you as relative to this order and your certificate.

Production may be made either by lodging the above at the said office of the sheriff clerk, or by registered or recorded delivery letter or registered postal packet enclosing the same, and addressed to the said sheriff clerk at said office.
(Signature and business address of the
solicitor of the party in whose favour
commission and diligence has been granted)
(Date) ....

Note: If you claim confidentiality for any of the documents produced by you, such documents must nevertheless be produced, but may be placed in a special sealed enclosure by themselves, marked "confidential".

CERTIFICATE

I hereby certify with reference to the order of the sheriff court at .... in the cause (reference No.) and the relative specification of documents, served upon me and marked respectively X.Y.—

(1) that the documents which are produced and which are enumerated in the inventory signed by me and marked Z, are the whole documents in my possession falling under the specification

or

that I have no documents in my possession falling within the specification.

(2) that, to the best of my knowledge and belief, there are in existence other documents falling within the specification, but not in my possession, namely (describe them by reference to one or more of the descriptions of documents in the specification), which were last seen by me on or about (date), at (place), in the hands of (name and address of the person)

or

that I know of the existence of no documents in the possession of any person, other than myself, which fall within the specification.

(Signed)

FORM Q

[Revoked by S.I. 1992 No. 249 (effective 4th May 1992).]

FORM R

[Revoked by S.I. 1992 No. 249 (effective 4th May 1992).]

FORM S

I, E.F., hereby claim to be preferred on the fund in the multiplepoinding raised in the name of A.B. against C.D. for £......... of principal due to me by [state the ground of claim, including a reference to any document founded upon in support thereof] with interest from .... with expenses.

To be signed by claimant or his solicitor.

[1] FORM T

A.B., pursuer, or C.D., defender, in the summary cause at the instance of A.B. against C.D. hereby moves the sheriff principal to certify that the cause is suitable for appeal to the Court of Session.

To be signed by the party or his solicitor.

NOTE

[1] As substituted by S.I. 1980 No. 455.

[1] FORM U1

(Extract decree for payment)

(Place, date) In this summary cause summons at the instance of the said pursuer(s) against the defender(s)(name) .... the Sheriff granted decree .... against the .... defender(s) for payment to the pursuer(s) of the sum of £...... with interest at the rate of ....% annually from .... until payment and £...... of expenses: and granted Warrant for all lawful execution hereon.

Date of Extract Decree Sheriff Clerk

NOTE

[1] As amended by S.I. 1978 No. 112.

Rule 89(2)

[1] FORM U2

(Extract Decree for Payment (Instalments)

At (*place*), (*date*). In this summary cause summons at the instance of the pursuer(s) (*name*) against the defender(s) (*name*), the Sheriff granted decree against the defender(s) for payment to the pursuer(s) of the sum of £ with interest at the rate of % annually from until payment and £ of expenses; the court under section 1(1) of the Debtors (Scotland) Act 1987 directed that said sums, and interest be payable by instalments of £ per . The first instalment being payable within after intimation of an extract of this decree and continuing thereafter by regular payment of the instalments until the whole of the sums be paid. If the defender allows a sum amounting to not less than the aggregate of two instalments to remain unpaid at the date when the next instalment becomes due, or if any sum is outstanding three weeks after the date on which the last instalment becomes due, then the right to pay by instalments shall cease; and, in that event, the Sheriff granted warrant for all lawful execution hereon for the whole sums and interest for which decree was granted so far as unpaid.

(*Signed*)

Sheriff Clerk

(*Date of Extract Decree*)

NOTE

[1] As substituted by S.I. 1988 No. 1978.

[THE NEXT PAGE IS D 290/3]

Rule 89(2) [1] FORM U2A

(Extract Decree for Payment by Lump Sum—Time to Pay Direction)

At (*place*), (*date*). In this summary cause summons at the instance of the pursuer(s) (*name*) against the defender(s) (*name*), the Sheriff granted decree against the defender(s) for payment to the pursuer(s) of the sum of £ with interest at the rate of % annually from until payment and £ of expenses; the court under section 1(1) of the Debtors (Scotland) Act 1987 directed that the sums, and interest, be payable within from the date of intimation of an extract of this decree. If any sum payable remains unpaid 24 hours after the end of the period specified in this extract, the right to pay by a lump sum shall cease to have effect; and in that event, the Sheriff granted warrant for all lawful execution hereon for the whole sums and interest for which decree was granted so far as unpaid.

(Signed)

Sheriff Clerk

(Date of Extract Decree)

NOTE
[1] Substituted by S.I. 1988 No. 1978.

---

[1] FORM U3

(Extract decree for recovery of possession of heritable property)

(Place, date) In this summary cause summons at the instance of the said pursuer(s) against the defender(s) (name) .... the Sheriff granted Warrant for Ejecting the defender [and others mentioned in the summons] from the subject specified, such Ejection not being sooner than (date) at 12 noon: and granted decree against the defender for payment to the pursuer of £......... of expenses: and granted Warrant for all lawful execution hereon.
Date of Extract Decree Sheriff Clerk

NOTE
[1] As amended by S.I. 1978 No. 112.

---

[1] FORM U4

(Extract decree and warrant to sell in sequestration and sale)

(Place, date) In this summary cause summons at the instance of the said pursuer(s) against the defender(s)(name) .... the Sheriff granted Decree against the defender for payment to the pursuer of £...... and £...... of expenses: and granted Warrant for all lawful execution hereon: and further, the Sheriff granted Warrant to any officer of Court or to A.B. (design) .... to sell, by Public Roup, at .... as much of the Sequestrated Effects as shall satisfy and pay the said sum of rent with the Expenses.

Date of Extract Decree Sheriff Clerk

NOTE
[1] As substituted by S.I. 1980 No. 455.

---

[1] FORM U5

(Extract warrant for ejection and warrant to re-let (sequestration and sale)

**(Place, date) In this summary cause summons at the instance of the said pursuer(s) against the defender(s) (name) ....
the Sheriff granted Warrant for ejecting the defender from the premises specified, they being displenished, and granted Warrant to the puruer to re-let the said premises: and granted decree against the defender for payment to the pursuer of £.......... of expenses: and granted Warrant for all lawful execution hereon.**
Date of Extract Decree **Sheriff Clerk**

NOTE
[1] As amended by S.I. 1978 No. 112.

FORM U6

(Extract decree (multiplepoinding etc.))

**(Place, date) In this summary cause summons at the instance of the said pursuer(s) against the defender(s) (name) ....
the Sheriff.**
Date of Extract Decree **Sheriff Clerk**

[THE NEXT PAGE IS D 291]

[1] FORM U7

Extract Decree against Arrestee for the Principal Sum and Expenses (Furthcoming)
(Place, date) In this summary cause summons at the instance of the said pursuer(s) against the Arrestee (name) ....
and the Common Debtor (name) ....
the Sheriff granted decree against the Arrestee to make furthcoming, pay and deliver to the pursuer the sum of £...... and £...... of expenses: and granted Warrant for all lawful execution hereon.
Date of Extract Decree Sheriff Clerk

NOTE
[1] As amended by S.I. 1978 No. 112.

[1] FORM U8

Extract Decree against Arrestee for the Principal Sum and against Common Debtor for Expenses (Furthcoming)
(Place, date) In this summary cause summons at the instance of the said pursuer(s) against the Arrestee (name) ....
and the Common Debtor (name) ....
the Sheriff granted decree against the Arrestee to make furthcoming, pay and deliver to the pursuer the sum of £......: and granted decree against the Common Debtor for £........ of expenses: and granted Warrant for all lawful execution hereon.
Date of Extract Decree Sheriff Clerk

NOTE
[1] As amended by S.I. 1978 No. 112.

[1] FORM U9

Extract Decree of Delivery
(Place, date) In this summary cause summons at the instance of the said pursuer(s) against the defender(s) (name) ....
the Sheriff granted decree against the defender for delivery to the pursuer of ....
....
and granted decree against the defender for payment to the pursuer of £........ of expenses: and granted Warrant for all lawful execution hereon.
Date of Extract Decree Sheriff Clerk

NOTE
[1] As amended by S.I. 1978 No. 112.

[1] FORM U10

Extract Decree of Delivery and Warrant to search and open lockfast places
(Place, date) In this summary cause summons at the instance of the said pursuer(s) (name)
....
against the defender(s) (name) ....
the Sheriff granted decree against the defender for delivery to the pursuer of ....
....
and granted decree against the defender for payment to the pursuer of £........ of expenses: and granted Warrant for all lawful execution hereon and further, the Sheriff granted Warrant to Officers of Court to search for and take possession of goods in the possession of the defender and to open shut and lockfast places occupied by the defender.
Date of Extract Decree Sheriff Clerk

NOTE
[1] As amended by S.I. 1978 No. 112.

[1] FORM U11

Extract Decree for payment failing delivery

(Place, date) In this summary cause summons at the instance of the said pursuer(s) against the defender(s) (name) ....
the Sheriff, in respect that the defender has failed to deliver in accordance with the preceding decree, granted decree against the defender for payment to the pursuer(s) of the sum of £...... claimed as the alternative crave with interest at the rate of ....% annually from .... until payment with expenses as previously decerned for and granted Warrant for all lawful execution hereon.

Date of Extract Decree Sheriff Clerk

NOTE

[1] As amended by S.I. 1978 No. 112.

[1] FORM U12

Extract Decree for Interim Aliment

(Place, date) In this summary cause summons at the instance of the said pursuer against the defender (name) ....
the Sheriff granted decree ....
against the defender for payment to the pursuer of aliment *ad interim* at the rate of .... and granted Warrant for all lawful execution hereon.

Date of Extract Decree Sheriff Clerk

NOTE

[1] As amended by S.I. 1978 No. 112.

[1] FORM U13

Extract Decree of Dismissal

(Place, date) In this summary cause summons at the instance of the said pursuer(s) (name) ....
against the defender(s) (name) ....
the Sheriff dismissed the cause ....
and granted decree against the said pursuer(s) for payment to the said defender(s) of the sum of £........ of expenses: and granted Warrant for all lawful execution hereon.

Date of Extract Decree Sheriff Clerk

NOTE

[1] As amended by S.I. 1978 No. 112.

[1] FORM U14

Extract Decree of Absolvitor

(Place, date) In this summary cause summons at the instance of the said pursuer(s) (name) ....
against the defender(s) (name) ....
the Sheriff assoilzed the .... defender(s) from the cause and granted decree against the said pursuer(s) for payment to the said defender(s) of the sum of £ .... of expenses: and granted Warrant for all lawful execution hereon.

Date of Extract Decree Sheriff Clerk

NOTE

[1] As amended by S.I. 1978 No. 112.

[1] FORM V

SHERIFF COURT

MINUTE SHEET

SUMMARY CAUSE PAYMENT SUMMONS

for the Court of.. 197....
197 . The pursuer craves the Court to grant decree or other Order in terms of the following Minute(s).
Pursuer/Solicitor/Authorised lay representative

Case No.	Name of Defendant(s)	Minute

NOTE
[1] Added by S.I. 1978 No. 1805. As amended by S.I. 1991 No. 821.

Rule 72 [1] FORM W

(Sequestration for Rent—Notice informing Defender of Right to Apply for Certain Orders under the Debtors (Scotland) Act 1987)

Where articles are sequestrated for rent you have the right to apply to the sheriff for certain orders under the Debtors (Scotland) Act 1987.

1. You may apply to the sheriff within 14 days from the date articles are sequestrated for an order releasing any article on the ground that:
   (*a*) it is exempt from sequestration for rent. (Articles which are exempt are listed in section 16 of the Debtors (Scotland) Act 1987.); or
   (*b*) its inclusion in the sequestration for rent or its subsequent sale is unduly harsh.

2. Where a mobile home, such as a caravan, is your only or principal residence and it has been sequestrated for rent you may apply to the sheriff before a warrant to sell is granted for an order that for a specified period no further steps shall be taken in the sequestration.

Any enquiry relating to the above rights should be made to a solicitor, Citizens Advice Bureau or other local advice centre or to the sheriff clerk at (*address*).

NOTE
[1] Inserted by S.I. 1988 No. 1978.

Proceedings under Sex Discrimination Act 1975 (No. 2) 1976

(S.I. 1976 No. 1851)

[3rd November 1976]

The Lords of Council and Session, under and by virtue of the powers conferred upon them by section 32 of the Sheriff Courts (Scotland) Act 1971 and section 66(7) of the Sex Discrimination Act 1975 and of all other powers competent to them in that behalf, do hereby enact and declare:—

Citation, commencement and interpretation

1.—(1) This Act of Sederunt may be cited as the Act of Sederunt (Proceedings under Sex Discrimination Act 1975) No. 2 1976 and shall come into operation on 26th November 1976.

(2) The Interpretation Act 1889 shall apply for the interpretation of this Act of Sederunt as it applies for the interpretation of an Act of Parliament.

Appointment of Assessors

2. In any proceedings brought under section 66(1) of the said Act of 1975 (reparation for breach of statutory duty by commission of certain acts of discrimination) the sheriff may *ex proprio motu*, or on the application of any party, appoint as an assessor any person whom he considers to have special qualifications likely to be of assistance in determining those proceedings.

Fatal Accidents and Sudden Deaths Inquiry Procedure (Scotland) Rules 1977

(S.I. 1977 No. 191)

[7th February 1977]

In exercise of the powers conferred on me by section 7(1) of the Fatal Accidents and Sudden Deaths Inquiry (Scotland) Act 1976 and of all other powers enabling me in that behalf I hereby make the following rules:—

Citation and commencement

1. These rules may be cited as the Fatal Accidents and Sudden Deaths Inquiry Procedure (Scotland) Rules 1977 and shall come into operation on 1st March 1977.

Interpretation

2.—(1) In these rules, unless the context otherwise requires,—

"the Act" means the Fatal Accidents and Sudden Deaths Inquiry (Scotland) Act 1976;

"inquiry" means an inquiry under the Act;

"officer of law" has the meaning assigned to it by section 462 of the Criminal Procedure (Scotland) Act 1975;

"procurator fiscal" has the meaning assigned to it by section 462 of the Criminal Procedure (Scotland) Act 1975;

"sheriff clerk" includes sheriff clerk depute and any person duly authorised to execute the duties of sheriff clerk.

(2) In these rules, unless the context otherwise requires, a reference to any enactment shall be construed as a reference to that enactment as amended or re-enacted by any subsequent enactment.

(3) The Interpretation Act 1889 shall apply for the interpretation of these rules as it applies for the interpretation of an Act of Parliament.

Application for holding of inquiry

3. The application for the holding of an inquiry in accordance with section 1(1) of the Act and the sheriff's first warrant thereon shall be in the case of such a death as is referred to in section 1(1)(*a*) of the Act in the form as nearly as may be of Form 1 of the Schedule to these rules, and in the case of such a death as is referred to in section 1(1)(*b*) of the Act in the form as nearly as may be of Form 2 of the said Schedule.

Notice of holding of inquiry

4.—(1) Intimation of the holding of an inquiry in accordance with section 3(2)(*a*) of the Act shall be made by notice in writing in the form as nearly as may be of Form 3 of the Schedule to these rules, given not less than 21 days before the date of the inquiry.

(2) Such notice shall be given to the following persons, besides those specified in the said section 3(2)(*a*),—

(*a*) in the case of such a death as is referred to in section 1(1)(*a*)(i) of the Act, to the Health and Safety Commission;

(*b*) in the case of such a death as is referred to in section 1(1)(*a*)(ii) of the Act, to any minister, government department or other authority in whose legal custody the person who has died was at the time of his death;

(*c*) in the case of a death occurring in the circumstances specified in section 9 of the Act, or a death resulting from an accident occurring in those circumstances, to the Secretary of State for Energy;

(*d*) in any case where it is competent for a minister or government department under any statute other than the Act to cause public inquiry to be made into the circumstances of the death, to such minister or government department.

(3) Public notice of the holding of an inquiry in accordance with section 3(2)(*b*) of the Act shall be given by publishing in at least two newspapers circulating in the sheriff court district where the inquiry is to be held, not less than 21 days before the date of the inquiry, an advertisement in the form as nearly as may be of Form 4 of the Schedule to these rules.

Custody of productions

5. The sheriff may at the time of making an order for the holding of an inquiry or at any time thereafter, upon the application of the procurator

[THE NEXT PAGE IS D 294/1]

fiscal, or of any other person entitled to appear at the inquiry or at his own instance, grant warrant to officers of law to take possession of anything connected with the death which is the subject of inquiry and which it may be considered necessary to produce at the inquiry and to hold any such thing in safe custody, subject to inspection by any persons interested.

Inspection of land, premises, etc.

6. The sheriff may at the time of making an order for the holding of an inquiry or at any time thereafter, upon the application of the procurator fiscal or of any other person entitled to appear at the inquiry or at his own instance, inspect or grant warrant for any person to inspect any land, premises, article or other thing the inspection of which the sheriff considers desirable for the purposes of the inquiry.

Representation

7.—(1) The procurator fiscal may appear on his own behalf at an inquiry or be represented by an assistant or depute procurator fiscal or by Crown counsel.

(2) Any person entitled to appear at an inquiry in terms of section 4(2) of the Act may appear on his own behalf or be represented by an advocate or a solicitor or, with the leave of the sheriff, by any other person.

Citation of witnesses or havers

8. The citation of a witness or haver to appear at an inquiry shall be in the form as nearly as may be of Form 5 of the Schedule to these rules, and an execution of citation in the form as nearly as may be of Form 6 of the said Schedule shall be sufficient evidence of such citation.

Adjournment of inquiry

9. The sheriff may at any time adjourn the inquiry to a time and place specified by him at the time of adjournment.

Written statements

10.—(1) The sheriff may admit in place of oral evidence by any person in an inquiry, to the like extent as such oral evidence, a written statement by that person signed by that person and sworn or affirmed to be true by that person before a notary public, commissioner for oaths or justice of the peace, or before a commissioner appointed by the sheriff for that purpose:

Provided that such a statement may only be admitted if—

(*a*) all persons who appear or are represented at the inquiry agree to its admission; or

(*b*) the sheriff considers that its admission will not result in unfairness in the conduct of the inquiry to any person who appears or is represented at the inquiry.

(2) A certificate that the statement has been so sworn and affirmed, annexed to the statement and signed by the person making the statement and by the person before whom it is sworn or affirmed, shall be sufficient evidence that it has been so sworn or affirmed.

(3) Any statement which is admitted in evidence by virtue of this rule shall, unless the sheriff otherwise directs, be read aloud at the inquiry; and where the sheriff directs that a statement or any part of it shall not be read aloud he shall state his reason for so directing and, where appropriate, an account shall be given orally of what the sheriff has directed not to be read aloud.

(4) Any document or object referred to as a production and identified in a written statement tendered in evidence under this rule shall be treated as if it had been produced and had been identified in court by the maker of the statement.

Sheriff's determination

11.—(1) The sheriff's determination shall be in writing and shall be signed by him.

(2) The sheriff's determination shall, except in the circumstances specified in paragraph (3) of this rule, be read out by him in public.

(3) Where the sheriff requires time to prepare his determination and considers that in the circumstances it is not reasonable to fix an adjourned sitting of the inquiry for the sole purpose of reading out the determination, the sheriff shall not be required to read out the determination, but the sheriff clerk shall send free of charge a copy of the determination, to the procurator fiscal and to any person who appeared or was represented at the inquiry and shall allow any person to inspect a copy of the determination at the sheriff clerk's office free of charge during the period of three months after the date when the determination was made.

Assessors

12.—(1) A request to the sheriff to summon a person to act as an assessor in terms of section 4(6) of the Act shall be made by written motion lodged with the sheriff clerk not less than seven days before the date of the inquiry.

(2) The appointment of an assessor shall not affect the admissibility of expert evidence in the inquiry.

Recording of evidence

13. Evidence given in an inquiry shall be recorded in the same manner as evidence given in an ordinary civil cause in the sheriff court:

Provided that where the evidence shall have been taken down in shorthand it shall not be necessary to extend such evidence unless the sheriff shall so direct or unless a copy of the transcript of evidence shall be duly requested by any person entitled thereto in terms of the Act and these rules.

Time-limit for obtaining copy of transcript of evidence

14. A person shall be entitled to obtain a copy of the transcript of the evidence in accordance with section 6(5)(*b*) of the Act only if he makes application therefor to the sheriff clerk within a period of three months after the date when the sheriff's determination was made.

Fee on obtaining copy of determination, or of transcript of evidence

15.—(1) The fee payable upon obtaining a copy of the sheriff's determination in accordance with section 6(5)(*a*) of the Act shall be such fee as is payable to sheriff clerks for copying documents relating to civil proceedings in the sheriff court.

(2) The fee payable upon obtaining a copy of the transcript of the evidence in accordance with section 6(5)(*b*) of the Act shall be—

(*a*) where the copy is made by a shorthand writer, such copying fee as is payable by the sheriff clerk to the shorthand writer;

(*b*) where the copy is made by the sheriff clerk, such fee as is payable to sheriff clerks for copying documents relating to civil proceedings in the sheriff court.

Service of documents

16.—(1) The notice intimating the holding of an inquiry in accordance with section 3(2)(*a*) of the Act, the citation of a witness for precognition by the procurator fiscal, the citation of a witness or haver to attend at an inquiry, and any interlocutor, warrant or other order of the sheriff or writ following thereon issued in connection with an inquiry may be served on a person in any of the following manners:–

(*a*) the procurator fiscal or the solicitor for any person entitled to appear at the inquiry, as appropriate, may post the document in a registered or recorded delivery letter addressed to the person on whom the document requires to be served at his residence or place of business or at any address specified by him for the purpose of receiving documents;

(*b*) a police officer (where the document is issued by the procurator fiscal) or a sheriff officer may—

(i) serve the document personally on the person on whom it requires to be served; or

(ii) leave the document in the hands of an inmate or employee at that person's residence or place of business or any address specified by him for the purpose of receiving documents;

(iii) introduce the document into that person's residence or place of business or any address so specified by means of a letterbox or other lawful means; or

(iv) affix the document to the door of that person's residence or place of business or any place so specified;

Provided that when it proves difficult for any reason to serve any document on any person the sheriff, on being satisfied that all reasonable steps have been taken to serve it, may dispense with service of such document or order such other steps as he may think fit.

Dispensing power of sheriff

17. The sheriff may in his discretion relieve any person from the consequences of any failure to comply with the provisions of these rules if the failure resulted from mistake, oversight or any cause other than wilful non-observance of these rules and in granting such relief may impose such terms and conditions as appear to him to be just; and in any such case the sheriff may make such order as appears to him to be just regarding extension of time, lodging or amendment of papers or otherwise, so as to enable the inquiry to proceed as if such failure had not happened.

SCHEDULE

Rule 3

Form 1

UNDER THE FATAL ACCIDENTS AND SUDDEN DEATHS INQUIRY (SCOTLAND) ACT 1976

To the Sheriff of at (*place of court*)

The APPLICATION of the Procurator Fiscal for the District of

From information received by the applicant it appears that (*narrate briefly the apparent facts of the death*);

In terms of the said Act an inquiry requires to be held into the circumstances of said death.

May it therefore please your Lordship to fix a time and place for the holding by your Lordship of such in inquiry; to grant warrant to cite witnesses and havers to attend at such inquiry, at the instance of the applicant, and of any other person who may be entitled by virtue of said Act to appear thereat; to grant warrant to officers of law to take possession of, and hold in safe custody, subject to inspection by any person interested, anything which it may be considered necessary to produce at the inquiry.

According to Justice, &c.

(*Signature*)
Procurator Fiscal

(*Place and date*). The Sheriff having considered the foregoing application orders that inquiry into the circumstances of the death of within designed, be held on the day of 19 , at (*time*), within the Sheriff Court House at ; grants warrant to cite witnesses and havers as craved; also grants warrant to officers of law to take possession of, and to hold in safe custody, subject to the inspection by any person interested, anything which it may be considered necessary to produce at the inquiry.

(*Signature*)

Rule 3 FORM 2

UNDER THE FATAL ACCIDENTS AND SUDDEN DEATHS INQUIRY (SCOTLAND) ACT 1976

To the Sheriff of at (*place of court*)

The APPLICATION of the Procurator Fiscal for the District of

From information received by the applicant is appears that (*narrate briefly the apparent facts of the death*);

and it appears to the Lord Advocate to be expedient in the public interest that an inquiry under the said Act should be held into the circumstances of said death.
May it therefore please your Lordship to fix a time and place for the holding by your Lordship of such an inquiry; to grant warrant to cite witnesses and havers to attend at such inquiry, at the instance of the applicant and of any other person who may be entitled by virtue of said Act to appear thereat; to grant warrant to officers of law to take possession of, and hold in safe custody, subject to inspection by any person interested, anything which it may be considered necessary to produce at the inquiry.

According to Justice, &c.

(*Signature*)
Procurator Fiscal

(*Place and date*). The Sheriff having considered the foregoing application orders that inquiry into the circumstances of the death of within designed, be held on the day of 19 , at (*time*) within the Sheriff Court House at ; grants warrant to cite witnesses and havers as craved; also grants warrant to officers of law to take possession of, and to hold in safe custody, subject to the inspection by any person interested, anything which it may be considered necessary to produce at the inquiry.

(*Signature*)

Rule 4(1) FORM 3

(*Address of procurator fiscal*)

(*Date*)

(*Name and address of person to whom notice is given*)

Dear Sir

DEATH OF (*insert name of deceased*)

I have to intimate that an inquiry under the Fatal Accidents and Sudden Deaths Inquiry (Scotland) Act 1976 into the circumstances of the death of (*insert name and address of deceased*) will be held on the day of at (*time*) within the Sheriff Court House at (*address*).

* [You have the right to appear, call witnesses and lead evidence at the inquiry. You may attend in person or be represented by an advocate or a solicitor instructed by you or, with the leave of the sheriff, by some other person.]

Yours faithfully,

(*Signature*)
Procurator Fiscal

* To be inserted only when the person to whom notice is given is the wife, husband or nearest known relative, or the employer, of the deceased.

Rule 4(3) FORM 4

ADVERTISEMENT

Under the Fatal Accidents and Sudden Deaths Inquiry (Scotland) Act 1976

The Sheriff of

will hold an inquiry on the day of (*month*) 19 at (*time*) within the Sheriff Court House at (*address*) into the circumstances of the death of (*name, occupation, address*).

(*Signature*)
Procurator Fiscal for the District of

Rule 8 FORM 5

To (*name and designation*).

YOU are cited to attend at the Sheriff Court House at (*address*) on (*date*) at (*time*) as a witness at the instance of (*insert* "the Procurator Fiscal for the District of " *or name and address of person calling witness*) at the INQUIRY then to be held into the circumstances of the DEATH of (*name and address of deceased*) [and are required to bring with you] and if you fail to attend you may be ordered to pay a penalty not exceeding*

(*Signature and designation of procurator fiscal, police officer, sheriff officer or solicitor*)

* (Insert penalty specified in rule [74(2)] of the First Schedule to the Sheriff Courts (Scotland) Act 1907 [as amended]).

Rule 8 FORM 6

I certify that on (*date*) I lawfully cited (*name and designation*) to attend at the Sheriff Court House at (*address*) on (*date*) at (*time*) as a witness at the instance of (*insert* "the Procurator Fiscal for the District of " *or name and address of person calling witness*) at the INQUIRY then to be held into the circumstances of the DEATH of (*name and address of deceased*) [and I required him to bring with him].

This I did by (*specify exactly how served*).

(*Signature and designation of procurator fiscal, police officer, sheriff officer or solicitor*)

Proceedings under Sex Discrimination Act 1975, 1977

(S.I. 1977 No. 973)

[31st May 1977]

The Lords of Council and Session, under and by virtue of the power conferred on them by section 32 of the Sheriff Courts (Scotland) Act 1971 and section 66 (5)A of the Sex Discrimination Act 1975 as inserted by paragraph 5(2) of Schedule 4 of the Race Relations Act 1976 and of all other powers competent to them in that behalf do hereby enact and declare:—

Citation, commencement and interpretation

1.—(1) This Act of Sederunt may be cited as the Act of Sederunt

[THE NEXT PAGE IS D 295]

(Proceedings under Sex Discrimination Act 1975) 1977 and shall come into operation on 21st June 1977.

(2) In this Act of Sederunt "the Act" means the Sex Discrimination Act 1975, and "the Commission" means the Equal Opportunities Commission established under section 53 of the Act.

(3) The Interpretation Act 1889 shall apply for the interpretation of this Act of Sederunt as it applies for the interpretation of an Act of Parliament.

Intimation of proceedings

2. When any proceedings are brought under section 66 of the Act the applicant shall send by recorded delivery post a copy of the summons or initial writ initiating the action to the Commission.

Proceedings under Race Relations Act 1976, 1977

(S.I. 1977 No. 975)

[31st May 1977]

The Lords of Council and Session, under and by virtue of the powers conferred on them by section 32 of the Sheriff Courts (Scotland) Act 1971, sections 57(6) and 66 of the Race Relations Act 1976 and of all other powers competent to them in that behalf to hereby enact and declare:—

Citation, commencement and interpretation

1.—(1) This Act of Sederunt may be cited as the Act of Sederunt (Proceedings under Race Relations Act 1976) 1977 and shall come into operation on 21st June 1977.

(2) In this Act of Sederunt "the Act" means the Race Relations Act 1976, and "the Commission" means the Commission for Racial Equality established under section 43 of the Act.

(3) The Interpretation Act 1889 shall apply for the interpretation of this Act of Sederunt as it applies for the interpretation of an Act of Parliament.

Procedure

2. The following proceedings under the Act shall be commenced by initial writ under the Sheriff Courts (Scotland) Acts 1907 and 1913 and shall be disposed of as summary applications as defined in those Acts, namely:—

(*a*) an application by the Commission under section 50(4) of an order requiring a person to comply with a notice served on him under section 50(1);

(*b*) an appeal by a person under section 59(1) against the requirement of a non-discrimination notice served on him under section 58;

(*c*) an application by the Commission under section 62(1) for an order restraining a person from doing any of the acts referred to in that section;

(*d*) an application by the Commission under section 63(2) for a decision whether an alleged contravention of section 29, 30 or 31 has occurred;

(*e*) an application by the Commission under section 63(4) for an order restraining a person from doing any of the acts referred to in that section; and

(*f*) an application by a person under section 72(5) for an order removing or modifying any term of a contract made unenforceable by section 72(2).

Intimation of proceedings

3. When any proceedings are brought under section 57 of the Act the applicant shall send by recorded delivery post a copy of the summons or initial writ initiating the action to the Commission.

Taxation

4. The expenses incurred by the Commission within the meaning and for the purposes of section 66(5) of the Act, shall be taxed or assessed by the auditor of the sheriff court in which proceedings under the Act were taken or would have been taken but for any compromise or settlement, as if they were outlays incurred by a solicitor on behalf of the applicant.

Appeals under the Licensing (Scotland) Act 1976, 1977

(S.I. 1977 No. 1622)

[6th October 1977]

The Lords of Council and Session under and by virtue of the powers conferred upon them by section 32 of the Sheriff Courts (Scotland) Act 1971 and by section 39(9) of the Licensing (Scotland) Act 1976 and of all other powers enabling them in that behalf, do hereby enact and declare:—

Citation, commencement and interpretation

1.—(1) This Act of Sederunt may be cited as the Act of Sederunt (Appeals under the Licensing (Scotland) Act 1976) 1977 and shall come into operation on 29th October 1977.

(2) In this Act of Sederunt—

(*a*) "the 1976 Act" means the Licensing (Scotland) Act 1976; and

(*b*) the Interpretation Act 1889 shall apply to the interpretation of this Act of Sederunt as it applies to the interpretation of an Act of Parliament.

Appeals procedure

2. Any appeal to the sheriff under section 39 of the 1976 Act against a decision of a licensing board shall be made by way of initial writ under the Sheriff Courts (Scotland) Acts 1907 and 1913 and such appeal shall be disposed of as a summary application as defined in the said Acts.

[1] **3.** At the same time as the initial writ is lodged with the sheriff clerk or as soon as may be thereafter, the appellant shall serve a copy of the initial writ—

(*a*) on the clerk of the licensing board; and

[THE NEXT PAGE IS D 299]

(*b*) if he was the applicant at the hearing before the licensing board, on all other parties who appeared (whether personally or by means of a representative) at the hearing; and

(*c*) if he was an objector at that hearing, on the applicant.

NOTE

[1] As substituted by S.I. 1979 No. 1520.

4. Where the appellant has received a statement of reasons for its decision from the licensing board he shall lodge a copy thereof with the sheriff clerk.

5. Where an appeal is made to the sheriff against a decision of a licensing board and that board has given as reasons for its decision one or more of the statutory grounds of refusal, the sheriff may, at any time prior to pronouncing a final interlocutor request the licensing board to give their reasons for finding such ground or grounds of refusal to be established.

Presumption of Death 1978

(S.I. 1978 No. 162)

[1st February 1978]

The Lords of Council and Session under and by virtue of the powers conferred on them by section 32 of the Sheriff Courts (Scotland) Act 1971 and by section 15 of the Presumption of Death (Scotland) Act 1977 and of all other powers enabling them in that behalf do hereby enact and declare:—

Citation, commencement and interpretation

1.—(1) This Act of Sederunt may be cited as the Act of Sederunt (Presumption of Death) 1978 and shall come into operation on 1st March 1978.

(2) The Interpretation Act 1889 shall apply to the interpretation of this Act of Sederunt as it applies to the interpretation of an Act of Parliament.

Service and advertisement

2.—(1) The pursuer in an action of declarator under section 1 of the Presumption of Death (Scotland) Act 1977 shall serve a copy initial writ and the applicant in an application for a variation order under section 4 (1) of that Act shall serve a copy application on the following persons:—

(*a*) the husband or wife of the missing person,

(*b*) any child including an illegitimate or adopted child of the missing person, or if the missing person has no children, the nearest known relative of that person,

(*c*) any person, including insurers, who as far as the pursuer is aware has any interest in the action,

(*d*) the Lord Advocate.

(2) The sheriff may on the motion of the pursuer or the applicant dispense with service on any of the persons referred to in sub-paragraph 1 (*a*) (*b*) and (*c*) above.

(3) In every action of declarator and every application referred to in sub-paragraph (1) above the sheriff shall order advertisement which shall be in such form as the sheriff thinks fit and shall call for information about the survival or death of the missing person.

Betting and Gaming Appeals 1978

(S.I. 1978 No. 229)

[17th February 1978]

The Lords of Council and Session under and by virtue of the powers conferred on them by section 32 of the Sheriff Courts (Scotland) Act 1971 and of the provisions of the Betting, Gaming and Lotteries Act 1963 and the Gaming Act 1968 as detailed in the Schedule hereto, and of all other powers enabling them in that behalf, do hereby enact and declare:—

Citation and commencement

1. This Act of Sederunt may be cited as the Act of Sederunt (Betting and Gaming Appeals) 1978 and shall come into operation on 13th March 1978.

Interpretation

2.—(1) In this Act of Sederunt the following expressions shall have the following meanings unless the context otherwise requires—

(*a*) " appropriate authority " shall mean an authority responsible for the grant or renewal in any area of a permit for the provision of amusements with prizes or of machines for amusement purposes;

(*b*) " appropriate collector of duty " shall mean the Collector of Customs and Excise for the area in which the relevant premises are or are to be situated;

(*c*) " appropriate officer of police " shall mean the chief constable for the area in which the relevant premises are or are to be situated;

(*d*) " the Gaming Board " shall mean the Gaming Board for Great Britain, established under section 10 (1) of the Gaming Act 1968;

(*e*) " licensing board " shall mean an authority responsible for the grant or renewal of bookmakers' permits, betting agency permits, betting office licences and licences for gaming in any area;

(*f*) " relevant premises " shall mean premises in respect of which a licence for gaming is for the time being in force or premises to which an application for a licence for gaming relates;

(*g*) " section 34 " shall mean section 34 of the Gaming Act 1968;

(*h*) " section 49 " shall mean section 49 of the Betting, Gaming and Lotteries Act 1963 as amended by section 53 of and Schedule 11 to the Gaming Act 1968.

(2) The Interpretation Act 1889 shall apply to the interpretation of this Act of Sederunt as it applies to the interpretation of an Act of Parliament.

Procedure

3. Any appeal mentioned in the following provisions of this Act of Sederunt shall be made by initial writ under the Sheriff Courts (Scotland) Acts 1907 and 1913, and shall be disposed of as a summary application as defined in those Acts.

4.—(1) An appeal against the decision of a licensing board—

(*a*) refusing to grant or renew a bookmaker's permit, betting agency permit or betting office licence, or

(*b*) ordering that a bookmaker's permit be forfeited or cancelled,

shall be made within 14 days after notice of such decision has been given to the applicant for such licence or permit, or the holder of such licence or permit, as the case may be.

(2) At the same time as the initial writ is lodged with the sheriff clerk or as soon as may be thereafter, the appellant shall serve a copy thereof on—

(*a*) the clerk to the licensing board;

(*b*) all the other parties who appeared at the hearing before the licensing board;

(*c*) in the case of an appeal against the forfeiture and cancellation of a bookmaker's permit, the applicant for forfeiture and cancellation.

5.—(1) An appeal against the decision of a licensing board—

(*a*) refusing to grant or renew a licence for gaming to take place on premises, or

(*b*) imposing restrictions upon such a licence, or

(*c*) cancelling such a licence,

shall be made within 14 days after notice of such decision has been given to the applicant for such grant or renewal.

(2) At the same time as the initial writ is lodged with the sheriff clerk or as soon as may be thereafter, the appellant shall serve a copy thereof on

(*a*) the clerk to the licensing board,

(*b*) all the other parties who appeared at the hearing before the licensing board,

(*c*) the Gaming Board,

(*d*) the appropriate collector of duty,

(*e*) the appropriate officer of police.

6.—(1) Where a licensing board after hearing any objections or representations made by or on behalf of the Gaming Board or any other person—

(*a*) grants or renews a licence for gaming to take place on premises, with or without imposing restrictions, or

(*b*) refuses an application for the cancellation of such a licence,

the clerk to the licensing board shall forthwith give notice of the decision of the licensing board to the Gaming Board.

(2) An appeal by the Gaming Board against any such decision as is referred to in sub-paragraph (1) shall be made within 14 days after notice of such decision has been given to the Gaming Board.

(3) At the same time as the initial writ is lodged with the sheriff clerk or as soon as may be thereafter, the appellant shall serve a copy thereof on—

(*a*) the clerk to the licensing board,

(*b*) the applicant,

(*c*) all the other parties who appeared at the hearing before the licensing board,

(*d*) the appropriate collector of duty,

(*e*) the appropriate officer of police.

7. Within seven days after service on the clerk to the licensing board of a copy of the initial writ in terms of paragraphs 4, 5 or 6 he shall send to the sheriff clerk, and to each of the persons on whom service of the copy initial writ has been made as aforesaid, a written statement setting out the reasons for the decision of the licensing board.

8.—(1) An appeal against a decision of an appropriate authority—

(*a*) refusing to grant or renew a permit for the provision of amusements with prizes under section 49, or

(*b*) for the provision of machines for amusement purposes under section 34 on any premises, or

(*c*) granting or renewing a permit for the provision of machines for amusement purposes subject to a condition,

shall be made within 14 days after notice of such decision has been given to the applicant for such grant or renewal.

(2) At the same time as the initial writ is lodged with the sheriff clerk or as soon as may be thereafter, the appellant shall serve a copy thereof on the clerk to the licensing board.

Revocation

9. The Act of Sederunt (Betting and Gaming Appeals and Fees of Clerks to the Licensing Authorities) 1970 is revoked.

Statutory Appeals 1981

(S.I. 1981 No. 1591)

[3rd November 1981]

The Lords of Council and Session under and by virtue of the powers conferred upon them by section 32 of the Sheriff Courts (Scotland) Act 1971 and of all other powers enabling them in that behalf, and after consultation with the Sheriff Court Rules Council, do hereby enact and declare:—

Citation and commencement

1.—(1) This Act of Sederunt may be cited as the Act of Sederunt (Statutory Appeals) 1981 and shall come into operation on 5th January 1982.

(2) This Act of Sederunt shall be inserted in the Books of Sederunt.

Time Limits

2.—(1) All statutory appeals and applications of the nature of appeals to the sheriff (other than appeals under section 27 of the Sheriff Courts (Scotland) Act 1907 and section 38 of the Sheriff Courts (Scotland) Act 1971 against a decision of a Minister, a department, statutory tribunal, referee or authority shall be taken within such time as may be prescribed by statutory enactment under which the appeal is presented, or, if no time is prescribed, not later than 21 days after the date on which the decision, order, scheme, determination, refusal, or other act of the authority or person complained of was intimated to the appellant.

(2) On special cause shown the sheriff may in his discretion hear an appeal to which this paragraph applies notwithstanding that it was not lodged within the time prescribed in sub-paragraph (1) of this paragraph.

Method of Appeal

3. Unless otherwise provided by statutory enactment an appeal or application under sub-paragraph (1) of paragraph 2 shall be made by initial writ under the Sheriff Courts (Scotland) Acts 1907 and 1913 and shall be disposed of as a summary application as defined in those Acts.

Applications under the Matrimonial Homes (Family Protection) (Scotland) Act 1981, 1982

(S.I. 1982 No. 1432)

[7th October 1982]

The Lords of Council and Session, under and by virtue of the powers conferred on them by section 32 of the Sheriff Courts (Scotland) Act 1971 and of all other powers competent to them in that behalf do hereby enact and declare:—

Citation and commencement

1. This Act of Sederunt may be cited as the Act of Sederunt (Applications under the Matrimonial Homes (Family Protection) Act 1981) 1982 and shall come into operation on 29th October 1982.

Interpretation

2.—(1) In this Act of Sederunt, unless the context otherwise requires:—

"the 1981 Act" means the Matrimonial Homes (Family Protection) (Scotland) Act 1981.

(2) Unless the context otherwise requires, words and expressions used in these rules and in the 1981 Act shall have the same meaning in these rules as they have in the Act.

Intimation to third parties

3.—(1) The applicant shall intimate a copy of the application or the terms of the motion by which the application is made—

(*a*) in an application under sections 2(1)(*e*) and 2(4)(*a*) (authorisation of non-essential repairs etc.), 4 (exclusion orders), 7 (dispensation with consent to dealing), 13 (transfer of tenancy) and 18 (occupancy rights of cohabiting couples) of the 1981 Act, to the landlord if the entitled spouse is a tenant of the matrimonial home;

(*b*) in an application under sections 2(1) (rights consequential to occupancy), 2(4)(*a*), 3(1) and (2) (rights of occupancy), 4, 7 and 18 of the 1981 Act, to the third party if the entitled spouse is permitted by a third party to occupy the matrimonial home;

(*c*) to any person as the sheriff may order in any application.

(2) A person to whom intimation of an application has been made in terms of this paragraph may lodge answers within such period as the sheriff may allow or if the application is made by motion may appear or be represented and may oppose the motion.

4. An order for intimation to be made under the last foregoing paragraph may be contained in the original warrant for citation or intimation may be appointed to be made at a later date.

Form of applications

5.—(1) Except as otherwise provided in this Act of Sederunt an application under the 1981 Act shall be brought as an ordinary cause except where the application falls within the definition of a summary cause in section 35 of the Sheriff Courts (Scotland) Act 1971 in which case it shall be brought as a summary cause.

(2) Where civil proceedings to which this paragraph refers (hereinafter referred to as "the principal proceedings") have been raised it shall be competent for a defender in the principal proceedings or other person who is entitled to make an application under the 1981 Act to lodge such an application in the process of the principal proceedings.

(3) An application lodged in terms of this paragraph shall be by minute signed by the applicant or his solicitor, shall be served upon the pursuer in the principal proceedings and shall contain:

(*a*) a crave or craves in a form which, if the application had been made by way of a separate action would have been appropriate in such separate action;

(*b*) a statement of facts setting out in numbered paragraphs the facts on which the application is founded; and

(*c*) a note of the pleas-in-law which are necessary to support the application.

(4) In any application lodged in terms of this paragraph the sheriff may make such order for any warrant for intimation, service or arrestment and may regulate the procedure as he thinks fit and may dispose of the application as if it had been stated in a substantive action.

(5) The principal proceedings are:

(i) an action of separation and aliment;

(ii) an action of adherence and aliment;

(iii) an action of interim aliment;
(iv) an action of affiliation and aliment;
(v) any application under the 1981 Act.

6.—(1) Applications for the variation or recall of orders which have been made under sections 3 or 4 of the 1981 Act shall be made by minute lodged in the original process in which the order was made.

(2) The sheriff shall order that any minute lodged in terms of this paragraph be served on the opposite party or parties and be intimated to—

(*a*) the landlord if the entitled spouse is a tenant of the matrimonial home,

(*b*) the third party if the entitled spouse is permitted to occupy the matrimonial home by a third party.

(*c*) any other person as the sheriff may order.

(3) The sheriff shall appoint answers to be lodged to any minute lodged in terms of this paragraph within a specified time and shall thereafter, without closing the record, and after such proof or other procedure as he may deem necessary, dispose of the application.

7. An application for an order under section 7 of the 1981 Act shall be made by initial writ under the Sheriff Courts (Scotland) Acts 1907 and 1913 and such application shall be dealt with as a summary application as defined in those Acts:

Provided that in any civil proceedings which involve proceedings in relation to a matrimonial home an application for an order under section 7 of the 1981 Act, by any party to such proceedings entitled to make such an application, shall be made by motion.

8. An application under section 11 (poinding) for a declarator or order of the 1981 Act shall be made by initial writ under the Sheriff Courts (Scotland) Acts 1907 and 1913 and such application shall be dealt with as a summary application as defined in those Acts.

[1]**9.** Where a matrimonial interdict, to which there is attached a power of arrest, is varied or recalled or the power of arrest ceases to have effect by reason of decree of divorce being granted, the spouse who applied for variation or recall, or in whose favour decree of divorce has been granted, shall ensure that there is delivered as soon as possible—

(*a*) to the chief constable of the police area in which the matrimonial home is situated; and

(*b*) if the spouse who applied for the interdict resides in another police area, to the chief constable of that other police area,

a copy of the application for variation or recall and of the interlocutor granting variation or recall or, as the case may be, a copy of the interlocutor granting decree of divorce and shall immediately thereafter lodge with the sheriff clerk a certificate of delivery.

NOTE

[1] Added by S.I. 1984 No. 255.

Variation and Recall of Orders in Consistorial Causes 1984

(S.I. 1984 No. 667)

[9th May 1984]

The Lords of Council and Session, by virtue of the powers conferred upon them by section 32 of the Sheriff Courts (Scotland) Act 1971, section 8(4) of the Law Reform (Miscellaneous Provisions) (Scotland) Act 1966 and of all other powers competent to them in that behalf, after consultation with the Sheriff Court Rules Council, do hereby enact and declare:—

Citation and commencement

1.—(1) This Act of Sederunt may be cited as the Act of Sederunt (Variation and Recall of Orders in Consistorial Causes) 1984 and shall come into operation on 1st June 1984.

(2) This Act of Sederunt shall be inserted in the Books of Sederunt.

Procedure for variation and recall of orders under 1966 Act

2.—(1) This Act of Sederunt shall apply to applications to the sheriff for variation or recall of any order to which section 8 of the said Act of 1966 applies.

(2) All such applications shall be commenced by initial writ and, subject to the provisions of this Act of Sederunt, shall proceed as an ordinary cause and shall be subject to the same rights of appeal as any ordinary cause.

3.—(1) In all such applications there shall be lodged in the sheriff court along with the initial writ a copy of the interlocutor which it is sought to vary certified by the appropriate officer of the Court of Session.

(2) Before lodging the initial writ in terms of paragraph (1), a copy of the initial writ certified by the pursuer or his solicitor shall be lodged in or sent by first class recorded delivery post to the Court of Session to be lodged in the process of the Court of Session action in which the original order was made and the pursuer or his solicitor shall attach a certificate of execution of intimation to the principal initial writ lodged in the sheriff court.

(3) The sheriff may, on cause shown, prorogate the time for lodging such certified copy interlocutor.

4. Where no notice of intention to defend has been lodged, the cause shall be called on the next convenient court day when the sheriff shall hear the pursuer or his solicitor and thereafter may grant decree or make such other order as he thinks appropriate.

5. Where a notice of intention to defend has been lodged and no request is made under paragraph 8, the pursuer shall, within 14 days after tabling or within such period as the sheriff may order, lodge in process in the sheriff court the following documents (or copies) from the process in the Court of Session action in which the original order was made—

(*a*) the pleadings;
(*b*) the interlocutor sheets;
(*c*) any opinions of the court; and
(*d*) the inventory of productions together with any productions upon which he seeks to found.

6. Where a notice of intention to defend has been lodged and no request is made under paragraph 8, the sheriff may, on the joint motion of the parties made at any time after the lodging of the documents mentioned in paragraph 5, dispense with proof, and whether defences have been lodged or not hear the parties and thereafter may grant decree or otherwise dispose of the cause as he thinks appropriate.

7.—(1) Where decree has been granted or the cause otherwise disposed of and the days of appeal have elapsed, the sheriff clerk shall transmit to the Court of Session the sheriff court process together with those Court of Session documents which have been lodged in the sheriff court.

(2) A sheriff court process so transmitted shall form part of the process of the Court of Session action in which the original order was made.

8.—(1) A request for a remit to the Court of Session under section 8(3) of the said Act of 1966 shall be made by way of minute signed by the applicant or his solicitor and lodged at or before tabling.

(2) The sheriff shall in respect of any such minute at tabling order that the cause be remitted to the Court of Session and within four days after the date of such order the sheriff clerk shall transmit the whole sheriff court process to the Court of Session.

9.—(1) A cause remitted to the Court of Session in terms of paragraph 8 shall form part of the process of the Court of Session action in which the original order was made.

Revocation

10. The Act of Sederunt (Variation and Recall of Orders in Consistorial Causes) 1970 is revoked.

Consumer Credit Act 1974, 1985

(S.I. 1985 No. 705)

[2nd May 1985]

The Lords of Council and Session, under and by virtue of the powers conferred on them by sections 70(3), 73(8), 75(5) and 141(5) of the Consumer Credit Act 1974, section 32 of the Sheriff Courts (Scotland) Act 1971 and of all other powers competent to them in that behalf, do hereby enact and declare:—

Citation and commencement

1.—(1) This Act of Sederunt may be cited as the Act of Sederunt (Consumer Credit Act 1974) 1985 and shall come into operation on 19th May 1985.

(2) This Act of Sederunt shall be inserted in the Books of Sederunt.

Interpretation

2.—(1) In this Act of Sederunt, "the 1974 Act" means the Consumer Credit Act 1974.

(2) Expressions used in this Act of Sederunt which are used in the 1974 Act have the same meaning as in that Act.

Revocation

3. The Act of Sederunt (Sheriff Court Procedure, Consumer Credit) 1977 is revoked.

Part I

Ordinary and Summary Causes

4. In a cause relating to a regulated agreement, the sheriff may, on cause shown on the motion of any party to the cause before or at proof, in relation to any party to that agreement or any surety, dispense with the requirement in section 141(5) of the 1974 Act to make that party or surety a party to the cause.

5. In any cause relating to a regulated agreement brought by a person who has acquired rights or liabilities of a former creditor under the agreement by assignation or by operation of law, the requirement in section 141(5) of the 1974 Act that all parties to the regulated agreement shall be made parties to the cause shall not apply to the former creditor unless the sheriff so directs.

Part II

Summary Causes

6.—(1) Where, in a summary cause to which this sub-paragraph applies, a defender has a claim against a third party who is jointly and severally liable with the defender to the pursuer in respect of the subject-matter of the cause and who is not already a party to the cause or whom the pursuer is not bound to call as a defender, the defender may apply to the sheriff under rule 93 of the Act of Sederunt (Summary Cause Rules, Sheriff Court) 1976 (incidental applications) for an order making the third party a party to the cause.

(2) Sub-paragraph (1) applies to a cause in which an application is made by virtue of—

(*a*) section 70(3) of the 1974 Act (supplier may be made a party to proceedings against the creditor for recovery of money on cancellation of a regulated agreement);

(*b*) section 73(8) of the 1974 Act (negotiator may be made a party to proceedings against the creditor for recovery of money on cancellation of a regulated agreement where goods were taken in part-exchange); or

(*c*) section 75(5) of the 1974 Act (supplier may be made a party to proceedings against the creditor for misrepresentation or breach of contract by the supplier).

7. If an application under paragraph 6(1) is granted, the sheriff shall appoint a date on which he will regulate further procedure and shall grant warrant to the defender to serve on the third party—

(*a*) a copy of the summons;

(*b*) a copy of the statement of defence, which shall contain the grounds upon which it is claimed that the third party is liable; and

(*c*) a notice as nearly as may be in accordance with the form set out in the Schedule to this Act of Sederunt.

8. On, or after, the date appointed for the regulation of further procedure under paragraph 7, the sheriff may—

(*a*) regulate procedure; or

(*b*) grant such degree, interlocutor or order as he considers appropriate.

9. A decree or other interlocutor granted against a third party under this

Part shall take effect and be extractable in the same way as a decree or other interlocutor against a pursuer or defender.

Paragraph 7(c) SCHEDULE

NOTICE TO THIRD PARTY

Third Party Notice in the case of

A.B., Pursuer v. C.D., Defender
and
E.F., Third Party

To E.F. (*name and address*)
This Notice is served upon you by C.D. by virtue of an order granted by the Sheriff of at on in the action raised against C.D., defender, by A.B., pursuer. The pursuer claims against the defender for (*describe pursuer's claim*) in respect of (*describe contract*) as more fully appears in the summons.

The defender admits [*or* denies] liability to the pursuer but [*or* and] claims that [if he is found liable to the pursuer] you are liable to relieve him wholly [*or* in part] of his liability for the reasons set out in the statement of defence enclosed herewith.

Take notice that if you wish to resist either the claim of the pursuer against the defender or the claim of the defender against you or to make an offer in settlement you are required to appear at the Sheriff Court House at (*address*) on (*day and date*) at (*time*).

If you do not appear decree may be granted against you in your absence.

Dated this day of 19 .

(*Signed*)
Solicitor for Defender

NOTES:
1. You may attend court in person or be represented by an advocate or a solicitor.
2. If you are ordered to pay a sum of money by instalments any failure to pay such instalments at the proper time may result in your forfeiting the right to pay by instalments and the whole amount outstanding will then become due.
3. If decree is granted against you this may, among other possible steps, lead to the arrestment of your wages and/or seizure of your possessions.

Mental Health (Scotland) Act 1984, 1986

(S.I. 1986 No. 545)

[14th March 1986]

The Lords of Council and Session, under and by virtue of the powers conferred on them by section 32 of the Sheriff Courts (Scotland) Act 1971 and of all other powers enabling them in that behalf, do hereby enact and declare:—

Citation and commencement

1.—(1) This Act of Sederunt may be cited as the Act of Sederunt (Mental Health (Scotland) Act 1984) 1986 and shall come into operation on 7th April 1986.

(2) This Act of Sederunt shall be inserted in the Books of Sederunt.

(3) The words and expressions used in this Act of Sederunt which are also used in the Mental Health (Scotland) Act 1984 (referred to in this Act of Sederunt as "the 1984 Act") shall, unless the context otherwise requires, have the same meaning as in that Act.

Service of notice

2.—(1) In an application to the sheriff for admission of a patient to a hospital under section 21, or of a patient into guardianship under section 40, of the 1984 Act—

(*a*) the sheriff shall appoint a hearing; and
(*b*) the sheriff clerk shall serve or cause to be served upon the person who is the subject of such proceedings a copy of the application (with the exception of any medical recommendations) together with a notice as nearly as may be in accordance with form 1 in the Schedule to this Act of Sederunt.

(2) The sheriff may appoint that the hearing of an application to which paragraph 2(1) applies shall take place in a hospital or other place, where he considers this to be appropriate in all the circumstances.

3.—(1) Where the person who is the subject of the application is not already a patient in a hospital, the notice and copy application referred to in paragraph 2(1) shall be served on him personally by a sheriff officer.

(2) Where the person who is the subject of the application is a patient in a hospital, the notice and copy application referred to in paragraph 2(1) shall be served—
(*a*) by recorded delivery post by the sheriff clerk; or
(*b*) personally by a sheriff officer,
on his responsible medical officer and shall be accompanied by a further notice as nearly as may be in accordance with form 2 in the Schedule to this Act of Sederunt addressed to the responsible medical officer.

(3) Where the person who is the subject of the application is already the subject of a guardianship order, the notice and copy application (including any medical recommendations) shall, in addition to any other service required by this paragraph, be served on the guardian—
(*a*) by recorded delivery post by the sheriff clerk; or
(*b*) personally by a sheriff officer.

Duties of responsible medical officer

4.—(1) On receipt by him of a notice under paragraph 3(2), the responsible medical officer shall, subject to paragraph 5(1)—
(*a*) deliver the notice referred to in paragraph 2(1) to the patient; and
(*b*) as soon as practicable thereafter, complete and return to the court a certificate of such delivery as nearly as may be in accordance with form 3 in the Schedule to this Act of Sederunt.

(2) Where, in the opinion of the responsible medical officer, it would be prejudicial to the patient's health or treatment if the patient were to be present during the proceedings, he shall set forth his reasons for his opinion in the certificate referred to in sub-paragraph (1).

Appointment of curator ad litem

5.—(1) Where, in an application to which paragraph 2(1) applies, two medical certificates are produced stating that it would be prejudicial to the health or treatment of the person who is the subject of the application if personal service were effected upon him in terms of paragraph 3(1) or 4(1), the sheriff—
(*a*) may dispense with such service; and
(*b*) if he does so, shall appoint a curator *ad litem* to receive the application and represent the interests of that person.

(2) Where, in an application to which paragraph 2(1) applies, the sheriff is satisfied that—
(*a*) the person who is the subject of the application should be excluded from the whole or any part of the proceedings under section 113(2) of the 1984 Act; or
(*b*) in any other case, it is in all the circumstances appropriate for him to do so,
he may appoint a curator *ad litem* to represent the interests of the person who is the subject of the application.

(3) Service of an application upon a curator *ad litem* shall be effected by the sheriff clerk handing, or sending by recorded delivery post, to him a copy of the application (including any medical recommendations) and of the order appointing him.

Appointment of solicitor by court

6. Where in an application to which paragraph 2(1) applies, the person who is the subject of the application has indicated that he wishes to be represented at the hearing but has not nominated a representative, the sheriff may appoint a solicitor to take instructions from that person.

Intimation to representatives

7. Where in any proceedings under the 1984 Act, the sheriff clerk is aware that the person who is the subject of the application is represented by any person and that representative would not otherwise receive intimation of any diet, a copy of the notice served on the person who is the subject of the application shall be intimated to the representative by the sheriff clerk by recorded delivery post.

Service by sheriff officer

8.—(1) Where a copy of an application and any notice has been served personally by a sheriff officer under this Act of Sederunt, he shall prepare and return to the court an execution of such service setting forth in detail the manner and circumstances of such service.

(2) Where a sheriff officer has been unable to effect personal service under this Act of Sederunt, he shall report to the court the reason why service was not effected.

SCHEDULE

Paragraph 2(1) FORM 1

NOTICE TO BE SERVED ON PERSON WHO IS THE SUBJECT OF ADMISSION OR GUARDIANSHIP PROCEEDINGS

To [*name and address*]
Attached to this notice is a copy of—

an application to the managers of [*name of hospital*] for your admission to that hospital in accordance with Part V of the Mental Health (Scotland) Act 1984.

[or

an application to the [*name of local authority*] for your reception into guardianship in accordance with Part V of the Mental Health (Scotland) Act 1984.]

The hearing will be held at on 19 at

You may appear personally at the hearing of this application unless the court decides otherwise on medical recommendations.

In any event, if you are unable or do not wish to appear personally you may request any person to appear on your behalf.

If you do not appear personally or by a representative, the sheriff will consider the application in the absence of you or your representative.

[*Signed*]
Sheriff Clerk

[*Place and date*]

Paragraph 3(2) FORM 2

NOTICE TO RESPONSIBLE MEDICAL OFFICER

To [*name and address*]

In accordance with the Mental Health (Scotland) Act 1984 a copy of the application and notice of hearing is sent with this notice.

1. You are requested to deliver it personally to .... [*name of patient*] and to explain the contents of it to him.

2. You are also required to arrange if the patient so wishes, for the attendance of [*name of patient*] at the hearing at [*place of hearing*] on [*date*] so that he may appear and be heard in person.

3. You are further requested to complete and return to me in the enclosed envelope the certificate appended hereto before the date of the hearing.

If in your opinion it would be prejudicial to the patient's health or treatment for him to appear and be heard personally you may so recommend in writing, with reasons on the certificate.

[*Signed*]
Sheriff Clerk

[*Place and date*]

Paragraph 4(1) FORM 3

CERTIFICATE OF DELIVERY BY RESPONSIBLE MEDICAL OFFICER

I, [*name and designation*] certify that—

1. I have on the day of personally delivered to [*name of patient*] a copy of the application and the intimation of the hearing; and have explained the contents or purport to him [*or her*].
2. The patient does [not] wish to attend the hearing.
3. The patient does [not] wish to be represented at the hearing [and has nominated [*name and address of representative*] to represent him].
4. I shall arrange for the attendance of the patient at the hearing [*or* in my view it would be prejudicial to the patient's health or treatment for him [*or* her] to appear and be heard in person for the following reasons [*give reasons*]].

[*Signature and designation*]

[*Address and date*]

Enforcement of Judgments under the Civil Jurisdiction and Judgments Act 1982 1986

(S.I. 1986 No. 1947)

[13th November 1986]

The Lords of Council and Session, under and by virtue of the powers conferred on them by section 32 of the Sheriff Courts (Scotland) Act 1971, section 48 of the Civil Jurisdiction and Judgments Act 1982 and of all other powers enabling them in that behalf, do hereby enact and declare:—

Citation and commencement

1.—(1) This Act of Sederunt may be cited as the Act of Sederunt (Enforcement of Judgments under the Civil Jurisdiction and Judgments Act 1982) 1986 and shall come into operation on 1st January 1987.

(2) This Act of Sederunt shall be inserted in the Books of Sederunt.

Interpretation

2.—(1) In this Act of Sederunt—

"the 1982 Act" means the Civil Jurisdiction and Judgments Act 1982;

"Ordinary Cause Rules" means the First Schedule to the Sheriff Courts (Scotland) Act 1907.

(2) A form referred to by number means the form so numbered in the Schedule to this Act of Sederunt or a form substantially to the same effect, with such variation as circumstances may require.

Enforcement of sheriff court judgments in other parts of the United Kingdom (Money provisions)

3.—(1) An application for a certificate under paragraph 2 of Schedule 6 to the 1982 Act shall be made in writing to the sheriff clerk and shall be accompanied by an affidavit—

(*a*) stating the sum or aggregate of the sums, including expenses, payable and unsatisfied;

(*b*) verifying that the time for bringing an appeal against the judgment has expired and no appeal has been brought within that time, or that any appeal has been finally disposed of; and that enforcement of the judgment has not been suspended and the time available for the enforcement has not expired; and

(*c*) stating the address of the party entitled to enforce, and the usual or last known address of the party liable to execution on, the judgment.

(2) A certificate under paragraph 4 of Schedule 6 to the 1982 Act shall be in Form 1 and be signed by the sheriff clerk.

Enforcement of sheriff court judgments in other parts of the United Kingdom (Non-money provisions)

4.—(1) An application for a certified copy of an interlocutor or extract decree and, where appropriate, a copy of the note or opinion of the sheriff under paragraph 2 of Schedule 7 to the 1982 Act shall be made in writing to the sheriff clerk and shall be accompanied by an affidavit—

(*a*) verifying that the time for bringing an appeal against the judgment has expired and no appeal has been brought within that time, or any appeal has been finally disposed of; and that enforcement of the judgment has not been suspended and the time available for the enforcement has not expired; and

(*b*) stating the address of the party entitled to enforce, and the usual or last known address of the party liable to execution on, the judgment.

(2) A copy of an interlocutor, decree, note or opinion issued under paragraph 4 of Schedule 7 to the 1982 Act shall have appended to it a certificate in Form 2 signed by the sheriff clerk.

Enforcement of sheriff court interlocutors and decrees in another Contracting State

5.—(1) Before an application is made under section 12 of the 1982 Act for a copy of a judgment or a certificate giving particulars relating to the judgment and the proceedings in which it was given, the party wishing to enforce the judgment shall serve the judgment on all parties against whom the judgment has been given in accordance with rule 10 or 12 of the Ordinary Cause Rules, as the case may be, accompanied by a notice in Form 4; and the execution of such service shall be in Form 5 unless a form of execution of service is provided by the person effecting service in the other Contracting State where service was effected.

(2) An application under section 12 of the 1982 Act shall be made in writing to the sheriff clerk for—

(*a*) a certificate in Form 3;
(*b*) a certified copy interlocutor; and
(*c*) if required, a certified copy of the opinion of the sheriff.

(3) A certificate shall not be issued under sub-paragraph (2)(*a*) unless there is produced and lodged in the process of the cause an execution of service required under sub-paragraph (1).

Recognition and enforcement in Scotland of foreign maintenance orders

6.—(1) An application under section 5 of the 1982 Act shall be in writing addressed to the Secretary of State, signed by—

(i) the applicants, or
(ii) a solicitor or professional person qualified to act in such matters in the Contracting State of origin, on his behalf,

and shall specify—

(*a*) an address within Scotland for service on the applicant;
(*b*) the usual and last known address of the person against whom judgment was granted;
(*c*) the place where the applicant seeks to enforce the judgment;
(*d*) whether at the date of the application the judgment has been satisfied in whole or in part;
(*e*) whether interest is recoverable on the judgment in accordance with the law of the country in which it was granted and, if so, the rate of interest and the date from which interest became due; and
(*f*) whether the time for bringing an appeal against the judgment has expired without an appeal having been brought, or whether an appeal has been brought against the judgment and is pending or has been finally disposed of.

(2) An application under sub-paragraph (1) shall be accompanied by—

(*a*) a copy of the judgment authenticated by the court which made the order;
(*b*) documents which establish that, according to the law of the country in which the judgment has been given, the judgment is enforceable and has been served;
(*c*) in the case of a judgment given in default, documents which establish that the party in default was served with the documents instituting the proceedings;
(*d*) where appropriate, a document showing that the applicant is in receipt of legal aid in the country in which the judgment was given; and
(*e*) a translation, certified as correct by a person qualified to make it, of the judgment and any documents referred to in heads (*a*) to (*d*) where they are in a language other than English.

(3) Where the applicant does not produce a document required under sub-paragraph (2), the sheriff clerk may—

(*a*) fix a time within which the document is to be produced;
(*b*) accept an equivalent document; or
(*c*) dispense with production of the document.

(4) Where the sheriff clerk is informed by a solicitor practising in Scotland that he is acting on behalf of the applicant, the business address of the solicitor shall thereafter be treated as the address for service on the applicant.

(5) A maintenance order authorised to any extent to be enforced under section 5 of the 1982 Act shall, to that extent, be registered by the sheriff clerk in a register to be kept for the purpose in each sheriff court district.

(6) Where a maintenance order registered under section 5 of the 1982 Act is superseded by a subsequent order registered under that Act, the sheriff clerk shall make an appropriate entry against the entry for the original order.

(7) The applicant may obtain an extract of an order under sub-paragraph (5) or (6) and proceed to arrest in execution, to inhibit and to charge and poind thereon, but may not proceed to an action of furthcoming in respect of an arrestment, adjudication in respect of an inhibition, or sale in respect of a poinding until the time for appeal against the determination of the sheriff clerk under sub-paragraph (10) or (11) has elapsed and any appeal has been disposed of.

(8) The sheriff clerk shall, immediately after registering, or refusing to register, an order under sub-paragraph (5) or (6) to any extent, serve a notice on the applicant, and on the person against whom enforcement is sought, in Form 6.

(9) Service by the sheriff clerk of a notice under sub-paragraph (8) shall be as nearly as may be in accordance with rule 10 or 15 of the Ordinary Cause Rules, and where service is by post the notice shall be posted by the sheriff clerk.

(10) Where enforcement of a maintenance order is authorised, the party against whom enforcement is sought may appeal by way of summary application to the sheriff against the decision of the sheriff clerk—

(*a*) within one month of service; or,

(*b*) if the person against whom enforcement is sought is domiciled in a Contracting State other than the United Kingdom, within two months of service,

and a single further appeal to the Inner House of the Court of Session on a point of law shall proceed in accordance with the rules of procedure for such appeals in the Ordinary Cause Rules.

(11) Where the application for enforcement of a maintenance order is refused, the applicant may appeal by way of summary application to the sheriff within one month, and a single further appeal to the Inner House of the Court of Session on a point of law shall proceed in accordance with the rules of procedure for such appeals in the Ordinary Cause Rules.

Consequential amendments

7.—(1) In paragraph 2 of the Act of Sederunt (Enforcement Abroad of Sheriff Court Judgments) 1962, for the word "abroad" wherever it occurs, substitute the words "in a country other than a country to which Parts I and II of the Civil Jurisdiction and Judgments Act 1982 applies".

(2) In rule 13(1) of the Act of Sederunt (Maintenance Orders (Reciprocal Enforcement) Act 1972 Rules) 1974, after the word "Act", where it second and third appears in that rule, insert the words "or any other enactment".

SCHEDULE

Paragraph 3(2) FORM 1

CERTIFICATE BY SHERIFF CLERK UNDER SECTION 18 OF, AND PARAGRAPH 4(1) OF SCHEDULE 6 TO, THE CIVIL JURISDICTION AND JUDGMENTS ACT 1982

Sheriff Court (*address*)

.... (Pursuer) v. ....(Defender)

I, Sheriff Clerk at Sheriff Court,
hereby certify:—

1. That [AB] obtained judgment against [CD] in the above sheriff court on (*date*) for payment of with of expenses of which is unsatisfied.

2. That the money provision in the judgment carries interest at the rate of *per centum per annum* from the day of 19 until payment.

3. That the time for appealing against the judgment has expired [and no appeal has been brought within that time] [*or* and an appeal having been brought within that time has been finally disposed of].

4. That enforcement of the judgment has not for the time being been suspended and that the time available for its enforcement has not expired.

5. That this certificate is issued under section 18 of, and paragraph 4(1) of Schedule 6 to, the Civil Jurisdiction and Judgments Act 1982 and paragraph 3(2) of the Act of Sederunt (Enforcement of Judgments under the Civil Jurisdiction and Judgments Act 1982) 1986.

Dated at (*place*) this day of 19 .

(*Signed*)
Sheriff Clerk

Paragraph 4(2) FORM 2

CERTIFICATE BY SHERIFF CLERK UNDER SECTION 18 OF, AND PARAGRAPH 4(1)(*b*) OF SCHEDULE 7 TO, THE CIVIL JURISDICTION AND JUDGMENTS ACT 1982

Sheriff Court (*address*)

I, Sheriff Clerk at Sheriff Court,
hereby certify:—

1. That [AB] obtained judgment against [CD] in the above sheriff court on (*date*).

2. That the copy of the interlocutor attached is a true copy of the decree [*or other order*] [and that the copy of the note or opinion of the sheriff attached is a true copy thereof].

3. That the time for appealing against the interlocutor has expired [and no appeal has been brought within that time] [*or* and an appeal having been brought within that time has been finally disposed of].

4. That enforcement of the decree [*or other order*] has not for the time being been suspended and that the time available for its enforcement has not expired.

5. That this certificate is issued under section 18 of, and paragraph 4(1)(*b*) of Schedule 7 to, the Civil Jurisdiction and Judgments Act 1982 and paragraph 4(2) of the Act of Sederunt (Enforcement of Judgments under the Civil Jurisdiction and Judgments Act 1982) 1986.

Dated at (*place*) this day of 19 .

(*Signed*)
Sheriff Clerk

Paragraph 5(2) FORM 3

CERTIFICATE BY SHERIFF CLERK UNDER SECTION 12 OF THE CIVIL JURISDICTION AND JUDGMENTS ACT 1982

Sheriff Court (*address*)

.... (Pursuer) v. ....(Defender)

I, Sheriff Clerk at Sheriff Court,
hereby certify:—

1. That the initial writ raised by the pursuer, [AB] (*address*), was executed by citation of the defender, [CD] (*address*), served on him on the day of 19 by (*state mode of service*).

2. That in the initial writ the pursuer sought [payment of the sum of £ in respect of (*state briefly the nature of the claim*) [and (*state other craves of the writ*)].

3. That [no] notice of intention to defend the action was lodged by the defender [on the day of 19] [and lodged defences on the day of 19].

4. That decree [*or other order*] was granted against the defender by the Sheriff of at for payment of the sum of £ [*or state briefly the terms of the interlocutor or opinion of the sheriff*] [and (*state briefly any other craves of the initial writ*)] together with expenses of the action in the sum of £ , all in terms of the certified copy interlocutor attached hereto.

5. That [no] objection to the jurisdiction of the court has been made [on the grounds that].

6. That the decree includes interest at the rate of *per centum per annum* on the total of the sum of £ and expenses of £ from the day of 19 until payment.

7. That the interlocutor containing the decree has been served on the defender.

8. That the time within which an appeal may be brought against the interlocutor [expires on [*or* has expired]].

9. That an [*or* no] appeal against the interlocutor has been brought [and has been finally disposed of].

10. That enforcement of the decree has not for the time being been suspended and the time available for its enforcement has not expired.

11. That the whole pleadings of the parties are contained in the closed record [*or* initial writ] a copy of which is attached.

12. That the pursuer [*or* defender] benefited from legal aid.

13. That this certificate is issued under section 12 of the Civil Jurisdiction and Judgments Act 1982 and paragraph 5(2) of the Act of Sederunt (Enforcement of Judgments under the Civil Jurisdiction and Judgments Act 1982) 1986.

Dated at (*place*) this day of 19

(*Signed*)
Sheriff Clerk

Paragraph 5(1) FORM 4

NOTICE TO ACCOMPANY SERVICE COPY OF JUDGMENT

To [AB] (*address*)

You are hereby served with a copy of the interlocutor of the Sheriff of at given on the day of 19 . [In terms of this interlocutor you are required to (*state requirements of interlocutor*). Your failure to do so may result in further steps being taken to enforce the interlocutor.]

(*Signed*)
(*Address*)
Solicitor [*or* Sheriff Officer]

(*Place and date*)

Paragraph 5(1) FORM 5

EXECUTION OF SERVICE OF JUDGMENT AND NOTICE WHERE SERVICE EFFECTED BY OFFICER OF COURT OR SOLICITOR IN SCOTLAND

(*place and date*)

I, [AB] (*address*), hereby certify that upon the day of 19 , I duly served a copy of this judgment together with notice in terms of paragraph 5(1) of the Act of Sederunt (Enforcement of Judgments under the Civil Jurisdiction and Judgments Act 1982) 1986 upon [CD], defender. This I did by posting (*set forth mode of service; if by officer and not by post, add* in presence of EF (*address*) witness, hereto with me subscribing).

(*Signed*)
(*Address*)
Solicitor for Pursuer
[*or* Defender]

[or

(*Signed*)
Sheriff Officer

(*Signed*)
Witness]

Paragraph 6(8) FORM 6

NOTICE OF DETERMINATION BY SHERIFF CLERK OF APPLICATION UNDER SECTION 5 OF THE CIVIL JURISDICTION AND JUDGMENTS ACT 1982

Sheriff Court (*address*)

.... (Appellant) v.................................... (Respondent)

TAKE NOTICE that the application by (*name and design*), for the recognition and/or enforcement of a maintenance order granted by (*state court or tribunal*) on the day of 19 ; has been GRANTED [*or* REFUSED] (*state reasons in brief for refusal*); and [has been registered in the Books of Court] [*or* has been registered in the Books of Court to the extent that (*state the extent*).].

(*Signed*)
Sheriff Clerk
(*date*)

NOTE:

1. If your application has been granted, the person against whom enforcement is sought may appeal against this decision within one month of service on him, unless he is domiciled in another Contracting State in which case he may appeal within two months of the date of service on him.

2. If your application has been refused you may appeal against the decision within (*insert months*). You should consult a solicitor qualified in Scots law for this purpose.

Small Claim Rules 1988

(S.I. 1988 No. 1976)

[10th November 1988]

The Lords of Council and Session, under and by virtue of the powers conferred on them by section 32 of the Sheriff Courts (Scotland) Act 1971 and of all other powers enabling them in that behalf, do hereby enact and declare:—

Citation and commencement

1.—(1) This Act of Sederunt may be cited as the Act of Sederunt (Small Claim Rules) 1988 and shall come into force on 30th November 1988.

(2) This Act of Sederunt shall be inserted in the Books of Sederunt.

Small Claim Rules

2.—(1) The provisions of the Schedule to this Act of Sederunt shall have effect for the purpose of providing rules for the form of summary cause process known as a small claim under section 35(2) of the Sheriff Courts (Scotland) Act 1971.

(2) The provisions of the Schedule to this Act of Sederunt shall not apply to a summary cause commenced before 30th November 1988.

Consequential amendment

3. [The amendment to para. 3(1) of the Act of Sederunt (Summary Cause Rules, Sheriff Court) 1976 is included in the print of that Act, *supra.*]

Paragraph 2(1) SCHEDULE

SMALL CLAIM RULES 1988

Arrangement of Rules

Part I

Introductory

Part II

Rules for Small Claims for Payment of Money Only

PART III

SPECIAL RULES FOR SMALL CLAIMS FOR DELIVERY OR RECOVERY OF POSSESSION OF MOVEABLE PROPERTY AND FOR IMPLEMENT OF AN OBLIGATION

PART I

INTRODUCTORY

Citation, application and interpretation

1.—(1) These rules may be cited as the Small Claim Rules 1988.

(2) These rules shall apply to a small claim, being such summary cause proceedings as may be prescribed by the Lord Advocate under section 35(2) of the Sheriff Courts (Scotland) Act 1971.

(3) In these rules—

(*a*) a form referred to by number means the form so numbered in Appendix 1 to these rules or a form substantially of the same effect with such variation as circumstances may require;

(*b*) a reference to the Ordinary Cause Rules means the rules in Schedule 1 to the Sheriff Courts (Scotland) Act 1907; and

(*c*) a reference to the Summary Cause Rules means the rules in the Schedule to the Act of Sederunt (Summary Cause Rules, Sheriff Court) 1976.

[1] 1A. In these rules, unless the context otherwise requires, "authorised lay representative" means a person to whom section 32(1) of the Solicitors (Scotland) Act 1980 (offence to prepare writs) does not apply by virtue of section 32(2)(*a*) of that Act.

NOTE

[1] Inserted by S.I. 1991 No. 821.

Application of certain Ordinary Cause, and Summary Cause, Rules

2.—(1) The provisions of the Ordinary Cause Rules specified in Appendix 2 to these rules shall apply to a small claim insofar as not inconsistent with these rules.

(2) The provisions of the Summary Cause Rules specified in Appendix 3 to these rules shall apply to a small claim insofar as not inconsistent with these rules.

PART II

RULES FOR SMALL CLAIMS FOR PAYMENT OF MONEY ONLY

3.—(1) A small claim for payment of money only shall be commenced by summons in form 1.

(2) A service copy summons in form 2 shall be served on the defender in a small claim for payment of money only in which a time to pay direction may be applied for; and the small claim shall be subject to the rules in this Part.

(3) A service copy summons in form 3 shall be served on the defender in a small claim for payment of money only in which a time to pay direction may not be applied for; and the small claim shall be subject to the rules in this Part except rules 9 and 11 below.

[1] (4) The pursuer shall give a statement of his claim in the summons to give the defender fair notice of the claim; and the statement shall include—

(*a*) details of the basis of the small claim including relevant dates;

(*b*) where the small claim arises from the supply of goods or services, a description of the goods or services and the date or dates on or between which they were supplied and, where relevant, ordered;

(*c*) a reference to any agreement which the pursuer has reason to believe may exist giving jurisdiction over the subject matter of the small claim to another court;

(*d*) a reference to any proceedings which the pursuer has reason to believe may be pending before another court involving the same cause of action and between the same parties as those named in the summons.

(5) A summons shall be signed—

(*a*) by the sheriff clerk; or

(*b*) by the sheriff, if he thinks fit, where—

(i) the defender's address is unknown; or

(ii) the sheriff clerk has for any reason refused to sign the summons.

(6) The signed summons shall be warrant for service on the defender and, where the appropriate warrant has been included in the summons, warrant for arrestment on the dependence or for arrestment to found jurisdiction, as the case may be.

NOTE

[1] As amended by S.I. 1992 No. 249 (effective 4th May 1992).

Period of notice

4.—(1) A small claim shall proceed after the appropriate period of notice of the summons has been given to the defender.

(2) The appropriate period of notice shall be—

(*a*) 21 days where the defender is resident or has a place of business within Europe; or

(*b*) 42 days where the defender is resident or has a place of business outwith Europe.

(3) Where a period of notice expires on a Saturday, Sunday, public or local holiday, the period of notice shall be deemed to expire on the first following day on which the sheriff clerk's office is open for civil court business.

[1] (4) Notwithstanding the terms of section 4(2) of the Citation Amendment (Scotland) Act 1882, where service is by post the period of notice shall run from the beginning of the day next following the date of posting.

(5) The sheriff clerk shall insert in the summons the date which is at the end of the period of notice being the last day on which the defender may return a response form to the sheriff clerk (the return date).

NOTE

[1] As amended by S.I. 1992 No. 249 (effective 4th May 1992).

Service of summons where address of defender is known

5.—(1) Subject to paragraph (7) of this rule, a service copy summons shall be served on the defender by the pursuer's solicitor, a sheriff officer or the sheriff clerk sending it by first class recorded delivery post, or by one of the methods specified in rule 6(1), (2) or (4) of the Summary Cause Rules (citation and service within Scotland by officer of court).

(2) Where the pursuer requires the sheriff clerk to effect service on his behalf by virtue of section 36A of the Sheriff Courts (Scotland) Act 1971 (pursuer not a partnership, body corporate or acting in a representative capacity), he may require the sheriff clerk to supply him with a copy of the summons.

(3) Subject to paragraph (7) of this rule, where service is to be effected by the sheriff clerk, he may do so by posting the service copy summons by first class recorded delivery post or, on

payment to the sheriff clerk by the pursuer of the fee prescribed by the Secretary of State by order, by sheriff officer.

(4) There shall be enclosed with the service copy summons a form of service in form 4.

(5) On the face of the envelope used for postal service in terms of this rule there shall be printed or written a notice in form 5.

(6) A certificate of service in form 6 shall be attached to the summons after service has been effected under this rule.

(7) Service on a defender who is outwith Scotland shall be effected in the manner prescribed by rule 9 of the Summary Cause Rules (citation of or service on persons outside Scotland).

(8) Where service is to be effected by the sheriff clerk under paragraph (7), any cost occasioned thereby shall be borne by the pursuer and no such service shall be instructed by the sheriff clerk until payment of such cost has been made to him by the pursuer.

Service where address of defender is unknown

6.—(1) Where the defender's address is unknown to the pursuer, the sheriff may grant warrant to serve the summons—

(*a*) by the publication of an advertisement in form 7 in a newspaper circulating in the area of the defender's last known address; or

(*b*) by displaying on the walls of court a copy of a notice in form 8,

and the period of notice, which shall be fixed by the sheriff, shall run from the date of publication of the advertisement or display on the walls of court, as the case may be.

(2) Where service is to be effected under paragraph (1) of this rule, the pursuer shall lodge a service copy of the summons with the sheriff clerk from whom it may be uplifted by the defender.

(3) Where the pursuer requires the sheriff clerk to effect service on his behalf under

[THE NEXT PAGE IS D 321]

paragraph (1) of this rule by virtue of section 36A of the Sheriff Courts (Scotland) Act 1971 (pursuer not a partnership, body corporate or acting in a representative capacity)—

(*a*) the cost of any advertisement required under paragraph (1)(*a*) of this rule shall be borne by the pursuer and no such advertisement shall be instructed by the sheriff clerk until such cost has been paid to him by the pursuer; and

(*b*) the pursuer may require the sheriff clerk to supply him with a copy of the summons.

(4) Where service by advertisement is made under paragraph (1)(*a*) of this rule, a copy of the newspaper containing the advertisement shall be lodged with the sheriff clerk unless advertisement is instructed by the sheriff clerk under paragraph (3) of this rule.

(5) Where display on the walls of court is required under paragraph (1)(*b*) of this rule, the pursuer shall supply to the sheriff clerk for that purpose a copy of form 8 duly completed unless service is to be effected by the sheriff clerk under paragraph (3) of this rule.

(6) Where service has been made under this rule and thereafter the defender's address becomes known, the sheriff may allow the summons to be amended and, if appropriate, grant warrant for re-service subject to such conditions as he thinks fit.

Return of summons

7.—(1) Where service has been effected other than by the sheriff clerk, the pursuer shall return the summons with a certificate of service to the sheriff clerk on or before the return date, failing which the sheriff may dismiss the small claim.

(2) Where the summons has been served by the sheriff clerk, he shall intimate to the pursuer, forthwith after the return date, whether or not a response to the summons has been tendered by the defender; and such intimation shall be made by the sheriff clerk sending to the pursuer by first class recorded delivery post a copy of form 9 (claim admitted; payment by instalments or lump sum), 10 (no response) or 11 (claim admitted and defender to appear or claim not admitted or jurisdiction challenged), as appropriate.

Response to summons where defender intends to appear

8.—(1) Where the defender intends—

(*a*) to challenge the jurisdiction of the court;

(*b*) to defend the small claim;

(*c*) to dispute the amount of the small claim; or

(*d*) to admit the small claim and make oral application for a time to pay direction (including, where appropriate, an application for recall or restriction of an arrestment),

he shall intimate his intention to appear by completing the appropriate part of the form of response attached to the service copy summons and shall lodge it with the sheriff clerk on or before the return date.

(2) A defender who intends to defend a small claim and has delivered a form of response to the sheriff clerk may, at any time prior to the date of the preliminary hearing of the small claim, lodge a written note of the defence which he proposes to state at the preliminary hearing.

(3) Where the defender has delivered a written note of his proposed defence to the small claim to the sheriff clerk, the defender shall, at the same time, send a copy of it to the pursuer.

Response to summons where defender does not intend to appear

9. Where the defender admits the small claim and does not intend to appear, he may, where competent, make an application for a time to pay direction (including, where appropriate, an application for recall or restriction of an arrestment) by completing the appropriate part of the form of response attached to the service copy summons and lodge it with the sheriff clerk on or before the return date.

No response by defender

10.—(1) Where a form of response has not been lodged by the defender in accordance with rule 8 or 9 above, the cause shall not be called in court and, if before noon on the day prior to the date for the preliminary hearing, the pursuer, his solicitor or his solicitor's authorised clerk enters a minute in the Book of Small Claims or lodges form 10 with the minute in box 1 or 2 duly signed, or a minute in form 12, as the case may be, decree or other order in terms of that minute may be granted on the date for the preliminary hearing.

(2) Where the pursuer does not enter a minute in the Book of Small Claims or lodge form 10 with the minute in box 1 or 2 duly signed, or a minute in form 12 in accordance with paragraph (1) of this rule, the court shall dismiss the small claim.

(3) A decree granted under paragraph (1) of this rule shall be subject to recall in accordance with the provisions of rule 27 below.

(4) The sheriff shall not grant decree under paragraph (1) of this rule unless it is clear from the terms of the summons that a ground of jurisdiction exists.

Consent to application for time to pay direction

11.—(1) Where the defender has delivered a form of response to the sheriff clerk in accordance with rule 9 above making application for a time to pay direction (including, where appropriate, an application for recall or restriction of an arrestment), the pursuer may intimate that he does not object to the application by—

(*a*) entering a minute in the Book of Small Claims stating that he does not object to the defender's application and for decree;

(*b*) lodging with the sheriff clerk a minute in form 12; or

(*c*) lodging with the sheriff clerk form 9 with a minute duly signed,

before noon on the day prior to the date for the preliminary hearing.

(2) Where the pursuer intimates under paragraph (1) of this rule that he does not object to the defender's application for a time to pay direction (including, where appropriate, an application for recall or restriction of an arrestment), the sheriff may grant decree on the date for the preliminary hearing and the parties shall not be required to attend and the cause shall not be called, in court.

Preliminary hearing

12.—(1) A preliminary hearing shall be held where—

(*a*) the defender has intimated his intention to appear in accordance with rule 8(1) above; or

(*b*) the defender has made an application for a time to pay direction (including, where appropriate, an application for recall or restriction of an arrestment) in accordance with rule 9 above which the pursuer does not accept.

(2) The preliminary hearing shall be held seven days after the return date, and may be continued to such other date as the court shall consider appropriate.

(3) The sheriff clerk shall insert in the summons the date for the preliminary hearing.

(4) Where the defender has delivered a form of response to the sheriff clerk in accordance with rule 8(1)(*a*), (*b*) or (*c*) above, he shall attend or be represented at the preliminary hearing and state his defence to the court (which shall be noted by the sheriff on the summons).

(5) Where the defender has delivered a form of response to the sheriff clerk in accordance with rule 8(1)(*d*) above, he shall attend or be represented at the preliminary hearing and may make oral representations in support of his application.

(6) Where the defender has delivered a form of response to the sheriff clerk in accordance with rule 9 above which the pursuer has not accepted, the sheriff shall make such order on the defender's application as he considers appropriate.

Conduct of preliminary hearing

13.—(1) Subject to paragraph (2) of this rule, where the defender has delivered a form of response to the sheriff clerk in accordance with rule 8(1) above but does not appear and has not stated a defence, decree may be granted against the defender in terms of the summons.

(2) The sheriff shall not grant decree until paragraph (1) of this rule unless it is clear from the terms of the summons that a ground of jurisdiction exists.

(3) Where the pursuer does not appear or is not represented at the preliminary hearing at which the defender is present or represented and if a defence has not been stated, the court shall grant decree absolving the defender.

(4) Where, at the preliminary hearing, the sheriff is satisfied that the small claim is incompetent or that there is a patent defect of jurisdiction, he may grant decree of dismissal in favour of the defender.

(5) At the preliminary hearing, the sheriff shall ascertain from the parties or their representatives what the disputed issues in the small claim are and shall make a note of them on the summons; and it shall thereafter be unnecessary for a party to satisfy the sheriff on any issue which is not noted as a disputed issue.

(6) Where the sheriff is satisfied that the facts are sufficiently admitted, he may decide the small claim on the merits at the preliminary hearing and if appropriate make an award of expenses.

(7) If, at the preliminary hearing or at any subsequent stage of the small claim, a disputed issue noted by the sheriff is the quality or condition of an object, the sheriff may inspect the object in the presence of the parties or their representatives in court or, if it is not practicable to bring the object to court, at the place where the object is located.

(8) The sheriff may, if he considers it appropriate, inspect any place material to the disputed issues in the presence of the parties or their representatives.

(9) The sheriff may, on the joint motion of the parties, if he considers it to be appropriate, remit to any suitable person to report on any matter of fact.

(10) Where a remit is made under paragraph (9) of this rule, the report of such person shall be final and conclusive with respect to the matter of fact which is the subject of the remit.

(11) A remit shall not be made under paragraph (9) of this rule unless parties have previously agreed the basis upon which the fees, if any, of such person shall be met by them.

(12) Where any issue of fact between the parties is still disputed, the sheriff shall appoint a date for a hearing.

Remit between rolls

14.—(1) Where a direction has been made by the sheriff under section 37(2B) of the Sheriff Courts (Scotland) Act 1971 that a small claim be treated as a summary cause or as an ordinary cause, the small claim shall be remitted to the summary cause roll or ordinary cause roll, as the case may be, first occurring not sooner than seven days after the date of that direction.

(2) Where a direction has been made under section 37 of the Sheriff Courts (Scotland) Act 1971 that a summary cause or an ordinary cause be treated as a small claim, the initial writ or summary cause summons, as the case may be, shall be treated as a small claim summons and the cause shall be remitted to the small claim roll occurring not more than seven days after the date of the direction; or, if there is no roll within that period, to the roll first occurring thereafter.

Alteration of summons, etc.

15. The sheriff may, on the motion of a party, allow amendment of the summons, statement of claim or note of defence and adjust the disputed issues at any time.

Witnesses

16.—(1) A party to a small claim shall be entitled to give and lead evidence but shall be responsible for securing the attendance of his witnesses at a hearing and shall be personally liable for their expenses (which shall form expenses in the cause only up to the limit prescribed in rule 26 below).

(2) The hearing of a small claim shall not be adjourned solely on account of the failure of a witness to appear unless the sheriff on cause shown so directs.

(3) Evidence by a party or witness shall be given on oath or affirmation.

Productions

17.—(1) A party who intends to found at a hearing (other than a preliminary hearing) upon any documents or articles in his possession, which are reasonably capable of being lodged with the court, shall lodge them with the sheriff clerk together with a list detailing the items no later than seven days before the hearing and shall at the same time send a copy of the list to the other party.

[1] (2) A party litigant or an authorised lay representative shall not borrow a production except with leave of the sheriff and subject to such conditions as the sheriff may impose, but may inspect them within the office of the sheriff clerk during normal business hours, and may obtain copies, where practicable, from the sheriff clerk.

(3) Only documents or articles—

(*a*) produced in accordance under paragraph (1) of this rule;

(*b*) produced at the preliminary hearing; or

(*c*) produced under rule 18 below,

may be used or put in evidence, unless with the consent of the parties or the permission of the sheriff.

NOTE

[1] As amended by S.I. 1991 No. 821.

Recovery of documents

18.—(1) Any party may apply to the sheriff for an order for recovery of such documents, referred to in a list of documents lodged by that party, as the sheriff considers relevant to the disputed issues.

(2) Where an order has been granted under paragraph (1) of this rule, a copy of it may be served by first class recorded delivery post on the person from whom the documents are sought to be recovered together with a certificate in form 13, and the order of the court shall be implemented in the manner and within the time specified in the order.

(3) Where the party in whose favour an order under paragraph (1) of this rule has been granted is not—

(*a*) a partnership or body corporate; or

(*b*) acting in a representative capacity,
and is not represented by a solicitor, service under paragraph (2) of this rule shall be effected by the sheriff clerk posting a copy of the order together with a certificate in form 13 by first class recorded delivery post or, on payment of the fee prescribed by the Secretary of State by order, by sheriff officer.

(4) Documents recovered in response to an order under paragraph (1) of this rule shall be sent to, and retained by, the sheriff clerk who shall, on receiving them, advise the parties that the documents are in his possession and (subject to rule 39 of the Summary Cause Rules (confidentiality)) may be examined within his office during normal business hours.

(5) In the event of a person, from whom documents are sought to be recovered, failing to implement an order of the court in the manner or within the time specified, the party seeking recovery may apply to the sheriff for an order requiring that person to appear before him to explain his failure; and if such person shall fail to appear he may be held in contempt of court.

(6) Documents recovered under this rule may be tendered as evidence at any hearing without further formality, and rule 17(2) above shall apply to such documents.

Hearing

19. Any hearing, including a preliminary hearing, shall be conducted in public in such manner as the sheriff considers best suited to the clarification of the issue before him; and shall, so far as practicable, be conducted in an informal manner.

Noting of evidence

20. The sheriff shall make notes of the evidence at a hearing for his own use and shall retain these notes until after any appeal has been disposed of.

Documents, etc., referred to during hearing

21. Documents or other productions referred to during a hearing, and a report of a person to whom a matter has been remitted, shall be retained in the custody of the sheriff clerk until any appeal has been disposed of.

Abandonment of small claim

22.—(1) At any time prior to decree being pronounced, the pursuer may offer to abandon the small claim.

(2) Where the pursuer offers to abandon, the sheriff clerk shall assess the sum of expenses payable by the pursuer to the defender calculated on such basis as the sheriff may direct (subject to section 36B of the Sheriff Courts (Scotland) Act 1971 and rule 26 below).

(3) The pursuer shall make payment to the defender of the assessed sum of expenses within 14 days of the date of assessment; and the court may thereafter dismiss the claim.

(4) Where the pursuer fails to make payment of the sum of assessed expenses within 14 days of the date of assessment, the court shall absolve the defender with expenses in favour of the defender.

Decree by default and dismissal

23.—(1) Where, after a defence has been stated, a party fails to appear or be represented at any hearing, a special hearing shall be fixed by the court to be held not earlier than 14 days after the date of such failure.

(2) Where a special hearing is fixed by the court under paragraph (1) of this rule, the sheriff clerk shall forthwith—

(*a*) intimate the date, time and place of the special hearing to the party who has failed to appear or to be represented;

(*b*) advise him of the reason for the special hearing; and

(*c*) advise him that decree may be granted against him if—

(i) he fails to appear or be represented at the special hearing; or

(ii) at the special hearing good cause is not shown for non-appearance at any prior hearing.

(3) Where a party—

(*a*) fails to appear or be represented at a special hearing;

(*b*) fails to show cause at a special hearing for his non-appearance at a prior hearing; or

(*c*) fails to appear or be represented at any hearing after a special hearing,

decree by default or decree absolving the defender may be granted.

(4) Where, after a defence has been stated, a party fails to implement an order of the court, the sheriff may, after giving him an opportunity to be heard, grant decree by default or absolve the defender.

(5) Where all parties fail to appear or be represented at any hearing, the sheriff shall, unless sufficient reason appears to the contrary, dismiss the small claim.

Application for a time to pay direction in defended small claims

24. A defender in a small claim which proceeds as defended may, where it is competent to do so, make a written or oral application to the court, at any time before decree is granted, for a time to pay direction (including where appropriate, an order recalling or restricting an arrestment).

Decree

25.—(1) The sheriff shall, where practicable, give his decision and a brief statement of his reasons at the conclusion of the hearing of a small claim or reserve judgment.

(2) Where the sheriff reserves judgment, he shall, within 28 days of the hearing give his decision in writing together with a brief note of his reasons; and the sheriff clerk shall forthwith intimate these to the parties.

(3) After giving his judgment, the sheriff shall—

(*a*) deal with the question of expenses and, where appropriate, make an award of expenses; and

(*b*) grant decree as appropriate.

(4) A decree of the sheriff in a small claim shall be a final decree.

Expenses

[1] 26. Subject to section 36B of the Sheriff Courts (Scotland) Act 1971 and to paragraph 4 of the Small Claims (Scotland) Order 1988, rule 88 (expenses) of the Summary Cause Rules shall apply to the determination of an award of expenses in a small claim as it applies to the determination of such an award in a summary cause.

NOTE

[1] As substituted by S.I. 1991 No. 821.

Recall of decree

27.—(1) A pursuer, at any time within 21 days of the grant of decree absolving the defender under rule 13(3) above, may apply for the recall of that decree by lodging with the sheriff clerk a minute for recall of the decree in form 14.

(2) A defender, at any time not later than 14 days after the execution of a charge or execution of arrestment, whichever first occurs, following on the grant of decree in terms of rule 10(1) or 13(1) above, may apply for the recall of that decree by lodging with the sheriff clerk a minute for recall of the decree in form 14.

(3) A party may apply for recall of a decree in the same small claims on one occasion only.

(4) Where the party seeking recall of a decree is not—

(*a*) a partnership or a body corporate; or

(*b*) acting in a representative capacity,

and is not represented by a solicitor, the sheriff clerk shall assist that party to complete and lodge a minute for recall of the decree.

(5) [Revoked by S.I. 1990 No. 2105.]

(6) On the lodging of a minute for recall of a decree, the sheriff clerk shall fix a date, time and place for a hearing of the minute; and a copy of the minute together with a note of the date, time and place of the hearing shall be served upon the other party not less than seven days before the date fixed for the hearing by the party seeking recall.

(7) Where the party seeking recall is not—

(*a*) a partnership or body corporate; or

(*b*) acting in a representative capacity,

and is not represented by a solicitor, service of the minute shall be effected by the sheriff clerk either by first class recorded delivery post or, on payment of the fee prescribed by the Secretary of State by order, by sheriff officer.

(8) At a hearing under paragraph (6) of this rule, the sheriff shall recall the decree so far as not implemented; and the small claim shall proceed in all respects as if the hearing were a preliminary hearing.

(9) [Revoked by S.I. 1990 No. 2105.]

(10) A minute for recall of a decree, when duly lodged and served in terms of this rule, shall have the effect of preventing any further action being taken by the other party to enforce the decree.

(11) On service of the copy minute for recall of a decree, any party in possession of the summons shall return it to the sheriff clerk.

Book of Small Claims

28.—(1) The sheriff clerk shall keep a book to be known as the Book of Small Claims in which shall be entered a note of all small claims, minutes under rule 27 above (recall of decree) and minutes under rule 92(1) of the Summary Cause Rules (applications in same cause for variation etc of decree), setting forth, where appropriate—

(*a*) the names, designations and addresses of the parties;
(*b*) whether the parties were present or absent at any hearing, including an inspection, and the names of their representatives;
(*c*) the nature of the cause;
(*d*) the amount of any claim;
(*e*) the date of issue of the summons;
(*f*) the method of service;
(*g*) the return date;
(*h*) whether a form of response was lodged, and details thereof;
(*i*) whether a statement of defence was lodged;
(*j*) details of any minute by the pursuer intimating that he does not object to an application for a time to pay direction, or minute by the pursuer requesting decree or other order;
(*k*) details of any interlocutors issued;
(*l*) details of the final decree and the date thereof; and
(*m*) details of any variation or recall of a decree by virtue of the Debtors (Scotland) Act 1987.

(2) The Book of Small Claims shall be signed in respect of each court day by the sheriff.

(3) The Book of Small Claims may be made up of separate rolls, each roll relating solely to proceedings of a particular description of small claim.

(4) The Book of Small Claims shall be open for inspection during normal business hours.

Appeals

29.—(1) An appeal to the sheriff principal, other than an appeal to which rule 85A of the Summary Cause Rules (appeals in relation to time to pay directions) applies, shall be by note of appeal—

(*a*) requesting a stated case;
(*b*) specifying the point of law upon which the appeal is to proceed; and
(*c*) lodged with the sheriff clerk not later than 14 days after the date of final decree.

(2) The appellant shall, at the same time as lodging a note of appeal, intimate its lodging to the other party.

(3) The sheriff shall, within 14 days of the lodging a note of appeal, issue a draft stated case containing—

(*a*) findings in fact and law or, where appropriate, a narrative of the proceedings before him;
(*b*) appropriate questions of law; and
(*c*) a note stating the reasons for his decisions in law,

and the sheriff clerk shall send a copy of the draft stated case to the parties.

(4) Within 14 days of the issue of the draft stated case—

(*a*) a party may lodge with the sheriff clerk a note of any adjustments which he seeks to make;
(*b*) the respondent may state any point of law which he wishes to raise in the appeal; and
(*c*) the note of adjustment and, where appropriate, point of law shall be intimated to the other party.

(5) The sheriff may, on the motion of a party or of his own accord, and shall where he proposes to reject any proposed adjustment, allow a hearing on adjustments and may provide for such further procedure under this rule prior to the hearing of the appeal as he thinks fit.

(6) The sheriff shall, within 14 days after—

(*a*) the latest date on which a note of adjustments has been or may be lodged; or
(*b*) where there has been a hearing on adjustments, that hearing,

and after considering such note and any representations made to him at the hearing, state and sign the case.

[1] (6A) Where the sheriff is temporarily absent from duty for any reason, the sheriff principal may extend any period specified in paragraphs (3) or (6) for such period or periods as he considers reasonable.

(7) The stated case signed by the sheriff shall include questions of law, framed by him, arising from the points of law stated by the parties and such other questions of law as he may consider appropriate.

(8) After the sheriff has signed the stated case, the sheriff clerk shall—

(*a*) place before the sheriff principal all documents and productions in the small claim together with the stated case; and
(*b*) send to the parties a copy of the stated case together with a written note of the date, time and place of the hearing of the appeal.

(9) In the hearing of an appeal, a party shall not be allowed to raise questions of law of which notice has not been given except on cause shown and subject to such conditions as to expenses or otherwise as the sheriff principal may consider appropriate.

NOTE
[1] Inserted by S.I. 1992 No. 249 (effective 4th May 1992).

[THE NEXT PAGE IS D 327]

Representation

[1] 30.—(1) A party may be represented by an advocate, solicitor or, subject to the following provisions of this rule, an authorised lay representative.

(2) Subject to the following provisions of this rule, an authorised lay representative may in representing a party do all such things for the preparation and conduct of a small claim as may be done by an individual conducting his own claim.

(3) An authorised lay representative shall cease to represent a party if the sheriff finds either that the authorised lay representative is not a suitable person to represent the party or that he is not authorised to do so.

NOTE

[1] As substituted by S.I. 1991 No. 821.

Application of rules to solicitors

31. Where a rule requires something to be done by, or intimated or sent to, a party, it shall be sufficient compliance with the rule if it is done by, or intimated or sent to, the solicitor acting for that party in the small claim.

Contents of envelope containing service copy summons

32. A document not forming part of the summons or any form of response or other notice in accordance with these rules shall not be included in the same envelope as the service copy summons.

Incidental applications

33.—(1) Except where otherwise provided, any incidental application in a small claim shall be lodged with the sheriff clerk and shall only be heard after two days' notice has been given to the other party.

(2) A party who is not—

(*a*) a partnership or a body corporate; or

(*b*) acting in a representative capacity,

and is not represented by a solicitor, may require the sheriff clerk to intimate to the other party a copy of an incident application.

(3) The sheriff clerk shall keep a book to be known as the Book of Incidental Applications in Small Claims in which shall be entered all applications incidental to a small claim, other than minutes under rule 10(1), 11(1) or 27(1) above or under rule 92(1) of the Summary Cause Rules (applications in same cause for variation etc of decree), and in which shall be set forth the following particulars, where appropriate—

(*a*) the names of the parties together with a clear reference to the entry in the Book of Small Claims;

(*b*) whether parties are present or absent at the hearing of the application, and the names of their representatives;

(*c*) the nature of the application; and

(*d*) the interlocutor issued or order made.

(4) The Book of Incidental Applications in Small Claims shall be—

(*a*) signed by the sheriff on each day on which incidental applications are heard; and

(*b*) be open for inspection during normal business hours to all concerned without fee.

Dispensing power of sheriff

34. The sheriff may relieve any party from the consequences of any failure to comply with the provisions of these rules which is shown to be due to mistake, oversight or other cause, not being wilful non-observance of the rules, on such terms and conditions as seem just; and in any such case the sheriff may make such order as seems just by way of extension of time, lodging or amendment of papers or otherwise so as to enable the small claim to proceed as if such failure had not occurred.

PART III

SPECIAL RULES FOR SMALL CLAIMS FOR DELIVERY OR RECOVERY OF POSSESSION OF MOVEABLE PROPERTY AND FOR IMPLEMENT OF AN OBLIGATION

Application

35.—(1) The provisions of Part II of these rules shall apply to a small claim for which rules are provided in this Part, except insofar as those provisions are inconsistent with the rules in this Part.

(2) The provisions of this Part of these rules shall apply to a small claim for delivery or recovery of possession of moveable property or for implement of an obligation to which article 2(*b*) or 3 of the Small Claims (Scotland) Order 1988 applies.

Summons for delivery or recovery of possession of moveable property

36.—(1) A small claim for delivery or recovery of possession of moveable property shall be commenced by summons in form 15.

(2) A service copy summons in form 16 shall be served on the defender in a small claim for delivery or recovery of possession of moveable property in which a time to pay direction may be applied for.

(3) A service copy summons in form 17 shall be served on the defender in a small claim for delivery or recovery of possession of moveable property in which a time to pay direction may not be applied for.

Summons for implement of an obligation

37.—(1) A small claim for implement of an obligation shall be commenced by summons in form 18.

(2) A service copy summons in form 19 shall be served on the defender in a small claim for implement of an obligation in which a time to pay direction may be applied for.

(3) A service copy summons in form 20 shall be served on the defender in a small claim for implement of an obligation in which a time to pay direction may not be applied for.

Service

38.—(1) Where service of the copy summons has been effected other than by the sheriff clerk, the pursuer shall return the summons together with a certificate of service in form 6 to the sheriff clerk at least 24 hours before the date of the preliminary hearing.

(2) Where paragraph (1) of this rule is not complied with, the sheriff may dismiss the small claim.

Time to pay directions

39.—(1) In a small claim where a service copy summons has been served under rule 36(2) or 37(2) above, the defender may, if he does not intend to defend, apply for a time to pay direction, where it is competent to do so, by—

(*a*) appearing at the preliminary hearing and making a motion for a time to pay direction; or

(*b*) completing and returning to the sheriff clerk, at least seven days before the date specified in the service copy summons for the preliminary hearing, the appropriate portion of form 16 or 19, as the case may be.

(2) In a small claim where a service copy summons has been served under rule 36(2) or 37(2) above which proceeds as defended, the defender may, where it is competent to do so, apply for a time to pay direction by written or oral application to the court at any time before final decree is granted.

(3) Where a defender applies for a time to pay direction under this rule, he may at the same time apply for an order recalling or restricting an arrestment on the dependence of the action or in security of the sum concerned by completing and delivering to the sheriff clerk the appropriate part of form 16 or 19, as the case may be.

Preliminary hearing

40.—(1) A preliminary hearing shall be held on the date specified in the summons.

(2) Where the defender does not appear or is not represented at the preliminary hearing, decree may be granted against him.

Decree for alternative claim for payment

41.—(1) Where decree for delivery or recovery of possession of moveable property or for implement of an obligation has been granted but the defender has failed to comply with that decree, the pursuer may lodge with the sheriff clerk an incidental application for decree in terms of the alternative crave for payment; and the incidental application shall be intimated to the defender.

(2) The pursuer shall appear at the hearing of an incidental application under paragraph (1) of this rule.

Rule 1(3)

APPENDIX 1

FORMS

Rule 3(1)

FORM 1

Form of summons in small claim for payment of money

SMALL CLAIM SUMMONS
CLAIM FOR PAYMENT
OF MONEY

Official Use Only
Summons No.
Return date
Preliminary hearing date

Sheriff Court (name and address and tel. no.)	1		Name, full address and tel. no. of pursuer's solicitor (if any)	2	
Name and address of person making the claim (PURSUER)	3				
Name and address of person from whom money is claimed (DEFENDER)	4				

5

CLAIM
1. The pursuer claims from the defender the sum of £... with interest on that sum at the rate of % annually from the date of service and expenses.

6

RETURN DATE	19		
PRELIMINARY HEARING DATE	19	at	am

The pursuer is authorised to serve (insert as appropriate form 2 or form 3), which is a service copy summons, on the defender not less than 21 days before the RETURN DATE shown in the box above. The summons is warrant for arrestment on the dependence (and for arrestment to found jurisdiction).

Sheriff Clerk Depute Date ....19......

The person making the claim (the pursuer) should complete boxes 1, 2, 3, 4 and 5 on this page and the statement of claim on page 2 and the sheriff clerk will complete box 6 when he receives this form from the pursuer.

STATE CLAIM HERE OR ATTACH A STATEMENT OF CLAIM
(to be completed by the pursuer)

1. The defender has refused or delayed to pay the sum claimed.

2. The details of the claim are*

*If necessary attach a separate sheet.

FOR OFFICIAL USE ONLY

Defence (to be noted by the sheriff)

Disputed issues (to be noted by the sheriff)

Rule 3(2) FORM 2

Form of service copy summons in small claim for payment of money where time to pay direction may be applied for

SMALL CLAIM SUMMONS
CLAIM FOR PAYMENT
OF MONEY

Summons No.

DEFENDER'S COPY

Sheriff Court (name and address and tel. no.)	1	
Name, full address and tel. no. of pursuer's solicitor (if any)	2	
Name and address of person making the claim (PURSUER)	3	
Name and address of person from whom money is claimed (DEFENDER)	4	

5 **CLAIM**

1. The pursuer claims from you the sum of £...... (you will find details of the claim on page 2).
   and
2. The pursuer claims interest on that sum at the rate of % annually from the date on which this summons was served on you.
   and
3. The pursuer also claims from you the court expenses.

6				
	RETURN DATE	19		
	PRELIMINARY HEARING DATE	19	at	am

The pursuer has been authorised by the court to serve this summons on you.

The pursuer should complete boxes 1, 2, 3, 4, 5 and 6 on this page, the statement of claim on page 2 and section A on page 4 before service on the defender.

STATEMENT OF CLAIM

1. The defender has refused or delayed to pay the sum claimed.

2. The details of the claim are*

*If necessary attach a separate sheet.

WHAT CAN I DO ABOUT THIS SUMMONS?

Decide whether you admit owing the money or not and what you want to do about it. Then look at the section on this page which covers your decision and follow the instructions in that section. You will find the RETURN DATE and the PRELIMINARY HEARING DATE on page 1. A leaflet "Small Claims in the Sheriff Court" can be obtained from the sheriff clerk. If you wish further advice contact any Citizens Advice Bureau, Consumer Advice Centre, Trading Standards or Consumer Protection Department or a solicitor.

DO NOTHING
If you do nothing about this summons the court may order you to pay the pursuer the sum claimed including interest and expenses.

ADMIT THE CLAIM and pay in full
If you want to avoid a court order against you, the whole sum claimed including interest and any expenses due should be paid **to the pursuer or his solicitor** in good time before the return date.

ADMIT THE CLAIM and make written application to pay by instalments or by deferred lump sum
Complete and sign box 1 opposite on page 3 and section B on page 4, and return pages 3 and 4 to the court to arrive **on or before the return date.** If the pursuer does not accept your offer, the court will decide how the amount claimed is to be paid.

ADMIT THE CLAIM and attend court to make application to pay by instalments or deferred lump sum
Complete and sign box 2 opposite on page 3. Return pages 3 and 4 to the court to arrive **on or before the return date. You must attend or be represented at court on the preliminary hearing date.** Your representative may be a solicitor or someone else having your authority. It may help you or your representative to bring pages 1 and 2 to the court. If you fail to return pages 3 and 4 as directed or if having returned them, you fail to attend or be represented, the court may decide the claim in your absence.

DENY THE CLAIM and attend court to dispute the sum claimed or state a defence or challenge the jurisdiction of the court
Complete and sign box 3 opposite on page 3. Return pages 3 and 4 to the court to arrive **on or before the return date. You must attend or be represented at court on the preliminary hearing date.** Your representative may be a solicitor or someone else having your authority. It may help you or your representative to bring pages 1 and 2 to the court. **If you fail to return pages 3 and 4 as directed or if having returned them, you fail to attend or be represented, the court may decide the claim in your absence.**

WRITTEN NOTE OF PROPOSED DEFENCE—You may also send to the court a written note of the defence you propose to state at the preliminary hearing. You can send this note at any time **before the date of the preliminary hearing.** However you must still attend or be represented at court on the preliminary hearing date.
If you decide to send a note you must send a copy of it to the pursuer.

KEEP PAGES 1 AND 2—YOU MAY NEED THEM AT A LATER STAGE

YOUR RESPONSE TO THE SUMMONS

CLAIM ADMITTED—Under the Debtors (Scotland) Act 1987

The Act gives you the right to apply to the court for a "time to pay direction" which is an order saying that you can pay any sum you are ordered to pay to the pursuer either in instalments or by deferred lump sum. A deferred lump sum means that you must pay all the amount at one time within a specified period set by the court.

In addition when making a "time to pay direction" the court may recall or restrict an arrestment made on your property by the pursuer in connection with the action or debt (for example your bank account may have been frozen).

If the court makes a "time to pay direction" a copy of the court order (called an extract decree) will be served on you by the pursuer telling you when payment should start or when it is you have to pay the lump sum.

If the court does not make a "time to pay direction" and makes an order for immediate payment against you, an order to pay (called a charge) may be served on you if you do not pay.

Box 1

ADMIT THE CLAIM and make written application to pay by instalments or deferred lump sum

I do not intend to attend court but admit the claim and wish to make a WRITTEN APPLICATION about payment.

I have completed the application form in section B on page 4.

Signature ....

Box 2

ADMIT THE CLAIM—INTENTION TO APPEAR

I admit the claim and INTEND TO APPEAR OR BE REPRESENTED IN COURT.

Signature ....

Box 3

DENY THE CLAIM—INTENTION TO APPEAR

I do not admit the claim. I intend to appear or be represented in court to state my defence.

*I intend to challenge the jurisdiction of the court.
*I attach a note of my proposed defence which has been copied to the pursuer.

Signature.................................... *Delete as necessary

PLEASE REMEMBER

Send pages 3 and 4 to the court to arrive **on or before the return date** if you have signed any of the responses above. If you have admitted the claim do not send any payment to the court.

Sheriff Court
(including address)

Summons No. ....
Return date ....
Preliminary
hearing date ....

SECTION A
This section must be completed before service

Pursuer's full name and address

Defender's full name and address

SECTION B

APPLICATION IN WRITING FOR A TIME TO PAY DIRECTION UNDER THE DEBTORS (SCOTLAND) ACT 1987
(payment by instalments or deferred lump sum)

CLAIM ADMITTED—I admit the claim and make application
(1) To pay by instalments of £..........

(Tick one box only)

EACH.... WEEK ☐ FORTNIGHT ☐ MONTH ☐

OR

(2) To pay the sum ordered in one payment within .... WEEKS/MONTHS

Signature ....

TO HELP THE COURT PLEASE PROVIDE DETAILS OF YOUR FINANCIAL POSITION IN THE BOXES BELOW

IF NECESSARY ATTACH A SEPARATE SHEET

My outgoings are:	Weekly ☐	Fortnightly ☐	Monthly ☐
Rent/Mortgage	£		
Heating	£		
Food	£		
HP	£		
Other	£		
Total	£		

My income is:	Weekly ☐	Fortnightly ☐	Monthly ☐
Wages/Pensions	£		
Social Security	£		
Other	£		
Total	£		

Dependants: Children—how many ☐ Dependent relatives—how many ☐

Here list all capital (if any) for example value of house; amount in bank/building society account, shares or other investments:

APPLICATION FOR RECALL OR RESTRICTION OF AN ARRESTMENT

I seek the recall or restriction of the arrestment of which the details are as follows:—

Signature ....

Rule 3(3)

FORM 3

Form of service copy summons in small claim where time to pay direction may not be applied for

SMALL CLAIM SUMMONS CLAIM FOR PAYMENT OF MONEY	Summons No.

DEFENDER'S COPY

Sheriff Court (name and address and tel. no.)	1		Name, full address and tel. no. of pursuer's solicitor (if any)	2	
Name and address of person making the claim (PURSUER)	3				
Name and address of person from whom money is claimed (DEFENDER)	4				

5

CLAIM

1. The pursuer claims from you the sum of £...... (you will find details of the claim on page 2).
and
2. The pursuer claims interest on that sum at the rate of % annually from the date on which this summons was served on you.
and
3. The pursuer also claims from you the court expenses.

6				
	RETURN DATE	19		
	PRELIMINARY HEARING DATE	19	at	am

The pursuer has been authorised by the court to serve this summons on you.

The pursuer should complete boxes 1, 2, 3, 4, 5 and 6 on this page, the statement of claim on page 2 and section A on page 3 before service on the defender.

STATEMENT OF CLAIM

1. The defender has refused or delayed to pay the sum claimed.

2. The details of the claim are*

*If necessary attach a separate sheet.

WHAT CAN I DO ABOUT THIS SUMMONS?

Decide whether you admit owing the money or not and what you want to do about it. Then look at the section on this page which covers your decision and follow the instructions in that section. You will find the RETURN DATE and the PRELIMINARY HEARING DATE on page 1. A leaflet "Small Claims in the Sheriff Court" can be obtained from the sheriff clerk. If you wish further advice contact any Citizens Advice Bureau, Consumer Advice Centre, Trading Standards or Consumer Protection Department or a solicitor.

DO NOTHING
If you do nothing about this summons the court may order you to pay the pursuer the sum claimed including interest and expenses.

ADMIT THE CLAIM and pay in full
If you want to avoid a court order against you, the whole sum claimed including interest and any expenses due should be paid **to the pursuer or his solicitor** in good time before the return date.

DENY THE CLAIM and attend court to dispute the sum claimed or state a defence or challenge the jurisdiction of the court
Complete and sign section B opposite on page 3. Return pages 3 and 4 to the court to arrive **on or before the return date. You must attend or be represented at court on the preliminary hearing date.** Your representative may be a solicitor or someone else having your authority. It may help you or your representative to bring pages 1 and 2 to the court.

If you fail to return pages 3 and 4 as directed or if having returned them, you fail to attend or be represented, the court may decide the claim in your absence.

WRITTEN NOTE OF PROPOSED DEFENCE—You may also send to the court a written note of the defence you propose to state at the preliminary hearing. You can send this note at any time **before the date of the preliminary hearing.** However you must still attend or be represented at court on the preliminary hearing date.
If you decide to send a note you must send a copy of it to the pursuer.

KEEP PAGES 1 AND 2—YOU MAY NEED THEM AT A LATER STAGE

Sheriff Court
(including address)

SECTION A
This section must be completed before service

Summons No. ....
Return date ....
Preliminary hearing date.......

Pursuer's full name and address

Defender's full name and address

Return date: Preliminary hearing date:

YOUR RESPONSE TO THE SUMMONS

SECTION B

DENY THE CLAIM—INTENTION TO APPEAR

I do not admit the claim. I intend to appear or be represented in court to state my defence.

*I intend to challenge the jurisdiction of the court.

*I attach a note of my proposed defence which has been copied to the pursuer.

Signature .... * delete as necessary

PLEASE REMEMBER

Send this page to the court to arrive **on or before the return date** if you have signed the above box.

If you have admitted the claim do not send any payment to the court.

Rule 5(4)

FORM 4

Form of service

[CD], defender, you are served with this summons.
Dated the day of 19

(*Signed*)
Solicitor for Pursuer
[*or* Sheriff Officer *or* Sheriff Clerk Depute]

Rule 5(5)

FORM 5

Form of notice on envelope used for postal service

This letter contains a citation to or intimation from Sheriff Court. If delivery of the letter cannot be made it is to be returned immediately to the sheriff clerk at (*insert address*).

Rule 5(6)

FORM 6

Form of certificate of service

(*Place and date*). I, , hereby certify that upon the day of I duly cited [CD], the defender, to answer to the foregoing summons. This I did by (*set forth the method of service*).

(*Signed*)
Solicitor for Pursuer
[*or* Sheriff Officer *or* Sheriff Clerk Depute]

Rule 6(1)(a)

FORM 7

Form of advertisement

In Sheriff Court

[AB] against [CD]

Summons No.

A small claim has been raised in Sheriff Court by [AB] pursuer calling as a defender [CD] whose last known address was

If [CD] wishes to respond to the claim he should immediately contact the sheriff clerk (*insert address*), Tel. No. from whom the service copy summons may be obtained.

(*Signed*)
Solicitor for Pursuer
[*or* Sheriff Officer *or* Sheriff Clerk Depute]

Rule 6(1)(b)

FORM 8

Form of display on the walls of court

[AB] against [CD]

Summons No.

A small claim has been raised in Sheriff Court by [AB] pursuer calling as a defender [CD] whose last known address was

If [CD] wishes to respond to the claim he should immediately contact the sheriff clerk (*insert address*), Tel. No. from whom the service copy summons may be obtained.

(*Signed*)
Solicitor for Pursuer
[*or* Sheriff Officer *or* Sheriff Clerk Depute]

Rule 7(2)

FORM 9

Form of notice to pursuer where claim admitted and defender offers to pay by instalments or lump sum

....	Sheriff Court ....
	Summons No. ....
....	Return date ....
	Preliminary hearing date ... at (*insert time*)
....	
....	
Pursuer's Name and Address	

Dear Sir/Madam

RESPONSE TO SMALL CLAIM SUMMONS

The enclosed response has been received from the defender in connection with your claim.

*Delete as necessary

The defender has admitted the claim and has applied to pay by *instalments of £ .... per week/fortnight/month* within......................

*The defender has also applied for the recall or restriction of an arrestment.

If you do not object to the defender's application sign box 1 below.

If you object to the application and wish the court to decide how your claim is to be paid you should attend or be represented at court on the PRELIMINARY HEARING DATE given above and sign box 2 below. Your claim may be dismissed if you fail to attend or be represented at court.

Once you have signed either box you should return this letter to the court so that it is received by 12 noon on 19

Yours faithfully

Sheriff Clerk Depute

1	I do not object to the defender's application and request the court to make an order against the defender for the sum claimed with interest and expenses payable in terms of said application. Signature ....

2	I object to the defender's application and will attend or be represented at court on the PRELIMINARY HEARING DATE. Signature ....

If you prefer you may attend at the sheriff clerk's office and enter a minute in the Book of Small Claims or lodge a separate minute in form 12 instead of returning this letter to court.

Rule 7(2) FORM 10

Form of notice to pursuer where defender does not respond

.... Sheriff Court ....
Summons No. ....
.... Return date ....
Preliminary hearing date ... at

....

....
Pursuer's Name and
Address

Dear Sir/Madam

RESPONSE TO SMALL CLAIM SUMMONS

The defender has not responded to your claim.

If you wish the court to make an order for payment of your claim with interest and expenses, sign box 1 below.

If you wish the court to continue the case to another date specify the reasons in box 2 below.

In any event you should return this letter to the court so that it is received by 12 noon on .... 19 . If you prefer you may attend at the sheriff clerk's office and enter a minute in the Book of Small Claims or lodge a separate minute in form 12 instead of returning this letter to court.

If you do not return this letter to court or enter a minute in the Book of Small Claims or lodge a separate minute in form 12 the court will dismiss your claim.

Yours faithfully

Sheriff Clerk Depute

1	I request the court to make an order against the defender for the sum claimed with interest and expenses. Signature ....
2	I request a continuation of the case for .... The reasons for the continuation are .... (*please specify*) Signature ....

Rule 7(2)

FORM 11

Form of notice to pursuer where defender (a) admits claim and intends to appear, (b) does not admit claim or (c) challenges jurisdiction

.... Sheriff Court ....
Summons No. ....
.... Return date ....
Preliminary hearing date ..... at (*insert time*)

....

....
Pursuer's Name and Address

Dear Sir/Madam

RESPONSE TO SMALL CLAIM SUMMONS

The following response has been received from the defender in connection with your claim.

*Delete as necessary

*The defender has admitted the claim and intends to appear or be represented in court on the PRELIMINARY HEARING DATE to apply to pay the claim by instalments or be deferred lump sum *(and to apply for the recall or restriction of an arrestment).

OR

*The defender does not admit the claim. He intends to appear or be represented in court on the PRELIMINARY HEARING DATE to dispute the amount claimed/to state a defence to the claim.

OR

*The defender intends to appear or be represented in court on the PRELIMINARY HEARING DATE to challenge the jurisdiction of the court.

You must attend or be represented at court on the PRELIMINARY HEARING DATE shown above. Your representative may be a solicitor or someone else having your authority.

If you fail to appear or be represented on that date the court may dismiss your claim or you may lose the right to pursue your claim and the court may order you to pay expenses to the defender.

Yours faithfully

Sheriff Clerk Depute

Rule 10(1) FORM 12

Form of minute sheet

Small Claim Summons

for the Sheriff Court of (*insert date*). The pursuer requests the court to grant decree or other order in terms of the following minute(s).

(*Signed*)
Pursuer [*or* Solicitor for Pursuer *or* authorised lay representative (if any)]

Case No.	Name of Defender	Minute

NOTE
[1] As amended by S.I. 1991 No. 821.

Rule 18(2) FORM 13

Form of order of court and certificate for recovery of documents

Order by the Sheriff Court at
In the Small Claim Summons No.
in which
[AB] (*design*) is Pursuer
and
[CD] (*design*) is Defender

To (*name and designation of person from whom the documents are sought to be recovered*).

TAKE NOTICE that you are hereby required to produce to the sheriff clerk at within 7 days of the service upon you of this order—

(1) this order itself which must be produced intact;
(2) a certificate signed and completed in terms of the form appended hereto; and
(3) all documents in your possession falling within the list enclosed herewith, together with a list or inventory of such documents signed by you as relative to this order and your certificate.

Production may be made either by lodging the above at the said office of the sheriff clerk at the court, or by registered or recorded delivery letter or registered postal packet enclosing the same, and addressed to the said sheriff clerk at the court.

Date (*Signed*)
Solicitor for Pursuer
.... [*or* Sheriff Officer *or* Sheriff Clerk Depute]

NOTE: If you claim confidentiality for any of the documents produced by you, such documents must nevertheless be produced, but may be placed in a sealed envelope by themselves, marked "confidential".

CERTIFICATE

I certify with reference to the order of the sheriff court at in the Small Claims Summons No. and the relative list of documents, served upon me and marked respectively XY—

(1) that the documents which are produced and which are numbered in the list signed by me and marked Z are the whole such documents in my possession

or

(2) that I have no such documents in my possession. That, to the best of my knowledge and belief, there are in existence other such documents, but not in my possession, namely (describe them by reference to one or more of the descriptions of documents), which were last seen by me on or about (*date*), at (*place*), in the hands of (*name and address of the person*)

or

(3) that I know of the existence of no such documents in the possession of any person, other than myself.

(*Signed*)

Rule 27(1) and (2) FORM 14

Form of minute for recall of decree

Sheriff Court ....

Summons No. ....

[AB] against [CD]
The pursuer [*or* defender] asks the court to recall the decree pronounced on
19 in this case [and in which execution of the charge/arrestment was effected on 19].

(*Signed*)
Pursuer
[*or* Defender *or* Solicitor for Pursuer *or* authorised lay representative (if any)]

NOTE
[1] As amended by S.I. 1991 No. 821.

Rule 36(1)

FORM 15

Form of summons on small claim for delivery or recovery of possession of moveable property

SMALL CLAIM SUMMONS
CLAIM FOR DELIVERY OR
RECOVERY OF POSSESSION
OF MOVEABLE PROPERTY

Official Use Only
Summons No.
Preliminary hearing date

Sheriff Court (name and address and tel. no.)	1	
Name, full address and tel. no. of pursuer's solicitor (if any)	2	
Name and address of person making the claim (PURSUER)	3	
Name and address of person from whom delivery is claimed (DEFENDER)	4	

5 **CLAIM**

1. The pursuer claims that in the circumstances set out in his statement of claim on page 2, he is entitled to possession of the article mentioned in that statement of claim.
2. The pursuer asks the court to order the defender to deliver that article to the pursuer.
3. Should the defender fail to deliver the article, the pursuer **alternatively** claims from the defender the sum of £........with interest on that sum at the rate of % annually from
4. The pursuer claims from the defender the court expenses.

6 PRELIMINARY HEARING DATE 19 at am

The pursuer is authorised to serve (insert as appropriate form 16 or form 17), which is a service copy summons, on the defender not less than 21 days before the preliminary hearing date shown in the box above. The summons is warrant for arrestment on the dependence (and for arrestment to found jurisdiction).

Sheriff Clerk Depute .... Date............19

The person making the claim (the pursuer) should complete boxes 1, 2, 3, 4 and 5 on this page and the statement of claim on page 2 and the sheriff clerk will complete box 6 when he receives this form from the pursuer.

STATE CLAIM HERE OR ATTACH A STATEMENT OF CLAIM
(to be completed by the pursuer)

1. The defender has refused to deliver the article to the pursuer or has delayed in doing so.

2. The details of the claim are*

*If necessary attach a separate sheet.

FOR OFFICIAL USE ONLY

Defence (to be noted by the sheriff)

Disputed issues (to be noted by the sheriff)

Rule 36(2)

FORM 16

Form of service copy summons in small claim for delivery or recovery of possession of moveable property where time to pay direction may be applied for

SMALL CLAIM SUMMONS
CLAIM FOR DELIVERY OR RECOVERY OF POSSESSION OF MOVEABLE PROPERTY

Summons No.

DEFENDER'S COPY

Sheriff Court (name and address and tel. no.)	1		Name, full address and tel. no. of pursuer's solicitor (if any)	2	
Name and address of person making the claim (PURSUER)	3				
Name and address of person from whom delivery is claimed (DEFENDER)	4				

5 **CLAIM**

1. The pursuer claims that he is entitled to possession of the article mentioned in the statement of claim (you will find details of the claim on page 2).
and
2. The pursuer asks the court to order you to deliver that article to him.
3. Should you fail to deliver that article, the pursuer **alternatively** claims from you the sum of £........and claims interest on that sum at the rate of % annually from
4. The pursuer also claims from you the court expenses.

6 PRELIMINARY HEARING DATE 19 at am

The pursuer has been authorised by the court to serve this summons on you.

The pursuer should complete boxes 1, 2, 3, 4, 5 and 6 on this page, the statement of claim on page 2 and section A on page 4 before service on the defender.

STATEMENT OF CLAIM

1. The defender has refused to deliver the article to the pursuer or has delayed in doing so.

2. The details of the claim are*

*If necessary attach a separate sheet.

WHAT CAN I DO ABOUT THIS SUMMONS?

Decide whether you admit the claim or not and what you want to do about it. Then look at the section on this page which covers your decision and follow the instructions in that section. You will find the PRELIMINARY HEARING DATE on page 1. A leaflet "Small Claims in the Sheriff Court" can be obtained from the sheriff clerk. If you wish further advice contact any Citizens Advice Bureau, Consumer Advice Centre, Trading Standards or Consumer Protection Department or a solicitor.

DO NOTHING
If you do nothing about this summons the court may order you to deliver the article in question to the pursuer within a specified period. Then if you fail to deliver the article the court may order you to pay the pursuer the alternative amount claimed including interest and expenses.

ADMIT THE CLAIM and deliver the article or pay the alternative amount
If you wish to avoid a court order against you, you should deliver the article claimed and pay any expenses due to the pursuer or his solicitor in good time before the PRELIMINARY HEARING DATE. Or you may offer to pay the alternative amount claimed including interest and expenses. If this offer is not accepted you must attend court on the PRELIMINARY HEARING DATE. If you prefer you may ask a solicitor or someone else to appear for you.

ADMIT THE CLAIM and attend court to make representations either about the article or the alternative amount
You must attend court on the PRELIMINARY HEARING DATE.

If you prefer you may ask a solicitor or someone else to appear for you.

ADMIT THE CLAIM and apply for a "time to pay direction"
You may apply for a "time to pay direction" in the event of a decree being granted for the alternative amount claimed. **Please read the next page which will explain this and tell you how to apply.**

DENY THE CLAIM and attend court to state a defence or dispute the alternative amount claimed or challenge the jurisdiction of the court
You must attend court on the PRELIMINARY HEARING DATE.

If you prefer you may ask a solicitor or someone else to appear for you.

YOUR RIGHTS UNDER THE DEBTORS (SCOTLAND) ACT 1987

(1) The Act gives you the right to apply to the court for a "time to pay direction" which is an order saying that you can pay any sum you are ordered to pay to the pursuer either in instalments or by deferred lump sum. A deferred lump sum means that you must pay all the amount at one time within a specified period set by the court.

(2) In addition, when making a "time to pay direction" the court may recall or restrict an arrestment made on your property by the pursuer in connection with the action or debt (for example your bank account may have been frozen).

HOW TO APPLY FOR A TIME TO PAY DIRECTION WHEN CLAIM ADMITTED AND YOU DO NOT WANT TO DEFEND THE ACTION

(1) You may apply for a "time to pay direction" by EITHER

(*a*) attending court on the PRELIMINARY HEARING DATE and asking the court to make a "time to pay direction". If you prefer you may ask a solicitor or someone else to appear for you;

OR

(*b*) completing page 4 of this form and returning it to the sheriff clerk to arrive at least seven days before the PRELIMINARY HEARING DATE.

(2) No court fee is payable when making an application for a "time to pay direction" whether you apply by appearing in court or by written application.

(3) The court will decide what order is to be made and if a "time to pay direction" is made a copy of the court order (called an extract decree) will be served on you by the pursuer telling you when payment should start or when it is you have to pay the lump sum.

If the court does not make a "time to pay direction" and makes an order for immediate payment against you, an order to pay (called a charge) may be served on you if you do not pay.

HOW TO COMPLETE THE APPLICATION

(1) Section A has been filled in already.

(2) (*a*) If you wish to apply to pay by instalments put in the amount you are proposing and tick the appropriate box in section B.

(*b*) If you wish to apply to pay the full sum due in one deferred payment enter the period of deferment you propose.

(3) You should give full details of your financial position in the appropriate boxes in section B.

(4) If an arrestment has been made in connection with this action and you wish the court when making a "time to pay direction" to recall or restrict the arrestment enter the appropriate details in section B about what has been arrested and the place and date and attach a schedule of arrestment or a copy.

(5) Sign the application where indicated. Keep pages 1 and 2. Return pages 3 and 4 to the court to arrive at least seven days before the PRELIMINARY HEARING DATE.

Sheriff Court
(including address)

SECTION A
This section must be completed before service

Summons No. ....

Preliminary hearing date ....

Pursuer's full name and address

Defender's full name and address

SECTION B

APPLICATION IN WRITING FOR A TIME TO PAY DIRECTION UNDER THE DEBTORS (SCOTLAND) ACT 1987
(payment by instalments or deferred lump sum)

CLAIM ADMITTED—I admit the claim and make application
(1) To pay by instalments of £..........

(Tick one box only)

EACH.... WEEK ☐ FORTNIGHT ☐ MONTH ☐

OR

(2) To pay the sum ordered in one payment within .... WEEKS/MONTHS

Signature ....

TO HELP THE COURT PLEASE PROVIDE DETAILS OF YOUR FINANCIAL POSITION IN THE BOXES BELOW

IF NECESSARY ATTACH A SEPARATE SHEET

My outgoings are:	Weekly ☐	Fortnightly ☐	Monthly ☐
Rent/Mortgage	£		
Heating	£		
Food	£		
HP	£		
Other	£		
Total	£		

My income is:	Weekly ☐	Fortnightly ☐	Monthly ☐
Wages/Pensions	£		
Social Security	£		
Other	£		
Total	£		

Dependants: Children—how many ☐ Dependent relatives—how many ☐

Here list all capital (if any) for example value of house; amount in bank/building society account, shares or other investments:

APPLICATION FOR RECALL OR RESTRICTION OF AN ARRESTMENT

I seek the recall or restriction of the arrestment of which the details are as follows:—

Signature ....

Rule 36(3) FORM 17

Form of service copy summons in small claim for delivery or recovery of possession of moveable property where time to pay direction may not be applied for

SMALL CLAIM SUMMONS
CLAIM FOR DELIVERY OR
RECOVERY OF POSSESSION
OF MOVEABLE PROPERTY

Summons No.

DEFENDER'S COPY

Sheriff Court (name and address and tel. no.)	1	
Name, full address and tel. no. of pursuer's solicitor (if any)	2	
Name and address of person making the claim (PURSUER)	3	
Name and address of person from whom delivery is claimed (DEFENDER)	4	

5 **CLAIM**

1. The pursuer claims that he is entitled to possession of the article mentioned in the statement of claim (you will find this on page 2).
   and
2. The pursuer asks the court to order you to deliver that article to him.
3. Should you fail to deliver that article, the pursuer alternatively claims from you the sum of £........and claims interest on that sum at the rate of % annually from
4. The pursuer also claims from you the court expenses.

6 PRELIMINARY HEARING DATE 19 at am

The pursuer has been authorised by the court to serve this summons on you.

The pursuer should complete boxes 1, 2, 3, 4, 5 and 6 on this page, and the statement of claim on page 2 before service on the defender.

STATEMENT OF CLAIM

1. The defender has refused to deliver the article to the pursuer or has delayed in doing so.

2. The details of the claim are*

*If necessary attach a separate sheet.

WHAT CAN I DO ABOUT THIS SUMMONS?

Decide whether you admit the claim or not and what you want to do about it. Then look at the section on this page which covers your decision and follow the instructions in that section. You will find the PRELIMINARY HEARING DATE on page 1. A leaflet "Small Claims in the Sheriff Court" can be obtained from the sheriff clerk. If you wish further advice contact any Citizens Advice Bureau, Consumer Advice Centre, Trading Standards or Consumer Protection Department or a solicitor.

DO NOTHING
If you do nothing about this summons the court may order you to deliver the article in question to the pursuer within a specified period. Then if you fail to deliver the article the court may order you to pay the pursuer the alternative amount claimed including interest and expenses.

ADMIT THE CLAIM and deliver the article or pay the alternative amount
If you wish to avoid a court order against you, you should deliver the article claimed and pay any expenses due to the pursuer or his solicitor in good time before the PRELIMINARY HEARING DATE. Or you may offer to pay the alternative amount claimed including interest and expenses. If this offer is not accepted you must attend court on the PRELIMINARY HEARING DATE. If you prefer you may ask a solicitor or someone else to appear for you.

ADMIT THE CLAIM and attend court to make representations either about the article or the alternative amount
You must attend court on the PRELIMINARY HEARING DATE.

If you prefer you may ask a solicitor or someone else to appear for you.

DENY THE CLAIM and attend court to state a defence or dispute the alternative amount claimed or challenge the jurisdiction of the court
You must attend court on the PRELIMINARY HEARING DATE.

If you prefer you may ask a solicitor or someone else to appear for you.

Rule 37(1)

FORM 18

Form of summons in small claim for implement of an obligation

SMALL CLAIM SUMMONS
CLAIM FOR IMPLEMENT
OF AN OBLIGATION

Official Use Only Summons No.
Preliminary hearing date

Sheriff Court (name and address and tel. no.)	1		Name, full address and tel. no. of pursuer's solicitor (if any)	2	
Name and address of person making the claim (PURSUER)	3				
Name and address of person from whom performance of duty is claimed (DEFENDER)	4				

5

CLAIM

1. The pursuer claims that in the circumstances set out in his statement of claim on page 2, the defender is required to perform the duty mentioned in that statement of claim.
2. The pursuer asks the court to order the defender to perform that duty.
3. Should the defender fail to perform that duty, the pursuer **alternatively** claims from the defender the sum of £........with interest on that sum at the rate of % annually from
4. The pursuer claims from the defender the court expenses.

6

PRELIMINARY HEARING DATE 19 at am

The pursuer is authorised to serve (insert as appropriate form 19 or form 20), which is a service copy summons, on the defender not less than 21 days before the preliminary hearing shown in the box above. The summons is warrant for arrestment on the dependence (and for arrestment to found jurisdiction).

Sheriff Clerk Depute .... Date.............19.....

The person making the claim (the pursuer) should complete boxes 1, 2, 3, 4 and 5 on this page and the statement of claim on page 2 and the sheriff clerk will complete box 6 when he receives this form from the pursuer.

STATE CLAIM HERE OR ATTACH A STATEMENT OF CLAIM
(to be completed by the pursuer)

1. The defender has refused to perform the duty specified below or has delayed in doing so.

2. The details of the claim are*

*If necessary attach a separate sheet.

FOR OFFICIAL USE ONLY

Defence (to be noted by the sheriff)
Disputed issues (to be noted by the sheriff)

Rule 37(2) FORM 19

Form of service copy summons in small claim for implement of an obligation where time to pay direction may be applied for

SMALL CLAIM SUMMONS
CLAIM FOR IMPLEMENT
OF AN OBLIGATION

Summons No.

DEFENDER'S COPY

Sheriff Court (name and address and tel. no.)	1		Name, full address and tel. no. of pursuer's solicitor (if any)	2	
Name and address of person making the claim (PURSUER)	3				
Name and address of person from whom performance of duty is claimed (DEFENDER)	4				

5 **CLAIM**

1. The pursuer claims that you are required to perform the duty mentioned in the statement of claim (you will find details of the claim on page 2).
and
2. The pursuer asks the court to order you to perform that duty.
3. Should you fail to perform that duty, the pursuer **alternatively** claims from you the sum of £........ with interest on that sum at the rate of % annually from

4. The pursuer also claims from you the court expenses.

6	PRELIMINARY HEARING DATE	19	at	am

The pursuer has been authorised by the court to serve this summons on you.

The pursuer should complete boxes 1, 2, 3, 4, 5 and 6 on this page, the statement of claim on page 2 and section A on page 4 before service on the defender.

STATEMENT OF CLAIM

1. The defender has refused to perform the duty specified below or has delayed in doing so.

2. The details of the claim are*

*If necessary attach a separate sheet.

WHAT CAN I DO ABOUT THIS SUMMONS?

Decide whether you admit the claim or not and what you want to do about it. Then look at the section on this page which covers your decision and follow the instructions in that section. You will find the PRELIMINARY HEARING DATE on page 1. A leaflet "Small Claims in the Sheriff Court" can be obtained from the sheriff clerk. If you wish further advice contact any Citizens Advice Bureau, Consumer Advice Centre, Trading Standards or Consumer Protection Department or a solicitor.

DO NOTHING
If you do nothing about this summons the court may order you to perform the duty in question within a specified period. Then if you fail to perform that duty the court may order you to pay the pursuer the alternative amount claimed including interest and expenses.

ADMIT THE CLAIM and perform the duty in question or pay the alternative amount
If you want to avoid a court order against you, you should perform the duty claimed and pay any expenses due to the pursuer or his solicitor in good time before the PRELIMINARY HEARING DATE. Or you may offer to pay the alternative amount claimed including interest and expenses. If this offer is not accepted you must attend court on the PRELIMINARY HEARING DATE. If you prefer you may ask a solicitor or someone else to appear for you.

ADMIT THE CLAIM and attend court to make representations either about the duty in question or the alternative amount
You must attend court on the PRELIMINARY HEARING DATE.

If you prefer you may ask a solicitor or someone else to appear for you.

ADMIT THE CLAIM and apply for a "time to pay direction"
You may apply for a "time to pay direction" in the event of a decree being granted for the alternative amount claimed. **Please read the next page which will explain this and tell you how to apply.**

DENY THE CLAIM and attend court to state a defence or dispute the alternative amount claimed or challenge the jurisdiction of the court
You must attend court on the PRELIMINARY HEARING DATE.

If you prefer you may ask a solicitor or someone else to appear for you.

YOUR RIGHTS UNDER THE DEBTORS (SCOTLAND) ACT 1987

(1) The Act gives you the right to apply to the court for a "time to pay direction" which is an order saying that you can pay any sum you are ordered to pay to the pursuer either in instalments or by deferred lump sum. A deferred lump sum means that you must pay all the amount at one time within a specified period set by the court.

(2) In addition, when making a "time to pay direction" the court may recall or restrict an arrestment made on your property by the pursuer in connection with the action or debt (for example your bank account may have been frozen).

HOW TO APPLY FOR A TIME TO PAY DIRECTION WHEN CLAIM ADMITTED AND YOU DO NOT WANT TO DEFEND THE ACTION

(1) You may apply for a "time to pay direction" by EITHER

(*a*) attending court on the PRELIMINARY HEARING DATE and asking the court to make a "time to pay direction". If you prefer you may ask a solicitor or someone else to appear for you;

OR

(*b*) completing page 4 of this form and returning it to the sheriff clerk to arrive at least seven days before the PRELIMINARY HEARING DATE.

(2) No court fee is payable when making an application for a "time to pay direction" whether you apply by appearing in court or by written application.

(3) The court will decide what order is to be made and if a "time to pay direction" is made a copy of the court order (called an extract decree) will be served on you by the pursuer telling you when payment should start or when it is you have to pay the lump sum.

If the court does not make a "time to pay direction" and makes an order for immediate payment against you, an order to pay (called a charge) may be served on you if you do not pay.

HOW TO COMPLETE THE APPLICATION

(1) Section A has been filled in already.

(2) (*a*) If you wish to apply to pay by instalments put in the amount you are proposing and tick the appropriate box in section B.

(*b*) If you wish to apply to pay the full sum due in one deferred payment enter the period of deferment you propose.

(3) You should give full details of your financial position in the appropriate boxes in section B.

(4) If an arrestment has been made in connection with this action and you wish the court when making a "time to pay direction" to recall or restrict the arrestment enter the appropriate details in section B about what has been arrested and the place and date and attach a schedule of arrestment or a copy.

(5) Sign the application where indicated. Keep pages 1 and 2. Return pages 3 and 4 to the court to arrive at least seven days before the PRELIMINARY HEARING DATE.

Sheriff Court (including address)

SECTION A
This section must be completed before service

Summons No. .....

Preliminary hearing date.......

Pursuer's full name and address

Defender's full name and address

SECTION B

APPLICATION IN WRITING FOR A TIME TO PAY DIRECTION UNDER THE DEBTORS (SCOTLAND) ACT 1987
(payment by instalments or deferred lump sum)

CLAIM ADMITTED—I admit the claim and make application
(1) To pay by instalments of £..........

(Tick one box only)

EACH.... WEEK ☐ FORTNIGHT ☐ MONTH ☐

OR

(2) To pay the sum ordered in one payment within .... WEEKS/MONTHS

Signature ....

TO HELP THE COURT PLEASE PROVIDE DETAILS OF YOUR FINANCIAL POSITION IN THE BOXES BELOW

IF NECESSARY ATTACH A SEPARATE SHEET

My outgoings are:	Weekly ☐ Fortnightly ☐ Monthly ☐
Rent/Mortgage	£
Heating	£
Food	£
HP	£
Other	£
Total	£

My income is:	Weekly ☐ Fortnightly ☐ Monthly ☐
Wages/Pensions	£
Social Security	£
Other	£
Total	£

Dependants: Children—how many ☐ Dependent relatives—how many ☐

Here list all capital (if any) for example value of house; amount in bank/building society account, shares or other investments:

APPLICATION FOR RECALL OR RESTRICTION OF AN ARRESTMENT

I seek the recall or restriction of the arrestment of which the details are as follows:—

Signature..

Rule 37(3)

FORM 20

Form of service copy summons in small claim for implementation of an obligation where time to pay direction may not be applied for

SMALL CLAIM SUMMONS
CLAIM FOR IMPLEMENT
OF AN OBLIGATION

Summons No.

DEFENDER'S COPY

Sheriff Court (name and address and tel. no.)	1		Name, full address and tel. no. of pursuer's solicitor (if any)	2	
Name and address of person making the claim (PURSUER)	3				
Name and address of person from whom performance of duty is claimed (DEFENDER)	4				

5

CLAIM

1. The pursuer claims that you are required to perform the duty mentioned in the statement of claim (you will find this on page 2).
and
2. The pursuer asks the court to order you to perform that duty.
3. Should you fail to perform that duty, the pursuer **alternatively** claims from you the sum of £........ with interest on that sum at the rate of % annually from
4. The pursuer also claims from you the court expenses.

6 PRELIMINARY HEARING DATE 19 at am

The pursuer has been authorised by the court to serve this summons on you.

The pursuer should complete boxes 1, 2, 3, 4, 5 and 6 on this page, and the statement of claim on page 2, before service on the defender.

STATEMENT OF CLAIM

1. The defender has refused to perform the duty specified below or has delayed in doing so.

2. The details of the claim are*

*If necessary attach a separate sheet.

WHAT CAN I DO ABOUT THIS SUMMONS?

Decide whether you admit the claim or not and what you want to do about it. Then look at the section on this page which covers your decision and follow the instructions in that section. You will find the PRELIMINARY HEARING DATE on page 1. A leaflet "Small Claims in the Sheriff Court" can be obtained from the sheriff clerk. If you wish further advice contact any Citizens Advice Bureau, Consumer Advice Centre, Trading Standards or Consumer Protection Department or a solicitor.

DO NOTHING
If you do nothing about this summons the court may order you to perform the duty in question within a specified period. Then if you fail to perform that duty the court may order you to pay the pursuer the alternative amount claimed including interest and expenses.

ADMIT THE CLAIM and perform the duty in question or pay the alternative amount
If you wish to avoid a court order against you, you should perform the duty claimed and pay any expenses due to the pursuer or his solicitor in good time before the PRELIMINARY HEARING DATE. Or you may offer to pay the alternative amount claimed including interest and expenses. If this offer is not accepted you must attend court on the PRELIMINARY HEARING DATE. If you prefer you may ask a solicitor or someone else to appear for you.

ADMIT THE CLAIM and attend court to make representations either about the duty in question or the alternative amount
You must attend court on the PRELIMINARY HEARING DATE.

If you prefer you may ask a solicitor or someone else to appear for you.

DENY THE CLAIM and attend court to state a defence or dispute the alternative amount claimed or challenge the jurisdiction of the court
You must attend court on the PRELIMINARY HEARING DATE.

If you prefer you may ask a solicitor or someone else to appear for you.

Rule 2(1)

[1] APPENDIX 2

Rules of the Ordinary Causes Rules which Apply to Small Claims

rule 13A (service of charge where defender's address is unknown).
rule 14 (persons carrying on business under a trading or descriptive name).
rule 60 (transfer of causes on death of party).
rule 89(4) (correction of clerical or incidental error in interlocutor).
rule 111 (service of schedule of arrestment).
rule 128 (disposal of money payable to persons under legal disability).
rule 134 (reference to the Court of Justice of the European Communities).
form P (receipt for a payment into court).
form Q (letter intimating payment).
form R (additional particulars of receipt).
form U (request for preliminary ruling of the Court of Justice of the European Communities).

NOTE
[1] As amended by S.I. 1990 No. 661.

Rule 2(2)

[1] APPENDIX 3

Rules of the Summary Cause Rules which Apply to Small Claims

rule 3A (information on summons).
rule 6(1), (2) and (4) (citation and service within Scotland by officer of court).
rule 9 (citation of or service on persons outwith Scotland).
rule 11 (endorsation of summons by sheriff clerk of defender's residence not necessary).
rule 12 (re-service).
rule 13 (defender appearing barred from objecting to citation).
rule 18(8) (sheriff to be satisfied that defender outwith Scotland also to receive summons).
rule 18A (decree in causes to which the Hague Convention applies).
rule 21A (party minuter).
rule 22 (transfer to another court).
rule 24A(1) and (2) (borrowing of productions).
rule 26 (documents lost or destroyed).
rule 29 (citation of witnesses).
rule 30 (form of citation and execution thereof).
rule 31 (failure to answer citation).
rule 32 (witnesses failing to attend).
rule 39 (confidentiality).
rule 47 (arrestment).
rule 48 (recall and restriction of arrestment).
rule 71 (diligence of decree in action of delivery).
rule 82 (effect of and abandonment of appeal).
rule 83(1), (3) and (4) (hearing of appeal).
rule 85 (sheriff to regulate interim possession).
rule 85A (appeal in relation to time to pay direction).
rule 89 (extract of decree).
rule 92 (applications in same cause for variation, etc, of decree).
form N (citation of witness).
form O (execution of citation of witness).
forms U1, U2, U2A, U9, U10, U11, U13 and U14 (extract decrees).

NOTE
[1] As amended by S.I. 1992 No. 249 (effective 4th May 1992).

Small Claims (Scotland) Order 1988

(S.I. 1988 No. 1999)

15th November 1988

The Lord Advocate, in exercise of the powers conferred on him by sections 35(2) and 36B(1) and (2) of the Sheriff Courts (Scotland) Act 1971, and of all other powers enabling him in that behalf, hereby makes the following Order, a draft of which has been laid before and approved by resolution of each House of Parliament:

Citation and commencement

1. This Order may be cited as the Small Claims (Scotland) Order 1988 and shall come into force on 30th November 1988.

Proceeding to be small claims

2. The form of summary cause process, to be known as a "small claim", shall be used for the purposes of summary cause proceedings of one or other of the following descriptions, namely—

(*a*) actions for payment of money not exceeding £750 in amount (exclusive of interest and expenses), other than actions in respect of aliment and interim aliment and actions of defamation;

(*b*) actions *ad factum praestandum* and actions for the recovery of possession of moveable property where in any such action *ad factum praestandum* or for recovery there is included, as an alternative to the claim, a claim for payment of a sum not exceeding £750 (exclusive of interest and expenses).

3. For the purpose of article 2, actions *ad factum praestandum* include actions for delivery and actions for implement but do not include actions for count, reckoning and payment.

Limit on award of expenses in small claims

4.—(1) The provisions of this article are without prejudice to the provisions of section 36B(3) of the Sheriff Courts (Scotland) Act 1971.

(2) No award of expenses shall be made in a small claim as specified in article 2 of this Order in which the value of the claim does not exceed £200.

(3) In the case of any small claim other than a small claim to which paragraph (2) applies, the sheriff may award expenses not exceeding £75.

[THE NEXT PAGE IS D 364]

Proceedings in the Sheriff Court under the Debtors (Scotland) Act 1987, 1988

(S.I. 1988 No. 2013)

[16th November 1988]

Arrangement of Rules

Part I

Introductory

Part II

Extension of Time to Pay Debts and Related Matters

Part III

Poindings and Warrant Sales

PART IV

DILIGENCE AGAINST EARNINGS

PART V

WARRANTS FOR DILIGENCE

PART VI

MISCELLANEOUS

SCHEDULE

FORMS

The Lords of Council and Session, under and by virtue of the powers conferred on them by section 97 of the Debtors (Scotland) Act 1987 and of all other powers enabling them in that behalf, do hereby enact and declare:—

Part I

Introductory

Citation and commencement

1.—(1) This Act of Sederunt may be cited as the Act of Sederunt (Proceedings in the Sheriff Court under the Debtors (Scotland) Act 1987) 1988 and shall come into force on 30th November 1988.

(2) This Act of Sederunt shall be inserted in the Books of Sederunt.

Interpretation

2. In this Act of Sederunt—

(*a*) "the Act" means the Debtors (Scotland) Act 1987; and

(*b*) a reference to a "form" means the form so numbered in the Schedule to this Act of Sederunt or a form substantially to the same effect with such variation as circumstances may require.

Part II

Extension of Time to Pay Debts and Related Matters

Notice of interest claimed

3.—(1) A creditor wishing to recover interest under a decree of the sheriff court shall serve on the defender the notice referred to in sections 1(7) and 5(7) of the Act (notice claiming and specifying amount of interest), either by posting it by recorded delivery post or by having it served personally by an officer of court—

(*a*) in the case of a decree requiring payment by instalments, no later than 14 days before the date on which the last instalment is due to be paid; or

(*b*) in the case of a decree requiring payment by lump sum within a certain period, no later than 14 days before the last day of such period.

Applications for variation or recall of time to pay directions or for recall or restriction of arrestments

4.—(1) An application under section 3(1) of the Act for an order for variation or recall of a time to pay direction, or where appropriate, for recall or restriction of an arrestment, shall be in form 1.

(2) An application to which paragraph (1) of this rule applies shall be lodged with the sheriff clerk who shall—

(*a*) fix a date for the hearing of the application (which date shall be not less than seven days from the date of intimation made under sub-paragraph (*c*) of this paragraph);

(*b*) obtain from the sheriff a warrant to intimate the application to the debtor and the creditor;

(*c*) intimate the application and warrant to the debtor and the creditor; and

(*d*) complete a certificate of intimation.

Applications for time to pay orders

5.—(1) A party who intends to apply for a time to pay order under section 5 of the Act shall complete and lodge with the sheriff clerk an application in form 2.

(2) An order by the sheriff under section 6(4) of the Act (creditor to furnish particulars of decree or other document) shall require a creditor to furnish the following information—

(*a*) the date of the decree or other document;

(*b*) the parties named in it;

(*c*) where appropriate, the court which granted it;
(*d*) details of the debt and any interest due; and
(*e*) any further information, relating to the decree or other document, as the sheriff shall consider necessary to enable him to determine the application.

(3) Service by the sheriff clerk of an application under paragraph (1) of this rule, or of any *interim* order of the sheriff under section 6(3) of the Act, shall be by recorded delivery post and the sheriff clerk shall serve, in like manner and at the same time, a copy of any *interim* order upon the applicant.

(4) Where a creditor fails to comply with an order referred to in sub-paragraph (2) of this rule, any order giving him an opportunity to make representations under section 6(5) of the Act shall be intimated to him by the sheriff clerk.

(5) A creditor may, within 14 days after the date of service of an application under paragraph (1) of this rule, object to the granting of the application by lodging with the sheriff clerk the appropriate portion of form 2 or a letter specifying his objections, including any counter-proposals on it.

(6) If no written objections are received from the creditor within the time specified in paragraph (5) of this rule, the sheriff shall make a time to pay order in accordance with the application.

(7) If written objections are received from the creditor within the time specified in paragraph (5) of this rule, the sheriff clerk shall—
(*a*) appoint a date for the hearing of the application;
(*b*) intimate that date to the parties and a copy of the written objections to the applicant; and
(*c*) advise the applicant that he may accept any counter-proposal prior to the date fixed for the hearing.

(8) Where the debtor accepts counter-proposals made by the creditor in accordance with paragraph (5) of this rule, he shall intimate his acceptance to the sheriff clerk who shall intimate the acceptance to the creditor and advise parties that the hearing of the application will not proceed; and the sheriff shall make a time to pay order in terms of the counter-proposals.

(9) The sheriff clerk shall intimate the decision of the sheriff on the application and any order relating to it to the parties by first class post and at the same time shall advise the creditor of the date when intimation was made to the debtor.

Applications for variation or recall of time to pay orders, poindings or arrestments

6.—(1) An application under section 10(1) of the Act for an order for variation or recall of a time to pay order or, where appropriate, for recall of a poinding or for recall or restriction of an arrestment shall be in form 3.

(2) An application to which paragraph (1) of this rule applies shall be lodged with the sheriff clerk who shall—
(*a*) fix a date for the hearing of the application (which date shall be not less than seven days from the date of intimation made under sub-paragraph (*c*) of this paragraph);
(*b*) obtain from the sheriff a warrant to intimate the application to the debtor and the creditor;
(*c*) intimate the application and warrant to the debtor and the creditor; and
(*d*) complete a certificate of intimation.

(3) The sheriff may, where he considers it appropriate, make an order requiring any person in possession of a summons or other writ or who holds an execution of diligence in respect of the debt to deliver it to the court.

Consumer Credit Act 1974

7.—(1) In any proceedings by a creditor or owner to enforce a regulated agreement or any related security within the meaning of the Consumer

Credit Act 1974, the pursuer shall lodge a copy of any existing or previous time order relating to the debt.

(2) Where a time to pay order is applied for, the applicant shall specify in his application whether a time order, within the meaning of the Consumer Credit Act 1974, relating to the debt has been made.

(3) Where a time order is applied for under the Consumer Credit Act 1974, the applicant shall specify whether a time to pay direction or order relating to the debt has been made.

PART III

POINDINGS AND WARRANT SALES

Applications for releasing poinded articles

8.—(1) An application under section 16(4) of, or paragraph 1(4) of Schedule 5 to, the Act for an order that an article be released from a poinding shall be made within 14 days after the date of execution of the poinding and shall be in form 4.

(2) An application to which paragraph (1) of this rule applies shall specify—

(*a*) the name and address of the person to whom the sheriff clerk will require to intimate the application under paragraph (3)(*c*) of this rule;

(*b*) the court which granted the original decree and the date of that decree, or details of the summary warrant or other document, upon which the poinding proceeded;

(*c*) the date and place of execution of the poinding;

(*d*) the poinded article sought to be released;

(*e*) the reasons for seeking release of the poinded article; and

(*f*) any competent crave for expenses.

(3) On the lodging of such an application the sheriff clerk shall—

(*a*) fix a date for a hearing;

(*b*) obtain from the sheriff a warrant for intimation;

(*c*) intimate the application and warrant to—

(i) the applicant, the creditor and the officer of court who executed the poinding; and

(ii) as appropriate, the debtor, any person who the applicant informs the sheriff clerk claims to own the poinded article in common with the debtor and any person having possession of the poinded article; and

(*d*) complete a certificate of intimation.

(4) The officer of court who executed the poinding shall, whether or not he appears to oppose the application, lodge with the court a copy of the poinding schedule before the date fixed for hearing under paragraph (3)(*a*) of this rule.

(5) The sheriff clerk shall intimate the sheriff's decision on such an application to any person to whom intimation of the application was made but who was not present when the application was determined.

(6) This rule shall apply to the release of an article from arrestment (other than an arrestment of a debtor's earnings in the hands of his employer), or from a sequestration for rent under a landlord's right of hypothec, as it applies to the release of an article from poinding.

Applications for extension of hours of poinding

9.—(1) An application by an officer of court under section 17(2) of, or paragraph 2(2) of Schedule 5 to, the Act (extension of hours of poinding) shall be made by endorsing a minute on the extract decree, summary warrant, or other document, upon which the poinding has proceeded.

(2) A minute under paragraph (1) of this rule shall specify—
(*a*) the extension sought; and
(*b*) the reason for the extension.

(3) A minute under paragraph (1) of this rule shall not be required to be intimated to any party and the sheriff may grant or refuse it without a hearing.

(4) The terms of the sheriff's decision on an application under this rule shall be endorsed on the extract decree, summary warrant or other document, as the case may be, and may be authenticated by the sheriff clerk.

Access to premises

10.—(1) An application by an officer of court under section 18(2) of, or paragraph 3(2) of Schedule 5 to, the Act to dispense with service of a notice of entry shall be made by endorsing a minute on the extract decree, summary warrant, or other document, upon which the poinding has proceeded.

(2) A minute under paragraph (1) of this rule shall specify the reason why notice might prejudice the execution of the poinding.

(3) A minute under paragraph (1) of this rule shall not be required to be intimated to any party and the sheriff may grant or refuse it without a hearing.

(4) The terms of the sheriff's decision on an application under this rule shall be endorsed on the extract decree, summary warrant or other document, as the case may be, and may be authenticated by the sheriff clerk.

Poinding schedule

11. A poinding schedule under section 20(5) of, or paragraph 5(5) of Schedule 5 to, the Act shall be in form 5.

Applications for security of poinded articles

12.—(1) An application for an order under section 21(1)(*a*) of, or paragraph 6(1)(*a*) of Schedule 5 to, the Act for the security of a poinded article shall be in form 6.

(2) The sheriff shall, on the lodging of an application under paragraph (1) of this rule, decide upon the further procedure in respect of it as he may consider appropriate, and may dispose of it without intimation to any party or without a hearing.

(3) Where the sheriff considers it appropriate, a date for a hearing of an application under paragraph (1) of this rule shall be fixed; and the sheriff clerk shall intimate a copy of the application together with a warrant for intimation to the applicant and as appropriate to the debtor, the creditor and the officer of court who executed the poinding, and shall thereafter complete a certificate of intimation.

(4) Where a hearing has been fixed under paragraph (3) of this rule, the officer of court who executed the poinding shall lodge with the court a copy of the poinding schedule before the date of the hearing.

(5) The sheriff clerk shall intimate the sheriff's decision on such an application to any person to whom intimation of the application was made but who was not present when the application was determined.

Applications for immediate disposal of poinded articles

13.—(1) An application for an order under section 21(1)(*b*) of, or paragraph 6(1)(*b*) of Schedule 5 to, the Act for immediate disposal of a poinded article shall be in form 7.

(2) In the case of an application by the debtor under paragraph (1) of this rule, intimation to the creditor or the officer of court as required by section 21(2)(*b*) of, or paragraph 6(2)(*b*) of Schedule 5 to, the Act shall be made by the sheriff clerk.

(3) On being satisfied that such an application has been intimated as

required by section 21(2) of, or paragraph 6(2) of Schedule 5 to, the Act the sheriff shall determine the further procedure in respect of the application as he considers appropriate.

Receipt of redemption of pointed articles

14. A receipt granted by an officer of court for payment in respect of a poinded article redeemed under section 21(4) of, or paragraph 6(4) of Schedule 5 to, the Act shall be in form 8.

Reports of execution of poindings

15.—(1) A report under section 22(1) of the Act by an officer of court of the execution of a poinding shall be in form 9 and shall state—

(*a*) the court which granted the original decree and the date of that decree, or details of the document upon which the poinding proceeded, and the date of any charge;

(*b*) that he did, before executing the poinding—

(i) exhibit to any person present the warrant to poind and the certificate of execution of charge;

(ii) demand payment of the sum recoverable from the debtor, if he was present, or any person present appearing to the officer to be authorised to act for the debtor; and

(iii) make enquiry of any person present as to the ownership of the articles proposed to be poinded, and in particular whether there were any persons who own any article in common with the debtor;

(*c*) if appropriate, that he informed the debtor of his right to redeem poinded articles, and whether any articles have been redeemed;

(*d*) if appropriate, that he informed any person present who owns any poinded article in common with the debtor of his right to redeem poinded articles;

(*e*) if appropriate, that he informed the debtor and any person present who owns any poinded article in common with the debtor, or who is in possession of the poinded article, of his right to apply for an order releasing articles from poinding under section 16(4), 23(1) or 41(3)(*b*) of the Act;

(*f*) whether he has carried out any of the actions mentioned in section 20(7) of the Act;

(*g*) the articles poinded and their respective values;

(*h*) the sum due by the debtor, including the fees, mileage charges or outlays which have been incurred in serving the charge and executing the poinding, and the amount of each; and

(*i*) in the case of a further or second poinding, the circumstances justifying the poinding.

(2) A report to which paragraph (1) of this rule applies shall be retained by the sheriff clerk.

(3) An application by an officer of court under section 22(1) of the Act to extend the time for lodging a report shall be made by endorsing a minute to that effect on the extract decree or other document upon which the poinding has proceeded stating the reasons for seeking the extension; and the terms of the sheriff's decision shall be endorsed on the extract decree or other document, as the case may be, and may be authenticated by the sheriff clerk.

Release of poinded articles on ground of undue harshness

16.—(1) An application by a debtor or person in possession of a poinded article for an order under section 23(1) of, or paragraph 7(1) of Schedule 5 to, the Act for release of an article from poinding on the ground of undue harshness shall be made in form 10 within 14 days after the date of the execution of the poinding.

(2) An application to which paragraph (1) of this rule applies shall specify—

(*a*) the name and address of the persons to whom the sheriff clerk will require to intimate the application under paragraph (3)(*c*) of this rule;

(*b*) the court which granted the original decree and the date of that decree, or details of the summary warrant or other document, upon which the poinding proceeded;

(*c*) the date and place of the execution of the poinding;

(*d*) the poinded article sought to be released;

(*e*) the reasons for seeking release of the poinded article; and

(*f*) any competent crave for expenses.

(3) On the lodging of such an application the sheriff clerk shall—

(*a*) fix a date for a hearing;

(*b*) obtain from the sheriff a warrant for intimation;

(*c*) intimate the application and warrant to the applicant, the creditor, the officer of court who executed the poinding and, as appropriate, the debtor or any person having possession of the poinded article; and

(*d*) complete a certificate of intimation.

(4) The officer of court who executed the poinding shall, whether or not he appears to oppose the application, lodge with the court a copy of the poinding schedule before the date fixed for hearing under paragraph (3)(*a*) of this rule.

(5) The sheriff clerk shall intimate the sheriff's decision on such an application to any person to whom intimation of the application was made but who was not present when the application was determined.

(6) Where an application to which paragraph (1) of this rule applies has been granted by the sheriff, an application under section 23(2) of, or paragraph 7(2) of Schedule 5 to, the Act (poinding of other articles belonging to debtor on the same premises) may be made by the creditor or the officer of court—

(*a*) orally at the time of granting of the application for release of an article; or

(*b*) endorsing a minute on the order granted.

(7) This rule shall apply to the release of an article from a sequestration for rent under a landlord's right of hypothec as it applies to the release of an article from poinding.

Invalidity, cessation and recall of poindings

17.—(1) An application by a debtor—

(*a*) for an order under section 24(1) of, or paragraph 8(1) of Schedule 5 to, the Act (poinding invalid or has ceased to have effect); or

(*b*) for recall of a poinding under section 24(3) of, or paragraph 8(3) of Schedule 5 to, the Act (undue harshness; aggregate value of articles low; aggregate proceeds of sale would not exceed expenses),

shall be in form 11.

(2) An application to which paragraph (1) of this rule applies shall specify—

(*a*) the name and address of the creditor, the officer of court who executed the poinding and any other person having an interest;

(*b*) the court which granted the original decree and the date of that decree, or details of the summary warrant or other document, upon which the poinding proceeded;

(*c*) the date and place of execution of the poinding;

(*d*) the reasons for the application and the order sought; and

(*e*) if appropriate, any competent crave for expenses.

(3) On the lodging of such an application the sheriff clerk shall—

(*a*) fix a date for a hearing;

(*b*) obtain from the sheriff a warrant for intimation;
(*c*) intimate the application and warrant to the applicant, the creditor and any other party having an interest;
(*d*) intimate the application to the officer of court who executed the poinding with an order that he deliver to the court before the date fixed for the hearing a copy of the poinding schedule; and
(*e*) complete a certificate of intimation.

(4) The sheriff clerk shall intimate the sheriff's decision on such an application to any person to whom intimation of the application was made but who was not present when the application was determined.

Sist of proceedings in poinding of mobile homes

18.—(1) An application by a debtor, or another person, whose only or principal residence is a caravan, houseboat or other moveable structure under section 26(1) of, or paragraph 10(1) of Schedule 5 to, the Act for an order that no further steps be taken in the poinding of such residence shall be in form 12.

(2) An application to which paragraph (1) of this rule applies shall specify—
(*a*) the name and address of, the debtor or other person whose only or principal residence is the subject of the poinding, the creditor and the officer of court who executed the poinding;
(*b*) the court which granted the original decree and the date of that decree, or details of the summary warrant or other document, upon which poinding proceeded;
(*c*) the date and place of execution of the poinding; and
(*d*) any competent crave for expenses.

(3) On the lodging of such an application the sheriff clerk shall—
(*a*) fix a date for a hearing;
(*b*) obtain from the sheriff a warrant for intimation;
(*c*) intimate the application and warrant to the debtor, the creditor, the officer of court who executed the poinding and any person whose only or principal residence is the subject of the poinding; and
(*d*) complete a certificate of intimation.

(4) The officer of court who executed the poinding shall, whether or not he appears to oppose the application, lodge with the court a copy of the poinding schedule before the date fixed for the hearing under paragraph (3)(*a*) of this rule.

(5) The sheriff clerk shall intimate the sheriff's decision on such an application to any person to whom intimation of the application was made but who was not present when the application was determined.

(6) This rule shall apply to the release of an article from a sequestration for rent under a landlord's right of hypothec as it applies to the release of an article from poinding.

Applications for extension of period of poindings

19.—(1) An application by a creditor or an officer of court under section 27(2) or (3) of, or paragraph 11(2) or (3) of Schedule 5 to, the Act for an extension of the duration of a poinding shall be in form 13.

(2) An application to which paragraph (1) of this rule applies shall specify—
(*a*) the name and address of the debtor, and where appropriate, the creditor and the officer of court who executed the poinding;
(*b*) the court which granted the original decree and the date of that decree, or details of the summary warrant or other document, upon which the poinding proceeded;
(*c*) the date and place of execution of the poinding;
(*d*) the period of extension sought;

(*e*) the reasons for making the application; and
(*f*) where appropriate, any competent crave for expenses.

(3) On the lodging of such an application the sheriff clerk shall—
(*a*) fix a date for a hearing;
(*b*) obtain from the sheriff a warrant for intimation;
(*c*) intimate the application and warrant to the applicant, the debtor and, where appropriate, the officer of court who executed the poinding; and
(*d*) complete a certificate of intimation.

(4) The officer of court who executed the poinding shall lodge with the court a copy of the poinding schedule before the date fixed for the hearing under paragraph (3)(*a*) of this rule.

Applications for removal of poinded articles

20.—(1) An application by a debtor or the person in possession of poinded articles under section 28(1)(*b*) of, or paragraph 12(1)(*b*) of Schedule 5 to, the Act for authority to remove a poinded article shall be in form 14.

(2) An application to which paragraph (1) of this rule applies shall specify—
(*a*) the name and address of the creditor, the officer of court who executed the poinding and, as appropriate, the debtor or the person having possession of the poinded article;
(*b*) the court which granted the original decree and the date of that decree, or details of the summary warrant or other document, upon which the poinding proceeded;
(*c*) the date and place of execution of the poinding;
(*d*) the poinded article to be removed and its present location;
(*e*) the reasons for seeking removal of the poinded article and the order sought; and
(*f*) any competent crave for expenses.

(3) On the lodging of such an application the sheriff clerk shall—
(*a*) fix a date for a hearing;
(*b*) obtain from the sheriff a warrant for intimation;
(*c*) intimate the application and warrant to the applicant, the creditor, the officer of court who executed the poinding and, as appropriate, the debtor or any person having possession of the poinded article; and
(*d*) complete a certificate of intimation.

(4) The officer of court who executed the poinding shall, whether or not he appears to oppose the application, lodge with the court a copy of the poinding schedule before the date fixed for the hearing under paragraph (3)(*a*) of this rule.

(5) The sheriff clerk shall intimate the sheriff's decision on such an application to any person to whom intimation of the application was made but who was not present when the application was determined.

Unauthorised removal of poinded articles

21.—(1) An application under section 28(4) of, or paragraph 12(4) of Schedule 5 to, the Act for an order for the restoration of a poinded article to the premises from which it was removed shall be in form 15.

(2) An application to which paragraph (1) of this rule applies shall specify—
(*a*) the name and address of the debtor, the officer of court who executed the poinding and the person having possession of the poinded article;
(*b*) the court which granted the original decree and the date of that decree, or details of the summary warrant or other document, upon which the poinding proceeded;

(*c*) the date and place of execution of the poinding;
(*d*) the article removed;
(*e*) the present whereabouts of the article, if known;
(*f*) the order sought; and
(*g*) any competent crave for expenses.

(3) On the lodging of such an application the sheriff clerk shall—
(*a*) fix a date for a hearing;
(*b*) obtain from the sheriff a warrant for intimation;
(*c*) intimate the application and warrant to the applicant, the officer of court who executed the poinding, the debtor and, where his identity is known, the person in possession of the poinded article; and
(*d*) complete a certificate of intimation.

(4) The officer of court who executed the poinding shall lodge with the court a copy of the poinding schedule before the date fixed for the hearing under paragraph (3)(*a*) of this rule.

(5) An application under section 28(5) of, or paragraph 12(5) of Schedule 5 to, the Act shall be made by motion at the hearing fixed under paragraph (3)(*a*) of this rule.

(6) Where the sheriff makes an order under section 28(4) of, or paragraph 12(4) of Schedule 5 to, the Act for restoration of a poinded article, the sheriff clerk shall serve a certified copy of the order on the person in possession of the article, if known, and shall complete a certificate of service and attach to it the form of application.

(7) Service in accordance with paragraph (6) of this rule shall be by recorded delivery post or by officer of court on payment of his fee by the applicant.

(8) Where an order under section 28(4)(*a*) of, or paragraph 12(4)(*a*) of Schedule 5 to, the Act for restoration of a poinded article has not been complied with, an application for a warrant under section 28(4)(*b*) of, or paragraph 12(4)(*b*) of Schedule 5 to, the Act may be made by endorsing a minute specifying the warrant craved on the form of application made under paragraph (1) of this rule.

(9) A minute under paragraph (8) of this rule shall be placed before the sheriff who may, where service of the order has been effected in accordance with paragraphs (6) and (7) of this rule, grant the warrant craved without further intimation, service or a hearing.

Pointed articles acquired for value without knowledge of poinding

22.—(1) Where, in an application to which rule 21 applies, the sheriff has made an order for restoration of a poinded article, an application under section 28(5)(*b*) or (*c*) of, or paragraph 12(5)(*b*) or (*c*) of Schedule 5 to, the Act to recall an order for restoration shall be in form 16.

(2) An application to which paragraph (1) of this rule applies shall specify—
(*a*) the name and address of the creditor, the debtor, any other person having an interest in the article known to him and the officer of court who executed the poinding;
(*b*) the court which granted the order for restoration and the date of that order;
(*c*) where known, the date and place of execution of the poinding;
(*d*) a description of the article concerned, details of the circumstances of its acquisition for value and without knowledge of the poinding and the applicant's interest in it;
(*e*) the order sought; and
(*f*) any competent crave for expenses.

(3) On the lodging of such an application the sheriff clerk shall—
(*a*) fix a date for a hearing;
(*b*) obtain from the sheriff a warrant for intimation;

(*c*) intimate the application and warrant to the applicant, the creditor, the debtor, the officer of court who executed the poinding and any other person known to the applicant as having an interest in the article or whom the sheriff may name in the warrant; and

(*d*) complete a certificate of intimation.

(4) The officer of court who executed the poinding shall lodge with the court a copy of the poinding schedule before the date fixed for the hearing under paragraph (3)(*a*) of this rule.

(5) The sheriff clerk shall intimate the sheriff's decision on such an application to any person to whom intimation of the application was made but who was not present when the application was determined.

Further poinding in same premises

23.—(1) An application under section 28(6) of, or paragraph 12(6) of Schedule 5 to, the Act for authority to poind another article in premises from which a poinded article has been removed shall be made—

(*a*) by oral motion in proceedings relating to the poinding; or

(*b*) in form 17.

(2) Where an application is made in accordance with paragraph (1)(*b*) of this rule, the application shall specify—

(*a*) the name and address of the debtor;

(*b*) the court which granted the original decree and the date of that decree, or details of the summary warrant or other document, upon which the poinding proceeded;

(*c*) the date and place of execution of the poinding;

(*d*) the grounds for the application including reasons for alleging that the debtor is at fault; and

(*e*) any competent crave for expenses.

(3) On the lodging of an application in accordance with paragraph (1)(*b*) of this rule, the sheriff clerk shall—

(*a*) fix a date for a hearing;

(*b*) obtain from the sheriff a warrant for intimation;

(*c*) intimate the application and warrant to the debtor and the applicant; and

(*d*) complete a certificate of intimation.

(4) The officer of court who executed the poinding shall lodge with the court a copy of the poinding schedule before the date fixed for the hearing under paragraph (3)(*a*) of this rule.

(5) The sheriff clerk shall intimate the sheriff's decision on such an application to any person to whom intimation of the application was made but who was not present when the application was determined.

Damage or destruction of poinded articles

24.—(1) An application under section 29(2) of, or paragraph 13(2) of Schedule 5 to, the Act for authority to poind another article where a poinded article has been damaged or destroyed or to revalue damaged articles shall be in form 18.

(2) An application to which paragraph (1) of this rule applies shall specify—

(*a*) the name and address of the debtor;

(*b*) the court which granted the original decree and the date of that decree, or details of the summary warrant or other document, upon which the poinding proceeded;

(*c*) the date and place of execution of the poinding;

(*d*) the poinded article alleged to have been damaged or destroyed;

(*e*) where appropriate, the reasons for alleging that the debtor is at fault;

(*f*) where appropriate, the alleged reduction in value;

(g) the order sought; and
(h) any competent crave for expenses.

(3) On the lodging of such an application the sheriff clerk shall—
(a) fix a date for a hearing;
(b) obtain from the sheriff a warrant for intimation;
(c) intimate the application and warrant to the applicant, the debtor, the officer of court who executed the poinding and any other party whom the sheriff may name in the warrant; and
(d) complete a certificate of intimation.

(4) The officer of court who executed the poinding shall lodge with the court a copy of the poinding schedule before the date fixed for the hearing under paragraph (3)(*a*) of this rule.

(5) The sheriff clerk shall intimate the sheriff's decision on such an application to any person to whom intimation of the application was made but who was not present when the application was determined.

Applications for consignation by third party

25.—(1) An application under section 29(3) of, or paragraph 13(3) of Schedule 5 to, the Act for an order against a third party to consign a sum of money shall be in form 19.

(2) An application to which paragraph (1) of this rule applies shall specify—
(a) the name and address of the creditor, the debtor, the person in respect of whom an order for consignation is sought and the officer of court who executed the poinding;
(b) the court which granted the original decree and the date of that decree, or details of the summary warrant or other document, upon which the poinding proceeded;
(c) the date and place of execution of the poinding;
(d) the article damaged, destroyed, lost, stolen or sold;
(e) details of the sum for which consignation is sought; and
(f) any competent crave for expenses.

(3) On the lodging of such an application the sheriff clerk shall—
(a) fix a date for a hearing;
(b) obtain from the sheriff a warrant for intimation;
(c) intimate the application and warrant to the applicant, the officer of court who executed the poinding, the person in respect of whom an order for consignation is sought and, as appropriate, the debtor or creditor; and
(d) complete a certificate of intimation.

(4) The officer of court who executed the poinding shall lodge with the court a copy of the poinding schedule before the date fixed for the hearing under paragraph (3)(*a*) of this rule.

(5) Where an application under paragraph (1) of this rule is granted, the sheriff clerk shall serve a certified copy of the sheriff's order upon the person concerned and shall complete a certificate of service.

(6) Service under paragraph (5) of this rule shall be by recorded delivery post or by officer of court on payment of his fee by the applicant.

Applications for warrants of sale

26.—(1) An application by a creditor or officer of court under section 30(1) of the Act for a warrant of sale shall be in form 20.

(2) An application to which paragraph (1) of this rule applies shall specify—
(a) the name and address of the applicant, the creditor, any person in possession of the poinded article, the debtor and the auctioneer or officer of court or other person who is to conduct the sale;
(b) the date of the report of execution of poinding to the sheriff;

(*c*) the name and address of the officer of court who will make the arrangements for the sale in accordance with the warrant;
(*d*) the intended location of the sale;
(*e*) the applicant's proposals for public notice of the sale where it will not be held in an auction room;
(*f*) the applicant's proposals for the period within which the sale is intended to take place; and
(*g*) any release or redemption of a poinded article.

(3) There shall be produced with such an application—
(*a*) where the sale is to be held in a dwellinghouse, the consent of the occupier, and, if he is not the occupier, of the debtor, to the sale being held in a dwellinghouse; or
(*b*) where the sale is to be held in premises other than a dwellinghouse or auction room, the consent of the occupier of the premises.

(4) No warrant for service of such an application shall be required.

(5) The notice to be served by the creditor or officer of court under section 30(3) of the Act shall be in form 21.

(6) The creditor or officer of court shall serve on the debtor a copy of any consents referred to in rule 27 with a copy application and notice under this rule.

(7) Service of the copy application and notice under this rule shall be by recorded delivery post or by officer of court; and the applicant shall thereafter complete an execution of service.

(8) A debtor may object to an application to which paragraph (1) of this rule applies by—
(*a*) completing and returning the appropriate portion of form 21 to; or
(*b*) lodging written objections with,
the sheriff clerk, within 14 days after the date of making of the application.

(9) Where a debtor lodges an objection under paragraph (8) of this rule, the sheriff clerk shall fix a date for a hearing and intimate it to the parties.

(10) Subject to section 30(4) of the Act, if no objection to an application under paragraph (1) of this rule is lodged, the sheriff may dispose of the application without a hearing.

Location of sales

27.—(1) The forms of consent, required under section 32(1) and (4) of, or paragraph 14(2) and (3) of Schedule 5 to, the Act, to a warrant sale being held in a dwellinghouse or in premises other than a dwellinghouse or an auction room, shall be in form 22.

(2) An application under paragraph 14(4) of Schedule 5 to the Act by the creditor or officer of court for an order that a warrant sale be held in the premises where the poinded article is situated shall be made in writing and may be determined by the sheriff after such procedure as appears to him appropriate.

Receipts for redemption of poinded articles after application for warrant of sale

28. A receipt granted by an officer of court on the redemption by the debtor of a poinded article under section 33(2) of, or paragraph 15(2) of Schedule 5 to, the Act shall be in form 23.

Intimation and publication of warrants of sale

29.—(1) A copy of every warrant of sale granted under section 30(1), or a variation of a warrant of sale under section 35(1) or 36(3)(*b*), of the Act shall be displayed on the walls of the court which granted it until the sale has been concluded.

(2) In the case of a sale of a poinded article which proceeds upon a summary warrant, the particulars to be sent to the sheriff clerk by the officer of court under paragraph 16(2) of Schedule 5 to the Act, shall be—

(*a*) the name and address of the debtor, the creditor and the officer of court who is making the arrangements for the sale; and
(*b*) the date, time and place of the sale.

Alteration of arrangements for warrant sales

30.—(1) An application under section 35(1) or 36(3)(*b*) of the Act for variation of a warrant of sale shall be in form 24.

(2) An application to which paragraph (1) of this rule applies shall specify—

(*a*) the name and address of the applicant, the creditor, the debtor, any person in possession of the poinded article, and the auctioneer or officer of court who is to conduct the sale;
(*b*) the date of the original warrant of sale;
(*c*) details of any steps of diligence taken;
(*d*) the applicant's proposals for variation and his reasons for seeking such variation;
(*e*) any release or redemption of a poinded article;
(*f*) details of any agreement between creditor and debtor to pay the debt by instalments or otherwise and any breach of it;
(*g*) details of any cancellation of warrant sale; and
(*h*) any additional powers sought by the applicant in the event of the application being granted.

(3) There shall be produced with such an application the original warrant of sale.

(4) No warrant for service of such an application shall be required.

(5) The notice to be served by the creditor or officer of court under section 35(5)(*a*) of the Act shall be in form 25.

(6) The creditor or officer of court shall, after effecting service, complete an execution of service and lodge the principal application and original warrant of sale with the sheriff clerk.

(7) Service of the copy application to which paragraph (1) applies may be by recorded delivery post or by officer of court.

(8) A debtor may object to an application to which paragraph (1) of this rule applies by—

(*a*) completing and returning the appropriate part of form 25 to; or
(*b*) lodging written objections with,

the sheriff clerk within seven days after the date of service of the application.

(9) Where a debtor lodges an objection under paragraph (8), the sheriff clerk shall fix a date for a hearing and intimate it to the parties.

(10) Subject to section 35(6) of the Act, if no objection to an application under paragraph (1) of this rule is lodged, the sheriff may dispose of the application without a hearing.

Reports of warrant sales

31.—(1) A report of sale, under section 39(1) of, or paragraph 20(1) of Schedule 5 to, the Act shall be in form 26.

(2) A report of sale shall specify—

(*a*) the name and address of the creditor, the debtor and any person, other than the debtor who had possession of the poinded article;
(*b*) the date of the decree, summary warrant or other document, upon which the sale proceeded, the date of issue of any extract decree and the prior steps of diligence;
(*c*) details of the warrant of sale and any variation of it;
(*d*) any intimation, service and notices given by the officer of court in respect of the sale;
(*e*) when and where the sale took place and the persons who arranged and conducted the sale;

(*f*) the articles which have been sold and the amount for which they have been sold;
(*g*) any articles which were not sold and whether their ownership passed to the creditor or reverted to the debtor;
(*h*) the sum which was due by the debtor and the expenses chargeable against the debtor under Schedule 1 to the Act;
(*i*) the amount of any surplus paid or to be consigned in court;
(*j*) any balance of the debt due by the debtor;
(*k*) any release or redemption of a poinded article whether or not otherwise reported to the court or specified in a warrant of sale or for variation of it; and
(*l*) any article damaged, destroyed, lost or stolen, any sum consigned by a party in connection with it and any balance of that sum due to the creditor or debtor.

(3) There shall be lodged with the report of sale the extract decree or other document upon which diligence proceeded, the original warrant of sale and any variation of it, any executions or certificates of intimation, service, copies of public notices required by the Act or these rules and vouchers for relevant outlays.

Modification of sale balance and declaration that poinding and sale void

32.—(1) Where the sheriff, after the receipt of the auditor of court's report, considers—
(*a*) that a balance due to or by the debtor should be modified; or
(*b*) that the poinding and sale may be void,
he shall before making an order under section 39(5)(*b*) or (*c*) of the Act fix a date for a hearing; and the sheriff clerk shall intimate such hearing to the creditor, the officer of court who prepared the report of sale, the debtor and any other person having or having had an interest in or possession of, the poinded article as the sheriff may specify.

(2) Where the sheriff has made an order modifying a sale balance or declaring a poinding and sale to be void, the sheriff clerk shall intimate that order and any consequential order of the sheriff to those persons to whom intimation was made under paragraph (1) of this rule.

Retention of reports of sales

33. A report of sale shall be retained by the sheriff clerk in accordance with section 39(8) of the Act for a period of five years from the date of its being lodged with the court.

Release from poinding of articles belonging to third party

34.—(1) An application under section 40(2) of, or paragraph 21(2) of Schedule 5 to, the Act for release from poinding of an article belonging to a third party shall be in form 27.

(2) An application to which paragraph (1) of this rule applies shall specify—
(*a*) where known, the name and address of the creditor, the debtor, the officer of court who executed the poinding and any person other than the debtor having possession of the poinded article;
(*b*) where known, the court which granted the original decree and the date of that decree, or details of the summary warrant or other document, upon which the poinding proceeded;
(*c*) the date and place of execution of poinding;
(*d*) if appropriate, where and when the warrant sale is to be held;
(*e*) the article which is sought to be released; and
(*f*) any competent crave for expenses.

(3) On the lodging of such an application the sheriff clerk shall—
(*a*) fix a date for a hearing;
(*b*) obtain from the sheriff a warrant for intimation;

(*c*) intimate the application and warrant to the applicant, the creditor, the debtor, the officer of court who executed the poinding and any person having possession of the article; and

(*d*) complete a certificate of intimation.

(4) The officer of court who executed the poinding shall, whether or not he appears to oppose the application, lodge with the court a copy of the poinding schedule before the date fixed for the hearing under paragraph (3)(*a*) of this rule.

(5) The sheriff clerk shall intimate the sheriff's decision on such an application to any person to whom intimation of the application was made but who was not present when the application was determined.

Release from poinding of articles in common ownership

35.—(1) An application under section 41(3), or paragraph 22(3) of Schedule 5 to, the Act for release from poinding of an article in common ownership shall be in form 28.

(2) An application to which paragraph (1) of this rule applies shall specify—

(*a*) the name and address of the creditor, the debtor, the officer of court who executed the poinding, any person who owns or claims to own the article in common with the debtor and any person other than the debtor having possession of the poinded article;

(*b*) the court which granted the original decree and the date of that decree, or details of the summary warrant or other document, upon which the poinding proceeded;

(*c*) the date and place of execution of poinding;

(*d*) if appropriate, where and when the warrant sale is to be held;

(*e*) the nature and extent of the applicant's ownership of the article;

(*f*) the nature and extent of the debtor's and any other person's ownership of the article;

(*g*) whether an undertaking has been or is made to pay a sum equal to the debtor's interest in the article;

(*h*) whether and, if so, why the continued poinding or sale of the article would be unduly harsh to the applicant; and

(*i*) any competent crave for expenses.

(3) On the lodging of such an application the sheriff clerk shall—

(*a*) fix a date for a hearing;

(*b*) obtain from the sheriff a warrant for intimation;

(*c*) intimate the application and warrant to the applicant, the creditor, the debtor, the officer of court who executed the poinding, any person named in the application who owns or claims to own the article in common with the debtor and any person having possession of the poinded article; and

(*d*) complete a certificate of intimation.

(4) The officer of court who executed the poinding shall, whether or not he appears to oppose the application, lodge with the court a copy of the poinding schedule before the date fixed for the hearing under paragraph (3)(*a*) of this rule.

(5) The sheriff clerk shall intimate the sheriff's decision in such an application to any person to whom intimation of the application was made but who was not present when the application was determined.

Applications for finding of common ownership of poinded article

36.—(1) An application under section 41(7)(*b*) of, or paragraph 22(6)(*b*) of Schedule 5 to, the Act for a finding that a poinded article is owned in common shall be in form 29.

(2) An application to which paragraph (1) of this rule applies shall specify—

(*a*) the name and address of the creditor, the debtor, the officer of court who executed the poinding and any person who owns or claims to own the article in common with the debtor;
(*b*) where known, the court which granted the original decree and the date of that decree, or details of the summary warrant or other document, upon which the poinding proceeded;
(*c*) the date and place of execution of poinding;
(*d*) if appropriate, where and when a warrant sale is to be held;
(*e*) the article in respect of which the application is made and the nature and extent of the applicant's ownership of it;
(*f*) the nature and extent of the debtor's and any other person's ownership of the article;
(*g*) the order sought; and
(*h*) any competent crave for expenses.

(3) On the lodging of such an application the sheriff clerk shall—
(*a*) fix a date for a hearing;
(*b*) obtain from the sheriff a warrant for intimation;
(*c*) intimate the application and warrant to the applicant, the creditor, the debtor, the officer of court who executed the poinding and any other person who the sheriff clerk is informed by the applicant also owns or claims to own the article in common with the debtor;
(*d*) complete a certificate of intimation.

(4) The officer of court who executed the poinding shall, whether or not he appears to oppose the application, lodge with the court a copy of the poinding schedule before the date fixed for the hearing under paragraph (3)(*a*) of this rule.

(5) The sheriff clerk shall intimate the sheriff's decision on such an application to any person to whom intimation of the application was made but who was not present when the application was determined.

Conjoining of poindings

37.—(1) An application under section 43(1) of the Act for an order conjoining poindings shall be made by the creditor or officer of court who executed the later poinding endorsing a minute to that effect on the later report of poinding.

(2) A minute to which paragraph (1) of this rule applies shall specify—
(*a*) that no warrant of sale has been granted in respect of either poinding;
(*b*) the date of execution of each poinding;
(*c*) whether any proceedings are subsisting in respect of the later poinding;
(*d*) whether any proceedings in respect of the later poinding have been disposed of by the sheriff and whether and by whom any leave to appeal has been sought or appeal taken in respect of any such proceedings.

Part IV

Diligence Against Earnings

Earnings arrestment schedules

38.—(1) An earnings arrestment schedule under section 47(2)(*a*) of the Act shall be in form 30.

(2) An earnings arrestment schedule shall state—
(*a*) the name, designation and address of the creditor, the debtor, the employer and any person residing in the United Kingdom to whom payment under the arrestment is to be made;

(*b*) the decree or other document constituting the debt and when, where and by whom it was granted or issued;
(*c*) the date on which any charge for payment was served; and
(*d*) the debt outstanding and the manner of its calculation.

(3) There shall be attached to or reproduced upon the earnings arrestment schedule, and any copy intimated to the debtor, the terms of section 49(1) to (6) of, and Schedule 2 to, the Act.

Intimation of regulations made under section 49(7) of the Act

39.—(1) The form of intimation to an employer under section 49(8) of the Act of regulations under section 49(7) of the Act varying Tables A, B or C of Schedule 2 to the Act or the percentages specified in section 49(5) or (6)(*a*)(ii) of the Act shall be in form 31.

(2) The form of intimation required under paragraph (1) of this rule shall specify—
(*a*) the date of service of the earnings arrestment schedule;
(*b*) the name and address of the creditor, the debtor and the employer;
(*c*) that changes in the tables or percentages, as the case may be, have been made by regulations made by the Lord Advocate, the date when they were made and the date of their coming into force.

(3) There shall be attached to or reproduced upon such a form of intimation the full text of the statutory deduction tables as varied by the regulations.

Applications for orders that earnings arrestments invalid etc.

40.—(1) An application under section 50(1) of the Act for declarator that an earnings arrestment is invalid or has ceased to have effect shall be in form 32.

(2) An application to which paragraph (1) of this rule applies shall state—
(*a*) the name and address of the creditor, the debtor, the officer of court who served the earnings arrestment schedule and the person on whom the schedule was served;
(*b*) the court which granted the original decree and the date of that decree, or details of the summary warrant or other document, upon which the earnings arrestment proceeded;
(*c*) the date of service of the earnings arrestment schedule;
(*d*) the form of order sought;
(*e*) the reasons for the application; and
(*f*) any competent crave for expenses.

(3) A copy of the earnings arrestment schedule shall, where practicable, be attached to such an application.

(4) On the lodging of such an application the sheriff clerk shall—
(*a*) fix a date for a hearing;
(*b*) obtain from the sheriff a warrant for intimation;
(*c*) intimate the application and warrant to the applicant, the creditor and, as appropriate, the debtor or the person on whom the earnings arrestment schedule was served; and
(*d*) complete a certificate of intimation.

Determination of disputes as to operation of earnings arrestment

41.—(1) An application under section 50(3) of the Act for determination of any dispute as to the operation of an earnings arrestment shall be in form 33.

(2) An application to which paragraph (1) of this rule applies shall specify—
(*a*) the name and address of the creditor, the debtor, the officer of court who served the earnings arrestment schedule and the employer;

(*b*) the court which granted the original decree and the date of that decree, or details of the summary warrant or other document, upon which the earnings arrestment proceeded;
(*c*) the date of service of the earnings arrestment schedule;
(*d*) the subject matter of the dispute;
(*e*) the form of order sought, including any sum sought to be reimbursed or paid;
(*f*) any claim for interest and the date from which such interest should run; and
(*g*) any competent crave for expenses.

(3) A copy of the earnings arrestment schedule shall, where practicable, be attached to such an application.

(4) On the lodging of such an application the sheriff clerk shall—
(*a*) fix a date for a hearing;
(*b*) obtain from the sheriff a warrant for intimation;
(*c*) intimate the application and warrant to the applicant and, as appropriate, the creditor, the debtor and the employer; and
(*d*) complete a certificate of intimation.

(5) The sheriff clerk shall intimate the sheriff's decision on such an application to any person to whom intimation of the application was made but who was not present when the application was determined.

Current maintenance arrestment schedules

42.—(1) A current maintenance arrestment schedule under section 51(2)(*a*) of the Act shall be in form 34.

(2) A current maintenance schedule shall state—
(*a*) the name, designation and address of the creditor, the debtor, the employee and any person residing in the United Kingdom to whom payment under the arrestment is to be made;
(*b*) the maintenance order constituting the current maintenance, when and by whom it was granted or issued, and, where appropriate, details of its registration or confirmation;
(*c*) the maintenance payable under the maintenance order by the debtor expressed as a daily rate;
(*d*) where appropriate, the date of intimation made to the debtor under section 54(1) of the Act and particulars of default; and
(*e*) whether or not income tax falls to be deducted from the maintenance payable by the debtor.

(3) There shall be attached to or reproduced upon the current maintenance schedule, and any copy intimated to the debtor, the terms of section 53(1) and (2) of the Act.

Intimation of regulations made under section 53(3) of the Act

43.—(1) The form of intimation to an employer under section 53(4) of the Act of regulations under section 53(3) of the Act varying the sum specified in section 53(2)(*b*) of the Act shall be in form 35.

(2) The form of intimation required under paragraph (1) of these rules shall state—
(*a*) the date of service of the current maintenance arrestment schedule;
(*b*) the name and address of the creditor, the debtor and the employer; and
(*c*) the new sum which is applicable in accordance with regulations made by the Lord Advocate, the date when they were made and the date of their coming into force.

Intimation of changes in small maintenance payments limits

44.—(1) The form of intimation to an employer under section 53(5) of the Act of a change in the small maintenance payments limits shall be in form 36.

(2) The form of intimation required under paragraph (1) of this rule shall specify—

(*a*) the date of service of the current maintenance arrestment schedule;

(*b*) the name and address of the creditor, the debtor and the employer; and

(*c*) that changes have been made to section 351(2) of the Income and Corporation Taxes Act 1988, what these changes are and the date of their coming into force.

(3) There shall be attached to or reproduced upon such a form of intimation the full text of section 351(2) of the Income and Corporation Taxes Act 1988.

Notice to debtor prior to service of current maintenance arrestment

[1] **45.**—(1) Intimation to a debtor under a maintenance order required by section 54(1)(*a*) of the Act prior to service of a current maintenance arrestment shall be given by intimating to him a notice in form 37 together with a copy of the relevant maintenance order.

(2) The notice referred to in paragraph (1) of this rule shall contain—

(*a*) the name and address of the creditor and of the debtor;

(*b*) details of the making, registration or confirmation of the maintenance order;

(*c*) guidance as to the manner in which payment may be made; and

(*d*) a statement of the consequences of failure to comply with the maintenance order.

(3) Intimation in accordance with this rule shall—

(*a*) where the debtor resides in the United Kingdom, be by recorded delivery post; and

(*b*) where the debtor resides outside the United Kingdom, be by any competent method of service appropriate to that place.

(4) The creditor shall prepare a certificate that intimation has been made in accordance with this rule and shall retain the certificate while the current maintenance arrestment is in force.

(5) Where, in the exercise of his powers under section 24B of the Social Security Act 1986, the Secretary of State seeks to enforce a maintenance order on behalf of a claimant, the following notice shall be appended to form 37:—

"The Secretary of State for Social Security ('the creditor') intends to enforce this maintenance order under the powers conferred on him by section 24B of the Social Security Act 1986.".

NOTE

[1] Substituted by S.I. 1991 No. 1920.

Applications for orders that current maintenance arrestments are invalid etc.

46.—(1) An application under section 55(1) of the Act for declarator that a current maintenance arrestment is invalid or has ceased to have effect shall be in form 38.

(2) An application to which paragraph (1) of this rule applies shall specify—

(*a*) the name and address of the creditor, the debtor, the officer of court who served the current maintenance arrestment schedule and the person on whom the schedule was served;

(*b*) the maintenance order and when, where and by whom it was granted or issued and, where appropriate, details of its registration or confirmation;

(*c*) the date of service of the current maintenance arrestment schedule;

(*d*) the reasons for seeking the order;

(*e*) the form of order sought; and

(*f*) any competent crave for expenses.

(3) A copy of the current maintenance arrestment schedule shall, where practicable, be attached to such an application.

(4) On the lodging of such an application the sheriff clerk shall—

(*a*) fix a date for a hearing;

(*b*) obtain from the sheriff a warrant for intimation;

(*c*) intimate the application and warrant to the applicant, the creditor and, as appropriate, the debtor or the person on whom the current maintenance arrestment schedule was served; and

(*d*) complete a certificate of intimation.

[THE NEXT PAGE IS D 385]

Recall of current maintenance arrestments

47.—(1) An application under section 55(2) of the Act for a recall of a current maintenance arrestment shall be in form 39.

(2) An application to which paragraph (1) of this rule applies shall specify—

(*a*) the name and address of the creditor, the debtor, the officer of court who served the current maintenance arrestment schedule and the employer;

(*b*) the maintenance order and when, where and by whom it was granted or issued and, where appropriate, details of its registration or confirmation;

(*c*) the date of service of the current maintenance arrestment schedule;

(*d*) such information as the applicant considers appropriate to satisfy the sheriff that he will not default again in paying maintenance;

(*e*) the order sought; and

(*f*) any competent crave for expenses.

(3) A copy of the current maintenance arrestment schedule shall, where practicable, be attached to such an application.

(4) On the lodging of such an application the sheriff clerk shall—

(*a*) fix a date for a hearing;

(*b*) obtain from the sheriff a warrant for intimation;

(*c*) intimate the application and warrant to the applicant and the creditor; and

(*d*) complete a certificate of intimation.

Determination of disputes as to operation of current maintenance arrestments

48.—(1) An application under section 55(5) of the Act for determination of any dispute as to the operation of a current maintenance arrestment shall be in form 40.

(2) An application to which paragraph (1) of this rule applies shall specify—

(*a*) the name and address of the creditor, the debtor, the officer of court who served the current maintenance arrestment schedule and the employer;

(*b*) the maintenance order and when, where and by whom it was granted or issued and, where appropriate, details of its registration or confirmation;

(*c*) the date of service of the current maintenance arrestment schedule;

(*d*) the subject matter of the dispute;

(*e*) the form of order sought, including any sum sought to be reimbursed or paid;

(*f*) any claim for interest and the date from which such interest should run; and

(*g*) any competent crave for expenses.

(3) A copy of the current maintenance arrestment schedule shall, where practicable, be attached to such an application.

(4) On the lodging of such an application the sheriff clerk shall—

(*a*) fix a date for hearing;

(*b*) obtain from the sheriff a warrant for intimation;

(*c*) intimate the application and warrant to the applicant and, as appropriate, the creditor, the debtor and the employer; and

(*d*) complete a certificate of intimation.

Intimation by sheriff clerk where non-Scottish maintenance order ceases to have effect

49. Where a maintenance order pronounced outwith Scotland and registered in a sheriff court for enforcement in Scotland ceases to have effect because the debtor no longer resides in Scotland, the sheriff clerk of that court shall, so far as reasonably practicable, intimate those facts—

(*a*) where a current maintenance arrestment is in force, to the person upon whom the current maintenance arrestment schedule was served; and

(*b*) where a conjoined arrestment order is in force, to the sheriff clerk to whom payments require to be made by the employer in terms of such order.

Intimation by creditor under section 57(4) of the Act

50. Intimation by the creditor to an employer required by section 57(4) of the Act shall be in writing.

Applications by debtors for payment by creditors

51.—(1) An application under section 57(6) of the Act by a debtor for an order requiring a creditor to pay an amount not exceeding twice the amount recoverable by the debtor under section 57(5) of the Act shall be in form 41.

(2) An application to which paragraph (1) of this rule applies shall specify—

(*a*) the name and address of the debtor, the creditor, the officer of court who served the arrestment and the employer;

(*b*) the court which granted the original decree and the date of that decree, or details of the summary warrant or other document, upon which arrestment proceeded;

(*c*) the amount of the debt or the sum to be deducted from the debtor's earnings;

(*d*) where appropriate, the expenses of diligence;

(*e*) where appropriate, whether the debt recoverable under the earnings arrestment is paid or otherwise extinguished and, if so, from what date and in what circumstances;

(*f*) where appropriate, whether the current maintenance arrestment has ceased to have effect and, if so, from what date and in what circumstances;

(*g*) where appropriate, whether the debt being enforced by the earnings arrestment has ceased to be enforceable by diligence and, if so, from what date and in what circumstances;

(*h*) the calculation showing the sum alleged to have been received by the creditor in excess of entitlement;

(*i*) the sum sought from the creditor and the grounds for seeking such sum; and

(*j*) any competent crave for expenses.

(3) A copy of the relevant arrestment schedule shall, where practicable, be attached to such an application.

(4) On the lodging of such an application the sheriff clerk shall—

(*a*) fix a date for a hearing;

(*b*) obtain from the sheriff a warrant for intimation;

(*c*) intimate the application and warrant to the applicant and to the creditor; and

(*d*) complete a certificate of intimation.

(5) The sheriff clerk shall intimate the sheriff's decision in such an application to the creditor if the creditor was not present when the application was determined.

Applications by second creditors for information

52.—(1) An application by a second creditor under section 59(5) of the Act for an order to ordain an employer to give information relating to any other earnings arrestment or current maintenance arrestment to the second creditor shall be in form 42.

(2) An application to which paragraph (1) of this rule applies shall specify—

(*a*) the name and address of the applicant, the debtor, the employer and the officer of court who served the arrestment schedule in respect of the debt due to the applicant;

(*b*) the date of service of the applicant's earnings arrestment or current maintenance arrestment schedule;

(*c*) that the arrestment did not come into effect by virtue of section 59 of the Act;

(*d*) the information required by the applicant and which he alleges has not been provided by the employer;

(*e*) the order sought; and

(*f*) any competent crave for expenses.

(3) On the lodging of such an application the sheriff clerk shall—

(*a*) fix a date for a hearing;

(*b*) obtain from the sheriff a warrant for intimation;

(*c*) intimate the application and warrant to the applicant and the employer; and

(*d*) complete a certificate of intimation.

(4) The sheriff clerk shall intimate the sheriff's decision in such an application to the employer if the employer was not present when the application was determined.

Applications for conjoined arrestment orders

53.—(1) An application under section 60(2) of the Act by a qualified creditor for a conjoined arrestment order shall be in form 43.

(2) An application to which paragraph (1) of this rule applies shall specify—

(*a*) the name and address of the applicant, the debtor, the employer and any person residing in the United Kingdom to whom payment is to be made in respect of the applicant's debt;

(*b*) such information relating to the debt due to the applicant as would require to be specified in an earnings arrestment schedule or, as the case may be, a current maintenance arrestment schedule;

(*c*) in respect of each earnings arrestment or current maintenance arrestment already in effect against the debtor in the hands of the same employer—

(i) the name and address of the creditor;

(ii) the date and the place of the execution of such arrestments; and

(iii) the debt recoverable specified in the earnings arrestment schedule or, as the case may be, the daily rate of maintenance specified in the current maintenance Schedule; and

(*d*) the expenses of the application.

(3) On the lodging of such an application the sheriff clerk shall—

(*a*) intimate the application, together with a form of notice and response in form 44, to the debtor and any other creditor of the debtor already enforcing a debt by an earnings arrestment or current maintenance arrestment in the hands of the same employer; and

(*b*) complete a certificate of intimation.

(4) Where a creditor or the debtor intends to object to such an application, he shall complete and lodge with the sheriff clerk the form of notice and response in form 44 within 14 days after the date of intimation.

(5) On receipt of such a form of notice and response the sheriff clerk shall fix a date for a hearing and intimate the date to the applicant and any person who received intimation of the application.

(6) Where such a form of notice and response is not timeously lodged with the sheriff clerk, the sheriff may grant the application or may make such other order as he considers appropriate.

Conjoined arrestment orders

54.—(1) A conjoined arrestment order shall be in form 45.

(2) A conjoined arrestment order shall—

(*a*) specify any earnings arrestment or current maintenance arrestment in effect against the earnings of the debtor in the hands of the same employer;

(*b*) notify the employer that he must deduct a sum calculated in accordance with section 63 of the Act from the debtor's net earnings on any pay day and to pay the sum deducted to the sheriff clerk as soon as is reasonably practicable for so long as the order is in effect;

(*c*) specify, as appropriate, the amount recoverable in respect of the debt or debts and maintenance, expressed as a daily rate or aggregate of the daily rates;

(*d*) state the address of the sheriff clerk to whom payments are to be sent and, where appropriate, a court reference number; and

(*e*) if appropriate, include an award of expenses.

(3) The sheriff clerk shall serve a copy of the conjoined arrestment order (or such final order of the sheriff in an application under rule 53 above) on the applicant, the employer, the debtor and the creditors in any earnings arrestment or current maintenance arrestment recalled by the order.

(4) There shall be attached to or reproduced upon every copy conjoined arrestment order as served on any person the full text of section 63(1) to (6) of the Act.

(5) There shall be enclosed with a conjoined arrestment order served on any person a notice in form 46 which shall require all creditors whose arrestments have been recalled to inform the sheriff clerk, within 14 days of the date of service of the notice, of the name and address of the person within the United Kingdom to whom payments should be made in respect of his debt.

(6) Subject to paragraphs (7) and (8) of this rule, service under this rule shall be by recorded delivery post.

(7) Where such service has been unsuccessful, reservice—

(*a*) in the case of service on the employer, shall be effected by an officer of court on payment of his fee by the applicant; and

(*b*) in any other case of service on a person within the United Kingdom, shall be by ordinary first class post.

(8) Service under this rule on a person outside the United Kingdom which cannot be effected by recorded delivery post shall be by any other competent method of service.

Applications by sheriff clerks for warrants for diligence

55.—(1) An application by a sheriff clerk under section 60(9)(*c*) of the Act for a warrant for diligence against an employer for recovery of sums which are claimed to be due shall be in form 47.

(2) An application to which paragraph (1) of this rule applies shall specify—

(*a*) the name and address of the sheriff clerk, the employer, the debtor and the creditors under the conjoined arrestment order;

(*b*) the date of the conjoined arrestment order and details of its service on the employer;

(*c*) the sum claimed to be due by the employer and details of its calculation; and

(*d*) the circumstances in which the sum is said to be due and, if appropriate, any reasons given to the sheriff clerk for its not having been paid.

(3) On preparing such an application the sheriff clerk shall—

(*a*) fix a date for a hearing;

(*b*) obtain from the sheriff a warrant for intimation;

(*c*) intimate the application and warrant to the employer, the debtor and the creditors under the conjoined arrestment order; and
(*d*) complete a certificate of intimation.

Applications by creditors for information under section 62 of the Act

56.—(1) An application by a creditor under section 62(4) of the Act for an order for information which an employer requires to provide in accordance with section 62(2) or (3) of the Act shall be in form 48.

(2) An application to which paragraph (1) of this rule applies shall specify—
(*a*) the name and address of the applicant, the debtor, the employer and the officer of court who served the arrestment schedule in respect of the debt due to the applicant;
(*b*) the date of service of the applicant's earnings arrestment or current maintenance arrestment schedule;
(*c*) the reason for that arrestment not coming into effect or ceasing to have effect;
(*d*) the information required by the applicant and which he alleges has not been provided by the employer; and
(*e*) any competent crave for expenses.

(3) On the lodging of such an application the sheriff clerk shall—
(*a*) fix a date for a hearing;
(*b*) obtain from the sheriff a warrant for intimation;
(*c*) intimate the application and warrant to the applicant and the employer; and
(*d*) complete a certificate of intimation.

(4) The sheriff clerk shall intimate the sheriff's decision on such an application to the employer if the employer was not present when the application was determined.

Application for variation of conjoined arrestment orders

57.—(1) An application under section 62(5) of the Act for variation of a conjoined arrestment order by a creditor whose debt is not being enforced under a conjoined arrestment order but would, but for the order, be entitled to enforce the debt by an earnings arrestment or current maintenance order shall be in form 49.

(2) An application to which paragraph (1) of this rule applies shall specify—
(*a*) the name and address of the applicant, the debtor, the employer and any person residing in the United Kingdom to whom payment is to be made in respect of the applicant's debt;
(*b*) the date of the conjoined arrestment order;
(*c*) such information relating to the debt due to the applicant as would require to be specified in an earnings arrestment schedule or, as the case may be, a current maintenance arrestment schedule; and
(*d*) the expenses of the application.

(3) On the lodging of such an application the sheriff clerk shall—
(*a*) intimate the application together with a form of notice and response in form 50 to the debtor and any creditor whose debt is being enforced under the conjoined arrestment order; and
(*b*) complete a certificate of intimation.

(4) Where a creditor or the debtor wishes to object to such an application, he shall complete and lodge with the sheriff clerk the form of notice and response in form 50 within 14 days after the date of intimation.

(5) On receipt of such a form of notice and response, the sheriff clerk shall fix a date for a hearing and intimate the date to the applicant and to those who received intimation of the application.

(6) Where such a form of notice and response is not timeously lodged

with the sheriff clerk, the sheriff may grant the application or may make such other order as he considers appropriate.

(7) Where an application to which paragraph (1) of this rule applies has been granted, there shall be served by the sheriff clerk with the sheriff's decision—

(*a*) a copy of the conjoined arrestment order as varied; and
(*b*) a notice in form 51.

(8) Subject to paragraphs (9) and (10) of this rule, service under this rule and section 62(6) of the Act shall be by recorded delivery post.

(9) Where such service has been unsuccessful, reservice—

(*a*) in the case of service on the employer, shall be effected by an officer of court on payment of his fee by the applicant; and
(*b*) in any other case of service on a person within the United Kingdom, shall be by ordinary first class post.

(10) Service under this rule and section 62(6) of the Act on a person outside the United Kingdom which cannot be effected by recorded delivery post shall be by any other competent method of service.

Intimation of changes to calculation of sum payable by employer

58.—(1) Intimation by the sheriff clerk to an employer operating a conjoined arrestment order—

(*a*) under section 63(7) of the Act, shall be in form 52; or
(*b*) under section 63(8) of the Act, shall be in form 53.

(2) A form of intimation required under paragraph (1) of this rule shall state—

(*a*) the date of the conjoined arrestment order and any variation of it and the date of service of it on the employer;
(*b*) the name and address of the debtor, the employer and the sheriff clerk; and
(*c*) that changes to—
(i) Tables A, B and C of Schedule 2 to the Act;
(ii) the percentages specified in section 49(5) and (6)(*a*)(ii) of the Act;
(iii) the sums specified in section 63(4)(*b*) of the Act; or
(iv) the small maintenance payments limits mentioned in section [351(2)] of the Income and Corporation Taxes Act [1988] have been made and the date when they were made and of their coming into force.

(3) There shall be attached to or reproduced upon form 52 the full text of the appropriate provisions of the Act.

(4) There shall be attached to or reproduced upon form 53 the full text of section 351(2) of the Income and Corporation Taxes Act 1988.

Determination of disputes as to operation of conjoined arrestment orders

59.—(1) An application under section 65(1) of the Act for determination of any dispute as to the operation of a conjoined arrestment order shall be in form 54.

(2) An application to which paragraph (1) of this rule applies shall specify—

(*a*) the name and address of the applicant, the debtor, the creditors whose debts are being enforced by the conjoined arrestment order, the employer and the sheriff clerk;
(*b*) the date of the conjoined arrestment order and the court which made the order;
(*c*) the subject matter of the dispute;
(*d*) the order sought, including details of any sum for which reimbursement or repayment is sought;
(*e*) any claim for interest and the date from which such interest shall run; and

(*f*) any competent crave for expenses.

(3) On the lodging of such an application the sheriff clerk shall—

(*a*) fix a date for a hearing;

(*b*) obtain from the sheriff a warrant for intimation;

(*c*) intimate the application and warrant to the applicant and, as appropriate, the debtor, the creditors whose debts are being enforced by the conjoined arrestment order and the employer; and

(*d*) complete the certificate of intimation.

(4) The sheriff clerk shall intimate the sheriff's decision on such an application to any person to whom intimation of the application was made but who was not present when the application was determined.

Applications for payment by creditors to debtors

60.—(1) An application under section 65(7) of the Act for an order requiring the creditor to pay to the debtor a sum not exceeding twice the sum recoverable by the sheriff clerk in accordance with section 65(6) of the Act shall be in form 55.

(2) An application in which paragraph (1) of this rule applies shall specify—

(*a*) the name and address of the debtor and creditor;

(*b*) the date of the conjoined arrestment order and the court which made the order;

(*c*) whether, in the case of an ordinary debt, the debt has been paid, otherwise extinguished or has ceased to be enforceable by diligence and also why and from what date;

(*d*) whether, in the case of current maintenance, the obligation to pay maintenance has ceased or has ceased to be enforceable by diligence and if so why and from what date;

(*e*) the calculation showing the sum alleged to have been received by the creditor in excess of entitlement;

(*f*) the sum sought from the creditor;

(*g*) the applicant's grounds for seeking such sum;

(*h*) any competent crave for expenses.

(3) On the lodging of such an application the sheriff clerk shall—

(*a*) fix a date for a hearing;

(*b*) obtain from the sheriff a warrant for intimation;

(*c*) intimate the application and warrant to the applicant and the creditor; and

(*d*) complete a certificate of intimation.

(4) The sheriff clerk shall intimate the sheriff's decision on such an application to the creditor if the creditor was not present when the application was determined.

Recall of conjoined arrestment orders under section 66(1)(a) of the Act

61.—(1) An application under section 66(1)(*a*) of the Act by a debtor, creditor, employer, sheriff clerk or interim, or permanent, trustee in the debtor's sequestration for recall of a conjoined arrestment order shall be in form 56.

(2) An application to which paragraph (1) of this rule applies shall specify—

(*a*) the name and address of the debtor, the creditors whose debts are being enforced under the conjoined arrestment order, the person on whom a copy of the order or an order varying the order was served under section 60(7) or 62(6) of the Act, any trustee in the debtor's sequestration and the sheriff clerk to whom payment is made under the order;

(*b*) the date of the conjoined arrestment order and the court which made the order;

(*c*) if appropriate, that the conjoined arrestment order is invalid and why it is claimed to be invalid;

(*d*) if appropriate, that all ordinary debts enforced by the order have been paid or otherwise extinguished or have ceased to be enforceable and in each case when and how this occurred;

(*e*) if appropriate, that all obligations to pay current maintenance enforced by the order have ceased or have ceased to be enforceable by diligence and in either case when and how this occurred;

(*f*) if appropriate, that the debtor's estate has been sequestrated and when this occurred;

(*g*) the order sought and any consequential order; and

(*h*) any competent crave for expenses.

(3) Subject to paragraph (4) of this rule, on the lodging of such an application the sheriff clerk shall—

(*a*) fix a date for a hearing;

(*b*) obtain from the sheriff a warrant for intimation;

(*c*) intimate the application and warrant to the applicant and, as appropriate, the debtor, the creditors whose debts are being enforced under the order, the person on whom a copy of the order or an order varying the order was served under section 60(7) or 62(6) of the Act and the interim, or permanent, trustee in the debtor's sequestration; and

(*d*) complete a certificate of intimation.

(4) Where such an application has been made by all of the creditors whose debts are being enforced by the conjoined arrestment order or where the sheriff clerk has previously received intimation from all of those creditors as to the matters referred to in section 66(1)(*a*)(ii) of the Act, the sheriff may grant the application without requiring intimation or any hearing of the application.

Recall of conjoined arrestment orders under section 66(1)(b) of the Act

62.—(1) An application under section 66(1)(*b*) of the Act by all creditors whose debts are being enforced for recall of a conjoined arrestment order shall be in form 57.

(2) An application to which paragraph (1) of this rule applies shall specify—

(*a*) the names and addresses of the applicants and the debtors; and

(*b*) the date of the conjoined arrestment order and the court which made the order;

(*c*) the reasons for the application; and

(*d*) any consequential order sought.

(3) On the lodging of such an application the sheriff may grant it immediately or may make such other order as he considers appropriate.

Applications for variation of conjoined arrestment orders

63.—(1) An application under section 66(4) of the Act for variation of a conjoined arrestment order shall be in form 58.

(2) An application to which paragraph (1) of this rule applies shall specify—

(*a*) the name and address of the debtor, the employer, the creditors whose debts are being enforced by the conjoined arrestment order and the sheriff clerk;

(*b*) the date of the conjoined arrestment order and the court which made the order;

(*c*) if appropriate, that any ordinary debt being enforced by the order has been paid, otherwise extinguished or has ceased to be enforceable by diligence and in each case when and how this occurred;

(*d*) if appropriate, that an order or decree varying, superseding or recalling any maintenance order has come into effect and when and by whom the order or decree was granted;

(*e*) if appropriate, that an obligation to pay maintenance has ceased or has ceased to be enforceable in Scotland and in either case when or how this occurred;

(*f*) the order sought; and

(*g*) any competent crave for expenses.

(3) On the lodging of such an application the sheriff clerk shall—

(*a*) fix a date for a hearing;

(*b*) obtain from the sheriff a warrant for intimation;

(*c*) intimate the application and warrant to the applicant and, as appropriate, to the debtor, the creditors whose debts are being enforced by the conjoined arrestment order and the employer; and

(*d*) complete a certificate of intimation.

Requests by creditors to cease enforcement of debts by conjoined arrestment orders

64.—(1) A request by a creditor to the sheriff under section 66(6) of the Act to vary a conjoined arrestment order, by ordering that a debt being enforced by him under it shall cease to be so enforced, shall be in writing.

(2) The sheriff may grant or refuse such a request or may make such order as he considers appropriate.

Service of sheriff's decision in applications for recall or variation of conjoined arrestment orders

65.—(1) Subject to the following paragraphs of this rule, the final order of the sheriff in an application to which rule 61, 62, 63 or 64 applies shall be served upon the applicant, the employer, the debtor and the creditors whose debts are being enforced under the conjoined arrestment order by recorded delivery post.

(2) Where such service has been unsuccessful, reservice—

(*a*) in the case of service on the employer, shall be effected by an officer of court on payment of his fee by the applicant; and

(*b*) in any other case of service on a person within the United Kingdom, shall be by ordinary first class post.

(3) Where an application for variation of a conjoined arrestment order to which rule 63 above applies has been granted, there shall be served by the sheriff clerk with the final order—

(*a*) a copy of the conjoined arrestment order as varied; and

(*b*) a notice in form 59.

(4) Service under this rule on a person outwith the United Kingdom which cannot be effected by recorded delivery post shall be by any other competent method of service.

Service by post of arrestments against earnings

66. On the face of the envelope used for service of an earnings arrestment schedule, a current maintenance arrestment schedule or a conjoined arrestment order there shall be written or printed the following notice—

"ARRESTMENT OF EARNINGS OF AN EMPLOYEE

This letter contains an earnings arrestment schedule/current maintenance arrestment schedule/conjoined arrestment order. If delivery of the letter cannot be made at the address shown it is to be returned immediately to (*name and address*).".

Certificates of execution

67. The certificate of execution of an earnings arrestment or a current maintenance arrestment shall be in form 60.

PART V

WARRANTS FOR DILIGENCE

Summary warrants

68.—(1) A summary warrant for recovery of—

(*a*) arrears of rates under section 247 of the Local Government (Scotland) Act 1947; or

(*b*) arrears of community charge under paragraph 7 of Schedule 2 to the Abolition of Domestic Rates Etc. (Scotland) Act 1987,

shall be in form 61.

(2) A summary warrant for recovery of arrears of rates under section 250 of the Local Government (Scotland) Act 1947 shall be in form 62.

(3) A summary warrant for recovery of—

(*a*) any tax in accordance with section 63 of the Taxes Management Act 1970 or of earnings-related contributions under that section as read with regulation 28 of the Income Tax (Employments) Regulations 1973;

(*b*) car tax in accordance with paragraph 3(3) of Schedule 1 to the Car Tax Act 1983; or

(*c*) value added tax in accordance with the Value Added Tax Act 1983,

shall be in form 63.

Applications by creditors for warrants to enforce acquired rights

69.—(1) An application to the sheriff clerk under section 88(2) of the Act by a person, who has acquired a right by assignation, confirmation as executor or otherwise to a decree, obligation, order or determination referred to in section 88(1) of the Act for a warrant authorising diligence, shall be made by minute endorsed on the extract decree or other document.

(2) The sheriff clerk shall, where he is satisfied that the applicant's right is established, endorse the warrant sought in such an application on the extract decree or other document.

PART VI

MISCELLANEOUS

Representation

70. A party to any proceedings under the Act shall be entitled to be represented by a person other than an advocate or a solicitor if the sheriff is satisfied that such person is a suitable representative and is duly authorised to represent the party.

Powers of sheriff

71. Without prejudice to any other powers competent to him, the sheriff, in the exercise of the powers conferred on him by these rules, shall have the same powers as regards the summoning and examination of witnesses, the production of documents, the administration of oaths and the correcting of interlocutors as those which he has in an ordinary cause to which the Ordinary Cause Rules in Schedule 1 to the Sheriff Courts (Scotland) Act 1907 apply.

Appeals

72.—(1) An application for leave to appeal from a decision of the sheriff under the Act shall be made in writing to the sheriff clerk within seven days of the making of the decision and shall specify the question of law upon which the appeal is to proceed.

(2) The sheriff may consider such an application without hearing parties unless it appears to him to be necessary to hold a hearing on the application in which case the sheriff clerk shall intimate the date, place and time of the hearing to the parties.

(3) Subject to section 103(2) of the Act, an appeal shall—

(*a*) be made by note of appeal written by the appellant on the written record containing the order appealed against or on a separate sheet lodged with the sheriff clerk;

(*b*) be as nearly as may be in the following terms—
"The applicant [*or* respondent *or other*] appeals to the sheriff principal/Court of Session";

(*c*) be signed by the appellant or his representative and bear the date on which it is signed; and

(*d*) where appeal is made to the Court of Session, bear the name and address of the solicitors in Edinburgh who will be acting for the appellant.

(4) The appellant shall, at the same time as marking his appeal under paragraph (3) of this rule, intimate that he is doing so to the other parties.

(5) The sheriff shall, on an appeal being marked under paragraph (3) of this rule, state in writing the reasons for his original decision.

(6) Where an appeal is marked, the sheriff clerk shall transmit the process within four days to the sheriff principal or to the Deputy Principal Clerk of Session, as the case may be.

Intimation

73.—(1) A warrant for intimation referred to in these rules shall be in form 64.

(2) The sheriff may order intimation to persons other than those to whom intimation is required under these rules as he considers appropriate.

Hearings

74. At any hearing (other than the hearing of an appeal) fixed under these rules the cause to be dealt with may be—

(*a*) determined;

(*b*) continued for such further procedure as the sheriff considers appropriate; or

(*c*) if no party appears, dismissed.

Dispensing power of sheriff

75. The sheriff may relieve any party from the consequences of any failure to comply with the provisions of these rules which is shown to be due to mistake, oversight or other cause, not being wilful non-observance of the same, on such terms and conditions as seem just; and in any such case the sheriff may make such order as seems just by way of extension of time, lodging or amendment of papers or otherwise so as to enable the cause to proceed as if such failure had not happened.

SCHEDULE

FORMS

Arrangement of Forms

EXTENSION OF TIME TO PAY AND RELATED MATTERS

Form No.	*Title*	*Rule*
1	Application for variation or recall of a time to pay direction and arrestment	4(1)
2	Application for time to pay order	5(1)

Form No.	Title	Rule
3	Application for variation or recall of a time to pay order, arrestment and poinding	6(1)
	Poindings and warrant sales	
4	Application for release of poinded article	8(1)
5	Poinding schedule	11
6	Application for security of poinded article	12(1)
7	Application for immediate disposal of perishable poinded article	13(1)
8	Receipt under s.21(5) of, and paragraph 6(5) of Schedule 5 to, the Debtors (Scotland) Act 1987	14
9	Report of poinding	15(1)
10	Application for release of poinded article on ground of undue harshness	16(1)
11	Application for declarator that poinding invalid or ceased to have effect or for recall of poinding	17(1)
12	Application for sist of proceedings in poinding of mobile home	18(1)
13	Application for extension of duration of poinding	19(1)
14	Application for authority to move poinded article	20(1)
15	Application for an order for restoration or removed article	21(1)
16	Application for recall of an order for restoration of removed article	22(1)
17	Application for authority to execute further poinding	23(1)(b)
18	Application for authority to execute further poinding and/or to revalue damaged article	24(1)
19	Application for an order for consignation by third party	25(1)
20	Application for warrant of sale of poinded article	26(1)
21	Note to debtor of application for warrant of sale	26(5)
22	Consent under sections 32(1) and 32(4) of, and paragraph 14(2) and (3) of Schedule 5 to, the Debtors (Scotland) Act 1987	27(1)
23	Receipt under section 33(3) of, and paragraph 15(3) of the Schedule 5 to, the Debtors (Scotland) Act 1987	28
24	Application for variation of a warrant of sale of poinded article	30(1)
25	Notice to debtor of application for variation of a warrant of sale	30(5)
26	Report of sale	31(1)
27	Application for release of poinded article belonging to third party	34(1)
28	Application for release of poinded article in common ownership	35(1)
29	Application for finding of common ownership of poinded article	36(1)
	Diligence against earnings	
30	Earnings arrestment schedule	38(1)
31	Intimation to employer under section 49(8) of the Debtors (Scotland) Act 1987	39(1)
32	Application for declarator that earnings arrestment invalid or ceased to have effect	40(1)
33	Application for determination of dispute in operation of earnings arrestment	41(1)
34	Current maintenance arrestment schedule	42(1)
35	Intimation to employer under section 53(4) of the Debtors (Scotland) Act 1987	43(1)
36	Intimation to employer under section 53(5) of the Debtors (Scotland) Act 1987	44(1)
37	Intimation to debtor under section 54(1)(*a*) of the Debtors (Scotland) Act 1987	45(1)
38	Application for declarator that current maintenance arrestment invalid or ceased to have effect	46(1)
39	Application for recall of a current maintenance arrestment	47(1)
40	Application for determination of dispute in operation of current maintenance arrestment	48(1)
41	Application for payment by creditor to debtor of penalty sum	51(1)
42	Application for order on employer to provide information	52(1)
43	Application for conjoined arrestment order	53(1)
44	Form of notice of application for a conjoined arrestment order	53(4)

Form No.	*Title*	*Rule*
45	Conjoined arrestment order	54(1)
46	Notice of service of conjoined arrestment order	54(5)
47	Application for warrant for diligence against employer	55(1)
48	Application for order on employer to provide information	56(1)
49	Application for variation of a conjoined arrestment order	57(1)
50	Form of notice of application for variation of a conjoined arrestment order	57(3)(a)
51	Notice of service of an order varying a conjoined arrestment order in terms of section 62(5) of the Debtors (Scotland) Act 1987	57(7)(b)
52	Intimation to employer in terms of section 63(7) of the Debtors (Scotland) Act 1987	58(1)(a)
53	Intimation to employer in terms of section 63(8) of the Debtors (Scotland) Act 1987	58(1)(b)
54	Application for determination of dispute in operation of conjoined arrestment order	59(1)
55	Application for payment by creditor to debtor of penalty sum (conjoined arrestment order)	60(1)
56	Application for recall of conjoined arrestment order	61(1)
57	Application for recall of conjoined arrestment order by all creditors whose debts are being enforced by it	62(1)
58	Application for variation of conjoined arrestment order	63(1)
59	Notice of service of an order varying a conjoined arrestment order in terms of section 66 of the Debtors (Scotland) Act 1987	65(3)(b)
60	Certificate of execution of earnings arrestment schedule/current maintenance arrestment schedule	67
Warrants for diligence		
61	Summary warrant for recovery of rates or community charge	68(1)
62	Summary warrant for recovery of rates	68(2)
63	Summary warrant for recovery of taxes etc.	68(3)
	Miscellaneous	
64	Warrant for intimation	73(1)

Rule 4(1)

FORM 1

The Debtors (Scotland) Act 1987, section 3

Sheriff Court .... 19......
(Court Ref. No.)

APPLICATION FOR VARIATION OR RECALL OF A TIME TO PAY DIRECTION AND ARRESTMENT

BY..
....
....
.... Applicant

against

....
....
....
.... Respondent

*delete as appropriate

The sheriff on 19 granted an order for payment by the defender to the pursuer of the sum of £ along with expenses amounting to £ and interest and made a time to pay direction directing that the total sum ordered be paid by

*(a) Instalments of £ each which started on 19 .
*(b) A deferred lump sum which became payable by 19

To the best of the applicant's knowledge and belief the amount which remains outstanding under the said direction at the date of this application is £ .

The applicant who is the defender/pursuer wishes the time to pay direction recalled or varied as follows (*please give details including reasons for application*):—...........................
....
....

or

seeks to have recalled or restricted an arrestment made on (*give details*)
19 at in respect of

Therefore the applicant asks the court:
*(a) To recall or vary the time to pay direction as sought.
*(b) To recall/restrict the arrestment referred to.

Date .... 19......

(*signed*)
Applicant

Rule 5(1) FORM 2

The Debtors (Scotland) Act 1987

Sheriff Court ....

.... 19......
(Court Ref. No.)

PART A

APPLICATION FOR TIME TO PAY ORDER

BY ....
....
.... Applicant

PERSON TO WHOM DEBT DUE
....
....
.... Creditor

PART B

*delete as appropriate

*(a) The applicant is the defender in an action raised in this Sheriff Court/Court of Session by the creditor in which decree was granted on 19 for £ ;

or

*(b) The debt due by the applicant is payable under a document bearing a warrant for diligence (*give details of this document*):—

The applicant states that to the best of his knowledge and belief that no time to pay direction or order relating to the debt has been made and that at the date of this application the amount outstanding is £ (*this figure should take account of interest, court expenses and any payments made to account*).

The applicant states that the following steps have been taken in respect of the debt, namely
*(a) A charge for payment has been served on the applicant;
*(b) An arrestment has been carried out;
*(c) An action for adjudication of debt has been commenced.

PART C

The applicant offers to pay the outstanding amount
*(a) By instalments of £ each

(*Tick one box only*) Week ☐ Fortnight ☐ Month ☐

or

*(b) In one payment within weeks/months

The applicant's financial position is:—

	Weekly	Fortnightly	Monthly		Weekly	Fortnightly	Monthly
My outgoings are:	☐	☐	☐	My income is:	☐	☐	☐
Rent/Mortgage	£			Wages/Pensions	£		
Heating	£			Social Security	£		
Food	£			Other	£		
HP	£						
Other	£						
Total	**£**			**Total**	**£**		

Dependants: Children—how many ☐ Dependent relatives—how many ☐

Here list all capital (if any) e.g. value of house; amount in bank/building society account; shares or other investments:—

Here list any outstanding debts:—

Here specify any action taken by creditor to enforce the debt (*e.g. arrestment; poinding; etc*):—

The applicant asks the court—

1. To make a "time to pay order"

*2. To make an order recalling the following poinding (*give details*):—

*3. To recall or restrict the following arrestment(s) (*give details*):—

*delete as appropriate

or

*4 To order that no further steps shall be taken by the creditor in the diligence concerned other than in the case of a poinding, applying for an order under section 21(1) of Debtors (Scotland) Act 1987 or making a report of the execution of the poinding under section 22 of that Act.

Date 19 .... (*signed*) Applicant

EXTRACT FROM SECTION 5(4) AND (5) OF THE DEBTORS (SCOTLAND) ACT 1987

"(4) It shall not be competent for the sheriff to make a time to pay order:—

(*a*) where the amount of the debt outstanding at the date of the making of the application under subsection (2) above (exclusive of any interest) exceeds £10,000 or such amount as may be prescribed in regulations made by the Lord Advocate;

(*b*) where, in relation to the debt, a time to pay direction or a time to pay order has previously been made (whether such direction or order is in effect or not);

(*c*) where, in relation to the debt, a summary warrant has been granted;

(*d*) in relation to a debt including any sum recoverable by or on behalf of the Inland Revenue in respect of tax or as if it were tax;

(*e*) in relation to a debt including rates payable to a rating authority;

(*ee*) in relation to a debt including any sum due to—

(i) a levying authority in respect of any community charge or community water charge within the meaning of section 26 of the Abolition of Domestic Rates Etc. (Scotland) Act 1987 (which defines terms used in that Act) or any amount payable under section 18(3) (payment of community charges in respect of back-dated period, with surcharge and interest) of that Act; or

(ii) a regional or islands council in respect of any amount payable as a civil penalty under section 17(10) or (11) (failure to provide information to a registration officer) of that Act; or

(*f*) in relation to a debt including—

(i) any duty due under the Betting and Gaming Duties Act 1981;

(ii) car tax due under the Car Tax Act 1983; or

(iii) value added tax due under the Value Added Tax Act 1983 or any sum recoverable as if it were value added tax.

(5) Where in respect of a debt to which this section applies:—

(*a*) there has been a poinding of articles belonging to the debtor and a warrant of sale has been granted in respect of them but has not been executed;

(*b*) moveable property of the debtor has been arrested and in respect of the arrested property—

(i) a decree in an action of forthcoming has been granted but has not been enforced; or

(ii) a warrant of sale has been granted but the warrant has not been executed; or

(*c*) a decree in an action of adjudication for debt has been granted and the creditor has, with the debtor's consent or acquiescence, entered into possession of any property adjudged by the decree or has obtained a decree of maills and duties, or a decree of removing or ejection, in relation to any such property,

it shall not be competent for the sheriff to make a time to pay order in respect of that debt until the diligence has been completed or has otherwise ceased to have effect."

The sheriff having considered the foregoing application and being satisfied that it is properly made, meantime sists all diligence in terms of section 8(1) of the Debtors (Scotland) Act 1987 pending the disposal of the application.

Appoints the creditor to furnish the sheriff with particulars of the decree or other document under which the debt is payable within days of intimation hereof.

Appoints the sheriff clerk to intimate a copy of the application and this interlocutor to the creditor; appoints him if he objects to the granting of this application to make written representations to the court within 14 days of the date of intimation hereof.

Sheriff

(Court Ref. No.)
.... 19......

To: The Sheriff Clerk
Sheriff Court ....

I have read the application for a "Time to Pay Order" by ....

*1. I do not object to the proposal made and agree to the making of a "Time to Pay Order".

*2. I object to the granting of the application for the following reasons:—

*delete as appropriate

*3. I object to the making of a "Time to Pay Order" as proposed, and wish to make the following alternative proposals:—

4. I intend/do not intend to appear at the hearing.

Date 19 .... (*Signed*) Creditor

Please Note:—This form (or if you wish, a letter with the same information) should be returned by .... 19......

Rule 6(1)

FORM 3

The Debtors (Scotland) Act 1987, section 10

Sheriff Court ....

....
(Court Ref. No.)

APPLICATION FOR VARIATION OR RECALL OF A TIME TO PAY ORDER, ARRESTMENT AND POINDING

BY..
....
....
.... Applicant

Against

....
....
....
.... Respondent

*delete as appropriate

1. *(a) On (*date*) decree was granted in this Sheriff Court/Court of Session for payment by the defender to the pursuer of the sum of £ along with expenses of £ and interest.
   *(b) The debt due by the applicant/respondent is payable under a document bearing a warrant for diligence (*give details of this document*):—

2. The sheriff on (*date*) made a time to pay order, that the debt outstanding amounting to £ be paid:—
   *(a) By instalments of £ each which started on
   *(b) As a lump sum which became payable by

   To the best of the applicant's knowledge and belief the amount which remains outstanding under the said order at the time of this application is £

3. The applicant who is the debtor/creditor:—
   *(a) Wishes the time to pay order recalled or varied as follows (*specify order sought*):— ....
   ....
   *(b) Seeks the recall or restriction of an arrestment (*give details of arrestment served, person on whom served, and date, and specify order sought*):— ....
   ....
   *(c) Seeks the recall of the poinding carried out on the instructions of the creditor at (*place of poinding*) on (*date of poinding*).

   Give reasons for this application:— ....
   ....

4. The applicant asks the court:—
   *1. To recall or vary the time to pay order as requested.
   *2. To recall or restrict the arrestment referred to.
   *3. To recall the poinding referred to
   *4. (*Specify any other order sought and the diligence to which it relates*).
   ....

Date ....   Signed ....
Applicant

Rule 8(1) FORM 4

The Debtors (Scotland) Act 1987, section 16(4)/Schedule 5, paragraph 1(4)

Sheriff Court ....

APPLICATION FOR RELEASE OF POINDED ARTICLE (1) .... 19......
(Court Ref. No.)
APPLICANT

*delete as appropriate

A. The applicant is
*(a) The debtor
*(b) The person claiming ownership in common with the debtor
*(c) A person having possession of the pointed article(s)

(1) Insert name and address

B. Other persons having an interest are
*(d) The creditor (1)
*(e) The debtor (1)
*(f) (Other) person(s) claiming ownership in common with the debtor (1)
*(g) A person having possession to the pointed article(s) (1)

(2) Insert name

C. Decree was granted in an action by the pursuer(s) (2)

in the Court of Session/Sheriff Court at
on 19
against the defender(s) (2)
(*or give details of other document or summary warrant upon which the poinding proceeded*):—

(3) Insert address

D. A poinding of the debtor's belongings was carried out by (1)

sheriff officer/messenger-at-arms on the instructions of the creditor on 19 at (3)

E. Among the articles poinded were the following:—

The(se) article(s) is/are exempt from poinding. (*Give reasons for claiming exemption*):—

This application is made under section 16(4) of the Debtors (Scotland) Act 1987/paragraph 1(4) of Schedule 5 to the Debtors (Scotland) Act 1987.

F. The applicant asks the court:—
1. To fix a hearing.
2. To order the sheriff clerk to intimate this application and the date of the hearing to the applicant to those persons stated above as having an interest and to the officer of court who carried out the poinding.
3. To order that said article(s) be released from the poinding on the ground that they are exempt.
4. To award expenses (if competent).

Date .... 19...... (*Signed*) ....
Applicant

IF YOU WISH FURTHER ADVICE CONTACT ANY CITIZENS ADVICE BUREAU/ LOCAL ADVICE CENTRE/SHERIFF CLERK OR SOLICITOR

Rule 11 **FORM 5**

*The Debtors (Scotland) Act 1987, *section 20(5)/Schedule 5, paragraph 5(5)*

*delete as appropriate

Poinding Schedule

To (*name and address of debtor*)

On (*date*) a decree was granted in the *Sheriff Court, (*place*)/*Court of Session in an action by (*name and address*)

Pursuer(s)

against (*name and address*) Defender(s)

(*or give details of other document or summary warrant upon which the poinding proceeds*)

*in which you were ordered to pay (*specify amounts*) to the said (*name of creditor*)
*On (*date*) a charge for payment of these sums (under deduction of £ paid to account since the date of the decree) was served on you.
I, (*name and address*), messenger-at-arms/*sheriff officer on the instructions of the said (*name of creditor*) poind at (*address*) the articles belonging to you specified in the list attached.
The sum now due by you is

Principal sum	£	(Further interest may accrue if the debt is not paid immediately)
Interest to date	£	
Expenses or other sum (*specify*)	£	
Less paid to account	£	
Charge Fee	£	
Poinding Fee	£	
Other Fee (*specify*)	£	
Travelling	£	
Other Outlays (*specify*)	£	
TOTAL		

If this sum is not paid *an application will be made to the sheriff for a warrant to sell the poinded articles/*arrangements will be made for the sale of the poinded articles.
Payment should be made to (*name and address*).
*I am removing the poinded articles to (*address of premises*) because (*officer of court to specify reasons for removal*).
You may move the poinded articles to another location only if the creditor or the officer of court has consented in writing to this or the sheriff has authorised their removal.

This poinding is carried out by me today (*date*) and is witnessed by (*name and address*).

I *deliver/*leave this poinding schedule *to/*for you (*name*) today at (*address*).

Witness Officer of court

WARNING: Any unauthorised removal of the poinded articles or any wilful damage or destruction of them by the debtor or persons who know the articles have been poinded shall be a breach of poinding and may be dealt with as a contempt of court.

LIST SPECIFYING POINDED EFFECTS

ARTICLE(S) POINDED	**VALUE FIXED**

Witness Officer of Court

YOUR RIGHTS UNDER THE DEBTORS (SCOTLAND) ACT 1987

To (a) the debtor, (b) any person who owns any pointed article in common with the debtor, (c) any person who is in possession of any poinded article, (d) any person whose only or principal residence has been poinded.

(1) *The debtor, any person who owns any poinded article in common with the debtor* and *any person in possession of a poinded article* may apply to the sheriff within 14 days from the date of the poinding for an order releasing the article on the ground that it is exempt from poinding. Articles which are exempt are listed in *section 16 of the Act/*paragraph 1 of schedule 5 to the Act.

(2) *The debtor* may at any time after the poinding apply to the sheriff for an order for the security of any of the poinded articles or where they are perishable or likely to diminish in value for their immediate disposal.

(3) *The debtor* may redeem any poinded article by paying the officer of court who carried out the poinding the amount fixed by him for the article at the poinding and stated in the poinding schedule. Payment must be made within 14 days from the date of the poinding. This right is subject to the power of the Sheriff to order immediate disposal of poinded articles in certain circumstances.

(4) *The debtor* or *any person in possession of a poinded article* may apply to the sheriff within 14 days from the date of the poinding for an order releasing the article on the ground that its inclusion in the poinding or its subsequent sale is unduly harsh.

(5) *The debtor* may apply to the sheriff on certain grounds stated in the Debtors (Scotland) Act 1987 for an order recalling the poinding or declaring that it is invalid or has ceased to have effect.

(6) Where a mobile home, such as a caravan, is the residence of the debtor [or] another person and it has been poinded, an application may be made by such person to the sheriff for an order that for a specified period no further steps shall be taken in the poinding.

(7) *Any person claiming to own any poinded article in common with the debtor* may at any time after the poinding and before *the warrant sale/*sale of the poinded articles apply to the officer of court for its release from poinding on payment to him of a sum equal to the value of the debtor's interest in the article.

In addition an application may be made to the sheriff within the same period for the release of the article from poinding. The sheriff will release the article if he is satisfied that it is owned in common and either the applicant undertakes to pay to the officer of court the value of the debtors interest in the article or the sheriff is satisfied that the inclusion of the article in the poinding or its subsequent sale is unduly harsh.

Any enquiry relating to the above rights should be made to a solicitor, Citizens Advice Bureau or other local advice centre or to the Sheriff Clerk at

Rule 12(1) FORM 6

The Debtors (Scotland) Act 1987, section 21(1)/Schedule 5, paragraph 6(1)(a)

Sheriff Court ....

APPLICATION FOR SECURITY OF POINDED ARTICLE (1) .... 19......
(Court Ref. No.)
APPLICANT

*delete as appropriate

A. The applicant is
*(a) The creditor
*(b) The officer of court who carried out the poinding
*(c) The debtor

(1) Insert name and address

B. Other persons having an interest are
*(d) The creditor (1) and the officer of court who carried out the poinding
*(e) The debtor (1)

(2) Insert name

C. Decree was granted in an action by the pursuer(s) (2)
in the Court of Session/Sheriff Court at
on 19
against the defender(s) (2)
(*or give details of other document or summary warrant upon which the poinding proceeded*):—

(3) Insert address

D. A poinding of the debtor's belongings was carried out by (1)
sheriff officer/messenger-at-arms on the instructions of the creditor
on 19 at (3)

E. Among the articles poinded were the following:—
It is necessary that an order be made for the security of the poinded article(s) (*give reasons why such an order should be made and proposed security arrangements*):—

This application is made under section 21(1)(*a*) of the Debtors (Scotland) Act 1987/paragraph 6(1)(*a*) of Schedule 5 to the Debtors (Scotland) Act 1987.

F. The applicant asks the court:—
1. To order such intimation (if any) and further procedure as the court considers appropriate.
2. To make such order as thought appropriate for the security of the poinded article(s) referred to.
3. To award expenses (if competent).

Date .... 19...... (*Signed*) ....
Applicant

IF YOU WISH FURTHER ADVICE CONTACT ANY CITIZENS ADVICE BUREAU/ LOCAL ADVICE CENTRE/SHERIFF CLERK OR SOLICITOR

Rule 12(1)

FORM 7

The Debtors (Scotland) Act 1987, section 21(1)/Schedule 5, paragraph 6(1)(b)

Sheriff Court ....

APPLICATION FOR IMMEDIATE DISPOSAL OF PERISHABLE POINDED ARTICLE

(1)

.... 19.....
(Court Ref. No.)
APPLICANT

*delete as appropriate

A. The applicant is
*(a) The creditor
*(b) The officer of court who carried out the poinding
*(c) The debtor

(1) Insert name and address

B. Other persons having an interest are
*(d) The creditor (1) and the officer of court who carried out the poinding
*(e) The debtor (1)

(2) Insert name

C. Decree was granted in an action by the pursuer(s) (2)

in the Court of Session/Sheriff Court at
on 19
against the defender(s) (2)
(*or give details of other document or summary warrant upon which the poinding proceeded*):—

(3) Insert address

D. A poinding of the debtor's belongings was carried out by (1)

sheriff officer/messenger-at-arms on the instructions of the creditor
on 19 at (3)

E. Among the articles poinded were the following:—

The(se) article(s) are of a perishable nature or are likely to deteriorate substantially and rapidly in condition or value (*give reasons for making application*):—

This application is made under section 21(1)(*b*) of the Debtors (Scotland) Act 1987/paragraph 6(1)(*b*) of Schedule 5 to the Debtors (Scotland) Act 1987.

F. The applicant asks the court:—
1. To order such further procedure as the court considers appropriate.
2. To make an order for the immediate disposal of the article(s) referred to.
3. If the article(s) is/are sold, to order payment of the proceeds of sale to the creditor or consignation of the proceeds in court until the diligence is completed or otherwise ceases to have effect.
4. To award expenses (if competent).

Date .... 19..... (*Signed*) ....
Applicant

IF YOU WISH FURTHER ADVICE CONTACT ANY CITIZENS ADVICE BUREAU/ LOCAL ADVICE CENTRE/SHERIFF CLERK OR SOLICITOR

Rule 14 FORM 8

Receipt under the Debtors (Scotland) Act 1987, section 21(5)/Schedule 5, paragraph 6(5)

In respect of the poinding executed on (*date*) at the instance of A (*design*) against B (*design*), received in the sum of £ in redemption of the following article(s) viz: (*specify*)

.... (*Signature of officer of court and date*)

Rule 15(1) FORM 9

The Debtors (Scotland) Act 1987, section 22(1)

Report of Poinding

Date of execution of the poinding—(*specify*)

On (*date*) a decree was granted in the Sheriff Court, (*place*)/Court of Session in an action by (*name and address*)

Pursuer(s)

against (*name and address*) Defender(s)

in which the defender(s) were ordered to pay to the pursuer(s)
(*specify amounts*)
*(*or give details of other document upon which the poinding proceeded*)

On (*date*) a charge for payment of these sums (under deduction of £ paid to account since the date of the decree) was served on the said (*name of debtor*)
The sum now due by the debtor is

Principal sum	£
Interest	£
Expended	£
Less paid to account	£__________
Charge fee	£
Poinding fee	£
Travelling	£
Other outlays (*specify*)	£__________
	__________

I, (*name and address*) messenger-at-arms/sheriff officer

attended at (*address*) along with the witness (*name and address*)

on the instructions of the creditor(s) (*name and address*)

exhibited the warrant to poind with certificate of execution of charge relating thereto to person(s) present *demanded payment of the sum due from the debtor/a person who in the debtor's absence appeared to be authorised to act for him. The said sum not being paid, and having made enquiry of those present as to the ownership of the articles I proposed to poind,* and in particular whether there were any persons who owned any of the articles in common with the debtor, I thereafter poinded the articles, belonging to the said (*name of debtor*), specified in the list attached at the valuations contained therein.

* delete if appropriate

I then advised person(s) present of their rights to redeem poinded article(s) or to apply for their release from poinding in terms of sections 16(4), 21(4), 23(1), 41(2) and (3)(a) and 41(3)(b) of the Debtors (Scotland) Act 1987.

I left/removed the poinded articles at/to
meantime and warned those present that any unauthorised removal of the poinded article(s) or any wilful damage or destruction of them by the debtor or persons who knew the article(s) had been poinded would be a breach of poinding and could be dealt with as a contempt of court.

Witness Officer of court

ARTICLE(S) POINDED	**VALUE FIXED BY ME/OR OTHERWISE**

I delivered/left a poinding schedule signed by myself and the witness to the poinding to/for (*name of debtor/person in possession of articles*)
at on the
day of
*and served a copy of it by first class post on the said debtor(s)

*delete if appropriate

Witness Officer of court

Note: (i) Any assertion made before the submission of this report to the sheriff, that any pointed article does not belong to the debtor(s), must be noted in the report.
(ii) Any redemption of poinded articles by the debtor before the submission of this report to the sheriff must be mentioned in the report.
(iii) Where the report relates to a further or second poinding to enforce the same debt, the officer of court must specify in the report the circumstances justifying the further or second poinding.

Rule 16(1) FORM 10

The Debtors (Scotland) Act 1987, section 23(1)/Schedule 5, paragraph 7(1)

Sheriff Court ....

APPLICATION FOR RELEASE OF POINDED ARTICLE ON GROUND OF UNDUE HARSHNESS (1) [ ] .... 19..... (Court Ref. No.)

APPLICANT

*delete as appropriate

A. The applicant is
*(a) The debtor
*(b) A person having possession of the pointed article(s)

(1) Insert name and address

B. Other persons having an interest are
*(c) The creditor (1)
*(d) The debtor (1)
*(e) A person having possession of the poinded article(s) (1)

(2) Insert name

C. Decree was granted in an action by the pursuer(s) (2)
in the Court of Session/Sheriff Court at
on 19
against the defender(s) (2)
(*or give details of other document or summary warrant upon which the poinding proceeded*):—

(3) Insert address

D. A poinding of the debtor's belongings was carried out by (1)
sheriff officer/messenger-at-arms on the instructions of the creditor on 19 at (3)

E. Among the articles poinded were the following:—
The(se) article(s) should be released from the poinding (*state why poinding of article(s) is said to be unduly harsh*):—

This application is made under section 23(1) of the Debtors (Scotland) Act 1987/paragraph 7(1) of Schedule 5 to the Debtors (Scotland) Act 1987.

F. The applicant asks the court:—
1. To fix a hearing.
2. To order the sheriff clerk to intimate this application and the date of the hearing to the applicant, to those persons stated above as having an interest and to the officer of court who carried out the poinding.
3. To order the said article(s) be released from poinding.
4. To award expenses (if competent).

Date .... 19..... (*Signed*) ....
Applicant

IF YOU WISH FURTHER ADVICE CONTACT ANY CITIZENS ADVICE BUREAU/ LOCAL ADVICE CENTRE/SHERIFF CLERK OR SOLICITOR

Rule 17(1)

FORM 11

The Debtors (Scotland) Act 1987, section 24/Schedule 5, paragraph 8

Sheriff Court ....

APPLICATION FOR DECLARATION THAT POINDING INVALID OR CEASED TO HAVE EFFECT OR RECALL OF POINDING

(1) [ ] .... 19.....
(Court Ref. No.)
APPLICANT

A. The applicant is
The debtor

(1) Insert name and address

B. Other persons having an interest are
The creditor (1)
*A person having an interest (1) (*specify nature of interest*):—

(2) Insert name

C. Decree was granted in an action by the pursuer(s) (2)
in the Court of Session/Sheriff Court at
on 19
against the defender(s) (2)
(*or give details of other document or summary warrant upon which the poinding proceeded*):—

(3) Insert address

D. A poinding of the debtor's belongings was carried out by (1)
sheriff officer/messenger-at-arms on the instructions of the creditor
on 19 at (3)

*delete as appropriate

E. *(a) Sale of pointed articles has not yet taken place.
*(b) An application for a warrant to sell the poinded articles has not yet been made.
*(c) Intimation has not been given to the debtor under paragraph 16 of schedule 5 to the Act of the date arranged for the removal of the poinded articles for sale or if the articles are to be sold in the premises where they are situated, of the date arranged for the sale.
*(d) The poinding is invalid/has ceased to have effect.
*(e) The poinding should be recalled.
(*Give reasons for application*):—

This application is made under section 24 of the Debtors (Scotland) Act 1987/paragraph 8 of Schedule 5 to the Debtors (Scotland) Act 1987.

F. The applicant asks the court:—
1. To fix a hearing.
2. To order the sheriff clerk to intimate this application and the date of the hearing to the applicant, to those persons stated above as having an interest, and to the officer of court who carried out the poinding.
*3. To make an order declaring that the poinding is invalid or has ceased to have effect.
*4. To recall the poinding.
5. To make the following consequential order (*give details*):—
6. To award expenses (if competent).

Date .... 19...... (*Signed*) ....
Applicant

IF YOU WISH FURTHER ADVICE CONTACT ANY CITIZENS ADVICE BUREAU/ LOCAL ADVICE CENTRE/SHERIFF CLERK OR SOLICITOR

Rule 18(1) FORM 12

The Debtors (Scotland) Act 1987, section 26(1)/Schedule 5, paragraph 10(1)

Sheriff Court ....

APPLICATION FOR SIST (1) .... 19......
OF PROCEEDINGS IN (Court Ref. No.)
POINDING OF MOBILE APPLICANT
HOMES

*delete as appropriate

A. The applicant is
*(a) The debtor
*(b) A person whose only or principal residence is a pointed mobile home

(1) Insert name and address

B. Other persons having an interest are
(c) The creditor (1)
*(d) The debtor (1)
*(e) A person whose only or principal residence is a poinded mobile home (1)

(2) Insert name

C. Decree was granted in an action by the pursuer(s) (2)
in the Court of Session/Sheriff Court at
on 19
against the defender(s) (2)
(*or give details of other document or summary warrant upon which the poinding proceeded*):—

(3) Insert address

D. A poinding of the debtor's belongings was carried out by (1)
sheriff officer/messenger-at-arms on the instructions of the creditor on 19 at (3)

E. Among the articles poinded was a mobile home (*state whether caravan, houseboat, or other moveable structure*) namely:—

This is the only principal residence of the applicant.

*A warrant of sale has not been granted in respect of the "mobile home".
*Intimation has not been given to the debtor under paragraph 16 of schedule 5 to the Act of the date arranged for the removal of the poinded articles for sale or if the articles are to be sold in the premises where they are situated of the date arranged for the sale.

This application is made under section 26(1) of the Debtors (Scotland) Act 1987/paragraph 10(1) of Schedule 5 to the Debtors (Scotland) Act 1987.

F. The applicant asks the court:—
1. To fix a hearing.
2. To order the sheriff clerk to intimate this application and the date of the hearing to the applicant to those persons stated above as having an interest and to the officer of court who carried out the poinding.
3. To order that for such period as the court shall specify, no further steps shall be taken in the poinding.
4. To award expenses (if competent).

Date .... 19...... (*Signed*) ....
Applicant

IF YOU WISH FURTHER ADVICE CONTACT ANY CITIZENS ADVICE BUREAU/ LOCAL ADVICE CENTRE/SHERIFF CLERK OR SOLICITOR

Rule 19(1)

FORM 13

The Debtors (Scotland) Act 1987, section 27/Schedule 5, paragraph 11

Sheriff Court ....

APPLICATION FOR (FURTHER) EXTENSION OF DURATION OF POINDING

(1) [ ] .... 19......
(Court Ref. No.)
APPLICANT

*delete as appropriate

A. The applicant is
*(a) The creditor
*(b) An officer of court on behalf of a creditor

(1) Insert name and address

B. Other persons having an interest are
*(c) The debtor (1)

(2) Insert name

C. Decree was granted in an action by the pursuer(s) (2)
in the Court of Session/Sheriff Court at
on 19
against the defender(s) (2)
(*or give details of other document or summary warrant upon which the poinding proceeded*):—

(3) Insert address

D. A poinding of the debtor's belongings was carried out by (1)
sheriff officer/messenger-at-arms on the instructions of the creditor on 19 at (3)

E. *(a) The poinding ceases to have effect on ....

or

*(b) An extension of duration of poinding was granted on .... extending the poinding so that it ceases to have effect on ....

No application has been made under section 30(1) of the Act for warrant of sale.

(*Narrate ground(s) for (further) extension*):—

This application is made under section 27 of the Debtors (Scotland) Act 1987/paragraph 11 of Schedule 5 to the Debtors (Scotland) Act 1987.

F. The applicant asks the court:—
1. To fix a hearing.
2. To order the sheriff clerk to intimate this application and the date of the hearing to the applicant, to the debtor and to the officer of court who carried out the poinding, (if not the applicant).
3. To (further) extend the duration of the poinding for (*state period proposed*).
4. To award expenses (if competent).

Date .... 19...... (*Signed*) ....
Applicant

IF YOU WISH FURTHER ADVICE CONTACT ANY CITIZENS ADVICE BUREAU/ LOCAL ADVICE CENTRE/SHERIFF CLERK OR SOLICITOR

Rule 20(1) FORM 14

The Debtors (Scotland) Act 1987, section 28(1)(b)/Schedule 5, paragraph 12(1)(b)

Sheriff Court ....

APPLICATION FOR AUTHORITY TO MOVE POINDED ARTICLES (1) .... 19...... (Court Ref. No.) APPLICANT

*delete as appropriate

A. The applicant is
*(a) The debtor
*(b) A person having possession of the pointed articles

(1) Insert name and address

B. Other persons having an interest are
*(c) The creditor (1)
*(d) The debtor (1)
*(e) A person having possession of the poinded articles (1)

(2) Insert name

C. Decree was granted in an action by the pursuer(s) (2)
in the Court of Session/Sheriff Court at on 19
against the defender(s) (2)
(*or give details of other document or summary warrant upon which the poinding proceeded*):—

(3) Insert address

D. A poinding of the debtor's belongings was carried out by (1)
sheriff officer/messenger-at-arms on the instructions of the creditor on 19 at (3)

E. Among the articles poinded were the following:—
These articles are presently situated at ....
The applicant wishes authority to move these articles to ....
(*give reasons for removal*):—

This application is made under section 28(1)(*b*) of the Debtors (Scotland) Act 1987/paragraph 12(1)(*b*) of Schedule 5 to the Debtors (Scotland) Act 1987.

F. The applicant asks the court:—
1. To fix a hearing.
2. To order the sheriff clerk to intimate this application and the date of the hearing to the applicant, to those persons stated above as having an interest and to the officer of court who carried out the poinding.
3. To authorise removal of the poinded articles.
4. To award expenses (if competent).

Date .... 19...... (*Signed*) ....
Applicant

IF YOU WISH FURTHER ADVICE CONTACT ANY CITIZENS ADVICE BUREAU/ LOCAL ADVICE CENTRE/SHERIFF CLERK OR SOLICITOR

Rule 21(1) FORM 15

The Debtors (Scotland) Act 1987, section 28(4)(a)/Schedule 5, paragraph 12(4)(a)

Sheriff Court ....

APPLICATION FOR AN ORDER FOR RESTORATION OF REMOVED ARTICLES (1) [ ] .... 19......
(Court Ref. No.)
APPLICANT

A. The applicant is
*(a) The creditor

(1) Insert name and address

B. Other persons having an interest are
(b) The debtor (1)
(c) A person having possession of the poinded articles (1)

(2) Insert name

C. Decree was granted in an action by the pursuer(s) (2)
in the Court of Session/Sheriff Court at
on 19
against the defender(s) (2)
(*or give details of other document or summary warrant upon which the poinding proceeded*):—

(3) Insert address

D. A poinding of the debtor's belongings was carried out by (1)
sheriff officer/messenger-at-arms on the instructions of the creditor on 19 at (3)

E. Among the articles poinded were the following:—
The(se) article(s) has/have been removed from premises situated at (3) .... otherwise than in accordance with Part II of or Schedule 5 to the Debtors (Scotland) Act 1987 and are now in the possession of (1) ....
(*State whereabouts of articles if known*):—

This application is made under section 28(4)(*a*) of the Debtors (Scotland) Act 1987/paragraph 12(4)(*a*) of Schedule 5 to the Debtors (Scotland) Act 1987.

F. The applicant asks the court:—
1. To fix a hearing.
2. To order the sheriff clerk to intimate this application and the date of the hearing to the applicant to the debtor, the person in possession of the poinded articles and to the officer of court who carried out the poinding.
3. To order that the person(s) in possession of the poinded articles restore them to the premises from which they were removed within a specified period.
4. To award expenses (if competent).

Date .... 19...... (*Signed*) ....
Applicant

IF YOU WISH FURTHER ADVICE CONTACT ANY CITIZENS ADVICE BUREAU/ LOCAL ADVICE CENTRE/SHERIFF CLERK OR SOLICITOR

Rule 22(1) FORM 16

The Debtors (Scotland) Act 1987, section 28(5)(b) and (c)/Schedule 5, paragraph 12(5)(b) and (c)

Sheriff Court ....

APPLICATION FOR RECALL OF AN ORDER FOR RESTORATION OF REMOVED ARTICLES

(1) [ ] .... 19......
(Court Ref. No.)
APPLICANT

A. The applicant is
*(a) A person having an interest (*state nature of interest*)

(1) Insert name and address

B. Other persons having an interest are
(b) The creditor (1)
(c) The debtor (1)
(d) Any other person having an interest (1)

(2) Insert name

C. Decree was granted in an action by the pursuer(s) (2)
in the Court of Session/Sheriff Court at
on 19
against the defender(s) (2)
(*or give details of other document or summary warrant upon which the poinding proceeded*):—

(3) Insert address

D. A poinding of the debtor's belongings was carried out by (1)
sheriff officer/messenger-at-arms on the instructions of the creditor on 19 at (3)

E. Among the articles poinded were the following:—

These articles were removed from the premises where they were situated and an order for their restoration to said premises was made by the court, in terms of section 28(4)(*a*)/Schedule 5, paragraph 12(4)(*a*) of the Debtors (Scotland) Act 1987 on .... Such order should be recalled (*give reasons for this including circumstances under which articles acquired*):—

The articles have been acquired for value and without knowledge of the poinding.

This application is made under section 28(5)(*b*) and (*c*) of the Debtors (Scotland) Act 1987/paragraph 12(5)(*b*) and (*c*) of Schedule 5 to the Debtors (Scotland) Act 1987.

F. The applicant asks the court:—
1. To fix a hearing.
2. To order the sheriff clerk to intimate this application and the date of the hearing to the applicant, to the creditor, the debtor, the officer of court who carried out the poinding and to such other person as the court may require.
3. To recall the order made.
4. To order that said article(s) be released from the poinding
5. To award expenses (if competent).

Date .... 19...... (*Signed*) ....
Applicant

IF YOU WISH FURTHER ADVICE CONTACT ANY CITIZENS ADVICE BUREAU/ LOCAL ADVICE CENTRE/SHERIFF CLERK OR SOLICITOR

Rule 23(1)(b)

FORM 17

The Debtors (Scotland) Act 1987, section 28(6)/Schedule 5, paragraph 12(6)

Sheriff Court ....

APPLICATION FOR AUTHORITY TO EXECUTE FURTHER POINDING

(1) [ ] .... 19......
(Court Ref. No.)
APPLICANT

*delete as appropriate

A. The applicant is
*(a) The creditor
*(b) An officer of court on behalf of the creditor

(1) Insert name and address

B. Other persons having an interest are
(c) The debtor (1)

(2) Insert name

C. Decree was granted in an action by the pursuer(s) (2)
in the Court of Session/Sheriff Court at
on 19
against the defender(s) (2)
(*or give details of other document or summary warrant upon which the poinding proceeded*):—

(3) Insert address

D. A poinding of the debtor's belongings was carried out by (1)
sheriff officer/messenger-at-arms on the instructions of the creditor on 19 at (3)

E. Among the articles poinded were the following:—
These articles were removed from premises at (3) .... otherwise than in accordance with Part II of or Schedule 5 to the Debtors (Scotland) Act 1987. The debtor was at fault for their removal and authority should be given for the poinding of other articles belonging to him in the same premises (*give reasons for the application including reasons for alleging debtor at fault*):—

This application is made under section 28(6) of the Debtors (Scotland) Act 1987/paragraph 12(6) of Schedule 5 to the Debtors (Scotland) Act 1987.

F. The applicant asks the court:—
1. To fix a hearing.
2. To order the sheriff clerk to intimate this application and the date of the hearing to the applicant to the debtor and to the officer of court who carried out the poinding, (if not the applicant).
3. To authorise the poinding of other articles belonging to the debtor in the premises situated at (3).................... .
4. To award expenses (if competent).

Date .... 19..... (*Signed*) ....
Applicant

IF YOU WISH FURTHER ADVICE CONTACT ANY CITIZENS ADVICE BUREAU/ LOCAL ADVICE CENTRE/SHERIFF CLERK OR SOLICITOR

Rule 24(1) FORM 18

The Debtors (Scotland) Act 1987, section 29(2)/Schedule 5, paragraph 13(2)

Sheriff Court ....

APPLICATION FOR AUTHORITY TO EXECUTE FURTHER POINDING AND/OR TO REVALUE DAMAGED ARTICLE

(1) [ ] .... 19.....
(Court Ref. No.)
APPLICANT

*delete as appropriate

A. The applicant is
*(a) The creditor
*(b) An officer of court on behalf of the creditor

(1) Insert name and address

B. Other persons having an interest are
(c) The debtor (1)

(2) Insert name

C. Decree was granted in an action by the pursuer(s) (2)
in the Court of Session/Sheriff Court at
on 19
against the defender(s) (2)
(or give details of other document or summary warrant upon which the poinding proceeded):—

(3) Insert address

D. A poinding of the debtor's belongings was carried out by (1)
sheriff officer/messenger-at-arms on the instructions of the creditor on 19 at (3)

E. Among the articles poinded were the following which were damaged or destroyed as specified:—

The debtor has been at fault for this (*specify reasons*):—

(*Where articles have been damaged give details of the alleged reduction in value of the damaged articles*):—

This application is made under section 29(2) of the Debtors (Scotland) Act 1987/paragraph 13(2) of Schedule 5 to the Debtors (Scotland) Act 1987.

F. The applicant asks the court:—
1. To fix a hearing.
2. To order the sheriff clerk to intimate this application and the date of the hearing to the applicant, to the debtor and to the officer of court who carried out the poinding (if not the applicant).
3. To authorise the poinding of other articles belonging to the debtor in the premises in which the original poinding took place and/or
4. To authorise the revaluation of the damaged articles.
5. To award expenses (if competent).

Date .... 19...... (*Signed*) ....
Applicant

IF YOU WISH FURTHER ADVICE CONTACT ANY CITIZENS ADVICE BUREAU/ LOCAL ADVICE CENTRE/SHERIFF CLERK OR SOLICITOR

Rule 25(1)

FORM 19

The Debtors (Scotland) Act 1987, section 29(3)/Schedule 5, paragraph 13(3)

Sheriff Court ....

APPLICATION FOR AN ORDER FOR CONSIGNATION BY THIRD PARTY (1) [ ] .... 19...... (Court Ref. No.) APPLICANT

*delete as appropriate

A. The applicant is
*(a) The creditor/officer of court on behalf of the creditor
*(b) The debtor

(1) Insert name and address

B. Other persons having an interest are
(c) The person in respect of whom an order for consignation is requested (1)
*(d) The creditor (1)
*(e) The debtor (1)

(2) Insert name

C. Decree was granted in an action by the pursuer(s) (2)
in the Court of Session/Sheriff Court at
on 19
against the defender(s) (2)
(*or give details of other document or summary warrant upon which the poinding proceeded*):—

(3) Insert address

D. A poinding of the debtor's belongings was carried out by (1)
sheriff officer/messenger-at-arms on the instructions of the creditor
on 19 at (3)

E. Among the articles poinded was the following which was valued at £ :—

This article has been wilfully *damaged/*destroyed by (1) ....

or

This article having been removed from premises by (1) ....
in breach of poinding has been *damaged/*destroyed/*lost/*stolen/
*passed on to another person without knowledge of the poinding for value.
*The said article is now valued at £
The said (2) .... knew the article had been poinded.

This application is made under section 29(3) of the Debtors (Scotland) Act 1987/paragraph 13(3) of Schedule 5 to the Debtors (Scotland) Act 1987.

F. The applicant asks the court:—
1. To fix a hearing.
2. To order the sheriff clerk to intimate this application and the date of the hearing to the applicant, to those persons stated above as having an interest and to the officer of court who carried out the poinding.
3. To order the said (2) .... to consign £ in court being:
*(i) the difference between the value of the article fixed under section 20(4) of the Act/paragraph 5(4) of Schedule 5 to the Act and the value of the article as damaged or
*(ii) the value fixed under said section.
4. To award expenses (if competent).

Date .... 19...... (*Signed*) ....
Applicant

IF YOU WISH FURTHER ADVICE CONTACT ANY CITIZENS ADVICE BUREAU/ LOCAL ADVICE CENTRE/SHERIFF CLERK OR SOLICITOR

Rule 26(1)

FORM 20

The Debtors (Scotland) Act 1987, section 30

Sheriff Court ....

APPLICATION FOR WARRANT OF SALE OF POINDED ARTICLES

(*name and address*)

Applicant

The applicant is the creditor/an officer of court on behalf of the creditor.
A poinding of the belongings of the debtor (*name and address*) was carried out by (*name and address*)
sheriff officer/messenger-at-arms on (*date*) at (*place*)
on the instructions of the creditor (*name and address*)
and a report of the poinding was made to the Sheriff at
on (*date*)
The person who presently has possession of the poinded articles is (*name and address*)

*delete as appropriate

*The following articles to the value of £ have been released/redeemed from poinding, in terms of section 33 of the Debtors (Scotland) Act 1987:—

The place where it is intended to hold the warrant sale is
*(a) an auction room
*(b) a dwellinghouse
*(c) other premises (*state nature of premises*)
(*Give details of every person whose consent is required if the sale is to be held in a dwellinghouse/other premises*):—

The applicant asks the court:—

1. To grant a warrant of sale of the poinded articles by public auction at (*place*).
2. To appoint (*name and address*) officer of court to make arrangements for the warrant sale.
3. To direct that the warrant sale shall take place within (*state period of time*).
4. To grant warrant to said officer of court to open shut and lockfast places for the purpose of executing the warrant.
5. To appoint (*name and address*) auctioneer/officer of court other suitable person, to conduct the warrant sale.
*6. To grant warrant to said officer of court to remove the poinded articles to the premises at (*place*) for the sale.
*7. To direct the warrant sale shall be advertised by public notice by (*state method*).

Date .... 19...... (*Signed*) ....
Applicant

Rule 26(5) FORM 21

The Debtors (Scotland) Act 1987, section 30

NOTICE TO DEBTOR OF APPLICATION FOR A WARRANT OF SALE

*delete as appropriate

(*place and date*) To Debtor

You are served with a copy of the application for a warrant of sale of pointed articles* along with copies of consents obtained.

Creditor/Officer of Court

NOTICE TO DEBTOR

This is an application for warrant to sell poinded articles belonging to you. Please read notes A and B carefully.

A. You may object to the application

1. The grounds for objection are:—
   a. The poinding is invalid or has ceased to have effect.
   b. The total value fixed for the articles at the poinding is substantially below the total price which they would likely fetch if sold on the open market.
   c. The likely proceeds of the warrant sale will not exceed the expenses likely to be incurred in this application and in any steps required in execution of the warrant, on the assumption that the application and such steps are unopposed.
   d. The granting of this application will be unduly harsh.
2. IF YOU WISH TO OBJECT: you must complete and sign the notice of objection attached to this form and return it to the court within 14 days from (*officer of court to specify date*), or lodge separate written objections within the same period.
3. You will then be advised by the sheriff clerk of the date fixed for the hearing of the application when you should attend to be represented at court.
4. PLEASE NOTE. If you fail to return the said notice of objection to the court or lodge separate written objections as directed and if having objected you fail to attend or be represented at the hearing, the application may be dealt with in your absence.
5. If you oppose the application on frivolous grounds you may have to pay certain expenses.

B. You may redeem any poinded article

To do this you must pay the officer of court, within seven days from the date this application is served on you, the amount fixed for the article at the poinding and stated in the poinding schedule.

If you wish further advice contact any citizen advice bureau/local advice centre/sheriff clerk or solicitor.

The following expenses have been incurred by the creditor in making this application viz:—

The Debtors (Scotland) Act 1987, section 30

NOTICE OF OBJECTION

*To the Sheriff Clerk
Sheriff Court....................

*In an application by (*state name and address of applicant*) for warrant to sell articles poinded on (*date*) in which a report of the poinding was made to the sheriff at (*place*) or (*date*)

I, (*name and address*),
have read the application
I object to the granting of it

....
(*Date*) (*Signature*)

Please note: (1) This form or separate written objections must be returned to the sheriff clerk within 14 days from (*officer of court to specify date*) *but only if* you have grounds to object to the application.
(2) If you oppose the application on frivolous grounds you may have to pay certain expenses.

*To be completed by officer of court prior to service

Rule 27(1) FORM 22

The Debtors (Scotland) Act 1987
consent under section 32(1)/32(4)/Schedule 5, paragraph 14(2)/14(3)

*In respect of an application by A (*design*) for warrant of sale of poinded articles belonging to B (*design*)/*In respect of the sale of poinded articles belonging to B (*design*) under summary warrant dated (*specify*) I, (*design*), being the debtor/an occupier of (*the place where sale is to take place*) hereby give my consent to the sale of the articles poinded on (*date*) being held at (*place*)

*delete as appropriate

..............................(*Signature and date*)

Rule 28 FORM 23

Receipt under the Debtors (Scotland) Act 1987, section 33(3)/Schedule 5, paragraph 15(3)

In respect of the poinding executed on (*date*) at the instance of A (*design*) against B (*design*), received the sum of £ in redemption of the following article(s) viz: (*specify*)

..............................(*Signature of officer of court and date*)

Rule 30(1)

FORM 24

The Debtors (Scotland) Act 1987, section 35(1) or 36(3)(b)

Sheriff Court ....

APPLICATION FOR VARIATION OF A WARRANT OF SALE OF POINDED ARTICLES

(*name and address*)

Applicant

The applicant is the creditor/an officer of court on behalf of the creditor. A pointing of the belongings of the debtor (*name and address*) was carried out by (*name and address*)
sheriff officer/messenger-at-arms on (*date*) at (*place*) on the instructions of the creditor (*name and address*)
and a report of the poinding was made to the Sheriff at
on (*date*)
A warrant of sale was granted on (*date*) . This is returned for amendment. The person who presently has possession of the poinded articles is (*name and address*)

*delete as appropriate

*The following articles to the value of £ have been released/redeemed from poinding, in terms of sections 33, 40 and 41 of the Debtors (Scotland) Act 1987:—

The place where it is now intended to hold the warrant sale is different from that stated in the original warrant of sale and is
*(a) an auction room
*(b) a dwellinghouse
*(c) other premises (*state nature of premises*)
(*Give details of every person whose consent is required if the sale is to be held in a dwellinghouse/other premises*):—

The original warrant of sale should be varied
(*State variation required and reason for this*):—

The following additional powers are required (*state powers required*):—

The applicant asks the court:—

To vary the warrant of sale granted on (*date*) and to make order(s) in terms of this application.

Date .... 19...... (*Signed*) ....
Applicant

Rule 30(5) FORM 25

The Debtors (Scotland) Act 1987, section 35

NOTICE TO DEBTOR OF APPLICATION FOR VARIATION OF A WARRANT OF SALE

*delete as appropriate

(*place and date*) To Debtor

You are served with a copy of the application for a variation of warrant of sale of poinded articles* along with copies of consents obtained.

Creditor/Officer of Court

NOTICE TO DEBTOR

This is an application for variation of a warrant to sell poinded articles belonging to you. Please read the following notes.

You may object to the application

1. The grounds for objection are:—
   a. The poinding is invalid or has ceased to have effect.
   b. The proposed variation is unsuitable.
2. IF YOU WISH TO OBJECT: you must complete and sign the notice of objection attached to this form and return it to the court within seven days from the date this application is served on you, or lodge separate written objections within the same period.
3. You will then be advised by the sheriff clerk of the date fixed for the hearing of the application when you should attend to be represented at court.
4. PLEASE NOTE If you fail to return the said notice of objection to the court or lodge separate written objections as directed and if having objected you fail to attend or be represented at the hearing, the application may be dealt with in your absence.
5. If you oppose the application on frivolous grounds you may have to pay certain expenses.

IF YOU WISH FURTHER ADVICE CONTACT ANY CITIZENS ADVICE BUREAU/ LOCAL ADVICE CENTRE/SHERIFF CLERK OR SOLICITOR.

The Debtors (Scotland) Act 1987, section 35

NOTICE OF OBJECTION

*To the Sheriff Clerk
Sheriff Court....................

*In an application by (*state name and address of applicant*) for variation of a warrant to sell granted on (*date*) of articles poinded on (*date*) in which a report of the poinding was made to the sheriff at (*place*) on (*date*)

I, (*name and address*),
have read the application
I object to the granting of it

....
(*Date*) (*Signature*)

Please note: (1) This form or separate written objections must be returned to the sheriff clerk within seven days from the date the application is served on you, *but only if* you have grounds to object to the application.
(2) If you oppose the application on frivolous grounds you may have to pay certain expenses.

*To be completed by officer of court
prior to service

Rule 31(1) FORM 26

The Debtors (Scotland) Act 1987, section 39(1)/Schedule 5, paragraph 20(1)

Sheriff Court ....

Report of Sale

Details of parties and prior steps in diligence

1. The creditor : (*name and address*)
2. The debtor : (*name and address*)
3. The person who had possession of the pointed articles, if not the debtor : (*name and address*)

[extract decree and other documents on which the diligence proceeded to be produced]

4. Date of decree etc :
5. Date of extract :
6. Date of charge :
7. Date of poinding :
8. Date poinding reported :

[warrant of sale and any variation to be produced]

9. Date warrant of sale granted :
10. Date of any variation to warrant of sale :

Details of sale arrangements

11. Date of sale :
12. Location of sale :
13. Officer of court who made arrangements : (*name and address*)
14. Person who conducted sale (if different from 13) : (*name and address*)
15. Person who witnessed sale (if applicable) : (*name and address*)

[executions to be produced]

16. Intimations, services and public notices given by officer of court in respect of sale or removal of articles for sale :

Disposal of poinded articles and sale proceeds

LIST:—

17. Articles sold and amount for which sold
18. Articles unsold
19. Articles whose ownership passed to creditor
20. Articles whose ownership reverted to debtor
21. Articles otherwise disposed of (*specify*)

Specify each item under 17–21 and amount debtor was credited with.

22. Articles released/redeemed from poinding and value fixed at poinding.

DETAIL:—

23. Disposal of sale proceeds including any surplus paid to debtor.
24. Any monies consigned in court.

STATEMENT OF DEBT AND EXPENSES

Sums due by debtor

1. Sums in decree etc
   Principal ________
   Expenses ________
   Interest ________
   Etc ________ ________

2. Diligence expenses
   Charge ________
   Poinding ________
   Application for warrant of sale ________
   Etc ________ ________

[vouchers for outlays to be produced]

3. Sale expenses ________ ________ ________ ________ ________

Paid to account ________

Proceeds of sale (from 17–22) ________

Consignation on by ________

Balance due to/by debtor ________

This report is made by me (*specify name and address*) to the sheriff at (*place*) on (*date*)

(*Signed*) ....
Messenger-at-Arms/Sheriff Officer

....
Witness (if applicable)

Rule 34(1) FORM 27

The Debtors (Scotland) Act 1987, section 40(2)/Schedule 5, paragraph 21(2)

Sheriff Court ....

APPLICATION FOR RELEASE OF POINDED ARTICLE(S) BELONGING TO THIRD PARTY (1) .... 19.....
(Court Ref. No.)
APPLICANT

A. The applicant is
(a) A person claiming ownership of pointed articles

(1) Insert name and address

*delete as appropriate

B. Other persons having an interest are
(b) The creditor (1)
(c) The debtor (1)
*(d) Any person (other than the debtor) having possession of the poinded article(s) for which release is sought (1)

(2) Insert name

C. Decree was granted in an action by the pursuer(s) (2)
in the Court of Session/Sheriff Court at
on 19
against the defender(s) (2)
(*or give details of other document or summary warrant upon which the poinding proceeded*):—

(3) Insert address

D. A poinding of the debtor's belongings was carried out by (1)
sheriff officer/messenger-at-arms on the instructions of the creditor
on 19 at (3)

E. Among the articles poinded were the following:—

A (warrant of) sale of the poinded article(s) has not yet taken place (*specify details of where and when a (warrant of) sale is to be held if this has been fixed*):—
The(se) article(s) belong to the applicant and should be released from poinding.

This application is made under section 40(2) of the Debtors (Scotland) Act 1987/paragraph 21(2) of Schedule 5 to the Debtors (Scotland) Act 1987.

F. The applicant asks the court:—
1. To fix a hearing.
2. To order the sheriff clerk to intimate this application and the date of the hearing to the applicant to those persons stated above as having an interest and to the officer of court who carried out the poinding.
3. To order that said article(s) be released from the poinding.
4. To award expenses (if competent).

Date .... 19..... (*Signed*) ....
Applicant

IF YOU WISH FURTHER ADVICE CONTACT ANY CITIZENS ADVICE BUREAU/ LOCAL ADVICE CENTRE/SHERIFF CLERK OR SOLICITOR

Rule 35(1) FORM 28

The Debtors (Scotland) Act 1987, section 41(3)/Schedule 5, paragraph 22(3)

Sheriff Court ....

APPLICATION FOR RELEASE OF POINDED ARTICLE(S) IN COMMON OWNERSHIP (1) [ ] [ ] [ ] .... 19..... (Court Ref. No.) APPLICANT

A. The applicant is
*(a) A person claiming ownership of pointed article(s) in common with the debtor

(1) Insert name and address

*delete as appropriate

B. Other persons having an interest are
(b) The debtor (1)
(c) The creditor (1)
*(d) Any other person claiming common ownership of the poinded article(s) (1)
*(e) Any person (other than the debtor) having possession of the poinded article(s) for which release is sought (1)

(2) Insert name

C. Decree was granted in an action by the pursuer(s) (2)
in the Court of Session/Sheriff Court at
on 19
against the defender(s) (2)
(*or give details of other document or summary warrant upon which the poinding proceeded*):—

(3) Insert address

D. A poinding of the debtor's belongings was carried out by (1)
sheriff officer/messenger-at-arms on the instructions of the creditor
on 19 at (3)

E. Among the articles poinded were the following:—

A (warrant of) sale of the poinded article(s) has not yet taken place (*give details of where and when a (warrant of) sale is to be held if this has been fixed*):—
The applicant owns the poinded article(s) in common with the debtor (*state nature and extent of common interest and name and full address of any other common owner*):—
*(i) The applicant undertakes to pay the officer of court a sum equal to the value of the debtors interest in the article(s).
*(ii) The inclusion of the article(s) in the poinding or its/their subsequent sale would be unduly harsh to the applicant (*give reasons for application on this basis*):—

This application is made under section 41(3) of the Debtors (Scotland) Act 1987/paragraph 22(3) of Schedule 5 to the Debtors (Scotland) Act 1987.

F. The applicant asks the court:—
1. To fix a hearing.
2. To order the sheriff clerk to intimate this application and the date of the hearing to the applicant to those persons stated above as having an interest and to the officer of court who carried out the poinding.
*3. To find that the continued inclusion of the article(s) in the poindings or its/their sale under summary warrant/warrant of sale would be unduly harsh to the applicant.
4. To order that said article(s) be released from poinding.
5. To award expense (if competant).

Date .... 19...... (*Signed*) ....
Applicant

IF YOU WISH FURTHER ADVICE CONTACT ANY CITIZENS ADVICE BUREAU/ LOCAL ADVICE CENTRE/SHERIFF CLERK OR SOLICITOR

Rule 36(1) FORM 29

The Debtors (Scotland) Act 1987, section 41(7)(b)/Schedule 5, paragraph 22(6)(b)

Sheriff Court ....

APPLICATION FOR FINDING OF COMMON OWNERSHIP OF POINDED ARTICLE (1) [ ] .... 19.....
(Court Ref. No.)
APPLICANT

A. The applicant is
(a) A person claiming ownership of pointed article(s) in common with the debtor.

(1) Insert name and address

*delete as appropriate

B. Other persons having an interest are
(b) The debtor (1)
(c) The creditor (1)
*(d) Any other person claiming common ownership of the poinded article(s) (1)

(2) Insert name

C. Decree was granted in an action by the pursuer(s) (2)
in the Court of Session/Sheriff Court at
on 19
against the defender(s) (2)
(*or give details of other document or summary warrant upon which the poinding proceeded*):—

(3) Insert address

D. A poinding of the debtor's belongings was carried out by (1)
sheriff officer/messenger-at-arms on the instructions of the creditor on 19 at (3)

E. Among the articles poinded were the following:—
The applicant claims to own the poinded article(s) in common with the debtor. He does not seek release of the article(s) from poinding. The creditor and debtor do not admit this claim and a finding should be pronounced that a valid claim exists.
(*State nature and extent of the common interest and the name and full address of any other common owner*):—

This application is made under section 41(7)(*b*) of the Debtors (Scotland) Act 1987/paragraph 22(6)(*b*) of Schedule 5 to the Debtors (Scotland) Act 1987.

F. The applicant asks the court:—
1. To fix a hearing.
2. To order the sheriff clerk to intimate this application and the date of the hearing to the applicant, to those persons stated above as having an interest and to the officer of court who carried out the poinding.
3. To find that the applicant has common ownership in the article(s) to the extent of (specify).
4. To award expenses (if competent).

Date .... 19..... (*Signed*) ....
Applicant

IF YOU WISH FURTHER ADVICE CONTACT ANY CITIZENS ADVICE BUREAU/ LOCAL ADVICE CENTRE/SHERIFF CLERK OR SOLICITOR

Rule 38(1) FORM 30

The Debtors (Scotland) Act 1987, section 47

Earnings Arrestment Schedule

On the date of service of this schedule there comes into effect an earnings arrestment. Particulars of the arrestment and of the requirement on the employer on a pay-day to pay sums deducted from the debtor's earnings to the creditor are given in the schedule.

Particulars of earnings arrestment

Employer : (*name, designation and address*)
Debtor (employee) : (*name, designation and address*)
Creditor : (*name, designation and address*)

Where there is more than one debt state details relating to each separately

The debt recoverable: ordinary debt –
expenses –
interest –
less paid to account – ________

expenses of serving charge –
expenses of executing this earnings arrestment – ________
TOTAL ________

Particulars of decree: (*specify*)
or other document or summary warrant upon which this arrestment proceeds

Date of any charge:

(*Place and date*)
To (*name of employer*)
You are served with this earnings arrestment schedule along with a copy of sections 49(1) to (6) and Schedule 2 to the Debtors (Scotland) Act 1987.

(*Signed*) ....
Officer of Court
(*name, designation and address*)

NOTE TO OFFICER OF COURT:

A copy of this earnings arrestment schedule and a copy of section 49(1) to (6) and Schedule 2 to the Debtors (Scotland) Act 1987 is to be intimated to the debtor by you, if reasonably practicable.

EFFECT OF EARNINGS ARRESTMENT

An earnings arrestment has the general effect of requiring the employer of a debtor:—

(1) to deduct a sum calculated in accordance with the Debtors (Scotland) Act 1987 from the debtor's net earnings on every pay-day; and

(2) to pay any sum so deducted to the creditor as soon as is reasonably practicable.

The arrestment remains in effect until the debt has been paid or otherwise extinguished, the debtor has ceased to be employed by the employer or the arrestment has been recalled or abandoned by the creditor or has ceased to have effect.

Instructions to Employer

Please read these instructions carefully.

1. When this earnings arrestment schedule is served on you, you are required to make a deduction from your employee's net earnings on every pay-day *unless* you are already making deductions from his earnings under a previous earnings arrestment or a conjoined arrestment order in which case read sections 59 and 62 of the Debtors (Scotland) Act 1987.

2.
   (1) You must begin deducting on the first pay-day occurring after a period of seven days after the date of service of this schedule on you.

   (2) Where any pay-day occurs within this seven day period you are entitled but not required to begin deducting.

3. The sum to be deducted is calculated in accordance with section 49 of the Debtors (Scotland) Act 1987. (A copy of section 49(1) to (6) and Schedule 2 to the Act is attached) [*officer of court to attach*].

4. As soon as is reasonably practicable you must pay the sum deducted to [*officer of court to insert name and address of a person in the United Kingdom to whom payment is to be made*].

5. You must continue to make deductions and payments until:—
   (1) the debt recoverable has been paid or otherwise extinguished;
   (2) the debtor has ceased to be employed by you or;
   (3) the arrestment has been recalled or abandoned by the creditor or has for any other reason ceased to have effect.

6. You are entitled to charge your employee a fee (at present) on each occasion you make a payment to the creditor.

7. For further information read the following notes.

NOTES

(1) The debt recoverable by the arrestment consists of the sums as set out in section 48 of the Act.

(2) "Earnings" and "net earnings" from which deductions are to be made, are defined in section 73 of the Act.

(3) You are also referred to the following sections of the Act:—

50(1):	Sheriff's power on an application by the debtor or the person on whom the earnings arrestment schedule was served to make an order declaring that the earnings arrestment is invalid or has ceased to have effect.
50(3):	Sheriff's power on an application by the debtor, the creditor or the employer to determine any dispute as to the operation of an earnings arrestment.
57(1):	Employer's liability where he fails to comply with an earnings arrestment.
58(1):	Provisions regarding the simultaneous operation of one earnings arrestment and one current maintenance arrestment.
59(1):	While an earnings arrestment is in effect, no other earnings arrestment against the earnings of the same debtor payable by the same employer is competent.

59(4): Employer's duty, on receipt of a second earnings arrestment schedule to give certain information to the "second creditor".

62(2) and (3): Employer's duty, when a conjoined arrestment order is in effect, to give certain information to a creditor who is not included in the conjoined arrestment order and who has served or has in effect an earnings arrestment.

69(3): If deductions are not made on the first pay-day after the service of the earnings arrestment schedule in accordance with section 69(2) of the Act, deductions made on a subsequent pay-day are not to include any deductions in respect of the first pay-day.

69(5)(*a*): Intimations the employer may expect to receive from the creditor or the sheriff clerk.

Further information and advice about the Act is available from solicitors' offices, Citizens' Advice Bureaux and other local advice centres and sheriff clerks' offices.

Rule 39(1)

FORM 31

The Debtors (Scotland) Act 1987

Intimation to employer in terms of section 49(8)

The employer : (*name and address*)
The debtor (employee) : (*name and address*)
The creditor : (*name and address*)
Date earnings arrestment schedule served on employer: (*specify*)

To the employer—Take note that on (*date*) the Lord Advocate made regulations which varied

*delete as appropriate

*(a) Tables, A, B and C of Schedule 2 to the Debtors (Scotland) Act 1987 (the statutory deduction tables)

*(b) the percentage specified in subsection (5) and (6)(*a*)(ii) of section 49 of the Debtors (Scotland) Act 1987 to (*specify change*)

The regulations come into force on (*date*)

Date .... (*Signed*) ....
Creditor/Debtor

(i) This intimation should be considered carefully by the employer as the variation referred to may affect the sum to be deducted by him under the earnings arrestment (see further section 69(1), (2) and (3) of the Debtors (Scotland) Act 1987).

(ii) The person intimating this form to the employer must attach the statutory deduction tables as revised where these have been varied by the regulations.

Rule 40(1)

FORM 32

The Debtors (Scotland) Act 1987, section 50(1)

Sheriff Court ....

APPLICATION FOR DECLARATION THAT EARNINGS ARRESTMENT INVALID OR CEASED TO HAVE EFFECT

(1) [ ] .... 19......
(Court Ref. No.)
APPLICANT

*delete as appropriate

A. The applicant is
*(a) The debtor
*(b) The person on whom the earnings arrestment schedule was served

(1) Insert name and address

B. Other persons having an interest are
(c) The creditor (1)
*(d) The debtor (1)
*(e) The person on whom the earnings arrestment schedule was served (1)

(2) Insert name

C. Decree was granted in an action by the pursuer(s) (2)
in the Court of Session/Sheriff Court at
on 19
against the defender(s) (2)
(*or give details of other document or summary warrant upon which the earnings arrestment proceeded*):—

D. An earnings arrestment schedule against the earnings of the debtor (2) was served on (2) by (1) sheriff officer/messenger-at-arms on the instructions of the creditor (2) on 19
A copy of the said schedule is attached.

E. The earnings arrestment is invalid/has ceased to have effect because (*Give reasons for application*):—

This application is made under section 50(1) of the Debtors (Scotland) Act 1987.

F. The applicant asks the court:—
1. To fix a hearing.
2. To order the sheriff clerk to intimate this application and the date of the hearing to the applicant and to those persons stated above as having an interest.
3. To make an order declaring that the earnings arrestment is invalid or has ceased to have effect.
4. To make the following consequential order (*give details*).
5. To award expenses (if competent).

Date .... 19..... (*Signed*) ....
Applicant

IF YOU WISH FURTHER ADVICE CONTACT ANY CITIZENS ADVICE BUREAU/ LOCAL ADVICE CENTRE/SHERIFF CLERK OR SOLICITOR

Rule 41(1)

FORM 33

The Debtors (Scotland) Act 1987, section 50(3)

Sheriff Court .. ..

APPLICATION FOR DETERMINATION OF DISPUTE IN OPERATION OF EARNINGS ARRESTMENT

(1) [ ] [ ] [ ]

APPLICANT

.... 19......
(Court Ref. No.)

*delete as appropriate

A. The applicant is
*(a) The debtor
*(b) The creditor
*(c) The employer

(1) Insert name and address

B. Other persons having an interest are
*(d) The debtor (1)
*(e) The creditor (1)
*(f) The employer (1)

(2) Insert name

C. Decree was granted in an action by the pursuer(s) (2)
in the Court of Session/Sheriff Court at
on 19
against the defender(s) (2)
(*or give details of other document or summary warrant upon which the poinding proceeded*):—

D. An earnings arrestment schedule against the earnings of the debtor (2)
was served on the employer (2)
by (1) sheriff officer/messenger-at-arms on the instructions of the creditor (2)
on 19
A copy of the said schedule is attached.

E. The following dispute as to the operation of the earnings arrestment requires to be determined (*specify nature of the dispute*):—

This application is made under section 50(3) of the Debtors (Scotland) Act 1987.

F. The applicant asks the court:—
1. To fix a hearing.
2. To order the sheriff clerk to intimate this application and the date of the hearing to the applicant and to those persons stated above as having an interest.
3. To make an order determining the dispute (*specify order sought*):—
*4. To order the reimbursement by (*name person*) to (*name person*) of £ with interest thereon at the rate of (*specify rate*) from (*specify date*) or such other date as the court may consider appropriate.
*5. To order the payment by (*name person*) to (*name person*) of £ with interest thereon at the rate of (*specify rate*) from (*specify date*) or such other date as the court may consider appropriate.
6. To award expenses (if competent).

Date .... 19..... (*Signed*) ....
Applicant

IF YOU WISH FURTHER ADVICE CONTACT ANY CITIZENS ADVICE BUREAU/ LOCAL ADVICE CENTRE/SHERIFF CLERK OR SOLICITOR

Rule 42(1)

FORM 34

The Debtors (Scotland) Act 1987, section 51

Current Maintenance Arrestment Schedule

On the date of service of this schedule there comes into effect a current maintenance arrestment. Particulars of the arrestment and of the requirement on the employer on a pay-day to pay sums deducted from the debtors earnings to the creditor are given in the schedule.

Particulars of current maintenance arrestment

Employer : (*name, designation and address*)
Debtor (employee) : (*name, designation and address*)
Creditor : (*name, designation and address*)

Particulars of maintenance order(s) upon which this arrestment proceeds: (*specify*)

Maintenance payable by the debtor expressed as a daily rate (see section 51(5)): (*state*)

Date of any intimation made under section 54(1):

The debtor has defaulted in his payments under the maintenance order(s): (*give particulars of default with reference to either subsection (1) or (2) of section 54 of the Act*)

*delete as appropriate

The debtor *is/*is not entitled to deduct income tax from the maintenance payable to the creditor:

(*Place and date*)
To (*name of employer*)
You are served with this earnings arrestment schedule along with a copy of sections 53(1) to (2) of the Debtors (Scotland) Act 1987.

(*Signed*) ....
Officer of Court
(*name, designation and address*)

NOTE TO OFFICER OF COURT:

A copy of this current maintenance arrestment schedule and a copy of section 53(1) to (2) of the Debtors (Scotland) Act 1987 is to be intimated to the debtor by you, if reasonably practicable.

EFFECT OF CURRENT MAINTENANCE ARRESTMENT

A current maintenance arrestment has the general effect of requiring the employer of a debtor:—

(1) to deduct a sum calculated in accordance with the Debtors (Scotland) Act 1987 from the debtor's net earnings on every pay-day; and

(2) to pay any sum so deducted to the creditor as soon as is reasonably practicable.

The arrestment remains in effect until the debtor has ceased to be employed by the employer or the arrestmment has been recalled or abandoned by the creditor or has ceased to have effect.

Instructions to employer

Please read these instructions carefully.

1. When this current maintenance arrestment schedule is served on you, you are required to make a deduction from your employee's net earnings on every pay-day *unless* you are already making deductions from his earnings under a previous current maintenance arrestment or a conjoined arrestment order in which case read sections 59 and 62 of the Debtors (Scotland) Act 1987.

2. (1) You must begin deducting on the first pay-day occurring after a period of seven days after the date of service of this schedule on you.

   (2) Where any pay-day occurs within this seven day period you are entitled but not required to begin deducting.

3. (1) The sum to be deducted is calculated in accordance with section 53 of the Debtors (Scotland) Act 1987. (A copy of sections 53(1) and (2) is attached) [*officer of court to attach*].

   (2) You may be required to make deductions under both an earnings arrestment and a current maintenance arrestment. If this is the case an on any pay-day the net earnings of your employee are less than the total sums to be deducted by you, you must first deduct under the earnings arrestment and then under the current maintenance arrestment on the balance of the net earnings in accordance with section 53(1) of the Act.

4. As soon as is reasonably practicable you must pay the sum deducted to [*officer of court to insert name and address of a person in the United Kingdom to whom payment is to be made*].

5. You must continue to make deductions and payments until:—

   (1) the debtor has ceased to be employed by you;
   (2) the arrestment has been recalled or abandoned by the creditor;
   (3) the arrestment has ceased to have effect under section 55(8) of the Act or for any other reason.

6. You are entitled to charge your employee a fee (at present   ) on each occasion you make a payment to the creditor.

7. For further information read the following notes.

NOTES FOR EMPLOYER

(1) "Earnings" and "net earnings" from which deductions are to be made, are defined in section 73 of the Act.

(2) You are also referred to the following sections of the Act:—

55(1): Sheriff's power on an application by the debtor or the person on whom the current maintenance arrestment schedule was served to make an order declaring that a current maintenance arrestment is invalid or has ceased to have effect.

55(2): Sheriff's power on an application by the debtor to recall a current maintenance arrestment if satisfied that the debtor is unlikely to default again in paying maintenance.

55(5): Sheriff's power on an application by the debtor, the creditor or the employer to determine any dispute as to the operation of a current maintenance arrestment.

57(1): Employer's liability where he fails to comply with a current maintenance arrestment.

58: Provisions regarding the simultaneous operation of one earnings arrestment and one current maintenance arrestment.

59(2): While a current maintenance arrestment is in effect, no other current maintenance arrestment against the earnings of the same debtor payable by the same employer is competent.

59(4): Employer's duty, on receipt of a second current maintenance arrestment schedule to give certain information to the "second creditor".

62(2) and (3): Employer's duty, when a conjoined arrestment order is in effect, to give certain information to a creditor who is not included in the conjoined arrestment order and who has served or has in effect a current maintenance arrestment.

68: Creditor's power to authorise the Secretary of State to receive any sums payable under the current maintenance arrestment direct from the employer.

69(3): If deductions not made on the first pay-day after service of the schedule in accordance with section 69(2) of the Act, deductions made on subsequent pay-day not to include any deductions in respect of first pay-day.

69(5)(6): Intimations the employer may expect to receive from the creditor or the sheriff clerk.

Further information and advice about the Act is available from solicitors' offices, Citizens' Advice Bureaux and other local advice centres and sheriff clerks' offices.

Rule 43(1) FORM 35

The Debtors (Scotland) Act 1987

Intimation to employer in terms of section 53(4)

The employer	: (*name and address*)
The debtor (employee)	: (*name and address*)
The creditor	: (*name and address*)
Date current maintenance arrestment schedule served on employer	: (*specify*)

To the employer: Take note that on (*date*) the Lord Advocate made regulations which varied the sum specified in subsection 2(*b*) of section 53 of the Debtors (Scotland) Act 1987 to £

The regulations come into operation on (*date*)

Date .... (*Signed*) ....
Creditor/Debtor

This intimation should be considered carefully by the employer as the variation referred to may affect the sum to be deducted by him under the current maintenance arrestment (see further section 69(1), (2) and (3) of the Debtors (Scotland) Act 1987).

Rule 44(1) FORM 36

The Debtors (Scotland) Act 1987

Intimation to employer in terms of section 53(5)

The employer	: (*name and address*)
The debtor (employee)	: (*name and address*)
The creditor	: (*name and address*)
Date current maintenance arrestment schedule served on employer	: (*specify*)

To the employer: Take note that on (*date*) the small maintenance payment limits mentioned in section 65(1A) of the Income and Corporation Taxes Act 1970 were changed to (*specify changes*)

The changes come into operation on (*date*)

Date .... (*Signed*) ....
Creditor/Debtor

(i) This intimation should be considered carefully by the employer as the changes made may affect the sum to be deducted by him under the current maintenance arrestment.
(ii) The person intimating this form to the employer must attach a copy of section 65(1A) of the Income and Corporation Taxes Act 1970 as amended or varied.

Rules 45(1) and 45(5) [1]FORM 37

The Debtors (Scotland) Act 1987

Intimation to debtor in terms of section 54(1)(a)

To (*name and address of debtor*)

Take note that a maintenance order, in which you are ordered to make payments to (*name and address*) was [granted/made/registered/confirmed] on (*date*) by/in (*name of court*). A copy of the order is attached. [Here insert reference to enforcement by Secretary of State for Social Security if appropriate]

Date .... (*Signed*) ....
[Creditor/Solicitor/Sheriff Officer/Authorised lay representative]

GUIDANCE ABOUT THE PAYMENT OF MAINTENANCE

(You should read this section carefully)

WHAT CAN HAPPEN IF YOU DO NOT MAKE REGULAR PAYMENTS?

If you do not make regular payments and get into arrears amounting in value to three instalments of maintenance, a document called a Current Maintenance Arrestment Schedule (referred to here as an arrestment) may be sent to your employer.

The arrestment will instruct your employer to make deductions from your net earnings on every pay day, and pay these sums over to the creditor (i.e. the person to whom the payment of maintenance is due).

The arrestment of your earnings will remain in force for so long as you are employed by your current employer or until the arrestment is recalled or abandoned by the creditor or ceases to have effect.

If an arrestment is sent to your employer you have the right to apply to the sheriff for the order to be recalled. If the sheriff is satisfied that you are unlikely to default in paying maintenance again he may recall the order.

HOW CAN YOU PAY MAINTENANCE?

To avoid the risk of an arrestment it is best to make arrangements to pay the maintenance regularly. This can be done in various ways, including

—by cash payment
—by standing order through a bank or building society
—by personal cheque
—by bank giro credit

Probably the simplest way to make payments is by standing order. This will also provide you with a clear record of payments made. Any bank or building society will give you further advice on this.

WHERE CAN YOU GET ADVICE?

FURTHER ADVICE MAY BE OBTAINED BY CONTACTING ANY CITIZENS ADVICE BUREAU, OTHER LOCAL ADVICE CENTRE, SHERIFF CLERK OR SOLICITOR

PAYMENT ARRANGEMENTS

The debtor : (*name and address*)
The creditor : (*name and address*)
*Creditor's agent : (*name and address*)

To the debtor: Take note that payment of sums due under this maintenance order should be sent to * the creditor at the above address/the account number referred to below/the creditor's agent at the above address.

*** PAYMENT TO BANK, BUILDING SOCIETY OR OTHER ACCOUNT**

To the debtor: Payment should be made direct to the following account—

ACCOUNT NUMBER:
SORT CODE:
NAME OF BANK, BUILDING SOCIETY, ETC:
ADDRESS:

(*Details to be inserted by or on behalf of the creditor*)

To debtor: If it is not possible for payment by standing order to start on the due date you must ensure that payment is made direct to the creditor until such time as the standing order comes into operation.

Do not delay in making payments while you are making arrangements with your own bank or building society. Otherwise you may inadvertently breach the terms of the court order. This could result in a current maintenance arrestment order being served on your employer.

* Delete as appropriate.

NOTE
[1] As substituted by S.I. 1991 No. 1920.

[THE NEXT PAGE IS D 441]

Rule 46(1)

FORM 38

The Debtors (Scotland) Act 1987, section 55(1)

Sheriff Court ....

APPLICATION FOR DECLARATION THAT CURRENT MAINTENANCE INVALID OR CEASED TO HAVE EFFECT

(1) [ ] .... 19.....
(Court Ref. No.)
APPLICANT

* delete as appropriate

A. The applicant is
*(a) The debtor
*(b) The person on whom the current maintenance arrestment schedule was served

(1) Insert name and address

B. Other persons having an interest are
(c) The creditor (1)
*(d) The debtor (1)
*(e) The person on whom the current maintenance arrestment schedule was served (1)

C. Specify details of maintenance order and when and by whom granted or issued and where appropriate details of its registration or confirmation:—

(2) Insert name

D. A current maintenance arrestment schedule against the earnings of the debtor (2) was served on (2) by (1) sheriff officer/messenger-at-arms on the instructions of the creditor (2)
on 19 . A copy of the said schedule is attached

E. The current maintenance arrestment is invalid/has ceased to have effect because (*give reasons for application*):—

This application is made under section 55(1) of the Debtors (Scotland) Act 1987.

F. The applicant asks the court:—
1. To fix a hearing.
2. To order the sheriff clerk to intimate this application and the date of the hearing to the applicant, and to those persons stated above as having an interest.
3. To make an order declaring that the current maintenance arrestment is invalid or has ceased to have effect.
4. To make the following consequential order (*give details*):
5. To award expenses (if competent).

Date .... 19...... (*Signed*) ....
Applicant

IF YOU WISH FURTHER ADVICE CONTACT ANY CITIZENS ADVICE BUREAU/ LOCAL ADVICE CENTRE/SHERIFF CLERK OR SOLICITOR

Rule 47(1)

FORM 39

The Debtors (Scotland) Act 1987, section 55(2)

Sheriff Court ....

APPLICATION FOR RECALL OF A CURRENT MAINTENANCE ARRESTMENT (1)

.... 19.....
(Court Ref. No.)
APPLICANT

A. The applicant is
The debtor

(1) Insert name and address

B. Other persons having an interest are
The creditor (1)

C. Specify details of maintenance order and when and by whom granted or issued and where appropriate details of its registration or confirmation:—

(2) Insert name

D. A current maintenance arrestment schedule against the earnings of the debtor (2) was served on the employer (1) by (1) sheriff officer/messenger-at-arms on the instructions of the creditor (2) on 19 . A copy of the said schedule is attached

E. The current maintenance arrestment should be recalled (*state why you say that you are unlikely to default again in payment maintenance*):—

This application is made under section 55(2) of the Debtors (Scotland) Act 1987.

F. The applicant asks the court:—
1. To fix a hearing.
2. To order the sheriff clerk to intimate this application and the date of the hearing to the applicant and to the creditor.
3. To recall the current maintenance arrestment.
4. To award expenses (if competent).

Date .... 19...... (*Signed*) ....
Applicant

IF YOU WISH FURTHER ADVICE CONTACT ANY CITIZENS ADVICE BUREAU/ LOCAL ADVICE CENTRE/SHERIFF CLERK OR SOLICITOR

Rule 48(1) FORM 40

The Debtors (Scotland) Act 1987, section 55(5)

Sheriff Court ....

APPLICATION FOR DETERMINATION OF DISPUTE IN OPERATION OF CURRENT MAINTENANCE ARRESTMENT

(1) [ ] APPLICANT

.... 19......
(Court Ref. No.)

*delete as appropriate

A. The applicant is
*(a) The debtor
*(b) The creditor
*(c) The employer

(1) Insert name and address

B. Other persons having an interest are
*(d) The debtor (1)
*(e) The creditor (1)
*(f) The employer (1)

C. Specify details of maintenance order and when and by whom granted or issued and where appropriate details of its registration or confirmation:—

(2) Insert name

D. A current maintenance arrestment schedule against the earnings of the debtor (2) was served on the employer (2) by (1) sheriff officer/messenger-at-arms on the instructions of the creditor (2) on 19 . A copy of the said schedule is attached

E. The following dispute as to the operation of the current maintenance arrestment requires to be determined (*specify nature of the dispute*):—

This application is made under section 55(5) of the Debtors (Scotland) Act 1987.

F. The applicant asks the court:—
1. To fix a hearing.
2. To order the sheriff clerk to intimate this application and the date of the hearing to the applicant, and to those persons stated above as having an interest.
3. To make an order determining the dispute (*specify order sought*):—
*4. To order the reimbursement by (*name person*) to (*name person*) of £ with interest thereon at the rate of (*specify rate*) from (*specify date*) or such other date as the court may consider appropriate.
*5. To order the payment by (*name person*) to (*name person*) of £ with interest thereon at the rate of (*specify rate*) from (*specify date*) or such other date as the court may consider appropriate.
6. To award expenses (if competent).

Date .... 19...... (*Signed*) ....
Applicant

IF YOU WISH FURTHER ADVICE CONTACT ANY CITIZENS ADVICE BUREAU/ LOCAL ADVICE CENTRE/SHERIFF CLERK OR SOLICITOR

Rule 51(1)

FORM 41

The Debtors (Scotland) Act 1987, section 57(6)

Sheriff Court ....

APPLICATION FOR PAYMENT BY CREDITOR TO DEBTOR OF PENALTY SUM (1)

.... 19......
(Court Ref. No.)
APPLICANT

A. The applicant is
The debtor

(1) Insert name and address

B. Other persons having an interest are
The creditor (1)

(2) Insert name

C. Decree was granted in an action by the pursuer(s) (2)
in the Court of Session/Sheriff Court at
on 19
against the Defender(s) (2)
(*or give details of other document or summary warrant or maintenance order upon which earnings arrestment or current maintenance arrestment proceeded*):—

D. An earnings arrestment schedule/a current maintenance arrestment schedule against the earnings of the debtor (2)
was served on the employer (2) by (1)
sheriff officer/messenger-at-arms on the instructions of the creditor (2) on 19
A copy of the said schedule is attached

*delete as appropriate

E. The amount of the debt or the sum to be deducted from the earnings of the debtor was (*specify*):—
The expenses of diligence were (*specify*):—
The creditor failed to intimate to the debtor's employer that
*(a) the debt recoverable under the earnings arrestment had been paid or otherwise extinguished (*specify from what date and in what circumstances*):—
*(b) the current maintenance arrestment has ceased to have effect under section 55(8) of the Debtors (Scotland) Act 1987 (*specify from what date and in what circumstances*):—
*(c) the debt being enforced by the earnings arrestment had ceased to be enforceable by diligence (*specify from what date and in what circumstances*):—
The employer overpaid £ as a result of this failure. (*Give details of the calculation of this sum and grounds for seeking the sum sought from the creditor*):—

This application is made under section 57(6) of the Debtors (Scotland) Act 1987.

F. The applicant asks the court:—
1. To fix a hearing.
2. To order the sheriff clerk to intimate this application and the date of the hearing to the applicant and to the creditor.
3. To order the creditor to pay to the debtor £ (*specify amount requested*).
4. To award expenses (if competent).

Date .... 19...... (*Signed*) ....
Applicant

IF YOU WISH FURTHER ADVICE CONTACT ANY CITIZENS ADVICE BUREAU/ LOCAL ADVICE CENTRE/SHERIFF CLERK OR SOLICITOR

Rule 52(1) FORM 42

The Debtors (Scotland) Act 1987, section 59(5)

Sheriff Court ....

APPLICATION FOR ORDER ON EMPLOYER TO PROVIDE INFORMATION (1) [ ] .... 19......
(Court Ref. No.)
APPLICANT

A. The applicant is
A second creditor in terms of section 59(4) of the Debtors (Scotland) Act 1987

(1) Insert name and address

B. Other persons having an interest are
The employer (1)

C. An earnings arrestment schedule/a current maintenance arrestment schedule against the earnings of the debtor (1) was served on the said employer by (1) sheriff officer/messenger-at-arms on the instructions of the applicant on 19

D. The arrestment did not come into effect because of the terms of section 59 of the Debtors (Scotland) Act 1987
The employer has failed without reasonable excuse to give the following information to the applicant (*specify information not given*):—

The applicant is entitled to this information.

This application is made under section 59(5) of the Debtors (Scotland) Act 1987.

E. The applicant asks the court:—
1. To fix a hearing.
2. To order the sheriff clerk to intimate this application and the date of the hearing to the applicant and to the employer.
3. To order the employer to give the information requested to the applicant within such period as the court may order.
4. To award expenses (if competent).

Date .... 19...... (*Signed*) ....
Applicant

IF YOU WISH FURTHER ADVICE CONTACT ANY CITIZENS ADVICE BUREAU/ LOCAL ADVICE CENTRE/SHERIFF CLERK OR SOLICITOR

Rule 53(1)

FORM 43

The Debtors (Scotland) Act 1987, section 60(2)

Sheriff Court ....

Application for a conjoined arrestment order

1. The applicant : (*name and address*)
   The debtor (employee) : (*name and address*)
   The employer : (*name and address*)
2. The applicant is a creditor of the debtor and wishes to enforce his debt by executing an earnings arrestment and/or a current maintenance arrestment against earnings payable to the debtor by the employer.
3. The applicant cannot execute this arrestment as there is already an earnings arrestment and/or a current maintenance arrestment in effect against these earnings.
4. No conjoined arrestment order has been made against these earnings.
5. The applicant's debt consists of

ORDINARY DEBT		*CURRENT MAINTENANCE*	
(Where there is more than one ordinary debt state details relating to each separately.)		Maintenance payable by debtor expressed as a daily rate	:
Sum due under decree or other: document or summary warrant		Is the debtor entitled to deduct income tax from maintenance payable?	: Yes/No
expenses	:	Particulars of maintenance order(s) which constituted the obligation to pay maintenance	:
interest	:	Date of any intimation made under section 54(1) of the Act	:
less paid to account	: ———	Specify particulars of debtors default in his payments under the maintenance order(s) with reference to either subsection (1) or (2) of section 54 of the Act	:
expenses of executing current maintenance arrestment	:		
expenses of serving charge	:		
expenses of executing	:		
earnings arrestment expenses of this application	:		
TOTAL AMOUNT RECOVERABLE	———		
Particulars of decree or other document or summary warrant upon which the poinding proceeded: (*specify*)			
Date of any charge	:		

6. The person within the United Kingdom to whom payments are to be made is: (*name and address*).
7. Specify the following information for each of the earnings and/or current maintenance arrestments already in effect against the earnings payable to the debtor by the employer.
   The creditor: (*name and address*)
   Date and place of execution of the arrestment:
   Debt recoverable or daily rate of maintenance as specified in the arrestment:

   The applicant asks the court to make a conjoined arrestment order which
   a. Recalls the earnings and/or current maintenance arrestment(s) presently in effect against earnings payable to the debtor by the employer.
   b. Orders the employer, while the conjoined arrestment order is in effect to deduct a sum calculated in accordance with section 63 of the Debtors (Scotland) Act 1987 from the debtors net earnings on any pay-day and to pay this sum as soon as is reasonably practicable to the sheriff clerk at (*place*).

Date .... Signed ....
Applicant

Rule 53(4) FORM 44

The Debtors (Scotland) Act 1987

Sheriff Court: .... Court Ref. No. ....

Form of notice of application for a conjoined arrestment order

1. (*Place and date*)
To (*name and address of person to whom intimation given*).
This application for a conjoined arrestment order by (*name and address of applicant*) is intimated to you this date.

....
Sheriff Clerk

2. IF YOU WISH TO OBJECT to the granting of the application you must fill in the box below

I intend to object to the granting of the application
Date .... Signature ....

3. If you have filled in the box above you must return this form to the court within 14 days from the date of this intimation
The address of the court is: THE SHERIFF CLERK, ...
4. You will then be advised by the sheriff clerk of the date fixed for the hearing of the application when you should attend or be represented at court.
5. PLEASE NOTE if you fail to return this form to the court as directed or if having returned it you fail to attend or be represented at the hearing the application may be dealt with in your absence.

IF YOU WISH FURTHER ADVICE CONTACT ANY CITIZENS ADVICE BUREAU/ LOCAL ADVICE CENTRE, SHERIFF CLERK OR SOLICITOR

Rule 54(1) FORM 45

SHERIFF COURT, (*Place*)

UNDER THE DEBTORS (SCOTLAND) ACT 1987, SECTION 60

CONJOINED ARRESTMENT ORDER

IN THE

APPLICATION

BY

(*name and address*)

(*Place and date*). The Sheriff RECALLS the following arrestment(s) which have been served on (*name and address of employer*), the employer of the debtor (*name and address of debtor*) on the following dates:—

1. On (*date*), for (*amount*), on behalf of (*name*)
2. Etc.

SPECIFIES the amount(s) recoverable under this order as:—

(a) Ordinary debt(s)

Name of creditor — Amount recoverable

(b) Current maintenance

Name of each maintenance creditor — Daily rate £

Aggregrate daily rate £

REQUIRES the said employer of the debtor, while this order is in effect to deduct a sum calculated in accordance with section 63 of the Debtors (Scotland) Act 1987 from the said debtor's net earnings on any pay-day and to pay it as soon as is reasonably practical to the sheriff clerk, (*address of sheriff clerk's office*);

Sheriff

INSTRUCTIONS TO EMPLOYER

Please read these instructions carefully

1. As soon as this conjoined arrestment order comes into effect, any earnings arrestment and/or current maintenance arrestment against earnings payable by you to your employee is recalled and you must stop making deductions under the(se) arrestments.

2. While this conjoined arrestment order is in effect you are required to deduct a sum from your employee's net earnings on any pay-day and to pay it as soon as is reasonably practicable to the sheriff clerk at (*address of sheriff clerk's office*).

3. When making payment to the sheriff clerk you are required to supply him with the following information:—
   (1) Name and address of your employee
   (2) Date of the conjoined arrestment order
   (3) Sum deducted from his earnings for ordinary debt(s)
   (4) Sum deducted from his earnings for current maintenance
   (5) Total sum being paid to the sheriff clerk
   (6) Whether income tax was deducted from the sum due for current maintenance

4. The sum to be deducted is calculated in accordance with section 63 of the Debtors (Scotland) Act 1987 (a copy of sections 63(1) to (6) is attached) (*sheriff clerk to attach*).

5. You must continue to make these deductions and payments until either—
   (1) a copy of an order recalling the conjoined arrestment order has been served on you under section 66(7) of the Debtors (Scotland) Act 1987; or
   (2) the debtor ceases to be employed by you.

   You should notify the sheriff clerk in writing immediately if the debtor ceases to be employed by you.

6. You are entitled to charge your employee a fee (at present) on each occasion you make a payment to the sheriff clerk under the conjoined arrestment order.

7. For further information read the following notes.

NOTES

(1) "Earnings" and "net earnings" from which deductions are to be made are defined in section 73 of the Act.

(2) You are also referred to the following sections of the Act:—

60(9): employer's liability where he fails to comply with a conjoined arrestment order

62(2) and (3): employer's duty, when a conjoined arrestment order is in effect, to give certain information to a creditor who is not included in the conjoined arrestment order and who has served or has in effect an earnings arrestment or a current maintenance arrestment.

65(1): Sheriff's power on an application by the debtor, a creditor whose debt is being enforced by a conjoined arrestment order, the employer or the sheriff clerk to determine any dispute as to the operation of a conjoined arrestment order.

66(1): Sheriff's power to recall a conjoined arrestment order where, in particular, all ordinary debts have been paid and all obligations to pay current maintenance have ceased.

66(4): Sheriff's power to vary a conjoined arrestment order where, for example an ordinary debt is paid or a maintenance order being enforced is varied or recalled.

69(3): If deductions are not made on the first pay-day after service of the conjoined arrestment order in accordance with section 69(2) of the Act, deductions made on a subsequent pay-day are not to include any deductions in respect of the first pay-day.

Further information and advice about the Act is available from solicitors' offices, Citizens' Advice Bureaux and other local advice centres and sheriff clerks' offices.

Rule 54(5) FORM 46

SHERIFF COURT:

NOTICE OF SERVICE OF CONJOINED ARRESTMENT ORDER

To , the debtor's employer.

To , debtor.

To , creditor.

You are served with a copy of the foregoing conjoined arrestment order along with a copy of sections 63(1) to (6) of the Debtors (Scotland) Act 1987. It comes into effect seven days after service of the copy order on the employer and remains in effect until a copy of an order recalling it is served on the employer under section 66(7) of the Debtors (Scotland) Act 1987 or the debtor ceases to be employed by him. The employer should notify the Sheriff Clerk in writing immediately if the debtor ceases to be employed by him.

Sheriff Clerk
Sheriff Clerk's Office
(*Address and date*)

Officer of Court
(*name and address, designation*)

All creditors whose arrestments have been recalled by the foregoing conjoined arrestment order and are included in it must inform the sheriff clerk in writing within 14 days of receiving this notice of the name and address of a person within the United Kingdom to whom payments are to be made by him under the order.

Rule 55(1)

FORM 47

The Debtors (Scotland) Act 1987, section 60(9)(c)

Sheriff Court ....

APPLICATION FOR WARRANT FOR DILIGENCE AGAINST EMPLOYER

(1) [ ] .... 19.....
(Court Ref. No.)
APPLICANT

A. The applicant is
(a) The sheriff clerk

(1) Insert name and address

B. Other persons having an interest are
(b) The employer (1)
(c) The debtor (1)
(d) The creditors whose debts are being enforced by the conjoined arrestment order (1)

(2) Insert name

C. A conjoined arrestment order against the earnings of the debtor (2) was made on (*date*) by the sheriff at (*place*) and was served on the employer (2) by or on the instructions of the sheriff clerk (*place*) on (*date*)

D. The employer has failed to comply with the conjoined arrestment order (*specify manner and circumstances of this failure*):—

The employer is accordingly liable to pay to the sheriff clerk £ which he would have paid if he had complied with the order.

This application is made under section 60(9)(*c*) of the Debtors (Scotland) Act 1987.

E. The applicant asks the court:—
1. To fix a hearing.
2. To order the sheriff clerk to intimate this application and the date of the hearing to the employer, the debtor and the creditors whose debts are being enforced by the conjoined arrestment order.
3. To order the employer to pay to the sheriff clerk (*place*) £
4. To grant warrant for diligence against the employer for recovery of this sum or such other sum as appears to the court to be due.
5. To award expenses (if competent).

Date .... 19...... (*Signed*) ....
Applicant

IF YOU WISH FURTHER ADVICE CONTACT ANY CITIZENS ADVICE BUREAU/ LOCAL ADVICE CENTRE/SHERIFF CLERK OR SOLICITOR

Rule 56(1)

FORM 48

The Debtors (Scotland) Act 1987, section 62(4)

Sheriff Court ....

APPLICATION FOR ORDER ON EMPLOYER TO PROVIDE INFORMATION	(1)		.... 19..... (Court Ref. No.) APPLICANT

A. The applicant is
The creditor who requires information under section 62(2) or (3)

(1) Insert name and address

B. Other persons having an interest are
The employer (1)

* delete as appropriate

C. *An earnings arrestment schedule/*a current maintenance arrestment schedule against the earnings of the debtor (1)
was served on the said employer by (1)
sheriff officer/messenger-at-arms on the instructions of the applicant on

D. The arrestment *did not come into effect/*has ceased to have effect as a conjoined arrestment order is in effect.
The employer has failed without reasonable excuse to inform the applicant which court made the conjoined arrestment order.
The applicant is entitled to this information.

This application is made under section 62(4) of the Debtors (Scotland) Act 1987.

E. The applicant asks the court:—
1. To fix a hearing.
2. To order the sheriff clerk to intimate this application and the date of the hearing to the applicant and to the employer.
3. To order the employer to inform the applicant which court made the conjoined arrestment order within such period as the court may order.
4. To award expenses (if competent).

Date .... 19..... (*Signed*) ....
Applicant

IF YOU WISH FURTHER ADVICE CONTACT ANY CITIZENS ADVICE BUREAU/ LOCAL ADVICE CENTRE/SHERIFF CLERK OR SOLICITOR

Rule 57(1)

FORM 49

The Debtors (Scotland) Act 1987, section 62(5)

Sheriff Court ....

Application for variation of a conjoined arrestment order

1. The applicant : (*name and address*)
   The debtor (employee) : (*name and address*)
   The employer : (*name and address*)
2. The applicant is a creditor of the debtor and wishes to enforce his debt by executing an earnings arrestment and/or a current maintenance arrestment against earnings payable to the debtor by the employer.
3. The debt cannot be enforced by executing an earnings arrestment or a current maintenance arrestment as a conjoined arrestment order is in effect against these earnings.
4. The conjoined arrestment order was made on (*date*) by the court at (*address of court*).
5. The applicant's debt consists of

ORDINARY DEBT

(Where there is more than one ordinary debt state details relating to each separately.)
Sum due under decree or other document or summary warrant :
expenses :
interest :
less paid to account : ______

expenses of executing current maintenance arrestment :
expenses of serving charge :
expenses of executing earnings arrestment :
expenses of this application :
TOTAL AMOUNT RECOVERABLE ______

Particulars of decree or other document or summary warrant which constituted the debt (*specify*) :
Date of any charge :

CURRENT MAINTENANCE

Maintenance payable by the debtor expressed as a daily rate :
Is the debtor entitled to deduct income tax from maintenance payable? : Yes/No
Particulars of maintenance order(s) which constituted the obligation to pay maintenance :
Date of any intimation made under section 54(1) of the Act :
Particulars of debtors default in his payments under the maintenance order(s) with reference to either subsection (1) or (2) of section 54 of the Act :

6. The person within the United Kingdom to whom payments are to be made is: (*name and address*).

The applicant asks the court:—
To vary the conjoined arrestment order granted on (*date*) to include the applicant's debt among the debts being enforced by the conjoined arrestment order.

Date .... Signed ....
Applicant

Rule 57(3)(a) **FORM 50**

The Debtors (Scotland) Act 1987

Sheriff Court: .... Court Ref. No. ....

Form of notice of application for variation of a conjoined arrestment order

1. (*Place and date*)
   To (*name and address of person to whom intimation given*).
   This application for a variation of a conjoined arrestment order by (*name and address of applicant*) is intimated to you this date.

....
Sheriff Clerk

2. IF YOU WISH TO OBJECT to the granting of the application you must fill in this box below

I intend to object to the granting of the application
Date .... Signature ....

3. If you have filled in the box above you must return this form to the court within 14 days from the date of this intimation
   The address of the court is: THE SHERIFF CLERK, ...
4. You will then be advised by the sheriff clerk of the date fixed for the hearing of the application when you should attend or be represented at court.
5. PLEASE NOTE if you fail to return this form to the court as directed or if having returned it, you fail to attend or be represented at the hearing, the application may be dealt with in your absence.

IF YOU WISH FURTHER ADVICE CONTACT ANY CITIZENS ADVICE BUREAU/ LOCAL ADVICE CENTRE, SHERIFF CLERK OR SOLICITOR

Rule 57(7)(b) FORM 51

SHERIFF COURT:

Notice of Service of an Order Varying a Conjoined Arrestment Order under Section 62(5) of the Debtors (Scotland) Act 1987

To , the debtor's employer.

To , debtor.

To , creditor.

You are served with (1) copy of an order dated varying a conjoined arrestment order made on

(2) a copy of the conjoined arrestment order as varied

(3) a copy of subsections (1) to (6) of section 63 of the Debtors (Scotland) Act 1987.

The employer is required to operate the conjoined arrestment order as varied seven days after service of the copy order on him, although he may operate it on any pay-day occurring within this seven day period. The conjoined arrestment order as varied remains in effect until a copy of an order recalling it is served on the employer under section 66(7) of the Debtors (Scotland) Act 1987 or the debtor ceases to be employed by him. The employer should notify the sheriff clerk in writing immediately if the debtor ceases to be employed by him.

Sheriff Clerk
Sheriff Clerk's Office
(*Address and date*)

Officer of Court
(*Name, designation and address*)

Rule 58(1)(a) FORM 52

The Debtors (Scotland) Act 1987

Intimation to employer under section 63(7)

The employer	: (*name and address*)
The debtor (employee)	: (*name and address*)
The sheriff clerk	: (*name and address*)
Date of conjoined arrestment order	: (*specify*)
Date order served on employer	: (*specify*)
Date of order varying the conjoined arrestment order	: (*specify*)
Date varied order served on employer	: (*specify*)

To the employer—Take note that on (*date*) the Lord Advocate made regulations which varied

*(a) Tables A, B and C of Schedule 2 to the Debtors (Scotland) Act 1987 (the statutory deduction tables)

*(b) The percentage specified in subsection (5) and (6)(*a*)(ii) of section 49 of the Debtors (Scotland) Act 1987 to (*specify change*)

*(c) The sum specified in subsection 4(*b*) of section 63 of the Debtors (Scotland) Act 1987 to £

The regulations come into operation on (*date*)

*delete as appropriate

Date .... (*Signed*) ....
Sheriff Clerk

(i) This intimation should be considered carefully by the employer as the variation(s) made by regulations referred to may affect the sum to be deducted by him under the conjoined arrestment order (see further section 69(1), (2) and (3) of the Debtors (Scotland) Act 1987).

(ii) The sheriff clerk must attach to this intimation the statutory deduction tables as revised where these have been varied by the regulations.

Rule 58(1)(b)

FORM 53

The Debtors (Scotland) Act 1987

Intimation to employer under section 63(8)

The employer	: (*name and address*)
The debtor (employee)	: (*name and address*)
The sheriff clerk	: (*name and address*)
Date of conjoined arrestment order	: (*specify*)
Date order served on employer	: (*specify*)
Date of order varying the conjoined arrestment order	: (*specify*)
Date varied order served on employer	: (*specify*)

To the employer—Take note that on (*date*) the small maintenance limits mentioned in section 351(2) of the Income and Corporation Taxes Act 1988 were changed to (*specify change*):—

The changes come into operation on (*date*)

Date .... (*Signed*) ....

Sheriff Clerk

(i) This intimation should be considered carefully by the employer as the change made may affect the sum to be deducted by him under the conjoined arrestment order.
(ii) The sheriff clerk must attach to this intimation a copy of section 351(2) of the Income and Corporation Taxes Act 1988.

Rule 59(1) FORM 54

The Debtors (Scotland) Act 1987, section 65(1)

Sheriff Court ....

APPLICATION FOR DETERMINATION OF DISPUTE IN OPERATION OF CONJOINED ARRESTMENT ORDER (1) [ ] .... 19.....
(Court Ref. No.)
APPLICANT

*delete as appropriate

A. The applicant is
*(a) The debtor
*(b) A creditor whose debt is being enforced by the conjoined arrestment order
*(c) The employer
*(d) The sheriff clerk (1)

(1) Insert name and address

B. Other persons having an interest are
*(e) The debtor (1)
*(f) (Other) creditors whose debts are being enforced by the conjoined arrestment order (1)
*(g) The employer (1)
*(h) The sheriff clerk (1)

C. A conjoined arrestment order against the earnings of the debtor (1) was made on (*date*) by the sheriff at (*place*)

D. The following dispute as to the operation of the conjoined arrestment order requires to be determined (*specify nature of the dispute*)

This application is made under section 65(1) of the Debtors (Scotland) Act 1987.

E. The applicant asks the court:—
1. To fix a hearing.
2. To order the sheriff clerk to intimate this application and the date of the hearing to the applicant and to those persons stated above as having an interest other than himself.
3. To make an order determining the dispute (*specify order sought*).
*4. To order the reimbursement by (*name person*) to (*name person*) of £ with interest thereon at the rate of (*specify rate*) from (*specify date*) or such other date as the court may consider appropriate.
*5. To order the payment by (*name person*) to (*name person*) of £ with interest thereon at the rate of (*specify rate*) from (*specify date*) or such other date as the court may consider appropriate.
6. To award expenses (if competent).

Date .... 19..... (*Signed*) ....
Applicant

IF YOU WISH FURTHER ADVICE CONTACT ANY CITIZENS ADVICE BUREAU/ LOCAL ADVICE CENTRE/SHERIFF CLERK OR SOLICITOR

Rule 60(1) FORM 55

The Debtors (Scotland) Act 1987, section 65(7)

Sheriff Court ....

APPLICATION FOR PAYMENT BY CREDITOR TO DEBTOR OF PENALTY SUM (CONJOINED ARRESTMENT ORDER) (1) [ ] .... 19.....
(Court Ref. No.)
APPLICANT

A. The applicant is
The debtor

(1) Insert name and address

B. Other persons having an interest are
The creditor (1)

C. A conjoined arrestment order against the earnings of the debtor was made on (*date*) by the sheriff at (*place*)

(2) Insert name
*delete as appropriate

D. *An ordinary debt/*current maintenance due to the said creditor (2) was included in the conjoined arrestment order.
The creditor failed to intimate to the sheriff clerk (*place*) that:—
*(a) The debt recoverable had been paid or otherwise extinguished.
*(b) The debt had ceased to be enforceable by diligence.
*(c) The obligation to pay the current maintenance had ceased.
*(d) The obligation to pay the current maintenance had ceased to be enforceable by diligence.
(*Specify when and how (a), (b), (c) or (d) occurred*):—
The debtor overpaid £ as a result of this failure. (*Give details of the calculation of this sum and grounds for seeking the sum sought from the creditor*):—

This application is made under section 65(7) of the Debtors (Scotland) Act 1987.

E. The applicant asks the court:—
1. To fix a hearing.
2. To order the sheriff clerk to intimate this application and the date of the hearing to the applicant and to the creditor.
3. To order the creditor to pay to the debtor £ (*specify amount requested*).
4. To award expenses (if competent).

Date .... 19..... (*Signed*) ....
Applicant

IF YOU WISH FURTHER ADVICE CONTACT ANY CITIZENS ADVICE BUREAU/ LOCAL ADVICE CENTRE/SHERIFF CLERK OR SOLICITOR

Rule 61(1)

FORM 56

The Debtors (Scotland) Act 1987, section 66(1)(a)

Sheriff Court ....

APPLICATION FOR RECALL OF CONJOINED ARRESTMENT ORDER (1) [ ] [ ] [ ] APPLICANT

.... 19.....
(Court Ref. No.)

*delete as appropriate

A. The applicant is
*(a) The debtor
*(b) A creditor whose debt is being enforced by the conjoined arrestment order
*(c) The person on whom a copy of the conjoined arrestment order or an order varying the order was served under section 60(7) or 62(6) of the Act
*(d) The sheriff clerk
*(e) An interim/permanent trustee of the debtor

(1) Insert name and address

B. Other persons having an interest are
*(f) The debtor (1)
*(g) (Other) creditors whose debts are being enforced under the conjoined arrestment order (1)
*(h) (Other) persons on whom a copy of the conjoined arrestment order or an order varying the order was served under section 60(7) or 62(6) of the Act (including the employer) (1)
*(i) The sheriff clerk (1)
*(j) An interim/permanent trustee of the debtor (1)

(2) Insert name

C. A conjoined arrestment order against the earnings of the debtor (2) was made on (*date*) by the sheriff at (*place*)

D. *(a) The conjoined arrestment order is invalid. (*Specify why it is claimed to be invalid*):—
*(b) All the ordinary debts being enforced by the conjoined arrestment order have been paid or otherwise extinguished or have ceased to be enforceable by diligence and all the obligations to pay current maintenance being so enforced have ceased or have ceased to be enforceable by diligence. (*Specify when and how these matters occurred*):—
*(c) The debtor's estate has been sequestrated (*specify date of sequestration*)

This application is made under section 66(1)(*a*) of the Debtors (Scotland) Act 1987.

E. The applicant asks the court:—
1. To fix a hearing.
2. To order the sheriff clerk to intimate this application and the date of the hearing to the applicant and to those persons stated above as having an interest other than himself.
*3. To dispense with a hearing and intimation.
4. To recall the conjoined arrestment order.
*5. To make the following consequential order (*specify order sought*).
6. To award expenses (if competent).

Date .... 19.....

(*Signed*) ....
Applicant

IF YOU WISH FURTHER ADVICE CONTACT ANY CITIZENS ADVICE BUREAU/ LOCAL ADVICE CENTRE/SHERIFF CLERK OR SOLICITOR

Rule 62(1)

FORM 57

The Debtors (Scotland) Act 1987, section 66(1)(b)

Sheriff Court ....

APPLICATION FOR RECALL OF CONJOINED ARRESTMENT ORDER (BY ALL CREDITORS WHOSE DEBTS ARE BEING ENFORCED BY IT)

(1) [ ] [ ] [ ]

.... 19.....
(Court Ref. No.)
APPLICANT

A. The applicants are
The creditors whose debts are being enforced by a conjoined arrestment order (1)

(1) Insert name and address

B. Other persons having an interest are
The debtor (1)

(2) Insert name

C. A conjoined arrestment order against the earnings of the debtor (2) was made on (*date*) by the sheriff at (*place*)

D. The conjoined arrestment order should be recalled (*specify reasons for application and any consequential order sought*)

This application is made under section 66(1)(*b*) of the Debtors (Scotland) Act 1987.

E. The applicants ask the court:—

1. To order such intimation (if any) and further procedure that the court considers appropriate.
2. To recall the conjoined arrestment order.
3. To make the following consequential order (*specify order sought*).
4. To award expenses (if competent).

Date .... 19..... (*Signed*) ....
Applicant

IF YOU WISH FURTHER ADVICE CONTACT ANY CITIZENS ADVICE BUREAU/ LOCAL ADVICE CENTRE/SHERIFF CLERK OR SOLICITOR

Rule 63(1)

FORM 58

The Debtors (Scotland) Act 1987, section 66(4)

Sheriff Court ....

APPLICATION FOR VARIATION OF CONJOINED ARRESTMENT ORDER

(1) [ ] .... 19.....
(Court Ref. No.)
APPLICANT

*delete as appropriate

A. The applicant is
*(a) The debtor
*(b) A creditor whose debt is being enforced by the conjoined arrestment order
*(c) The employer
*(d) The sheriff clerk

(1) Insert name and address

B. Other persons having an interest are
*(e) The debtor (1)
*(f) (Other) creditors whose debts are being enforced by the conjoined arrestment order (1)
*(g) The employer (1)
*(h) The sheriff clerk (1)

(2) Insert name

C. A conjoined arrestment order against the earnings of the debtor (2) was made on (*date*) by the sheriff at (*place*)

D. *(a) An ordinary debt being enforced by the conjoined arrestment order has been paid or otherwise extinguished or has ceased to be enforceable by diligence (*give details of when and how this occurred*):—
*(b) An order or decree has come into effect which varies/supersedes/recalls a maintenance order being enforced by the conjoined arrestment order (*give details of the order or decree which varied, superseded or recalled the maintenance order*):—.
*(c) An obligation to pay maintenance being enforced by the conjoined arrestment order has ceased to be enforceable in Scotland (*give details of when and how this occurred*):—
The conjoined arrestment order should accordingly be varied (*specify variation required*):—

This application is made under section 66(4) of the Debtors (Scotland) Act 1987.

E. The applicant asks the court:—
1. To fix a hearing.
2. To order the sheriff clerk to intimate this application and the date of the hearing to the applicant and to those persons stated above as having an interest other than himself.
3. To vary the conjoined arrestment order as requested.
4. To award expenses (if competent).

Date .... 19..... (*Signed*) ....
Applicant

IF YOU WISH FURTHER ADVICE CONTACT ANY CITIZENS ADVICE BUREAU/ LOCAL ADVICE CENTRE/SHERIFF CLERK OR SOLICITOR

Rule 65(3)(b) FORM 59

SHERIFF COURT:

Notice of Service of an Order Varying a Conjoined Arrestment Order under Section 66 of the Debtors (Scotland) Act 1987

To (*Name and address of persons upon whom service is made*)

You are served with (1) a copy of an order dated varying a conjoined arrestment order made on

(2) a copy of the conjoined arrestment order as varied

(3) a copy of subsections (1) to (6) of section 63 of the Debtors (Scotland) Act 1987.

The variation comes into effect seven days after service of the copy order on the employer and the conjoined arrestment order as varied remains in effect until a copy of an order recalling it is served on the employer under section 66(7) of the Debtors (Scotland) Act 1987 or the debtor ceases to be employed by the employer. The employer should notify the sheriff clerk in writing immediately if the debtor ceases to be employed by him.

Sheriff Clerk
Sheriff Clerk's Office
(*Address and date*)

Officer of Court
(*Name, designation and address*)

Rule 67 FORM 60

Certificate of execution of earnings arrestment schedule/current maintenance arrestment schedule

(*Place and date*)
I certify that on (*date*) I served the foregoing earnings arrestment schedule/current maintenance arrestment schedule on (*name and address of employer*) employer of the debtor (*name and address of debtor*). This I did by (*state method of service*).

Officer of Court
(*Name, designation and address*)

Rule 68(1) [1] FORM 61

SUMMARY WARRANT FOR THE RECOVERY OF

1. Rates under section 247 of the Local Government (Scotland) Act 1947.

2. Community charges under paragraph 7 of Schedule 2 to the Abolition of Domestic Rates Etc. (Scotland) Act 1987.

(*Place and date*)

The Sheriff having considered the application dated (*date*) by (*name and address of applicant*) along with certificate produced and it being stated in the application that an action has not been commenced for the recovery of any amount due, Grants a Summary Warrant authorising recovery of the amount remaining due and unpaid by each person specified in the application along with a surcharge of 10 *per cent* of that amount by:—

(a) a poinding and sale in accordance with Schedule 5 to the Debtors (Scotland) Act 1987;
(b) an earnings arrestment;
(c) an arrestment and action of furthcoming or sale;

and Grants Warrant to enter premises in the occupancy of any person specified in the application in order to execute a poinding or sale or the removal and sale of the poinded articles and, for any of those purposes, to open shut and lockfast places.

NOTE
[1] As substituted by S.I. 1991 No. 1920.

Rule 68(2) [1] FORM 62

SUMMARY WARRANT FOR THE RECOVERY OF RATES UNDER SECTION 250 OF THE LOCAL GOVERNMENT (SCOTLAND) ACT 1947

(*Place and date*)

The Sheriff having considered the application dated (*date*) by (*name and address of applicant*) and being satisfied that the person specified in the application has removed/is about to remove/that there is reason to suspect his removal from the land and heritages referred to in the application, Grants a Summary Warrant authorising the recovery of the amount remaining due and unpaid by such person by:—

(a) a poinding and sale in accordance with Schedule 5 to the Debtors (Scotland) Act 1987;
(b) an earnings arrestment;
(c) an arrestment and action of furthcoming or sale;

and Grants Warrant to enter premises in the occupancy of any person specified in the application in order to execute a poinding or sale or the removal and sale of the poinded articles and, for any of those purposes, to open shut and lockfast places.

NOTE
[1] As substituted by S.I. 1991 No. 1920.

Rule 68(3) [1] FORM 63

SUMMARY WARRANT FOR THE RECOVERY OF

1. Tax under section 63 of the Taxes Management Act 1970.

2. Car tax under paragraph 3(3) of Schedule 1 to the Car Tax Act 1983.

3. Value added tax under paragraph 6(5) of Schedule 7 to the Value Added Tax Act 1983.

(*Place and date*)

The Sheriff having considered the application dated (*date*) by (*name and address of applicant*) along with certificate produced, Grants a Summary Warrant authorising the recovery of the amount remaining due and unpaid by each person specified in the application by:—

(*a*) a poinding and sale in accordance with Schedule 5 to the Debtors (Scotland) Act 1987;

(*b*) an earnings arrestment;

(*c*) an arrestment and action of furthcoming or sale;

and Grants Warrant to enter premises in the occupancy of any person specified in the application in order to execute a poinding or sale or the removal and sale of the poinded articles and, for any of those purposes, to open shut and lockfast places.

NOTE

[1] As substituted by S.I. 1991 No. 1920.

[THE NEXT PAGE IS D 463]

Rule 73(1)

FORM 64

WARRANT FOR INTIMATION

(*Place and date*)

The sheriff grants warrant to intimate the foregoing application and this warrant to the applicant, to the other person(s) stated in the application as having an interest [or to the therein designed] and *to the sheriff officer/messenger-at-arms named in the application.†

*delete as appropriate
†state other person(s) as the Sheriff may direct

Fixes as a hearing (*date*) at (*time*) within the Sheriff Court House (*address of court*).

1. *Requires the applicant* to appear or be represented at the hearing to show why the application should be granted.
2. *Requires the other persons to whom intimation is given* to appear or be represented at the hearing if they intend to oppose the application.

*3. *Directs the sheriff officer/messenger-at-arms* to send a copy of the poinding schedule to the sheriff clerk before the date of the hearing.

Sheriff

To (*name of person receiving intimation*)

The application and warrant is hereby intimated to you.

Sheriff Clerk Depute
Date

TAKE NOTE

To the applicant
If you fail to appear or be represented at the hearing fixed your application may be dismissed.

To the other persons to whom intimation is given
If you fail to appear or be represented at the hearing fixed the application may be dealt with in your absence.

Form of Charge for Payment

(S.I. 1988 No. 2059)

[24th November 1988]

The Lords of Council and Session, under and by virtue of the powers conferred on them by section 5 of the Court of Session Act 1988, section 32 of the Sheriff Courts (Scotland) Act 1971 and of all other powers enabling them in that behalf, do hereby enact and declare:—

Citation and commencement

1.—(1) This Act of Sederunt may be cited as the Act of Sederunt (Form of charge for payment) 1988 and shall come into force on 30th November 1988.

(2) This Act of Sederunt shall be inserted in the Books of Sederunt.

Form of charge for payment

2. The form of charge for payment of money to be used by a messenger-at-arms or a sheriff officer under section 90 of the Debtors (Scotland) Act 1987 shall be in the form in the Schedule to this Act of Sederunt or a form substantially to the same effect with such variation as circumstances may require.

Paragraph 2 SCHEDULE

FORM OF CHARGE FOR PAYMENT OF MONEY

CHARGE FOR PAYMENT OF MONEY

in

[AB] (*address*)
PURSUER

against

[CD] (*address*)
DEFENDER

To (*name and address or debtor*)

On (*date*) a decree against you was granted in the Court of Session [*or* the sheriff court at (*place*)] for payment of a sum of money in the above action by (*name and address*), Pursuer(s) [*or give details of other document upon which charge proceeds*].

The decree was extracted on (*date*).

I, (*name and address*), messenger-at-arms [or sheriff officer], by virtue of the extract decree, in Her Majesty's name and authority and in the name and authority of the Lords of Council and Session [*or* the sheriff], charge you to pay the total sum due as set out below [together with any further interest] within [14] days after the date of this charge to (*name and address of person to whom payment to be made*).

If you do not pay this sum within [14] days you are liable to have further action taken against you including arrestment of your earnings and the poinding and sale of articles belonging to you. You are also liable to be sequestrated (declared bankrupt).

This charge is served on you today by me by (*state method of service*) and is witnessed by (*name and address of witness*).

Dated the day of 19

(*Signed*) (*Signed*)
Witness Messenger-at-arms [or sheriff officer]

The sum now due by you is:—	
Principal sum	£
Interest to date	£
Expenses	£
TOTAL	£
Less paid to account	£
Agent's fee	£
Expenses of messenger-at-arms [*or* sheriff officer]	£
Charge fee	£
Travelling	£
Witness fee	£
Other outlays in connection with service of charge (*specify*)	£
TOTAL SUM DUE	£
[Interest on the principal sum will continue to run until the date of payment.]	

IF YOU ARE NOT SURE WHAT TO DO YOU SHOULD CONSULT A SOLICITOR, CITIZENS ADVICE BUREAU OR OTHER LOCAL ADVICE CENTRE IMMEDIATELY.

Applications under the Social Security Act 1986

(S.I. 1990 No. 2238)

[8th November 1990]

The Lords of Council and Session, under and by virtue of the powers conferred on them by section 32 of the Sheriff Courts (Scotland) Act 1971 and of all other powers enabling them in that behalf, having approved, with modifications, draft rules submitted to them by the Sheriff Court Rules Council in accordance with section 34 of that Act, do hereby enact and declare:

Citation, commencement and interpretation

1.—(1) This Act of Sederunt may be cited as the Act of Sederunt (Applications under the Social Security Act 1986) 1990 and shall come into force on 3rd December 1990.

(2) This Act of Sederunt shall be inserted in the Books of Sederunt.

(3) In this Act of Sederunt, "the 1986 Act" means the Social Security Act 1986, and, unless the context otherwise requires, words and expressions used in this Act of Sederunt which are also used in the 1986 Act shall have the meaning assigned to them by that Act.

Applications under section 24 of the 1986 Act

2.—(1) An application to the sheriff under section 24(1) of the 1986 Act (recovery of expenditure on benefit from person liable for maintenance) shall be by summary application.

(2) Where, in such an application, a sum is craved which represents or includes a personal allowance element, that element shall be identified separately in the application.

Transfer of rights under section 24A of the 1986 Act

3.—(1) The sheriff clerk, on receiving notice from the Secretary of State of a transfer of rights to an order by virtue of section 24A(3) or (7) of the

1986 Act, shall endorse on the interlocutor sheet a certificate as nearly as may be in accordance with the form set out in the Schedule to this Act of Sederunt.

(2) Where, following a transfer by virtue of section 24A(3) or (7) of the 1986 Act, the dependent parent or the Secretary of State requests an extract of the order originally granted, the sheriff clerk shall issue an extract with a certified copy of the latest certificate referred to in sub-paragraph (1) of this paragraph endorsed on it.

Notice to Secretary of State under section 24B(5) of the 1986 Act

4. The notice required to be given to the Secretary of State by the sheriff clerk in accordance with section 24B(5) of the 1986 Act (notice of application to vary etc. a maintenance order) as read with regulation 3 of the Income Support (Liable Relatives) Regulations 1990, shall—

(*a*) be in writing;
(*b*) specify any date assigned for the hearing of the application;
(*c*) be accompanied by a copy of the application; and
(*d*) be sent by recorded delivery post.

Notice to Secretary of State of making of maintenance order

5. Where an order granted by the sheriff in favour of the Secretary of State under section 24(4) of the 1986 Act has been transferred to the dependent relative in accordance with section 24A(3) of that Act and a maintenance order is subsequently granted by the sheriff in favour of the dependent relative, the sheriff clerk shall forthwith notify the Secretary of State in writing and by recorded delivery post of the granting of the maintenance order.

Amendment of Ordinary Cause Rules

6. [New rule 132G in the Sheriff Courts (Scotland) Act 1907, Sched. 1, has been inserted in the print of that Act, *supra*.]

SCHEDULE

Form of certificate of a transfer of rights to an order by virtue of section 24A of the 1986 Act

(*Place*) (*date*)

I certify that notice has today been received from the Secretary of State under section 24A of the Social Security Act 1986 of a transfer of rights under an order granted on (*date*) from (*name and design*) to (*name and design*) with effect from (*date*).

(*Sgd*) Sheriff Clerk [Depute]

Copyright, Designs and Patents 1990

(S.I. 1990 No. 380)

[27th February 1990]

The Lords of Council and Session, under and by virtue of the powers conferred on them by section 32 of the Sheriff Courts (Scotland) Act 1971, section 58C of the Trade Marks Act 1938 and sections 114, 204 and 231 of the Copyright, Designs and Patents Act 1988, and of all other powers enabling them in that behalf, do hereby enact the following Act of Sederunt which embodies, with modifications, draft rules submitted by the Sheriff Court Rules Council under section 39 of the said Act of 1971:

Citation and commencement

1.—(1) This Act of Sederunt may be cited as the Act of Sederunt (Copyright, Designs and Patents) 1990 and shall come into force on 26th March 1990.

(2) This Act of Sederunt shall be inserted in the Books of Sederunt.

(3) In this Act of Sederunt—

"the 1938 Act" means the Trade Marks Act 1938; and

"the 1988 Act" means the Copyright, Designs and Patents Act 1988.

Orders for delivery up, forfeiture, destruction or other disposal

2.—(1) An application to the sheriff made under section 58C of the 1938 Act shall be made by summary application.

(2) An application to the sheriff made under section 99, 114, 195, 204, 230, 231 or 298 of the 1988 Act shall be made—

(*a*) by motion or incidental application, as the case may be, where proceedings have been commenced; or

(*b*) by summary application where no proceedings have been commenced.

Service of notice on interested persons

3.—(1) Where an application has been made to the sheriff under section 58C of the 1938 Act or section 114, 204 or 231 of the 1988 Act, the sheriff shall order that there be intimated to any person who has an interest in the goods, material, copy, recording, article or other thing which forms the subject matter of the application—

(*a*) a copy of the pleadings in the principal proceedings and a copy of the motion or incidental application; or

(*b*) the summary application,

as the case may be.

(2) In any such application the applicant shall—

(*a*) specify the name and address of any person known or believed by him to have such an interest; or

(*b*) state that to the best of his knowledge and belief no other person has any such interest.

Leave of the court for certain actions to proceed

4.—(1) Where, in an action for infringement of copyright or for infringement of design right, leave of the sheriff is required before the action may proceed the pursuer shall lodge along with the initial writ or summons a written motion or incidental application, as the case may be, seeking such leave and stating the grounds upon which it is sought.

(2) The sheriff may hear the pursuer on the motion or incidental application and may grant or refuse it or may make such other order in relation to it as he considers appropriate prior to such determination.

(3) Where such a motion or application is granted, a copy of the sheriff's interlocutor shall be served upon the defender along with the warrant of citation.

Applications under section 57C of the Social Security Pensions Act 1975, 1990

(S.I. 1990 No. 2116)

[23rd October 1990]

The Lords of Council and Session, under and by virtue of the powers conferred on them by section 32 of the Sheriff Courts (Scotland) Act 1971 and of all other powers enabling them in that behalf, having approved, with modifications, draft rules submitted to them by the Sheriff Court Rules Council under section 34 of that Act, do hereby enact and declare:

Citation and commencement

1.—(1) This Act of Sederunt may be cited as the Act of Sederunt (Applications under section 57C of the Social Security Pensions Act 1975) 1990 and shall come into force on 12th November 1990.

(2) This Act of Sederunt shall be inserted in the Books of Sederunt.

(3) In this Act of Sederunt, the expression "acting as an insolvency practitioner" has the meaning assigned to it by section 57C(8) of the Social Security Pensions Act 1975.

Application

2. This Act of Sederunt applies to applications under section 57C(6) of the Social Security Pensions Act 1975 for an order requiring a person acting as an insolvency practitioner to discharge his duties under section 57C(2) of that Act.

Procedure

3. An application to which this Act of Sederunt applies shall be made—

(*a*) by note in the process of the proceedings by virtue of which or in relation to which the person acting as insolvency practitioner was appointed; or

(*b*) where there have been no such proceedings, by summary application.

Applications in the Sheriff Court in respect of Defective Company Accounts

(S.I. 1991 No. 24)

[4th February 1991]

The Lords of Council and Session, under and by virtue of the powers conferred on them by section 32 of the Sheriff Courts (Scotland) Act 1971 and of all other powers enabling them in that behalf, having approved draft rules submitted to them by the Sheriff Court Rules Council under section 34 of that Act, do hereby enact and declare:

Citation and commencement

1.—(1) This Act of Sederunt may be cited as the Act of Sederunt (Applications in the Sheriff Court in respect of Defective Company Accounts) 1991 and shall come into force on 4th February 1991.

(2) This Act of Sederunt shall be inserted in the Books of Sederunt.

Applications under section 245B of the Companies Act 1985

2.—(1) An application to the sheriff under section 245B of the Companies Act 1985 (application for declarator that annual accounts of a company do not comply with the requirements of that Act) shall be made by summary application.

(2) A copy of such an application shall be intimated to every director of the company at the time the accounts are approved.

Applications under Part VII of the Companies Act 1989

(S.I. 1991 No. 145)

[25th February 1991]

The Lords of Council and Session, under and by virtue of the powers conferred on them by section 32 of the Sheriff Courts (Scotland) Act 1971 and of all other powers enabling them in that behalf, having approved draft rules submitted to them by the Sheriff Court Rules Council in accordance with section 34 of that Act, do hereby enact and declare:

Citation and commencement

1.—(1) This Act of Sederunt may be cited as the Act of Sederunt ("Applications under Part VII of the Companies Act 1989) 1991 and shall come into force on 25th February 1991.

(2) This Act of Sederunt shall be inserted in the Books of Sederunt.

(3) In this Act of Sederunt, "insolvency proceedings" means proceedings commenced by a petition in accordance with rules 10 (administration orders), 15 (appointment of receiver) or 18 (winding up of a company) of the Act of Sederunt (Sheriff Court Company Insolvency Rules) 1986, a petition for sequestration under sections 5 or 6 of the Bankruptcy (Scotland) Act 1985 or a summary petition under section 11A of the Judicial Factors (Scotland) Act 1889.

Applications under Part VII of the Companies Act 1989

2.—(1) An application for an order or direction under the provisions of the Companies Act 1989 ("the Act") specified in sub-paragraph (2) below shall be made:

(*a*) where there are before the sheriff insolvency proceedings to which the application relates, by note in the process of those proceedings; or

(*b*) where there are no such proceedings before the sheriff, by summary application.

(2) The provisions of the Act referred to in sub-paragraph (1) above are—

(*a*) section 161(1) (interim order in relation to party to market contract dissipating or applying assets to prevent recovery by relevant office-holder);

(*b*) section 161(3) (order altering or dispensing from compliance with duties of relevant office-holder);

(*c*) section 163(4) (direction that profit arising from a sum is not recoverable by relevant office-holder);

(*d*) section 164(4) (direction that profit from a market contract or the amount or value of a margin is not recoverable by relevant office-holder);

(*e*) section 175(2) (order to ensure that charge under a prior or *pari passu* ranked charge is not prejudiced by enforcement of market charge);

(*f*) section 175(5) (direction that profit from a property disposition is not recoverable by relevant office-holder); and

(*g*) section 182(4) (order to achieve same result as if provisions of Schedule 22 to the Act had been in force).

Intimation

3. Without prejudice to any other order in respect of intimation which the sheriff may make, he shall not make an order under section 175(2) of the Act unless intimation has been made to such persons having an interest as he considers necessary and any such person has had an opportunity to be heard.

Proceedings in the Sheriff Court under the Model Law on International Commercial Arbitration 1991

(S.I. 1991 No. 2214)

[2nd October 1991]

The Lords of Council and Session, under and by virtue of the powers conferred on them by section 32 of the Sheriff Courts (Scotland) Act 1971 and of all other powers enabling them in that behalf, having approved, with modifications, draft rules submitted to them by the Sheriff Court Rules Council in accordance with section 34 of that Act, do hereby enact and declare:

Citation and commencement

1.—(1) This Act of Sederunt may be cited as the Act of Sederunt (Proceedings in the Sheriff Court under the Model Law on International Commercial Arbitration) 1991 and shall come into force on 28th October 1991.

(2) This Act of Sederunt shall be inserted in the Books of Sederunt.

(3) In this Act of Sederunt, "the Model Law" means the United Nations Commission on International Trade Law Model Law on International Commercial Arbitration as set out in Schedule 7 to the Law Reform (Miscellaneous Provisions) (Scotland) Act 1990.

Form of application

2.—(1) Subject to sub-paragraph (2), any request or application which may be made to the sheriff under the Model Law shall be made by summary application.

(2) Where proceedings involving the same arbitration and the same parties are already pending before the sheriff under this Act of Sederunt, a further application or request may be made by note in the same process.

(3) The sheriff shall order service of such summary application or note to be made on such persons as he considers appropriate.

Recognition and enforcement of awards

3.—(1) There shall be lodged along with an application under Article 35 of the Model Law—

(*a*) the original arbitration agreement or certified copy thereof; and

(*b*) the duly authenticated original award or certified copy thereof; and

(*c*) where appropriate, a duly certified translation in English of the agreement and award.

(2) An application under this paragraph shall specify whether to the knowledge of the applicant—

(*a*) the arbitral award has been recognised, or is being enforced, in any other jurisdiction; and

(*b*) an application for setting aside or suspension of the arbitral award has been made to a court of the country in which or under whose law the award was made.

(3) Where the sheriff is satisfied that an arbitral award should be recognised and enforced, he shall so order and shall instruct the sheriff clerk to register the award in the Books of the Sheriff Court for execution.

[THE NEXT PAGE IS D601]

Acts of Court and Practice Notes

NOTE

This section reprints the current Acts of Court and Practice Notes of the sheriffdoms of Scotland, so far as notified to the publishers, other than transient measures relating to court sessions and holidays, etc. For court days, see the Courts, Offices, etc. Division, *supra*. Measures now spent although not formally repealed, such as those relating to small debt courts or the suspension of court business during industrial action, have not been reprinted.

Sheriffdom of Glasgow and Strathkelvin

Revised Practice Notes

[August 1982]

I, John Alexander Dick, Q.C., Sheriff Principal of Glasgow and Strathkelvin, for the purpose of regulating practice in the sheriff court at Glasgow, in pursuance of the powers conferred by section 15(2) of the Sheriff Courts (Scotland) Act 1971 and all common law powers enabling in that behalf order and direct as follows:

Section 1—Civil Actions

1.01. The contents of a judicial tender shall not be brought to the notice of a sheriff except at the stage of a cause when he is finally dealing with expenses.

1.02. A tender may be withdrawn before it is accepted only by a minute of withdrawal of tender lodged in process and duly intimated to the agents for the other party or parties forthwith. No minute of judicial tender or minute of withdrawal of such tender may be borrowed by any party from process.

1.03. In all actions in which expenses are awarded against an assisted person it shall not be necessary for the court, unless it thinks fit to order otherwise, to remit the account of expenses of the party in whose favour the award is made to the auditor of court for taxation but the court may, on the motion of any party to the cause, proceed forthwith to determine to what extent the liability of the assisted person for such expenses shall be modified; and where the account of expenses of the party in whose favour the award was made has been remitted for taxation, the case shall call before the sheriff not sooner than the second day after the solicitor has lodged the auditor's report on taxation for approval. The solicitor lodging the report shall simultaneously inform the solicitor of the party liable and both solicitors shall attend such diet.

Conveyancing and Feudal Reform (Scotland) Act 1970

1.04.—(1) The initial writ in an application brought under Part II of the Conveyancing and Feudal Reform (Scotland) Act 1970 and where that is the only crave shall be dealt with as a summary application. It should be headed and backed with the name of the Act and should specify in the crave the section of the Act upon which the remedy sought depends.

(2) An initial writ bearing to be under Part II of the Act but containing a crave for declarator (other than that of declarator for rights under said Part II of the Act) or ejection or interdict or interim interdict shall proceed as an ordinary action.

Section 2—Appeals

2.01. If an appeal is taken against an interlocutor to which the sheriff has not appended a note, the person taking the appeal shall, at the time when he marks the appeal, add a request that the sheriff write a note.

2.02. When, following a proof, an appeal is marked against an interlocutor of a sheriff which has been issued before the notes of evidence are extended and lodged in process, the appellant's solicitor shall inform the shorthand writer forthwith that the notes of evidence are required, and ascertain from him the date when they will be available. When the appeal is to the sheriff principal, the appellant's solicitor shall thereafter inform the sheriff principal's clerk of the date when the notes of evidence will be available in order that an appropriate diet may be fixed for hearing the appeal.

Failure by the appellant or his solicitor to comply with the terms of the two preceding rules, so that there is undue delay in hearing an appeal, or a diet fixed for a hearing is rendered abortive, may be taken into account in determining liability for payment of the expenses of the appeal.

Section 3—Extracts

3.01. All orders for extracts shall be made by written application. Applications for extracts in cases in the ordinary court will be lodged in the general civil department and in other cases in the office of the appropriate department and shall specify the dates of the interlocutors to be extracted. Extracts may be ordered at any time after decree has been pronounced but will not be issued until after the appropriate statutory period has elapsed. The party applying for extract shall be responsible for lodging the process if it is not in the custody of the sheriff clerk at the time when extract may lawfully be issued. The extractor shall not be bound to issue extract if the whole process is not in his hands, but he may do so if he thinks fit.

3.02. Since the sheriff clerk can repay fees only with the authority of H.M. Exchequer, any application for repayment of a fee must be made in writing, giving full particulars and the reason why repayment is desired.

Section 4—Diligence

4.01. The sheriff clerk will cause the backing of each extract decree accompanying a report of poinding to be marked with the date of the poinding to which the report relates, and an entry recording the date of the poinding and the court reference number of the case will also be made in a register of poindings. Before presenting a report of poinding to the sheriff for approval, the sheriff clerk will verify that no earlier poinding has occurred following the decree, and, if there has been an earlier poinding, he will report that fact to the sheriff.

4.02. If warrant of sale is applied for within six months of the date of execution of the poinding, it may be granted, if otherwise lawful, without special inquiry as to whether there has been undue delay in applying for the warrant. If warrant of sale is applied for more than six months after the date of execution of the poinding, application shall be made by minute setting forth the reasons for the delay. The first deliverance on such a minute shall require service on the debtor and appoint objections, if so advised, within seven days. If so required by the sheriff, the solicitor instructing the diligence, or an accredited representative for the creditor, shall appear personally before the sheriff to give such additional information as may be necessary in support of the application.

4.03. Every sheriff officer shall, before carrying out a poinding, inquire of the debtor or other occupier of the premises if any of the goods proposed to be poinded are the subject of a hire purchase agreement or are otherwise the property of a third party and no fee shall be allowed for poinding goods which are not the property of the debtor except on cause shown.

4.04. Where a debtor claims that goods are subject to a hire purchase agreement but refuses, or is unable, to produce evidence to that effect, the sheriff officer may poind the goods but, in that event, shall add a note on the schedule of the poinding to the effect that the debtor has claimed that the goods are subject to a hire purchase agreement.

4.05. A sheriff officer shall not execute a second poinding in the same premises under the same decree on the instructions of the same creditor, unless, in the special circumstances of the case, the sheriff has granted leave to do so. Application for leave will be made by the sheriff officer by minute signed by him and lodged with the sheriff clerk, and the sheriff officer shall appear personally before the sheriff, if so required, to give such additional explanations as may be necessary. The special circumstances which would justify the granting of such leave include—

(*a*) the fact that the debtor has brought into the premises poindable goods which were not in the premises when the first poinding was executed; and

(*b*) the fact that, for reasons beyond the control of the creditor or of the sheriff officer instructed by him, it was impossible to complete the poinding by sale.

4.06. All minutes craving sale of poinded effects shall contain the name and address of the defender, and where the defender resides in premises where several houses are described by the same street number, the house shall be particularised by position and the name of the defender stated.

4.07. When the sheriff grants a warrant of sale, the auctioneer appointed by him shall be a person who, alone or with others, carries on business as an auctioneer, and who is not a whole time employee of the sheriff officer executing the diligence or of any partner or employer of such sheriff officer or of the creditor. If such a person is not available or in warrants of sale proceeding on a decree in a summary cause the sheriff may appoint the sheriff officer acting as judge of the roup or such person as seems to him to be suitably qualified to perform the duties of auctioneer.

4.08. When the sheriff grants a warrant of sale he may appoint as the judge of the roup a sheriff officer, and the sheriff officer so appointed may be the sheriff officer who has executed the poinding.

4.09. When a report of sale is lodged with the sheriff clerk, there shall be written upon the report of sale and signed by the sheriff an interlocutor in the following or similar terms:

"The sheriff remits the report of sale and the documents attached thereto to the auditor of court to tax the account contained therein, to state the balance due to or by the defender as a result of the sale and/or delivery of the poinded goods, and to report."

If, after considering the report of sale, and the auditor's report and any objections thereto, the sheriff approves of the report of sale as taxed, he will sign a docquet "Approved as taxed" which will be written upon the report of sale.

4.10. The report of sale shall state the date when the sale took place.

4.11. When poinded goods of a debtor are exposed for sale and are not sold but are adjudged to the poinding creditor, the debt shall be reduced by the appraised value of such goods, albeit such goods are not removed from the premises by the poinding creditor.

[1] Section 5—Affidavits in Undefended Actions of Divorce other than Simplified Divorces, and of Separation and Aliment and in Opposed Interim Orders under the Matrimonial Homes (Family Protection) (Scotland) Act 1981

NOTE

[1] Added by Practice Note 1984 No. 1, 2 April 1984. The terms of this section have been repeated in Acts of Court or Practice Notes for the other sheriffdoms, but without reference to opposed interim orders under the 1981 Act. Reference should be made also to p.D1011, *infra*, for the sheriffdom of Lothian and Borders.

Precognition

5.01. An affidavit is no substitute for a reliable and adequate precognition though a precognition may eventually be the basis for an affidavit.

Form and content

5.02. The affidavit should be typed on substantial paper, should be backed up longways, and should be stitched or stapled. It must commence with the words "At the day of 19 , in the presence of
Compeared who being solemnly sworn, Depones as follows ". The full name, age, address and occupation must be given, and it must thereafter proceed in the first person and should take the form of numbered paragraphs. The witness should be made to appreciate the importance of the affidavit. The witness must be placed on oath, or must affirm, and each page will require to be signed by both the witness and the notary. It is not essential that it should be sealed by the notary. The document should be of a shape and size convenient to be lodged as part of the process. The affidavit should end with the words "All of which is truth as the Deponent shall answer to God," or "All of which is affirmed to be true," as appropriate.

5.03. Affidavits of parties and witnesses should follow step by step the averments in the initial writ. The drafter of an affidavit should provide himself, before drawing it, with a copy of the initial writ, a copy of the appropriate precognition, and the relative productions. The affidavit to be taken from a witness should follow the averments in the initial writ to the extent that these are within the knowledge of that particular witness. It is not a requirement that the wording of an affidavit should follow exactly the wording of the initial writ.

[*Hearsay*]

[1] **5.04.** [*No hearsay.*] The drafter must take care that an affidavit [contains only matters of fact to which the party or the witness in question can testify, and that it] is correct at the date at which it is sworn.

NOTE

[1] Words in square brackets deleted by practice note, June 1991, by the Sheriff Principal of Glasgow and Strathkelvin.

Person before whom taken

5.05. On the matter of the qualification of the person before whom the affidavit is taken, the rules provide that the affidavit is admissible if it is duly emitted before a notary public or other competent authority. This means a notary public, justice of the peace, commissioner for oaths or other statutory authority within the meaning of the Statutory Declarations Act 1835. In the examples given hereafter, it is assumed that the affidavit is in fact taken before a solicitor who is a notary public and therefore the references to the party before whom the affidavit is sworn are "the notary". The solicitor acting in the action may well be called also to act in a notarial capacity when the affidavit is subsequently sworn. This is permissible. In acting in a notarial capacity he must, however, as a competent authority, observe all the normal rules in this connection, and must satisfy himself as to the capacity of the witness to make the statement, and ensure that the witness understands that it constitutes his or her evidence in the case.

Productions

5.06. On the matter of productions, those required, when an affidavit is being taken, may already have been lodged in process, but there may be some productions (such as photographs) which are produced by the witness to the notary when the affidavit is sworn, and which may not by that time have been lodged in process.

5.07. Productions already lodged in process must be borrowed up, and put to the party or the witness who makes them part of his or her evidence in the appropriate part of the affidavit. Each production will require to be referred to in the affidavit by its number of process and must be docqueted and signed by the party or witness and the notary. If a production has not yet been lodged when the affidavit is being taken, it will require to be identified by the witness in his evidence in the affidavit, and will then be docqueted with regard to the affidavit and signed by the party or witness and the notary. It will then be lodged as a production. Obviously, certain productions will be docqueted with regard to more than one affidavit.

[1] **5.08.** In adultery cases, photographs of both the pursuer and the defender will require to be produced, put to the appropriate party or witnesses in the affidavit, and signed and docqueted with reference thereto in the manner already described. [In certain circumstances, a photograph may have to be identified and docqueted by more than one person, as in the case of the photograph of a party requiring to be spoken to by the pursuer and two inquiry agents.]

NOTE

[1] Words in square brackets deleted by practice note, June 1991, by the Sheriff Principal of Glasgow and Strathkelvin.

Date of affidavit

5.09. All affidavits lodged must be of as recent a date as is possible in the circumstances. This factor is particularly important in (1) cases involving children; (2) those in which financial craves are involved; or (3) in any other circumstances where the evidence of a party or witness is liable to change through the passage of time. The notary will require to ensure, therefore, that an affidavit represents the deponent's evidence on such matters at the time the affidavit is sworn.

Custody of or access to children

5.10. In actions of divorce or separation and aliment involving custody of or access to children, an affidavit or affidavits providing corroborating evidence about the welfare of the children should be provided. The evidence of that witness must present the court with a full picture of the position regarding the child or children. It is, however, clear that such independent evidence in no way relieves the pursuer from testifying fully the position regarding the children in his or her own affidavit, so far as within his or her knowledge. Whatever else the affidavits of the pursuer and the independent witness contain, their evidence should certainly include the following:–

(*a*) the qualifications of the witness, if not a parent, to speak about the child; how often, for example, and in what circumstances, does the witness normally see the child;

(*b*) a description of the home conditions in which the child lives;

(*c*) observations upon the child's general appearance, interests, state of health and well being;

(*d*) information, where relevant, about the school the child attends; whether and to what extent he has contact with other children and relatives;

(*e*) observations on the relationship between the child and the person in whose care he or she lives, on the child's attitude towards each of the parents and on the extent of contact with the parent or parents with whom the child is not living;

(*f*) details of child care arrangements at all times including arrangements during working hours (outwith school hours);

(*g*) the means and status of the person craving custody with a view to enabling him or her to maintain and bring up the child in a suitable manner.

5.11. The attention of solicitors is drawn to the provisions of the Matrimonial Proceedings (Children) Act 1958. The court will not (unless the provisions of section 8(2) are shown to apply) grant decree of divorce until the court is satisfied as respects every child for whose custody, maintenance and education the court has jurisdiction to make provision in that action (a) that arrangements have been made for the care and upbringing of the child and that those arrangements are satisfactory or are the best which can be devised in the circumstances; or (b) that it is impracticable for the party or parties appearing before the court to make any such arrangements.

Financial craves

5.12 Where financial craves are involved, it is even more important that the evidence is full, accurate and up to date. In parole proofs the evidence of the pursuer and the witnesses on these matters can be supplemented at the proof by questions from the bench or from the solicitor for the pursuer. This will not be possible where evidence is taken by affidavit, and the affidavits must be so framed as to exclude the necessity for supplementary questions. Failure to do so may result in the sheriff requiring the attendance of the solicitor in court. If, after an affidavit has been taken, and the solicitor concerned has parted with it, a material change of circumstances occurs, it is essential that the court be immediately informed, and where necessary, that a further affidavit be sworn.

5.13. Where the pursuer in an action is speaking in the affidavit of the financial position of the defender, it is essential that the affidavit should state the date, as precisely as possible, at which that information was valid. Otherwise it may be assumed by the court that the pursuer is speaking to the defender's position at the date of the affidavit. The court must be provided with as up to date information as possible about the defender's ability to pay the sums the pursuer is seeking, and these sums should be such as that evidence justifies. The pursuer must, of course, speak also to his or her own financial position, at the date of the affidavit. Where the pursuer cannot obtain recent information as to the defender's means, it is suggested that, if the pursuer's advisers approve, assessment should be left to the sheriff, and in such cases it may be that the solicitors representing the pursuer would be willing to incorporate in the terms of the minute for decree, after the words "in terms of the crave of the initial writ" the words "or such other sum (or sums) as the court may think proper."

Minute for decree

5.14. The minute for decree in actions of divorce and separation and aliment must be signed by a solicitor who has examined the affidavits and other documents and takes responsibility therefor, whether or not he is the person who drew the initial writ or affidavits.

Consents

5.15. In consent cases, the defender's written consent form will also have to be borrowed up, put to the pursuer in his or her affidavit, and docqueted and identified in the same way as other productions.

Joint minutes

5.16. Affidavit procedure will not prevent the parties to the action agreeing the financial or other ancillary craves by joint minute. For so long as these ancillary craves are opposed, the affidavit procedure cannot be used for them, but it can be used for the merits of the action. If a joint minute is signed before an affidavit or supplementary affidavit is emitted by the pursuer, that affidavit must refer to the arrangements in the joint minute. Decree of divorce will not be granted before any issues relating to financial provisions consequent upon the divorce which require to be decided by the court, have been so decided.

5.17. Where the pursuer has craved a capital allowance, a periodical allowance, aliment for the child or children, or expenses, and in the minute for decree does not seek decree for one or any of these, it is essential that the reasons for this are fully narrated in the affidavit. Where these reasons are capable of corroboration by witnesses, they should be dealt with in the witnesses' affidavits.

5.18. Solicitors are reminded that the normal rules of evidence about corroboration still apply except in actions of divorce where—

(*a*) the action is brought in reliance on the facts set out in section 1(2)(*d*) (two years' non-cohabitation and the defender's consent to decree) or in section 1(2)(*e*) (five years' non-cohabitation) of the Divorce (Scotland) Act 1976;

(*b*) no other proceedings are pending in any court which could have the effect of bringing the marriage to an end;

(*c*) there are no children of the marriage under the age of 16 years;

(*d*) neither party applies for an order for financial provision on divorce; and

(*e*) neither party suffers from mental disorder within the meaning of section 6 of the Mental Health (Scotland) Act 1960.

Practice by Solicitors which would Assist the Running of the Sheriff Court at Glasgow

1. Solicitors who appear professionally at the bar of all courts in open session are expected to wear gowns.

2. That where solicitors are engaged in two or more summary trials on the same day, if they inform the procurator fiscal by letter of that fact at least 14 days before the date of the diets of trial setting out (1) the full names of the party or parties whom they represent and (2) in criminal prosecutions where their client or clients are charged with others, the full name of the accused first named in the complaint, the procurator fiscal, whenever possible, will arrange to allocate these trials to the same sheriff.

3. That it would be helpful to the sheriff if solicitors, at the time they lodged documentary productions in process, lodged, if possible, for the use of the sheriff, one copy of each production clearly marked with the number of the process not later than 48 hours before the debate or proof at which said productions are to be referred to or put in evidence.

4. All processes must be returned to the sheriff clerk and all adjustments marked on the process not later than 12 o'clock noon of the day preceding any diet or the date on which they appear on the rolls of the court if the court is to function properly.

5. It is helpful if the solicitor for each party to an action in which a debate has been fixed, not later than 10 a.m. on the day before a debate, lodges with the sheriff clerk a note of all authorities to which reference is to be made in the course of the argument for the party whom he represents.

6. When moving for a date to be fixed for a proof or debate, solicitors at that time should be prepared, so far as possible, to inform the court of the reasonably estimated duration of said proof or debate.

7. That it is helpful and facilitates the reading of records, that when records are prepared, that the answers for the defender should be inset from the margin used for the pleadings of the pursuer and that all interlocutors in the cause to the date of making up the record should be reproduced.

8. Solicitors engaged in two or more civil proofs on the same day before different sheriffs, should inform the sheriff clerk by letter of that fact at least 14 days before the date of the diets or proof setting out (1) the full names of the party or parties whom they represent and (2) the full names of the other party or parties. The sheriff clerk will, wherever possible and convenient, then arrange to allocate these proofs and debates to the same sheriff.

9. When, in any action in which a diet of proof or debate or appeal has been fixed, a solicitor for any party is no longer prepared to act for his client and has so informed his client, it would be helpful if, at the same time, he would also intimate that fact in writing to the solicitors for all parties to the action or appeal and also to the sheriff clerk.

10. When a settlement has been reached in any case and as a result of that settlement a proof or debate or appeal will not proceed on the date which has been fixed, it would be helpful if the solicitors acting in the case would, at once, intimate the position by telephone to the sheriff clerk and confirm such intimation in writing.

11. Where there is an appeal to the sheriff principal, any parts of process in a case on appeal must be returned to the sheriff principal's clerk not later than 10 a.m. on the day before the diet of hearing.

12. The solicitors for each party to an action under appeal, should, if possible, not later than 10 a.m. on the day before the diet of hearing, lodge with the sheriff principal's clerk a note of all authorities to which reference is to be made in the course of the argument for the party he represents.

Practice Note

[25th April 1990]

I, Norman Donald MacLeod, Q.C., Sheriff Principal of Glasgow and Strathkelvin, for the purpose of regulating practice in the Sheriff Court at Glasgow, in exercise of the powers conferred by section 15(2) of the Sheriff Courts (Scotland) Act 1971 and all common law powers enabling in that behalf, hereby recall paragraph 1.04, "Conveyancing and Feudal Reform (Scotland) Act 1970," and paragraph 4, "Diligence," of the practice note issued on 1 June 1982.

This Note shall come into force on 1 May 1990.

Any act done in accordance with the provisions of said paragraphs prior to said date shall continue to have effect as if the same had not been recalled.

Norman D. MacLeod,
Sheriff Principal of Glasgow and Strathkelvin

[THE NEXT PAGE IS D 701]

Sheriffdom of North Strathclyde

Practice Note

[23rd December 1976]

SUMMARY CAUSE—EXPENSES

This practice note is directed to ensure that the determination of awards of expenses in actions of delivery in summary causes shall proceed on a uniform basis throughout the Sheriffdom of North Strathclyde.

The Act of Sederunt (Alteration of Sheriff Court Fees) 1971 as amended by subsequent Acts of Sederunt and in particular by the Act of Sederunt (Solicitors Fees) 1976, section 2(*f*), requires a reduction in the solicitors' fees prescribed of 25 per cent. when the action is of a value from £50 to £250 and 50 per cent. when the action is of a value of less than £50 and makes special provisions for certain specified forms of action which do not include actions for delivery.

Where the pursuer fails to specify a value for the article or articles which he seeks to have delivered it is not possible to comply with the provision in the act of sederunt. Therefore I hereby direct that:

(i) in an action of delivery the value of the article or articles should be stated at the market value of the articles having regard to depreciation or appreciation from the value as new;

(ii) the reduction of 50 per cent. of fees shall apply in all cases of delivery where the value of the article is not stated;

(iii) in summonses where the crave for delivery is accompanied by alternative or ancillary craves for payment and the value of the article or articles sought to be delivered is not specified, the basis for calculation of fees shall be the amount of the alternative or ancillary craves;

(iv) where the value of the article is specified and there are in addition craves for payment the basis for calculation of fees shall be the aggregate of the value of the article and the total of the sums on the additional craves.

F. W. F. O'Brien,
Sheriff Principal of North Strathclyde

Practice Note

[23rd May 1977]

UNDEFENDED CONSISTORIAL PROOFS—RECORDING OF EVIDENCE

This practice note is directed to ensure that the practice in regard to recording of evidence in undefended consistorial actions shall apply uniformly throughout the Sheriffdom of North Strathclyde. I accordingly direct as follows, viz:

In any undefended consistorial action it shall not be necessary to have the evidence recorded by a shorthand writer unless the sheriff in his interlocutor allowing proof appoints the evidence to be so recorded either *ex proprio motu* or on the motion of the pursuer.

F. W. F. O'Brien,
Sheriff Principal of North Strathclyde

Act of Court

[18th November 1977]

PRACTICE—CONVEYANCING AND FEUDAL REFORM (SCOTLAND) ACT 1970

I hereby direct as follows:-

1. The initial writ in any application under Part II of the Conveyancing and Feudal Reform (Scotland) Act 1970 shall be dealt with as a summary application. It should be headed and backed with the name of the Act, and should specify in the crave the section of said Act upon which the remedy sought depends.

2. An initial writ bearing to be under the said Part of the abovementioned Act but containing a crave for interdict or interim interdict or other crave ancillary to the specific remedy provided in the said Act shall not be entitled to a first deliverance as a miscellaneous application without the prior approval of the Sheriff.

F. W. F. O'Brien,
Sheriff Principal of North Strathclyde

Practice Note

[1] [20th November 1978]

APPEALS

NOTE
[1] As amended, 23rd December 1983 and 6th April 1989.

This practice note is directed to ensure that when an appeal is marked against an interlocutor to which the sheriff has not appended a note that he may be given the opportunity of providing such a note following that interlocutor as soon as possible and that diets of appeal are assigned to suit, so far as possible, both the convenience of parties to the cause and the court. I accordingly direct as follows, viz:

(1) That when an appeal is marked against an interlocutor to which the sheriff has not appended a note, the person marking the appeal shall, at the time of marking, add a request that the sheriff should write a note. The sheriff shall thereafter provide such note as may be appropriate in terms of rule 82 of the Sheriff Courts (Scotland) Act 1907 [rule 89 of the Schedule as amended—Ed.]; and

(2) That, within 10 days of marking an appeal or receiving intimation that an appeal has been marked, parties shall provide the Secretary to the Sheriff Principal, Sheriff Court House, St James Street, Paisley, with a note of any dates within the ensuing six week period (excluding periods of court vacation) on which they, or their legal representatives, do not wish the appeal to be heard. Reasons must be given in support of such representations. When assigning the diet of appeal the sheriff principal will take into account, but not be bound by, such representations, particularly as regards urgent matters.

(3) Not later than two clear working days prior to the diet of hearing, the solicitors for each party to an action under appeal shall lodge a note of all authorities to which reference is to be made in the course of argument for the party he represents with the Secretary to the Sheriff Principal, Sheriff Court House, St James Street, Paisley, and shall send a copy of said note to the sheriff clerk of the court where the appeal is to be heard.

John A. Dick,
Sheriff Principal of North Strathclyde

Act of Court

[6th August 1979]

Practice—Petitions for Admission as Sheriff Officer

I, John Alexander Dick, M.C., Q.C., Sheriff Principal of North Strathclyde, considering that it is desirable that the business interests in debt collecting, if any, of a petitioner for admission as an officer of the sheriff court should be ascertained prior to admission, hereby direct:

1. That where a petitioner has any business interest in debt collecting, direct or indirect, present or prospective, or an intention to acquire any such interest at the date of the petition, he shall include in his petition for admission detailed averments of the nature and extent of that interest or proposed interest.

2. That where a petitioner has no such business interest, direct or indirect as aforesaid, he shall include such an averment in his petition for admission and produce therewith a certificate signed by him to that effect and containing an undertaking that in the event of his forming an intention in the future to acquire any such interest he shall inform the court before doing so or in the event of his succeeding to or however acquiring any such interest he shall inform the court thereof as soon as possible.

Act of Court

[21st September 1979]

Commissary Business

I, John Alexander Dick, M.C., Q.C., Sheriff Principal of North Strathclyde, considering that it is necessary and desirable for the purpose and the application of the Act of Sederunt (Commissary Business) 1975 to make further provision for the efficient administration of the commissary business arising in the sheriffdom after 1st October 1979, direct that:—

1. With effect from 1st October 1979 the inventories of the estates of deceased persons should be presented to the sheriff court of the sheriff court district in which they were last ordinarily resident; or if presented elsewhere forwarded to that court for issue of confirmation and recording. This shall apply whether the death occurred prior to or after 1st October 1979. The exceptions to the foregoing general direction are in respect of the sheriff court districts of Dunoon, Rothesay, Oban and Campbeltown. Inventories of the estates of deceased persons who resided in the sheriff court districts of Dunoon and Rothesay should be lodged at Greenock Sheriff Court; inventories of the estates of deceased persons who resided in the sheriff court district of Oban should be lodged at Dumbarton Sheriff Court; and inventories of the estates of deceased persons who resided in the sheriff court district of Campbeltown should be lodged at Paisley Sheriff Court; or if such inventories are presented elsewhere forwarded to the appropriate above court for issue of confirmation and recording.

2. Petitions for appointment of executors-dative should be lodged and published in the sheriff court of the district in which the deceased last ordinarily resided.

. . . . . .

4. Subject to the following provisions of this order, all additional and corrective inventories, inventories *ad non executa*, inventories *ad omissa* and additional oaths shall be considered as steps in the original confirmation and shall be lodged in the sheriff court in the commissariot in which the confirmation was granted, or the sheriff court which holds the records of the original application for confirmation.

5. The sheriff of any court in which a commissary application is made (a) may remit that application to another court, and (b) may require an applicant who has applied as executor-dative in any other court within the sheriffdom to produce an extract decree of the appointment.

6. In the oath to an inventory or in a petition for appointment of executor it shall be sufficient to refer to the deceased's domicile as being within the Sheriffdom of North Strathclyde in Scotland.

Act of Court

[28th February 1980]

I, John Alexander Dick, Esquire, M.C., Q.C., Sheriff Principal of North Strathclyde, by virtue of the provisions of section 17(1)(*c*) of the Sheriff Courts (Scotland) Act 1971, do hereby prescribe arrangements for registering deeds in the court books of the Sheriffdom of North Strathclyde as follows, viz:

Protests of bills of exchange and deeds shall be registered relative to the sheriff court districts of Paisley and Campbeltown at Paisley Sheriff Court; to the sheriff court districts to Greenock, Dunoon and Rothesay at Greenock Sheriff Court; to the sheriff court districts of Dumbarton and Oban at Dumbarton Sheriff Court; to the sheriff court district of Kilmarnock at Kilmarnock Sheriff Court.

Act of Court

[12th November 1980]

I, John Alexander Dick, M.C., Q.C., Sheriff Principal of North Strathclyde, considering that it is desirable to achieve and maintain a reasonable degree of uniformity in the administration and practice in the separate courts of this sheriffdom, hereby constitute a committee to be known as the "North Strathclyde Sheriff Clerks' Committee" which shall have the constitution, functions and procedural rules prescribed in the Schedule annexed hereto.

SCHEDULE

Constitution

1. The committee shall consist of the sheriff clerks of Paisley, Kilmarnock, Dumbarton and Greenock. The chairman shall be the sheriff clerk at Paisley.

Dates and places of meetings etc.

2. Meetings shall be held once during each session of court at Paisley or at one of said other courts at said places and on dates to be mutually agreed and arranged by the sheriff clerk at Paisley. Additional meetings, if necessary, may be held if the committee so resolves.

Functions of the committee

3. The committee shall take into consideration any matter affecting all the courts in the sheriffdom referred to it by the sheriff principal or raised by any of its members at any meeting concerning the efficiency and uniformity overall of the administration of the sheriff courts in North Strathclyde and such administrative arrangements or requirements arising from new legislation or decisions as may be necessary with a view to achieving reasonable uniformity in practice throughout the courts in the sheriffdom; and shall make agreed recommendations as they think proper from time to time to the sheriff principal for the achievement, so far as reasonable and possible, of these ends.

Practice Note

[1st April 1983]

Diligence—Poinding and Sale

This practice note is directed to ensure that the procedures of poinding and sale shall apply in a uniform manner throughout the Sheriffdom of North Strathclyde.

I hereby direct as follows:

Poinding

1.—(*a*) It is not necessary to obtain a warrant of concurrence under section 13 of the Debtors (Scotland) Act 1838 on a decree granted by a court within the sheriffdom for the purpose of poinding moveables of the defender named in said decree where the moveables are situated in another sheriff court district of the sheriffdom.

(*b*) Every report of a poinding and all applications for orders or warrants relating to poinded moveables and the report of any sale thereof shall be lodged with or made to the court of the sheriff court district in which the poinded moveables are situated.

(*c*) There shall be discontinued any practice whereby the sheriff clerk of a court which has received the report of a poinding proceeding on a decree granted outwith the sheriffdom is required to notify the court which granted the decree of the receipt of the report.

2.—(*a*) Every sheriff officer shall, before carrying out a poinding, inquire of the debtor if any of the goods proposed to be poinded are the subject of a hire purchase agreement or are otherwise the property of a third party and no fee shall be allowed for poinding goods which are not the property of the debtor except on cause shown.

(*b*) Where a debtor claims that goods are subject to a hire purchase agreement but refuses, or is unable, to produce evidence to that effect, the sheriff officer may poind the goods, but, in that event, shall add a note on the schedule of the poinding to the effect that the debtor has claimed that the goods are subject to a hire purchase agreement. No fee shall be allowed for poinding the goods if the debtor subsequently establishes that the goods were so subject.

Duration of poinding

3.—(*a*) If warrant to sell is applied for within six months of the date of execution of the poinding it may be granted, if otherwise lawful, without enquiry as to whether there has been undue delay in applying for the warrant.

(*b*) If warrant to sell is applied for more than six months after the date of execution of the poinding, said application shall be made by the creditor or his solicitor in the form of a minute which shall set forth the circumstances of the reasons for the delay. The first deliverance on such a minute shall require service on the debtor and appoint objections, if so desired, within seven days. If so required by the sheriff, the solicitor instructing the diligence, or an authorised representative of the creditor, shall appear personally before the sheriff to give additional information as may be necessary in support of the application.

Second poinding

4. A sheriff officer shall not execute a second poinding in the same premises under the same decree on the instructions of the same creditor unless the debtor has brought into the premises poindable goods which were not in the premises when the first poinding was executed.

Appointment of judge of roup

5. When the sheriff grants a warrant of sale he may appoint as the judge of the roup a sheriff officer, and the sheriff officer so appointed may be the sheriff officer who has executed the poinding.

Appointment of auctioneer

6. In granting a warrant of sale, the sheriff shall have a discretion to appoint an auctioneer. In summary causes a sheriff officer may be appointed and in ordinary actions if an auctioneer is appointed by him, the auctioneer shall be a person who, alone or with others, carries on business as an auctioneer, and who is not a whole time employee of the sheriff officer executing the diligence or of any partner or employer of such sheriff officer or of the creditor. If such a person is not available the sheriff may appoint such person as seems to him to be suitably qualified to perform the duties of auctioneer.

Date of sale

7. The report of sale will state the date when the sale took place.

Report of sale

8. When a report of sale is lodged with the sheriff clerk, there shall be written upon the report of sale and signed by the sheriff an interlocutor in the following or similar terms:—

> "The sheriff remits the report of sale and the documents attached thereto to the auditor of court to tax the account contained therein, to state the balance due to or by the defender as a result of the sale and/or delivery of the poinded goods, and to report".

The remit to the auditor of court which, under existing practice, is included at the end of the warrant of sale, shall in future be deleted therefrom. If, after considering the report of sale, and the auditor's report and any objections thereto, the sheriff approves of the report of sale as taxed, he will sign a docquet "Approved as taxed" which will be written upon the report of sale.

Unsold poinded goods

9. When poinded goods of a debtor are exposed for sale and are not sold but are delivered to the poinding creditor, the debt shall be reduced by the appraised value of such goods, albeit such goods are not removed from the premises by the poinding creditor.

R. A. Bennett,
Sheriff Principal of North Strathclyde

Practice Note

[14th March 1984]

CITATION

I, Philip Isaac Caplan, Q.C., Sheriff Principal of North Strathclyde, in order to put an end to the practice in civil proceedings of attaching a variety of unauthorised notices to service documents prior to service or enclosing such notices with the service document in the citation envelope, do hereby direct in respect of civil proceedings within the Sheriffdom of North Strathclyde that as from the date hereof no document shall be served on or transmitted to the defender or respondent along with the service document other than such notice as is prescribed or required by law.

Practice Note

[30th March 1984]

Notes by the Sheriff Principal of North Strathclyde for the guidance of solicitors in relation to affidavit evidence in undefended divorce actions other than simplified divorces.

[The terms of the Notes are identical to Section 5 of the Practice Notes of Glasgow and Strathkelvin (p. **D** 604, *supra*).]

Act of Court

[14th June 1988]

COMMISSARY BUSINESS

I, Philip Isaac Caplan, Q.C., Sheriff Principal of North Strathclyde, considering that it is necessary and desirable for the purpose and the application of the Act of Sederunt (Commissary Business) 1975 to make further provision for the efficient administration of the commissary business arising in the sheriffdom after 1st July 1988, direct that:—

1. With effect from 1st July 1988 the inventories of the estates of deceased persons should be presented to the sheriff court of the sheriff court district in which they were last ordinarily resident; or if presented elsewhere forwarded to that court for issue of confirmation and recording. This shall apply whether the death occurred prior to or after 1st July 1988. The exceptions to the foregoing general direction are in respect of the sheriff court districts of Dunoon, Rothesay, Oban and Campbeltown. Inventories of the estates of deceased persons who resided in the sheriff court districts of Dunoon and and Rothesay should be lodged at Greenock Sheriff Court; inventories of the estates of deceased persons who resided in the sheriff court districts of Campbeltown and Oban should be lodged at Dumbarton Sheriff Court, or, if such inventories are presented elsewhere, forwarded to the appropriate above court for issue of confirmation and recording.

[The subsequent terms of this Act of Court are identical to sections 2–6 of the Act of Court of 21st September 1979 (p. **D** 703, *supra.*)]

Act of Court

[14th June 1988]

Registration of Deeds

I, Philip Isaac Caplan, Q.C., Sheriff Principal of North Strathclyde by virtue of the provisions of section 17(1)(*c*) of the Sheriff Courts (Scotland) Act 1971, do hereby prescribe arrangements for registering deeds in the court books of the Sheriffdom of North Strathclyde as follows, viz.:

Protests of bills of exchange and deeds shall be registered relative to the sheriff court district of Paisley at Paisley Sheriff Court; to the sheriff court districts of Greenock, Dunoon and Rothesay at Greenock Sheriff Court; to the sheriff court districts of Campbeltown, Dumbarton and Oban at Dumbarton Sheriff Court; to the sheriff court district at Kilmarnock at Kilmarnock Sheriff Court.

Practice Note

[13th December 1989]

This practice note is directed to ensure that the court can ascertain at any time whether or not a party to a civil cause is legally represented and, if so, by whom. Accordingly I direct as follows, viz:

1. The name and address of the *principal agent(s)* shall be stated on each part of process lodged in court.

2. When, in the course of litigation, a solicitor either withdraws from acting for a party to a cause or accepts instructions to act for a party to a cause, he shall notify immediately that fact *in writing* to the sheriff clerk of the relevant court. Such notice shall specify (a) the process number; (b) the names of the litigants; and (c) the particular litigant to whom the notice relates.

3. On receipt of such notice the sheriff clerk shall attach it to the interlocutor sheets, failing which to the initiating document, i.e. the initial writ, summary application, petition, summary cause summons, small claims summons, etc.

R. C. Hay,
Sheriff Principal of North Strathclyde

Practice Note

[18th May 1990]

Notice of Authorities for Proofs or Debates

This practice note is directed to ensure that sufficient notice of authorities to which reference is to be made is given to the court. I accordingly direct as follows, viz:

Not later than two clear working days prior to the diet the solicitor for each party to an action in which a proof or debate has been fixed shall lodge with the sheriff clerk a note of all authorities to which reference is to be made in the course of the argument for the party whom he represents.

R. C. Hay,
Sheriff Principal of North Strathclyde

Practice Note

[18th May 1990]

SHERIFF COURT, PAISLEY: AVOIDANCE OF CONGESTION IN CORRIDORS

This practice note is directed to ensure that congestion in the corridors of Paisley Sheriff Court is kept to a minimum. I accordingly direct as follows, viz.

1. Interviews between solicitors and clients should not take place in the main hall and corridors of the sheriff court, Paisley. Use should be made of the interview rooms provided.

2. Members of the public attending the court must not loiter in corridors, but should make their way to court rooms or witness rooms as directed.

R. C. Hay,
Sheriff Principal of North Strathclyde

[THE NEXT PAGE IS D 801]

Sheriffdom of South Strathclyde, Dumfries and Galloway

Act of Court No. 1 of 1977

[23rd November 1977]

PRACTICE—CONVEYANCING AND FEUDAL REFORM (SCOTLAND) ACT 1970

I, Charles Hampton Johnston, Q.C., Sheriff Principal of South Strathclyde, Dumfries and Galloway, hereby direct as follows:—

1. The initial writ in any application under Part II of the above-mentioned Act shall be headed and backed with the name of the Act, and shall be dealt with as a summary application.

2. An initial writ bearing to be under the said Part of the above-mentioned Act but containing a crave for interdict or interim interdict alone or along with other craves shall not be accepted for warranting without the approval of the sheriff.

Act of Court No. 1 of 1978

[15th February 1978]

HAMILTON SHERIFF COURT STANDING ADVISORY COMMITTEE

I, Charles Hampton Johnston, Q.C., Sheriff Principal of South Strathclyde, Dumfries and Galloway, after consultation with the Dean of the Society of Solicitors of Hamilton, the regional procurator fiscal of South Strathclyde, Dumfries and Galloway and the sheriff clerk of Hamilton, hereby constitute a committee to be known as the "Hamilton Sheriff Court Standing Advisory Committee", which shall have the constitution, functions and procedural rules prescribed in the schedule annexed hereto.

[1] SCHEDULE

NOTE

[1] As amended, 31st May 1983.

Constitution

1. The committee shall consist of one sheriff nominated by the sheriff principal, two solicitors nominated by the Dean of the Society of Solicitors of Hamilton, two persons of the rank of assistant procurator fiscal or procurator fiscal depute nominated by the regional procurator fiscal of South Strathclyde, Dumfries and Galloway and the heads of each of the criminal and civil departments, for the time being, of the sheriff clerk at Hamilton. The chairman shall be the nominated sheriff. Failing the attendance of the chairman at any meeting, a person shall be elected to act as chairman by the members present at the meeting. In the event of equality of votes with regard to any proposed recommendation, the chairman for the time being shall have a casting vote in addition to his deliberative vote. The secretary of the committee shall be a sheriff clerk depute not being already a member of the committee and shall be appointed by the sheriff clerk to perform that office. It shall be open to the sheriff clerk to nominate a sheriff clerk depute other than the secretary to attend to the functions of secretary if the secretary is for any reason not available. The sheriff principal, the Dean of the Society of Solicitors of Hamilton, the regional procurator fiscal of South Strathclyde, Dumfries and Galloway and the sheriff clerk of Hamilton are hereinafter referred to as "the constituents".

Appointment of secretary and nomination and period of service of members

2. The name of the person appointed to be the secretary shall be intimated to the constituents on or before 28th February 1978 by the sheriff clerk of Hamilton, and similar intimation will be made on the occasion of any change in the appointment.

The names and addresses of the persons nominated as members of the committee shall be sent to the secretary by the constituents on or before 31st March 1978 and on or before 31st March in each year thereafter. The members will serve for one year from 1st May following their nomination and they may be renominated for further periods of service. In the event of the death or resignation of a member during such period of service, another person shall be nominated by the appropriate constituent to replace such member for the remainder of the period. In the event of a member being unable to attend any meeting, such member may be represented by a nominee of the affected constituent for the purposes of that meeting only and shall have the same rights at that meeting as if such nominee were a full member of the committee.

Dates and place of meetings, etc.

3. Meetings of the committee will be held as necessary and at least once a year.

Members of the committee will inform the secretary, a fortnight before each meeting, of matters to be included in the agenda, and the secretary will send a copy of the agenda, together with a draft minute of any previous meeting, to each member a week before the meeting. The committee may appoint sub-committees from time to time to perform specific functions delegated to them by the committee. Persons other than members may be invited to attend meetings of the committee or of sub-committees and to take part in their discussions.

Functions of the committee

4. The committee shall take into consideration any matter affecting the efficiency of the administrative arrangements of the sheriff court in Hamilton, which they are asked by any of the constituents or by any member of the committee to take into consideration, and shall make such recommendations as they think proper from time to time with regard to such matters to the constituents or to any of them. A recommendation of the committee shall require the approval of a meeting attended by at least one nominee of each constituent. Any such recommendation shall be communicated in writing by the secretary to constituents.

Act of Court No. 4 of 1981

[18th August 1981]

Practice—Sterling Equivalent of Foreign Currency

I, Frederick William Fitzgerald O'Brien, Q.C., Interim Sheriff Principal of South Strathclyde, Dumfries and Galloway, in view of the decision of the

First Division of the Court of Session in the case of *Commerzbank Aktiengesellschaft* v. *Large*, 1977 S.L.T. 219, hereby direct as follows:

Where in any action payment is craved of a sum of money in a foreign currency or the sterling equivalent thereof at the date of payment or at the date of extract, whichever is the earlier, with or without interest, and decree has been granted in these terms, an extract may proceed upon a minute by the party in whose favour decree has been granted or his agent, endorsed on or annexed to the summons or initial writ, stating the rate of exchange prevailing at the close of business on the preceding day and the sterling equivalent at that rate of the sum decerned for in foreign currency, craving extract accordingly and accompanied by a certificate, which may be in the form provided in the schedule hereto, from one of the Scottish clearing banks certifying the said rate and sterling equivalent; and the extract shall bear a reference to said certificate.

SCHEDULE

Form of Certificate

I (*designation and address*) certify that the rate current in London for the purchase of (state the unit of the foreign currency in which the decree is expressed) at the close of business on the . . . . day of . . . . 19 (being the date preceding that on which extract of the decree is requested) was . . . . to the £ sterling and at this rate the sum of (state the amount of the sum in the decree) amounts to £ . . . .

Dated the . . . . . . day of . . . . 198 .

Signed for or on behalf of the Bank

Manager or other official

Act of Court No. 4 of 1982

[25th May 1982]

Taxation of Professional Accounts

I, Ronald Alistair Bennett, Q.C., Sheriff Principal of the Sheriffdom of South Strathclyde, Dumfries and Galloway, hereby direct that it shall not be necessary for solicitors suing for the recovery of professional fees to have their accounts taxed by the auditor of court before decree, except when the account is challenged by the defender(s).

Act of Court No. 5 of 1982

[25th May 1982]

Reports of Sale of Poinded Effects

I, Ronald Alistair Bennett, Q.C., Sheriff Principal of South Strathclyde, Dumfries and Galloway, hereby direct that upon a report of sale being lodged, the sheriff shall remit the account of expenses of the poinding and sale to the sheriff clerk for assessment and report and no fee shall be exigible from any party in respect of such assessment and report.

Act of Court No. 7 of 1982

[4th June 1982]

Summary Cause—Form Q—Inquiries from Solicitors

I, Ronald Alistair Bennett, Q.C., Sheriff Principal of South Strathclyde, Dumfries and Galloway, hereby direct that there shall be no obligation upon sheriff clerks to make provision for dealing with telephone inquiries from solicitors in relation to the lodging of Forms Q in summary causes, but it shall be within the discretion of the sheriff clerk to answer such inquiries where he is satisfied that to do so would not impair the service normally provided to solicitors and to the public.

Practice Note

[25th June 1982]

I, Ronald Alistair Bennett, Q.C., Sheriff Principal of South Strathclyde, Dumfries and Galloway, direct that the rules contained in the schedule annexed hereto, shall come into force and have effect in all sheriff courts in the Sheriffdom of South Strathclyde, Dumfries and Galloway from and including 1st July 1982; and I hereby revoke all practice notes issued prior to the date of this order.

SCHEDULE

General—Civil and Criminal Causes

Gowns to be worn

1. Solicitors appearing at the bar of all courts (other than summary cause courts) shall wear gowns.

Civil Causes—Ordinary Actions

Return of process

1. All processes must be returned to the sheriff clerk not later than 12 o'clock noon of the second day preceding any diet or the date on which they appear on the rolls of the court.

Anticipated duration of proof or trial

2. When moving for a date to be fixed for a proof or debate, solicitors shall be prepared to inform the court of the anticipated duration of the proof or debate.

Retirals and settlements

3.—(1) When, in any action in which a diet of proof, or debate, has been fixed, the solicitor of any party decides to retire from the action, he shall at once intimate in writing the fact of his retirement to the solicitors for all other parties to the action and also to the sheriff clerk.

(2) When in any such case a settlement has been reached or it is probable that the proof or debate will not proceed on the date which has been fixed,

the solicitors acting in the case shall at once intimate the position, in writing, to the sheriff clerk.

Note of authorities for debate

4. The solicitor for each party to an action in which a debate has been fixed shall, not later than 10 a.m. on the day of the debate, lodge with the sheriff clerk a note of all authorities to which reference is to be made in the course of the argument for the party whom he represents.

Copies of productions to be provided

5. Solicitors shall, at the time they lodge documentary productions in process, lodge for the use of the court one copy of each production clearly marked with the number of process.

Appeals—Ordinary Actions

6. [Revoked by Practice Note No. 1 of 1989.]

Note of authorities for hearing of appeal

7. The solicitors for each party to an action under appeal shall, not later than two clear working days prior to the day of the diet of hearing, lodge with the sheriff clerk of the court where the hearing of the appeal is to take place, a note of all authorities to which reference is to be made in the course of the argument for the party he represents, and shall send a copy of said note to the sheriff clerk at Airdrie.

Notes by the Sheriff Principal for the Guidance of Solicitors in Relation to Affidavit Evidence in Undefended Divorce Actions other than Simplified Divorces

[30th January 1984]

[The terms of the Notes are identical to Section 5 of the Practice Notes of Glasgow and Strathkelvin (p. **D** 604), *supra*.]

Act of Court No. 6 of 1988

[18th August 1988]

Transfer of Administrative Responsibility

I, Maurice Gordon Gillies, Q.C., Sheriff Principal of South Strathclyde, Dumfries and Galloway, hereby direct that as from 1st September 1988 the sheriff court at Kirkcudbright shall, for administrative purposes, cease to be a depute court of Stranraer and shall become a depute court attached to the sheriff court at Dumfries.

Practice Note No. 2 of 1988

[25th November 1988]

This practice note has been made to ensure that parties' solicitors have the opportunity of being heard on the question of expenses after judgment on the merits has been issued in a defended ordinary action in which a party has been successful in obtaining decree for payment of a sum of money, other than expenses.

I, John Stuart Mowat, Q.C., Sheriff Principal of the Sheriffdom of South Strathclyde, Dumfries and Galloway, hereby direct as follows:

1. When a sheriff issues an interlocutor in a defended action in which a party has obtained judgment on the merits for a sum of money and which, if it dealt also with liability for expenses, would be a final judgment, he shall not in that interlocutor deal with the question of expenses, but shall, after giving judgment on the merits of the action, appoint the case to his first procedure roll thereafter for a hearing on the question of expenses.

2. Unless the sheriff for special reasons decides to do otherwise, he shall in all such interlocutors *ex proprio motu* suspend extract thereon until the expiry of 14 days from the date on which the question of expenses shall be decided.

3. This practice note comes into force on 1st December 1988 and applies to the whole sheriffdom.

Note.—Solicitors are reminded that an interlocutor such as that referred to in the foregoing practice note in which expenses have been reserved and extract suspended, may not be appealed without leave of the sheriff.

After the liability for expenses has been dealt with, the interlocutor dealing with the merits and the interlocutor determining liability for expenses will together constitute a final judgment which may be appealed, without leave, in the usual way.

Practice Note No. 1 of 1989

[14th December 1989]

Appeal Against an Interlocutor to which the Sheriff has not Appended a Note

I, John Stuart Mowat, Q.C., Sheriff Principal of South Strathclyde, Dumfries and Galloway, hereby direct as follows:

Where an appeal is marked against an interlocutor to which the sheriff has not appended a note as required by rule 89(1) of the First Schedule to the Sheriff Courts (Scotland) Act 1907, the sheriff clerk, or one of his deputes, shall ascertain from the sheriff concerned, before transmission of the process to the sheriff principal, whether the sheriff wishes to add to such interlocutor a note setting out the grounds upon which he has proceeded.

This practice note supersedes para. 6 of the practice note dated 25th June 1982 and comes into force on 3rd January 1990 and applies to the whole sheriffdom.

[THE NEXT PAGE IS D 901]

Sheriffdom of Tayside, Central and Fife

Practice Note

[26th January 1983]

Duration of poinding

If warrant to sell is applied for within six months of the date of execution of the poinding, it may be granted, if otherwise lawful, without special enquiry as to whether there has been undue delay in applying for the warrant.

If warrant to sell is applied for more than six months after the date of execution of the poinding, it shall be done by the creditor or his solicitor in the form of a minute which shall set forth the reasons for the delay. The first deliverance on such a minute shall require service on the debtor and appoint objections, if so advised, within seven days. If so required by the sheriff, the solicitor instructing the diligence, or an accredited representative for the creditor, shall appear personally before the sheriff to give such additional information as may be necessary in support of the application.

Second poinding

A sheriff officer shall not execute a second poinding in the same premises under the same decree on the instructions of the same creditor unless of poindable goods which were not in the premises when the first poinding was executed.

Noting of poindings by sheriff clerk—ordinary action

The sheriff clerk will cause the backing of each extract decree accompanying a report of poinding to be marked with the date of the poinding to which the report relates, and an entry recording the date of the poinding and the "A" number of the case will also be made in a register of poindings, indexed by defenders' names which will be kept for this purpose. Before presenting for approval, the sheriff clerk will verify that no earlier poinding has occurred following the decree, and, if there has been such an earlier poinding, he will report the fact to the Sheriff.

Appointment of auctioneer

When the sheriff grants a warrant of sale, the auctioneer appointed by him shall be a person who, alone or with others, carries on business as an auctioneer, and who is not a whole time employee of the sheriff officer executing the diligence or of any partner or employer of such sheriff officer or of the creditor. If such a person is not available, or in warrants of sale proceeding on a decree in a summary cause, the sheriff may appoint the sheriff officer acting as judge of the roup or such person as seems to him to be suitably qualified to perform the duties of auctioneer.

Appointment of judge of roup

When the sheriff grants a warrant of sale he may appoint as the judge of the roup a sheriff officer and the sheriff officer so appointed may be the sheriff officer who has executed the poinding.

Unsold pointed goods

When poinded goods of a debtor are exposed for sale and are not sold and are adjudged to the poinding creditor, the debt shall be reduced by the appraised value of such goods, albeit such goods are not removed from the premises by the poinding creditor.

Date of sale

The report of sale in an ordinary action will state the date when the sale took place.

Report of sale—ordinary action

When a report of sale is lodged with the sheriff clerk, there shall be written upon the report of sale and signed by the sheriff an interlocutor in the following or similar terms:—

> "The Sheriff remits the report of sale and the documents attached thereto to the Auditor of Court to tax the account contained therein, to state the balance due to or by the defender as a result of the sale and/or delivery of the poinded goods, and to report".

The remit to the auditor of court which, under existing practice, is included at the end of the warrant of sale, shall in future be deleted therefrom. If, after considering the report of sale, and the auditor's report and any objections thereto, the sheriff approves of the report of sale as taxed, he will sign a docquet "Approved as taxed" which will be written upon the report of sale. A record of the sale will be made in the register of poindings.

Warrants of concurrence

It is not necessary to obtain a warrant of concurrence under section 13 of the Debtors (Scotland) Act 1838 on a decree granted by a court within the sheriffdom for the purpose of poinding moveables of the defender named in said decree where the moveables are situated in another sheriff court district of the sheriffdom.

Reports of poindings and sales—where to be made

Every report of a poinding and all applications for orders or warrants relating to poinded moveables and the report of any sale thereof shall be lodged with or made to the court of the sheriff court district in which the poinded moveables are situated.

There shall be discontinued any practice whereby the sheriff clerk of a court which has received the report of a poinding proceeding on a decree granted outwith the sheriffdom is required to notify the court which granted the decree of the receipt of the report.

R. R. Taylor,
Sheriff Principal of Tayside,
Central and Fife.

Practice Note

[February 1984]

Notes by the Sheriff Principal for the guidance of solicitors in relation to affidavit evidence in undefended divorce actions other than simplified divorces.

[The terms of the Notes are identical to Section 5 of the Practice Notes of Glasgow and Strathkelvin (p. **D**604, *supra*).]

[THE NEXT PAGE IS D 1001]

Sheriffdom of Lothian and Borders

Act of Court (Consolidation, etc.) 1990 No. 1

[4th April 1990]

ARRANGEMENT OF RULES

I, Gordon Nicholson, Q.C., Sheriff Principal of Lothian and Borders, in respect that many of the Acts of Court in force within the Sheriffdom are spent or are in need of modernisation, hereby repeal all acts of court presently in force within the Sheriffdom other than those listed in the Schedule hereto, and direct that the following will be given effect on and after 1 May 1990:

Part I—Civil Procedure

Civil jurisdiction

1.—(1) Where a pursuer in an ordinary cause, summary cause or small claim is unaware of any agreement to prorogate jurisdiction over the subject matter of the cause to another court, no averment to that effect need be made in the initial writ or summons as the case may be.

(2) Where a pursuer in an ordinary cause, summary cause or small claim is unaware of any proceedings pending before another court involving the same cause of action and between the same parties as those named in the initial writ or summons as the case may be, no averment to that effect need be made in the initial writ or summons.

Caveats

2. A caveat intended to give a person notice of "any application" made in respect of him in proceedings before the court will not be accepted automatically by the sheriff clerk. Any caveat in such terms will be put before a sheriff for consideration and, after hearing the person seeking to lodge the caveat, or his representative, the sheriff may allow the caveat to be lodged with or without modification.

Borrowing, return and inspection of processes

[1] **3.**—(1) Where a process or a part thereof has been borrowed it must be returned to the sheriff clerk not later than 4p.m. on the second working day before the date on which it is required in court.

(2) No process or part thereof may be borrowed, nor will it be available for inspection, during the period from the foresaid time and day until the day after the date on which it is required in court.

NOTE

[1] Substituted, 15th August 1991.

Lodging of initial writs, etc.

[1] **3A.** All initial writs, petitions, summonses, motions and minutes must be lodged with the sheriff clerk not later than 4p.m. on the second working day before the date on which they are to appear on the appropriate rolls of the court.

NOTE

[1] Inserted, 15th August 1991.

Summary cause and small claim causes—incidental applications and sist of procedure

4.—(1) Any incidental application under Rule 93 of the Act of Sederunt, (Summary Cause Rules, Sheriff Court) 1976, or under Rule 33 of the Act of Sederunt (Small Claim Rules) 1988, shall be lodged with the sheriff clerk along with two copies thereof. The sheriff clerk shall appoint the application to be heard at a sitting of the summary cause court or, as the case may be, the small claim court on a date which will allow notice to be given before the hearing to the other party or parties as required by said Rules, and shall mark the date and time appointed on the backing of the application and on the copies. The application and one copy will then be returned to the applicant or his representative, the remaining copy being retained by the sheriff clerk.

(2) Not later than the time fixed for the hearing of the application the applicant or his representative shall, except in a case where intimation has been made by the sheriff clerk under Rule 33(2) of the Act of Sederunt (Small Claim Rules) 1988, return the application to the sheriff clerk along with evidence of notice having been duly given which may be

(*a*) a certificate by a solicitor of posting a copy by (i) ordinary first class post, or (ii) recorded delivery first class post, or (*b*) a holograph acceptance of notice.

(3) Failure to follow the above procedure may result in dismissal of the application.

(4) Any motion to sist procedure in a summary cause or in a small claim shall be considered by the sheriff, and the sheriff clerk shall if necessary arrange for the cause to be called in court for that purpose.

[THE NEXT PAGE IS D 1003]

Ordinary cause—motions

5.—(1) The following provisions will apply in regard to cases where all parties to an action are legally represented:

(*a*) In all defended ordinary actions a party, before presenting any motion at the sheriff clerk's office, may transmit the principal motion to all the other parties in the action inviting them, if so advised, to mark the motion as consented to or to mark it as unopposed. Upon the motion being so marked, dated and signed, it must be returned to the originator. The motion, so docquetted, may then be presented at the civil department of the sheriff clerk's office to be laid before a sheriff in chambers.

(*b*) The sheriff when considering the motion may grant the same and sign the appropriate interlocutor, or, if he sees fit, direct that the presenter appear in support of the motion.

(*c*) Where the sheriff instructs a hearing, the motion will be put on the motion roll of the first convenient ordinary court and the date thereof be given to the presenter by a member of the sheriff clerk's staff. The presenter of the motion shall advise all other parties to the action of the date fixed for the hearing.

(2) Except as provided in paragraph (1)(*b*) above the following motions shall not be enrolled for calling in the ordinary court, but shall be considered in chambers:

(*a*) Any motion in an undefended action, (other than a motion in terms of Rule 22 of the first schedule to the Sheriff Courts (Scotland) Act 1907);

(*b*) Any motion which is endorsed as unopposed in accordance with paragraph (1)(*a*) above other than a motion under paragraph (5) below;

(*c*) Any joint motion which disposes of an action including all questions of expenses.

(3) Any other written motion presented in an ordinary action shall be enrolled for calling in an appropriate ordinary court. The solicitor presenting the motion shall intimate the date of calling to all other interested parties in the action by lodging the motion with the sheriff clerk, obtaining a date for calling, and intimating said date to all other interested parties in the action.

(4) All motions under paragraph (3) above must be intimated to all other interested parties in the action before noon on the day before the motion is called in court.

(5) Except in the event of an unforeseeable emergency, a motion to discharge a diet of proof, whether made of consent or not, shall be lodged in time to be heard not less than two clear days before the diet of proof.

Affidavit evidence in undefended actions of divorce, other than simplified divorces, and in undefended actions of separation and aliment

6.—(1) An affidavit is no substitute for a reliable and adequate precognition though a precognition may eventually be the basis for an affidavit.

(2) The affidavit should be typed on substantial paper, should be backed up longways, and should be stitched or stapled. It must commence with the words "At..........., the...........day of........... 19.., in the presence of............ Compeared............, who being solemnly sworn, Depones as follows...........,". The full name, age, address and occupation must be given, and it must thereafter proceed in the first person and should take the form of numbered paragraphs. The witness should be made to appreciate the importance of the affidavit. The witness must be placed on oath, or must affirm, and each page will require to be signed by both the witness and the notary. It is not essential that it should be sealed by the notary. The document should be of a shape and size convenient to be lodged as part of the process. The affidavit should end with the words "All of which is truth as the deponent shall answer to God", or "All of which is affirmed to be true" as appropriate.

(3) Affidavits of parties and witnesses should follow step by step the averments in the initial writ. The drafter of an affidavit should provide himself, before drawing it, with a copy of the initial writ, a copy of the appropriate precognition, and the relative productions. The affidavit to be taken from a witness should follow the averments in the initial writ to the extent that these are within the knowledge of that particular witness. It is not a requirement that the wording of an affidavit should follow exactly the wording of the initial writ.

(4) On the matter of the qualifications of the person before whom the affidavit is taken, the Ordinary Cause Rules provide that the affidavit is admissible if it is duly emitted before a notary public or other competent authority. This means a notary public, Justice of the Peace, Commissioner of Oaths, or other statutory authority within the meaning of the Statutory Declarations Act 1835. In the examples given hereafter, it is assumed that the affidavit is in fact taken before a solicitor who is a notary public, and thereafter the references to the party before whom the affidavit is sworn are to "the notary". The solicitor acting in the action may well be called on also to act in a notarial capacity when the affidavit is subsequently sworn. This is permissible. In acting in a notarial capacity he must, however, as a competent authority, observe all the normal rules in this connection, and must satisfy himself as to the capacity of the witness to make the statement, and ensure that the witness understands that it constitutes his or her evidence in the case.

(5) On the matter of productions, those required, when an affidavit is being taken, may already have been lodged in process, but there may be some productions (such as photographs) which are produced by the witness to the notary when the affidavit is sworn, and which may not by that time have been lodged in process.

(6) Productions already lodged in process must be borrowed up, and put to the party or the witness who makes them part of his or her evidence in the appropriate part of the affidavit. Each production will require to be referred to in the affidavit by its number of process and must be docquetted and signed by the party or witness and the notary. If a production has not yet been lodged when the affidavit is being taken, it will require to be identified by the witness in his evidence in the affidavit, and will then be docquetted with regard to the affidavit and signed by the party or witness and the notary. It will then be lodged as a production. Obviously, certain productions will be docquetted with regard to more than one affidavit.

(7) In adultery cases, photographs of both the pursuer and the defender normally require to be produced, put to the appropriate party or witnesses in the affidavit, and signed and docquetted with reference thereto in the manner already described. In certain circumstances, a photograph may have to be identified and docquetted by more than one person, as in the case of the photograph of a party requiring to be spoken to by the pursuer and two inquiry agents.

(8) After the expiry of the period of notice and no notice of intention to defend or minute in terms of rule 34 having been lodged, affidavits may be prepared and lodged without first seeking the authority of the court. All affidavits lodged must be of as recent a date as is possible in the circumstances. This factor is particularly important in (1) cases involving children, (2) those cases in which financial craves are involved or (3) any other cases where the evidence of a party or witness is liable to change through the passage of time. The notary will require to ensure, therefore, that an affidavit represents the deponent's evidence on such matters at the time the affidavit is sworn. Any affidavit which is more than three months old is likely to be regarded as unacceptable.

(9) In cases involving custody of or access to children, an affidavit or affidavits providing corroborating evidence about the welfare of the children should be provided. The evidence of that witness must present the

court with a full picture of the position regarding the child or children. It is, however, clear that such independent evidence in no way relieves the pursuer from testifying fully to the position regarding the children in his or her own affidavit, so far as within his or her knowledge. Whatever else the affidavits of the pursuer and the independent witness contain, their evidence should certainly include the following:

(*a*) the qualifications of the witness, if not a parent, to speak about the child; how often, for example, and in what circumstances, does the witness normally see the child;
(*b*) a description of the home conditions in which the child lives;
(*c*) observations upon the child's general appearance, interests, state of health and well being;
(*d*) information, where relevant, about the school the child attends; whether and to what extent he has contact with other children and relatives;
(*e*) observations on the relationship between the child and the person in whose care he or she lives, on the child's attitude towards each of the parents, and on the extent of contact with the parent or parents with whom the child is not living;
(*f*) details of child care arrangements at all times including arrangements during working hours (outwith school hours);
(*g*) the means and status of the person craving custody with a view to enabling him or her to maintain and bring up the child in a suitable manner.

(10) The attention of solicitors is drawn to the provisions of the Matrimonial Proceedings (Children) Act 1958. The court will not (unless the provisions of section 8(2) are shown to apply) grant decree of divorce until the court is satisfied as respects every child for whose custody, maintenance and education the court has jurisdiction to make provision in that action (a) that arrangements have been made for the care and upbringing of the child and that those arrangements are satisfactory or are the best which can be devised in the circumstances; or (b) that it is impracticable for the party or parties appearing before the court to make any such arrangements.

(11) Where financial craves are involved, it is even more important that the evidence is full, accurate and up-to-date. In parole proofs the evidence of the pursuer and the witnesses on these matters can be supplemented at the proof by questions from the bench or from the solicitor for the pursuer. This will not be possible where evidence is taken by affidavit, and the affidavit must be so framed as to exclude the necessity for supplementary questions. Failure to do so may result in the sheriff requiring the attendance of the solicitor in court. If, after an affidavit has been taken, and the solicitor concerned has parted with it, a material change of circumstances occurs, it is essential that the court be immediately informed, and where necessary, that a further affidavit be sworn.

(12) Where the pursuer in an action is speaking in the affidavit of the financial position of the defender, it is essential that the affidavit should state the date, as precisely as possible, at which that information was valid. Otherwise it may be assumed by the court that the pursuer is speaking to the defender's position at the date of the affidavit. The court must be provided with as up-to-date information as possible about the defender's ability to pay the sums the pursuer is seeking, and these sums should be such as that evidence justifies. The pursuer must, of course, speak also to his or her own financial position, at the date of the affidavit. Where the pursuer cannot obtain recent information as to the defender's means, it is suggested that, if the pursuer's advisers approve, assessment may be left to the sheriff, and in such cases it may be that the solicitors representing the pursuer would be willing to incorporate in the terms of the minute for decree, after the words "in terms of the crave of the initial writ" the words "or such other sum (or sums) as the court may think proper".

(13) Where the pursuer has craved a capital sum, a periodical allowance, aliment for the child or children, or expenses, and in the minute for decree does not seek decree for one or any of these, it is essential that the reasons for this are fully narrated in the affidavit. Where these reasons are capable of corroboration by witnesses, they should be dealt with in the witnesses' affidavits.

(14) The minute for decree must be signed by a solicitor who has examined the affidavits and other documents and takes responsibility therefor, whether or not he is the person who drew the initial writ or affidavits.

(15) In consent cases, the defender's written consent form will also have to be borrowed up, put to the pursuer in his or her affidavit, and docquetted and identified in the same way as other productions.

(16) Affidavit procedure will not prevent the parties to the action agreeing the financial or other ancillary craves by joint minute. For so long as these ancillary craves are opposed, the affidavit procedure cannot be used for them, but it can be used for the merits of the action. If a joint minute is signed before an affidavit or supplementary affidavit is emitted by the pursuer, that affidavit must refer to the arrangements in the joint minute. Decree of divorce will not be granted before any issues relating to financial provisions consequent upon the divorce which require to be decided by the court have been so decided.

(17) While it is no longer necessary to corroborate any fact, proof of which is required to establish a ground of divorce or any other matter, solicitors are nonetheless reminded that any affidavit or affidavits must satisfy the requirements of section 8 of the Civil Evidence (Scotland) Act 1988.

(18) The foregoing provisions shall apply *mutatis mutandis* to undefended actions of separation and aliment as they apply to undefended actions of divorce.

Conveyancing and Feudal Reform (Scotland) Act 1970

7. An initial writ bearing to be under Part II of the abovementioned Act but containing a crave for interdict or interim interdict alone or along with other craves shall not be accepted for warranting without the approval of the sheriff.

Copy productions for use by sheriff

8.—(1) Where documentary productions have been lodged in process, and are to be referred to in the course of a proof or a debate, copies of all such productions, for use by the sheriff, shall, whenever practicable, be lodged with the sheriff clerk not less than two days prior to the diet of proof or debate.

(2) All such copy productions shall be clearly marked with their process number.

(3) Where copies of productions are lodged with the sheriff clerk in terms of paragraph (1) above, he shall forthwith docquet the inventory of productions to show that copies have been lodged and to show the date of their lodging.

Authorities to be referred to at appeal hearing, proof or debate

9. Where authorities are to be referred to in the course of an appeal hearing, a proof or a debate, a list of those authorities shall, whenever practicable, be given to the sheriff clerk at least 24 hours prior to the diet in question so that copies of those authorities may be made available for use by the sheriff principal or sheriff in the court where the hearing is to take place.

Appeals

10.—(1) When an appeal is marked, the note of appeal or the entry in the interlocutor sheet must specify the interlocutor which is to be the subject of the appeal. In a case where there is an interlocutor dealing with the merits of a case and a subsequent interlocutor dealing with the question of expenses, an appeal marked thereafter in respect of "the foregoing interlocutor" will be taken to be an appeal in respect only of the interlocutor dealing with the question of expenses.

(2) When an appeal is marked against an interlocutor to which the sheriff has not appended a note, the person marking the appeal shall, at the time of marking, add a request that the sheriff should write a note.

(3) When, following a proof, an appeal is marked against an interlocutor which has been issued by the sheriff before the notes of evidence are extended and lodged in process, the appellant or his solicitor shall, except in a case to which paragraph (5) below applies, inform the shorthand writer forthwith that the notes of evidence are required, and ascertain from him the date when the notes of evidence will be available. When the appeal is to the sheriff principal, the appellant or his solicitor shall thereafter inform the sheriff clerk of the date when the notes of evidence will be available in order that the diet for hearing the appeal may be fixed for a later date.

(4) Failure by the appellant or his solicitor to comply with the above provisions, so that there is undue delay in hearing the appeal, or a diet fixed for the hearing is rendered abortive, may affect the question of expenses.

(5) Where the appeal is to the sheriff principal, and it appears to the appellant or his solicitor that the ground of appeal is such that it may be unnecessary to have the notes of evidence available for the hearing of the appeal, a motion to dispense with the requirements of paragraph (3) above may be made to the sheriff principal. Any such motion shall be made as soon as possible after the marking of the appeal, and shall be intimated to all other parties. The sheriff principal's decision on any such motion shall be final.

Part II—Criminal Procedure

Judicial examinations

11.—(1) All judicial examinations should be put out before a full time or floating sheriff, and not before an honorary or temporary sheriff.

(2) In the event of a full time sheriff not being available, application should be made to the sheriff clerk at Edinburgh, who will endeavour to arrange for a full time sheriff from another court, whom failing a floating sheriff, to attend the court in question.

(3) In the last resort the sheriff principal should be notified with a view to dispensing with the foregoing requirements if so advised.

(4) In this context the expression "full time" sheriff includes an honorary sheriff who holds or has held office as a full time sheriff.

Part III—Edinburgh Sheriff Court Standing Advisory Committee

The Edinburgh Sheriff Court Standing Advisory Committee shall have the following constitution, functions and procedural rules:

Constitution

12.—[1] (1) The committee shall consist of three sheriffs nominated by the Sheriff Principal of Lothian and Borders, three solicitors nominated by the President of the Edinburgh Bar Association, two persons of the rank of assistant procurator fiscal or procurator fiscal-depute nominated by the Regional Procurator Fiscal of Lothian and Borders, two persons nominated by the Chief Constable of Lothian and Borders Police, those persons to be the Chief Inspector in charge of the Court and Records Department and the Sheriff Court Sergeant, and three persons of the rank of assistant sheriff clerk or sheriff clerk-depute nominated by the

Regional Sheriff Clerk of Lothian and Borders. The chairman shall be the senior sheriff present at any meeting and, failing the attendance of a sheriff, the person elected to act as chairman by the members present at the meeting. In the event of equality of votes with regard to any proposed recommendation, the chairman for the time being shall have a casting vote. The secretary of the committee shall be a member of the sheriff clerk's staff appointed by the Regional Sheriff Clerk of Lothian and Borders to perform that office. The Sheriff Principal of Lothian and Borders, the President of the Edinburgh Bar Association, the Regional Procurator Fiscal of Lothian and Borders, the Chief Constable of Lothian and Borders Police, and the Regional Sheriff Clerk of Lothian and Borders are hereinafter referred to as "the constituents".

Appointment of Secretary and Nomination and Period of Service of Members

(2) Whenever there is any change in the appointment as secretary, the Regional Sheriff Clerk of Lothian and Borders shall intimate to the other constituents the name of the person appointed to act as secretary.

The names and addresses of the persons nominated as members of the committee shall be sent to the secretary by the constituents on or before 31 October each year. The members will serve for one year from the first day of November following their nomination and they may be re-nominated for further periods of service. In the event of the death or resignation of a member during his period of service, another person shall be nominated by his constituent to replace him for the remainder of the period.

Dates and Place of Meetings, etc.

(3) Meetings of the committee will be held during each session of the court on the last Monday of every session, or, if this is a public holiday, upon the last Tuesday. Each meeting shall commence at 4 p.m. in the Conference Room, Sheriff Court House, Lawnmarket, Edinburgh. Members of the committee will inform the secretary, a fortnight before each meeting, of matters to be included in the agenda, and the secretary will send a copy of the agenda, together with a draft minute of any previous meeting, to each member a week before the meeting. Additional meetings may be held if the committee so resolves, and the committee may appoint sub-committees from time to time which will exercise the functions delegated to them by the committee. Persons other than members may be invited to attend meetings of the committee or of sub-committees and to take part in their discussions but shall have no voting rights.

Functions of the Committee

(4) The committee shall take into consideration any matter affecting the efficiency of the administrative arrangements of the sheriff court in Edinburgh which they are asked by any of the constituents or by any member of the committee to take into consideration, and shall make such recommendations as they think proper from time to time with regard to such matters to the constituents or to any of them. A recommendation of the committee shall require the approval of a meeting attended by at least one nominee of each constituent. Any such recommendation shall be communicated in writing by the secretary to the constituents or constituent concerned.

NOTE

[1] Amended, 15th August 1991.

PART IV—MISCELLANEOUS

Representation and wearing of gowns

13.—(1) Any solicitor appearing professionally at the Bar of any sheriff court in the sheriffdom shall wear a gown.

(2) Except in accordance with rule 17(2) of the Schedule to the Act of Sederunt (Summary Cause Rules, Sheriff Court) 1976, or rule 30 of the

Schedule to the Act of Sederunt (Small Claim Rules) 1988, no person other than a qualified solicitor holding a practising certificate, or a member of the Faculty of Advocates, shall be permitted to appear on behalf of a litigant at any stage of procedure.

(3) When a trainee solicitor is allowed to represent a party in terms of the said rule 17(2) or the said rule 30 he shall not wear a gown.

(4) Any party not personally present or represented in accordance with these directions at any diet shall be deemed to be absent.

Sterling equivalent of foreign currency

14. Where in any action payment is craved of a sum of money in a foreign currency or the sterling equivalent thereof at the date of payment or at the date of extract, whichever is the earlier, with or without interest, and decree has been granted in these terms, an extract may proceed upon a minute by the party in whose favour decree has been granted or his agent, endorsed on or annexed to the summons or initial writ, stating the rate of exchange prevailing at the close of business on the preceding day and the sterling equivalent at that rate of the sum decerned for in foreign currency, craving extract accordingly and accompanied by a certificate, which may be in the form provided in the schedule hereto, from one of the Scottish clearing banks certifying the said rate and sterling equivalent; and the extract shall bear a reference to said certificate.

SCHEDULE

Form of Certificate—

I (designation and address) certify that the rate current in London for the purchase of (state the unit of the foreign currency in which the decree is expressed) at the close of business on the .... day of .... 19.. (being the date preceding that on which extract of the decree is requested) was .... to the £ sterling and at this rate the sum of (state the amount of the sum in the decree) amounts to £.....

Dated the .... day of .... 19..

Signed for or on behalf of the Bank

Manager or other official

Commissary: Applications

15. Where a deceased had his last place of residence within a Sheriff Court District of the Sheriffdom of Lothian and Borders, any commissary application, including an application for the appointment of executor dative relative to the said death, shall, if presented to the Commissariot of the said sheriffdom, be presented only at the sheriff court of the said district.

Commissary: Re-sealing (Southern Rhodesia and Zimbabwe)

16. Considering that by virtue of an Ordinance of the Governor of Southern Rhodesia enacted on 7 December 1979, following the Southern Rhodesia Constitution (Interim Provisions) Order 1979, provision was made for the recognition of any act done in Southern Rhodesia in reliance upon any law or purported law in operation in that country from 11 November 1965 onwards until its independence, the re-sealing under the Colonial Probates Act 1892 of grants of representation issued by the courts in Southern Rhodesia, irrespective of the date of issue, and of like grants issued by courts in Zimbabwe on and after 18 April 1980, the date on which Southern Rhodesia became an independent country known as Zimbabwe, are hereby permitted.

PART V—EXTENT

17. The forgoing Directions, with the exception of Direction number 12, shall apply in all the sheriff courts within the sheriffdom. Direction number 12 shall apply in the sheriff court at Edinburgh only.

I appoint this Act of Court to be inserted in the Act Books of all the sheriff courts in the Sheriffdom of Lothian and Borders and to be posted on the notice boards in said sheriff courts for publication to the lieges.

Gordon Nicholson,
Sheriff Principal of Lothian and Borders

SCHEDULE

The following Acts of Court are not repealed by this Act of Court:

The Acts of Court specified relate to the then current dates of court sittings and holidays.

Notes for Guidance

Sheriff Court of Chancery

Guidance

1.1. The following notes, which have the general approval of the Sheriff of Chancery, are designed to give guidance to solicitors dealing with chancery petitions.

Advisory service

2.1. The depute sheriff clerk of chancery (tel. 031–226 7181, ext. 207) is available to discuss particular cases and will suggest revisals to any petitions submitted in draft. Advice will be given as to the type of petition best suited to particular circumstances.

Publication

3.1. An abstract of the particulars in each chancery petition is published on the walls of the appropriate court having jurisdiction over the subjects or over the domicile of the ancestor. No further procedure will take place until the induciae, which varies according to where the deceased died, has expired. It is generally inadvisable to take evidence from witnesses before the expiry of the induciae.

Proof form

4.1. The normal form of proof is by corroborated affidavit evidence. The affidavits should not be sworn before a notary public, acting as a commissioner, who is a partner or employee of the firm acting for the petitioner.

Designation

5.1. The full name, age and occupation of the witness must be given and the full designations of both the ancestor and petitioner must be included in the depositions, the heading to the affidavit being no part of the depositions.

5.2. In special services, the designation and address of the ancestor, as stated in the deed founded on, must be given as well as a designation and address as stated in the petition, when they differ.

Subscription

6.1. The usual practice is for the first deponent to testify to the facts in detail signing each page of his deposition, while the second deponent signs a form of concurrence. The second deponent must sign each page of the deposition of the first deponent as well as his own, unless both are wholly contained on one page. The deponents are, however, speaking to the facts within the knowledge of each, and where their evidence does not coincide there should be separate depositions.

Evidence

7.1. The evidence in the proof should speak to all material facts in the petition. It is not necessary or advisable for deponents to speak to such facts as intestacy or as to the contents of deeds. Probative deeds are their own evidence.

Difficulty in obtaining evidence

7.2. Where there is difficulty in obtaining the evidence of two independent witnesses the Sheriff of Chancery has discretion to allow the evidence of a single witness and, under the Civil Evidence (Scotland) Act 1988, to allow hearsay evidence to be led. It may be that the only witness available is the petitioner, and in that event his evidence is admissible. In all these circumstances the evidence will only be accepted provided that cause is shown why the normal level of proof is unavailable (cf. *Burke* v. *Burke*, 1983 S.L.T. 331 at p. 332).

Mandate

8.1. At present mandates are required where solicitors are to sign petitions. If a mandate is not produced the petitioner must sign the petition. Mandates need not be tested or holograph but should be specific to the purpose of the petition.

Productions—inventory

9.1. A complete inventory of documents produced must be made out. This should be lodged, together with the productions, along with the affidavits. The inventory does not require to be signed by the petitioner or his mandatory. A property search should be produced in petitions for special service and in petitions under s. 10 of the Conveyancing (Scotland) Act 1874.

Minutes of amendment

10.1. Minutes of amendment may be lodged. Depending on the extent of the amendment, republication may be necessary or the sheriff may on cause shown dispense with republication.

Error in type of petition

10.2. Amendment is inappropriate if the wrong type of petition has been lodged, e.g., if a petition for service has been presented in place of a petition for completion of title. Under these circumstances the petition should be withdrawn and a fresh one lodged. If publication of the original petition has already taken place there will have to be publication of new in respect of the second petition.

Decree

11.1. When decree has been granted, the petitioner's agent will be informed by letter. Productions will be returned at this point but the process will be transmitted to the Keeper of the Registers of Scotland.

Extract decree

12.1. Extracts are prepared for the petition by the Keeper of the Registers. The extract is issued, along with a fee note, to the petitioner's agent.

Process

13.1. All parts of process, petitions, mandates, affidavits and inventory of productions should be stiff-backed and headed up "Sheriff Court of Chancery".

Fee

14.1. The correct fee for lodging a chancery petition is £36.